THE OXFORD HANDBOOK OF

MUSIC PERFORMANCE

THE OXFORD HANDBOOK OF

MUSIC

PERFORMANCE

DEVELOPMENT AND LEARNING, PROFICIENCIES, PERFORMANCE PRACTICES, AND PSYCHOLOGY

VOLUME 1

Edited by

GARY E. MCPHERSON

OXFORD

UNIVERSITY PRESS

OXFORD
UNIVERSITY PRESS

Oxford University Press is a department of the University of Oxford. It furthers the University's objective of excellence in research, scholarship, and education by publishing worldwide. Oxford is a registered trade mark of Oxford University Press in the UK and certain other countries.

Published in the United States of America by Oxford University Press
198 Madison Avenue, New York, NY 10016, United States of America.

Library of Congress Cataloging-in-Publication Data
Names: McPherson, Gary E., editor.
Title: The Oxford handbook of music performance : development and learning, proficiencies, performance practices, and psychology / editor: Gary E. McPherson.
Description: New York : Oxford University Press, 2021–2022. |
Series: Oxford handbooks series | Includes index. |
Identifiers: LCCN 2021046050 | ISBN 9780190056285 (hardback : volume 1) |
ISBN 9780190058869 (hardback : volume 2) | ISBN 9780190056308 (epub : volume 1) |
ISBN 9780190058883 (epub : volume 2) | ISBN 9780190056292 (volume 1) |
ISBN 9780190056315 (volume 1) | ISBN 9780190058890 (volume 2) |
ISBN 9780190058876 (volume 2)
Subjects: LCSH: Music—Performance. | Music—Performance—Psychological aspects. |
Music—Instruction and study—Psychological aspects. |
Music—Performance—Research. | Performance practice (Music) |
Musicians—Health and hygiene. | Practicing (Music)
Classification: LCC ML457 .O95 2021 | DDC 780.78—dc23
LC record available at https://lccn.loc.gov/2021046050

DOI: 10.1093/oxfordhb/9780190056285.001.0001

The manufacturer's authorised representative in the EU for product safety is Oxford University Press España S.A. of El Parque Empresarial San Fernando de Henares, Avenida de Castilla, 2 – 28830 Madrid (www.oup.es/en or product.safety@oup.com). OUP España S.A. also acts as importer into Spain of products made by the manufacturer.

Contents

PART II PROFICIENCIES—PART EDITOR PETER MIKSZA

PART III PERFORMANCE PRACTICES— PART EDITOR JANE W. DAVIDSON

PART IV PSYCHOLOGY— PART EDITOR PAUL EVANS

ACKNOWLEDGMENTS

DRAFTS of each chapter were reviewed by the editor, the part editor, and at least one other independent expert on the topic, either an author in the same or another part of the handbook, or an external scholar. With regard to external assistance, I am particularly grateful to the following for either providing a blind review or helpful feedback for chapter authors: Robert Adlington, Jesper Andersen, David Ashby, Birgitta Burger, Christine Carter, Roger Chaffin, Timothy Cleary, Andrea Creech, Paul Draper, Timothy Dugan, Anders Friberg, Andrew Goldman, Stephen Grant, Björn Heile, Brita Heimarck, Don Hodges, Alexander Refsum Jensenius, Daniela Kaleva, Satoshi Kawase, Andrew King, Jessandra Kono, Andrew Lynch, Isaac Malitz, Chanel Marion-St-Onge, Catherine Massie-Laberge, J. Matt McCrary, Christopher Mesagno, Miriam Mosing, Mark Montemayor, Samuel Nelson, Donald Nicolson, Christianne Orto, Maurizio Ortolani, Raôul Oudejans, Matt Parkin, Eva Moreda Rodriguez, Alex Ruthmann, Amanda Schlegel, Erwin Schoonderwaldt, Dale Schunk, Ronald C. Scherer, Gregory Springer, Gregory Squire, Johan Sundberg, Laura Talbott-Clark, Bill Thompson, Marc Thompson, Justin Trieger, Amanda Tumbleson, Gregor Widholm, Clemens Wöllner, and Harvey Young. I am also grateful to Daniel Yeom for providing valued comments on a number of chapters and for his help in the final stages when we were formatting chapters ready to be sent off to OUP.

I take this opportunity to thank the various representatives at Oxford University Press, especially our commissioning editor Suzanne Ryan, whose enthusiasm and support for this handbook throughout the process leading up to a decision to move forward with a contract was invaluable. I am also grateful to Norman Hirschy who managed all of the details after submission.

I am indebted to the authors who have contributed, and the enormous effort they gave to dealing with reviews and requests for revision over a long period leading up to finalizing each individual chapter. Most important, I thank the Part Editors Peter Miksza, Jane W. Davidson, Paul Evans, Reinhard Kopiez, Eckart Alternmüller, Jim Woodhouse, and Aaron Williamon, without whom the various parts could not have been designed and then completed.

The hard work of many marvelous and valued colleagues helped to create this handbook. All of us hope that you enjoy the results of a project that has taken over four years to complete.

Gary E. McPherson
December 2020

LIST OF CONTRIBUTORS

Jennifer Blackwell studied music education at the University of Western Ontario, before completing master's degrees in saxophone performance and music education at Central Michigan University, and a PhD in music education at the Indiana University Jacobs School of Music. She currently serves as Assistant Professor of Music at the University of Hawai'i at Mānoa, where she teaches coursework in instrumental music education, popular music pedagogy, assessment, learning theory, and research methods, in addition to supervision of student teachers. Her research interests include applied music teaching expertise (from behavioral, cognitive, social, cultural, and affective perspectives), the development of music performance expertise, applications of authentic context learning paradigms, popular music education, and music teacher training.

Arielle Bonneville-Roussy obtained her PhD in social and developmental psychology at the University of Cambridge, researching age differences in musical preferences. She is also a classically trained musician, having gained her bachelor's and master's degrees in clarinet performance from the Université de Montréal. She was a Senior Lecturer (Associate Professor) of education at the University of Roehampton, United Kingdom, and also a board member of the Society for Education, Music and Psychology Research (SEMPRE). She has received many prizes and awards for her work in music psychology research including the Reg and Molly Buck award from SEMPRE and the certificate of excellence from the Canadian Psychological Association. Her research aims to examine the motivational factors that predict performance, persistence, and wellbeing of musicians of all ages, from childhood up to retirement. She also has published widely on the factors associated with age differences in musical preferences. She is now Professor of Lifespan Developmental Psychology at the University of Quebec in Montreal, Canada.

Mary C. Broughton holds a PhD in music psychology from Western Sydney University, focusing on expressive body movement in musical performance. She a senior lecturer in music psychology, having established and leading the psychology of music program area at The University of Queensland's School of Music. Prior to this, she held a research associate position at the School of Music, University of Western Australia where she worked with Jane W. Davidson on a number of music and gesture projects. Her key research areas include performer-audience communication, audience engagement and development, and promoting individual and community wellbeing through active participation in music performance. Mary is also a percussionist who has performed with orchestras such as the Queensland Symphony Orchestra and West Australian Symphony Orchestra, and has performed nationally and internationally as a chamber and solo musician.

Alexander P. Burgoyne earned his PhD in cognition and cognitive neuroscience at Michigan State University. He is currently a post-doctoral researcher in the Attention & Working Memory Laboratory at the Georgia Institute of Technology. His work with David Z. Hambrick has been published in the *New York Times, Scientific American,* and *Slate.* During his time as a graduate student he was awarded the Rasmussen Fellowship, the Future Academic Scholars in Teaching Fellowship, and the College of Social Sciences' Research Scholars Award. His research focuses on individual differences in skill acquisition and expertise, academic achievement, and intelligence. His latest projects investigate the interplay between nature and nurture and the relative contribution of these factors to individual differences in achievement.

Jane W. Davidson studied for undergraduate and master's degrees in music and dance in the UK and Canada and holds a PhD from City University of London. She is currently Professor of Creative and Performing Arts and Head of Performing Arts, Faculty of Fine Arts and Music at the University of Melbourne and Chair of the University's Creativity and Wellbeing Hallmark Research Initiative. From 2011 to 2018 she was Deputy Director of the Australian Research Council's Centre of Excellence for the History of Emotions and is the current President of the Australian Society for Music Psychology. Her research spans music psychology, history of emotions, and performance. Her work contributes to the study of musical skill, music as social interaction, arts for wellbeing outcomes, music and emotion, and opera performance. Her most recent outputs include a major six-volume series *A Cultural History of Emotions* (with Susan Broomhall and Andrew Lynch, Bloomsbury, 2019), the coauthored *Music Nostalgia and Memory* (with Sandra Garrido, Palgrave, 2019), and the two-volume series *Opera, Emotion and the Antipodes* (with Stephanie Rocke and Michael Halliwell, Routledge, 2020).

Paul Evans is an Associate Professor of Educational Psychology in the School of Education at the University of New South Wales, Sydney, Australia. He completed a Doctor of Philosophy in Music Education at the University of Illinois at Urbana-Champaign, a Master of Music Education from the University of Western Australia, and a Bachelor of Music and Bachelor of Education (Hons I) at the University of New South Wales, Sydney. Paul conducts research and teaches in educational psychology, motivation, instruction, music education, and teacher education. His music education research has focused on why children begin learning an instrument, the factors that lead to them persisting or dropping out, their motivation and wellbeing, and the way all of these change throughout adolescence and in the early stages of professional music performance careers.

Dorottya Fabian studied musicology at the Liszt Ferenc Music Academy in Budapest, obtaining a bachelor's of music with honors. After migrating to Australia, she completed a master's of music and a PhD at the University of New South Wales, Sydney. She is Professor of Music at UNSW Sydney and a Fellow of the Australian Academy of Humanities. Previously she served as National Secretary of the Australian Musicological Society and on the International Advisory Panel of the Centre for the History and Analysis of Recorded Music (CHARM, Royal Holloway, UK). Her research embraces historical, empirical, and experimental approaches to address questions of aesthetics, performance, and perception. Her most important investigations focus on performances of J. S. Bach's music in modern times as evidenced in sound recordings.

Jane Ginsborg studied music at the University of York and singing at the Guildhall School of Music and Drama in London before, having established a successful career as a freelance concert singer specializing in twentieth-century and contemporary music, she took a bachelor's degree in psychology with the Open University and a PhD at Keele University. She won the British Voice Association's Van Lawrence Award in 2002 for her research on singers' memorizing strategies and was shortlisted for a Times Higher Education award in 2013 for research on musicians with hearing impairments. She is Professor of Music Psychology and Associate Director of Research at the Royal Northern College of Music in Manchester, where she has worked since 2005, and has served as President of the European Society for the Cognitive Sciences of Music (2012–2015) and Managing Editor of the journal *Music Performance Research* (2010–2018). She is currently Editor-in-Chief of *Musicae Scientiae*. She has many publications to her name; recent and current research interests include expert individual and collaborative practice, rehearsal and performance, particularly involving singing; musicians' health, wellbeing, literacy and resilience; practice-led research; and virtuosity.

Solange Glasser studied violin performance and musicology at the Queensland Conservatorium of Music (Australia), obtaining her bachelor's of music (Hons) with first-class honors in musicology. Solange went on to complete both a licence and a master's in music and musicology at the University of Paris IV Sorbonne, a diploma of orchestral conducting at the Municipal Conservatorium of Paris XIX (France), and a PhD at the University of Melbourne (Australia). Now based at the Melbourne Conservatorium of Music, she is the University of Melbourne's inaugural Lecturer in Music Psychology, with a broad and interdisciplinary range of teaching areas that encompass music psychology, performance science, creativity, and expertise. Her research interests include multisensory perception, prodigious development, and exceptional abilities, with a particular interest in understanding the impact of synesthesia and absolute pitch on musical development.

Susan Hallam studied the violin at the Royal Academy of Music, subsequently working as a professional musician with the BBC before studying for a BA in psychology externally with London University, and completing a MSc and PhD at the Institute of Education UCL, where she became an academic in 1991 and is now Emerita Professor of Education and Music Psychology. She was awarded an MBE for her services to music education in 2015, a lifelong achievement music and drama education award in 2020, and honorary life membership of the British Psychological Society, the International Society for Music Education, and SEMPRE. Her research interests include psychological and educational issues (e.g., ability grouping, disaffection from school, homework), while in music she has focused on the effects of music on a wide range of human activity across the lifespan and how the whole range of musical skills are acquired and maintained.

David Z. Hambrick completed his PhD in experimental (cognitive) psychology at the Georgia Institute of Technology in 2000. He is a Professor in the Department of Psychology at Michigan State University, Co-Founding Editor of the *Journal of Expertise*, and a Fellow of the Association for Psychological Science. His research examines the nature of expertise and expert performance, with a focus on the origins of individual differences. His work has examined the relative contributions of both domain-general and domain-specific factors to individual differences in complex task performance in music, among other domains. Findings from this research have challenged the conclusion that individual differences in expertise can largely be explained by training history. At a general level, Hambrick's research has helped to move expertise research beyond an outmoded nature vs. nurture perspective and toward a multifactorial view that takes into account all relevant explanatory constructs.

Lauren Julius Harris studied piano and cello as a Chicago native through his teens and regularly attended Chicago Symphony concerts. At the University of Illinois, he majored in psychology, followed by graduate study in the Institute of Child Development at the University of Minnesota. He also took courses at the Minnesota Center for the Philosophy of Science and continued going to concerts. Conveniently, the Minneapolis (now Minnesota) Symphony performed right on campus. In 1965, he went to Michigan State University, where he is a Professor of Psychology and teaches courses in child psychology, history of psychology, neuropsychology, and psychology of the arts. In his research, he tries bringing them together as in his 2019 article, "Does Music Matter?" (*Developmental Neuropsychology*). He is a Fellow of the American Psychological Association and the American Association for the Advancement of Science and serves on the editorial boards of *Laterality*, and *Developmental Neuropsychology*. He still practices the piano (fitfully) and attends concerts.

Warren Haston holds a doctorate in philosophy in music education from Northwestern University, and a master's of music in performance-conducting and a bachelor's of music education, with high honors, from the University of Texas–El Paso. He taught all levels of band in Texas and Virginia for nine years. He is Associate Professor and Director of the Music Education Division, and summer term Director at the Hartt School, University of Hartford, where he oversees undergraduate and graduate degree programs. His research interests include teacher education, teacher identity, and instrumental pedagogy. He has presented papers at regional, national, and international conferences, published in leading music education journals, and served on the editorial boards of the *Music Educators Journal* and the *Journal of Music Teacher Education*.

John Hattie completed his bachelor's of education and master's of education at the University of Otago (New Zealand) and his doctor of philosophy at the University of Toronto. He is a Laureate Professor at the Melbourne Graduate School of Education at the University of Melbourne, and has served as Head of Department or Associate Dean in four universities (Western Australia, North Carolina, Auckland, Melbourne) over more than twenty years. He is Chair of the Board of the AITSL (a Federal Government agency), Co-Director of the ARC–Science of Learning Center, and advisor to various Ministers of Education. John has supervised over 200 thesis students, directed $70m in research grants, been invited to more than 200 keynote conference sessions, and published over 550 articles and 51 books. He is known for the series of books on *Visible Learning*, which have sold more than one million copies and are based on probably the largest database on education influences in the world.

Karin S. Hendricks studied cello performance and German studies at the Oberlin College–Conservatory of Music, and received a PhD in music education from the University of Illinois at Urbana Champaign. She is Associate Professor and Chair of Music Education at Boston University and has served the American String Teachers Association (ASTA) as National Secretary and on its national Collegiate, Content, and Research Committees. She has received local, state, and national music teaching awards and was given the 2018 ASTA "String Researcher" award for promising contributions to the field of string education and performance. Karin's research interests include social psychology and social justice in music learning contexts, with a particular focus on student motivation and musical engagement. She has authored numerous research papers and has published four books, including *Performance Anxiety Strategies* and *Compassionate Music Teaching*.

Emese Hruska completed her PhD in music psychology at the University of Roehampton, London, focusing on self-concept, perfectionism, music performance anxiety, and the impact of parents and teachers on classical musicians' development. Having a varied background, she studied and taught classical violin and traditional Hungarian folk music, and obtained a master's degree in journalism. She is an Assistant Professor of Applied Psychology at the Faculty of Education and Psychology, Eötvös Loránd University, Hungary. Previously, she worked as a Research Fellow at the Social and Cultural Psychology Research Group at the Hungarian Academy of Sciences. Related to her doctoral research, she won numerous scholarships and awards from British and Hungarian organizations. Her research interests lie in applied music psychology, aiming to assist musicians in developing healthy practices, and achieving high-quality performances in challenging situations.

Frederic Kiernan holds a PhD in music (musicology) from the University of Melbourne, as well as a BA/BMus and MMus from the same university. He is an early-career researcher and current Research Fellow at the Creativity and Wellbeing Hallmark Research Initiative at the University of Melbourne and Secretary of the Musicological Society of Australia. His research uses methods from historical musicology, the history of emotions, psychology and sociology to explore the intersections of music, creativity, emotion and wellbeing, both presently and in the past. He has published a critical edition of six works (dated 1737) by the Bohemian composer Jan Dismas Zelenka with A-R Editions (Wisconsin) in 2018, and coauthored the revised article on Zelenka for *Grove Music Online* (Oxford University Press). He has also published numerous peer-reviewed articles, and a monograph on Zelenka is forthcoming.

Aaron Kozbelt is a Professor of psychology at Brooklyn College and the Graduate Center of the City University of New York. His research focuses on creativity and cognition in the arts. He has published more than eighty peer-reviewed articles and book chapters, and is a Co-Editor of the *Cambridge Handbook of Expertise and Expert Performance* (2nd ed., 2018). He serves on several editorial boards and has received several national and international awards for his research, including the Daniel Berlyne Award from APA Division 10 and the Alexander Gottlieb Baumgarten Award from the International Association of Empirical Aesthetics.

Raymond MacDonald obtained a BSc and PhD in psychology from the University of Glasgow. He then worked as Artistic Director for a music company, Sounds of Progress, specializing in working with people with disabilities. He is currently Professor of Music Psychology and Improvisation at University of Edinburgh, where he was Head of the School of Music between 2013 and 2016. He is a past Editor of journal *Psychology of Music* and has co-edited texts such as *The Handbook of Musical Identities, Music Health and Wellbeing, Musical Imaginations, Musical Communication, Musical Identities*, and coauthored *The Art of Becoming: How Group Improvisation Works*. His ongoing research focuses on issues relating to improvisation, psychology of music, music health and wellbeing, musical identities, and music education. His work includes studying the processes and outcomes of music participation and music listening, and he is also a saxophonist and composer.

Andrew J. Martin, PhD, is Scientia Professor, Professor of Educational Psychology, and Co-Chair of the Educational Psychology Research Group in the School of Education at the University of New South Wales, Australia. He is also Honorary Research Fellow in the Department of Education at the University of Oxford. He specializes in motivation, engagement, achievement, and quantitative research methods. Although the bulk of his research focuses on these areas, Andrew is also published in important cognate topics such as Aboriginal/Indigenous education, ADHD, academic resilience and academic buoyancy, adaptability, goal setting, pedagogy, and teacher-student relationships. Andrew's research also bridges other disciplines through assessing motivation and engagement in sport, music, and work.

Gary E. McPherson studied music education at the Sydney Conservatorium of Music, before completing a master's of music education at Indiana University, a doctorate of philosophy at the University of Sydney, and a Licentiate and Fellowship in trumpet performance through Trinity College, London. In 2021, he was the recipient of an Honorary Doctorate - *Artium Doctorem Honoris Causa* - from Lund University Sweden. He is the Ormond Professor of Music at the Melbourne Conservatorium of Music and has served as National President of the *Australian Society for Music Education* and President of the *International Society for Music Education*. His research interests are broad and his approach interdisciplinary. His most important research examines the acquisition and development of musical competence, and motivation to engage and participate in music from novice to expert levels. With a particular interest in the acquisition of visual, aural, and creative performance skills, he has attempted to understand more precisely how music students become sufficiently motivated and self-regulated to achieve at the highest level.

Peter Miksza completed his bachelor's of music degree at the College of New Jersey and his master's of music education and PhD in music education at the Indiana University Jacobs School of Music, where he currently serves as Professor of music education and an affiliate member of the IU Cognitive Science Program. His research emphasizes the social- and cognitive-psychological dimensions of musical skill acquisition (e.g., practicing, expertise, musical expression, musical memory). He also conducts research on music teacher preparation policy issues relevant to music education. He is a regular presenter at national and international conferences and has articles published many prominent peer-reviewed publications. Miksza has also published a book titled *Design and Analysis for Quantitative Research in Music Education*, with coauthor Dr. Ken Elpus, as well as several book chapters in edited volumes. He is also Co-Director of the IU JSOM Music and Mind Lab.

Steven J. Morrison holds an undergraduate degree in music education from Northwestern University, a master's of music education from the University of Wisconsin–Madison, and a PhD in music education from Louisiana State University. He is Professor of Music at Northwestern University's Henry and Leigh Bienen School of Music and co-directs the Center for the Study of Education and the Musical Experience. He served as editor of the *Journal of Research in Music Education* and was a visiting fellow at the Centre for Research in the Arts, Social Sciences, and Humanities at the University of Cambridge. His research addresses cognitive aspects of music teaching and learning, including the integration of auditory and visual processing of expressive gesture and modeling in large ensembles. Recognizing the importance of studying music as a global phenomenon, he has also worked to understand variability of musical responses across diverse cultural contexts.

Daniel Müllensiefen studied systematic musicology at the universities of Hamburg (Germany) and Salamanca (Spain) and obtained his PhD from the University of Hamburg. He joined the computing department at Goldsmiths', University of London, and later the Goldsmiths' psychology department where he is now a Professor and Co-Director of the MSc in Music, Mind and Brain. In 2016 he was awarded the prestigious Anneliese-Maier research prize by the German Humboldt foundation and since then is also affiliated with the University of Music, Drama and Media, Hannover, Germany. He is the current Editor of the open-access peer commentary journal *Empirical Musicology Review*.

Jane Oakland studied at the Guildhall School of Music in London, after which she pursued a career as an opera singer for thirty-five years. During this time she completed a master's in psychology for musicians at Sheffield University and a PhD at Glasgow Caledonian University. She is Psychology Module Lead (Performing Arts Medicine MSC) at University College London, a former practitioner and trainer with British Association of Performing Arts Medicine, and a member of the British Psychological

Society. Her research interests are concerned with understanding the nuances of a musical identity, specifically in the context of voluntary and involuntary career transition for musicians. As a performance psychologist she currently works with professional musicians on all aspects of career stress and anxiety management.

Paula M. Olszewski-Kubilius is the director of the Center for Talent Development at Northwestern University and a professor in the School of Education and Social Policy. Over the past thirty-six years, she has created programs for all kinds of gifted learners and written extensively about talent development. She has served as the editor of *Gifted Child Quarterly*, as Co-Editor of the *Journal of Secondary Gifted Education*, and on the editorial boards of *Gifted and Talented International, Roeper Review*, and *Gifted Child Today*. She is Past President of the National Association for Gifted Children and received the NAGC Distinguished Scholar Award in 2009.

Ian Pace studied at Chetham's School of Music; Queen's College, Oxford; the Juilliard School, where he was a Fulbright Scholar; and Cardiff University, where he completed his PhD on new music and its infrastructure in early occupied West Germany. He has combined parallel careers as a pianist specializing in new music and a musicologist, having held positions at the University of Southampton, Dartington College, and since 2010 at City University of London, where he is currently Reader in Music and Head of Department. He has published a monograph on Michael Finnissy's *The History of Photography in Sound*, co-edited five other books, and published many articles and book chapters on diverse subjects. As a pianist, he has played in 25 countries, given over 300 world premieres, and recorded 35 CDs. His specialist areas include nineteenth- and twentieth-century performance practice, modernist/avant-garde aesthetics, music in Germany after 1918, practice-as-research, and critical musicology.

Kelly A. Parkes studied music performance at the Australian National University before completing a second master's degree at Florida International University and a PhD at the University of Miami, Florida. She is currently Program Director and Professor of the Music and Music Education Program at Teachers College, Columbia University. Previously, as Program Leader of the Music Education program in the School of Education at Virginia Tech, she was awarded both the University Research Award for Research in Teaching and Learning and the University Teaching Award for Excellence in Teaching with Technology. She has served as Chair of the National Association for Music Education Special Research Interest Group in Assessment and served on the Editorial Board of the *Journal of Research in Music Education*. Her research interests focus on assessment in all settings, teaching and learning in the applied studio, and music teacher preparation.

Neal Peres Da Costa graduated with a BMus Hons (Class 1) at the University of Sydney before completing a Postgraduate Diploma in Early Music at the Guildhall School of Music and Drama and a Master of Music Performance at the City University in London. He was subsequently awarded a PhD from the University of Leeds. He is Associate Dean (Research) and Professor of Historical Performance at the Sydney Conservatorium of

Music, University of Sydney. Peres Da Costa is recipient of two Australian Research Council Discovery Project grants, is an Australian Recording Industry Association winner, and has an exemplary track record in traditional and non-traditional research. As a performing scholar and world-recognized authority in historical performing practice, his particular specialty is eighteenth- and nineteenth-century piano playing. He has applied data embedded in written sources and early recordings in several performance and recording projects that combine practice-led and cyclical research processes and recording emulation to reimagine interpretations of music spanning from Mozart to Brahms.

Franzis Preckel studied psychology at the University of Münster, Germany, and at the St. Norbert College in Green Bay, Wisconsin. She received a doctorate of philosophy from the University of Münster. For two years, she was head of the Counseling Center for the Gifted and Talented at the University of Munich before she became Full Professor for Giftedness Research and Education at the University of Trier, Germany. Her main research interests are intelligence and giftedness, talent development, personality factors related to achievement, and psychological assessment including test construction. Preckel has published her research in top-ranked journals including *Psychological Bulletin, Perspectives on Psychological Science, Journal of Personality and Social Psychology*, and *Intelligence*. In 2017, she received the Path Breaker Award of the AERA special interest group on Research on Giftedness, Creativity, and Talent.

Stephanie Rocke studied flute and musicology at the University of Melbourne, completing master's and doctoral degrees at Monash University. She is currently a research associate at the University of Melbourne and was a postdoctoral researcher with the Centre of Excellence for the History of Emotions. She was Secretary of the Musicological Society of Australia from 2012 to 2016 and Treasurer from 2016 to 2019. Her primary interests revolve around investigating and analyzing music-related cultural change across long time spans, particularly but not exclusively from the perspectives of emotion, secularization, and pluralism. Her most recent publications include a monograph *The Origins and Ascendancy of the Concert Mass* (Routledge 2020) and multiple chapters in a two-volume series *Opera, Emotion and the Antipodes* (Routledge 2020), of which she is also Co-Editor.

Richard M. Ryan is a Professor at the Institute for Positive Psychology and Education at Australian Catholic University. He is a clinical psychologist and co-developer of self-determination theory, with over 400 papers and books in the areas of human motivation, personality, and psychological wellbeing. He earned his PhD in clinical psychology from the University of Rochester and a BA in philosophy from the University of Connecticut. Ryan has lectured in hundreds of universities worldwide, received many distinguished career awards, held several editorial posts, consulted with numerous organizations, schools, and clinics, and served as an expert on health care and education initiatives. He is a Fellow of the American Psychological Association, the American Educational Research Association, and the Society for Self and Identity, among others, and is an Honorary Member of the German Psychological Society (DGP). He has also been a James McKeen Cattell and Leverhulme Fellow and a visiting scientist at the National Institute of Education in Singapore, the University of Bath, UK, and the Max Planck Institute, Berlin. Ryan is among the most cited and influential researchers in psychology and social sciences today, and many of his research papers have been cited in prominent media outlets such as the *New York Times, Washington Post, Huffington Post*, BBC News, and CNN.

Andrea Schiavio studied philosophy, musicology, classical guitar, and music composition in Milan, before completing a PhD in music psychology at the University of Sheffield. After his doctoral studies, he held post-doctoral positions in the United States, Turkey, and Austria. He currently works at the University of Graz, where he leads an interdisciplinary research project on musical creativity and embodied cognitive science. Schiavio serves as Vice President of ESCOM—the European Society for the Cognitive Sciences of Music. He gave keynote addresses as well as invited talks at institutions in Finland, Germany, Austria, Italy, United States, Spain, Norway, Switzerland, and Poland. His research focuses on the relationship between creative cognition and musical skill acquisition, the embodied and enactive roots of human musicality, and the development of musical expertise in early infancy.

Emery Schubert is a Professor in Music at the University of New South Wales Australia. He has held a number of fellowships, including the Australian Research Council Future Fellowship. Among his over 150 peer-reviewed publications, he has contributed a number book chapters including for the OUP volumes *Emotion in Music* (2001 and 2010) edited by Patrik Juslin and John Sloboda, as well as co-editing a volume on *Expressiveness in Music Performance*, also published by OUP. He is a foundation member of the Australian Music and Psychology Society (AMPS), serving as Secretary (until 2007) and President (2008–2009) and in 2004 he co-founded the Empirical Musicology Laboratory. He is or has been on the editorial board for nearly all the major international music psychology journals. His research specializes in the continuous response, wellbeing, and the psychology of emotion and aesthetics in music.

Brian A. Silvey has degrees in music education from Morehead State University (BME), Wichita State University (MME), and the University of Texas at Austin (PhD). He is Professor of Music Education and Director of Bands at the University of Missouri. He serves as the Editor of the National Association for Music Education journal *Update: Applications of Research in Music Education* and on the editorial board of the *College Band Directors National Association Research Journal*. He previously was Editor of the *Missouri Journal of Research in Music Education* and served on the *Journal of Research in Music Education* editorial board. His most extensive research involvement involves perceptions of conducting expressivity and effectiveness, instrumental conducting pedagogy, and novice conductor development.

Mark Slater studied music at the University of Sheffield before completing a postgraduate certificate in higher education and a PhD that focused on the relationship between composition and improvisation. He is a Senior Lecturer in Music at the University of

Hull. He has served as articles editor for the *Journal on the Art of Record Production* and has published in *Popular Music*, the *Journal of the Royal Musical Association*, and *Music Analysis* on topics relating to production, collaboration, and ontology in the digital era. As a composer and producer, his works span broad stylistic and sonic terrains. He has a particular interest in the intersections between the familiar and the unpredictable, the stable and the volatile, and between improvised spontaneity and forensic manipulation in technology-mediated collaborative contexts. His compositions and production projects have been performed, released, and broadcast internationally.

Tawnya D. Smith received a PhD in curriculum and instruction from the University of Illinois at Urbana–Champaign and a certificate of advanced graduate study in expressive arts therapy from Lesley University in Cambridge, Massachusetts. She is Assistant Professor of Music Education at Boston University and Music Area Editor for the *International Journal of Education and the Arts*. Smith has published numerous research articles and book chapters and is coauthor of the book *Performance Anxiety Strategies* and lead editor of *Narratives and Reflections in Music Education: Listening to Voices Seldom Heard*. She is an integrative researcher who explores expressive arts principles to promote holistic learning. Her background in music education has led her to experiment with free improvisation and multi-modal art response as a means for learners to explore the self in community settings. Her recent work focuses on arts integration and social justice.

Rena F. Subotnik, PhD is Director of the Center for Psychology in Schools and Education at the American Psychological Association. The Center promotes high-quality application of psychology to programs and policies for schools and education. One of the Center's missions is to generate public awareness, advocacy, clinical applications, and cutting-edge research ideas that enhance the achievement and performance of children and adolescents with gifts and talents in all domains. Subotnik has been supported in this work by the National Science Foundation, the American Psychological Foundation, the Association for Psychological Science, the Camille and Henry Dreyfus Foundation, and the Jack Kent Cooke Foundation.

Dylan van der Schyff holds master's degrees in humanities (Simon Fraser University) and music psychology (University of Sheffield). He received his PhD from Simon Fraser University in 2017. His postdoctoral work was hosted by the University of Oxford and was funded by a full fellowship from the Social Sciences and Humanities Research Council of Canada. He is currently Senior Lecturer in music at the Melbourne Conservatorium of Music, University of Melbourne. His scholarship draws on cognitive science, phenomenological philosophy, and musicology to explore questions related to how and why music is meaningful for human beings. Much of this research develops possibilities for thought and action in practical areas such as music performance and music education, with a special focus on creativity and improvisation. As a performer, he has toured extensively throughout North America and Europe, and appears on numerous recordings, spanning the fields of jazz, free improvisation, and experimental music.

Frank C. Worrell is a Professor of School Psychology in the Graduate School of Education and an Affiliate Professor in the Department of Psychology at the University of California, Berkeley. His areas of expertise include talent development, cultural identities, scale development, time perspective, and the translation of psychological research findings into practice. Worrell is a Fellow of the Association for Psychological Science, the American Educational Research Association, and the American Psychological Association (APA). He was a 2018 recipient of the Outstanding International Psychologist Award from Division 52 of APA (International Psychology) and the 2019 recipient of the Palmarium Award in Gifted Education from the Morgridge College of Education, University of Denver.

Katie Zhukov received her bachelor's of music (honours) from the Elder Conservatorium of Music, Adelaide, before completing a master's of music degree at the Juilliard School of Music, New York, and a PhD at the University of New South Wales Sydney. Prior to working at Monash University, she had been a music research fellow at the University of Queensland School of Music for eleven years. In 2019 she was the Chair of Australasian Piano Pedagogy Conference in Brisbane, and she has served on the Editorial Board of the *International Journal of Music Education*. Her publications demonstrate a strong record of interdisciplinary research across music education, psychology, and science, and include topics such as eye movement during music sight-reading, performance anxiety, skills for classical music careers, innovative approaches to teaching music sight-reading, and teaching and learning in the studio setting, including gender issues.

....

CHAPTER 1

CONTEXTUALIZING THE STUDY OF MUSIC PERFORMANCE

....

GARY E. MCPHERSON

In the years leading up to 2002, I worked with Richard Parncutt to co-edit *The Science and Psychology of Music Performance: Creative Strategies for Teaching and Learning.* The challenge we set ourselves and the authors was to produce a publication that would provide practical applications of cutting-edge research to further understand the practice of music performance. At that time, our interdisciplinary approach envisioned a music psychologist working with a music educator or practicing musician on each chapter within the volume. We wanted to produce something that was fresh and different from any other publication in the area, and a book that was unprecedented for the time in either music psychology or music education.

By the time this new compendium is published, it will have been twenty years since *The Science and Psychology of Music Performance* was released. Since that time, there have been many publications in music psychology and music education, but few focused exclusively on music performance. To fill this gap, the *Oxford Handbook of Music Performance* (OHMP) updates the 2002 publication and provides a resource that is distinctive as a result of the significant number of international experts who have contributed and the breadth of topics and issues addressed. Our aim has been to produce a resource that scholars and practitioners can use as a comprehensive overview of work within the area of music psychology and performance science.

The eighty scholars from thirteen countries who prepared the fifty-four chapters in this two-volume handbook are leaders in the fields of music psychology, performance science, musicology, psychology, education, music medicine, science, and music education. They include academics who hold prominent positions in music institutions worldwide, emerging early careers researchers who have begun to make their mark through publications of international stature, and leaders outside the field of music whose work deserves to be adapted, understood, and applied within the field of music performance.

I hope that readers will agree that this unique combination of authorities has resulted in a publication of real significance and impact that will stand the test of time.

Many of the chapters in the OHMP are focused on "classical" music partly because most literature currently available focuses on this genre of performance and because it represents how music performance is often taught in many formal institutions around the world. Musicians and music students will find many specific recommendations and understandings of issues related specifically to pursuing careers and experiencing music in this tradition. But many of the chapters and the ideas contained within them clearly extend and apply well to other genres, including traditional music, jazz, as well as popular and folk music, speaking to the universality of music and the experience of becoming a musician or music performer regardless of the musical tradition itself.

Chapters in the OHMP provide a broad coverage of the area with considerable expansion of the topics that most would normally expect to be covered in a resource of this type. In this way, the range and scope of the content is much wider than other publications by virtue of the inclusion of chapters from related disciplines such as performance science (e.g., optimizing performance, mental techniques, talent development in non-music areas) and education (e.g., human development, motivation, learning and teaching styles), as well as the attention given to emerging critical issues in the field (e.g., wellbeing, technology, gender, diversity, inclusion, identity, resilience and buoyancy, diseases, and physical and mental disabilities).

Within all chapters of this handbook, authors have selected what they consider to be the most important scientific and artistic material relevant to their topic. The authors begin their chapters by surveying theoretical views on each topic and then, in the final part of the chapter, highlight practical implications of the literature that performers will be able to apply within their daily musical lives.

The book is intended for a range of different types of readers. It is aimed primarily for practicing musicians, particularly those who are preparing for a professional career as performers and are interested in practical implications of psychological and scientific research for their own music performance development. The second target group comprises educators with a specific interest or expertise in music psychology, who will wish to apply the concepts and techniques surveyed in their own teaching. The third group consists of advanced undergraduate and postgraduate students, particularly those starting to specialize in music performance science who understand the potential of music psychology for informing music education, and vice versa. Last but not least, we are writing for researchers in the area of music performance who consider it important for the results of their research to be practically useful for musicians and music educators. To aid each group of readers, all chapters include up to five key sources for readers who want to broaden their reading on the topic, and five reflective questions that aim to help focus attention on how the concepts surveyed are useful when applied in various practical ways. In that sense, we are hoping that musicians, music educators, music psychologists, and others may benefit from a broader perspective that goes beyond their own particular area of expertise.

The OHMP was designed around eight distinct parts. Volume 1 is subdivided into parts for Development and Learning, Proficiencies, Performance Practices, and

Psychology. Volume 2 covers Enhancements, Health and Wellbeing, Science, and Innovations.

As the title suggestions, the opening part—Development and Learning—opens with four chapters that cover the origins of musical expertise, music potential, readiness to start learning an instrument or voice, and more broadly, a framework for conceptualizing talent development in the domain of music. This part is rounded off with two chapters dealing with learning strategies; the first from a self-directed student learning perspective and the second dealing with high-impact teaching mindframes.

Part II—Proficiencies—covers some of the most essential competencies involved in efficient music performance from effective practice habits, through to the abilities of being able to play by ear, sight-read, improvise, memorize repertoire, and conduct. Moreover, this part includes a chapter that details the highly personalized forms of musical expression that go beyond the printed notation or stylistic convention of the repertoire being performed. The last chapter in this part deals with the central role of body movement in the production and perception of musical performance.

The first three chapters of Part III—Performance Practices—cover some of the most fundamental aspects of performance practices from Baroque through to New Music repertoire. In these chapters the authors stress that knowledge of these genres relies largely on written documents. Consequently, performers today, as they have in the past, will inevitably interpret works across these periods with the aesthetic preferences of their own time. Because there are often no definitive appropriate interpretations, performers are encouraged to study the original historical sources as a means of developing their own understanding of the repertoire and how it might be performed. The part continues with a chapter dealing with how emotions—both felt and portrayed— might be generated as a form of historically informed performance practice, while another chapter focuses on how creativity unfolds in the real-time dynamics of musical performance. A sixth chapter situates performance within the technological trappings of the studio and its associated social and musical processes, and the seventh and final chapter of the part explores music performance in terms of power, marginalization, inclusiveness, and empowerment, to provide a way for classical music stakeholders to envision new possibilities for music learning and performance.

Part IV—Psychology—concerns characteristics and individual differences in human behavior, cognition, emotion, and wellness. These features of the human condition are relevant for expertise in any domain, but they are particularly intertwined with the phenomenon of music itself. The "why" of music is explored in chapters on why people experience and perform music, how individuals sustain the difficult work required to become musicians (motivation), and how they experience their relationships with music and the social role of being a musician (identity). The "how" of music is addressed by chapters on how musicians can regulate their practice and rehearsal behavior to best develop and refine their performance abilities (self-regulated learning), and how musicians respond to setbacks, adversity, and change (buoyancy, resilience, and adaptability). A key theme in psychology that is relevant to music performance is personality, and the study of personality and other features that are common to musicians, different between musicians, and that change over time. These topics are addressed in a general review (individual differences), as well as a close examination of a particularly inter-esting neurological condition that occurs much more frequently in musicians than in the general population (synesthesia). Across these chapters, several common threads and themes are evident: our relationships with music itself and what it means to become and to be a musician, the tensions that can arise between the joy of music and the hard work required to develop musical skills, and the intimate connection between music performance and our social and emotional lives.

Part V—Enhancements—covers the popular Feldenkrais method and Alexander technique, and how these experiential learning processes that employ movement and guided attention can be used to develop and refine self-awareness to either re-educate or develop one's awareness of body and self to perform in a more relaxed, effortless manner. These lead to chapters titled "Peak Performance" and "Mindfulness," which cover, from two different perspectives, the psychological skills of goal setting, arousal regulation, concentration, and imagery. A chapter titled "Stage Behavior, Impression Management, and Charisma," plus another covering "Enhancing Music Performance Appraisal," provide a wealth of information on the need for performers to be aware of how to model their playing to provide enhanced, persuasive performances and ensure their performances are well received and appreciated by others. All of these chapters are about building a career and the skills and competencies needed to be successful. The complexity surrounding the ways in which performance careers are defined, developed, and sustained forms the basis of the last chapter in this part—"Creating Sustainable Performance Careers"—which provides a discussion on the elements and contexts that impact on musicians' experiences as they attempt to forge a career in musical perfor-mance and explore ways in which the transition into professional life can be smoothed and optimized.

No handbook of this type would be complete without a part dealing with health and wellbeing within the context of music performance. For this reason, Part VI—Health and Wellbeing—outlines the brain mechanisms involved in music learning and performing as the foundation for the following chapters dealing with musical ac-tivities in people with disabilities, performance anxiety, disease and health risks in instrumentalists, hearing and voice, and finally, a discussion of how to promote a healthy related lifestyle. Authors within this part are eminently qualified, with either medical or clinical psychology qualifications, in addition to their musical qualifications. Together, they provide a unique perspective on these fundamentally important topics.

Part VII—Science—contains material that may be less familiar to musicians, drawing upon the scientific literature of musical acoustics. The first six chapters cover the basic science underlying the operation of wind, brass, and string instruments, and the piano. They also summarize what science has to say about the player-instrument interactions in these instruments, ranging from embouchure to string choice to the physiology and psychology of piano fingering. The two chapters that follow cover the solo voice and vocal ensembles. They describe the anatomical and physiological background of the vocal mechanism, as well as the impact of room and stage design, reflectors, and the deployment of sound equipment to control the sound in choirs. The chapter on instrumental ensembles extends these descriptions with comments on the creative challenges facing ensemble musicians, the psychological mechanisms underpinning coordination among players, the anticipatory and reactive processes involved when performing in an ensemble, and the attentional strategies that allow performers to move between effortful and automatic levels of coordination. The penultimate chapter explains digital musical instruments in terms of the design of computer-based technologies in commonly used electronic synthesizers. The final chapter focuses on motion capture, and the practical issues that researchers and performers face when studying movement during musical performances using this rapidly developing technology.

The four chapters in Part VIII—Innovations—address the types of technological and social and wellbeing innovations that are reshaping how musicians conceive their performances in the twenty-first century. Advances in synchronous online learning, teaching, and performance, as well as the types of technology that can enhance the learning of performance, are described in the first half, while the final two chapters in the part cover the types of interdisciplinary experiential learning and rethinking of musicians' wellbeing that are exerting a profound impact on contemporary practice.

In the past thirty years, scientific interest in music psychology and performance science has thrived, with empirical research generating a wealth of new information that clarifies, enhances, explains, and sometimes even contradicts many aspects of performing music. Although in many areas there is still a rainbow of ideas and explanations, researchers are beginning to more fully illuminate elements of performance that have rarely if ever been discussed in training programs aimed at developing elite-level music performers. We are on the cusp of huge advances in our understandings of how musicians develop their art, and this handbook aims to foster even greater interest in our rapidly evolving discipline.

It is my hope, and that of the authors who have contributed to the OHMP, that our work will help move us closer to understanding the nature and scope of music performance in a way that satisfies both scientists who want robust, empirically validated evidence, and practical musicians and teachers of music performance who want clear, easy-to-digest explanations of the many and varied processes related to refining expertise in music performance.

It is my hope also that in the years to come, readers will enjoy reading and applying the concepts and ideas suggested in each chapter of this new publication.

Gary E. McPherson
June 2021

PART I

DEVELOPMENT AND LEARNING

CHAPTER 2

THE ORIGINS OF MUSICAL EXPERTISE

ALEXANDER P. BURGOYNE, DAVID Z. HAMBRICK, AND LAUREN JULIUS HARRIS

"I have wept only three times in my life: the first time when my earliest opera failed, the second time when, with a boating party, a truffled turkey fell into the water, and the third time when I first heard Paganini play."
—Gioachino Rossini (quoted in Amis & Rose, 1992, p. 175)

NATURE VS. NURTURE

ROSSINI's weeping over a lost turkey sounds like a joke—and may well have been—although as is well known, after retiring from opera composing at age thirty-seven, he devoted the last thirty-nine years of his life to culinary and other pleasures. His remark about Paganini, however, was surely no joke: others were no less astonished whenever they heard him play. For many, he was and remains the personification and mystery of the "expert," someone whose skill seems to defy explanation.

With prodigies as the most extreme example, some people acquire musical skill much faster than others and attain a higher level of performance. What accounts for this variability? Could anyone, given the right conditions, reach a level of skill necessary to play for a first-rank orchestra? As a more extreme example, could anyone compose a masterpiece of the kind that Mozart wrote, or play the piano like Vladimir Horowitz? Or did these extraordinary musicians already have traits that facilitated their pursuit of excellence and set them apart from the rest?

The perennial debate in the psychology of expertise is whether experts are born or made. That is, to what extent do *nature* (hereditary and constitutional factors) and *nurture* (the totality of environmental factors) contribute to expertise? We define *expertise* here as a person's level of performance in a task (Macnamara, Hambrick, Frank, King, Burgoyne, & Meinz, 2018). Some have argued for a strict environmentalist view, suggesting that virtually anyone can become highly skilled in a domain with enough practice. Others, while acknowledging the importance of practice, argue that heritable individual differences—talents, proclivities, and predispositions—make expertise more attainable for some than for others (for a discussion, see Hambrick, Burgoyne, Macnamara, & Ullén, 2018). The debate was ignited by the publication of Francis Galton's *Hereditary Genius* (1869) over 150 years ago and has raged on ever since.

For this chapter on the origins of musical expertise, rather than champion any one class of factors, we favor a multifactorial approach. As advances in behavioral genetics have shown, nature and nurture are not independent (Plomin, 2017). Genetic and environmental factors are entwined, and it is their joint product that gives rise to expertise. Heritable traits such as height, intelligence, and personality are influenced by one's environment, and in music as in other domains, many environmental factors are influenced by genetics. For instance, children genetically predisposed to grow tall will not do so without adequate nutrition. Likewise, evidence indicates that musicians' genetic makeup will influence their propensity to practice and the amount of skill they acquire (Mosing, Madison, Pedersen, Kuja-Halkola, & Ullén, 2014a).

Practice

> "There is nothing remarkable about it. All you have to do is hit the right notes at the right time, and the instrument plays itself."
> —J. S. Bach (quoted in Amis & Rose, 1992, p. 186)

Among the environmental factors contributing to musical expertise, no one can reasonably doubt the importance of practice. We are not born knowing how to play the A harmonic minor scale on the euphonium, a six-stroke roll on the drums, or an organ cantata with the requisite speed, accuracy, and style. We therefore need not take seriously Bach's droll remark opening this section; like any musician, he had to practice hitting the right notes at the right time.

Nevertheless, some musicians practice far more than others. One of the most surprising discoveries from recent music research is that the propensity to practice has strong genetic underpinnings. This finding comes from a study of 10,500 identical and fraternal Swedish twins (Mosing et al., 2014a). Twin studies allow researchers to investigate the contribution of genes to between-person variation in a *phenotype* (i.e., observed characteristic) because identical twins share 100 percent of their genes, whereas fraternal twins share only 50 percent, on average. The extent to which identical twins are more similar than fraternal twins for a given trait indicates its degree of heritability. The results of the twin study revealed that the propensity to practice is substantially heritable, with genetic effects accounting for approximately half the variance across individuals. Thus, variation in what many consider a purely environmental factor underlying expertise—practice—is influenced by heritable characteristics.

The story gets more complicated, however, because some musicians require less practice than others to reach an equivalent level of skill. Stated differently, given the same amount of practice, individuals will attain different levels of expertise. As a case in point, we recently examined individual differences in the early stages of learning to play the piano (Burgoyne, Harris, & Hambrick, 2019). We had 161 undergraduates with little or no experience spend 12 minutes with a digital piano while they watched an animated video lesson on how to play "Happy Birthday," displayed on a computer monitor above the piano. Their task was to perform the 25-note song from memory, using the practice time however they wished. We tested them prior to practice (pre-test), halfway through practice (mid-test), and after practice (post-test). Three graduate students in piano performance rated the performances based on their melodic and rhythmic accuracy.

The results revealed striking differences in the students' skill acquisition trajectories, as shown in Figure 2.1. Some learned quickly, earning perfect marks within the first 6 minutes of practice. Others performed poorly in the early stages but improved substantially from mid-test to post-test. By contrast, a few seemed to fade from mid-test to post-test as if they had lost their motivation. And some never improved, performing poorly throughout the practice session.

What could explain this variability in skill acquisition? Anticipating this question, we also gave the students tests of *cognitive ability* (e.g., tests of reasoning, perceptual speed,

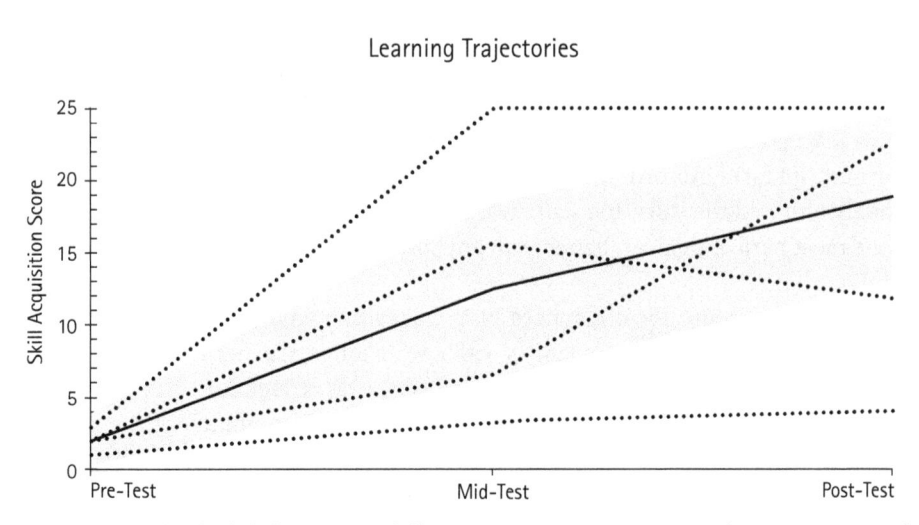

FIGURE 2.1. Individual differences in skill acquisition over 12 minutes of piano practice. The solid line represents the mean skill acquisition trajectory of 161 students. The shaded region represents one standard deviation above and below the mean. The dotted lines represent four students selected for comparison.

working memory, and word knowledge), *music aptitude* (e.g., on listening tests, are two melodies the same or different?), and *non-ability factors* (e.g., growth mindset).

We found that cognitive ability and music aptitude significantly predicted individual differences in skill acquisition. Students with more cognitive ability and better auditory discrimination skills performed better after practice than those with lesser abilities. *Growth mindset*, reflecting whether students believed they could improve their music ability, did not predict performance. This is perhaps unsurprising; as popular as growth mindset has been in the educational sphere, its effects appear to be overstated and its impact on achievement is weak (Burgoyne, Hambrick, & Macnamara, 2020; Sisk, Burgoyne, Sun, Butler, & Macnamara, 2018).

Our study, however, examined only the earliest stage of skill acquisition. Although early success or failure on an instrument might be a formative experience, to what extent will these results generalize to higher-skill musicians? For example, if our students had been musically trained and were auditioning for admission to a music school, one might expect that higher-order skills such as musicality would be more important. (For further discussion on the importance of practice, see Miksza, this volume).

SIGHT-READING

Along with practice, sight-reading has long been valued for rapid, efficient preparation, and before composer-performers like Mendelssohn and Clara Schumann began the tradition of publicly performing what we now call "repertoire," new scores were sight-read, and extensive rehearsing was uncommon (Lehmann & McArthur, 2002, p. 138). Certain performers, Franz Liszt perhaps most famously, were known to be remarkable sight-readers. Among the many accounts attesting to his skill is Mendelssohn's description of how Liszt played his, that is, Mendelssohn's, Piano Concerto in G Minor when still in manuscript form. According to conductor and composer Ferdinand Hiller, to whom Mendelssohn told the story, the score was hardly legible, but Liszt "played it at sight . . . in the most perfect manner, better than anybody else could play it" (Schonberg, 1963, p. 165).

What could account for differences in sight-reading among skilled musicians? To find out, we studied fifty-seven pianists with a wide range of experience practicing and performing (Meinz & Hambrick, 2010). Their task was straightforward: to play three pieces of unfamiliar music after reviewing each for only one minute. Each piece was 12–16 measures long. Following each attempt, they were given another minute to review before playing the piece again. This format is often used in auditions for university music programs. Two university piano teachers rated the performances based on their technical proficiency, musicality, and overall quality.

The strongest predictor of sight-reading performance was accumulated hours of what Ericsson and colleagues call *deliberate practice* (Ericsson, Krampe, & Tesch-Römer,

1993). The definition of deliberate practice, however, has shifted throughout the years, posing issues for the falsifiability of Ericsson and colleagues' theory (see Macnamara et al., 2018). For example, Ericsson has sometimes argued that deliberate practice must be designed by a teacher (e.g., Ericsson & Lehmann, 1996; Ericsson, 2020) but other times has stated that it can be designed by a teacher or by "performers themselves" (e.g., Ericsson, 1998, p. 84). (For an account of the variety of definitions of deliberate practice, see the presentation on the Open Science Framework: https://osf.io/buqsk/.) This issue aside, deliberate practice can broadly be thought of as practice activities that are designed (by someone) to improve performance, require concentration, incorporate immediate feedback, and are not inherently enjoyable. In general, deliberate practice and other experiential factors such as years of piano lessons positively correlated with performance. However, a measure of cognitive ability, *working memory capacity*, also positively predicted performance, even after accounting for deliberate practice. This suggests that given two musicians with equivalent amounts of deliberate practice, the one with greater working memory would outperform the other. *Working memory capacity* refers to one's ability to keep goal-relevant information in an active state and is often conceptualized as one's "mental workspace" (Logie, 2003). It could play a role in sight-reading because while pianists look at the score, they must keep track of upcoming notes so that their hands are in position to play what comes next. Those with greater working memory capacity could keep larger "chunks" of the score in mind with each look, allowing them to direct their eyes and attention elsewhere as needed (Meinz & Hambrick, 2010).

PRACTICE (REPRISE)

In two studies we have shown that individual differences in musical expertise cannot fully be explained by training. Obviously practice is important, but how important is it? Practice effects can be evaluated from two perspectives. The first is *intra-individual*: how much does practice help a musician improve? The second is *inter-individual*: how much does practice account for differences in skill across individuals? We focus on the latter question here.

Nearly thirty years ago, Ericsson, Krampe, and Tesch-Römer (1993) claimed that individual differences in skill could "largely be accounted for by differential amounts of past and current levels of practice" (p. 392). Today, we know this claim is likely false. As a case in point, we conducted a *meta-analysis* (i.e., a quantitative synthesis of studies) to determine how much practice accounts for individual differences in performance in music, games, and sports (Macnamara, Hambrick, & Oswald, 2014; see also the 2018 corrigendum to this study). We surveyed the literature and found sixteen music studies with a total of 1,259 participants. Averaging across studies, deliberate practice correlated with musical skill but accounted for only about one-quarter of the variance (23%) across individuals. Stated differently, practice *did not* largely account for individual differences in skill; it left over half the variance unexplained, and this was true even after liberal corrections for the unreliability of the measures. The results were similar for games (24%) and sports (20%).

As we stated in a commentary (Hambrick, Altmann, Oswald, Meinz, & Gobet, 2014), "The bottom line is that, in all major domains in which deliberate practice has been studied, most of the variance in performance is explained by factors other than deliberate practice (Macnamara et al., 2014). These factors may include starting age (Gobet & Campitelli, 2007), working memory capacity (Meinz & Hambrick, 2010), and genes (Hambrick & Tucker-Drob, 2014)" (p. 2). Results from other studies support this conclusion. Most notably, in their own meta-analysis of music studies, Platz, Kopiez, Lehmann, and Wolf (2014) found that deliberate practice explained 37 percent of the reliable variance in music achievement (i.e., corrected meta-analytic $r = .61$), leaving 63 percent unexplained. Platz et al. declared that this estimate should be regarded as a "theoretically lower bound of the true effect of DP [deliberate practice]" (p. 11), given that retrospective estimates of deliberate practice may be inaccurate. However, as pointed out in our response to Platz et al. (Hambrick et al., 2014), this estimate could just as well be regarded as an *upper bound* on the true effect of deliberate practice. For example, using retrospective estimates of deliberate practice could lead to inflated correlations between deliberate practice and performance if people base practice estimates on their skill rather than accurate recollections of practice activity. In short, the available evidence indicates that deliberate practice is an important piece of the expertise puzzle, but it is neither the only piece, nor necessarily the largest. What else might contribute?

Intelligence

Just over a century ago, Seashore (1919) argued that intelligence is critical for musical greatness: "It is possible for a person, strong in other capacities, but with relatively low intellectual power, to assume fairly important roles in music within restricted fields of activity; but the great musician is always a person of great intellect" (p. 253). By *intelligence*, we mean "a very general mental capability that, among other things, involves the ability to reason, plan, solve problems, think abstractly, comprehend complex ideas, learn quickly and learn from experience" (Gottfredson, 1997, p. 13). Although often treated as a single factor, this definition shows that intelligence includes a number of different cognitive abilities.

Each of these cognitive ability factors may contribute to musical skill acquisition and performance (see, e.g., Gagné & McPherson, 2016). For instance, we have already discussed how individual differences in working memory capacity predicted sight-reading performance in one of our studies, and how cognitive ability predicted beginners' skill acquisition in another. Perceptual speed has also been implicated in sight-reading (Kopiez & Lee, 2008). Because sight-reading is a fast-paced task, musicians with greater *perceptual speed*—those quicker to perceive and respond to information in their environment—have an advantage. Another factor to consider is *reasoning ability*. It refers to the ability to recognize patterns and solve novel problems, and it has been found to predict students' music achievement (Ruthsatz, Detterman, Griscom, & Cirullo, 2008). Conceivably, greater reasoning ability helps students solve the problem of learning their instrument and applying their knowledge to new challenges. Although few studies have examined the cognitive abilities of expert musicians, studies of young students have reliably found that individual differences in cognitive ability predict individual differences in musical skill acquisition (e.g., Hufstader, 1974; Klinedinst, 1991; McCarthy, 1980).

We also know, however, that musicians face selection processes early in their careers that might make individual differences in cognitive ability more consequential. For example, high school students typically earn a chair position (e.g., principal violinist) based on their skill relative to their peers, which in turn might dictate the difficulty of the parts they are assigned, whether they are given solos, and the amount of attention they receive from the conductor. After graduation, admission to a music program will depend in part on their expertise relative to other applicants. Because cognitive ability exerts a strong influence early in training, more intelligent music students are more likely to be selected for greater opportunities, which leads to a self-reinforcing feedback loop of favorable outcomes for the student.

The contribution of intelligence to achievement extends beyond the musical domain. In non-music professions, cognitive ability is the single best predictor of performance within one's chosen job (Schmidt & Hunter, 2004). Moreover, its effects on performance are mitigated only slightly by job experience, if at all (Hambrick, Burgoyne, & Oswald, 2019). People with greater cognitive ability will still have an advantage years after taking up a domain.

Music Aptitude

Another factor that may play a role in developing expertise is *music aptitude*. The term has been defined in different ways. Seashore (1960) and others have defined it as one's potential for auditory sensory discrimination (Seashore, 1960). Although music aptitude tests appear to measure basic perceptual abilities, some researchers have argued that differences in basic abilities might have important consequences for higher-order musical skills. For example, referring to his measure of music aptitude, Gordon (1989) stated: "Audiation leads to understanding" (p. 19). Music aptitude has also been defined as a measure of an individual's "innate capacity for musical success" (p. 2, Harrison, Collins, & Müllensiefen, 2017; see also McPherson, Blackwell, & Hallam, this part).

In one popular test, the Advanced Measures of Music Audiation (Gordon, 1989), listeners are presented two melodies and must determine whether they are the same or different in tone or rhythm. As another example, the Swedish Music Discrimination Test (Ullén, Mosing, Holm, Eriksson, & Madison, 2014) includes melody, rhythm, and tonal subtests. Tests of music aptitude often use auditory stimuli that are stripped of musical meaning so that less acquired knowledge can be brought to bear on the task (Gembris, 1997; Mishra, 2014).

Melodic, rhythmic, and tonal aptitudes are correlated with one another and with general intelligence (McGrew, 2009; Mosing, Pedersen, Madison, & Ullén, 2014b). We have found that students who performed well on the melody subtest of the Swedish Music Discrimination Test also performed well on the rhythm and tonal subtests (Burgoyne et al., 2019). But despite these relationships, individuals can still have specific strengths, with possible consequences for specialization. For example, a musician who excels at rhythmic auditory discrimination may be better suited for percussion than strings. Of course, melodic and tonal aptitudes are still important for percussionists (e.g., playing the vibraphone or tuning marching tenor drums), and a musician with well-rounded auditory abilities will benefit from them. Music aptitude also correlates with measures of working memory capacity (Burgoyne et al., 2019). Because music aptitude tests require listeners to keep in mind and compare two stimuli, these tests tap domain-general working memory in addition to domain-specific auditory ability.

Music aptitude is related to music achievement in elementary school students, fifth and sixth graders, high school band members, and university wind players, although the correlations are typically small to moderate in size (Froseth, 1971; Hayward & Gromko, 2009; Ruthsatz et al., 2008; Schleuter, 1978). Fewer studies have examined music aptitude in highly skilled musicians. Music aptitude also predicts sight-reading accuracy, but this may be because music aptitude correlates with general intelligence and experience; these third-variable explanations have not been ruled out (Mishra, 2014).

One interesting finding is that the perceptual abilities measured by tests of music aptitude are difficult to improve with training. Perhaps the most compelling evidence comes from the study of Swedish twins cited previously (Mosing et al., 2014a). Along with showing that the propensity to practice is partly heritable, it revealed that music aptitude is influenced by genetic effects. Furthermore, once genetic and shared environmental influences were accounted for within a twin pair, the twin who practiced more did not have better music aptitude than the twin who practiced less. In one case the twins differed by over 20,000 hours of music practice, roughly equivalent to three hours per day, every day, over nineteen years!

Despite their frequent use, tests of music aptitude are not without their critics. This may be because musicality is multifaceted, yet music aptitude ostensibly captures only basic sensory discrimination abilities. As Gembris (1997) stated, tests of music aptitude "are very reductionistic and restrict themselves to measure only a few receptive aspects of musicality" (p. 20). Indeed, these tests do not capture many attributes important for musicianship and expertise, such as "musical responsiveness, creative and re-creative abilities, and musical interests and motivation" (p. 20). In the next section, we discuss a relatively new construct that has been developed to capture some of these untapped facets of musicality, namely, *musical sophistication*.

MUSICAL SOPHISTICATION

Musical sophistication refers to one's "ability to engage with music in a flexible, effective and nuanced way" (gold.ac.uk/music-mind-brain/gold-msi). One measure of it is the Goldsmiths Musical Sophistication Index (Gold-MSI; Müllensiefen, Gingras, Musil, & Stewart, 2014), which consists of listening tests and a self-report questionnaire on perceptual abilities, singing abilities, musical training, active engagement, and emotional engagement with music. The Gold-MSI has high test-retest reliability and demonstrates moderate to strong correlations with music aptitude, openness to aesthetics, and musician vs. non-musician status (Greenberg, Müllensiefen, Lamb, & Rentfrow, 2015; Müllensiefen et al., 2014).

Using unpublished data from our study of novices' piano skill acquisition (Burgoyne et al., 2019), we found that musical sophistication correlated significantly with piano performance after 12 minutes of practice ($r = .34$). It also explained 6.1 percent of the variance in piano skill acquisition after accounting for music aptitude, suggesting that the predictive validity of musical sophistication was not driven entirely by perceptual abilities tapped by the construct.

MOTIVATION

All musicians will probably agree that motivation is important in the pursuit of expertise. As the psychologist Ellen Winner (2000) said of the gifted young musicians and artists she studied, they all display a "rage to master" (p. 163) and a "deep intrinsic motivation to master the domain in which they have high ability" (p. 162).

Research by Elliot and colleagues also points to distinct *achievement goal orientations*, reflecting differences in how individuals interpret, experience, and behave in pursuit of their goals (Elliot & Church, 1997; Elliot & McGregor, 2001). Competence is central to this achievement goal framework. Musicians with *mastery goals* are intrinsically motivated to develop intrapersonal competency (i.e., improvement relative to oneself), whereas those with *performance goals* are extrinsically motivated toward normative competency (i.e., superior ability relative to others). A further distinction concerns the positive or negative valence of the musician's goal pursuit. For example, musicians with *mastery-approach goals* seek to improve their abilities, whereas those with *mastery-avoidance goals* do not want to regress. On the other hand, musicians with *performance-approach goals* seek to demonstrate their ability relative to others, whereas those with *performance-avoidance goals* are driven to avoid performing poorly.

Committed musicians may find that they strongly endorse all four goals. For example, fear of failure (a performance-avoidance goal) might motivate many students to practice intensively before auditioning for a music school. Once admitted, a desire to outperform their peers (a performance-approach goal) might lead them to spend long hours in the practice room. And, after reaching a stable point in their careers, mastery-approach goals might drive them to learn new styles of music, even those unrelated to their performance repertoire, to broaden their musical horizons. By contrast, mastery-avoidance goals might drive them to continue practicing so as not to lose ability in their later years.

Research shows that musicians' goals are linked to their ensemble commitment, practice behaviors, and achievement. For example, Miksza, Tan, and Dye (2016) found that among band students in the United States and Singapore, mastery goals correlated significantly with commitment to band. In another study, Miksza (2009) found that mastery goals (but not performance goals) correlated with etude performance achievement over the course of three 25-minute practice sessions. Furthermore, musicians who strongly endorsed mastery goals were more likely to focus on critical sections of the piece during their practice sessions.

Performance goal orientations can have maladaptive consequences. For instance, a student with performance-avoidance goals may shy away from challenges to avoid failure, but as a result, miss opportunities to learn new skills. This may explain why some students seem to practice only what they already play well. In practice, working on weaknesses is an effective way to improve one's abilities. Performance-approach goals can also have negative consequences; individuals strongly motivated by performance-approach goals but not given opportunities to showcase their ability may lose interest in developing expertise.

There are, of course, exceptions: the great pianist Van Cliburn provides a notable example. His spectacular early success in winning the Tchaikovsky Competition in Moscow in 1958—for the finale, he played Tchaikovsky's Piano Concerto No. 1 and Rachmaninoff's Piano Concerto No. 3—brought him instant fame, but after that, audiences wanted to hear him perform only those and other works from the Romantic repertoire. He obliged, and as a result, his repertoire remained narrow over the course of his career. When asked why he played the same pieces all the time, he countered, "In classical music, there is no such thing as a twice-told tale" (quoted by Vittes, 2017).

STARTING AGE

To acquire any motor or cognitive skill, early is generally better, whether one starts as a child or an adult (Noble, Baker, & Jones, 1964; Voelcker-Rehage, 2008). Many accomplished musicians began their studies when very young. Mozart is among the most prominent examples. He began picking out tunes on the clavier when he was only about three, apparently inspired by watching Nannerl (Maria Anna), his seven-year-old sister, taking lessons from their father, Leopold (Solomon, 1995, p. 38). He spent "endless hours at the keyboard, particularly delighting in 'picking out thirds and sounding them'" (p. 38). By age four, he was using Nannerl's music book of minuets and other short pieces arranged by Leopold in progressive order of difficulty, and within a few weeks, his own compositions were entered into the book.

There are several reasons why starting early could be beneficial for developing expertise. In this section, we discuss two of them: first, the brain is especially malleable during childhood, with evidence suggesting that early musical experiences can have lasting effects on brain function; and second, the earlier one starts, the more time there is to sample instruments and practice before selection processes take effect.

Psychologists have long been interested in critical periods for the acquisition of various skills, that is, whether certain skills can be acquired only before a certain age. The hypothesis rests on the premise that beyond that age, the brain's period of malleability, its "window of time," has passed. A weaker version of the hypothesis holds that because malleability declines with age, the "window" remains open but learning is more difficult. Today, we know there are critical periods for aspects of visual functioning and language acquisition (Hensch, 2005; Johnson & Newport, 1989).

There also appears to be a critical period for the acquisition of *absolute pitch*—the ability to identify or produce a given pitch without an external referent (Gervain et al., 2013; Takeuchi & Hulse, 1993). Absolute pitch is rare; it has an estimated prevalence of .01 percent in the general population (Takeuchi & Hulse, 1993), but it is somewhat more common (~9%) among university music students (Gregersen, Kowalsky, Kohn, & Marvin, 1999). Evidence suggests that people who possess absolute pitch typically begin formal music training early, at or before age seven (Levitin & Zatorre, 2003), and those who start later than age nine are increasingly unlikely to develop it (Levitin & Rogers, 2005). Keenan, Thangaraj, Halpern, and Schlaug (2001) found that among musicians with absolute pitch, asymmetry in the planum temporale, a region just posterior to the auditory cortex, was more asymmetric (larger on the left than the right) than in musicians without absolute pitch. This suggests that early musical experiences can have lasting effects on brain function.

This point is supported by a landmark study of string players that compared representations of digits (fingers and thumbs) in the *somatosensory cortex* (responsible for processing sensory information) between musicians who started practicing at different ages and non-musicians (Elbert, Pantev, Wienbruch, Rockstroh, & Taub, 1995). Magnetic source imaging was used to measure the size and strength of their cortical response to stimulation of digits on the left and right hands. Compared with non-musicians, string players showed enhanced activity in response to stimulation of left-hand digits (used for fingering the strings) but not right-hand digits. The strength of the response was greater for those who started practicing at an earlier age, but it was unrelated to overall amount of practice. Thus, the effects of early musical experiences on cortical organization were not made up for by later practice. Because left-hand digital dexterity and tactile sensitivity are critical for string players, this difference in brain function could be adaptive for music making. Since this early study, there have been many further demonstrations of the effects of musical training on the development of auditory cortical-evoked fields. For young children, even a single year of training can make a difference (Fujioka, Ross, Kakigi, Pantev, & Trainor, 2006).

Generally speaking, aspiring musicians report being heavily influenced by their childhood environment. As Igor Stravinsky recounted: "I was brought up in an atmosphere of musical achievement, and inherited a natural capacity for transmitting my feelings into music and a keen interest in the study of technique" (Gramophone, 1934).

Further support for the importance of the childhood environment is provided by a study investigating the relationship between enrichment in childhood and music achievement in over 6,000 twins (Wesseldijk, Mosing, & Ullén, 2019). Music enrichment was measured by the number of records in the home, the number of family members who played an instrument, the frequency of concert visits, and music education before age twelve. Participants reported their level of music achievement, with responses ranging from *not at all engaged in the domain* to *award-winning professional*. Childhood musical enrichment proved to be a major predictor of achievement. Enrichment also *amplified* individual differences in achievement, mainly due to an increase in genetic effects. This result is consistent with the idea that early musical experiences allowed for the activation of genetic predispositions favorable to music achievement.

Starting early also lets students acquire more experience before selection processes take effect. Musicians can practice only so many hours per day without risking injury. Simply put, musicians who start practicing when young can accumulate more hours of practice than musicians who start at a later age. Starting young also allows students to try different instruments and find one that best suits their strengths and interests before specializing. Mozart, for example, started on the clavier but by age six had taught himself to play the violin (Solomon, 1995, p. 39). The keyboard, however, remained his favorite. Taken together, these advantages could have a substantial impact on the opportunities young musicians receive. For example, they might garner positive attention from competition judges, teachers, and local directors who wish to feature them as performers. As discussed in the section on intelligence, this self-reinforcing cycle of opportunity paves the way for developing musical expertise.

PERSEVERANCE

The road to musical expertise is long and filled with setbacks. Perseverance, resilience, and determination are important personality traits for aspiring musicians as they are for most anyone wanting to achieve mastery in a domain. These personality traits may be especially important when performers are met with failure, challenges, or plateaus in progress, and must decide whether to continue pursuing their goal.

There are many examples of perseverance in musicians, with some of the most notable stemming from their injuries or illnesses. One prominent example is the Russian composer and pianist Alexander Scriabin. At age twenty, he suffered an overuse injury of his right hand while trying to improve the sound quality of his touch at the piano. The pain endured throughout his career, but he continued to play, and in his compositions, he incorporated unusual and virtuosic use of the left hand (Altenmüller, 2015). For the American pianist Leon Fleisher, one of the more remarkable child prodigies in musical history, the challenge was perhaps even greater. At age thirty-six, he lost all use of his right hand due to focal task-specific dystonia. He too persevered, performing the left-hand literature, conducting, commissioning, and performing new works for the left hand, and never ceasing in his search for a cure. Finally, decades later, he was able to play with both hands after treatment with botulinum toxin (Botox) injections. He continued to perform up to his death at age ninety-two (Brubach, 2007; Frucht, 2009). One last example, this one of perseverance beyond all measure, is Beethoven. In his letter to his brothers Carl and Johann, written in 1802 at age thirty-two, he told of his sorrow in realizing that his deafness might keep him from realizing his profoundest ambitions. The letter ("The Heiligenstadt Testament") has been called, with good reason, "one of the most tragic documents in the history of music" (Amis & Rose, 1989, p. 378). He too searched for a cure; it never came.

All three, against all odds, persevered and achieved their goals, but success can never be guaranteed. This poses a hidden cost of extreme perseverance. Individuals must be able to recognize when their goals are not realistically attainable. After all, not every musician will make it to Carnegie Hall. Perseverance in the extreme could lead to a dogged pursuit of an unattainable goal when effort may better be allocated elsewhere.

It should also be noted that not all struggles are as extreme as the examples described here. Although overuse injuries are common among musicians (Fry, 1986), other challenges include searching for work in a new city, studying with a new teacher, coping with a poor performance, and so on. Each of these can cause musicians to question their goals and abilities, and require perseverance and determination to be overcome. (For further discussion, see chapters by Martin and Evans, and by Hruska and Bonneville-Roussy, both this volume.)

THE ROLE OF PARENTS

For the development of expertise, we must not forget the essential role of parents. Most musicians have the advantage of growing up hearing music at home, whether performed by their parents or other family members. Along with providing economic resources, parents of children who take lessons are more likely to have *openness to experience* (Corrigall & Schellenberg, 2015), a personality characteristic associated with aesthetic sensitivity, creativity, interest in and enjoyment of intellectual activities, and notably a liking for new activities and learning new skills, including playing a musical instrument (McCrae, 1996). Parents also must be invested. Davidson, Howe, Moore, and Sloboda (1996) showed this in interviews with fifty-seven children and their parents. All the children had studied an instrument but differed in level of mastery, and the parents of the most able were those most involved in the earliest stages, involvement that tended to increase over time (for further examples, see Harris, 2019).

THE ROLE OF TEACHERS

For the development of expertise, we also must not forget the essential role of teachers. Some musicians are said to have been self-taught. The usual examples are rock and jazz musicians, perhaps most famously Jimi Hendrix, Paul McCartney, and Ornette Coleman (Chlasciak, 2017). On the other hand, legendary jazz drummer Gene Krupa was significantly influenced by his teacher Sanford Moeller—namesake of the "Moeller Method," which uses a whipping motion to play fast with ease (see Figure 2.2)—as well as by musicians he heard playing in New York City at age twenty:

> I felt the need to really know my instrument and became deeply involved in studies with Sanford "Gus" Moeller—one of the great drum teachers—while simultaneously learning more and more about jazz by playing and listening in Harlem. I'd practice on the rubber pad six, seven, eight hours during the day. Go out and work. Then, after hours, I'd play uptown . . . and watch tap dancers and great drummers like George Stafford and Sonny Greer. I learned a lot of rhythmic beats that way. It was a wonderful, exciting period of discovery. (Klauber, 1990, p. 24)

Informal learning, that is, the acquisition of musical skill outside of school or without the help of a teacher, has garnered attention in recent years (Green, 2017). Green

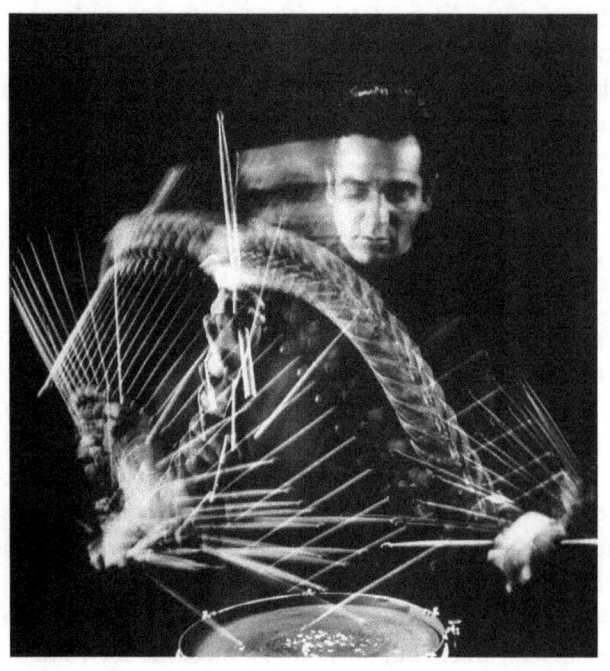

FIGURE 2.2. Drummer Gene Krupa at Gjon Mili's studio, 1941. Gjon Mili/The LIFE Picture Collection via Getty Images. Reproduced with permission.

(2005) describes the many ways in which aspiring musicians develop competence informally at home and in groups. For example, listening to recordings, experimenting with instruments, imitating familiar songs, composing, working with peers, learning through observation, and improvising are all activities that can proceed without formal guidance or supervision. Moreover, all these activities allow emerging musicians to acquire competency in a natural way by pursuing their interests wherever they may lead.

Generally, however, teachers are beneficial, and certainly many of the greatest performers were all fortunate to have had great teachers: As we noted, Mozart's first teacher was his father, Leopold; Scriabin's were Nikolai Zverev, a strict disciplinarian, and later, as a student at the Moscow Conservatory, a trio of prominent pedagogues: Anton Arensky, Sergei Taneyev, and Vasily Safonov. Sergei Rachmaninoff, just a year younger, was a classmate. Vladimir Horowitz's teachers at the Kiev Conservatory were equally distinguished, as were Jascha Heifetz's and Nathan Milstein's, both of whom studied with the great Leopold Auer at the St. Petersburg Conservatory; Milstein also studied with the great violinist Eugène Ysaÿe in Belgium; Leon Fleisher with Artur Schnabel, one of the few child prodigies he accepted; and the long list goes on.

It is less clear what qualities great teachers have in common. We are told that Leopold Mozart was "a supreme teacher who understood how to inspire gifted children to great effort and achievement, instilling a drive for excellence" (Solomon, 1995, p. 39). It is less clear whether, like Leopold, they also should "[awaken] in them a sense of unlimited devotion to his person and a desire to obtain his approval above all else" (Solomon, 1995, p. 39). Nor is it clear that parents are necessarily the best teachers for their own children. Their more important role instead may be to find the right teachers for their children, and for teachers themselves to know the right time for the child to move on to someone better and more qualified.

PRACTICAL IMPLICATIONS

What does all this mean for aspiring musicians? First, the "nature vs. nurture" debate is over. World-class performers are not born or made, they are born *and* made (Plomin, 2017). That is, both genetic and environmental factors contribute substantially to music achievement, as shown in Figure 2.3. Genetic potential will not be fully realized in an unsupportive environment, and a lifetime of training may not overcome deficits associated with heritable traits. Expertise may be attainable for many hard-working performers, but musical genius is probably reserved for only a few. Truly exceptional musicians are the product of talent and hard work, and both are required for greatness in an increasingly competitive domain.

Second, pick your parents. Or rather, recognize that certain factors underpinning expertise are within musicians' control and other factors are not. Rather than dwell on immutable shortcomings, musicians should focus on building skill and well-being. For example, practice can be made more effective by spacing repetitions and paying close

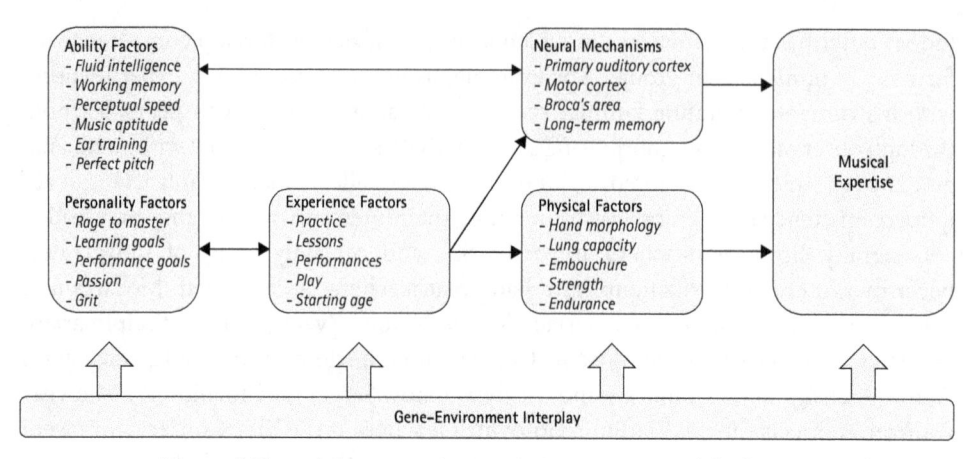

FIGURE 2.3. The multifactorial gene-environment interaction model of expert performance applied to musical expertise. Psychological traits such as abilities and personality are associated with music experience factors and neural mechanisms. Music experience can lead to neural and physical adaptations. The joint product of these factors results in musical expertise. Gene-environment interplay is assumed to play a role throughout the model. Specific examples of each factor are listed in italics under the bolded headings. For more information on neural mechanisms, see Ullén, Hambrick, and Mosing (2016), listed under "Key sources."

attention to detail (Lee & Genovese, 1988; see also Miksza, this volume). Performers should prioritize sleep because it is critical for strengthening motor skills acquired through practice (Stickgold, 2005). And musicians should be mindful of their motivation, because some reasons for pursuing expertise foster greater resilience than others.

Third, musicians should play to their strengths. We have already discussed how music aptitudes are correlated yet distinct, with some performers having greater rhythmic abilities than melodic abilities, and vice versa. However, individuals differ in other ways that might support different career paths. Knowledgeable musicians with a knack for communication may make effective instructors, and those who are outgoing and especially patient may gravitate toward working with children. Musicians who love to play but do not enjoy performing in public may prefer to compose, orienting toward a career producing scores for films, television programs, video games, and so on. Many paths are available to aspiring musicians, and finding one that aligns with one's strengths and interests is worthwhile.

CONCLUSION

The psychology of expertise has moved beyond the "nature vs. nurture" debate and toward a multifactorial perspective. Still, much work remains to understand the interplay between heritable traits and experience factors as they contribute to skill acquisition and expertise. Although we have described some of these factors underlying musical skill, the domain is far too complex to be summarized in a single chapter. Other chapters in this two-volume publication, however, also speak to these issues, including the next chapter on musical potential, giftedness and talent development (see McPherson, Blackwell, & Hallam, this part). Understanding the origins of musical expertise will allow aspiring performers to match their strengths to their pursuits and come closer to maximizing their potential.

KEY SOURCES

Hambrick, D. Z., Burgoyne, A. P., Macnamara, B. N., & Ullén, F. (2018). Toward a multifactorial model of expertise: Beyond born versus made. *Annals of the New York Academy of Sciences, 1423*, 284–295. https://doi.org/10.1111/nyas.13586.

Harris, L. J. (2019). Does music matter? A look at the issues and the evidence. *Developmental Neuropsychology, 44*, 104–145. https://doi.org/10.1080/87565641.2016.1274316.

Macnamara, B. N., Hambrick, D. Z., & Oswald, F. L. (2014). Deliberate Practice and Performance in Music, Games, Sports, Education, and Professions: A Meta-Analysis. *Psychological Science, 11*, 1608–1618. https://doi.org/10.1177%2F0956797614535810.

Ullén, F., Hambrick, D. Z., & Mosing, M. A. (2016). Rethinking expertise: A multifactorial gene-environment interaction model of expert performance. *Psychological Bulletin, 142*, 427–446. http://dx.doi.org/10.1037/bul0000033.

REFLECTIVE QUESTIONS

1. Do you think that anyone can become an expert musician? Why or why not?
2. Looking back on your own development as a musician, which aspects would you change if you could start over knowing what you know now? Which aspects would you keep?
3. *Transfer of training* refers to the idea that training in one domain facilitates performance or skill acquisition in another. Which aspects of musical training do you think would transfer to other domains, and why?
4. What are the merits and potential consequences of starting music at an early age?
5. List some of the differences between *music aptitude* and *ear training*.

REFERENCES

Altenmüller, E. (2015). Alexander Scriabin: His chronic right-hand pain and its impact on his piano compositions. *Progress in Brain Research, 216*, 197–215. https://doi.org/10.1016/bs.phr.2014.11.031.

Amis, J., & Rose, M. (1992). *Words about music: A treasury of writings*. New York: Paragon House.

Beethoven, L. van (1802). *The Heiligenstadt Testament*. Letter to his brothers Carl and Johann, October 6, 1802. Reprinted in J. Amis & M. Rose (Eds.), *Words about music: A treasury of writings (1989)* (pp. 378–380). New York: Paragon House.

Brubach, H. (2007). *The pianist Leon Fleisher: A life-altering debility, reconsidered. The New York Times*, Arts, June 12 – see https://www.nytimes.com/2007/06/12/arts/12iht-pianist.1.6104272.html [accessed October 24, 2019].

Burgoyne, A. P., Hambrick, D. Z., & Macnamara, B. N. (2020). How firm are the foundations of mindset theory? The claims appear stronger than the evidence. *Psychological Science, 31*(3). https://doi.org/10.1177/0956797619897588.

Burgoyne, A. P., Harris, L. J., & Hambrick, D. Z. (2019). Predicting piano skill acquisition in beginners: The role of general intelligence, music aptitude, and mindset. *Intelligence, 76*. https://doi.org/10.1016/j.intell.2019.101383.

Chlasciak, M. M. (2017). *Dispelling the myth of being self-taught*. Guitar World – see http://www.guitarworld.com/metalmike-dispelling-myth-being-self-taught.

Corrigall, K. A., & Schellenberg, E. G. (2015). Predicting who takes music lessons: Parent and child characteristics. *Frontiers in Psychology, 6*, article 282. https://doi.org/10.3389/fpsyg.2015.00282.

Davidson, J. W., Howe, M. J. A., Moore, D. G., & Sloboda, J. A. (1996). The role of parental influences in the development of musical performance. *British Journal of Developmental Psychology, 14*, 399–412. https://doi.org/10.1111/j.2044-835X.

Elbert, T., Pantev, C., Wienbruch, C., Rockstroh, B., & Taub, E. (1995). Increased cortical representation of the fingers of the left hand in string players. *Science, 270*(5234), 305–307. https://doi.org/10.1126/science.270.5234.305.

Elliot, A. J., & Church, M. A. (1997). A hierarchical model of approach and avoidance achievement motivation. *Journal of Personality and Social Psychology, 72*, 218–232. https://doi.org/10.1037/0022-3514.72.1.218.

Elliot, A. J., & McGregor, H. A. (2001). A 2× 2 achievement goal framework. *Journal of Personality and Social Psychology, 80*(3), 501–519.

Ericsson, K. A. (1998). The scientific study of expert levels of performance: General implications for optimal learning and creativity. *High Ability Studies, 9*, 75–100.

Ericsson, K. A. (2020). Towards a science of the acquisition of expert performance in sports: Clarifying the differences between deliberate practice and other types of practice. *Journal of Sports Sciences, 38*, 159–176. https://doi.org/10.1080/02640414.2019.1688618.

Ericsson, K. A., Krampe, R. T., & Tesch-Römer, C. (1993). The role of deliberate practice in the acquisition of expert performance. *Psychological Review, 100*, 363–406. https://psycnet.apa.org/doi/10.1037/0033-295X.100.3.363.

Ericsson, K. A., & Lehmann, A. C. (1996). Expert and exceptional performance: Evidence of maximal adaptation to task constraints. *Annual Review of Psychology, 47*, 273–305.

Froseth, J. O. (1971). Using MAP scores in the instruction of beginning students in instrumental music. *Journal of Research in Music Education, 19*, 98–105. https://psycnet.apa.org/doi/10.2307/3344119.

Frucht, S. J. (2009). Focal task-specific dystonia of the musicians' hand" A practical approach for the clinician. *Journal of Hand Therapy, 22*, 136–142. https://doi.org/10.1016/j.jht.2008.11.006.

Fry, H. J. (1986). Overuse syndrome of the upper limb in musicians. *Medical Journal of Australia, 144*, 182–185. https://doi.org/10.5694/j.1326-5377.1986.tb128353.x.

Fujioka, T., Ross, B., Kakigi, R., Pantev, C., & Trainor, L. J. (2006). One year of musical training affects development of auditory cortical-evoked fields in young children. *Brain, 129*, 2593–2608. https://doi.org/10.1093/brain/awl247.

Gagné, F., & McPherson, G. E. (2016). Analyzing musical prodigiousness using Gagné's Integrative Model of Talent Development. In G. E. McPherson (Ed.) *Musical prodigies: Interpretations from psychology, education, musicology, and ethnomusicology* (pp. 3–114). Oxford: Oxford University Press.

Galton, F. 1869. *Hereditary genius*. London: Macmillan. https://psycnet.apa.org/doi/10.1037/13474-000.

Gembris, H. (1997). Historical phases in the definition of musicality. *Psychomusicology: A Journal of Research in Music Cognition, 16*(1–2), 17–25.

Gervain, J., Vines, B. W., Chen, L. M., Seo, R. J., Hensch, T. K., Werker, J. F., & Young, A. H. (2013). Valproate reopens critical-period learning of absolute pitch. *Frontiers in Systems Neuroscience, 7*, 102. https://doi.org/10.3389/fnsys.2013.00102.

Gobet, F., & Campitelli, G. (2007). The role of domain-specific practice, handedness, and starting age in chess. *Developmental Psychology, 43*, 159–172. https://doi.org/10.1037/0012-1649.43.1.159.

Gordon, E. (1989). *Manual for the advanced measures of music audiation*. Chicago: GIA Publications.

Gottfredson, L. S. (1997). Mainstream science on intelligence: An editorial with 52 signatories, history, and bibliography. *Intelligence, 24*, 13–23. https://psycnet.apa.org/doi/10.1016/S0160-2896(97)90011-8.

Gramophone (1934). *Stravinsky: As I see myself*. Gramophone – see https://www.gramophone.co.uk/feature/stravinsky-as-i-see-myself, accessed on 28.09.2019.

Green, L. (2005). The music curriculum as lived experience: Children's "natural" music-learning processes. *Music Educators Journal, 91*(4), 27–32.

Green, L. (2017). *Music education as critical theory and practice: Selected essays*. Routledge.

Greenberg, D. M., Müllensiefen, D., Lamb, M. E., & Rentfrow, P. J. (2015). Personality predicts musical sophistication. *Journal of Research in Personality, 58*, 154–158. https://doi.org/10.1016/j.jrp.2015.06.002.

Gregersen, P. K., Kowalsky, E., Kohn, N., & Marvin, E. W. (1999). Absolute pitch: prevalence, ethnic variation, and estimation of the genetic component. *American Journal of Human Genetics, 65*, 911–913. https://doi.org/10.1086/302541.

Hambrick, D. Z., Altmann, E. M., Oswald, F. L., Meinz, E. J., & Gobet, F. (2014). Facing facts about deliberate practice. *Frontiers in Psychology, 5*, 751. https://doi.org/10.3389/fpsyg.2014.00751.

Hambrick, D. Z., Burgoyne, A. P., Macnamara, B. N., & Ullén, F. (2018). Toward a multifactorial model of expertise: Beyond born versus made. *Annals of the New York Academy of Sciences, 1423*, 284–295. https://doi.org/10.1111/nyas.13586.

Hambrick, D. Z., Burgoyne, A. P., & Oswald, F. L. (2019). Domain-general models of expertise: The role of cognitive ability. In P. Ward, J. M. Schraagen, J. Gore, & E. M. Roth (Eds.), *The Oxford handbook of expertise* (pp. 56–84). Oxford: Oxford University Press. https://doi.org/10.1093/oxfordhb/9780198795872.013.3.

Hambrick, D. Z., & Tucker-Drob, E. (2014). The genetics of music accomplishment: evidence for gene-environment correlation and interaction. *Psychonomic Bulletin & Review, 22,* 112–120. https://doi.org/10.3758/s13423-014-0671-9.

Harris, L. J. (2019). Does music matter? A look at the issues and the evidence. *Developmental Neuropsychology, 44,* 104–145. dhttps://doi.org/10.1080/87565641/2016.1274316.

Harrison, P. M., Collins, T., & Müllensiefen, D. (2017). Applying modern psychometric techniques to melodic discrimination testing: Item response theory, computerised adaptive testing, and automatic item generation. *Scientific Reports, 7,* 1–18. https://doi.org/10.1038/s41598-017-03586-z.

Hayward, C. M., & Gromko, J. (2009). Relationships among music sight-reading and technical proficiency, spatial visualization, and aural discrimination. *Journal of Research in Music Education, 57,* 26–36. https://doi.org/10.1177%2F0022429409332677.

Hensch, T. K. (2005). Critical period plasticity in local cortical circuits. *Nature Reviews Neuroscience, 6,* 877–888. https://doi.org/10.1038/nrn1787.

Hufstader, R. A. (1974). Predicting success in beginning instrumental music through use of selected tests. *Journal of Research in Music Education, 22,* 52–57. https://doi.org/10.2307%2F3344618.

Johnson, J. S., & Newport, E. L. (1989). Critical period effects in second language learning: The influence of maturational state on the acquisition of English as a second language. *Cognitive Psychology, 21,* 60–99. https://doi.org/10.1016/0010-0285(89)90003-0.

Keenan, J.P., Thangaraj, V., Halpern, A. R., & Schlaug, G. (2001). Absolute pitch and planum temporale. *Neuroimage, 14,* 1402–1408. doi:10.1006/nimg.2001.0925

Klauber, B. H. (1990). *World of Gene Krupa: That legendary drummin' man.* Ventura, CA: Pathfinder Publishing.

Klinedinst, R. E. (1991). Predicting performance achievement and retention of fifth-grade instrumental students. *Journal of Research in Music Education, 39,* 225–238. https://doi.org/10.2307%2F3344722.

Kopiez, R., & In Lee, J. (2008). Towards a general model of skills involved in sight reading music. *Music Education Research, 10,* 41–62. https://doi.org/10.1080/14613800701871363.

Lee, T. D., & Genovese, E. D. (1988). Distribution of practice in motor skill acquisition: Learning and performance effects reconsidered. *Research Quarterly for Exercise and Sport, 59,* 277–287. https://doi.org/10.1080/02701367.1988.10609373.

Lehmann, A. C., & McArthur, V. (2002). Sight-reading. In R. Parncutt & G. E. McPherson (Eds.), *The science and psychology of music performance: Creative strategies for teaching and learning* (pp. 135–150). Oxford: Oxford University Press.

Levitin, D. J., & Rogers, S. E. (2005). Absolute pitch: perception, coding, and controversies. *Trends in Cognitive Sciences, 9,* 26–33. https://doi.org/10.1016/j.tics.2004.11.007.

Levitin, D. J., & Zatorre, R. J. (2003). On the nature of early music training and absolute pitch: A reply to Brown, Sachs, Cammuso, and Folstein. *Music Perception: An Interdisciplinary Journal, 21,* 105–110. https://doi.org/10.1525/mp.2003.21.1.105.

Logie, R. H. (2003). Spatial and visual working memory: A mental workspace. In D. E. Irwin & B. H. Ross (Eds.), *Psychology of learning and motivation* (Vol. 42, pp. 37–78). Cambridge, MA: Academic Press.

Macnamara, B. N., Hambrick, D. Z., Frank, D. J., King, M. J., Burgoyne, A. P., & Meinz, E. J. (2018). The deliberate practice view: An evaluation of definitions, claims, and empirical evidence. In D. Z. Hambrick, G. Campitelli, & B. N. Macnamara (Eds.), *The science of expertise: Behavioral, neural, and genetic approaches to complex skill* (pp. 151–168). New York: Routledge.

Macnamara, B. N., Hambrick, D. Z., & Oswald, F. L. (2014). Deliberate practice and performance in music, games, sports, education, and professions: A meta-analysis. *Psychological Science, 11*, 1608–1618. https://doi.org/10.1177%2F0956797614535810.

McCarthy, J. F. (1980). Individualized instruction, student achievement, and dropout in an urban elementary instrumental music program. *Journal of Research in Music Education, 28*, 59–69. https://doi.org/10.2307%2F3345053.

McCrae, R. R. (1996). Openness to experience as a basic dimension of personality. *Imagination, Cognition and Personality, 13*, 39–55. https://doi.org/10.2190/H8H6=QYKR-KEU8-GAQ0.

McGrew, K. S. (2009). CHC theory and the human cognitive abilities project: Standing on the shoulders of the giants of psychometric intelligence research. *Intelligence, 37*, 1–10. https://doi.org/10.1016/j.intell.2008.08.004.

Meinz, E. J., & Hambrick, D. Z. (2010). Deliberate practice is necessary but not sufficient to explain individual differences in piano sight-reading skill: The role of working memory capacity. *Psychological Science, 21*, 914–919. http://doi.org/10.1177/0956797610373933.

Miksza, P. (2009). Relationships among impulsivity, achievement goal motivation, and the music practice of high school wind players. *Bulletin of the Council for Research in Music Education, 180*, 9–27. https://www.jstor.org/stable/40319317.

Miksza, P., Tan, L., & Dye, C. (2016). Achievement motivation for band: A cross-cultural examination of the 2 × 2 achievement goal motivation framework. *Psychology of Music, 44*, 1372–1388. https://doi.org/10.1177%2F0305735616628659.

Mishra, J. (2014). Factors related to sight-reading accuracy: A meta-analysis. *Journal of Research in Music Education, 61*, 452–465. https://doi.org/10.1177%2F0022429413508585.

Mosing, M. A., Madison, G., Pedersen, N. L., Kuja-Halkola, R., & Ullén, F. (2014a). Practice does not make perfect: no causal effect of music practice on music ability. *Psychological Science, 25*, 1795–1803. https://doi.org/10.1177%2F0956797614541990.

Mosing, M. A., Pedersen, N. L., Madison, G., & Ullén, F. (2014b). Genetic pleiotropy explains associations between musical auditory discrimination and intelligence. *PLoS ONE, 9*, e113874. https://doi.org/10.1371/journal.pone.0113874.

Müllensiefen, D., Gingras, B., Musil, J., & Stewart, L. (2014). The musicality of non-musicians: An index for assessing musical sophistication in the general population. *PLoS ONE, 9*(2), e89642. https://doi.org/10.1371/journal.pone.0089642.

Noble, C. E., Baker, B. L., & Jones, T. A. (1964). Age and sex parameters in psychomotor learning. *Perceptual and Motor Skills, 19*, 935–945. https://doi.org/10.2466/pms.1964.19.3.935.

Platz, F., Kopiez, R., Lehmann, A. C., & Wolf, A. (2014). The influence of deliberate practice on musical achievement: A meta-analysis. *Frontiers in Psychology, 5*, 646. https://doi.org/10.3389/fpsyg.2014.00646.

Plomin, R. (2017). Foreword. In D. Z. Hambrick, G. Campitelli, & B. N. Macnamara (Eds.), *The science of expertise: Behavioral, neural, and genetic approaches to complex skill* (pp. xiv–xvii). New York: Routledge.

Ruthsatz, J., Detterman, D., Griscom, W. S., & Cirullo, B. A. (2008). Becoming an expert in the musical domain: It takes more than just practice. *Intelligence, 36*, 330–338. https://doi.org/10.1016/j.intell.2007.08.003.

Schleuter, S. L. (1978). Effects of certain lateral dominance traits, music aptitude, and sex differences with instrumental music achievement. *Journal of Research in Music Education, 26*, 22–31. https://doi.org/10.2307%2F3344786.

Schmidt, F. L., & Hunter, J. (2004). General mental ability in the world of work: occupational attainment and job performance. *Journal of Personality and Social Psychology, 86*, 162–173. https://psycnet.apa.org/doi/10.1037/0022-3514.86.1.162.

Schonberg, H. C. (1963). *The great pianists from Mozart to the present*. New York: Simon & Schuster.

Seashore, C. E. (1919). *The psychology of musical talent*. Boston: Silver, Burdett.

Seashore, C. E. (1960). *Manual of instructions and interpretations for measures of musical talent*. New York: Psychological Corporation. (Originally published 1919.)

Sisk, V. F., Burgoyne, A. P., Sun, J., Butler, J. L., & Macnamara, B. N. (2018). To what extent and under which circumstances are growth mind-sets important to academic achievement? Two meta-analyses. *Psychological Science, 29*, 549–571. https://doi.org/10.1177%2F0956797617739704.

Solomon, M. (1995). *Mozart: A life*. New York: HarperCollins.

Stickgold, R. (2005). Sleep-dependent memory consolidation. *Nature, 437*(7063), 1272–1278. https://doi.org/10.1038/nature04286.

Takeuchi, A. H., & Hulse, S. H. (1993). Absolute pitch. *Psychological Bulletin, 113*, 345–361. https://psycnet.apa.org/doi/10.1037/0033-2909.113.2.345.

Ullén, F., Hambrick, D. Z., & Mosing, M. A. (2016). Rethinking expertise: A multifactorial gene-environment interaction model of expert performance. *Psychological Bulletin, 142*, 427–446. http://dx.doi.org/10.1037/bul0000033.

Ullén, F., Mosing, M. A., Holm, L., Eriksson, H., & Madison, G. (2014). Psychometric properties and heritability of a new online test for musicality, the Swedish Musical Discrimination Test. *Personality and Individual Differences, 63*, 87–93. https://doi.org/10.1016/j.paid.2014.01.057.

Vittes, L. (2017). Van Cliburn in Moscow, 1958: When classical music made the world stand still. Huffington Post, December 26 – see https://www.huffpost.com/entry/van-cliburn-in-moscow-1958-when-classical-music-made_b_5a423c5de4b0dfode8b066d7 [accessed September 25, 2019].

Voelcker-Rehage, C. (2008). Motor-skill learning in older adults: A review of studies on age-related differences. *European Review of Aging and Physical Activity, 5*, 5–16. https://doi.org/10.1007/s11556-008-0030-9.

Wesseldijk, L. W., Mosing, M. A., & Ullén, F. (2019). Gene-environment interaction in expertise: The importance of childhood environment for musical achievement. *Developmental Psychology, 57*, 1473–1479. https://psycnet.apa.org/doi/10.1037/dev0000726.

Winner, E. (2000). The origins and ends of giftedness. *American Psychologist, 55*, 159–169. https://psycnet.apa.org/doi/10.1037/0003-066X.55.1.159.

CHAPTER 3

MUSICAL POTENTIAL, GIFTEDNESS, AND TALENT DEVELOPMENT

GARY E. MCPHERSON, JENNIFER BLACKWELL, AND SUSAN HALLAM

INTRODUCTION

"THAT performer was so musical!" . . . "She was born with a special talent for music" . . . "I'm tone deaf, I have no ear for music." How often have you heard comments similar to these? To what extent might any be true? At their heart, statements like these open up questions surrounding "nature" versus "nurture" and the roles of the natural abilities humans are born with as compared to the host of other influences that can impact on potential, giftedness, and talent. To understand whether any of these statements has any factual basis, we will survey what we consider to be the most authoritative research evidence available at the time of writing this chapter, and in so doing, try to dispel some of the myths and misconceptions that pervade our discipline.

GENERAL OBSERVATIONS: ARE WE ALL BORN MUSICAL?

The issue of whether everyone is born with equal potential certainly applies to music. In our area, people tend to hold firm views, often without any real evidence other than their basic instincts. So, then, what does research tell us?

Beyond any doubt, the vast majority of any population will possess the capacity to succeed and do well in music if they so choose (see Figure 3.1; Peretz, 2020). At the

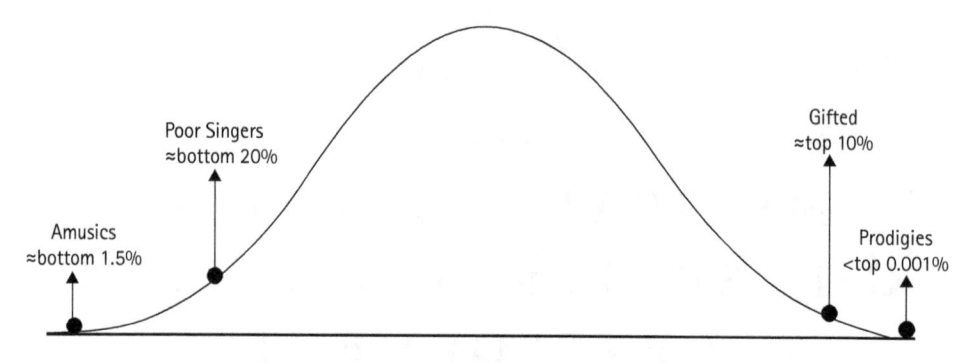

FIGURE 3.1. Musical ability across the population.

extreme, only about 1.5 percent display *congenital amusia*, in that they lead normal lives, but have difficulty processing pitch (Peretz & Vuvan, 2017). About half of these are able to enjoy music, while the other half struggle to appreciate music (Omigie, Müllensiefen, & Stewart, 2012).

About 20 percent of the population can be labeled "off-key singers"; in contrast to those with congenital amusia, these individuals are not amusic and can therefore benefit from a music education and even be successful at playing an instrument.

Contextualizing Musical Potential, Giftedness, and Talent

There are a number of explanations of what constitutes musical potential and the many different terms that have been used to refer to it, including musical aptitude, musical potential, musical ability, musical achievement, musical giftedness, musical talent, and musicality. To a large extent, the meanings attributed to these terms are socially constructed and reflect the cultural, political, economic, and social factors pertaining to where and when they were adopted. For us, however, there is some value in trying to at least provide a starting point for thinking about the difference between each of these terms, and what they might imply when used in music.

The term *musical aptitude* is generally used when trying to estimate a person's overall capacity to learn or develop musically before any type of formal education or training has begun. To do this, researchers have devised different types of aptitude profiles to try to measure an individual's capacity to benefit from formal learning of music. Thus, we should use the term *musical aptitude* (or the more vernacular term *musical potential*) to refer to an individual's currently unrealized capacity to learn or develop within an area of music, such as playing the violin or trombone.

The term *gifts* denotes the specific mental and physical natural abilities—shown in Figure 3.2—that are evident in the early years of life and that give learners an advantage

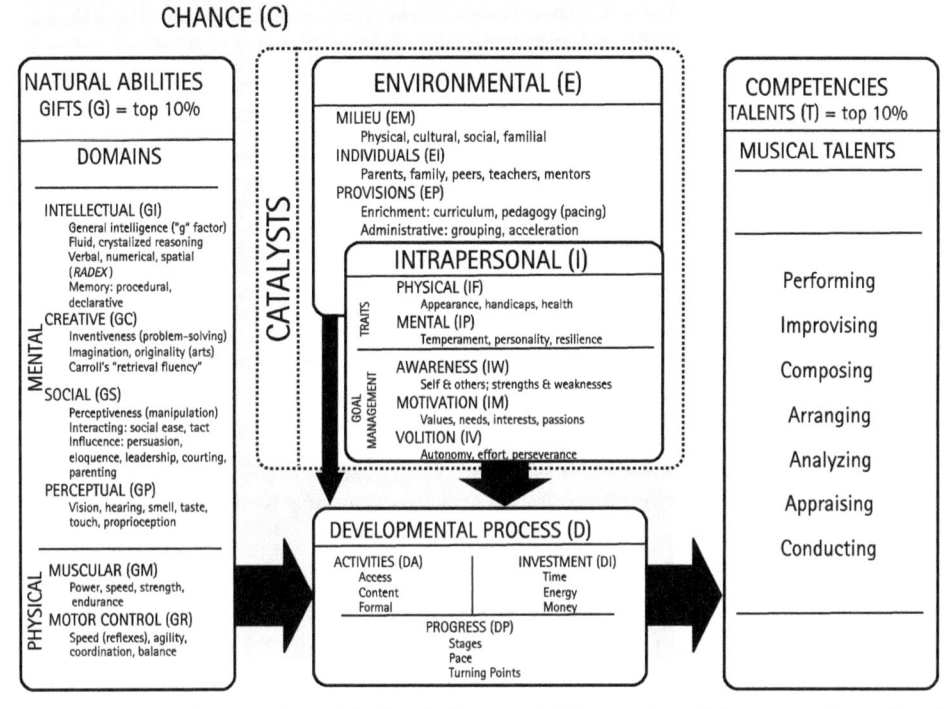

FIGURE 3.2. *Differentiated Model of Giftedness and Talent.* Adapted for music from Gagné (2009, p. 64).

if they were to become involved in learning music (or any other area of learning) at some point in their lives (Gagné & McPherson, 2016). These natural abilities develop during childhood through maturation and informal exercise, even though they are partially controlled by one's genetics. Broadly speaking, these natural abilities fit into four *mental processes* (intellectual, creative, social, and perceptual) and two *physical abilities* (muscular and motor control).

The right side of Figure 3.2 indicates that about 10 percent of the population display evidence of being musically gifted. Within this top 10 percent, the labels *mildly* (top 10%), *moderately* (top 1%), *highly* (1; 1,000), *exceptionally* (top 1:10,000), or *profoundly* (top 1: 100,000) can be used to describe their level of giftedness (Gagné & McPherson, 2016). Prodigies are even more rare, with examples like Mozart, Mendelssohn, Clara Schumann, and many other important musicians throughout history (both in classical music and in other genres), probably being at the extreme top of the tip of profoundly gifted individuals (Gagné & McPherson, 2016).

Musical talent is a term used to describe how musicians demonstrate competence in an area of music after their natural abilities and a host of intrapersonal, environmental, and developmental processes have exerted influence and led to some level of achievement. In this way, the term *musical talent* can be used to describe a host of different ways of displaying competence in music, such as performing a violin concerto with an orchestra, playing a simple melody by ear on the piano, composing a new song, or analysing the chords in a piece of music.

Within our explanations, we prefer to use the term *musical talent* rather than *musical ability* as for us, the word *ability* refers to a more generalized concept. Likewise, instead of saying *musical giftedness*, we would just refer to *gifts* as natural abilities evident in individuals to varying degrees that are independent of any specific musical connotation. All of this becomes clear in Figure 3.2, where we have adapted Gagné's (2009) model by adding seven types of musical talent in order to differentiate between *giftedness*, encompassing a range of mental and physical natural abilities that are evident from birth and that people can develop during childhood and general maturation, from *talents*, which refer to a host of developed abilities such as being able to perform, compose, improvise, arrange, analyse or appraise music, or conduct an ensemble (Gagné & McPherson, 2016).

Before we go on, four additional terms deserve to be defined; two associated with music (*musicality, musical sophistication*), and two referring to development (*competence, expertise*).

Any internet search will result in a very general statement about how the term *musicality* is used and defined. Most use this term to describe a person's sensitivity to music or as depicting some special attribute that distinguishes the individuals from others, such as the quality or pleasantness of their sound, or the sense of phrasing and expression they project when performing. In some situations, the term *innate musicality* is used to denote something that seems mysterious or unexplainable, as though the person is hard-wired with some sort of musical gene that makes them uniquely different. As shown in the opening chapter of this handbook (see Burgoyne, Hambrick, & Harris, this part), this type of thinking is simplistic, because genetic and environmental influences are entwined, such that the vast majority of the population (with the possible exception of individuals with congenital amusia) have various genetically predetermined abilities that can be further developed through an education in music.

Musical sophistication is a label described in more recent research that refers to the ability of highly musically sophisticated individuals "to respond to a greater range of musical situations" because they "are more flexible in their responses, and possess more effective means of achieving their goals when engaging with music" (Müllensiefen, Gingras, Musil, & Stewart, 2014, p. 2). Using this concept, researchers at the University of London have devised the *Goldsmiths Musical Sophistication Index* (Gold-MSI), which attempts to measure, through a self-report inventory, differences among individuals, in terms of their active musical engagement (time and resources they devote to music), perceptual abilities (music listening skills), singing abilities, and ability to identify emotions that are expressed by music. Research using the Gold-MSI has found links between personality traits and musical sophistication (Greenberg, Müllensiefen, Lamb, & Rentfrow, 2015), and musical self-concept and musical achievement (Müllensiefen, Harrison, Caprini, & Fancourt, 2015), and highlighted how it can be used as a measure of musical sophistication for "non-musicians" (Müllensiefen, Gingras, Musil, & Stewart, 2014).

Competence refers to a number of "related and systematically developed abilities, knowledge, and skills that enable a person to act effectively in a situation and that result from systematic training" (Preckel et al., 2020). As individuals engage in an activity, they typically improve, and this sets them apart from their peers because of the high level of competence they display compared to others.

Finally, *expertise* is a term used to describe consistently high levels of superior achievement. Experts are typically committed to the activity and have acquired a knowledge-base and set of domain-specific skills that facilitate accurate, consistent levels of performance each time they demonstrate their expertise. As an example, expert musicians are able to perform the same work accurately across multiple performances in close proximity to each other (Preckel et al., 2020).

MUSICAL POTENTIAL AS SPECIES-SPECIFIC

Music is a universal feature of human culture and plays a central role in people's lives (McDermott & Hauser, 2005). Humans have the potential to listen to, appreciate, and make music without formal training. The capacity for processing sound develops before birth, ensuring that a newborn infant has well-developed systems to support the acquisition of spoken language, systems that also process musical sounds (Parncutt, 2016). Despite the consensus that as a species, humans have the capacity to engage with music, there continues to be debate about the extent to which there are individual differences in musical potential and whether these are underpinned by genetic inheritance, learning, or an interaction between the two. Although some extreme positions have been articulated, overall, the research suggests that there are complex interactions between genetic and environmental factors underlining musical potential.

Absolute pitch

An example of the role of genes in musical ability relates to absolute pitch (for further discussion of absolute pitch and synesthesia, see Glasser, this volume). This is generally defined as the ability to identify or produce isolated pitches in the absence of a reference pitch. Absolute pitch is rare in the general population (between 0.01% and 1%, see Dowling, 1999; Profita, Bidder, Optiz, & Reynolds, 1988; Loui, 2016) but somewhat more common among professional musicians. Within musically trained populations, reported estimates range from around 4 percent in some orchestras to 15 percent in some music conservatoires (Gregersen et al., 2013). Early research assumed that having absolute pitch was an all-or-nothing skill, but it has become increasingly apparent that there is variability in the extent to which it applies. For instance, some people are only able to identify pitches from the sounds of specific instruments, familiar sounds, or within specific pitch ranges. This suggests that knowledge of absolute pitch may be acquired incrementally over time as the result of ongoing experience (Bahr et al., 2005).

Gagné and McPherson (2016) report that every one of the prodigies they studied had absolute pitch, and therefore music seems to be more accessible for this rare group of musicians than the general population. Ockelford (2016) noted that absolute pitch is also a key factor in the identification and emergence of savant prodigies.

Available evidence suggests that absolute pitch is also shaped by genetic predisposition (Bahr et al., 2005; Wilson et al., 2012; Szyfter & Witt, 2020), with one study even reporting on an adult absolute pitch possessor with minimal training who could perform a pitch memory task at the same level as trained AP musicians. There is some evidence that "High Accuracy" individuals, people who can identify many pitches without meeting the threshold for true AP, have an intermediate genetic predisposition for AP, which can be strengthened by musical training (Chavarria-Soley, 2016).

Absolute pitch aggregates in families, with a sibling occurrence risk ratio of 7.5 to 15.1 when controlling for musical training (Baharloo et al., 2000). Absolute pitch is more common in autistic children (Heaton, 2009) and is found more frequently in people of East Asian ethnic decent. Interestingly, not everyone who receives equivalent musical training at an early age will acquire absolute pitch (Bermudez & Zatorre, 2009). It may be that, as a species, we are predisposed to develop absolute pitch (Saffran, 2003), but that we require an appropriate environment and exposure at the right time for it to develop (Takeuchi & Hulse, 1993), particularly with regard to "finding the note" forms of tonal training (Vitouch, 2003). Interestingly, a kind of residual absolute pitch seems to be present in adults, many of whom can typically approximate the pitch of familiar songs (Levitin, 1994).

It is also possible that individuals who do not possess absolute pitch may use different pitch-processing mechanisms (McLachlan et al., 2013) that indicate genetically influenced neuroanatomical differences. Ross and Marks (2009) tested children before they had been exposed to musical training and found two children who possessed elevated levels of being able to perceptually encode pitch. This suggests the possibility of "an innate perceptual process that may precede (if not predetermine) the traditionally defined [absolute pitch] skill of note naming" (p. 204), and leaves open the question of whether early onset of music education or any form of training is actually necessary for absolute pitch to emerge (Ross, Olson, & Gore, 2003).

Tone deafness (congenital amusia)

Another approach to exploring the role of genes in musical development has been to study adults who have congenital amusia, or what is known colloquially as "tone deafness" (Peretz, 2020). In her extensive research on this topic, Peretz (2020) suggests that individuals who possess congenital amusia are "deaf" to aspects of pitch. They sing out of tune, but do not hear this themselves (even though others will), and typically find it hard to sing without words or some sort of syllable (such as "la, la, la"). They also find it difficult to recognize familiar tunes unless they are accompanied by lyrics, or to detect wrong notes in a performance. Even though they find little pleasure in listening to music, these individuals lead normal lives, as evidenced in some who have achieved at an exceptional level in other pursuits.

Whereas most of the research on congenital amusia has been focused on pitch, another form of *beat deafness* to time has been found that is believed to be even more rare in the population. Individuals who display this form of beat deafness are unable to synchronize movements with music, or detect whether another person is moving in time with the same music, even though their motor and auditory systems are intact (Phillips-Silver et al., 2011). In short, their beat impairment seems to be related to an imprecise internal timekeeping mechanism (Tranchant & Peretz, 2020).

Peretz's research has shown that *amusics* make up less than 1.5 percent of the population (Peretz & Vuvan, 2017), depending on the criteria used, and that their brains and genetic make-up explain their deficiencies in music. Because this condition is hereditary, it tends to aggregate in families, with approximately half the offspring possessing amusia (Peretz, 2020). Amusia is also found in communities that speak tonal languages such as Mandarin, where, even though they have difficult identifying these linguistic tones, are not significantly handicapped because their brains are able to resolve ambiguities on the basis of multiple clues, such as the context and meaning of the sentence (Nan, Sun, & Peretz, 2010).

Finally, if not begun before six or seven years of age, musical training does not seem to be effective in attenuating amusia, a finding that further strengthens its genetic underpinnings (Peretz & Vuvan, 2017; Peretz, 2020).

"Off-key" or out-of-tune singers

People with congenital amusia can be distinguished from those who simply struggle to match or identify pitches. These individuals—often referred to as "off-key singers"—make up roughly 20 percent of the population and are able to improve with training at virtually any age. Because it is so challenging to diagnose amusia in very young children, Peretz (2020) suggests that early music education for all children helps amusics to experience some enjoyment in music. Even though they may never reach a high level of singing ability, this early musical experience may still offer them pleasure as well as academic benefits (Peretz, 2020). Importantly also, being part of this population does not preclude these individuals from experiencing success if they choose to learn a musical instrument.

HERITABILITY STUDIES

The question of whether musical potential is heritable has, in the past, been hotly contested, despite the fact that any genetically determined musical potential will not express itself unless the individual spends a great deal of time engaging with music. The Matthew Effect (Stanovich, 1986) suggests that those who have greater inherited potential in a field learn more quickly than others, and thus individual experience leads to a pattern of differential accrual of skill over time (for support on this effect in music, see Mosing, Hambrick & Ullén, 2019). This has been interpreted in relation to prior knowledge, where the greater the prior knowledge in a field, the easier it is to learn other material in the field (i.e., "the rich get richer"). This may also be thought of in terms of a scaffolding metaphor: early training develops the scaffold for building a skyscraper-like level of expertise later in life, while a late start allows for only moderate results because they have had less time to develop a similar type of scaffolding (Steele et al., 2013). This process is particularly complex in music because of the wide range of skills required and differences between genres and instruments. These skills may rely on different but overlapping brain networks (see Altenmüller & Furaya, 2018). As an example, in their analyses about how high the bar needs to be to produce a musician of exceptional talent, Gagné and McPherson (2016) provided an analysis of four genes or traits theorized to influence the development of a musical prodigy. They explain that falling outside the top 1 percent for any of the traits/genes mathematically pushes the individual quickly out of the top tier of the musically talented (see also Simonton, 2001).

Musical training during childhood, a period in one's life where greater brain plasticity occurs, can lead to long-term changes in the brain that support skilled behavior well into adulthood (Steele & Zatorre, 2018). These changes appear to be greater than if the same amount of training occurs later in life, a finding that led Steele and Zatorre (2018) to conclude that "musical training induces white matter plasticity in children and that white-matter structure and performance in adult musicians is enhanced in those who began training earlier in life, even after controlling for total amount of practice" (pp. 1645–1646). As explained by these authors, at the beginning of any training program, no two individuals will be exactly the same, and experience alone cannot account for how they will turn out as a result of training. For example, not everyone who learns a musical instrument will reach the level of a professional musician, partly because individual brains differ so widely due to genetic and environmental factors. For Steel and Zatorre (2018), "there is clear evidence from twin studies that genetic factors account for a large part of the variance in ability; yet at the same time, if one twin receives musical training and the other does not, structural differences can be seen in relevant brain areas. Thus, genetic predispositions interact with environmental factors to influence training, which in turn changes brain structure" (p. 1646).

Steel and Zatorre's (2018) findings highlight a major confounding issue in understanding heritability: namely, the commonly held view that the more an individual engages with music, the higher their assessed level of musical potential will be. Even so, research is still trying to identify which elements of musical potential are determined by genetics and which by the environment. And a further complication is that genetic factors may also be important in determining interests, motivations, goals, and attitudes for the skills being acquired and learn from practice (Tucker-Drob, 2017). Examples where genetic factors are clearly demonstrated are those of savants, children with Williams syndrome, and prodigies.

Musical Savants

In the literature, prodigies and savants are sometimes discussed together, but the distinguishing factor is that savants have deficiencies that severely impact on their daily lives and social development even though they possess high ability in a domain, as compared to prodigies, who are normal functioning individuals with exceptional talent in one or more domains.

Savants are people whose general cognitive functioning is well below normal levels, but who nevertheless are able to undertake some activities with ease and exceptional skill, for instance drawing, calculating calendar dates, or making music. Whatever the particular savant skill, it is always linked to exceptional memory (Treffert, 2009). Another distinguishing feature of savants is that absolute (or perfect) pitch and synesthesia are common within their population (see Glasser, this volume). Moreover, savants who are blind seem to have a particular interest in everyday sounds, as sound becomes a source of stimulation—and sometimes fixation—due to their lack of sight (Ockelford, 2016).

One of the main authorities on savants is Treffert (2012a, 2012b), who has spent much of his professional life describing this type of individual. He considers their abilities to be innate because they can appear suddenly and their "instant talent" can reach very high levels in childhood with minimal systematic training (see also Gagné & McPherson, 2016). Further research is needed to confirm much of Treffert's assertions, but what can be said is that up to 10 percent of individuals on the autism spectrum exhibit savant-like exceptional skills.

Autism is known to relate to enhanced perceptual processing in low-level cognitive operations, for instance, discrimination in the visual and auditory modalities. This may be why many musical savants exhibit absolute pitch (Bonnel et al., 2003; Heaton, 2003), which enables them to make confident, rapid judgements about individual pitches and complex chords. Mottron and colleagues (2009) suggest that in autistic children, enhanced detection of patterns, including similarity within and among patterns, is one of the mechanisms responsible for their abilities, as they easily process highly structured material such as music (see also Mottron & Bouvet, 2016). They go on to suggest that processing in pattern-rich, highly structured domains is emotionally rewarding for people with autism.

While people with autism often struggle with sensory integration (connecting information from their different senses), their ability to hyper-focus on auditory data gives them a unique advantage in musical contexts, and particularly in the development of absolute pitch (Ockelford, 2016). Additionally, Ockelford (2016) notes that with an "exceptional early cognitive environment" (EECE) typical of those with autism and particularly those with additional challenges (such as blindness or learning challenges), sounds that would typically be heard as functional (for example, the whir of a fan or tick of a clock) do not acquire these functional attributions and are simply pleasing to the individual, and thus these sounds are processed for their sounding qualities, meaning that they are heard musically rather than "functionally." Additionally, there is some evidence suggesting that savant syndrome may be a distinct sub-group of autism with a unique cognitive and behavioral profile, including heightened sensory sensitivity, obsessional behaviors, unique technical and spatial abilities, systemizing, and different approaches to task learning (Hughes et al., 2018).

While there is an underlying genetic basis for savant skills, environmental influences should not be underestimated, not least in explaining the range of different skills that savants can exhibit. As Mottron and Bouvet (2016) note, "savantism combines altered neurobiological constraints on early learning abilities with favourable environmental conditions" (p. 498). Many musical savants have sight and language disorders, which may lead to increased development of auditory processing skills. Over time, such conditions can lead to the development of high levels of musical skill, but only if appropriate opportunities are available.

Williams Syndrome

Children with Williams syndrome (alternatively known as Williams-Beuren syndrome) possess a genetic abnormality where around twenty-seven of their genes are deleted from a specific region of chromosome 7 (Mosing, Peretz & Ullén, 2018). These individuals often experience difficulties with mathematical and spatial reasoning and have low measured intelligence but are more adept than might be expected in language and musical skills.

Levitin and colleagues (Levitin & Bellugi, 1998; Levitin et al., 2003; Levitin et al., 2007) have shown that children with Williams syndrome are typically as musically accomplished, engaged, and interested as ordinary children, but display greater emotional responses to music, become interested at a younger age, spend more time listening to music, and possess a highly sensitive emotional attachment to music. While children with Williams syndrome show great variability in musical skills, their musical strengths often come in the form of expressivity and sensitivity to music. Children with Williams syndrome seem to retain the overall structure of musical phrases better than they can reproduce them, suggesting that musical skill and musical understanding are not synonymous. Their strong affinity for music may be rooted in atypical auditory processing, in autonomic irregularities, or in their atypical neurobiology (Thakur, Martens, Smith, & Roth, 2018).

In contrast, another different type of mutation on chromosome 7 has been shown to cause speech and language difficulties and alter musicality, again suggesting that genes on chromosome 7 are in some way involved in various forms of musical development (Mosing, Peretz, & Ullén, 2018).

MUSICAL PRODIGIES

A widely cited definition of a prodigy is "a child (typically younger than 10 years old) who is performing at the level of a highly trained adult in a very demanding field of endeavour" (Feldman, 1993, p. 188). In our view, this definition is deficient in a number of ways (see Gagné & McPherson, 2016). Even though there is wide variability, boys and girls tend to reach puberty at different ages (boys around 9–14 and girls 8–13), meaning that coordination issues may be apparent during this timeframe (Khan, 2019). It is also difficult to define exactly what is meant by performing at "the level of a highly trained adult." Furthermore, why would music prodigies be restricted to a "very demanding field of endeavour," especially if this is used to imply Western art music? For Gagné and McPherson (2016), a more constructive way is to move from this "product" emphasis to a "process" emphasis that examines the level of musical competence according to the length of time that it took this person to reach this level of achievement. When we use these criteria to establish the threshold of a true musical prodigy, we see that the bar is extremely high.

Within this perspective, prodigies can be distinguished by their unusual precociousness, as the rate at which prodigious children learn is highly accelerated (Comeau et al., 2017; Geake, 2009; Howard, 2008; Jenkins, 2005; McPherson, 2007). For example, Ruthsatz and Detterman (2003) describe a six-year-old boy who in their opinion possessed high musical ability because he could copy others, improvise his own musical pieces, sing in two languages, and play numerous instruments. These skills are remarkable given that he had received no formal musical tuition and seemed to have acquired these skills entirely through his own motivation to engage with music in these ways. Another musical prodigy, Alma Deutscher, began to play the piano at two years of age, the violin aged three, and by the age of four had started composing at which age she wrote her first opera about a pirate. She has given numerous concert performances, often of her own works, and her opera, *Cinderella*, has been performed in various venues across the world.

Musically gifted children tend to be particularly sensitive to the structure of music, its tonality, key, harmony, and rhythm, and its expressive properties, and can remember songs much earlier than other children. Whatever the underlying genetic makeup that facilitates these phenomena, appropriate environmental conditions need to be present such as supportive parents and teachers and a high level of motivation of the type that Winner (1996) describes as a "rage to master."

McPherson and Lehmann (2012) describe a young female pianist, Tiffany, who at the age of two was observed copying, on a toy piano, music played on her father's hi-fi system. At the age of four and a half she began formal piano lessons, and after three years of learning she was practising for three or four hours a day and capable of performing at Grade 8 Associated Board Standard. Her mother reported that during the early stages of learning, she would play games with her daughter that helped her to focus on repetition and mastery. This provided a playful learning environment in which there was frequent positive verbal feedback. The mother-child relationship supported the development of motivation to achieve at a continually higher level. Tiffany also had a high level self-regulatory skills and acquired an aural representation of the music before playing it, selecting repertoire that she wanted to learn. Her primary motivation was being able to play particular pieces of music (McPherson & Lehmann, 2012).

It seems that the key factors for the accelerated development seen in prodigies are general intelligence; the ability to mimic others; auditory memory for melodies; manual dexterity; motor memory; intense, purposeful practice; autonomy; a passionate involvement and love of music; and a willpower and perseverance to succeed (Gagné & McPherson, 2016). As these children develop, they respond to stimuli in ways that heighten their cognitive, emotional, and social sensitivities, thereby providing a foundation for their accelerated learning (Shavinina, 2016).

There are some similarities in the development and overt musical behaviors of savants, Williams syndrome individuals, and prodigies, even though their neuro-developmental trajectories differ. Neuro-constructivists suggest that typical and atypical development can be viewed as different trajectories in a continuum of possibilities. Typical and atypical development trajectories impact the interactions of others with the child, and the kind of experiences that the child seeks out, which further impacts their trajectory (Mareschal et al. 2007). For example, when parents believe that their child has musical ability, whether as a prodigy, savant, or Williams syndrome child, they are more likely to support musical activities by providing opportunities and rewarding engagement. This, in turn, encourages further musical activity, supporting skill development and consequent changes in neural structures, which facilitate future learning (Altenmüller & Gruhn, 2002; Hodges, 2006).

It is difficult to disentangle the complex relationships between genetic and environmental factors. Passive gene-environment correlation refers to situations in which offspring inherit genes from their biological parents that also influence those parents to provide a particular environment for their children. For example, musical parents tend to provide a musical environment and also pass on genetic dispositions toward musical activities. Active gene-environment correlations refer to situations in which individuals seek out environmental experiences based on genetically influenced characteristics: for instance, a child with a passion for music will seek out musical training. Evocative gene-environment correlation refers to situations in which individuals evoke environmental experiences based on genetically influenced traits from the people and institutions around them. For example, children showing an aptitude for playing an instrument may be encouraged by their peers or teachers to further engage in music making. Active and evocative gene-environment correlations may serve to explain how individuals select and evoke environments on the basis of their genetically influenced characteristics. These experiences in turn affect the development of expert skills, while also reinforcing the genetic characteristics that drove the selection and evocation. These dynamic relationships have come to be termed *gene-environment transactions* (Tucker-Drob, Briley, & Harden,

2013). Characteristics that lead people to differentially select and evoke environmental experiences have been termed *experience-producing drives* (Bourchard, 1997; Johnson, 2013). These may include their interests, motivations, goals, and aptitudes for the skills being acquired (Tucker-Drob, 2017). As these processes unfold, experience and the skills developing from these relationships are likely to become increasingly differentiated by genotype, producing a Matthew Effect. The amount of experience comes to be correlated with genotype, such that environmental experience itself is heritable.

Environmental Catalysts

In Figure 3.2, three basic forms of environmental catalysts are depicted. In many ways these are fairly straightforward, given that the social environment or milieu in which a child is raised impacts the path to acquiring talent because of the people they come in contact with, the emotions they experience while engaged in music, the attitudes they develop about music, and the physical settings to which they are exposed. For children, the way that parents and significant others mentor, educate, and inculcate values, in addition to the environment they provide through early exposure to a music education, high-quality models, professional level concerts, and various enrichment activities, can all act together to accelerate musical learning.

Intrapersonal Catalysts

Intrapersonal catalysts include the physical and mental traits that can impact positively or negatively on the development of musical talent. Physical traits would include a musician's physical health, such as the repertoire decisions pianists make based on their own personal finger span (Parncutt & Troup, 2002). The mental traits shown in Figure 3.2 include temperament, which impacts a musician's behavioral predisposition, and personality, which are often defined in terms of five attributes: *Openness, Conscientiousness, Agreeableness, Extraversion,* and *Neuroticism* (see further Hruska & Bonneville-Roussy, this volume).

A second category of intrapersonal catalysis includes those goal management attributes that are integral to success in music, such as a personal sense of one's strengths and weaknesses, and the volition, or autonomy that drives a musician to persist and apply effort. With regard to the musical values, needs, interests, and passion of each individual—that is, their motivation—the literature in music is vast, with much of this topic covered in other sections of this handbook (especially the opening two chapters of Part IV).

CHANCE

In any part of Figure 3.2, *chance* will play a role. As Gagné and McPherson (2016) suggest, chance is not strictly a causal factor, but it will, to a certain extent, help predict all of the elements in the components of giftedness, environmental and intrapersonal catalysts, and developmental processes. This is because personal accomplishment depends on "two crucial rolls of the dice over which no individual exerts any personal control. These are the accidents of birth and background. One roll of the dice determines an individual's heredity; the other his formative environment" (Atkinson, 1978, p. 221). An example, from countless others, would be a child born in a developing country who might never have the opportunity to touch an instrument, let alone be allowed to pursue music as a career because of a lack of access and opportunity to a music education.

DEVELOPMENTAL PROCESSES

The greatest challenge to the notion of musical potential being an inherited, immutable characteristic has come from research within the expertise paradigm. This perspective suggests that the level of expertise an individual attains in a field of study depends on the amount of deliberate practice undertaken in that field, as well as a variety of other environmental factors. Some of earliest research on this topic was conducted by Ericsson and colleagues (1993, 2019), who argued that there was a direct relationship between the amount of deliberate practice undertaken by young musicians and the level of expertise that they attained. While subsequent research has supported the importance of practice in attaining high levels of expertise, there has been little support for this relationship being the sole determinant in the development of expertise.

In particular, Ericsson's theory cannot account for wide individual differences in the amount of practice undertaken to achieve similar levels of expertise (Ericsson et al., 1993, 2019; Sloboda et al., 1996; Hallam et al., 2012), especially given that retrospective estimates of the amount of practice undertaken in learning to perform are notoriously unreliable (Madsen, 2004). More recently, Ericsson and Harwell (2019) have claimed that these estimate issues should be "less problematic for practice activities meeting the criteria for deliberate practice in domains with an established curriculum that prescribes a particular progression of mastery" (p. 9), but this is based on the largely unsupported assumption that teachers of elite performers are providing an "established curriculum" or "particular progression of mastery." This is a tenuous claim in the field of elite music performance, given that performance staff in music schools are typically hired because of exceptional performance skills, not for any systematic training in or evidence of the ability to provide excellent teaching (Parkes, 2009/2010).

Even where there are statistically significant relationships between deliberate practice, level of expertise, or performance on particular tasks, the amount of variance explained varies considerably (McPherson, 2005; Macnamara, Hambrick, & Oswald, 2014; Macnamara, Hambrick, & Moreau, 2016; Platz, Kopiez, Lehmann & Wolf, 2014). There are also differences in the amount of practice undertaken between those playing different instruments (Jørgensen, 2002; Hallam, et al., 2019). In addition, the amount of practice undertaken is not a strong predictor of the quality of the musical outcomes (Hallam, 1998; 2013; Hallam et al., 2012; Williamon & Valentine 2000). Students differ in the practice strategies that they adopt, their meta-cognitive skills, and levels of concentration. Typically, the quality of practice improves as higher levels of expertise are attained, and beginners in particular tend to adopt ineffective strategies, wasting time on unproductive activities (McPherson & Renwick, 2001; Hallam et al., 2012). The emphasis in the paradigm on deliberate practice means that no account is taken of other musical activities in which a learner may engage, for instance, listening, improvising, and participating in group activities where learning and the consolidation of skills occurs in an informal learning context (e.g., Kokotsaki & Hallam, 2011). Zatorre and colleagues' findings show that musical training in sensitive periods during childhood supports skilled behavior well into adulthood, suggesting that early study is important in achieving high-level skill (Steele & Zatorre, 2018). Recently, the role of interest has been shown to be a major contributing factor in the development of expertise (Hambrick, Burgoyne, & Oswald, 2019; Ullén, Hambrick, & Mosing, 2016). Thus, it is likely that a wide range of musical activities contribute to the development of expertise, not only deliberate practice (Macnamara, Hambrick, & Moreau, 2016; Macnamara, Hambrick, & Oswald, 2014).

While there may be flaws in Ericsson's paradigm in terms of its narrow focus on individual deliberate practice, the notion of active engagement with musical activities contributing to musical achievement and ongoing musical potential is supported by research from neuroscience. Many brain regions are involved in making music (see Brown, Zatorre & Penhume, 2015, for a review), and changes occur as expertise develops. As the individual engages with different musical learning experiences over long periods of time, permanent changes occur in the brain. The longer the engagement with music, the greater the neurological change. The changes are also specific to the particular musical learning undertaken. For example, different parts of the brain respond to the processing of pitch in string players when compared with the complex memory for rhythm acquired by drummers. Musical training, when undertaken over extended periods of time, can potentially change brain functioning as well as brain structure. Thus, the interaction between genes and environmental factors provides a compelling explanation for individual differences in the realization of musical potential.

TALENT DEVELOPMENT IN MUSIC

What are some of the most basic principles underpinning the development of the types of musical talents depicted in Figure 3.2? Very recent research has begun to distinguish some of these:

1. *Abilities are important for high achievement.* Individuals differ in both the general and domain-specific abilities they possess, even though they are malleable and need to be developed for musicians to achieve their own individual goals.
2. *In music, as in other domains, there are different beginnings, peaks and end points for development.* Examples in music performance include boy sopranos who specialize and peak in childhood and end their careers in early adolescence. Violinists typically start in early childhood, peak in early adulthood, and end their careers in late adulthood. Flute performers start in middle adolescence, peak in middle adulthood, and end in late adulthood. Vocal arts performers often begin in late adolescence, peak in middle adulthood, and end in late adulthood.
3. *Abilities need to be deployed to develop.* Providing opportunities to learn an instrument/voice is important for individuals to realize their own musical potential. In parallel, the role of teachers, parents, and peers changes across time as the musician becomes competent and seeks to develop further expertise.
4. *Mental and social skills transform abilities into competencies, expertise, and creative productivity.* Abilities will not develop unless the individual is receptive to the opportunities that may be provided for them. Development depends therefore on possessing the confidence and motivation to take advantage of the opportunities that might be provided, plus also the autonomy to seek these out. The degree of mental and social skills that people possess also helps determine whether they will persevere despite obstacles and setbacks, invest sufficient resources to continuing to improve, and maintain a healthy long-term commitment to their own musical development.
5. *Talents can be development in both formal and informal settings.* Many developing musicians extend their formal music education through a variety of enhancement activities that they seek outside of these formal settings. These include a variety of extracurricular and cocurricular activities that extend and serve them as they seek to meet their individual goals (see Preckel et al., 2020, pp. 3–5, Subotnik et al., 2011).

Aligned with these principles are at least four successive levels of talent development: *aptitude, competence, expertise,* and *transformational achievement*. These four developmental levels are shown in Figure 3.3. *Aptitudes* refer to the types of mental and physical natural abilities shown in Figure 3.2 that can be developed further and that underpin successful musical learning. Music learners start to gain in *competence* after they have acquired a number of skills and become invested in their own learning to the degree that they can independently invest time practicing in order to broaden their musical repertoire and expressive abilities. *Expertise* refers to being able to demonstrate a superior level of musical skill that others notice, such as in public performances or the types of talents listed in Figure 3.2. Groundbreaking achievement of the highest order that is distinguished by huge output, creative productivity, commercial success, artistic recognition by experts, and influential to other musicians is the hallmark of *transformational achievement.*

The increasing specialization of talent are shown in the second column of Figure 3.3, which indicate the roles of high general ability (what we refer to as natural abilities) that are related to and predict achievement more generally because they are, to a certain extent, malleable and variable across the lifespan. This column also depicts increasing specialization over time, and how ability relates to the development of the individual's personality, which eventually characterizes one's identity-personality profile of abilities, interests and valuing, motivation to persist, and self-concepts within that domain. Each of these informs subsequent talent development toward higher levels of achievement (Preckel, et al., 2020). As these processes begin to unfold, one of the most fundamental transformations involves moving from a personal belief of "I learn music" to "I am a musician" (or, more specifically, for example, "I learn violin" to "I am a violinist").

Finally, in the right-hand side of Figure 3.3, we see the level-dependent predictors and indicators of talent development. Each of these boxes outlines the main variables that

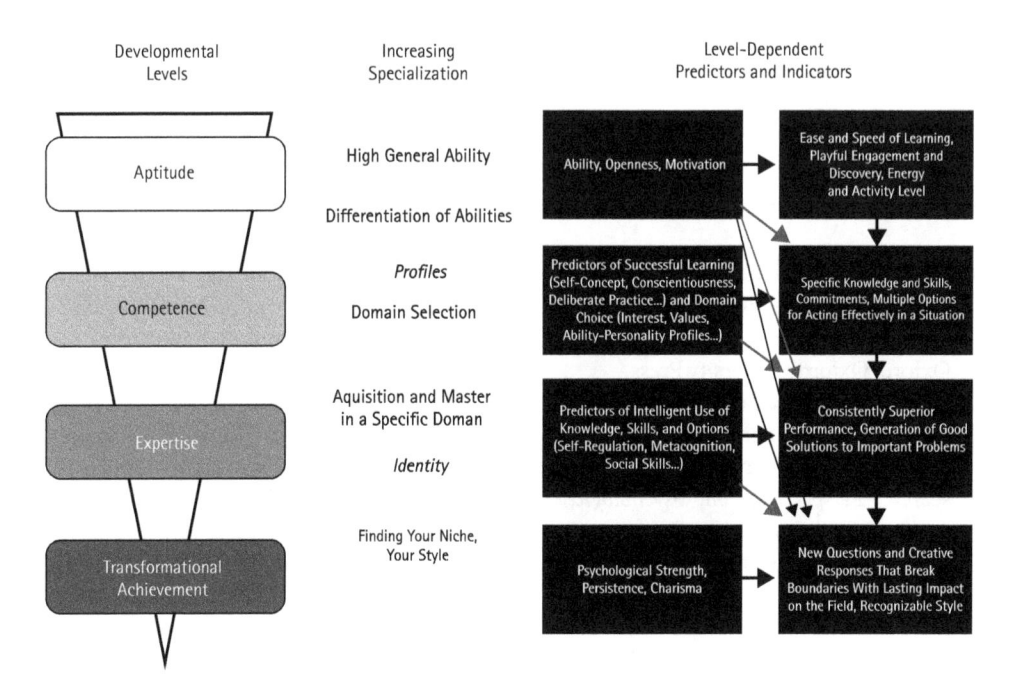

FIGURE 3.3. The Talent-Development-in-Achievement-Domains (TAD) Framework. Reproduced with permission from Preckel et al., 2020, p. 7.

separately and cumulatively act on talent development over time. Importantly, some of these variables (e.g., general cognitive ability, motivation) impact throughout an individual's development, whereas others increase over time. A good example are the social skills needed to succeed as a performer as one moves to an advanced student or professional level of playing ability.

CONCLUSION

In this chapter, we have shown that music is a universal feature of our human design and that virtually everyone can successfully engage with music, if they so choose. Even individuals with amusia, who may never reach a high level of performance, can benefit from a music education if only for the academic benefits associated with music learning (Peretz, 2020). With modern teaching techniques and unprecedented access to technology, people are able to learn music through a multitude of avenues. With this in mind, the best recommendation we can offer readers is to pursue those musical endeavors that are of most interest to them!

For musicians who wish to take their talent development to a much higher level, the framework outlined in this final part of our chapter may provide greater awareness of what exactly is taking place on this road to developing expertise, from the earliest stages of learning right through to the types of transformational achievement that distinguishes the world's leading exponents of music.

Music produces a kind of pleasure that none of us can afford to live without.

KEY SOURCES

Gagné, F., & McPherson, G. E. (2016). Analyzing musical prodigiousness using Gagné's Integrative Model of Talent Development. In G. E McPherson (Ed.), *Music prodigies: Interpretations from psychology, education, musicology and ethnomusicology* (pp. 3–114). Oxford: Oxford University Press.

Preckel, F., Folle, J., Grabner, R., Jarvin, L., Kozbelt, A., Müllensiefen, D., Olszewski-Kubilius, P., Scheider, W., Subotnick, R., Vock, M., & Worrell, F. C. (2020). Talent development in achievement domains: A psychological framework for within- and cross-domain research. *Perspectives on Psychological Science*, 15(3), 519–543. https://doi.org/10.1177/1745691619895030.

For video footage relating to the protegee Alma Deutscher, go to www.youtube.com/user/AlmaDeutscher.

For an account of the life of Derek Paravicini, a British musical savant, see Ockelford, A. (2008). *In the key of genius: The extraordinary life of Derek Paravicini*. London: Arrow. For examples of Derek's playing, see www.youtube.com/user/derekparavicini.

To download the musical sophistication questionnaire, go to www.gold.ac.uk/music-mind-brain/gold-msi/download.

To pursue issues about your own personal development, refer to Hallam, S & Gaunt, H. (2012). *Preparing for success: A practical guide for young musicians*. London: Institute of Education Press.

GLOSSARY OF TERMS

Musical aptitude:	A term used to describe a person's overall capacity to learn or develop musically before any form of education or training.
Giftedness:	The natural abilities (mental, physical) evident in the early years that underpin future development.
Musical talent:	Being able to demonstrate competence (e.g., performing, composing, improvising) after one's natural abilities, intrapersonal, environmental, and developmental processes have all facilitated development.
Musicality:	Demonstrating a sensitivity to music (e.g., pleasant sound, phrasing, expression when performing) of a type that distinguishes the person from other individuals.
Musical sophistication:	The ability of individuals to engage with music in a flexible, effective and nuanced way.
Competence:	Systematically developed abilities, knowledge, and skills resulting from systematic training that enable individuals to act effectively in a specific situation.
Expertise:	Being able to display high levels of superior achievement in an area. Musical experts are able to perform at the same level across multiple performances of the same repertoire.

REFLECTIVE QUESTIONS

1. What do you consider to be your finest musical attributes? How do these impact your daily engagement with music, how you perceive yourself as a "performer," or the pathways and influences that have shaped your development as a musician?

2. Do you know anyone who claims to be "unmusical" or "tone deaf"? If so, how might you use the information in this chapter to counter or justify their claims?

3. Do you know anyone who appears to be extraordinarily musically talented? How does the information surveyed in this chapter help you more precisely explain this person's talent?

4. To what degree do you come from a "musical family"? How were your own interests and abilities fostered during your childhood?

5. What strategies might you use as a teacher to foster your students' interest in music?

6. What strategies might you use to foster your child's interest in music?

References

Altenmüller, E. O., & Furaya, S. (2018). Brain changes associated with the acquisition of musical expertise. In A. Ericsson, R. R. Hoffman, A. Kozbelt & M. Williams (Eds.), *The Cambridge handbook of expertise and expert performance* (pp. 550–575). Cambridge, UK: Cambridge University Press.

Atkinson, J. W. (1978). Motivational determinants of intellective performance and cumulative achievement. In J.W. Atkinson & J.O. Raynor (Eds.), *Personality, motivation, and achievement* (pp. 221–242). New York: Wiley.

Baharloo, S., Service, S. K., Risch, N., Gitschier, J., & Freimer, N. B. (2000). Familial aggregation of absolute pitch. *American Journal of Human Genetics, 67*, 755–758. https://doi.org/10.1086/303057.

Bahr, N., Christensen, C. A., Bahr, M. (2005). Diversity of accuracy profiles for absolute pitch recognition. *Psychology of Music, 33*, 58–93. https://doi.org/10.1177/0305735605048014.

Bermudez, P., & Zatorre, R. J. (2009). A distribution of absolute pitch ability as revealed by computerized testing. *Music Perception, 27*(2), 89–101. https://doi.org/10.1525/mp.2009.27.2.89.

Bonnel, A., Mottron, I. L., Peretz, L., Trudel, M., Gallun, E., & Bonnel, A. M. (2003). Enhanced pitch sensitivity in individuals with autism: A signal detection analysis. *Journal of Cognitive Neuroscience, 15*, 226–35. https://doi.org/10.1162/089892903321208169.

Brown, R. M., Zatorre, R. J., & Penhume, V. B. (2015). Expert music performance: Cognitive, neural and developmental bases. *Progress in Brain Research, 217*, 57–86. https://doi.org/10.1016/bs.pbr.2014.11.021.

Burgoyne, A. P., Harris, L. J., & Hambrick, D. Z. (2019). Predicting piano skill acquisition in beginners: The role of general intelligence, music aptitude, and mindset. *Intelligence, 76*, 1–8. https://doi.org/10.1016/j.intell.2019.101383.

Chavarria-Soley, G. (2016). Absolute pitch in Costa Rica: Distribution of pitch identification ability and implications for its genetic basis. *Journal of the Acoustical Society of America, 140*(2), 891–897. https://doi.org/10.1121/1.4960569.

Comeau, G., Vuvan, D. T., Picard-Deland, C., & Peretz, I. (2017). Can you tell a prodigy from a professional musician? *Music Perception, 35*(2), 200–210. https://doi.org/10.1525/MP.2017.35.2.200.

Dowling, W. J. (1999). The development of music perception and cognition. In D. Deutsch (Ed.), *The psychology of music* (2nd ed., pp. 603–627). Amsterdam: Academic Press.

Ericsson, A. K., & Harwell, K. W. (2019). Deliberate practice and proposed limits on the effects of practice on the acquisition of expert performance: Why the original definition matters and recommendations for future research. *Frontiers in Psychology, 10*, 2396. https://doi.org/10.3389/fpsyg.2019.02396.

Ericsson, K. A., Krampe, R. T., & Tesch-Romer, C. (1993). The role of deliberate practice on the acquisition of expert performance. *Psychological Review, 100*(3), 363–406.

Feldman, D. H. (1993). Child prodigies: A distinctive form of giftedness. *Gifted Child Quarterly, 37*, 188–193. https://doi.org/10.1177%2F001698629303700408.

Gagné, F. (2009). Building gifts into talents: Detailed overview of the DMGT 2.0. In B. MacFarlane & T. Stambaugh (Eds.), *Leading change in gifted education: The festschrift of Dr. Joyce VanTassel-Baska* (pp. 61–80). Waco, TX: Prufrock Press.

Gagné, F., & McPherson, G. E. (2016). *Analyzing musical prodigiousness using Gagné's Integrative Model of Talent Development.* In G. E. McPherson (Ed.), *Music prodigies: Interpretations from psychology, education, musicology and ethnomusicology*(pp. 3–114). Oxford: Oxford University Press.

Geake, J. G. (2009). Neuropsychological characteristics of academic and creative giftedness. In L. A. Shavinina (Ed.), *International handbook on giftedness* (pp. 261–273). Gatineau, Quebec: Springer.

Greenberg, D. M., Müllensiefen, D., Lamb, M. E., & Rentfrow, P. J. (2015). Personality predicts musical sophistication. *Journal of Research in Personality, 58*, 154–158. http://dx.doi.org/10.1016/j.jrp.2015.06.002.

Gregersen, P. K., Kowalsky, E., Lee, A., Baron-Cohen, S., Fisher, S. E., Asher, J. E., Ballard, D., Freudenberg, J., & Li, W. (2013). Absolute pitch exhibits phenotypic and genetic overlap with synesthesia. *Human Molecular Genetics, 22*(10), 2097–2104. https://doi.org/10.1093/hmg/ddt059.

Hallam, S. (1998). The predictors of achievement and dropout in instrumental tuition. *Psychology of Music, 26*(2), 116–132. https://doi.org/10.1177%2F0305735698262002.

Hallam, S. (2013). What predicts level of expertise attained, quality of performance, and future musical aspirations in young instrumental players? *Psychology of Music, 41*(3), 265–289. https://doi.org/10.1177%2F0305735611425902.

Hallam, S., Creech, A., Varvarigou, M., & Papageorgi, I. (2019). Are there differences in practice depending on the instrument played? *Psychology of Music, 48*(4), 745–765. https://doi.org/10.1177/0305735618816370.

Hallam, S., Rinta, T., Varvarigou, M., Creech, A., Papageorgi, I., & Lani, J. (2012). The development of practising strategies in young people. *Psychology of Music* 40, 652–680. https://doi.org/10.1177/0305735612443868.

Heaton, P. (2009). Assessing musical skills in autistic children who are not savants. *Philosophical Transactions of the Royal Society B: Biological Sciences, 364*, 1443–1447. https://doi.org/10.1098/rstb.2008.0327.

Heaton, P. F. (2003). Pitch memory, labeling and disembedding in autism. *Journal of Child Psychology and Psychiatry, 44*(4), 543–551. https://doi.org/10.1111/1469-7610.00143.

Hodges, D. A. (2006) The musical brain. In G. E. McPherson (Ed.), *The child as musician: A handbook of musical development* (pp. 51–68). Oxford: Oxford University Press.

Howard, R. W. (2008). Linking extreme precocity and adult eminence: A study of eight prodigies at international chess. *High Ability Studies, 19*, 117–130. https://doi.org/10.1080/13598130802503991.

Hughes, J. E. A., Ward, J., Gruffydd, E., Baron-Cohen, S., Smith, P., Allison, C., & Simner, J. (2018). Savant syndrome has a distinct psychological profile in autism. *Molecular Autism, 9*, 53. https://doi.org/10.1186/s13229-018-0237-1.

Jenkins, J. S. (2005). Prodigies of nature. *Journal of the Royal Society of Medicine, 98*, 277–280. https://doi.org/10.1258/jrsm.98.6.277.

Johnson, W. (2013). Greatness as a manifestation of experience-producing drives. In S. B. Kaufman (Ed.), *The complexity of greatness* (pp. 3–16). Oxford: Oxford University Press.

Jørgensen, H. (2002). Instrumental performance expertise and amount of practice among instrumental students in a conservatoire. *Music Education Research, 4*(1), 105–119. https://doi.org/10.1080/14613800220119804.

Khan, L. (2019). Puberty: Onset and progression. *Pediatric Annals, 48*(4), 141–145. http://dx.doi.org/10.3928/19382359-20190322-01.

Kokotsaki, D., & Hallam, S. (2011). The perceived benefits of participative music making for non-music university students: A comparison with music students. *Music Education Research, 13*(2), 149–72. https://doi.org/10.1080/14613808.2011.577768.

Levitin, D. J. (1994). Absolute memory for musical pitch: Evidence from the production of learned melodies. *Perception & Psychophysics, 56,* 414–423. https://doi.org/10.3758/BF03206733.

Levitin, D. J., & Bellugi, U. (1998). Musical abilities in individuals with Williams syndrome. *Music Perception, 15*(4), 357–89. https://doi.org/10.2307/40300863.

Levitin, D. J., Cole, K., Chiles, M., Lai, Z., Lincoln, A., & Bellugi, U. (2007). Characterizing the musical phenotype in individuals with Williams syndrome. *Child Neuropsychology, 10*(4), 223–247. https://doi.org/10.1080/09297040490909288.

Levitin, D. J., Menon, V., Schmitt, J. E., Eliez, S., White, C. D., Glover, G. H., & Kadis, J. (2003). Neural correlates of auditory perception in Williams syndrome: An fMRI study. *NeuroImage, 18,* 74–82. https://doi:10.1006/nimg.2002.1297.

Loui, P. (2016). Absolute pitch. In S. Hallam, I. Cross & M. Thaut (Eds.), *Oxford handbook of music psychology* (pp. 81–94). Oxford: Oxford University Press.

Macnamara, B. N., Hambrick, D. Z., & Moreau, D. (2016). How important is deliberate practice? A reply to Ericsson (2016). *Perspectives in Psychological Science, 11*(3), 355–358. https://doi.org/10.1177/1745691616635614.

Macnamara, B. N., Hambrick, D. Z., & Oswald, F. L. (2014). Deliberate practice and performance in music, games, sports, education, and professions: A meta-analysis. *Psychological Science, 25*(8), 1608–1618. https://doi.org/10.1177/0956797614535810.

Mareschal, D., Johnson, M. H., Sitois, S., Spratling, M. W. Thomas, M. S. C., & Westerman, G. (2007). *Neuroconstructivism: How the brain constructs cognition, Vol. 1.* Oxford: Oxford University Press.

McDermott, J., & Hauser, M. D. (2005). The origins of music: Innateness, uniqueness and evolution. *Music Perception, 23*(1), 29–59. https://doi.org/10.1525/mp.2005.23.1.29.

McLachlan, N. M., Marco, D. J., & Wilson, S. J. (2013). Pitch and plasticity: Insights from the pitch matching of chords by musicians with absolute and relative pitch. *Brain Sciences, 3*(4), 1615–1634. https://doi.org/10.3390/brainsci3041615.

McPherson, G. E. (2005). From child to musician: Skill development during the beginning stages of learning an instrument. *Psychology of Music, 33*(1), 5–35. https://doi.org/10.1177%2F0305735605048012.

McPherson, G. E. (2007). Diary of a child musical prodigy. In A. Williamon & D. Coimbra (Eds.), *Proceedings of the International Symposium on Performance Science* (pp. 213–218). Utrecht: European Association of Conservatoires (AEC).

McPherson, G. E. & Lehmann, A. (2012). Exceptional musical abilities—child prodigies. In G. E. McPherson & G. Welch (Eds.), *Oxford handbook of music education* (Vol. 2, pp. 31–50). New York: Oxford University Press.

Mosing, M. A., Hambrick, D. Z., & Ullén, F. (2019). Predicting musical aptitude and achievement: Practice, teaching, and intelligence. *Journal of Expertise, 2*(3), 184–197.

Mottron, L. & Bouvet, L. (2016). Veridical mapping in the development of autistic musical savants. In G. E. McPherson (Ed.), *Musical prodigies: Interpretations from psychology, education, musicology, and ethnomusicology* (pp. 496–508). Oxford: Oxford University Press.

Mottron, L., Dawson, M., & Soulieres, I. (2009). Enhanced perception in savant syndrome: Patterns, structure and creativity. *Philosophical Transactions of the Royal Society, 364,* 1385–1391. https://doi.org/10.1098/rstb.2008.0333.

Müllensiefen, D., Gingras, B., Musil, J., & Stewart, L. (2014). The musicality of non-musicians: An index for assessing musical sophistication in the general population. *PLoS ONE 9*(2), e89642. https://doi.org/10.1371/journal.pone.0089642.

Müllensiefen, D., Harrison, P., Caprini, F., & Fancourt, A. (2015). Investigating the importance of self-theories of intelligence and musicality for students' academic and musical achievement. *Frontiers in Psychology, 6,* 1702. https://doi.org/10.3389/fpsyg.2015.01702.

Nan, Y., Sun, Y., & Peretz, I. (2010). Congenital amusia in speakers of a tone language: Association with lexical tone agnosia. *Brain, 133*(9), 2635–2642. https://doi.org/10.1093/brain/awq178.

Ockelford. A. (2016). Prodigious musical talent in blind children with autism and learning difficulties: Identifying and educating potential musical savants. In G. E. McPherson (Ed.), *Musical prodigies: Interpretations from psychology, education, musicology, and ethnomusicology* (pp. 471–495). Oxford: Oxford University Press.

Parkes, K. A. (2009/2010). College applied faculty: The disjunction of performer, teacher, and educator. *College Music Symposium, 49/50,* 65–76. http://www.jstor.org/ stable/41225232.

Parncutt, R. (2016). Prenatal development. In G. E. McPherson (Ed.)., *The child as musician: A handbook of musical development* (2nd ed., pp. 3–30). Oxford: Oxford University Press.

Parncutt, R., & Troup, M. (2002). Piano. In R. Parncutt & G. E. McPherson (Eds.), *The science and psychology of music performance* (pp. 286–302). Oxford: Oxford University Press. http://doi.org/10.1093/acprof:oso/9780195138108.001.0001.

Peretz, I. (2020). Congenital amusia (tone deafness). In *How music sculpts our brain* (pp. 61–66). Paris: Editions Odile Jacob.

Peretz, I., & Vuvan, D. T. (2017). Prevalence of congenital amusia. *European Journal of Human Genetics, 25*(5), 625–630. https://doi.org/10.1038/ejhg.2017.15.

Phillips-Silver, J., Toivianen, P., Gosselin, N., Piché, O., Nozaradan, S., Palmer, C., & Peretz, I. (2011). Born to dance but beat deaf: A new form of congenital amusia. *Neuropsychologia, 49,* 961–969. https://doi.org/10.1016/j.neuropsychologia.2011.02.002.

Platz, F., Kopiez, R., Lehmann, A., & Wolf, A. (2014). The influence of deliberate practice on musical achievement: A meta-analysis. *Frontiers in Psychology, 5,* 646. https://doi.org/10.3389/fpsyg.2014.00646.

Preckel, F., Folle, J., Grabner, R., Jarvin, L., Kozbelt, A., Müllensiefen, D., Olszewski-Kubilius, P., Scheider, W., Subotnick, R., Vock, M., & Worrell, F. C. (2020). Talent development in achievement domains: A psychological framework for within- and cross-domain research. *Perspectives on Psychological Science, 15*(3), 691–722. https://doi.org/10.1177/1745691619895030.

Profita, J., Bidder, T. G., Optiz, J. M., & Reynolds, J. F. (1988). Perfect pitch. *American Journal of Medical Genetics, 29,* 763–771. https://doi.org/10.1002/ajmg.1320290405.

Ross, D. A., & Marks, L. E. (2009). Absolute pitch in children prior to the beginning of musical training. *Annals of the New York Academy of Sciences, 1169,* 199–204. https://doi.org/10.1111/j.1749-6632.2009.04847.x.

Ross, D. A., Olson, I. R., & Gore, J. C. (2003). Absolute pitch does not depend on early musical training. *Annals of the New York Academy of Sciences, 999*(1), 522–526. https://doi.org/10.1196/annals.1284.065.

Ruthsatz, J. & Detterman, D. K. (2003). An extraordinary memory: The case study of a musical prodigy. *Intelligence, 31*(6), 509–518. https://doi.org/10.1016/S0160-2896(03)00050-3.

Saffran, J. R. (2003). Absolute pitch in infancy and adulthood: The role of tonal structure. *Developmental Science, 6*(1), 35–47. https://doi.org/10.1111/1467-7687.00250.

Shavinina, L. V. (2016). On the cognitive-developmental theory of the child prodigy phenomenon. In G. E. McPherson (Ed.), *Musical prodigies: Interpretations from psychology, education, musicology and ethnomusicology* (pp. 259–278). Oxford: Oxford University Press.

Simonton, D. K. (2001). Talent development as a multidimensional multiplicative, and dynamic process. *Current Directions in Psychological Science, 10*, 39–43. https://doi.org/10.1111/1467-8721.00110.

Sloboda, J. A., Davidson, J. W., Howe, M. J. A., & Moore, D. G. (1996). The role of practice in the development of performing musicians. *British Journal of Psychology, 87*, 287–309. https://doi.org/10.1111/j.2044-8295.1996.tb02591.x.

Stanovich, K. E. (1986). Matthew Effects in reading: Some consequences of individual differences in the acquisition of literacy. *Reading Research Quarterly, 21*(4), 360–407.

Steele, C. J., Bailey, J. A., Zatorre, R. J., & Penhune, V. B. (2013). Early musical training and white-matter plasticity in the corpus callosum: Evidence for a sensitive period. *Journal of Neuroscience, 33*(3) 1282–1290. https://doi.org/10.1523/JNEUROSCI.3578-12.2013.

Steele, C. J., & Zatorre, R. J. (2018). Practice makes plasticity. *Natural Neuroscience 21*(12), 1645–1646. https://doi.org/10.1038/s41593-018-0280-4.

Subotnik, R. F., Olszewski-Kubilius, P., & Worrell, F. C. (2011). Rethinking giftedness and gifted education: A proposed direction forward based on psychological science. *Psychological Science in the Public Interest, 12*(1), 3–54. https://doi.org/10.1177/1529100611418056.

Szyfter, K., & Witt, M. P. (2020). How far musicality and perfect pitch are derived from genetic factors? *Journal of Applied Genetics, 61*, 407–414. https://doi.org/10.1007/s13353-020-00563-7.

Takeuchi, A. H., Hulse, S. H. (1993). Absolute pitch. *Psychological Bulletin, 113*(2), 345–361. https://doi.org/10.1037/0033-2909.113.2.345.

Thakur, D., Martens, M. A., Smith, D. S., & Roth, E. (2018). Williams Syndrome and music: A systematic integrative review. *Frontiers in Psychology, 9*, 1–22. https://doi.org/10.3389/fpsyg.2018.02203.

Tranchant, P., & Peretz, I. (2020). Basic timekeeping deficit in the beat-based form of congenital amusia. *Scientific Reports, 10*(1), 1–10. https://doi.org/10.1038/s41598-020-65034-9.

Treffert, D. A. (2009). The savant syndrome: An extraordinary condition. A synopsis: Past, present, future. *Philosophical Transactions of the Royal Society B, 364*(1522), 1351–1357. https://doi.org/10.1098/rstb.2008.0326.

Treffert, D. A. (2012a). *Islands of genius: The bountiful mind of the autistic, acquired, and sudden savant*. London: Jessica Kingsley.

Treffert, D. A. (2012b). Savant syndrome: A compelling case for innate talent. In S. B. Kaufman (Ed.), *The complexity of greatness: Beyond talent or practice* (pp. 103–18). Oxford: Oxford University Press.

Tucker-Drob, E. M. (2017). Motivational factors as mechanisms of gene-environment transactions in cognitive development and academic achievement. In A. J. Elliot, C. S. Dweck, & D. S. Yeager (Eds.), *Handbook of competence and motivation: Theory and application* (pp. 471–486). New York: Guilford Press.

Tucker-Drob, E. M., Briley, D. A., & Harden, K. P. (2013). Genetic and environmental influences on cognition across development and context. *Current Directions in Psychological Science*, 22(5), 349–355. https://doi.org/10.1177%2F0963721413485087.

Ullén, F., Hambrick, D. Z., & Mosing, M. A. (2016). Rethinking expertise: A multifactorial gene-environment interaction model of expert performance. *Psychological Bulletin*, 142(4), 427–446. https://psycnet.apa.org/doi/10.1037/bul0000033.

Vitouch, O. (2003). Absolutist models of absolute pitch are absolutely misleading. *Music Perception: An Interdisciplinary Journal*, 21(1), 111–117. https://doi.org/10.1525/mp.2003.21.1.111.

Williamon, A. & Valentine, E. (2000). Quantity and quality of musical practice as predictors of performance quality. *British Journal of Psychology*, 91(3), 353–376. https://doi.org/10.1348/000712600161871.

Wilson, S. J., Lusher, D., Martin, C. L., Rayner, G., & McLachlan, N. (2012). Intersecting factors lead to absolute pitch acquisition that is maintained in a "fixed do" environment. Music Perception, 29(3), 285–296. https://doi.org/10.1525/mp.2012.29.3.285.

Winner, E. (1996). *Gifted children: Myths and realities*. New York: Basic Books.

CHAPTER 4

···

READINESS FOR LEARNING
TO PERFORM MUSIC

···

JENNIFER BLACKWELL AND GARY E. MCPHERSON

INTRODUCTION

FOR many children, music lessons are a normal part of their childhood. But how do we know when a child is ready to start learning? For us, a good starting point is to consider the concept of "readiness" as an entry point to an area of learning that goes well beyond the child needing to "know about" or being able to "do" things before learning commences. Rather, we are attracted to the advice of Dan Gartrell (2020), a child development expert, who stresses the need for the child to possess a "willing attitude and confidence in the process of learning: a healthy state of mind" (p. 66).

This view provides a quite different perspective from the focus most instrumental and vocal teachers give to thinking about how to introduce a child to music. Indeed, as we began writing this chapter, we undertook an internet search to see what information is readily available regarding an appropriate age for beginning piano studies. One of the top hits included the recommendation that if a child can recognize numbers 1 through 5, letters A through G, and focus on one activity for ten minutes, then that child may be ready for piano lessons as young as two years old. Others suggest that lessons should not start until the child has started formal schooling and become used to a structured learning environment.

As we searched the literature further, we realized that there is a multitude of advice about when children are ready to begin learning a musical instrument or voice, and the types of issues that need to be sorted through before their first lessons. For this reason, our chapter does discuss a number of developmental factors associated with the child's physical, cognitive, affective, and social maturation, all in the context of neurotypical children with typical development patterns. Although not the focus of our chapter, many of the comments we make are relevant for understanding how to accommodate children with neurodiversity based on our view that all children should be encouraged—if they wish—to pursue their interests in music.

Our chapter should be read in conjunction with our parallel chapter on musical potential, giftedness and talent development (see McPherson, Blackwell, & Hallam, this part) where many of the issues we mention here are dealt with in more detail. The present chapter begins with a discussion of prominent learning theories to contextualize aspects of development and then drills down to individual components that are relevant to learning to perform music. However, in the final section dealing with practical applications, we return to the broader definition of readiness as a "healthy state of mind" to provide a set of principles that can be used to guide the types of environments, approaches and beliefs that best cater for the individual needs of each child. One of the main points of our chapter, however, is that there are no definitive rules as to when a child is ready to commence the formal study of music. Determining readiness is highly contextual and will vary from child to child.

Developmental Considerations: Learning Theories

To understand developmental readiness, it is important to explore the ways in which learning has been conceptualized. Over the past century, a number of highly respected theories of learning have emerged to explain the most important aspects of how we learn, and in turn, these have helped to expand our knowledge of how to teach students. Among the most relevant for music are those proposed by Piaget, Vygotsky, and Bruner.

Piaget

Jean Piaget (1929; 1936) was a psychologist with a perspective that was somewhat unusual for his time: rather than viewing intelligence as a fixed trait, he believed children developed their cognitive skills as a result of both their maturation and interactions with their environment. His "stage theory of cognitive development" proposes discrete stages of development based on age. Piaget's theory has three relevant components: the idea of a schema, adaptation processes for changing schema over time, and his proposed stages of cognitive development.

Broadly speaking, *schema* comprise our mental models of the world. Schema act as a type of building block for intelligent behaviors, in that they help us to organize our knowledge. For example, a child may have a schema for "drum," which includes the head of the drum, the stick used to hit them, the loud, banging sound made after striking them, and perhaps a stand to hold the drum, all of which come together to form the child's understanding of what a drum is. This schema becomes the basis for which the child compares any new information they learn about drums.

The child's "drum schema" may be challenged by new information, which is the process of changing schema. This can happen in two ways: *assimilation* and *accommodation*. For example, when children are presented with the idea that a bongo is also a drum, despite the lack of stick and stand, they may accept this into their schema about drums; this is a form of assimilation. Children may also develop an incorrect idea that a violin is also a percussion instrument, because they saw a violinist strike the strings with their bow in a concert. When an existing schema does not continue to "hold water" with the introduction of new information, a process of accommodation occurs, in which a schema is adapted, and perhaps new schemas—such as one for string instruments—are formed. This occasionally difficult shift of understanding is called *disequilibrium*, meaning the learner has new information that cannot fit into their existing schemas.

Piaget proposed that humans have a powerful urge to categorize the information around them, and thus go through a process of *equilibration*. Equilibration drives the learning process because learners seek to restore balance in their understandings, thereby mastering new intellectual challenges and skills. Moreover, as schemas expand through these processes, learners are more able to adapt in the future.

Piaget also proposed four discrete stages of development, called the *sensorimotor stage* (typically from birth to age 2), the *preoperational stage* (from age 2 to age 7), the *concrete operational stage* (from age 7 to age 11), and the *formal operational stage* (from age 11 through adulthood). According to this view, each child goes through these stages in the same order, because development is determined by biological maturation and interaction with the environment. The sensorimotor stage is characterized through interacting with the environment via the senses. In the preoperational stage, children start to be able to think symbolically, meaning they can understand that one thing can stand for another (for example, the word "cat" and an actual cat). The concrete operational stage is characterized by the ability to think logically and figure things out in their heads, rather than exclusively through interaction with the world. Finally, the formal operational stage is characterized by the ability to think abstractly. It is important to note that, while Piaget's ideas still have relevance today, his stages have not been supported by empirical evidence.

Because Piaget's based his ideas on the idea of biological maturation and stages, the notion of *readiness* is important. From Piaget's perspective, readiness concerns when certain skills or concepts should, or indeed can, be taught. According to Piaget's theory, children should not be taught certain concepts until they have reached the appropriate stage of cognitive development. Though Piaget's theory has not stood the test of time in terms of the absolute nature of the stages and their implications for learner readiness, he has been extremely influential in the development of educational policy and teaching practices for young children. Perhaps the most important educational idea derived from his theory is that of discovery learning, meaning that children learn best by actively exploring their environments.

Vygotsky

Though a contemporary of Piaget, Lev Vygotsky's (1978) theory, often regarded as a social development theory or a sociocultural theory, differs in a number of key aspects. Perhaps most important, Vygotsky stressed the importance of the social component of learning, and particularly how children's own cultural community shapes how they will understand the world. This cultural component manifests in two main ways: the importance of language for shaping thought, and the importance of support from others in learning new material.

Vygotsky proposed that language has a powerful influence on learning, because it develops through interactions with others and shapes how we can understand new ideas. He further differentiates between social speech, private speech, and inner speech. Social speech is simply communication used to talk to others. Private speech is typically seen in young children, is directed to the self, and serves a function in completing tasks. For example, children might quietly verbalize the steps in tying their shoes to themselves in order to help complete the task. As they become more proficient, their private speech decreases in audibility as it takes on a self-regulating function, eventually becoming silent inner speech. Interestingly, even older children and adults use private speech when engaging in new or challenging activities that require a focus on a series of steps, for example, learning to put together a clarinet or to parallel park a car.

The *Zone of Proximal Development* (ZPD) refers to the difference between what a child can achieve independently and what a child can achieve with support from a more knowledgeable other. The more knowledgeable other can be an adult, or a more proficient child who has a better understanding or a higher ability level than the learner. For example, a child may struggle to perform a tricky rhythm, but can do so with a teacher's support and guidance when attempting to clap the passage. The ZPD is important to understanding learning because it helps to pinpoint where learners need additional support. As the learner progresses, the ZPD will shift to accommodate the additional skills the child can accomplish without help. Thus, with the support of teachers and peers in the learning environment, learners develop increasingly complex skills and understandings.

Bruner

Jerome Bruner's theory of learning is considered to be a constructivist learning theory, meaning that learners build their understanding through active participation in the world around them. One of the most common methods for introducing complex material is the spiral curriculum model, which was first articulated by Bruner in 1960. As Bruner (1960) suggests, a spiral curriculum involves the iterative revisiting of topics, subjects, or themes throughout learning. Importantly, a spiral curriculum does not constitute simple repetition of a topic; rather, it requires more depth of investigation and understanding with each spiral, and each spiral builds on those previous. Bruner (1960) disagreed with Piaget's conception of learning readiness and believed that any subject could be "taught effectively in some intellectually honest form to any child at any stage of development" (p. 33). Rather than waiting for the child to be ready for the subject, Bruner proposed that the material be made accessible to the child, including beginning at the simplest information in the field of study. Bruner (1978) also highlighted the importance of scaffolding, which is the process of simplifying or streamlining a task to help children focus on the skills they are acquiring. For example, to teach articulation on the saxophone, a teacher might start by having the child perform articulations on the neck and mouthpiece alone, so as to allow them to focus on the task and avoid any confusion about how to hold the instrument or perform specific fingerings that might disrupt their learning.

Bruner's theory of learning also includes three different ways of thinking, called "modes of representation": *enactive representation*, which is action-based; *iconic representation*, which is image-based; and *symbolic representation*, which is language-based. Enactive representation involves thinking-as-doing, meaning that the learner understands new information through physical activity. For example, a child might understand the concept of a steady beat by marching to the beat of a drum provided by a teacher. Iconic representation involves the use of visual representations of information. Continuing with the steady beat example, the students might be shown pictures of a heart to explain the idea of a "heartbeat" (a commonly used term for steady beat with children) and be asked to represent how many steady beats they hear using these icons. Symbolic representation involves encoding information in symbolic ways, such as language. The child might learn later that the "heartbeat" is called a quarter note and begin to both write a quarter note in the staff to represent the steady beat, and to spell the words themselves. Rather than being age-related, Bruner's modes of representation are only loosely sequential, and apply to all learners, including adults.

In understanding developmental readiness, learning theories provide a useful tool for understanding how children learn, and thus when a skill or idea may be appropriate for the child. Moreover, learning theories provide guidance on how new material might be introduced to enhance student understanding (see further, Ormrod, 2019).

Readiness from a Developmental Perspective

Developmental factors

In a field where children can be labeled as musically precocious at a very young age, it is important to understand how age and maturation play a role in this identification. Literature about talent identification in sport provides a useful caution on this subject. In this area, studies exploring the identification of talent in young athletes have highlighted maturation as a key confounding variable, as these athletes are typically identified either before or during puberty. Because of the unpredictability of growth and change during this period, children may be identified as particularly coordinated or uncoordinated due to developmental differences, known as *relative age effects*. Relative age effects, in turn, produce a learning environment that provides advantages to some children while disadvantaging others (Baker, Schorer, & Cobley, 2010). Physiological testing during this time may thus provide results that are neither reliable nor valid (Pearson, Naughton, & Torode, 2006; Preckel et al., 2020).

An overemphasis on early identification, rather than the development of skill in individuals, results in an environment that does not consider readiness to learn as an important variable (Abbott, Button, Pepping, & Collins, 2005). As Jaap and Patrick (2014) note, the careless or inconsistent use of terms such as *gift* or *talent* can create "havoc" in educational policy because children identified as gifted are given access to additional resources, including teacher time and access to expertise through specialist instruction. When children fulfill their potential, the tendency is to cite their "innate talent" as the reason for their achievement, rather than recognizing the important role played by the additional educational resources. In music, where they can begin lessons as young as two years of age for some instruments, an age difference of six months between infants could mean marked differences in their readiness to perform the motor and cognitive tasks essential for performing music. Thus, great caution is needed when identifying children as musically inclined—or not—without first considering how their age and maturation might play a role in their readiness for musical activities.

Distinguishing giftedness from talent

There continues to be a huge degree of misunderstanding about whether the precocious giftedness shown by some children learning music is the result of nature, nurture, or both genetic influences and environmental factors. Many everyday explanations are outdated and would benefit from teachers and musicians using terms in a more consistent way to explain development, from before formal learning begins until a learner has acquired some level of ability on an instrument.

We choose to draw on Gagné's (2009, 2013; Gagné & McPherson, 2016) explanations, where *gifts* refer to those natural abilities or aptitudes that a child possesses before instruction begins, as compared to the types of *talents* that can be developed as a result of exposure to a variety of environmental, personal catalysts, and developmental processes that impact on musical development (see further, McPherson, Blackwell & Hallam, this part). These natural abilities are evident in all children, and because they are not innate, continue to develop during childhood as a result of maturation and informal use (Gagné & McPherson, 2016).

Parents and teachers can observe these mental and physical natural abilities in children in a variety of ways, such as when they display unusually precocious *intellectual abilities* of the type that allow for rapid development when learning how to read and comprehend music; the *creative abilities* that convey a mature interpretation when performing or improvising music; the *social abilities* that allow them to communicate and interact with others in a way that appear to be well beyond their years; the *perceptual abilities*—especially aural and visual—for learning to think in sound and read notation; and the *physical abilities*—especially coordination and flexibility—that make performing music look so effortless (Gagné & McPherson, 2016). Gagné (2009) suggests that these four forms of natural ability serve as the *raw material* for subsequent learning, and that it is the ease and speed of learning new skills that distinguishes the level of these *gifts* or natural abilities (Gagné & McPherson, 2016).

Attributes affecting readiness

In terms of readiness for learning an instrument or voice, some of the main attributes that impact on development include:

Predispositions to learn

In the first *Harry Potter* book, students began their schooling by placing on themselves a magical "sorting hat" that looked inside their minds and then determined their individual predispositions and untapped abilities to assign them to a "house" that would best develop their tendencies (see Herholz, 2013). Although nothing like this exists in real life, a growing body of neurological research has increased knowledge of how "individual brain characteristics underlie the huge variability in behaviors and abilities" (Herholz, 2013, p. 15321). Some of this rapidly growing body of research has begun to document the functional and structural brain characteristics that help determine our potential to learn, especially in the auditory domain, and the types of training-induced change that arises from individual predispositions for learning. Such predispositions do not infer that everything we do is predetermined, because "Even if our brains are not optimally wired to learn a certain task, we may still invest our motivation and energy into activities of our choice and compensate by increased effort and training intensity" (Herholz, 2013, p. 15323). This has been shown in studies of twins where genetic factors account for a large part of their abilities. When only one of the twins is exposed to music training, structural differences become evident in particular brain areas. In this way, genetic predispositions interact with a host of environmental factors to impact on learning and development, and this leads to changes in brain structure (Steele & Zatorre, 2018). For example, Corrigall and Schellenberg (2015) found that the parental personal characteristic openness-to-experience predicted children's duration of musical training, even when the child's characteristics (demographic variables, intelligence, and personality) were controlled for. These findings suggest both passive and active gene-environment interactions, such that genetic predispositions influence the likelihood that a child will have the environmental experience of music training. Research by Herholz and others moves us beyond the belief that "practice makes perfect," to a more sophisticated understanding of the forces that will impact on a child's potential to learn music.

Sensitive and critical periods

In the general psychological literature, *sensitive periods* are defined as the limited time window in development when the effects of a form of experience or learning are heightened and particularly strong and impactful, and *critical periods* as the particular experiences that are crucial for normal development in an area without which the learner's abilities may be permanently impacted (Knudsen, 2004).

There is general agreement in the scientific literature that starting to learn a musical instrument early has benefits for a person's overall development, as well as musical development, and that these benefits last well into adulthood, even if the child ceases instruction after a few years (Bailey & Penhune, 2012). In fact, there is now quite conclusive evidence that "training before the age of 7 years results in changes in white-matter connectivity that may serve as a scaffold upon which ongoing experience can build" (Steele, Bailey, Zatorre & Penhune, 2013, p. 1282). In other words, particularly strong effects occur in the brain's ability to rewire itself—what scientists refer to as brain plasticity or neuroplasticity—if children start learning an instrument before the age of ten.

A parallel approach to discussing *sensitive periods* suggests that these can change with age, and that there are special windows when the child experiences a heightened sensitivity that can have extraordinary, long-lasting benefits (Shavinina, 1990, 2016). Sensitive periods are thought to accelerate a child's mental development through the realization of intellectual capacities and strengthening of cognitive resources. This then leads to a unique framework of cognitive experience for the learner in which their unique intellectual understandings help explain their exceptional achievement (Shavinina, 2016). As Peretz (2020) states: "With equal amounts of practice, musicians who start early (before the age of 7) have better sensorimotor integration and greater temporal accuracy than those who start later. However, not all skills develop at the same pace. The more sophisticated the learning is and the more it involves different brain systems, the later the stabilization of neural networks will be, as they depend on prior learning" (p. 48). This does not mean, however, that learning later is pointless, as the incredible adaptability of the brain allows for learning across the lifespan.

In contrast, once a *critical period* finishes, is it more difficult for new skills related to certain attributes to be acquired, perhaps because the neural networks that facilitate development have already formed and become more stable. A good example is perfect pitch, which often reveals itself before the age of six (Peretz, 2020).

Perceptual abilities

Throughout the history of music psychology, there has been a continual stream of researchers who have asserted the importance of sensory discrimination abilities for children to be able to discern differences in pitch, loudness, rhythm, time, and timbre; from Carl Seashore's pioneering (but now outdated) *Tests of Musical Abilities* (1919/1960, 1939) through to Edwin Gordon's (2007) more recent concept of *audition* to describe how individuals comprehend music by "performing" and "imagining" music in their minds. According to Gordon, better *audiators* are more quickly able to process music that they are listening to. In some ways, this is similar to what Winner and Martino (2000) feel is a core ability of musically gifted children—that is, their "*sensitivity* to the structure of music—tonality, key, harmony, and rhythm, and the ability to hear the expressive properties of music" (p. 102). At a much more sophisticated level than their peers, gifted children are able to notice and then later *audiate* structural aspects of music that facilitate how they remember, play back, transpose, improvise, and create music.

To extend this line of thinking, Andrew Solomon (2012) suggests that music utilizes three important capacities: the physical (or athletic), the ability to mimic others, and the ability to interpret. *Mimicry* involves the auditory capacity to be able to perceive a specific musicality or interpretation, and motor aptitude, an ability to be able to reproduce this through singing or playing. These processes appear to be similar to how some people are born with a natural inclination that enables them to pick up (or mimic) new languages easily throughout their lives (Harris, 1998).

Perhaps the most distinctive feature of the most capable music learners is that they are able to memorize large bodies of repertoire easy and rapidly (Gagné & McPherson, 2016), so it is not unreasonable to assume that memory plays an important part of how fast a young child will be able to perceive the musicality and interpretation of the literature being learned and reproduce this on an instrument in the way we have described. This is exactly what McPherson (2005) found in his longitudinal study of young beginners who were learning an instrument. Testing their ability to play rehearsed music, sight-read, play from memory, play by ear, and improvise at the end of their first, second, and third years of learning, he reports distinctly different approaches to perceiving and reproducing music on the children's instruments. For example, when reproducing short musical examples from memory, some would employ a *conceptual* approach (independent of the instrument and how the melody would sound; chanting of rhythm or letters/names of the notes; trying to sing the melody but not explicitly linking this with instrumental fingerings), others a *kinesthetic* emphasis (trying to chant the rhythm or pitch while fingering the melody through on the instrument), while the most proficient students employed a *musical* strategy (processing the score holistically by working from the beginning to the end of the piece while mentally rehearsing the melody). Across the first three years of learning, distinct differences were observed in the children's progress, with successful and more capable learners employing more sophisticated mental strategies for each of the five styles of performance much earlier in their development. Importantly, these students went on in the second and third years of their learning to achieve at a much higher level than their peers. Even children who were exposed to the same method of instruction at the same school reported vastly different mental strategies for the tasks set, which further strengthens the possibility that the strategies they employed were in some ways shaped by natural abilities that more generally impacted on their overall learning.

Extending this, we also recognize the importance of motor control abilities in performing music. Motor dexterity controls all aspects of being able to reproduce music:

pitch, dynamics, timing, and others. Psychomotor abilities underlie the technical aspects of performing music and conveying expression. These are closely linked with two related perceptual abilities: *proprioception* (awareness of the body's position in space) and *kinesthesia* (awareness of the body's movements) (Gagné & McPherson, 2016). Teachers are able to gauge a child's motor and physical abilities very soon after they start to learn an instrument (McPherson & Williamon, 2016), yet to date, these two psychomotor abilities have been largely ignored in explanations aimed at understanding children's readiness to learn music or even their ongoing progression.

Physical maturation

During childhood, children experience significant physical growth. In a later section, we have framed these physical considerations in terms of how teachers commonly discussed the potential advantages or disadvantages of certain physiological characteristics for playing some instruments.

MATCHING STUDENTS WITH INSTRUMENTS

In previous sections we have alluded to some of the ways that music educators have advised learners based on a philosophy that they will be more successful on instruments that "match" their physiological makeup, aptitudes, timbre preferences, personality, and/or musical background. Regarding choosing students for instruments based on their physiological characteristics, the most commonly considered factors are the lips, teeth and jaw alignment, hand size, and overall body size. Lip size is most commonly considered for brass instruments and flute, as these instruments require the use of the lips to change registers (Bayley, 2004; Bazan, 2005).

On the topic of teeth and jaw alignment, the literature is both contradictory and outdated. Perhaps the most important consideration is malocclusion, such as an overbite or underbite, when either the top teeth or bottom jaw protrudes excessively. Jaw disorders such as Temporomandibular Disorder (TMD) have been associated with a variety of instruments, including all brass and woodwind instruments, violin, and viola, but the evidence is weak in terms of a causal link between TMD and playing these instruments (Attallah, Visscher, van Selms, & Lobbezoo, 2014). Risk factors for TMD include physical trauma from playing posture for the instrument and the presence of parafunctional habits such as bruxism (clenching or grinding the teeth) or tongue tension (Amorim & Jorge, 2016). Thus, playing an instrument that forces the musician into a physical position that deviates significantly from their natural position (for example, a student with an extreme overbite would struggle to align the jaws to play trumpet or flute) may increase the risk of developing a TMD disorder.

When considering hand size, three factors are worth considering: (a) overall hand size; (b) the width of the finger pads; and (c) hypermobility or "double jointed" fingers. A number of instruments require hands large enough to reach extended finger positions, including double bass, oboe, and bassoon. Finger width is an important consideration for instruments with open holes, but particularly the clarinet due to the size of the holes; conversely, narrow fingers may be an advantage for high string instruments such as violin and viola. Hypermobility has been cited as an issue for a number of instruments, including flute and saxophone, due to the need to support the instrument and manipulate a variety of keys (Millican, 2017).

In terms of body size, recommendations have also been mixed regarding its relative importance in choosing instruments. Fortney, Boyle, and DeCarbo (1993) found that students may be apprehensive about selecting larger instruments. Practitioners have suggested that larger body sizes are useful for large instruments and instruments that require significant reach (such as trombone or double bass), but apart from students who are not large enough to reach the appropriate positions for instruments, there does not appear to be any research evidence that larger body sizes provide any advantage. Moreover, there have been some adaptive tools developed to assist children with smaller body sizes in playing such instruments until they are large enough to play full size instruments, such as ¼-, ½-, and ¾-sized string instruments, curved flute head joints, and extension tools for reaching positions on trombone. Indeed, in the case of large string instruments such as bass, the "standard" professional size is considered to be ¾, with some professionals playing ½-size instruments to accommodate a smaller body size, suggesting that these large instruments can still be played successfully by people of a smaller stature.

Interestingly, advice from practitioners on choosing instruments based on physical characteristics has often been contradictory; for example, as Millican (2017) notes, various sources have recommended choosing students with thin lips, full lips, or that any lip thickness could be appropriate for flute (see further, Millican, 2017). Needless to say, and based on our previous comments, such considerations of basic physical factors such as slender fingers, lip thickness, and evenness of teeth appear to be completely unreliable at predicting success on string, brass, and woodwind instruments.

Motor Development

Playing an instrument requires a number of fine and gross motor skills, including arm movements, grasping, fine movements in fingers and wrists, maintaining posture, and more. During early childhood, children make significant strides in their ability to perform fine motor skills requiring manual dexterity, including improvements in steadiness, progress in grasping, and carrying small objects (Czajka, Kołodziej, Kochan, & Sławińska, 2019; Michel, Molitor, & Schneider, 2018). There is a strong link between age and motor proficiency, meaning that children become increasingly coordinated as they grow older (Barnett, Lai, Veldman, Hardy, Cliff, Morgan, & Okely, 2016; Kakebeeke, Knaier, Chaouch, Caflisch, Rousson, Largo, & Jenni, 2018; Xu, Morse, Lacy, Baggett, & Gogola, 2011). Children typically develop wrist stability between three and six years of age (Czajka et al., 2019), suggesting they may be able to start learning instruments in this age range.

Some gender differences are evident in early childhood in terms of motor development and coordination, with girls typically able to outperform boys in motor skills (dos Santos, Nevill, Buranarugsa, Pereira, Gomes, Reyes, & Maia, 2018; Luz, Cumming, Duarte, Valente-Dos-Santos, Almeida, Machado-Rodrigues, & Coelho-E-Silva, 2016). As children age, this trend begins to reverse, but this may be due to increased opportunities to engage in physical activities in the socialization of boys (Luz, Cumming, Duarte, Valente-Dos-Santos, Almeida, Machado-Rodrigues, & Coelho-E-Silva, 2016).

It seems that physical activity is also important in the development of motor skills, as children who are more fit have consistently better gross motor control (Henrique, Bustamante, Freitas, Tani, Katzmarzyk, & Maia, 2018; Lopes, Maia, Malina, de Souza, de Chaves, Seabra, & Garganta, 2014). Thus, providing a variety of opportunities to engage in activities that require both fine and gross motor skills during childhood may lead to stronger motor abilities as children grow up, allowing success in performing the complex movements necessary in playing most musical instruments.

Teeth

Because a number of instruments require the use of the front teeth to anchor or support the instrument during performance, understanding the development of permanent teeth is an important consideration for working with young students. Typically, teeth begin to emerge for babies between six and twelve months of age. Most children will have permanent teeth before starting wind instruments, as they typically begin to emerge by age seven or eight and are complete by age thirteen, with the exception of wisdom teeth, which may erupt as late as twenty-one years of age (American Dental Association Eruption Chart, 2012). Because the "front teeth," including central incisors, lateral incisors, and canines, are the first to emerge and have typically erupted by ten years of age, missing teeth should only be a consideration for teachers working with very young wind instrumentalists. In particular, missing teeth would pose a challenge for young reed players and may preclude brass playing until the permanent central incisors, lateral incisors, and canines have erupted. Interestingly, professional clarinetist Julian Bliss, who was known as a child prodigy and earned a performer diploma from the Jacobs School of Music by age twelve, was warned not to play with baby teeth, only to later perform comfortably with the clarinet mouthpiece wedged where his missing front teeth should be!

It is important to consider the impact that the pressure exerted to play instruments may have on the teeth and jaws of young children. Less than 100g of pressure is required to orthodontically move a tooth, while the force many instruments exert on oral tissues has been measured to be as high as 500g of pressure (Guzmán-Valderrábano, Durán-Gutiérrez, Hernández-Carvallo, & Gómez, 2018). Instruments such as the saxophone, clarinet, flute, oboe, trumpet, horn, trombone, and tuba can negatively impact the front teeth as well as the jaw joint, while the violin and viola can place significant pressure on both the teeth and jaw through the use of a chin rest. Because these tissues are particularly sensitive to damage while they are still developing, researchers have recommended that beginning musicians visit an orthodontist regularly for prevention and control of dental and jaw issues to prevent the development of dysfunctions that may subsequently result in an inability to play (Guzmán-Valderrábano, Durán-Gutiérrez, Hernández-Carvallo, & Gómez, 2018).

There is limited research literature relating to the impact of braces on playing musical instruments. Recommendations from practitioners typically advise changes to practice or playing routines, such as the use of wax or other protective materials, rather than avoiding certain instruments while wearing braces (Whitis, 2014).

Sex differences

From a developmental perspective, there are some documented differences in males and females. In physical development, the primary differences have to do with the size of bodies and when certain characteristics develop. Females tend to reach their full adult height at approximately sixteen years of age, while males continue to grow until approximately eighteen years of age. Females typically experience their adolescent growth spurt earlier than males, though the duration for both males and females are approximately two years (Becklake & Kauffman, 1999).

In terms of lung development, females typically have smaller lungs at birth, and they tend to be smaller throughout their lifespan. Moreover, while female lung capacity ceases to develop when they reach their full adult height, males continue to develop into their mid-twenties. Females generate lower respiratory pressures than males at all ages, but females produce higher forced expiratory flow rates, meaning that their maximum speed of expiration is faster (Becklake & Kauffman, 1999). It is important to note, however, that there is no known evidence that smaller lungs in females means they should be restricted from playing instruments that require a significant amount of air to play (for example, tuba or flute); rather, female musicians breathe efficiently for their lung capacity.

When considering cognitive development, there are also some notable differences between males and females. Evidence shows that females mature faster and have greater verbal and non-verbal abilities at a very young age, but that these differences are no longer evident by fourteen to sixteen years of age (Toivainen, Papageorgiou, Tosto, & Kovas, 2017). Differences in brain development include the frontal, parietal, and temporal lobes showing larger surface area in males between eight and fifteen years of age, indicating prolonged surface area expansion in boys. Girls' surface area expansion seems to be slower, or perhaps already completed, as they show slower rates of developmental change in the brain (De Bellis, Keshavan, Beers, Hall, Frustaci, Masalehdan, Noll, & Boring, 2001; Koolschijn & Crone, 2013). Through childhood and adolescence, boys show greater loss of grey matter volume, and an increase in white matter volume and corpus callosal area compared with girls over a similar age range (De Bellis, et al, 2001). This evidence suggests that, while males and females essentially "even out" by their preteen years, girls tend to develop faster, and may thus be more show readiness for more complex tasks at younger ages. In a systematic review of sex differences in childhood brain development, Etchell and colleagues (2018) found inconsistent evidence of any differences in brain structure and function related to language. Despite statistically significant differences, they suggest that structure and function of these differences seems to be negligible, though boys and girls may employ different cognitive strategies. These differences may be due to their brain structure, or even aspects of socialization.

Gender bias

Gender associations, and thus gender bias, have been associated with a number of musical instrument choices; evidence suggests that students develop gender associations with various instruments as early as the third grade (Abeles & Porter, 1978). These gender associations influence students' instrument choices (Delzell & Leppla, 1992; Fortney et al., 1993; Cramer et al., 2002; Payne, 2009; Cooper & Burns, 2021) and may even prevent students from selecting instruments that they may otherwise enjoy playing (Cooper & Burns, 2021) or from singing (Elpus & Abril, 2019). When presented with information that either reinforces or thwarts stereotypes surrounding the gender of instruments, students can be strongly influenced in their decisions about what instruments are "appropriate" for them to play. For example, when presented with images of female performers on all instruments, female students have been shown to show much higher preference for playing instruments that are typically considered to be "more for boys," such as drum set (Cooper & Burns, 2021). In a similar way to these results, a recent national sampling of high school choir participation in the United States revealed that the female-to-male ratio was 70:30, suggesting that students have a perception of choir as feminine or inappropriate for boys (Elpus & Abril, 2019). Music teachers have the power to influence instrument choice such that students might choose to participate in music less along traditional sex-based lines, and more in line with their true preferences and interests (O'Neill and Boulton, 1996; Harrison and O'Neill, 2000; Eros, 2008; Cooper & Burns, 2021).

MEASURES FOR PREDICTING FUTURE SUCCESS

Tests of aural acuity

Historically, there have been a number of aurally based attempts to predict whether students will be successful in studying music (Gordon, 1965/1995, 1969, 1979, 1982, 1984; Karma, 1983; Seashore, 1919, 1939; Wing, 1961). While the Wing (1961) and Seashore

(1939) tests are no longer in common use, their legacy continues to shape both popular perceptions of musicality and educational practices. The idea that these tests are useful in determining which students would benefit most from instruction or that future success can be predicted based on a set of skills that exist prior to any formalized musical training is pervasive, despite the fact that there is little evidence for any sort of predictive validity in these tests (Mitchum, 1971; Mills, 2007; Preckel et al., 2020). And because the focus of these tests is on aural discrimination (e.g., being able to recognize differences in pitch or differences in loudness) rather than the individual's sensitivity to the structural and expressive qualities of music we have described, none are able to predict an individual's musical progress (Hallam, 2016), and probably are no more predictive of musical potential than possessing good eyesight is predictive of good reading ability (Winner & Martino, 2000).

Perhaps the most unreliable of all is the Selmer music guidance measure, which, although no longer in print, is still used in many school music systems internationally to select students for entry into music programs or to guide student choice of instruments. Such measures tell us nothing about whether a child will succeed in music and therefore lack any credibility for use in educational settings.

Tests of timbre preference

When it comes to students making choices about which instrument to select, the instrument's timbre or quality of sound may have some influence in making a decision (Fortney et al., 1993; O'Neill & Boultona, 1996; Taylor, 2009). Students may choose based on their prior experience hearing different instruments, or they may show interest in particular sounds on a standardized test such as Gordon's (1984) Instrument Timbre Preference Test. Our view, however, is that firsthand practical exposure to both seeing and hearing instruments is more valuable in the selection of an instrument than is taking a measure that consists of synthesized sounds to determine some sort of timbral preference. Moreover, researchers have raised concerns about the validity of Gordon's use of synthesized sounds as the basis for determination of listener preference of actual instrument timbres (Williams, 1996).

Examining physical characteristics

A far less studied area of testing, although one that has research going back to the first half of last century, has tried to determine whether physical characteristics can be used to predict success to learn certain instruments.

Before embarking on their landmark study, Lamp and Keys (1935) had observed teachers on the west coast of the United States discouraging children from learning an instrument they really wanted to play, because they felt the child did not have the physical characteristics to succeed on the instrument. As a result, they searched for evidence that physical characteristics might predict success on particular instruments. Their research design sought to test three commonly held teacher assumptions: that string instruments require slender fingers; that success on a brass instrument depends on the thickness of lips in proportion to the size of the mouthpiece; and that woodwind and brass instruments require even teeth. Painstaking efforts to accurately measure and document the physical characteristics of 150 children before they began instruction resulted in a huge amount of data that they then compared with the progress of the children across the first years of their learning. None of the commonly held views was supported. The slender fingers of string players in no way predicted success on the violin (in fact, evenness of teeth was just as predictive of the violinist's success); there was no relationship between success and evenness of teeth for brass and woodwind players, and students with thin and thick lips were able to go on to become successful French horn players. Based on these results, and for a period of time, the school system in San Francisco allowed children to learn instruments that they most wanted to learn, rather than being assigned to particular instruments based on physical attributes. Unfortunately, this is no longer the norm internationally, as literature in use even today still details the types of physical attributes that teachers mistaken believe are needed to be successful on particular instruments.

Obviously, a severe underbite, seriously misaligned teeth, or challenges such as needing braces are factors to be considered when advising students of the types of instrument in which they might flourish. But stereotyping children based on general physical characteristics deserves to be seriously questioned in contemporary music education practice.

Other comments on physical attributes

These discussions show that physical attributes *are not* good predictors of success in music performance; in professional practice there are many exceptions to the norm in terms of ideal physical attributes for certain instruments. For example, renowned jazz trumpeter Dizzy Gillespie struggled to control his buccinator muscles, and international violin virtuoso Itzhak Perlman is known to have unusually large, thick fingers for a violinist. Imagine what the musical world would have lost if a well-meaning music teacher had barred these artists from their chosen instruments!

Perhaps the most important point to stress for a music teacher is the importance of understanding the available literature, and to use this information wisely to advise (but not definitively assign) instruments to children. As an example, for children who are having problems because of a significant underbite or other physical attribute, teachers can explain why they might be having difficulty, and give them choices so they feel supported and understand why they might be struggling. Then, the teacher can give the child opportunities to move to another instrument or persevere through the challenges. But, short of any physical barriers to performance, physical pain, or damage caused by playing a certain instrument (in which case, a medical professional should be consulted!), we do not recommend prohibiting students from playing instruments they are excited to learn simply because they do not have the perceived ideal physical attributes to play that instrument.

Of course, there are physical attributes that definitely need to be considered. For example, having missing teeth or braces may impede playing for a specific period, and prior injuries to any body part involved in playing an instrument should be considered. However, it is important to provide an autonomy supportive environment and balance between advising students on options from an information basis and allowing students to try out a few instruments (perhaps a restricted range of instruments such as the basic wind or brass instruments) before settling on one. It is important to remember how central motivation is to success in musical learning, and thus providing students with autonomy and choice may prove more important than any instrument-specific factor.

Practical Implications

Having surveyed available evidence on the range of issues discussed in the previous sections, we can now turn our attention to outlining twelve general principles that can be applied to guide efforts for those of us who provide instrumental and vocal lessons to children.

Principle 1: Everyone can benefit from a music education

In her book *How music sculpts our brain*, Isabelle Peretz (2020) shows how genetic and environmental forces interact to facilitate or impede musical development. One area of understanding she has pioneered is a neural disorder called *congenital amusia*, or in lay terms what is commonly called *tone deafness* or *beat deafness* (see further, McPherson, Blackwell, & Hallam, this part). About 1.5 percent of the population experience this type of severe difficulty with music, such that they find it impossible to sing in tune, have trouble recognizing familiar tunes (unless sung with lyrics), cannot recognize wrong notes, and usually do not gain much pleasure from music, or, in more rare instances struggle to keep up with rhythms, be it when clapping or dancing with a partner (Peretz, 2020). In every other sense they lead normal lives, with some having exceptional careers in other pursuits (several have won Nobel prizes).

Amusia should not be confused with inaccurate, out-of-tune singing, which is evident in about 20 percent of the population. People who sing out of tune can hear the difference between what they produce and an in-tune model. Their problem is largely motor control as they try to control and adjust the pitch of their voice. And unlike people with *amusia*, they will benefit from a music education. A key finding of all the research that has been undertaken in this area is that over 95 percent of the population can benefit from systematic music education, and with sufficient practice and systematic training can even develop their musical potential to a professional level (see further, McPherson, Blackwell & Hallam, this part).

When considering whether a child is ready to undertake musical study, remember that there are no definitive rules for when a child is ready to learn. Determining readiness is highly contextual and will vary from child to child. There are, however, some key ideas to keep in mind.

Principle 2: Start early

Research consistently shows that an early start in musical learning is advantageous in developing musical skills. It is well documented that musical training, particularly during sensitive periods (i.e., periods where greater brain plasticity occurs during development), will lead to long-term changes in the brain that support an individual's overall development well into adulthood (Peretz, 2020). It is important to note, however, that this early music learning need not be overly structured or rigorous. Rather, children should have the opportunity to engage with music playfully, perhaps playing multiple instruments before committing to one, and that a musically enriching environment for very young children should include listening and moving to music. That said, this should not be taken as discouraging for musicians who are not able to start musical training at a young age, as a later start does not necessarily preclude high-level achievement. Moreover, people can find value and enjoyment in engaging with music in a variety of ways, regardless of their skill level or professional status.

Principle 3: Immerse the child in other aspects of music, beyond learning to perform

For the purposes of maximizing musical potential, the question of whether biology or the learning environment is more important is essentially moot, as we can only control the environmental factors surrounding music learning. As we have noted, any preexisting musical potential will not come to fruition unless the individual spends a great deal of time engaging with music, as these potentially genetic musical traits will not express themselves outside of a musically stimulating environment. Thus, caregivers who seek to maximize musical potential should provide children with ample opportunities to engage in musical activities. For example, parents can play music in their homes, sing along to the radio, or play instruments themselves to show musical pursuits as engaging and worthwhile. Parents can sit or be close to their young children as they practice, plus provide encouragement and some direction when they struggle to organize their practice. In all instances, fostering a home environment in which musical pursuits are encouraged, celebrated, and supported will help to maximize a child's potential.

Principle 4: Allow choice when selecting and choosing to change instruments

Many teachers give informal playing tests, instrument tryouts at exploration nights, or "instrument petting zoos" for their learners. Provided that the goal of these activities is to make sure a child does not choose an instrument on which they cannot make an appropriate sound due to some physical limitation, we would encourage this practice. Children should also be encouraged to sing throughout their childhood, regardless of any preconceived notion about their vocal abilities.

We recognize also that some instruments are more appropriate for an early start than others. In particular, instruments that allow for adaptations to accommodate smaller body sizes, such as ¼-sized violins, one-handed piano playing, or curved head joints for flute, provide opportunities for earlier study. Conversely, most wind instruments require a later start, primarily due to the physical demands of holding the instruments and coordinating air, articulation, and technical challenges such as hitting correct notes on brass instruments or finger coordination on woodwinds. That said, all children will develop at different rates, and such decisions are best made in collaboration between caregivers and qualified music teachers to determine an appropriate age to start each child.

In terms of choosing students for instruments, due to the often-contradictory nature of advice from both researchers and practitioners, it seems most appropriate to recommend avoiding specific physical characteristics that may cause unnecessary limitations or challenges and therefore potential frustration in a student's playing, rather than trying to select students who will be most successful. As a general guide we would advise as follows: students should be encouraged to choose instruments for which they are most interested or most motivated to play, providing that they are not more likely to incur any injury on that specific instrument.

Principle 5: Consider the developmental appropriateness of the learning environment

The learning environment, be it a school ensemble, studio, or community setting, is an important consideration. While some children may thrive with the individualized attention afforded by private lessons, others may find more appeal in the excitement and social aspects that group learning can offer. In either case, where possible, the child should make the choice whether to play a particular instrument or sing, rather than a teacher using a test result. Allowing tryouts with some reasonable opportunities to change instruments provides the fairest and most equitable solution for all children who wish to learn an instrument or voice.

Principle 6: Motivation is the key to success

Motivation is central to success in all forms of learning. No matter what the form and level of pertinent predispositions and natural abilities (gifts), when individuals are not motivated to learn, they will not realize that potential. Thus, providing an autonomy supportive, musically stimulating, and encouraging environment may prove more important than any predispositions to musical learning. As Herholz (2013) notes, "Even if our brains are not optimally wired to learn a certain task, we may still invest our motivation and energy into activities of our choice and compensate by increased effort and training intensity" (p. 15323). Thus, the focus of fostering musicianship should be on helping each child to find the types of musical pursuits in which they are most motivated.

Principle 7: Understand how students learn

Several important theories of learning have emerged to explain key aspects of how we learn, and in turn, these have resulted in more knowledge about how we might teach students. Understanding schemas helps teachers to understand how students make sense of new information; spiral curriculum provides guidance on how to introduce new material; and the Zone of Proximal Development shows how teachers might scaffold students to learn ever more complex material. Understanding such theories allows caregivers and educators to cater for the needs of each individual child, rather than seeing children as all the same. By providing a framework for general principles of effective teaching and learning, these theories guide adults to make educational decisions that foster the musical development of children.

Principle 8: Make the learning journey "visible" in order to foster a sense of musical identity

When children choose to study musical instruments, they often do so without any sense of where the journey will take them. Their image of trumpet players, for example, are other members in the band or their teacher, rather than images outside school; they rarely see trumpeters on TV or in everyday life, so probably find it hard to imagine what they might be able to do with the instruments beyond playing in the band, while at school. Thus, teachers need to make these instrument and vocal roles clear from the outset such as by providing images that include a variety of genders, genres, and contexts. Preliminary experiences (or pre-learning experiences) can also be provided so that learners gain a sense of what music learning is, what certain instruments do, and how they can use these instruments now and into the future. In this way, providing clear information on how the child might apply their new musical skills in a variety of contexts, both now and into the future, is paramount to sustaining long-term involvement on an instrument.

As discussed in our chapter "Musical Potential, Giftedness, and Talent Development" (McPherson, Blackwell & Hallam, this part), moving from a conception of "I learn piano . . ." to "I am a pianist . . ." is an important transformational change that shows that young learners are starting to move away from viewing their learning as something that is similar to other areas in which they may not be fully personally invested, to a more intrinsic desire to make music part of their everyday lives. To this we would even suggest that many students tend to neglect their future musical selves because of some failure of belief or imagination about how they might project themselves into the future. In this sense, the most successful musicians (and music learners) are those who can imagine themselves as musicians into the future.

Principle 9: Do not use tests of music aptitude to determine who learns music

In her book *Instrumental teaching*, Mills (2007) discusses studies she and her colleagues have undertaken on this subject. In particular, she devotes pages to explaining how a number of other commonly used techniques for assigning children to instruments are flawed, such as "musicality tests" that assess children's capacity to hum, sing, or whistle common melodies in tune and identify the sound of particular instruments, and concludes by emphatically stating:

> There is nothing, of which I am aware, in personality research that could fairly or reasonably be used to prevent a student who is eager to learn a particular instrument from undergoing the best test of potential: having some lessons from a flexible and sympathetic teacher, and seeing how he or she gets on. (Mills, 2007, p. 94)

For Mills, it is important for beginner learners to become familiar with several instruments before choosing to focus on one, and not become discouraged from taking lessons if they fail to immediately make a good sound. She believes also that teachers should give more weight to the child's motivation than their physical attributes, not discourage children who take more time to choose their instrument, and realize that children who struggle on one instrument can become highly capable on another. In some ways these suggestions echo research in other areas of learning such as sport, where successful Olympians in team sports have often played a variety of sports before focusing on one, and in music, where some of the best students in instrumental music programs had learned other instruments outside of school but quit this instrument before starting their school instrument (McPherson, Davidson & Faulkner, 2012).

Principle 10: Design learning to minimize biases and stereotypes

Given the potential connection between physical fitness and motor skills, it would seem advisable to engage children in a number of activities, such as sports and play, to develop the skills necessary for playing musical instruments. Teachers also have the power to shape student perceptions about gender associations with instruments and can thus help to prevent gender bias in relation to instrument choices. Showing both male and female performers on "non-traditional" instruments (such as male flautists or female electric guitarists) can help students to choose instruments that match their interest, rather than their gender.

Principle 11: Focus on a love of music, and avoid external rewards, pressures, and controls

A huge amount of evidence across various disciplines now shows that external rewards, pressures, and controls tend to impede a child's intrinsic motivation and desire to continue. In fact, in a longitudinal study of learning instruments undertaken by the second author (McPherson, Davidson & Faulkner, 2012), all of the children who received pocket money to do their practice ceased learning fairly soon after receiving this form of extrinsically based incentive. External rewards (e.g., allowances or pocket money), pressures (e.g., demands to do practice), or controls (e.g., not allowing a child to do something else until practice is finished) might have short-term effects but seriously undermine intrinsic motivation, as well as reducing free-choice behavior and interest (see further, Evans & Ryan, this volume; also McPherson & Hattie, this part).

Principle 12: Develop a healthy state of mind through support, love, and encouragement

Avoid any tendency to give up on your child's music learning. In McPherson's longitudinal study (McPherson, Davidson & Faulkner, 2012), the second author observed many instances where a mother and/or father came to believe that their child was struggling with music learning so started to steer them toward other activities, often well before the child began to feel the same way. No child's progress will be a straight line, and admittedly there may be times when a child shows no interest in music over an extended period, so reluctantly, ending musical participation might be the right choice. However, most successful music learners will experience periods when they struggle, feel frustrated, or experience low levels of motivation. These are the times when children depend most on their parents, who can help by being involved, being supportive, providing love and understanding, and encouraging their child to view music learning as a series of challenges and a worthwhile journey that will ultimately be rewarding. In this way of thinking, readiness has much to do with how the child develops a healthy state of mind as a consequence of appropriate adult guidance (Gartrell, 2020). Adults are most effective when they nurture their children's unexpressed potential instead of ignoring it, rejecting it, or trying to train it. Readiness and healthy musical development depend on secure, responsive adult-child relationships (Gartrell, 2020).

Conclusion

As we stated in this chapter's opening paragraphs, the concept of "readiness" can best be thought of as teacher and parent practices that develop in the child, a "willing attitude and confidence in the process of learning: a healthy state of mind" (https://www.naeyc. org/our-work/families/readiness-not-state-knowledge-state-mind). Within such a philosophy, the emphasis is on fostering student autonomy, helping students to be successful, and providing a non-judgmental learning environment, rather than direction or control of student choices.

Aligned with this perspective is a growing literature from experts on talent development who have come to believe something that we stressed in an earlier part of this chapter. That is, an overemphasis on early identification, rather than the development of skill in individuals, leads to many of the misconceptions that pervade talent development in areas such music, particularly the view that some form of "innate talent" underlies musical achievement. Such beliefs distract us from a broader understanding of how children can be taught and come to love music.

As adults, we can all celebrate just how miraculous it is that all children are born with potential to learn and grow. While they each may have different kinds of interests and abilities, individually and collectively, they constitute what Gartrell (2020) refers to as the "the miracle of humanity." We do our best for the children we come in contact with when we nurture their unexpressed potential, and we achieve this goal by fostering a responsive adult-child relationship as an important way of ensuring their healthy development.

Key Sources

Millican, S. (2012). *Starting out right: Beginning band pedagogy*. Lanham, MD: Scarecrow Press.
Ormrod, J. E. (2019). *Human Learning*. 8th ed. Boston: Pearson Education. For information on learning theories.
Peretz, I. (2020). *How music sculpts our brain*. Paris: Odile Jacob.

Preckel, F., Folle, J., Grabner, R., Jarvin, L., Kozbelt, A., Müllensiefen, D., Olszewski-Kubilius, P., Scheider, W., Subotnick, R., Vock, M., & Worrell, F. C. (2020). Talent development in achievement domains: A psychological framework for within- and cross-domain research. *Perspectives on Psychological Science*, 15(1), 691–722. https://doi.org/10.1177/1745691619895030.

REFLECTIVE QUESTIONS

1. How do you define musical success in terms of the children you teach? Above all else, what do you wish to achieve as a musician who might teach your instrument?
2. What factors might you take into consideration when advising a parent about the best time for their child to start learning music?
3. Looking back on your own development as a musician, what might you change about your learning experiences? What might you keep?
4. What are the potential consequences of attempting to identify potential for learning music in young children?
5. How important is it to consider potential for success when assigning students to instruments?
6. How might you foster student autonomy with your own students? Do you have any current teaching practices that may inadvertently undermine student autonomy and choice?

REFERENCES

Abbott, A., Button, C., Pepping, G., & Collins, D. (2005). Unnatural selection: Talent identification and development in sport. *Nonlinear Dynamics, Psychology, and Life Sciences*, 9(1), 61–88.

Abeles, H. F., & Porter, S.Y. (1978). The gender-stereotyping of musical instruments in the Western tradition. *Journal of Research in Music Education*, 26(2), 65–75. https://doi.org/10.7202/1014420ar.

American Dental Association, (2012). Eruption charts. Retrieved from https://www.mouthhealthy.org/~/media/MouthHealthy/Files/Kids_Section/ADAPermanentTeethDev_Eng.pdf?la=en.

Amorim, M. I. T., & Jorge, A. I. L. (2016). Association between temporomandibular disorders and music performance anxiety in violinists. *Occupational Medicine*, 66(7), 558–563. https://doi.org/10.1093/occmed/kqw080.

Attallah, M. M., Visscher, C. M., van Selms, M. K., & Lobbezoo, F. (2014). Is there an association between temporomandibular disorders and playing a musical instrument? A review of literature. *Journal of Oral Rehabilitation*, 41(7), 532–541. https://doi.org/10.1111/joor.12166.

Bailey, J., & Penhune, V. B. (2012) A sensitive period for musical training: Contributions of age of onset and cognitive abilities. *Annals of the New York Academy of Sciences*, 1252, 163–170. https://doi.org/10.1111/j.1749-6632.2011.06434.x.

Baker, J., Schorer, J., & Cobley, S. (2010). Relative age effects: An inevitable consequence of elite sport? *Sportwissenschaft, 40*, 26–30. https://doi.org/10.1007/s12662-009-0095-2.

Barnett, L. M., Lai, S. K., Veldman, S. L. C., Hardy, L. L., Cliff, D. P., Morgan, P. J., & Okely, A. D. (2016). Correlates of gross motor competence in children and adolescents: A systematic review and meta-analysis. *Sports Medicine, 46*(11), 1663–1688. https://doi.org/10.1007/s40279-016-0495-z.

Bayley, J. G. (2004). The procedure by which teachers prepare students to choose a musical instrument. *Update: Applications of Research in Music Education, 23*(2), 23–34. http://doi.org/10.1177/87551233040220020104.

Bazan, D. E. (2005). An investigation of the instrument selection processes used by directors of beginning band. *Contributions to Music Education, 32*(1), 9–31.

Becklake, M. R., & Kauffmann, F. (1999). Gender differences in airway behaviour over the human life span. *Thorax, 54*, 1119–1138. http://doi.org/10.1136/thx.54.12.1119.

Bruner, J. S. (1960). *The process of education*. Cambridge, MA: Harvard University Press.

Bruner, J. S. (1978). The role of dialogue in language acquisition. In A. Sinclair, R., J. Jarvelle, & W. J. M. Levelt (Eds.), *The child's concept of language* (pp. 241–256). New York: Springer.

Cooper, P. K., & Burns, C. (2021). Effects of stereotype content priming on fourth and fifth grade students' gender-instrument associations and future role choice. *Psychology of Music, 49*(2), 246–256. https://doi.org/10.1177%2F0305735619850624.

Corrigall, K. A., & Schellenberg, E. G. (2015). Predicting who takes music lessons: parent and child characteristics. *Frontiers in Psychology, 6*, 282. https://doi.org/10.3389/fpsyg.2015.00282

Cramer, K. M., Million, E., & Perreault, L. A. (2002). Perceptions of musicians: Gender stereotypes and social role theory. *Psychology of Music, 30*(2), 164–174. https://doi.org/10.1177%2F0305735602302003.

Czajka, K., Kołodziej, M., Kochan, K., & Sławińska, T. (2019). Development of manual dexterity in preschool children. *Human Movement, 19*(4), 79–86. https://doi.org/10.5114/hm.2018.79735.

De Bellis, M. D., Keshavan, M. S., Beers, S. R., Hall, J., Frustaci, K., Masalehdan, A., Noll, J., & Boring, A. M. (2001). Sex differences in brain maturation during childhood and adolescence. *Cerebral Cortex, 11*(6), 552–557. https://doi.org/10.1093/cercor/11.6.552.

Delzell, J. K. & Leppla, D. A. (1992). Gender association of musical instruments and preferences of fourth-grade students for selected instruments. *Journal of Research in Music Education, 40*(2), 93–103. https://doi.org/10.2307%2F3345559.

dos Santos, M. A. M., Nevill, A. M., Buranarugsa, R., Pereira, S., Gomes, T. N. Q. F., Reyes, A., . . . & Maia, J. A. R. (2018). Modeling children's development in gross motor coordination reveals key modifiable determinants: An allometric approach. *Scandinavian Journal of Medicine and Science in Sports, 28*(5), 1594–1603. https://doi.org/10.1111/sms.13061.

Elpus, K., & Abril, C. R. (2019). Who enrolls in high school music? A national profile of U.S. students, 2009–2013. *Journal of Research in Music Education, 67*(3), 323–338. https://doi.org/10.1177/0022429419862837.

Eros, J. (2008). Instrument selection and gender stereotypes: A review of recent literature. *Update: Applications of Research in Music Education, 27*(1), 57–64. https://doi.org/10.1177%2F8755123308322379.

Etchell, A., Adhikari, A., Weinberg, L. S., Choo, A. L., Garnett, E. O., Chow, H. M., & Chang, S.-E. (2018). A systematic literature review of sex differences in childhood language and brain development. *Neuropsychologia, 114*, 19–31. https://doi.org/10.1016/J.NEUROPSYCHOLOGIA.2018.04.011.

Fortney, P. M., Boyle, J. D., & DeCarbo, N. J. (1993). A study of middle school band students' instrument choices. *Journal of Research in Music Education, 41*, 28–39. https://doi.org/10.2307/3345477.

Gagné, F. (2009). Building gifts into talents: Detailed overview of the DMGT 2.0. In B. MacFarlane & T. Stambaugh (Eds.), *Leading change in gifted education: The festschrift of Dr. Joyce VanTassel-Baska* (pp. 61–80). Waco, TX: Prufrock Press.

Gagné, F. (2013). The DMGT: Changes within, beneath, and beyond. *Talent Development and Excellence, 5*, 5–19.

Gagné, F., & McPherson, G. E. (2016). *Analyzing musical prodigiousness using Gagné's Integrative Model of Talent Development.* In G. E McPherson (Ed.), *Music prodigies: Interpretations from psychology, education, musicology and ethnomusicology* (pp. 3–114). Oxford: Oxford University Press.

Gartrell, D. (2020). *A guidance guide for early childhood leaders: Strengthening relationships with children, families, and colleagues.* St. Paul, MN: Redleaf Press.

Gordon, E. E. (1965/1995). *Music Aptitude Profile.* Chicago: GIA Publications.

Gordon, E. E. (1969). Intercorrelations among Musical Aptitude Profile and Seashore measures of musical talents subtests. *Journal of Research in Music Education, 17*, 263–271.

Gordon, E. E. (1979). *Primary measures of music audiation.* Chicago: GIA Publications.

Gordon, E. E. (1982). *Intermediate measures of music audiation.* Chicago: GIA Publications.

Gordon, E. E. (1984). *Instrument timbre preference test.* Chicago: GIA Publications.

Gordon, E. E. (2007). *Learning sequences in music: A contemporary music learning theory.* Chicago: GIA.

Guzmán-Valderrábano, C. P., Durán-Gutiérrez, A., Hernández-Carvallo, J. R., & Gómez, I. G. V. (2018). Musical instruments as etiologic factors for malocclusions. *Revista Mexicana de Ortodoncia, 6*(1), 33–42.

Hallam, S. (2016). Musicality. In G. E. McPherson (Ed.), *The child as musician: A handbook of musical development* (2nd ed., pp. 67–80). Oxford: Oxford University Press.

Harris, J. R. (1998). *The nurture assumption: Why children turn out the way they do.* New York: Free Press.

Harrison, A. C., and O'Neill, S. (2000). Children's gender-typed preferences for musical instruments: An intervention study. *Psychology of Music, 28*, 81–97. https://doi.org/10.1177%2F0305735600281006.

Henrique, R. S., Bustamante, A. V., Freitas, D. L., Tani, G., Katzmarzyk, P. T., & Maia, J. A. (2018). Tracking of gross motor coordination in Portuguese children. *Journal of Sports Sciences, 36*(2), 220–228. https://doi.org/10.1080/02640414.2017.1297534.

Herholz, S. C. (2013). Individual predispositions for learning and neuroplasticity. *Journal of Neuroscience*, September 25, 2013, *33*(39), 15321–15323. https://doi.org/10.1523/JNEUROSCI.3197-13.2013.

Jaap, A. & Patrick, F. (2014). Teachers' concepts of musical talent and nurturing musical ability: Music learning as exclusive or as opportunity for all? *Music Education Research, 17*(3), 262–277. https://doi.org/10.1080/14613808.2014.950559.

Kakebeeke, T. H., Knaier, E., Chaouch, A., Caflisch, J., Rousson, V., Largo, R. H., & Jenni, O. G. (2018). Neuromotor development in children. Part 4: New norms from 3 to 18 years. *Developmental Medicine and Child Neurology, 60*(8), 810–819. https://doi.org/10.1111/dmcn.13793.

Karma, K. (1983). Selecting students to music instruction. *Bulletin for the Council for Research in Music Education, 75*, 23–32.

Knudsen E. I. (2004). Sensitive periods in the development of the brain and behavior. *Journal of Cognitive Neuroscience, 16*(8), 1412–1425. https://doi.org/10.1162/0898929042304796.

Koolschijn, P. C. M. P., & Crone, E. A. (2013). Sex differences and structural brain maturation from childhood to early adulthood. *Developmental Cognitive Neuroscience, 5,* 106–118. https://doi.org/10.1016/j.dcn.2013.02.003.

Lamp, C. J., & Keys, N. (1935). Can aptitude for specific musical instruments be predicted? *Journal of Educational Psychology, 26*(8), 587–596. https://psycnet.apa.org/doi/10.1037/h0060956.

Lopes, V. P., Maia, J., Malina, R. M., de Souza, M. C., de Chaves, R. N., Seabra, A., & Garganta, R. (2014). Motor coordination, activity, and fitness at 6 years of age relative to activity and fitness at 10 years of age. *Journal of Physical Activity and Health, 11*(6), 1239–1247. https://doi.org/10.1123/jpah.2012-0137.

Luz, L. G. O., Cumming, S. P., Duarte, J. P., Valente-Dos-Santos, J., Almeida, M. J., Machado-Rodrigues, A., . . . & Coelho-E-Silva, M. J. (2016). Independent and combined effects of sex and biological maturation on motor coordination and performance in prepubertal children. *Perceptual and Motor Skills, 122*(2), 610–635. https://doi.org/10.1177/0031512516663773.

McPherson, G.E. (2005). From child to musician: Skill development during the beginning stages of learning an instrument. *Psychology of Music, 31,* 5–35. https://doi.org/10.1177/0305735605048012

McPherson, G. E. & Williamon, A. (2016). Building gifts into musical talents. In G. E. McPherson (Ed.), *The child as musician: A handbook of musical development* (2nd ed.) (pp. 340–60). New York: Oxford University Press.

McPherson, G. E., Davidson, J. W., & Faulkner, R. (2012). *Music in our lives: Rethinking musical ability, development and identity.* Oxford: Oxford University Press.

Millican, J. S. (2017). Band instrument selection and assignment: A review of the literature. *Update: Applications of Research in Music Education, 35*(2), 46–53. https://doi.org/10.1177%2F8755123315610174.

Mills, J. (2007). *Instrumental teaching.* Oxford: Oxford University Press.

Mitchum, J. P. (1971). The Wing standardised tests of musical intelligence: An investigation of predictability with selected seventh-grade beginning-band students. *Bulletin of the Council for Research in Music Education, 25,* 74–78.

O'Neill, S. A., & Boulton, M. J. (1996). Boys' and girls' preferences for musical instruments: A function of gender? *Psychology of Music, 24*(2), 171–183. https://doi.org/10.1177/0305735696242009.

Ormrod, J. E. (2019). *Human learning.* 8th ed. Boston: Pearson Education.

Payne, P. D. (2009). *An investigation of relationships between timbre preference, personality traits, gender, and music instrument selection of public school band students.* Unpublished doctoral dissertation, University of Oklahoma, 227; 3366051.

Pearson, D. T., Naughton, G. A., & Torode, M. (2006). Predictability of physiological testing and the role of maturation in talent identification for adolescent team sports. *Journal of Science and Medicine in Sport, 9*(4), 277–287. https://doi.org/10.1016/j.jsams.2006.05.020.

Peretz, I. (2020). *How music sculpts our brain.* Paris: Odile Jacob.

Piaget, J. (1929). *The language and thought of the child.* London: Routledge & Kegan Paul.

Piaget, J. (1936). *Origins of intelligence in the child.* London: Routledge & Kegan Paul.

Preckel, F., Folle, J., Grabner, R., Jarvin, L., Kozbelt, A., Müllensiefen, D., Olszewski-Kubilius, P., Scheider, W., Subotnick, R., Vock, M., & Worrell, F. C. (2020). Talent development in achievement domains: A psychological framework for within- and cross-domain research. *Perspectives on Psychological Science, 15*(1), 691–722. https://doi.org/10.1177/1745691619895030.

Seashore, C. E. (1919). *The psychology of musical talent.* Boston: Silver Burdett Company.

Seashore, C. E. (1919/1960). *Measures of musical talent.* New York: Psychological Corporation.

Seashore, C. E. (1939). *The Seashore measures of musical talents.* Camden, NJ: RCA Manufacturing Co.

Shavinina, L. (1990). The psychological essence of the child prodigy phenomenon: Sensitive periods and cognitive experience. *Gifted Child Quarterly, 43*(1), 25–38. https://doi.org/10.1177%2F001698629904300104.

Shavinina, L. V. (2016). On the cognitive-developmental theory of the child prodigy phenomenon. In G. E. McPherson (Ed.), *Musical prodigies: Interpretations from psychology, education, musicology and ethnomusicology* (pp. 259–278). Oxford: Oxford University Press.

Solomon, A. (2012). *Far from the tree: Parents, children, and the search for identity.* New York: Scribner.

Steele, C. J., Bailey, J. A., Zatorre, R. J., & Penhune, V. B. (2013). Early music training and white-matter plasticity in the corpus callosum: Evidence for a sensitive period. *Journal of Neuroscience, 33*(3), 1282–1290. https://doi.org/10.1523/JNEUROSCI.3578-12.2013.

Steele, C. J., & Zatorre, R. J. (2018). Practice makes plasticity. *Nature Neuroscience, 21,* December 2018, 1645–1650. https://doi.org/10.1038/s41593-018-0280-4.

Taylor, D. M. (2009). Support structures contributing to instrument choice and achievement among Texas all-state male flutists. *Bulletin of the Council for Research in Music Education, 179,* 45–60.

Toivainen, T., Papageorgiou, K. A., Tosto, M. G., & Kovas, Y. (2017). Sex differences in non-verbal and verbal abilities in childhood and adolescence. *Intelligence, 64,* 81–88. https://doi.org/10.1016/j.intell.2017.07.007.

Vygotsky, L. S. (1978). *Mind in society: The development of higher psychological processes.* Cambridge, MA: Harvard University Press.

Whitis, J. (2014). Insights on dealing with braces. *SBO School Band & Orchestra, 17*(9), 36–46.

Williams, D. A. (1996). A study of internal validity of the instrument timbre preference test. *Journal of Research in Music Education, 44*(3), 268–277. https://doi.org/10.2307%2F3345599.

Wing, H. D. (1981). *Standardized tests of musical intelligence.* Windsor, UK: NFER-Nelson.

Winner, E., & Martino, G. (2000). *Giftedness in non-academic domains: The case of the visual arts and music.* In K. A. Heller, F. J. Mönks, R. J. Sternberg, & R. Subotnik (Eds.), *International handbook of giftedness and talent* (2nd ed., pp. 95–110). Oxford: Pergamon.

Xu, S., Morse, A. M., Lacy, B., Baggett, L. S., & Gogola, G. R. (2011). Peg Restrained Intrinsic Muscle Evaluator (PRIME): Development, reliability, and normative values of a device to quantify intrinsic hand muscle strength in children. *Journal of Hand Surgery, 36*(5), 894–903. https://doi.org/10.1016/j.jhsa.2011.01.006.

CHAPTER 5

TALENT DEVELOPMENT IN MUSIC

DANIEL MÜLLENSIEFEN, AARON KOZBELT,
PAULA M. OLSZEWSKI-KUBILIUS,
RENA F. SUBOTNIK, FRANK C. WORRELL,
AND FRANZIS PRECKEL

INTRODUCTION

TALENT development is a complex long-term process. It can generally be defined as the transformation of a person's potential for achievement into actual achievement in a domain (Subotnik, Olszewski-Kubilius, & Worrell, 2011). Accordingly, musical talent development can be defined as the transformation of a person's potential for musical achievement into actual achievement in the musical domain. The relevance of musical potential and its development has been recognized for a long time (e.g., Seashore, 1919). Musical potential is commonly understood as an individual differences trait, that is, one that differs between individuals (e.g., McPherson & Hallam, 2016; see also McPherson, Blackwell, & Hallam, this part). This trait describes the scope of what an individual might be able to achieve musically under suitable conditions. In circumstances where resources for music instruction were scarce, the identification of musical potential was historically suggested as a selection criterion for deploying these resources most efficiently (e.g., Seashore, 1947). This resulted in the development of several test batteries for assessing musical talents (Seashore, 1919; Seashore, Lewis, & Saetveit, 1960) or musical potential in children (e.g., Gordon, 1965) over the course of the twentieth century. But in recent decades the use of these tests to select children for music instruction has been largely discredited as discriminatory and of little use, partly due to the low predictive validity of most test batteries (Hallam 2016; Winner & Martino, 2000).

Beyond allocating musical resources, knowing one's musical potential can also be important for personal development. Developing in a domain where continuous learning and progress is possible can be highly satisfying for an individual, regardless of the level of proficiency that is achieved eventually. Conversely, trying to develop in a domain that permits an individual to learn and progress only very little because of personal physical or psychological or opportunity constraints can be a source of frustration. Finally, identifying potential can also serve societal and cultural functions and contribute to the economic role of music. Listening to or watching the display of music can provide great joy to audiences and, of course, this joy can also be turned into economic value.

Despite the obvious relevance of musical potential as a concept for musical achievement, it has been surprisingly difficult to develop rigorous empirical evaluations of models of musical talent development. On the one hand, are prominent models of musical talent development (e.g., Davidson & Faulkner, 2013; Gagné & McPherson, 2016; Kirnarskaya, 2009); on the other hand, most musical talent development models are not specified at a level that allows for empirical validation. There is widespread use of teacher checklists for talent identification (Heller & Perleth, 2008; Ohio Department of Education, 2004; Wisconsin Music Educators Association, 2009), and there is also a long tradition of perceptual tests that purport to measure musical potential (Bentley, 1966; Gordon, 1989; Seashore, 1919; Wing, 1968). However, the empirical evaluation of various models is hindered by their complexity and the inclusion of a large number of (non-psychological) variables that are costly or difficult to measure, such as a person's genotype. Also, because most models describe musical talent development from a young age to adulthood, longitudinal data across extended time periods would be necessary to assess these models. But so far, it has been fairly difficult to find convincing evidence for specific predictors of musical talent development that have substantial predictive power for long-term musical success (e.g., Howe, 1998; Manturzewska, 1990; Norton, Winner, Cronin, Lee, & Schlaug, 2005).

Hence, with this chapter, we aim to sketch out how the application of a general talent development framework, the Talent Development in Achievement Domains (TAD, Preckel et al., 2020) framework, can be applied to the musical domain. The resulting talent development model in the musical domain (TAD music model) should allow for empirical testing of model-derived hypotheses and should integrate existing evidence while also highlighting open research questions. Thus, the model can act as a tool to guide empirical investigations of musical talent development, it can inform the construction of diagnostic material and the training of music teachers' diagnostic skills, and it can support the identification and promotion of children with high musical potential.

The TAD Framework

The TAD framework (Figure 5.1) is a general talent development framework that offers a common set of concepts and definitions that can be used across several domains. Therefore, the TAD framework can be used for constructing domain-specific talent development models like the TAD music model. The TAD framework builds on existing formulations and especially on the talent development megamodel by Subotnik, Olszewski-Kulilius, and Worrell (2011).

The TAD framework describes the talent development process in successive levels, following the notion of a trajectory in talent development moving from general abilities to highly specific skills, competencies, and expertise. It conceptualizes talent

Developmental levels	Increasing specialization	Level–dependent predictors and indicators

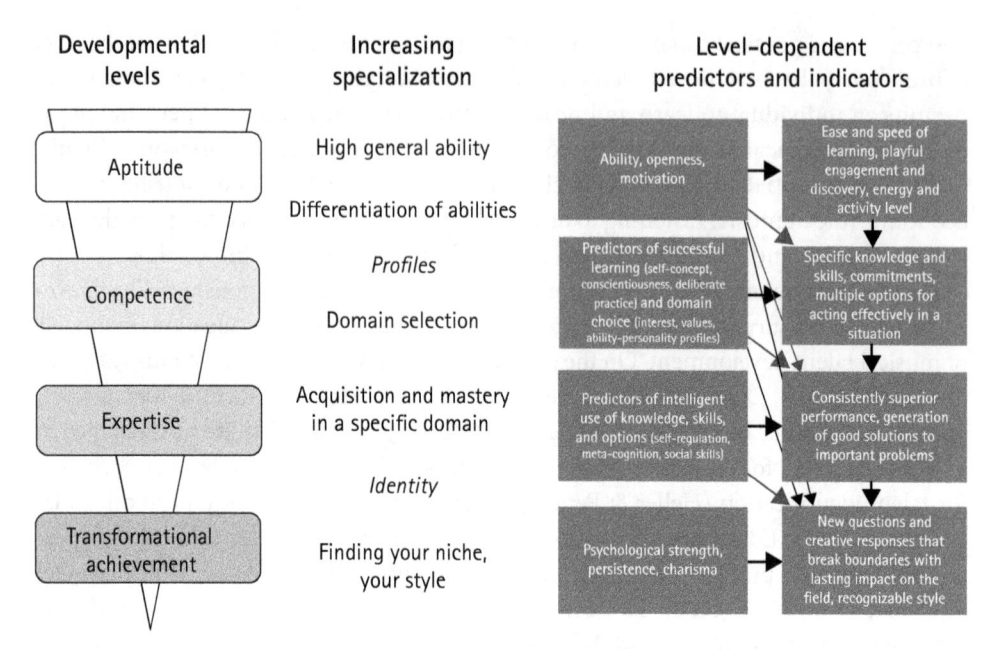

FIGURE 5.1. The Talent-Development-in-Achievement-Domains (TAD) framework. Adapted from Preckel et al., 2020, p. 697.

development as dependent on multiple factors (i.e., predictors), with a focus on measurable person-related psychological variables (i.e., abilities, personality traits, as well as psychosocial skills). In the following, we outline the main concepts and ideas of the framework by introducing its three columns: developmental levels, increasing specialization, and level-dependent predictors and indicators.

Developmental levels

Within the TAD framework the talent development process is described within four successive levels:

1. *Aptitude* refers to variations in individuals' constellations of psychological factors that are predictive of a positive development of achievement or future performance. It reflects individual differences in psychological variables (e.g., the abilities for precise pitch encoding, fine pitch, and time discrimination, or the ability to identify and express emotional meaning in music) that would predispose a person to becoming interested in or to engage in activities relevant to a particular kind of achievement domain like music. These tend to have the quality of a natural fit between the person and the content or challenges of that domain. Aptitude is indicated by the ease and speed of learning of new content and frequently by high levels of activity in the form of playful engagement and discovery.

2. *Competence* refers to a cluster of related and systemically developed abilities, knowledge, and skills that enable a person to act effectively in a situation (e.g., as a pianist, flautist, violinist) with multiple options. Usually, competence is acquired by successful and systematic learning under formal tutelage (Gagné & McPherson, 2016).

3. *Expertise* refers to a high level of consistently superior achievement; experts have a strong grasp of their field and are capable of generating good solutions to important domain problems (Subotnik, Olszewski-Kubilius, & Worrell, 2019). Expertise is acquired through lots of particularized education, constant investment, and the intelligent application of gained knowledge and skills.

4. *Transformational achievement* refers to levels of accomplishment that go beyond mere expertise and established practices by generating creative responses or interpretations that require breaking domain boundaries, combining different domains, or setting new questions. These can be single high-impact innovations or multiple achievements that span an entire career. Making a transformational achievement requires creative problem formulation, persistent motivation, and psychological strength, to make one's work visible and to convince others of its value.

It is worth noting that, within the TAD framework, these four levels are suggested as a theoretical guidance for structuring the different phases of the talent development process. While the aptitude level describes a phase without any formal instruction in an achievement domain, the competence level describes a phase in which someone acquires the knowledge and skills related to a domain, frequently with formal instruction and extensive practice. The expertise level represents a phase in which this competence is applied and further refined to solve important questions within a domain. Finally, the transformational achievement level marks a phase in which someone uses and communicates his or her expertise in a way that influences others and moves the field forward. That is, the levels can be distinguished by the respective demands of talent development. However, transitions between levels are assumed to be continuous and each level can be considered a developmental process, but a rather short-term one compared with the overall talent development process.

Increasing specialization

The TAD framework follows the notion of a trajectory in talent development, moving from general abilities to specific skills and competencies. To describe this process of specialization, the TAD framework focuses on internal processes that lead to interest and success in a domain. General abilities are invested into the acquisition of specific knowledge or skills by taking advantage of available learning opportunities, which leads to the development of more specific abilities or specialized knowledge structures (i.e., process of ability differentiation). Ability and personality factors, like domain-related self-concepts or interests, develop along mutually causal lines within the process of talent development, and this process results in specific ability-personality profiles (i.e., interplay of ability development and personality development). These ability-personality profiles are important to understand the process of specialization that occurs on the talent development journey.

Investment and success in a domain reinforce personal identification with the domain, which, in turn, enhances investment and success (i.e., profiles inform talent development). Overall, the process of increasing specialization outlines how ability development and the development of the individual's personality relate to each other over time. This process will eventually produce an individual's ability-personality profile (i.e., constellation of an individual's abilities, interests and values, motivation, and self-concepts) and identity within that domain, which informs subsequent talent development toward higher levels of achievement (Preckel et al., 2020).

Level-dependent predictors and indicators

The TAD framework conceptualizes talent development as dependent on multiple factors. Its focus is on measurable person-related psychological variables (i.e., abilities, personality traits, and psychosocial skills). While acknowledging the important role of environmental and genetic factors for talent development, they are not specified within the TAD framework depiction. The impact of these factors can be seen through the psychological lens of the person, as for example by the way individuals engage with the opportunities they receive and the support they gain from others (for models including environmental and genetic factors, see Gagné & McPherson, 2016, and Ullén, Hambrick, & Mosing, 2016).

The TAD framework further states that the relative importance of each variable depends on the level of talent development. Some variables, such as general cognitive ability, domain specific abilities, and achievement motivation, can be important from early on and remain important throughout the person's development. Others, especially social skills or charisma, can gain in importance as the individual transitions from being a novice student to becoming an advanced student or professional (Jarvin & Subotnik, 2010). Accordingly, the TAD framework suggests predictors and indicators of talent development at the four different levels that can be used to identify achievement potential and to track progress in an achievement domain. By doing so, the TAD framework aims to describe which predictors and indicators should be assessed empirically at various levels. These indicators serve to identify *potential as an individual's constellation of psychological factors that impact the likelihood of successfully progressing to the next level within the talent domain.*

A MUSIC MODEL OF TALENT DEVELOPMENT

One important reason for the lack of a robust model of musical talent development is the scarcity of longitudinal studies that would provide the data necessary for specifying and testing talent development models. Longitudinal studies are expensive and complex (e.g., Little, 2013), and funding opportunities for longitudinal studies are comparatively rare. Hence, the few longitudinal studies in the music research literature lack standardized quantitative assessment of psychological variables but rely largely on qualitative research techniques (e.g., McPherson, Davidson, & Faulkner, 2012) or use only small samples with a distribution of musical abilities in the normal range and without special consideration of high ability levels (Gordon, 1975). In the latter studies, the subsample of individuals with exceptional musical trajectories is often too small to provide adequate empirical data for statistical model construction and evaluation.

A further challenge to the empirical modeling of talent development is the definition of a meaningful and measurable criterion for achievement in music or music performance. Often, professional engagement with music as an adult (e.g., as solo performer, being a member of a professional orchestra or ensemble) is taken as the sole criterion for high musical achievement. But the decision to end formal musical training and to change career focus despite a promising musical career trajectory is fairly common (McPherson et al., 2012). At higher levels of talent development, criteria and opportunities for success as performers become more exclusive, and some individuals may refocus their efforts toward other career options—as composers, well-regarded educators, or artistic directors and other kinds of "gatekeepers" (Knotek et al., 2020)— or they may abandon the domain of music entirely.

A final problem for modeling musical talent concerns predictor variables that might explain and predict musical development as an instrumentalist or musical engagement in different ways. Many who study this area assume—often implicitly—that quantitative features such as intelligence, emotional engagement with music (Kirnaskaya, 2009), musical discrimination ability, and musical memory ("audiation", Gordon, 1986) can serve as predictors for long-term musical development. Although these psychological factors might all have predictive value for a certain period of musical development, the assumption that they might serve as sole predictors of long-term musical success has not yet been empirically validated. It is an open question whether such psychological variables, assessed at an early age, enjoy long-term predictive power for the development of musical talent, beyond very early levels.

Applying the TAD Framework to the Music Domain: The TAD Music Model

The TAD framework has several features that address the challenges of talent modeling and, therefore, holds promise to provide the necessary theoretical orientation for the development of an evidence-based model of musical talent development. Such a model should allow for rigorous testing as well as provide useful predictions and indicators for the musical trajectory of individuals. First, TAD focuses on measurable psychological constructs, and developing additional measurable constructs when needed. Second, by breaking up the developmental trajectory into different levels as guided by theory, models from the TAD framework do not necessarily rely on the assumption that individual psychological variables need to have strong and sustained predictive power across long periods of musical talent development (for a distinction of effect sizes of predictors for short vs. longer term outcomes, see Kraft, 2020). Model predictions are mainly intended to predict development within each of the four levels of the TAD framework. These four levels can be linked to Levels I to IV in Manturzewska's (1990) model of lifespan development of professional musicians that she developed from a large interview study with professional as well as artistically eminent musicians. Third, in line with the concept of musical sophistication (Müllensiefen, Gingras, Musil, & Stewart, 2014), the TAD framework does not prescribe only a single prototypical musical trajectory (e.g., as performer of Western art music), but also allows for considering high musical achievements in other forms, including music composition or music production and musical achievements in genres and styles other than Western art music.

Finally, the TAD framework helpfully distinguishes between indicators of achievement and predictors of talent development. Indicators are measurable variables that reflect a current level of achievement in the domain of interest (here, music performance), such as scores on a musical ability test, a checklist of achieved instrumental skills, music examination grades, or volume of professional engagements as a music performer. Although predictors are also measurable variables, their function is to predict the absolute level of future achievement after a defined time interval. Predictors can be general psychological features such as intelligence, working memory, conscientiousness, a growth mindset (i.e., the belief that one's own cognitive abilities can change through learning), or measures of the current musical skill level. Hence, the same variable (e.g., technical competence on primary instrument) can act as an indicator of current musical achievement as well as a predictor of future musical development. The distinction between predictors and indicators is illustrated in Figure 5.2, which contains examples of predictors and indicators associated with different developmental levels in the musical domain. These are discussed in the following section.

Figure 5.2 shows how different predictors can have their strongest effect at a specific developmental level (as indicated by the thickness of the arrows). For example, working memory and general intelligence might be strong predictors at the early stages of

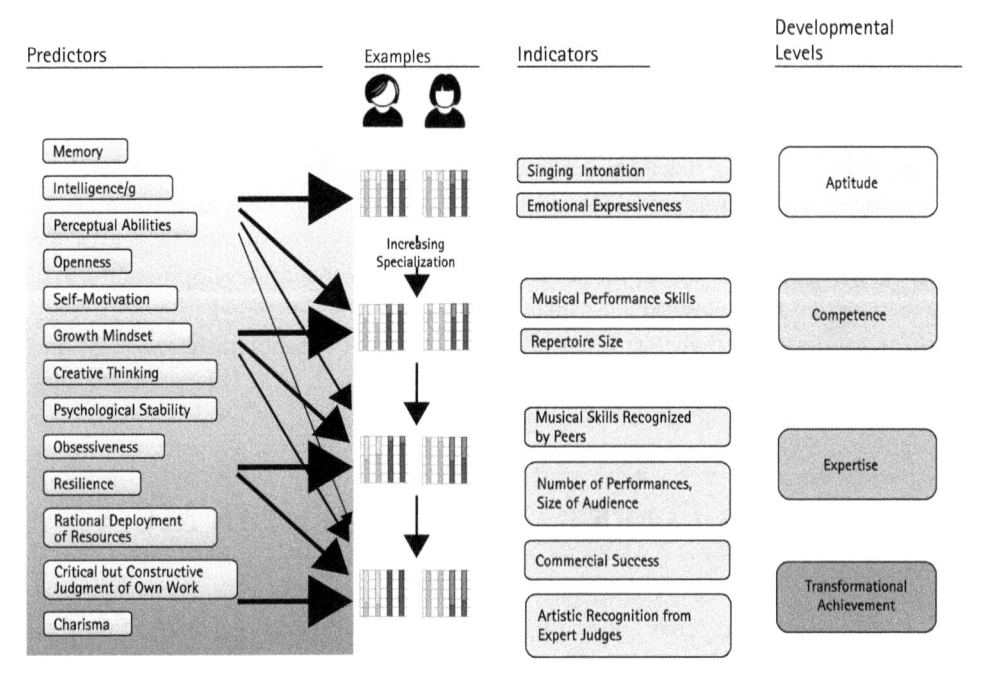

FIGURE 5.2. The TAD music model with examples for predictors and indicators of musical talent.

> Note: The associations of predictors and indicators with the four developmental levels shown in the figure are only
> hypothetical and serve as an illustrative example. They are not the result of empirical research yet. Also note that the
> relationships between predictors and developmental levels as represented by the arrows are only suggestions. The precise
> impact and strength of predictor variables needs to be determined empirically. See explanations in the text.

instrumental learning, but less predictive at the expert and creative contribution levels. However, some other predictors like self-motivation predict development across several levels.

The examples of performers in the second column represent two musical performers who develop differently over time and specialize in different skill sets. The dark grey bars on the bar chart represent hypothetical aspects of technical performance skills on an instrument relative to the data norms from the musical peer group. The light grey bars represent hypothetical aspects of improvisation skills relative to the peer group. Hence in this example, the performer on the left-hand side develops into an expert improviser with relatively low technical skills (compared to fellow expert music performers), whereas the performer on the right-hand side becomes an instrumental virtuoso with relatively low improvisation skills.

The Indicators column suggests possible measures that may indicate the degree of achievement at a specific age or developmental level. Obviously, the more that performers specialize in a specific musical genre, style, or niche, the more these indicators have to be adapted to reflect the corresponding comparison group. For example, Singing Intonation and Rhythmic Accuracy can be employed as fairly general indicators of musical achievement at the Aptitude level, but measures such as recognition by peers, commercial success, and the size of audiences will have to be adapted according to whether the performer is an expert in, say, improvisational jazz, Western classical, or electronic DJ music.

Note that Figure 5.2 does not contain a timeline linking developmental levels to chronological age. Developmental trajectories differ greatly between instruments (e.g., Subotnik et al., 2011) and even more for developments in different musical genres and styles. Hence, the TAD music model is formulated in terms of developmental levels, not in terms of chronological age. This choice enables the researcher to model developmental trajectories that start relatively late in terms of chronological age (e.g., Jimi Hendrix starting to play the guitar at age fifteen) or very early (e.g., Hilary Hahn beginning violin instruction at age three).

LEVELS OF TALENT DEVELOPMENT IN MUSIC

Following Preckel et al. (2020), we outline in this section the nature of each of the four developmental levels of the TAD framework and describe corresponding predictors and indicators in the domain of music.

Aptitude. Within the TAD model of musical talent development, high musical aptitude is defined as general mental and physical potential to process, learn, and produce music expressively at a high achievement level in the future. Therefore, musical aptitude is present, if latent, before the start of any systematic music instruction, which might be the first course of systematic music instruction received from a teacher or the initial phase of self-directed music learning. The term *aptitude* describes the potential to go through the initial levels of systematic music learning. High musical aptitude would be predictive of measurable high musical achievements after an initial learning phase (i.e., after a few music/instrumental lessons or after a few sessions of self-directed music learning). For musicians engaged in Western art music, the start of systematic music instruction can begin as early as age three in some cases. However, for many self-taught musicians within the popular music genre as well as for players of wind instrument or voice, the start of systematic music learning can be later, during the adolescent years. Thus, the TAD music model avoids any general association of windows of chronological age with developmental levels.

According to the literature, general psychological features that might be linked to high musical aptitude and short-term musical achievements are intelligence (Schellenberg, 2011), working memory (Vandervert, 2016), and gross and fine motor skills relevant for the particular form of instrumental learning. In addition, skills associated with high aptitude that are thought to be music-specific include sensory sensitivity and emotional understanding of music (Kirnarskaya & Winner, 1997; MacGregor & Müllensiefen, 2019); cognitive auditory skills, including sequence memory and perceptual discrimination skills (Gordon, 1986; Harrison, Collins, & Müllensiefen, 2017; Larrouy-Maestri,

Harrison, & Müllensiefen, 2019; Lee & Müllensiefen, 2020); singing ability (Howe, Davidson, Moore, & Sloboda, 1995); rhythmic skills (Kirnarskaya, 2009; Zuk, Andrade, Andrade, Gardiner, & Gaab, 2013); and the development of musical imagination and spontaneous musical activity (Manturzewska, 1990).

To use the TAD model empirically at the aptitude level, these psychological predictor variables should ideally be assessed before the first music lesson or first self-directed practice session. Achievement should then be assessed after a period of several lessons or practice sessions. Achievement can be determined through structured reports from multiple observers (e.g., instrumental teacher, class teacher, parents, peers) following the guidelines suggested by Haroutounian (2000). In addition, the development of music perception abilities can also be measured via an increase in tonal, rhythmic, and harmonic abilities on standardized listening tests. Musical achievements after the aptitude level should reflect the ability to benefit from instruction and feedback, the cognitive and sensory-motor mastery of basic musical elements, the command of means of musical expression (i.e., dynamics and articulation), memory for musical patterns, the ability to combine mastered elements to more complex musical objects, and the ability to self-learn and self-correct during music production to a certain degree.

In sum, musical aptitude according to the TAD music model comprises psychological factors that are beneficial to the first stage of musical learning. It permits the prediction of musical achievements after units of initial instruction or self-directed teaching. Phrased in terms of a simple hypothetical example: if several children start taking initial piano lessons at the same time and with the same teacher, the TAD music model aims to predict the progress of these children over, for example, the first six months from their psychological profiles (e.g., general cognitive ability, working memory, perceptual acuity, prior musical skills, and musical expressiveness or musicality).

Competence. Musical competence describes the cumulative acquisition of skills necessary for widening the musical repertoire as well as the range of expressive scenarios and musical contexts within which an individual can contribute. For music performers, indicators of competence include the mastery of increasingly complex pieces and the ability to perform in different settings (e.g., solo, or with other performers as part of a small ensemble or a band) and to change expressivity at will and independent from musical structure. In addition, the ability to make aesthetic and creative decisions independently and implement these aesthetic decisions in one's own performances also ranks among the achievements at the competence level. Depending on the genre of music, competence includes an understanding of harmony, rules for the generation of melodic lines, complex rhythmical patterns, and the links between emotional expressivity and sound texture and dynamics, as well as the rules for the interaction of multiple voices and instruments.

These achievements can be assessed through structured reports by multiple observers (Haroutounian, 2000) and through self-report. The predictors frequently suggested as contributing to high achievement at the competence level are a growth mindset (Dweck, 2000; Müllensiefen, Harrison, Caprini, & Fancourt, 2015); the ability to self-motivate, a positive musical self-concept (Spychiger & Hechler, 2014); the integration of musicality into self-concepts (Müllensiefen et al., 2015); superior motor skills (Kopiez & Lee, 2006); teachability; the ability to cope with failure; self-motivation to learn (Jarvin & Subotnik, 2010); and the "rage to master"; that is, a high level of intrinsic motivation to perform exceptionally well in the domain (Winner, 1996).

The transition from the aptitude to the competence level is continuous and hence there is no clear starting point for the competence level. However, most authors (Gembris, 2009; Manturzewska, 1992) agree that the time deliberately (and without external pressures) invested in musical learning marks the transition from the aptitude to the competence level. Hence, the beginning of the competence level could be defined as the point in time where a substantial increase in the time dedicated to musical learning is discernible. Taken together, the competence level is the period when individuals master increasingly complex musical materials and broaden their musical repertoires and expressive scenarios to a considerable degree. Thus, an increase in competence is reflected in the cumulative acquisition of skills necessary for mastering a broader musical repertoire. This increase in competence will go hand in hand with a substantial increase of the time deliberately dedicated to musical learning and practice.

The following might serve as a simple hypothetical example for the application of the TAD music model at the competence level: can we predict the time it takes different performers to master a selection of pieces for a concert program? It would be necessary to include the individual level of technical proficiency at the start of the observation period and the estimated difficulty of the pieces. But the main focus of the prediction model would be on the contribution of candidate psychological predictors such as a growth mindset, self-motivation abilities, and the ability to cope with failure. Practice time in the observation period would also be an important predictor to record, but the TAD music model hypothesizes that practice time would act as a variable that mediates or moderates the effect of the psychological predictors on the preparation of the concert program.

Expertise. The expertise level is characterized by a superior level of musical skill that is recognized by peers and allows an individual to act within professional contexts. In music performance, expertise can be indicated, for example, by regular performances for larger audiences. Achievements at the expertise level might be measured by the number, frequency and complexity, quality, creativity, and diversity of performances. Although number and frequency of musical productions can be easily measured objectively, judging the complexity, quality, creativity, and diversity will usually require some form of peer expert judgment.

The transition from competence to expertise level is also a continuous process, and marking the starting point of the expertise level for the assessment of psychological features is difficult. But part of the expert status is the recognition that an individual's work reflects a strong grasp of the domain such that the performer is capable of generating good solutions to important domain problems (Subotnik et al., 2019). Therefore, a marker of entering the expertise level in music performance can be the noticeable increase in time invested in outward facing musical activities compared with private musical engagement such as deliberate practice and exercising.

Predictors relevant for the development of musical expertise should be assessed at the beginning of the expert level; they include relative psychological stability, openness to experience, conscientiousness, resilience, obsessiveness (Winner, 1996), rational deployment of time as well as mental and monetary resources, strategic risk taking and mastering the "game" (Jarvin & Subotnik, 2010) capitalizing on strengths and the ability for critical but constructive judgment of one's own work (Sternberg, 1999). In summary, the level of musical expertise is often characterized by the increasing amount of musical activity that is outward facing and directed toward an audience. Experts in the domain of musical performance are usually able to act within professional contexts and to provide good solutions to difficult musical problems (e.g., the execution and interpretation of highly difficult pieces and the consistent delivery of high-quality performances under difficult constraints) as recognized by their peers.

The following can serve as an example application of the TAD music model at the expert level: consider students in the final year of a music performance degree. Can we predict from psychological predictors (such as psychological stability, openness to experience, resilience, obsessiveness, and the ability to judge one own's work critically) the increase in frequency, complexity, diversity, and audience size of their musical performances over the subsequent year after their graduation from music college?

Transformational achievement. Musical achievements at the level of transformational achievement are characterized by the volume of professional artistic output, commercial success, artistic recognition from expert judges and a wide audience, influence on other musicians, and the freedom to make aesthetic and creative choices at the highest level. Predictors for achievements at this level include that elusive attribute, charisma, as well as other factors that are only partially psychological (Jarvin & Subotnik, 2010). Chance, context, and intuitive aesthetic choices are important factors for creative productivity, which include preparing for opportunities and events that are outside an individual's control, such as filling in for an ailing performer or responding to novel nuances of an ongoing ensemble performance on the fly. Hence, detailed statistical modeling of high musical achievements at this level might be less feasible because of the large number of potential predictors, the difficulties associated with their measurement, and the relatively small number of individuals who reach this level. Indeed, at the transformational achievement level, available data may be highly idiosyncratic. Therefore, more varied methods, including qualitative research (Folkestad, 2004; Jarvin & Subotnik, 2010), archival analyses of historic individuals (e.g., Kozbelt, 2008; Simonton, 1977, 1996), retrospective self-reports (Krampe, 1994, 2006), and biographical case studies (Manturzewska, 1992) might be more appropriate at this elite level.

Constructing a meaningful general example of a hypothetical research application of the TAD music model at this level is difficult, but not impossible. Indeed, in the realm of classical musical composition, researchers have successfully modeled many aspects of high-level creative output over the lifespan. These include composers' average overall career path (Simonton, 1977, 1997), as well as finer distinctions rooted in variables like creative potential (Simonton, 1991), approaches to the creative process (Kozbelt, 2014), and musical forms (Kozbelt, 2008). Such variables are useful for assessing a composer's prospects for sustained creative development, versus creative burnout or "one-hit wonder" status. These core ideas can be readily extended to musical performance and improvisation (Kozbelt, 2018).

IMPLEMENTING A MODEL OF MUSICAL TALENT DEVELOPMENT WITHIN THE TAD FRAMEWORK

The descriptions of the four developmental levels highlight the core principle of an empirical implementation of the TAD music model: prospects for future musical achievements at the end of a developmental level are predicted from current musical achievements and from a set of psychological features. Hence, the main task for the construction of an empirical test of the TAD model is to define suitable assessment measures of musical achievement and sets of psychological features that might have predictive power for specific levels and phases of musical talent development. According to the general TAD framework (Preckel et al., 2020), there are domain-general predictors of talent development (e.g., general cognitive ability, conscientiousness, self-regulatory skills) but also domain-specific predictors of talent development (e.g., auditory skills for music, spontaneous focusing on numerosity for math). Domain specificity of predictors further includes that the set of suitable assessment measures and psychological features chosen as predictors also depends on the respective type of music education.

An implementation of a TAD music model could take the form of a regression model that aims to explain musical talent development over time. Predictors of the developmental model are the psychological variables that are assessed at the beginning of a developmental level. Outcome variables are measures of musical achievements (e.g., indicators of competence or expertise). Model testing then consists in investigating how much variability in later outcomes can be explained by earlier interindividual differences in predictors. Additionally, the predictive value of variables can be compared for different levels (e.g., the aptitude level or the competence level) to test the assumption that the importance of a predictor changes with talent development level (e.g., that general cognitive ability is more important at earlier than at later levels).

At the core of the TAD music model is the relation between time and achievement that differs among individuals and where the notion of (high) potential is closely associated with accelerated learning (Winner, 1996). Formally, accelerated learning can be described as learning curves with growth coefficients that model the progress of individual learners. Positive and above-average growth curve coefficients are then indicative of individuals with high potential in the respective domain.

Two different types of models describe the relationship between time and achievement or performance, and these two types are already reflected across the hypothetical examples given in the previous section. In a time-to-performance model, the time it takes an individual to perform at a predefined next level from the initial level of his or her performance is estimated based on the set of psychological predictors measured at the beginning. An example of a time-to-performance model would be the prediction of the time needed for a piano student to go from passing one level of piano examination (e.g., Grade 5 on the British Associated Board of the Royal Schools of Music examination system) to passing the next level.

In a performance-after-time-interval model, the performance level after a fixed time interval is predicted from the initial level of performance and the psychological predictors at the start of the time interval. An example of a performance-after-time-interval model could be the prediction of achievement or performance in year $n + 1$ of a recurring annual examination or competition (such as the round and points achieved at the annual "Jugend Musiziert" competition for young amateur music performers in Germany) from the performance level, as well as psychological predictors assessed in year n.

The accuracy of the model can be expressed in terms of model fit measures. Model predictions are likely to be more accurate for shorter time intervals (performance-after-time-interval model) and for more fine-grained increases in competence (time-to-performance model). Hence, choosing shorter time intervals and a fine-grained scale of musical performance can be beneficial for model construction and will enable researchers to employ identical or highly similar assessment procedures for evaluating musical performance at the start and end of the observation period. Alternatively, in longitudinal models with multiple waves of measurement, predictions can be tested for the varying time slots and predictive validity of a variable can be estimated over different time intervals.

In either case, the most principled way of testing the TAD music model empirically is the analysis of longitudinal data over a specific period (e.g., initial exposure, competence, or expertise, which would vary with age depending on the instrument and musical genre) that allows for the comparisons of musical achievements at later time points with achievements and psychological profiles at earlier points in time. The implementation of longitudinal studies that allow for a rigorous quantitative evaluation of the TAD music model assumptions at different developmental levels is a primary item on the future research agenda for the TAD music model.

Note that the idea to use the time it takes to go from one level of instrumental performance to the next one as an index of musical potential has been formulated before, for example, in the *musical progress quotient* defined by Gagné and McPherson (2016). What is specific to the TAD music model is a set of psychological variables that are relevant at a specific developmental level. Hence, once an empirically robust TAD music model for a particular developmental level and musical genre/instrument has been constructed, musical potential is represented by the profile of psychological variables at this specific level. Therefore, musical potential exists and can be expressed in quantitative terms (e.g., operationalized as a constructive or reflective latent variable; Bollen &

Diamantopoulos, 2017), regardless of whether this potential is actualized or whether the musical performer decides to give up music.

PRACTICAL IMPLICATIONS

The primary motivation for constructing the TAD music model is to understand and subsequently foster and enable talent development in an achievement domain, in this case talent development in music. Importantly, this applies not only to the development of exceptional achievements but also to individuals who achieve at ordinary musical levels. Perceiving oneself as being able to continuously develop as a musical performer is one important cause for sustained and joyful engagement with music. Although this chapter has mainly focused on quantitative implementations of the TAD music model, the basic principles of the model also apply to qualitative observations and can guide the work of music teachers and instrumental instructors with their students. Some examples follow.

Different musical learners progress at different rates

The core idea of the TAD music model is that there are individual differences in the tempo at which different learners make progress. Observing these differences in musical progress in a fair and—as far as possible—objective way is a first and necessary step to exploit these differences in a way that is beneficial to the musical learner. Differential ability to progress can be evidenced, for example, by the time it takes a student to learn and master a new piece or in the level of performance proficiency of a given piece after, for example, a week. Instrumental teachers will be able to draw on a repertoire of standard pieces suitable for instrumental skill levels where they can compare the progress of a new student to the majority of students they have taught in the past. Is this new student much quicker or much slower than the bulk of the students in mastering a particular piece to a given standard? Is the learning advantage/disadvantage of a particular student specific to pieces of a particular kind or visible as a general advantage across pieces with specific musical challenges (e.g., technical, rhythmic, melodic, or expressive)?

Differences in the musical progress need to be observed among students of same developmental level

When differences in musical progress are observed, it is necessary to match musical learners with regards to their developmental levels. Progress at earlier levels often seems more rapid than at later ones, and different factors are potentially relevant at different levels. Hence, from progress at the aptitude level it is difficult to predict progress in the same individual at the expert level or to predict whether a musical performer will reach the expert level at all. Conversely, an important distinction is to be observed among learners at the same developmental level (e.g., 4-to-7-year-olds starting to play the violin, 22-year-olds starting lessons on the clarinet). Adults differ from children in most psychological variables relevant for musical learning (e.g., working memory, general intelligence, conscious strategies, transfer skills, but also sensory-motor integration and motor skills). Hence, during the earliest stages of music learning adults might show comparatively quick progress, similar to the advantage at the earliest stages of second language learning where adults can usually benefit from an acquired set of learning strategies (e.g., Huang, 2015). In essence, it is important to choose the comparison group carefully against which individual progress is judged.

Distinguish between psychological predictors and indicators of musical achievement and recognize the differential importance of predictors at different levels

For instrumental teachers, it is natural to observe indicators of present musical achievement and predict musical learning progress from these. In short, if a student plays exceptionally well, within a defined developmental level, it is reasonable to predict exceptional progress for the future. However, future progress might also depend on psychological variables that only start to matter from a certain level. For example, psychological stability, resilience, and the ability to judge one's own work critically and constructively might become important predictors for progress at the expert level but are of comparatively little importance at the aptitude and competence level (Jarvin & Subotnik 2010; Subotnik et al., 2011). It is therefore important for music teachers to recognize and identify the psychological variables that are conducive for progress over the next developmental phase.

Working with differences in musical talent profiles

Once a teacher has observed the profile of psychological variables relevant for musical learning and progress over the next developmental level, there are different options for how to leverage this knowledge. We now turn to briefly outlining two opposing strategies.

The first strategy uses musical learning to target limitations in the profile of psychological predictors. Here, a key assumption is that musical and psychological development can be a cyclic process of mutual influences, especially over the course of childhood and adolescence where neural plasticity of the brain is high and many psychological abilities and traits are formed (e.g., Seither-Preisler, Parncutt, & Schneider, 2014). Hence, the intrinsic motivation and joy to engage in musical learning can affect important psychological constructs, such as one's own lay theory of intelligence (i.e., growth mindset; Dweck 2000; Müllensiefen & Harrison, 2020). The strong belief that the personal levels of intelligence and musicality are fixed (i.e., the entity view of intelligence) can be an impediment to motivation and successful musical learning, especially among adult learners. But music can be an excellent domain to show novice music learners that new skills (e.g., playing a song on the piano) can be developed in a relatively short amount of time, which might contribute to changing self-beliefs of musicality and general learning and intelligence (e.g., Müllensiefen et al., 2015). Hence, limitations in the profile of psychological talent predictors can potentially be amended through addressing and conscious reflection of a musical learner's progress. The focus of this strategy is improving areas of personal weakness through musical learning.

In contrast, a second strategy aims to compensate for limitations in the profile of psychological variables. If certain psychological variables can be expected to affect musical development negatively and cannot be influenced substantially by musical learning (e.g., emotional stability), it is beneficial for teachers to recognize and respect these limitations, provide advice about addressing the concern (e.g., seeing a therapist or first providing non-therapeutic coaching on breath control for performance anxiety), and adjust the planned teaching program accordingly. Depending on the developmental level, it can be helpful to develop a musical or creative niche that suits the psychological profile of the musical performer and focuses on his or her strengths rather than weaknesses (Subotnik, Jarvin, Moga, & Sternberg, 2003). Rather than considering a surrender to one's deficiencies, carving a niche for a musical performer can be viewed as an important decision for enabling personal success. Such decisions can be suitable at all developmental levels, from suggesting a suitable instrument for beginners at the aptitude level with perceptual difficulties (e.g., pitch-based amusia or tone-deafness) to eminent performers at the creative contribution level (e.g., turning Glenn Gould's social awkwardness into a unique career as a recording studio pianist).

Conclusion

Musical talent development represents a long-term process that can start at different chronological ages and be observed across different developmental levels. To understand this process, to make it open for empirical investigations, and to make it applicable for musicians and music teachers in practice, it is helpful to focus on measurable psychological variables and to structure the talent development process into different levels that entail different relationships between psychological variables and indicators of musical achievement. Within the TAD framework presented in this chapter, musical talent is seen as a dynamic concept where predictors as well as indicators of musical talent can change over time. This means that assessments like "this child is (or is not) highly musically talented" might change over time as well. The TAD music model also shows that musical talent development requires not only special perceptual and motor abilities but also a range of personality traits and psychosocial skills, and that these skills might be trained as well. Furthermore, the TAD model shows how identity formation is an important part of musical talent development, in particular at the later stages of the talent development process. Finally, the model makes it clear that it is helpful to decouple the talent development process from chronological age and offers an architecture for investigating as well as recognizing and supporting musical talent development in different musical fields. Available evidence as well as new research findings can be integrated within the TAD music model. Over time, the knowledge base resulting from the accumulation of evidence within this model framework will be able to offer very specific and practically relevant information for the assessment and fostering of talent in music.

Key Sources

Gagné, F., & McPherson, G. E. (2016). Analyzing musical prodigiousness using Gagné's integrative model of talent development. In G. E. McPherson (Ed.), *Musical prodigies* (pp. 3–114). New York: Oxford University Press. https://doi.org/10.1093/acprof:oso/9780199685851.003.0001.

Haroutounian, J. (2000). Perspectives of musical talent: A study of identification criteria and procedures. *High Ability Studies, 11*, 137–160. https://doi.org/10.1080/13598130020001197.

Müllensiefen, D., Gingras, B., Musil, J., & Stewart, L. (2014). The musicality of non-musicians: An index for assessing musical sophistication in the general population. *PLoS ONE, 9*, e89642. https://doi.org/10.1371/journal.pone.0089642.

Preckel, F., Golle, J., Grabner, R., Jarvin, L., Kozbelt, A., Müllensiefen, D., Olszewski-Kubilius, P., Subotnik, R., Schneider, W., Vock, M., & Worrell, F. C. (2020). Talent development in achievement domains: A psychological framework for within and cross-domain research. *Perspectives on Psychological Science, 15*, 691–722. https://doi.org/10.1177/1745691619895030.

Subotnik, R. F., Olszewski-Kubilius, P., & Worrell, F. C. (2019). High performance: The central psychological mechanism for talent development. In R. F. Subotnik, P. Olszewski-Kubilius, & F. C. Worrell (Eds.), *The psychology of high performance: Developing human potential into domain specific talent* (pp. 7–20). Washington, DC: American Psychological Association. https://doi.org/10.1037/0000120-002.

Reflective Questions

1. In your own words, how would you describe the main differences between aptitude, competence, expertise, and transformational achievement in music?
2. Do you think that potential can get lost and/or can be built up during the talent development process?

3. Is it possible that exceptional musical potential can go completely unrecognized? Could there be a hidden Mozart living among us without anyone being aware of it?
4. Describe ways in which music educators can make best use of the concept of "talent."
5. What are the ethical implications if you discover that someone close to you possesses a great potential for music? How do you act on this information?

References

Bentley, A. (1966). *Bentley measures of musical abilities*. London: Harrap.

Bollen, K. A., & Diamantopoulos, A. (2017). Notes on measurement theory for causal-formative indicators: A reply to Hardin. *Psychological Methods, 22*(3), 605–608. https://doi.org/10.1037/met0000149.

Davidson, J., & Faulkner, R. (2013). Music in our lives. In S. B. Kaufmann (Ed.), *The complexity of greatness: Beyond talent or practice* (pp. 367–389). New York: Oxford University Press. https://doi.org/10.1093/acprof:oso/9780199794003.003.0017.

Dweck, C. S. (2000). *Self-theories: Their role in motivation, personality, and development*. Philadelphia: Psychology Press.

Folkestad, G. (2004). A meta-analytical approach to qualitative studies in music education: A new model applied to creativity and composition. *Bulletin of the Council for Research in Music Education, 161/162*, 83–90.

Gagné, F., & McPherson, G. E. (2016). Analyzing musical prodigiousness using Gagné's integrative model of talent development. In G. E. McPherson (Ed.), *Musical prodigies: Interpretations from psychology, education, musicology and ethnomusicology* (pp. 3–114). New York: Oxford University Press. https://doi.org/10.1093/acprof:oso/9780199685851.003.0001.

Gembris, H. (2009). *Entwicklungsperspektiven zwischen Publikumsschwund und Publikumsentwicklung: Empirische Daten zur Musikausbildung, dem Musikerberuf und den Konzertbesuchern* [Development perspectives between decline in audience and audience development: Empirical data on music education, the music profession and concertgoers]. In M. Tröndle (Ed.), *Das Konzert. Neue Aufführungskonzepte für eine klassische Form* (pp. 61–82). Bielefeld, Germany: Transcript. https://doi.org/10.14361/transcript.9783839416174.61.

Gordon, E. (1965). *Musical aptitude profile*. Boston: Houghton Mifflin.

Gordon, E. E. (1975). Fifth-year and final results of a five-year longitudinal study of the musical achievement of culturally disadvantaged students. *Experimental Research in the Psychology of Music: Studies in the Psychology of Music, 10*, 24–52.

Gordon, E. (1986). *Intermediate measures of music audiation*. Chicago: Gia Publications.

Gordon, E. (1989). *Advanced measures of music audiation*. Chicago: Gia Publications.

Hallam, S. (2016). Musicality. In G. E. McPherson (Ed.), *The child as musician: A handbook of musical development* (2nd ed., pp. 67–80). Oxford: Oxford University Press.

Haroutounian, J. (2000). Perspectives of musical talent: A study of identification criteria and procedures. *High Ability Studies, 11*, 137–160. https://doi.org/10.1080/13598130020001197.

Harrison, P., Collins, T., & Müllensiefen, D. (2017). Applying modern psychometric techniques to melodic discrimination testing: Item response theory, computerised adaptive testing, and automatic item generation. *Scientific Reports, 7*. https://doi.org/10.1038/s41598-017-03586-z.

Heller, K. A., & Perleth, C. (2008). The Munich High Ability Test Battery (MHBT): A multidimensional, multimethod approach. *Psychology Science Quarterly, 50*(2), 173–188.

Howe, S. W. (1998). Reconstructing the history of music education from a feminist perspective. *Philosophy of Music Education Review, 6*(2), 96–106.

Howe, M. J. A., Davidson, J. W., Moore, D. G., & Sloboda, J. A. (1995). Are there early childhood signs of musical ability? *Psychology of Music, 23*(2), 162–176. https://doi.org/10.1177/0305735695232004.

Huang, B. H. (2015). A synthesis of empirical research on the linguistic outcomes of early foreign language instruction. *International Journal of Multilingualism, 13*(3), 257–273. http://dx.doi.org/10.1080/14790718.2015.1066792.

Jarvin, L., & Subotnik, R. F. (2010). Wisdom from conservatory faculty: Insights on success in classical music performance. *Roeper Review, 32*(2), 78–87. https://doi.org/10.1080/02783191003587868.

Kirnarskaya, D. (2009). *The natural musician: On abilities, giftedness, and talent.* Oxford: Oxford University Press.

Kirnarskaya, D., & Winner, E. (1997). Musical ability in a new key: Exploring the expressive ear for music. *Psychomusicology, 16*(1-2), 2–16. https://doi.org/10.1037/h0094071.

Knotek, S. E., Foley-Nicpon, M., Kozbelt, A., Olszewski-Kubilius, P., Portenga, S., Subotnik, R. F., & Worrell, F. C. (2020). Gatekeeping in high-performance settings. *Review of General Psychology, 24*(3), 254–267. https://doi.org/10.1177/1089268020905578.

Kopiez, R., & Lee, J. I. (2006). Towards a dynamic model of skills involved in sight reading music. *Music Education Research, 8*(1), 97–120. https://doi.org/10.1080/14613800600570785.

Kozbelt, A. (2008). One-hit wonders in classical music: Evidence and (partial) explanations for an early career peak. *Creativity Research Journal, 20*(2), 179–195. https://doi.org/10.1080/10400410802059952.

Kozbelt, A. (2014). Musical creativity across the lifespan. In D. K. Simonton (Ed.), *Handbook of genius* (pp. 451–472). Hoboken, NJ: Wiley-Blackwell.

Kozbelt, A. (2018). Musicians' strategies for sustaining creativity over the lifespan. In N. Donin (Ed.), *The Oxford handbook of the creative process in music.* Oxford Handbooks Online. Oxford: Oxford University Press. https://doi.org/10.1093/oxfordhb/9780190636197.013.13.

Kraft, M. A. (2020). Interpreting effect sizes of education interventions. *Educational Researcher, 49*(4), 241–253. https://doi.org/10.3102%2F0013189X20912798.

Krampe, R. T. (1994). *Maintaining excellence: Cognitive-motor performance in pianists differing in age and skill level.* Berlin: Edition Sigma.

Krampe. R. T. (2006). Musical expertise from a lifespan perspective. In H. Gembris (Ed.), *Musical development from a lifespan perspective* (pp. 91–105). Frankfurt: Peter Lang. https://doi.org/10.1017/s0265051708007936.

Larrouy-Maestri, P., Harrison, P., & Müllensiefen, D. (2019). The mistuning perception test: A new measurement instrument. *Behavior Research Methods, 51*(2), 663–675. https://doi.org/10.3758/s13428-019-01225-1.

Lee, H., & Müllensiefen, D. (2020). The Timbre Perception Test (TPT): A new interactive musical assessment tool to measure timbre perception ability. *Attention, Perception, & Psychophysics, 82*, 3658–3675. https://doi.org/10.3758/s13414-020-02058-3.

Little, T. D. (2013). *Longitudinal structural equation modeling.* New York: Guilford Press.

MacGregor, C., & Müllensiefen, D. (2019). The Musical Emotion Discrimination Task: A new measure for assessing the ability to discriminate emotions in music. *Frontiers in Psychology, 10.* https://doi.org/10.3389/fpsyg.2019.01955.

Manturzewska, M. (1990). A biographical study of the life-span development of professional musicians. *Psychology of Music, 18*(2), 112–139. https://doi.org/10.1177/0305735690182002.

Manturzewska, M. (1992). Identification and promotion of musical talent. *European Journal for High Ability, 3*(1), 15–27. https://doi.org/10.1080/0937445920030102.

McPherson, G. E., Davidson, J. W., & Faulkner, R. (2012). *Music in our lives: Rethinking musical ability, development, and identity.* New York: Oxford University Press. https://doi.org/10.1093/acprof:oso/9780199579297.001.0001.

McPherson, G., & Hallam, S. (2016). Musical potential. In S. Hallam, I. Cross & M. Thaut (Eds.), *Oxford handbook of music psychology,* 2nd ed. (pp. 443–448). Oxford: Oxford University Press.

Müllensiefen, D., Gingras, B., Musil, J., & Stewart, L. (2014). The musicality of non-musicians: An index for assessing musical sophistication in the general population. *PLoS ONE, 9,* e89642. https://doi.org/10.1371/journal.pone.0089642.

Müllensiefen, D., & Harrison, P. (2020). The impact of music on adolescents' cognitive and socio-emotional learning. In J. Harrington, J. Beale, A. Fancourt, & C. Lutz (Eds.), *The "BrainCanDo" handbook of teaching and learning: Practical strategies to bring psychology and neuroscience into the classroom* (pp. 222–239). Abington: Routledge.

Müllensiefen, D., Harrison, P., Caprini, F., & Fancourt, A. (2015). Investigating the importance of self-theories of intelligence and musicality for students' academic and musical achievement. *Frontiers in Psychology, 6,* Article ID 1702. https://doi.org/10.3389/fpsyg.2015.01702.

Norton, A., Winner, E., Cronin, K., Lee, D., & Schlaug, G. (2005). Are there pre-existing neural, cognitive, or motoric markers for musical ability? *Brain and Cognition, 59*(2), 124–134. https://doi.org/10.1016/j.bandc.2005.05.009.

Ohio Department of Education (2004). *Identification of children who are gifted in music: Implementation handbook for educations* – see https://files.eric.ed.gov/fulltext/ED491926.pdf.

Preckel, F., Golle, J., Grabner, R., Jarvin, L., Kozbelt, A., Müllensiefen, D., Olszewski-Kubilius, P., Subotnik, R., Schneider, W., Vock, M., & Worrell, F. C. (2020). Talent development in achievement domains: A psychological framework for within and cross-domain research. *Perspectives on Psychological Science, 15,* 691–722. https://doi.org/10.1177/1745691619895030.

Schellenberg, E. G. (2011). Examining the association between music lessons and intelligence. *British Journal of Psychology, 102*(3), 283–302. https://doi.org/10.1111/j.2044-8295.2010.02000.x.

Seashore, C. E. (1919). *Manual of instructions and interpretations for measures of musical talent.* New York: Columbia Graphophone Company.

Seashore, C. E. (1947). *In search of beauty in music: A scientific approach to musical esthetics.* Westport, CT: Greenwood Press.

Seashore, C., Lewis, D., & Saetveit, J. (1960). *Seashore measures of musical talents: Manual.* New York: Psychological Corp.

Seither-Preisler, A., Parncutt, R., & Schneider, P. (2014). Size and synchronization of auditory cortex promotes musical, literacy, and attentional skills in children. *Journal of Neuroscience, 34*(33), 10937–10949. https://doi.org/10.1523/JNEUROSCI.5315-13.2014.

Simonton, D. K. (1977). Creative productivity, age, and stress: A biographical time-series analysis of 10 classical composers. *Journal of Personality and Social Psychology, 35*(11), 11: 791–804. https://psycnet.apa.org/doi/10.1037/0022-3514.35.11.791.

Simonton, D. K. (1991). Emergence and realization of genius: The lives and works of 120 classical composers. *Journal of Personality and Social Psychology, 61*(5), 829–840. https://psycnet.apa.org/doi/10.1037/0022-3514.61.5.829.

Simonton, D. K. (1996). Creative expertise: A life-span developmental perspective. In K. A. Ericsson (Ed.), *The road to excellence: The acquisition of expert performance in the arts and sciences, sports, and games* (pp. 227–253). Mahwah, NJ: Lawrence Erlbaum Associates.

Simonton, D. K. (1997). Creative productivity: A predictive and explanatory model of career landmarks and trajectories. *Psychological Review, 104*(1), 66–89.

Spychiger, M., & Hechler, J. (2014). Musikalität, Intelligenz und Persönlichkeit: Alte und neue Integrationsversuche [Musicality, intelligence, and personality]. In W. Gruhn & A. Seither-Preisler (Eds.), *Der musikalische Mensch: Evolution, Biologie und Pädagogik musikalischer Begabung* (pp. 23–68). Hildescheim: Olms. https://doi.org/10.1177/1029864915595793.

Sternberg, R. J. (1999). Intelligence as developing expertise. *Contemporary Educational Psychology, 24*(4), 359–375. https://doi.org/10.1006/ceps.1998.0998.

Subotnik, R. F., Jarvin, L., Moga, E., & Sternberg, R. J. (2003). Wisdom from gatekeepers: Secrets of success in music performance. *Bulletin of Psychology in the Arts, 4*, 5–9.

Subotnik, R. F., Olszewski-Kubilius, P., & Worrell, F. C. (2011). Rethinking giftedness and gifted education: A proposed direction forward based on psychological science. *Psychological Science in the Public Interest, 12*(1), 3–54. https://doi.org/10.1037/e665862012-001.

Subotnik, R. F., Olszewski-Kubilius, P., & Worrell, F. C. (2019). High performance: The central psychological mechanism for talent development. In R. F. Subotnik, P. Olszewski-Kubilius, & F. C. Worrell (Eds.), *The psychology of high performance: Developing human potential into domain specific talent* (pp. 7–20). Washington, DC: American Psychological Association. https://doi.org/10.1037/0000120-002.

Ullén, F., Hambrick, D. Z., & Mosing, M. A. (2016). Rethinking expertise: A multifactorial gene-environment interaction model of expert performance. *Psychological Bulletin, 142*(4), 427–446. https://doi.org/10.1037/bul0000033.

Vandervert, L. R. (2016). Working memory in musical prodigies. In G. E. McPherson (Ed.), *Musical prodigies: Interpretations from psychology, education, musicology, and ethnomusicology* (pp. 223–244). Oxford: Oxford University Press. https://doi.org/10.1093/acprof:oso/9780199685851.003.0008.

Wing, H. D. (1968). *Tests of musical ability and appreciation* (2nd ed.). Cambridge, UK: Cambridge University Press.

Winner, E. (1996). *Gifted children* (Vol. 1). New York: Basic Books.

Winner, E., & Martino, G. (2000). Giftedness in non-academic domains: The case of the visual arts and music. In K. A. Heller, F. J. Mönks, R. J. Sternberg, & R. Subotnik (Eds.), *International handbook of giftedness and talent* (2nd ed., pp. 95–110). Oxford: Pergamon.

Wisconsin Music Educators Association (2009). *Music identification handbook for educators, coordinator, and administrators in Wisconsin Public Schools* – see https://www.maine.gov/doe/sites/maine.gov.doe/files/inline-files/WMEAGiftedandTalentedHandbook.pdf.

Zuk, J., Andrade, P. E., Andrade, O. V. C. A., Gardiner, M., & Gaab, N. (2013). Musical, language, and reading abilities in early Portuguese readers. *Frontiers in Psychology, 4*, Article ID 288. https://doi.org/10.3389/fpsyg.2013.00288.

CHAPTER 6

SELF-DIRECTED LEARNING STRATEGIES

KELLY A. PARKES

INTRODUCTION

HAVE you ever practiced at home, repeatedly attempting to learn music, only to stop and say, "I'll have to wait until my next lesson to figure this out"? Perhaps you aren't sure whether you are playing correctly or whether it sounds the way it is supposed to. This can be frustrating for any musician. So how do musicians learn to control, moderate, and evaluate their own learning to gain independence from their teacher? Why would a musician want to gain independence from their teacher? Successful musicians are those who can move on from their teachers and take charge of their careers.

This chapter provides an overview of self-directed learning (SDL) frameworks with a synthesis of the latest research. It also explores the connections SDL has to constructivism, to learner-centered teaching, and the differences observed between SDL and self-regulation. Methods for measuring SDL are also described and suggestions given for implementing various learning strategies within musical settings. The final section discusses implications for musicians.

SELF-DIRECTED LEARNING

Self-directed learning (SDL) is essentially how individuals moderate, control, and evaluate their learning so that they can learn on their own. Broadly speaking, SDL includes goal setting and task analyses, implementation of a plan that is self-constructed, and self-evaluation of learning along with the processes experienced. Over the past two decades, researchers have identified cognitive processes present in musical learning. These are grouped into salient areas of research (such as motivation, self-efficacy, self-regulation, and practice) and given specific attention in this volume (Parts II and IV, this volume). For the purposes of this chapter, I will focus on literature outside of music, examining what Garrison (1997) proposed as contextual control, cognitive responsibility, and motivational dimensions. This is what has more recently been labeled as "self-managing, self-monitoring, and self-modifying" behaviors in both learners and teachers (Costa & Kallick, 2004, p. 37). My purpose is to examine theory and findings from research that are related, along with practical applications that the literature suggests are warranted for music instruction.

THEORETICAL MODEL OF SDL

SDL is a framework that allows musicians to understand how they can be more proactive with their learning, by taking more control of the processes involved. When learners take responsibility for their learning, they can develop and evaluate their processes more effectively. Knowing the background theories of this model allows musicians to be familiar with the overall approach. SDL lets musicians make decisions that will impact their performance.

The theories about SDL are generally similar to each other. There are many situations within music where musicians need to take responsibility for their own learning, as they develop and evaluate the thoughts and actions they implement during the act of performing. Rogers (1969) suggested that learners take responsibility for the cognitive and motivational facets of learning, and several researchers such as Brookfield (1986) and Knowles (1975, 1990) have also provided useful ideas. A formal theoretical model of SDL was posed specifically for adult education (Garrison, 1997), and this model of SDL extends from the original work of Knowles (1975). Knowles defined SDL as "a process in which individuals take the initiative, with or without help from others, in diagnosing their learning needs, formulating goals, identifying human and material resources, choosing and implementing appropriate learning strategies, and evaluating learning outcomes" (p. 18).

SDL is a process comprising personal autonomy, self-management of learning, the independent pursuit of learning, and learner control (Candy, 1991; 2004); it can be helpful for adolescent through adult learners (Gibbons, 2002). In his model, Garrison (1997) integrates self-management (contextual control), self-monitoring (cognitive responsibility), and motivation (entering and task). In some ways, these overlap with the constructs found in self-regulated learning (SRL; see also Part IV, this volume). An overview of the theoretical concept of SDL is warranted as many of the core constructs are based in external control and management of learning (and a detailed examination of SRL can be found in Parts II and IV, this volume).

Individuals who are self-directed in their learning might be seen as simply independent, or as being able to learn on their own; that is, musicians who are able to practice at home without their teacher and make consistent progress. SDL has been described from a "collaborative constructivist perspective" (Garrison, p. 19), and in that sense we see the merging of psychological cognitive motivational constructs with some of the more social elements of the constructivist theory. A main tenet of constructivism is that individuals learn themselves by doing, by experiencing, and consequently are able to construct new knowledge and meaning. Constructivism in action (while not specifically being a formal pedagogy) might include collaboration and learning from others, whether from a teacher or from a peer, while also learning from oneself. Constructivism is not only a social theory because there are ostensibly two strands of constructivist thinking, social and cognitive, and Garrison makes connections between both of these in the model of SDL.

In the twenty-first century, a constructivist worldview has appeared, explaining how individuals learn and how knowledge is produced (Gordon, 2008). It can also be seen as a paradigm, with social constructivism taking an ontological position with epistemological implications.

The presence of constructivism in SDL models should be noted because early constructivist thinkers (such as Dewey, Piaget, and Vygotsky) were largely interested in describing how learning happens. Learning occurs internally (as Piaget suggested) via experiences (as Dewey noted), and/or as mediated by the environment or social interactions (as Vygotsky believed). The inclusion of a constructivist approach in Garrison's model signals the learner's role and their responsibility to create, interpret, and reorganize knowledge for themselves.

Three overlapping dimensions are stressed in the Garrison (1997) model. These are "self-management (contextual control), self-monitoring (cognitive responsibility) and motivational (entering and task)" (p. 21), and all three are closely connected (see Figure 6.1).

The three dimensions are not presented in a hierarchical or linear manner; rather, they should be considered together. Self-management can be seen as task control issues, such as enacting learning goals and managing learning resources and support. In Garrison's model, the learner assesses these continuously and negotiates what they need. It is beneficial for learners to have choices with how they conduct their learning process. Garrison uses self-management to describe external control (which is still linked to motivation and self-monitoring). It is clear that the concept of self-management is also seen in the SRL literature; however, Garrison posits that self-management is more focused on resource management (the context) and the activities learners are undertaking. The context of the learning can be shaped or managed toward the learners' goals. Garrison states that self-management does not mean isolated, but instead that teachers (what he calls "facilitators") give direction and support, therefore making it a collaborative experience. The key concept here is that the communication between teacher and learner is imperative to balance control and the degree to which learners are self-managed.

The second dimension, self-monitoring, seems to align with what we now know about cognition and metacognition. This essentially means thinking about learning and

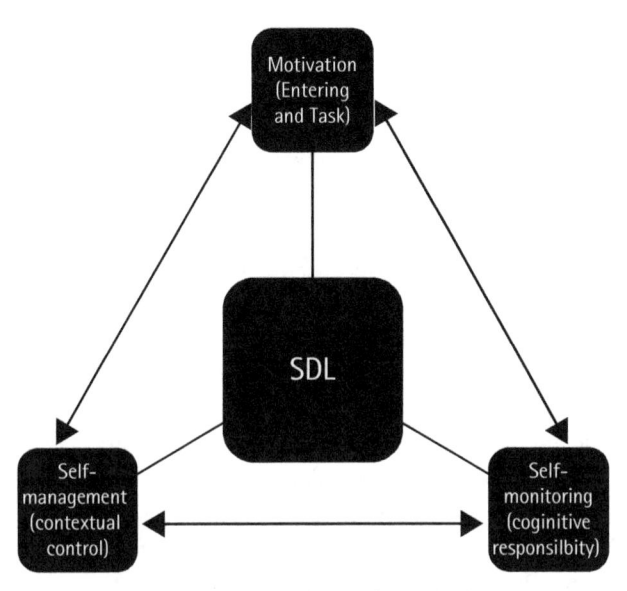

FIGURE 6.1. Visual representation of Garrison's SLD framework.

learning strategies. Garrison maintains that self-monitoring is also where the learner takes responsibility for constructing learning and constructing meaning via the paths of reflection and collaboration. Self-monitoring, in Garrison's model, is dependent on contextual or environmental effects and on internal/external feedback. Garrison notes the similarities to SRL with "observing, judging, and reacting" (p. 25) to learning tasks and activities and articulates the associations between metacognitive skills and reflection along with critical thinking. Feedback from the teacher assists in meaning making so learners can form their thinking and further learning strategies. For students to assume self-monitoring responsibility, they must have choice and collaboration (Garrison, 1997).

The third, and final, dimension in Garrison's model is motivation (see Müllensiefen et al., this part). Garrison notes the important effects of motivation factors, choosing to focus on the process individuals take at the decision to start a learning task (entering) and also on the process of staying with the task. Current psychological literature (e.g., expectancy-value framework, fixed-growth mindset theory) indicates that there are several constructs within motivation theories that can predict both why individuals choose a particular task and why they may or may not choose to persist with a task. Garrison's model, in this dimension, shows the early influence of motivational theories such as attribution theory, self-determination theory, expectancy-value theory, and self-efficacy theory. In summary, SDL in Garrison's model seems to privilege the notion of continuous, lifelong learning, along with individual learning, in collaboration with a facilitator or teacher.

RECENT EXTENSIONS OF SDL

Current views on SDL continue Garrison's initial ideas but seat them in modern learning contexts by incorporating technology (Rashid & Asghar, 2016; Teo, Tan, Lee, Chai, Koh, Chen, & Cheah, 2010;) and situating SDL within problem-based learning contexts (Loyens, Magda, & Rikers, 2008). SDL in problem-based learning has an interesting corollary with music. Music instruction might be seen as almost exclusively problem-based; however, the traditionally teacher-directed nature of music instruction is inherited from the master-apprentice applied model (Daniel & Parkes, 2019). Learners are rarely afforded the opportunity to solve musical problems, technical problems, or music environment problems even when teachers take an individualized approach. In problem-based learning, musician learners can typically collaborate over problems that stem from professional practices or problems that are typical in a certain area of study. The goal is for musicians to understand the problem via discussion and then create solutions. Problem-based learning relies on what we already know about an issue, so in the initial phase of solving a problem, learners need to plan and monitor what they are doing in order to find gaps in their knowledge before they seek the assistance of a facilitator, coach, or teacher. Planning and monitoring are markers of SDL. Van den Hurk (2006) investigated how SDL strategies (self-monitoring and time planning) worked in a problem-based learning setting and found that self-monitoring had a relationship with higher levels of performance. Garrison (1997), Knowles (1975, 1990), and Candy (1991) all suggest that in SDL, learning takes place with others so problem-based approaches that include SDL may perhaps best be undertaken in music ensemble settings.

Musicians can become disappointed when they are not able to see the relevance of their training in real life (Loyens et al., 2008). This can be seen in theories that stress learners' beliefs, such as the expectancy-value theory of Wigfield and Eccles (2000). The constructs of utility value or task usefulness certainly impact student motivation. We see this in music when younger musicians are not aware of the value, or usefulness of developing a particular technical skill. Beginner musicians may be reluctant to learn scales because they do not see the relationship between being able to play G and D scales and being able to play a piece of music in G major.

Technology can play an important part in SDL. It has similarities to music instruction if we consider one-to-one teaching in applied studio settings where musicians work independently for most of their time, practicing, until they meet with their teacher or ensemble once a week. There are two factors, as studied by Teo et al. (2010), related to learning with technology: self-management and intentional learning, especially when measuring SDL with younger children (ages 10–12). If we consider that young music students may be practicing at home unsupervised, because many parents do not have a background in or knowledge about music to support them (McPherson & Zimmerman, 2011), then these two aspects of SDL become important. If music students were to engage in self-management with technology, they might contact their teacher via the phone, video call, or email to ask questions about their practice, posture, or music. They might also keep a practice journal on their tablet device or computer, noting what they are having difficulty with or what is working well, or keep a e-journal or blog/vlog about their learning. They might make a recording of their practice session. If music students engage in intentional learning with technology, they might find out more information about a piece of music by using the internet, or texting/emailing a friend, or they might seek out other ideas from the internet via a search engine. They might also find other recordings of their music via YouTube.

The relationship between undergraduate university students' SDL and other variables (technology use, student engagement, and academic achievement) was examined by Rashid and Asghar (2016). Using Williamson's (2007) instrument to measure SDL, they found that SDL had a positive relationship with technology and engagement, indicating that SDL improved academic performance when technology use supported the SDL strategies. Positive technology predictors of SDL were email, smartphone usage, internet use, and social media use. This supports the ideas of Teo et al. (2010) that SDL strategies employed via technology may be useful to all learners, even musicians.

SDL and Learner-Centeredness

The learner-centered framework holds similar notions of SDL theory, sharing Rogers's (1969) early concept of the learner taking responsibility for their learning. However, the learner-centered framework suggests that the learner and teacher roles in the learning setting are changed from traditional structures of teacher control. Learner-centered approaches (Weimer, 2002) focus not only on what is being learned but also on the conditions in which the learning is occurring, how the learning is applied and retained, and to what level the learning has occurred. As with SDL theory, the focus is on the learner. Weimer's framework is instructional for the teacher, holding five tenets: the balance of power, the function of content, the role of the teacher, the purpose and processes of evaluation, and one tenet that resonates with the SDL theory—responsibility for learning. Weimer suggests that the responsibility for learning rests with the learner and that to achieve this, the learning setting and climate need to be optimal. Weimer's practical strategies for teachers include involving students in the process of setting a learning climate, getting feedback from students about the climate, allowing students choice in assigned work or deadlines, clarifying their responsibilities, and empowering students to fix problems.

Encouraging learners to take responsibility starts first with the climate of the learning environment where, Weimer suggests, they should be told that the teaching learning setting is a shared space, one where both learner and teacher are responsible for what occurs. Weimer suggests teachers can show learners the value of the content and create environmental conditions where learners are empowered to take responsibility for their learning. Weimer suggests that students be included in the process of articulating the class climate, so perhaps this suggestion makes the most sense for music ensembles. Asking a student ensemble to participate in a discussion where principles are suggested (for behavior, processes, physical setup of the room, group work), discussed, and agreed upon for implementation. Giving learners this opportunity to contribute to their learning setting conditions can signal to them that their ideas are welcome and equally as valid as the teacher's. In the SDL theoretical model of Garrison (1997), this type of responsibility can be seen as contextual control.

Allowing students to articulate their perceived strengths and weaknesses can indicate that the teacher values students' ideas about themselves and about their learning (Doyle, 2008). Doyle recommends the giving of responsibility to students and also suggests that the more control that is offered to students, the more motivated they will become. In this sense, he advocates for giving students choices over their learning processes, the rationale being that when students have choice and control over how they learn, they will discover their strengths and weaknesses. This can be seen as parallel to what Garrison sees as cognitive responsibility. The notion of general responsibility for learning in learner-centered frameworks perhaps can therefore be seen as the preparatory step in encouraging the cognitive responsibility proposed by Garrison (1997) in SDL.

DIFFERENCES BETWEEN SRL AND SDL

Self-regulation was initially proposed as having a beneficial effect on academic outcomes. Researchers suggested that learners can monitor and control their thoughts and become active participants in their own learning (e.g., Zimmerman, 1986; 1989; 2000). Broadly speaking, self-regulation includes processes such as goal setting, metacognition, and self-assessment, so it is related to SDL. Self-regulated learning has been examined by researchers recently in several music learning contexts such as higher education and middle school instrumental classes (e.g., de Bézenac, & Swindells, 2009; Leon-Guerrero, 2008; McPherson & McCormick, 1999; McPherson, Osborne, Evans, & Mikszo, 2017; McPherson & Renwick, 2001; Mikszo, Blackwell, & Roseth, 2018; and Nielsen, 2001; for review, see Varela, Abrami, & Upitis, 2016). Self-regulation is most often studied in music during the practice of musicians and involves a collection of context-specific behavioral, cognitive, metacognitive, and affective phenomena.

In medical education, there is confusion between SDL and SRL (Gandomkar & Sandars, 2018). There are similarities in that learners are actively engaged in setting their learning goals, they choose and implement suitable learning strategies, and they evaluate their learning outcomes. Gandomkar and Sandars suggest, however, that SDL "describes the general approach to learning adopted by the learner, whereas SRL has a specific focus on the key learning processes, in relation to a clearly defined task" (p. 862). Moreover, they articulate the differences as follows: A self-directed learner takes responsibility for their own learning and has internal motivation to develop, implement, and evaluate their approach to learning. An SRL process, on the other hand, is highly strategic and uses a variety of key cognitive and metacognitive processes to ensure that the intended learning is achieved, including enhancing motivation through increasing their self-efficacy beliefs, self-monitoring of the progress of selected goals, and making adaptive changes to goals and motivational and attribution beliefs. At its core, SRL involves a dynamic feedback loop in relation to achieving a specific task within a particular context (p. 862).

Although there are similarities between the SDL and SRL models, SDL researchers measure self-reported information about less narrowly defined elements such as overarching awareness, learning strategies, learning activities, evaluation, and interpersonal skills (e.g., Williamson, 2007). SDL researchers examine the many choices students make in their learning by "diagnosing their learning needs, formulating goals, identifying human and material resources, choosing and implementing appropriate learning strategies, and evaluating learning outcomes" (Knowles, 1975, p. 18).

One similarity between SDL and SRL is that the ultimate goal is to have learners who are autonomous, but researchers suggest the two should be seen and conceptualized differently (e.g., Gandomkar & Sandars, 2018; Jossberger, Brand-Gruwel, Boshuizen, & Wiel, 2010; and Pilling-Cormick & Garrison, 2007). SDL and SRL can perhaps be seen at two contrasting levels, whereby SDL is placed at what has been labeled the macro level and SRL is placed at the micro level (Jossberger et al., 2010). Pilling-Cormick and Garrison (2007) suggest that SDL skills are the overt management of the external learning environment, whereas they see SRL as the covert management of the internal learning environment, with internal cognitive and motivational constructs at play. SRL might also be seen as a resource for the psychological dimensions of SDL (Garrison, 1997).

Current research in music education with SRL, using microanalysis, delivers important information about how learners approach, perform, and reflect, as noted in the studies by McPherson, Osborne, Evans and Miksza (2017) and Miksza, Blackworth, and Roseth (2018). This is illustrated as forethought, performance, and self-reflection phases with specific tasks. This is different to SDL, which is characterized as an overarching learning approach (regardless of the task), one in which the learner conceptualizes, designs, conducts, and evaluates their learning; the assumption in SDL is that in order to become autonomous, these elements are, or will be, within the learner's control.

Clearly it is advantageous for learners to be autonomous as well as self-dependent. In SDL the learner exhibits independence by deciding what to learn and how to learn it by self-managing, self-monitoring, and self-modifying. The ability to learn on one's own is a lifelong learning trait and one that is tacitly considered to be a common human goal. SDL also relies on resources, supports, and assistance found in the educational setting. SDL occurs when learners take responsibility to construct their learning, which happens when learners and teachers co-construct or negotiate a shared purpose. Ultimately, individuals engaging in SDL should see results in improved learning outcomes. In the twenty-first century, education should be preparing students to resolve problems encountered in an increasingly complex society (Costa & Kallick, 2004). As noted earlier in the chapter, SDL can be seen as an asset in problem-based learning settings and a general step toward independence.

Measuring the Components of SDL

SDL is important for music learners to consider, and it is also important to know when it is happening and when it is not. Attempts at measuring SDL in other domains outside music were developed as early as the 1970s (see Guglielmino, 1977) and other researchers have since developed Likert-type instruments to identify domains within SDL (e.g., Fisher, King, & Tague; 2001; Hendry & Ginns, 2009; Oddi, 1986; Shen, Chen, & Hu, 2014; Stockdale & Brockett, 2010). These instruments typically include items (questions) that lead to the identification of constructs semi-consistent with self-regulated learning processes, self-efficacy, self-determination, and motivation. Guglielmino (1977) identified eight components of SDL: self-concept as an effective and independent learner, initiative in learning, informed acceptance of responsibility for one's own learning, love of learning, risk and complexity tolerance in learning, positive orientation to lifelong learning, creativity, and self-understanding. Fisher et al. (2001) found three components (self-management, desire for learning, and self-control) with principal component factor analysis. Williamson (2007) created a self-rating scale of SDL in measuring early adult individuals' SDL domains: awareness, learning strategies, learning activities, evaluation, and interpersonal skills. Cheng, Kuo, Lin, and Lee-Hsieh (2010) created a SDL instrument (SDLI) specifically for nursing students. They found four important domains: learning motivation, planning and implementing, self-monitoring, and interpersonal communication. Shen, Chen, and Hu (2014) used the work of Cheng et al. (2010) and found further support for these four dimensions. Musicians don't need to measure these constructs formally in their day-to-day routine in the way these researchers have, but musicians should be able to recognize these areas and how they work. Example includes recognizing when we are open to learning opportunities, considering what is our own self-concept as an effective learner, taking initiative and independence in our learning, being accepting of responsibility for our own learning, consciously enjoying or loving learning, taking creative or new approaches, staying positive to the future, and trying to use problem-solving skills rather than waiting for the next lesson with the teacher. Increasing awareness of these areas may allow music learners to identify their learning motivations, leading to improvements in their planning and in their self-monitoring.

Practical Implications

SDL strategies provide a way of helping music students (adolescents through to adults) (a) identify and set goals; (b) analyze the tasks that will be needed to meet these goals by; (c) planning and managing the work needed, and monitoring for changes that also might be needed; and (d) self-evaluate or reflect on their learning strategies to ensure they are aware of their learning (also known as elements of metacognition). For adolescents, Gibbons (2002) suggests that SDL is useful in developing responsibility for learning and decision-making skills.

There are various strategies that musicians may undertake (Candy, 1991, 2004) and several strategies describe how learners process information. These are directly relevant for music students. There are different levels of processing, deep and surface. Deep-level processing allows for strategies that find meaning, such as reflection, whereas surface-level processing only allows for strategies such as rote rehearsal. If we consider both classroom and applied studio settings, the performance teacher typically makes most of the decisions: what to play, how to sit/stand, when to breathe in a phrase, when to warm up, when to play, when to stop, etc. Musicians can be self-directed when they are responsible for and take ownership of their learning. The teacher should allow for students to have autonomy and foster an environment where students can have some choice. Deep-level processing is more likely to occur when learners can choose what they learn and how they learn it (Candy, 1991, 2004). Independent learning with only moderate involvement from the teacher allows for this sense of ownership of the learning. As such, teachers might consider allowing greater choice for students and releasing some control within the teaching/learning transaction (Georgii-Hemming, & Westvall, 2010). It is important to point out here that SDL is not only about freedom of learning, where teachers and students simply take an "everything works" approach. Rather, learners need to consider their choice of strategies, with their teacher, in line with the SDL framework to purposefully aim toward their specific and individualized goals.

When ensemble members self-select musical parts (as part of a mature adult learning ensemble opportunity), they exercise control over the musical tasks (Harrington, 2018). This also affects the learning opportunities they face during ensemble rehearsals and performances. By making this choice, musicians can control the rate of their musical learning. "Individuals who prefer to review and solidify music performance skills before increasing the overall difficulty of their musical materials may select less-demanding parts, while those who desire more challenging musical materials may select parts that require more advanced performance skills" (Harrington, 2018, p. 192).

SDL strategies in informal, popular music settings include interactions with peers and group activities (Lebler, 2008), and these are activities that rarely receive direction from an expert mentor or teacher. Students can record the music they create and critically reflect on the performance, alone and/or with peers more than once if desired. This, according to Lebler, allows for immediate feedback and the application of knowledge, which should result in improved performances.

Self-directed learners control and monitor not only their behavior and thinking, but also their environment. This means that in the ensemble setting, students need to be able to find and choose spaces for group work, as well as have the necessary materials available to problem-solve such as white boards and markers for idea sharing, or notation paper for working through tasks. In the applied setting, learners should be encouraged to move the music stand and chair in any given studio, to make decisions about where their sound might project, and to move their physical location in the room. Additionally, learners should make these decisions in their practice room locations and have choices about when and where they practice.

SELF-MANAGING, SELF-MONITORING, AND SELF-MODIFYING

Self-managing means that musicians can approach tasks with outcomes clearly defined, form a strategic plan, and collect any information or data needed; after establishing indictors of success, they move toward accomplishing their goal (Costa & Kallick (2004). *Self-monitoring* means that individuals can create metacognitive strategies to assess whether their plan is working or not. Decisions may need to be made about altering the plan. *Self-modifying* includes reflection, evaluation, analysis, and making meaning from the experience, which is then applied to future activities, tasks, and challenges. In any typical learning situation these three components may often occur simultaneously for the learner (Garrison, 1997). Figure 6.2 illustrates these three areas.

To elaborate the preceding paragraph, there are seven principles that musicians might find helpful to help focus a cycle of SDL. These are modeled on work by Costa and Kallick, (2004, pp. 28–29), whose comments are reinterpreted here for music learning and teaching:

(a) *Clarify goals and purposes*: What is the purpose for what you are doing? What beliefs or values does this plan of action reflect? What outcomes would you expect as a result of your actions? Both teachers and students can ask these questions of themselves and each other at the start of a lesson or series of lessons.

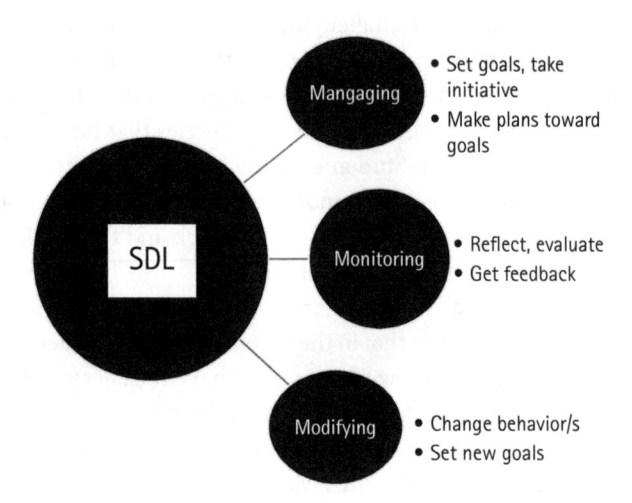

FIGURE 6.2. Components of SDL

(b) *Planning*: What actions would you take to achieve the desired outcomes? How would you set up a learning environment to test your ideas? What evidence would you collect to help to inform you about the results of your actions? What would you look for as indicators that your outcomes were or were not achieved? And how will you leave the door open for other discoveries and possibilities that were not built into the original design? What process will you put in place that will help you describe what actually happened? This might allow space for students to decide to record a lesson or make notes directly afterward.

(c) *Take action/implement*: Execute the plan by taking action; the teacher and student can agree to always clarify goals at the start of each lesson and set up a recording device to record each lesson in the future.

(d) *Assess/gather evidence*: The student is then ready to assess and gather evidence about their learning. They implement the assessment strategy by recording the lessons and making notes afterward.

(e) *Study, reflect, evaluate/derive meaning*: What meaning can be made of the data? Who might serve as critical friends to coach, facilitate, or mediate your learning from this experience? Students are able to ask themselves, "What have I learned from my recordings and notes?" They can listen back to the recording after each lesson and then study, reflect, evaluate, and derive meaning, which in turn may lead to an improved performance and a stronger sense of ownership over the improvements. Perhaps they may need assistance with what meaning can be made of the recordings or notes. They might need assistance to find critical friends, such as a peer musician, to help with what can be learned from the recordings and notes.

(f) *Modify actions based on new knowledge*: What will be done differently in the future as a result of reflection and integration of new knowledge? Is it worth trying again? Musicians might notate what they have learned in a reflective journal and modify their future practice sessions based on new knowledge. They may plan different actions.

(g) *Revisit/redefine*: Do the goals still make sense? Are they still of value or do they need to be redefined, refocused, refined? After a month, or semester, of recording lessons and reflecting, it is important to revisit and redefine. Musician-learners may need to check if their goals still make sense. Are they still of value or do they need to be redefined, refocused, refined? Do they need to keep recording their lessons or are the notes made after each lesson enough? This perhaps returns to the first step in the spiral of goal clarification but relies on the teacher to provide key scaffolds and supports to the students.

This cycle can also be seen from two perspectives: (a) the music classroom and (b) the applied studio. In the music classroom, where students make and create music, this cycle presents an opportunity for problem-based or inquiry-based group work activities, facilitated by the teacher to develop SDL opportunities. Teachers could consider giving students time during class to work together on small group projects, to rehearse chamber music or trios/quartets, or to create compositions that illustrate a particular message or theme. Posing the questions as cited by Costa and Kallick (2004) would assist students in developing their SDL strategies. For example, in working in a small group for chamber rehearsal, the teacher would ask the students several questions (potential student responses are in italics):

"What is your goal for the rehearsal (today, this week, this month) and how do you expect to get there?" *We need to talk to each other to decide which piece we will play and how far we want to get in the piece by next week based on how difficult our parts are. We need to set up a rehearsal schedule for our group.*

"How are you planning to be able to perform the piece the goal date and have you set up a rehearsal schedule?" *We want to be able to play the first movement by the end of the month. We have set up a rehearsal schedule to make sure we focus on several areas we know will be hard for us.*

"What will happen if you are not making progress with learning the music? Who will you ask for help?" *We will know if we are not making progress because we will hear that some notes are not correct, or that we cannot play it at the marked tempo.*

"How will you know if you are playing it correctly?" *We will record ourselves and compare our recording to our parts.*

From the second perspective, a student learning in an applied one-to-one studio may also be able to engage in SDL strategies by being encouraged with similar questions but with the teacher providing more assistance with choices for the student to consider individually in the home learning environment.

"What is your goal for the week and how will you get there?" *I am going to choose two pieces to practice, pieces that use G major scales in them, but I need to make sure I can practice at home for 1 hour each day. It depends on when my baby sister needs to sleep. I can plan a schedule with my parents, or perhaps I can practice at my aunt's house two days a week. I will need to set up a rehearsal schedule once I talk to my parents.*

"How are you planning to be able to perform the piece the goal date? Have you set up a practice plan?" *I want to be able to play the first section by the end of the month. I set up a plan with my aunt and my parents to make sure I will have a place to practice each afternoon after school.*

"How will you know you are making progress with learning the music? Who will you ask for help?" *I will make notes on the areas in the music that are difficult for me or that don't sound right to me. If they are still giving me trouble at the middle of the week, I will check with you by calling or emailing to ask for help.*

"How will you know if you are playing it correctly?" *I could compare my recording to the one my teacher provided or I will find one on YouTube that I like.*

In general, teachers need to facilitate and support learners in developing these self-directed strategies. Knowles (1975) suggested that the learner will continue to need several key supports from their teachers. Most important, willingness and ability are needed to enter into a respectful learning relationship with learners to provide an environment that is physically and psychologically comfortable, open to interaction, and based on cooperation. Teachers can acknowledge that they are continuing to learn about their students and therefore teachers can take responsibility for determining their own learning needs as well. Teachers can collaboratively set goals with their students, using their knowledge and experience but also taking their students' goals and interests into account. Teachers can plan for, implement, and evaluate the learning activities of their students, and this will allow them to help learners self-direct. Essentially, the teacher is ultimately a facilitator and a resource. Knowing how to effectively use small-group processes would be helpful for teachers in classroom settings, and all teachers need to be able to evaluate learning processes and outcomes with their students.

SDL can be seen as an individual's efforts to manage, monitor, and modify their learning, with an ultimate goal of becoming independent of the teacher. The strategies relevant to SDL include goal setting and task analyses, implementation of a plan constructed by the learner, and self-evaluation of learning along with the processes experienced. The overarching factors (learning motivation, planning and implementing, self-monitoring, and interpersonal communication) support general domains such as awareness, learning strategies, learning activities, evaluation, and interpersonal skills as essential for a self-directed learner. There is a need for future research in this area, to develop the potential empirical and practical connections between SDL and SRL (self-regulated learning). Current SDL strategies encourage students to conceptualize, design, conduct, and evaluate their learning in tandem with their teacher, leading eventually to independence.

KEY SOURCES

Brookfield, S. D. (2009). Self-directed learning. In R. Maclean & D. Wilson (Eds.), *International handbook of education for the changing world of work* (pp. 2615–2627). Dordrecht: Springer.

Candy, P. C. (1991). *Self-direction for lifelong learning.* San Francisco: Jossey-Bass.

Candy, P. C. (2004). *Linking thinking: Self-directed learning in the digital age.* Commonwealth of Australia: Department of Education, Science and Training.

Garrison, D. R. (1997). Self-directed learning: Toward a comprehensive model. *Adult Education Quarterly, 48*(1), 18–33. https://doi.org/10.1177%2F074171369704800103.

Knowles, M. (1975). *Self-directed learning: A guide for learners and teachers.* New York: Cambridge University Press.

Reflective Questions

1. How would a teacher improve the outcomes of their students' performance using the self-directed learning approach?
2. What would be the first step a musician could take toward being more self-directed in their practice sessions?
3. What do you consider to be the most helpful SDL strategy for a beginning music learner?
4. How could a performer use the self-managing and self-modifying steps to prepare for an audition?
5. In what ways could a classroom music teacher incorporate SDL strategies and problem-solving activities together?

References

Brookfield, S. (1986). *Understanding and facilitating adult learning.* San Francisco: Jossey-Bass.

Candy, P. C. (1991). *Self-direction for lifelong learning.* San Francisco: Jossey-Bass.

Candy, P. C. (2004). *Linking thinking: Self-directed learning in the digital age.* Commonwealth of Australia: Department of Education, Science and Training.

Cheng, S. F., Kuo, C. L., Lin, K. C., & Lee-Hseih, J. (2010). Development and preliminary testing of a self-rating instrument to measure self-directed learning ability of nursing students. *International Journal of Nursing Studies, 47*(9), 1152–1158. https://doi.org/10.1016/j.ijnurstu.2010.02.002.

Costa, A. L., & Kallick, B. (2004). *Assessment strategies for self-directed learning.* Thousand Oaks, CA: Corwin Press.

Daniel, R. & Parkes, K. A. (2019). Applied music studio teachers in higher education: Evidence of learner-centred teaching. *Music Education Research, 21*(3), 269–281. https://doi.org/10.1080/14613808.2019.1598345.

de Bézenac, C., & Swindells, R. (2009). No pain, no gain? Motivation and self-regulation in music learning. *International Journal of Education and the Arts, 10*(16), 1–33.

Doyle, T. (2008). *Helping students take charge of their learning: A guide to facilitating learning in higher education.* Sterling, VA: Stylus. https://doi.org/10.1111/j.1467-9647.2010.00659.x.

Fisher, M., King, J., & Tague, G. (2001). Development of self-directed learning readiness scale for nursing education. *Nurse Education Today, 21*(7), 516–525. https://doi.org/10.1054/nedt.2001.0589.

Gandomkar, R., & Sandars, J. (2018) Clearing the confusion about self-directed learning and self-regulated learning, *Medical Teacher, 40*(8), 862–863. https://doi.org/10.1080/0142159X.2018.1425382.

Garrison, D. R. (1997). Self-directed learning: Toward a comprehensive model. *Adult Education Quarterly, 48*(1), 18–33. https://doi.org/10.1177%2F074171369704800103.

Georgii-Hemming, E., & Westvall, M. (2010). Music education—a personal matter? Examining the current discourses of music education in Sweden. *British Journal of Music Education, 27*(1), 21–33. https://doi.org/10.1017/S0265051709990179.

Gibbons, M. (2002). *The self-directed learning handbook: Challenging adolescent students to excel*. San Francisco: Jossey-Bass.

Gordon, M. (2008). Between constructivism and connectedness. *Journal of Teacher Education*, 59(4), 322–331. https://doi.org/10.1177%2F0022487108321379.

Guglielmino, L. M. (1977). *Development of the self-directed learning readiness scale*. Unpublished doctoral dissertation, University of Georgia. Dissertation Abstracts International. 38(11a): 6467.

Harrington, A. M. (2018). An exploration of the self-selection of musical parts by members of a New Horizons concert band. *International Journal of Community Music*, 11(2), 183–198. https://doi.org/10.1386/ijcm.11.2.183_1.

Hendry, G. D., & Ginns, P. (2009). Readiness for self-directed learning: Validation of a new scale with medical students. *Medical Teacher*, 31(10), 918–920. https://doi.org/10.3109/01421590802520899.

Jossberger, H., Brand-Gruwel, S., Boshuizen, H., & Wiel, M. (2010). The challenge of self-directed and self-regulated learning in vocational education: A theoretical analysis and synthesis of requirements. *Journal of Vocational Education and Training*, 62(4), 415–440. https://doi.org/10.1080/13636820.2010.523479.

Knowles, M. S. (1975). *Self-directed learning: A guide for learners and teachers*. New York: Association Press.

Knowles, M. S. (1990). *The adult learner: A neglected species*. 4th ed. Houston: Gulf.

Lebler, D. (2008). Popular music pedagogy: Peer learning in practice. *Music Education Research*, 10(2), 193–213. https://doi.org/10.1080/14613800802079056.

Leon-Guerrero, A. (2008). Self-regulation strategies used by student musicians during music practice. *Music Education Research*, 10(1), 91–106. https://doi.org/10.1080/14613800701871439.

Loyens, S. M. M., Magda, J. & Rikers, R. M. J. P. (2008) Self-directed learning in problem-based learning and its relationships with self-regulated learning. *Educational Psychology Review*, 20(4), 411–427. https://doi.org/10.1007/s10648-008-9082-7.

McPherson, G. E., & McCormick, J. (1999). Motivational and self-regulated components of musical practice. *Bulletin of the Council for Research in Music Education*, 141, 98–102.

McPherson, G. E., Osborne, M. S., Evans, P., & Miksza, P. (2017). Applying self-regulated learning microanalysis to study musicians' practice. *Psychology of Music*, 47(1), 18–32. https://doi.org/10.1177/0305735617731614.

McPherson, G. E., & Renwick, J. M. (2001). A longitudinal study of self-regulation in children's musical practice. *Music Education Research*, 3(2), 169–186. https://doi.org/10.1080/14613800120089232.

McPherson, G. E. & Zimmerman, B. J. (2011). Self-regulation of musical learning: A social cognitive perspective on developing performance skills. In R. Colwell & P. Webster (Eds.), *MENC handbook of research on music teaching and learning* (pp. 130–175). New York: Oxford University Press.

Miksza, P., Blackwell, J., & Roseth, N. E. (2018). Self-regulated music practice: Microanalysis as a data collection technique and inspiration for pedagogical intervention. *Journal of Research in Music Education*, 66(3), 295–319.

Nielsen, S. (2001). Self-regulating learning strategies in instrumental music practice. *Music Education Research*, 3(2), 155–167. https://doi.org/10.1080/14613800120089223.

Oddi, L. F. (1986). Development and validation of an instrument to identify self-directed continuing learners. *Adult Education Quarterly*, 36(2), 97–107. https://doi.org/10.1177%2F0001848186036002004.

Pilling-Cormick, J., & Garrison, D. R. (2007). Self-directed and self-regulated learning: Conceptual links. *Canadian Journal of University Continuing Education, 33*(2), 13–33. https://doi.org/10.21225/D5S01M.

Rashid, T. & Asghar, H. M. (2016). Technology use, self-directed learning, student engagement and academic performance: Examining the interrelations. *Computers in Human Behavior, 63,* 604612. https://doi.org/10.1016/j.chb.2016.05.084

Rogers, C. R. (1969). *Freedom to learn.* Columbus, OH: Charles E. Merrill.

Shen, W., Chen, H., & Hu, Y. (2014). The validity and reliability of the self-directed learning instrument (SDLI) in mainland Chinese nursing students. *BioMed Central Medical Education, 14*(1), 108. https://doi.org/10.1186/1472-6920-14-108.

Stockdale, S. L., & Brockett, R. G. (2010). Development of the PROSDLS: A measure of self-direction in learning based on the personal responsibility orientation model. *Adult Education Quarterly, 20,* 1–20. https://doi.org/10.1177/0741713610380447.

Teo, T., Tan, S. C., Lee, C. B., Chai, C. S., Koh, J. H. L., Chen, W. L., & Cheah, H. M. (2010). The self-directed learning with technology scale (SDLTS) for young students: An initial development and validation. *Computers and Education, 55*(4), 1764–1771. https://doi.org/10.1016/j.compedu.2010.08.001.

van den Hurk, M. M. (2006). The relation between self-regulated strategies and individual study time, prepared participation and achievement in a problem-based curriculum. *Active Learning in Higher Education, 7,* 155—169. doi:10.1177/1469787406064752.

Varela, W., Abrami, P. C., & Upitis, R. (2016). Self-regulation and music learning: A systematic review. *Psychology of Music, 44*(1), 55–74. https://doi.org/10.1177%2F0305735614554639.

Weimer, M. (2002). *Learner-centered teaching: Five key changes to practice.* San Francisco: Jossey-Bass.

Wigfield, A. & Eccles, J. S. (2000). Expectancy-value theory of achievement motivation. *Contemporary Educational Psychology, 25*(1), 68–81. https://doi.org/10.1006/ceps.1999.1015.

Williamson, S. N. (2007). Development of a self-rating scale of self-directed learning. *Nurse Researcher, 14*(2), 66–83. https://doi.org/10.7748/nr2007.01.14.2.66.c6022.

Zimmerman, B. J. (1986). Becoming a self- regulated learner: Which are the key subprocesses? *Contemporary Educational Psychology, 11*(4), 307–313. https://doi.org/10.1016/0361-476X(86)90027-5.

Zimmerman, B. J. (1989). A social cognitive view of self-regulated academic learning. *Journal of Educational Psychology, 81*(3), 329–339. https://psycnet.apa.org/doi/10.1037/0022-0663.81.3.329.

Zimmerman, B. J. (2000). Attaining self-regulation: A social cognitive perspective. In M. Boekaerts, P. R. Pintrich & M. Zeidner (Eds.), *Handbook of self-regulation* (pp. 13–39). New York: Academic Press.

....

CHAPTER 7

HIGH-IMPACT TEACHING MINDFRAMES

....

GARY E. MCPHERSON AND JOHN HATTIE

INTRODUCTION

CHANCES are that if you are reading this chapter, you share a love of performing and teaching music. But how did you get to this point in your career, and what influences were formative in helping you get there? Most likely there were people in your life whose influence was pivotal in giving direction to your love of music and what you hoped to achieve as a musician. This might have been a family member, a friend, or one of your teachers.

When we remember back on those people who have changed our lives, many of us will recall a single teacher and how this person changed us forever. What did this teacher do, and why was this person so influential? And while this teacher stood out, we could equally remember a number whom we would rather erase from our memory. Why?

In this chapter we focus on the first type of teachers. Those teachers who, because of their passion for imparting knowledge and their unique ways of thinking, supported and challenged us to achieve our personal best, and inspired us to achieve more than we could previously have imagined possible. They were able to do this because they saw something in us that we were unable to see ourselves or could previously imagine possible (Clinton, Hattie, & Nawab, 2018). In short, these teachers were able to bring out the best in us because their passion for music inspired us to develop our own love of learning and desire to excel as a musician.

To understand why these teachers left such a positive impact on our love for performing music we draw on the second author's extensive research within education that has created a powerful explanation of how to make learning visible, according to ten mindframes that explain successful learning and inspirational teachers (Hattie & Zierer, 2018). Because this chapter is placed within a book on music performance, our adaptation of the ten mindframes relates to how they might be relevant within the context of studio (i.e., one-to-one) instrumental and vocal teaching, which are typical in many music institutions internationally.

Setting the Scene

Like successful leaders in business, impactful teachers know how to challenge and encourage us to the greatest possible extent. Simon Sinek (2009), the American motivator and writer, provides one of the most insightful reflections into how they do this. If we think about Sinek's ideas on leadership and how they might relate to impactful teaching, we can glean two major points. First, great teachers are able to inspire their students to act; and second, they do this because they know there are only two ways of changing behavior: manipulating the learner's behavior or inspiring the learner to strive even harder.

When our focus is on telling learners what we want them to learn and how they can go about learning it, we are essentially manipulating their behavior. The goals we set are typically about something external to the learner, such as succeeding in a specific performance, solving a technical challenge, or gaining a position in a professional ensemble. On the other hand, when we start by explaining why we are introducing a new idea, strategy, or technique, then we are contextualizing learning, by placing the emphasis on the *purpose*, *cause*, or *belief* inherent in the learning event. For example, starting with *why* would include discussing the *purpose* of the task being assigned, or how mastering the skill would *cause* change by allowing the musician to be able to tackle or solve other technical or musical challenges. Starting with *why* also focuses the learner on bolstering their own personal *belief* in themselves and what they can achieve into the future (see Figure 7.1).

This explanation shows how inspirational teachers think about their goals as professionals. At the heart of this form of reflection is our desire for wanting to make a

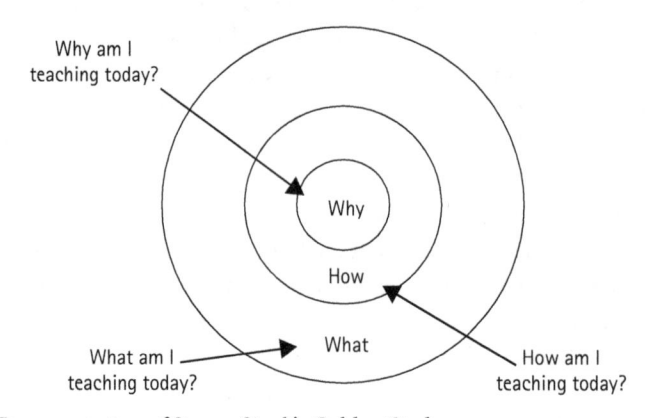

FIGURE 7.1. Representation of Simon Sinek's *Golden Circle*.

difference to the musical development of the musicians we teach and how our aspirations as performance teachers are based upon a simple philosophy of action. Inherent within this perspective is the critical role of evaluating the effect we have on our students, such that learning is seen as a journey, and development as a particular point that has been reached along that journey.

All of the foregoing has been encapsulated by Hattie and Zierer (2018), who have compiled a set of ten mindframes that epitomize highly impactful teaching, each of which is based on extensive research. Reproduced here, they are as follows (Hattie & Zierer, 2018, p. xv):

A. Impact
   1. I am an evaluator of my impact on student learning.
   2. I see assessment as informing my impact and next steps.
   3. I collaborate with my peers and my students about my conceptions of progress and my impact.
B. Change and Challenge
   4. I am a change agent and believe all students can improve.
   5. I strive for challenge and not merely "doing your best."
C. Learning Focus
   6. I give and help students understand feedback and I interpret and act on feedback given to me.
   7. I engage as much in dialogue as monologue.
   8. I explicitly inform students what successful impact looks like from the outset.
   9. I build relationships and trust so that learning can occur in a place where it is safe to make mistakes and learn from others.
   10. I focus on learning and the language of learning.

The extensive body of research that underpins these mindframes provides the basis for citing them as distinguishing characteristics of what successful teachers do. Essentially, these mindframes are about how teachers "think about what they do that matters most, how they understand their impact, and their search for feedback to improve the positive impact they have on their students" (p. xv). In studio teaching, this would mean that teaching expertise includes more than the competence of being able to demonstrate a skill or body of musical repertoire to a learner (i.e., *what*), or the learner's willingness (i.e., *how*) to follow their teacher's directions in order to master a certain skill or repertoire. Of crucial importance is the performance teacher's ability to contextualize the learning so it is clear to both the teacher and the student *why* this new skill or piece of music is being learned, knowing and communicating to the student what the next level of success looks like, and how this newly developed knowledge or competency can be applied in other musical situations (transfer). According to Hattie and Zierer (2018), "Ability is based on knowledge that can be retrieved only when there is a will to do so, and since there are always reasons for doing so, this will is based on judgments" (pp. xv–xvi). It follows from this explanation that being a highly competent musician is not enough to be a successful, impactful teacher. To impart your knowledge to others, you not only need to be competent at what you do, but willing to adopt and refine the mindframes listed earlier. Although one's musical competence is relatively stable over time, will and judgment are tested every time we try to impart our knowledge to a learner.

With this as our context, the following explanation focuses on each of the ten mindframes and the thinking and research that underpins them.

IMPACT

I am an evaluator of my impact on student learning.

The first mindframe places an emphasis on a core skill for teachers; that is, to constantly reflect on what they do, to see themselves through the eyes of the student, and to systematically aim to understand the impact they have on their students. It begs the question as to what the teacher means by *impact* (which can include not only enhanced musical competence, but enhanced motivation to invest in learning, enhanced aspiration or exceeding personal bests, and respect for other musicians and the audience for any performance). Evaluating our impact on a student can have a number of benefits to their learning: higher achievement and more positive attitudes and dispositions, a sense of belonging, an increased willingness and passion for performing music at a higher level, and a respect for themselves and for others that we can observe among our student cohort.

A problem with many music situations is that achievement is stressed over progress—whereas the act of teaching primarily relates to enhancing progress through to achievement. Figure 7.2 shows this relationship in terms of the types of

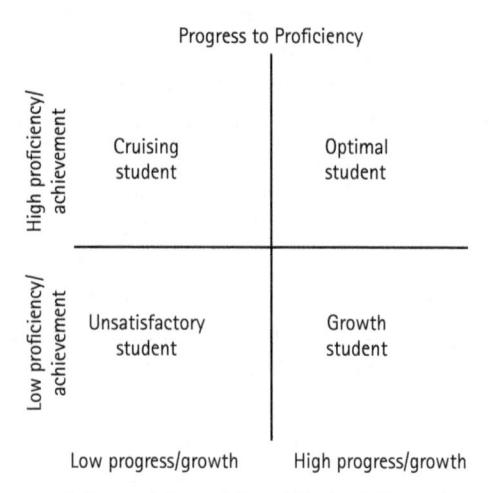

FIGURE 7.2. Progress to proficiency. Adapted from Hattie & Zierer (2018, p. 4).

student profiles evident in formal music learning environments. On the x-axis is achievement and the y-axis growth or progress. Importantly, within this explanation, successful learning can be seen not only in high-achieving students (i.e., top right-hand quadrant) but also in students who may have low proficiency compared to others, but whose progress has been substantial (i.e., bottom right-hand quadrant). Moving all students to the right, no matter where they start, is how we might define successful teaching.

The typical studio teaching environment includes a range of ongoing formal and informal assessments as teachers try to improve their students' performance abilities. Often such assessment comprises formative feedback through comments by the teacher in ways that aim to monitor and steer the learner's progress. This type of feedback can occur from teacher to student. A more powerful means of informing the teacher about the optimal next steps in teaching and learning, however, is from student to teacher. Every time a student performs, we should be making evaluations to help us work out where to go next in our teaching. While feedback can be focused on any aspect of teaching, formative evaluations focus on the goals of the learning process, with the aim of determining whether or not the learner has reached a certain milestone in their learning. The point of such feedback is to reduce the gap between where the student is now relative to the success criteria of the lesson(s). This type of evaluation can help steer students in the right direction as they seek to improve and refine their playing.

Feedback that provides information back to the teacher about the success of their teaching is of more consequence and therefore of greater impact than most other forms of feedback. When teachers say: "I was wrong in the way I advised you to correct this deficiency in your technique" or instead, "I correctly now chose the best approach to correct this deficiency in your technique," they are making appraisals that lead them to being able to successfully engage in a collaborative enquiry with their students. They also position themselves to avoid thinking that their students are unable to achieve a learning goal because they lack ability or did not commit themselves fully to the task. This mindframe therefore places an emphasis on being able to:

1. diagnose what students brings to their lesson, their motivation for learning, and their willingness to actively learn;
2. incorporate a variety of interventions during lessons and changing direction if some of these do not work;
3. not lay blame on students when they are unable to meet the challenge;
4. apply multiple methods for tackling a learning task; and
5. work collaboratively with each student by discussing the impact of the magnitude of improvement (if any) that resulted from the intervention. This approach involves the students in the teaching act, ensures co-construction of learning and performance, and privileges the expertise of the teaching in being adaptable, reflective, and sensitive to the motives and skills of the student.

I see assessment as informing my impact and next steps

Just as students use assessment to provide important feedback on their progress, so too can teachers use assessment to determine how well and to what extent their students have achieved the learning goal, were able to apply the technique in their playing, and have found the strategies they were given to be useful. In this way, assessment can be any task or assignment that a teacher sets to provide both themselves and the learner with information about how the learning is going, how much has been achieved, whether the learning is moving forward, and what should be covered next.

Too often students see assessment as evidence that the task is over, and this is why it is important to ensure there is a high degree of "where to next" feedback, preferably based on feedback about goal attainment, and how well the student is moving from their current achievement to mastery.

Extending the time practicing an instrument will not in and of itself effect learning. Of more importance from the teacher's perspective is how challenged the learner is, and how well the teacher can make learning visible to the student by implementing a variety of approaches and applying these appropriately, in addition to believing in these methods sufficiently to systematically apply them during teaching. This mindframe is therefore about valuing student assessments as feedback about oneself. This is because students can find it frustrating within their lessons when they can clearly hear or see the difference between their playing and that of the teachers in a particular section but do not quite know how to get there. They may have been told to workshop the section by "separating the parts," "breaking it down," or "repeating the section," but these suggestions do not always convey the teacher's knowledge and skill.

To break this cycle, learners need to be willing to invest in their own learning but open also to new experiences that might contradict what they already know, or the ways in which they normally learn. Assigning clear, goal-directed tasks, or working with students so they understand the next best success criteria to be learned within a set period, allows a teacher to gauge the suitability of the learning goals, the nature and content of what is to be learned, and the methods that are appropriate to learn the new material and reach the success criteria. Assessment not only provides indications of what a student has and has not learned, but also an opportunity for a teacher to reflect on and interpret information that aids the devising of the next task or skill to be learned.

In summary, student assessment provides opportunities for feedback about the teacher and for the teacher. It is an opportunity to link the learning process with the teaching process, and information gained from assessment can be used as the scaffolding to devise what comes next in the learning cycle. To do this effectively, studio teachers keep track of their student's progress by writing down what has and has not yet been achieved and encouraging students to monitor their progress and exceed their personal bests. Teachers and students can reflect on this information and use it to devise tasks for the next stage of learning. Just as a practice diary can be beneficial for allowing a student to keep track of what has and needs to be learned, similarly a written log of progress can help a teacher collect and reflect on the individual needs of each student. The types of questions that teachers should ask themselves include, therefore: "What does it mean to be successful in the next series of lessons and where is the student now relative to their success criteria?," "Which of my goals did I achieve in the lesson?," "What material did I successfully get across to the learners?," "What evidence would I accept that there is a lack of successful teaching?," "Which methods turned out to be useful for fostering learning?," and "Which resources or techniques were useful for fostering learning?" (Hattie & Zierer, 2018, p. 22). These types of questions allow a teacher to feel more confident that a student has in fact learned the material (in comparison to believing this to be possibly the case), as well as better informed when determining the next teaching acts and lesson direction.

I collaborate with my peers and my students about my conceptions of progress and my impact

When lawyers deal with a case that seems hopeless, journalists lack options for dealing with seemingly contradictory information, and scientists reach a dead end in their experiments, they typically try to resolve their problems by entering into a dialogue and cooperating with others. But in many instrumental and vocal teaching studios, we often do not see teachers exchanging ideas and cooperating with other musicians. This is a shame, because substantial changes can occur when teachers work together to build their confidence to enhance their impact on students (Bandura, 1976; 1977). In the visible learning literature, conversing and critiquing a student's progress with colleagues has been found to be among the most powerful ways of enhancing teachers' impact on their learners' skills and motivations (Donohoo, 2019). It really does make a difference!

What does a year's worth of growth mean for an undergraduate performance major, and are we even aware of what this might look (or sound) like? For a studio teacher, collaborating with peers and students about their notions of growth means that the teacher is willing to believe that all students can gain more than a year's growth for a year's input, that this is visible within the setting (including to the student), and that the organizational climate of the educational institution is built on norms about what is to be learned, and clear expectations about progress. The type of organizational climate that helps to create this comes about when institutions encourage teachers to collaborate and discuss their student's progress within an environment built on a sense of confidence, high levels of trust, and high expectations about making a difference. The important point here is to believe that teachers can and do "cause learning." We are not detached onlookers who stand on the side; we are active and deliberate instructional coaches tasked with maximizing our impact on student's growth and success.

Students progress only to the extent that the environment demands they progress, so setting high expectations is integral to achieving an environment in which all students can have experiences that allow them to reach their personal best. This can be contrasted with a "do your best" approach, which, in stark contrast, research shows has a low impact on learning because it is too vague and lacking sufficient detail for a student to evaluate their own progress.

Instead of encouraging students to "do your best," our role should be to appropriately challenge them to exceed the personal expectations they set for themselves by using terms such as "personal best," which more aptly conveys a sense of accomplishment the learner can use to reference their learning. Andrew Martin and Paul Evans in their chapter (see Martin & Evans, this volume) suggest that the major value of "personal best" is that the learner "owns" the goals, and by thinking in this way, they are more likely to strive to push themselves to outperform their previous best, direct their attention and effort toward goal-relevant tasks, and achieve at a higher level because they are more aroused and energized to persevere and focus on the task even when faced with failure.

Ensuring that challenges are "not too high, and not too boring" lies at the art of applying this concept. An appropriate narrative within a studio setting therefore is not about "how to teach" but instead one's personal "impact as a teacher." Not what it means to be good as a performance major, but what does it mean to grow *at least* one year in any particular year of a music degree. The collective efficacy of a studio of like instruments, or for an entire music school, can therefore benefit when teachers take the view that:

a) they cause learning;
b) they are all jointly responsible for each student;
c) they believe in the value of evaluating the impact of their learning;
d) they work with others to seek evidence of their impact;
e) high levels of growth for a learning period can be defined, shared, and evaluated; and
f) working with colleagues will help establish a shared pride in the positive impact they are all having on their students.

Obviously, of fundamental importance to the foregoing is the role of leadership within the organization, without which the legitimization, support, esteem, and trust for developing a collective efficacy are not possible. The greatest power of leaders is the narrative they legitimize among their staff, and the recommendation is that this narrative be about impact (what is taught, how many students benefit from this teaching, and the acceptable magnitude of this impact in terms of annual growth).

CHANGE AND CHALLENGE

I am a change agent and believe all students can improve

Consider the implications of making these two comments to a student:

> "I wouldn't advise you to do this yet, it's too hard."
> "Believe in yourself. I know you can do this."

It is self-evident from the first statement that whether the learner achieves at the level required hangs in the balance. Will the learner just give up? Does the learner have the will power, motivation, skills, or strength to succeed? These are natural consequences when teachers' comments are similar to the first statement. In comparison, the second is more likely to spark an interest and determination, increase motivation, and possibly unleash powers that learners did not necessarily know they had. Hence, the fourth mindframe is about learners seeing themselves as consumers or producers of their own learning. When they are not learning, it is because they have not yet found a suitable strategy to make learning happen.

The most successful positive learning environments are built on a collective responsibility of everyone who comes in contact with a learner—their teacher, parents, peers—holding a positive perspective about what can and might be achieved by the learner. Everyone, including learners themselves, see themselves as a "change agent."

A prominent motivation expert, Carol Dweck (2012; 2015; 2017), coined the terms *fixed mindset* and *growth mindset* to distinguish between individuals who see their abilities and potentials as fixed and unchangeable, versus those who view their abilities and potentials as fluid and within their control. The two types of guidance to students that open this section characterize these two positions. If teachers see student ability as fixed or something that they can have little impact on, then they are probably more likely to make the first rather than the second statement. It is imperative, claims Dweck, that students be taught when to invoke these growth mindsets, as they are not generic skills. The optimal moments for this are when they lack confidence, when they are making errors, and when they do not know what to do next. This is when teachers need to focus their thinking on a belief that these problems are not a function of their ability or lack of competence but because they have not yet learned them, and that they need to seek feedback and be open to teaching.

For teachers, encouraging a "growth mindset" in students and believing that all students can improve entails establishing a learning environment that is conducive to the development of these attributes. These ideas are visible in private or group lessons when a musician's teaching is distinguished by five management processes:

1. *Focus and Presence*: Making sure that the student knows that you are focused on the lesson and not distracted by other things that can be distracting to you or the learner.
2. *Constructing Success Criteria*: Making it clear with the student what the notions of success look like for the lesson(s) and regularly providing feedback of their journey from where they start (their prior achievement) to these criteria of success;
3. *Smoothness and Pace*: Avoiding wasted time and setting a work ethic that demands that the student fully concentrate. This also involves pacing the lesson so that there are periods of intense concentration and lesson pace followed by short intuitively timed breaks where the teacher can contextualize what is or has been learned, or performing the work being learned in a more complete fashion (Duke & Simmons, 2006).

4. *Group Focus*: This management strategy refers most to group situations (e.g., masterclasses, instrumental workshops) and the desirability of focusing on all learners rather than just the performers, especially when asking questions, soliciting feedback, or asking the group to reflect on aspects covered during the lesson.

5. *Avoidance of Tedium*: Boredom is a stand-out negative influence on learning in any situation, so engaging students in appropriately challenging tasks and making them aware of their incremental successes and gradual or rapid progress will foster attention to detail. An environment that accepts that we learn from errors and offers mastery experiences aimed at celebrating progress can also help avoid periods when students are not concentrating on what is being learned.

Aligned with these ideas, it is important for the performance teacher to be specific about what is to be learned and make this clear to the student in the beginning stages of a lesson. Learning intentions and success criteria involve an awareness by the teacher and student of what is to be covered in the lesson, what is being learning today, and how we would know that this has been achieved once we get there. For performance teaching this would involve setting additional goals for a student to practice for the next lessons, and approaching development within a teacher-student dynamic that focuses on (a) what is already known; (b) what needs to be learned; (c) what gaps exist between what is known and needs to be known; and (d) what can be done to reduce this gap.

Inspirational teachers set the tone within their lessons by trying different strategies for students who are struggling, regarding the learner's failure as their own failure, and adopting the view that difficulties are challenges waiting to be solved. It is not possible, however, to reach every learner in a group performance such as an ensemble all of the time, because their motivation can be constantly changing. However, for conductors and performance teachers, making themselves aware of and using the range of motivational strategies shown in Table 7.1 can help.

All of this encourages us to view lessons as opportunities for teachers to monitor the impact of their teaching and for changing the teaching approach when the impact of an approach is not obvious. This is more important than having a lesson go smoothly, keeping student busy, or blindly following a particular methodology without serious questioning of how this impacts the learner.

I strive for challenge and not merely "doing your best"

Inspirational teaching is not just challenge-focused but also emotionally rewarding for the student. When challenge and skill come together in optimal ways, musicians can experience a sense of *flow*, which Mihaly Csikszentmihalyi (2008) suggests is a mental

Table 7.1. Action, Relevance, Confidence, and Satisfaction Model.

Attention	*Perceptual Arousal*	*Inquiry Arousal*	*Variability*
	Provide novelty and surprise	Stimulate curiosity by posing questions or problems to solve	Incorporate a range of methods and media to meet students' varying needs
Relevance	*Goal Orientation*	*Motive Matching*	*Familiarity*
	Present objectives and useful purpose of instruction and specific methods for successful achievement	Match objectives to student needs and motives	Present content in ways that are understandable and that are related to the learners' experiences and values
Confidence	*Learning Requirements*	*Successful Opportunities*	*Personal Responsibility*
	Inform students about learning and performance requirements and assessment criteria	Provide challenging and meaningful opportunities for successful learning	Link learning success to students' personal effort and ability
Satisfaction	*Intrinsic Reinforcement*	*Extrinsic Rewards*	*Equity*
	Encourage and support intrinsic enjoyment of the learning experience	Provide positive reinforcement and motivational feedback	Maintain consistent standards and consequences for success

Reprinted with permission from Hattie & Zierer (2018, p. 51).

state in which the learner is immersed in the activity, feels energized, and enjoys the process of playing and performing. This state of being in *flow*, and the resultant emotions typically experienced when there is a misalignment between challenge and skill, are depicted in Figure 7.3.

The mindframe of setting challenges for students can become more visible when the teacher plans ahead and sets clear goals for each lesson. One way of making goals explicit for students is to ask your students to reflect on the learning experience they have just been exposed to and reflect on what they mention happened in the lesson or what was achieved. Did the students talk about how challenging the tasks were or the degree to which they have mastered these new skills? Or alternatively, do they talk about where they made errors, or the misconceptions and things they still do not understand? Or perhaps they talk about the strategies they applied when they were successful as compared to unsuccessful? Moving students from feeling "this is hard, I can't do it" to "I see this as a challenge" is at the heart of this mindframe. Of course, they may need to appreciate and realize that they need a teacher to help them reach the next level of challenge.

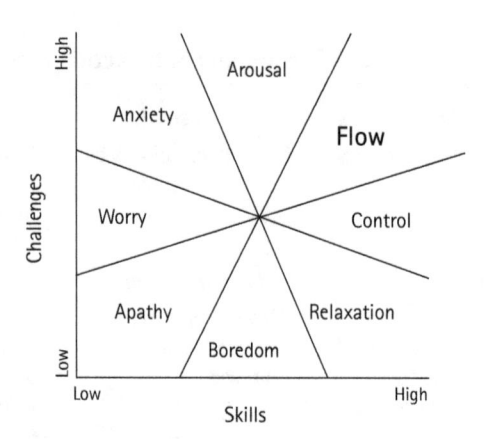

FIGURE 7.3. Csikszentmihalyi's model of flow. Adapted from Nakamura & Csikszentmihalyi (2002, p. 95).

This mindframe is exemplified when teachers are willing to:

1. be mindful of the steps needed for students to reach their goals and making these explicit for the student, including the observable skills the learner should be able to demonstrate by the end of the lesson;
2. explain the types of exercises and practice habits required to master a new learning challenge, plus conveying a sense of how long the skill will take to learn; and
3. specify the standard required, either through practical demonstration or analysis of the performance for determining the extent to which the learner has achieved each learning goal.

Obviously, within any performance studio, students will progress at different rates, which is why it is important for performance teachers to focus their students' attention on aspects of mastery learning such as advancing the standard of repertoire to be learned, encouraging them to think about how they can "self-pace" their own progress, and fostering a sense of achievement through use of transparent and challenging goals.

Figure 7.3 shows the optimal flow balance between skill and challenge and the negative emotions when these are not aligned. Opportunities for students to experience flow therefore occur when the task assigned by the teacher is not too demanding, but also not overly easy or boring. Getting the right amount of challenge is fundamental to students' experiencing an optimal learning environment, which is the reason why teachers should do everything they can to develop their ability to formulate and communicate clear, differentiated goals for each individual student, monitor the dosage and fidelity of their teaching, and understand what optimally motivates the students.

One further point related to this teacher ability is that students thrive when they are allowed to be involved in the choices about their own learning and progression. This does not mean students are "in control of their learning," as too often they do not know what they do not know, do not know the optimal next steps compared to the expert teacher, and sometimes need to be taught more efficient and effective ways to improve. Developing musicians are more likely to flourish, however, when they are given opportunities to set high expectations for themselves, choose repertoire that challenges them, and feel that they want to master a new skill rather than that their teacher wants them to master the new skill (these points will be further expanded and are illustrated in Figure 7.4).

In summary, performance teachers can optimize their instruction by:

1. making the goals they set for the student clear to themselves and for the student;
2. allowing some degree of autonomy for the student to co-construct, choose, or enhance the goals established;
3. demonstrating and explaining what learning success involves and implies;
4. analyzing each student's skill level and using this information as the basis for formulating new goals;
5. tailoring appropriately challenging goals to meet the needs and expectations for each student;
6. differentiating between goals to ensure a balance between difficulty level and achievement level;
7. comparing their assessment of the level of the goals achieved with similar assessment interpretations made by the student; and
8. aiming to formulate goals that describe observable behavior and that identify ways these behaviors can be monitored and evaluated.

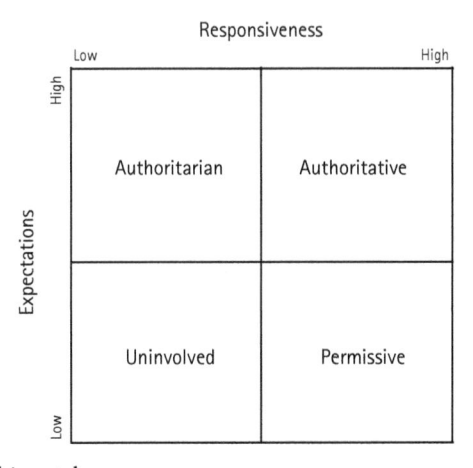

FIGURE 7.4. Four teaching styles.

LEARNING FOCUS

I give and help students understand feedback and I interpret and act on feedback given to me

In recent decades, the master-apprentice style of performance studio teaching has been criticized as being overly teacher- rather than student-focused, with an emphasis on authoritarian styles of instruction. In some traditional music studio settings, knowledge is seen as a flow of information from teacher to student, yet in contemporary education, there is a realization that feedback is a two-way process and that some of the most powerful exchanges occur when students give their teacher feedback about the impact of their teaching. By listening to student comments and observing the student's behavior, teachers are able to understand more fully whether the lesson was successful, the degree to which the student clearly understood the material covered, whether the student was able to connect what has been learned previously with the new material, and whether the strategies employed by the teacher develop a deeper understanding of the content covered, in addition to whether the student actually gained in confidence and enjoyed the learning experience. Four factors that help make learning visible to the teacher and to the student can be derived from reinterpreting educational research to music performance studio settings:

Questioning: Asking students questions is one of the most common techniques used in all educational settings, yet research shows that around 90 percent of questions within school education settings relate to factual information that can be regarded as surface-level rather than deeper, more penetrating questions. A good general guide is that if a student is at a basic level, one should ask questions just above this level, intermixed with questions that occasionally probe the student to think at a much deeper level. Once the student has attained a deeper level of understanding, this can be refined to questions that require relating ideas and transferring the knowledge being learned to other situations such as different repertoire that the learner might learn at some point in the future.

Metacognition: When students think about their own thought process they are thinking metacognitively. Students do this when they attempt to make learning visible to themselves, ask questions about their own learning, and use mistakes to reflect upon the logic and coherence of their own actions. Each of these types of metacognition has been found to be highly influential in learning, because they provide opportunities for dialogue between the learner and their teacher. Encouraging students to think metacognitively has a number of major benefits on learning. Importantly, it leads students to critically examine their own learning, makes what is known and unknown visible to the learner, and provides high-quality feedback for the teacher about what to cover next, and in what way. Students who self-regulate in these ways are also typically good at seeking and reacting to feedback, which is why metacognitive strategies are now seen as a vital part of how students learn and what teachers should actively encourage.

Practice Skills: It is self-evident that the sophistication of practice skills is a major determining factor in students' progress, given that they typically have one lesson with their studio teacher each week and are then left to their own devices for the following six days. The important claim is that it is not practice, but deliberate practice—which involves seeking, receiving, and learning from feedback and renewed instruction during the practice.

Study Skills: When students actively keep track of their own learning by maintaining a practice diary, seeking out information, listening to recordings of works they are learning, regulating their motivation, setting goals, and structuring their practice sessions, they are displaying attributes associated with taking charge of their own learning and "learning to learn."

Feedback

Important for this mindframe, and indeed embedded in all of the mindframes, is the overarching need for teachers to understand and incorporate into their teaching the use of high-quality feedback. Understanding how to maximize feedback within a teaching setting implies being able to focus each students' attention on where they are going, how they are going, and what they will need to do next.

In educational settings, research suggests that teachers tend to focus almost all of their feedback on questions associated with the first two of these: "Where am I going?" and "How am I going?," in contrast to students, who overwhelmingly prefer feedback associated with the question "Where to next?" (Hattie & Clarke, 2019). Feedback based on the "Where to next?" can and should be based on feedback related to the first two questions. To achieve this, and to maximize its impact, feedback can be focused on two dimensions:

Person-Based Feedback: The Self. Feedback aimed at the individual often involves praise or criticism such as "That was great," "You're really good at this," or "No, that's not right." Research shows that this type of feedback has virtually no impact on learning (and sometimes a negative impact) because the focus on the individual does not include information about the learning process. Excessive, ongoing praise can also lead to a reduction in one's willingness to try in some learners, especially those who are reluctant to put a positive image of themselves on display too often. In a similar way, criticism can lead other students to develop a negative self-concept for performing, especially in situations where they feel their abilities are not being recognized. For highly motivated students, praise can act as a form of extrinsic motivation, and thus undermine intrinsic motivation. Praise and criticism are therefore problematic because they reduce students' focus on the task.

Research evidence in education and music does not suggest, however, that teachers should not give any praise or criticism. Duke and Simmons (2006), for example, studied the studio lessons of renowned artist-teachers and found there were infrequent, intermittent, and often unexpected instances within lessons when these teachers provided negative feedback that was clearly directed to improving the quality of the performance. Importantly, though, there were also other moments in the lesson where "intense praise" was used to convey how excited they were that the student had been able to master a new learning challenge. This is consistent with the recommendation of Hattie and Zierer (2018) that "less is more" regarding when and how often a teacher should provide self-feedback and research showing that constant praise can act as a diluter when it is mixed with feedback about the work.

Performance-Based Feedback: Task, Process, and Self-Regulation. Providing information to a learner about what they can and cannot do can occur in many forms, such as when a teacher assigns a new piece to be learned and then provides feedback at the next lesson about how well the piece has been learned. Such feedback can be in the form of identifying parts that have already been mastered or nearly mastered, or parts where a student is using the wrong fingering or needs to rethink an interpretation. This type of feedback is therefore focused on how the student has worked since the last lesson, but will also occur in the lesson when the teacher focuses on specific musical or technical details that need to be mastered in order to perform the piece.

Another form of performance-based feedback involves providing information to learners about the mechanics they can apply to regulate their own learning. As an example, teachers can encourage their students to reflect upon the effectiveness of their practice strategies or technical approach to a specific part of a piece they are learning, or evaluate their own interpretation of the piece. Feedback that is focused on encouraging and making explicit to the student how they can monitor and control their own learning helps students develop the types of self-regulated learning skills that equip them to be much more productive in their individual practice outside of lessons.

Effective, beneficial feedback is not a matter of quantity, but of quality. It is about the timing of feedback relative to where the student is in the instructional cycle (learning content, processes, or self-regulation), and is most powerful when it is formative, leading to improvements. For a student, feedback that provides clear information on how to correct errors and how these errors can be avoided in the future is obviously more effective than feedback that merely identifies errors, especially when the same errors are mentioned repeatedly by the teacher without a solution. Hence, the more students and teachers see errors as opportunities to learn, the more opportunities there are for effective feedback. The most impactful forms of feedback identify errors but also focus on the process whereby the error can be corrected, and the self-regulatory mechanisms needing to be employed by a learner in order for them to have some ability to monitor and control their own mastery of the skill.

To motivate students upward in their learning, a general rule is to provide feedback that is pitched at the level where the student is currently working but also to include some feedback at the next level. In this way, various types of feedback are interconnected with the basic rule being to pitch feedback at an appropriate level for the student, while also trying to focus on moving upward through the various levels required to achieve mastery of the learned material. In summary, the most powerful forms of feedback are given at or just above the level where the student is working and are focused on the task process and self-regulatory mechanisms required to develop mastery. It is best to avoid repetitive comments that merely identify errors, and instead provide a clear indication to the student about "where to next."

Another obvious consideration is that feedback needs to be tailored to the level of the student. Feedback that works for one student may not work for another. Evidence shows, however, that in virtually all cases, feedback that includes at least some "Where to next?" information will enhance the impact of the feedback.

Within the explanation of visible learning, each level of feedback is viewed from the perspectives of "feed up," "feed back," and "feed forward". Reinterpreting these for music learning, "feed up" feedback involves comparing the learner's current state with a desired target state. It is focused on the present. An example would be critiquing a student's playing and comparing this with a desired performance once the work has been mastered. "Feed back" compares a learner's current state with previous performance, such as pointing out improvements in the playing of repertoire since the previous lesson. "Feed forward" feedback illustrates the desired target state and, because it is aimed at what a student will be able to do in the future, is the most desired form of feedback for students. When implemented appropriately in teaching, these three forms of feedback emphasize past, present, and future perspectives. They are most successful when they lead to students understanding how they are going now, where they are going next, and how they might get to the next level.

Table 7.2 provides a summary of the main points we have highlighted.

As mentioned earlier, in most teaching situations feedback occurs mainly from the teacher to learner. Within this context, the teacher is seen as the person who is most

Table 7.2. Levels of feedback

		Task	Process	Self-Regulation
Perspectives of Feedback	Past ("feed back")	What progress has the learner made in goals and content?	What progress has the learner made on task completion? Is there evidence of improvement?	What progress has the learner made on self-regulation strategies?
	Present ("feed up")	What goals did the learner reach? What content did the learner understand?	How did the learner complete the task? Is there evidence of how the learner worked?	What self-regulation strategies did the learner successfully apply?
	Future ("feed forward")	What goals should be set next? What content should be learned next?	What tips on task completion should the learner be given next?	What self-regulation strategies should the learner apply next?

Reprinted with permission from Hattie & Zierer (2018, p. 89).

responsible for providing comprehensive feedback of the type we have outlined. However, a learning environment focused on this type of one-way interaction is far from optimal. Learner-to-teacher feedback is now viewed within contemporary educational settings as fundamentally important for effective learning, because teachers cannot always answer questions about whether their students have achieved their goals, whether they fully understood what was being taught, and the degree to which they considered the methods suggested by the teacher for improving the quality of a performance to be helpful. All of these are questions that only a learner can answer, especially given that only about 20 percent of what happens in a lesson is observable; the other 80 percent is often not immediately apparent and therefore needs to be made visible. When teachers make themselves aware of what their student is thinking; their appraisal of the effectiveness of a method or technique for mastering a musical challenge; and how they feel about themselves, their learning, and the task being mastered, then they employ a cyclic process whereby learning objectives, goals, and progress are made visible to both the teacher and the student as they jointly negotiate a pathway forward.

Teachers who give and help students understand their feedback, and in turn interpret and act on the feedback students give to them, foster a powerful learning environment in which mistakes are seen as a positive force within the learning environment and a learning context whereby learning and teaching both involve making errors, with high-quality feedback helping the learner to feed off errors and misconceptions.

The subtle difference between correcting mistakes (i.e., slips-ups and accidents while playing a piece through) as compared to errors (i.e., things that a student cannot yet do, or has not yet learned) is something an experienced music teacher understands. Stopping to work on or correct mistakes is pointless and can waste a great deal of time during a performance lesson.

In summary, cultivating the mindframe "I give and help students understand feedback and I interpret and act on feedback to me" involves a willingness to critically evaluate one's own feedback and a willingness also to engage students in a two-way feedback dialogue throughout each lesson. It can be seen in the way that teachers provide feedback at different levels (task, process, and especially self-regulation), avoid repetitive superficial praise and extrinsic rewards, and reflect on their own teaching by inviting feedback from the learner in ways that help make learning visible.

I engage as much in dialogue as monologue

A key concept within the visible learning literature is that "although teachers matter, it is how they think, how they foster students becoming their own teachers, and how they can see the impact of their efforts through the eyes of the students that matters more" (Hattie & Zierer, 2018, p. 101). This mindframe therefore focuses on the need for teachers to achieve a balance between talking and explaining or modeling and listening and fostering student discussion. In educational settings, teacher talk tends to dominate classrooms, and this is similar in music where conductors simply tell the ensemble what they want, rather than asking musicians for their ideas or collaboration. This also happens in the applied studio when teachers tell students how to play expressively, or demonstrate how to play expressively, without asking for musical ideas and explanations/conversations from the students. In school classrooms and in music studios, dialogically organized instruction, where the teacher uses authentic questioning in which there are no right and wrong answers, helps to stimulate and extend student thinking, and allows the student and teacher to diagnose what they might know or misunderstand, as together they search for the best way forward.

Dialogically organized instruction involves not only listening to what students are saying or how they are performing but demonstrating that you have listened and understood what they have said or played. It also involves deliberate teaching to the student about how to think aloud and use their voice as part of the teaching and learning process. The focus is on teaching via listening, prompting, and reacting to how students are thinking. This can be fostered through *interactions* that encourage the learner to think in different ways, *questions* that require more than simple recall, *answers* that are followed up rather than merely received, *feedback* that informs and leads to thinking forward and perceived by the learner as encouraging, *contributions* that are extended rather than fragmented, *exchanges* that chain together coherent and deepening lines of enquiry, and a *studio learning environment* that makes all of these possible. Other factors include *uptake*, where either the learner or teacher responds to or takes forward the ideas of another; *scaffolding*, which helps learners bridge the gap between their current and intended level of performance; and *handover*, which involves the successful transfer of skills, knowledge, and understanding to new situations and higher levels of performance.

Dialogue within a lesson is important, especially in situations where the learner is encouraged to engage in a verbal think-aloud explanation of what they are doing, thinking, and feeling. Research shows that the optimal time for dialogue within a lesson is after the student has sufficient surface-level content knowledge and is ready to make more sophisticated connections between ideas (Donohoo & Katz, 2019; Donohoo, Hattie & Eells, 2018) They can do this by discussing what they can and cannot do as they transfer their newly acquired abilities to another context or a deeper level of understanding. When used appropriately, discussion within a lesson can foster self-regulation and much deeper understandings in the student.

Apart from dialogue, through their instruction teachers can foster less one-way monologue in their lessons by (a) making clear to the student what their learning intensions are; (b) knowing and informing students what successful criteria are expected for mastering the new skill; (c) building a commitment to, and engagement with, the learning task; (d) using modeling to check for understanding and to provide exemplars of the required performance; (e) incorporating guided practice into the lesson so students can demonstrate that they understand how to practice the material when on their own; (f) providing closure by helping students to bring together the knowledge and skills they have acquired during the lesson; and (g) encouraging independent practice that is shaped around a clear sense of what is expected to have been achieved by the next lesson.

I explicitly inform students what successful impact looks like from the outset

A principle for this mindframe is the need for teachers to continually articulate the criteria needing to be fulfilled in order for the learner to succeed; this is a teaching principle that is backed up by extensive research indicating that successful learning occurs when there is a clarity of purpose for the lesson, and it is based on explicit learning objectives.

One of the main ways of enacting this mindframe is by adopting a *mastery learning* approach. Providing adequate explanations about what is required to be learned and ensuring that the student has achieved at least around 85 percent mastery of the skills before proceeding to the next challenge is a general guide advocated by education experts who study learning. They consider learning objectives and success criteria to be two sides of a coin, especially in situations where the objective of the lesson is made clear at the outset of the learning process and the goal of the learning is revealed and made visible during the lesson as students fulfill each learning goal. Enacting this mindframe also involves making the challenge visible so that the learner understands they have strengths and weaknesses and what the difference is between what they can and cannot yet do. The level of challenge needs to be above current performance and neither too hard nor too boring.

When learning criteria and lesson goals are clear to learners, they are in a better position to take more responsibility for their learning and embark on achieving personal bests. This can be reinforced through social contacts and peer influences that lead to high levels of commitment. In situations where all of this has been achieved, an added bonus is that learners become more self-confident and trust their own abilities, because they are able to assess their own progress and set realistic expectations for the future. In this way, they are also able to move from superficial levels of understanding or skill to deeper levels of understanding or skill. Consequently, making learning objectives visible and discussing success criteria along the journey are seen in educational settings as essential tools for teachers to acquire. Discussions with students in a cohort and with colleagues within and across differing instrumental and vocal groupings can also help focus everyone on the most important "goals" and "success criteria" for a music program year level and help inculcate a culture wherein everyone pulls in the same direction.

I build relationships and trust so that learning can occur in a place where it is safe to make mistakes and learn from others

Self-determination theory shows that humans have a number of psychological needs that can be satisfied through relationships between individuals that are built on trust.

The intimate nature of one-to-one studio performance lessons suggests that close ties between teacher and student that are built on a safe and trusting environment are essential for fostering productive learning. The educational literature is replete with concepts surrounding this mindframe from Herbart's (1808) "pedagogical rhythm," Nohl's (1970) "pedagogical reference," through to Bollnow's (2001) "pedagogical love." All of these and many others stress the importance of a strong teacher-student relationship in relation to successful learning.

A key feature of this mindframe are the expectations teachers place on their students. The Pygmalion effect in which positive or negative expectations placed on a person can affect that person's performance has been substantiated in much educational literature. Students thrive in studios where their teacher has high expectations for all students, not just the star performers (Rubie-Davies, 2017). Findings of research show that teachers who hold high expectations for all of their students tend to produce students whose attainment is higher. The reverse has also been shown consistently within a number of educational settings. A key implication therefore is that variations in teacher expectation explain a large part of the variance among teachers regarding their effectiveness in enabling students to succeed. When the environment is conducive, students come to believe their teachers' expectations for them. It is important, however, that such perceptions be based on a mindframe from both the teacher and the student that the student has produced a year's growth for a year's work, and not an ability attribution that the student is "good" at certain parts of their playing and "poor" at others.

Establishing and maintaining a healthy, productive teacher-student relationship involves a delicate balance between being demanding versus being responsive to the student's needs and interests. This relationship is shown in Figure 7.4, with four types of teaching profiles relating to these two dimensions. The master-apprentice model of instrumental/vocal teaching has often occurred within a studio setting where teachers are highly demanding and give their students little choice in the literature they learn or the techniques they adapt to their technical and musical development. In the model, this is depicted as an "authoritarian" style of teaching, in contrast to what research would suggest is a much more effective relationship—the "authoritative" style shown in the top right-hand quadrant—where the teacher holds high expectations but is willing to negotiate with the student an appropriate pathway forward. An authoritative style of teaching holds the greatest potential for optimizing learning, because it helps to create an environment based on fairness, predictability, and risk taking in which making errors, seeking help, and working with others are seen as natural parts of the learning process.

The authoritative style of teaching has also been shown to help reduce anxiety in students, particularly in situations where they feel they are in control of their learning rather than having external factors such as examinations, performances, and teacher pressure controlling them. Teachers who reduce anxiety in their students by engaging them in the challenge of learning inspire confidence and trust. Most important, however, is that students should always be encouraged to attribute their successes to controllable causes such as effort, persistence, and mastery learning rather than on things they cannot change such as their perception of their own ability.

One of the most intriguing studies in education had a simple design: to see if providing feedback to student through statements such as "You can't do it" versus "You can't do it yet" made any difference to their motivation to learn (Dweck, 2012). Results were startling. The comment "You can't do it" reinforced perceptions that the student lacks ability and produced students who were less motivated and more frustrated. "You can't do it yet" resulted in the opposite effect. Students felt more confident and more willing to exert effort, and this approach produced far better results. The reason we observe such results is that comments such as "not yet" signals to learners that they can achieve a goal if they put in sufficient effort, and that they are at a particular point along the path required to master the skill or concept. The important consideration, as Dweck has often claimed, is that these perceptions are situation-specific and not necessarily generalized mindsets. When students are confused, make mistakes, lack confidence, or feel challenged is when this high sense of confidence, resilience, and growth is most essential.

A certain amount of humor and cheerfulness can do wonders within a teaching studio to brighten up a lesson. When used effectively, humor helps promote those aspects of a lesson when everyone involved can have a chance to laugh at themselves and about what they are learning. Humor also helps to take the pressure off when students are sitting at the edge of their ability levels, or are making mistakes and not knowing where to go next. Likewise, a smile when genuinely given can be contagious, settle nerves, and conveys positive signs to learners that build relationships and inculcate a sense of direction for where to go next, particularly when learning is challenging.

Research literature demonstrates the power of the "chameleon effect" such that learners will often mimic the body language, posture, facial expressions, and speech tempo of their teacher (Hattie & Yates, 2015). For example, teachers who ask lots of questions that the students already know produce students who likewise ask questions they already know the answer to. This type of ritual leads to lessons looking more like an act of performance around the known rather than a search or inquiry toward the unknown. Importantly, the more intense our relationships are, the more likely we are to imitate each other. Within music, this important principle is evident every time we interact with a musician or performance teacher who acts passionately and shows their love for music and for learning. This type of approach is also infectious because subjective norms such as perceived social pressure to engage or not engage in a behavior (e.g., working hard or meeting a challenge) are often acquired by students through vicarious observation of others, such as their teacher.

A final dimension of the mindframe of building relationships and trust is built around credibility as the core of an intact teacher-student relationship. Students respond more positively to teachers who are fair in their judgments and sincere in their criticism. In terms of Dweck's "not yet" study (2012), this means taking students and their work seriously, giving them the attention they deserve, and keeping their learning journey straightforward by avoiding superficial feedback and working with them to master specified elements of their technical and musical skill sets. Similarly, credibility involves not playing down the significance of mistakes and helping students to focus on those aspects of their playing that need further development. All of this is achieved when teachers provide students with differentiated feedback. What matters to students, therefore, is not only *what* teachers say but also *how* and *why* they say it.

I focus on learning and the language of learning

The final mindframe reminds us that no student is a blank slate. Each student comes to lessons with a certain degree of prior knowledge, skill, and willingness to learn. Across more than the last century of educational research, various theories about learning and especially its relationship to the age of the learner have populated many courses offered in universities. Each of the main theories characterizes the learner and teachers in various roles. One that has been particularly influential, however, is the notion, proposed by Piaget and others, that across time learners change in the way they process information and that thinking develops in qualitative ways according to distinct stages that are influenced by maturation and the social and physical environment. A key concept within this body of research concerns how to assess and teach at an appropriate pace for the learner—not too fast and not too slow—in order to avoid stress or boredom. Within such theories the notion of "cognitive acceleration" has gained in prominence. This is based on three ideas. First, that the mind develops in response to challenge, or to disequilibrium, so teaching should provide at least some cognitive conflict. Second, learning that encourages metacognition helps build a growing ability for learners to become conscious of what they are learning and able to control their own thought processes. Finally, cognitive development is seen as a social process that blooms when high-quality discussion among peers is structured within the teaching process. Teacher predictions of their students' future achievement are generally reliable, but this does not mean that all learners follow a similar path toward their goals. Focusing on learning implies that the we remind ourselves that our most talented students are not always the most successful, and that our job is to provide them with the support they need to cope with the challenges of learning music.

A parallel issue is the mindframe of the student. Of the "big five" factors that researchers use to define people's personality, "conscientiousness" or the capacity to act in a purposeful, controlled way, is the one most cited as critical to learning, mainly in situations where the learner experiences tension and is making mistakes, or alternatively, when overlearning something, such as a technical skill that needs to be secure, is important (Hattie & Zierer, 2018). Knowing when to help students to be aware that they need to apply themselves and be conscientious is critical to effective teaching.

Teachers shouldn't just see their role as only to stand alongside the student, or to guide their development. Instead they should adopt the role of helping the student "feed back," "feed up," and "feed forward" as discussed earlier in this chapter. Students are more likely to thrive when they are challenged, when they are at the edge of their understanding, and are taught in a way that encourages them to do things they would not have been able to manage on their own. This "zone of proximal development" is what Vygotsky (1978) described as the difference between what learners can do by themselves, versus what they can do with a supportive, knowledgeable other helping to focus their efforts.

Studies of university students' estimates of their own scores before they undertake a test often show that low-achieving students overestimate their score by up to 20 percent, in contrast to high-achieving students who underestimate their score by around 5 percent (Hattie & Yates, 2015). In a very general way, we could interpret these results in one of two ways: first, that low-achieving students find it hard to assess their level of competence, or second, from a Socratic perspective, that high-achieving students are better able to know what they still do not know. The main point of this research, however, is that student assessments of their own abilities are not always accurate, so an important role for teachers is to remain in the background and intervene whenever they are expected to make such judgments. The additional finding that low-achieving students tend to choose tasks that are too difficult and that high-achieving students tend to choose tasks that are too easy reinforces the need for teachers to help their students to make better judgments of whether their learning has been successful.

A huge amount of research has also studied cognitive load (i.e., the level of thinking and problem solving required to successfully accomplish a task) and found that learners can overlook many important aspects of their learning because they are too focused on other associated aspects that take up most of their working memory (see Sweller, 1988, 1999). In other words, when learning is particularly challenging, students might be unable to see all of the forest because they are focusing on only some of the trees. Cognitive load theory suggests that this problem can occur when a student feels overwhelmed by other factors (e.g., an impending examination or recital, inaccurate self-assessments) or being overwhelmed by an overuse of methodology (e.g., directions that are overly complicated and that do not fully reveal to the leaner what the true intensions of the learning task is, and how it might lead to the next step in the learning journey). Thus, constantly keeping an eye on the extent to which the student is clear about the intentions of the learning exercise and focused on the aspect of their learning being dealt with at that particular point in the lesson or learning cycle is critical to effective teaching.

The adage that learners retain 20 percent of what they read, 20 percent of what they hear, 30 percent of what they see, 50 percent of what they see and hear, 70 percent of what they present themselves, and 90 percent of what they do themselves has no empirical basis. It is simply not true. What research shows instead is the value for teachers of using multiple ways of engaging students' thinking strategies in their teaching (Hattie & Donoghue, 2016). No student has a single dominant way of thinking, and the most successful and productive are those who are more capable of choosing appropriate learning strategies depending on where they are in the learning cycle. Within this conception, learning is effective to the extent that it is enjoyable. The best way of making it enjoyable is by designing a learning situation that takes into account the learners' prior knowledge and experiences, and one that ties in with their existing thinking to present them with a challenge. Joyful emotions emerge when learning is successful, just as success breeds joy. Engagement typically follows successful learning that precedes it.

One other aspect needs to be taken into account when focusing on learning and its language. Our self-concept—how we think about and evaluate or perceive ourselves in relation to others—plays a major role in determining how we view our own learning. Some learners tend to attribute their success to luck and their deficiencies to a flaw in their personality, while others attribute their success to effort and their failures to not enough hard work. Students' differing motivational profiles play out within learning environments in many varied ways, which reinforces the need for teachers to know how their students process information relating to their own personal beliefs. To what extent do they believe in themselves, persist when faced with challenges, or feel proud when they see themselves flourishing? The principles outlined in this chapter suggest that how students think about themselves and the beliefs they hold about their own abilities as musicians are just as important as the amount of time they spend learning a new piece of music or the amount of effort they put into refining their instrumental or vocal technique.

CONCLUSION

Just as music is a performing art, so too is teaching a performing art. Great musicians are not necessarily inherently great performance teachers. Great musicians have typically worked hard to reach their level of performance ability, and while in some ways this might provide a solid foundation for developing into a high-impact performance teacher, this ability will only become evident if the musician is willing to develop the types of teaching skills that can shape an impactful career as a mentor, coach, and inspirer of young musicians who seek them out for lessons.

None of us are miracle workers. But by applying the mindframes outlined in this chapter, teachers of music performance will be in a much better position to cater for the needs of the diverse range of student abilities we observe in music institutions internationally. And by recalibrating their teaching to focus on questions of *why* as well as *what* and *how*, they position themselves to take on a much wider and more impactful role as a performer-teacher who really cares about students, who wants to spark their interest, who encourages them to live their musical dreams, and who helps them exceed what they think is their full potential.

KEY SOURCES

Duke, R. A., & Simmons, A. (2006). The nature of expertise: Narrative descriptions of 19 common elements observed in the lessons of three renowned artist-teachers. *Council for Research in Music Education*, *170*, 7–19.

Dweck, C. (2017). *Mindset: Changing the way you think to fulfil your potential.* New York: Hachette.

Hattie, J., & Zierer, K. (2018). *10 mindframes for visible learning: Teaching for success.* New York: Routledge.

Sinek, S. (2009). *Start with why: How great leaders inspire everyone to take action.* New York: Penguin.

Personal Reflections

1. *Mindframe 1*: Assess the degree to which you are very good at (a) applying multiple strategies to make your impact on students visible; and (b) regularly and systematically evaluating your impact on your students' learning.

2. *Mindframe 2*: Assess the degree to which you are very good at (a) adapting your teaching when your students haven't met their learning goals; (b) using the achievement of your students to draw conclusions about the goals, content, and methods you set for their learning; and (c) using objective methods to measure your students' achievement in order to assess the success of your teaching.

3. *Mindframe 3*: Assess the degree to which you are very good at (a) sharing ideas with other teachers; and (b) using new ideas obtained from other teachers to continue your own development as a teacher.

4. *Mindframe 4*: Assess the degree to which you are very good at (a) applying successful strategies to make your teaching more differentiated; (b) using different strategies to enhance your students' motivation; and (c) teaching in a way that has a positive impact on your students, based on a belief that continuously questioning of the impact of your teaching is fundamental to effective teaching.

5. *Mindframe 5*: Assess the degree to which you are very good at setting challenging assignments for your students that are based on their individual learning needs and level of development.

6. *Mindframe 6*: Assess the degree to which you are very good at (a) obtaining feedback from your students; (b) using this feedback to improve your own teaching; (c) acting on the feedback obtained from your students; and (d) reflecting on the feedback obtained from your students.

7. *Mindframe 7*: Assess the degree to which you are very good at (a) encouraging your students to discuss the content of lessons and what they have learned; (b) encouraging your students to work cooperatively with others; (c) providing instruction that is clear; and (d) encouraging your students to present their thinking about solutions to problems/challenges within the dialogue you encourage during each lesson.

8. *Mindframe 8*: Assess the degree to which you are very good at (a) making it clear to your students what the goal of the lesson is and what the successful criteria of learning are; and (b) making the objectives of your lessons clear, challenging, and

transparent so that your students understand the criteria you have established for success.

9. *Mindframe 9*: Assess the degree to which you are very good at (a) establishing a feeling of belonging within your lessons; (b) fostering a positive relationship with your students; and (c) getting your students to trust you (and you to trust them).

10. *Mindframe 10*: Assess the degree to which you are very good at (a) identifying the strengths and the weaknesses of your students; (b) diagnosing the prior knowledge or skills your students possess before beginning a challenging task; and (c) designing your tuition in ways that take into account the prior knowledge or skills your students possess.

11. How might you go about improving any of these aspects in which you feel less competent?

REFERENCES

Bandura, A. (1976). Social learning perspective on behavior change. In A. Burton (Ed.), *What makes behavior change possible?* (pp. 34–57). New York: Brunner/Mazel.

Bandura, A. (1977). Self-efficacy: Toward a unifying theory of behavior change. *Psychological Review, 84*, 191–215.

Bollnow, O. F. (2001). *Die pädagogische Atmosphäre: Untersuchungen über die gefühlsmäßigen zwischenmenschlichen Voraussetzungen der Erziehung.* Essent: Die blaue Eule. Originally published 1964.

Clinton, J., Hattie, J. A. C., & Nawab, D. (2018). The good teacher—Our best teachers are inspired, influential and passionate. In M. Gläser-Zikuda, M. Harring, & C. Rohlfs (Eds.), *Handbuch Schulpädagogik* (pp. 880–888). Stuttgart: UTB GmbH.

Csikszentmihalyi, M. (2008). *Flow: The psychology of optimal experience.* New York: Harper.

Donohoo, J. (2019). *Collective efficacy: Together we can make a difference.* Thousand Oaks, CA: Corwin.

Donohoo, J., Hattie, J., & Eells, R. (2018). The power of collective efficacy. *Educational Leadership, 75*(6), 40–44.

Donohoo, J., & Katz, S. (2019). What drives collective efficacy? Four ways educators gain the power to make a difference. *Educational Leadership, 76*(9), 24–29.

Duke, R. A., & Simmons, A. (2006). The nature of expertise: Narrative descriptions of 19 common elements observed in the lessons of three renowned artist-teachers. *Bulletin of the Council for Research in Music Education, 170*, 7–19.

Dweck, C. (2012). *Mindset: How you can fulfill your potential.* New York: Random House.

Dweck, C. (2015). Carol Dweck revisits the "growth mindset." *Educational Week, 35*(5), 20–24.

Dweck, C. (2017). *Mindset: Changing the way you think to fulfil your potential.* New York: Hachette.

Hattie, J. A. C., & Clarke, A. (2019). *Visible learning: Feedback.* New York: Routledge.

Hattie, J. A. C., & Donoghue, G. (2016). Learning strategies: A synthesis and conceptual model. *Nature: Science of Learning, 1*(1), 1–13. https://doi.org/10.1038/npjscilearn.2016.13.

Hattie, J. A. C., & Yates, G. (2015). *Visible learning and the science of how we learn.* New York: Routledge.

Hattie, J. A. C., & Zierer, K. (2018). *10 mindframes for visible learning: Teaching for success*. New York: Routledge.

Herbart, J.-F. (1808). *Allgemeine Pädagogik aus dem Zweck der Erziehung abgeleitet*. Bochum: Kamp.

Nakamura, J., & Csikszentmihalyi, M. (2002). The concept of flow. In C. R. Snyder & S. J. Lopez (Eds.), *Handbook of positive psychology* (pp. 89–105). Oxford University Press.

Nohl, H. (1970). *Die pädagogische Bewegung in Deutschland und ihre Theorie*. 7th ed. Frankfurt: Schulte-Bulmke.

Rubie-Davies, C. M. (2017). *Teacher expectations in education*. London: Routledge.

Sinek, S. (2009). *Start with why: How great leaders inspire everyone to take action*. New York: Penguin.

Sweller, J. (1988). Cognitive load during problem solving: Effects on learning, *Cognitive Science*, 12(2), 257–285. https://doi.org/10.1016/0364-0213(88)90023-7.

Sweller, J. (1999). *Instructional design in technical areas*, Camberwell, Victoria, Australia: Australian Council for Educational Research.

Vygotsky, L. S. (1978). *Mind in society: The development of higher psychological processes*. Cambridge, MA: Harvard University Press.

PART II

PROFICIENCIES

CHAPTER 8

....

PRACTICE

....

PETER MIKSZA

Those who fall in love with practice without knowledge are like a sailor
who gets into a ship without rudder or compass and who never can be certain whither he is going. Practice must always be founded on sound theory.

—Leonardo da Vinci (quoted in Suh, 2005, p. 389)

INTRODUCTION

ENGAGING in extended periods of isolated practice is a rite of passage for nearly
all musicians seeking performance expertise. Although there is variation across
individuals, it is commonly understood that acquiring and refining music performance skills requires devoting an enormous amount of time, energy, and motivational
resources to practice (Jørgensen & Hallam, 2016; Miksza, 2011a). More important,
advances in performance science have shown that the *efficient* acquisition of music performance expertise requires a disciplined learning approach that involves a focused application of strategies that maximize human learning potentials.

Since music learners spend nearly all of their practice time working alone, it is especially critical that they have a clear understanding of how to design and execute effective practice methods. Unlike other disciplines in which high-level performance skill
is sought (e.g., athletics, medicine, dance, chess), musicians rarely have opportunities
for coaching beyond the typical hour-long, one-on-one meeting per week they may
spend with their private teachers. In contrast, a developing athlete may only practice
in the presence of a coach, or even several coaches, who attend to the learner's mental,
physical, and emotional states. Regrettably, most developing musicians have relatively
few external resources available to them for structure, guidance, and feedback when
practicing. It is perhaps not surprising, then, that even relatively advanced musicians
have been found to be ineffective with the time they devote to individual practice (e.g.,
Miksza, 2011b; Miksza, Blackwell, & Roseth, 2018).

Musicians cannot afford to be ill-informed when it comes to practice. Meandering and wandering through learning via trial and error can lead to plateaus in achievement as well as emotional or motivational burnout. At best, such practices can be inefficient and result in lost opportunities to improve performance. At worst, haphazard approaches to practice can result in the internalization of improper techniques, poor habits, and performance errors. Having to work to overcome such challenges can consume tremendous amounts of time as well as emotional and motivational resources, forcing learners to spend time on remediating their technique or relearning fundamental skills rather than advancing in ability. More than simply time lost, inefficient practice can result in negative net gains in skill acquisition.

One partial remedy for this current state of affairs is for music learners and their teachers to become knowledgeable of the many theory-driven, evidence-based approaches that have emerged from the scientific study of motor skill acquisition. As the quote from Leonardo da Vinci in the epigraph implies, "fall(ing) in love with practice" and committing time and energy to learning are not sufficient for those who wish to achieve performance success. Developing musicians can also benefit from an understanding of a "theory" of learning regarding how skill acquisition occurs. Then, they will be able to focus their efforts on systematically implementing intentional practice techniques that will help them be "more certain of whither they are going." Accordingly, practice methods derived from an understanding of psychological processes involved in motor skill learning can be particularly useful for musicians. The purposes of this chapter are, therefore: (a) to describe selected theoretical frameworks that are particularly useful for characterizing how practice and human learning potential are intertwined; and (b) to present several evidence-based strategies and techniques that researchers have identified as efficient and effective approaches for skill acquisition.

This chapter is arranged in two main sections. The first section serves as the theoretical framework for the practical recommendations presented in the second section of the chapter. I will first present the concept of deliberate practice as theorized by the cognitive psychologist K. Anders Ericsson and colleagues and discuss some of the most compelling evidence for and against the contributions of deliberate practice to the development of musical expertise. I will then briefly describe some of the critical elements of the human cognitive system involved in motor skill acquisition. In the second section, I will describe some of the most reliable generalizations that can be drawn from the extant motor learning and music psychology literature while providing brief examples for how they are relevant to music practice.

Theoretical Foundations

Deliberate practice

Many scientists have contributed to our understanding of how people achieve expert performance (see Ericsson, Hoffman, Kozbelt, & Williams, 2018); Ericsson and colleagues' concept of deliberate practice, however, has been highly influential in the music performance science literature[1] while also infiltrating popular culture (Ericsson & Pool, 2016a; Gladwell, 2008). In their landmark study of violinists and pianists, Ericsson, Krampe, and Tesch-Römer (1993) described deliberate practice as teacher-prescribed, goal-directed learning activities that students engage in during the time between their meetings with their private instructor. In contrast to other, less formal types of activities, deliberate practice is characterized as being intentional, effortful, and not necessarily intrinsically fun. In their 1993 study, Ericsson et al. found that the highest-achieving musicians also reported the greatest amounts of accumulated deliberate practice throughout their development, whereas those only achieving amateur status or those preparing to be music teachers (as opposed to preparing to be performers) had accumulated less. This finding, among others like it, led the researchers to theorize that individual differences in achievement among elite performers are likely to be the result of individuals' efforts in practice rather than immutable talents or gifts.

Ericsson and colleagues also, however, recognize that individuals negotiate key constraints of resources, effort, and motivation in addition to partaking in large amounts of deliberate practice to achieve expertise (Ericsson & Harwell, 2019; Ericsson et al., 1993; Ericsson & Lehmann, 1996; Lehmann & Ericsson, 1997a). *Resource constraints* refer to access to high-quality instructors, training facilities, and training materials. Without access to these resources at critical points in development, learners would be much less likely to receive the guidance they need to enact effective strategies during individual practice. *Effort constraints* are a recognition of the limits of human attention, energy expenditure, and memory formation, as they refer to the need for learners to balance their effort with rest and regular attention to recuperation. Effort constraints highlight the fact that developing expertise typically requires extended periods of intense engagement across many years, which requires careful management of mental and physical exhaustion and strategic avoidance of burnout. *Motivational constraints* are important to consider, given that deliberate practice is primarily valued by a learner for the growth that results from it rather than from the inherent enjoyment of the act itself. As such, musicians typically need to develop and/or find motivation to improve prior to engaging in deliberate practice and for reasons beyond the act of practice itself.

The acquisition of expertise involves not only technical mastery of a craft (e.g., fluidity and automaticity of musical performance), but also the refinement of several forms of mental representations that provide experts with increased amounts of control over their performance such that they can be lithe and reactive in the moment. Lehmann and Ericsson (1997a) pithily describe how three types of mental representations are particularly important for the development of musical skill and the type of control of performance that experts can demonstrate: desired performance representations, production representations, and current performance representations. A *desired*

---

[1] As of the time of this writing, Ericsson, Krampe, and Tesch-Römer's (1993) paper on deliberate practice has amassed over 10,250 citations according to Google scholar.

performance representation is a mental concept of how the music a performer wishes to convey should sound. In other words, it is the goal of the performance. *Production representations* consist of the knowledge and skill components necessary for the control of the musician's instrument and are drawn upon when acting to achieve the desired performance goal. Last, *current performance representations* refer to the musician's conceptions of their performance in the moment, which are used to monitor their performance as it unfolds. Evidence for these cognitive mediators of performance comes from experts' verbal reports and experiments in which experts maintain high-level performance amid changes in performance contexts and constraints (Lehmann & Ericsson, 1997b).

Critique of the deliberate practice account

The relatively extreme perspective that achievement disparities among individuals is due mostly to differences in cumulative quantities of deliberate practice has received much criticism in recent years. Macnamara, Hambrick, and Oswald (2014) and Macnamara, Hambrick, and Moreau (2016) have conducted meta-analyses of studies that examined relationships between accumulated amounts of practice and indicators of performance achievement. Their meta-analyses revealed that reported accumulated amounts of practice did indeed correlate with performance achievement, but that a good deal of the variation in performance achievement remained unexplained. For example, one study found that only 23 percent of the variation in performance achievement could be explained by accumulated amount of deliberate practice. Most recent critiques of the deliberate practice account have put forth evidence of genetic contributions to individual differences in performance acquisition as well as the impact of gene-environment interactions (e.g., Hambrick, Campitelli, & Macnamara, 2017; Hambrick, Macnamara, Campitelli, Ullén, & Mosing, 2016; Hambrick & Tucker-Drob, 2015).

In response to these critiques and newly found evidence, Ericsson and Harwell (2019) conceded that genetic differences and gene-environment interaction effects explain some of the variation among individuals in performance attainment. However, they disagreed with the relatively conservative limits that critics have proposed for the role that deliberate practice serves (e.g., Macnamara et al., 2014; Ullén, Mosing, & Madison, 2015). Instead, Ericsson and colleagues have pointed out that those critical of the deliberate practice account of expertise have been too lax in their definition of deliberate practice and have not adhered to the specific conception of deliberate practice as described in the original Ericsson et al. (1993) article (Ericsson & Harwell, 2019, Ericsson & Pool, 2016b). As a result, they claim that the estimates of how much variation in performance achievement could be explained by accumulated deliberate practice are artificially low. In an effort to clarify and revise their claims as well as to guide future research, Ericsson and Harwell (2019) have described a continuum of individual practice archetypes ranging from the most unstructured and least goal-oriented to the most structured and intentional: naïve practice, purposeful practice, and deliberate practice, respectively.

A musician is engaging in *naïve practice* when practicing for some purpose other than the explicit aim of improving a particular aspect of performance (Ericsson & Harwell, 2019). For example, playing individually for fun, engaging in uncoached chamber music practice, or participating in a performance (i.e., working) could each be considered instances of naïve practice. Although these types of activities are important and can often be educative, they are not within the bounds of the definition of deliberate practice. Ericsson and Harwell (2019) describe *purposeful practice* as engaging in the same sort of individualized, goal-oriented behavior as is typical of *deliberate practice*, only without regular access to guidance and feedback from a coach/teacher. For example, a musician working to explicitly improve their individual performance during solitary practice without sufficiently periodic meetings with a teacher might be described as engaging in purposeful rather than deliberate practice. Although the definitional difference between purposeful and deliberate practice would be subtle, their potential impact on performance achievement is thought to differ significantly. Ericsson and Harwell (2019) also specify that goal-oriented, supervised group activities such as conductor-led rehearsals do not qualify as deliberate practice. Instead, they call such activity structured practice and explain that structured practice activities are typically aimed at increasing specific aspects of group performance (e.g., ensemble goals) as opposed to being tailored to individuals' performance challenges.

The fluid skills and variety of flexible mental representations that emerge from accumulated deliberate practice are critical to developing performance expertise. However, it is necessary to recognize that there is much more that goes into becoming a skilled, committed, and satisfied musician than deliberate practice alone. A number of chapters in this two-volume handbook address other important aspects of musical development and learning (see, for example, chapters on self-regulated learning, motivation, self-directed learning, memorization methods, peak performance, and musician health). The remainder of this chapter is delimited specifically to the discussion of theoretical frameworks and research-based approaches that are relevant to the sorts of deliberate music practice undertaken when seeking to develop efficient and effective methods for learning skilled movements.

A cognitive model of information processing

It is necessary to briefly consider the human cognitive architecture that learners possess when exploring what sorts of approaches may most effectively lead to efficient learning during deliberate practice. Working from a theoretical model of how learners attend to, encode, store, and retrieve information and recognizing the constraints upon such processes can be valuable when designing learning strategies. In this section, my discussion is limited to several critical aspects of the prevailing model of human information processing. Each of these outlines important theoretical constructs and processes that are relevant to understanding the motor skill learning and music psychology research literature that follow in the next section of the chapter. These include attention; working memory, the central executive, and cognitive load; and long-term memory and memory consolidation (e.g., Baddeley, Eysenck, & Anderson, 2019). However, the reader can find detailed treatments of the complete information processing model in nearly any introductory psychology of learning text; see, for example, Ormrod (2020).

Attention

If information is to be processed by a learner, then it must first be attended to. Attention is often drawn to stimuli in an environment via automatic subconscious means—consider the human startle response when encountering sudden loud sounds. However, it is also possible, more or less, to direct one's attention to particular stimuli via conscious will. A key element of motor learning is attending to the appropriate and relevant features of a task when engaging in practice. Unfortunately, attentional capacity is limited, and the potential for distraction during learning or learners inadvertently attending to irrelevant features of a task is high. Considering learners' focus of attention is always important, although it is especially important when applying slow practice, modeling strategies, mental rehearsal strategies, and choosing whether to emphasize internal (e.g., bodily/technical mechanics of performance) or external (e.g., aural goal outcomes) targets when engaging in practice. The necessity of maintaining high levels of attention during learning also informs the relative benefits of massed and distributed practice schedules.

Working memory, central executive, and cognitive load

Once attended to, an individual can begin encoding information, which entails processing it in the working memory for storage in long-term memory. Information is thought to last in working memory for approximately 1 minute or less, and capacity is limited to about 4 or so "chunks" of novel material (Cowan, 2010; Miller, 1956). In order to keep information in working memory and prolong encoding and storage processes, it needs to be continuously attended to and rehearsed in some manner, which is typically a conscious process. The quality of the encoding and storage that occurs is largely determined by the quality of the rehearsal that is undergone in working memory. Rote methods of rehearsal (e.g., mindless repetition) are generally much less effective for encoding information into long-term memory (i.e., learning) compared to methods that involve assigning meaning to the information being rehearsed or elaborating upon the information in some way. As such, applying a variety of repetition strategies through which learners can make meaningful associations among chunks of information and perform in a variety of elaborative methods can be particularly beneficial.

The mechanism that governs how well individuals can maintain focus upon and negotiate the complexity of information being rehearsed in working memory is called the *central executive*. Learners can benefit from understanding that the control processes that the central executive performs are sensitive to the complexity and size of the informational load (i.e., cognitive load) being rehearsed (Sweller, 1988, 2011; Sweller, Ayres, & Kalyuga, 2011). All learning tasks can be described as having some theoretical quantity of intrinsic, extraneous, and germane cognitive load.

Intrinsic cognitive load refers to the difficulty (e.g., amount and complexity of information) inherent to a task. For example, for a particular student, a passage of music might present a particular amount of intrinsic cognitive load based on their current performance ability. *Extraneous cognitive load* refers to unnecessary cognitive burdens a learner experiences from aspects external to the task itself—often due to the instructional methods used. For example, a teacher might not provide much instruction for students on how to practice, and the student would need to devise the structure and content of practice activities for themselves. Because the act of devising the structure and content of their practice activities does not directly contribute to their music learning or performance, it is considered extraneous cognitive load. Practice activities can be designed for learners such that the intrinsic load of learning objectives is recognized (e.g., by selecting repertoire appropriate to the student's ability), extraneous load is reduced as much as possible (e.g., by providing scaffolding and structure to students' practice and by removing distractions that divert attention and consume cognitive resources), and *germane cognitive load* is optimized. Germane cognitive load refers to cognitive resources necessary for processing the information to be learned and storing it in long-term memory. Slow practice, chunking, and mental rehearsal strategies can be effective methods for managing the cognitive load a learner encounters when working on materials that are initially too challenging for their current level of skill.

Long-term memory and memory consolidation

Information that is effectively encoded and stored is thought to then be moved to long-term memory, which is hypothesized to be potentially permanent and have virtually limitless capacity. Information stored in long-term memory is thought to be structured as an associative network with hierarchical organizational properties. As such, the relative security of information storage and flexibility of information retrieval can depend on the degree to which information was encoded and processed in a meaningful way. When information in long-term memory is retrieved into working memory, it consumes virtually no cognitive resources, and can be embellished and built upon with new information, providing the mechanism by which learning can continually improve performance abilities.

Knowledge that exists in long-term memory can be of two types, explicit or implicit. Generally speaking, *explicit* types of knowledge are described as declarative forms that can be consciously recalled, e.g., the phenomenon of "knowing what", whereas *implicit* types of knowledge are described as procedural forms of "knowing how" to do something even when it is not declarable, such as is the case with many aspects of performing complex motor skills.

Motor learning theorists have proposed that skill development can begin with explicit, declarative forms of knowledge that are gradually transformed or serve as transitional scaffolds toward the development of implicit, procedural knowledge over time as practice ultimately leads to the automation of movement. Fitts and Posner's (1967) classic three-stage model is helpful for describing this process. The first stage is called the *cognitive stage*, in which initial attempts at learning a movement are guided primarily through conscious attention, trial and error, and perhaps even assisted with verbalization.

Although learners show much improvement across this stage, performance tends to remain inconsistent. The second stage is the *associative stage*, wherein learners are still applying some conscious effort at controlling their performance, but tend to make small gains in achievement and still demonstrate some inconsistency in performance. The last stage, which is typically reached only after much practice, is the *autonomous stage*. In this stage, the learner operates from implicit, procedural knowledge in a seemingly automatic way and executes the skill with fluency and consistency. Conscious efforts to control performance are no longer necessary in the autonomous stage.

The distinction between explicit, declarative knowledge of performance and implicit, procedural knowledge of how to perform, and being sure to focus learning on the appropriate type of knowledge at critical points, is important. For example, once a learning objective has been mastered and can be executed with relative automaticity, directing learners to maintain an external focus of attention (e.g., aural goal outcomes) to draw from implicit procedural knowledge can be beneficial, whereas learners who work from an internal focus of attention (e.g., explicit declarative knowledge of bodily/technical mechanics of performance), despite having already achieved automaticity, can often "choke" and fail to perform with accuracy and fluency (e.g., Beilock & Carr, 2001).

Last, information of any type that is encoded and moved to long-term memory also undergoes a process of memory consolidation. *Memory consolidation* is the refinement of networks of information over time that can occur naturally by virtue of appropriate rest and sleep. Learners could experiment, therefore, with practice schedules that optimize the quality of their sleep as well as rest and recuperation efforts.

Music teachers and learners can benefit from asking the following series of information processing theory-informed questions when considering the design of deliberate practice activity: To what extent is the learner attending? What meaningful physical or mental activities are the learners engaging in when processing information? What is the difficulty/complexity of the information the learner is dealing with? How securely and flexibly has the information been stored in long-term memory?

PRACTICAL APPLICATIONS

There is a substantial legacy of research regarding musicians' practice methods, with some of the earliest examples being studies of how pianists commit pieces to memory appearing alongside the emergence of psychology as a discipline (e.g., Brown, 1928; Rubin-Rabson, 1939). More recent research in music practice methods has been based in the cognitive information processing framework of learning presented in the previous section and influenced by more recent developments emerging from the motor learning research community (e.g., Altenmüller & McPherson, 2007, Schmidt, Lee, Winstein, Wulf, & Zelaznik, 2019). In this section, I will present research generalizations pertaining to effective and efficient practice that have emerged from the motor learning and music psychology literature. My goal is to provide the reader with information about general types of strategies and behaviors that musicians can employ when engaging in deliberate practice.

Massed vs. distributed practice schedules, rest, and sleep

The manner in which learners schedule their practice sessions over time is critical for their learning in many ways. Researchers have found that practicing for relatively short sessions distributed across time is more effective than scheduling massed, long sessions (e.g., Donovan & Radosevich, 1999; Duke, Allen, Cash, & Simmons, 2009). "Cramming" learning into long sessions can be exhausting and is likely to result in degraded information processing and limited memory consolidation. There is also a growing body of research that emphasizes the importance of rest (e.g., Cash, 2009) and sleep (e.g., Duke & Davis, 2006), specifically, for procedural memory consolidation in music learning. These studies have revealed that it can be more beneficial to introduce rest relatively earlier in a practice schedule rather than later, and that learning can be enhanced through consolidation following a good night's sleep. Moreover, in their seminal study introducing the term *deliberate practice*, Ericsson et al. (1993) also found that relatively high-performing musicians were more likely to take naps in the afternoon during an average week and were less likely to cram practice time in on weekends, as compared to relatively lower-performing musicians.

Exactly how long a learner should engage in practice prior to taking a break, however, is relative to a learner's experience/skill level, attentional capacity, general stamina, and their typical needs for recovery—as well as the challenge the learning objective poses (i.e., the cognitive load). For example, a beginning musician might be expected to engage in concentrated practice for 15 minutes at a stretch prior to a break, whereas an advanced musician might easily be able to manage a longer practice session without a serious loss of learning efficiency. Ultimately, learners need to become sensitized to their personal limits and monitor the efficacy of their practice to determine the appropriate schedule of distributed practice. Monitoring one's attentional limits is also consistent with Ericsson and colleagues' assertion that effort and motivational constraints must be considered when gauging the potential for deliberate practice to impact one's skill development (also see Evans & Ryan, this volume).

Modeling

The effects of observing a model have been studied extensively (McCullagh & Weiss, 2001), and modeling is a strategy that most teachers and learners engage in intuitively. As one might expect, having a positive exemplar of a learning objective in mind while practicing can be helpful. This is consistent with the need for experts to develop what Lehmann and Ericsson (1997a) describe as desired performance representations. Modeling is also a key element of Bandura's (1986) social-cognitive learning theory in which he proposes that the most effective modeling occurs when learners (a) are attentive to the relevant features of the modeled behavior; (b) actively work to retain the information the model is demonstrating; (c) engage in the modeled behavior themselves; and (d) are motivated to achieve the behavior the model is demonstrating. Bandura also states that a model that is perceived by the learner as competent, prestigious in some way, and relatable is more likely to lead to beneficial effects than otherwise.

There are a number of studies that have demonstrated the positive effects of audio- and video-recorded models such as would be typically employed during individual music practice (e.g., Hewitt, 2001; Rosenthal, 1984). Observing an aural-visual model seems to be more effective than a model presented in either modality alone (Linklater, 1997). In addition, combining modeling with having students self-evaluate their own subsequent performance while attending to specific criteria may enhance the effect of the model (Hewitt, 2011). There is also evidence to suggest that having students of similar skill levels model for each other in dyadic pairs can be beneficial (Granados & Wulf, 2007).

Focus of attention

Managing central executive processing through maintaining concentration and directing one's attention during deliberate practice is critical. One study has demonstrated that maintaining concentration while practicing might be as simple as noting when one experiences distraction so that it is possible to self-correct and re-focus (Madsen & Geringer, 1981). However, there is a large body of research that has sought to determine whether focusing one's attention on internal (e.g., bodily/technical mechanics of performance) or external (e.g., goal outcomes) targets would be most beneficial for developing motor skills (Wulf, 2013). Many researchers have compared internal vs. external foci of attention while studying a wide range of skills, and the consensus of the findings is that instruction and feedback that direct learners to maintain an external focus of attention are more effective than those which emphasize an internal focus of attention. Inducing external foci of attention leads to more effective (e.g., accuracy, consistency) and efficient (e.g., easier production, less tiring) skill execution (Wulf, 2013). Wulf, McNevin, and Shea (2001) suggest that focusing on external outcomes allows learners to access automatic control processes from memory (i.e., procedural knowledge) and enhance the efficiency of the motor system, whereas a focus on internal processes can disrupt automatic control processes and constrain the motor system.

Inducing an external focus of attention has also been found to be beneficial for music learning outcomes, specifically. Duke, Cash, and Allen (2011) found that the common music instruction of "listen to your sound" helped students learn and perform simple keyboard tasks more than instructions to focus attention on their fingers, the piano keys, or the piano hammers. Similarly, Mornell and Wulf (2019) found that inducing an external focus of attention led to better technical precision and ratings of musical expression as compared to an internal focus of attention among instrumentalists as well as singers. As such, directing attention toward products rather than processes seems to be an advantageous strategy for musicians to engage in during deliberate practice.

Mental practice

Mental practice refers to the covert (i.e., cognitive) rehearsal of a skill in absence of any overt physical movement or audible sound (Coffman, 1990; Driskell, Copper, & Moran, 1994). For example, musicians engaging in imagery of physical movements relevant to executing skills, aural aspects of the sounds they wish to produce, or even the entirety of approaching a performance (e.g., moving from backstage to onstage, imagining an audience, initiating a performance) are engaging in mental practice. Mental practice is typically found to be more beneficial than no practice but not quite as beneficial as physical practice, suggesting that a combination of mental and physical practice with a relatively larger proportion of physical practice could be an optimal approach (Lotze & Halsband, 2006). However, in the absence of the opportunity to physically practice due to injury or other setbacks, mental practice may be a productive substitute. Mental practice has been shown to result in brain activation and plasticity similar to that which results from physical practice, and as such it is likely valuable for the formation of the mental representations Lehmann and Ericsson (1997a) describe as critical to expertise. It is also a form of practice that can reduce cognitive load for difficult tasks, help individuals focus attention, and serve dually as a form of rest, since actually producing physical movement is not required.

Several studies have revealed benefits of combinations of physical and mental practice in a variety of music learning contexts (Cahn, 2007; Ross, 1985; VanderArk & Murphy, 1998). Highben and Palmer's (2004) study of pianists is of particular interest because their experiment showed that musicians with strong aural skills were more likely to benefit from mental practice. This suggests that musicians engaging in mental practice for the purpose of improving aural learning targets should first have a strong auditory image in mind. Therefore, combining mental practice with aural models for those with less developed aural skills would be particularly important to consider.

Repetition

Repetition is the *sine qua non* of music practice and there is a good deal of literature documenting just how heavily musicians rely upon repetition strategies (Chaffin & Logan, 2006; Gruson, 2001; Maynard, 2006). However, repetition in and of itself is a double-edged sword since it is an easy strategy to use carelessly and can result in the inadvertent reinforcement of poor performance. Fortunately, there are many approaches for musicians to use that can help them engage in repetition behavior with mindful intentionality.

Speed vs. accuracy, chunking, chaining, and overlearning

Errors in practice are inevitable during skill development and necessary since an essential aspect of human learning is recognizing discrepancies between attempts and ideal outcomes and adjusting behavior accordingly (Hamilton, 2017). Despite this reality, it is beneficial for repetitions in practice to be accurate whenever possible, so that strong habits of movement can be formed. However, human beings have limited information processing capacities and can struggle to repeat musical tasks that require complex coordination and/or rapid movement accurately. In recognition of these limitations, foundational motor learning theorists have emphasized that there is a speed vs. accuracy trade-off that occurs in skill execution (e.g., Fitts, 1954). For example, since individuals can only process so much information at once, learners often find that they can either execute a movement they are learning slowly and accurately or quickly and inaccurately—but not quickly and accurately. As would be expected, systematically varying tempo to repeat passages more slowly than the target tempo is a practice behavior that has been found to be positively associated with performance achievement (Duke, Simmons, & Cash, 2009; Miksza, 2007; Sikes, 2013). As such, musicians' and teachers' intuitions that practice should proceed at a slow tempo until mastery is achieved and only then gradually increase in tempo is consistent with theory as well as empirical evidence.

One relatively obvious approach to intentional and accurate repetitions while practicing is for musicians to analyze materials and break them into chunks that are suitable for their information processing capacity at the moment (Williamon & Valentine, 2000). Once broken down, the chunks can be practiced independently until mastered and then gradually pieced back together—or chained together—increasing the size of the newly formed chunk according to the levels of complexity and difficulty the learner can handle (i.e., repeat with accuracy). This is a strategy that can be beneficial for encoding information and that has been found to be correlated with achievement in several studies of instrumental musicians' practicing (Miksza, 2007, 2011b; Nielsen, 1999).

Moreover, continuing to repeat accurate material once mastery has been achieved at the target tempo (and perhaps even beyond it) can be beneficial as well. Motor learning theorists describe this sort of behavior as overlearning—when learners continues to practice a task even after it has been mastered to achieve a "ceiling" in their performance (Driskell, Copper, & Willis, 1992; Schmidt et al., 2019). Overlearning can free up a learner's attentional space and allow them to be more flexible in the moment of performance or more able to react to secondary tasks. It can also lead to being able to perform with more efficiency of movement/less effort and result in an ability to recall information from memory more quickly. Last, overlearning can also result in better long-term retention and thus allow a learner to refresh a skill to regain mastery more quickly after a period of time away.

Whole-part practice

Whole-part practice is a specific type of chunking behavior wherein a musician rehearses a passage, identifies a specific learning objective to isolate within the passage, rehearses the specific learning objective, and then re-contextualizes the specific learning objective within the whole passage with further repetition. Like chaining, whole-part practice tends to be correlated with performance achievement (Miksza, 2006, 2007, 2011b). This strategy may be beneficial because it recognizes the oftentimes serial nature of memory. For example, one way to conceive of the ability to perform a passage of music is to imagine it as a series of motor programs that have been stored as procedural memories and are recalled and executed in a particular order (i.e., from beginning to end). If the passage is repeated from beginning to end often enough, then executing the first bits of the series can become memory cues for recalling the next bits, and so on. If an error in the middle of the passage has been stored in memory, it is likely to be stored in such a way that it is associated with the materials that immediately precede and follow it. Executing repetitions and correcting the isolated bit that was performed wrong without also rehearsing it again within the broader context of the passage would fail to account for the serial nature of how the passage is stored in memory. Therefore, it's possible that when the performer returns to the beginning of the passage, the materials immediately preceding the error would cue the "old" error again rather than the more recently stored "corrected" version of the skill.

The contextual interference effect

Musicians often strive for a path of least resistance via the reduction of cognitive load when it comes to repetitive practice. However, researchers have found that it can sometimes be beneficial for the retention of skill to actually introduce additional challenge when engaging in repetitive practice—a phenomenon motor learning theorists call the *contextual interference effect*. For example, a musician aiming to master three tasks might intuitively schedule their practice of these tasks in bundles of repetitions, or what researchers would refer to as blocks of repetitions, such that they engaged in a block of repetitions of task A first, then a block of task B second, and a block of task C third. However, the contextual interference effect suggests that mixing repetitions of these tasks up, that is, interleaving them by repeating sequences of task A, task B, and task C contiguously rather than multiple repetitions of each task before moving on to the next, could be more beneficial for long-term retention (J. B. Shea & Morgan, 1979; Stambaugh, 2011). For example, a blocked pattern could be represented as "AAA BBB CCC," whereas an interleaved pattern could be represented as "ABC ABC ABC." Interestingly, blocked practice seems to lead to quicker, more immediate skill acquisition than interleaved practice—and therefore can be tempting—but interleaved practice leads to better long-term retention. See Figure 8.1 for a visualization of this effect based on exaggerated hypothetical data.

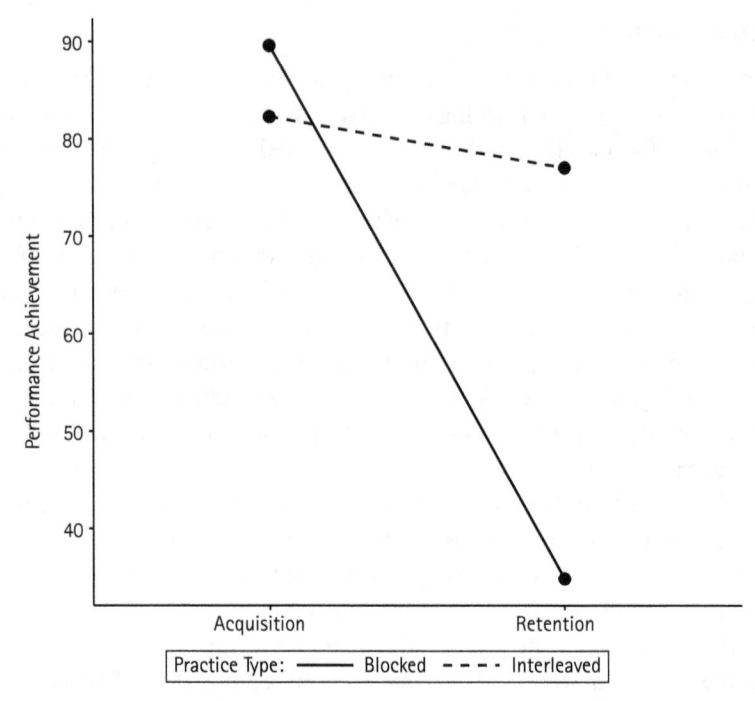

FIGURE 8.1. An illustration of the relative benefits of blocked vs. interleaved practice on performance achievement with hypothetical exaggerated data.

One possible reason for the benefits of interleaved practicing for retention is that switching tasks forces a learner to compare and contrast the tasks in their memory when processing and encoding information, and therefore leads them to build a more robust mental representation of each—an explanation referred to as the *elaboration hypothesis*. Another view, known as the *reconstruction hypothesis*, is that the task switching may be beneficial simply because it forces the learner to retrieve and reconstruct the task more often in working memory. For example, the information for planning and executing task A held in working memory will be abandoned and replaced when switching to task B when interleaving tasks, whereas that is not the case with blocked practice repetitions. It is important to note that the contextual interference effect and the benefits of interleaved practice are sensitive to the cognitive load required for the tasks being practiced and the skill level of the learner. After all, if tasks are already too difficult for a learner, then adding more difficulty or extra processing demands would not likely be helpful.

Variation during practice

The benefits of task variation during practice repetition is not necessarily obvious, since musicians might wish to practice passages in their idealized forms (e.g., as written, as expected by an audience) in order to match the context of a future performance situation. However, researchers have demonstrated fairly clear and robust effects of varying the parameters of a task when repeating it (Miksza, 2006, 2011b; Nielsen, 1999; Shea & Kohl, 1990; Van Rossum, 1990; Welch, 1985). Theorists suggest that variation during practice facilitates the development of generalized motor programs that can be used to execute both the specific practice target that an individual is concerned with as well as a variety of other similar movements (Schmidt, 1975; Schmidt et al., 2019). There are many parameters that musicians could consider varying during repetitive practice that could be more or less suitable for specific learning objectives such as tempo, rhythm, articulation patterns, fingering patterns, dynamic patterns, and octave placement. Combining variation strategies with efforts to reduce cognitive load demands is also likely to be beneficial. For example, engaging in repetitions of only the rhythm of a passage while performing on one constant note or removing text from vocal passages and singing on a constant syllable are activities that could help to develop generalized motor programs while also reducing the complexity of tasks.

Conclusion

Seeking musical performance excellence requires a serious commitment to engaging in many hours of practice. Musicians looking to maximize the benefits they accrue through practice would be well-advised to consider the characteristics of deliberate practice and design their activities such that they are intentional and goal-directed with opportunities for feedback from knowledgeable others. Moreover, considering the nature and constraints of the human cognitive architecture when deciding how to apply such strategies and approaches is essential. Choosing to practice intelligently by selecting strategies and approaches for which empirical evidence exists can enhance the effectiveness of one's practice and result in more robust skill sets. Ultimately, exploiting the theories and research generalizations scientists have put forth can enable a learner to apply their efforts in much more directed and effective manner and, consequently, make it more likely that they will reach their goals.

Key Resources

Baddeley, A., Eysenck, M. W., & Anderson, M. C. (2019). *Memory* (2nd ed.). London: Taylor & Francis.

Ericsson, K. A., Hoffman, R. R., Kozbelt, A., & Williams, A. M. (Eds.). (2018). *The Cambridge handbook of expertise and expert performance.* New York: Cambridge University Press.

Schmidt, R. A., Lee, T. D., Winstein, C. J., Wulf, G., & Zelaznik, H. N. (2019). *Motor control and learning: A behavioral emphasis.* Champaign, IL: Human Kinetics.

Ward, P., Schraagen, J. M., Gore, J., & Roth, E. M. (2019). *The Oxford handbook of expertise.* New York: Oxford University Press.

Reflective Questions

1. How has the way you engage in practice evolved throughout your learning as a musician thus far, and to what extent do you believe your practice has reflected Ericsson and colleagues' definition of deliberate practice?

2. Given what you've learned about the way that human beings process information and learn, what aspects of your typical practice activities might not be as effective as you previously thought?

3. How have you worked to mitigate the cognitive load demands you've faced in the past? In what ways have you broken down difficult and complex tasks for more efficient practice?

4. Consider whether you maintain a disciplined, consistent schedule of distributed practice sessions with adequate rest. If you do not, what are the barriers that are preventing you from doing so and how could you change your habits?

5. Identify a set of learning objectives and design practice strategies that you could employ that are informed by motor learning principles described in the second main section of this chapter.

References

Altenmüller, E., & McPherson, G. E. (2007). Motor learning and instrumental training. In W. Gruhn & F. H. Rauscher (Eds.), *Neurosciences in Music Pedagogy* (pp. 121–142). New York: Nova Science Publishers. https://doi.org/10.1146/annurev.bioeng.6.040803.140223.

Baddeley, A., Eysenck, M. W., & Anderson, M. C. (2019). *Memory* (2nd ed.). London: Taylor & Francis.

Bandura, A. (1986). *Social foundations of thought and action: A social-cognitive theory*. Upper Saddle River, NJ: Prentice-Hall.

Beilock, S. L., & Carr, T. H. (2001). On the fragility of skilled performance: What governs choking under pressure? *Journal of Experimental Psychology: General, 130*, 701–725. https://doi.org/10.1037/0096-3445.130.4.701.

Brown, R. W. (1928). A comparative study of the "whole," "part" and "combination" methods of learning piano music. *Journal of Experimental Psychology, 11*, 235–247. https://doi.org/10.1037/h0071327.

Cahn, D. (2007). The effects of varying ratios of physical and mental practice, and task difficulty on performance of a tonal pattern. *Psychology of Music, 36*, 179–191. https://doi.org/10.1177/0305735607085011.

Cash, C. D. (2009). Effects of early and late rest intervals on performance and overnight consolidation of a keyboard sequence. *Journal of Research in Music Education, 57*, 252–266. https://doi.org/10.1177/0022429409343470.

Chaffin, R., & Logan, T. (2006). Practicing perfection: How concert soloists prepare for performance. *Advances in Cognitive Psychology, 2*, 113–130. https://doi.org/10.2478/v10053-008-0050-z.

Coffman, D. D. (1990). Effects of mental practice, physical practice, and knowledge of results on piano performance. *Journal of Research in Music Education, 38*, 187–196. https://doi.org/10.2307/3345182.

Cowan, N. (2010). The magical mystery four: How is working memory capacity limited, and why? *Current Directions in Psychological Science, 19*(1), 51–57. https://doi.org/10.1177/0963721409359277.

Donovan, J. J., & Radosevich, D. J. (1999). A meta-analytic review of the distribution of practice effect: Now you see it, now you don't. *Journal of Applied Psychology, 84*, 795–805. https://doi.org/10.1037/0021-9010.84.5.795.

Driskell, J. E., Copper, C., & Moran, A. (1994). Does mental practice enhance performance? *Journal of Applied Psychology, 79*, 481–492. https://doi.org/10.1037/0021-9010.79.4.481.

Driskell, J. E., Copper, C., & Willis, R. P. (1992). Effects of overlearning on retention. *Journal of Applied Psychology, 77*, 615–622. https://doi.org/10.1037/0021-9010.77.5.615.

Duke, R. A., Allen, S. E., Cash, C. D., & Simmons, A. L. (2009). Effects of early and late rest breaks during training on overnight memory consolidation of a keyboard melody. *Annals of the New York Academy of Sciences, 1169*, 169–172. https://doi.org/10.1111/j.1749-6632.2009.04795.x.

Duke, R. A., Cash, C. D., & Allen, S. E. (2011). Focus of attention affects performance of motor skills in music. *Journal of Research in Music Education, 59*, 44–55. https://doi.org/10.1177/0022429410396093.

Duke, R. A., & Davis, C. M. (2006). Procedural memory consolidation in the performance of brief keyboard sequences. *Journal of Research in Music Education, 54*, 111–124.

Duke, R. A., Simmons, A. L., & Cash, C. D. (2009). It's not how much; it's how: Characteristics of practice behavior and retention of performance skills. *Journal of Research in Music Education, 56*, 310–321. https://doi.org/10.1177/0022429408328851.

Ericsson, K. A., & Harwell, K. W. (2019). Deliberate practice and proposed limits on the effects of practice on the acquisition of expert performance: Why the original definition matters and recommendations for future research. *Frontiers in Psychology, 10*, 1–19. https://doi.org/10.3389/fpsyg.2019.02396.

Ericsson, K. A., Hoffman, R. R., Kozbelt, A., & Williams, A. M. (Eds.). (2018). *The Cambridge handbook of expertise and expert performance.* New York: Cambridge University Press.

Ericsson, K. A., Krampe, R., & Tesch-Römer, C. (1993). The role of deliberate practice in the acquisition of expert performance. *Psychological Review, 100*, 363–406. https://doi.org/10.1098/rsos.190327.

Ericsson, K. A., & Lehmann, A. C. (1996). Expert and exceptional performance: Evidence of maximal adaptation to task constraints. *Annual Review of Psychology, 47*, 273–305. https://doi.org/10.1146/annurev.psych.47.1.273.

Ericsson, K. A., & Pool, R. (2016a). *Peak: Secrets from the new science of expertise.* New York: Houghton-Mifflin.

Ericsson, K. A., & Pool, R. (2016b, April 10). Malcom Gladwell got us wrong: Our research was key to the 10,000-our rule, but here's what got oversimplified. *Salon* – see https://www.salon.com/2016/04/10/malcolm_gladwell_got_us_wrong_our_research_was_key_to_the_10000_hour_rule_but_heres_what_got_oversimplified/.

Fitts, P. M. (1954). The information capacity of the human motor system in controlling the amplitude of movement. *Journal of Experimental Psychology, 47*(6), 381–391.

Fitts, P. M., & Posner, M. I. (1967). *Human performance.* Oxford: Brooks/Cole.

Gladwell, M. (2008). *Outliers: The story of success.* New York: Hachette.

Granados, C., & Wulf, G. (2007). Enhancing motor learning through dyad practice: Contributions of observation and dialogue. *Research Quarterly for Exercise and Sport, 78*(3), 197–203. https://doi.org/10.1080/02701367.2007.10599417.

Gruson, L. M. (2001). Rehearsal skill and musical competence: Does practice make perfect? In J. A. Sloboda (Ed.), *Generative processes in music: The psychology of performance, improvisation, and composition* (pp. 1–33). New York: Oxford University Press. https://doi.org/DOI:10.1093/acprof:oso/9780198508465.003.0005.

Hambrick, D. Z., Campitelli, G., & Macnamara, B. N. (Eds.) (2017). *The science of expertise: Behavioral, neural, and genetic approaches to complex skill.* New York: Routledge.

Hambrick, D. Z., Macnamara, B. N., Campitelli, G., Ullén, F., & Mosing, M. A. (2016). Beyond born versus made: A new look at expertise. In B. H. Ross (Ed.), *Psychology of learning and motivation: Advances in research and theory* (Vol. 64, pp. 1–55). Oxford: Elsevier Ltd. https://doi.org/10.1016/bs.plm.2015.09.001.

Hambrick, D. Z., & Tucker-Drob, E. M. (2015). The genetics of music accomplishment: Evidence for gene-environment correlation and interaction. *Psychonomic Bulletin and Review, 22,* 112–120. https://doi.org/10.3758/s13423-014-0671-9.

Hamilton, L. M. (2017). *Perceptions of discrepancies between intentions and outcomes during music practice: Differences among musicians with varied levels of experience and expertise.* (Doctoral dissertation). University of Texas at Austin, Austin, TX. Retrieved from: https://repositories.lib.utexas.edu/handle/2152/62193.

Hewitt, M. P. (2001). The effects of modeling, self-evaluation, and self-listening on junior high instrumentalists' music performance and practice attitude. *Journal of Research in Music Education, 49,* 307–322. https://doi.org/10.2307/3345614.

Hewitt, M. P. (2011). The impact of self-evaluation instruction on student self-evaluation, music performance, and self-evaluation accuracy. *Journal of Research in Music Education, 59,* 6–20. https://doi.org/10.1177/0022429410391541.

Highben, Z., & Palmer, C. (2004). Effects of auditory and motor mental practice in memorized piano performance. *Bulletin of the Council for Research in Music Education, 159,* 58–65.

Jørgensen, H., & Hallam, S. (2016). Practicing. In S. Hallam, I. Cross, & M. Thaut (Eds.), *The Oxford handbook of music psychology* (2nd ed., pp. 449–462). New York: Oxford University Press.

Lehmann, A. C., & Ericsson, K. A. (1997a) Research on expert performance and deliberate practice: Implications for the education of amateur musicians and music students. *Psychomusicology: A Journal of Research in Music Cognition, 16,* 40–58. https://doi.org/10.1037/h0094068.

Lehmann, A. C, & Ericsson, K. A. (1997b). Expert pianists' mental representations: Evidence from successful adaptation to unexpected performance demands. In A. Gabrielsson (Ed.), *Proceedings of the 3rd triennial ESCOM conference* (pp. 165–169). Uppsala University, Sweden.

Linklater, F. (1997). Effects of audio- and videotape models on performance achievement of beginning clarinetists. *Journal of Research in Music Education, 45,* 402–414. https://doi.org/10.2307/3345535.

Lotze, M., & Halsband, U. (2006). Motor imagery. *Journal of Physiology–Paris, 99*(4–6), 386–395. https://doi.org/10.1016/j.jphysparis.2006.03.012.

Macnamara, B. N., Hambrick, D. Z., & Moreau, D. (2016). How important is deliberate practice? Reply to Ericsson (2016). *Perspectives on Psychological Science, 11,* 355–358. https://doi.org/10.1177/1745691616635614.

Macnamara, B. N., Hambrick, D. Z., & Oswald, F. L. (2014). Deliberate practice and performance in music, games, sports, education, and professions: A meta-analysis. *Psychological Science, 25*(8), 1608–1618. https://doi.org/10.1177/0956797614535810.

Madsen, C., & Geringer, J. (1981). The effect of a distraction index on improving practice attentiveness and musical performance. *Bulletin of the Council for Research in Music Education, 66/67*, 46–52.

Maynard, L. M. (2006). The role of repetition in the practice sessions of artist teachers and their students. *Bulletin of the Council for Research in Music Education, 167*, 61–72.

McCullagh, P., & Weiss, M. (2001). Modeling: Considerations for motor skill performance and psychological responses. In R. N. Singer, H. A. Hausenblas, & C. M. Janelle, (Eds.), *Handbook of sport psychology* (pp. 205–238). New York: Wiley.

Miksza, P. (2006). Relationships among impulsiveness, locus of control, sex, and music practice. *Journal of Research in Music Education, 54*, 308–323. https://doi.org/10.1177/002242940605400404.

Miksza, P. (2007). Effective practice: An investigation of observed practice behaviors, self-reported practice habits, and the performance achievement of high school wind players. *Journal of Research in Music Education, 55*, 359–375. https://doi.org/10.1177/0022429408317513.

Miksza, P. (2011a). A review of research on practicing: Summary and synthesis of the extant research with implications for a new theoretical orientation. *Bulletin of the Council for Research in Music Education, 190*, 51–92.

Miksza, P. (2011b). Relationships among achievement goal motivation, impulsivity, and the music practice of collegiate brass and woodwind players. *Psychology of Music, 39*, 50–67. https://doi.org/10.1177/0305735610361996.

Miksza, P., Blackwell, J., & Roseth, N. E. (2018). Self-regulated music practice: Microanalysis as a data collection technique and inspiration for pedagogical intervention. *Journal of Research in Music Education, 66*(3), 295–319. https://doi.org/10.1177/0022429418788557.

Miller, G. A. (1956). The magical number seven, plus or minus two: Some limits on our capacity for processing information. *Psychological Review, 63*, 81–97.

Mornell, A., & Wulf, G. (2019). Adopting an external focus of attention enhances musical performance. *Journal of Research in Music Education, 66*, 375–391. https://doi.org/10.1177/0022429418801573.

Nielsen, S. G. (1999). Learning strategies in instrumental music practice. *British Journal of Music Education, 16*(3), 275–291. https://doi.org/10.1080/14613800120089223.

Ormrod, J. E. (2020). *Human learning* (8th ed.). Pearson.

Rosenthal, R. K. (1984). The relative effects of guided model, model only, guide only, and practice only treatments on the accuracy of advanced instrumentalists' musical performance. *Journal of Research in Music Education, 32*, 265–273. https://doi.org/10.2307/3344924.

Ross, S. L. (1985). The effectiveness of mental practice in improving the performance of college trombonists. *Journal of Research in Music Education, 33*, 221–230. https://doi.org/10.2307/3345249.

Rubin-Rabson, G. (1939). Studies in the psychology of memorizing piano music. IV. The effect of incentive. *Journal of Educational Psychology, 30*(5), 321–345. https://doi.org/10.1037/h0061124.

Schmidt, R. A. (1975). A schema theory of discrete motor skill learning. *Psychological Review, 82*(4), 225–260. https://doi.org/10.1037/h0076770.

Schmidt, R. A., Lee, T. D., Winstein, C. J., Wulf, G., & Zelaznik, H. N. (2019). *Motor control and learning: A behavioral emphasis*. Champaign, IL: Human Kinetics.

Shea, C. H., & Kohl, R. M. (1990). Specificity and variability of practice. *Research Quarterly for Exercise and Sport, 61*(2), 169–177. https://doi.org/10.1080/02701367.1990.10608671.

Shea, J. B., & Morgan, R. L. (1979). Contextual interference effects on the acquisition, retention, and transfer of a motor skill. *Journal of Experimental Psychology: Human Learning and Memory, 5*(2), 179–187. https://doi.org/10.2466/pms.1999.88.2.437.

Sikes, P. L. (2013). The effects of specific practice strategy use on university string players' performance. *Journal of Research in Music Education, 61*, 318–333. https://doi.org/10.1177/0022429413497225.

Stambaugh, L. A. (2011). When repetition isn't the best practice strategy: Effects of blocked and random practice schedules. *Journal of Research in Music Education, 58*, 368–383. https://doi.org/10.1177/0022429410385945.

Suh, H. A. (Ed.) (2005). *Leonardo's notebooks*. New York: Black Dog & Leventhal.

Sweller, J. (1988). Cognitive load during problem solving: Effects on learning. *Cognitive Science, 12*(2), 257–285. https://doi.org/10.1016/0364-0213(88)90023-7.

Sweller, J. (2011). Cognitive load theory. In J. P. Mestre & B. H. Ross (Eds.), *The psychology of learning and motivation* (Vol. 55, pp. 37–76). https://doi.org/10.1016/B978-0-12-387691-1.00002-8.

Sweller, J., Ayres, P., & Kalyuga, S. (2011). *Cognitive load theory*. New York: Springer.

Ullén, F., Mosing, M. A., & Madison, G. (2015). Associations between motor timing, music practice, and intelligence studied in a large sample of twins. *Annals of the New York Academy of Sciences, 1337*(1), 125–129. https://doi.org/10.1111/nyas.12630.

VanderArk, S., & Murphy, E. (1998). Effects of traditional physical, mental, mental with physical, and physical with singing practice on instrumental music performances. *Southeastern Journal of Music Education, 10*, 50–55.

Van Rossum, J. H. A. (1990). Schmidt's schema theory: The empirical base of the variability of practice hypothesis. A critical analysis. *Human Movement Science, 9*(3–5), 387–435. https://doi.org/10.1016/0167-9457(90)90010-B.

Welch, G. F. (1985). Variability of practice and knowledge of results as factors in learning to sing in tune. *Bulletin of the Council for Research in Music Education, 85*, 238–247.

Williamon, A., & Valentine, E. (2000). Quantity and quality of musical practice as predictors of performance quality. *British Journal of Psychology, 91*, 353–376. https://doi.org/10.1348/000712600161871.

Wulf, G. (2013). Attentional focus and motor learning: A review of 15 years. *International Review of Sport and Exercise Psychology, 6*(1), 77–104. https://doi.org/10.1080/1750984X.2012.723728.

Wulf, G., McNevin, N., & Shea, C. H. (2001). The automaticity of complex motor skill learning as a function of attentional focus. *Quarterly Journal of Experimental Psychology Section A: Human Experimental Psychology, 54*(4), 1143–1154. https://doi.org/10.1080/713756012.

CHAPTER 9

··

PLAYING BY EAR

··

WARREN HASTON AND GARY E. MCPHERSON

INTRODUCTION

WHEN musicians play "by ear," they are reproducing music they have learned aurally, without having seen or read the notation in any form of visual representation. In this way, playing by ear is different from playing from memory, where the musician learns the piece from written notation, and then performs this work without the aid of notation at the time of the performance.

It is self-evident that Western art music relies heavily on written notation, and that this aspect of literacy is fundamental when performing within this genre of music. This is not the case in many other genres of music or musical cultures, however, where the process of learning to perform repertoire is focused on mimicking other musicians and listening to live or recorded models in preparation for reproducing this on an instrument. Throughout the world, there are a number of musical cultures in which performing "by ear" is the sole means of learning and performing music.

The basic differences between playing music by ear and other forms of performance are shown in Figure 9.1. In many forms of playing by ear, the musician reproduces an existing piece of repertoire, or a variation of the original. Thus, an important distinction to consider when conceptualizing how musicians play music by ear is the degree to which they change the aural model when performing the piece back on their instrument. The distinction between improvising (creating something new) or extemporizing (elaborating or embellishing an existing version of a work) is much harder to define, because most performances "by ear" inevitably encompass at least some variation of the music into a distinctly individual style, whether by performing with a different interpretation or feel, embellishing the melodic line, or changing the accompaniment or key/register in which the performance takes place. Because no notation is used during the process of learning or performing the work, playing by ear involves an aural emphasis in which the performer transfers an aural representation into appropriate instrumental

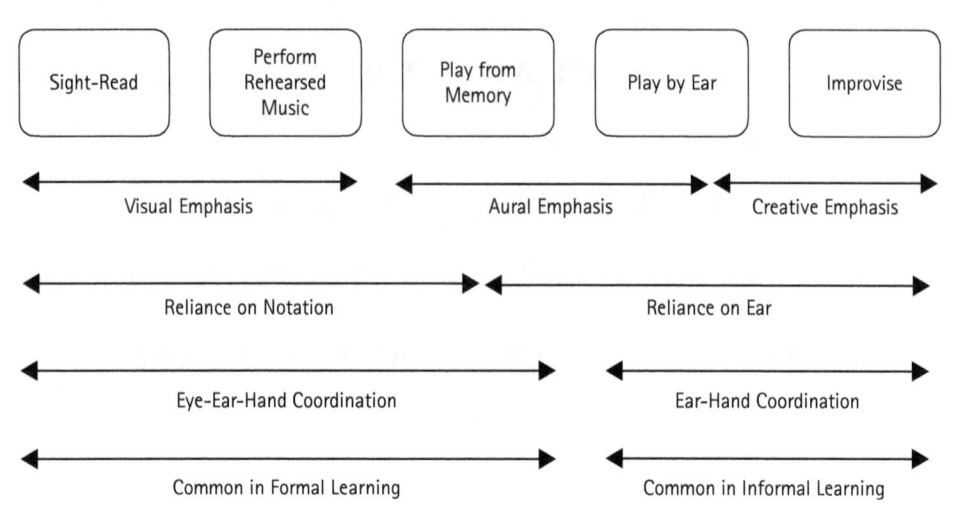

FIGURE 9.1. Modes of performing music.

fingerings and techniques, a skill music educators sometimes refer to as ear-to-hand co-ordination (Froseth, 1985; Humphreys, 1984, 1986; Markovich, 1985).

Much of the literature on informal musical learning processes shows that the music performed "by ear" is most often already familiar to musicians before they start learning it, either through being surrounded by other musicians who perform the particular reper-toire, as a result of participating in some sort of social grouping who are enthusiastic about that style of music, by listening to the music individually on the radio or in recordings, by being a member of a friendship group who choose some and not other styles of music, or through individual choices made by musicians about the particular types of music they wish to perform (Green & Smart, 2017). Another key distinction is that the social group within which the musician is a member typically experience high levels of enjoyment and appreciation for the music being performed. Typically, they display a strong affinity and identity with this style of music by listening first, and then aurally copying it by piecing it together using a call-and-response format after a more stable mental blueprint has been formed (Green & Smart, 2017). This distinction is markedly different from scenarios where students learn instruments within formal settings where the focus is on an organ-ized curriculum, syllabi, examinations, gaining formal qualifications; or where learning occurs with a specialist teacher who provides individual or small group lessons.

Informal approaches to learning and performing music often rely on "ear playing" and paying close attention to musical parameters that are often not addressed in learning via notation, such as "playing with 'feel,' 'swing,' 'sensitive phrasing,' 'sensitive touch,' or just the ephemeral notion of 'playing musically'" (Green & Smart, 2017 p. 431).

In this chapter we will discuss the value of playing by ear both as a skill that musicians can gain in competence and apply within their practice and performing, and as a tool for enhancing the learning of a musical instrument or voice, no matter what genre of music is being learned.

HISTORICAL OVERVIEW

The value of playing by ear as a pedagogical tool can be seen in the evolution of Western art music, particularly up until the mid-nineteenth century when the teaching of instruments was passed from one generation of musicians to the next through a form of musical apprenticeship that did not separate technical practice from more general musical skills. Developing an all-round musician occurred through the integration of technique with other aspects of general musicianship (Gellrich & Parncutt, 1998), with scales and arpeggios serving as a means of learning the common vocabulary of the musical language. In cases where passages were practiced in isolation from the music, it was for the purpose of developing a range of musical skills, such as sight-reading, improvisation, or composition. Beginners were typically taught pieces "by ear," rather than by reading musical notation through rote learning and imitating the teacher's model, or through the reconstruction of familiar music that had been internalized by repeated hearings or singing. As skills developed, learners were encouraged to invent their own passages in order to develop the expressive and technical skills needed to master the musical language of the repertoire being learned (Gellrich & Sundin, 1993; McPherson & Gabrielsson, 2002).

This system of learning music was disrupted in the early to mid-1800s when high-speed printing machines made it possible for the production of relatively cheap scores to be produced in large numbers. From the second half of the nineteenth century, these publications became commercially available, with the result that the nature of learning to perform changed dramatically. The previous emphasis on developing skills in interpretation, improvisation, and composition swiftly changed to music as a reproductive art in which technique, interpretation, and reproducing music directly from the written notation were emphasized (Gellrich & Parncutt, 1998). The result was a rapid expansion of published exercise and methods books, an emphasis on technical skills, and approaches to practice that focused on the repetition of exercises during practice.

Even today, many beginning instrumental books stress drill and technical material such as scales, rhythms, articulations, and finger exercises rather than material of real melodic interest (Haston, 2007; Musco, 2010; Schleuter, 1997). Another common trend across more than the past 150 years was to organize beginning method books according to the proportionality of note values whereby students were first taught a series of whole notes and whole note rests, before graduating to half notes/rests, quarter notes/rests, and eventually eighth and sixteenth notes and rests (Schleuter, 1997). Thankfully, most contemporary method books now emphasize the learning of repertoire, even though the predominant approach is focused on the re-creation of music through a process of learning to read and develop technical skill from the very first lesson. Much current beginner pedagogy, however, is still focused on associating fingerings with notation rather than fingerings with sound, emphasizing note naming and theoretical concepts more than perceptual understandings, and separating technical skill from the process of learning to play actual music (McPherson & Gabrielsson, 2002). All of this tends to reinforce the notion of performance as a specialist craft in which technical development and knowledge of notation are valued above all else, and this has led to the unfortunate consequence that musical practice and the learning process have become visually dominant rather than aurally based. Some student flourish in this context, but many have found this emphasis boring and uninspiring (McPherson & Gabrielsson, 2002).

A Natural Learning Process

In the twentieth century, Suzuki (1983) developed his *mother tongue* pedagogical approach, which sought to parallel language acquisition, whereby students learn songs by ear in the beginning stages of their learning, and only after achieving some technical facility on their instrument begin to combine this with decoding notation and reading pieces from traditional staff notation. This approach has been extended and advocated by a number of prominent music educators who support the idea that removing the complication of learning to decode notation from the already complicated task of learning to physically manipulate an instrument will enhance the learning process, and lead to better outcomes because of a focus on reinforcing sound rather than the connection between notated symbols and fingerings (Kohut, 1985; Schleuter, 1997).

To explain this further, we can think of music and language sharing four types of vocabularies: listening, speaking, reading, and writing (Gordon, 2012). Children listen to language for many months and then draw upon this information when they begin to speak. After many more months, they begin to read and then write. It is their familiarity with language from years of listening and speaking that enables them to more efficiently learn to read and write more efficiently. "Just as listening to language prepares children to speak, listening and speaking prepare them to read and write. The four vocabularies form a chain, with proficiency at the earlier levels giving the learner stress-free entry to the next level" (Liperote, 2006, p. 47). As language readers hear in their heads what they are reading, so too musicians can hear in their heads what they are visually decoding. Music literacy is achieved and maintained at all levels of skill development by following this same sequence. Following the language learning sequence allows students to engage in aural activities that focus, for example, on tonality, meter, style, and patterns prior to the added complication of physically manipulating an instrument. Both language and music listeners perceive patterns, not individual letters and words or notes and rhythms (Dowling & Harwood, 1986). Once they have developed a good vocabulary from listening, a learner is able to comprehend music by associating each new visual symbol with a recognizable aural experience (Liperote, 2006, p. 51).

To extend this point further, we might consider the challenges beginners face as they attend to integrate knowledge from a number of sources. Like reading text, learning to decode musical notation is a complex skill that in the beginning stages involves processes that are not instant and automatic but rather conscious and deliberate

(Samuels, 1994). However, unlike reading, in which a novice can focus on decoding the visual symbols, learning to perform music involves two competing and non-automated tasks: learning to read musical notation at the same time as learning to manipulate an instrument. In this type of situation, there are constraints on the amount of information a beginner can think about at any one time, how long they will be able to hold it in their mind before it is lost, and how quickly they can process new information (Shaffer, 1999; Sweller, van Merrienboer, & Paas, 1998). To complicate this even further, vision tends to dominate and inhibit the processing of signals from other modalities (Posner, Nissen, & Klein, 1976; Witten & Knudsen, 2005; Stokes, Matthen, & Biggs, 2014). Consequently, when children's attention is focused on notation reading, they may have few cognitive resources left to devote to manipulating their instrument and listening to what they are playing.

READINESS TO LEARN NOTATION

The foregoing ideas can be contrasted with teaching that introduces notation from the earliest lessons. Children as young as three can develop a basic understanding of the pitch elements of musical notation and relate this to the piano keyboard (Tommis & Fazey, 1999), so the issue is not whether young children can learn to read notation at an early age, but whether they should learn it so early.

Again, by comparing the acquisition of literacy skills in language with music, we can see that no sensible person would consider teaching children to read while they are still learning to speak, yet this occurs often in teaching children to play an instrument (Sloboda, 1978). By the time children enter year one at school, they are typically in command of their own language to the extent that they are able to perceive and use a vocabulary in excess of 5,000 words, which they can use as the basis from which to begin associating familiar words with the symbols that represent them (Bruning, Schraw, & Norby, 2011; McGeown, Osborne, Warhurst, Norgate, & Duncan, 2016). Learning typically starts with the child "sounding out" individual letters, spelling patterns and words, and then beginning to recognize the spelling, sound, and meaning of particular words. Over time they are able to comprehend the meaning of complex sentences (Adams, 1994). Adopting the same process in music learning would involve teaching children to perform familiar tunes "by ear" before they learn to "sound out" tunes they already know using notation. This is why many music educators advocate teaching known tunes "by ear" in familiar keys before the notation of these melodies are introduced to the child (e.g., Mainwaring, 1951; Kohut, 1985; Schleuter, 1997; Suzuki, 1983).

As a final comparison between language and music literacy, we can highlight the importance of metalinguistic abilities of children who are learning to read. Before they start to read, children possess a huge knowledge about the uses of print, including how sounds can be represented in letters and words, how letters and words can be put together to form sentences, and how these sentences can convey information or tell a story

(Bruning, Schraw, & Norby, 2011). Such awareness enables them to create meaning by mapping the visual symbols of written language onto their oral language.

Similarly, before children are able to fully process and comprehend musical notation, they need to have developed an awareness of why notation is important, how sound is represented by symbols, how phrases are formed and flow on from each other, and how melodies function within the larger landscape of a musical work. In this way, learning to play a musical instrument involves more than linking visual cues with instrumental fingerings, to avoid producing button-pushers "to whom notation only indicates what fingers to put down rather than what sounds are desired" (Schleuter, 1997, p. 48). The effective learning of an instrument therefore involves teaching notation as a decoding process rather than recognition process (Spears, 2014).

This point was highlighted by Mainwaring (1951), who proposed a simple but powerful model depicting how literacy should be developed (see Figure 9.2). For Mainwaring, most teaching of literacy skills occurs by seeing the symbol, reacting to this symbol by moving the fingers on the instrument, and then hearing the sound. Instead, "true" musicianship occurs when a musician is able to see the symbol, hear the sound, and then move the fingers (see also Odam, 1995). The two contrasting cycles of symbol-action-sound versus symbol-sound-action are depicted in Figure 9.2.

All of these points have been reinforced by Bamberger's (1996, 1999, 2006) studies with instrumentalists who are learning to reproduce songs "by ear." In her groundbreaking work, Bamberger observed that when learning to play "by ear," musicians tend to perform the work according to structural units, such as an entire phrase. They do not construct the piece note by note. Instead, they rewind their mental tape recorders to the beginning of a phrase every time they make a mistake or try to piece the tune together. Because of this, Bamberger (1996, 2006) advocates that young learners should first gain experience in playing musical patterns before they learn to decontextualize these patterns into individual notes. This is because the "units of perception" that these beginning instrumentalists intuitively attend to when processing music are "structurally meaningful entities such as motives, figures, and phrases," not individual notes (p. 42).

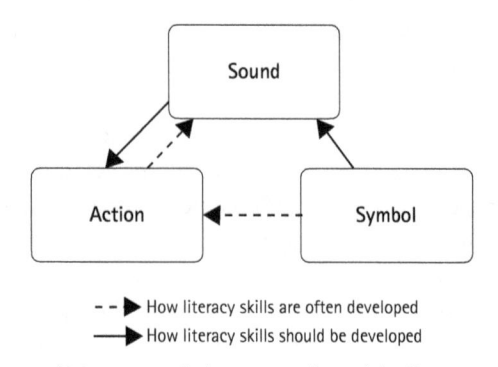

— ▶ How literacy skills are often developed
──▶ How literacy skills should be developed

FIGURE 9.2. Illustration of Mainwaring's (1951, p. 201) model of literacy development.

This evidence can be compared with how beginners taught using a method book approach typically correct performance errors when reading notation. In the earliest stages of learning a new piece, they will often stumble over individual notes and continue playing, sometimes so slowly or hesitantly that they no longer perceive the music they are attempting to play as a complete phrase (McPherson, 1993; McPherson & Renwick, 2000). These types of beginners find it confusing and frustrating to learn music in this way, especially in situations where they are taught to "start out by listening for, looking at, and identifying the smallest, isolated objects" and to "classify and measure with no context or functional meaning" (Bamberger, 1996, p. 43). Asking beginners to focus on notation too early, according to Bamberger (1996), means asking them to "put aside their most intimate ways of knowing—figures, felt paths, context and function" (p. 44). In this way, too early an emphasis on notation can lead to a decreased aural sensitivity for the natural musical "Gestalts" or unified patterns that children spontaneously observe when listening to music.

MOTOR PRODUCTION

To this point, our discussion has emphasized the value for musicians to learn to coordinate their ears and their fingers. Playing by ear requires aural discrimination skills and the alignment of concomitant motor skills: goal imaging, motor production, and self-monitoring. Linking that goal image to motor production is key. When reading notation, the visual cues should bring to mind sounds that are already cognitively linked to the instrumental action needed" (Woody, 2012, p. 85). With this in mind, a number of studies have examined whether goal image or motor production was the cause of ear-playing difficulties for a musician. These examine whether musicians who have learned in a formal manner (i.e., classically trained, one-on-one studio lessons, traditional methods books) are any different from musicians who have learned more informally (i.e., learning to play by ear and improvise, less emphasis on notation). In one of these studies comparing both groups learning pieces by ear, informally trained musicians employed a more automatic process, required fewer repetitions, and relied on harmonic knowledge to repeat melodies they described as predictable or typical. Classically trained musicians, on the other hand, thought more in terms of melodic intervals and committed more conscious attention to how the melodies would be fingered and physically reproduced on their instrument (Woody & Lehmann, 2010). Results of these types of studies reinforce the importance for musicians to aurally represent sound so that they can generate goal images that can guide the way they coordinate their ear and their hands.

Similarly, formal musicians tend to consciously focus on the mechanics of playing the melody such as the fingerings, slide positions, or mallet strokes when playing back short melodies by ear (Woody, 2012). In contrast, informal musicians tend to move more automatically from the mental image to motor production. And finally, vocally reproducing melodies by ear is also easier than instrumental reproduction, because it is more closely connected to the musicians' goal images and therefore requires one fewer step as compared to performing the musical image on an instrument (Woody & Lehmann, 2010). The creation of a mixed model teaching culture—capitalizing on the advantages of both formal and informal music practices—may encourage more people to make music (Green, 2002).

AURAL IMAGERY

What musicians hear inwardly when reading music—aural imagery—has some parallels to what they hear inwardly when they read words (Drai-Zerbib et al., 2011). When we silently read words, we see and then hear them inwardly to ourselves. Subconsciously, we practice aural imagery of words almost constantly, and that improves our reading and speaking skills. Musicians develop aural imagery of music when reading music, and practicing that skill improves their playing-by-ear ability because they become increasingly able to develop aural images without the aid of notation. Neuroimaging research shows similar brain activity when music is being heard and imagined, thus suggesting that a musician can "hear" correct pitches and "feel" correct muscular movements when practicing music mentally (Alluri, et al., 2017; Gordon, Cobb, & Balasubramaniam, 2018). This combination of hearing the note in combination with feeling how it would be performed on an instrument reminds us of the continual cross-modal processing that occurs in instrumental performance (Woody, 2012; Ross, 1985). Further research has shown that mental practice away from an instrument can be as productive as physical practice (see Miksza, this part).

AN INTEGRATED MODEL

Our review has focused on studies that provide evidence of the importance of learning to play by ear in the beginning stage of learning an instrument. Other research helps to clarify the beneficial effects of ear playing on subsequent development. In a series of longitudinal studies, McPherson (McPherson, 1993; McPherson, Bailey, & Sinclair, 1997; McPherson, Davidson, & Faulkner, 2012) examined the relationship among five different aspects of musical performance and environmental variables that prior research suggested may influence their development. The instrumentalists he worked with were beginners through to advanced-level high school students. In the earliest part of his research, McPherson (1993) employed a particular form of statistical analysis called "path analysis" to bring together information he had collated through detailed interviews with the learners, their teachers, and their parents, with evaluation of their progress as musicians according to five distinct aspects of performing: sight-reading, performing rehearsed music, playing from memory, playing by ear, and improvising.

Interviews with and surveys of the students, teachers, and parents focused on four types of information. *Early Exposure* described variables related to the quality and quantity of the students' early exposure to music, such as when and how they started learning, how long they had been playing, and whether they had learned another instrument before commencing. *Enriching Activities* grouped variables associated with reports of how frequently the learners played "by ear," improvised, as well as whether they were taking classroom music at school in which composing was an important component. Students who reported higher average levels of daily practice were more likely to report higher levels of these types of "informal" activities. *Length of Study* included variables associated with the period the student had been playing their instrument and taking private lessons. Finally, *Quality of Study* included the subjects' report of their interest and participation in various forms of singing, the number of ensembles they were performing with, and a report of how often they mentally rehearsed music in their minds away from their instruments.

McPherson reviewed available literature in order to develop a theoretical model that he could test empirically using results from the school students' performances and interviews (see Figure 9.3).

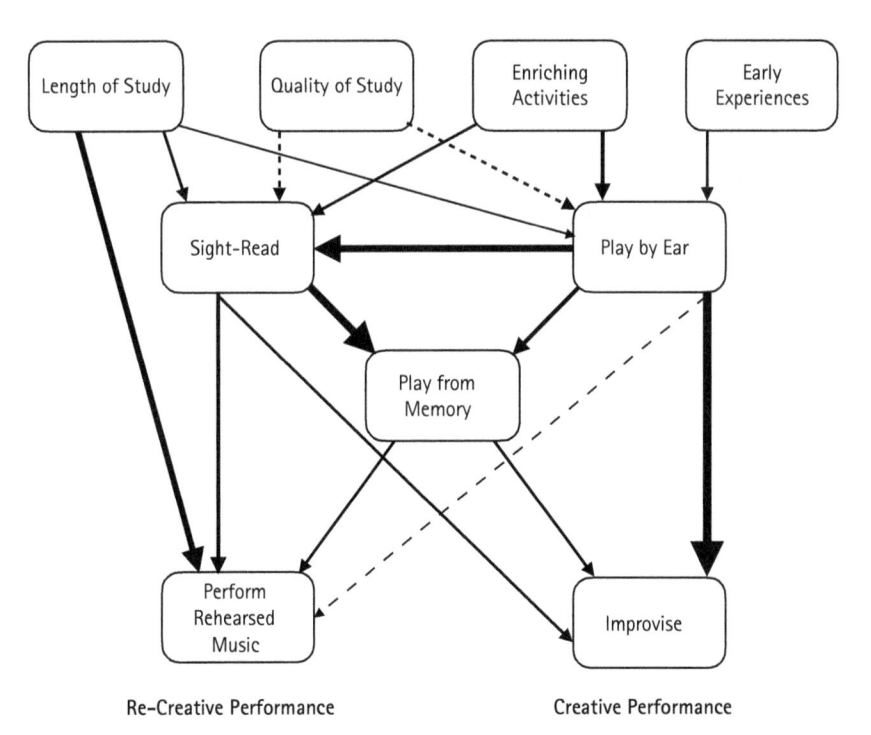

FIGURE 9.3. Path analysis of the McPherson (1993) theoretical model. In the simplified path diagram, path coefficients have been replaced by lines of differing thickness. Thicker lines represent stronger influences and thinner lines weaker relationships from one variable to the next, as shown by the direction of the arrow (see McPherson & Gabrielsson, 2002).

Results from the analysis and related literature indicated that the model was robust and defensible and fits nicely with the data he obtained. As shown in Figure 9.3, the model implies both direct and indirect effects. Direct effects are the unmediated relation between two variables (e.g., the influence of playing "by ear" on improvising is shown by a direct arrow). Indirect effects are the relation between two variables that are mediated by one or more other variables (e.g., the influence of playing by ear on improvising is also mediated through its effect on sight-reading and playing from memory). (A complete explanation is available in McPherson, 1993; McPherson, Bailey, & Sinclair, 1997.)

Early Exposure exerted a positive influence on the instrumentalists' ability to play "by ear" but far less impact on their ability to sight-read. *Enriching Activities*, which included variables concerned with how often the instrumentalists played "by ear" and improvised during their practice, had a stronger impact on the skill of playing "by ear" than for sight-reading. *Quality of Study* had only a weak influence on the abilities of playing "by ear" and sight-reading. Likewise, *Length of Study* had a consistently moderate influence on performing rehearsed music, sight-reading, and playing music "by ear".

The relationships shown in Figure 9.3 indicate that the skill of improvising was most strongly influenced by the capacity of the musicians to play "by ear." In contrast, performing rehearsed music was most heavily influenced by the variables associated with *Length of Study*, plus the players' ability to sight-read.

Analysis of comments made by the less capable players show that they tended to use strategies that were independent of their instrument when preparing to play "by ear" (e.g., "While I listened to the tape I was trying to think in terms of what letter names the notes might be"). In contrast, more capable musicians were able to connect what they heard on the taped performances with the instrumental fingerings needed to execute these thoughts (e.g., "I just sing it in my head while I finger it through on my instrument").

The strong relationship McPherson (1993) reports between the students' ability to play "by ear" and sight-read is consistent with previous evidence (Luce, 1965; Priest, 1989) and the assertion that ear-playing may be more beneficial to the development of musicianship than sight-reading and also more receptive to training. These results also support psychological and pedagogical assertions that the skill of playing "by ear" helps student musicians learn to coordinate ear, eye, and hand, and to perform on their instrument what they see in notation and hear or imagine in their mind.

PRACTICAL IMPLICATIONS

Two broad practical implications flow from this section's discussion. The first relates to the value of playing by ear in the early stages of learning to perform music, and benefits that can occur when learners are exposed to a "sound before sign" approach. The second concerns the value of playing by ear for experienced, capable musicians, and how the further development of this skill can enrich a performer's musical abilities beyond the focus of playing music from notation.

Developmental level

Since children start learning an instrument at widely different ages, at least some comments are appropriate about developmental issues. Bruning, Schraw, and Norby (2011) explain that there are obvious developmental limits to how early children can be taught to read their language, but that most children start formal reading around the age of six, after they have gained a great deal of prior experience in the use of their native tongue and reached the mental age necessary to maximize their success as readers. By this time their home experiences will have typically prepared them through hundreds of hours of storybook experience and general guidance about the form and nature of print, and since the advent of the digital age, many more hours of written text through their exposure to electronic devices such as iPads and computers (Adams, 1994; Rideout, 2014).

Obviously, a great deal of music learning takes place prior to formal lessons, and even very young children will come to their lessons having heard a vast amount of music in their everyday lives. However, the extent of a six-year-old child's knowledge about how music can be represented in notation will typically be nowhere near the level of their understanding for how language can be represented in print. For this reason, there appears to be enough evidence to speculate that an emphasis on reading musical notation should not occur until a child is at least six or seven. Up until this age, it is best for teachers to emphasize rote teaching of pieces learned "by ear" in order to establish the important ear-to-hand coordination skills that provide a foundation for introducing notation later. In general, we believe that this rule should be extended to older age groups, although the length of time before introducing notation can be shortened, depending on how quickly the learner develops the necessary aural awareness and technical security on their instrument for them to be able to comprehend notation.

Pre-notation activities

In our view, two types of activities provide the foundation from which literacy skills can be developed. First, during the early months (or weeks for older learners) of training, familiar pieces can be introduced by rote and repeated listening. At this stage, singing and then playing familiar repertoire is an important developmental activity for beginners. Singing (either mentally or aloud) is useful because it helps to establish a correct mental model that can guide the translation from what has been memorized to the instrumental fingerings needed to perform the work on an instrument. Singing should occur often and form a natural part of all early lessons. However, it should be noted that students need to progress from singing to linking singing with the fingerings needed to perform the piece on their instrument. Mentally and outwardly rehearsing (singing and fingering) a piece "by ear" develops a child's ability to experience sounds through gestures and touch, as well as helps to integrate the body with the mind (Galvao & Kemp, 1999). The use of solfège can also be useful in reinforcing this transition from memorization (i.e., singing to a neutral syllable such as "la") to comprehension (i.e., singing using sol-fa syllables and/or instrumental fingerings).

Introducing notation

An appropriate sequence of introducing notation is to start with melodies the child has already learned by ear and then move to melodies that they have not learned but already know, before moving on to new unfamiliar repertoire that demands more sophisticated levels of processing. Notation should be introduced gradually, however, and in ways that challenge the child to consider how and why notation is used in music.

To elaborate further on all of these points, six general principles can be used to develop the wide range of skills needed for children to become musically literate. (These principles are modeled on the work of Bruning, Schraw, & Norby, 2011, pp. 255–256, whose comments on teaching children to read are reinterpreted here for beginning instrumental instruction):

1. *Approach the reading of notation as a meaningful activity*: Reading musical notation is a "meaning-making" act. Although children need to learn to decode notation, and know, for example, that a quarter note is one beat in length, their developing skills need to be linked to structurally meaningful entities such as phrases and melodies rather than to individual notes. Children can lose track of the purpose of learning to read notation when the focus of their attention is on decoding signs and visual representations, in terms of individual note values and theoretical relationships (e.g., understanding the proportions of note values or scale-pitch relationships). They need to be continually reminded of the basic reasons for acquiring music reading skills—learning, communicating, and enjoyment.

2. *Take a broad perspective on literacy development*: Functional literacy, in terms of knowing where to put one's fingers as a result of seeing a visual cue on the score, represents only a limited understanding of how to comprehend musical notation. Our goal should be to instill competence in the use of notation for all forms of thinking and expression. Focusing the child's attention on the flow of a melody, the expressive detail in a composition, or simply how to make a passage sound different helps to foster a more sophisticated awareness of the broader purpose of musical notation, and how it can be used to help an instrumentalist think, reason, and communicate musically. An important dimension of teaching, therefore, is to focus on meaningful tasks that help develop both musical and cognitive competencies.

3. *Help young readers move toward automatic decoding*: Skilled readers are able to quickly and accurately discern key features in the visual appearance of the score, and then instigate the required motor action to perform them on their instruments. When these actions are automatic, it is easier to direct attention to higher-level expressive elements that enhance one's performance. Explicit instruction in how to decode notation is important. Replaying passages to improve fluency is obviously important to improving performance ability, but it does not follow that drilling activities and endless repetition will lead to automaticity. Guided meaningful reading of a range of musical pieces in which the teacher directs a student's attention to the relevant technical and expressive characteristics embedded in the work itself helps to instill confidence in performance and knowledge that can be applied when performing other literature.

4. *Draw on children's domain and general knowledge*: All children have knowledge about music before they commence instruction. Reading notation is more likely to be meaningful when it connects with prior experiences of music. For example, introducing the notation for a piece a child already knows and wishes to learn can provide a powerful incentive that helps the student learn to read more quickly, as well as decipher any new elements that are being introduced by the teacher. Encouraging young beginners to invent their own notations to represent pieces they can already perform provides them with the meta-musical awareness that will enhance their progress toward understanding why traditional notation looks and works the way it does. Providing multiple ways for young learners to interact with and learn about notation helps make notation meaningful.

5. *Encourage children to develop their musical knowledge*: Effective teachers draw their students' attention to the many dimensions of musical notation. They encourage them to reflect on their performance and to come up with different interpretations. Learning to read musical notation is a multifaceted process that hinges on knowledge activation, memory, and attention. Aural awareness enables students to map the visual symbols of the musical notation into the required actions that produce the sounds on their instruments. Memory facilitates comprehension of the larger-scale structures of what is being performed, and attention enables the musician to focus on individual signs, phrases, and expressive detail in order to perform musically.

6. *Expect children to vary widely in their progress toward fluent reading*: No two children will ever be at exactly the same level of musical development. Some will struggle with learning to read notation, while others will pick up notational skills relatively easily. Unfortunately, children who do not pick up reading skills early in their development are often not given the types of remedial attention needed to correct their deficiencies. It does not mean, however, that they cannot develop into competent musicians. As with any complex skill, learning a musical instrument involves a complex mix of abilities. Every student will have strengths and weaknesses that impact on the rate, and in turn, the likelihood that they will continue learning.

Teaching and learning

Modeling is a common strategy for teaching play-by-ear skills. Modeling occurs when the teacher sings or plays a pattern and the student vocally/instrumentally echoes the pattern, and this has been found to be an effective strategy for improving play-by-ear skills (Dickey, 1988; Haston, 2010). Musicians who sing and finger as part of the model/echo teaching sequence establish stronger connections between ears and fingers, that is, multimodal learning (Wilkinson, n.d.). Any performance concept can be taught with a well-sequenced teacher modeling strategy (Haston, 2007).

The following strategies can be used to incorporate more playing by ear into an instrumentalist's regular practice routines: following a more haphazard manner of learning pieces rather than using a systematic approach of scales and etude exercises, fiddling around with musical ideas until the melody is worked out, and working with peers and in small groups to help others (as we saw in the reports about the success of informal music practice and training) (see further, Spears, 2014).

The value of playing by ear within contemporary practice

Inner hearing

Advocates of playing by ear suggest that it promotes inner hearing through the enhancement of an internal representation of what the music sounds like before the musician attempts to reproduce this model (Woody, 2012). Engaging in playing-by-ear activities allows musicians to enhance not only their aural and creative abilities to imitate sounds, but also to adapt and respond to changes in these sounds. Sometimes these changes are a result of a co-performer's musical interpretation, memory slip, or a response to an improvised phrase (Varvarigou, 2017b). Performers who develop inner hearing feel it helps them learn to listen with expectation—an essential skill set for listening to music—and performing music by eye or by ear, alone or in a group (Varvarigou & Green, 2015).

Aural database—expanding memory (aurally)

When musicians play by ear, sight-read, and interact with each other, they are building their own aural database by expanding their aural capacities to memorize larger amounts of music (Fine et al., 2006; Odam, 1995). As musicians form aural images, they develop and store mental warehouses of melodic and harmonic patterns. Future learning is therefore more efficient because they can draw from and build upon those stored aural images (Freymuth, 1999). Memorization depends on acquiring aural, visual, and kinesthetic codes (Hallam, 1998). Playing by ear develops aural and kinesthetic codes, and perhaps also visual, as many musicians visualize notation (or some personal image) of what they are playing. This multimodal (aural, kinesthetic, visual) encoding allows instrumentalists to more efficiently play by ear (Woody & Lehmann, 2010; Woody, 2019).

Practicing with recordings

One particular way to improve playing-by-ear skills is to use recordings, either in real time or using a call-and-response format. The instant digital availability of recordings has increased this already common practice, both in solo practice sessions and om private lessons. Twenty-first-century musicians use recordings to develop skills—artistic imagination, personal flexibility, lifelong enjoyment of music making, and aural skills (Varvarigou, 2017a, p. 7). Some musicians even claim that listening to recordings and interacting with fellow musicians during group listening enhances their freedom to be creative when imitating, inventing, and improvising (Varvarigou, 2017b). One might also consider the prospect that too much listening is detrimental to the development of individual musicianship. However, relying on aural models in order to develop an understanding of tone, timbre, and musicality is essential, and imitating those models is an important step in developing a performer's musicality and music literacy.

Conclusion

We end our chapter with two comments. First, it is important to address criticism by some sectors of the music community that children who start off with a focus on "sound before sign" will have difficulty integrating the knowledge required to read music when notation is introduced and therefore never achieve the same level of reading fluency as do children exposed to notation from their first lesson. This view appears to be wrong, given the literature cited earlier as well as the results of a growing body of research showing that children who learn "by ear" do not typically become less successful sight-readers (Haston, 2010; Hayward & Gromko, 2009; Luce, 1965; McPherson, 1993; Sperti, 1970). Second, many musicians lament opportunities of not having learned to play by ear in their private instrumental lessons (Varvarigou, 2017b). In our view, the skill of being able to play by ear can have considerable benefits for developing musicians who are able to cope with the wide variety of playing techniques and demands required of contemporary musicians. This is why we advocate that strengthening one's ear-to-hand coordination skills should be a prime aim of all musicians whatever their specialization.

KEY SOURCES

Green, L. (2002). *How popular musicians learn: A way ahead for music education*. London: Routledge.

Mainwaring, J. (1951). Psychological factors in the teaching of music: Part II: Applied musicianship. *British Journal of Educational Psychology, 21*(3), 199–213.

Varvarigou, M., & Green, L. (2015). Musical "learning styles" and "learning strategies" in the instrumental lesson: The ear playing project (EPP). *Psychology of Music, 43*, 705–722. https://doi.org/10.1177/0305735614535460.

REFLECTIVE QUESTIONS

1. Reflect back on your own musical development. To what extend were you encouraged to "play by ear"?
2. How might your development be different if playing by ear had been a normal part of your training?
3. How might you take the ideas in this chapter to develop further your own philosophy of performing music and learning to "become" a musician?
4. What are the similarities between learning a language and learning music? How can music teachers and musicians capitalize on those similarities?
5. List some ways you could change your practice by focusing on moving from notation, to sound, to action (rather than notation, to action, to sound)?
6. To what extent do you use mental and aural imagery in your music practice?

AUTHOR NOTE

The content of this chapter is drawn from McPherson, G. E., & Gabrielsson, A. (2002). From sound to sign (pp. 99–115). In R. Parncutt & G. E. McPherson (Eds.), *The science and psychology of musical performance: Creative strategies for music teaching and learning.* Oxford: Oxford University Press. Our intention is to provide an update of this publication.

REFERENCES

Adams, M. J. (1994). *Beginning to read: Thinking and learning about print*. Cambridge, MA: MIT Press.

Alluri, V., Toiviainen, P., Burunat, I., Kliuchko, M., Vuust, P., & Brattico, E. (2017). Connectivity patterns during music listening: Evidence for action-based processing in musicians. *Human Brain Mapping, 38*, 2955–2970. https://doi.org/10.1002/hbm.23565.

Bamberger, J. (1996). Turning music theory on its ear. *International Journal of Computers for Mathematical Learning, 1*(1), 33–55.

Bamberger, J. (1999). Learning from the children we teach. *Bulletin of the Council for Research in Music Education, 142*, 48–74.

Bamberger, J. (2006). What develops in musical development? In G. E. McPherson (Ed.), *The child as musician: A handbook of musical development* (pp. 69–92). Oxford: Oxford University Press.

Bruning, E. H., Schraw, G. J., & Norby, M. N. (2011). *Cognitive psychology and instruction* (5th ed.), Boston: Pearson Higher Education.

Dickey, M. R. (1988). *A comparison of the effects of verbal instruction and nonverbal teacher-student modeling on instructional effectiveness in instrumental music ensembles.* Doctoral Dissertation, University of Michigan.

Dowling, W. J., & Harwood, D. L. (1986). *Music cognition.* Orlando, FL: Academic Press.

Drai-Zerbib, V., Baccino, T., & Bigand, E. (2011). Sight-reading expertise: Cross-modality integration investigated using eye tracking. *Psychology of Music, 40*, 216–235. https://doi.org/10.1177/0305735610394710.

Fine, P., Berry, A., & Rosner, B. (2006). The effect of pattern recognition and tonal predictability on sight-singing ability. *Psychology of Music, 34*, 431–447. https://doi.org/10.1177/0305735606067152.

Freymuth, M. (1999). *Mental practice and imagery for musicians: A practical guide for optimizing practice time, enhancing performance, and preventing injury.* Boulder, CO: Integrated Musician's Press.

Froseth, J. O. (1985). *A longitudinal study of the relationship of melodic ear-to-hand coordination and selected indices of musical achievement at the University of Michigan School of Music.* Research presented to the Dean and Executive Committee of the School of Music: University of Michigan, Ann Arbor.

Galvao, A., & Kemp. A. (1999). Kinaesthesia and instrumental music instruction: Some implications. *Psychology of Music, 27*, 129–137. https://doi.org/10.1177%2F0305735699272004.

Gellrich, M., & Parncutt, R. (1998). Piano technique and fingering in the eighteenth and nineteenth centuries: Bringing a forgotten method back to life. *British Journal of Music Education, 15*(1), 5–24. https://doi.org/10.1017/S0265051700003739.

Gellrich, M., & Sundin, B. (1993). Instrumental practice in the 18th and 19th centuries. *Bulletin of the Council for Research in Music Education, 119*, 137–145.

Gordon, C. L., Cobb, P. R., & Balasubramaniam, R. (2018). Recruitment of the motor system during music listening: An ALE meta-analysis of fMRI data. *PLoS ONE 13*(11): e0207213. https://doi.org/10.1371/journal.pone.0207213.

Gordon, E. E. (2012). *Learning sequences in music: A contemporary music learning theory.* Chicago: GIA Publications.

Green, L. (2002). *How popular musicians learn: A way ahead for music education.* London: Routledge.

Green, L., & Smart, T. (2017). Learning music: Informal processes and their outcomes. In R. Ashley & R. Timmers (Eds.), *The Routledge companion to music* cognition (pp. 427–440). New York: Routledge.

Hallam, S. (1998). *Instrumental teaching: A practical guide to better teaching and learning.* Oxford: Heinemann Educational Publishers.

Haston, W. (2007). Teacher modeling as an effective teaching strategy. *Music Educators Journal, 93*(4), 26–30. https://doi.org/10.1177/002743210709300414.

Haston, W. (2010). Beginning wind instrument instruction: A comparison of aural and visual approaches. *Contributions to Music Education*, 37(2), 9–28.

Hayward, C. M., & Gromko, J. E. (2009). Relationships among music sight-reading and technical proficiency, spatial visualization, and aural discrimination. *Journal of Research in Music Education*, 57, 26–36. https://doi.org/10.1177/0022429409332677.

Humphreys, J. T. (1984). *An investigation of an experimental harmonic audiation skills testing and training program for instrumental music education majors*. Doctoral Dissertation, University of Michigan.

Kohut, D. (1985). *Musical performance: Learning theory and pedagogy*. Englewood Cliffs, NJ: Prentice-Hall.

Liperote, K. A. (2006). Audiation for beginning instrumentalists: Listen, speak, read, write. *Music Educators Journal*, 93(1), 46–52. https://doi.org/10.1177%2F002743210609300123.

Luce, J. R. (1965). Sight-reading and ear-playing abilities as related to instrumental music students. *Journal of Research in Music Education*, 13, 101–109. https://doi.org/10.2307%2F3344447.

Mainwaring, J. (1951). Psychological factors in the teaching of music: Part II: Applied musicianship. *British Journal of Educational Psychology*, 21(3), 199–213. https://doi.org/10.1111/j.2044-8279.1951.tb02789.x.

Markovich, V. A. (1985). *An investigation of the effects of matching timbre and training on melodic ear-to-hand coordination of college music majors*. Doctoral Dissertation, University of Michigan.

McGeown, S. P., Osborne, C., Warhurst, A., Norgate, R., & Duncan, L. G. (2016). Understanding children's reading activities: Reading motivation, skill and child characteristics as predictors. *Journal of Research in Reading*, 39(1), 109–125. https://doi.org/10.1111/1467-9817.12060.

McPherson, G. E. (1993). Factors and abilities influencing the development of visual, aural and creative performance skills in music and their educational implications. Doctoral dissertation, University of Sydney, Australia.

McPherson, G. E., Bailey, M., & Sinclair, K. (1997). Path analysis of a model to describe the relationship among five types of music performance. *Journal of Research in Music Education*, 45, 103–129. https://doi.org/10.2307%2F3345469.

McPherson, G. E., Davidson, J. W., & Faulkner, R. (2012). *Music in our lives: Rethinking musical ability, development and identity*. New York: Oxford University Press.

McPherson, G. E., & Gabrielsson, A. (2002). From sound to sign. In R. Parncutt & G. E. McPherson (Eds.), *The science and psychology of music performance* (pp. 99–115). New York: Oxford University Press.

McPherson, G. E., & Renwick, J. (2000). Self-regulation and musical practice. In C. Woods, G. B. Luck, R. Brochard, F. Seddon, & J. A. Sloboda (Eds.), *Proceedings of the Sixth International Conference on Music Perception and Cognition*. Keele, UK: Keely University, Department of Psychology. CD-ROM.

Musco, A. M. (2010). Playing by ear: Is expert opinion supported by research? *Bulletin of the Council for Research in Music Education*, 184, 49–64.

Odam, G. (1995). *Sounding the symbol: Music education in action*. Cheltenham, UK: Stanley Thornes (Publishers) Ltd.

Posner, M. I., & Nissen, M. J. (1976). Visual dominance: An information-processing account of its origins and significance. *Psychological Review*, 83(2), 157–171. https://psycnet.apa.org/doi/10.1037/0033-295X.83.2.157.

Priest, P. (1989). Playing by ear: Its nature and application to instrumental learning. *British Journal of Music Education*, 6, 173–191. https://doi.org/10.1017/S0265051700007038.

Rideout, V. (2014). *Learning at home: Families' educational media use in America*. A report of the Families and Media Project: New York: Joan Ganz Cooney Center at Sesame Workshop.

Ross, S. L. (1985). The effectiveness of mental practice in improving the performance of college trombonists. *Journal of Research in Music Education, 33*, 221–230. https://doi.org/10.2307%2F3345249.

Samuels, S. J. (1994). Toward a theory of automated information processing in reading, revisited. In R. B. Ruddell, M. R. Ruddell, & H. Singer (Eds.), *Theoretical models of processes of reading* (4th ed.), 816–837. Newark, DE: International Reading Association.

Schleuter, S. (1997). *A sound approach to teaching instrumentalists* (2nd ed.). New York: Schirmer Books.

Shaffer, D. R. (1999). *Developmental psychology: Childhood and adolescence* (5th ed.). Pacific Grove, CA: Brooks/Cole.

Sloboda, J. (1978). The psychology of music reading. *Psychology of Music, 6*(2), 3–20. https://doi.org/10.1177/030573567862001.

Spears, A. (2014). *Constructivism in the band room: Facilitating high school band students' playing by ear through informal, student-led practices*. Doctoral Dissertation, Arizona State University.

Sperti, J. (1970). *Adaptation of certain aspects of the Suzuki method to the teaching of the clarinet: An experimental investigation testing the comparative effectiveness of two different pedagogical methodologies*. Unpublished Doctoral dissertation. New York University.

Stokes, D., Matthen, M., & Biggs, S. (2014). The dominance of the visual. In D. Stokes & M. Matthen (Eds.), *Perception and its modalities*. Oxford: Oxford University Press. https://doi.org/10.1093/acprof:oso/9780199832798.001.0001.

Suzuki, S. (1983). *Nurtured by love* (2nd ed.). New York: Smithtown.

Sweller, J., van Merrienboer, J. J. G., & Paas, F. G. W. C. (1998). Cognitive architecture and instructional design. *Educational Psychology Review, 10*(3), 251–296.

Tommis, Y., & Fazey, D. M. A. (1999). The acquisition of the pitch element of music literacy skills by 3–4-year-old pre-school children: A comparison of two methods. *Psychology of Music, 27*, 230–244. https://doi.org/10.1177/0305735699272016.

Varvarigou, M. (2017a). Nurturing the twenty-first century musician through playing by ear from recordings in one to one and small group instrumental lessons. In E. Lopes (Ed.), *Research themes for the learning of musical instruments* (pp. 171–196). Goiânia: Kelps.

Varvarigou, M. (2017b). Group playing by ear in higher education: The processes that support imitation, invention and group improvisation. *British Journal of Music Education, 34*, 291–304. https://doi.org/10.1017/S0265051717000109.

Varvarigou, M., & Green, L. (2015). Musical "learning styles" and "learning strategies" in the instrumental lesson: The ear playing project (EPP). *Psychology of Music, 43*, 705–722. https://doi.org/10.1177/0305735614535460.

Witten, I. B., & Knudsen, E. I. (2005). Why seeing is believing: Merging auditory and visual worlds. *Neuron, 48*, 489–496. https://doi.org/10.1016/j.neuron.2005.10.020.

Woody, R. H. (2012). Playing by ear: Foundation of frill? *Music Educators Journal, 99*(2), 82–88. https://doi.org/10.1177/0027432112459199.

Woody, R. H. (2019). Musicians' use of harmonic cognitive strategies when playing by ear. *Psychology of Music, 48*, 1–19. https://doi.org/10.1177/0305735618816365.

Woody, R. H, & Lehmann, A. (2010). Student musicians' ear-playing ability as a function of vernacular music experiences. *Journal of Research in Music Education, 58*, 101–115. https://doi.org/10.1177/0022429410370785.

CHAPTER 10

....

SIGHT-READING

....

KATIE ZHUKOV AND GARY E. MCPHERSON

It's easy to play any musical instrument: all you have to do is touch the
right key at the right time and the instrument will play itself.

—Johann Sebastian Bach

INTRODUCTION

JUST as literacy and fluency in reading text are central to success in academic achievement,
so too are musical literacy and fluency in reading music central to being able to perform
effectively within the Western art music tradition. While contemporary, popular, and jazz
performers tend to rely on improvisatory and aural skills in their repertoire learning, for
classical musicians the ability to read a score and rapidly decode the notation into appropriate instrumental fingerings is of paramount importance. The initial speed and efficiency of learning new repertoire depends largely on one's ability to process the musical
notation accurately during an initial "sight-reading" of the work being learned. But to
"touch the right key at the right time," as Bach suggests, involves a number of processes
that all come together to help us understand how musicians are able to sight-read music. It
is the purpose of this chapter to explain these processes and to offer some suggestions that
musicians might like to consider for improving their ability to sight-read music.

WHAT IS SIGHT-READING?

The first step in learning to play any notated musical work is to read through the
score for the first time—prima vista or music sight-reading. Sight-reading can

therefore be thought of as anything from the initial playing of music from a printed score after a brief perusal but prior to actual practicing (Gabrielsson, 1999), right through to being given the music and being expected to reproduce it correctly at the time of a performance. One definition of sight-reading describes this as "the execution—vocal or instrumental—of longer stretches of non- or under-rehearsed music at an acceptable pace and with adequate expression" (Lehmann & Kopiez, 2009, p. 344). To do this at sight without any prior rehearsal requires rapid information processing and highly developed motor responses. These abilities allow musicians to sight-read music quickly and efficiently and are an invaluable aid when learning new repertoire and participating in ensembles (Zhukov & Ginsborg, 2021).

BRIEF HISTORY OF MUSIC NOTATION

The earliest known example of music notation (ca. 1400–1250 BC) was found on a clay tablet from Ugarit, Babylonia (Burkholder, Grout, & Palisca, 2010). Systems of music notation and music theory were also evolved by the ancient Greeks and Romans, who devised concepts based around intervals and scales, with rhythm linked to speech patterns. Music notation became more precise during the Early Music period (ca. 590–1025) when Gregorian chants were notated using lines, clefs, and staff but without pitch duration. Eventually this led to the codification of church modes and solmization of A-B-C-D-E-F-G that are still used today to notate musical pitch.

Musicians of the Notre Dame introduced the rhythmic notation in the early thirteenth century by distinguishing between long and short notes. This allowed for notation of polyphonic music and co-ordination of multiple vocal parts in motets. The Franconian notation (ca. 1280) further developed rhythmic notation into four signs for single notes: double long, long, breve, and semibreve. Ars Nova notation (ca. 1300–1425) introduced a minim, and Renaissance notation (ca. 1450–1600) subdivided this into shorter notes of semiminim, fusa, and semifusa (Burkholder, Grout, & Palisca, 2010). These are the modern-day equivalents of the quarter note, eighth note, and sixteenth note.

After centuries of handwritten scores that were in turn copied by hand, the printing of music flourished from the sixteenth century onward and brought church and court music into the lives of ordinary people. Celebrated composers such as Vivaldi, Handel, Haydn, and Beethoven were highly sought after by music publishers. As public concerts became popular in the eighteenth century and amateurs began playing contemporary works at home, the demand for printed music rapidly expanded. The nineteenth century witnessed a boom in music publishing as vast quantities of music were composed for domestic consumption, and orchestral and chamber works were arranged for piano solo or duet to promote music that could only be heard live in concerts.

Over the centuries, the printing of musical scores led to further consolidation of universal musical notation, and today musicians have a range of music software available to notate and hear their compositions. Despite the technological advances in the twenty-first century, the ability to fluently decode musical notation remains an important skill for classically trained musicians. While most of music education literature discusses approaches for introducing music notation to beginners (Mills & McPherson, 2016), little has been written about how musicians gain fluency in reading notation as their performance skills develop, and how the gap between performance skills and music reading skills could be narrowed.

Sight-Reading Research

Research into sight-reading has focused on three main areas: eye movement, structural perception, and training approaches (see Hodges, 1992; Lehmann & Kopiez, 2009; Lehmann & McArthur, 2002; Lehmann, Sloboda, & Woody, 2007; Thompson & Lehmann, 2004; Wristen, 2005). Eye movement experiments have investigated sight-readers' responses to visual stimuli and demonstrate that the eyes of accomplished sight-readers tend to move further ahead than the eyes of slow readers (Goolsby, 1994; Truitt et al., 1997). Studies focusing on structural perception report that skilled sight-readers tend to look further ahead and process larger stretches of music as compared to slower readers (Goolsby, 1994; Penttinen & Huovinen, 2011).

Much work has been carried out to clarify the skills involved in music reading and the predictors of accomplished sight-reading. These studies suggest that reading comprehension, rhythmic audiation, visual perception, and spatial reasoning all contribute to expertise (Gromko, 2004). Aural-spatial patterning and technical proficiency interact when reading music notation to help players transfer their mental representations of music into sounds (Hayward & Gromko, 2009). All these elements combined suggest that high-level fluent music reading ability is an acquired skill that relies on how quickly the player can process information and respond physically on their instrument.

Score difficulty impacts the skills needed to realize music through playing. For example, when pianists are sight-reading examples that are easy, general instrumental accomplishment is usually sufficient. At the intermediate levels of difficulty, factors such as psychomotor skills, speed of information processing, inner hearing, and sight-reading experience become more important, while in the most complex tasks psychomotor skill (measured by the speed of trilling) has been found to be the dominant factor (Kopiez & Lee, 2006). This suggests that sight-reading accomplishment is heavily dependent on each musician's physical motor control, as evidenced in their ability to perform with speed, agility, coordination, and balance.

FACTORS CONTRIBUTING TO FLUENT SIGHT-READING

Eye movement

In recent decades, sophisticated eye movement devices have been developed to track the eyes when involved in reading anything from a web page, through to text and music notation. Because of ophthalmologist Louise Émile Javal, we have known since the late nineteenth century that the eyes make short, rapid forward and backward movements (*saccades*) and short stops at a particular point (*fixations*) rather than move continuously along a line of text when reading. *Regressions* (or *backward saccades*) occur when the eyes re-read information that was not fully comprehended on the first reading.

Using modern eye movement tracking technology, a visual map of *fixations* and *saccades* can be generated that provides accurate indications on what an individual sees, and what they attend to (as determined by the length of their *fixation durations*). Measurements of pupil dilation even provides indications of their emotional stage, arousal, and cognitive load (Krejtz et al., 2018). In music research, eye-tracking equipment is being used to detect each of these types of eye movement during music sight-reading and then produce highly detailed graphs of the musician's eye movements. It can also map the type of information people acquire, what they might be focusing on, and how they are feeling emotionally (Wang, 2011).

We know from eye movement literature that accomplished text readers move their eyes approximately four times a second with the average fixation about 200–250 ms. Each movement (or *saccade*) can vary between 1 and 20 characters with an average of around 7–9 characters. The period of time for each *saccade* is generally between 20–40 ms, a period when no new information is acquired by the reader. Although this can vary depending on the sophistication of the text, accomplished readers typically make *regressions* back to previously read material about 15 percent of the time. As compared to slow readers, accomplished readers have shorter *fixation durations* (because they are able to process and encode information more quickly), *longer saccades* (because their eyes are moving greater distances to the next piece of information), and *fewer regressions* (because their processing capacity is more efficient) (Rayner et al., 2010).

These general points also apply to reading music notation, but whereas reading text may involve reading aloud, the complexity of performing music means that the musician also has to transfer the information gleaned from the score into the instrumental fingerings and expressive intensions needed to bring off a successful performance.

Focus of attention

Where do musicians look when they are sight-reading music? Early research has demonstrated that accomplished music readers tend to look further ahead than slow readers (Goolsby, 1994; Truitt et al., 1997). Even during silent music reading where the technical challenges of playing the instrument are removed, the eye movement of accomplished sight-readers is different from slow sight-readers, with skilled professionals being able to grasp the similarities and differences in rhythmic patterns much faster than novice musicians (Silva & Castro, 2019). At the same time, accomplished music readers are less dependent on looking at their hands and are able to maintain their gaze on the score for longer periods (Banton, 1995).

Eye-hand span versus perceptual span

Investigating eye movement during music reading is a special area of sight-reading research that has focused largely on the *eye-hand span* and *perceptual span* of musicians (Madell & Hébert, 2008; Puurtinen, 2018). Eye-hand span refers to the number of notes a musician is able to remember and keep playing when the score is suddenly covered up. Accomplished sight-readers can usually recall up to seven notes, while less capable sight-readers can only remember around four notes (Sloboda, 1985). Several studies have confirmed that accomplished piano sight-readers demonstrate larger eye-hand spans than less skilled readers (Penttinen et al., 2015; Truitt et al., 1997), and that eye-hand span is a unique characteristic of musicians' ability that is developed over a long period of time (Rosemann et al., 2016). Short-term interventions aimed at improving sight-reading are therefore unlikely to have an immediate impact on one's sight-reading ability.

Perceptual span is somewhat different, because it involves focusing on the distance between the notes the musician's eyes are looking at and the notes being played at that moment. Importantly, accomplished musicians not only look further ahead but their eyes also tend to move toward and even search out musical boundaries such as ends of phrases, sections, and other structural elements of the score that can aid their performance (Sloboda, 1985).

Eye movement mechanisms

Sight-reading skill and score difficulty both impact on the efficiency of a musician's reading capacity. *Saccades* are affected by the complexity of music being played, with accomplished performers being able to look further ahead by lengthening the distance of their saccades (Huovinen et al., 2018), even though more complex scores result in a tendency to look back more often (Wurtz et al., 2009). In singing, accomplished sight-singers tend to scan the entire piece searching for information, backtracking to double check particular details (*regressing*), in contrast to slow readers who tend to only look at the next note (Goolsby, 1994). Similarly, more experienced musicians demonstrate longer saccades than slow readers when silently reading melodies (Penttinen et al., 2013).

There is clear evidence that eye fixations vary depending on the level of skill. In general, however, accomplished sight-readers need and utilize fewer fixations than less-capable readers even when reading examples of increasing difficulty (Zhukov, Khuu, & McPherson, 2019). This is because their speed of processing each element in the score is faster, and thus they are able to quickly process more information. Accomplished sight-readers also utilize shorter fixations when silently reading notation (Penttinen et al., 2013) and when playing altered versions of familiar tunes (Penttinen et al., 2015). Overall, they need less time to process musical notation.

In recent years, the use of eye-tracking devices has enabled researchers to undertake more sophisticated studies than at any time in the past. As an example, Figure 10.1 illustrates the difference in eye movement of adult clarinet players during the first 5 seconds of score perusal prior to sight-reading the music (Zhukov, Khuu, & McPherson, 2019):

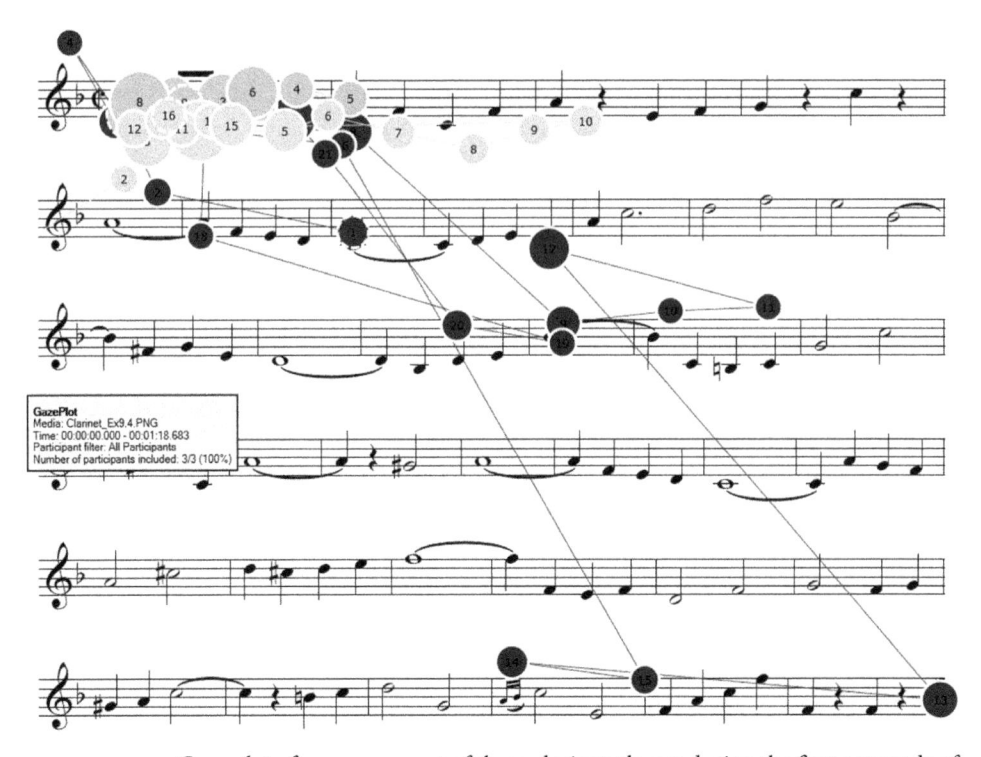

FIGURE 10.1. Gaze plot of eye movement of three clarinet players during the first 5 seconds of perusal.

Participant A (Black): quickly scans the entire score to the end and identifies unusual elements such as tied notes and ornaments;

Participant B (Medium Grey): only manages to preview the first two measures of the music;

Participant C (Light Grey): only processes the first measure of the score.

Differences in eye movement during perusal before commencing to perform correspond to the overall sight-reading accuracy of each participant for the entire experiment as rated by two independent music educators. On the overall sight-reading measure (with a ceiling of 133 points), Participant A scored 98.5, Participant B scored 90, and Participant C was the slowest sight-reader with only 74.5 points. This demonstrates that accomplished sight-readers use perusal time much more efficiently by scanning the score for difficulties, in contrast to less capable sight-readers who process far less relevant information.

Perceptual skills

Another approach to studying music reading abilities is to focus on the amount of information musicians are able to immediately recognize and process when confronted with a new piece of music. Sight-reading research investigating structural perception during music reading has shown that when reading music, beginner instrumentalists tend to focus on individual notes and on intervallic leaps rather than rhythmical units (Penttinen & Huovinen, 2011). Accomplished sight-readers are able to realize longer segments of the score than less experienced sight-readers (Waters et al., 1997). This is because they are more capable of *chunking* information into larger units when sight-reading. The chunking process is typically described as breaking down the score into meaningful units and appears to apply to the rhythmic components of music in particular (Halsband et al., 1994). These ideas make sense, as groupings of individual notes into rhythmic patterns governed by meter and pulse/beat rules allow players to process more notes at a glance instead of reading one note at a time. Similarly, with pitch, recognizing several notes as belonging to a known chord (e.g., tonic and dominant), or to a scale, facilitates the grouping and processing of pitch. While it might appear to be logical that training in chunking might facilitate more fluent sight-reading, this has not been shown in research, where studies show few differences between those who are trained in rhythm and pitch drills and those who did not receive the same training (Pike & Carter, 2010).

How can pattern recognition and prediction skills be developed? The ability to "guess" or predict where the music is likely to go is dependent on how well the musician understands the different musical styles and their structure, typical formulas, harmony, and phrasing (Sloboda, 1984; Thompson & Lehmann, 2004). Musicians are more likely to sight-read a new piece by the same composer with a higher level of accuracy when they become familiar with the composer's melodic shapes, choices of harmony, and compositional style from having learned other pieces by the same composer. This is because accumulated experience allows musicians to predict upcoming material when reading a new (yet similar) work for the first time (Thompson & Lehmann, 2004). Similarly, musicians will have more difficulty in sight-reading a work by a composer they have never played before. This point has also been shown in choral singing, where, in one study, altering the melody and disrupting the underlying harmony in four obscure Bach chorales impaired the sight-singing performance of experienced choral singers (Fine, Berry, & Rosner, 2006). This type of findings suggests that musical accomplishment leads to the accumulation of knowledge of melodic patterns and harmony pertinent to a particular musical period/style and that these play an important role in sight-reading performance. Violating these expectations affects the accuracy of sight-reading (and in a similar manner, sight-singing).

Another important yet basic dimension of pattern recognition is the ability to fully comprehend the key in which the work is notated. Simply knowing the sharps or flats in the key signature does not guarantee accurate score reading, as the errors played when first sight-reading a piece tend to be imprinted into the brain and therefore can take time to be erased. It is self-evident that sight-reading accuracy is affected by the complexity of the key, with more errors occurring as the number of sharps or flats in the key signature increases (Alexander & Henry, 2012).

As an extension of these findings, Edwin Gordon's music learning theory (2012) explains that true comprehension comes when the musician is able to bring meaning to sound through a process he defines as *audiation*. Being able to audiate or comprehend individual pitches involves not only identifying each note but also possessing a sense of the register in which they appear and the key in which they will be performed. Likewise, audiating rhythm involves being able to feel the pulse and understand the meter of the pattern being performed. For Gordon and many others, poor sight-reading skills are often due to poor aural skills rather than poor instrumental technique.

Auditory skills

A fundamental difference between sight-reading and sight-singing is that when sight-singing, the musician needs to process and comprehend both pitch and rhythm, but when sight-reading musicians can respond when seeing a sequence of pitches by pressing down the finger without fully comprehending (audiating) the pitch beforehand. The demands of comprehending pitch when sight-reading are therefore lower. As explained in the previous chapter in this handbook on playing by ear (see Haston & McPherson, this part), one indication of the level of musicianship is how well a musician is able to see the symbol, hear the sound, and then react by moving the fingers to the correct note placement. Ideally, musicians should be able to see the note—hear it in their mind—then play it, but this is not always the case, or always evident to the same degree across musicians of varying levels of ability.

The long-held belief that auditory skills play an important role in accomplished sight-reading has been stressed in a number of research findings. One study demonstrated that at least one out of three musicians with advanced formal training is able to hear in their mind a familiar melody that has been hidden inside a newly composed piece of music (Brodsky et al., 2003). However, this research used a range of distractions to evaluate participants' auditory skills, and the authors acknowledged that the ability to recognize an embedded theme did not produce conclusive evidence of whether audiation occurs during silent music reading. To investigate this issue further, in the next experiment the same research team added a biomonitor attached to the participant's throat to record vocal chord activity that is beyond our hearing range and also measured muscle movement in the larynx using electromyography (Brodsky et al., 2008). The second study replicated initial results, confirming that musicians' inner hearing processes do occur when silently reading scores. It also showed that hearing a melody in one's mind cues motor sequences in one's fingers. This is why it is important to sight-sing music as well as sight-read music through, for example, practice routines that move from *notation—to sound—to action* (rather than from *notation—to action—to sound*; cf. Figure 9.2).

To aid the forming of auditory representations of music before sight-singing and sight-reading, it is best not to be distracted by other forms of music. One study asked undergraduate students to sight-sing two simple tonal melodies, once after a silent perusal and second time with a blues piece played as a rhythmic and harmonic distraction during perusal and performance (Wöllner et al., 2003). Unsurprisingly, the participants found it much more difficult to form auditory representations of the test melodies during perusal with interference, and their inner hearing difficulties led to more sight-reading errors. Recent brain research has confirmed this finding, demonstrating how pianists try to resolve conflicting information when hearing irrelevant sounds while preparing to sight-read. In another study, different parts of the brain were activated, suggesting that hearing "wrong" sounds before sight-reading interferes with the musicians' overall visual processing and conflicts with their monitoring mental processes, thus affecting their sight-reading performance (Delogu et al., 2019).

Memory

Performing from memory and performing by sight-reading might appear to be different types of skills. Performance from memory aims at a faultless execution and is achieved through many hours of deliberate practice, supplemented by score analysis and listening. Sight-reading is considered to be an impromptu realization of the score when a flowing performance is more important than playing every note perfectly. However, both have much in common.

Sight-reading literature discusses working memory (a fairly new term replacing the older concept of short-term memory) and long-term memory. Short-term memory typically refers to a small amount of information (seven items, plus or minus two) that can be retained for a short time (10–60 seconds). The concept of working memory is slightly different and is commonly defined as a process, an executive function that controls our capacity to remember different types of information. Working memory is specific to particular areas. For example, a musician might recall a tune easily but may not remember the words of the song, demonstrating a skilled memory for melodies but a poor memory for text. To retain specific information, we tend to make a conscious effort to transfer this from working memory to long-term memory by linking it to our previous knowledge and experience.

Memory for motor tasks is held in our long-term memory, where it is reinforced by many hours of music practice. This allows musicians to utilize automatic playing processes stored in long-term memory without conscious effort. Accomplished music sight-readers, as well as accomplished readers in other domains, appear to be able to access their long-term memory faster than others in their field, with the result that their performances are superior (Thompson & Lehmann, 2004). Because they are more efficient in their retrieval processes, they are able to maintain a more flowing performance, a steadier overall tempo, and take more time to attend to the additional musical markings such as dynamics and phrasing as they generate a more musical performance (Herrero & Carriedo, 2019).

Another skill of accomplished sight-readers is that they are flexible in their intake of visual information and able to suppress irrelevant information from their working memory such as by ignoring unsuitable fingerings (Drai-Zerbib, Baccino, & Bigand, 2012). They also use their perusal time to locate potential difficulties, suppress unhelpful information from their working memory, and access established fingering patterns in their long-term memory that facilitate a fluent rendition of their music sight-reading. The level of musicians' sight-reading proficiency is evidenced in the accuracy of their performance, which is dependent on fingering consistency and a reliance on overlearned, rule-governed sequences that are triggered by familiarity with visual patterns within the notation (Sloboda et al., 1998). When sight-reading music for the first time, accomplished pianists typically fall back on automated fingering patterns that they have used many times previously, and may omit certain notes, simplify passages, privilege aspects of melody or harmonic progression, and the overall musical effect over ornamentation. They are forced to do this because the time constraints of on-the-spot music reading do not allow sufficient time for them to plan their fingering movements just before they begin playing.

New frontier—neuroscience

New insights into the brain processes during sight-reading is emerging through advances in brain-monitoring technology. For example, when classical musicians are presented with scores only versus scores with recordings of familiar melodies with notated diatonic violations, reading and listening to the same errors in music does not seem to trigger the same electrophysiological activations in the brain (Gunter, Schmidt, & Besson, 2003). This suggests that reading of music and listening to music may have less in common neurologically than previously thought. Despite this difference, brain research shows that musicians tend to process the visual score as an auditory prompt when sight-reading, storing this in working memory and comparing it to the sound they are producing immediately following (Simoens & Tervaniemi, 2013). In addition, the commonly held view that pianists who experience difficulties during sight-reading frequently omit playing some of the notes in the left hand has been validated by research showing hemispheric brain asymmetries during sight-reading of musical notation that indicate a bias toward the right hand when playing both hands together (D'Anselmo et al., 2015).

ACQUISITION OF SIGHT-READING SKILLS

Reviews of sixty years of sight-reading research have shown that stable characteristics such as musical aptitude, IQ, and personality correlate *less* strongly with sight-reading accomplishment than do a number of musical skills that can be improved through targeted practice and that effective interventions for improving sight-reading would include aural skills training (particularly solfège), as well as sight-reading works with others (Mishra, 2014). Particularly strong evidence has been found that "interventions that included a counting system, movement, or rhythmic drill effectively enhanced rhythmic sight-reading," and that melodic sight-reading could be improved with collaborative playing and general instrumental training (Mishra, 2016, p. 9). This research supports the view that sight-reading skill can be enhanced utilizing targeted methodologies that focus on a number of specific factors contributing to fluent sight-reading, and that developing these skills individually and in combinations is likely to lead to an improved overall performance on sight-reading tasks.

Other training interventions aimed at enhancing sight-reading ability including scanning the score before commencing to play, mentally rehearsing the score in one's mind (while silently going over the keys), collaborative playing activities such as accompanying, and efforts aimed at improving an understanding of musical style (Lehmann & McArthur, 2002; McPherson, 1994; Wristen, 2005). Three strategies in particular—rhythm training, understanding of musical style, and collaborative playing—have been identified as useful training approaches (Zhukov, 2006).

Rhythm training to improve sight-reading

It is self-evident that fluent sight-reading depends on both pitch and rhythmic accuracy. However, McPherson (1994) found, for the reasons we discussed when comparing sight-reading and sight-singing, that school-aged instrumentalists tend to make about twice as many errors in rhythm as they do in pitch. In general, though, musicians who are able to perform rhythms accurately are more likely to demonstrate pitch accuracy as well (Henry, 2011). However, the reverse is not always found in musicians. Musicians who can accurately sight-read pitch (e.g., those who possess absolute pitch) do not necessarily produce more accurate rhythms. Paying attention to rhythm first and pitch afterward improves the accuracy of notating music dictation (Beckett, 1997). Recent research has confirmed that performing rhythm alone and pitch alone requires different cognitive processes than simultaneously sight-reading rhythm and pitch together (Russel, 2019).

Given the challenges inherent in decoding rhythm and the percentage of errors that occur in this area compared to other factors within the sight-reading process, it would seem important for training programs to start by identifying where performers are having problems and then develop targeted exercises aimed at improving these deficiencies. For example, if a young player cannot feel the pulse or meter of a work, then exercises should be devised to help develop this facets of rhythmic comprehension, such as conducting while singing the pattern through, or moving to the pulse while performing the work at a slower pace. The most appropriate interventions start by diagnosing the problem, then tailoring the training program to focus on improving this aspect of the learner's playing abilities.

Knowledge of musical styles to improve sight-reading

Possessing an understanding of the differences between compositional styles in terms of structure, texture, harmony, melody, and rhythm of the genre of music being performed helps musicians recognize patterns that are linked to the features of the particular musical style (Palmer & van de Sande 1993, 1995). For example, works written in a polyphonic style are more likely to contain imitations between voices and heavy ornamentation, while repertoire from the Classical style tend to have a simple melody with chordal accompaniment. Typical sonata-form structures of the Classical period give way to the more complex forms during the Romantic era, while greater chromaticism of the Romantic period is replaced with non-standard scales of the Impressionist and twentieth-century compositional styles.

Sight-reading errors can be related to the musical units characteristic of a particular style. Skilled sight-readers tend to process the notes more rapidly because they recognize familiar patterns as groups of notes (Waters et al., 1998). Recognition of such patterns during sight-reading results in the usage of standard fingering patterns, which in turn produces greater consistency and accuracy of playing (Sloboda et al., 1998). Training musicians to focus on the characteristics of the musical style being performed would appear to also help develop sight-reading skills.

Collaborative playing to improve sight-reading

Vocal and instrumental accompanying involves fine co-ordination between the soloist and the accompanist, and requires superior prediction skills (Palmer, 1997). Accompanists tend to be accomplished sight-readers because they have accumulated a great deal of experience reading three or more lines of music when playing, often due to having limited rehearsal time (Lehmann & Ericsson, 1996). Furthermore, the amount of accompanying experience and varied repertoire learned have been identified as important factors in sight-reading ability (Lehmann & Ericsson 1993, 1996). The findings from studies of accompanying suggest that playing with someone forces pianists to keep going as they play through errors and maintain the tempo of the work. For pianists, accompanying also involves reading more than two lines of music and can therefore lead to improved horizontal and vertical eye movement across the staves.

Collaborative playing for single-line instrumentalists includes playing duets with other musicians and participating in small and large ensembles and orchestras, each of which can contribute to the development of sight-reading skills. Therefore, augmenting musical training with additional playing activities that build musicians' collaborative repertoire can be an effective strategy for improving sight-reading ability.

A holistic approach to improving sight-reading

In order to assess the effectiveness of approaches for improving sight-reading suggested by previous research—rhythm training, understanding of musical styles, and accompanying—three new training programs were developed and trialed by Zhukov (2014a) in a large group of advanced pianists versus a control group. Results showed some improvement in pitch and rhythm accuracy in each of these training groups. The greatest progress was made by the rhythm training group, while the control group made no gains in rhythm accuracy. This research demonstrated that additional training in accompanying, rhythm training, and understanding of musical styles does impact participants' sight-reading skills immediately.

Since sight-reading is a complex issue where many factors interact simultaneously, the findings of Zhukov's (2014a) study suggested that combining all three training programs into one holistic curriculum might help target diverse sight-reading weaknesses across a range of musical abilities. Consequently, a new program was developed in collaboration with piano lecturers from four universities and trialed with two student cohorts (Zhukov et al., 2016). This consisted of ten weeks of materials, with each week containing rhythm training, solo repertoire, and duet playing. Given that only pianists participated in this study, the accompanying experienced were restricted to duet playing. The pieces consisted of examples from the traditional repertoire and were greatly varied in style. Artistically rich musical examples rather than sight-reading exercises were used to increase student engagement with the process.

The rhythm training section contained scales and arpeggios in varied rhythmic patterns to practice the application of basic rhythms to simple musical materials. The solo section consisted of four short pieces each week from the Baroque, Classical, Romantic, and twentieth-century style periods. The aim of the solo work was to develop analytical and practical understandings of the characteristics of each style with regard to the development of structural, harmonic, and melodic pattern recognition and prediction skills.

The participants receiving this training were tested on sight-reading before and after training, and their results were compared to the earlier single-focus training programs (i.e., accompanying, rhythm training, understanding of musical styles, and control). The combined curriculum group outstripped the other programs in both pitch and rhythm accuracy improvement, showing that this hybrid approach to training sight-reading was an effective way to improve sight-reading skills in a mixed cohort of advanced pianists. While this approach is yet to be tested in other instrumental teaching settings and with students of different skill levels—beginner and intermediate—instrumental teachers could trial such a combined approach or its individual components with their students using their own materials.

Practical Implications

Research into the acquisition of sight-reading skills has been rather patchy, making it difficult to define clear practical suggestions for musicians (Hodges, 1992; Lehmann & Kopiez, 2009). There is still little "compelling evidence about how best to assist students in acquiring music-reading skills" (Hodges & Nolker, 2011, p. 81). In higher music education, teachers tend to believe they can do little to improve their students' sight-reading, with the topic largely absent from studio lessons (Kornicke, 1995; Zhukov, 2014b). Simply practicing sight-reading regularly, as advocated by many studio teachers, does not guarantee improvement (Zhukov, 2017). For this reason, attempts to improve sight-reading abilities need to be purposeful, and take into account the types of strategies listed below.

Based on literature discussed in this chapter, we can propose several general and specific strategies to improve sight-reading skills in musicians of all instruments and levels.

General Strategies

(1) *Make sight-reading a regular activity.* Consistent and systematic sight-reading each week can produce beneficial gains in music reading fluency, which in the long term will save time, as new repertoire will be learned more quickly.

(2) *Where appropriate, employ duet playing in music activities.* Playing with another performer encourages musicians to keep going and counter the stop-and-start

nature of typical sight-reading. It could also improve counting and eye movement. Playing duets motivates practice and provides further opportunities to read new music.

(3) *Locate suitable materials for sight-reading practice.* Trying to sight-read repertoire at your current playing level (as opposed to your current sight-reading level) is difficult and may lead to frustration and disappointment. A better strategy is to choose pieces that are below your current playing level to build confidence in being able to read simpler music fluently.

(4) *Spend more time preparing to read than correcting reading errors.* It is far too easy to simply start playing and then note every mistake made. This leads to negative attitudes toward sight-reading and lack of confidence in this skill. Implement specific training strategies *before* sight-reading (see following section).

(5) *Be positive in your evaluation.* Start with finding something positive about sight-reading of a particular example, such as, "I kept going and did not stop" or "My rhythm was much better today." Try to focus on the progress being made rather than solely on the accuracy of your performance.

(6) *Be constructive and try to find solutions.* For example, ask yourself, "Where exactly did things go wrong?" and think about why or how any faults occurred. This will help focus your attention on habitual problems such as missed key signature, time signature, lack of counting (often on longer notes and rests), and accidentals.

(7) *End your sight-reading session on an overall positive note, even if your sight-reading performance was below par on this particular occasion.* It is important to maintain a positive long-term outlook in your skill development and keep engaged in sight-reading practice.

SPECIFIC STRATEGIES

Experienced sight-readers will apply certain types of cueing mechanisms immediately before performing from sight, such as scanning the music to observe the hardest section to perform, checking the tempo, and making oneself aware of the key and time signatures and other expression markings (McPherson, 1994, 2005). To facilitate the development of such positive pre-sight-reading habits:

(1) *Scan the entire example to decipher the length of phrases*; note any repetition or variation of previous material. This will focus your attention on structural elements of the work and assist in pattern recognition. Identify any unusual elements—accidentals, irregular rhythms, and rests. This highlights potential trouble spots that will typically require additional attention when playing.

(2) *Understand the key signature.* Go beyond naming sharps or flats and identify the key in which the example is written (major; minor—what type?). Play this scale and tonic/dominant triads—you need to be sure you are capable of playing all notes before you try to play the piece of music and confirm sound production before music reading.

(3) *Understand the time signature.* Go beyond the basic answer like, "Four quarter notes per bar." Ask yourself rhythm questions, for example, "How many eighth notes will fit into this bar?" Make up some short 1-bar rhythmic patterns in this time signature and clap those, for example, "I'll do two quarter notes and four eighth notes." Once you fully understand the time signature, clap the rhythm of the entire example. Most important, make sure you feel the pulse and the meter of the work you are about to perform before commencing your performance, and note any changes of time signature or tempo during the piece.

(4) *Focus on the melodic shape.* Instead of reciting the names of the notes, it is more beneficial for reading to follow the linear movement. To reinforce this approach, simply name the first note and then focus on where the melody is going (ascending/descending, step movement, leaps, etc.). If a particular note is difficult to execute on your instrument (e.g., different string, tricky fingering, large leap), do identify and play this note.

(5) *Sing the melody even if you are not a confident singer.* This helps to form a mental representation of what your playing should sound like and focuses yet again on the rhythmical elements and linear movement of the melody. For intermediate pianists, when sight-reading involves two staves of music to be played simultaneously with two hands, sing the melody of the right hand while playing the left hand. This helps you to pay more attention to the left-hand part, which pianists tend to omit when sight-reading becomes too difficult.

(6) *If there are tempo and dynamic markings on the score, note these and aim for a comfortable performance speed with expression.* Musical playing involves greater sensitivity to all musical concepts, and playing expressively is more beneficial in the long term than fast but mechanical playing. The positive emotions associated with an expressive musical performance will go a long way in nurturing positive attitudes toward sight-reading and building confidence in this skill.

(7) *If there is anything else on the score that you are not sure about, clarify this before playing.* Tell yourself you are confident in your ability to sight-read this unfamiliar music well and accompany this with a positive body language (nodding and smiling) before you start. Give a positive evaluation of your attempt.

(8) *Focus on similarities and variations between different composers of the same period/ style not only through performance but also through listening and score analysis.* This can assist in developing pattern recognition and prediction skills. Analyzing the overall structure, melodic shape, phrase length, harmonic progressions, and rhythmic patterns, and referencing the works previously learned when starting new repertoire is a productive way of facilitating this form of knowledge transfer.

Developing fluency in music reading is a crucial part of instrumental/vocal music learning that directly impacts musicians' enjoyment of music making and their life-long engagement with music performance. Some musicians manage to acquire music reading fluency effortlessly, while others hit stumbling blocks once or twice in their learning journey. The most important consideration for any musician, however, is to gauge the level of one's own sight-reading ability at various stages of their development and to take appropriate targeted training where necessary to develop their ability to the level needed to perform confidently in various musical situations.

Key Sources

Hodges, D. A., & Nolker, D. B. (2011). The acquisition of music reading skills. In R. Colwell & P. R. Webster (Eds.), *MENC handbook of research on music learning* (vol. 2, pp. 61–91). Oxford: Oxford University Press.

Lehmann, A. C., & Kopiez, R. (2009). Sight-reading. In S. Hallam, I. Cross, & M. Thaut (Eds.), *The Oxford handbook of music psychology* (pp. 344–351). Oxford: Oxford University Press.

McPherson, G. E. (2005). From child to musician: Skill development during the beginning stages of learning an instrument. *Psychology of Music, 33*(1), 5–35. https://doi.org/10.1177/0305735605048012.

Puurtinen, M. (2018). Eye on music reading: A methodological review of studies from 1994 to 2017. *Journal of Eye Movement Research, 11*(2), 1–16. https://doi.org/10.16910/jemr.11.2.2.

Thompson, S., & Lehmann, A. C. (2004). Strategies for sight-reading and improvising music. In A. Williamon (Ed.), *Musical excellence* (pp. 143–159). Oxford: Oxford University Press.

Reflective Questions

(1) Reflect on your own abilities as a sight-reader. What are your strengths and what are your weaknesses?

(2) How might you use the information in this chapter to devise a targeted training program aimed at improving your own sight-reading abilities?

(3) What do you notice when performing with other more accomplished musicians? When they sight-read music, what do they do differently from you?

(4) What genres of music or stylistic characteristics do you have most difficulty sight-reading? Knowing this, what could you do to improve your performances in these genres?

(5) What approaches or techniques would you employ to train one of your students to be a better sight-reader?

REFERENCES

Alexander, M. L., & Henry, M. L. (2012). The development of a string sight-reading pitch skill hierarchy. *Journal of Research in Music Education, 60*(2), 201–216. https://doi.org/10.1177%2F0022429412446375.

Banton, L. J. (1995). The role of visual and auditory feedback during the sight-reading of music. *Psychology of Music, 23*(1), 3–16. https://doi.org/10.1177%2F0305735695231001.

Beckett, C. A. (1997). Directing student attention during two-part dictation. *Journal of Research in Music Education, 45*(4), 613–625. https://doi.org/10.2307%2F3345426.

Brodsky, W., Henik, A., Rubinstein, B-S., & Zorman, M. (2003). Auditory imagery from musical notation in expert musicians. *Perception and Psychophysics, 65*(4), 602–612.

Brodsky, W., Kessler, Y., Rubinstein, B-S., Ginsborg, J., & Henik, A. (2008). The mental representation of music notation: Notational audiation. *Journal of Experimental Psychology: Human Perception and Performance, 34*(2), 427–445. https://doi.org/10.1037/0096-1523.34.2.427.

Burkholder, J. P., Grout, D. J., & Palisca, C. V. (2010). *A history of Western music* (8th Ed). New York: W. W. Norton.

D'Anselmo, A., Giuliani, F., Marzoli, D., Tommasi, L., & Brancucci, A. (2015). Perceptual and motor laterality effects in pianists during sight-reading. *Neuropsychologia, 71,* 119–125. https://doi.org/10.1016/j.neuropsychologia.2015.03.026.

Delogu, F., Brunetti, R., Inuggi, A., Campus, C., Del Gatto, C., & D'Ausilio, A. (2019). That does not sound right: Sounds affect visual ERPs during a piano sight-reading task. *Behavioural Brain Research, 367,* 1–9. https://doi.org/10.1016/j.bbr.2019.03.037.

Drai-Zerbib, V., Baccino, T., & Bigand, E. (2012). Sight-reading expertise: Cross-modality integration investigated using eye tracking. *Psychology of Music, 40*(2), 216–235. https://doi.org/10.1177%2F0305735610394710.

Fine, P., Berry, A., & Rosner, B. (2006). The effect of pattern recognition and tonal predictability on sight-singing ability. *Psychology of Music, 34*(4), 431–447. https://doi.org/10.1177%2F0305735606067152.

Fourie, E. (2004). The processing of music notation: Some implications for piano sight-reading. *Journal of Musical Arts in Africa, 1*(1), 1–23. https://doi.org/10.2989/18121000409486685.

Gabrielsson, A. (1999). The performance of music. In D. Deutch (Ed.), *The psychology of music* (2nd ed, pp. 501–602). New York: Academic Press.

Goolsby, T. W. (1994). Profiles of processing: Eye movements during sight-reading. *Music Perception, 12*(1), 97–123. https://doi.org/10.2307/40285757.

Gordon, E. E. (2012). *Learning sequences in music: A contemporary music learning theory.* Chicago: GIA Publications.

Gromko, J. E. (2004). Predictors on music sight-reading ability in high school wind players. *Journal of Research in Music Education, 52*(1), 6–15. https://doi.org/10.2307%2F3345521.

Gunter, T. C., Schmidt, B-H., & Besson, M. (2003). Let's face the music: A behavioral and electrophysiological exploration of score reading. *Psychophysiology, 40,* 742–751. https://doi.org/10.1111/1469-8986.00074.

Halsband, U., Binkofski, F., & Camp, M. (1994). The role of perception of rhythmic grouping in musical performance: Evidence from motor-skill development in piano playing. *Music Perception, 11*(3), 265–288. https://doi.org/10.2307/40285623.

Hayward, C. M., & Gromko, J. E. (2009). Relationships among music sight-reading and technical proficiency, spatial visualization and aural discrimination. *Journal of Research in Music Education, 57*(1), 26–36. https://doi.org/10.1177%2F0022429409332677.

Henry, M. L. (2011). The effect of pitch and rhythm difficulty on vocal sight-reading performance. *Journal of Research in Music Education, 59*(1), 72–84. https://doi.org/
10.1177%2F0022429410397199.

Herrero, L., & Carriedo, N. (2019). The contributions of updating in working memory sub-
processes for sight-reading music beyond age and practice effects. *Frontiers in Psychology,
10*, 1080. https://doi.org/10.3389/fpsyg.2019.01080.

Hodges, D. A. (1992). The acquisition of music reading skills. In R. Colwell (Ed.), *Handbook of
research on music teaching and learning* (pp. 466–471). New York: Schirmer Books.

Hodges, D. A., & Nolker, D. B. (2011). The acquisition of music reading skills. In R. Colwell & P.
R. Webster (Eds.), *MENC handbook of research on music learning* (vol. 2, pp. 61–91). Oxford,
UK: Oxford University Press.

Huovinen, E., Ylitalo, A.-K., Puurtinen, M. (2018). Early attraction in temporarily controlled
sight reading of music. *Journal of Eye Movement Research, 11*(2), 3. https://doi.org/10.16910/
jemr.11.2.3.

Kopiez, R., & Lee, J. I. (2006). Towards a dynamic model of skills involved in sight-reading
music. *Music Education Research, 8*(1), 97–120. https://doi.org/10.1080/14613800600570785.

Kopiez, R., & Lee, J. I. (2008). Towards a general model of skills involved in sight-reading
music. *Music Education Research, 10*(1), 41–62. https://doi.org/10.1080/14613800701871363.

Kopiez, R., Weih, C., Ligges, U., & Lee, J. I. (2006). Classification of high and low
achievers in music sight-reading task. *Psychology of Music, 34*(1), 5–26. https://doi.org/
10.1177%2F0305735606059102.

Kornicke, E. (1995). An exploratory study of individual difference variables in piano sight-
reading achievement. *Quarterly Journal of Music Teaching and Learning, 6*(1), 56–79.

Kostka, M. J. (2000). The effects of error-detection practice on keyboard sight-reading achievement of undergraduate music majors. *Journal of Research in Music Education, 48*(2), 114–122.
https://doi.org/10.2307%2F3345570.

Krejtz, K., Duchowski, A. T., Niedzielska, A., Biele, C., & Krejtz, I. (2018). Eye tracking cognitive load using pupil diameter and microsaccades with fixed gaze. *PLoS ONE 13*(9):
e0203629. https://doi.org/10.1371/journal.pone.0203629.

Lehmann, A. C., & Ericsson, K. A. (1993). Sight-reading ability of accomplished pianists in the
context of piano accompanying. *Psychomusicology, 12*, 122–136. https://psycnet.apa.org/doi/
10.1037/h0094108.

Lehmann, A. C., & Ericsson, K. A. (1996). Performance without preparation: Structure and acquisition of accomplished sight-reading and accompanying performance. *Psychomusicology,
15*, 1–29. https://psycnet.apa.org/doi/10.1037/h0094082.

Lehmann, A. C., & Kopiez, R. (2009). Sight-reading. In S. Hallam, I. Cross, & M. Thaut (Eds.),
The Oxford handbook of music psychology (pp. 334–351). Oxford: Oxford University Press.

Lehmann, A. C., & McArthur, V. (2002). Sight-reading. In R. Parncutt & G. E. McPherson
(Eds.), *The science and psychology of music performance: Creative strategies for teaching and
learning* (pp. 135–150). Oxford: Oxford University Press.

Lehmann, A. C., Sloboda, J. A., & Woody, R. H. (2007). *Psychology for musicians*. Oxford:
Oxford University Press.

Madell, M., & Hébert, S. (2008). Eye movements and music reading: Where do we look next?
Music Perception, 26(2), 157–170. https://doi.org/10.1525/MP.2008.26.2.157.

McPherson, G. E. (1994). Factors and abilities influencing sightreading skill in music. *Journal
of Research in Music Education, 42*(3), 217–231. https://doi.org/10.2307%2F3345701.

McPherson, G. E. (2005). From child to musician: Skill development during the beginning stages of learning an instrument. *Psychology of Music, 33*(1), 5–35. https://doi.org/10.1177/0305735605048012.

Meinz, E. J., & Hambrick, D. Z. (2010). Deliberate practice is necessary but not sufficient to explain individual differences in piano sight-reading skill: The role of working memory capacity. *Psychological Science, 21*(7), 914–919. https://doi.org/10.1177%2F0956797610373933.

Mills, J., & McPherson, G. E. (2016). Music literacy: Reading traditional clef notation. In G. E. McPherson (Ed.), *The child as musician: A handbook of musical development* (2nd ed., pp. 177–191). Oxford: Oxford University Press.

Mishra, J. (2014). Factors related to sight-reading accuracy: A meta-analysis. *Journal of Research in Music Education, 61*(4), 452–465. https://doi.org/10.1177%2F0022429413508585.

Mishra, J. (2016). Rhythmic and melodic sight-reading interventions: Two meta-analyses. *Psychology of Music, 44*(5), 1082–1094. https://doi.org/10.1177%2F0305735615610925.

Palmer, C. (1997). Music performance. *Annual Review of Psychology, 48*, 115–138. https://doi.org/10.1146/annurev.psych.48.1.115.

Palmer, C. & van de Sande, C. (1993). Units of knowledge in music performance. *Journal of Experimental Psychology: Learning, Memory, Cognition, 19*(2), 457–470. https://doi.org/10.1037//0278-7393.19.2.457.

Palmer, C. & van de Sande, C. (1995). Range of planning in skilled music performance. *Journal of Experimental Psychology: Human Perception and Performance, 21*(5), 947–62. https://doi.apa.org/doi/10.1037/0096-1523.21.5.947.

Penttinen, M., & Huovinen, E. (2011). The early development of sight-reading skills in adulthood: A study of eye movements. *Journal of Research in Music Education, 59*(2), 196–220. https://doi.org/10.1177%2F0022429411405339.

Penttinen, M., Huovinen, E., & Ylitalo, A.-K. (2013). Silent music reading: Amateur musicians' visual processing and descriptive skills. *Musicae Scientiae, 17*(2), 198–216. https://doi.org/10.1177/1029864912474288.

Penttinen, M., Huovinen, E., & Ylitalo, A.-K. (2015). Reading ahead: Adult music students' eye movements in temporally controlled performances of a children's song. *International Journal of Music Education, 33*(1), 36–50. https://doi.org/10.1177/0255761413515813.

Pike, P. D., & Carter, R. (2010). Employing cognitive chunking techniques to enhance sight-reading performance of undergraduate group-piano students. *International Journal of Music Education, 28*(3), 231–246. https://doi.org/10.1177%2F0255761410373886.

Puurtinen, M. (2018). Eye on music reading: A methodological review of studies from 1994 to 2017. *Journal of Eye Movement Research, 11*(2), 1–16. https://doi.org/10.16910/jemr.11.2.2.

Rayner, K., Slattery, T. J., Belanger, N. N. (2010). Eye movements, the perceptual span, and reading speed. *Psychonomic Bulletin & Review, 17*(6), 834–39. https://doi.org/10.3758/PBR.17.6.834.

Rosemann, S., Altenmüller, E., & Fahle, M. (2016). The art of sight-reading: Influence of practice, playing tempo, complexity and cognitive skills on the eye-hand span in pianists. *Psychology of Music, 44*(4), 658–673. https://doi.org/10.1177/0305735615585398.

Russell, C. R. (2019). Effects of pitch and rhythm priming tasks on accuracy and fluency during sight-reading. *Journal of Research in Music Education, 67*(3), 252–269. https://doi.org/10.1177%2F0022429419851112.

Silva, S., & Castro, S. L. (2019). The time will come: Evidence for an eye-audiation span in silent reading of music. *Psychology of Music, 47*(4), 504–520. https://doi.org/10.1177/0305735618765302.

Simoens, V. L., & Tervaniemi, M. (2013). Auditory short-term memory activation during score-reading. *PLoS One, 8*(1), e53691. https://doi.org/10.1371/journal.pone.0053691.

Sloboda, J. A. (1984). Experimental studies of music reading: A review. *Music Perception, 2*(2), 222–236. https://doi.org/10.2307/40285292.

Sloboda, J. A. (1985). *The musical mind: The cognitive psychology of music.* Oxford: Oxford University Press.

Sloboda, J. A., Clarke, E. F., Parncutt, R., & Raekallio, M. (1998). Determinants of finger choice in piano sight-reading. *Journal of Experimental Psychology: Human Perception and Performance, 24*(1), 185–203. https://psycnet.apa.org/doi/10.1037/0096-1523.24.1.185.

Thompson, S., & Lehmann, A. C. (2004). Strategies for sight-reading and improvising music. In A. Williamon (Ed.), *Musical excellence* (pp. 143–159). Oxford: Oxford University Press.

Truitt, F. E., Clifton, C., Pollatsek, A., & Rayner, K. (1997). The perceptual span and the eye-hand span in sight-reading of music. *Visual Cognition, 4*(2), 134–161. https://doi.org/10.1080/713756756.

Wang, J. (2011). Pupil dilation and eye-tracking. In M. Schulte-Mecklenbeck, A. Kühberger, & R. Ranyard (Eds.), *A handbook of process tracing methods for decision research: A critical review and user's guide* (pp. 185–204). Society for Judgment and Decision Making Series. Abingdon: Routledge.

Waters, A. J., Townsend, E., & Underwood, G. (1998). Expertise in musical sight-reading: A study of pianists. *British Journal of Psychology, 89*(1), 123–149. https://doi.org/10.1111/j.2044-8295.1998.tb02676.x.

Waters, A. J., Underwood, G., & Findlay, J. M. (1997). Studying expertise in music reading: Use of a pattern-matching paradigm. *Perception and Psychophysics, 59*(4), 477–488. https://doi.org/10.3758/BF03211857.

Wöllner, C., Halfpenny, E., Ho, S., & Kurosawa, K. (2003). The effects of distracted inner hearing on sight-reading. *Psychology of Music, 31*(4), 377–389. https://doi.org/10.1177%2F03057356030314003.

Wristen, B. (2005). Cognition and motor execution in piano sight-reading: A review of literature. *Update: Applications of Research in Music Education, 24*(1), 44–56. https://doi.org/10.1177%2F87551233050240010106.

Wurtz, P., Mueri, R., & Wiesendanger, M. (2009). Sight-reading of violinists: Eye movements anticipate the musical flow. *Experimental Brain Research, 194*(3), 445–450. https://doi.org/10.1007/s00221-009-1719-3.

Zhukov, K. (2006). Skilled sight-readers: Born or bred? *Proceedings of the 7th Australasian Piano Pedagogy Conference,* 12–16 July 2005, Adelaide, Australia. www.appca.com.au/proceedings.

Zhukov, K. (2014a). Evaluating new approaches to teaching of sight-reading skills to advanced pianists. *Music Education Research, 16*(1), 70–87. https://doi.org/10.1080/14613808.2013.819845.

Zhukov, K. (2014b). Exploring advanced piano students' approaches to sight-reading. *International Journal of Music Education, 32*(4), 487–498. https://doi.org/10.1177/0255761413517038.

Zhukov, K. (2017). Experiential (informal/non-formal) practice does not improve sight-reading skills. *Musicae Scientiae, 21*(4), 418–429. https://doi.org/10.1177/1029864916684193.

Zhukov, K., & Ginsborg, J. (2021). Time for practice: Implications of undergraduate pianists' choice of repertoire. *British Journal of Music Education.* https://doi.org/10.1017/S0265051720000315.

Zhukov, K., Khuu, S., & McPherson, G. (2019). Eye movement efficiency and sight-reading expertise in woodwind players. *Journal of Eye Movement Research*, *12*(2), 6. https://doi.org/10.16910/jemr.12.2.6.

Zhukov, K., Viney, L., Riddle, G., Teniswood-Harvey, A., & Fujimura, K. (2016). Improving sight-reading skills in advanced pianists: A hybrid approach. *Psychology of Music*, *44*(2), 155–67. https://doi.org/10.1177/0305735614550229.

CHAPTER 11

··

IMPROVISATION

··

RAYMOND MACDONALD

Improvisation is the art of becoming sound. It is the only art in which a human being can and must become the music he or she is making. It is the art of constant, attentive and dangerous living in every moment. It is the art of stepping outside of time, disappearing in it, becoming it. It is both the fine art of listening and responding and the more refined art of silence. It is the only musical art where the entire "score" is merely the self and the others, and the space and moment where and when this happens. Improvisation is the only musical art which is predicated entirely on human trust and love.

—Alvin Curran[1]

INTRODUCTION

IMPROVISATION is a defining aspect of music making. No longer a musical skill conceptualized as the preserve of elite jazz musicians, improvisation is now taught and researched as a creative, universally accessible musical skill at universities, conservatories, and music schools around the world. Pioneering composer and improviser Alvin Curran signals these post-genre aspects of improvisation in the epigraph, and in this chapter I will offer a broad definition of improvisation that encompasses genre-based approaches and also non-idiomatic improvisation. The chapter reviews major theories of improvisation and summarizes a model proposing that improvisation proceeds via a series of creative choices made during real-time music making. The chapter then discusses implications of these observations, highlighting educational and performance-based issues with a focus upon skill acquisition.

---

[1] http://www.alvincurran.com/writings/spontaneous.html.

IMPROVISATION AS A UNIVERSAL CAPACITY

Over the past twenty years there has been an explosion of interest around improvisation, and we now see festivals, venues, radio programs, and higher education courses dedicated to improvisation as a non-idiomatic type of musical engagement. The influential English guitarist Derek Bailey once described improvisation as "the most widely practised of all music activities but the least acknowledged or understood" (Bailey, 1993, p. ix). While this quote has long been explicitly used as a point of departure for countless research projects, this is no longer the case, and improvisation is now widely accepted as a key skill for the contemporary musician, as well as a part, to a greater or lesser extent, of all music making (MacDonald & Wilson, 2020). While there is no doubt that there has been increased research interest, there is still much to learn about the processes and outcomes of improvisational practices around the world (Bertinetto, 2013; Lewis & Piekut, 2016a, 2016b).

We are all improvisers. Not only is improvisation a key musical process, it is a fundamental life process. The earliest communication between a parent and a newborn baby is musical and improvisatory. The cooing and the babbling and the playful interactions that take place in those early days and months of a baby's life involve basic musical and improvisatory processes (Trevarthen, 2002). These patterns of interaction will have an important influence on a baby's developing personality; therefore, musical improvisation plays an essential role in the earliest and most important bonding relationship of our life—that with our parents. Of course, this is a very broad definition of improvising, but we can see it manifested on conventional musical instruments. Think of a young child's first experiences of playing a piano. The child may explore the piano for its sonic possibilities: pressing keys, maybe hitting the lid or banging the side of the piano. Less concerned with playing the piano correctly, a child playfully improvises with the piano, coaxing new sounds and experiences from the interaction. These improvisational gestures of babies and children contain many of the key creative, psychological, and decision-making processes of what we might want to call mature improvisers, and this is an important point. While many musicians claim they are not able to improvise (Bernhard & Stringham, 2016), I contend this belief is born of a socially constructed and possibly elitist view of what improvisation is.

Attempting to unambiguously define improvisation is difficult, and perhaps a distraction from more important surrounding questions; however, broadening what we consider to be improvisation opens up possibilities for practitioners seeking to explore new ways of working and collaborating. This is particularly important if we are interested in how musicians develop skills and proficiencies in improvising. On the one hand, we all have improvisational proficiencies and skills, since we are using them as we navigate and negotiate our way through daily life. A breakfast chat with our family, ordering food in a café, meeting a friend in the street, all involve improvisational skills that we take for granted. These proficiencies include choices about stopping, starting, responding, listening, and selecting what to say and do. However, when musicians are improvising they deploy these precise skills in choosing what and when to play. On the other hand, musicians are also deploying a vast repertoire of situationally specific improvisation skills that are learned and developed over months, years, and decades of creative activities. Therefore, improvisation is both a universal proficiency, accessible to all, and a series of skills that can be taught, developed, and honed to virtuosic levels, as I will discuss later in the chapter.

TALKING ABOUT IMPROVISATION

Adopting a social constructionist view leads on to one of the key issues in this chapter, namely, the importance of language in terms of how we talk about improvisation. How we talk about music influences how we hear music, how we play music, and the type of musical proficiencies we may develop. In this sense, talking about music is a key part of the overall music communication process (Miell et al., 2005). For example, two musicians discussing a concert they have just performed may talk about the types of chords, scales, soundscapes, and textures they used during the concert. Of course, there is a limitless list of possibilities in terms of what the musicians discuss, but what is clear is that the nature of this discussion can influence their aesthetic judgement of the concert and also their improvisational choices for future performances. Talking about music can therefore be just as important as the moment-to-moment decisions made during an improvisation since these discussions will influence the music performed (MacDonald & Wilson, 2020). In terms of the development of musical proficiency, how we talk about our musical lives will influence the development of specific musical proficiencies since our conversations can influence confidence levels and choices about what to play and with whom. Talking about improvising not only describes the process, but it also actively constructs improvisational moments in our memory via the discussions we may have with colleagues, family, and friends about the nature of music making and listening. These discussions function as psychological negotiations as we formulate and reformulate our musical views and plans based upon these crucial interactions.

IMPROVISATION AS REAL-TIME DECISION-MAKING

One way of conceptualizing improvisation is to view it as real-time decision-making in the sense that musicians are required to make choices about when to play and what to play, when to change what they are playing, and when to respond to others around them by contrasting or developing what they hear (Berkowitz, 2010). We developed a model for describing the type of creative decisions musicians make when improvising (Wilson & MacDonald, 2016) by asking musicians to improvise in trios, and then inviting the same musicians to listen to these recordings and discuss what they hear and the type of decisions they made.

One of the primary decisions an improviser has to make is what they wish to communicate. With this in mind, one of the often-quoted functions of music is the expression and communication of emotion (Juslin 2019; MacDonald, in press). Improvising musicians are also concerned with the communication of emotion, but just how this is achieved is unclear. McPherson et al. (2014) investigated how jazz musicians make decisions around structural features such as tonality (major and minor keys), tempo, articulation, and so on, in order to communicate emotion. These authors conclude that there is no simple relationship between structural features and particular emotions. Rather, musicians should be able to deploy a wide range of structural features in order to convey emotions (Johansen, 2018; Johansen, et al., 2019). It is also important to note that regardless of the emotion an improviser intends with a musical gesture, all music is heard through the listener's own experience and is therefore, to some extent, ambiguous (Born et al., 2017; MacDonald et al., 2017). Meaning is ascribed along a number of dimensions of which one is structural, the other two being cultural and associative (Wilson & MacDonald, 2019).

Another way to conceptualize the decision-making processes at the heart of improvisation is to think of it as real-time composition. In some respects, when we engage in improvisation we are creating on-the-spot compositions with no time to go back and edit, particularly when these choices are made in public (Toop, 2016). However, some of the creative choices to be made when improvising are exactly the same when composing. This suggests that to view improvisation as an all-or-nothing category is what might be termed a "false binary." It makes more sense to conceptualize improvisation as existing along a continuum with completely planned-out compositional processes at one end and completely spontaneous improvisational processes at the other. In addition, all musical activities involve an element of improvisation. For example, a violinist reading the score of Beethoven's Fifth Symphony will still be making in-the-moment decisions about volume, attack, length of note, and a host of other aspects of interpretation based on a set of variables such as the acoustics of room, proximity of other musicians and instruments, and the tempo set by the conductor. Granted, these decisions may not seem as significant as the type of choices a free improviser makes when beginning a performance with no preconceived plan, or a blues musician making note choices from within a specific scale. However, all these examples involve improvisational choices that have some similarity between them.

In an often-quoted anecdote, the composer and pianist Frederic Rzewski, who met saxophonist Steve Lacy in Rome, asked the following question: "Steve, in 15 seconds, what is the difference between composition and improvisation?" Rzewski was prescient enough to take out a tape recorder and record the response which was: "In 15 seconds, the difference between composition and improvisation is that in composition you have all the time you want to think about what to say in 15 seconds, while in improvisation you have only 15 seconds." The story goes that when Rzewski listened back to the recording, he observed that Lacy's answer took exactly 15 seconds. While we cannot be sure of the exact details of this anecdote, the point was brilliantly made that the differences between improvisation and composition are not as clear as one might expect.

This anecdote does hint at a number of differences between the processes. Biasutti (2015) discusses these differences in detail. For example, compositions can be edited, whereas improvisations are irreversible. In compositions, composers can have more control over what other musicians play, whereas in improvisation there is less implicit control and individuals have a greater degree of choice over what they play. In improvisation, performers have a more direct means of communication with the audience, whereas in composition, the composer has less direct connection with the audience (unless they are also performing). Improvisation also provides more opportunities for interactive communication with audiences as well as between performers, whereas composers have little or no chance to interact with audiences or the performers. There are also opportunities for immediate feedback from an infinite variety of sources when improvising (audience, colleagues, performance location, etc.), whereas with composition, unless the composer is present at the performance, these opportunities are much diminished.

The desire to offer a definitive description that can function as a conclusive all-encompassing definition for improvisation can be perplexing. Some authors discuss improvisation as something we do rather than something that is: in other words, a verb rather than a noun (Morris, 2012). This foregrounds the active aspects of improvising in the same way that Christopher Small's definition of music as *Musicking* emphasizes that music is also something we do (Small, 1998). While a conclusive definition may be beyond us right now, and is indeed limiting, it is important to attempt to outline what we see as key features, and perhaps problematize them, as they help us to understand in more detail the basic processes involved in improvisation.

IMPROVISATION AND CROSS-CULTURAL, INDIGENOUS, OR FIRST NATION MUSIC MAKING

When considering the utility of improvisation and how it can be developed, it is important to note that it plays a central role in music making around the world and that ethnomusicologists have long studied its prevalence and nature (Nettl, 2012). The crucial point from this work is that improvisation exists in all musical cultures and how it is conceptualized and performed is inextricably linked to its social context. While observing the ubiquitous presence of improvisation across musical cultures, Nettl and Russell (2008) note that improvisation has played a minor role in the ethnomusicological analyses of global music making. *Die Improvisation in der Musik* a book in German by Ernest Ferand (Ferand, 1938) is regarded as one of the first.

From an ethnomusicological perspective, the relationship between improvising and wider cultural practices is crucial, and improvised music plays a central role in religious and social rituals around the world (Blum, 1998). Inuit cultures use music events with improvisation at its heart to resolve grievances. People will improvise songs and melodies in public that outline the nature of their dispute, and friends and members of the public who listen are involved in helping resolve the dispute (Nettl & Russell, 2008). Recent years have seen the development of "complaints choirs" around the world, where people will sing their complaints, often improvised, as part of a community choir in public. These complaints choirs have echoes of Inuit improvised cathartic musical activity.[2]

Altered states of consciousness influenced by improvised music in native American social rituals are outlined by Nettl and Russell (2008). Improvisation also plays a central role in Indian and Iranian musical traditions, where musicians develop spontaneous melodies and rhythms based upon agreed scales and overarching structures (Nooshin, 2003). A study of Cuban flute playing by Miller (2013) also highlights similar approaches to improvisation.

Improvised music and dance play an important role in the social rituals of the indigenous peoples of Australia. Aboriginal culture utilizes improvised music and dance in such a way that they are woven into everyday life and are also part of key ceremonies and rituals called *corroborees* (Bradley & Mackinlay, 2007). These ethnomusicological studies signal the wide range of social situations into which improvisation is woven in complex and subtle ways. These studies also demonstrate the significance of a wider social and cultural context when studying improvisation (Novack, 1990).

All these examples demonstrate the importance of viewing improvisation as a social, collaborative, and universal form of music making, since its practice can be seen as a fundamental feature of music making around the world. John Blacking's groundbreaking book *How Musical Is Man* highlighted this idea of universal musicality, when he noted that every member of the Venda Society in Africa is viewed as musical and took part in many improvised music and dancing events that were inextricably woven into everyday life (Blacking, 1974).

PREVIOUS MODELS OF IMPROVISATION

There have been a number of approaches to developing overarching models of improvisation. Pressing (1988) developed an information processing account—a model that involves a number of discrete processes: sensory input (auditory, visual,

---

[2] http://www.complaintschoir.org/index.html.

proprioception), information processing (recognizing rhythms, scales, etc.), decision-making (what to play), and motor output (coordinating hand and fingers on a guitar fret board). Pressing's account outlines physiological processes, including neurological and hormonal systems. This account also includes motor coordination tasks involving muscles, bones, and connective tissue executing electrical instructions from the brain. Physiological feedback mechanisms then facilitate a constant flow of ideas to be executed as musicians use auditory, visual, and proprioceptive information to evaluate and generate new ideas (Beaty, 2015). Feedback is important, as it allows musicians to evaluate material that has just been played and make decisions about how to proceed, how to modify what they played, and how to continue within any given context (Keller et al., 2011). A key feature of Pressing's model is how these processes are integrated to produce improvised melodies, harmonies, rhythms, and textures. Repeated performance and practice allow the experienced improviser to execute these processes quickly and autotomize their responses (Wopereis et al., 2013). This process is sometimes called developing "muscle memory"—an ability to execute motor coordination tasks without being consciously aware of the fine-grained detail. There is some evidence that the concept of muscle memory is not purely a metaphor, as repeating specific tasks may produce a thickening of myelin sheaths around the axons of neurons, producing more efficient conduction of electrical impulses and greater ease of execution of coordinated movement (Takeuchi et al., 2010). Earlier work in this area (Johnson-Laird, 1988, 1991, 2002) highlights that a particular type of specialized knowledge related to genre and context also needs to be learned and accessed easily, almost unconsciously, in order for idiomatic improvisation to be proceed efficiently.

Kenny and Gellrich (2002) elaborated upon these ideas to present a model of mental processes implicated in improvisation that involves planning (decisions about what to play), recall (remembering what has been played), and feedback (judging what has just occurred in the improvisation). Biasutti and Frezza (2009) also present a cognitive model of improvisation that utilizes these features. A key element of their model is the development of knowledge around repertoire. Effective genre-based improvisers develop a knowledge of key repertoire that is shared, and this becomes a cornerstone of effective improvising. In one of the most in-depth studies of how jazz musicians describe their music practice and learning, Berliner (1994) highlights the importance of not only individual learning but also of collaborative practices in the development of improvisation skills. Monson (1996) also signals the importance of collaborative practice in her influential book that includes interviews with well-known jazz musicians.

A particularly innovative approach, drawing on cognitive theory, emphasizing group processes and the metaphor of the brain as a computing system, was outlined by Borgo (2006). This idea of group processes being important in the development of improvisation skills is developed by Keith Sawyer in a series of books (Sawyer, 2006, 2008, 2012, 2013), in which he discusses the social nature of improvisation. He describes how improvisation skills rely upon a group process where creativity is distributed across the group rather than residing purely within individual players. Ashley (2016) discusses key themes when considering how musicians develop improvisation skills. He notes that there are a number of constraints that influence the extent to which musicians can produce ideas spontaneously. The restrictions of real-time processing, both in terms of how fast our bodies can react and the reservoir of knowledge (both conscious and unconscious), and the embodied nature of improvising, all place certain constraints on how we improvise (Hamilton & Pearson, 2020).

Much of the cognitive approach to improvising focuses upon how jazz musicians develop specific genre-based skills including learning repertoire, scales, structures, and being able to spontaneously recreate music that adheres to the these broad, what one might call, "rules" (Caines & Heble, 2015). Also, other cognitive and neuroscientific research seeks to be generalizable to other improvisatory domains of behavior. For example, Goldman (2016), outlining a cognitive approach to studying improvisation, draws an analogy between musical improvisation and reaching out for a glass of water (drawing a similarity from music to everyday life in the generalization of certain motor behaviors).

However, if improvisation is a fundamental feature of life, as per Alvin Curran's quote at the start of this chapter, then our concept of improvisation must be broad enough to capture these specialist examples such as virtuosic jazz, folk, or Indian improvisations and also the cooing and babbling interactions of a newborn baby and its parents. The question remains: is John Coltrane really doing something similar to a newborn baby reaching out to its parents? Here I will say the answer is an emphatic yes! The social and creative decisions underlying Coltrane's choices are similar to those of a newborn baby: when to start, when to stop, evaluating what has just occurred, and choosing to maintain or change or stop. If there is to be a change, what will that change be? Will it be a development of something that has gone before? Or will it be complete contrast to what has gone before? These creative decisions underlie all improvisation. The nature of these decisions emerged from a series of studies that I and my colleague Graeme Wilson worked on over a number of years while investigating how musicians talk about improvisation.

This work was influenced by theories of identity and, in particular, musical identities (MacDonald et al., 2002). Identity has become a key concern for modern society in terms of our life choices (Giddens & Sutton, 2017); political identity, professional identity, and gender identity are understood to be much more fluid than they have been in previous times (MacDonald et al., 2002). For performing musicians, their professional identity is a central part of their practice as a musician, and in particular for musicians who improvise, their improvisational identities are a fundamental part of their lives (MacDonald et al., 2017). For example, jazz musicians' ability to work and support themselves and their families may rest upon their improvisational skills. Therefore, their views of improvisation become fundamentally important and, in turn, inform how they improvise. We reported that musicians did not have any agreed definition of jazz music or improvisation, and that they often have very different interpretations of the same improvisational moment. Indeed, the belief that musicians share a similar interpretation of the music they perform is a common trope or even cliché.

Schober and Spiro (2014) and Pras et al. (2017) have also shown that jazz musicians can interpret different meanings from music they have just performed. Importantly, these differing meanings do not suggest that the improvisation is viewed as unsuccessful. Often musicians will be very positive about the music they play but report different interpretations of what happened during the performance. This points toward the conclusion that the meaning of any improvisation is a social construction influenced by a range of variables. We took this social constructionist approach in a study investigating how musicians use different repertoires of talk when describing improvisational activities. For example, a repertoire of *mastery* was used by musicians when they wanted to emphasize that knowledge and technical skill were important features of an improvising musician's skill base. On the other hand, a repertoire of *mystery* was deployed when they wanted to foreground the more ineffable and soulful aspects of improvising. Here musicians emphasize the unlearnable, almost esoteric aspect of improvising. Importantly, we do not suggest that these repertoires are in any way a reflection of an objective truth, but more that musicians use these repertoires at particular times in order to fulfill particular identity needs. Very often we see musicians deploy both repertoires at same time.

PRACTICAL IMPLICATIONS

Given that this section has made a case for improvisation being a universal, creative, and spontaneous form of creativity, the next question we must turn to is: "What are the implications of these findings?" Below I set out a number of key implications for this work.

New virtuosities

Many of the proficiencies or skills of an improviser can be viewed as pertaining to what we might consider conventional virtuosity: for example, highly advanced motor coordination facilitating the execution of real-time decision making, acute aural skills allowing for recognition of scales and chords and rhythms, and advanced repertoire of songs memorized that can be performed readily. These skills foreground the type of technical mastery that is viewed as virtuosic.

One of the criticisms leveled at music education is that it focuses upon a narrow definition of virtuosity (Higgins & Campbell, 2010). Emphasizing technical mastery exclusively draws us away from broader creative skills that may also be viewed as virtuosic. For example, a key skill not just for improvisers, but indeed for all musical engagement, is listening. Developing improvisation skills necessitates developing listening skills, not just skills relating to assessing tonality or melody, but also skills regarding texture, timbre, as well as social aspects of the music such as what other musicians might need, want, or expect.

Listening skills facilitate improvisational decisions, so in this sense we can think of listening as a type of virtuosity. Influential composer and improviser Pauline Oliveros certainly believed in this skill, and her writings around *deep listening* foregrounded the importance of sensitive, reflective detailed listening (Oliveros, 2005). Related to these ideas is another type of virtuosity, a social virtuosity that may also come with increased experience of improvisation. Here a social virtuosity would include an understanding of ensemble musical decision making, and the types of material required within group situations. In this instance, musical decisions merge with broader creative and social decisions such as eye contact, nonverbal communication, when to stop playing and leave space for others, or when to support another musician with an emphatic musical gesture. These types of behaviors and decisions are ones that experienced improvisers can make with confidence, and importantly these actions can be conceptualized as proficiencies that can be learned and developed in the same way that learning a blues scale can be learned.

Improvising vocalist Maggie Nicols coined the term *social virtuosity* to include the types of social creative musical skills involved in improvising. Taken together, these ideas could be summarized to what we might believe to be a creative virtuosity, one that goes beyond technical mastery to include broader socio-musical skills. Although this chapter outlines a claim for the universality and accessibility of improvisation skills, many musicians will claim not to be able to improvise, perhaps due to a narrow definition of improvisation and an overt reliance upon the particular types of technical mastery most often seen in genre-specific improvising.

New education techniques

There is a vast and easily accessed literature focusing upon developing specific skills of improvisation within the jazz idiom. Many of these texts are instrument-specific, and perhaps the most well-known of these instructional guides is the Jamey Aebersold series of instructional texts (Aebersold, 1967). These approaches help musicians to gain skills in playing rhythmic and melodic patterns in different keys, developing fluid phrasing and learning the specifics of different types of jazz improvising (bebop, Latin, swing, etc.). An influential and different account of learning to improvise is presented by Sudnow (2001), who describes in significant detail how his hands and body move and seem to learn while improving. With detailed descriptive precision of his own piano playing, this phenomenological account focuses upon the embodied nature of improvising. It highlights the fundamental importance of being aware of how our body moves when improvising, and its very personal and physiological provides unique and important insights.

Utilizing a broad definition of improvisation affords significant educational implications beyond genre-specific approaches (Beegle, 2010; Campbell, 2009; Hickey,

2015). Hickey (2009) outlined ways in which free improvisation can be utilized in classroom activities. In this paper she discusses the proposition "can improvisation be taught?" and outlines a number of ways in which classroom teachers can teach children to develop improvisational skills that move beyond a conventional jazz-based approach, once again emphasizing that improvisation can be universally accessed. Siljamäki and Kanellopoulo (2020) undertook a systematic literature review revealing that different practices and theories are employed in the teaching of improvisation. These authors report that educators see improvisation teaching as enabling a deeper understanding of musical traditions along with specific skill development. Their participants also reported that teaching improvisation could enhance creativity generally, developing new music making and also cultivating social relationships that other researchers have suggested as well (e.g., Wall, 2018).

In terms of specific approaches that can be adopted, specialized conduction techniques can be employed to help novice improvisers develop skills. Holding out the palm of your hand and instructing children to play a long note when your finger touches your hand is a simple way of generating a series of improvised long notes and textures. This can be contrasted with short notes, obtained by clenching one's hand into a fist and tapping the other hand's index finger off the knuckles. Participants are invited to play a short note whenever the finger touches a knuckle. These two signs alone can create a rich textured piece of long notes and short notes and could form the basis of longer conducted improvisations. This approach, called *conduction* (a term taken from physics), was pioneered by American musician Butch Morris in 2010 as a means of structuring free improvisation. Conduction within improvisation has some similarities with conventional classical conduction techniques, in that one person gives specific instructions to a group of musicians regarding what to play. Hand gestures have specific meanings (e.g., long notes, short notes, loops, etc.). The key difference is that the musicians in improvised conduction make important choices about the material they play and they have no prewritten notes to guide them. The musicians can play any long note or any short note. The unique textures spontaneously created in these situation can be quite thrilling to experience, and often novice improvisers will be surprised at how conventionally "beautiful" a series of spontaneously and randomly created long-note harmonies can sound. An example of spontaneously created improvised textures with a large group of around can be seen at 14 minutes into the Ted talk in the footnote link.[3] A similar technique called *sound painting* was developed by Walter Thompson (Thompson, 2006) and is more frequently used to facilitate cross-disciplinary improvisation. This approach introduces young children to structured improvisation, and it can develop specific proficiencies with musical decision-making and enhance confidence in those decisions. Importantly, it can have exactly the same results

---

[3] https://www.youtube.com/watch?v=p4-g4FPJA_8.

for experienced musicians who may lack confidence or experience in improvisation. Teachers can also be taught this technique and it can be quickly and efficiently utilized in classroom contexts. Conduction can also be an excellent way of scaffolding people's early experiences of improvising. *Scaffolding* refers to types of support and facilitating a teacher can give students when helping them learn via instructions or encouragement (Leman et al., 2019). Improvised conduction is also utilized by experienced groups and large ensembles around the world, such as the Glasgow Improvisers Orchestra, London Improvisers Orchestra, and St. Petersburg Improvisers Orchestra. These groups all use this technique as means of exploring improvisation in large ensembles, sometimes with more than forty individuals.[4]

Other ways in which individuals can be introduced to improvisation include graphic scores and non-conventional music notation. Graphic scores represent music using visual images outside the realm of traditional music notation.[5] These can be independent works of visual art in their own right; however, the images function as musical scores to be read by musicians. Explanatory notes can direct the reading of each image. For example, color and shape might denote instrumentation, texture of music, pitch, and tone. Time can be expressed through horizontal and vertical lines. The images are then the base for unique musical explorations and improvisations. Modernist composers such as Cornelius Cardew, Iannis Xenakis, Earle Brown, John Cage, and Krzysztof Penderecki also utilized nonconventional notation in the form of graphic scores and embraced improvisational approaches in their work. Similar to conduction techniques, graphic notation can be used to enhance musical proficiencies in young children and experienced musicians who lack experiences in improvisation. The translation of shapes to music can be a simple instruction to comprehend. For example, a long thick blank line on a page can represent a long note, any long note, of the musician's choosing. A black dot can represent a short note. Thus, a drawing such as Figure 11.1 becomes an easily interpretable musical score that can be performed by groups of musicians of varying experience and varying instrumentation.

More complex instructions and images can also be developed, as in Figure 11.2.

Text-based approaches to improvising, where musicians are asked to respond to written material, can also be an excellent way to develop improvisation skills and create new work. Here musicians can be asked to respond to single words (or more complex sentences or paragraphs) with musical gestures. A piece may involve a series of flash cards with single words written on them such as "happy," "sad," "angry," "loud," "quiet" and "strange," and musicians are invited to respond to these words as the cards are turned over. Once again, this approach, although straightforward, can be used with musicians of all ages, experiences, and instrumentation to create complex and highly nuanced improvised music.

---

[4] https://www.youtube.com/watch?v=lFdHksQedA8.
[5] http://www.woodstockguild.org/PDFs/DrawingSoundCatalog.pdf.

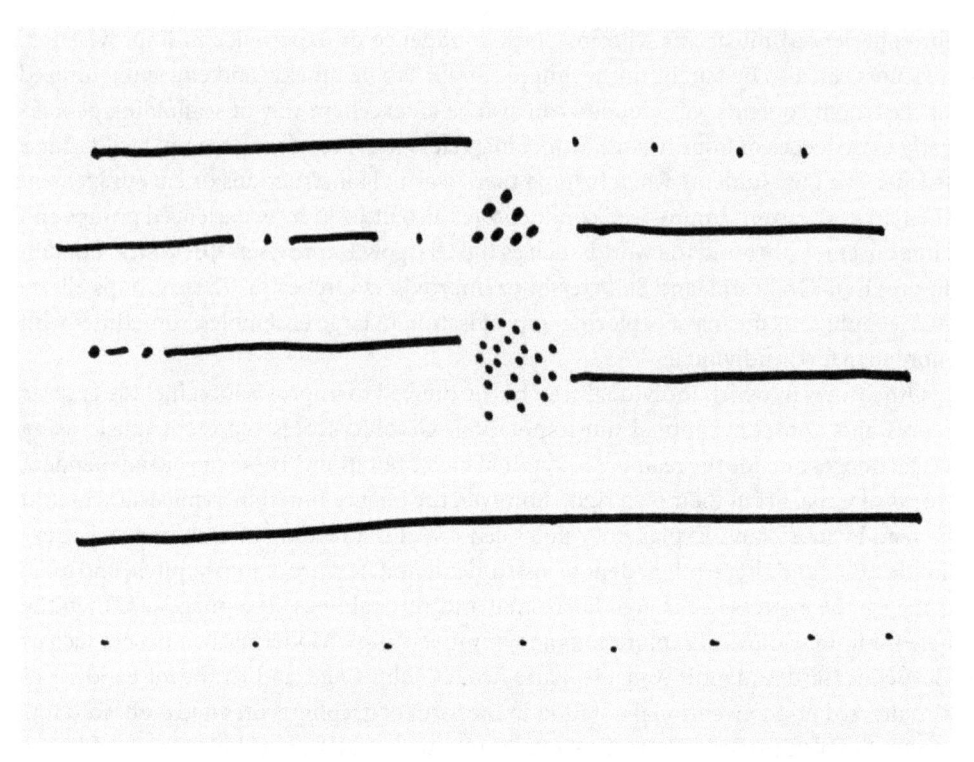

FIGURE 11.1. Long horizonal lines denote long notes of varying length. Dots represent short notes.

The development of improvisation skills

Another implication of the research I have outlined concerns the nature of improvisation and its relationship to skill development. Improvisation is not an all-or-nothing capacity. On the contrary, it can be developed incrementally over time (Chandler, 2018). Socio-musical skills learned during improvisation may generalize to other contexts (Kalmanovitch, 2016). Therefore, learning to improvise in some settings may enhance improvisation in another setting (Higgins & Mantie, 2013). Developing socio-musical skills that facilitate the ability to undertake in-the-moment creative choices while under pressure (e.g., in public or with others) may be transferable to other contexts (Currie, 2016). This is important when we consider that improvisation is taught in universities and conservatories globally, since we suggest that learning to improvise over a jazz standard, play a graphic score, or spontaneously collaborate with a dancer or artist helps develop skills and techniques that can have utility across a range of different situations (Martin & Minors, 2020; Wilson & MacDonald, 2019. In other words, learning to improvise fosters the development of transferable skills, the ability to collaborate, cooperate, compromise, and help reach solutions, and to do these things quickly and efficiently. These are skills an improvising musician must learn to develop.

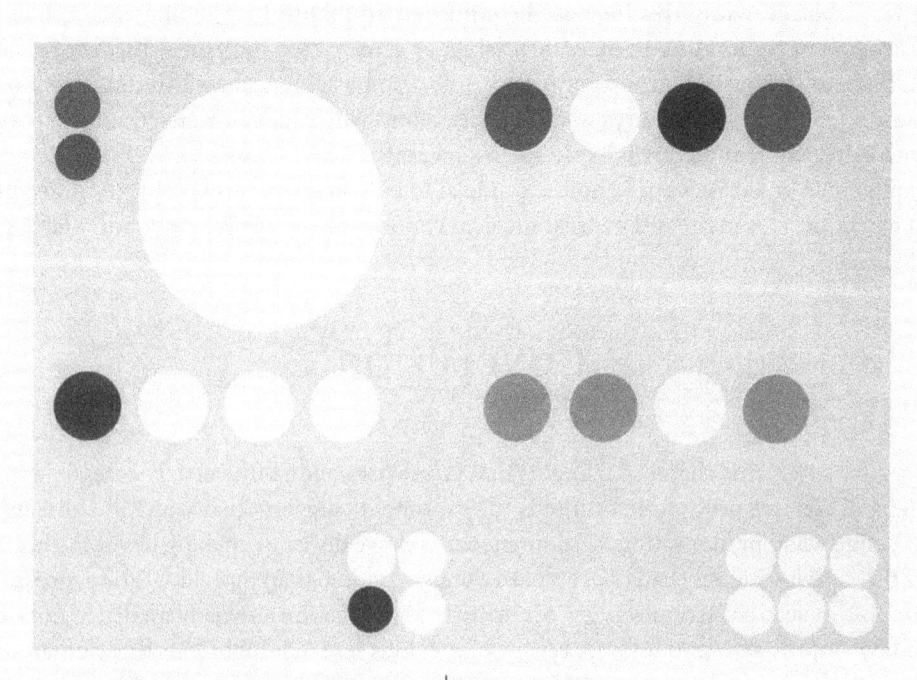

FIGURE 11.2. Initial instructions for improvised graphic score

The circles' sizes indicate the duration of the musical incidents to be played

Color indicates instrumentation and is also suggestive of pitch.

For example, the saxophone plays crimson circles circle while the greens, light and dark played by the bass. (Note: original poster was in color and the darkest circles are red and the lighter circles are green).

The background texture should be played quietly by a different instrument. Drums/percussion will keep time.

In terms of this discussion, we might conclude that a new conception of virtuosity in improvisation would include enhanced confidence in real-time decision-making in terms of choosing what to play, and a strong belief in the conceptual underpinnings of why those choices have been made. Over time, those choices would display nuance, complexity, and sophistication and would be coherent. There would also be an advanced ability to discriminate between available choices and a discernment for the type of choices made. This increased confidence would produce competence and decisiveness in responding to new, surprising, or unexpected moments. Incorporating all these examples into group contexts would also be achievable within this new virtuosity. These are all features and qualities along which performers could improve with experience, and there is evidence to suggest that this is possible (Virkkula, 2016). Confidence in performance choices can lead to enhanced musical identities in terms of career development and general musical confidence (Heble & Laver, 2016; Hickey et al., 2016).

Conclusion

To summarize, this chapter highlights that improvisation is a universally accessible social and creative process that unfolds in real time. It suggests that while it is difficult to define what improvisation is, spontaneous creative decision-making lies at the heart of this activity. Rather than conceptualize improvisation as an individualistic process, I propose instead a distributed view of creativity focused upon a socially mediated notion of how improvisation unfolds. A review of previous research highlights that numerous cognitive and neural processes are implicated as central to improvisation. These include memory, attention, retention, and motor coordination. Within genre-specific contexts this also includes the development of a knowledge of specific repertoires. Regardless of genre, a knowledge and understanding of the social context of improvisation is important for practitioners.

Improvisation can also foster cross-disciplinary collaborations in terms of facilitating conceptual breakthroughs and new work. The chapter also discusses various cross-cultural practices within improvisation, highlighting its ubiquitous presence globally and historically. Implications suggest that a new conception of musical virtuosities could include such issues as virtuosic listening, social virtuosity, and creative virtuosity. The chapter also discusses various teaching implications in connection with these findings, including conduction techniques, graphic scores, and text and multidisciplinary approaches. Finally, a discussion of development issues and the progressive accretion of skills related to improvisation is also highlighted.

Improvisation as an artistic process is enjoying an explosion of interest from practitioners and researchers around the world. Once central to classical music, it all but disappeared, with one or two exceptions (chiefly organists) at the end of nineteenth century (Moore, 1992). Prior to this, classical musicians would routinely incorporate improvisation into their performances. For example, cadenzas—usually the most technically elaborate passage of a classical soloist's performance—would be improvised. The advent of recording technology and listeners' desire to hear the same cadenza performed repeatedly was one factor in the gradual disappearance of improvisation from classical music, while it became prominent within jazz music during the twentieth century (Borio & Carone, 2018; Gooley, 2018). While twentieth-century Modernist classical composers such as Percy Grainger, Karlheinz Stockhausen, Milton Babbitt, and Henry Cowell, among many others, included improvisation in their scores, improvisation became viewed as the defining aspect of a jazz musician's technical repertoire. However, over the past twenty years we have seen a wave of interest with new festivals and academic societies dedicated to the study of improvisation as a uniquely creative and social process, applicable not only to all musical contexts but to all artistic endeavors.

As I write this chapter in 2020, I am reminded that this year has proven to be a year of change with a global pandemic radically shifting our priorities and forcing an evaluation of what society should look like. The tectonic plates of communication are shifting and necessitate a reimagining of how we exist together, locally and globally. Despite the need for physical distancing during the COVID-19 pandemic, music and improvisation have helped people stay connected. Whether it's music therapists using online improvised music to help clients adjust to the psychological stresses of social isolation, or residents singing from their home on balconies in Sicily, or playing dance music in high-rise apartments in Glasgow, or engaging in online group improvisations that include participants from across the world,[6] improvisation has helped people to stay connected and sustain their communities in life-threatening and troubling times. What is clear is that improvisation is a process whose time has come, and although we cannot be sure what the future holds for us, one thing is certain—the future will be improvised.

KEY SOURCES

Ashley, R. (2016). Musical improvisation. In S. Hallam, I. Cross, & M. Thaut (Eds.), *The Oxford handbook of music psychology* (2nd ed, pp. 336–378). Oxford: Oxford University Press.

Biasutti, M. (2015) Pedagogical applications of cognitive research on musical improvisation. *Frontiers in Psychology, 6*, 614. https://doi.org/10.3389/fpsyg.2015.00614.

Lewis, G. E., & Piekut, B. (Eds.). (2016a). *The Oxford handbook of critical improvisation studies* (Vols. 1&2). New York: Oxford University Press.

MacDonald, R., & Wilson, G. (2020). *The art of becoming: How group improvisation works.* New York: Oxford University Press.

Siljamäki, E., & Kanellopoulos, P. A. (2020). Mapping visions of improvisation pedagogy in music education research. *Research Studies in Music Education, 42*(1), 113–139. https://doi.org/10.1177%2F1321103X19843003.

---

[6] https://www.youtube.com/watch?v=sYpMSrpgg4Q.

REFLECTIVE QUESTIONS

1. Reflect on an instance where you have been required to improvise. How did you react, and what did you do, think, and feel at the time of improvising?
2. How, and in what ways, might your understanding of improvisation as an important part of performing have been shaped by reading this chapter?
3. With reference to this chapter, what particular skills do you feel you need to enhance within your own improvisational practice?
4. If you were asked to teach a class on improvisation, what activities would you use?
5. What do you think is happening musically, psychologically, and socially when you improvise?

REFERENCES

Aebersold, J. (1967). *How to play jazz and improvise.* New York: Jamey Aebersold Jazz.

Ashley, R. (2016). Musical improvisation. In S. Hallam, I. Cross, & M. Thaut (Eds.), *The oxford handbook of music psychology* (2nd ed., pp. 336–378). Oxford: Oxford University Press.

Bailey, D. (1993). *Improvisation: Its nature and practice in music.* Boston: Da Capo.

Beegle, A. C. (2010). A classroom-based study of small-group planned improvisation with fifth-grade children. *Journal of Research in Music Education, 58*(3), 219–239. https://doi.org/10.1177/0022429410379916.

Berkowitz, A. L. (2010). *The improvising mind: Cognition and creativity in the musical moment.* New York: Oxford University Press.

Berliner, P. F. (1994). *Thinking in jazz: The infinite art of improvisation.* Chicago: University of Chicago Press. ISBN 0-226-04380-0.

Bernhard, H. C., & Stringham, D. A. (2016). A national survey of music education majors' confidence in teaching improvisation. *International Journal of Music Education. 34*(4), 383–390. doi:10.1177/0255761415619069

Biasutti, M. (2015). Pedagogical applications of cognitive research on musical improvisation. *Frontiers in Psychology, 6,* 614. https://doi.org/10.3389/fpsyg.2015.00614.

Biasutti, M., & Frezza, L. (2009). The dimensions of music improvisation. *Creative Research Journal, 21,* 232–242. https://doi.org/10.1080/10400410902861240.

Beaty, R. E. (2015). The neuroscience of musical improvisation. *Neuroscience & Biobehavioral Reviews, 51,* 108–117. https://doi.org/10.1016/j.neubiorev.2015.01.004.

Bertinetto, A. (2013). Musical ontology: A view through improvisation. *Cosmo: Comparative Studies in Modernism, 2,* 81–101. https://doi.org/10.13135/2281-6658/316.

Blacking, J. (1974). *How musical is man?* Seattle: University of Washington Press.

Borgo, D. (2006). Sync or swarm: Musical improvisation and the complex dynamics of group creativity. *Algebra, Meaning and Computation, 4060,* 1–24. DOI: 10.1007/11780274_1

Blum, S. (1998). Recognizing improvisation. In B. Nettl & M. Russell (Eds.), *In the course of performance: Studies in the world of musical improvisation* (pp. 27–45). Chicago: University of Chicago Press.

Borio, G., & Carone, A. (Eds.). (2018). *Musical improvisation and open forms in the age of Beethoven.* London: Routledge.

Born, G., Lewis, E., & Straw, W. (Eds.). (2017). *Improvisation and social aesthetics*. Durham, NC: Duke University Press.

Bradley, J., & Mackinlay, E. (2007). Singing the land, singing the family: Song, place and spirituality amongst the yanyuwa. In F. Richards (Ed.), *The soundscapes of Australia: Music, place and spirituality* (pp. 75–91). London: Routledge. ISBN 9780754640721

Caines, R., & Heble, A. (Eds.). (2015). *The improvisation studies reader: Spontaneous acts*. London: Routledge.

Campbell, P. S. (2009). Learning to improvise music, improvising to learn music. In G. Solis & B. Nettl (Eds.), *Musical improvisation: Art, education, and society* (pp. 119–142). Chicago: University of Chicago Press.

Chandler, M. D. (2018). Improvisation in elementary general music: A review of the literature. *Update: Applications of Research in Music Education*, 37(1), 42–48. https://doi.org/10.1177%2F8755123318763002.

Currie, S. (2016). Improvise globally, strategize locally: Institutional structures and ethnomusicological agency. In A. Heble & M. Laver (Eds.), *Improvisation and music education: Beyond the classroom* (pp. 153–163). New York and London: Routledge.

Giddens, A., & Sutton, P. W. (2017). *Sociology*, (8th ed.), John Wiley and Sons Ltd. ISBN: 9780745696683

Goldman, A. (2016). Improvisation as a way of knowing. *Music Theory Online*, 22(4). Retrieved from: http://mtosmt.org/issues/mto.16.22.4/mto.16.22.4.goldman.html.

Gooley, D. (2018). *Fantasies of improvisation: Free playing in nineteenth-century music*. Oxford: Oxford University Press.

Hamilton, A., & Pearson, L. (2020). *The aesthetics of imperfection in music and the arts spontaneity, flaws and the unfinished*. London: Bloomsbury Academic.

Heble, A. & Laver, M. (Eds.). (2016). *Improvisation and music education: Beyond the classroom*. New York and London: Routledge.

Hickey, M (2015). Learning from the experts: A study of free-improvisation pedagogues in university settings. *Journal of Research in Music Education*, 62(4), 425–445. https://doi.org/10.1177%2F0022429414556319.

Hickey, M., Ankney, K., Healy, D., & Gallo, D. (2016). The effects of group free improvisation instruction on improvisation achievement and improvisation confidence. *Music Education Research*, 18(2), 127–141. https://doi.org/10.1080/14613808.2015.1016493.

Higgins, L., & Campbell, P. S. (2010). *Free to be musical: Group improvisation in music*. Lanham, MD: Rowman & Littlefield.

Higgins, L., & Mantie, R. (2013). Improvisation as ability, culture, and experience. *Music Educators Journal*, 100(2), 38–44. https://doi.org/10.1177%2F0027432113498097.

Johansen, G. G. (2018). Explorational instrumental practice: An expansive approach to the development of improvisation competence. *Psychology of Music* 46(1), 49–65. https://doi.org/10.1177/0305735617695657.

Johansen, G. G., Holdhus, K. C., Larsson, C., & MacGlone, U. (Eds.). (2019). *Expanding the space for improvisation pedagogy in music: A transdisciplinary approach*. London: Routledge.

Johnson-Laird, P. N. (1988). Freedom and constraint in creativity. In R. J. Sternberg (Ed.), *The nature of creativity* (pp. 202–219). Cambridge, UK: Cambridge University Press.

Johnson-Laird, P. N. (1991). Jazz improvisation: A theory at the computational level. In P. Howell, R. West & D. Cross (Eds.), *Representing musical structure* (pp. 291–325). New York: Academic Press.

Johnson-Laird, P. N. (2002). How jazz musicians improvise. *Music Perception, 19*(3), 415–442. https://doi.org/10.1525/mp.2002.19.3.415.

Juslin, P. N. (2019). *Musical emotions explained: Unlocking the secrets of musical affect.* Oxford: Oxford University Press.

Kalmanovitch, T. (2016). Teaching the "complete musician": Contemporary improvisation at New England Conservatory. In A. Heble & M. Laver (Eds.), *Improvisation and music education: Beyond the classroom* (pp. 164-175). New York and London: Routledge.

Keller, P., Weber, A., & Engel, A. (2011). Practice makes too perfect: Fluctuations in loudness indicate spontaneity in musical improvisation. *Music Perception, 29*(1), 109–114. https://doi.org/10.1525/mp.2011.29.1.109.

Kenny, B. J., & Gellrich, M. (2002). Improvisation. In R. Parncutt & G. E. McPherson (Eds.), *The science and psychology of music performance: Creative strategies for teaching and learning* (pp. 117–134). New York: Oxford University Press.

Leman, P. Bremner, A. J. Parke, R. D. & Gauvain, M. (2019) *Developmental psychology.* New York: McGraw-Hill Education.

Lewis, G. E., & Piekut, B. (Eds.). (2016a). *The Oxford handbook of critical improvisation studies* (Vol. 1). New York: Oxford University Press.

Lewis, G. E., & Piekut, B. (Eds.). (2016b). *The Oxford handbook of critical improvisation studies* (Vol. 2). New York: Oxford University Press.

MacDonald, R. A. R. (2021). The social functions of music: Communication, wellbeing, art, ritual, identity and social networks (C-WARIS). In A. Creech, D. Hodges, & S. Hallam (Eds.), *Routledge international handbook of music psychology in education and the community* (pp. 5–20). London: Routledge.

MacDonald, R. A. R., Miell, D., & Hargreaves, D. J. (Eds.). (2017). *The Oxford handbook of musical identities.* Oxford: Oxford University Press.

MacDonald, R., Miell, D., & Hargreaves, D. J. (2002). *Musical Identities.* Oxford University Press. https://doi.org/10.1093/oxfordhb/9780199298457.013.0043

MacDonald, R. & Wilson, G. (2020). *The art of becoming: How group improvisation works.* New York: Oxford University Press.

Martin, B., & Minors, H, J. (Eds.). (2020). *Artistic research in performance through collaboration.* Cham: Palgrave Macmillan.

McPherson, M. J., Lopez-Gonzalez, M., Rankin, S. K., & Limb, C. J. (2014). The role of emotion in musical improvisation: An analysis of structural features. *PLoS ONE, 9*(8), e105144. https://doi.org/10.1371/journal.pone.0105144.

Miell, D., MacDonald, R., & Hargreaves, D. J. (2005). (Eds.), *Musical communication.* Oxford University Press. ISBN 0-19-852935X

Miller, S. (2013). *Cuban flute style: Interpretation and improvisation.* Lanham: MD: Scarecrow Press: ISBN 978-0-8108-8441-0.

Monson, I. (1996). *Saying something: Jazz improvisation and interaction.* Chicago: University of Chicago Press.

Moore, R. (1992). The decline of improvisation in Western art music: An interpretation of change. *International Review of the Aesthetics and Sociology of Music, 23*(1), 61–84.

Morris, J. (2012). *Perpetual frontier: The properties of free music.* Stony Creek, CT: Riti Publishing.

Nettl, B. (2012). Some contributions of ethnomusicology. In G. E. McPherson, & G. F. Welch (Eds.), *The Oxford handbook of music education* (Vol. 1, pp. 105–124). New York: Oxford University Press.

Nettl, B., & Russell, M. (Eds.). (2008). *In the course of performance: Studies in the world of musical improvisation*. Chicago and London: University of Chicago Press.

Nooshin, L. (2003). Improvisation as "other": Creativity, knowledge and power—The case of Iranian classical music. *Journal of the Royal Musical Association, 128*(2), 242–296. https://doi.org/10.1093/jrma/128.2.242.

Novack, C. J. (1990). *Sharing the dance: Contact improvisation and American culture*. Madison: University of Wisconsin Press.

Oliveros, P. (2005). *Deep listening: A composer's sound practice*. New York and Lincoln, NE: iUniverse.

Pras, A., Schober, M. F., & Spiro, N. (2017). What about their performance do free jazz improvisers agree upon? A case study. *Frontiers in Psychology, 8*, 966. https://doi.org/10.3389/fpsyg.2017.00966.

Pressing, J. (1988). Improvisation: Methods and models. In J. A. Sloboda (Ed.), *Generative processes in music: The psychology of performance, improvisation, and composition* (pp. 129–178). Oxford: Clarendon Press.

Sawyer, R. (2006). Group creativity: Musical performance and collaboration. *Psychology of Music, 34*(2), 148–165. https://doi.org/10.1177/0305735606061850.

Sawyer, R. (2012). *Explaining creativity: The science of human innovation* (2nd ed). Oxford: Oxford University Press.

Sawyer, R. (2013). *Zig zag: The surprising path to greater creativity*. New York: Wiley.

Schober, M. F., & Spiro, N. (2014). Jazz improvisers' shared understanding: A case study. *Frontiers in Psychology, 5*, 808. https://doi.org/10.3389/fpsyg.2014.00808.

Sudnow, D. (2001). *Ways of the hand: A rewritten account*. Cambridge, MA: MIT Press.

Takeuchi, H., Sekiguchi, A., Taki, Y., Yokoyama, S., Yomogida, Y., Komuro, N., Yamanouchi, T., Suzuki, S., & Kawashima, R. (2010). Training of working memory impacts structural connectivity. *J Neurosci., 30*(9), 3297–303. doi: 10.1523/JNEUROSCI.4611-09.2010. PMID: 20203189; PMCID: PMC6634113.

Thompson, W. (2006). *Soundpainting: The art of live composition*. New York: Walter Thompson.

Thompson, W. F. (2003). A matter of taste: Evaluating improvised music. *Creativity Research Journal, 15*(2-3), 287–296. https://doi.org/10.1080/10400419.2003.9651421.

Toop, D. (2016). *Into the maelstrom: Music, improvisation and the dream of freedom, before 1970*. London: Bloomsbury.

Trevarthen, C. (2002). Origins of musical identity: Evidence from infancy for musical social awareness. In R. MacDonald, D. Miell, & D. Hargreaves (Eds.), *Musical identities* (pp. 21–38). Oxford: Oxford University Press.

Virkkula, E. (2016). Informal in formal: The relationship of informal and formal learning in popular and jazz music master workshops in conservatoires. *International Journal of Music Education, 34*(2), 171–185. https://doi.org/10.1177/0255761415617924.

Wall, M. P. (2018). Improvising to learn. *Research Studies in Music Education, 40*(1), 117–135. https://doi.org/10.1177%2F1321103X17745180.

Wilson, G. B., & MacDonald, R. A. R. (2019). "It's got a life of its own": Teaching group improvisation through responsive choices. In G. G. Johansen, K. M. Holdhus, C. Larsson, & U. MacGlone (Eds.), *Expanding the space for improvisation* (pp. 211–222). London: Routledge.

Wopereis, I. G. J. H., Stoyanov, S., Kirschner, P. A., & Van Merriënboer, J. J.G. (2013). What makes a good musical improviser? An expert view on improvisational expertise. *Psychomusicology: Music, Mind, and Brain, 23*(4), 222–235. https://psycnet.apa.org/doi/10.1037/pmu0000021.

CHAPTER 12

···

MEMORIZATION

···

JANE GINSBORG

INTRODUCTION

···

HAVE you ever witnessed a performance in which a musician experienced a memory lapse? Have you ever given a performance in which you forgot the words of a song, missed an entry, or simply "blanked out"? If so, you are not alone. Very few performers have *not* had this experience, whether the audience knew it at the time or not. For example, the celebrated singer Kiri Te Kanawa lost her place while performing "Dove sono" from Mozart's *Le nozze di Figaro* at the Metropolitan Opera Centennial Gala in 1983, broadcast to a huge audience around the world. She was only adrift from the orchestra for five measures lasting no more than 14 seconds, but it must have felt to her and the conductor, James Levine, like minutes if not hours (you can search for and watch a recording of this performance via online video-sharing platforms; the lapse occurs between 5′29″ and 5′43″). Most musicians who perform from memory—although this is a convention that applies only to a small proportion of singers and instrumentalists—are familiar with the fear of forgetting on stage. Knowledge is a powerful tool for reducing fear. In this chapter you will learn how memory is currently understood, how music is memorized both spontaneously and deliberately, and about a range of strategies for memorizing music that have been used successfully by musicians and that are also supported by the findings of empirical research.

HOW MEMORY IS CURRENTLY UNDERSTOOD

···

Stores and processes

Memory used to be thought of as a series of stores, but more recently it has also come to be understood as a series of processes. It can be helpful for musicians who memorize and perform from memory to think of it in both ways. For example, when we have memorized a piece of music and performed it successfully from memory several times or perhaps, indeed, many times, we can think of that piece of music as being stored in our long-term memory, much as an album of treasured family photographs might be stored in an attic. Retrieving the music so that we can recall it when we perform it again is a process, rather like the process of climbing into the attic, finding the photograph album, and bringing it downstairs when it is wanted. Unlike an album, however, music requires a great deal of processing before it can be stored and retrieved from long-term memory.

Sensory and short-term memory stores

The performer's first encounter with the piece of music to be memorized and performed from memory is likely to involve hearing a live or recorded performance or reading a notated score. This can be thought of as the stimulus that enters the sensory store in the form of auditory or visual information (the sensory store also holds tactile and olfactory information) but which remains there only as long as it takes for the performer to pay attention to it—by listening rather than hearing, by reading rather than by seeing. Once the performer has registered the stimulus by paying attention to it, it can be thought of as entering the short-term memory store. While long-term memory has infinite capacity and can last a lifetime, short-term memory has the capacity for only five to nine items, or chunks of information, which are retained for one or two minutes at the most. Short-term memory can be thought of as a form of temporary storage.

It is no coincidence that when telephone numbers were first introduced by the Bell Telephone Company (a year after George Miller's seminal article "The magic number seven, plus or minus two" was published in 1956), they consisted of seven digits, so that they would be easy to remember for just long enough to be written down from memory. In the very early stages of learning to play an instrument or to read music, the items that can be stored in short-term memory consist of single elements such as notes or very small groups of elements such as chords, but it is not long before they begin to be combined and encoded as larger groups or chunks such as scales, arpeggios, and chord progressions. Nevertheless, unless these items—whether single elements or chunks—are processed in such a way that they can be stored in long-term memory, they are forgotten just as a telephone number is forgotten once it has been recorded, whether in writing or by being added to a list of contacts in a cellular phone directory.

Long-term memory store

The processes that enable information in short-term memory to be stored in long-term memory, which has infinite capacity for knowledge that can be stored indefinitely, are known as *rehearsal* and *elaboration*. We can remember telephone numbers for long enough to record them by rehearsing them, or repeating them over and over again, just as we can train ourselves to play scales and arpeggios by practicing them repeatedly. We can memorize long telephone numbers by elaborating them or making sense of them by reference to information that is already stored in our long-term memory. A digit string such as 0033493860508 can be broken down into five easily remembered chunks if 00 is associated with a country code, 334 with France, 93 with the area code for the Alpes-Maritimes department of France, and 86 05 08 with a unique telephone number. Just as telephone numbers can be memorized if they are grouped meaningfully, so three kinds of knowledge stored in long-term memory can be used to group the notes and chords as scales, arpeggios, and chord progressions. These three kinds of knowledge are described as semantic, episodic, and procedural.

Semantic and episodic knowledge

Semantic knowledge is knowledge *about* something, while episodic knowledge is *of* something: information that has not been learned but experienced personally. The two kinds of knowledge do, of course, interact; I have semantic knowledge of France and French telephone numbers, but I have episodic memories of regular visits to the Alpes-Maritimes, and indeed this particular telephone number was that of my late parents for twenty years. Similarly, when we memorize a piece of music we may draw on our semantic knowledge of the composer, the context of the piece within the composer's output, and its performance and recording history, but we also draw on our episodic memories of having heard performances of the piece by other people and of having given performances of it ourselves. If we have performed it many times, one or more performances may be particularly memorable for a variety of reasons such as their circumstances, venue, or outcome.

Procedural knowledge

Semantic and episodic knowledge interact with each other, and also with the third kind of knowledge—procedural knowledge of *how to do* something such as tying a shoelace, riding a bicycle, skateboarding, yodeling, or playing a scale, arpeggio, or chord progression. We all have episodic memories of the first or the most recent times we did these things, although it can be difficult—even sometimes for teachers—to articulate them in words using their semantic knowledge. Procedural knowledge is intrinsic to playing an instrument, to singing, and to memorizing music in such a way that it can be performed both accurately and fluently from memory.

Working memory

The account of memory as a series of three stores—sensory, short-term, and long-term, holding semantic, episodic, and procedural knowledge—and the concepts of attention, rehearsal, and elaboration that link them, are derived from Atkinson and Shiffrin's (1968) *modal model*. This model continues to be useful for explaining that we store different kinds of information for different lengths of time, from fleeting moments in the sensory store, through 90 seconds or so in the short-term store, to indefinitely in the long-term store; the latter explains, for example, why music we may not have heard for years, if not decades, can evoke vivid memories, and how it is that we can even summon the long-forgotten lyrics or melodies of songs in certain contexts. The modal model is less useful for explaining the processes whereby we are able to encode information for storage or how we can retrieve it at will, as musicians must do when they memorize a piece of music and recall it for performance from memory. These tasks are typical of human problem solving in domains other than music, of course. To begin to explain problem-solving processes, Baddeley and Hitch (1974) proposed their model of *working memory*. These processes were thought to occur once information has been received from the senses, but before it is stored in long-term memory. For this reason, working memory is illustrated in Figure 12.1 within the short-term memory store.

Baddeley and Hitch have now been developing and testing the working memory model for nearly half a century. Its original three components were the *central executive*, which allocates attentional resources to different kinds of information: visual/spatial, encoded on the *visuo-spatial sketchpad*, and verbal/acoustic, encoded via the *phonological* (previously the *articulatory*) loop. Baddeley (2000) proposed a fourth component, the *episodic buffer*, which is currently conceived as a means of combining these different kinds of information, and others, and making them available to conscious awareness (Baddeley, 2012; Baddeley et al., 2019). These other kinds of information include color and shape as characteristics of visual information; kinesthetic and tactile aspects of haptic information (i.e., touch and feel); smell and taste; the comprehension of sign language and lip reading as well as speech; and music and sound.

Long-term working memory

On its own, however, the working memory model does not explain how we can learn to encode, store, and—above all—retrieve at will much more information than would be expected on the basis of what is known about the capacity of short-term memory, nor how we can make use of it for planning and reasoning. Building on both the modal model and the working memory model, Ericsson and Kintsch (1995) proposed a link between them known as *long-term working memory* (LT-WM). This explains how we make use of knowledge stored in long-term memory to group items of information held in short-term memory—whether numbers or elements of music, as described earlier— and, by so doing, encode them and store them in long-term memory in such a way that they can be recalled both quickly and reliably. Ericsson and Kintsch based their model on evidence from research on expertise in a range of domains, from chess (e.g., Chase & Simon, 1973) to restaurant orders (Ericsson & Polson, 1988). Three principles underlie LT-WM: first, the ability to encode new information using existing knowledge to make the new knowledge meaningful and therefore memorable; second, the use of a well-learned retrieval framework; and third, extended practice to make retrieval faster

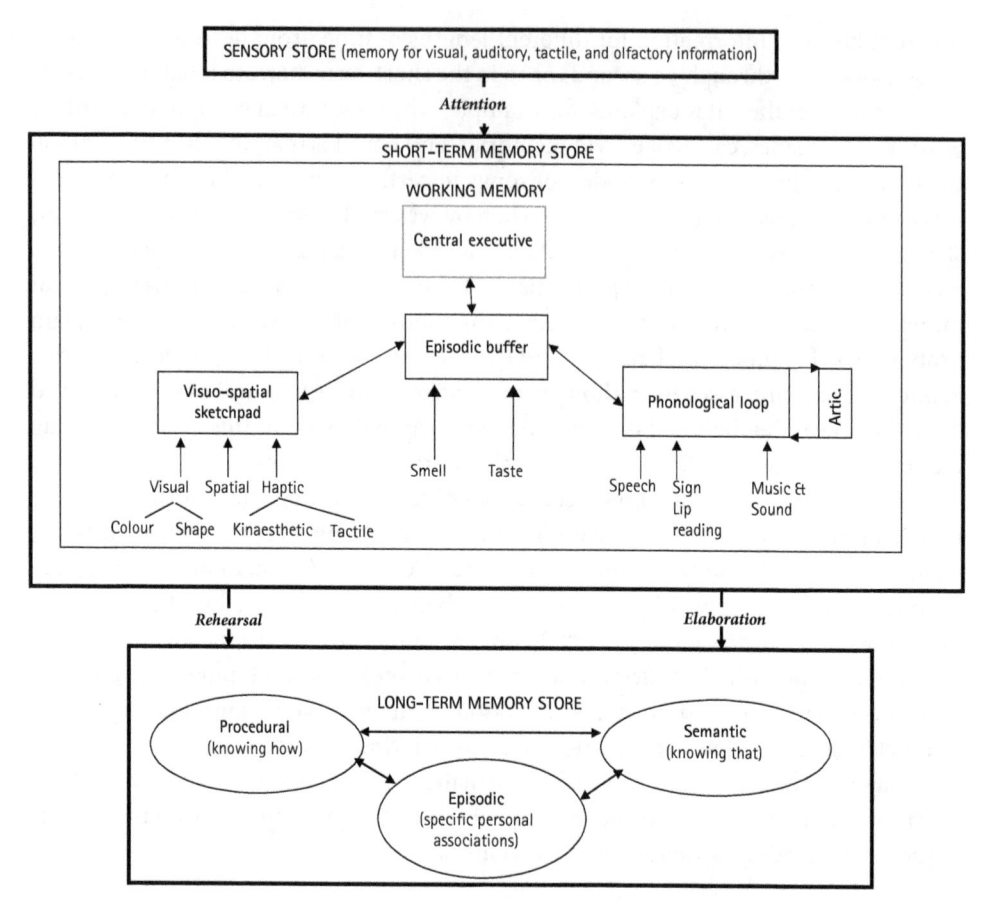

FIGURE 12.1. Updated model of memory adapted from Eysenck and Keane (2000) and Baddeley et al. (2019).

and more efficient. The first two principles clearly depend on the use of semantic and episodic information that has been stored and organized hierarchically in long-term memory, while extended practice makes use, in addition, of procedural knowledge.

The application of LT-WM to expert memorization and recall for music

These three principles underlie expert musicians' memorization and recall for music. First, musical information must be encoded meaningfully. In the case of notated music, the musician starts by decoding the score; in the case of music that is listened to, the musician makes sense of it in terms of its most salient characteristics (such as its key, chord progressions, or verse-chorus structure). Meaningful encoding involves chunking, with reference to knowledge stored in long-term memory as the result of repeated past experiences of reading, listening to, and playing music. Second, the formal or compositional structure of the music provides a retrieval framework whereby the musician can access and retrieve chunks of musical information from long-term memory. Third, extended practice, including mental practice, reinforces the musician's memory for each chunk of musical information and each larger chunk as the musician combines them while memorizing.

MEMORIZING MUSIC SPONTANEOUSLY AND DELIBERATELY

Roger Chaffin and his colleagues, many of whom are expert musicians, have been studying memorization and the performance of music from memory for more than twenty-five years. They have concluded that successful memorization is typically the result of two processes, one spontaneous and the other deliberate (Chaffin et al., 2016).

Serial cuing

The spontaneous process is known as *serial cuing*.[1] It occurs automatically while we are engaging in the earliest stages of meaningful encoding and extended practice, and is experienced when what we are about to play or sing serves as a cue for the next bit of music that we need to play or sing (this is known as *prospective memory*). We know what comes next because it is stored in our long-term memory, either because we have heard it, played it, or sung it before, or because we can draw on *schemas* (items of relevant information, grouped together in long-term memory) presenting a range of possibilities— within constraints imposed by the music such as its tonality and meter—from which we can choose the most appropriate one. It is difficult to articulate how we choose the most appropriate possibility, however, since the kind of information we memorize through serial cuing tends to be procedural: playing scales, arpeggios, or a series of familiar chord progressions. It is vital, of course, for musicians to be able to group these and other kinds of musical sequences together to form longer passages that can be played automatically, so that they do not need to expend any effort on trying to recall what comes next. When preparing to perform a piece of music from memory, however, it is dangerous to rely solely on the serial cuing produced by rote repetitive practice, since the sequence can easily be interrupted. We experience disruptions as memory lapses. When they occur,

---

[1] Until relatively recently this process was called *associative chaining* (e.g. Chaffin et al., 2016). The term has been replaced by *serial cuing* because it has fewer theoretical connotations than associative chaining, which typically refers to a particular explanation for serial position effects in serial recall based on item-to-item associations (see Lindsey & Logan, 2019). In music performance, serial cuing occurs on multiple time scales, not just note-to-note (beat-to-beat, bar-to-bar; phrase-to-phrase, etc.).

it can be difficult to continue; we have to go back to the beginning of the piece and hope that the sequence will have mended itself, somehow, by the time we arrive at the place where it broke, so that we can carry on to the end without further mishap.

Content-addressable memory

Content-addressable memory, by contrast, can only be established in the course of deliberate and thoughtful practice, defined by Ericsson (2013), specifically in relation to music making, as "the engagement with full concentration in a training activity designed to improve a particular aspect of performance with immediate feedback, opportunities for gradual refinement by repetition and problem-solving" (p. 534)—in other words, to make use of LT-WM. To have content-addressable memory for a piece of music is to be able to retrieve it from long-term memory in such a way that it is possible to start playing or singing at locations other than the beginning of the piece, such as the beginning of the second verse or the start of the coda.

The development of content-addressable memory for music has been demonstrated in a series of longitudinal case studies investigating how expert musicians go about the task of memorizing and performing from memory, carried out by Roger Chaffin and colleagues including the pianists Gabriela Imreh (e.g., Chaffin et al., 2005; Chaffin et al., 2003; Chaffin, 2007) and Cristina Capparelli Gerling (Chaffin et al., 2013), the cellist Tânia Lisboa (Chaffin et al., 2010; Lisboa et al., 2018), and the singer Jane Ginsborg (e.g., Ginsborg et al., 2012). In these studies, the musicians tracked their learning and memorization of the works they were to perform from memory. They did so by recording and transcribing their practice and annotating their musical scores to indicate the locations and nature of their thoughts about the music during practice and performance. Their thoughts were found to function as cues for prospective memory. These cues can be seen as landmarks in their *mental representations* or maps of the piece of music. They have come to be known as *performance cues*, even though they cannot be shown to serve as cues for retrieval in performance until there is evidence of their doing so in repeated performances.

Performance cues

Converging evidence from these and other studies suggest that the most useful cues are those provided by our understanding of the compositional structure of the piece, whether this is a 32-bar song in AABA form, the first movement of a Classical sonata, or a four-movement Romantic symphony. Since memory for the musical figures that form the building blocks of phrases is nested within memory for phrases within sections, sections within movements, and movements within larger works, we can see that compositional structure provides an invaluable *hierarchical retrieval organization* enabling content-addressable access. It is important to note that there is no single correct understanding of the structure of a particular piece of music; it is the musician's own representation of the structure that provides the framework for retrieval. Accordingly, a variety of other cues can serve as landmarks. They can be conceptualized as *basic* (e.g., to do with fingering, bowing, pedaling, breathing, phrasing), *interpretive* (e.g., dynamics, tempo, rubato), and *expressive* (e.g., how to implement interpretive decisions). Many of these originate in decisions made while learning and practicing the piece alone or rehearsing it with others.

Spontaneous insights in performance

As musicians know only too well, not everything that happens during a performance has been prepared during practice; as Emil Gilels states, "It is different each time I play" (Mach, 1991, p. 123, quoted by Chaffin et al., 2007, p. 455). The LT-WM model was developed, in part, to explain how we can make use of the knowledge stored in long-term memory for planning and reasoning, which—in relation to music—we might think of as *interpretation* or the ability to improvise, coupled with the flexibility to respond to unexpected events during performance.

Ginsborg et al. (2012) explored the role of prepared and unprepared thoughts during performance as cues in subsequent performances and found that performance can be a valuable source of spontaneous, new insights. Geeves et al. (2013) developed an alternative model derived from interviews with professional performers in a range of musical genres: the Applying Intelligence to the Reflexes (AIR) approach. They argued that expert skill in music performance is apparently paradoxical in that it relies on "mindedness characterized by flexibility" (p. 688), enabling musicians to allocate their attention where it is most needed so they can respond to the moment-by-moment demands of the performance situation. The work of Chaffin and his colleagues has been criticized for emphasizing the role of deliberate preparation for performance, but it is worth remembering that it derives largely from research with classical soloists; spontaneity in performance is a theme in Ginsborg's research, which has been carried out with classical singer-pianist (e.g., Ginsborg, Chaffin, & Nicholson, 2006) and singer-viola player duos (e.g., Ginsborg & Bennett, 2021), while the ten performers interviewed by Geeves et al. (2013) included just one classical musician. Musicians do, of course, differ in their approaches to memorization and performance from memory, and these may well vary not only from genre to genre and, indeed, piece to piece, but also because they have been taught—or at least encouraged—to memorize using different strategies.

Musicians' Memorization Strategies

A brief history of the pedagogy of memorizing

The history of the pedagogy of memorizing is brief because—as I pointed out at the beginning of this chapter—performance from memory is a convention that has applied only to a comparatively small proportion of professional Western classical musicians for a relatively short period of time. Until well into the nineteenth century, it was much more important for musicians to be able to improvise than to memorize (Ginsborg, 2017; Kopiez, Wolf & Platz, 2017; Mishra, 2010). Although being able to memorize is important for those musicians who are required to perform from memory—typically solo pianists, singers who perform in opera or give song recitals, and concerto soloists—it is rarely taught formally. According to the master-apprentice model of teaching prevalent in music conservatories and schools of music, teachers pass on the knowledge they learned from their teachers to their students. The recommendations of the earliest pedagogues were thus what we would now call "anecdotal," based on experience rather than evidence from research. Yet much of the evidence, from the experiments designed by psychologists to test the general theories of memory outlined earlier in this chapter to the studies of different strategies for music memorization discussed later, supports those early recommendations, so it is well worth reviewing them.

Pedagogical recommendations: visual, auditory, kinesthetic, and analytic memory

Shinn (1898), for example, identified four "forms of memory belonging respectively to the ear, the fingers, the eye, and the intellect employed more or less continuously throughout the progress of a piece" (p. 1). Like Shinn, Hughes (1915) referred to the ear, fingers, eye, and intellect, but he extended the last category to encompass knowledge of formal structure and the ability consciously to draw on that knowledge, if not actually to be able to articulate it in words:

> Piano music may be memorized in three ways: by ear, visual memory, either of the notes on the printed page or the notes on the keyboard, and by finger memory or reflex action.[2] On one or both of the first two ways are dependent the very useful and important methods of learning the harmonic and formal structure of the composition to be memorized and of being able to *say* the notes, or at least to bring up a very distinct mental picture of them. (Hughes, 1915, p. 595)

Pedagogical recommendations: mental strategies

The great piano teacher Leschetizky, however, recommended the use of what we would now call *mental practice*:

> Thought is indispensable in the study of pieces, as they are learned first by the brain, and from that by the fingers. . . . To memorize a piece, read it through at the keyboard

---

[2] On the previous page of the article, Hughes had strongly discouraged the use of "finger memory or reflex action."

only once, to get its outline without creating any faulty habits of fingering. Then take one or two measures at a time . . . analyze the harmonies and decide upon the fingering and pedalling. (Brée & Bernstein, 1913/1997, p. 57)

Two pedagogues of singing concurred with Leschetizky's view. Taylor (1914) wrote: "In studying a song, the first thing to do is memorize it, so that the mind will not be taxed with trying to recall the words and the melody" (p. 26); and Curtis (1914) proposed that "all work of learning and memorizing music should be mental. When the mind is concentrated upon learning the melody, rhythm and construction of a composition, the voice should not be used" (p. 207).

Summary of pedagogical recommendations

To summarize these early examples of pedagogical recommendations, memorizing requires the use of auditory, visual, and kinesthetic strategies to answer questions such as: What should the music sound like? What is meant by the information on the page? How does it feel to play or sing the music? and How many times do I have to repeat it before my fingers or lips will be able to do it automatically? Above all, however, what Hughes (1915) had dubbed the "intellect"—what we might now define as the application of knowledge to a problem-solving task—is needed for analyzing the music so that it can be memorized reliably and, of course, for making the decisions that will create a convincing performance, whether or not it is given from memory. The process of analyzing a piece of music requires the musician to draw on their general knowledge of compositional structures, which is already stored in long-term memory, so as to create a mental representation of the compositional structure of the music to be memorized. This representation takes the form of a hierarchical retrieval organization, enabling content-addressable access to the music when the performer is playing or singing from memory.

Evidence from research: the inseparability of visual, auditory and kinesthetic strategies

While both the working memory model shown in Figure 12.1 and the early pedagogues distinguish between different forms of memory (visuo-spatial and phonological; visual, auditory, kinesthetic, analytic), the findings of empirical research suggest that they are, in practice, inseparable. Although some musicians say they can "see" the score in their mind's eye when playing from memory (e.g., Marcus, 1979), there is little reliable evidence to suggest that this is a useful strategy, on its own, for memorizing. One study claimed to show that piano and composition students who reported using a visual strategy were quicker to memorize a newly composed piece of music than students who reported using kinesthetic, auditory, or combined strategies (Nuki, 1984). It transpired first, however, that these students were also the best sight-readers, scoring high in their solfège examinations, and, second, that the term *visual strategy* had been inferred to mean the use of the so-called inner ear or *notational audiation* (Gordon, 1976). In a more recent comparison of student pianists' memorizing strategies, as recommended by the early pedagogues, Herrera and Cremades (2014) administered the Musical Memorization Inventory (Mishra, 2007) to student pianists and found that visual memory was the strategy reported least often (analytic was the most popular, followed by auditory and kinesthetic memory respectively).

There is empirical evidence to suggest that developing auditory strategies, such as listening to recorded performances (Rosenthal, 1984; Rosenthal et al., 1988; Bernardi et al., 2013), may be useful for memorizing music. For example, in an experiment carried out by Highben and Palmer (2004) in which sixteen pianists practiced specially composed short pieces of music with and without auditory and motor feedback, recall from memory was best when the pianists practiced as normal and worst when they were imagining both the feel of playing the keyboard and the sound of the music they were playing. Pianists who scored high on a test of aural imagery and described themselves as being able to play by ear well were least affected by not being able to hear the sound of the music they were playing.

The reported use of auditory strategies can thus be seen to represent a form of mental practice, as recommended by the early pedagogues. In a review of research on the use of mental imagery in music performance, Keller (2012) points out that "musical imagery involves the interplay of brain regions implicated in auditory and motor processing" (p. 207) and concludes that "the deliberate use of anticipatory auditory (and/or motor and visual) imagery during performance may assist in planning and executing one's own actions . . . and predicting others' actions with a view to optimizing ensemble coordination" (p. 211).

The effects of mental and physical practice on memory for music were explored by Bernardi et al. (2013) in another experiment involving sixteen pianists. Each pianist took part in two experimental sessions; in one they memorized an unfamiliar piece by the Baroque composer Domenico Scarlatti using mental practice, and in the other they memorized another unfamiliar piece by the same composer using physical practice. The findings of the experiment suggested a link between the use of auditory imagery and greater anticipation of movement, as proposed by Keller (2012); the findings also showed that memorization was most effective when the pianists had used auditory imagery for pitch, and when they were accustomed to carrying out formal/structural analysis of the pieces they were memorizing. Different kinds of imagery may be used when memorizing music in different genres and styles; for example, Loimusalo and Huovinen (2018) showed, in a mixed-methods study of silent memorization for tonal and nontonal music, involving the participation of thirty pianists, that imagery for pitch was more likely to be used in tonal music, while imagery for rhythm was more likely to be used in atonal music.

Young children and even older beginners learning to play a musical instrument often associate the term *practice* with repetition, particularly if they are not given explicit instruction on how to practice or memorize. Repetition (*rehearsal*) is necessary both for transferring sensory information from short-term memory into long-term memory and, according to the principles of LT-WM, reinforcing procedural memory for chunks of musical information that can be combined into longer and longer sequences. Repetition thus produces the spontaneous memory described earlier as serial cuing, but it can also be used as a kinesthetic strategy explicitly to develop procedural (*tactile*, *motor*, *finger*, or *muscular*) memory so that the musician can play as though automatically, focusing attention on other aspects of the performance.

The findings of research involving the participation of thirty-seven student pianists at university suggest that they may favor physical strategies such as practicing slowly, with hands separately, and varying the notated rhythms, over mental strategies such as analyzing and memorizing the music before beginning to play it (Davidson-Kelly et al., 2012), perhaps because they are accustomed to repetitive physical practice, or because they are deliberately developing their procedural memory at the keyboard, and of the keyboard. In a study in which nine student pianists were introduced to the development and use of performance cues while memorizing Classical and Romantic works (Gerling & Dos Santos, 2017), the pianists referred not only to kinesthetic cues such as awareness of the direction in which the hand moved at given locations in the music but also to their procedural knowledge of what they called the *topography* of the keyboard and its association with the type and direction of their body movements.

In short, musicians may think they are using strategies for developing visual, auditory, and kinesthetic memory independently, but they are in fact inseparable; repetition is an important contributor to musicians' mental representations for music, which are, inevitably and necessarily, multidimensional.

Learning styles and music memorization

It is worth noting that efforts to link the perceptual learning modalities or *learning styles* that are popularly observed in classroom teaching (i.e., visual, aural, and kinesthetic; Barbe, 1979) with preferences for using visual, auditory, and kinesthetic strategies when memorizing music have, to date, been unsuccessful. Mishra (2007) found small correlations between eighty-two respondents' scores on the Learning Styles Test (LdPride, n.d.); the Visual, Aural, Read/Write, Kinesthetic (VARK) Questionnaire (Fleming, n.d.); and her own Musical Memorization Inventory. Having carried out a series of studies using a range of empirical methods, Odendaal (2013, 2016) found no evidence to support the applicability of perceptual learning style theory to musicians' memorization.

Analytic strategies and the development of content-addressable memory

Analytic or conceptual strategies are, however, vital to the development of content-addressable memory. As we have seen, the early pedagogues suggested that analysis can take place before a musician begins to learn and memorize a piece, as recommended by Taylor (1914) and Curtis (1914); early in the process (Leschetizky, in Brée & Bernstein, 1913/1997); and/or throughout the whole period of preparation (Shinn, 1898). The ability to apply analytic strategies relies on musicians' semantic knowledge and particularly—in the context of Western classical music—familiarity with its tonal, harmonic, and compositional structures. The latter is invaluable for developing the ability to divide ("chunk") a piece into sections so that each can be learned and memorized separately before being recombined into longer sections (Bernardi et al., 2013).

Solfège—assigning syllables (e.g., *do re mi*) to either the degrees of the scale (*movable* do) or specific pitches (*fixed* do)—is one way of conceptualizing music. Nuki (1984), as we have already seen, showed that its use was beneficial for both sight-reading and memorizing, and Apostolaki (2013) proposed the theory that solfège is useful for musicians because—as Hughes (1915) had argued nearly a century earlier—it provides one way of verbalizing musical material.

The effectiveness of another way of verbalizing was tested by Timperman and Miksza (2019), who asked twenty student string players to learn an 18-bar piece of music and then, after an initial learning period, to discuss its musical character and high points, characteristic phrase structures and rhythmic motives, state its keys or tonal centers, and provide a detailed analysis from beginning to end before playing the piece from memory. There was no difference between these players' short-term recall for the piece and that of a control group who did not verbalize, but they had more accurate recall after 24 hours.

Mental practice is perhaps the analytic strategy most frequently investigated, although this can be understood in different ways (see Mielke & Comeau, 2019, who have produced a useful taxonomy of terms). We have already considered how different forms of imagery—auditory, visual, kinesthetic, conceptual—can be employed in mental practice, together with the use of structural analysis. Ultimately, however, mental practice is inherent in physical practice, and they would seem to be most effective when they are combined (Bernardi et al., 2013).

Practical Implications

Much of the advice of the pedagogues writing more than a century ago is as relevant to musicians now as it was at the time. Taylor (1914) and Curtis (1914), writing for singers, and Leschetizky (in Brée & Bernstein, 1913/1997) and Hughes (1915), writing for pianists, did not use or even know the terms *deliberate practice* (Ericsson et al., 1993) or *content-addressable memory* (Chaffin et al., 2005), as they were introduced comparatively recently. Nevertheless, these concepts are implicit in the learning and memorizing strategies recommended by the early pedagogues.

The practical advice that follows is based on the pedagogical and research literature discussed earlier but is not designed to be prescriptive; individuals differ, as do musical genres and particular pieces of music, and what is effective for one musician may not be effective for another.

While musicians—particularly young musicians—do memorize spontaneously, as the result of repeatedly hearing, singing, playing, and/or imagining the works to be performed from memory, their recall, especially under performance conditions, may not be reliable. Spontaneous memorization may be inevitable, and for this reason it is worth remembering the well-known saying that *practice makes permanent* (i.e., rather than *perfect*). It is better to repeat what has been learned accurately in the first place than to have to unlearn it for the purposes of deliberate memorization.

The aim of deliberate practice should be to memorize both accurately and securely, developing content-addressable memory so that it is possible for the musician to start playing or singing at a range of locations. A first step could be to identify the locations that represent the musician's understanding of the compositional structure of the work or, if they prefer, its "story" or emotional journey. There is no right or wrong way to do this. As Ginsborg et al. (2006) showed, two musicians performing the same work may conceptualize it in different ways, depending on their individual performance needs. The process of identifying structural boundaries enables musicians to develop a mental representation of the whole work divided into sections, chunks, or chapters that can be further subdivided, memorized separately, and recombined as necessary.

Note that it is important to practice and memorize the links between sections, as it is at these locations that memory lapses are most likely to occur and, conversely, where the musician is most likely to be able to recover. And it can be helpful to employ the *backward-chaining* strategy of working backward, section by section, from the end of the work (or, in a longer piece, a movement), rather than always starting at the beginning. This has two advantages: when musicians recombine two sections they are working forward again toward the end, and as they play the just-learned section preceded by the previous section, they are reinforcing their practice of the links between them.

A second step could be to make basic decisions (Chaffin et al., 2005), since these are likely to be assimilated and automatized during the course of practice and rehearsal. Once automatic, they can be hard to change, so while they can be provisional at first they should be fixed as soon as possible. These vary from instrument to instrument; singers and wind players make decisions about phrasing and where to breathe, for example, while pianists decide on fingering, and where and how to pedal, and string players choose when to use up-bows and when to use down-bows. Singers need to memorize lyrics as well as melodies; it can be more effective—at least for expert singers—to memorize them simultaneously than separately (Ginsborg, 2002; Ginsborg & Sloboda, 2007), while Gruson (1988) showed that pianists benefit from practicing the left and right hand parts separately before practicing and memorizing them together.

These first two steps are conceptual. A third step can be to deploy the auditory, visual, and kinesthetic strategies that seem most appropriate to the music and the musician. Auditory memory is both retrospective (i.e., memory for what has just been played) and prospective (i.e., memory for what is about to be played). Listening to recordings of the work to be performed can be useful for developing spontaneous auditory memories, as can—for instrumentalists or singers performing with accompaniment—imagining or playing along with a recording of the accompaniment alone, if this is available. Musicians can develop their auditory skills for deliberate use by reading music and simultaneously hearing it in their imagination. Paradoxically, this technique underlies the skill of reading music (i.e., translating visual information into sound and "feel") and it was therefore known by Gieseking and Leimer (1932/1972) as *visualization*, although it was renamed *audiation* by Gordon (1976). It is one of the most powerful tools musicians possess for mental practice, memorizing away from their instrument, since it can be undertaken anywhere, any time.

Musicians often report spontaneous recall for the visual appearance of the notated score while performing (e.g., whether they are playing or singing from top or bottom of the *recto* or *verso* page, and where the page turns are), which can be valuable for preventing or recovering from memory lapses. They can reinforce their visual memory by marking the score in pencil or with colored pens. Visual memory can also be for the position of the fingers, hands, or body in relation to the topography of the instrument (Gerling & Dos Santos, 2017) and/or for cues and signals from other performers including the conductor.

Once the musician has made the decisions that shape their conception and ultimate performance of the work, repetition (but, ideally, not by rote) produces the kinesthetic, procedural memory that enables both stability and flexibility. In other words, recall for all sections of the work and the links between them, independently and combined, is so secure in both body and mind that the musician can safely respond spontaneously "in the moment" to whatever happens during performance, from an unexpected disturbance in the audience, a co-performer's flight of musical fancy, or the musician's own new insight into the music while performing.

Although interpretative and expressive decisions may be made earlier, they often emerge during this stage of repetitive practice and rehearsal, sometimes known as *overlearning*, while the musician is undertaking mental practice and even when they are not even thinking about the piece consciously. It can be helpful to note these decisions and their locations in the music, as they may well become performance cues, adding to the musician's repertoire of landmarks for retrieval, to guard against and help recovery from memory lapses.

Conclusion

Some general points can be made about memorizing and recalling music from memory. Whatever material is to be memorized, a great deal of research has shown that it is more efficient to divide it into small chunks and memorize it in several short sessions rather than trying to memorize a whole piece of music, for example, in one long session (e.g., Donovan & Radosevich, 1999). Memories are consolidated during rest periods, especially sleep (Fischer et al., 2005), so musicians often find that passages they struggled to memorize one day are recalled with ease the next. Once a work is memorized, it is well worth practicing it as though performing, for example by giving practice performances, so that the feelings associated with singing or playing in public are already familiar. Every opportunity to practice in the venue where the performance is to take place should be taken—although it should be borne in mind that the acoustics are likely to be different when the audience is present—and if the musician rarely wears formal concert attire, it is always helpful to ensure in advance that it fits and is comfortable for playing or singing.

Finally, it should be remembered that performing notated music from memory is a convention, for many but not all musicians, in Western classical music. It is not an immutable law that music *has* to be performed from memory, and there are plenty of examples of well-known performers who take the view that they—and their audiences—gain more enjoyment from their playing when they perform with rather than without the score. If musicians do memorize and perform from memory, however, the more strategies they have used while practicing and rehearsing, the more secure they will feel. If one form of memory—conceptual, auditory, visual, or kinesthetic—fails, the others remain, enabling the performance to continue. Few professional musicians have not experienced either memory lapses or the fear of forgetting. Most audiences do not notice or do not care, provided the performer does not indicate by their demeanor that an error has been made (Waddell & Williamon, 2017). Provided that recovery is swift or the musician can improvise with conviction, the overall quality of the performance is what matters.

Key Sources

Baddeley, A. D., & Hitch, G. J. (2019). The phonological loop as a buffer store: An update. *Cortex*, 112, 91–106. https://doi.org/10.1016/j.cortex.2018.05.015

Chaffin, R., Demos, A. P., & Logan, T. (2016). Performing from memory. In S. Hallam, I. Cross, & M. Thaut (Eds.), *The Oxford handbook of music psychology* (2nd ed., pp. 559–571). Oxford: Oxford University Press.

Ginsborg, J. (2017). Memory in music listening and performance. In P. Hansen & B. Blaesing (Eds.), *Performing the remembered present: The cognition of memory in dance, theatre and music* (Chapter 3, pp. 69–96). London: Bloomsbury.

Mishra, J. (2010). A century of memorization pedagogy. *Journal of Historical Research in Music Education*, 32(1), 3–18. https://doi.org/10.1177%2F153660061003200102.

Reflective Questions

1. How is your everyday use of memory reflected in the theoretical models presented in the first section of this chapter? Can you think of examples illustrating, for example, episodic, procedural, and semantic memory, or of how you use elaboration and rehearsal to remember information?

2. Consider the extent to which you used serial cuing and content-addressable access when giving a recent performance from memory. If you do not typically memorize pieces of music for performance, try singing the last phrase of "Happy Birthday" (or any other song you know well). Do you have to start from the beginning to be able to do so?

3. In what ways do (or could) you use visual, auditory, kinesthetic, and analytic strategies when memorizing a work for instrument or voice? Do you use any other strategies?

4. If you play more than one instrument, or play an instrument and also sing from memory (either separately or together), to what extent do you use strategies that are similar and different? Are they transferable between instruments, or between instrument and voice? If you are a singer, what are your strategies for memorizing lyrics?

5. Think about the last piece of music or song that you memorized for performance. What were the basic, interpretive, and expressive dimensions to which you attended while practicing and rehearsing? Which were the ones you drew on when performing from memory? Did you have other thoughts while performing, and if so, what were they? Might they serve as retrieval cues in future performances?

6. How many of the strategies that you have read about in this chapter do you already use? How many are unfamiliar to you? Experiment by introducing new strategies into your memorizing practice and try to assess the extent to which they are effective for you.

References

Apostolaki, A. (2013). The significance of familiar structures in music memorisation and performance. In E. King & H. Prior (Eds.), *Music and familiarity* (pp. 238–283). Farnham: Ashgate.

Atkinson, R. C., & Shiffrin, R. M. (1968). Human memory: A proposed system and its control processes. In K. W. Spence & J. T. Spence (Eds.), *The psychology of learning and motivation* (Vol. 2, pp. 89–195). New York: Academic Press.

Baddeley, A. D. (1990). *Human memory: Theory and practice*. Boston: Allyn & Bacon.

Baddeley, A. D. (2000). The episodic buffer: A new component of working memory? *Trends in Cognitive Sciences, 4*(11), 417–423. https://doi.org/10.1016/S1364-6613(00)01538-2.

Baddeley, A. D. (2012). Working memory: Theories, models, and controversies. *Annual Review of Psychology, 63*, 1–29. https://doi.org/10.1146/annurev-psych-120710-100422.

Baddeley, A. D., & Hitch, G. J. (1974). Working memory. In G. H. Bower (Ed.), *The psychology of learning and motivation: Advances in research and theory* (Vol. 8, pp. 47–89). New York: Academic Press.

Baddeley, A. D., Hitch, G. J., & Allen, R. J. (2019). From short-term store to multicomponent working memory: The role of the modal model. *Memory & Cognition, 47*(4), 575–588. https://doi.org/10.3758/s13421-018-0878-5.

Barbe, W. B. (1979). *Swassing-Barbe modality index*. Columbus, OH: Zaner-Bloser.

Bernardi, N. F., Schories, A., Jabusch, H.-C., Colombo, B., & Altenmüller, E. (2013). Mental practice in music memorization: An ecological-empirical study. *Music Perception, 30*(3), 275–290. https://doi.org/10.1525/mp.2012.30.3.275.

Brée, M., & Bernstein, S. (1913/1997). *The Leschetizky Method: A guide to fine and correct piano playing.* North Chelmsford, MA: Courier Corporation.

Chaffin, R. (2007). Learning "Clair de Lune": Retrieval practice and expert memorization. *Music Perception, 24*(4), 377–393. https://doi.org/10.1525/mp.2007.24.4.377.

Chaffin, R., Gerling, C., Demos, A. P., & Melms, A. (2013). Learning Chopin's "Barcarolle": Performance cues as a mental map for performance. In A. Williamon & W. Goebl (Eds.), *Proceedings of the International Symposium on Performance Science* (pp. 21–26). Brussels: European Association of Conservatoires.

Chaffin, R., Imreh, G., & Crawford, M. (2005). *Practicing perfection: Memory and piano performance* (2nd ed.). New York: Psychology Press.

Chaffin, R., Imreh, G., Lemieux, A. F., & Chen, C. (2003). "Seeing the Big Picture": Piano practice as expert problem solving. *Music Perception, 20*(4), 465–490. https://doi.org/10.1525/mp.2003.20.4.465.

Chaffin, R., Lemieux, A. F., & Chen, C. (2007). "It is different each time I play": Variability in highly prepared musical performance. *Music Perception, 24*(5), 455–472.

Chaffin, R., Lisboa, T., Logan, T., & Begosh, K. T. (2010). Preparing for memorized cello performance: The role of performance cues. *Psychology of Music, 38*(1), 3–30. https://doi.org/10.1177%2F0305735608100377.

Chase, W. G., & Simon, H. A. (1973). The mind's eye in chess. In A. Newell & W. G. Chase (Eds.), *Visual information processing* (pp. 215–281). New York: Academic Press.

Curtis, H. H. (1914). *Voice building and tone placing, showing a new method of relieving injured vocal cords by tone exercises* (3rd edition). D. Appleton and Co.

Davidson-Kelly, K., Moran, N. & Overy, K. (2012). Learning and memorisation amongst advanced piano students: A questionnaire study. In E. Cambouropoulos, C. Tsougras, C. P. Mavromatis, & K. Pastiadis (Eds.), *Proceedings of the 12th International Conference on Music Perception and Cognition and the 8th Triennial Conference of the European Society for the Cognitive Sciences of Music* (pp. 248–249). Thessaloniki, Greece, 23–28 July.

Donovan, J. J., & Radosevich, D. J. (1999). A meta-analytic review of the distribution of practice effect: Now you see it, now you don't. *Journal of Applied Psychology, 84*(5), 795–805. https://psycnet.apa.org/doi/10.1037/0021-9010.84.5.795.

Ericsson, K. A. (2013). Training history, deliberate practice and elite sports performance: An analysis in response to Tucker and Collins review—what makes champions? *British Journal of Sports Medicine, 47*(9), 533–35. http://dx.doi.org/10.1136/bjsports-2012-091767.

Ericsson, K. A., & Kintsch, W. (1995). Long-term working memory. *Psychological Review, 102*(2), 211–245. https://psycnet.apa.org/doi/10.1037/0033-295X.102.2.211.

Ericsson, K. A., Krampe, R. T., & Tesch-Römer, C. (1993). The role of deliberate practice in the acquisition of expert performance. *Psychological Review, 100*(3), 363–406.

Ericsson, K. A., & Polson, P. G. (1988). A cognitive analysis of exceptional memory for restaurant orders. *The Nature of Expertise, 1*, 23–70.

Eysenck, M. W., & Keane, M. T. (2000). *Cognitive psychology: A student's handbook.* London: Psychology Press.

Fischer, S., Nitschke, M. F., Melchert, U. H., Erdmann, C., & Born, J. (2005). Motor memory consolidation in sleep shapes more effective neuronal representations. *Journal of Neuroscience, 25*(49), 11248–11255. https://doi.org/10.1523/JNEUROSCI.1743-05.2005.

Fleming, N. D. (n.d.) VARK: A guide to learning styles. Retrieved August 2, 2020, from http://www.varklearn.com/english/index.asp.

Geeves, A., McIlwain, D., Sutton, J. & Christensen, W. (2013). To think or not to think: The apparent paradox of expert skill in music performance. *Educational Philosophy and Theory*, *46*(6), 674–691. https://doi.org/10.1080/00131857.2013.779214.

Gerling, C. C., & Dos Santos, R. A. T. (2017). How do undergraduate piano students memorize their repertoires? *International Journal of Music Education*, *35*(1), 60–78. https://doi.org/10.1177%2F0255761415619427.

Gieseking, W., and Leimer, K. (1932/1972). *Piano technique*. New York: Dover.

Ginsborg, J. (2002). Classical singers memorising a new song: An observational study. *Psychology of Music*, *30*(1), 56–99. https://doi.org/10.1177%2F0305735602301007.

Ginsborg, J., & Bennett, D. (2021). Developing familiarity in a new duo: Rehearsal talk and performance cues. *Frontiers of Psychology: Performance Science*, *12*. https://doi.org/10.3389/fpsyg.2021.590987.

Ginsborg, J., Chaffin, R., & Demos, A. P. (2012). Different roles for prepared and spontaneous thoughts: A practice-based study of musical performance from memory. *Journal of Interdisciplinary Music Studies*, *6* (2), 201–232. https://doi.org/10.4407/jims.2014.02.005.

Ginsborg, J., Chaffin, R., & Nicholson, G. (2006). Shared performance cues in singing and conducting: A content analysis of talk during practice. *Psychology of Music*, *34*(3), 167–194.

Ginsborg, J., & Sloboda, J. (2007). Singers' recall for the words and melody of a new, unaccompanied song. *Psychology of Music*, *35*(3), 421–440. https://doi.org/10.1177%2F0305735607072654.

Gordon, E. (1976). *Tonal and rhythm patterns: An objective analysis*. Albany: State University of New York Press.

Gruson, L. M. (1988). Rehearsal skill and musical competence: Does practice make perfect? In J. A. Sloboda (Ed.), *Generative processes in music: The psychology of performance, improvisation, and composition* (pp. 91–112). Oxford: Clarendon Press.

Herrera, M., & Cremades, R. (2014). Memorisation in piano students: A study in the Mexican context. *Musicae Scientiae*, *18*(2), 216–231. https://doi.org/10.1177%2F1029864914527105.

Highben, Z., & Palmer, C. (2004). Effects of auditory and motor mental practice in memorized piano performance. *Bulletin-Council for Research in Music Education*, *159*, 58–67.

Hughes, E. (1915). Musical memory in piano playing and piano study. *The Musical Quarterly*, *1*, 601.

Keller, P. E. (2012). Mental imagery in music performance: Underlying mechanisms and potential benefits. *Annals of the New York Academy of Sciences*, *1252*(1), 206–213. https://doi.org/10.1111/j.1749-6632.2011.06439.x.

Kopiez, R., Wolf, A., & Platz, F. (2017). Small influence of performing from memory on audience evaluation. *Empirical Musicology Review*, *12*(1-2), 2–14. http://dx.doi.org/10.18061/emr.v12i1-2.5553.

LdPride. (n.d.). Learning Styles Test. Retrieved August 2, 2020, from http://www.ldpride.net/learningstyles.MI.htm.

Lindsey. R. B., & Logan, G. D. (2019). Item-to-item associations in typing: Evidence from spin list sequence learning. *Journal of Experimental Psychology: Learning, Memory, and Cognition*, *45*(3), 397–416. http://dx.doi.org/10.1037/xlm0000605.

Lisboa, T., Demos, A., & Chaffin, R. (2018). Training thought and action for virtuoso performance. *Musicae Scientiae*, *22*(4), 519–538. https://doi.org/10.1177%2F1029864918782350.

Loimusalo, N. J., & Huovinen, E. (2018). Memorizing silently to perform tonal and non-tonal notated music: A mixed-methods study with pianists. *Psychomusicology: Music, Mind, and Brain, 28*(4), 222. https://psycnet.apa.org/doi/10.1037/pmu0000227.

Marcus, A. (1979). *Great pianists speak.* Neptune, NJ: Paganiniana Publications.

Mielke, S., & Comeau, G. (2019). Developing a literature-based glossary and taxonomy for the study of mental practice in music performance. *Musicae Scientiae, 23*(2), 196–211. https://doi.org/10.1177%2F1029864917715062.

Miller, G. A. (1956). The magical number seven, plus or minus two: Some limits on our capacity for processing information. *Psychological Review, 63*(2), 81. https://psycnet.apa.org/doi/10.1037/h0043158.

Mishra, J. (2007). Correlating musical memorization styles and perceptual learning modalities. *Visions of Research in Music Education, 9*(1), 1–19.

Nuki, M. (1984). Memorization of piano music. *Psychologia, 27*(3), 157–163.

Odendaal, A. (2013). Perceptual learning style as an influence on the practising of instrument students in higher music education. Unpublished doctoral dissertation, University of the Arts, Helsinki.

Odendaal, A. (2016). (Mis)matching perceptual learning styles and practicing behavior in tertiary level Western Classical instrumentalists. *Psychology of Music, 44*(3), 353–368. https://doi.org/10.1177%2F0305735614567933.

Rosenthal, R. K. (1984). The relative effects of guided model, model only, guide only, and practice only treatments on the accuracy of advanced instrumentalists' musical performance. *Journal of Research in Music Education, 32*(4), 265–273. https://doi.org/10.2307%2F3344924.

Rosenthal, R. K., Wilson, M., Evans, M., & Greenwalt, L. (1988). Effects of different practice conditions on advanced instrumentalists' performance accuracy. *Journal of Research in Music Education, 36*(4), 250–257. https://doi.org/10.2307%2F3344877.

Shinn, F. G. (1898). The memorizing of piano music for performance. *Proceedings of the Musical Association, 1898–1899, 25th Session* (pp. 1–25). Taylor & Francis, Ltd., on behalf of the Royal Musical Association.

Taylor, D. C. (1914). *Self-help for singers; a manual for self-instruction in voice culture based on the old Italian method.* H. W. Gray Co.

Timperman, E., & Miksza, P. (2019). Verbalization and musical memory in string players. *Musicae Scientiae, 23*(2), 212–230. https://doi.org/10.1177%2F1029864917727332.

Waddell, G., & Williamon, A. (2017). Eye of the beholder: Stage entrance behavior and facial expression affect continuous quality ratings in music performance. *Frontiers in Psychology: Performance Science, 8*, 513. https://doi.org/10.3389/fpsyg.2017.00513.

CHAPTER 13

··

CONDUCTING

··

STEVEN J. MORRISON AND BRIAN A. SILVEY

INTRODUCTION

> There's the physical element, of course: the ability to communicate the rhythm, flow, texture and shifting moods of a piece of music through a set of traditional (yet freely elaborated) gestures. Conducting is a kind of strange, proactive dance. You move your body not in response to music but in anticipation of it. (Phillips, 2018)

CONDUCTING is a performative act. Although it constitutes a well-defined skill set and is often considered, at least at a rudimentary level, fundamental knowledge for practicing musicians, it also stands alone as a recognized form of artistic expression in and of itself. Unlike most of the other proficiencies of "musicianship" covered in this part of the volume, the particular proficiency of conducting has evolved through Western classical music tradition into a distinctive performance area, personified in the familiar figure of the conductor. Conducting is not a skill to be executed in isolation, however. The act of conducting requires the presence of an ensemble to be conducted and, to only a slightly lesser extent, the presence of an audience for whom such coordinated performances are presented. In this chapter, we will first focus on the specific skills expected of, and necessary to be developed by, conductors and the manner in which these skills figure into the conductor's interactions with an ensemble. As a performance-oriented skill, however, conducting also actively engages audience members through its embodied distillation of temporal, structural, and expressive information. The dynamic interaction among these will be the focus of the second section of this chapter.

Conductors are unique individuals. In the strict sense of the word, they are unique because there is only one. Ensembles may engage a team—or, more often, a hierarchy—of conductors, but there is only one in front of the ensemble at any given time. The size of the ensemble may vary considerably, but not so the number of conductors on the podium. The uniqueness of the conductor is underscored in ways ranging from the obvious (they face a different direction) to the subtle (their attire may be a bit more distinctive) to the functional (for conductors of instrumental ensembles, they are usually the only performers with the full score). The conductor is also unique in that they are the sole member of a performance ensemble whose contribution does not involve the direct creation of sound. Nevertheless, they are considered a performer. This begs the question, as posed by *Washington Post* music critic Anne Midgette (2019), "What does a conductor do, anyway?" This is a surprisingly difficult question to answer when contrasting what it may be believed that a conductor does with evidence gathered from controlled or systematic observation. Recognizing the complex and interactive context in which conducting skills are deployed, we will approach the topic from the perspective of relationships: that between the conductor and the ensemble, and that between the audience and the conductor/ensemble entity.

Between the Conductor and the Ensemble

> All of these players are individuals, with personalities, talents, ideas and brains that have had their own experiences. There is just this enormous potential and, definitely, the secret of a good conductor, to put it one way, is using this potential to finding ways to awaken in them the best they have, in a way that serves them best. (Mirga Grazinyte-Tyla, quoted in O'Reilly, 2017)

Conducting is a form of music performance. By virtue of its position within the context of formal music study, it is an enterprise generally grouped within the same collection of concentrations as the study of voice or an instrument, often leading to the same performance-oriented degree or credential. Unlike the case with other performance areas, the relative scarcity of undergraduate conducting degree programs suggests that it is viewed as a more advanced area of study that necessitates prior accomplishment in a specific vocal or instrumental performance medium. Moreover, when it appears within undergraduate programs of study, conducting tends to show up later rather than sooner in the curriculum, certainly after the completion of implicitly or explicitly prerequisite courses. Again, this is unlike other performance study, which typically is undertaken from the very first term of matriculation.

Conducting is also a temporal act. As such, the conductor is a focal point in synchronizing musicians' performances. On a rudimentary level, the conductor aims to influence the ensemble through a variety of nonverbal conducting behaviors such as gesture, facial expression, and eye contact, the greater usage and variety of which have been found to differentiate expert from novice conductors (Byo & Austin, 1994). Therefore, an important aspect of the complex interaction between conductor and ensemble centers on what the conductor shows while on the podium (i.e., nonverbal mechanical skills) and how the musicians in the ensemble perceive and interpret that visual information to produce a unified performance (i.e., synchronization).

Nonverbal mechanical skills

Given that learning the basic physical skills necessary to lead an ensemble is central to coordinating ensemble performances, much time is devoted by conducting instructors to the development and refinement of such competencies. Keeping a steady beat, getting an ensemble to start and stop, and learning how to give cues are practiced by conductors who must learn to automatize these newly learned motor skills. However, the initial learning of basic nonverbal skills usually occurs without any sound to guide students' efforts, perhaps emphasizing the notion that conducting is a largely mechanical enterprise, one in which conducting technique supersedes all else. Regardless of the manner in which these skills are attained, there are three general domains in which conductors are taught to use their bodies to communicate with the musicians in their ensembles—gesture, eye contact, and facial expression.

Gesture

Gesture is the most important skill for a conductor to develop. Nearly all of the synchronization efforts that emanate from the conductor are from the movement of their arms and hands. Although the unique physical characteristics of each conductor lead individual gestures to be executed and viewed somewhat differently, specific gestures (referred to as conducting *emblems*) are often taught such that they can be transmitted to a group of musicians and experienced similarly (Sousa, 1988). For example, gesture itself is typically learned through the grouping of movements into beat patterns suggestive of particular time signatures. An additional layer of musical information is often placed upon this information by applying motions that are indicative of specific musical markings such as marcato, tenuto, or staccato. Although perhaps not explicitly stipulated to novice conductors by their teachers, these articulation markings—along with other aspects of the music score—should help to inform the expressivity of the gesture itself. This framework provides a template for applying future learned conducting skills. Nevertheless, focusing predominately on isolated patterns of gesture may limit the importance and functions of gesture in that they could also indicate more complex features of expressive intent, phrasing, form, and dynamic variation. Expressive aspects of conducting tend to be characterized by variability of and contrast between aspects of movement including speed, size, and acceleration: for example, between smooth and sharp hand gestures or between use of larger or smaller areas of space (Byo & Austin, 1994; Luck et al., 2010). Because these differential aspects of movement are discernable to observers (Wanderley et al., 2005), it is sensible that gesture could and should assist performers' and listeners' understanding of the music that is being performed.

Regardless of the similarity of fundamental conducting gestures, there is a lack of evidence for a direct causal relationship between specific nonverbal conducting behaviors and ensemble sound. In other words, no one-to-one or cause-and-effect relationship has been found to associate particular conducting gestures with performer outcomes. Rather, there appear to be many movements that may be associated with a given aspect of performance and a variety of outcomes resulting from a particular gesture. The gestural vocabulary of a particular conductor may not be interpreted in the same manner by a different group of musicians or have the intended effect. A notable and interesting exception was found in the context of choral music by Manternach (2016), who reported that vocalists' laryngeal muscle activity and resultant sound quality varied in a consistent manner on the basis of a conductor's preparatory gestures. Whether or not instrumentalists' muscle usage or performance responses might differ in a similar manner on the basis of gesture has yet to be explored.

Eye contact

Eye contact with ensemble musicians can also help conductors increase their communicative ability through the recognition and validation of musical content. For example, looking at a section of string players before a critical entrance can boost their confidence to perform accurately and increase their comfort about the synchronization of a particular musical phrase. Maintaining eye contact with musicians while gesturing intensifies the connection between the conductor and the ensemble. Conductors who maximize eye contact with their ensembles are viewed more positively than those who do not (Fredrickson et al., 1998).

Facial expression

The use of engaging and varied facial expressions (e.g., smiling, frowning, raising eyebrows, opening mouth, furrowing brow) is often related to musicians' positive perceptions of and preferences for conductors (Yarbrough, 1975). Facial expression is a powerful tool for conductors when conveying the emotion of the music they are conducting because the intent behind many facial expressions is often shared across cultures. Similar to the multiple functions that conducting gestures can and should transmit, facial expressions communicate musical intention and emotion, and alert musicians to information such as musical structure and form (Livingstone et al., 2009). Paired with the information gleaned from gesture and eye contact, facial expression serves to amplify the overall musical message being conveyed by the conductor.

   The use of gesture, facial expression, and eye contact are seen as essential skills for all conductors to develop and cultivate at high levels. In isolation without sound, however, the use of these behaviors carries no intent about the music itself. Only in conjunction with a thorough knowledge of the musical score can conductors use these skills to communicate fully, the power of which increases when these nonverbal behaviors are used in combination with one another.

Synchronization

By employing an established set of mechanical skills, conductors play a central role in getting the ensemble to perform together. The focus on the "conductor-as-synchronizer" is reinforced early in the skill development process through the content of basic conducting textbooks, which prioritize coordination over expressivity (Pasquale, 2008). Although the responsibility of timekeeper is an important one, evidence suggests that the conductor does not hold this role exclusively (D'Ausilio et al., 2012). In this case, it seems vital to consider the multiple ways in which an ensemble might achieve and maintain synchrony.

Entrainment

One way is through the process of musical entrainment, the interaction and consequent synchronization of two or more rhythmic processes. Entrainment has been observed in groups ranging from two up to thousands of individuals (McNeill, 1997). This phenomenon is of particular importance to musicians, as it represents the coordination of temporally structured events through interactive means. Some basic examples found in music performance settings include tapping one's foot to the beat, performing a note at the same time as the surrounding musicians, or releasing a note together at the end of a phrase.

In order to achieve entrainment, Levitin et al. (2018) suggest that "an internal representation of the beat must exist, so that the individual can initiate their movements in synchrony with the beat rather than reacting to each beat" (p. 56). Instead of waiting to perform based upon the conductor's ictus, or relying exclusively on other external visual signals, performers are constantly adjusting and coordinating their physical actions with one another based upon the nature and performance of the music itself. More specifically, models of rhythmic entrainment (e.g., Toiviainen & Snyder, 2003) help to illuminate how, through interaction with the musical information available, multiple musicians are able to identify and lock into specific aspects of rhythm such as downbeats, obviously an important aspect of aligning group performance across time. As the difficulty of the music grows and the number of performers increases, entrainment becomes more difficult because each individual ensemble member is part of a much larger and more complicated entity, and the available information may be both dense and widely distributed.

Dynamic attending theory

Other underlying aspects of synchronization have been proposed through the concept of dynamic attending theory. Jones (1976) hypothesized that listeners made sense out of complex auditory sequences by processing them preferentially in relationship to their importance within a given temporal structure. That is, a large collection of auditory events can be more efficiently understood when viewed as combinations of smaller events (beats grouped into measures, for example) or subdivisions of events (for instance, beats divided into halves and quarters). In an ensemble context, with so much sonic information being produced and heard at any given time, musicians' attention is drawn to the most salient and identifiable melodic and rhythmic aspects of what is being performed to identify patterns of temporal regularity. These auditory markers help musicians synchronize their performances with one another. Conducting is an efficient and effective means of visually highlighting such high-level auditory markers.

The concept of future-oriented attending (Jones & Boltz, 1989) extends understanding of dynamic attending theory insofar as musicians not only identify temporal markers but are able to make predictions about the timing of upcoming events. Because musicians have expectations about how time should unfold while performing, anticipating their own performance within structured temporal events can help them to predict with greater accuracy what will happen next. In this way, musicians are better able to make judgments about their timing during future performance, thus improving their synchronization.

Beat induction

In conducted large ensembles, however, musicians cannot rely exclusively on what they hear to coordinate their own performances, but instead must also process the visual information that is provided from the conductor. Beat induction, or the skill that allows one to hear a regular pulse in music to which one can synchronize, helps to explain how musicians translate conducting gestures into information that promotes entrainment. Similar in nature to future-oriented attending—which involves prediction through aural means—visual beat induction provides a framework demonstrating that musicians also predict and synchronize their performances based upon visual means (i.e., gesture).

As an example of this phenomenon, a conductor's rate of acceleration along a trajectory within a conducting gesture can influence their musicians' perception of visual beat induction (Luck & Sloboda, 2009). It is not surprising, then, that musicians synchronize more consistently with conducting gestures performed in a marcato style than they do with gestures performed in a legato style (Wöllner et al., 2012). More pronounced movements required for marcato—which produces more extreme acceleration peaks and troughs—are easier to synchronize with than smoother movements and decreased extremes in acceleration for legato gestures (Wöllner et. al., 2012). Velocity and change of direction provided through conducting gestures are more responsible for musicians' synchronization than the actual placement of the beat itself in space.

As tempting as it may be to suggest that conductors play the most important role in synchronizing their ensemble members' performance, evidence suggests that this process is more fluid and complex than once imagined, and involves cognitive, physiological, and neurological processes (Ono et al., 2015). As highlighted by Meals (2018), "the degree of congruence between conductor gesture to ensemble response is potentially a negotiated, or at least dynamic, property" (p. 46). It appears that musicians must adjust the timing of their performance to both what they see and what they hear in order to best maintain the temporal structure of the music being performed.

The Conductor, the Ensemble, and the Audience

> Joana Carneiro is a conductor who makes us listen. She focuses our concentration as listeners, just as she focuses an orchestra's performance. She shapes the music with grace and precision. (Scheinin, 2009)

The attention given to the relationship between a conductor and an ensemble emphasizes the conductor's presumed role in the development of the ensemble's sound and the interpretation of the ensemble's music selections all while maintaining temporal synchronization among the ensemble members. As it is traditionally held, the conductor examines formal structures and expressive potentials of a composition (often with an effort to ascertain the composer's original intentions) through careful study of a musical score. This knowledge and these creative decisions are then taken into a sequence of ensemble rehearsals leading to a public performance. The performance, in turn, provides an audience with a sonic realization of the composer's ideas imbued with the interpretive nuances of the performers as guided by the conductor through sequences of movement and gesture. This linear relationship—from composer, to conductor, to ensemble, to audience—serves as the foundation of conducting practice and pedagogy in which emphasis is placed on the reflective connection between conductor and score and the resultant physical act of gestural communication to the ensemble. The audience apprehends and evaluates the music content presumably based on the sounds made by the ensemble. The success or failure of a performance might be attributed to how well an ensemble executed the tasks presented by the conductor ("The orchestra was not up to the conductor's demands") or the way in which a conductor deployed the ensemble's skills ("The conductor evoked an imaginative and exuberant performance"), or a combination of both. Nevertheless, in the end, it is generally the playing of the ensemble that is ultimately judged, regardless of whether it is considered to be the result of, in spite of, or apart from the conductor's actions.

Investigations into the listener's experience of music performances, however, suggest a more complex relationship among the components in play, particularly that between the conductor's movements and the ensemble's performance. The manner in which the conductor deploys skills of gesture and movement has a notable effect on listeners' broad judgments of a performance's overall quality and level of expressivity (Morrison et al., 2009; Morrison & Selvey, 2014). On a more fine-grained level, evaluations of specific expressive aspects of a performance have been found to be related to specific components of the conducting gestural repertoire (Morrison et al., 2014). Even the way that listeners describe music may be connected to movement-related decisions made by the conductor (Kumar & Morrison, 2016). In other areas of music performance, visual information has been observed to be more salient than aural information when individuals have been asked to make decisions about performance quality (Tsay, 2014).

This raises the question, then, of the degree to which conducting is more useful than—or at least integral to—ensemble sound in shaping listeners' opinions about the music being performed.

Admittedly, the term "listener" indicates a particular hearing-centric perspective on the manner in which musical encounters are described and suggests the predominance of auditory information in one's interaction with music. Given the focus in this section on interactive aspects of auditory and visual information, "listener" is a misleading and arguably inaccurate choice of words. However, there is no other word in common usage that as efficiently encapsulates the active and intentional witnessing of a musical event in its many forms—audience member, adjudicator, critic, observer, or bystander, among others. We will continue to use the term "listener" throughout, keeping this significant caveat in mind.

Expressivity and quality

The connection between the quality of conducting and the quality of ensemble performance has generally been believed to reside in the way in which assured, precise, and expressive conducting can evoke stronger, more technically exact, and more expressively compelling responses from the assembled performers. However, Price and Chang (2005) found no relationship between conductors' perceived level of accomplishment and the quality of wind band performances. Skilled, expressive conductors did not necessarily lead the most precise, expressive groups. To be sure, the complex array of teaching skill, rehearsal pedagogy, and interpersonal interaction implemented over an extended number of rehearsals or period of instruction interact with in-the-moment gestures and movements to give rise to any specific performance (for an extensive discussion of the conductor's role in the teaching and rehearsal setting, see Price & Byo, 2002).

By manipulating performances to keep either the visual component (the conductor) or the auditory component (the ensemble) constant, it is possible to get a clearer picture of the relationship one component has with the other, at least in the listener's judgment. When identical band and choir performances were matched with video of either expressive or neutral conductors—that is, conductors who demonstrated either a high or low degree of gestural variability, independence between right and left hands, use of horizontal and vertical space, contrasting velocity and weight of hand movement, and facial expression—listeners evaluated the performances paired with expressive conductors as more expressive (Morrison et al., 2009; Morrison & Selvey, 2014). At least among these advanced-level performances, neutral conducting appeared to exert a negative influence on evaluations of the ensemble's performances. From an alternate perspective, videos of conductors paired with high-quality, more expressive ensemble performances were judged more expressive than the same videos paired with lower-quality performances (Silvey, 2011).

It is not only ensemble performance evaluations that appear to vary depending on the conductor's actions. Evaluations of teaching episodes have been found to be more positive when those episodes included skillful, expressive conducting (Montemayor & Silvey, 2019). Notably, participants in Montemayor and Silvey's (2019) study were specifically directed to focus on aspects of teaching effectiveness entirely apart from those associated with the teacher's conducting skill or manner. Findings such as these lend weight to the inclusion of conducting skill requirements for aspiring music educators and to the assumption that skillful conducting is a vital component of good teaching. At the same time, the apparent interaction of conducted and verbalized elements of teaching episodes raises important questions about instructional evaluation and the degree to which the perceptions of one element are influenced by the other.

Components of expressivity and structure

Although the concept of expressivity is a meaningful and powerful component of musical interactions and the extent to which listeners deem a performance as successful or competent, it is not a term that lends itself easily to definition or measurement. Musical expressivity consists of multiple components, the balance and interaction among which vary considerably from piece to piece and performance to performance. In notated music traditions, it is a performer's decisions regarding these very components that give rise to interpretation—that is, distinctive and idiosyncratic realizations of a given score. Among group music performances, these decisions may be the result of a collective effort. Among large group performances, the conductor tends to guide such decision-making.

Given the relationship between a conductor's gestural choices and the perceived expressivity of an ensemble's performance, a subsequent question is whether and which specific aspects of a conductor's gestural repertoire are more salient to such perceptions. In other words, is the impact of "expressive" conducting evident when constrained to specific individual musical parameters? Morrison et al. (2014) isolated conductor gestures specifically indicative of contrasting articulations (staccato, legato) or dynamics (loud, soft). Adult listeners with varied levels of music experience evaluated these features of instrumental performances as more effective in the presence of conductors who demonstrated corresponding clear visual contrasts. For example, an ensemble's performance of dynamics was judged as more successful when the conductor clearly depicted dynamic contrasts. Differences in judgments were evident even in the absence of variability within the ensemble's actual performance (i.e., the ensemble played with no dynamic contrast), suggesting that the addition of a visual depiction of contrast was enough to influence perception.

Despite the emphasis on specific elements of musical expression, evaluations of these elements as well as of the overall performances were quite similar. Listeners found it difficult (or perhaps unnecessary) to disentangle isolated aspects of a music performance from its expressive whole. Much like with the broad evaluations of ensemble performances or teaching episodes described in the previous section, an individual's demonstration of skillful conducting appears to convey a general sense of accomplishment and artistry that permeates even seemingly unrelated elements of the musical context.

Conducting conveys information about time as well as about general and specific aspects of expression. As a skill that is deployed over time, musicians' movements communicate information about how music coheres and contrasts within and between larger units such as phrases and sections (Ceaser et al., 2009; Wanderley et. al., 2005). Conductors use gestural character and contrast to depict the form and trajectory of music, if not in whole, then at least through delineation of formal boundaries. Amid the considerable volume of information being generated by a large ensemble at any given point in time, conducting gestures and movement can draw an audience member's attention to a subset of that information, such as a specific line or part.

When encountering music that included both a connected song-like line and a rhythmic ostinato, adult listeners' descriptions of the music varied depending on which of these two elements the conductor reflected in gesture (Kumar & Morrison, 2016). Listeners selected words such as "smooth" and "flowing" to describe the music in instances when the conducting was congruent with the connected line; in contrast, they chose words like "angular" and "rough" as descriptors when the conducting was congruent with the ostinato. If the choice of descriptors is a valid indication of the way an individual is experiencing a piece of music, it is striking that identical performances might be experienced differently depending on the gestural choices made by a conductor. Such a finding underscores the notion that movement—even soundless movement—can be a salient element of music performance.

PRACTICAL IMPLICATIONS

> What I can't teach people, however, is intention. If you have a clear intention, if the stereo inside your head is clicking along and giving you something that's exactly what you want, then it almost doesn't matter what you do with your hands. (Robert Spano, quoted in Davidson, 2006)

Conducting is a multifaceted skill in which movement and gesture are used to depict musical interpretation. Conducting occupies a vital role in group leadership and coordination. The conductor is the performer at the nexus of the musical score, the ensemble, and the audience, and makes a contribution that is central, but also soundless. It is not surprising that conducting skills and the function of the conductor have been the focus of research in fields as diverse as music, psychology, neuroscience, and sociology. As a more detailed picture emerges of the complexity of conducting and its functions, it is worth considering how this knowledge may serve the ways by which this skill set is taught and learned, and how it is applied by those who inhabit this role.

Skill development

As evidenced by many of the materials devoted to the topic (for example, Green & Gibson (2004)), the development of conducting skills traditionally begins with the accrual of a set of basic competencies. Skills related to conveying timekeeping—preparatory gestures, location of pulse, metric patterns, fermatas—are emphasized first, followed by accrual of gestural vocabulary pertaining to specific expressive elements (e.g., articulation, dynamics). These are complemented by skills that support organizational aspects of performance such as cues and releases. Combinations of these components add layers of complexity and introduce demands for independence among the various sources of nonverbal information, such as between right and left hands or between hands and face. (See Madsen & Yarbrough, 1985, for a thorough examination and assessment of one possible path of skill development.)

Established pedagogies of conducting skill development—from fundamental time-related skills through more expressive and organizational aspects—are arguably at odds with at least two important characteristics of expert conductors, specifically, and expert musicians, broadly. In the first instance, individuals who demonstrate a high level of conducting skill are characterized by a commensurately high degree of variability. Expert conductors deploy a remarkable variety and range of movements and gestures across time; they also tend to be very different from one another (Byo & Austin, 1994; Wöllner, 2012). In other words, although the study of conducting is often construed as centered around sequential skill-building, it is the variability within and among conductors that has been identified as an indicator of expertise. This raises the question, Is gestural conformity a prerequisite for gestural creativity? A similar question has been raised about music improvisation; compared to those with less experience, advanced jazz improvisers have been found to engage a qualitatively different set of cognitive processes based on novel arrangements of an extensive vocabulary of musical ideas (Norgaard, 2011).

Undoubtedly there is a need for particular threads of consistency to run through the fabric of all variants of conducting. Given the conductor's critical role in ensemble synchronization, this is arguably most evident in the way gesture clearly communicates pulse. It seems sensible that the specific aspects of movement that performers recognize as conveying the metrical passage of time (Luck & Sloboda, 2009) must be discernable. Indeed, artificially decreased levels of variability in conducting patterns have been associated with more precise beat-keeping, although at the expense of perceived expressivity (Wöllner et al., 2012). Even in the case of timekeeping, however, the ability to recognize and respond to conductor gesture appears to be learned (Ono et al., 2015). Individuals with experience performing with conducted groups are more accurate at synchronizing with a conductor, suggesting that while conducting gestures may be particularly effective at relaying temporal information, their meaning is not intrinsic.

Other gestural skills, even those that are "emblematic" in nature (Sousa, 1988)—recognizable as referring to specific aspects of performance—appear to accommodate a greater degree of variability, perhaps due to the broader character of the performance element when compared to time-keeping (e.g., articulation style) or due to the longer timespan across which the element occurs (e.g., a change in dynamic that could span multiple beats or measures). More broadly expressive gestures, those not bound by the necessary precision of time-keeping, may need only fit within a general characterization of congruence, a plausible connection between action and sound, to be effective or informative. Indeed, it may be that unexpected or novel associations between patterns of movement and musical outcomes underlie attributions of a conductor's creativity or artistry.

In the second instance, expert musicians tend to begin their exploration of repertoire to be performed with the development of a rich, expressive internal representation of each piece. Only after creating a vision and an understanding of the musical outcome do they set about addressing technical hurdles that exist along the way (Chaffin et al., 2005). Technical skills are employed as needed to achieve the expressive or interpretive outcome that the performer has deemed desirable. The performer's musical decisions create a "need to know" toward which technique is applied.

In contrast, skill-building for novice conductors tends to focus on the application of discrete skills (changes of meter, for example) within the context of brief purpose-composed or -selected excerpts that highlight the particular challenge in question. In this context, the need to know is part and parcel of the excerpt itself, the musical goal rather than a means toward the musical goal. Novices acquire a vocabulary of movement, whereas experts use movement as a means of artistic or technical problem-solving. Expert conductors are quick to identify their own conducting movements, even when depicted in the visually austere format of a set of light points (Wöllner, 2012). This suggests not only the underlying distinctiveness of each conductor's movement repertoire, but also the agency and deep-seated musical intentionality that drives movement decisions. In these cases, gesture reflects embodied knowledge of a piece's structural and expressive dimensions.

Given that experts imbue their mechanical conducting behaviors with expressivity at multiple levels, it may be advantageous for developing conductors to encounter these elements in a simultaneous and holistic manner. For example, rather than starting exclusively with pattern learning and recognition, students could experiment with gestures (e.g., shaping, molding) that represent the intent (or interpreted intent) of a specific musical phrase. Next, they could apply those shapes into the context of a specific time pattern. Recalling that conducting study often occurs after one attains skill as a vocalist or instrumentalist, the performance expertise a student has already achieved suggests a capability to set artistic goals and identify intervening challenges. Even at the earliest stages of skill learning, novices can be challenged to conceptualize conducting as an intentional act with multiple functions, one in which an internalized musical message can be delivered more powerfully when timekeeping, mechanical, and expressive gestures are demonstrated together.

Ensemble dynamics

Because conducting is not a solitary endeavor, it is important to consider other practical applications and implications that embrace the ensemble at large. Conducting is a skill that invokes the relationship between a conductor and an ensemble. In order to maximize the efficacy of the conductor, it may be beneficial to address the way in which the conductor and ensemble members interact.

The ability to synchronize is not derived solely from watching the conductor; therefore, it may be beneficial to afford ensemble members opportunities to rehearse and perform with minimal gesture or without any gesture from the conductor. Skilled ensembles are characterized by tiers of musical leadership within their group (Dineen, 2011), thus it may be useful to recognize these structures and to find ways of making such internal structures more overt. Among developing ensembles where internal dynamics have yet to form, tasking a principal player with providing a preparatory gesture such as a head nod to indicate the tempo of a predetermined passage or the end of a phrase could highlight the multiplicity of places from which temporal and formal information might emanate. Ongoing similar experiences will allow ensemble members multiple opportunities to tune in to their fellow musicians and discover ways to monitor and refine pulse accuracy and rhythmic precision within sections and across the ensemble. Far from stepping aside entirely, conductors could provide feedback after such internally guided segments to help direct performers' attention to important musical lines, harmonies, or rhythmic features that might be helpful in synchronizing group performance and cohering disparate performance elements into a cohesive whole.

Expressivity, too, has been observed to have a positive effect on the attitude of ensemble members and, among less experienced musicians, on their perceptions of the group's performance (Silvey & Koerner, 2016). Although the rehearsal context could be construed as demanding a more utilitarian and less artistic approach to conducting, the conveyance of information regarding expression and nuance appears to evoke, among the performing musicians, a more positive view of the conductor and a stronger (if not necessarily more accurate) sense of the ensemble's accomplishment. Among professional musicians, the conductor's attention to expressive and interpretive elements—including through gesture—is particularly well received when it is responsive to and reflective of suggestions and decisions that emanate from the group (Khodyakov, 2014).

Conducting as performance

Returning to an initial point of this chapter, conducting is a performative act. It functions not only to evoke a performance, but also as part of the performance itself. Yet it is rarely discussed as such. In the case of a vocal or instrumental performance, much of a musician's attention and preparation centers on whether and how an internal musical image can be effectively communicated. Conductors, like other performers, expend considerable effort to develop their own interpretation of a musical score. Yet their efforts at effective communication are typically focused on their interactions with other performing musicians, not with an observing audience. Communicating a musical image to an audience may be viewed more as a second-order process that occurs by virtue of the ensemble performance.

Expert conductors are self-aware in regards to their manner of movement and use of gesture (Wöllner, 2012). Though this may be, in part, due to the intentionality of their actions as a depiction of musical goals, it may also be due to careful attention given to the way they appear to observers, be they performers or audience members. Although it is commonly held that a conductor's interpretation is mediated by the ensemble performance, for a listener, the ensemble's performance is also mediated by the conductor's movements. Given this function, it may be beneficial to consider how one's conducting choices appear and how they interact with the musical sounds, as well as how they assist with the making of those sounds. Movement can evoke expressive performance, but it is also itself expressive and, arguably, worthy of attention and practice as such. The way in which conducting movements draw attention to, amplify, or are congruent with aspects of the music being performed appears central to the conductor/audience dynamic.

"What Does a Conductor Do, Anyway?"

Despite the central role that conducting holds within the large ensemble context and the long-standing presence of conducting study within programs of formal music study, there is much still to be learned about the nature of this set of skills, about what conducting is, and what a conductor does. In this chapter we have focused on movement and gesture and the ways these can function both within the ensemble and between the ensemble and audience. Beyond the technical and expressive aspects of conducting, the interpersonal complexities of the conductor-ensemble interactions, an understanding of the way these interactions effect an observing audience, and the extent to which conducting skills and their function in music performances are evident in other music traditions are only partially understood.

Within the ensemble setting, there is still much to be learned about potential intersections between the musical and social aspects of the rehearsal and performance environment. The power of shared musical activity has been suggested by work proposing links between interpersonal synchronization (keeping a beat together) and empathic and prosocial behavior among children (Kirschner & Tomasello, 2010). Pairs of adults demonstrated heightened levels of synchronized brain activity—an indicator associated with prosocial behavior—during an imitative song-learning activity (Pan et al., 2018). In what way might outcomes associated with small-scale interpersonal synchronization, such as those between two people keeping a beat together, be evident in the large-scale and long-term synchronized contexts of large ensembles? And, considering conducting as an abstract representation of music rather than a strictly imitative action, what role might a conductor play in promoting and supporting an environment of heightened interpersonal interaction?

The manner in which conductor-oriented functions are taken up by singers and instrumentalists in smaller conductor-less groups could provide insight into the real or perceived utility of these functions. Alternatively, to what extent does a conductor's detachment from the rest of the performing ensemble enhance, amplify, or liberate the efficacy of their actions? And in cases where a conductor's imprecision or inaccuracy compromises the cohesion, consistency, and effectiveness of an ensemble's performance, evidence could be gathered that identifies essential, rather than simply complementary, elements of the conducting act.

Considering the audience, data are compelling that a relationship exists between a conductor's movements—their quality, congruence, and timing—and a listener's response. Yet, it is not known whether this response is indicative of bias or of a more deeply altered experience of the musical interaction. It may be that a conductor who demonstrates a high level of expressivity, clarity, and precision—in other words, a high level of overall accomplishment—raises the expectations of listeners and, in so doing, inclines them toward a more positive reaction to the performance. Alternatively, creative and accomplished juxtapositions of ensemble sound and conductor movement may result in variations of perceptual input that lead listeners to divergent cognitive experiences in terms of affective response, pattern recognition, and the various other ways in which one gives meaning to musical encounters.

At the outset of this chapter we emphasized the uniqueness of the conductor. We also posed the question of what it is, exactly, that a conductor does. While the formal *role* of conductor and its familiar trappings of the baton, podium, and formal attire may be exclusive to large and generally Western or Western-oriented concert ensembles, it is unlikely that the *functions* of the conductor are unique to this setting. One would predict that the vital elements fundamental to conducting—synchronization, organization, expression—would be in evidence across music performance traditions, particularly those featuring larger groups of musicians and necessitating some sort of centralized coordination. More thorough understanding of leadership in time-keeping, interpretive, structural, and expressive functions within group music performance can be gained by examination of the various manifestations of these roles in ensembles across music cultures and traditions. Is there any evidence that can be drawn from a broader number of music types that would yield insight into the functional basis of conducting? Although conducting is in a particular sense genre-bound, it is unlikely that the functional contributions of the conductor only exist within a small number of very historically and culturally specific practices.

Key Resources

Green, E. A. H., & Gibson, M. (2004). *The modern conductor* (7th ed.). New York: Pearson.

Levitin, D., Grahn, J., & London, J. (2018). The psychology of music: Rhythm and movement. *Annual Review of Psychology, 69,* 51–75. https://doi.org/10.1146/annurev-psych-122216-011740.

Price, H. E., & Byo, J. L. (2002). Rehearsing and conducting. In R. Parncutt & G. McPherson (Eds.), *The science and psychology of music performance: Creative strategies for teaching and learning* (pp. 335–351). New York: Oxford University Press.

Reflective Questions

1. What are the most important mechanical skills for a conductor to demonstrate? How might the order in which one approaches or masters these skills potentially affect a conductor's development?

2. Given that musical synchronization is a shared property between conductor and ensemble, how can this aid our understanding of ensemble music making?

3. Watch video performances of at least three expert conductors. What aspects of movements and gestures are common across all three? What aspects are distinctive or idiosyncratic? To what extent do common and unique features differ across functions of synchronization, expression, and organization?

4. Are there aspects of music that are more useful or consequential for informing the conductor's choices of gesture, eye contact, and facial expression? Do these vary with different music styles or ensemble settings?

5. In what ways can a conductor share control during rehearsals or performances in order to heighten musicians' sensitivity to the music that is being performed?

References

Byo, J. L., & Austin, K. R. (1994). Comparison of expert and novice conductors: An approach to the analysis of nonverbal behaviors. *Journal of Band Research, 30*(1), 11–34.

Ceaser, D. K., Thompson, W. F., & Russo, F. (2009). Expressing tonal closure in music performance: auditory and visual cues. *Canadian Acoustics, 37*(1), 29–34. https://jcaa.caa-aca.ca/index.php/jcaa/article/view/2113.

Chaffin, R., Imreh, G., & Crawford, M. (2005). *Practicing perfection: Memory and piano performance.* New York: Psychology Press.

D'Ausilio, A., Badino, L., Tokay, S., Craighero, L., Canto, R., Aloimonos, Y., & Fadiga, L. (2012). Leadership in orchestra emerges from the causal relationships of movement kinematics. *PLoS One, 7*(5), e35757. https://doi.org/10.1371/journal.pone.0035757.

Davidson, J. (2006, August 21). Measure for measure: Exploring the mysteries of conducting. *New Yorker, 82*(25), 34–44.

Dineen, P. M. (2011). Gestural economies in conducting. In A. Gritten & E. King (Eds.), *New Perspectives on Music and Gesture* (pp. 131–157). Farnham, Surrey: Ashgate Publishing, Ltd.

Fredrickson, W. E., Johnson, C. E., & Robinson, C. R. (1998). The effect of pre-conducting and conducting behaviors on the evaluation of conductor competence. *Journal of Band Research, 33*(2), 1–13.

Green, E. A. H., & Gibson, M. (2004). *The modern conductor* (7th ed.). New York: Pearson.

Jones, M. R. (1976). Time, our lost dimension: Toward a new theory of perception, attention, and memory. *Psychological Review, 83,* 323–355. https://dx.doi.org/10.1037/0033-295X.83.5.323.

Jones, M. R., & Boltz, M. (1989). Dynamic attending and responses to time. *Psychological Review, 96*(3), 459–491. https://dx.doi.org/10.1037/0033-295X.96.3.459.

Khodyakov, D. (2014). Getting in tune: A qualitative analysis of guest conductor-musicians relationships in symphony orchestras. *Poetics, 44,* 64–83. https://dx.doi.org/10.1016/j.poetic.2014.04.004.

Kirschner, S., & Tomasello, M. (2010). Joint music making promotes prosocial behavior in 4-year-old children. *Evolution and Human Behavior, 31*(5), 354–364. https://doi.org/10.1016/j.evolhumbehav.2010.04.004.

Kumar, A. B., & Morrison, S. J. (2016). The conductor as visual guide: Gesture and perception of musical content. *Frontiers in Psychology, 7,* 1049. https://doi.org/10.3389/fpsyg.2016.01049.

Levitin, D., Grahn, J., & London, J. (2018). The psychology of music: Rhythm and movement. *Annual Review of Psychology, 69,* 51–75. https://doi.org/10.1146/annurev-psych-122216-011740.

Livingstone, S. R., Thompson, W. F., & Russo, F. A. (2009). Facial expressions and emotional singing: A study of perception and production with motion capture and electromyography. *Music Perception, 26*(5), 475–488. https://doi.org/10.1525/mp.2009.26.5.475.

Luck, G., & Sloboda, J. A. (2009). Spatio-temporal cues for visually mediated synchronization. *Music Perception, 26*(5), 465–473. https://doi.org/10.1525/mp.2009.26.5.465.

Luck, G., Toiviainen, P., & Thompson, M. R. (2010). Perception of expression in conductors' gestures: A continuous response study. *Music Perception, 28*(1), 47–57. https://doi.org/10.1525/mp.2010.28.1.47.

Madsen, C. K., & Yarbrough, C. (1985). *Competency-based music education.* Raleigh, NC: Contemporary Publishing.

Manternach, J. N. (2016). Effects of varied conductor prep movements on singer muscle engagement and voicing behaviors. *Psychology of Music, 44*(3), 574–586. https://doi.org/10.1177/0305735615580357.

McNeill, W. H. (1997). *Keeping together in time.* Cambridge, MA: Harvard University Press.

Meals, C. D. (2018). *Questions of gesture and sound: Temporal interactions in conducted ensembles. A multiple study dissertation.* Doctoral thesis. Retrieved from ProQuest Dissertations and Theses Global. (2125484156).

Midgette, A. (2019). *What does a conductor do, anyway? A music critic lays it out. Washington Post* – see https://www.washingtonpost.com/entertainment/music/what-does-a-conductor-do-anyway-a-music-critic-lays-it-out/2019/10/01/5205df24-decb-11e9-be96-6adb81821e90_story.html.

Montemayor, M., & Silvey, B. A. (2019). Conductor expressivity affects evaluation of rehearsal instruction. *Journal of Research in Music Education, 67*(2), 133–152. https://doi.org/10.1177/0022429419835198.

Morrison, S. J., Price, H. E., Geiger, C. G., & Cornacchio, R. A. (2009). The effect of conductor expressivity on ensemble performance evaluation. *Journal of Research in Music Education, 57*(1), 37–49. https://doi.org/10.1177/0022429409332679.

Morrison, S. J., Price, H. E., Smedley, E. M., & Meals, C. D. (2014). Conductor gestures influence evaluations of ensemble performance. *Frontiers in Psychology, 5*(e35757), 806. http://doi.org/10.3389/fpsyg.2014.00806.

Morrison, S., & Selvey, J. (2014). The effect of conductor expressivity on choral ensemble evaluation. *Bulletin of the Council for Research in Music Education, 199,* 7–18. https://doi.org/10.5406/bulcouresmusedu.199.0007?ref=no-x-route:952ab0b6c558cb426fe8d3396f4984cb.

Norgaard, M. (2011). Descriptions of improvisational thinking by artist-level jazz musicians. *Journal of Research in Music Education, 59*(2), 109–127. https://doi.org/10.1177/0022429411405669.

Ono, K., Nakamura, A., & Maess, B. (2015). Keeping an eye on the conductor: Neural correlates of visuo-motor synchronization and musical experience. *Frontiers in Human Neuroscience, 9,* 154. https://doi.org/10.3389/fnhum.2015.00154.

O'Reilly, S. (2017, August 30). *The conductor who prefers to work with silence. Irish Times.* https://www.irishtimes.com/culture/music/the-conductor-who-prefers-to-work-with-silence-1.3197114.

Pan, Y., Novembre, G., Song, B., Li, X., & Hu, Y. (2018). Interpersonal synchronization of inferior frontal cortices tracks social interactive learning of a song. *Neuroimage, 183,* 280–290. https://doi.org/10.1016/j.neuroimage.2018.08.005.

Pasquale, J. D. (2008). *Directed listening for wind ensemble conductors: A pedagogy for developing aural analysis and effective rehearsal strategy* Doctoral thesis. Retrieved from ProQuest Dissertations & Theses Global. (304486848).

Phillips, B. (2018, November 1). *What makes superstar conductor Gustavo Dudamel so good? New York Times* – see https://www.nytimes.com/2018/11/01/magazine/gustavo-dudamel-los-angeles-philharmonic.html.

Price, H. E., & Byo, J. L. (2002). Rehearsing and conducting. In R. Parncutt & G. McPherson (Eds.), *The science and psychology of music performance: Creative strategies for teaching and learning* (pp. 335–351). New York: Oxford University Press.

Price, H. E., & Chang, E. C. (2005). Conductor and ensemble performance expressivity and state festival ratings. *Journal of Research in Music Education, 53*(1), 66–77. https://doi.org/10.1177/002242940505300106.

Scheinin, R. (2009, October 16). *Review: Joana Carneiro makes impressive debut as Berkeley Symphony's new music director. Mercury News* – see https://www.mercurynews.com/2009/10/16/review-joana-carneiro-makes-impressive-debut-as-berkeley-symphonys-new-music-director/.

Silvey, B. A. (2011). The effect of ensemble performance quality on the evaluation of conducting expressivity. *Journal of Research in Music Education, 59*(2), 162–173. https://doi.org/10.1177/0022429411406173.

Silvey, B. A., & Koerner, B. D. (2016). Effects of conductor expressivity on secondary school band members' performance and attitudes toward conducting. *Journal of Research in Music Education, 64*(1), 29–44. https://doi.org/10.1177/0022429415622451.

Sousa, G. D. (1988). *Musical conducting emblems: An investigation of the use of specific conducting gestures by instrumental conductors and their interpretation by instrumental performers* (Doctoral dissertation, Ohio State University).

Toiviainen, P., & Snyder, J. (2003). Tapping to Bach: Resonance-based modeling of pulse. *Music Perception, 21*(1), 43–80. https://doi.org/10.1525/mp.2003.21.1.43.

Tsay, C. J. (2014). The vision heuristic: Judging music ensembles by sight alone. *Organizational Behavior and Human Decision Processes, 124*(1), 24–33. https://doi.org/10.1016/j.obhdp.2013.10.003.

Wanderley, M. M., Vines, B. W., Middleton, N., McKay, C., & Hatch, W. (2005). The musical significance of clarinetists' ancillary gestures: An exploration of the field. *Journal of New Music Research, 34*(1), 97–113.

Wöllner, C. (2012). Self-recognition of highly skilled actions: A study of orchestral conductors. *Consciousness and Cognition, 21*(3), 1311–1321. https://doi.org/10.1016/j.concog.2012.06.006.

Wöllner, C., Deconinck, F. J. A., Parkinson, J., Hove, M. J., & Keller, P. E. (2012). The perception of prototypical motion: Synchronization is enhanced with quantitatively morphed gestures of musical conductors. *Journal of Experimental Psychology: Human Perception and Performance, 38*(6), 1390–1403. https://dx.doi.org/10.1037/a0028130.

Yarbrough, C. (1975). Effect of magnitude of conductor behavior on students in selected mixed choruses. *Journal of Research in Music Education, 23*(2), 134–146. https://doi.org/10.2307/3345286.

CHAPTER 14

....

MUSICAL EXPRESSION

....

EMERY SCHUBERT

INTRODUCTION

....

THE art of performing music involves shaping the piece being performed through highly personalized, ongoing changes to the dynamics, phrasing, timbre, and articulation, as well as other musical dimensions that go beyond the printed notation or stylistic convention of the repetoire being performed. Experienced musicians understand that performing expressively is more engaging for the listener, and can intensify the affective qualities of the music, bringing it to life, so to speak. As will become evident in this chapter, being able to perform music expressively is an indispensible skill for any high-level musician.

To make a piece of music sound expressive requires the musician(s) to manipulate loudness, timing, pitch, and timbre in a special way while performing. Technically this manipulation, if done successfully, is referred to as *musical expression*. Expressiveness is a term that crosses over in important and complex ways with rhetoric, authenticity, and creativity, themselves being intuitively understood concepts, while without contradiction also quite nebulous. Musical expression is both complex and central to music making; it is often seen as the aspect of music performance that takes music above and beyond the mechanics of "just playing or singing notes." It is also indicative of numerous artistically pleasing and successful options.

Expressiveness is thought to occur within a range of options in a given genre or style of music—outside this range, expressiveness stops or becomes inappropriate (Clarke, 1995). Sometimes, the phrase "expressive playing" connotes that the sound signal produced by the musicians is elevated to a special, higher status that a Western listener may refer to as "true art." The idea of expressive playing, however, has been appropriated by musicians outside Western art-music traditions, and so accordingly its meaning differs depending on the genre or style of music being performed.

A key concern for high-level performers is how their performance can be distinguished from other performances (such as their own earlier performances and those of others). For example, two highly skilled performers of the same genre will often be diffi-cult to tell apart in terms of technical expertise, and so adjudicators—be they an audition panel, or a concert audience—may end up relying almost exclusively upon "successful" expressive communication to determine which is the better or more satisfying perfor-mance (should that be the listener's aim). Such judgments involve decisions that are aes-thetic and subjective to varying extents. Ranking two or more highly skilled performers, for example in a competition or audition, therefore creates enormous challenges, and so makes the understanding of expressiveness all the more critical.

The sections that follow in this chapter present an overview of the nature and meaning of expression in music performance. Music expression will be broken into three components to help understand how expression is created, perceived, and acquired, the components being labeled: *Performance* (the act of playing), *Affect* (reception of the playing by the audience), and *Knowledge* (understanding the links between the act of performing and its impact on the listener). We will see how these three components, referred to as the KPA process model (Figure 14.1), cycle through a process of music ex-pressiveness. After summarizing the main body of literature regarding the performance and affect components, the bulk of the chapter turns attention to the knowledge com-ponent, since this is the area that musicians and students can do much about in terms of interrogating their own approaches to musical expression, and furthermore the addi-tional space devoted here to knowledge reflects a need to compensate for some neglect

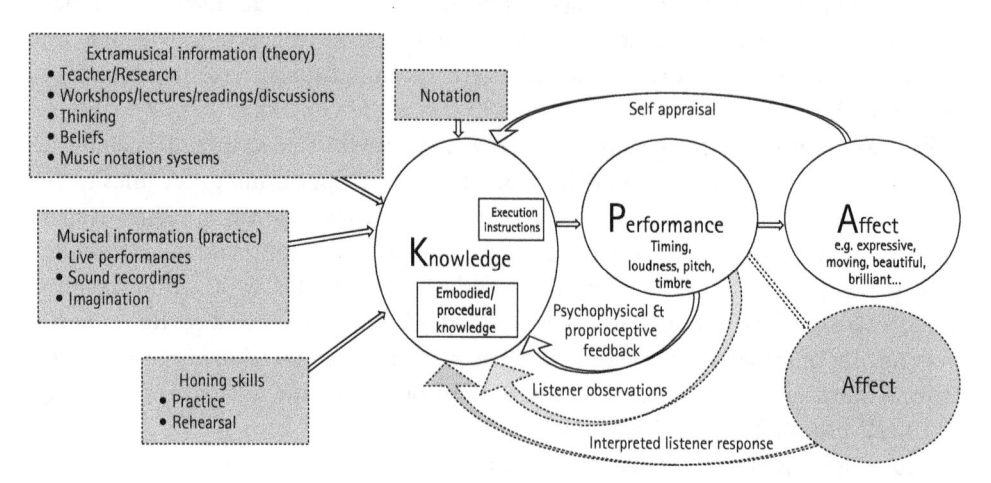

FIGURE 14.1. Knowledge-Performance-Affect (KPA) process model of musical expression.

Note: KPA refers to the three processing blocks (components) that are essential for musical expression. Performer knowledge (K) is central and the starting point of expressive performance, being a repository of knowledge on all aspects of musical expression, which is then applied during performance (P) through physical interaction with the musical instrument, which then produces an affect (aesthetic) experience in the performer/listener (A). Boxes and arrows in the lower part of the diagram focus on the music sound world; upper parts are more theory-driven. Dotted shapes are from the external world (e.g., audience affect is the dotted circle); solid line shapes are the internal world of the performer. The performer is influenced by all three processes, while the non-performing listener is influenced by K and A components only. The listener can also be the performer and make direct observations about their performance, without "affect" (as is the case for the dotted arrow "Listener observations"). The process with multiple performers is not shown here (but see Keller, 2014; Novembre & Keller, 2014).

that this component suffers in the musicological and pedagogical literature. Indeed, the Knowledge component is the first component of musical expression, but here is left to the end to allow the reader to understand how it brings the other two components together in important ways.

The Performance Component of Musical Expression

Rules of expressive performance

The sound of a musically expressive performance emanates from the musical instrument while the performer manipulates the instrument, converting carefully controlled and coordinated physical actions into musical/psychophysical signals. These signals are often described by musicians in terms of timing, loudness, pitch, and timbre, depending on the style of the music and the instruments (Clarke, 1991). The musculoskeletal motor actions that generate these manipulations may be thought of as the act of performance because they constitute the *performance component* of musical expression. The performance component therefore occurs at the interface between musical instruction execution and the corresponding formation of musical/psychoacoustic information.

A number of researchers have mapped out specific rules of expressive performance that describe how to execute a musically expressive performance. Most notably, the "KTH" rules, which bear the name of the institution where they were discovered (i.e., KTH Royal Institute of Technology, Stockholm), have been frequently applied both in codifying expressive rules, and in generating convincing robotic performances of music (De Poli, 2004; Friberg, Bresin, & Sundberg, 2006; Katayose, Hashida, De Poli, & Hirata, 2012).

In an overview of the "KTH rules, Friberg, et al. (2006) suggest that those most researched in Western classical music of the common practice period (MCPP) and jazz include:

1. *Phrasing*—such as getting louder and faster in the middle of a musical phrase.
2. *Micro-level timing*—exaggerating length of notes, for example double- or overdotting a dotted eighth note.
3. *Metrical patterns and grooves*—playing a series of evenly notated duration pitches with a rhythmic bias, such as lengthening the first note of each pair of equal-duration notes.
4. *Articulation*—for example, grouping together a melodic fragment using a micropause at the end of a fragment.
5. *Tonal tension*—such as emphasizing a non-chord tone of a melody.

6. *Intonation*—such as sharpening the leading tone in preparation for its resolution to the tonic.
7. *Ensemble timing*—being the adjustment of a group of players to ensure synchronization in part playing, to counter loss of timing synchronization that would have occurred had variation in interpretations in the prior six groups been left unchecked.

These "rules" may be thought of as performance execution strategies rather than rules per se. Furthermore, some, such as duration contrasts—that require the player to contrast duration of consecutive pairs of pitches even when they are notated as being of equal duration—are more in the realm of performance practice in general, rather than being necessary for producing expressive playing. The so-called rules are evident in performances of certain styles of music, but do not cover all aspects of expressive playing that are quantifiable at a physical level (e.g., Clarke & Doffman, 2014). Indeed, the awareness of such rules, and other technical developments particularly since World War II may in part contribute to their growing prevalence in performance. That is, some have hypothesized that performances in the first half of the twentieth century and earlier were more expressively flexible because principles of expressive playing had not been codified to the extent they have been in recent decades by the academy (for further discussion, see Cook, 2013; Leech-Wilkinson, 2009; Sung & Fabian, 2011).

It is worth remembering that performance science researchers tend to track elements of music that are reasonably easy to quantify, with timing (from which tempo, rhythm, and articulation can be calculated), intensity (related to dynamics and loudness), and pitch being the most common (Gabrielsson, 2003). More challenging to quantify is timbre, which can change as a result of expressive intention, the human voice being the most obvious and important example. Timbre itself is physically a multidimensional construct, deriving physically from the energy spectrum and short-timescale transients of the music, and being correlated with other features, such as loudness and pitch (Melara & Marks, 1990; Schubert & Wolfe, 2006). Therefore, timbre is not easily reducible to a single physical measure to the extent that timing and intensity are. This explains why timbre manipulation is not as well understood as a performance parameter in relation to musical expression. Nevertheless, one should keep in mind its potential influence.

Noise and reliability of expressive intent

An eighth group of rules that form the KTH rule set is performance "noise" (or what Juslin, 2003 refers to as "random," but see also Juslin et al., 2001). From the performer's perspective the "noise" aspect of expressiveness, and any uncontrolled physical variability, is antithetical to expressiveness. So, even though listed as performance information related to musical expressiveness, it is an aspect of playing that a performer seeks to minimize to the extent humanly possible, or to allow under certain discretionary conditions (e.g., as a result of some kind of knowledge about random physical information). Robot performances may include some such "noise" in order to make the robot sound more convincingly human. But this should not be confused with an explicit goal of music performance by a human.

Noise also provides an opportunity for researchers to better understand the nature of expressive performance. Assuming a performer seeks to eliminate noise as an element of expressive variation, one could analyze a repeated performance by the same musician under similar conditions applying same expressive intention each time. The variations found between the two performances can then be used to provide empirical evidence of the amount of noise that cannot easily be controlled by the performer. If an expressive performance can be reproduced with precision, then it means that the "noise" component is small. There exists compelling evidence that expert performers are able to execute the physical expressive performance properties more or less identically even when the work in question is played years after an earlier performance (Gabrielsson, 1999; Margulis, 2014; Sung & Fabian, 2011). This is not to say that performers always interpret music the same way over time. But such change, when it occurs, is likely to be an intentional decision or a natural development. From a psychological perspective, this strengthens the idea that expert performers are able to create, store, and reproduce physical actions with a high level of intentionality and precision.

Expression in music—a more technical definition

The KTH rules provide concrete examples of how musical expression comes into existence from the performance component perspective. For each rule, some parameter of music is varied with respect to an underlying reference or norm. This allows us to propose a more technical definition of music expression than that presented at the opening of the chapter, and one in terms of the performance component. In the broadest sense, expression is the "modulation of" or "deviation from" a stylized set of physical actions (that is, the act of playing the musical instrument in a typical manner). This modulation or deviation is driven by a goal of communicating musically with one or more individuals and is often achieved with or without the deliberate attention of the performer. For example, to achieve greater expressiveness, a performer may play slightly faster and louder at a certain part of a piece or add some additional ornaments during a vocal passage. The "faster and louder" and the "more ornaments" instruction is in comparison to some norm. It is a modulation because it can be viewed as signal being manipulated over another signal—the normal tempo, loudness, or ornamentation, whatever they may be, being modulated with some additional adjustment of tempo, loudness, or ornamentation. Determining this "norm" has challenged musicians and researchers alike, and it is a matter to which we return.

Performance linked to perception

Performance is inextricably linked with perception (Novembre & Keller, 2014). For example, the motor cortex (the part of the brain involved in executing musculoskeletal actions) is activated by the perception of familiar music in expert musicians even when they listen to the music, rather than play it (Haueisen & Knösche, 2001). This is why, for example, expert pianists, even when they are not playing the piano, may need to inhibit finger motion that involuntarily corresponds to the music to which they are listening. This mirroring behavior reminds us that the "component" of musical expression proposed here, like each component, is as much a convenient label as is it a clearly demarcated boundary. With this limitation in mind, we now turn our attention to the Affect component.

THE AFFECT COMPONENT
OF MUSICAL EXPRESSION

The concept of "affect valence" for understanding the end-product of musical expression

The experience of expressive playing from a listener's perspective is usually seen as a qualitative aspect of expressive communication, in contrast to the performance component, which is frequently defined quantitatively (e.g., playing at this point of the music takes place at x beats per minute, and with an intensity of y). Responses to musical expression often take place using words such as that performance was beautiful, moving, or highly expressive. With this in mind, we can try to better understand musical experience by categorizing the verbal descriptions used. Two broad categories of words tend to be used when describing musical expression (Schubert & Fabian, 2014): *emotion expression* and *musical expression.*

While expressing specific emotions (*emotion* expression) such as sadness, joy, anger, and so on can be goals of a performer (Juslin & Laukka, 2003), in MCPP these specific emotions are more or less prescribed by the musical structures created by the composer (Gabrielsson & Lindström, 2010). They are coded into the music by the composer using increasingly well understood relationships between emotion and musical structure, such as minor mode and slow tempo being suited for the expression of sadness.

The more ethereal goal of expressive performance, as in "playing with feeling," is *musical* expression, and is a distinctly different kind of expressive content to (though sometimes confused with) expression of emotion. This kind of "musical" expressive content produces reactions that are more general, and more connected with the aesthetic outcome of the expression in comparison to emotional expression. To help more clearly partition *musical* expression content from *emotional* expression content, the term *positive affect valence* can be used to describe the former, to distinguish it from specific emotions and at the same time to distinguish it from *negative affect valence*, which refers to *unsuccessful* musical expression in performances (disliked, poorly executed, unsettling, and so on) (Schubert, North, & Hargreaves, 2016).

Positive affect valence terms are the descriptions made in response to performances that are successful in musical expressive performance, such as beautiful, moving, powerful, and convincing. In addition to assessment of the performance, musical expression can also generate internal feelings such as being satisfied, moved, impressed, or exhilarated (Schubert, et al., 2016). What the assessed and the felt descriptions have in common is that they express a positive state (affect) that is qualitatively different from specific emotions such as happiness and joy ("emotion valence"). Positive affect valence is the desired, endpoint aesthetic outcome of musical expressiveness.

But so-called affect valence is not by any means an exclusive category for describing musical expression. Musical expression may be described via the technical characteristics of the performance features (discussed earlier in the performance component section of this chapter) and musical expression is also frequently described via metaphor (e.g., Wolfe, 2018), which may or may not involve affect valence. To summarize, Table 14.1 illustrates the distinctions between acclamations of positive affect valence (for describing

Table 14.1. Sample of expressive content and affect terms.

Expressive content type	Sample terms for the affective experience of musical expression (positive affect valence)	Sample affective experience terms indicative of lacking expression in performance (negative affect valence)
Musical expression (affect valence) terms	Expressive, beautiful, moving, powerful, feelingful, flexible, consoling, musical, outstanding, convincing, high quality, (good) quality, magnificent*, exuberant*, impressive*, brilliant*	Inexpressive, lackluster, boring, mechanical, inflexible, robotic, "expressionless," low quality, deadpan, mediocre, nominal, norm, normal, and to use De Poli's (2004) terminology, "reference"
	Emotional expression (emotion valence) sample words	
Emotional expression (emotion valence) terms	Happy, joyous, calm, sad, tender, angry, scared	

Note:

The table shows selected words exemplifying the affect categories for different kinds of affect content: those concerned with successful musical expression (positive affect valence), those concerned with unsuccessful musical expression (negative affect valence), and those concerned with emotion expression (emotion valence).

* affect words indicative of musical expression that are more likely to describe successful performances that are technically challenging.

successful musical expression) and negative affect valence (for describing unsuccessful musical expression), as well as examples of emotion valence showing descriptions that may be used to describe music, but are not typically used to describe *musical* expression.

Organizing terms for describing affect information about successful musical expressiveness helps us to understand the aesthetic goal to which the performer aims and to ignite positive affect valence experience that may even be indescribable, producing an ineffable experience, which is nevertheless, and indeed a pinnacle of, positive affect valence. Positive affect valence experienced as a result of musical expression may itself be subdivided. In Table 14.1, some of the positive-valence words (those marked with an asterisk) are noted for being more suitable for well-expressed performances that are perceived as technically challenging. Further subdivisions will no doubt emerge as we learn more about how affect responses are related more specifically to particular characteristics of expressive performance.

Prototype theory: Optimizing performance to achieve positive affect valence

Bruno Repp (1997) showed that the "typical" performance is rated with positive affect valence more than are atypical performances even when all performances are by expert pianists. In one experiment, Repp (1997, Study 2) collected ratings of expert and student performances of a Chopin étude extract, but also included artificially constructed performances that consisted of averaging preexisting performance timing values (performance information). An artificial "expert average" performance was created by using the averaged note by note timing patterns of eleven expert performances. This "average of experts" performance received among the highest overall rating in performance quality. The affect valence rating of quality was made on a 10-point scale ranging from a lowest score of "mediocre" through to highest score of "outstanding" by those judging the sound recordings.

The idea that an average is most preferred is prevalent outside the reception of music expression. Evidence exists that people are attracted to the most typical objects among a class of objects, and so a kind of mental statistical averaging seems to take place when casting judgement. For example, if one grows up in a particular culture and ethnicity, that person will be exposed to a particular range of people's facial features (this is their "class" of human faces), of which the average will be the most expected (such as eye, mouth, and nose positions relative to each other, and in terms of their individual shapes). This kind of mental average is referred to as a *prototype* (Rosch, 1978). Evidence suggests that an individual face that most resembles the prototypical (average) face is most preferred (Rhodes, 2006). Repp's study, which supports this finding in musical expression, has also been confirmed by other findings that the most typical expressive rendering of a piece of music is the most preferred (Wolf, Kopiez, Platz, Lin, & Mütze, 2018).

Research on the prototypical performance has important implications for understanding musical expressiveness, implications that are pertinent to the most important, but often neglected, psychological component in musical expression: knowledge. However, the prototype understanding of musical expression appears to contradict the above proposed definition of musical expressiveness concerned with deviation from some norm, a matter to which we shall return (see section on the theories of musical expression)

THE KNOWLEDGE COMPONENT OF MUSICAL EXPRESSION

Types of musical expression knowledge

Up to this point we have discussed two self-evident components of music expression: (1) the motor aspects of performance that produce the expressive sounding music; and (2) the listeners' response, which can be thought of as the reception or the assessment of the performance—the affective response. The knowledge component links these two components together into a complete process of music expressiveness.

The knowledge component provides the necessary understandings and instructions for musically expressive actions and outcomes. The individual does not have to be aware of this knowledge, and it may be embodied or "procedural" (that is, highly automated; see Eichenbaum & Cohen, 1993) or "intuitive" (Bangert, Schubert, & Fabian, 2014b). We shall focus on four interrelated kinds of knowledge that a player needs to build for achieving a desired level of musical expression: *Notation, Honing skills, Proprioception,* and *Extramusical.*

Notation. Western music notation (see the Notation box in Figure 14.1) stores a limited set of musical instructions. To realize the instructions for the purpose of producing a musically satisfying or appropriate performance, knowledge about reading music is needed (part of the extramusical information box shown in Figure 14.1), and additional information is required by the player because the specific microinstructions that lead to expressive performance have not, to date, been notated in sufficient detail, or in a way that could reasonably easily be interpreted by an advanced human performer. Understanding how to convert the music notation system into sounded music is an aspect of the knowledge component. As a result, musical expression may be thought of as something that is only precisely documented as the *music* output, namely sound recordings and live performances, and in the mind of the performer (imagination) as shown in the dotted Musical information box of Figure 14.1. In the example of realizing a music score, it is the execution of the music score information that may or may not be a literal rendering of those instructions (and as we shall see, it is usually not). The performer must, in general, add information to the notated instructions to produce an expressive output.

Honing skills **or** *skill acquisition.* An important part of building knowledge is developing playing skill to an expert level (see dotted box labeled Honing skills in Figure 14.1), which itself is a major undertaking (Ericsson, 2014/1996). The skills built in this way directly and obviously impact on the Performance component of the KPA process. But there is more to playing in a musically expressive manner than honing skill through practice alone (see also McPherson & Lehmann, 2012 about this matter in regard to the developing musician).

Proprioception. Knowledge also develops through feedback from the individual's own experience of performing, with psychophysical/music feedback (the player hearing the sounds they are making), proprioceptive feedback of the musculoskeletal interaction with the musical instrument, and evaluation of the self-experienced affect component (that is, the affect the listener experiences in response to their own, live performance). These "internal" forms of feedback are shown as solid, curved arrows in Figure 14.1.

Extramusical. Additional sources that feed into the knowledge component can be organized into musical and extramusical information (see dotted boxes in Figure 14.1 with the corresponding titles). Here, musical information is the musical sound world to which the performer is exposed, including imagined performances (Hargreaves, 2012). Exposure to the musical sound world provides the source from which the prototype (discussed earlier) for a piece of music emerges, and includes focused listening to master performers and implicit learning that occurs through "mere" (unfocused) exposure to music (Burwell, 2013; Hallam, 2004).

Extramusical information usually comes from verbal sources, such as teacher explanations, books on music making, and other forms of study or experiences that are outside the music sound world itself. This includes explicit technical knowledge about music notation and even recording systems (understanding how sound is recorded, so that the musical sound world can be distinguished from technical matters concerning recording quality, such as microphone placement, audio editing, or noise). Extramusical information may also be gathered from listener feedback, be it from an audition panel, a teacher, a mentor, a master performer, concert audience, a trusted friend, and so on. A selection of different kinds of extramusical feedback are indicated by the dotted, curved arrows in Figure 14.1.

Sources of musical expression

From where do the approaches to musical expression come? The source of musical expression can be classified into universal, cultural, situational, and personal. Universal sources are those where an expressive gesture is understood or considered essential regardless of the situation or context or the performance. As we have seen, for certain pieces of music this may be a tempo rubato (slowing down and then speeding up) in the middle of a musical phrase. Cultural sources are those that are accepted or expected by a group of performers who share a particular approach, such as a school of musical practice. The "historically informed performance" practice movement is one such example, and within this movement there are different groups of people who share views about how particular pieces of music should be sounded to achieve a desired expressive goal (Fabian, 2003; Rink, 2002).

The individual's musical signature leads to eccentricities of a particular performer (Fabian & Ornoy, 2009; Gingras, 2014). Situational sources (Friberg & Battel, 2002) refer to where the expression used is dependent on the context in which it is being used—be it a particularly special performance, the performer being in a particular state or mood, a desire to satisfy a particular kind of audience, and so on. The four sources are exemplified in Table 14.2. These sources (cultural, universal, situational, individual) interact with each other, making it evident that the four-way distinction is useful for

Table 14.2. Source of musical expression.

Source	Explanation	Examples
Individual	Personal characteristics such as mood and predisposition of the performer, which may manifest as an individual's expressive "signature" (Fabian & Ornoy, 2009)	Unexpectedly fast performance; player holds the last chord longer than any other player; eccentricities that make it easy to identify the performer (e.g., Glenn Gould's vocalizations while playing the piano).
Situational	The environment of a performance	Performing in a manner thought appropriate: —for a critic who likes a particular style; —for an audience that is accustomed to a mainstream performance style
Cultural	Adopting expressive techniques from a tradition of playing	The performer's expressive approach resembles that of his teacher; the performer plays in a historically informed manner or that of a national tradition.
Universal	The most general "rules" of performance, most likely with origins in natural, evolutionarily based systems, for example: biomechanical kinematics such as the way a runner slows before stopping (Friberg & Sundberg, 1999); highlighting structural boundaries (Sloboda, 2000; Sloboda & Gregory, 1980; Todd, 1989); origins in the need to take a breath when speaking, while making communication meaningful "players slow down at phrase boundaries because of the perceptual biases they possess as listeners" (Sloboda, 2000, p. 401); speech structures (Brown, Pfordresher, & Chow, 2017); and other expressive phenomena that appear to be or do occur in nature.	Slowing down at the end of a phrase of slow, non-dance music.

understanding the sources of musical expression, but of limited value in understanding the detail.

THEORIES OF MUSICAL EXPRESSION

A fundamental challenge signaled by the knowledge component of musical expression is to establish how to control the performance parameters with the goal of producing a desired affect. Researchers deal with this matter by proposing and testing theories which can in turn inform the player. Such research aims to draw knowledge from the Performance and the Affect components of the process. In that light we turn our attention to the pertinent issue that ties in with the very definition of expressiveness presented at the opening of this chapter.

The definition that music expression is the deviation of musical features from some norm has an important implication as to how the knowledge component is psychologically grounded. To begin with, performance scientists have been attempting to ascertain what the norms are. One early attempt at defining the norm was proposed by a North American pioneer of quantitative research on musical expression, Carl Seashore (for non-American, earlier pioneers, see Kopiez, 1996), who stated that:

> artistic expression of feeling in music consists in esthetic deviation from the regular—from pure tone, true pitch, even dynamics, metronomic time, rigid rhythms, etc. (Seashore, 1938/1967, p. 9)

Seashore's approach has been interpreted to mean that the literal music score instructions dictate the nominal performance parameter values, which if actually performed might be described as "mechanical" or "unexpressive" (see section on the affect component), and that deviation from these score-based values, such as relatively speeding up, slowing down, playing louder, playing softer, at particular points in the score will lead to more expressive results. Seashore presents examples of how this deviation occurs by plotting performed note durations against score-based note durations, allowing quantification of expressive effects (see Figure 14.2 for an example).

Eric Clarke (1991) disputed considering the literal score as a basis against which to measure musical expression because of the difficulty in specifying the amount of deviation that is possible "before" a deviation is considered an error rather than expressive. Furthermore, as Clarke points out, for music that is not score based, a score-based assessment of expression is likely to fail. Consider music of many non-Western cultures and in particular those where improvisation plays a central role (Clarke, 1991) or when extreme specificity, for example in electronic dance music consisting of inflexible tempo and highly reproduceable digital sounds that may appear to stifle prospects for tempo-based expressiveness. In such cases, from what exactly are the musical features deviating?

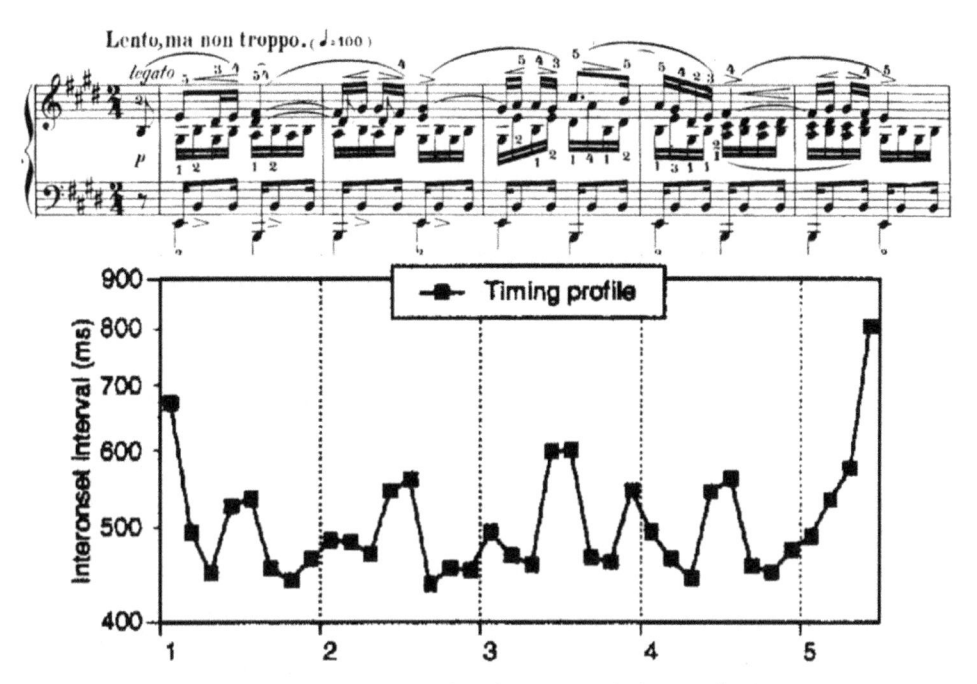

FIGURE 14.2. Score and typical timing profile of bars 1 to 5 of Chopin's Étude Op. 10, no. 3.

Note: This example is taken from a study of performances of the étude by a number of pianists, with the typical performance timing shown in the graph. Each dot in the graph represents a semiquaver (sixteenth-note) beat in the score, with the height of the dot indicating how long the beat is held for in milliseconds. Some semiquaver beats take over 700 ms, while faster playing is indicated by dots at around 450 ms. The figure is an adaptation of Figure 3C. "A typical timing profile for the Chopin 'theme,' shown on top," p. 797 from Repp (1998).

Some have proposed that tempo inflexibility does not alone prevent musical expressiveness. "Conventional" aspects of expressive playing such as rubato in MCPP are often replaced by manipulation of other aspects of timing in other styles, such as the use of syncopation in some popular and jazz music styles (Temperley, 2004). Ornamentation, which became less evident in MCPP during the nineteenth century (e.g., Butt, 2002, p. 98), is another example of how expressiveness is possible in musical forms with inflexible tempo (see Dibben, 2014). And so, this should remind us of the nuances of musical expression, particularly when the concept is applied beyond MCPP. It should also remind us that tempo is just one feature among many that are employed to control expression.

If musical expression does not stem from modulation of parameters indicated in the music score, what is the player doing to achieve an expressive performance? In other words, what is the "reference" against which the deviations occur (for an elegant overview of a range of theories on musical expression, see, e.g., Clarke, 1995)? The answer may lie in interrogating performances that are *not* expressive. Deliberately inexpressive performances may reflect the idealized reference performance of a piece. Considerable empirical evidence attests to the inability of players to perform in a strictly mechanical, "score-based" manner when asked to do so (Clarke & Baker-Short, 1987; Drake &

Palmer, 1993; Gabrielsson, 1974; Palmer, 1989; Seashore, 1938/1967). Players can be given explicit instructions to play without expression, and despite the instruction to play in a mechanical manner being issued to highly skilled musicians, and even when accounting for technical (not expressive) factors such as difficult leaps, and awkward fingering that may inhibit attempts to perform in a strictly mechanical way, literal, score-based timings and dynamics are not found. Such "literal" performances, rather than the music score, therefore provide aural data for the reference performance against which deviations for legitimately expressive performance could be made. That is, instead of using the literal score-based performance as the reference against which expression is generated, the reference is some imaginary, humanly performed, literal performance.

Another solution to identifying the reference performance against which to measure deviation in the performance is to again use data from the performance sound world, but to take the "average" of a number of "natural" performances in contrast to the more artificial, literal performance. This is the basis of the "prototype" view of expressive playing, discussed in this chapter's section on the affect component.

An alternate approach based on the results of Repp's (1997) study invokes quite a contrasting interpretation to these theories. With Repp's finding (discussed under the affect component section)—that the most average or "prototypical" performance is most preferred—optimal expression is obtained by the *removal* of deviations from the norm. That is, the norm itself produces optimal expression in contrast to previous prototype theory. These distinct, somewhat contradictory theories of how expressive knowledge is executed demonstrate the complexities of musical expression, and how limited our theoretical understanding of musical expression is at this point.

At this stage, the different theories can serve as provocative points of departure for performers seeking to explore different expressive solutions: removing expression as a pedagogical device, and the two approaches to deviation (levels of exaggeration in comparison to expectations of the typical) and matching (playing as closely as possible to the expected, typical performance). In the meantime, researchers continue to work on discovering good theoretical foundations.

Individual Differences in Approaches to Musical Expression

Understanding musical expressiveness as a process unfolding through the three KPA components has implications for the performer seeking to better understand expressive performance and to further master it.

Some performers may wish to focus on physical aspects of performance, dealing with expression at the timing, dynamic, intonation, and timbre levels. This type of focus is of particular interest to music psychologists and performance scientists.

Others may prefer to focus on the affective/aesthetic aspects of their performance, thinking in terms of the ethereal goal of the performance, and leaving the (highly developed) physical component to operate at a more automated level. Music pedagogy and philosophical investigations of aesthetics tend to be interested in understanding from this perspective.

Deliberate focus by the musician on either of these two processes is in itself a stance taken toward making decisions about musical expression. And those focusing on the knowledge process are taking an intellectual stance to their playing. This includes examining the score for signs of appropriate or successful interpretation and focusing on sound recordings to explicitly replicate or revolt against existing expressive performances.

Without taking a performance-focused stance or an affect-focused stance, the musician may also be taking in intuitive stance. Intuition is considered by psychologists as one of two thinking systems, the other being deliberate (Kahneman, 2011). Even those well versed in performance expression will agree that aspects of musical expression require some level of intuition (Bangert, Fabian, Schubert, & Yeadon, 2014a; Bangert, et al., 2014b; Rink, 2002).

Teachers inevitably use a variety of approaches that take different stances. For example, in a study by Meissner (2017), teaching techniques labeled "discussion of musical character" (affect component) and instruction about modifying expressive devices (performance component) were found to be linked to more successful performances by students. And so different combinations of thinking systems may be brought to a performance to help understand performance puzzles and to enhance the expressive outcomes.

The stance taken to deal with the execution of musical expressiveness may be related to the character of the individual. Simon Baron-Cohen proposed that some people have a propensity to engage with the world through objects (people with such propensity are referred to as systemizers), while others have a propensity to engage with people (so-called empathizers), but most excel in both of these "cognitive styles" (Baron-Cohen, 2002). This concept has been expanded to "music" systemizers who engage with musical objects and "music" empathizers who engage with the thoughts and feelings of people involved in music (Kreutz, Schubert, & Mitchell, 2008). One may speculate that those who are predominantly music systemizers will engage with the question of expression with a performance stance, whereas those with a propensity for music empathizing will engage with expressiveness with an affect stance, where the focus is in moving or affecting the listener. As with the findings on thinking systems in music performance, an expert most likely will move across the different music cognitive styles (and different stances) when dealing with challenges concerning musical expression.

Conclusion

In this chapter, musical expressiveness was defined and delimited. The three-component Knowledge-Performance-Affect process model was presented as a way of organizing and understanding musical expression.

The performance component of the KPA process refers to the musculoskeletal actions of producing musical features (pitch, loudness, timing, timbre) each at a desired level, and is seen by many as the necessary starting point of expression, because without the performance there can be no musical sound. A set of rules for how these features are manipulated to produce expressive output have been developed, with particular focus on achieving musical expressiveness in music of the common practice period.

The affect component of the KPA process refers to the expressive outcome of the performance component and is the human endpoint of expressive performance. A successful performance leads to a positive (affect valence) experience in the mind and body of the listener, and a number of verbal descriptions represent these positive experiences, culminating in experiences that may be ineffable. These were contrasted with the (negative) "affect" of unsuccessful performances, and with specific emotions that are concerned with a different kind of expressive content (emotional, rather than musical, expression). While researchers need to differentiate between descriptions such as "the music is sad" (specific emotion concerned with emotion expression) versus "the music is powerful" (affect valence concerned with musical expression), performers interested in more clearly defining the kind of expressive content they seek to communicate will find greater clarity in understanding this conceptual distinction in affect.

The third component of the KPA process, knowledge, encapsulates the cultures, skills, and theories of how expressive performance is planned, executed, and perceived. At the theoretical level, the knowledge component is concerned with deviation from some reference performance or communicating some expressive goal. Current explanations point to two contrasting, alternative theories of deviation-from-the-norm among many. One is that the reference performance is the most typical performance against which deviations produce musical expression. An alternative is that expressive performance is characterized by the extent to which it matches with, rather than deviates from, this idealized, typical performance. These contrasting alternatives make the idea of deviation from a reference problematic but may also inspire the performer to contemplate performances in different ways by exploring the "affect" of these contrasting perspectives. The knowledge component also deals with different approaches individuals take when planning and executing a performance. The stance taken by individuals to understanding and interpreting music may be tied to personality factors such as thinking systems (through intuitive and deliberate approaches) and cognitive styles (music systemizing and music empathizing).

It is worth noting that the KPA model, while representing as a cyclical process, can also be viewed in terms of three coexisting worlds as proposed by science philosopher Karl Popper (see also Parncutt, 1989; Popper & Eccles, 1977). World 1 consists of physical reality, and the Performance component of the KPA process model is its parallel. World 2 consists of sensory experience and has its parallel with the Affect component. World 3 consists of the world of ideas and knowledge, being a kind of (human) interface between the physical and experiential worlds (1 and 2), therefore paralleling the Knowledge component. The parallels between the KPA process model and Popper's three worlds is useful because it shows how in addition to being thought of a cycling process, the three processes can also be thought of as three coexisting "worlds."

The focus of the present chapter has been on musicians based in cultures of MCPP. However, the KPA process is psychologically founded, rather than culture-specific, so it will still apply to performances in different traditions. While this chapter has proposed some of the ways our understanding of the KPA process may assist the performer, it is important to note that developments in performing will dynamically continue to inform theory on expression in music, and it is the symbiotic relationship between performer, teacher, and researcher that will allow the knowledge component of the model to continue to grow, deepen, and be refined.

Key Sources

Cook, N. (2013). *Beyond the score: Music as performance.* New York: Oxford University Press.

Fabian, D., Timmers, R., & Schubert, E. (Eds.). (2014). *Expressiveness in music performance: A cross-cultural and interdisciplinary approach.* Oxford: Oxford University Press.

Friberg, A., Bresin, R., & Sundberg, J. (2006). Overview of the KTH rule system for musical performance. *Advances in Cognitive Psychology,* 2(2-3), 145–161. https://psycnet.apa.org/doi/10.2478/v10053-008-0052-x.

Gabrielsson, A. (2003). Music performance research at the millennium. *Psychology of Music,* 31(3), 221–272.

Leman, M. (2016). *The expressive moment: How interaction (with music) shapes human empowerment.* Cambridge, MA: MIT Press.

Reflective Questions

1. How might the Knowledge-Performance-Affect process of musical expression aid your approach as a musician trying to address an expressive musical performance challenge?

2. To what extent should musically expressive performance be a deliberate act, and how large is the role for intuition? Give examples.

3. Expressiveness can refer to matters other than playing the expressive content of the music. Indicate at least three of these other matters.

4. Reflect on the different meanings of the term *expressiveness* in regard to music and describe how each overlaps with the others.

5. Explain a psychological theory that helps us to understand how musical expression is learned, planned, and/or achieved. Describe the implications of the theory from your own perspective as a performer.

REFERENCES

Bangert, D., Fabian, D., Schubert, E., & Yeadon, D. (2014a). Performing solo Bach: A case study of musical decision-making. *Musicae Scientiae, 18*(1), 35–52. https://doi.org/10.1177/1029864913509812.

Bangert, D., Schubert, E., & Fabian, D. (2014b). A spiral model of musical decision-making. *Frontiers in Psychology, 5*. https://doi.org/10.3389/fpsyg.2014.00320.

Baron-Cohen, S. (2002). The extreme male brain theory of autism. *Trends in Cognitive Sciences, 6*(6), 248–254. https://doi.org/10.1016/s1364-6613(02)01904-6.

Brown, S., Pfordresher, P. Q., & Chow, I. (2017). A musical model of speech rhythm. *Psychomusicology, 27*(2), 95–112. https://doi.org/10.1037/pmu0000175.

Burwell, K. (2013). Apprenticeship in music: A contextual study for instrumental teaching and learning. *International Journal of Music Education, 31*(3), 276–291. https://doi.org/10.1177/0255761411434501.

Butt, J. (2002). *Playing with history: The historical approach to musical performance.* Cambridge, UK: Cambridge University Press.

Clarke, E. (1991). Expression and communication in musical performance. In J. Sundberg, L. Nord, & R. Carlson (Eds.), *Music, language, speech and brain* (pp. 184–193). London: Macmillan.

Clarke, E. (1995). Expression in performance: generativity, perception and semiosis. In J. Rink (Ed.), *The practice of performance: Studies in musical interpretation* (pp. 21–44). Cambridge, UK: Cambridge University Press.

Clarke, E., & Baker-Short, C. (1987). The imitation of perceived rubato: A preliminary study. *Psychology of Music, 15*(1), 58–75. https://doi.org/10.1177%2F0305735687151005.

Clarke, E., & Doffman, M. (2014). Expressive performance in contemporary concert music. In D. Fabian, R. Timmers & E. Schubert (Eds.), *Expressiveness in music performance: Empirical approaches across styles and cultures* (pp. 98–114). Oxford: Oxford University Press.

Cook, N. (2013). *Beyond the score: Music as performance.* New York: Oxford University Press.

De Poli, G. (2004). Methodologies for expressiveness modelling of and for music performance. *Journal of New Music Research, 33*(3), 189–202. https://doi.org/10.1080/0929821042000317796.

Dibben, N. (2014). Understanding performance expression in popular music recordings. In D. Fabian, R. Timmers, & E. Schubert (Eds.), *Expressiveness in music performance: Empirical approaches across styles and cultures* (pp. 117–132). Oxford: Oxford University Press.

Drake, C., & Palmer, C. (1993). Accent structures in music performance. *Music Perception, 10*(3), 343–378. https://doi.org/10.2307/40285574.

Eichenbaum, H., & Cohen, N. J. (1993). *Memory, amnesia, and the hippocampal system.* Cambridge: MIT Press.

Ericsson, K. A. (2014/1996). The acquisition of expert performance: An introduction to some of the issues. In K. A. Ericsson (Ed.), *The road to excellence: The acquisition of expert performance in the arts and sciences, sports, and games* (pp. 1–50). New York: Psychology Press.

Fabian, D. (2003). *Bach performance practice 1945–1975: A comprehensive review of sound recordings and literature.* Aldershot: Ashgate.

Fabian, D., & Ornoy, E. (2009). Identity in violin playing on records: Interpretation profiles in recordings of solo Bach by early twentiety-century violinists. *Performance Practice Review, 14*(1), Article 3. https://doi.org/10.5642/perfpr.200914.01.03.

Friberg, A., & Battel, G. U. (2002). Structural communication. In R. Parncutt & G. E. McPherson (Eds.), *The science and psychology of music performance: Creative strategies for teaching and learning* (pp. 199–218). New York: Oxford University Press.

Friberg, A., Bresin, R., & Sundberg, J. (2006). Overview of the KTH rule system for musical performance. *Advances in Cognitive Psychology*, 2(2–3), 145–161. https://psycnet.apa.org/doi/10.2478/v10053-008-0052-x.

Friberg, A., & Sundberg, J. (1999). Does music performance allude to locomotion? A model of final ritardandi derived from measurements of stopping runners. *Journal of the Acoustical Society of America*, 105(3), 1469–1484. https://doi.org/10.1121/1.426687.

Gabrielsson, A. (1974). Performance of rhythm patterns. *Scandinavian Journal of Psychology*, 15(1), 63–72. https://doi.org/10.1111/j.1467-9450.1974.tb00557.x.

Gabrielsson, A. (1999). The performance of music. In D. Deutsch (Ed.), *The psychology of music.* (2nd ed., pp. 501–602). Academic Press Series in Cognition and Perception. San Diego, CA: Academic Press.

Gabrielsson, A. (2003). Music performance research at the millennium. *Psychology of Music*, 31(3), 221–272. https://doi.org/10.1177%2F03057356030313002.

Gabrielsson, A., & Lindström, E. (2010). The role of structure in the musical expression of emotions. In P. N. Juslin & J. Sloboda (Eds.), *Handbook of music and emotion: Theory, research, applications* (pp. 367–399). Oxford: Oxford University Press.

Gingras, B. (2014). Individuality in music performance: Introduction to the research topic. [Editorial]. *Frontiers in Psychology*, 5(661). https://doi.org/10.3389/fpsyg.2014.00661.

Hallam, S. (2004). Learning in music: Complexity and diversity. In C. Philpott & C. Plummeridge (Eds.), *Issues in music teaching* (pp. 72–86). London: Routledge.

Hargreaves, D. J. (2012). Musical imagination: Perception and production, beauty and creativity. *Psychology of Music*, 40(5), 539–557. https://doi.org/10.1177%2F0305735612444893.

Haueisen, J., & Knösche, T. R. (2001). Involuntary motor activity in pianists evoked by music perception. *Journal of cognitive neuroscience*, 13(6), 786–792.

Juslin, P. N., Friberg, A., & Bresin, R. (2001). Toward a computational model of expression in music performance: The GERM model. *Musicae Scientiae*, 5(1 suppl), 63–122. https://doi.org/10.1177/10298649020050S104.

Juslin, P. N., & Laukka, P. (2003). Communication of emotions in vocal expression and music performance: Different channels, same code? *Psychological Bulletin*, 129(5), 770–814. https://psycnet.apa.org/doi/10.1037/0033-2909.129.5.770.

Kahneman, D. (2011). *Thinking, fast and slow*. New York: Farrar, Straus & Giroux.

Katayose, H., Hashida, M., De Poli, G., & Hirata, K. (2012). On evaluating systems for generating expressive music performance: the rencon experience. *Journal of New Music Research*, 41(4), 299–310. https://doi.org/10.1080/09298215.2012.745579.

Keller, P. (2014). Ensemble performance: Interpersonal alignment of musical expression. In D. Fabian, R. Timmers & E. Schubert (Eds.), *Expressiveness in music performance: Empirical approaches across styles and cultures* (pp. 260–282). Oxford: Oxford University Press.

Kopiez, R. (1996). Aspekte der Performanceforschung. In H. d. L. Motte-Haber, R. Kopiez, & G. Rötter (Eds.), *Handbuch der Musikpsychologie* (pp. 505–587). Laaber, Germany: Laaber Verlag.

Kreutz, G., Schubert, E., & Mitchell, L. A. (2008). Cognitive styles of music listening. *Music Perception*, 26(1), 57–73. https://doi.org/10.1525/mp.2008.26.1.57.

Leech-Wilkinson, D. (2009). Recordings and histories of performance style. In N. Cook, E. Clarke, D. Leech-Wilkinson, & J. Rink (Eds.), *The Cambridge companion to recorded music* (pp. 246–262). Cambridge, UK: Cambridge University Press.

Margulis, E. H. (2014). Verbatim repetition and musical engagement. *Psychomusicology*, 24(2), 157–163. https://doi.org/10.1037/pmu0000048.

McPherson, G. E., & Lehmann, A. C. (2012). Exceptional musical abilities: Musical prodigies. In G. E. McPherson & G. Welch (Eds.), *Oxford handbook of music education* (pp. 31–50). New York: Oxford University Press.

Meissner, H. (2017). Instrumental teachers' instructional strategies for facilitating children's learning of expressive music performance: An exploratory study. *International Journal of Music Education*, 35(1), 118–135. https://doi.org/10.1177%2F0255761416643850.

Melara, R. D., & Marks, L. E. (1990). Interaction among auditory dimensions: Timbre, pitch, and loudness. *Perception & Psychophysics*, 48(2), 169–178. https://doi.org/10.3758/BF03207084.

Novembre, G., & Keller, P. E. (2014). A conceptual review on action-perception coupling in the musicians' brain: What is it good for? *Frontiers in Human Neuroscience*, 8, 603. https://doi.org/10.3389/fnhum.2014.00603.

Palmer, C. (1989). Mapping musical thought to musical performance. *Journal of Experimental Psychology: Human Perception & Performance*, 15, 331–346. https://doi.org/10.1037/0096-1523.15.2.331.

Parncutt, R. (1989). *Harmony: A psychoacoustical approach*. Berlin: Springer.

Popper, K. R., & Eccles, J. C. (1977). *The self and its brain*. Heidelberg: Springer-Verlag.

Repp, B. H. (1997). The aesthetic quality of a quantitatively average music performance: Two preliminary experiments. *Music Perception*, 14(4), 419–444. https://doi.org/10.2307/40285732.

Repp, B. H. (1998). Variations on a theme by Chopin: Relations between perception and production of timing in music. *Journal of Experimental Psychology: Human Perception & Performance*, 24(3), 791–811. https://psycnet.apa.org/doi/10.1037/0096-1523.24.3.791.

Rhodes, G. (2006). The evolutionary psychology of facial beauty. *Annual Review of Psychology*, 57, 199–226. https://doi.org/10.1146/annurev.psych.57.102904.190208.

Rink, J. (2002). Analysis and (or?) Performance. In J. Rink (Ed.), *Musical performance: A guide to understanding* (pp. 35–58). Cambridge, UK: Cambridge University Press.

Rosch, E. (1978). Prototype classification and logical classification: The two systems. In E. Scholnik (Ed.), *New trends in conceptual representation: Challenges to Piaget's theory* (pp. 73–86). Hillsdale, NJ: Lawrence Erlbaum Associates.

Schubert, E., & Fabian, D. (2014). A taxonomy of listeners' judgments of expressiveness in music performance. In D. Fabian, R. Timmers, & E. Schubert (Eds.), *Expressiveness in pusic merformance: A cross-cultural and interdisciplinary approach* (pp. 283–303). Oxford: Oxford University Press.

Schubert, E., North, A. C., & Hargreaves, D. J. (2016). Aesthetic experience explained by the affect-space framework. *Empirical Musicology Review*, 11(3–4), 330–345. https://doi.org/10.18061/emr.v11i3-4.5115.

Schubert, E., & Wolfe, J. (2006). Does timbral brightness scale with frequency and spectral centroid? *Acta Acustica United with Acustica*, 92(5), 820–825.

Seashore, C. E. (1938/1967). *Psychology of music*. New York: McGraw-Hill.

Sloboda, J. A. (2000). Individual differences in music performance. *Trends in Cognitive Sciences*, 4(10), 397–403. https://doi.org/10.1016/S1364-6613(00)01531-X.

Sloboda, J. A., & Gregory, A. H. (1980). The psychological reality of musical segments. *Canadian Journal of Psychology*, 34(3), 274–280. https://psycnet.apa.org/doi/10.1037/h0081052.

Sung, A., & Fabian, D. (2011). Variety in performance: A comparative analysis of recorded performances of Bach's sixth suite for solo cello from 1961 to 1998. *Empirical Musicology Review*, 6(1), 20–42. https://doi.org/10.18061/1811/49760.

Temperley, D. (2004). Communicative Pressure and the Evolution of Musical Styles. *Music Perception*, 21(3), 313–337.

Todd, N. (1989). Towards a cognitive theory of expression: The performance and perception of rubato. *Contemporary Music Review*, 4(1), 405–416. https://doi.org/10.1080/07494468900640451.

Wolf, A., Kopiez, R., Platz, F., Lin, H.-R., & Mütze, H. (2018). Tendency towards the average? The aesthetic evaluation of a quantitatively average music performance: A successful replication of Repp's (1997) study. *Music Perception: An Interdisciplinary Journal*, 36(1), 98–108. https://doi.org/10.1525/mp.2018.36.1.98.

Wolfe, J. (2018). An investigation into the nature and function of metaphor in advanced music instruction. *Research Studies in Music Education*, 41(3), 280–292. https://doi.org/10.1177/1321103X18773113.

CHAPTER 15

....

BODY MOVEMENT

....

JANE W. DAVIDSON AND MARY C. BROUGHTON

INTRODUCTION

OUR bodies are critical to musical performance. At a physical level, when creating sung vocalization, sound originating from within the larynx and dependent on breath flow, is shaped via internal resonators, and also through mouth, tongue, and lip formations to produce not only sustained pitches, but also glides, hums, grunts, gurgles, laughs even screams. Further to this, we can use our own bodies as percussive instruments to click, slap, or tap out rhythms. We use our bodies to interact with musical instruments to blow, pluck, or strike them into action. When these processes are structured through musical systems, they can produce desired and highly specific powerful effects (consider, for example, the artistry of jazz performer Bobby McFerrin). This chapter investigates relevant research on instrumental skill development, musical expression, and expressive movement, acknowledging its base in previous endeavor (specifically Davidson & Broughton, 2016).

The growing research field of embodied cognition theorizes that the full range of perceptual, cognitive, and motor capacities we possess are dependent upon features of the physical body (Leman & Godøy, 2010; also van der Schyff & Schiavio, this volume). It has been argued that in addition to using our bodies to make musical sounds, we also tend to think about music itself as moving in particular directions or experience it in terms of movement-based concepts (Juslin & Västfell, 2008), so perceptually, we link music to movement. Of course, in today's society when most music is disseminated via listening devices, music is largely appreciated without "seeing" the musicians, and there is a significant body of evidence to show that listeners can perceive many structural and expressive aspects of the music in sound alone (for overviews, see Dahl et al., 2010; Fabian et al., 2014). Still, being able to see a performer most certainly influences perception of that performance (Davidson, 1993, Huang & Krumhansl, 2011; Juchniewicz, 2008; Platz & Kopiez, 2012; Thompson et al., 2005; Vines et al., 2006). A powerful piece of evidence on the interaction of visual and aural perception is the *McGurk effect*

(MacDonald & McGurk, 1978). Originally identified in speech, the effect occurs when there is a mismatch between visual and auditory components of a spoken sound. The listener imagines one sound based on the visual cues and unconsciously adjusts their perception of the sound to hear something that accords with the visual cue. In musical performance it has been demonstrated that facial expressions of singers influence the perception of pitch in listeners (Krahle et al., 2015; Thompson et al., 2010), and studies of string and percussion performance showed sound information was influenced by visual information (Saldaña & Rosenblum, 1993; Schutz & Lipscomb, 2007). For example, when percussionists made longer-duration arm gestures than the musical notes they were playing, these arm gestures contributed to the perception of longer-duration notes. Further studies have shown that visual information can dominate aural perception of musical intention (Tsay, 2013) and no sound is required to evaluate performance intention (Davidson, 1993).

Furthermore, neuroscientific evidence reveals that our understanding of another person's bodily actions is shaped by cognitive and neural processing that enables us to mirror and mimic the movements of others (Gallese & Goldman, 1998; Hommel et al., 2001; Leman, 2008; Leman & Godøy 2010; Molnar-Szakacs & Overy, 2006; Pfeifer & Dapretto, 2009). *Growth point theory* links the earliest beginnings of spoken utterances with the beginnings of mimetic physical movement, suggesting that both linguistic and movement processes emerge from a single source (McNeill, 1992). From the experience of everyday speech, we know that some kinds of bodily movements enable us to access and clarify thoughts, and music research suggests that similar principles are in operation when we are performing music (Argyle, 1988; Goldin-Meadow, 2003; Kendon, 2004; McNeill, 1992; Broughton & Davidson, 2016).

Knowing that body movements can shape our production and perception of music, it is important to understand them in detail. Overarchingly, the music performer is dealing both with technical concerns relating to sound production, such as hitting the correct keys on a piano, and with expression (see King, 2006). Key components of expression include interpretating the music's generative rules such as timing, dynamics, and articulation rules that group harmonic structures and communicate metrical accents. Motion principles also seem to shape some of this expression. For instance, phrase boundaries may be approached with a gradual slowing that follows the deceleration curve of an object coming to rest (Todd, 1995). Expressive performance also serves to communicate emotions, and the performer achieves this by infusing the performance with an emotional character (Juslin & Timmers, 2010, Rocke, Davidson, & Kiernan, this volume).

Refining these two elements of music performance movement further, the movements a performer makes can be grouped into four main categories:

1. sound-producing (blowing, striking, bowing instruments);
2. sound-facilitating (movements involved in shaping the resultant sound, such as muting the instrument);

3. sound-accompanying (movements that follow the music but are not used to produce sound, or that mimic sound-producing or sound-facilitating without producing sounds themselves); and

4. communicative (movements made between performers or to the audience such as eyes glances) (see Davidson, 2009; Jensenius et al, 2010; Nusseck et al, 2018; Wanderley et al., 2005; Wanderley & Vines, 2006).

The communicative aspects are shaped by socio-cultural practices, and individual differences and are susceptible to change over time. Comparing two performances given by experts of different generations can demonstrate this. Consider for example, renditions of Tchaikovsky's Violin Concerto in D major, Op. 35, many examples of which are readily found online. While there are certainly individual differences between performers, some of the aesthetic/social practices of the period in which the music is being performed are also apparent in the nature of the bodily presentation and the expressive focus on both musical structures and physicalized emotional expression. Consider, for instance, the restrained movement of Jascha Heifetz (1901–1974) as compared with the expansive movement of Joshua Bell (b. 1967). Drawing from such observations, the current chapter explores body movements inclusive of the socio-cultural factors that influence the performer generating them and the audience's perception of these performances.

The chapter begins by investigating the motor control (mental representations) required to carry out physical actions including the manipulation of musical instruments. These motor programs need to be refined and automated into sequences of coordinated thoughts and actions. This follows with a discussion of the aspects of the performance movement that are involved in both the production and perception of expert expressive performance in a given context by exploring solo and ensemble performances. The chapter concludes by offering practical information for today's Western art music performer.

MOTOR CONTROL

Understanding the infinite array of muscle and nerve impulses that stimulate bodily movement has been a significant scientific challenge, although there is strong evidence to show that impulses sent from the brain's motor cortex to its motor units engage a coordinated contraction of muscles that initiate and direct purposeful movement (Altenmüller & Gruhn, 2002). As the movement occurs, the nervous system assesses and adjusts force, timing, and tone, drawing on sensory information from visual and balance (vestibular) systems and our sense of body awareness that also detects/controls force and pressure in our muscles and joints (proprioception). The information acquired can be stored in memory for future performance of the same task, and through repetition a new skill can be learned (Jäncke, 2006).

Although musicians do not need to have a precise understanding of motor programming, they do need to understand that motor learning is vital to music making (Dahl, 2018). In fact, in order for skilled music performance movement to be achieved (e.g., playing scales in both hands simultaneously on a piano), a relatively permanent change in motor skills needs to be acquired through practice (Miksza, this part; Muratori et al., 2013).

The Three-Stage Model of Motor Learning has become a classical model to explain motor skill development (Fitts & Posner, 1967). In brief, the first is a *cognitive stage*, in which the learners make conscious effort to remember instructions for performing the desired skill. Next, in the *associative stage*, learners rely less on external instructions and become more adept at refining the reasonably familiarized skilled action in response to the demands of the situation. Finally, in the *autonomous stage*, learners perform the skills automatically without much reliance on conscious cognitive processes. This model is borne out if we consider the following desired outcomes that shape practice behaviors (for more detail see Miksza, this part):

Improvement: This involves looking for objective positive changes in skills over time. A typical example would be to become more accurate in achieving a musical outcome, such as making the appropriate embouchure and applying the necessary amount of breath pressure to achieve the target notes on a brass or woodwind instrument. By engaging in specific behaviors, the appropriate motor programs will develop and there will be a decrease in errors.

Consistency: This demands the individual to be able to reliably produce the desired performance output on multiple occasions. Thus, motor learning needs to occur, thereby enabling deep memory traces and automation of the action so that it is fluent and can be achieved without conscious thought.

Retention: This is to ensure permanent learning. This can be achieved through repetitive practice in order to embed the information in memory. Testing following a delay in practice will determine if permanent learning has occurred.

Transfer: This is the ability to perform a similar movement within a different context to the one in which it was initially learned, such as changing the amount of force or direction when a movement is employed.

Research has shown that if motor learning is approached too quickly, the capacity to process and establish the necessary mental representations may not increase in an expected progression (Guadagnoli & Lee, 2004). But what are the behaviors required to ensure these three stages of motor learning progress at an optimum pace? For the *cognitive stage* of motor learning to occur, attentional focus needs to be high and deliberate, the mental focus being on achieving the movements required. In this phase, movements are often stiff or cumbersome or overcorrected; they lack fluency and accuracy. The performer is often unable to consider other performance-related concerns such as adapting to new situations. Encountering a piano with squeaking pedal, or a trumpet with a faulty valve, for example, is likely to cause the musician to falter.

In the *associative phase*, the movements are more refined and not overcorrected, and through an internal feedback system, error can be corrected, and movement is made more effective. By the *autonomous phase*, the focus is not on the skill of execution, but on other strategies or different aspects of performance, such as the ability to improvise additional elements within the performance (Davidson & McPherson, 2017; MacDonald, this part). The coordination of the body to achieve a single note is vastly different to that necessary to play sequences of cascading high speed notes or achieving effects such as bringing out inner voicings when playing keyboard harmony, so that achieving fluency can take many years and needs to be maintained for optimal retention (Lehmann, Sloboda & Woody, 2007; Palmer, 2006). Additionally, and importantly, motor activity is both anticipatory and emergent during performance. Evidence of anticipatory action is shown in a study of skilled pianists who were found to move their fingers approximately three to four events ahead of time (Dalla Bella & Palmer, 2004; see also Goebl, 2018, for a review of the literature on piano movement and touch).

The acquisition of music performance motor skills has been investigated by a range of researchers. In one project, it was found that actions have specific timing effects reflecting task demand. For example, the amount of time required to press a particular configuration of piano keys, such as a chordal sequence, falls within a unique time profile that has a fixed minimum (Shaffer, 1984). This profile will vary further as different keyboard instruments are subtly different in touch; the amount of physical effort required will also vary according to the instrument's size and shape (Wiesendanger et al., 2006). Furthermore, the performer's own body will also inevitably affect the motor representations, with a smaller person playing a guitar in a slightly different assemblage of movements than that of a larger person. There are, of course, necessary moment-by-moment adaptations during the music performance, such as playing a note longer or sharper or flatter due to acoustic or ensemble concerns. Additional body-related skills required during performance might include eye-to-hand coordination if sight-reading from a score or coordinating movements with others in co-performance to enable a coherent approach to timing, dynamics, and overall expressive ideas.

In summary, the skills involved in performance are complex. The range of body movements that constitute a musical performance are durable indicators of the performer's motor, cognitive, and affective interpretations and are integral to humanly produced music (see Dalca et al., 2013). Working with this knowledge can assist the performer as they build their physical and musical skills. Musical style brings its own demands, with socio-cultural practices and performance conventions shaping the performer's approach, along with personal style and individual personality influences. In co-performance, these elements may require shared knowledge and spoken discussion to achieve interpretive consensus, but some elements rely on bodily signs. It is to these latter categories that the chapter will now turn, looking at singers, instrumentalists, and conductors.

Performer Movement, Expression and Style in Solo and Ensemble Performance

Soloists

To begin this exploration, consider a soloist playing the same piece of music on multiple occasions and asks: Will the musical sounds and body movements producing them be the same at each rendition? While the physical assemblage required to play the notes is nearly identical on multiple performances, there will be variation due to a range of factors. (There may be musical errors that require correction and adaption, but we shall discount them for now.) Even when playing the correct notes, there is bound to be "noise" where some of the moments involve microvariations, marking the individuality of the one-off performance. Also, while the performer may not deliberately intend to perform the piece differently, changing the performance features on which they focus in any given performance can bring this about. A case study of a solo pianist helps to understand the types of differences that occur across multiple performances of the same music (see Clarke & Davidson, 1998). When analyzing performances of Chopin's Étude in E major, it became apparent that the pianist presented different structural interpretations of the music in each, even though he never mentioned this when asked to comment on the different renditions. It became evident that he was not thinking about structural features; rather, different kinds of imagery and thoughts came into his mind during each rendition, such as imagining walking over moorland. The flow of movement offered an overall "feel" for each rendition, but specifically identifiable expressive movements were in the same locations within the music and were strongly related to key musical structures such as phrase peaks.

What might one deduce from a study such as this? Of particular note is that performers may not have conscious access to processes that underpin a particular interpretation. (The aforementioned pianist did not know he was highlighting different interpretations of the compositional structure.) Furthermore, evidence that the mind is free to attend to other information as well as bring new influencing factors to their performance, such as imagining walking over moorland, demonstrates that there is a high degree of automaticity in an expert's performance. Also, there is considerable variability in the types and forms of expressive movement within and across a performance.

Before delving further into understanding the types of expressive movements that occur within performance, the meaning of two common terms in relation to body movement needs to be clarified:

a *gesture* is "a movement of any part of the body: hand, foot head, chest, etc."
a *posture* is "a movement of the body as a block. Assuming a position; shifting position; a set posture; a pose, as in a photograph or sculpture" (see McGarrigle-Schlosser, 1994, p. 1).

It is also important to note that both continuous movement (such as swaying) or still-ness are also regarded as expressive actions. In the latter case, while the body may look static, there is work from the muscles to maintain this "posture."

A solo performer may be asked to play with consciously different expressive intentions. They might be asked to withhold or play with no expression at all, or to play according to the musical instructions interpreted within the context of their own per-formance ideas, or to present an exaggerated or overblown expression that goes beyond the score indications or the performer's ideal interpretation, or anywhere along this con-tinuum. Body movement research on this topic shows that performers move less when constraining their natural expressive interpretation and move more in other conditions (Davidson 1993, 1994; Thompson & Luck, 2012). For example, although the parts of the body required to execute the music may follow movement contours consistent with the biomechanical tasks of playing the correct notes, there may be significant differences in the amplitude of these movements. This can be illustrated by considering a pianist completing a scalic passage and then moving her hand two octaves up the keyboard to approach the next sequence of notes. In an exaggerated performance, this would be more typically achieved by the performer lifting the hand high and with a greater ges-tural flourish than the other conditions. One study found that such perceptions were available from only 2 seconds of visual information and could be detected not only from sound producing areas of the body but could be perceived from torso movements of a pianist (Davidson, 1991). In another case, a marimba player was asked to depict different emotional intention (to play happy, sad, angry, and afraid), and these differences could also be easily depicted from non-sound-producing areas of the body, for example the head of a marimba player (Dahl & Friberg, 2007). These examples show that all aspects of the performer's bodily movement are rich in information and contribute to the exe-cution of performance goals.

Another important finding that emerged from Davidson's studies is that even though performers attempted to play without expression in deadpan conditions, they found it almost impossible to achieve; in other words, purely functional movement alone just does not happen. Moreover, from various movement tracking studies, it has been demonstrated that performers not only adopt movement within minimal timing profiles, but they also produce movements that are sensitive to musical structures. Indeed, a performer may literally lean into a rising musical figure as it reaches a har-monic peak. Some responses to musical structure are reactive to the musical sound as it is being produced. For example, responding to the reverberations of a note by either mimicking the sound quality in some sort of shaking movement (see Broughton & Davidson, 2016; Shoda & Adachi, 2012). These findings together reveal that a musician is both generating and reacting to the sounds being produced through the body.

Jazz pianist Keith Jarrett is renowned for the extraordinary body movements he makes when performing, for example, sitting at the piano stool and raising his legs the height of the keyboard. When asked why his movements were so extreme, he commented that they are unconscious, his mental effort being focused on trying to release the mu-sical ideas from his mind through his body (Elsdon, 2006). In Jarrett's case, his body movements are reported to dominate audience perception of his performances, and some people prefer listening to him perform without watching his movements because they distract from their appraisal of the musical sounds. Another famous pianist known to have changed his body movements over his career was Glenn Gould, whose later-life studio performances were reported to comprise highly repetitive actions (Delalande, 1988). Gould's limited repertoire of movements in the studio suggests two possibilities. First, freed from the need to consider how his performance appeared to a live audience, he was focused entirely upon producing the best sound and that this was best achieved without flourish; and second, that pianists can and do adapt their bodily movements according to the performance context.

In combination, these findings suggest that movements are produced in part for audience effect, and they can and do influence audience perception of the quality of the performance (see also Glowinski et al., 2013). This is further borne out in a study that indicated that performances with too little, too much, or too stylized movement were perceived to impede the performance quality (Broughton & Davidson, 2016; Davidson & Coulam, 2006). If expressive body movements are vital to the generation and perception of performance, what form do they take, and do they appear commonly across instruments, musical styles, and individuals?

Singers

Like actors or public speakers, singers are relatively free to use their faces for expression (Davidson & Coulam, 2006); however, the facial expressions in singing are more restricted in range and scope than in speaking, owing to the requirements of producing the singing tone (Di Carlo & Guaïtella, 2004; Thompson & Russo, 2007). Nonetheless, singers do use smiles, raised eyebrows, frowns, furrowed brows, and a range of other facial gestures frequently in the delivery of their performance. These gestures can be directly related to the music, the text, or both, and can also refer to extra-musical matters such as responding to an audience member. Furthermore, glances are another key aspect of the singer's expressive repertoire, with eye contact being necessary for information exchange between collaborative performers, or as information to the audience. For example, a raised eyebrow might accompany a sung exclamation such as "Oh, really," adding a questioning meaning through the eye gesture (Thompson et al., 2008).

Unless singers are holding a score, they are also free to use hand and arm gestures as they sing. Research shows that they commonly use their hands to coordinate timing between themselves and their co-performers (referred to as regulatory gestures, see Davidson, 1997). For example, a singer might look to a co-performer and use a raised forearm with forefinger pointing gently toward them to gesture to "come in now," or use a cupping and closing hand gesture to close a phrase (Davidson, 2001). Additionally, singers often use illustrative gestures to express the textual narrative. For example, when singing about holding someone in their arms, they may illustrate this with a mimetic gesture similar to the real action, or use a so-called container gesture in which they might bring their hands into a palms-facing position as if describing the shape and action of "holding" (Davidson & Coulam, 2006; King & Ginsborg, 2011). They might also trace the melodic contour of their singing with their hands, rather like a speaker tracing the contour of their vocal utterance in order to give it emphasis or direction (Kendon, 1980). Similarly, they may employ "beat" gestures, which are commonly used in speech to track the rhythm of speech; in the case of singing, the rhythmic patterns of the music are marked out (Alibali et al., 2001; Davidson, 2001). In addition to these commonly used gestures, singers may also engage emblematic gestures, such as a thumbs up to signify that everything is going well. These gestures are highly cultur-ally determined, and/or may be developed within a very particular musico-dramatic context.

The use of choreographed movement follows a long-established historical tradition of the art of rhetoric (see also Rocke, Davidson, & Kiernan, this volume). In fact, the anon-ymous author of the theater treatise *Il Corago* (*c.* 1630) noted that:

> The manner of reciting is of great importance, because something said by a person who knows how to deliver it well and accompany it with gesture will make a much greater impression on the spirits of the listeners and will more easily stir in them the affections of anger, of hatred, of passion, of happiness, and the like. This will not happen when it is simply narrated by someone without gesture or modulation of the voice. (see Treitler, 1998, p. 633)

Two other key sources on the topic are John Bulwer's (1606–1656) *Chirologia, or the Naturall Language of the Hand* (1644), and *Chironomia, or the Art of Manuall Rhetorique* (1644). In his writing, Bulwer (1644) explains that gestures originate in natural commu-nication but are formalized to offer strong signs for interpretation. Bulwer notes that the hand offers the "universal character of reason," and hand gestures are described in great detail. Illustrations of the gestures required for specific affective outcomes are pro-vided; see Figure 15.1. Some were clearly being developed emblematically. For example, see image B, *Auditores mitigabit*:

> To apply the Middle-Finger to the Thumbe is the common way of gracing an exor-dium [an opening]. (p. 104)

Also, note image Y, *Dolobit*, "both hands clasped and wrung together is an Action on convenient to manifest griefe and sorrow."

Bulwer's instruction shows that it was historically well understood that gestures re-flected on a person's inner mental state. Bulwer offers the following advice:

> To play and fumble with the Fingers in speech is a simple and foolish habit of the Hand, condemned by the ancient Rhetoricians as an argument of a childish and ill-temper'd minde. (p. 119)

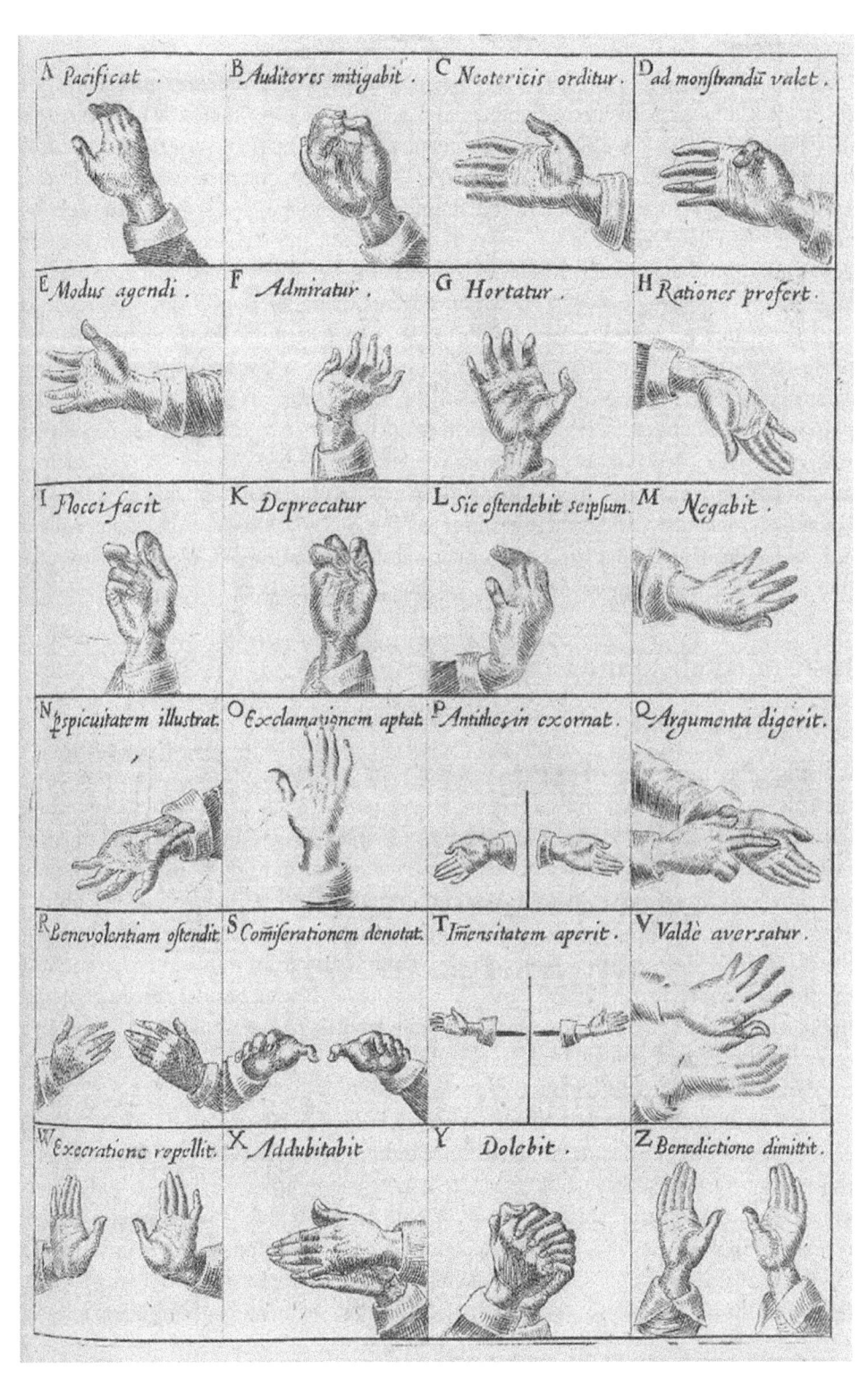

FIGURE 15.1. From Bulwer (1644, p. 65). This article image was published in The Public Domain Review under a Creative Commons Attribution-ShareAlike 3.0. See: https://publicdomainreview.org/legal/.

A detailed analysis of modern-day singers performing in different musical styles reveals that these socially learned emblematic gestures are used alongside both gestures that illustrate real actions (like holding someone in one's arms) and a series of postures that have been referred to as states of "display" (Davidson & Coulam, 2006). For example, a very expansive stance with chest raised, shoulder position low, and arms raised to elbow height is often used by opera singers, rock performers, and dancers when greeting or departing from the audience. Modern-day studies have also revealed that solo singers often adopt "adaptive gestures." These are movements undertaken by an individual to manage feelings or control responses during social interactions. They function to improve comfort or reduce stress and often happen at such a low level that they usually escape conscious awareness (Eaves & Leathers, 2017). Adaptors include behaviors like putting the hand under the chin and touching the face when speaking. It was noted that singers were regarded as more communicative if they employed adaptive gestures such as touching their own shoulder, or relaxing the arm down to touch their side, as well as illustrative, emblematic, and display gestures (Argyle, 1988; Davidson, 2001). Singers who only used "display" were regarded as unnatural or stiff and forced, seemingly because they used a restricted expressive range (Davidson & Coulam, 2006).

Instrumentalists and Conductors

Solo instrumentalists

Although the use of speech and facial gestures in singing is probably not surprising, their use in instrumental music may be less expected. Such usage varies depending upon the instrument. For example, where the face is engaged in making the musical sound, such as in the case of woodwind players who blow into their instruments, they can show very little facial expression, except through the eyes (Davidson & Broughton, 2016). By contrast, keyboardists are free to use their faces, as one case study involving the pianist Lang Lang reveals. Consider the examples taken from his interpretation of the climax of Franz Liszt's *Liebestraum* (Dream of Love), Nocturne no. 3 (1850), depicted in Figures 15.2–15.6 (see Davidson, 2012, for full details). The analysis stems from a live recorded concert at Carnegie Hall, New York, on November 7, 2003. (See https://youtu.be/2FqugGjOkQE, accessed 16 August 2020.)

The Nocturne was inspired by the poem *O lieb, so lang du lieben kannst (O love, as long as you can love)* by Ferdinand Freiligrath. It is unknown whether Liszt followed the narrative that lovers must love wholeheartedly as death soon brings separation and regret; nonetheless, the musical material follows a dramatic arc building to an intense climax created through a series of harmonic tensions and increasing tempi and dynamics. While Figures 15.2–15.6 show only snapshots taken from the overall movement at bars 55–59,[1] it seems that the facial expressions at the very least enact the expression of emotional release.

---

[1] Analysis and images taken from Davidson (2012, pp. 620–622). These figures and text are reprinted by permission of SAGE Publications.

FIGURE 15.2. Bar 55, playing the first chord of the bar.

Figure 15.2, showing bar 55, demonstrates muscular tension; with closed eyes and contracted facial muscles, Lang Lang's mouth is slightly opened. Figure 15.3 shows an open-mouthed release of tension.

In Figure 15.4, Lang Lang's eyes close and the slight opening mouth indicates a further release of tension.

Figure 15.5 shows the start of the new phrase at the end of bar 56, revealing a softer, more gentle facial appearance.

After this short musical and physical relaxation, the music builds again (bars 57–59), and in Figure 15.6 Lang Lang reveals an upward cheek movement causing the top lip to move downward into a sobbing appearance.

The individual style of the performer determines the outcome and while not everyone may support this interpretation, Lang Lang's example shows how biomechanical movement entwines with gestures to communicate expressive effects. The left hand, for example, traces the flow of the music in the air as the right hand executes the notes. While certain gestures and postural adjustments serve to accompany and illustrate the flow of musical ideas, other gestures help to regulate the performance timing. The overarching swaying captured in the snapshot images reflect other work on the expressive movement of pianists (Clarke & Davidson 1998; Davidson, 2002; Davidson, 2007), which indicates that this movement, although aligned to musical pulse, does not correlate smoothly to it. Rather, it contains elements that interact with all the movements found in the performance (Demos et al., 2014; Thompson & Luck, 2012). As noted earlier, some of these movements are quite possibly generated by the musical structures when others may be reactive to elements in the musical structure. Also, and critically

FIGURE 15.3. Bar 55, playing the octave Gs, the notes of the phrase climax.

FIGURE 15.4. Bar 56, playing the descending passage as the musical climax subsides.

FIGURE 15.5. The last two octaves of bar 56.

FIGURE 15.6. Showing bars 57–59.

given the narrative nature of this piece, the emotions depicted in performance are more likely portrayed rather than real, owing to the performer having to plan and control the predetermined arc of the piece (noted in MacDonald, this part). Nonetheless, the performance activity itself can generate a feedback loop in the moment and a real emotional response can be stimulated in the musician (Davidson, 2012).

Of course, musical style may also be influencing how Lang Lang is interpreting this piece by Liszt and his bodily movements may differ to some degree playing a work by a composer of a different period and style, especially in terms of achieving a balance between emotion portrayed and/or felt. Indeed, it is useful to return to the historical treatises on rhetoric to note that even where specific gestures are listed for use in specific circumstances, and thus subject to highly specific historical style, "naturalness" is always a strong goal. In other words, if the gestures (whatever the historical context) are too forced or over-exaggerated, they would lead to a lesser performance (recall the previous reference to Bulwer, 1644). One of the most celebrated authors on the topic was the flute player and composer Johann Joachim Quantz (1697–1773), who stated:

> [The] orator and the musician have, at bottom, the same aim, . . . namely to make themselves masters of the hearts of their listeners, to arouse or still their passions, and to transport them now to this sentiment, now to that. (Quantz, in Reilly, 1966, p. 119)

Lang Lang's example is testimony to the tradition's persistence. Modern research also shows that players of the same instrument type display similar repertoires of movements, in part due to the constraints imposed by their instrument. For example, a piano is positioned in front of the body and navigated by sitting at a stool or bench, thus the pianist needs to shift upper body weight to provide visually expressive cues, moving from the fulcrum of the hips to reach the extremities of the keyboard. In the case of flautists, who hold their instrument to the right of their body, one study found a tendency to lean to the right as well as an inclination to make circles in the air with the foot of the flute. Clarinetists raise and lower the bell of their instrument, and make circling movements with their elbows (Davidson, 2012; Nusseck & Wanderley, 2009; Nusseck et al., 2018; Teixeira et al., 2014; Vines et al., 2006; Wanderley et al., 2005). This movement also interacts with socio-cultural practice, with certain tropes having become extremely familiar; for instance, jazz saxophonists are known to raise the bell of their instruments as they play louder. While this may service audience effect—complying with the finding that bigger or louder musical production requires greater physical effort—it is also known that such a movement is not functionally useful. This is a practice, therefore, developed at least in part to make the musician appear as though they are performing with as much expression and/or dynamic volume as possible.

Despite the overarching similarities of bodily approach among players of the same instrument type, all still demonstrate a high degree of individuality in their movement style, even when playing the same music (Davidson, 2012; Palmer, 2013). For example, some flautists are much more still than others, and some move in a rocking back-and-forth movement while others move side to side. This point returns us to the opening section of this chapter, where it was noted that individual difference is also embedded in a historical context, and this factor will additionally shape performance outcome.

Research reveals that the number of distinct gestures in instrumental performance are relatively limited, though utilized in a fairly flexible manner within performances, indicating that the gestures are not tied to a single musical style or concept. A study of a pianist revealed a vocabulary of around twenty movement types, ranging from specific and distinctive hand lifts to more vague movements, and these could be associated with emblematic, illustrative, or display functions. For example, a nodding movement might be illustrative of musical closure or even an opening chord, if the chord is sustained and the nodding persists across the note duration. A rapid figure-of-eight movement in the upper torso ("wiggle"), might illustrate or indeed be reflective of the performer playing an ornament, but equally might be used at the start of a long phrase in a different work by a different composer (Davidson, 2007; see also Kendon, 2004, for more on speech gestures).

Ensembles

It has been shown that performers communicate between themselves through glances, movement, and gesture, and that this is vital to the musical cohesion (Chang et al., 2017; Davidson & Coulam, 2006; Goebl & Palmer 2009; Keller & Appel, 2010; King & Ginsborg, 2011; Palmer et al., 2019). Common moments for gestures included those where entrances and exits between performers needed to be managed (Davidson & Good, 2002; Davidson & Coulam, 2006),and also moments when regulation of tempo (King & Ginsborg, 2011) and the indication of phrasing (Williamon & Davidson, 2002) and structural boundaries (King & Ginsborg, 2011) were necessary. A study of flamenco ensembles revealed that the dancer conducted the musicians through expressive movements of her arms, head and torso, feet stumping, and hands clapping (Maduell & Wing 2007).

There are also performer-performer movements that are related to interpersonal exchanges outside of musical coordination. There may be facial expressions to communicate pleasure and encouragement, both in response to the unfurling music or in the creation or reaction to additional or complementary elements within the performance, such as managing an unexpected event like a sudden noise from behind the performance platform (Davidson, 1997). Performer-audience communicative processes also draw on similar kinds of gestural codes, and in genres of performance outside of the Western classical music tradition, these can be extremely elaborate. For example, an analysis of Robbie Williams and his band performing at a rock festival show how references to other genres including movies provide means for performer and audience to share in the enjoyment of the performance through interactivity and mimicry (see Davidson, 2006).

Some of the gestures any musician might use relate to memory recall (see work on performance cues and memory in Chaffin & Imreh, 2002; Chaffin & Logan, 2006; Chaffin et al., 2007; Ginsborg, 2018). Therefore, at times the function of musicians' bodily and facial behaviors may be unclear as they are not focused on communication per se, but rather on retrieval of information.

Conductors

When conductors coordinate ensemble performance, their physical directions have a dramatic effect on both the sound and visual display of the ensemble's performance. For example, a horizonal, phrase-shaping conducting movement might lead choristers to increase their bodily and head movements, as they follow the hand gesture. One study found that sharp, aggressive fist or stabbing movements resulted in a mirrored tension in the singers (Fuelberth, 2003). In fact, it has been demonstrated that the physical beat patterns conductors produce with their arms vary (Luck & Nte, 2007; Luck & Sloboda, 2007, 2008, 2009; Wöllner et al., 2012), as does how they use their hands to communicate the different musical expressions and the overall character (Maruyama & Thelen, 2004; Price & Mann, 2011; Wöllner, 2008; Wöllner & Auhagen, 2008).

Conductors use head nods and eye contact to assist in managing musical exchanges within an ensemble and spend most of their time looking at the performers they are guiding (Silvey, 2013). Ensemble musicians, on the other hand, make glances of about 1 second in duration toward the conductor approximately a third of the time they are playing (as observed by Fredrickson, 1994). But, ensemble members' overall eye-contact behavior does vary according to how essential the conductor's role is in the coordination of the musical event, with slower music providing more opportunities for performers to look at the conductor (Byo & Lethco, 2001).

At least some rehearsal time with a conductor involves musicians getting used to these gestural instructions (Durrant, 1994). It has been hypothesized, therefore, that the most successful conductors on the international professional circuit are those who focus on clear nonverbal interaction, being efficient in their use of illustrators and regulators, and keeping emblems to a minimum, given the time involved in learning their meanings (Davidson, 1997).

Movement Quality

Analysis and Training

In addition to identifying specific gestural repertoires, Laban effort-shape analysis has been used as an observational framework to describe actors' and musicians' expressive bodily movement, as it offers a movement meta-language to capture the expressive qualities of bodily movement and document *how* rather than *what* movement occurs (see

Adrian, 2008; Broughton & Davidson, 2016). The analysis technique is a systematic approach based on Rudolph Laban's (1879–1958) choreographic and dance notation work (*Labanotation*) and on studies of human movement including the development of Laban Movement Analysis (LMA) (Laban, 1988). LMA examines four main components of body movement: *effort, body, space,* and *shape*. Work using LMA in music performance is useful because the observational analysis requires visual inspection and requires the analyst to engage in a bodily/kinesthetic mirroring process to capture how expressive bodily actions both look and feel when performing them (Broughton & Davidson, 2014, 2016; Broughton & Stevens, 2012). Of direct relevance to performers, LMA has also been viewed as a way for musicians to understand how expressive movements function and thus be able to develop a performance movement plan to optimize expressive communication with an audience (see Broughton & Stevens, 2012).

One of the tools of LMA is effort-shape analysis. In this analytical framework, basic goal-directed "effort actions" include those labeled as *punch, dab, float, glide, press, slash, flick,* and *wring*. Non-goal-directed "transformation drives" are labeled *passion, vision,* and *spell*. "Shape" features include *rising, sinking, widening, narrowing, advancing,* and *retreating*. A study of marimbists that employed Laban effort-shape analysis uncovered a subset of goal-directed basic effort actions, non-goal-directed transformation drives, and shaping features. The *dab* goal-directed action with rising shape appeared across performances and performers. No *slash* or *wring* basic effort actions were observed, suggesting that these types of actions are not appropriate to marimba playing. The effort-shape actions were also found to be related to music structure, technique, and expressive musical interpretation and were shown to be manifest in highly individualistic ways, a glide action in one performer being different to a glide in another performer, though maintaining similar degree of effort and shape (see Broughton & Davidson, 2016).

There is a tradition of music teachers using bodily movements to enhance the execution of expressive musical sounds. For example, to achieve a smooth crescendo-diminuendo across a rising melody, a teacher might suggest that the student sing the melody while simultaneously co-creating the effect with an arm movement tracing the swelling and retreating (Davidson, 2009). Émile Jaques-Dalcroze (1865–1950) was one of the first modern music educators to place this sort of movement work at the core of teaching music concepts. Constructing goal-directed physical exercises for violinists, one teacher encourages players to stand in a group swaying rhythmically to a slow beat and passing a bow from player to player, the bow being handled in a precise and accurate hold and within the framework of the music—the lesson being to maintain a constant pulse across different aspects of bowing (Dell, 2010). The exercise is an adaptation of Dalcroze's original ball bouncing and passing game in which the speed of the bounce is determined by the group.

As the next sub-section reveals, musical clarity, technical fluency, and expressive goals relating to the communication of structure are not the only roles of bodily movement in musical performance.

Schismogenesis, Proxemics, and Mind and Body Alignment Techniques

Schismogenesis

In music ensembles, people need to collaborate, but the extent to which participants are able to do so varies due to a range of factors. What is common to all situations, however, is that appropriate bodily action has a significant impact on shaping the unfurling dynamics of an ensemble. One concept that helps understand this phenomenon is *schismogenesis*, which considers the power dynamics in relationships. Applying this theory to music ensembles, when individuals have the same aspirations, the dynamic is regarded as being "symmetric"; when they reveal different aspirations and behavioral patterns, the dynamic is regarded as being "complementary" (see full details of the theory in Bateson 1972, p. 68). A study of the rehearsal dynamics of a student string quartet by Davidson and Good (2002) was subsequently used in an application of schismogenesis theory that argued that aspirations might be determined by observing an ensemble's nonverbal, bodily interactions (Jensen & Marchetti, 2010). Davidson and Good had noted that the second violinist directed much bodily movement communication toward the cellist, yet was ignored, while the first violinist and violist turned toward one another to interact more strongly. There was also a great deal of tension and conflict manifested in the nonverbal behaviors of the first and second violinists. Analyzing the situation from the perspective of schismogenesis, Jensen and Marchetti concluded that the second violinist may have been wanting to take over the leadership of the group, and so his aspirations were symmetric to the first violinist's, whereas the aspirations of the other members of the quartet were complementary to the first violinist's as they accepted her legitimacy as the group's leader. While talk was evident in these rehearsals, it was the body movements that underpinned the dynamics of the interaction.

Thus, applying the theory of schismogenesis allows for a precise definition of "nonverbal interaction as an expression of the social dynamics emerging within the group, but functional to the artistic quality of group performances" (Jensen & Marchetti, 2010, p. 6). It reveals how important bodily movement is and how attuned to it musicians must be in the rehearsal and performance process. In this vein, it is necessary to highlight that the underlying social cues present in body movement are useful not only to co-performers, but to audiences too. They can inform the audience of expressive information related to the performance, such as outlined in many of the studies mentioned in this chapter. But it can also reveal a raft of information such as tension between co-performers and whether or not the performer is anxious, and this information can have a strong and enduring impact on the audience.

Proxemics

Another field of relevance to body movement and musical performance is *proxemics*, or the study of the spatial "zones" or distances that people need to maintain in order to feel comfortable in interactions. This behavior is dependent on social norms and individual variability (Hall, 1963). Proxemics influence us every day, including in ensemble music-making. Social distancing in a manner that fits the collaborative music-making context has consequential effects on body movement.

The piano duet is a very intimate seating arrangement where players need to share a bench and the music is written in such a way that arms often need to overlap briefly and so players reach into one another's most personal space. In one study of a piano duet who swapped between first and second parts, it was discovered that in practicing and then performing a concert, the pianist who moved most when playing solo modified his movements the most in the duet context, moving less and reducing the quantity of expressive movements employed. By contrast, the more restrained player actually increased the amount of expressive movement across the rehearsal period (Williamon & Davidson, 2002). Finding themselves in such close proximity—effectively in the same physical zone—the pianists began to move more as a unit, rather than two individuals.

In the string quartet study mentioned in the previous section (see Davidson & Good, 2002), it was found that it was much easier to achieve the canonical musical entries in Britten's *Rhapsody* (1929) if the players leaned across into one another's physical space. Over and above making the cueing more visually apparent, the rippling physical movement mirrored the musical effect, adding a further dimension to the performance. In another example, when choral singers stand in "cheek-by-jowl" proximity to each other, it not only facilitates a secure and tight musical ensemble, but affords opportunities to experience an emotional closeness and interpersonal "harmony" (Faulkner, 2013).

Some performers may enjoy close proximity, possibly being motivated toward ensemble activity for those reasons, but others may not feel comfortable and would probably steer away from this kind of contact (see Davidson, 2017, for a discussion of individual differences and the emergence of a performer identity).

Proxemics have effects on audiences too, such as when performers are too close to the audience. For example, a drawing room concert featuring a quartet of singers and pianists was scheduled for a well-known intimate concert venue in North London. Advertised to seat around thirty people, the concert room was at maximum capacity when the performance began. In combination, the relatively loud music and very tight seating arrangements, compounded by the low ceiling heights of the venue, led to a feeling of being overpowered by the sound and the physical presence of the performers. But, on the contrary, audiences can just as easily feel isolated from a performance if they are too far away from the performers. For example, attending a concert by world-renowned tenor Luciano Pavarotti, the current author found she was so far away from him that she could barely make his presence out on the stage. Consequently, her experience of the concert was very negative. A couple of years later, she attended a concert by pop singer Annie Lennox. Again, the singer was a far-distant speck, but clever use of strategically deployed projection screens and live-streamed film footage meant that the artist was much more visually proximate to audience members in the immediate vicinity of the screen. Thus, the audience members were able to direct their attention to the screen, leading them feeling much more included in the performance event. So, in exploring the critical role of body movement and bodily communication, it is necessary to consider the role of proxemics as another factor in shaping performance outcomes.

Alignment techniques

A number of postural techniques and pedagogical approaches have been developed to aid the performer in maintaining balance between the technical and expressive demands of playing and the psychological stressors, both social and personal, that come to bear on the performer in practice, rehearsal, and performance. Some of the most common practices in Western art music circles that explore body and mind are discussed in Part V of Volume 2, including the Alexander and Feldenkrais techniques, yoga, and mindfulness. All approaches aim to develop kinesthetic awareness and postural alignment. The Alexander and Feldenkrais techniques were both developed in the first half of the twentieth century in Europe and employ verbal instructions and hands-on manipulations to achieve a postural balance and produce an economy of movement to minimize both physical and psychological tension (Jain, Janssen, & DeCelle, 2004). Yoga originated in Ancient India and comprises a group of postures that are taught as a routine of exercises that are extremely physically demanding but also have a meditative, spiritual core. These self-managed movements and thoughts are developed under the direction of a teacher who introduces a series of increasingly demanding poses to augment suppleness and flexibility of the body while simultaneously focusing the mind on breath management and mental focus to calm mind and body and focus on the present (Olson, 2009). Mindfulness is the sustained, non-judgmental attention toward the world and the self (Lecuona & Rodríguez-Carvajal, 2014). Increasingly, instrumental and voice teachers are turning to these approaches to integrate them in their teaching (e.g., Grant, 2014; Neely, 2016; Olson, 2009). They show musicians how being attentive and actively in control of bodily movements can be key to developing a healthier and more effective use of their bodies in the production of music.

PRACTICAL APPLICATIONS

This chapter has revealed that for performers, bodily movement is tied to the mental representations required to develop musical performance skills. These skills involve the technical requirements of playing an instrument or singing and delivering the music with appropriate musical and personal expression and the need for bodily movements to be executed with overall fluency. Within fluent biomechanical and expressive movement are local specifically identifiable physical gestures that are not necessary for note execution but are essential for the communicative aspects of performance. These gestures give the music an immediate and communicative purpose, generating and responding to the musical sounds. They also provide co-performers with cues for regulating musical entrances and exits and enhancing the flow of content, as well as the expression of immediate and perhaps idiosyncratic moments that may unfurl in the moment of performance. The movements draw from each individual's movement repertoire, some of which reveals intimate personal states, others of which may serve a much more direct communicative end. Whether regulative, illustrative, or emblematic, the origin of these movements is similar to that of nonverbal communication in speech, making them more readily understood in the musical performance context. Overarchingly, social and cultural practices of the performance tradition influence the extent and types of communicative movement produced. These movements offer audiences access to critical information and also offer possibilities for sharing and participation, like tapping along to the music, or getting up and dancing (if the context is appropriate!). But, as pointed out, these movement are also very good sources of information about other internal states of the performer, such as if the performer is tense or anxious. These inner states can feed into further physical tensions, all negatively impacting performance coherence and communicability. A range of mind/body techniques are increasingly integrated into the training of performers to aid the optimal communication of their performance to the audience.

In order to highlight these different elements of body movement in musical performance, it is useful to offer the performer some practical suggestions.

Techniques to optimizing body fluency in performance

1. Aim for the highest level of movement skill—develop automated fluency and balance of movement through extensive practice, always applying best practice techniques for the voice/instrument.
2. Develop effective body alignment, especially in areas of the body where tension can build owing to how to stand or sit or how the musical instrument is held—shoulder, arm, neck and back. Take regular practice breaks to prevent strain.
3. Overall body techniques for physical alignment such as Alexander, Feldenkrais, or yoga might complement practice.

Techniques to clarify expressive use of the body to improve communication

1. Explore your own expressive parameters—exaggerate/underplay musical ideas and movement possibilities in order to find the right level of physical engagement to achieve optimal musical communication.
2. Explore historical/socio-cultural norms and additional meanings you might want to bring to your performance.

3. Clarify coordination between co-performers—explain/demonstrate the role of coordinating gestures such as nods and sways between co-performers.
4. Heighten the dramatic climax/tension of a musical/dramatic moment—explore the role and function of an expressive gesture, such as using a movement flourish or an open-armed gesture to the audience.

To undertake these explorations, videorecord your practice sessions to enable review and self-critique.

Conclusion

This chapter has illustrated that if equipped with knowledge of the types and origins of body movement in musical performance, a well-prepared performer can deliver fluent and expressive performances through the use of an engaged and aligned body (and mind). Increasing advances in technology will enable systematic study to detail the types and functions of performance movement. The practical implications of the work covered suggest that performers can experiment to optimize the range of movements they can draw upon in their musical performance for the benefit of themselves and audiences alike.

Key Sources

Davidson, J. W. (2017). Performance identity. In R. MacDonald, D. J. Hargreaves, & D. Miell (Eds.), *Handbook of musical identities* (pp. 364–382). Oxford: Oxford University Press.
Jäncke, L. (2006). From cognition to action. In E. Altenmüller, M. Wiesendanger, & J. Kesselring (Eds.), *Music, motor control and the brain* (pp. 25–37). New York: Oxford University Press.
Leman, M., & Godøy, R. I. (2010). Why study musical gestures? In R. L. Godøy & M. Leman (Eds.), *Musical gestures: Sound, movement, and meaning* (pp. 3–11). New York: Routledge.
Nusseck, M., Wanderley, M. M., & Spahn, C. (2018). Body movements in music performances: The example of clarinet players. In B. Müller & S. I. Wolf (Eds.), *Handbook of human motion* (pp 1789–1802). New York: Springer.
Schneider, A. (2010). Music and gesture: A historical introduction and survey of earlier research. In R. I. Godøy & M. Leman (Eds.), *Musical gestures: Sound, movement, and meaning* (pp. 69–100). New York: Routledge.

Key Questions

1. In what ways do the three stages of motor learning discussed in this chapter relate to your own approach to practicing and performing?

2. How might you rethink your approach to musical expression by optimizing your use of body movement?

3. Can you list a regulator, an illustrator, an emblem, and an adaptor gesture that might be used in your own performance? What is the context of each gesture and how might these vary across repeated renditions of the same piece of music?

4. What role does body movement have in the coordinative and collaborative concerns of performers?

5. What might you do to develop fluent and expressive body movement in your musical performance?

REFERENCES

Adrian, B. (2008). *Actor training the Laban way: An integrated approach to voice, speech, and movement*. New York: Allworth Press.

Alibali, M. W., Heath, D. C., & Myers, H. J. (2001). Effects of visibility between speaker and listener on gesture production: Some gestures are meant to be seen. *Journal of Memory and Language, 44*(2), 169–188. https://doi.org/10.1006/jmla.2000.2752.

Altenmüller, E., & Gruhn, W. (2002). Brain mechanisms. In R. Parncutt & G. E. McPherson (Eds.), *The science and psychology of music performance: Creative strategies for teaching and learning* (pp. 63–81). New York: Oxford University Press.

Argyle, M. (1988). *Bodily communication*. London: Methuin.

Bateson, G. (1972). *Steps to an ecology of mind*. New York: Chandler Publishing Company.

Broughton, M. C., & Davidson, J. W. (2014). Action and familiarity effects on self and other expert musicians' Laban effort-shape analysis of expressive bodily behaviors in musical performance: A case study approach. *Frontiers in Psychology, 5*, 1201. https://doi.org/10.3389/fpsyg.2014.01201.

Broughton, M. C. & Davidson, J. W. (2016). An expressive bodily movement repertoire for marimba performance, revealed through observers' Laban effort-shape analyses, and allied musical features: Two case studies. *Frontiers in Psychology, 7*, 1211. https://doi.org/10.3389/fpsyg.2016.01211.

Broughton, M. C., & Stevens, C. J. (2012). Analyzing expressive qualities in movement and stillness: Effort-shape analyses of solo marimbists' bodily expression. *Music Perception, 29*(4), 339–357. https://doi.org/10.1525/mp.2012.29.4.339.

Bulwer, J. (1644). *Chirologia, or the naturall language of the hand*. London: Privately published.

Bulwer, J. (1644). *Chironomia, or the art of manuall rhetorique*. London: Privately published.

Byo, J. L., & Lethco, L.-A. (2001). Student musicians' eye contact with the conductor: An exploratory investigation. *Contributions to Music Education, 28*(2), 21–35.

Chaffin, R., & Imreh, G. (2002). Practicing perfection: Piano performance as expert memory. *Psychological Science, 13*(4), 342–349. https://doi.org/10.1111/j.0956-7976.2002.00462.x.

Chaffin, R., Lemieux, A. F., & Chen, C. (2007). "It is different each time I play": Variability in highly prepared musical performance. *Music Perception: An Interdisciplinary Journal, 24*(5), 455–472. https://doi.org/10.1525/mp.2007.24.5.455.

Chaffin, R., & Logan, T. (2006). Practicing perfection: How concert soloists prepare for performance. *Advances in Cognitive Psychology, 2*(2–3), 113–130. https://doi.org/10.2478/v10053-008-0050-z.

Chang, A., Livingstone, S. R., Bosnyak, D. J., & Trainor, L. (2017). Body sway reflects leadership in joint music performance. *Proceedings of the National Academy of Sciences, 114,* E4134–E4141. https://doi:10.1073/pnas.1617657114.

Clarke, E. F., & Davidson, J. W. (1998). The body in performance. In W. Thomas (Ed.), *Composition-performance-reception: Studies in the creative process in music* (pp. 74–92). Aldershot: Ashgate.

Dahl, S. (2018). Movements, timing and precision of drummers. In B. Müller & S. I. Wolf (Eds.), *Handbook of human motion* (pp. 1840–1857). New York: Springer.

Dahl, S., Bevilacqua, F., Bresin, R., Clayton, M., Leante, L., Poggi, I., & Rasamimanana, N. (2010). Gestures in performance. In R. I. Godøy & M. Leman (Eds.), *Musical gestures: Sound, movement, and meaning* (pp. 36–68). New York: Routledge.

Dahl, S., & Friberg, A. (2007). Visual perception of expressiveness in musicians' body movements. *Music Perception, 24*(5), 433–454. https://doi.org/10.1525/mp.2007.24.5.433.

Dalca, I. M., Vines, B. W., Pearce, M. T., Wanderley, M. M. (2013). Expressivity as time-dependent movement for music performance: A statistical exploration. *Proceedings of the 10th International Symposium on Computer Music Multidisciplinary Research (CMMR2013),* 845–854, Marseille: France.

Dalla-Bella, S. & Palmer, C. (2004). Tempo and dynamics in piano performance: The role of movement and amplitude. In S. D. Lipscomb, R. Gjerdingen, & P. Webster (Eds.), *Proceedings of the International Conference on Music Perception and Cognition* (pp. 256–257). Adelaide: Causal Productions.

Davidson, J. W. (1991). *The perception of expressive movement in music performance* (Unpublished doctoral thesis). City University, London.

Davidson, J. W. (1993). Visual perception of performance manner in the movements of solo musicians. *Psychology of Music, 21*(2), 103–113. https://doi.org/10.1177/0305735693021002 01.

Davidson, J. W. (1994). Which areas of a pianist's body convey information about expressive intention to an audience? *Journal of Human Movement Studies, 26*(6), 279–301.

Davidson, J. W. (1997). The social psychology of performance. In D. J. Hargreaves & A. C. North (Eds.), *The social psychology of music* (pp. 209–226). Oxford: Oxford University Press.

Davidson, J. W. (2001). The role of the body in the production and perception of solo vocal performance: A case study of Annie Lennox. *Musicae Scientiae, 5*(2), 235–256. https://doi.org/10.1177/102986490100500206.

Davidson, J. W. (2002). Understanding the expressive movements of a solo pianist. *Musikpsychologie, 16,* 9–31.

Davidson, J. W. (2006). "She's the One": Multiple functions of body movement in a stage performance by Robbie Williams. In A. Gritten and E. C. King (Eds.), *Music and gesture* (pp. 208–226). Aldershot: Ashgate.

Davidson, J. W. (2007). Qualitative insights into the use of expressive body movement in solo piano performance: A case study approach. *Psychology of Music, 35*(3), 381–401. https://doi.org/10.1177/0305735607072652.

Davidson, J. W. (2009). Movement and collaboration in musical performance. In S. Hallam, I. Cross, & M. Thaut (Eds.), *Oxford handbook of psychology of music* (pp. 364–376). Oxford: Oxford University Press.

Davidson, J. W. (2012). Bodily movement and facial actions in expressive musical performance by solo and duo instrumentalists: Two distinctive case studies. *Psychology of Music, 40*(5), 595–633. https://doi.org/10.1177/0305735612449896.

Davidson, J.W., & Broughton, M. (2016). Bodily mediated coordination, collaboration, and communication in music performance. In S. Hallam, I. Cross & M. Thaut (eds.), The *Oxford handbook of music psychology, 2nd edition* (pp. 573–596). Oxford, UK: Oxford University Press.

Davidson, J. W. (2017). Performance identity. In R. MacDonald, D. J. Hargreaves, & D. Miell (Eds.), *Handbook of musical identities* (pp. 364–82). Oxford: Oxford University Press.

Davidson, J. W., & Broughton, M. (2016). Bodily mediated coordination, collaboration, and communication in music performance. In S. Hallam, I. Cross & M. Thaut (Eds.), *The Oxford handbook of music psychology* (2nd ed., pp. 573–596). Oxford: Oxford University Press.

Davidson, J. W., & Coulam, A. (2006). Exploring jazz and classical solo singing performance behaviours: A preliminary step towards understanding performer creativity. In I. Deliège & G. A. Wiggins (Eds.), *Musical creativity: Multidisciplinary research in theory and practice* (pp. 181–199). East Sussex, England: Psychology Press.

Davidson, J. W., & Good, J. M. M. (2002). Social and musical co-ordination between members of a string quartet: An exploratory study. *Psychology of Music, 30*(2), 186–201. https://doi.org/10.1177/0305735602302005.

Davidson, J. W, & McPherson, G. (2017). Learning to perform: From "gifts" and "talents" to skills and creative engagement. In J. Rink, H. Gaunt, & A. William (Eds.), *Musicians in the making: Pathways to creative performance* (pp. 7–27). Oxford: Oxford University Press.

Delalande, F. (1988). La gestique de Gould: Élements pour une sémiologie du geste musical. In G. Guertin (Ed.), *Glenn Gould pluriel* (pp. 85–111). Québec: Louise Courteau.

Dell, C. (2010). Strings got rhythm: A guide to developing rhythmic skills in beginners. *Music Educators Journal, 96*(3), 31–34. https://doi.org/10.1177/0027432109355635.

Demos, A. P., Chaffin, R., & Kant, V. (2014). Toward a dynamical theory of body movement in musical performance. *Frontiers in Psychology, 5*, 477. https://doi.org/10.3389/fpsyg.2014.00477.

Di Carlo, N. S., & Guaïtella, I. (2004). Facial expressions of emotion in speech and singing. *Semiotica, 149*(1/4), 37–55. https://doi.org/10.1515/semi.2004.036.

Durrant, C. (1994). Towards an effective communication: A case for structured teaching of conducting. *British Journal of Music Education, 11*, 56–76.

Elsdon, P. (2006). Listening in the gaze: The body in Keith Jarrett's solo piano improvisations. In A. Gritten & E. King (Eds.), *Music and gesture* (pp. 192–207). Abingdon: Ashgate.

Eaves, M., & Leathers, D. G. (2017). *Successful nonverbal communication: Principles and applications.* Oxford: Routledge.

Fabian, D., Timmers, R. & Schiubert, E. (Eds.). (2014). *Expressiveness in music performance: Empirical approaches across styles and cultures.* Oxford: Oxford University Press.

Faulkner, R. (2013). *Icelandic men and me: Songs, singing, self and everyday life.* Aldershot: Ashgate.

Fitts, P. M., & Posner, M. T. (1967). *Human performance.* Belmont, CA: Brooks/Cole.

Fredrickson, W. E. (1994). Band musicians' performance and eye contact as influenced by loss of a visual and/or aural stimulus. *Journal of Research in Music Education, 42*(4), 306–317. https://doi.org/10.2307/3345738.

Fuelberth, R. J. V. (2003). The effect of left hand conducting gesture on inappropriate vocal tension in individual singers. *Bulletin of the Council for Research in Music Education, 157*, 62–70.

Gallese, V., & Goldman, A. (1998). Mirror neurons and the simulation theory of mind-reading. *Trends in Cognitive Sciences, 2*(12), 493–501. https://doi.org/10.1016/S1364-6613(98)01262-5.

Ginsborg, J. (2018). Small ensembles in rehearsals. In J. Rink, H. Gaunt & A. Williamon (Eds.), *Musicians in the making* (pp. 164–185). New York: Oxford University Press.

Glowinski, D., Mancini, M., Cowie, R., Camurri, A., Chiorri, C., & Doherty, C. (2013). The movements made by performers in a skilled quartet: A distinctive pattern, and the function that it serves. *Frontiers in Psychology, 4*, 841. https://doi.org/10.3389/fpsyg.2013.00841.

Goebl, W. (2018). Movement and touch in piano performance. In B. Müller & S. I. Wolf (Eds.), *Handbook of human motion* (pp. 1821–1838). New York: Springer.

Goebl, W., & Palmer, C. (2009). Synchronization of timing and motion among performing musicians. *Music Perception, 26*(5), 427–438. https://doi.org/10.1525/mp.2009.26.5.427.

Goldin-Meadow, S. (2003). *Hearing gesture: How our hands help us think*. Cambridge, MA: Belknap Press of Harvard University.

Grant, S. J. (2014). Vocal pedagogy and the Feldenkrais method. In S. Harrison & J. O'Bryan (Eds.), *Teaching singing in the twenty-first century* (pp. 175–185). New York: Springer.

Guadagnoli, M. & Lee, T. (2004). Challenge point: A framework for conceptualizing the effects of various practice conditions in motor learning. *Journal of Motor Behavior, 36*, 212–224. https://doi.org/10.3200/JMBR.36.2.212-224.

Hall, E. T. (1963). A system for the notation of proxemic behaviour. *American Anthropologist, 63*(5), 1003–1026.

Hommel, B., Müsseler, J., Aschersleben, G., & Prinz, W. (2001). The theory of event coding (TEC): A framework for perception and action planning. *Behavioral and Brain Sciences, 24*(05), 849–878. https://doi.org/10.1017/s0140525x01000103.

Huang, J., & Krumhansl, C. L. (2011). What does seeing the performer add? It depends on musical style, amount of stage behavior, and audience expertise. *Musicae Scientiae, 15*(3), 343–364. https://doi.org/10.1177/1029864911414172.

Jain, S., Janssen, K. & DeCelle, S. (2004). Alexander technique and Feldenkrais method: A critical overview. *Physical Medicine and Rehabilitation Clinics of North America, 15*, 811–825. https://doi.org/10.1016/j.pmr.2004.04.005.

Jäncke, L. (2006). From cognition to action. In E. Altenmüller, M. Wiesendanger & J. Kesselring (Eds.), *Music, motor control and the brain* (pp. 25–37). New York: Oxford University Press.

Jensen, E., & Marchetti, K. (2010). A meta-study of musicians' non-verbal interaction. *International Journal of Technology, Knowledge & Society, 6*, 1–12. https://doi: 10.18848/1832-3669/CGP/v06i05/56143.

Jensenius, A. R., Wanderley, M. M., Godøy, R. I., & Leman, M. (2010). Musical gesture: concepts and methods in research. In: R. I. Godøy & M. Leman (Eds.), *Musical gestures: Sound, movement and meaning* (pp. 12–35). New York: Routledge.

Juchniewicz, J. (2008). The influence of physical movement on the perception of musical performance. *Psychology of Music, 36*(4), 417–427. https://doi.org/10.1177/0305735607086046.

Juslin, P. & Timmers, R. (2010). Expression and communication of emotion in music performance. In P. Juslin & J. A. Sloboda (Eds.), *Handbook of music and emotion: theory, research, applications* (pp. 453–489). New York: Oxford University Press.

Juslin, P. & Västfell, D. (2008). Emotional responses to music: The need to consider underlying mechanisms. *Behavioural and Brain Sciences, 31*, 559–575. https://doi.org/10.1017/S0140525X08005293.

Keller, P. E. & Appel, M. (2010). Individual differences, auditory imagery, and the coordination of body movements and sounds in musical ensembles. *Music Perception, 28*(1), 27–46. https://doi.org/10.1525/mp.2010.28.1.27.

Kendon, A. (1980). Gesticulation and speech: Two aspects of the process. In M. R. Key (Eds.), *The relation between the verbal and nonverbal communication* (pp. 207–227). The Hague: Mouton.

Kendon, A. (2004). *Gesture: Visible action as utterance*. Cambridge, UK: Cambridge University Press.

King, E. C. (2006). The roles of student musicians in quartet rehearsals. *Psychology of Music, 34*(2), 262–282. https://doi.org/10.1177/0305735606061855.

King, E. C., & Ginsborg, J. (2011). Gestures and glances: Interactions in ensemble rehearsal. In A. Gritten & E. King (Eds.), *New perspectives on music and gesture* (pp. 177–201). Surrey, England: Ashgate.

Krahle, C., Hahn, U. & Whitney, K. (2015). Is seeing (musical) believing? The eye versus the ear in emotional responses to music. *Psychology of Music, 43*(1), 140–148. https://doi.org/10.1177/0305735613498920.

Laban, R. (1988). *The mastery of movement* (4th ed., rev.). Plymouth, England: Northcote House Publishers Ltd.

Lehmann, A. C., Sloboda, J. A. & Woody, R. H. (2007). *Psychology for musicians: Understanding and acquiring the skills*. New York: Oxford University Press.

Leman, M. (2008). *Embodied music cognition and mediation technology*. Cambridge, MA: MIT Press.

Leman, M., & Godøy, R. I. (2010). Why study musical gestures? In R. L. Godøy & M. Leman (Eds.), *Musical gestures: sound, movement, and meaning* (pp. 3–11). New York: Routledge.

Luck, G., & Nte, S. (2008). An investigation of conductors' temporal gestures and conductor-musician synchronization, and a first experiment. *Psychology of Music, 36*(1), 81–99. https://doi.org/10.1177/0305735607080832.

Luck, G., & Sloboda, J. A. (2007). An investigation of musicians' synchronization with traditional conducting beat patterns. *Music Performance Research, 1*(1), 26–46.

Luck, G., & Sloboda, J. A. (2008). Exploring the spatio-temporal properties of simple conducting gestures using a synchronization task. *Music Perception, 25*(3), 225–239. https://doi.org/10.1525/mp.2008.25.3.225.

Luck, G., & Sloboda, J. A. (2009). Spatio-temporal cues for visually mediated synchronization. *Music Perception, 26*(5), 465–473. https://doi.org/10.1525/mp.2009.26.5.465.

MacDonald, J., & McGurk, H. (1978). Visual influences on speech perception processes. *Perception and Psychophysics, 24*(3), 253–257. https://doi.org/10.3758/BF03206096.

Maduell, M. & Wing, A.M. (2007). The dynamics of ensemble: The case for flamenco. *Psychology of Music, 35*, 591–627. https://doi.org/10.1177/0305735607076446.

Maruyama, S., & Thelen, E. (2004). Invariant timing structures of orchestra conductors' hand strokes. In S. D. Lipscomb, R. Ashley, R. O. Gjerdingen, & P. Webster (Eds.), *Proceedings of the 8th International Conference on Music Perception and Cognition* (pp. 523–526). Adelaide, Australia: Causal Productions.

McGarrigle-Schlosser, K. (1994). Definitions of gesture, posture and integrated movement. In *Action Profile System Trainer Guide* (pp. 1–2). New York: Laban/Bartenieff Institute of Movement Studies.

McNeill, D. (1992). *Hand and mind: What gestures reveal about thought*. Chicago and London: University of Chicago Press.

Molnar-Szakacs, I., & Overy, K. (2006). Music and mirror neurons: From motion to 'e'motion. *Social Cognitive and Affective Neuroscience, 1*(3), 235–241. https://doi.org/10.1093/scan/nsl029.

Muratori, L. M., Lamberg, E. M. Quinn, L. & Duff, S. V. (2013). Applying principles of motor learning and control to upper extremity rehabilitation. *Journal of Hand Therapy, 26*(2), 94–103. https://doi.org/10.1016/j.jht.2012.12.007.

Neely, D. W. (2016). Body consciousness and singers: Do voice teachers use mindbody methods with students and in their own practice? *Journal of Singing, 73*(2), 137–147.

Nusseck, M., & Wanderley, M. M. (2009). Music and motion: How musicrelated ancillary body movements contribute to the experience of music. *Music Perception, 26*(4), 335–353. https://doi.org/10.1525/mp.2009.26.4.335.

Nusseck, M. Wanderley, M. M., & Spahn, C. (2018). Body movements in music performances: The example of clarinet players. In B. Müller & S. I. Wolf (Eds.), *Handbook of human motion* (pp. 1789–1802). New York: Springer.

Olson, M. (2009). *Musician's yoga: A guide to practice, performance and inspiration*. Boston: Berklee College Press.

Palmer, C. (2006) The nature of memory for music performance skills. In E. Altenmüller, M. Wiesendanger, & J. Kesselring (Eds.), *Music, motor control and the brain* (pp. 109–123). New York: Oxford University Press.

Palmer, C. (2013). Music performance: Movement and coordination. In D. Deutsch (Ed.), *The psychology of music* (3rd ed., pp. 405–422). Amsterdam: Elsevier Press.

Palmer, C., Spidle, F., Koopmans, E., & Schubert, P. (2019). Ears, heads, and eyes: When singers synchronise. *Quarterly Journal of Experimental Psychology, 72*(9), 2272–2287. https://doi.org/10.1177/1747021819833968.

Pfeifer, J., H., & Dapretto, M. (2009). "Mirror, mirror, in my mind": Empathy, interpersonal competence, and the mirror neuron system. In J. Decety & W. Ickes (Eds.), *The social neuroscience of empathy* (pp. 183–197). Cambridge, MA: A Bradford Book, MIT Press.

Platz, F., & Kopiez, R. (2012). When the eye listens: a meta-analysis of how audio-visual presentation enhances the appreciation of music performance. *Music Perception, 30*(1), 71–83. https://doi.org/10.1525/mp.2012.30.1.71.

Price, H. E., & Mann, A. (2011). The effect of conductors on ensemble evaluations. *Bulletin of the Council for Research in Music Education, 189*, 57–72.

Quantz, J. J. (1966). *On playing the flute* (E. R. Reilly, Trans.). New York: Free Press.

Saldaña, H. M., & Rosenblum, L. D. (1993). Visual influences on auditory pluck and bow judgments. *Perception and Psychophysics, 54*(3), 406–416. https://doi.org/10.3758/BF03205276.

Schneider, A. (2010). Music and gesture: A historical introduction and survey of earlier research. In R. I. Godøy & M. Leman (Eds.), *Musical gestures: Sound, movement, and meaning* (pp. 69–100). New York: Routledge.

Schutz, M., & Lipscomb, S. (2007). Hearing gestures, seeing music: Vision influences perceived tone duration. *Perception, 36*(6), 888–897. https://doi.org/10.1068/p5635.

Shaffer, L. H. (1984) Timing in solo and duet piano performance. *Quarterly Journal of Experimental Psychology, 36*, 577–595. https://doi.org/10.1080/14640748408402180.

Shoda, H., & Adachi, M. (2012). The role of a pianist's affective and structural interpretations in his expressive body movement: A single case study. *Music Perception, 29*(3), 237–254. https://doi.org/10.1525/mp.2012.29.3.237.

Silvey, B. A. (2013). The role of conductor facial expression in students' evaluation of ensemble expressivity. *Journal of Research in Music Education, 60*(4), 419–429. https://doi.org/10.1177/0022429412462580.

Teixeira, E. C. F., Loureiro, M. A., Wanderley, M. M., & Yehia, C. H. (2014). Motion analysis of clarinet performers. *Journal of New Music Research*, *44*(2), 97–111. https://doi.org/10.1080/09298215.2014.925939.

Thompson, M. R., & Luck, G. (2012). Exploring relationships between pianist's body movements, their expressive intentions, and structural elements of the music. *Musicae Scientiae*, *16*(1), 19–40. https://doi.org/10.1177/1029864911423457.

Thompson, W. F., Graham, P., & Russo, F. A. (2005). Seeing music performance: Visual influences on perception and experience. *Semiotica*, *156*(1/4), 177–201.

Thompson, W. F., & Russo, F. A. (2007). Facing the music. *Psychological Science*, *18*(9), 756–757. https://doi.org/10.1111/j.1467-9280.2007.01973.x.

Thompson, W. F., Russo, F. A., & Livingstone, S. R. (2010). Facial expressions of singers influence perceived pitch relations. *Psychonomic Bulletin & Review*, *17*, 317–322. https://doi.org/10.3758/PBR.17.3.317.

Thompson, W. F., Russo, F. A., & Quinto, L. (2008). Audio-visual integration of emotional cues in song. *Cognition and Emotion*, *22*(8), 1457–1470. https://doi.org/10.1080/02699930701813974.

Todd, N. M. (1995). The kinematics of musical expression. *Journal of the Acoustial Society of America*, *97*(3), 1940–1949. https://doi.org/10.1121/1.412067.

Treitler, L. (Ed.) (1998). *Strunk's source readings in music history* (Rev. ed.). New York and London: W. W. Norton.

Tsay, C. J. (2013). Sight over sound in the judgment of music performance. *Proceedings of the National Academy of Sciences*, *110*(36), 14580–14585.

Vines, B. W., Krumhansl, C. L., Wanderley, M. M., & Levitin, D. J. (2006). Cross-modal interactions in the perception of musical performance. *Cognition*, *101*(1), 80–113. https://doi.org/10.1016/j.cognition.2005.09.003.

Wanderley, M. M., & Vines, B. W. (2006). Origins and functions of clarinettists' ancillary gestures. In A. Gritten & E. King (Eds.), *Music and gesture: New perspectives on theory and contemporary practice* (pp. 165–191). Aldershot: Ashgate.

Wanderley, M. M., Vines, B. W., Middleton, N., McKay, C., & Hatch, W. (2005). The musical significance of clarinetists' ancillary gestures: An exploration of the field. *Journal of New Music Research*, *34*(1), 97–113. https://doi.org/10.1080/09298210500124208.

Wiesendanger, M., Baader, A., & Kazennikov, O. (2006) Fingering and bowing in violinists: A motor control approach. In E. Altenmüller, M. Wiesendanger & J. Kesselring (Eds.), *Music, motor control and the brain* (pp. 109–123). New York: Oxford University Press.

Williamon, A., & Davidson, J. W. (2002). Exploring co-performer communication. *Musicae Scientiae*, *6*(1), 53–72. https://doi.org/10.1177/102986490200600103.

Wöllner, C. (2008). Which part of the conductor's body conveys most expressive information? A spatial occlusion approach. *Musicae Scientiae*, *12*(2), 249–272. https://doi.org/10.1177/102986490801200204.

Wöllner, C., & Auhagen, W. (2008). Perceiving conductors' expressive gestures from different visual perspectives: An exploratory continuous response study. *Music Perception*, *26*(2), 129–144. https://doi.org/10.1525/mp.2008.26.2.129.

Wöllner, C., Deconinck, F. J., Parkinson, J., Hove, M. J., & Keller, P. E. (2012). The perception of prototypical motion: Synchronization is enhanced with quantitatively morphed gestures of musical conductors. *Journal of Experimental Psychology: Human Perception and Performance*, *38*(6), 1390–1403. https://doi.org/10.1037/a0028130.

PART III

PERFORMANCE PRACTICES

CHAPTER 16

PERFORMANCE PRACTICES FOR BAROQUE AND CLASSICAL REPERTOIRE

DOROTTYA FABIAN

INTRODUCTION

BY the twenty-first century, Western art music had amassed a thousand years of written tradition, with much of the repertoire from the last 400 years still being performed in concert halls today. Such a large range of music across so many centuries may provide a considerable challenge for current-day musicians who choose to work within this tradition, if they wish to negotiate issues of style, authenticity, period versus modern performance practice, and the various aesthetic considerations that may arise when performing this repertoire. Styles of composed music change with historical periods and so do the conventions of performing practices and the meaning of signs and inscriptions in notated scores (Cook, 2014; Lawson & Stowell, 2012, 2018; Philip, 2004; Taruskin, 1995). It is therefore important that contemporary musicians become aware of differing traditions and gain a good understanding of the aesthetic principles and preferences of composers whose creative outputs they intend to perform as they develop their own artistic choices. This is not, as this chapter will argue, to stifle creativity or set up rigid rules but to the contrary: to enable musicians to have a broader palette of performing techniques and choices to create interpretations that may not only be personally authentic and convincing but may also better reflect the differences in compositional styles than a uniform way of playing that stems from mid-to-late-twentieth-century ideals of instrumental and vocal delivery. The goal is to be informed musicians in an environment of constantly changing aesthetics and creativity.

As much research into archival sources and sound recordings has shown, each generation of musicians tends to reinterpret their understanding of canonical composers and pieces. It is harder and harder to argue what might be a "correct" way of performing a particular composition, especially those from times prior to sound recording. And even if we had audio evidence of composers performing their own music, we might not conclude that this would be the only or best way of rendering the piece. What matters is lifelong curiosity about context: historical, biographical, aesthetic, practical, and so on. Essential questions to ask when considering the evidence, whether written or aural, include the nature of the instrument used, the circumstances of the performance, the esteem of the performer, the meaning of the signs in the score, the nature of the musical language and the aesthetics it reflects, the expression intended, and so on.

This chapter outlines current views and other relevant issues as they pertain to the performance of eighteenth-century Baroque and Classical music. It starts with a brief overview of this music's performance history, followed by a focus on the aesthetic ideals that permeated music making during the "long" eighteenth century (ca. 1680–1810) and their differences from the Romantic or Modern periods. The bulk of the chapter then provides more detailed information on the various technical aspects that contribute to stylistic differences in performance. In the final section examples illustrate the practical implications of the investigation.

Throughout the discussion it is important to keep in mind that our knowledge of eighteenth-century music relies exclusively on written documents and that each generation inevitably interprets these from the hindsight and aesthetic preferences of their own time. No absolute truths or verisimilitude can be claimed, and it is essential to study the original historical sources to develop a thorough and personally authentic understanding of how things might have been. The aim of this chapter is to provide an introduction to such a journey.

PERFORMANCE HISTORY OF
EIGHTEENTH-CENTURY MUSIC

As stated at the outset of this chapter, most twenty-first-century musicians of the European concert tradition perform music composed over a period of some 400 or more years. They learn from teachers and each-other's styles of performance handed down from one generation to another. So why do we need to study historical sources? The legacy of sound recordings shows a gradual but constant change in interpretative approaches to music of the past. The further away we get from the time of composition, the more pedagogical and aesthetic layers accumulate over our understanding of how to read and understand the music.

The performance of eighteenth-century music is not just vulnerable to these imperceptible layers of change, but it also lacks such a potentially unbroken tradition because until about 1800 composers and audiences were only interested in what was new. Music was always contemporary, fresh, usually composed and performed by local musicians for a specific occasion. Even compositions from two years earlier were considered old and hardly ever performed again. By the time of Mozart or Beethoven, the earlier Baroque conventions and aesthetic ideals were largely superseded by different ones.

The first major public instance of repertoire revival was led by Mendelssohn in 1829 when he conducted Bach's *St. Matthew Passion* in Berlin, although performances of Handel's oratorios were regular events in England even after Handel's death in 1759, and smaller works of Bach had been performed in private salons in Vienna and elsewhere during Mozart's and Beethoven's time. Mendelssohn adopted a modernizing attitude because he believed that music of the past had to be adjusted to be appealing to later audiences. Due to his influence, this resulted in Baroque and Classical pieces being performed first in a Romantic and later in a Modern style (Fabian, 2018, 2015; Philip, 2004; Taruskin, 1995). From around the mid-1960s, an alternative style has also developed that aimed to revive not just the compositions but also the performing practices of past eras. By the 2000s this historically informed performing practice (HIP) has largely become the mainstream when performing Baroque music. Table 16.1 summarizes the development of performing style pitted against our current knowledge of historical practices.

Table 16.1. General summary of the different approaches to performing eighteenth-century music (Haynes, 2007; Fabian, 2015).

Period	Stylistic characteristics
18th century	"Rhetorical": Baroque and Classical instruments and playing techniques (bowing, tonguing, fingering); small ensembles (1–3 players per parts), closely articulated and nuanced, harmony driven, with strongly projected pulse and rhythm; short melodic and rhythmic motives gradually getting longer and attaining a more singing quality. Vibrato is used to ornament longer or more important melodic notes.
1820–1920s	"Romantic": Enlarged ensembles, modern instruments, emotional projection of melody, wide range of tempo, ponderous slow movements, varied vibrato, sustained tone, legato articulation, long-range phrasing with fluctuating dynamics and tempo rubato. Highly edited and annotated scores by famous nineteenth-century musicians.
1930–1980s	"Modernist": literalist, monotonous rhythm, pulse not projected, steady, relatively fast tempos, homogeneous dynamics and tone, detached articulation, emotionally reserved, technical accuracy and brilliance emphasized. Continuous and well-regulated vibrato is part of tone production or completely eliminated. Urtext scores aiming at getting back to the composers' intentions and fostering to only play what the composer notated (i.e., no embellishments, no rhythmic flexibility, no nuance).
1990–2010s	"Post-modern and HIP-inspired": individuality and flexibility returns, some musicians perform on period instruments (or their copies), use different bowing, tonguing, fingering patterns; add ornaments and embellishments, use varied vibrato and not continuously but to color or decorate special moments, selectively adapt practices described in historical sources. More expressive performances than those from the "Modernist" period but differently expressive to those from the "Romantic" period.

Today it is more or less expected that musicians performing eighteenth-century music possess some familiarity with key historical resources. The next two sections discuss some of the aesthetic and practical questions that these resources pose for the contemporary performer and make a few recommendations.

AESTHETICS

During the Baroque and Classical periods, musicians were regarded as "orators in tone":

> Musical execution may be compared with the delivery of an orator. The orator and the musician have, at bottom, the same aim in regard to both the preparation and the final execution of their productions, namely to make themselves masters of the hearts of their listeners, to arouse or still their passions, and to transport them now to this sentiment, now to that. (Quantz, 1966/1752, p. 119)

It was the composers' and performers' duty to make music intelligible, clear, and affective, similar to a well-constructed and well-delivered speech that induced emotional states in the listener (Lawson & Stowell, 1999, pp. 28–33; Bonds, 1991, pp. 54–55; Barth, 1992; Beghin and Goldberg, 2007). This meant that musical gestures were short with frequent punctuation. A musical motif or unit might be only a few notes long, building to a measure or pair of measures. The direct and often symmetrical structure consisting of 2 + 2, 4 + 4, and 8 + 8 measures is familiar to anybody learning to perform the music of Johann Sebastian Bach or Wolfgang Amadeus Mozart. As we traversed ahead in time toward Beethoven and beyond, these structures became increasingly extended and often less symmetrically balanced; the emphasis shifted to longer, songful melody lines and eliciting inexpressible feelings. In contrast, eighteenth-century musicians, living as they were in the Age of Reason and the Enlightenment, wanted music to move the passions, to create particular mental states or idealized emotions such as anger, happiness, sadness, hate, joy, or melancholy and to depict the meaning of words with clarity.

Such basic differences in aesthetic outlook have influenced not just compositional style but also performing practice (Lawson & Stowell, 1999; Haynes, 2007). Modern musicians interested in gaining experiential knowledge of these differences can be greatly aided by studying the characteristics of, and/or learning to play, period instruments.

Practically all the instruments we associate with Western art music today had an earlier version in the eighteenth century. As examples, we speak of the Baroque violin, Baroque cello, and associated bows, the Baroque flute and oboe, the harpsichord, and the fortepiano, as well as the natural trumpet and horn. Their physical differences from their modern counterpart are considerable and both engender and require different techniques. These, in turn, make the realization of contemporaneous aesthetic ideals easier, while on modern instruments they can only be adapted and approximated.

Eighteenth-century instruments and their techniques

There are some excellent modern books on many Baroque instruments (Brown, 2003; Rowland, 2001; Stowell, 2001) and vocal performance (Potter, 1998, 2000; Toft, 2013). These complement the more detailed original eighteenth-century textbooks of Agricola (1995/1757), Bacilly (1968/1668), Hotteterre (1968/ca.1700), Leopold Mozart (1951/1756), Quantz (1966/1752), C. P. E Bach (1949/1753), Tosi (1968/1743), Tromlitz (1991/1791), Türk (1982/1789), and others, and provide further information. In this review I detail some of the basic issues and differences of the most relevant instruments from the period.

Voice

As there are obviously no surviving museum copies of eighteenth-century voices, period vocal techniques are difficult to establish. The nature of vocal production has been one of the most controversial and hotly contested topics of the period performance revival movement. Written sources are open to subjective interpretation and aesthetic ideals seem to change with each generation. What Tosi (1653–1732) might criticize in younger singers like Farinelli (1705–1782), Quantz (1697–1773), as a contemporary of such famous castrati, may praise enthusiastically. Regardless of contemporary aesthetic battles, we simply do not know what a castrato sounded like or how they may have compared to a modern countertenor or soprano. How much chest voice did they use? What technique and vocal practice might help a modern soprano to resemble the sound and artistry of an eighteenth-century singer?

What we do know for sure is the requirement of vocal expression, agility and control. Most operatic and sacred music of the time has extensive florid passages that presume agile coloratura technique, while the lyrical items have long-spun melodies and held notes that presuppose smooth breath-control and *port-de-voix*. In addition, singers had to express the text by highlighting and conveying the emotions of key words (Toft, 2013, 2015). Historical vocal treatises and exercise books provide further evidence for the importance of vocal agility and the ability to add expressive ornaments and melodic embellishments. Modern operatic vocal technique is not congenial to such delivery because it relies on a lower larynx position and aims to generate the "singer's formant" (Sundberg, 1987) that carries over a large symphonic orchestra. Instead, as John Potter (1998, pp. 52–54) argues, eighteenth-century singers sang with a higher larynx position closer to the position used in speaking. This limits the volume of sound produced, but enables greater clarity of text (easier distinguishing between vowels) and makes the voice light and agile.

Since both halls and orchestras were smaller in the eighteenth century than from about the 1830s onwards, and the instruments had less carrying power, singers were not required to sing loudly. On the other hand, good diction was important to ensure the performance was expressive and conveyed the minute meaning of the text (Toft, 2013, 2015). Singing with a higher larynx position fits these conditions and creates what historical singing authorities might be referring to as the "natural voice" (Tosi, 1743; Agricola, 1757), or the "*clair*/clear voice/*voix blanche*" (Garcia, 1840). In fact, we can probably learn most about the differences between "early" and "modern" singing by reading Garcia's scientifically inclined treatise. It is the first to discuss the new "*voix sombrée*," its characteristics and advantage for the new, heavier, and more dramatic nineteenth-century repertoire, and to contrast it to the earlier style of vocal production.

Violin

The most important physical differences between the modern and eighteenth-century violin are the shorter neck, lower bridge, and gut strings (Stowell, 2001). The flatter bridge and looser strings made string crossing easier and the sound more resonant, although softer. The shorter neck and different hold slightly below the collarbone (and without chin rest or shoulder pad) made shifting upward on the fingerboard risky, promoting the use of low positions. This, in turn, required frequent string crossing, creating varied colors (each string has a slightly different timbre due to varying thickness) and rich resonances due to the use of open strings rather than hand-position shifts. The hold of the violin and the frequency of open strings contributed to the prevailing aesthetic that limited vibrato to be a coloring and ornamenting technique on longer notes rather than a part of essential tone production, as is customary today.

Importantly, eighteenth-century violinists used shorter bows that were heavier at the frog than their modern counterparts. The shorter bow is not suitable for projecting long cantilenas but fitting for delineating shorter groups of notes. The uneven distribution of weight between frog and tip highlights the difference between an up-bow and a down-bow, with heavier down-bow accents. This constant chiaroscuro effect serves well the projection of meter and clarity of articulation, two essential techniques in conveying the "speaking" quality of eighteenth-century music.

> The bowing gives life to the notes; . . . it produces now a modest, now an impertinent, now a serious or playful tone; now coaxing, or grave and sublime; now a sad or merry melody; and is therefore the medium by the reasonable use of which we are able to rouse in the hearers the aforesaid affects. (Mozart, 1951/1756, p. 114)

Flute

Among woodwinds the flute (*traverso*) was the most common solo instrument (Brown, 2003). Like other eighteenth-century wind instruments, it had no keys (or just one until late into the century) or mouthpiece. The blow (embouchure) hole was relatively small, circular on earlier versions and more oval on later ones. Finger holes (usually six or seven) were also small and required a variety of cross-fingerings to create full scales. Some chromatic notes were only possible by using half-holes.

As a result, Baroque flutes have a supple and varied sound, generally airier, softer, and "darker" than their modern metal counterpart. Flipping between registers and creating nuances of dynamics are easier through flexible embouchure shapes that are not hindered by a fixed mouthpiece. However, tuning is delicate and each key sounds slightly different due to different cross-fingered notes. These can sound "hollow," adding to the palette of colors and key characteristics. The simple design and lack of mouthpiece also allow for intricate tonguing patterns that aid the articulation of musical contours. According to Quantz (1966/1752, pp. 70–84), *Ti* creates a short, sharp attack; *Di* a more legato attack; *Ti ri* helps shape dotted rhythms, with *ri* being long and *ti* short; and *Did'll* is used for double tonguing. Hotteterre (1968, pp. 36–40) recommended the alternation of *tu* and *ru*. This creates a natural long-short effect. These tonguing differences are much more audible on the wooden than on the metal flute and play a significant role in creating an expressive, "speaking" performance.

> The tongue is the means by which we give animation to the execution of the notes upon the flute. It is indispensable for musical articulation, and serves the same purpose as the bow-stroke upon the violin. . . . It is true that much also depends upon the fingers. . . . The liveliness of the execution, however, depends less upon the fingers than upon the tongue. It is the latter which must animate the expression of the passions in pieces of every sort, whatever they may be: sublime or melancholy, gay or pleasing. (Quantz, 1966/1752, p. 71)

> The appropriate tonguing for any note was dependent largely upon the speed and character of the movement and the position of that note in the hierarchy of the bar. (Lawson & Stowell, 1999, p. 49)

Harpsichord and fortepiano

There were a great variety of keyboard instruments in use during the eighteenth century (Komlós, 1995; Rowland, 2001; Rosenblum, 1988). Their constructions created different constraints and opportunities for performers. Apart from the organ, nowadays musicians tend to be concerned only with the harpsichord and fortepiano, although at the time the clavichord was equally important, albeit primarily in the home and as a practice instrument due to its soft sound and sensitiveness to touch.

The plucking action of the harpsichord does not allow for direct control of dynamics. Players created an illusion of dynamic nuance through articulation (e.g., by subtly delaying or hurrying notes and thus adding emphasis or prolonging the note decay to create a softening effect) and simple registration options (e.g., doubling at the octave). Terraced or flat dynamics come by naturally through use of register stops. These were adjusted by hand (not pedal) and therefore tended to be changed at section ends. Short, light, and smaller keys enabled a variety of fingering patterns that aided articulation. For instance, groups of two and three notes were highlighted by a series of 3-4, 2-3, 2-3-4, or 4-3-2 finger motions, rather than the modern fingering with tucking the thumb under. Using grace notes and arpeggiation were the common ways to sustain or increase sound, as it decays almost as soon as a note is plucked. These instrumental techniques align well with contemporaneous aesthetics as outlined earlier.

During the second half of the eighteenth century, the harpsichord was gradually replaced by the fortepiano as the most popular keyboard instrument. It proved more versatile and better suited the needs of the emerging bourgeoisie, their appetite for home music making, public concerts, and larger halls.

The fortepiano has a similar mechanism to the modern piano, enabling gradated dynamics, legato articulation, and *cantabile* playing, but its frame and action are lighter and the keys are smaller, making the sound less resonant and its decay more rapid. The various registers have quite different timbres; the bass is cleaner albeit sonorous and the treble somewhat clunky and drier than on the modern grand. The lighter action makes the performance of long scale passages easier. The smaller keys and lighter action also allow for varied fingering patterns (as with the harpsichord) in aid of closely nuanced articulation that maintains the desired speaking quality. Stronger accents and sudden dynamics in the left hand do not muffle the overall clarity of texture, enabling bold, rhetorical gestures (Komlós, 1995, pp. 33–52; Rosenblum, 1988, pp. 37–39). In earlier fortepianos the sustaining pedal was handled by the knee, lifting it to press a lever under the keyboard. This is more cumbersome than using a foot pedal and hindered the aesthetic shift toward favoring long, smoothly connected sounds.

As is evident in the following sections, these physical differences in instrument-making have implications for performance that can be further explored by examining eighteenth-century sources on the various elements and techniques of execution.

Performance Parameters

Articulation

As can be deduced from the discussion so far, articulation is perhaps the most important component of eighteenth-century music performance. It is intimately connected with the principles of rhetoric and was embedded in every player's technique through countless exercises of metric patterns with matching fingering, bowing, and tonguing drills (Houle, 1987, p. 85; Lawson & Stowell, 1999, pp. 47–53).

> Performers usually began their study of the instrument with simple pieces in which there was a close connection between the choice of fingers and the meter of the music. (Houle, 1987, p. 91)

Music of the first half of the eighteenth century was strongly influenced by contemporaneous dance music and used varied meters, each with its own accentual pattern and implied tempo, at times moderated by additional tempo words such as *andante, largo,* and *allegro* (see more on this under the section on tempo). Metric signatures with larger denominator values implied a weightier type of playing than signatures with small values. Familiar time signatures like C (Common time) meant something slightly different to an eighteenth-century musician than to a modern one. It was not the same as 4/4 because it only allowed a minor structural stress on the third beat and a main one on the downbeat. In contrast, 4/4 could be performed with four equally stressed beats. The different "flow" (or *movement*, to use Mattheson's [1981/1739] term) of C compared to 4/4 is especially important when the music comprises eighth to sixteenth notes. In C, these should be projected as groups of four (eighth notes) or eight (sixteenths) rather than beat by beat. Sources also discuss the difference between 3/4 with triplets and 9/8. In the latter it was possible to have a harmonic change on the last eighth note, unlike in the case of triplets (Kirnberger, 1982/1771–1776; Houle, 1987, p. 49).

In terms of early eighteenth-century music, articulation thus means the projection of pulse through delineation of metric groups that tend to reflect harmonic progression because much of the melodic detail is essentially figuration over a bass. The importance of pulse and metric structure is also discussed in sources with reference to the intrinsic values of "good" and "bad" notes: good notes occur in metrically important moments and have to be emphasized, while bad notes (on weak beats) should be passed over lightly (Houle, 1987, pp. 84–85; Quantz, 1966/1752). This principle lies at the heart of an uneven, bouncing-dancing sound, by creating a strong sense of pulse and guiding the shaping of motives and gestures (Donington, 1973; Haynes, 2007; Lawson & Stowell, 1999, pp. 55–58).

During the later Classical period of the eighteenth century, the importance of metric delivery receded to give way to a more *cantabile* style. Harmony was simplified and the differentiation and hierarchy between melody and accompaniment enhanced. Composers started to add many more articulation marks to their scores, and their sensitive realization became the hallmark of elite performers. The various tonguing and bowing patterns discussed in treatises were now indicated by signs (primarily slurs but also staccato dots and wedges and tenuto markings) and ensured the rhetorical, speech-like shaping of phrases and thus the intelligibility of the musical text.

Articulation in this more modern sense of staccato and legato execution still requires awareness of particular historical conventions. In the eighteenth century, slurs indicated the grouping of notes, rather than legato per se. The first note under a slur was held slightly longer to mark the beginning of a group of notes and the metric structure. In a series of notes paired with slurs, the first in each pair was slightly longer and the second slightly shorter and with softer dynamics, creating what is known as the "sigh effect" or "sigh-motif."

Because composers in the Baroque period conceived of their music primarily harmonically and rhythmically, rather than melodically as in later periods, it is important to recognize harmonic goals and potentially shifting accentual patterns. Uniform accenting can create monotony, and most composers would venture away from established patterns to cross measure boundaries and create instability before returning to base and restore order. These moments tend to be led by harmony, and musicians must recognize and project these shifts in their performance through articulation (Fabian, 2018, pp. 193–203).

Rhythm

Given the importance of meter and pulse in music of the earlier part of the eighteenth century, the articulation of rhythm is paramount. Rhythmic patterns tend to follow the metric structure and need to be performed in groups of metric units (Fabian, 2018, pp. 185–193). Early eighteenth-century theorists discussed the "intrinsic" and "extrinsic" values of notes and drew comparisons with Greek poetic meters and the distributions of long and short values (Houle, 1987). Toward the end of the century, composers started to push for longer melody lines and smother melodic flow, downplaying and simplifying the role of metric structures (Neumann, 1993, pp. 85–89; Komlós, 1995, p. 138; Rosenblum, 1988, pp. 144–147).

There are two special conventions of rhythmic performance worth mentioning: *notes inégales* and over-dotting. The former was a convention of French Baroque music that spread to Germany and England as well (Hefling, 1993, pp. 3–20, 37–64). It refers to the uneven (usually long-short) performance of an evenly notated series of eighth or sixteenth notes. Sometimes the notes are beamed or slurred in pairs to indicate *notes inégales* performance, but this does not mean unequal performance is not intended elsewhere. However, when dots are placed over a series of eighth or sixteenth notes, it is likely that they should be played evenly. Importantly, the convention of *notes inégales* should be distinguished from the general rhythmic flexibility (*inégalité*) that was common in all performances because of the strong projection of meter and grouping of notes according to pulse.

Over-dotting is not an exclusive eighteenth-century practice, although it is much discussed by historical and modern sources (Donington, 1973; Hefling, 1993; Lawson & Stowell, 1999; Neumann, 1993). Musicians all over the world and across time tend to use flexible dotting ratios to suit the character of the music. Festive, flamboyant music tends to inspire over-held dotted notes and delayed, truncated short notes, often with a slight rest in between. Performers of pastoral, lyrical, rocking music may lessen the ratio and connect the two notes more smoothly. Importantly, research has shown that tempo and articulation play crucial roles in our perception of dotting, and it is not always the change in ratio between the duration of the dotted note and its short pair that determines whether a listener perceives over-dotting or not (Fabian & Schubert, 2010).

Dynamics

The eighteenth century has to be separated into its earlier Baroque and later Classical periods when one is to examine dynamics. In Baroque music it is more common to encounter contrasting (or "terraced") dynamics. This is partly explained by the prevalence of harpsichord and organ music—two instruments with no capability for gradual change from soft to loud or vice versa. Another reason might lie in a general preference for contrast, manifesting in echo effects, in vividly distinctive colors and juxtaposed light and shade (as observed in contemporaneous painting), of pitting large ensembles against a smaller group of soloists, of vocalists against instrumentalists, of high sounds against low, and so on. However, instruments like the violin, flute, or oboe as well as the voice—all much loved and used throughout the century—are perfectly capable of gradated dynamics, and their expressive qualities were often set as examples for all musicians to strive for. Avoiding the use of gradated dynamics in Baroque music may therefore seem historically unfounded.

Dynamics in Baroque music are, in fact, far from static and change is not usually limited to contrast. Nuanced dynamic shifts are part and parcel of performing on eighteenth-century strings and winds because of bowing and tonguing characteristics, impacting the shaping of notes and aiding articulation by making certain notes in a group sound more defined or louder. Meanwhile, singers of the time are famed for their execution of *messa di voce*, a perfectly controlled crescendo and decrescendo on held notes. They are also upheld as musicians to be imitated by violinists, flautists, and other soloists.

From around the late 1770s these nuances at the local level were increasingly transferred to longer sections. One- or two-measure motives became eight-measure phrases shaped through fluctuating dynamics, creating an ebb and flow typical of Viennese classical music and beyond. Furthermore, varied and detailed dynamic signs were notated with increasing frequency as these effects could be produced on the new fortepiano.

Nevertheless, one can note that during the eighteenth century the standard volume was *forte*, and only indicated after a *piano* section. Generally, dynamic markings in manuscripts are sporadic and extreme dynamics are rare. Johann Sebastian Bach used *pp* only a handful of times and even in Mozart's output *ff* and *pp* markings are relatively uncommon. It is also noteworthy that for Leopold Mozart *f* meant "played rather more strongly" (cited in Houle 1987, p. 133), implying articulation rather than volume. Accents (*sf* or *fz*) tend to be indicated more frequently in music from around 1800, especially by Beethoven, or when the composer intends to disrupt the general accentual pattern indicated by the meter (Badura-Skoda and Badura-Skoda, 2008; Komlós, 1995, pp. 24–30; Neumann, 1993, pp. 169–184; Newman, 1988; Rosenblum, 1988, pp. 55–70).

Tempo

According to the majority of sources, the range of tempo was quite moderate throughout the eighteenth century; there was limited contrast in speed between a lively vivace and a tranquil adagio. Such terms indicated musical character primarily, as tempo was deciphered from the combination of meter and predominant rhythmic values, as discussed in the section on articulation. In general, time signatures with smaller denominators (9/16, 12/16, 24/16, or 6/8, 9/8, 12/8) are progressively faster versions of time signatures with 4 or 2 as denominator (2/4, 3/4, 4/4 or 2/2, 3/2, 4/2). Although some sources recommend a "natural" tempo for each, depending on the genre and its affect as well as the prevalent note values (Mattheson 1713), "these can be modified . . . by tempo words" (Houle, 1987, p. 47). This *tempo giusto* is

> best learned by studying all kinds of dance pieces, their meter signatures, and the note values used. Tempo words such as "*largo, adagio, andante, allegro, presto* (. . .)" modify this natural tempo, rather than set absolute tempos determined by the words alone. (Kirnberger 1982/1779 cited in Houle, 1987, p. 48)

Thus the tempo of each movement in a Baroque sonata might not differ as much as the basic character (e.g., lively versus tranquil), with most of the difference composed into the music through choice of meter, number of structural stresses per measure, prevailing note values, and different rhythmic patterns, harmonic rhythms, and the like. It is therefore important to know the meaning of these words in order to fully understand the additional information they contain regarding the underlying nature of a movement. They are described and explained in various old and modern sources (e.g. Kirnberger, 1982/1771–1779; Mattheson, 1713; Neumann, 1993; Houle, 1987; Donington, 1973, 1989) that can be synthesized like:

Adagio (comfortably, at your ease, without pressing on), required a slow somewhat dragging speed;

Largo (broad) directed the player to increase emphasis on the second half of the time unit and thus create a broadening of beats;

Lento (slowly) implied a not at all animated or lively movement;

Grave (serious), somewhat heavy and ponderous tempo

Maestoso (with majesty) required deliberate, not at all hurried playing;

Andante (walkingly) was used to encourage continuity of tone through a reduced emphasis on beats;

Allegretto (gaily, agreeably) indicated playing with a gracious, pretty gaiety;

Allegro (happy, cheerful) indicated fewer accents for a lighter effect, rather than faster pace; and

Presto (fast) implied very short beats to foster forward motion.

FIGURE 16.1. Bach, Concerto for two harpsichords BWV1061, 2nd movement, mm. 1–3.

FIGURE 16.2. Mozart, *Marriage of Figaro*, Act 2 Finale, mm. 121–129 (strings and vocal parts only).

A specific case may illustrate this different usage of "tempo words" well (see Figure 16.1). The second movement of Bach's Concerto for two harpsichords (BWV 1061) is inscribed "Adagio ovvero Largo" (Adagio or otherwise Largo). This makes little sense if we think of both adagio and largo to mean slow, even if one may be faster than the other. However, given the discussion of these words in historical sources, the inscription actually indicates that the movement can be performed either with normal accent patterns; that is, 6/8 with sixteenth notes and two accents per measure (i.e., adagio), or broadly (largo), with six accents per measure (Newman, 1985, p. 44).

Another example comes from Mozart's *The Marriage of Figaro* (see Figure 16.2). The Finale of Act II starts allegro (C) and the excitement intensifies as the Count accuses the Countess of hiding Cherubino, the pubescent page, in her walk-in wardrobe. As he opens the door, we hear the Count's and Countess's startled "Susanna?" exclamation (an upward leap of perfect fourths). After a general pause with fermata sign, the time signature is changed to 3/8 with the marking molto andante. Historically, editors changed this to andante con moto (e.g., in Peter's edition, number 8087) and most performances slow the tempo considerably at this point. Yet 3/8 indicates light forward motion with little accenting, and "molto andante" literally means "very walking," or "power walking," if you wish. It certainly implies a fast walking pace rather than a slower version of andante. The instruction of "much increased continuity of tone" (molto andante) makes even more sense when one considers not just the time signature (3/8) but especially the orchestral figures that accompany Susanna's entrance: repeated chords in sixteenths, marked *p*. Mozart obviously envisioned a completely different dramatic effect than what an andante con moto brings about in modern performance.

Rubato

In current times, musicians are expected to keep a steady tempo in performance. However, modern listeners are also accustomed to hearing slight tempo fluctuations. Performers speed into phrases and slow down toward the end of sections to give shape to the music. This kind of tempo rubato does not appear to be discussed in eighteenth-century sources except as a criticism. On the other hand, *rubato*, from the Italian word *rubare*, "to rob," is mentioned as an expressive device. It refers to a practice where the melody "frees itself" from the steady accompaniment to enhance expression through slight delaying or rushing of notes. What is "robbed" from one note (or measure) is given back to the next. This eighteenth-century rubato practice is different from its later *tempo rubato* version because the pulse does not change and the flexibility occurs over a short section (a group of notes, a measure or two) rather than longer phrases (Hudson, 1994). Eighteenth-century sources describe the difference and their preference for the local, decorative, "rhythmic" rubato thus:

> When a true virtuoso who is worthy of the title is to be accompanied, then one must not allow oneself to be beguiled by the postponing or anticipating of the notes, which he knows how to shape so adroitly and touchingly, into hesitating or hurrying, but must continue to play throughout in the same manner; else the effect which the performer desired to build up would be demolished by the accompaniment. (Mozart, 1951/1756, p. 224)

> What . . . people cannot grasp is that in tempo rubato in an Adagio, the left hand should go on playing in strict time. With them the left hand always follows suit. (Wolfgang Mozart's letter from October 1777, cited in Anderson, 1985, p. 340)

Given the earlier discussion of articulation and the importance of projecting meter and accentual groups, it is quite clear that this type of rubato is closely associated with the rhetorical principles of delivery. It assists the musical orator to clearly communicate the expressive content and move the listener's mental state.

Improvisation and ornamentation

Apart from the issue of articulation and rhythmic projection, the most important aspect of performing music from the eighteenth century is ornamentation and embellishment. Improvisation was a key feature of performance well into the Romantic period. In the Baroque and Classical periods the emphasis was on embellishments and ornamentation, although ex tempore improvising on themes was also held in high esteem. Singers and keyboard players in particular received systematic instructions in composition and had to practice various patterns and figurations suitable for particular harmonic progressions, melodic contours, and musical characters or moods. These could be freely and spontaneously called upon to decorate skeleton melodies, to improvise over a figured (or unfigured) bass line, to vary the music during repeats, or to develop a set of variations on a prescribed theme. For the most part, modern musicians have been focusing on simple ornamentation only. However, in more recent times, instrumentalists and vocalists have started to engage more broadly with eighteenth-century musical language and practice enabling them to explore the wider palette of embellishing and improvising (e.g., violinists Stefano Montenari, Victoria Mullova, Isabelle Faust; fortepianist Robert Levin). What they need to consider is whether the goal is to decorate, to show virtuosity, or to increase expression. Their choices will change accordingly (Lawson & Stowell, 1999, pp. 70–75).

Ornamentation as decoration refers to the use of grace notes such as trills, mordents, slides, appoggiaturas, and their various combinations and derivatives. They were particularly common in French harpsichord music. They tend to be indicated in scores by signs, and we have many original (and modern) tables of ornaments that explain the execution of these signs and the context in which the use of a particular ornament is recommended (Neumann, 1993; Zaslaw, 1996).

In contrast, *embellishment* refers to melodic decoration, the addition of notes to fill out leaps, to change melodic contours, to add figuration to plain accompaniment, and so on. The practice of embellishment was most common in Italian music. The added figures can serve virtuosity or enhance expression and are in effect miniature manifestations of improvisation that is called upon at a more complex or extended level during a cadenza in a concerto or at fermata signs. Such spontaneous additions are necessary in most Baroque compositions and are desirable in many Classical solo parts (Fabian, 2013; Levin, 1992).

Baroque composers tended to notate only a skeleton (bass and essential melodic pitches) and expected the performer to fill out the rest (see Figure 16.3). There are

FIGURE 16.3. Excerpt from "Corelli's Op. 5/1 Avec les Agréments" (Walsh, 1750), that is "with [performer's] embellishments" in the upper stave.

FIGURE 16.4. Bach, Sonata in G minor BWV 1001, 1st movement, mm. 1–3.

surviving "performer's copies" of Corelli's violin sonatas, for instance, that show this process (Walsh, 1750; Zaslaw, 1996).

We also have written-out embellishments of Handel opera arias that he prepared for some of his singers (Handel 1973), among other such resources. What is important to note, however, is that from J. S. Bach on, the norm has gradually become for composers to write out much more precisely what the performer should play. In these eighteenth-century scores, the modern performer must recognize what is essential melody and what is embellishment in order to communicate this to the listener. By performing ornamental figures in a gestural, lighter way, rhythmically freely as if spontaneously added in the spur of the moment, the performer avoids the possibility that the music may sound too calculated and melodically complex. Figure 16.4 shows the opening bars of Bach's G minor Violin Sonata (BWV 1001) and a reduction to highlight the written-out embellishment over the basic melody. The example also shows that slurs indicate note groups, not legato.

In Classical music, embellishment is more commonly called for at special moments, such as pauses and fermatas as well as before the return of a main theme (e.g., at the conclusion of an episode in a rondo). These moments break the narrative in the music and provide opportunity for showing spontaneous virtuosity and creativity. Again, the best way to approach an interpretation is to study written-out examples. There are many in Mozart's and Haydn's keyboard sonatas and fantasias, especially in the slow movements in minor keys (e.g., K475, K511; Hob.XVI:44 in G minor). Longer, more complex, and extended improvisation was called for at the final cadenzas of concertos. During the nineteenth and twentieth centuries, it became customary for prominent performers and pedagogues to compose cadenzas for Classical concertos and these have become part of the standard repertoire. However, studying the original cadenzas of Mozart (1965) allows a musician to immerse themselves in his compositional language and understand how to create their own. This is essentially what Friedrich Gulda did in the early 1960s and Robert Levin in the 2000s.

Rhetorical techniques

Apart from articulation and rhythmic projection, a further device aiding the "speaking" manner of performance was the convention of indicating hand distribution in linear passages of fantasias and other keyboard works through marking the stems of notes down for left-hand and up for right-hand performance. Combined with eighteenth-century fingering patterns, diligent observation and delivery of such indications (rather than aiming to even out the disruptive hand movements) will promote a more gestural, rhetorical rendering.

Another convention was the un-notated arpeggiation of chords. These can be delivered gently, slowly or abruptly and fast, creating a variety of effects according to the required rhetorical context. However, it is important to adapt these means to the modern instrument as not all performance conventions are equally effective due to the different physical parameters.

Virtuosity

At least since the rise of the concert hall and the advent of a paying public toward the end of the seventeenth century, musical performance functioned primarily as entertainment (as well as serving ceremonial or ecclesiastical functions and the accompanying of dance). The public attended concerts to see and hear a virtuoso performer and to be moved by the performance. However, eighteenth-century treatises tended to pay more attention to discussions of interpretation, taste, and means of expression than to the perfecting of technical skills. This does not mean that virtuosity was not valued but certainly implies that musicianship and a "functional" rather than "acrobatic" virtuosity is closer to the ideals of the Age of Reason and Classicism. Refinement, feeling, and sensitivity were more valued than fast fingers and the delivery of scales and leaps, especially in Vienna (Komlós, 1995).

To conclude this section, a summary of issues discussed is presented in Table 16.2.

Table 16.2. Summary of key eighteenth–century performing practices.

Issue	Early 18th-century practice	Late 18th-century practice	Current practice (not HIP)
General aesthetics	Musician as orator; music speaks, simple, balanced, easy to follow and "comprehend." Emphasis is on harmony and rhythm/meter—melody is just harmonic figuration on bass, often skeletal and needs to be embellished in performance.	Concept of rhetoric maintained but increasing importance of longer melodies. Harmony is subordinated to melody and tends to be fully notated.	Smooth, homogeneous sound, long-spun melodies. Playing all notes with equal importance, whether ornamental or essential (basic) pitch. Little regard for underlying harmonic structure and meter.
Voice, vocal production	Clear voices, higher larynx position, boy sopranos, falsettos, and castrati are more common than female singers; low voices are rare in operatic roles. Clarity of text, agility of voice are paramount. All instruments should aspire to sound like a good singer.	Castrati are the stars of opera, but the female soprano is on the rise; virtuosic, agile singing, higher larynx position, less vibrato. Instruments should imitate the singing voice.	Lower larynx position, darker tone, less frequent breathing and articulation; power-singing, less agility, less clear diction, more chest voice, smoothly integrated registers.
Violin playing (general)	Low positions, lots of open string and string crossing, varied timbre, little vibrato (limited to ornament longer notes).	Similar, but moving towards modern: longer neck, more shifts and focus on melody.	Position shifts to maintain playing on same string for homogeneous color.
Violin bow	Short, uneven weight distribution: rapid decay, contrast between up-bow and down-bow accent.	Longer bow, more even weight distribution, longer sustain and more even sound.	Up-bow and down-bow strokes are even, bow change seamless.
Flute	One or no keys, no mouthpiece, 6–7 finger holes: variety of colors, complex fingering, delicate tuning. Range of intricate tonguing patterns.		Homogeneous tone, fewer and simpler tonguing patterns
Keyboards	Harpsichord, clavichord. Smaller keys, lighter action, distinct registers, quick decay of sound, varied fingering (limited use of thumb), no direct control of dynamics through touch/playing but only through register stops.	Fortepiano. Smaller keys, lighter action, distinct registers, more sustained sound; tucking the thumb under is used increasingly by around 1810. Gradated dynamics, more legato tone. Introduction of foot pedals.	Piano. Larger and heavier, require more physical power; sustained tone, more resonance, less clear bass, more homogeneous tone throughout range.

Table 16.2. Continued

Issue	Early 18th-century practice	Late 18th-century practice	Current practice (not HIP)
Articulation	Detached, detailed, nuanced: "speaking" delineation of metric groups; influence of dance music; slur indicates grouping of notes with first note under slur played longer.	Move toward legato, longer singing lines, melody increasingly more important than meter or harmony; more use of articulation markings.	Long, uninterrupted, seamless lines.
Dynamics	Contrasting (terraced) or nuanced (through bowing, tonguing technique), few markings (*p* or *f* and word: *dolce*).	Gradated (crescendo-decrescendo) more common; more dynamic markings in scores (*pp* to *ff* plus *sf*, *fp*).	Gradated from *pppp* to *ffff*; constantly fluctuating ebb and flow.
Meter and pulse	Great variety of time signatures, their differences emphasized through articulation; carry meaning for tempo.	Reduced number of time signatures; differences in accentual patterns are de-emphasized for smoother melodic flow.	Rarely projected.
Rhythm	Groups and patterns follow metric structures and need to be articulated.	Rhythmic projection gives way to singing melodies.	Focus is mostly on melody lines.
Notes inégales	The French convention of playing paired notes in a lilted way (usually long-short); used outside of France as well.	Not common as a convention, but unequal playing of groups of notes is still practiced.	Commonly observed in jazz performance.
Tempo	Italian words refer more to affect, mood, or character than speed; they tend to qualify time signature.	Italian tempo words are increasingly used to indicate speed.	Tempo words indicate speed.
Rubato	Local timing flexibility, at level of note or measure; pulse (accompaniment) remains steady while melodic notes are played earlier or later for expression.		Long-range tempo flexibility: tempo speeds up and then slows down as phrase unfolds.
Ornamentation and improvisation	Adding grace notes, embellishing skeleton melodies, improvising over bass lines, harmonies and melodies.	Creating cadenzas (at fermata signs, in concertos), improvising sets of variations, fantasias, paraphrases.	Playing what is written in the score
Vibrato	Used for coloring and ornamenting.	Increasing use.	Part of basic tone production.

Practical Implications

There are a variety of sources at the disposal of today's musicians to learn about eighteenth-century aesthetics and means of expression: books and treatises, original scores and letters, and, most important, the instruments themselves. There are also recordings that provide aural evidence for the different interpretative approaches. So what are the problems we face?

One major challenge could be our enculturated readings of scores; we are accustomed to hearing pieces being performed in particular ways as in the case of the Aria from Bach's Goldberg Variations.

> [I]f it was meant to sound, as usual today, *andante, dolce, piano, affettuoso, cantabile e tenero*, it seems odd that none of these words (the first five of which were all used elsewhere by Bach) appears in the score. Furthermore, if the Aria were *affettuoso*, so would be its "prototype," the G major sarabande in the French Suites. So used now are listeners to being transported by the Aria's opening bars to a unique contemplative world, especially by modern pianists, that envisaging anything different, anything more "light and playful," is difficult. But not impossible. (Williams, 2007, pp. 296–297)

So how do we question the validity of what we are used to and how do we re-learn reading scores? Williams implies an answer: go study the scores, the context, the conventions, and the composer's notation practices and dare to draw conclusions even if these may rock the boat of the established tradition.

Similarly, particular recommendations may sound familiar, yet cannot be followed blindly, such as the frequently voiced advice in eighteenth-century treatises to emulate good singers. In the contemporary context, "good singers" might be replaced by "historically informed singers or performers of eighteenth-century music," rather than "good Wagner, Verdi, or contemporary music singers."

In the earlier discussion of articulation and rhetorical techniques, several conventions have been noted that demonstrate that notational signs currently in use often had different meaning back in the eighteenth century (e.g., slurs, time signatures). Being familiar with these differences and reading the score according to eighteenth-century conventions are thus essential for any "re-learning."

Regarding instruments, is not just the difference between modern and old versions that has to be pondered. Instruments were changing during the eighteenth century as well. One should also be mindful of the period, the particular instrument, the region of the composer and piece, and consider the relevance of advice regarding fingering, tempo, genre, and so on. The same composer's early work might require quite different techniques and aesthetics than his late pieces, for "[t]he instrument's sound production and the very keyboard itself had evolved towards making greater smoothness and sensitive touch possible, and so must have its playing" (Williams, 2004, p. 163).

Advice in treatises therefore should not be considered rules. Deep contextual knowledge and analytical as well as practical familiarity with repertoire and instruments enable musicians to experiment and create new readings. Performers must search and experiment with playing style, looking for the *sound* the music "must have had" and creating it anew on the instrument at hand.

The implications regarding ornamentation and embellishment are similar. One crucial lesson from reading the treatises is that moderation seems to be the guiding principle. If used too often, their purpose is lost; if never used (as in the case of vibrato in many contemporary performances of Baroque and Classical music), the composition may sound bare and colorless. Most sources discuss this fine balance between what is desirable and what is "too much" and appeal to the cultivated good taste of the musician— an ageless advice, equally relevant and applicable today (Fabian, 2013, 2015).

As a final example of differences between eighteenth-century and contemporary notation practices and their implication for performance, three excerpts from Classical keyboard works are worth considering: the opening theme (mm. 1–8) of Haydn's Sonata in B minor Hob. XVI/32 (c. 1776); the G minor episode (mm. 52–70) from the third movement of Mozart's Sonata in B flat major K281 (1774); and the opening of Mozart's Fantasie in C minor K475 (1785). All three bear obvious marks of rhetorical conceptions that are clearly indicated through notation (see Figure 16.5a, b, c).

FIGURE 16.5A. Haydn, Sonata in B minor Hob. XVI/32, 1st movement, mm. 1–8.

(b)

FIGURE 16.5B. Mozart, Sonata in B-flat major K281, 3rd movement, mm. 52–70.

In the first example, attention should be drawn to how Haydn establishes the pulse through rhythm and ornamentation. He ensures the second metrical accent (beat 3) is emphasized through written-out appoggiatura (mm. 3, 5, 6, 7) or coinciding with the end of gesture (mm. 4, 8). The sixteenth note figures in mm. 5, 6, 7 are carefully slurred and lead the music to the newly articulated appoggiatura on beat 3. If these articulation marks are not observed and the measures delivered in a continuous legato, both the speaking quality and the considerable drama are lost.

In the rondo episode of Mozart's K281 it is worth noting the many *fp* markings and the fragmented nature of the music. Alternation of hands, paired slurs, rests, contrasting note values, larger leaps, octaves, and louder dynamics alternate with soft linear legato

FIGURE 16.5C. Mozart, Fantasy in C minor K457, mm. 1–8.

melody. The flow is interrupted every two measures or so, ending on a general pause with fermata. A short cadenza seems appropriate, given the following cadential descent through small paired notes. The subsequent linking three measures (68–70) may also be decorated, or at least the final chord arpeggiated, as indicated in the Köhnemann Urtext edition (Budapest 1993) of the sonatas. Highlighting the fragmented nature of the music enhances the contrast this episode in the minor key provides in the overall jolly character of the movement. Enhancing these effects also contributes a sense of improvisation that is rounded off by the added cadenza and embellished measures that lead back to the return of the playful rondo theme. It would be quite in keeping with the aesthetics of an eighteenth-century rondo to make the episodes sound improvised (hear Malcolm Bilson's recording on Hungaroton 31009).

The Fantasia opens with contrasting measures and dynamics. The sigh effect of the eighth note chords in mm. 2 and 4 are indicated by the notation as well (shorter second notes under the slur). In performance it is important to observe the measure-long slurs and articulate each group anew to make the unfolding harmonic drama intelligible.

Some of these articulations are hard to execute convincingly on the heavy modern concert grand. But this does not mean the performer should not be aware of what is intended. Once the image is in the mind and ears, the fingers find a solution to create the sound. In each of these examples a keen awareness of the consonance/dissonance relations and harmonic goals of the music will aid the shaping of gestures whatever instrument is used.

KEY RESOURCES

Fabian, D. (2018). *Bach performance practice 1945–75: A comprehensive review of sound recordings and literature.* London: Routledge. (1st ed: Ashgate 2003.)

Houle, G. (1987). *Meter in music, 1600–1800: Performance, perception, and notation.* Bloomington: Indiana University Press.

Lawson, C., & Stowell, R. (1999). *The historical performance of music: An introduction.* Cambridge, UK: Cambridge University Press.

Neumann, F. (1993). *Performance practices of the seventeenth and eighteenth centuries.* New York: Schirmer.

Rosenblum, S. (1988). *Performance practices in classic piano music: Their principles and applications.* Bloomington: Indiana University Press.

REFLECTIVE QUESTIONS

1. What does historical performance practice mean for you? In what ways could you use the information in this chapter to enhance your abilities as a performer?
2. Taking a piece of eighteenth-century music as a case study, how would you communicate eighteenth-century aesthetics in performance on your own (modern) instrument?
3. How can articulation serve the projection of rhythm and meter in practical terms?
4. What information is disclosed in eighteenth-century "tempo" words like siciliano, largo, allegro, adagio, etc.?
5. What were the principles and types of improvisation during the seventeenth and eighteenth centuries, and how can we recreate these practices?

REFERENCES

Agricola, J. (1995/1757). *Introduction to the art of singing* (English trans. Baird, J.). Cambridge, UK: Cambridge University Press.

Anderson, E. (1985). *The letters of Mozart and his family* (3rd ed). London: Macmillan.

Bach, C. P. E. (1949/1753). *Essay on the true art of playing keyboard instruments* (English trans. Mitchell, W.). New York: W. W. Norton.

Bacilly, B. de (1968/1668). *Remarque curieuses sur l'art de bien chanter Paris* (Geneve: Minkoff, 1971); *Commentary upon the art of proper singing* (trans. Caswell). Brooklyn: Institute of Medieval Music.

Badura-Skoda, E., & Badura-Skoda, P. (2008). *Interpreting Mozart: The performance of his piano pieces and other compositions* (2nd ed.). New York: Routledge.

Barth, G. (1992). *The Pianist as orator: Beethoven and the transformation of keyboard style.* Ithaca, NY: Cornell University Press.

Beghin, T. and Goldberg, S. M. (eds.). (2007). Haydn and the performance of rhetoric. Chicago: Chicago University Press.

Bonds, M. (1991). *Wordless rhetoric: Musical form and the metaphor of the oration.* Cambridge, MA: Harvard University Press.

Brown, R. (2003). *The early flute: A practical guide.* Cambridge, UK: Cambridge University Press.

Cook, N. (2014). *Beyond the score.* New York: Oxford University Press.

Donington, R. (1973). *A performer's guide to Baroque music.* London: Faber & Faber.

Donington, R. (1989). *The interpretation of early music* (New edition). London: Faber & Faber.

Fabian, D. (2013). Ornamentation in recent recordings of J. S. Bach's solo sonatas and partitas for violin. *Min-Ad: Israeli Studies in Musicology Online* 11/2, 1–21.

Fabian, D. (2015). *A musicology of performance: Theory and method based on Bach's Solos for Violin.* Cambridge, UK: Open Book Publishers.

Fabian, D., & Schubert, E. (2010). A new perspective on the performance of dotted rhythms. *Early Music* 38(4), 585–588.

Garcia, M. (1840). *Mémoire sur la voix humaine.* Paris: Académie des Sciences.

Handel, G. F. (1973). *Three ornamented arias* (score). Dean, W. (Ed.). Oxford: Oxford University Press.

Haynes, B. (2007). *The end of early music: A period performer's history of music for the twenty-first century.* New York: Oxford University Press.

Hefling, S. E. (1993). *Rhythmic alteration in seventeenth- and eighteenth-century music.* New York: Schirmer.

Hotteterre, J. (1968/ca.1700). *Principles of the flute, recorder and oboe* (English trans. Marshall Douglass, P.). Mineola, NY: Dover.

Hudson, R. (1994). *Stolen time: The history of tempo rubato.* Oxford: Clarendon.

Kirnberger, J. P. (1982/1771–1776). *The art of strict musical composition* (English trans. Beach, D., & Thym, J.). New Haven: Yale University Press.

Komlós, K. (1995). *Fortepianos and their music: Germany, Austria, and England, 1760–1800.* Oxford: Clarendon Press.

Lawson, C., & Stowell, R. (2012). *The Cambridge history of musical performance.* Cambridge, UK: Cambridge University Press.

Lawson, C., & Stowell, R. (2018). *The Cambridge encyclopedia of historical performance in music.* Cambridge, UK: Cambridge University Press.

Levin, R. D. (1992). Improvised embellishments in Mozart's keyboard music. *Early Music,* 20(2), 221–236.

Mattheson, J. (1713). *Das neu-eröffnete Orchestre.* Hamburg: Bey Benjamin Schillers Wittwe im Thum.

Mattheson, J. (1981/1739). *Der vollkommene Capellmeister* (English trans. Harriss, E. C.). Ann Arbor, MI: UMI Research Press.

Mozart, L. (1951/1756). *A treatise on the fundamental principles of violin playing* (English trans. Knocker, E.). Oxford: Oxford University Press.

Mozart, W. (1965). *Konzerte für ein oder mehrere Klaviere und Orchester mit Kadenzen* (score). Badura-Skoda, E., & Badura-Skoda, P. (Eds.), Neue Mozart Ausgabe [NMA V/15/5], pp. 237–243. Kassel: Bärenreiter.

Newman, A. (1985). *Bach and the baroque: A performing guide to baroque music with special emphasis on the music of J. S. Bach.* New York: Pendragon Press.

Newman, W. S. (Ed.). (1988). *Beethoven on Beethoven: Playing his piano music his way.* New York: W. W. Norton.

Philip, R. (2004). *Performing music in the age of recording.* New Haven and London: Yale University Press.

Potter, J. (1998). *Vocal authority: Singing style and ideology.* Cambridge, UK: Cambridge University Press.

Potter, J. (Ed.) (2000). *The Cambridge companion to singing.* Cambridge, UK: Cambridge University Press.

Quantz, J. J. (1966/1752). *On playing the flute* (English trans. Reilly, E. R.). London: Faber.

Rowland, D. (2001). *Early keyboard instruments: A practical guide.* Cambridge, UK: Cambridge University Press.

Stowell, R. (2001). *The early violin and viola: A practical guide.* Cambridge, UK: Cambridge University Press.

Sundberg, J. (1987). *The science of the singing voice.* DeKalb: Northern Illinois University Press.

Taruskin, R. (1995). *Text and act: Essays on music and performance.* New York: Oxford University Press.

Toft, R. (2013). *Bel Canto: A performer's guide.* New York: Oxford University Press.

Toft, R. (2015). *With passionate voice: Re-creative singing in 16th-Century England and Italy.* New York: Oxford University Press.

Tosi, P. F. (1968/1743). *Observations on the florid song: Or sentiments on the ancient and modern singers* (English trans. Galliard, J. E.). New York: Johnson Reprint Corporation.

Tromlitz, J. G. (1991/1791). *The virtuoso flute player* (English trans. Powell. A.). Cambridge, UK: Cambridge University Press.

Türk, D. G. (1982/1789). *School of clavier playing* (English trans. Haggh, R.). Lincoln: University of Nebraska Press.

Walsh, J. (Ed.) (1750). Corelli's *12 Violin Sonatas Op. 5 Avec les Agréments* (score). Amsterdam.

Williams, P. (2004). *The life of Bach.* Cambridge, UK: Cambridge University Press.

Williams, P. (2007). *J. S. Bach: A life in music.* Cambridge, UK: Cambridge University Press.

Zaslaw, N. (1996). Ornaments for Corelli's violin sonatas, Op. 5. *Early Music 24*(1), 95–116.

CHAPTER 17

PERFORMANCE PRACTICES FOR ROMANTIC AND MODERN REPERTOIRE

NEAL PERES DA COSTA

INTRODUCTION

IN 1999, conductor Sir Roger Norrington, known for his groundbreaking historically-informed interpretations of canonical nineteenth-century orchestral works with London Classical Players, wrote an enthusiastic preface to Clive Brown's monumental *Classical and Romantic Performing Practice (1750–1900)*. Norrington's opening statement provides a useful point of departure for this chapter. He extols the fact that the previous thirty years had seen the forging of links between performers and scholars, producing exciting results (in the area of historically informed performance [HIP]) and leading to an accumulation of performing practice information for the sixteenth through eighteenth centuries. The nineteenth century, he notes "has been largely a closed book, assumed, perhaps dangerously, to be part of a received 'tradition,'" and he praises Brown's work for revealing "just how wrong that tradition can sometimes be" (Norrington, quoted in Brown, 1999, p. vii). Norrington's thoughts about the dangers of assuming a received tradition for the Romantic era ought to be extended to include at least the first half of the twentieth century—the rise of the Modern era, a time of rapid change in performance practices clearly captured in sound recording.

This chapter looks at the long nineteenth century roughly spanning 1800–1950. It is structured in three parts. The first explores important concepts about performance traditions and performance practices in the era. The second introduces key performance practices pertinent to vocal and/or instrumental repertoire, drawing on a rich tapestry of evidence. The third provides case studies demonstrating the author's utilization of pertinent performance practice information—expanding the palette of expressive means, to produce novel interpretations of canonical repertoire.

PERFORMANCE PRACTICES
TRAVERSING ERAS

Romantic and Modern

In music, the "Romantic" era started between c. 1800 and the end of the Beethoven/ Schubert era c. 1830. Its emergence is closely related to changes in European art, literature, and intellectual ideas, reflected in compositions that were increasingly individualistic, strongly imbued with dramatic, emotional, or programmatic content— foregrounded in the *Empfindsamer* (Sensitive) and *Sturm und Drang* (Storm and Stress) styles, harmonically complex and chromatic, and larger and more varied in instrumental forces than was previously the case.

The "Modern" era emerged from c. 1890 and was more firmly established by c. 1910, again following broad changes in society and other areas of culture. Key elements in musical compositions (melody, harmony, and rhythm) were dramatically reorganized, leading to new styles that rejected previous compositional conventions, for example, Impressionism, Expressionism, Serialism, and Atonality.

Changes in compositional style between the Romantic and Modern eras were not simultaneously reflected in changes to performance practices. An eye-opening example is seen in Hector Berlioz' protest in 1843 against what he considered an "old-fashioned style and an irritating mania for trills and mordents" ["un vieux style, et une manière de faire des trilles et des mordants"]—presumably a late-eighteenth-century style, in the third movement of his *Symphonie fantastique* Op. 14 by the first oboist in the Dresden Court Orchestra (Berlioz, 1870, vol. 2, p. 276).

During the Romantic era, musical tastes and performing practices evolved continuously. Less than twenty years after Beethoven's death, his pupil Czerny remarked that style had already changed somewhat and that Beethoven's "way of playing [...] could not always act as a model" (Czerny, 1846, vol. 4, p. 34). Nevertheless, such changes took place slowly and organically within a continuum of practice. Remnants at least of Baroque- and Classical-era performance practices will have continued on into the Romantic era (Peres Da Costa, 2012), just as remnants of Romantic performance practice continued on into the Modern era.

Performance practice traditions

Another interesting phenomenon is seen in the continuing traditions of performance associated with individual composers. A clear case is the application of un-notated piano arpeggiation and asynchrony (separating melody from accompaniment) in performances of Chopin's works (particularly his Nocturnes) by pianists of varying generations. Of the oldest generation on record, Leschetizky's (b. 1830) rendition of Nocturne Op. 27, no. 2 (1906) and of Saint-Saëns' (b. 1835) Nocturne Op. 15, no. 2 (1905)—both on Welte reproducing piano rolls (accessible on YouTube)—demonstrate these practices in ways that, if not exactly what Chopin expected, accord with a tradition of playing Chopin's works in the second half of the nineteenth century. These practices can also be heard on Chopin recordings by later generations throughout the first half of the twentieth century—a time when such practices were being generally suppressed (Peres Da Costa, 2012, pp. 47–50, 74–75, 132–139). These include recordings by Pugno (b. 1852), Pachmann (b. 1848), Paderewski (b. 1860), Rachmaninoff (b. 1873), Bartók (b. 1881), Koczalski (b. 1884)—a pupil of Chopin's favorite Polish student Mikuli (b. 1821)—and Michelangeli (b. 1920) in the 1960s, and Cicollini (b. 1925) as late as 2003 (albeit less noticeably).

An ongoing tradition is also noticeable in the recordings of Brahms's piano works (some as late as the 1950s) by pianists who studied with him. Davies (b. 1861), Friedberg (b. 1872), De Lara (b. 1872), Eibenschütz (b. 1872), and Freund (b. 1879) used arpeggiation and asynchrony, and modified rhythm and tempo in ways that are undoubtedly Brahmsian, but that had become unfashionable by the time they were recording.

Old practices and notational divergences

Contrary to popular belief, many composer/performers of the first half of the twentieth century did not notate exactly what they expected. Their own interpretations often highlight inconsistencies between notation and practice. Debussy's performances of his own piano music (on Welte piano rolls) reveal his use of asynchrony and arpeggiation (Langham Smith, 1999, pp. 21–22; see also Ho, 2014 and 2018; Buchanan, 2018). This is unsurprising, as he was trained by the Romantic French piano pedagogue Marmontel (b. 1816).

Bartók's recordings of his own piano compositions show that he employed a gamut of effects (including lyrical and percussive) and piano tone qualities that he learned from his teacher Thomán (b. 1862)—a pupil of Liszt. Bartók developed expressive notation using " 'tenuto,' 'portato,' half-tenuto signs, and verbal instructions such as espressivo and dolce" to indicate an old (Romantic) parlando style of rubato in many of his works, including those marked " 'sostenuto,' 'parlando,' 'rubato' or 'recitativo' " (Fischer, 1995, p. 292–293). Despite this level of fastidiousness his notation could not illustrate the myriad subtleties of rubato that "performances by Bartók of his own works provide" (Fischer, 1995, p. 296).

Rachmaninoff's performance of his Prélude in C sharp minor Op. 3, no. 2 (1919) is quite remarkable for the expressive effect he achieves in the opening Lento section through rhythmic and tempo changes, practices inherited from the late Romantic era. For example, in each of measures 3–6 he makes a noticeable agogic accent (lengthening) on the highest and most poignant chord on the third eighth-note beat. And, extraordinarily, he more or less doubles the pace in measure 7, then dramatically slows down through measure 8, continuing this pattern in the following measures. In measures 13 and 14, his ritardando before the Agitato section is effective but extreme by today's standards. The musical effect of his interpretation is individual, volatile, and improvisatory.

Even a staunchly modernist composer such as Stravinsky (b. 1882) did not adhere strictly in performance to his own published score markings. On several occasions, Stravinsky claimed that recordings that he conducted preserve the correct tempi for his works. But these often depart from the metronome markings in his published scores (Buxbaum, 1988, p. 61).

The meaning of musical notation

As the previous chapter (see Fabian, this part) put forward, performing practice conventions and the meaning of musical signs and symbols have evolved over time. The notation of Romantic and Modern repertoire (excluding music using new or idiosyncratic notation) draws from an armory of notational practices developed across several centuries. From Beethoven to Messiaen, composers have used the same types of notes and symbols to represent their musical creations, but their expectations for what these signaled to performers in terms of appropriate sound and expression have varied substantially. More to the point, their notation was incomplete. Prior to the Modern era, music scores were understood to be imperfect in conveying the subtleties of expressive interpretation that were requisite to breathe life into the "inexpressive notation" (Toft, 2000, p. 4). As the vocal pedagogue D. Corri (b. 1746) pointed out in c. 1781, an air or recitative sung exactly as noted would lead to a very inexpressive and uncouth performance (D. Corri, 1781, p. 2). A century later, the German composer and musical commentator Klauwell (b. 1851) posited that notation indicated "only measurable quantities, multiples and fractions of a fundamental unit." Highly artistic execution required reading between the lines of the notation to implement the "necessary deviations" including agogic accents, changes to dynamics and the "rubato of manifold variety" (Klauwell, 1883, trans. 1890, pp. 1–2). This attitude remained of paramount importance for many musicians in the early-twentieth century, but change was afoot.

Artistic agency

During the long nineteenth century, composers, if they were not the interpreters of their own works, relied on highly skilled performers (often members of their close circle) to supply expressive qualities that were essential but impractical to notate. The performer's agency, that is, the individuality of their artistry, was paramount. To that end, clear distinctions were articulated between a "correct" style of delivery—that which students were required to master, and a "beautiful" or "fine" style requisite of an accomplished artist. This was foregrounded in the mid-eighteenth century by C. P. E. Bach, who listed the constituents of performance including factors such as tempo modification, which, if missing or used incorrectly, would lead to "a bad performance style" (Mitchell, 1949, p. 148), and by Milchmeyer in 1797 in the first published treatise on piano playing (Rhein, 1993, p. 106).

An 1806 expanded version of L. Mozart's *Violinschule* by an anonymous author describes correct as "clean, exact, in tempo playing" ["Ein reines, genanes, taktmässiges Spiel"], which is "the student's chief duty" ["des Lehrings Hauptsorge"]. Once correct performance is mastered, the talented and feeling student "will gradually discover grace and expression" ["dann werden Zierlichkeit und Ausdruck sich nach und nach einfinden, wenn der Spieler Talent und Gefühl hat."] (Anon., 1806, pp. 68–69).

The pianist Hummel related the descriptive term *correct* with "the mechanism of playing" as indicated in the notation, while *beautiful* is playing "nicely rounded off" and well suited to all parts of the composition to include the "tasteful, pleasing and ornamental" (Hummel, 1828, vol. 3, pp. 39). For the violinist Spohr, correct equated with: (i) perfect intonation; (ii) notes given their exact notated duration; and, (iii) strict observance of tempo, notated dynamics, different kinds of bowing, slurs, and ornaments (Spohr, c. 1833, vol. 3, p. 179).

To these authors, a "beautiful" or "fine" style involved higher artistic practices. For Spohr these included: (i) fine bow management to achieve (a) varied tone colors— "strong, even, rough, soft, fluty" and (b) "the accentuation and separation of phrases; (ii) artificial shifts, not merely for ease but for expression and tone including *portamento* ("gliding from one note to another") and "the changing of the finger on the same tone; (iii) four types of vibrato; and, (iv) increase of speed in "furious, impetuous and passionate passages" and decrease of speed in passages of "tender, doleful or melancholy character" (Spohr, c. 1833, vol. 3, p. 179).

As late as 1906, the pianist Reinecke opined that "correctly regular performance in certain circumstances may be the exact opposite of beautiful; a beautiful performance may apparently offend against all rules" (Reinecke, 1906, p. xiii). As with other performance practice matters, nineteenth-century sources suggest that the most successful means to cultivate beautiful instrumental playing was to listen to the best singers "gifted with great powers of expression" (Hummel, 1828, vol. 2, 39). Of course, they meant the powers of expression that singers of their time employed, not of our time!

Instructive editions

From the second half of the nineteenth century, music editors (often celebrated performers), sometimes amplified dynamic nuances and accents, provided bowings and expressive fingerings, gave realisations of ornament signs, and gave verbal discussion on other performance practice issues. These provide a means of understanding some of what was expected in artistic performance at the time of the editions' publication. For example, some of the editions of Beethoven's Sonatas for Piano and Violin edited by musicians such as Speidel and Singer (1887), Rosé (1901), and Halir (1905), and who were closely connected with a Viennese tradition of performing Beethoven's music, provide prolific dynamic and accent markings showing how they conceived of such practices in a beautiful performance of these works (Brown & Peres Da Costa, 2020). While of a later era than Beethoven, study of these markings has potential to inspire ideas about what Beethoven may have expected from musicians of his day.

The modernist revolution

For Romantic-era musicians a beautiful performance relied on individual artistry to bring the score to life with a rhetorically-inspired delivery using a palette of largely un-notated expressive tools—the common language of an ongoing tradition. But this changed dramatically in the first decades of the twentieth century in large part due to a growing fixation with score fidelity. Already by 1870, the English composer G. A. Macfarren remarked tersely to G. A. Cussins that "the modern system of literal exactitude, at the cost of spiritual fidelity, ignores tradition, and stiff and clumsy are the results" (Cussins, 1874, quoted in Brown, 2012, p. 243). In a similar vein, Joachim remarked of Vieuxtemps, that in contrast to Spohr, "like most violinists of the Franco-Belgian school in recent times—he [Vieuxtemps] adhered too strictly to the lifeless note-heads when playing the classics, not understanding how to read between the lines"[[weil er [Vieuxtemps] sich, wie übrigens in neuerer Zeit die meisten Geiger der französisch-belgischen Richtung, beim Vortrag der Klassiker zu sehr an die leblosen Notenköpfe hielt, nicht zwischen den Zeilen zu lessen verstand] (Moser, 1908–1910, vol. 2, p. 292).

The upsurge of modernist aesthetics around the turn of the twentieth century led to the expunging—evidenced in sound recordings (Philip, 1992)—of long-established performing practices, previously considered indispensable. Within twenty years of Brahms's death in 1897, a widening chasm between his "expectations and the rapidly changing realities of early twentieth-century practice" (Brown, Peres Da Costa, & Bennett Wadsworth, 2015, p. viii) was already noted by Richard Barth—a member of Brahms's close circle. In performing Brahms's music, musicians were already ignoring the "incontrovertible tradition" ["unanfechtbaren Tradition"] which Barth considered absolutely essential "if a performance that is faithful to its content is to be achieved" [wenn es zu einer inhaltsgetreuen Wiedergrabe gelangen soll] (Hoffmann, 1979, quoted in Brown, Peres Da Costa, & Bennett Wadsworth, 2015, p. 34. The rejection of Romantic practices is strongly reflected in the violinist Flesch's advice in 1930 about recalling Spohr's compositions to life: "we must employ present day means of expression in their reproduction. [. . .] It is only that which is essential, the Spohrian spirit, that we must try to save and carry over without injury into our own time" (Flesch, 1930, vol. 2, p. 193). The Modern style that fully emerged by the mid-twentieth century and which continues seriously to influence Western art music performance today constituted an almost complete break with Romantic performance tradition.

The text-literal approach

As a pianist studying at university in the 1980s, I was instructed to follow the Urtext very carefully. The notes, signs, and symbols were to be meticulously observed; and apart from the addition, say, of ornaments on repeats in Baroque- and early Classical-era music, little else was permissible. Unwarranted (that is to, say un-notated) changes to the score were considered faulty and in bad taste. The modernist aesthetic saw the elevation of the score to the level of authoritative.

The result of this text-literal modernist approach is that musical works tend to sound the way their scores appear. For example, Bach and Mozart sound neat and tidy. The overall effect can range from restrained to full blooded depending on the work's style or character. But many interpretations (even today) conspicuously feature long-lined phrases with minimum sonic undulation; very stable (static) rhythm and tempo; and, lack of beat, bar, harmonic hierarchy or agogic accentuation. Other 'late-Romantic' expressive practices are minimised. The exception is vibrato, which for many singers and instrumentalists is a constant and relatively unvaried feature on notes long enough to accommodate it. The monochromatic look of the score and its markings are reflected in a rather neutral interpretation. Such a style is exemplified in the 1968 recording of Bach's Brandenburg Concerto No. 5 directed by Karl Richter from the harpsichord with the Munich Bach Orchestra on modern instruments (accessible on YouTube). Interestingly, the same work recorded in 1953 by a small ensemble from the Schola Cantorum Basiliensis on period instruments directed by August Wenziger (accessible on YouTube) reveals a similar style. The sound of the period instruments makes a noticeable tonal difference (lighter and more transparent), but the overall conception is text-literal and long-lined. A similar style is noticeable in Richter's recordings of Mozart, Gluck and Haydn in the 1960s (accessible on YouTube).

Later composers gave more directions in their scores; interpretations that follow these might therefore sound more varied than earlier compositions, but spontaneous artistic agency (personality) in the sense that undoubtedly existed in the nineteenth century is discouraged. Modern performers are charged not only with the job of realizing the score meticulously, but also with reverently upholding received notions of composers' character and musical epoch. For example, Classical-era music is generally considered to be contained in style and structure, therefore requiring a controlled manner of performance. Romantic-era music is seemingly less contained and can therefore admit of a more passionate performance style. The modern performer's role has become one of "a disappearing transmitter of canonic works and identities" (Scott, 2014, pp. 242–243). This together with "the deadly perfection of recording have helped to homogenize musical interpretation" (Dubal, 1992, p. xix).

The result is a predictability of interpretation; performances by different musicians of the same work tend to sound fairly similar. For example, many recordings from the

1930s to the present (including modern and period-instrument versions) of the slow movement from Mozart's Piano Concerto No. 23 K. 488 are characterized by a "modern" Mozartian style—neat and tidy execution with correct notes, rhythms performed precisely as notated, and a stable tempo throughout particularly with reference to the opening 12-bar solo piano sequence. These tend to project a similarly somber and static mood, a way of interpreting this particular movement that became set in stone during the course of the twentieth century (Peres Da Costa, 2019).

In the Romantic era (and before), this way of canonizing a composer's identity and a particular work's interpretation is less likely to have occurred. The recordings of musicians trained in the nineteenth century show that interpretations (even of the same work) were often quite individual and unpredictable. These musicians employ a common musical language, but they do so in idiosyncratic ways. In 1905, Reinecke (b. 1824)—the oldest pianist to have recorded—made a piano roll for Hupfeld of his own arrangement (1896) for solo piano of the slow movement from K. 488, which is enlightening in this respect. Trained in the first half of the nineteenth century, Reinecke was revered for upholding a tradition of Mozart performance that had all but disappeared by the time he came to make this recording (Peres Da Costa, 2019, p. 136). He employs arpeggiation, asynchrony, noticeable rhythm and tempo flexibility, and frequent note embellishment, in ways that render his interpretation improvisatory in feel and dramatic in mood, completely at odds with later interpretations, and very likely closer to what Mozart hand in mind (Peres Da Costa, 2019). In a similar vein, pianists of the Clara Schumann–Brahms school such as Eibenschütz and Friedberg employ un-notated tempo modification in Brahms's Ballade Op. 118, no. 3 to great effect but in highly individual ways that stem from the same tradition: "Friedberg's performance and Eibenschütz's are as different as night and day, but night and day in the same city" (Crutchfield, 1986, p. 18).

Early sound recordings

Recordings by Reinecke and others of his generation including the violinist Joachim (b. 1831) and the soprano Patti (b. 1843), as well as ensuing generations provide a window into the performance practices of Romantic-era musicians. They reveal the range of expressive devices employed (in many respects different to the present day), the places in which they ocurred, and their quality—how they sounded: fast, slow, loud, soft, and so on. As Haynes explains, these recordings evidence the "heavy, personal, organic, free, spontaneous, impulsive, irregular, disorganized and inexact" style of Romantic performance. Modern performance style is the reverse—"light, impersonal, mechanical, literal, correct, deliberate, consistent, metronomic, and regular". Haynes concludes that "Modernists look for discipline and line, while they disparage Romantic performance for its excessive rubato, its bluster, its self-indulgent posturing, and its sentimentality" (Haynes, 2007, p. 49).

Performance in the Romantic and Modern Eras

We turn our attention now to some of the key expressive practices that were character-istic of vocal and instrumental performance in the Romantic and Modern eras.

Legato and slurring

Legato

By the beginning of the Romantic era, legato (the smooth connection between tones) had become the default style of delivery for singers and instrumentalists. Throughout the era, composers generally marked slurs (both short and long) to indicate legato, but when these are absent legato can be assumed (Brown, 1999, pp. 172–173). Passages with consecutive slurs, often of varying length (see Beethoven's scores) implied continuous legato without any break in sound between slurs (Brown, 2020, p. xvii).

Pianists' legato

For pianists, a true legato involved the slight overholding of one note into the next—a technique essential on pre-modern pianos with relatively fast tonal decay. For sequences of notes forming a stable harmony (for example, a broken chord), holding the notes down (also called finger pedal or legatissimo) to create special resonance with or without the sustaining pedal was recommended as it had been for earlier keyboards (Milchmeyer, 1797, Trans. Rhein, 1993, pp. 18–19). These practices continued in piano playing into the Modern era (Peres Da Costa, 2016, p. 24) and are still used by some pianists today.

Slurs over a few notes and slurred pairs

Throughout the Romantic era, performers generally understood slurs over a small number of notes (two, three, or four) as signaling a slight tonal emphasis on the first note followed by diminuendo, the last note often shortened in piano playing (Brown, 2020, p. xiv). Slurred pairs of equal-valued notes could signal agogic accentuation (lengthening) of the first note and shortening of the second, as already recommended in the mid-eighteenth century (Peres Da Costa, 2020, pp. 133–134). Both practices continued to be used until the 1950s, after which they were generally abandoned. Since the rise of HIP, the first practice has come back into vogue, but few musicians engage with the rhythmic nuancing of slurred pairs.

Altering and adding slurs

Romantic performers had little compunction in adding slurs (among other things), or changing slurring patterns to suit musical goals. This is exemplified in the annotations by Spohr's pupil Ferdinand David (b. 1810) to the solo violin part of the first movement from Beethoven's Violin Concerto Op. 61 (Figure 17.1). Such practices became less acceptable in the Modern era.

FIGURE 17.1. Excerpt from Beethoven's Violin Concerto Op. 61, first movement, annotated by Ferdinand David (http://mhm.hud.ac.uk/chase/view/pdf/2122/1/).

Articulation

Staccato

Romantic composers used staccato dots and strokes (dashes) in individual ways according to musical context and requirements, generally to indicate shortened (sources give different lengths), separated, or accented notes (Brown, 2020, p. xxi).

Portato

In the first half of the nineteenth century, *portato* (slurs over staccato dots or dashes) signaled that each note be held almost full length with a pulsing effect (pressure) in singing, string, wind, and clavichord playing. While not possible to effect on the piano in this way, portato could alternatively imply an expressive separation playing the melody note very slightly after the accompaniment (Adam, 1804, quoted in Peres Da Costa, 2012, pp. 70–71), or in a chordal texture a very swift arpeggiation while holding the notes down for the length that the portato articulation requires (Moscheles, 1827, quoted in Peres Da Costa, 2012, pp. 111–112). Later in the century, portato was sometimes indicated with tenuto lines instead of staccato under slurs.

Tenuto

The word *tenuto* or the horizontal *tenuto line* instructed the performer to hold notes for full length and/or to make a very slight accent (Brown, 2020, p. xx). In the late-nineteenth century, some composers notated tenuto lines with dots to indicate holding notes for about half length.

Non-legato

For Romantic performers, an articulation something between legato and staccato (inherited from eighteenth-century practice) was also a choice, and occasionally indicated by composers (Brown, 1999, pp. 186–199).

In the early-twentieth century, Bartók provided explanations for various articulation signs (Table 17.1), which might serve as a model for their interpretation in Modern-era repertoire (Fischer, 1995, p. 288).

String bowing

From the beginning of the Romantic era until the early-twentieth century, string players (especially chamber and orchestral) in the Austro-German and Franco-Belgian traditions employed a predominantly on-string bowing style even in energetic passages marked with short or staccato notes. The upper half of the bow (from the middle to the tip) was much more employed than today. Broad legato was achieved with continuous bowstrokes, *detaché* in the middle of the bow, and *martelé* (hammered) toward the tip. Elastic strokes (like the French *sautillé*) in which the bow comes almost off the

Table 17.1. Transcription (by the author) of Fischer's table of signs and explanations drawn from the preface to the 1916 Rozsnyai edition (ed. Bartók) of *The Notebook for Anna Magdalena Bach.*

▼ ▼ ▼	Sharp staccato (staccatissimo), implying a certain accentuation and stronger tone color
● ● ●	The regular staccato, whereby the sounding of the note ranges from the shortest in value to one-half the value of the note
⌒••••	Portamento (portato), whereby the tones must be permitted to sound almost up to half of the note value in conjunction with a certain special coloring
▬•▬•▬•	The symbol for half-shortening (the tones should sound longer than half of the note value)
▬ ▬ ▬	The tenuto symbol above individual notes signifies that they must be held for their entire note value; when above each note of a group, that we must permit the notes to sound throughout their entire note value if possible, without linking them to one another
⌒	The well-known legato symbol, which we are also using, in the case of legato parts, for marking the phrase for lack of another symbol
sf	The strongest accentuation
∧	Accentuation still forceful enough
>	The weak accentuation
▬ ▬ ▬	The tenuto symbol above the different tones of the legato parts signifies delicately emphasizing the tone by way of a different tone coloring

string, but the hair remains in contact, were achieved a third of the way down the bow in moderately fast tempi and toward the tip for faster tempi (Brown, 1999, pp. 265–281). Bounced or jumping bow effects (*spiccato, saltato*) were employed almost exclusively by Franco-Belgian soloists in the second half of the nineteenth century. In 1887, the violinist Schröder explained that the bounced (light) bow that "has spread particularly from the newer French School is now an indispensable bowstroke for every violinist." In the "old Italian School and particularly in the German up to Louis Spohr," passages considered for the bounced bow were played "with short on-string bowing at the point" (Schröder, 1887, quoted in Brown, 1999, 273). By 1900, saltato was, according to modern taste, "absolutely indispensable" ["gar nicht zu entbehren ist"] for Classical works (for example Mozart) "where light grace and sparkling humour predominate" ["wo leichte Grazie und prikelnder Humor vorherrschend sind"], even though this was not known in Mozart's day (Jokisch, 1900, p. 141). By the middle of the twentieth century, spiccato was considered indispensable for passages marked staccato in *piano* or *forte*— particularly in Mozart's string music (Dounias, 1958, p. ix). At present, off-the-string strokes are generally used (even in HIP circles) in faster movements, for lively passage work, and wherever staccato is indicated in repertoire from the eighteenth century onwards.

Vibrato

In the Romantic era, singers, string, and wind players (including clarinettists) used vibrato (tremolo)—"the frequency modulation of fundamental frequency" (Chi-Ching Shih et al, 2017, p. 3) sparingly (like an expressive ornament) to color or to emphasize particular notes (Brown, 1999, 529–557; Milsom 2012; Toft, 2000 and 2013; Sarah Potter, 2014). The famous singing teacher García recommended it for depicting sentiments "of a poignant character" (anguish, anger, revenge, and the like), to be used with great moderation, warning that its exaggerated use would become "fatiguing and ungraceful" (García, 1857, p. 69). Spohr explains that vibrato use is guided by the best singers of his day who use it in "passionate passages," strongly to mark accents *sf* and >, and to animate and strengthen long sustained notes. He defines four types of vibrato in varying speeds (Figure 17.2): quick, slow, gradually increasing, and gradually decreasing (Spohr, 1833, vol. 2, p. 162), and his annotations of it in measures 1–26 of the second movement from his Ninth Violin Concerto Op. 55 (Figure 17.3) are telling about the sparseness of its use (Spohr, c. 1834, vol. 3, p. 212).

Notably, vibrato is not indicated in measures 1–4, probably because the music is soft and delicate. And it is also conspicuously missing in measures 21–25, very likely to enhance a dark tonal effect, which Spohr indicates by asking for the passage to be played entirely on one string ("sopra una corda"), in this case the G string. It is not indicated on many other notes including some on which it would be possible, and not on smaller-value notes. Table 17.2 lists where vibrato is notated including the type (speed) and probable intended effect. It is indicated on a total of eleven notes over twenty-five measures.

Spohr's advice is representative of the Austro-German tradition until the death of Joachim's favorite student Soldat (b. 1863) (Brown, 1999; Milsom 2003; Wilson, 2015), and of the Franco-Belgian tradition until at least the third quarter of the nineteenth century, if not a little later (Yeadon & Peres Da Costa, 2020). Recordings of the oldest generation, for example, Patti and indeed Joachim (accessible on YouTube), demonstrate a similar application of vibrato to Spohr in terms of frequency and variation of speed. The undulation of their vibrato is generally very narrow—like a quiver (in the case of string players, produced by the finger rather than the wrist or lower arm) (Philip, 1992, p. 103).

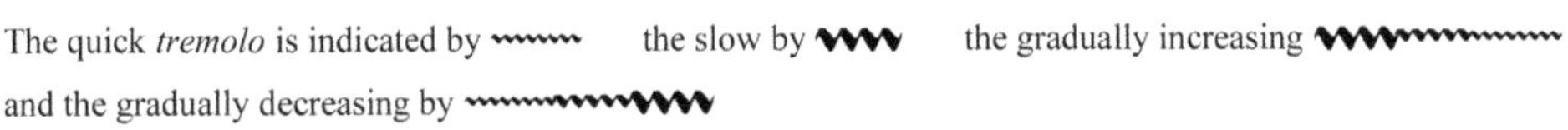

The quick *tremolo* is indicated by 〰〰〰   the slow by 〰〰   the gradually increasing 〰〰〰〰〰 and the gradually decreasing by 〰〰〰〰〰

FIGURE 17.2. Spohr's explanation of four types of vibrato (Spohr, 1833, vol. 2, p. 162).

FIGURE 17.3. Spohr's annotations of vibrato in the second movement of his Ninth Violin Concerto, Op. 55 (Spohr, 1833, vol. 3, p. 212).

Table 17.2. The places, speed, and probable intended effect of Spohr's vibrato signs annotated in the Adagio from of his Ninth Violin Concerto, Op. 55.

Bar	Note position	Speed	Intended intensification or emphasis
5	i	gradually increasing	long note matching the sudden shift to a high register and notated crescendo
6	i	quick	note at the height of the phrase marked *f*
8	i	gradually increasing	long note in tandem with an increase of dynamic from *pp* to *f*
9	ii	fast	highest note in the phrase
10	i	fast	dissonant note
13	i	gradually increasing	long note matching a notated crescendo
13	ii	fast	highest note within a notated crescendo
14	i	fast	long note marked *fz* at the height of a notated crescendo
15	iv	fast	short note marked *fz*
18	ii	fast	sudden high note marked *f* at the height of a crescendo
20	i	gradually increasing	high note marked *f*

By contrast, the vibrato generally employed in modern mainstream classical music performance today tends to be both slower in speed and wider in undulation. Significantly, Soldat recorded Spohr's Adagio in 1920. Her style of vibrato mimics Joachim's and she remains more or less faithful to Spohr's annotations, adding it in only a few other places (Milsom, 2012).

In the late nineteenth century, some singers and particularly Franco-Belgian string players used a more systematic vibrato (though still in the main fast in speed and narrow in undulation)—promoted by Belgian violinist Massart (b. 1811), who taught Kriesler, Ysaÿe, Wieniawski, and others (Milsom, 2013). With younger violinists (including Flesch, Kreisler, Hubermann, and Heifetz) in the 1920s and 1930s, vibrato intensity became more diverse including a wider and slower vibrato to complement differing emotional contexts in the music. (Leech-Wilkinson, CHARM, https://charm.rhul.ac.uk/studies/chapters/chap5.html#par10; Phillip, 1992, pp. 99–108). By the 1950s, a rich, sensual, and more or less continuous vibrato (generally unvarying in speed), particularly in singing and string playing, came to be considered essential for sound production and projection.

The influence of the HIP movement since the 1970s has encouraged a diversification of practices. A more ornamental application of vibrato (of varying intensities) has been adopted in wide-ranging repertoire up to the late nineteenth century in both the HIP and mainstream classical music arenas. These include instrumental soloists, chamber and orchestral ensembles, individual singers, and some vocal ensembles and choirs. But, in operatic repertoire and lieder, the use of a conspicuously continuous vibrato remains trenchant.

Portamento

Portamento, the audible shifting (sliding) between two adjacent notes, was a particularly expressive feature of Romantic performance in singing, string, and, to some extent, wind playing, which continued on into the Modern and post-Modern eras, albeit with substantially altered characteristics. Portamento is mentioned in written sources as early as the seventeenth century and with increasing frequency during the eighteenth century. Despite warnings against its use (other than occasionally by soloists), for example by Reichardt in 1776, portamento was becoming fairly widespread, even in orchestral playing (Brown, 1999, pp. 558–563). By the nineteenth century, many written sources recommend it to enhance smooth connection (legato) sounding the intermediate intervals between two slurred notes and to increase emotional effect between intervals of large or stepwise movement. In singing, García advises that the portamento occupies "the last portion of the note quitted," that its speed depends "on the kind of expression required," and that it assists "in equalizing the registers, timbres and power of the voice" (García, 1857, p. 13). He notes that it can sound: (i) "from weak to strong" ["du faible au fort"]; (ii) "from strong to weak" ["du fort au faible"]; (iii) "weak or strong" ["faible ou fort"]; and, (iv) "in different ways whether it be ascending or descending" ["de ces différentes manières, soit en montant, soit en descendant"] (García, 1847, p. 29).

In string playing, portamento was employed to preserve the tone quality of a melody by shifting position on the same string instead of conveniently crossing to a new string. Most effective for music in slower tempos, the portamento shift (slide) itself was often louder than the arrival note and was varied in terms of speed and weight (thickness of sound). The weight, and therefore the audibility, depended largely on the speed of the shift and the music's tempo. It could be used to increase the effect of crescendo, emphasize melodically or harmonically important notes, and give special color to the interval of a falling third. It was used equally for ascending and descending intervals (Wilson, 2015, pp. 256–258).

Nineteenth-century woodwind and brass players occasionally employed portamento, particularly between intervals of a semitone, but its use depended largely on the type of instrument and on whether the key mechanism (in the case of woodwinds) would permit it (Brown, 1999, pp. 573–574).

Patti's recordings serve as models for the application of portamento in singing in a nineteenth-century manner across different genres. In Mozart's "Voi che sapete" from *Le nozze di Figaro* K. 492, for example, portamenti can be heard frequently with a flexibility that is beautiful and touching. She, like the Italian castrato Moreschi (b. 1858), employed it between notes on different syllables, which appears to accord with instructions of D. Corri (1810, 8, quoted in Brown, 1999, pp. 566–567) handed down from the eighteenth century. These are the "anticipation grace" (sounding the second syllable's note with the first syllable very slightly before its notated arrival point), and the "leaping grace" (sounding the first syllable's note or another note concordant with the second syllable's harmony at the beginning of the second syllable). Both also employ portamento between notes on the same syllable (Brown, 1999, pp. 566–574).

Nineteenth-century instrumentalists imitated the portamento of singers, and two main types of portamento emerged. The violinist Flesch (1923, vol. 1, p. 30) coined terms for these. The A-Portamento involved sliding on the initial note ("Anfangsnote"), and the E-Portamento sliding on the second ("Endfinger") note. These were translated to B-portamento ("Beginning note") and the L-portamento ("Last finger") (Flesch, Trans. Martens, 1924, vol. 1, p. 30). Spohr explained the B-portamento (Figure 17.4) as "moving forward the first finger of the first tone, until the finger of the second tone can fall on its place" (Spohr, c. 1834, vol. 2, p. 107). This type remained the popular choice of Austro-German string players until the death of Joachim and his students. The L-portamento (Figure 17.5), sliding "with the finger of the high tone" (Spohr, c. 1834, vol. 2, p. 107), was a practice that the Austro-Germans up to Joachim advised was to be steadfastly avoided. However, Joachim sometimes used L-portamento, and it was the preference of Franco-Belgian string players. Flesch emphasized that "among the great violinists of our day"

FIGURE 17.4. Spohr's pictorial explanation of the B-portamento (Spohr, 1833, vol. 2, p. 106).

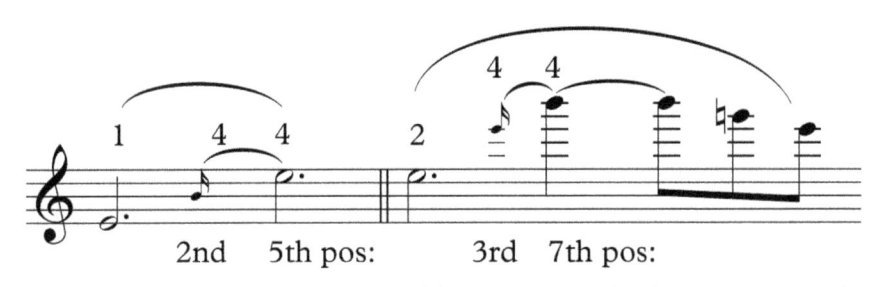

FIGURE 17.5. Spohr's pictorial explanation of the L-portamento (Spohr, 1833, vol. 2, p. 107).

from Ysaÿe onwards "there is not one who does not more or less frequently use the L-portamento (Flesch, Trans. Martens, 1924, vol. 1, p. 30).

In the mid-nineteenth century, the Franco-Belgian violin pedagogue De Bériot developed three symbols (Figure 17.6) encapsulating the varying speeds of the L-portamento to achieve a spectrum of effects from lively and light to tender, plaintive, sorrowful, and heartbreaking (Brown, 1999, p. 579, Peres Da Costa and Yeadon, 2020, pp. 6–7).

Recordings show that older and younger generations of musicians continued to employ portamento to great expressive effect well into the twentieth century. Patti used it equally in lieder, folk song, and opera. String players including Joachim (and Soldat), Sarasate, Ysaÿe, Kreisler, Heifetz, Flesch, and Austro-German and Franco-Belgian string quartets used it in repertoire spanning the eighteenth and nineteenth centuries. It is also a feature of German, French, and English orchestral recordings until the mid-twentieth century (Leech-Wilkinson, CHARM, https://charm.rhul.ac.uk/studies/chapters/chap5.html; Phillip, 1992, pp. 143–178). By this time, it was almost impossible on woodwind instruments with complex key systems, but some brass players continued to use it for special effect. Listen, for example, to the saxophone and trombone solos in Ravel's *Bolero* in a 1930 recording with the *Orchestre de L'Association de Concerts Lamoureux* conducted by Ravel himself (accessible on Spotify).

In the second half of the twentieth century, portamento was discouraged and went largely out of fashion in string playing, purportedly due to a change in pedagogical approach. However, in singing, portamento has remained an expressive device particularly in opera, though less so in lieder performance. Surprisingly, portamento has not generally been re-adopted in singing or instrumental performance by the HIP movement (Potter, 2006, p. 523), though in recent times some scholarly musicians have been experimenting with its use in Romantic repertoire (see, e.g., the performance of Schumann's *Dichterliebe* by tenor Koen van Stade and the author, accessible at https://www.sydney.edu.au/music/our-research/research-areas/artistic-research/reinvigorating-nineteenth-century-performance.html).

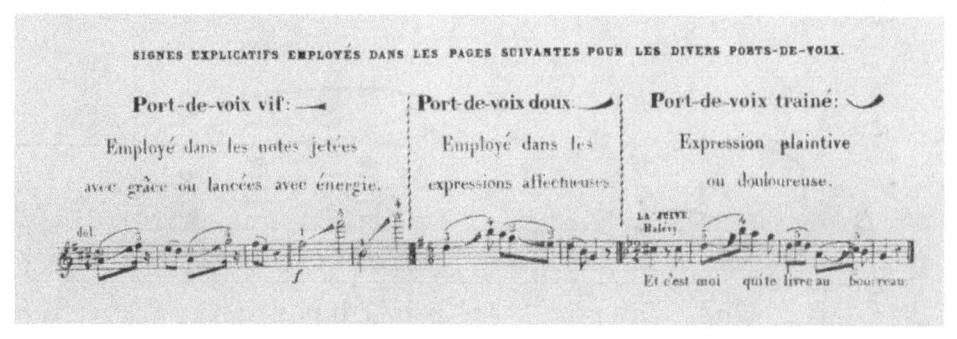

FIGURE 17.6. De Bériot's explanations of three types of portamento (De Bériot, 1858, vol. 3, p. 215).

Asynchrony and arpeggiation

Asynchrony

Romantic-era pianists often heightened the expressivity of melody notes through asynchrony—dislocation between melody notes and accompaniment (playing one hand after the other, usually melody note before accompaniment, or sometimes the reverse). This technique was handed down from seventeenth-century French keyboard playing, and earlier lute and guitar playing (Peres Da Costa, 2012, pp. 56–57. F. Couperin prescribes the *suspension* in harpsichord playing (with a special sign) as a way of intimating dynamic nuance, explaining that its use "in those places where the bowed instruments would increase [swell] their tone [. . .] by a contrary effect, seems to produce this desired result [en sorte que dans les occasions ou les instrumens à archet enflent leurs sons, la suspension de ceux du clavecin semble, par un éffet contraire, retracer au l'oreille la chose souhaitée] (F. Couperin, 1713, 16). The delay itself created an agogic accent that could be varied in length according to context and need, which in combination with dynamic nuance gave rise to a wide palette of expression and color. This method of emphasizing melody notes, especially those in the higher range, was particularly useful on pre-modern pianos, which often had a lighter, less powerful treble (Peres Da Costa, 2012, pp. 41–72). The pianist Thalberg recommended it as a great aid to singing at the piano, particularly in "a slow melody written in notes of long duration [. . .] above all on the first delivery of each measure, or at the commencement of each period or phrase" [Dans un mélodie lent écrite en notes de longues durée, il est d'un bon effet, surtout au premier temps de chaque mesure ou en començant chaque période de phrase"] (Thalberg, 1853, series 1, unpaginated 2). It was similarly described at the beginning of the twentieth century in the Leschetizky method (Brée, 1902, pp. 72–73) and indeed can be heard in the recordings of Leschetizky, Reinecke, and Saint-Saëns, and a later generation of pianists, revealing the wide-ranging contexts of its use that were not described in written sources (Peres Da Costa, 2012, pp. 72–100; Brown and Peres Da Costa 2020, p. 5). It continued to be employed by many pianists until the 1950s, and by a few until the early twenty-first century.

Arpeggiation

Allied with asynchrony, un-notated chordal arpeggiation was an equally important means of expression for pianists, guitarists, and harpists. Written sources make it clear that for much of the nineteenth century it was the default mode of playing chords, especially in slow movements. Thalberg stated that "The chords which carry a song or melody to the higher notes should always be played in arpeggio fashion, but very tight and almost together ["Les accords qui porteront un chant à la note supérieure devront toujours s'arpéger, mais très serrés, presque plaques"] (Thalberg, 1853, unpaginated 2). Tellingly, Hummel explained that on Viennese or German pianos "Full chords [. . .] are mostly broken very quickly, and are far more effective thus than if the notes were played together with the same degree of strength" ["Volle Akkorde werden [. . .] meist ganz rasch gebrochen vorgetragen, und wirken so weit mehr, als wenn die Töne zusammen auf einmal noch so stark angeschlagen werden'] (Hummel, 1827, vol. 3, p. 454). And Czerny gave specific rules for its use (Czerny, 1839, vol. 3, pp. 55–56). Given Hummel's, Czerny's, and Thalberg's pedigrees and their close connections with European centres such as Vienna, Paris, and London, the implications for the use of arpeggiation in the piano music of Mozart, Haydn, Beethoven, Schubert, and many other Classical and Romantic composers are clear.

The guitar methods of Molino (1813), Pelzer (1833), and Carcassi (1858) promote the use of chordal arpeggiation. Carcassi advises that chords are always arpeggiated swiftly and that in slow movements arpeggiations are made more slowly to suit character (Carcassi, 1858, p. 15). Arpeggiation of all chords (even when not marked) was already recommended for single-action-pedal harp playing by Meyer (1763 and 1774) to produce a more harmonious and gentle effect than if all notes are played together (Kanemitsu-Nagasawa, 2018, p. 42). This practice continued to be advocated in the nineteenth century by Butler Challoner, who warned that arpeggiation must be always observed "as the effect would be greatly injured if all the Strings were pulled exactly at once" (Challoner, 1816, p. 3). Further to this, Desargus explains that "when the musical expression requires it, even a chord of two-notes should almost always be arpeggiated" ["les accords composée seulement de deux notes ne doivent s'arpéger qu'autant que l'expression semble l'exiger"] (Desargus, 1821, p. 51), a practice also supported by Boscha, who explained that in slow movements, because the harp is unable to preserve the duration of long notes, arpeggiation is essential (Boscha, 1826, p. 7). Harp arpeggiation continued until at least the first half of the twentieth century, as evidenced, for example, in the recording by the French composer and harpist H. Renié (b. 1886) of her own composition *Contemplation* c. 1930 (accessible on YouTube) in which she used arpeggiation a great deal more than is notated.

Romantic pianists, guitarists, and harpists used arpeggiation:

(i)   to give special prominence to melody notes by delaying them;
(ii) to enhance texture by providing a cushion of sound, to prevent harshness when chords were to be accented; and
(iii) to produce a certain fire, energy, and brilliance.

In respect of the third point, De Bériot explained that "many notes played together [in a chord] do not produce, overall, an effect as brilliant as when a small interval is put between them, however small the interval" ["plusieurs notes frappées ensemble ne produisent pas à beaucoup près un effet aussi brillant qu'en mettant entr'elles un petit intervalle, quelque minime qu'il soit"] (De Bériot, 1858, part 2, p. 86).

More generally, it was recommended for main beats, chords of long duration, and whenever there was an important melody note or harmony, but to be avoided on chords of very short value or those marked staccato (Peres Da Costa, 2012, pp. 102–125; Brown and Peres Da Costa, 2020, pp. 3–5).

Importantly, certain terminology and signs inspired arpeggiation. P. A. Corri explained that "When the words 'con espressione, con Anima or Dolce etc.' are mark'd at a passage, it signifies that the appogiando [arpeggio] must be particularly and often used, and made as long as possible" (P. A. Corri, 1810, p. 77, quoted in Peres Da Costa, 2012, p. 124). And Moscheles advised its use for chords marked portato (Moscheles, 1827, book 1, p. 6; see also Peres Da Costa, 2012, pp. 111–112), a practice also implied by Desargus (1821, p. 51) in harp playing.

At the turn of the twentieth century, recordings reveal the plethora of ways in which performers employed arpeggiation that were not captured in written sources (Peres Da Costa, 2012, pp. 129–139). Tellingly, Reinecke, Leschetizky, and Saint-Saëns—the earliest pianists on record—use it the most, but it is present in the playing of younger generations until the 1950s, albeit in decreasingly conspicuous ways.

Asynchrony and arpeggiation were used in tandem with, and seen as equally important to, the practice of playing melody-notes at a higher volume level than the accompaniment to bring them out of the texture. Yet, there is little engagement with these two practices in piano, guitar, and harp circles (including HIP) at present; in general, the modernist aesthetic of vertical synchrony (alignment) still exerts its strong hold.

Dynamics, accentuation, and accent signs

Dynamics and accent marks

From the Romantic era onwards, dynamic and accent markings in scores began to increase in scope and detail; however, composers still expected performers to enhance the musical effect according to their artistic response within the boundaries of good taste. Milchmeyer's descriptions in 1797 of the effect of the various dynamics on the listener might serve as inspiration for their addition in Romantic repertoire (Table 17.3).

Accentuation

Until the end of the nineteenth century, accentuation was generally theorized under two broad categories:

(i) metrical accentuation connected with the metrical or measure structure within the various time signatures and "integral to the relationship between melodic figuration and harmony change and the positioning of dissonance and resolution"

(ii) rhetorical, oratorical, or expressive accentuation analogous to the accentuation in speech, which would often match that of metrical accentuation or else provide a higher more sophisticated level of accentuation (Brown, 1999, pp. 8–28).

Table 17.3. Milchmeyer's descriptions of dynamics (Rhein, 1993, pp. 112–120)

pianissimo	"the listener imagines hearing, at night under a clear, calm sky, from a distance of some hundred paces away, a conversation between two people"
piano	as with pianissimo, "though the expression must indeed be a little less extreme, as if the conversation were some 50 paces closer"
dolce	"indicates a conversation whose quality is gentleness and tenderness, and serves for the expression of sweet melancholy, of love, and ecstasy"
mezzo forte	"calls for the expression of a lively conversation, in which one speaks his words with more emphasis than usual"
forte	"does not express gentle emotions, but rather strong passions, defiance, and the like; one can also characterize the joy of the rabble with it"
fortissimo	"indicates violent passions, such as anger, or confused excitement, clash of weapons, the noise of a crowd of people, or of a field army"
crescendo	"is like the approach of several people, conversing amongst themselves, or like steadily approaching military music"
diminuendo, decrescendo, smorzando	"hearing the conversation of several people who are continually moving farther away"

In practice, nineteenth- and early-twentieth-century performers were expected to contribute much beyond what was notated by the composer to achieve a "beautiful" performance. Accentuation was implied by: certain symbols; articulations including among other things small groups of slurred notes; dissonant notes (for example, appoggiaturas) and chromatic notes; high and low notes, particularly if separated by a large interval from the preceding note; longer notes within a phrase; and syncopated notes (Brown, 1999, pp. 30–50).

Accent signs

Nineteenth-century sources describe gradations of accents implied by standard symbols (Brown, 2020, pp. xvi–xviii; Kim, 2012; see also Bartók discussion earlier in this chapter), which, however, will have varied to some extent from composer to composer:

(i) *sf* might be seen as the strongest (sharpest) of accents given to a single note, but will vary according to overall dynamic;

(ii) ^ is something slightly less than *sf*;

(iii) *rinzforzando* (*rf*) seems to have been used by some to mean an accent less powerful than *sf* and by others to swell a few notes or bring them out of the texture before returning to the previous dynamic;

(iv) *fp* signifies a less intense accent than *sf* and ^, and can be taken as indicating *forte* followed immediately by *piano*;

(v) repeated *fs* or *ffs* probably indicate equal force on each note marked thus;

(vi) > is perhaps the least intense accent and might also indicate a slight agogic accentuation;

(vii) < > could, in addition to dynamic nuance and according to context, indicate a gentle and/or agogic accent of a single tone, or, when placed across several notes, a speeding up toward and lingering at the apex, followed by a return to tempo afterward;

(viii) tenuto (both the term and the sign ‾), which initially meant holding a note for full length, but by the end of the nineteenth century could imply length and emphasis.

Rhythmic modification

Rhythmic flexibility was considered an essential element of "beautiful" performance throughout the Romantic era and to a great extent until the mid-twentieth century. Singers and instrumentalists gave rhetorically expressive deliveries by positioning notes more flexibly than indicated in the notation. This enhanced word stress or, in the case of purely instrumental music, helped to deliver the notes as if there were words, as well as to provide energy and feeling appropriate to individual musical thoughts.

Rhythmic freedom could be achieved in multiple ways:

(i) lengthening certain important notes in a phrase at the expense of others, which might be shortened in compensation;

(ii) enacting the practice of *notes inégales* usually associated with earlier music by playing unequally a succession of equal-valued notes (eighth and sixteenth notes), creating effects ranging from gently lilting (long-short) to triplet-like or back-dotted rhythms;

(iii) over- and under-dotting dotted figures;

(iv) making an agogic accent on the first of a slurred pair of equal-valued notes and shortening the second; and

(v) emphasizing single notes through agogic accentuation.

Such changes could be made on a small scale as local changes within a measure, or on a larger scale affecting multiple measures at a time.

Rhythmic alteration was closely associated with bel canto singing (emulated in instrumental performance) in which the singer would deliver the words rhetorically (moving the syllables earlier or later than notated) to underline the meaning and impact of the text, while the accompaniment remained "strictly" in time. This duality, already mentioned in the early-eighteenth century, was often ascribed to performances by Mozart, Chopin, and others (Hudson, 1994, pp. 43–65 and 189–197; Peres Da Costa, 2012, pp. 193–194 and 236–237; Brown, 1999, pp. 396–411).

Recordings from the first half of the twentieth century, particularly by the oldest generation of musicians such as Patti, Joachim, Reinecke, Saint-Saëns, and Leschetizky, reveal great flexibility with regard to rhythm (Peres Da Costa, 2012, pp. 191, 204–220, 223–224, 226–233). This is also true of string quartets and orchestras. For example, in the second movement of Beethoven's Fifth Symphony by the Berlin Philharmonic under Nikisch (1912), the woodwinds play a sequence based on the main theme (bars 127–143) with noticeable inequality of rhythm. Kreisler's and Zimbalist's (and their ensembles') inequality in the first and third movements of the Concerto for Two Violins in D minor BWV 1043 by J. S. Bach (1915) is striking, at times foreshadowing the "do-be-do" rhythms of jazz style that are demonstrated in the 1937 Eddie South and Stéphan Grapelli performance of the work accompanied by Django Reinhardt on guitar (both accessible on YouTube)

Often when the musical texture is melody against a simple accompaniment, rhythmic flexibility engenders particular expressive tension due to the asynchrony that occurs between the parts. A telling example of this is the 1935 rendition by Bazelaire and Philipp of measures 7–11 from the second movement of Saint-Saëns' Cello Sonata No. 1, Op. 32 (Peres Da Costa, 2012, pp. 245–246). Another is the opening sequence of the "Scène" from Tchaikovsky's *Swan Lake* in the 1933 recording by the London Philharmonic under Sir John Barbirolli (accessible on YouTube). The oboe soloist Goosens's flexibility in playing the haunting melody is extraordinary by today's standards. It provides a glimpse of what many performances would have sounded like in the pre-Modern era. In other recordings, it is clear that the accompaniment is not played absolutely strictly in time, though nevertheless a sense of the pulse prevails (Peres Da Costa, 2012, pp. 242–244). Remnants of a nineteenth-century style of rhythmic alteration were still heard as late as the 1950s. For example, the pianist Freund plays with lilting inequality in her 1953 recording of the slow movement from Brahms's Op. 5 Piano Sonata (Peres Da Costa, 2012, p. 249).

Since the 1950s, modernist aesthetics have dictated that notated rhythms be followed fairly closely. This led to a more rhythmically-rigid style of delivery in general in the second half of the twentieth century. More recently, some performers have begun to experiment with a freer approach to rhythm in certain musical styles and genres.

Tempo

Terms as tempo modifiers

As in previous eras, there were specific tempo conventions in the Romantic era, some inherited, some newly developing, and some associated with particular composers (Brown, 1999 pp. 336–372). Additionally, some terms were used to indicate a modification of tempo. In the first half of the nineteenth century, *amoroso* sometimes indicated a slowing down of tempo. Throughout the century, *sostenuto* meant several things including a fairly slow tempo and to take a slower tempo, while *cantabile* could indicate a slow tempo or a change of tempo or a singing style (Brown, 1998, pp. 372–374; Brown, 2020, pp. xvii–xviii).

Tempo modification

The unnotated modification of tempo (often quite noticeably) was, like rhythmic flexibility, absolutely essential to a "beautiful" performance in the Romantic era and by many musicians until the middle of the twentieth century. Performers modified tempo to enhance various musical effects (Peres Da Costa, 2012, pp. 251–304; Brown, 1999, pp. 375–395; Hudson, 1994 300–355) for example by:

(i)   getting noticeably faster with crescendo and slower with diminuendo;
(ii) broadening to underline a mood change or to create a special nuance including in music marked *sostenuto*, *espressivo*, *con anima* and so on; and
(iii) lingering on multiple notes or measures encircled by a double hairpin sign < >.

In this respect, Czerny advises that "there occurs almost in every line [of music] some notes or passages, where a small and almost imperceptible relaxation or acceleration of the movement is necessary, to embellish the expression and increase the interest" (Czerny, 1839, vol. 3, p. 31).

Frequency of tempo change

Some idea of the frequency with which performers in the first half of the nineteenth century changed tempo can be gauged from Hummel's advice to students in measures 120–215 of the first movement from his A minor Piano Concerto, Op. 85 (Hummel, 1828 vol. 3, pp. 43–47). Over the 95-bar sequence, Hummel annotates nine extra instructions indicating tempo modifications, which enhance the music's changes of mood. In general, when the texture is melody with accompaniment, the tempo is more relaxed than when fiery or energetic passage work is presented (Table 17.4). While Hummel, like Czerny, counsels performers not to carry to excess the degree of tempo change, this should not be taken to mean that changes were intended to be subtle in the sense that is understood now. Without audible evidence it is impossible to know how he expected these to sound in reality (Peres Da Costa, 2012, pp. 288–295).

Frequent tempo modification is discernible in recordings of nineteenth-century-trained singers and instrumentalists including in solo, chamber, and orchestral repertoire, but these often sound radical compared with present-day practices. For example, the first movement of Beethoven's Fifth Symphony Op. 67 in the first known recording (1910) by the Berlin *Grosse Odeon Streich Orchester* conducted by Kark (b. 1869) demonstrates wild tempo accelerations and retardations, which may or may not be similar to what Beethoven expected, but certainly enhance the dramatic content of this particular movement. In this respect, it is interesting to ponder the cellist Becker's (b. 1863) remarks about tempo modification to underline the narrative: "Animato is the marking for that feeling that makes us talk faster when relating events that affect us very strongly [. . .] Meno or più tranquillo, on the other hand, should check the flow of the narrative; it can be used either as a calming effect, or to underline the meaning of a particular place, in order to bring out something musically significant"

Table 17.4. Hummel's annotations of tempo modification to enhance mood change in measures 120–215 of the first movement from his Piano Concerto in A minor op. 85

Measure	Hummel's added instructions	Mood of music
120	with energy (perhaps a slightly faster tempo)	suddenly fiery and accented
131	in an expressive and melodious style	return to texture of melody with accompaniment like the opening
139	from here, something quicker and more marked	fast and energetic passage work
152	somewhat slower and in a singing style	return to melody with chordal accompaniment marked *portato*
168	somewhat accelerated	a return to fast passage work
185	the middle period somewhat slower and with tender feeling	return to melody with accompaniment marked *dolce*
193	quicker and with spirit	section marked *risoluto* alternating dotted texture and fast passage work
209	somewhat relaxing in time	passage preparing for the cadenza

("Das Animato ist die Bezeichnung für die Belebung, mit der wir Begebenheiten, die uns innerlich stärker angehen, in rascherem Zeitmass erzählen [. . .] Das Meno oder Più tranquillo soll dagegen den Fluss der Erzählung aufhalten; es kann sowohl zur Beruhigung gebraucht werden, als auch um die Bedeutung einer Stelle zu unterstreichen, um etwas musikalisch Gewichtiges hervorzuheben" (Becker, 1929, p. 159).

Such means of rhetorical expressivity was steadily outlawed during the first half of the twentieth century, when "new concepts of time and rhythm which involved a far greater adherence to strict tempo" began to dominate (Hudson, 1994, p. 356). But it is clearly historically appropriate for repertoire from the nineteenth and to some extent the first half of the twentieth centuries.

Ornaments and Ornamentation

Signs

Romantic-era composers continued to use ornament signs developed in previous centuries, including appoggiaturas (grace notes), trills, turns, mordents, and slides. Some of these retained the same meaning, while others such as trills changed. Written sources vary in advice, some still advocating for an upper auxiliary-note start (as was the case for much of the eighteenth century), others for a main-note start. Beethoven is known to have used both in different contexts throughout his lifetime (Brown, 2000, pp. xxiii–xxvi). By the second half of the nineteenth century, main-note starts were normal. Ornament signs are explained in written sources by Hummel, Czerny, and others and can sometimes be matched to specific composers or, at the very least, to a specific period and place.

Fioriturae

In the first half of the nineteenth century, florid ornamental figures remained fashionable, particularly in bel canto–type writing in slow expressive movements (Brown, 1999, pp. 411–414). These gave the music an improvised feeling and could be used to portray great pathos, passion, and a host of other sentiments. Their successful performance requires high levels of skill and it seems clear that flexibility in timing was a key to making them sound natural. In this respect, Czerny expressly advises that complex *fioriturae* should be allowed to take more time than the notation suggests (Czerny, 1839, vol. 3, p. 33ff).

Improvised ornaments and improvisation

Until the early-twentieth century, it remained the fashion for performers to add simple or at times more complex ornaments or, in the same vein, to make changes to the notation to achieve melodic or rhythmic variety according to their needs and taste (Baillot, 1834, pp. 136–137). Such additions or changes were particularly appropriate when the music repeated, for example, during the repeat of the exposition of a sonata form movement or for successive occurrences of a rondo theme (Brown and Peres Da Costa, 2020, pp. 58–59). Sometimes, the ornamentation amounted to substantial re-composition, as is evidenced in the variations to an aria in Meyerbeer's opera *Robert le diable* published in the mid-nineteenth century by the French singing teacher Laure Cinti-Damoreux (b. 1801) (Figure 17.7)

FIGURE 17.7. Cinti-Damoreu's variations to an extract from Meyerbeer's *Robert le Diable* showing her own version at the top, followed by five variations (Cinti-Damoreu, 1849, p. 97).

Related to these practices was the craft of improvisation, which soloists often introduced within performances. These might be in the form of extended cadenzas in concerto movements, or extemporized preludes, interludes, and postludes within multi-movement works, an art that went on until the early-twentieth century and is being revitalized at present (Hamilton, 2007, pp. 101–138).

Ensemble practices

One interesting aspect of recordings made around the turn of the twentieth century is that parts vertically aligned in the score (be it singer with piano accompaniment or orchestra, string quartet, symphony orchestra, choirs, or the pianists' left and right hands) are often conspicuously asynchronous by today's standards. Far from being the result of a cavalier or sloppy performance style or bad technique, such asynchrony was mainly the result of artistically spontaneous performance decisions, the expressive practices of the Romantic era that give these performances their free, blustery, and volatile character.

And speaking of ensemble, it is worth noting here that recordings of choirs and choruses at the turn of the twentieth century reveal styles of performance that are at odds with "the hallmarks of the modern choral aesthetic," which favors "acute rhythmic precision, seamless vocal blend, uniform tonal production and vowel shape." Instead, Romantic choral practice as evidenced in these recordings emphasizes "declamatory diction, tonal variation between voice parts, tempo rubato, choral ornamentation, and greater audible energy per singer." Choristers even made use of portamento and other expressive sliding effects resulting in "a less-refined yet more exuberant sound scape" (Bailey, 2017).

Due to the present-day insistence on "perfect" ensemble, practices such as these might be challenging to engage with, yet they would open up new expressive possibilities that pre-Modern musicians regarded as "beautiful."

Vocal and instrumental qualities

An important aspect of engagement with performing practices in Romantic and Modern repertoire is consideration of the quality of sound that vocalists and instrumentalists employed to support their delivery. In the bel canto tradition prior to marked changes that started to take place in the third quarter of the nineteenth century, singers focused on expressivity in communicating words and melodies so that they would "forcibly appeal" to a listener's feelings (Turner, 1833, p. 183).

Messa di voce

Among the many bel canto practices that helped singers to portray feelings was the technique of swelling and dying of the voice (*messa di voce*) on individual notes, which the singing teacher Nathan (b. c. 1791) explained "makes music respond to the various passions, and passes the feeling of one mind to another" (Nathan, 1836, p. 150). Nathan went to the trouble of describing with illustrations the variety of ways in which this could be achieved (Figure 17.8). Such nuances of volume are conspicuously missing in singing practice today.

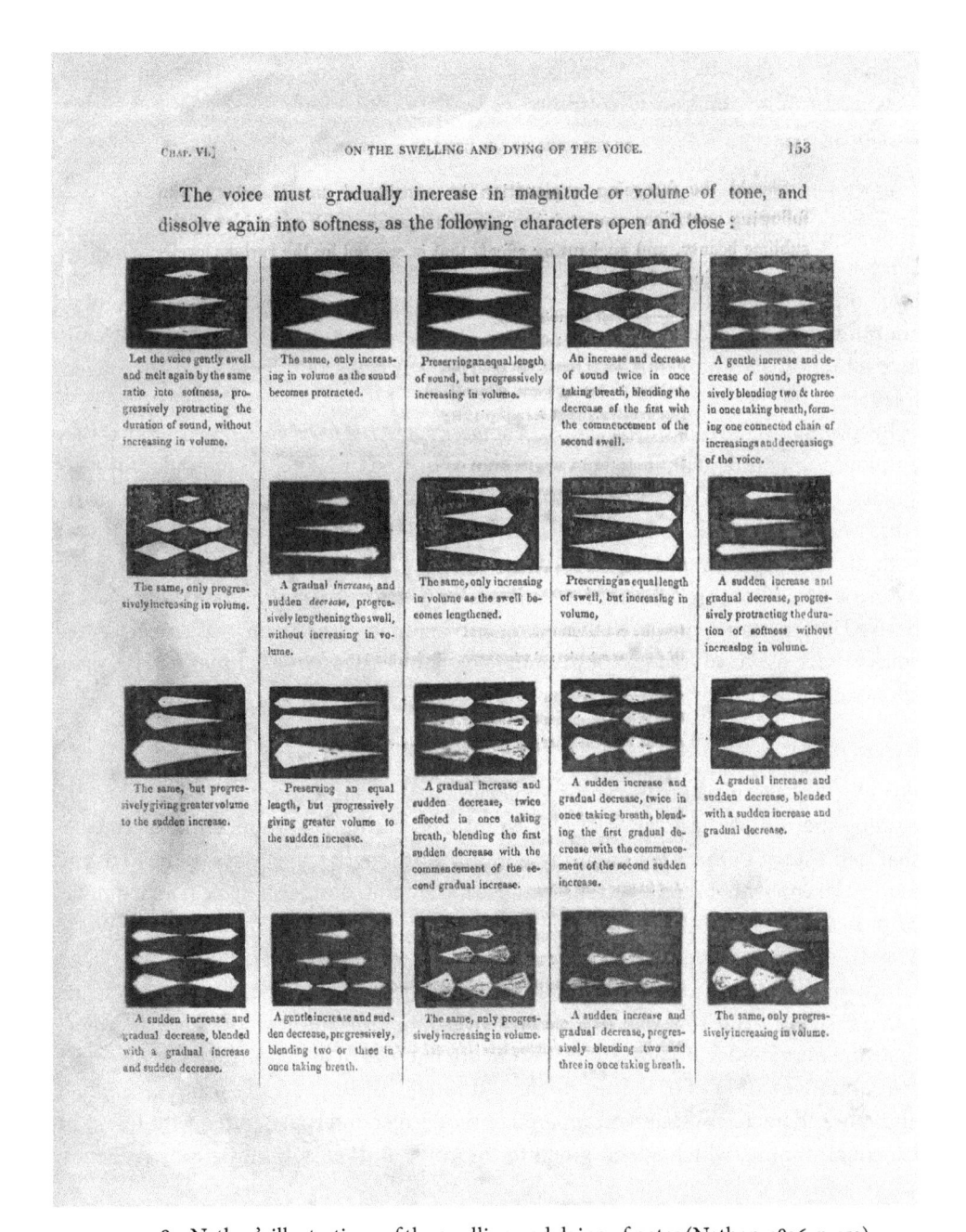

FIGURE 17.8. Nathan's illustrations of the swelling and dying of notes (Nathan, 1836, p. 153).

Modern bel canto

From the 1860s onwards, a modernist notion of bel canto steadily developed to include: (i) continual text emphasis, a practice already mentioned earlier in the century, in which all syllables receive equal weight (Kitchiner, 1821, p. 39); (ii) the "wobble" (Wood, 1927, vol. 4, p. 87), a generally wide, continuous vibrato of unvarying intensity, to maximize the richness of long, unarticulated vocal lines; and (iii) adherence to the "school of sensuously pretty voice-production" (Ffrangcon-Davies, 1905, pp. 14–16), a monochromatic approach to timbre, regardless of the emotional qualities of text and music.

Vocal projection

These notions have understandably become entrenched due to the modern concern (Potter, 2014, p. 49) for vocal projection in very large spaces, above the tonal heft of a large orchestra or grand piano—a modern phenomenon that has led to the general adoption (and staunch advocacy among vocal pedagogues) of a low larynx position to access more space and resonance and to increase energy around 3000 Hz (the singer's formant).

Recordings of the oldest generation of singers such as Patti reveal, however, that they employed a mixture of high and neutral larynx positions, much like in popular forms of singing today such as "chart pop" (Dibben, 2014, p. 120; Potter, 2014, p. 20; Toft, 2011), which naturally produces lighter, less powerful sounds than those usually associated with the use of the lowered larynx (Toft, 2000, pp. 25–26). Their singing is characterized by great flexibility through emphatically varied delivery, using multifaceted oration-derived interpretative means well documented in nineteenth-century historical written sources such as: vocal treatises, for example by Balfe (1857) and Kitchiner (1821); correspondence; concert reviews; and other information (Toft, 2000 and 2013).

Instrumental sounds

For much of the nineteenth century, instrumentalists emulated the best singers, including the use of the various practices outlined earlier, to produce interpretations that told a story. Perhaps the equivalent of the pre-Modern singer's use of the high and neutral larynx with its concomitant soundscape are the sounds of musical instruments prior to their modern standardization in the twentieth century. Until the end of World War II, string instruments were generally strung with pure gut or gut core strings, which produced both a lighter and more transparent sound at one end of the spectrum, and a raspy or gruff sound at the other. Until standardization, woodwind, and brass instruments varied from place to place and era in types of materials, sizes, joints, bore sizes, numbers of keys or valves, pitch, and range. These generally produced lighter and more characterful sounds compared to modern counterparts, often with irregular (unequal) tuning, which added much to the color and tension in the music. Pianos, too, came in varying constructions and types including concert instruments (grand pianos) and various forms of domestic instruments (for example, square pianos). In the first half of the nineteenth century, these were mainly associated with the Austro-Hungarian empire and German-speaking lands, France, and England; in the second half, the piano-making industry boomed in America and other countries. Over the course of the Romantic era, pianos evolved significantly from the lighter-sounding, wooden-framed, straight-strung instruments with varying hammer coverings, pedals (sometimes up to five or six including una corda and due corde shift, moderator, sustaining, and janissary effects), and actions (Brown and Peres Da Costa, 2020, pp. 5–8), to the more homogeneous and hefty-sounding grand piano with fully iron frame and over-stringing.

Pitch and temperament

Until the early-twentieth century, pitch varied (sometimes significantly) from city to city and country to country. Pitch has quite a significant influence on how music feels and sounds both to performers and audiences, and to some extent will influence the choice and use of expressive practices. No less important is the matter of temperament. Equal temperament in piano tuning did not become standard until the late-nineteenth century, and what was generally adopted in major centers may not reflect the choice of temperament in provincial places. Unequal temperaments will have affected the expression of music in different keys due to the varying sizes of intervals, in particular of the major and minor thirds.

The spaces of performance

In the nineteenth and early-twentieth centuries, many performances took place in spaces other than purpose-built concert halls. These included smaller spaces such as salons, rooms in grand houses and palaces, town and assembly halls, and churches. Recent studies show that the atmosphere in these spaces, their furnishings and decorative features, and, importantly, their acoustics with early reflections (sounds that the listener hears after being reflected of the rooms surfaces only once or twice) have a significant effect on performance, both physically and in the sense of feeling a deeper connection with the history of the time. It is richly rewarding to match repertoire with appropriate performing space (Peres Da Costa, Mitchell and Stephens, 2020), as a recent short documentary film—*Songs of Home: Exploring the Past through Music* (2019) focusing on nineteenth-century colonial Australian music-making—clearly demonstrates (https://sydneylivingmuseums.com.au/exhibitions/songs-home). Like the expressive practices I have outlined throughout this chapter, the consideration of performing space is a vital ingredient in approaching repertoire of the past.

PRACTICAL IMPLICATIONS:
THREE CASE STUDIES

We now turn our attention to three case studies in which I explore how various expressive practices might be applied in performance today in reaction to signals in the musical notation. These case studies are referenced with experimental recorded interpretations of the works.

Case Study 1: Tempo modification in the first movement of Beethoven's Piano Concerto No. 1, Op. 15.

In 2017, I had the opportunity to perform and record Beethoven's Piano Concerto Op. 15 (1795, revised 1800) with the Australian Haydn Ensemble using a beautiful fortepiano modeled on one by the Viennese maker Conrad Graf who made a piano for Beethoven (https://www.australianhaydn.com.au/beethovens-piano-concerto-1-3; also accessible on iTunes and Spotify). Most interpretations of this work do not experiment with the use of noticeable tempo modification. But, taking into account the character of the music, Beethoven's notation, and documented information about his own practices, suggests to me that he would have expected its use in several places.

For example, from measure 205 onwards in the first movement, Allegro con brio, character and mood can be enhanced through tempo modification, adopting Hummel's annotations in his Piano Concerto in A minor as a guide. After a very energetic passage (mm. 205–214), Beethoven suddenly changes character at measure 215 with a slurred ascending chromatic scale marked decrescendo (accompanied by strings playing a held chord pianissimo), which invites a significant slowing down (Figure 17.9). This is followed in measure 216 with four poignant repeated quarter notes marked portato during which time seems almost to stand still—an opportunity perhaps to play in as languishing a fashion as one dares. This is followed in measures 217–224 by an extraordinarily ethereal and dreamlike sequence in pianissimo dynamic, which traverses many distant harmonies and which cries out for slow arpeggiation of the chords to enhance expression. The section invited a significantly slower tempo with lingering on the important harmonies. In measure 22, the harmonic rhythm doubles in pace and Beethoven marks a crescendo, a signal that the drama is about to resume. Here the tempo might increase gradually over three measures until measure 225, where Beethoven suddenly gives the piano upward stomping quarter-note patterns marked *ben marcato*. These propel the music forward again, requiring a return to tempo for the build-up to the orchestral interlude at measure 237, heralded by the explosive cadential trill in measures 235–236.

E.E.3815

FIGURE 17.9. Beethoven, Piano Concerto, Op. 15, first movement, measures 214–237 (ed. Altmann, Eulenberg, c. 1930, p. 23).

Case Study 2: Chordal arpeggiation in Saint-Saëns' Piano Quintet Op. 14 in A minor

In 2020, the Australian-based chamber music ensemble Ironwood recorded Saint-Saëns' Piano Quintet in A minor (1855). On this recording the string players used gut-strung instruments and I used an original Paris Érard grand piano c. 1869, which is ideal for this work (Peres Da Costa & Ironwood, 2020) (https://www.abcmusic.com.au/discography/louise-farrenc-camille-saint-saëns-romantic-dreams-quintets-piano-and-strings-ironwood; also accessible on iTunes and Spotify). In preparation for this recording, I listened to Saint-Saëns' own piano playing preserved on wax disc and reproducing piano rolls. In his own music as well as in music by Chopin and Beethoven, he makes use of nineteenth-century piano practices discussed in this chapter including un-notated chordal arpeggiation. His manner of using arpeggiation is a great enhancement to character and texture and certainly accords with written evidence. In the opening of the first movement—Allegro moderato e maestoso measures 1–18 (Figure 17.10)—Saint-Saëns gives the piano sequences of powerful chords of long duration juxtaposed with sustained string unison notes of contrastingly ghostly effect. In all the recorded interpretations of this work that I have listened to, pianists play these chords with the notes strictly aligned. However, based on the evidence I decided to play each of the chords with a very quick (tight) arpeggiation, which I feel gives them a fire and energy that enhances Saint-Saëns' intended maestoso effect.

In the second movement, Andante sostenuto, Saint-Saëns again starts with solo piano, giving it a full chordal texture that supports the beautifully nostalgic melody (Figure 17.11). There can be little doubt that Saint-Saëns expected these chords to be arpeggiated in varying speeds within say a moderate range, even though he did not mark any arpeggio signs. This practice aligns with Thalberg's advice from just two years before the quintet's publication that all chords supporting a melody ought to be arpeggiated. And in any case, the term *sostenuto* might also signal its use to create a sustained texture by filling out the sound in the measure. So, I played measures 1–16 with all chords arpeggiated, varying the speeds in accordance with the length, position of the chord in the measure, the poignancy of the harmony and melody, the accentuation and the ebb and flow of dynamics, pace, and phrasing. When the theme returns in the solo piano at measure 114, Saint-Saëns marks *dolce*. Here, I took the opportunity to make the chordal arpeggiation even more poignant than at the opening, by spreading the notes even more luxuriously (slowly).

Case Study 3: Various practices in the first movement of Brahms's Piano Quartet in G minor Op. 25

In 2016, I recorded Brahms's Op. 25 Piano Quintet with Ironwood (Peres Da Costa & Ironwood, 2016) (https://www.abcmusic.com.au/discography/brahms---tones-romantic-extravagance-piano-quartet-no-1-piano-quintet; also accessible on iTunes

FIGURE 17.10. Saint-Saëns, Piano Quintet, Op. 14 in A minor, first movement, measures 1–18 (Leuchardt edition, c. 1877, p. 3).

and Spotify). For this recording the string players used gut strung instruments and I used a replica of the piano that Brahms owned and loved—a Viennese-action grand piano after J. B. Streicher and Sons (1868). Measures 1–20 of the first movement, Allegro (Figure 17.12), afforded several opportunities for us to experiment with the application of performing practices typical of Brahms and his circle. Brahms marks the opening section *espressivo*, an expression he used to encourage the use of asynchrony, chordal arpeggiation, portamento, and rhythmic and tempo modification, as evidenced in the playing and commentaries of those who knew, worked, and studied with him (Brown, Peres Da Costa, & Bennett Wadsworth, 2015). In measures 1–10, I applied noticeable asynchrony

FIGURE 17.11. Saint-Saëns, Piano Quintet, Op. 14 in A minor, second movement, measures 1–19 (Leuchardt edition, c. 1877, p. 26).

and arpeggiation on important notes in the unison texture as well as on certain important chords, to give them prominence. In measure 4, I interpreted Brahms's decrescendo hairpin to mean both decrescendo and a substantial slowing down in tempo to round off the phrase. From measures 5–10, the string players applied the Austro-German B-portamento in several places:

(i) measure 5—the descending 4th in the cello between beats 2 and 3;
(ii) measure 7—the descending 4th in the viola between beats 1 and 2;

FIGURE 17.12 Brahms, Piano Quartet in G minor, first movement measures 1–20, *Sämtliche Werke Band 8* (Leipzig: Breitkopf & Härtel, 1926–1927), pp. 69–70.

(iii) measure 8—the descending 4th in the violin and cello between beats 1 and 2; and

(iv) measure 9—the descending minor 3rd in the violin and cello between beats 3 and 4.

In measures 6–7, we interpreted Brahms's double hairpin (marked properly in the viola part) to mean a substantial lingering on the apex of the hairpin in measure 7. For the following section from measure 11, Brahms indicates *dolce*, a term that signifies both a change in sound world (through use of the soft pedal on the piano and a sweeter string tone) and a much slower expressive arpeggiation of the longer chords in measures 11 and 12.

From measure 13 onwards, Brahms's notation of slurred pairs of equal-valued notes elicited an unequal performance style as discussed in written sources and audible in early recordings. Accordingly, we lengthened the first note and correspondingly shortened the second note of each pair. In measure 17, we interpreted the crescendo-decrescendo hairpin in the violin, viola, and cello as a slight speeding up towards, and lingering at the apex, followed by a return to tempo. We repeated the effect in measure 18, even though Brahms does not mark another crescendo-decrescendo hairpin. The repetition of such nuances in parallel musical contexts was expected in Brahms's era. The collective effect of these practices is a fluidity of rhythm and tempo that supports the intensely sighing nature of this section of the movement and accords with reports of Brahms's own playing.

Conclusion

This chapter has provided an overview of the performance practices that are pertinent to vocal and instrumental repertoire in the period 1800–1950 and has shown that there is much interesting historical information with which to grapple if we are to keep the music of those eras fresh and alive. Readers are encouraged to engage with the concepts offered in the first section of the chapter, and to experiment with the performance practices introduced in the second section dealing with relevant performance practices. As the three case studies in the final section show, such experimentation can lead to very interesting results that are different and new, and stretch the boundaries of current musical practice. As a reviewer of the recording discussed in Case Study 1 exclaimed enthusiastically: "Here, indeed, is a "rhetorical Beethoven" [. . .] one with a more flexible approach to rhythm and tempo in order to advance the musical argument with improvisatory flair and panache. It's wonderful stuff: intimate, revelatory and highly enjoyable" (Yeoman, Limelight, 2018). And for the recording in Case Study 2, one reviewer hailed the performance as "revelatory" (Weretka, Music Trust, 2020), while another "a truly new recording" (Nolan, Sydney Arts Guide, 2020).

For performers, being informed about the performance practices discussed in this chapter would undoubtedly lead to an "educated flexibility" in performance (Donington, 1989, pp. 119–120) and a deeper connection with both the composer and the music (Peres

Da Costa 2012, p. xxvi). Most important, it would inspire "an imaginative re-creation in performance of the notes on the page" (Mayer Brown, 1988, p. 41). Engaging with performance practices of bygone eras can help reshape our musical instincts and inspire us to rethink what we do in performance. Reimagining the sounds of the past can help us to come up with novel results that shape and influence music making now (Taruskin, 1995, p. 102), the most modern of post-Modern performance styles.

KEY SOURCES

Brown, C. (1999). *Classical and Romantic performing practice 1750–1900*. Oxford: Oxford University Press.

Haynes, B. (2007). *The end of early music: A period performer's history of music for the twenty-first century*. New York: Oxford University Press.

Hudson, R. (1994). *Stolen time: The history of tempo rubato*. Oxford: Clarendon Press.

Peres Da Costa, N. (2012) *Off the record: Performing practices in Romantic piano playing*. New York: Oxford University Press.

Philip, R. (1992). *Early recordings and musical style: Changing tastes in instrumental performance 1900–1950*. Cambridge, UK: Cambridge University Press.

REFLECTIVE QUESTIONS

1. What do you understand to be the intention and meaning of the score when it comes to Romantic and Modern repertoire?
2. How would you approach the performance of melody notes and chords in piano repertoire from the nineteenth and early-twentieth centuries?
3. How would you approach the application of portamento and vibrato in string repertoire from the nineteenth and early-twentieth centuries?
4. How would you approach the performance of nineteenth-century expressive music in terms of rhythmic nuance?
5. In what ways can tempo modification be used to enhance changes of mood in nineteenth- and early-twentieth-century repertoire?

REFERENCES

Altmann, W. (Ed.). (1930). *Beethoven: Piano Concerto Op. 15*. Leipzig: Eulenberg.

Anon. (c. 1806). *Violinschule oder Anweisung die Violine zu spielen von Leopold Mozart: Neue umgearbeitete und vermehrte Ausgabe*. Vienna: Johann Cappi.

Bach, C. P. E. ([1753/1762] 1949). *Essay on the true art of playing keyboard instruments* (W. J. Mitchell, Trans.). New York: W. W. Norton.

Bailey, M. (2017). *Lost voices: The aesthetic and practices of Romantic-era choral performance* – see https://www.youtube.com/watch?v=dibLbpyKaQw.

Baillot, P. (1834). *L'Art du violon: Nouvelle méthode*. Paris: Depot Central de Musique.

Balfe, M. (1857). *A new universal method of singing*. London: Boosey.

Becker, H. (1929). *Mechanik und Aesthetik des Violoncellospiels*. Vienna: Universal Edition.

Berlioz, H. (1870). *Mémoires de Hector Berlioz*. 2 Vols. Paris: Michel Lévy Frères.

Boscha, N. C. (c. 1826). *L'Anima di Musica for the Harp*. London: Goulding & D'Almaine.

Brahms, J. (c. 1863). *Piano Quartet in G minor*. Bonn: Simrock.

Brée, M. (1902). *The groundwork of the Leschetizky Method* (T. H. Baker, Trans.). New York: Schirmer.

Brown, C. (1999). *Classical and Romantic performing practice 1750–1900*. Oxford: Oxford University Press.

Brown, C. (2012). Reading between the lines. In M. Harlow (Ed.), *Mozart's chamber music with keyboard* (pp. 235–264). Cambridge, UK: Cambridge University Press. https://doi.org/10.1017/CBO9780511751455.013.

Brown, C. (Ed.). (2020). *Beethoven Sonatas for Pianoforte and Violin Vol. 1*. Kassel: Bärenreiter. BA 9014.

Brown. C., & Peres Da Costa, N. (2020). *Beethoven Sonatas for Pianoforte and Violin Vol. 1: Performing practice commentary*. Kassel: Bärenreiter. BA 9014.

Brown, C., Peres Da Costa, N., & Bennett Wadsworth, K. (2015). *Performing practices in Johannes Brahms' chamber music*. Kassel: Bärenreiter. BA 9600.

Buchanan, V. (2018). *Evolving performance practice of Debussy's piano preludes*. Master's thesis, Louisiana State University.

Buxbaum, E. H. (1988). Stravinsky, tempo and Le Sacre. *Performance Practice Review*, *1*(1), 61–70. https://doi.org/10.5642/perfpr.198801.01.6.

Carcassi, M. (1858). *Méthode complète pour la guitare*. Mainz: B. Schott's Söhne.

Challoner, N. B. (1816). *A new preceptor for the harp*. London: Skillern.

Cinti-Damoreau, L. (1849). *Méthode de chant, composée pour ses classes du Conservatoire*. Paris: Heugel et Cie.

Corri, D. (c. 1779). *A select collection of the most admired songs, duetts &c.* 3 Vols. Edinburgh: John Corri.

Corri, D. (1810). *The singer's preceptor*. London: Chappell & Co.

Corri, P. A. (1810). *L'Anima di musica*. London: Chappell & Co.

Couperin, F. (1713). *Premier livre de pieces de clavecin*. Paris: L'auteur.

Crutchfield, W. (1986). Brahms, by those who knew him. *Opus*, *2*(5), 12–21.

Cussins, W.G. (1874). *Handel's Messiah. An examination of the original and some contemporary MSS*. London: Augener.

Czerny, C. (1839). *Theoretical and practical pianoforte school Op. 500* (J. A. Hamilton, Trans.). London: Cocks & Co.

Czerny, C. (1846). *The art of playing the ancient and modern piano forte works* (John Bishop, Trans.). London: Cocks.

de Bériot, C. (1858). *Méthode de violon*. 3 Vols. Paris and Mainz: Fils de B. Schott.

Desargus, F. X. (1821). *Traité générale, sur l'art de jouer de la harpe*. Paris: L'Auteur.

Dibben, N. (2014). Understanding performance expression in popular music recording. In D. Fabian, R. Timmers, & E. Schubert (Eds.), *Expressiveness in music performance: Empirical approaches across styles and cultures* (pp.117–132). Oxford: Oxford University Press.

Dounias, M. (Ed.). (1958). *Neue Mozart Ausgabe*. Kirchensonaten VI. Kassel: Bärenreiter. BA 4511.

Donington, R. (1989). The present position of authenticity. *Performance Practice Review*, vol. 2 no. 2, 117–125.

Dubal, D. (1992). *Evenings with Horowitz*. London: Robson Books Ltd.

Fischer, V. (1995). Articulation notation in the piano music of Béla Bartók: Evolution and interpretation. *Studia Musicologica Academiae Scientiarum Hungaricae, 36(3/4),* 285–301. https://doi.org/10.2307/902215.

Flesch, C. (1923). *Die Kunst des Violinspiels*. 2 Vols. Berlin: Ries & Erler.

Flesch, C. (1924). *The art of violin playing*. 2 Vols. (F. H. Martens, Trans). Boston: Carl Fischer.

Flesch, C. (1930). *The art of violin playing*. Vol. 2. *Artistic Realisation and Instruction*. New York: Carl Fischer Inc.

Ffrangcon-Davies, D. (1905). *The singing of the future*. London: John Lane.

García, M. (1847). *École de García, Traité complet de l'art du chant*. 2nd ed of Part 1 and 1st ed of Part 2. Paris: Chez L'auteur.

García, M. (1857). *García's new treatise on the art of singing: A compendious method of instruction*. London: Beale & Chappell.

Halir, C (Ed.). (1905). *Sonaten für Pianoforte und Violine von Ludwig van Beethoven*. Braunschweig: Litolff.

Hamilton, K. (2007). *After the Golden Age: Romantic pianism and modern performance*. New York: Oxford University Press.

Haynes, B. (2007). *The end of early music: A period performer's history of music for the twenty-first century*. New York: Oxford University Press.

Ho, J. (2014). Towards an embodied understanding of performing practices: A gestural analysis of Debussy's "Minstrels" according to the 1912 piano rolls. *La Revue Musicale OICRM, 2(1),* 40–58. https://doi.org/10.7202/1055845ar.

Ho, J. (2018). Debussy and late-Romantic performing practices: The *piano* rolls of 1912. In F. de Médicis & S. Huebner (Eds.) *Debussy's resonance*, 513–561. Rochester, NY: University of Rochester Press.

Hoffmann, K. (1979). Johannes Brahms in den Erinnerungen von Richard Barth. Hamburg: Schuberth.

Hudson, R. (1994). *Stolen time: The history of tempo rubato*. Oxford: Clarendon Press.

Hummel, J. N. (1827). *Ausführliche theoretische-praktische Anweisung zum Piano-Forte-Spiel*. Vienna: Tobias Haslinger.

Hummel, J. N. (1828). *Complete theoretical and practical course of instructions on the art of playing the pianoforte*. London: Boosey.

Jockisch, R. (1900). *Katechismus der violine*. Leipzig: J. J. Weber.

Kanemitsu-Nagasawa, M. (2018). *Understanding the characteristics of the single-action pedal harp and their implications for the performing practices of its repertoire from 1760 to 1830*. PhD dissertation. University of Leeds.

Kim, D. H. (2012). The Brahmsian hairpin. *19th-Century Music, 36(1),* 46–57. https://doi.org/10.1525/ncm.2012.36.1.046.

Kitchiner, W. (1821). *Observations on vocal music*. London: Hurst, Robinson, and Co.

Klauwell, O. (1890). On musical execution: An attempt at systematic exposition of the same primarily with reference to piano-playing. New York: G. Schirmer.

Langham Smith, R. (1999) Debussy on performance: Sound and unsound ideals. In J. R. Briscoe (Ed.), *Debussy in performance* (pp. 3–27). New Haven: Yale University Press.

Leech-Wilkinson, D. (2009). *The changing sound of music: Approaches to studying recorded musical performances*. CHARM – see https://charm.rhul.ac.uk/studies/chapters/chap5.html#par10.

Milsom, D. (2003). *Theory and practice in late nineteenth-century violin performance: An examination of style in performance, 1850–1900*. Aldershot: Ashgate Publishing Ltd.

Milsom, D. (2012). Practice and principle: Perspectives upon the German "Classical" school of violin playing in the late nineteenth century. *Nineteenth-Century Music Review*, 9(1), 31–52. https://doi.org/10.1017/S1479409812000067.

Milsom, D. (2013). The Franco-Belgian school of violin playing: Towards an understanding of chronology and characteristics, 1850–1925. *Ad Parnassum*, 11(20), 1–20.

Molino, F. (1813). *Nouvelle méthode pour la guitare*. Leipzig: Breitkopf & Härtel.

Moser, A. (1908-1910). *Joseph Joachim: Ein Lebensbild* (2nd ed). Berlin: Verlag der Deutschen Brahms-Gesellschaft.

Nathan, I. (1836). *Musurgia vocalis* (2nd ed). London: Fentum.

Nolan, P. (2020). *Ironwood – Farrenc & Saint-Saëns: Romantic Dreams – Quintets for Piano and Strings*. CD Review accessible at https://www.sydneyartsguide.com.au/ironwood-farrenc-saint-saens-romantic-dreams-quintets-for-piano-and-strings/

Pelzer, F. (1833). *Instructions for the Spanish Guitar*. 2nd edn. London: Chappell

Peres Da Costa, N. (2012). *Off the record: Performing practices in Romantic piano playing*. New York: Oxford University Press.

Peres Da Costa, N. (2015). Performing practices in piano playing. In Brown, C., Peres Da Costa N., and Bennett Wadsworth, K. *Performing practices in Johannes Brahms' chamber music* (pp. 15–26). Bärenreiter: Kassel. BA 9600.

Peres Da Costa, N. & Ironwood . (2016). *Brahms—Tones of Romanic extravagance: Piano quartet no. 1*. Australia: ABC Music https://www.abcmusic.com.au/discography/brahms---tones-romantic-extravagance-piano-quartet-no-1-piano-quintet.

Peres Da Costa, N. and Australian Haydn Ensemble (2017). *Beethoven Piano Concertos 1 & 3*. Sydney: Australian Haydn Ensemble https://www.australianhaydn.com.au/beethovens-piano-concerto-1-3.

Peres Da Costa, N. (2019). Carl Reinecke's performance of his arrangement of the second movement from Mozart's Piano Concerto K. 488: Some thoughts on style and the hidden messages in musical notation. In T. Gartmann and D. Allenbach (Eds.), *Rund um Beethoven: Interpretationsforschung heute* (pp. 114–149). Schliengen: Edition Argus.

Peres Da Costa, N. & Ironwood (2020). *Romantic dreams: Quintets for piano and strings by Farrenc and Saint-Saëns*. Australia: ABC Music: https://www.abcmusic.com.au/discography/louise-farrenc-camille-saint-saëns-romantic-dreams-quintets-piano-and-strings-ironwood.

Peres Da Costa, N. (2020). *Reinvigorating nineteenth-century performance: A collection of informed-practice experimental interpretations*. Sydney Conservatorium of Music, University of Sydney – see https://www.sydney.edu.au/music/our-research/research-areas/artistic-research/reinvigorating-nineteenth-century-performance.html.

Peres Da Costa, N., Mitchell, H., & Stephens, M. (2020). The Dowling Songbook Project: An uniquely Australian opportunity in HIP learning. In A. Reid, N. Peres Da Costa & J. Carrigan (Eds.), *Creative research in music: Informed practice, innovation and transcendence* (pp. 53-66). Abingdon: Routledge.

Peres Da Costa, N. & Yeadon, D. (2020). Liner notes to *Romantic dreams: Quintets for piano and strings by Farrenc and Saint-Saëns*, Australia: ABC Music.

Philip, R. (1992). *Early recordings and musical style: Changing tastes in instrumental performance 1900–1950*. Cambridge, UK: Cambridge University Press.

Potter, J. (2006). Beggar at the door: The rise and fall of portamento in singing. *Music and Letters*, 87(4), 523–550.

Potter, S. (2014). *Changing vocal style and technique in Britain during the long nineteenth century*. PhD dissertation. University of Leeds.

Reinecke, C (Ed.). (1906). *W.A. Mozart: Twenty Piano Compositions*. Boston: Oliver Ditson.

Rhein, R. (1993). *Johann Peter Milchmeyer's "Die wahre Art das Pianoforte zu spielen": An annotated translation*. Doctoral thesis, University of Nebraska.

Rosé, A (Ed.). (1901). *Sonaten für Pianoforte und Violine von Ludwig van Beethoven*. Vienna: Universal.

Saint-Saëns, C. (c. 1877). *Piano Quintet Op. 14 in A minor*. Leipzig: F. E. C. Leuchardt.

Schröder, H. (1887). *Die Kunst des Violinspiels*. Köln: P. J. Tonger.

Scott, A. (2014). Changing Sounds, Changing Meanings: How Artistic Experimentation Opens Up the Field of Brahms Performance Practice. In D. Crispin and B. Gilmore (Eds.). *Artistic Experimentation in Music: An Anthology* pp. 241–250. Leuven: Leuven University Press.

Shih, C., Li, P., Lin, Y., Wang, Y., & Su, A. W. Y. (2017). Analysis and synthesis of the violin playing of Heifetz and Oistrakh. In A. Torin, B. Hamilton, S. Bilbao, & M. Newton (Eds.), *Proceedings of the 20th International Conference on Digital Audio Effects (DAFx-17)* (pp. 466–473), University of Edinburgh.

Speidel, W. & Singer, E (Eds.). (1887). *Sonaten für Pianoforte und Violine von Ludwig van Beethoven*. Stuttgart und Berlin: J.G. Cotta.

Spohr, L. (1833). Louis Spohr's grand violin school (C. Rudolphus, Trans.). London: Wessel.

Thalberg, S. (1853). *L'Art du chant appliquée au piano*. Paris: Heugel.

Taruskin, R. (1995). *Text and act*. New York: Oxford University Press.

Toft, R. (2000). *Heart to heart: Expressive singing in England, 1780–1830*. Oxford: Oxford University Press.

Toft, R. (2011). Bel Canto: the unbroken tradition. In Singing music from 1500 to 1900: style, technique, knowledge, assertion, experiment. *Proceedings of the National Early Music Association International Conference*, in association with the University of York Music Department and the York Early Music Festival. John Potter and Jonathan Wainwright (Eds.). York: University of York.

Toft, R. (2013). *Bel canto*. New York: Oxford University Press.

Turner, J. A. (1833). *Manual of instruction in vocal music*. London: John W. Parker.

Weretka, J. (2020). *Romantic Dreams. Quintets for Piano and Strings by Louise Farrenc and Camille Saint-Saëns. Ironwood*. CD Review accessible at https://musictrust.com.au/loudmouth/romantic-dreams-quintets-for-piano-and-strings-by-louise-farrenc-and-camille-saint-saens-ironwood/

Wilson, R. (2015). *Style and interpretation in the nineteenth-century German violin school with particular reference to the Three Sonatas for Pianoforte and Violin by Johannes Brahms*. Doctoral thesis, Sydney Conservatorium of Music, University of Sydney.

Wood, H. (1927). *The gentle art of singing*. London: Oxford University Press.

Yeoman, W. (2018). *Beethoven: Piano Concertos Nos 1 and 3 (Neal Peres Da Costa, Australian Haydn Ensemble)* CD Review accessible at https://www.limelightmagazine.com.au/reviews/beethoven-piano-concertos-nos-1-and-3-neal-peres-da-costa-australian-haydn-ensemble/.

CHAPTER 18

NEW MUSIC

Performance Institutions and Practices

IAN PACE

INTRODUCTION

By the beginning of the twentieth century, concert programming had transitioned away from the mid-eighteenth-century norm of varied repertoire by (mostly) living composers to become weighted more heavily toward a historical and canonical repertoire of (mostly) dead composers (Weber, 2008). As a consequence, the focus in this chapter—"new music"—relates to music that did not then occupy as central a place in mainstream performance as the musical art works of prior centuries. Conversely, this degree of autonomy from mainstream performance support lent a greater freedom to composers, enabling them to establish a cultural field with different norms and assumptions, thereby creating what we now label "new music." From the period following the end of World War I, a distinct performance culture emerged, with its own gradually evolving infrastructure of specialized concert series, festivals, radio programs, recording labels, and some educational institutions, and which attracted the foundation of specialized ensembles and performers. This subculture of Western art music has been established for long enough for its identity to be palpable. To posit absolute divides and stark antagonisms between "new music" and mainstream music is relatively unproductive given the interactive relationship between the two manifested through the involvement of common players and, of course, some common musical provenance; nonetheless, the focus of this chapter is on the performance of the repertoire most readily associated with a new music subculture, rather than upon twentieth- and twenty-first-century Western art music in general. This focus is not to imply that music exhibiting radical and iconoclastic compositional approaches is aesthetically superior to or more significant than that embodying a more continuous or integrative relationship with existing traditions; rather, it enables a concentration on the specific new issues pertaining to performance of a repertoire whose demands differ in various respects from earlier traditions, such as those presented in the two preceding chapters (see Fabian and Peres Da Costa chapters, this part).

While it is tempting to overlay a somewhat uniform or homogeneous "modernist" model of the performance of all art music in the broad middle section of the twentieth century—mainstream, new, and historically informed—(see Cook, 2013; Haynes, 2007; Leech-Wilkinson, 2009a, 2009b; and various essays in Taruskin, 1995), there are enough counterexamples to falsify claims for such a model (see Pace 2017a; drawing in part upon Fabian, 2001, 2003, 2006). In allowing for a more heterogeneous history, I do not intend to supply instructions on the "correct" ways to perform a range of new music, as I believe such a task to be impossible and ineffective. Rather, I trace the history of the performance culture of new music, including the institutional and aesthetic contexts in which it has developed and the types of works that were performed, to identify key critical questions that are inevitable for any performer(s) intending to render various repertoire that can be categorized as such. Among the most important of these are the following:

1. In what context has such work previously been heard through programming?
2. Which institutions have nurtured and supported such work, and which continue to do so?
3. Who are the performers who have helped to forge a performance tradition for such work?
4. Does such music necessitate new techniques, skills, insights, competencies, and aesthetic attitudes?
5. To what extent should the performer(s) situate their interpretations so as to foreground continuities with earlier traditions, or conversely emphasize difference and uniqueness?

I divide the period from 1918 to the present day essentially into three sub-periods: 1918–1945, 1945–c. 1975, and c. 1975 to the present day. I concentrate particularly upon the first two periods because they witnessed extremely wide-ranging developments and transformations in performance culture, while the last period is characterized more by consolidation, assimilation, but also possible ossification, to which I will return in the conclusion.

The Concept of "New Music" and the Beginnings of a Performance Culture

It was in the German-speaking world after 1918 that the contemporary concept of "new music" first developed well beyond looser meanings encountered from the mid-nineteenth century (Blumröder, 1981; Dahlhaus, 1987). In 1919, music critic Paul Bekker called specifically for music to reflect the new times brought about by the war and its aftermath (Bekker, 1923). He looked for inspiration to movements in other arts such as futurism and expressionism, feeling music to lag behind these, while at the same time recognizing the potential of:

- microtonal instruments (as advocated by Ferruccio Busoni);
- the splintering of tonality (Liszt and the *Neudeutsche Schule*);
- whole-tone scales, (Debussy and Schoenberg);
- influences from non-Western-European traditions; and
- archaic modes from medieval music.

More than a decade earlier, Busoni had called for greater freedom from tradition (Busoni, 1962) employing near-atonality, archaic allusions undermined through semitonal progressions, parallel chords, whole-tone and other unusual scales, mirror structures, and quotations from Native American music in his own compositions (Samson, 1977). Profoundly opposed to Wagner, Busoni advocated classical ideals of beauty and simplicity in place of nineteenth-century profundity, and declared his objective to create a *Junge Klassizität*, in which melody would once again become the begetter of harmony, while music would eschew sensuousness and subjectivity (Busoni, 1987). Conductor Hermann Scherchen also favored an emphasis upon melody rather than harmony, which he found in Schoenberg's Five Orchestral Pieces, Op. 15 (Scherchen, 1919), while Bekker too urged a new approach to melody in which the relationship between individual pitches would become less dependent upon harmonic and more invested in linear counterpoint, as well as a freer approach to rhythmic diction unconstrained by unity and periodicity (Bekker, 1923), a significant shift in musical priorities from much nineteenth-century practice that would weaken the link to functional tonality.

The essays of Bekker, Scherchen, and Busoni initiated a vigorous and sometimes very heated debate (see Grues, Kruttge & Thalheimer, 1925; Cherney, 1974; Blumröder, 1981) conducted by a range of international musicians, especially following a counter-polemic by conservative composer Hans Pfitzner, who viewed Bekker in particular as representative of an "international Jewish tendency" that sought to destroy the essence of German music (Pfitzner, 1920). Throughout this period, these and other major aesthetic debates were conducted in particular in the pages of specialist journals for new music: the Berlin-based *Melos*, founded by Scherchen; the Viennese *Musikblätter des Anbruch*; and Prague-based *Der Auftakt* (Hass, 2004, 2005, 2019). Ultimately, such debates consolidated the "new music" concept as constituting a marked break with prewar traditions, especially with respect to Germanic models of musical subjectivity, profundity, and chromatic harmony. Nonetheless, this by no means betokened a new spirit of aesthetic unity, and in the second half of the 1920s the German new music world became more factionalized, especially among Schoenbergian and Stravinskian/Hindemithian partisans, as well as those who favored influences from jazz or moves toward mechanization.

Schoenberg's Verein and Donaueschingen

The other key event informing the development of a culture of new music was the foundation of Schoenberg's Verein für musikalische Privataufführungen in November 1918 in Vienna, an organization unashamedly presenting music for a relatively few dedicated individuals, excluding critics or members of the public who might disrupt proceedings. This presented a remarkable range of new music, by no means only or especially that from Schoenberg's own circle (see Stuckenschmidt, 1977, pp. 254–277; Smith, 1986, pp. 81–102, 245–268; Szmolyan, 1984, pp. 101–104). It also inspired a range of similar societies and other organizations throughout Germany (Pace, 2018, pp. 23–24), including the important concert series that was mounted from 1922 by the Novembergruppe, an artists' organization founded in 1918 that sought artistic radicalism to match the spirit of political revolution of the time (Kliemann, 1969; Kaes et al, 1994, pp. 477–478; Peters and Vogt, 1998). While many of the early interwar new music organizations were relatively short-lived, the Donaueschinger Kammermusiktage, established in 1921, did survive, with the help of aristocratic patronage and financial support from town, state, and national institutions, as well as the radio (Thrun, 1995). Running through to 1930 (relocating during this period to Baden-Baden, then Berlin), programs included only relatively few works that would become absorbed into a wider repertoire of new music (Zintgraf, 1987; Häusler, 1996); the majority—which included microtonal works, those for mechanical instruments, and film, radio, and gramophone composition—are today known primarily by aficionados. As such, the festival is more significant in terms of the consolidation of an arena devoted to new music than necessarily in bequeathing a new repertory.

International Society for Contemporary Music

Even more important, and not restricted to Germany, was the founding of the International Society for Contemporary Music (ISCM) in Salzburg in 1923 and its subsequent World Music Days, annual festivals hosted by branches across the globe. Some early members, especially those from Germany and Austria, hoped to make the Society into an organization specifically for the promotion of dodecaphonic and other avant-garde tendencies, but they were overruled by others from France, Britain, and the United States who preferred that all contemporary Western art music be welcomed (Haefeli, 1982). As such it became an organization that promoted a good deal of new music, but not exclusively that. Especially contentious for some was the lack of any particular favor toward music exhibiting clear "national" tendencies, even spurring the establishment of the oppositional Ständiger Rat für die internationale Zusammenarbeit der Komponisten, active for a short period from 1935 to 1939 (see Garberding, 2014; Martin, 2016; Pace, 2021–22 forthcoming). Conversely, the encouragement by the ISCM of national or regional branches was of immense, even decisive, importance in the expansion of a culture of new music performance in a great many developed countries.

National perspectives

Beyond Germany, new music had different meanings, especially where there was a less extensively developed and institutionalized earlier culture of symphonic repertoire, chamber music, or late Romantic composition, occasioning a less pronouncedly oppositional relationship of new music to tradition, which enabled some continuations even in some fascist regimes. Musical iconoclasm in Italy was initially focused around the Società Italiana di Musica Moderna, founded in 1917 by Alfredo Casella. The society presented a range of concerts that were often controversial, featuring Italian composers alongside international figures. The organization was succeeded in 1923 by the Corporazione delle Nuove Musiche, which was affiliated with the ISCM. They invited performers such as Scherchen, Walter Gieseking, Hindemith, and Bartók to perform in Italy for the first time (Waterhouse, 1999; Antokoletz, 2013; Nicolodi, 2011). In Venice, the longest-lasting continuous festival for new music, the Festival internazionale di musica contemporanea, was inaugurated in 1930. While less devoted to radical tendencies than that in Donaueschingen, the festival nonetheless featured advanced music by composers from across Europe and the United States. Despite wider attacks on futurism and atonality in 1932, a thriving culture of new music continued in Fascist Italy for most of the decade (Earle, 2013). By 1942 the Venice festival had narrowed somewhat as the Italian regime had become closer to Nazi Germany, yet one could still hear Stravinsky's *Petrushka* and Honegger's *Pacific 231* (Biennale Musica, n.d.).

In New York City, Leo Ornstein's individualistic piano recitals of 1910 and 1919 and Edgard Varèse's New Symphony Orchestra in 1919 signaled the beginning of a new music culture, but it would be the establishment of the International Composers Guild (ICG) in 1921 that would cement such a new direction in the United States. Over two thirds of the premieres hosted by the ICG comprised radical music of composers such as Schoenberg, Stravinsky, and Varèse himself. Some came to favor the greater assimilation of composers into a musical "mainstream"; as a result, the League of Composers split from the ICG in 1923 and a variety of other institutions branched out at the same time (Lott, 1983; Oja, 2000). A different direction was represented by the ICG-affiliated New Music Society, founded by Henry Cowell in 1925 in Los Angeles. This group favored works by American composers that "developed indigenous materials," although not completely excluding European music and influences (Mead, 1982; Oja, 2000). Also, in Hartford, Connecticut, Chick Austin created a series called *The Friends and Enemies of Modern Music*, in which new music was played in living rooms or other small venues, to stimulate debate among participants (Watson, 1995), a model later emulated around the American Zone of Occupied Germany (Beal, 2006; Pace, 2018). Somewhat distinct was the Berkshire Symphonic Festival, founded in 1934, from 1937 taking place at Tanglewood and presenting what would now be considered "mixed" programs of older and newer work (Howe, 1946), though this ultimately paved the way for the later contemporary music festival there.

French new music had become highly inwardly focused and nationalistic during the war, and some of this pattern continued after 1918, with some important exceptions, including concert series mounted by Serge Koussevitzky and Walther Staram (Fulcher, 2005). The Société musicale indépendante (SMI) (1909–1935) had been founded as a break-away from the highly nationalistic Société nationale de musique (Duchesneau, 1994), and the SMI resisted attempts to re-merge the two societies after the war (Fulcher, 2005), and instead presented both French and international new music (Orenstein, 1975; Duchesneau, 1997). Other concert series demonstrated a clearer break with prewar culture than those of the SMI, such as the chamber concerts mounted by Félix Delgrange from 1917 (Orledge, 1987), and especially the *concerts salades* that began in December 1921, organized by pianist and composer Jean Wiener. Intentionally oppositional to traditionalist culture and including both jazz and contemporary German music, this series was associated (pejoratively) in some of the French press with futurism and cubism. This characterization was far from inaccurate; the first concert featured the American jazz orchestra of Billy Arnold, alongside a player piano rendition of Stravinsky's *Le sacre du printemps*, and a sonata of Darius Milhaud (Fulcher, 2005; Milhaud, 1995).

Both Delgrange and Wiener's concerts played a significant role in propagating the work of Le Groupe des Six, the term first employed by Henri Collet to Georges Auric, Louis Durey, Arthur Honegger, Milhaud, Francis Poulenc, and Germaine Tailleferre in 1920. The Six had to varying degrees been programmed alongside, identified, and claimed the mantle of Satie, whose work, above all other prewar French composers, pointed to a new aesthetic direction and a new approach to performance (Brévignon 2020). Many of their works eschewed the romantic and sensuous trappings and chromatic harmony that were still a feature in the work of Debussy, Florent Schmitt, and others, in favor of clearer textures, rhythmic regularity, with plentiful use of irony and humor and allusions to popular musics, drawing upon the achievements of both Satie and Stravinsky.

Other important arenas for new music in France included the concert series associated with the journal *La revue musicale* (Kelly, 2018) and the concert series La Spirale. While running only between 1935 and 1937, the latter was a pivotal event for French music (Mawer, 2006), being run by the composers who would come together as La jeune France in 1936—Olivier Messiaen, André Jolivet, Daniel-Lesur, and Yves Baudrier. These four composers moved away from the irreverence, urbanity, and secular detachment of Les Six toward a more "spiritualist" and sometimes nationalist approach evident in programs that were French-dominated, although not entirely devoid of international composers (Simeone, 2002; Kelly, 2013; Fulcher, 2005).

More broadly, across Europe pockets of new music support was found in many countries. In Belgium the musicologist, pianist, and conductor Paul Collaer was a prime advocate, championing Milhaud in particular and supporting the Brussels-based Pro Arte Quartet (Hughes, 2015; Barker, 2017). In the Netherlands, Dutch composers were promoted in a 1919–1920 Concertgebouw series and a chamber music series featuring international composers, organized by Russian-Jewish émigré violinist Alexander Schmuller. Meanwhile, composer Daniel Ruijneman promoted the "most progressive" Dutch composers through the Verenigning tot Ontwikkeling der Moderne Scheppende Toonkunst from 1918 to 1923, after which it was subsumed into the ISCM (Samama, 2006; Braas, 2001) and was instrumental in the foundation of successor organizations, notably the Nederlandse Vereniging voor Hedendaagse Muzike (1930–1962) (Muziek Encyclopedie, n.d.; P.M. On the Coul, 2014). In addition, international new music was integrated within Concertgebouw Orchestra programs, particularly by conductor Pierre Monteux between 1924 and 1934, with the occasional individual concert devoted entirely to new music (Samama, 2006; Royal Concertgebouw Orchestra, n.d). In Scandinavian countries, new music organizations included Det Unge Tonekunstnerselskab (DUT), founded in Copenhagen in 1920 (Christensen, 2002); Fylkingen, founded in Stockholm in 1933 to present contemporary music alongside more traditional works (Fylkingen, n.d.); and in Norway, nyMusikk, founded in 1938 by composer Pauline Hall and run by her for more than twenty years (Herresthal & Pedersen, 2002). All three either became or were founded as branches of the ISCM in those countries. In Spain, activities were more limited, although Stravinsky's music enjoyed some support, not least thanks to the advocacy of Manuel de Falla and the small Residencia de Estudiantes, associated strongly with Ortega y Gasset, who also presented music of de Falla and Schoenberg (Hess, 2005; Levitz, 2013). The Grupo de los Ocho (very loosely modeled on the French Groupe des Six), including composers Rodolfo and Ernesto Halffter, presented their work at the Residencia from 1930 (Rodriguez, 2016; Hess, 2005). A wider initiative for the promotion of avant-garde music, especially that by Catalan composers, was taken in the 1930s by Roberto Gerhard (Perry, 2013), which included the organization of visits to Barcelona by Schoenberg and Webern (Pujadas & Quadreny, 2014).

A performance culture for new music had begun in pre-revolutionary Russia with the series of Evenings of Contemporary Music in St. Petersburg in 1901, and in Moscow from 1909, which provided the first outings for works of Stravinsky, Prokofiev, and Miaskovsky, as well as international figures including Debussy, Schoenberg, Ravel, and Schmitt (Schwarz, 1983). After the Revolution, composer Arthur Lourié, as head of the main state music organization Muzo, was able to promote a range of international music centered on his personal tastes (e.g., Debussy, Ravel, Scriabin), before he left the country for good in 1921 (Nelson, 2004), while some more radical experiments from Nikolai Roslavets and Arsenii Avraamov briefly flourished under the auspices of the Proletkult movement (Nelson, 2004; Fitzpatrick, 1992). But the closest thing to the wider European new music culture was found through the Assotsiatsiya Sovremennoy Muzyki (ASM) or Association for Contemporary Music, founded by Roslavets in 1923, which organized performances of such composers as Schoenberg, Berg, Webern, and Krenek as well as radical Russian works such as Aleksander Mosolov's *The Iron Foundry*. This competed for funds with the Rossiiskaia Assotsiatsiia Proletarskykh Muzykantov (RAPM) or Russian Association of Proletarian Musicians, founded the same year, fervently opposed to any aspects of Western modernism, folklore, jazz, spiritualism, primitivism, nationalism, mysticism, and eroticism in music, preferring mass choral music and other politicized songs. Some have argued that the RAPM were a much more influential force than the ASM in Soviet musical life in the 1920s (Nelson, 2004; Taruskin, 1997; Edmunds 2000; Frolova Walker & Walker, 2012), and that one should be wary of over-emphasizing aspects of Soviet musical life that adhered most closely to Western models. But both organizations were dissolved in 1932 and replaced by the Union of Soviet Composers, with the official adoption of an aesthetic policy of socialist realism (Frolova Walker & Walker, 2012). If RAPM can in some senses be considered as promoting a distinctly Soviet species of "new music," related to movements emphasizing workers' songs and choirs in Germany and elsewhere, this cannot be said of the USC after 1932. For at least two decades, even such hugely important composers as Shostakovich and Prokofiev (after his return to the Soviet Union in 1936) quickly fell afoul of the newly censorious climate toward work that demonstrated anything akin to a modernist break with traditional musical languages.

The establishment of new music organizations across Europe was influential, and a large section of the resulting infrastructure for new music performance was fundamentally indebted to Schoenberg's model, above all the need for contexts freed from popular taste and critical opinion, albeit applied in looser fashions. The Verein was not the first concert association devoted to new music, but as violinist Rudolf Kolisch observed, it was then unique in its attitudes toward audiences, critics, the close control exerted over the repertoire and types of performances, the attitude toward musical "texts" and composers, and the generation of a new canon (Kolisch, 2009c). The claims made for such a model, and associated culture, have certainly not gone unchallenged, on grounds of elitism, asociality, white male bias, and more, but at the time of writing, such a culture and its institutions certainly remain intact.

Objectivism and *Texttreue*

The period after 1918 witnessed a major growth in an "objectivist" approach to performance that was a logical consequence of wider aesthetic developments. Although not without earlier precedents (Oja, 2000), different manifestations of new music combined eschewal of overt manifestations of subjective expression, radical, discontinuous approaches to harmony, abrupt cuts in musical material without any transitions, the displacement of functional harmony through the assertion of a primary role to rhythm and timbre, a re-inscription of various classical principles of structural organization, and a cult of the machine and technology associated above all with the United States as an emblem of modernity (Saldern, 2013).

Nowhere were these ideas more explosive than in Germany, as the epicenter of late romanticism. One of the first clear articulations of a new credo came from the pianist and composer Eduard Erdmann in 1920, contrasting an "objective" *Es-Musik* with a subjective and egoistic *Ich-Musik* epitomized by the work of Wagner (Erdmann, 1920; cited in Rehding, 2006). This foreshadowed the priorities of the *Neue Sachlichkeit*, a term first applied to the visual arts in the early 1920s (Plumb, 2006; Kyora, 2013) and whose first known use in a musical context was in an article by Heinrich Strobel published in

1926. Discussing the folk-inspired work of Stravinsky, Bartók, and Janáček, Debussy's inspirations from painting, the rhythmic energy of jazz and other music inspired by dance, and the work of Hindemith (who would become most prominently associated with the new aesthetic), Strobel argued that this all pointed away from music of inner turmoil toward objectivity and craftsmanship more appropriate for a new age (Strobel, 1926), while he and others also linked this to attempts to communicate with a wider audience (Grosch, 2013). Both in Germany and beyond, these ideas assumed a new prominence, with regular talk of "Overcoming Romanticism" (Hill, 1994), and a perception that most aesthetic talk referred either positively or negatively to "expressive music" (Besseler, 1927; cited in Hinton, 1989).

A period in which many rejected older manifestations of subjectivity and expression was one which also fostered a new interest in mechanical instruments. Stravinsky, Casella, Gian Francesco Malipiero, George Antheil, Hindemith, Ernst Toch, and others all wrote works for player piano or mechanical organ, while the festivals at Donaueschingen and Baden-Baden championed mechanical composition in 1926–1927, at the behest of Hindemith (1994). A range of polemical articles proposing the demise of the human performer, whose imperfections would be superseded by mechanical devices, appeared in German and Czech new music journals (Stuckenschmidt, 1925; Toch, 1926; Schoenberg, 1975a). At the same time, the growth of recordings and especially the new medium of radio, with the relatively limited microphone technology of the time, led some to advocate the value of more "spiky" and clearly delineated timbres in place of richer string sonorities (Hailey, 1994; Schoenberg, 1975b), an approach to performance, as well as composition, which can be traced throughout the remainder of the century and beyond.

Many of the composers associated with this new movement made clear their preferences for performers who would eschew the stylistic norms of "expressive" music as well as personal caprice and individuation. Hindemith averred that all types of singers, players, and conductors were "nothing but an intermediate station, a road-side stop, a transformer house, and their duty is to pass along what they received from the generating mind," that "[c]overing a piece with a thick layer of the performer's so-called feelings means distorting, counterfeiting it," and was especially harsh on conductors in these respects (Hindemith, 1952, pp. 33–34, 104–106). Ravel retorted that "Interpreters *are* slaves!" when pianist Paul Wittgenstein claimed to the contrary (Ivry, 2000), Others such as pianist Vlado Perlemuter report less dogmatic utterances, but still confirm that that Ravel consistently warned against excess and sentimentality, preferring "exact interpretations" (Perlemuter & Jourdan-Morhange, 1988). Moreover, study of Ravel's piano roll of *Valses nobles et sentimentales* (Ravel, 2003) and a range of performances by other interpreters who are known to have met with Ravel's favor demonstrate a plurality of approaches, including stylistic indicators of an earlier period such as spread chords and desynchronization of hands, as well as a subtle rhythmic freedom not always deducible from the text (Woodley, 2000). Accordingly, Ravel's strictures should be understood as modifications relative to the norms of his time rather than absolutes.

Nonetheless, there is no doubt that he desired a considerably more "objective" approach than was common in prewar times.

Stravinsky was more emphatic about a new role for the performer, above all in his 1939–1940 Charles Eliot Norton lectures at Harvard, later published as *Poetics of Music*. Arguing that "Having been fixed on paper or retained in the memory, music exists already prior to its actual performance"; he finds that most of the problems in contemporary performance are rooted in a conflict between "execution and interpretation," the former involving "the strict putting into effect of an explicit will that contains nothing beyond what it specifically commands" (Stravinsky, 1947, pp. 121–122; see also Stravinsky, 1936). The composer recognized that no score could completely prescribe every possible detail of performance, which he clearly regretted, but insisted that "The sin against the spirit of the work always begins with a sin against its letter" (1947, p. 124), a reversal of the view expressed by Liszt to Richard Pohl in 1853, whereby "the letter killeth the spirit" (La Mara, 1894). Nonetheless, in the context of Stravinsky's own five recorded versions of *Le sacre du printemps*, any analysis of his conducting resists attempts to discern consistency of intention (Taruskin, 1995; see also Buxbaum, 1988), so the composer's ideals were to some extent belied by his actual practice.

The position Stravinsky articulates in his *Poetics* provides a clear case of an attitude now known as *Texttreue*. In contrast to the older concept of *Werktreue*, or faithfulness to the *work* (Danuser, 2002), that asserts an idealist concept of some "essence" that lies beyond either the written score or any particular performance, the ideas underpinning *Texttreue* incorporate a literal fidelity to the *text* of the score. Other musicians who adhered quite explicitly to the *Texttreue* principle include Arturo Toscanini (Marsh, 1962; Civetta, 2012) and pianists Walter Gieseking and his teacher Karl Leimer, who jointly published a treatise that dismissed such practices as playing equally notated rhythmic values "unevenly and strongly rubato," insisting that "*Absolutely correct execution* of a composition is the only foundation upon which a really excellent interpretation can be built" (Gieseking & Leimer, 1972, p. 43). One who adopted a position somewhere between *Werktreue* and *Texttreue* was conductor Bruno Walter, who claimed, "I have made only the music of others sound forth, I have been but a 're-creator'" (Walter 1948, p. vii) but also allows that the life experiences of some performers might make it impossible to disguise "the peculiarities of the interpreter's personality" (Walter 1948, p. 47). Accordingly, he recommends performing "as near as possible to the intentions of the composer" while acknowledging that "the spontaneity which is an indispensable quality of each musical performance" may result in variances (Ryding & Pechefsky, 2001, p. 347).

Continuities and *Werktreue*: Bartók, Schoenberg, Kolisch, Adorno

Not all composers prominent during this era espoused the types of objectivity I have described, however, and some clearly continued to adhere to aspects of older practices.

For example, despite some superficial similarities of Bartók's mid-period works to those of Stravinsky, a range of recordings of Bartók as pianist demonstrate a flexible approach to rhythm and tempo, a diaphanous range of touch over and above what is indicated, and more widely, frequent liberties taken with the score (see Garst, 1985; Suchoff, 2003).

Schoenberg wrote only occasionally about performance, but his ideas concur essentially with the ideal of *Werktreue*. In 1923–1924 he emphasized audibility of every note, and subtle reproduction of the musical ideas in preference to "obtrusive and gesticulating" types of performance. He cited Fritz Kreisler, Pablo Casals, and Bronisław Huberman as exemplary performers, while decrying "the fashionable need for interpretation" (Schoenberg, 1923/24). Elsewhere, he criticized sudden shifts of tempi without proper transitions, and exaggerated fermatas, also making a clear distinction between "subjective" and metronomic, "objective" performance styles (Schoenberg, n.d.a, b). In terms of conductors, Schoenberg found Mahler, Richard Strauss, Arthur Nikisch, and Furtwängler to be "perfect musicians in every respect," in stark contrast to Otto Klemperer, Koussevitzky, and especially Toscanini, variously described as incompetent, illiterate, uneducated, and metronomic. Schoenberg especially berated Toscanini's legendary memory, on the grounds that he could remember the exact letter of a score, but not recognize errors there that should be musically self-evident (Schoenberg, 1944), thus demonstrating the composer's contempt for *Texttreue*.

A more comprehensive theory of performance was developed by Kolisch, who studied composition privately with Schoenberg from 1919 and developed strong convictions of his own. Kolisch lectured on performance, applying his trenchant views equally to old and new music (Adorno & Kolisch, 2009), and advocating a consistent use of what he categorized as *espressivo* playing except when the composer explicitly stated otherwise (Kolisch, 1983). Like Schoenberg (and Brahms), he believed the ideal performance comes from silent contemplation of the score and was therefore skeptical about the value of recordings. He was also resistant to approaches that fetishized "[t]echnical perfection and brilliancy" (Kolisch, 2009a) and consistently advocated the projection of the *idea* behind the work rather than merely the details of the score (Shreffler and Trippett, 2009a).

Overarchingly, however, Kolisch's views make the *Werktreue/Texttreue* dichotomy problematic; he consistently emphasized the need for close reading of the score (Shreffler & Trippett, 2009b), but that the quest for the fundamental idea (and "work") can be understood as a quest to discover what the score *implies* rather than simply *states*. Nevertheless, there was no question to Kolisch (2009a) that this quest should lead to a singular result:

> [W]e have to decide whether such a thing as right interpretation exists at all! In other words, are the indications given through a score precise enough to guarantee a right; that means, only one interpretation? My answer is, YES. They are in all respects. We must only learn to understand these indications to their full extent. (p. 205)

As the leader of the Kolisch quartet, he advocated freedom for individual chamber group members, but all should be bound by the score ahead of the leader's dictates. Where the score is non-specific, it should be supplemented by an "espressivo-quality," which Kolisch defined in relatively general terms as entailing the use of vibrato, *rubato*—meaning some modification of rhythm, but not tempo—and the swell-tone (or *messa di voce*). Kolisch (2009b) even believed it could be possible to notate these with such specificity that "Espressivo could thus be transformed into an *objective* performance element" (p. 209). Ultimately this opens the way to a future *Texttreue*, even if the scores of Kolisch's time had not yet made this particular interpretation of such a concept into a meaningful reality.

Kolisch's (2009a) arguments for performance as "the realization of the objective contents of the text" rather than "an expression of the performer's personality" (p. 205) relate to those of Theodor Adorno, who planned a coauthored treatise on performance with Kolisch. Adorno held the performances of Kolisch and his quartet in high esteem, viewing him as having developed a new approach to performance that eschewed surface brilliance in favor of projection of musical context and structural/spiritual understanding (Adorno, 2009). Adorno articulated as a key challenge for the performer of any music the need to break habituated aspects of performance through addressing and re-addressing the specifics of individual works (Adorno 2006), but he rarely addressed the performance of new music specifically. Adorno's model arguably makes more room for a performer's subjective interaction with the text than does Kolisch, but rarely for any more autonomous subjective will (Pace, 2007). While only a relatively small number of performers could be said to have realized Adorno's ideals, their potential application to post-1945 new music in particular are limited anyway, in light of how many composers of that time did indeed respond positively to the objectivist aesthetics of the interwar period.

A Performance Culture for the Avant-Garde, 1945–1973

The postwar years witnessed the growth of a more permanent infrastructure specifically for new music. This was most prominent from an early stage in West Germany, sustained by the ideology of *Nachholbedarf*, the view (only partially true) that the country had been cut off from modernist and international developments for twelve years, and thus needed to "catch up" (Pace 2018; forthcoming 2021-22). The festival in Donaueschingen, which had been turned into a vehicle for nationalistic and militaristic music during the Nazi era, was relaunched for two years in 1946 and 1947 (before later being taken up by the Südwestfunk radio station), alongside a range of other comparable but mostly short-lived events in other regional centers (Häusler, 1996; Zintgraf, 1987; Pace, 2018). However, the hugely important summer courses of the Darmstädter Ferienkurse, which began in 1946 and combined teaching and a wide range of performances, have continued in a relatively unbroken fashion to the present day (Stefan et al, 1996; Borio & Danuser, 1997). Theories of these as a US- or even CIA-backed venture have been comprehensively refuted (Wellens, 2002; Beal, 2006; Custodis, 2010; Iddon, 2013; Pace, 2018), while the mythological view of the courses as a haven for hegemonic domination of serial music is not backed up by evidence of the programming, at least in the first decade (Borio & Danuser, 1997, vol. 3; Pace 2011). Nonetheless, the courses did provide a major opportunity for avant-garde composers to meet and exchange ideas, and the visit of Cage to the courses in 1958 served as a catalyst to stimulate wider indeterminate composition in Europe (Borio & Danuser, 1997, vol. 2).

National perspectives

German radio stations played a pivotal role in sustaining the performance culture of new music (Weißbach, 1986). What became known as the Woche für neue Musik, run by Radio Frankfurt (later Hessicher Rundfunk), beginning with a preliminary festival in Bad Nauheim in 1946, can be seen as a template for many later more extended festivals. Introducing little-known works, notably by composers of the occupying powers, the festival also offered lectures on issues of musical "progress," "world music" (*Weltmusik*), and the possibilities of twelve-tone technique (Pace, 2018). Equally archetypal was the regular concert series of new music founded in 1945 by Karl Amadeus Hartmann that came to be known as Musica viva (Hass, 2004; Arlt, 2010), supported by Radio Munich (later Bayerischer Rundfunk), which inspired a whole range of other comparable series around Germany (Pace, 2018), including the leading das neue werk in Hamburg and Musik der Zeit in Cologne, both launched from radio stations, which hosted major premieres of Pierre Boulez, Karlheinz Stockhausen, Luigi Nono, and others (Weißbach, 1986). The radio station Südwestfunk (SWF), headquartered in Baden-Baden, relaunched the Donaueschingen festival (now called Donaueschinger Musiktage für zeitgenössische Tonkunst) in 1950, under the direction of Heinrich Strobel, and built this into one of the most powerful and prominent new music events in the world. The radio stations supported new orchestras and choirs that could program more adventurously than their "philharmonic" counterparts, and the stations also commissioned many new works (especially SWF), at first from a wide range of different types of composers, then from the 1960s with an increasing concentration on the more radically inclined new work (Betz, 1977; Nauck, 2004). To this day, the radio orchestras in Frankfurt, Cologne, Baden-Baden, and to a lesser extent in Hamburg and Munich, have been among the most prominent institutions in the world for championing radical new music (Pace, 2018), alongside the BBC Symphony Orchestra in London and BBC Scottish Symphony Orchestra in Glasgow (Glock, 1991; Kenyon, 1981; Notlingk, 2017).

In the UK, a range of early postwar institutions, including the Cheltenham Music Festival and Aldeburgh Festival, demonstrated a modest commitment to new music. William Glock, a major enthusiast for interwar modernist music such as that of the Second Viennese School (especially Berg), Stravinsky, and Bartók, founded the Bryanston Summer School in Dorset in 1948, hosting visits from Nadia Boulanger, Hindemith, and Boris Blacher in the early years. In 1949, Glock also launched the important new music periodical *The Score* and in 1953 he moved the Summer School to the grandiose location of Dartington Hall in Devon, where he presented British premieres of major new works of Elliott Carter, Boulez, Nono, Stockhausen, Stefan Wolpe, and Peter Maxwell Davies, hosting visits from several of these figures and others (Glock, 1991). Then the representation of new music at the BBC was enhanced considerably by the appointment of Glock as Controller of Music in 1959. While Glock's actions generated resentment from more conservatively minded colleagues, composers, and others (Carpenter 1996), he had a significant effect in opening up British musical life to more radical developments.

In France, in the early period following the Libération in 1944, a comprehensive study of the next ten years demonstrates that new music could be located primarily in a few institutions, once again through radio, above all the Radiodiffusion de la Nation française and associated Orchestre national de la Radiodiffusion française. At the same time, avant-gardists such as René Leibowitz and Pierre Boulez had to operate in a country with significant support for the Parti communiste française and consequently the types of aesthetic doctrines propagated in Moscow and Prague in 1948 (Feneyrou & Poirier, 2018). But the major initiative for a performance culture in new music, indeed a seminal part of the history of the early post-1945 era in this respect, was the foundation of the Domaine musicale concert series in 1954 by Pierre Boulez, who remained its director until 1967, succeeded by Gilbert Amy for the series' final six years. The first concert, conducted by Scherchen, presented Nono's *Polifonica, Monodia, Ritmica* (1951), Stockhausen's *Kontra-Punkte* (1952–1953), Webern's Concerto, Op. 24, and Stravinsky's *Renard*, featured alongside Bach's *Das musikalische Opfer* (Aguila, 1992). Overall, the programming demonstrated a type of modernist focus that was unusual for its time (even at Darmstadt), and laid the foundations for what would become a canonical modernist repertoire in the decades to come. Over a third of the works programmed were contemporary "classics" of Stravinsky, Varèse, Bartók, Debussy, Ravel, Ives, and in particular the Second Viennese School, with a strong emphasis upon Webern (Aguila, 1992; Boulez, 1986). By no means was all or even most of the more recent music played at the Domaine serial in nature, but a clear majority was atonal, and only a tiny amount could be considered neo-tonal, neo-Classical, or neo-Romantic, or did not constitute a significant break with nineteenth-century traditions.

In the Netherlands, the major boost to a new music culture came about through the foundation of the Stichting Gaudeamus in 1945, which from 1947 ran an annual Muziekweek of concerts, at first alternately featuring national and international composers and from 1957 centered on a shortlist of works nominated for a Gaudeamus Award, which from 1959 was fully international (Peters, 1995). In Italy, the Venice festival began again in September 1946, and gave an early outing to the young Bruno Maderna as conductor and composer, while the first International Dodecaphonic Congress in Milan in 1949 created a new focus for the avant-garde (Roderick, 2010).

In the United States, the major organization presenting concerts of new music continued to be the League of Composers, which merged with the US branch of the ISCM in 1954. They presented a range of Schoenberg performances (Feisst, 2011), but was equally a vehicle for tonal composers or those pursuing forms of interwar modernism (Straus, 1999). A more forward-looking direction came about in Los Angeles, where in 1939 writer Peter Yates and his wife, pianist Frances Mullen, founded a new music concert series entitled Evenings on the Roof, in the tradition of the Verein, which was succeeded by the Monday Evening Concerts in 1954. Directed by Lawrence Morton, works by Stravinsky and Luigi Dallapiccola dominated programs that also included Renaissance and early Baroque music from Gesualdo to Purcell, but also the likes of Leibowitz, Nono, and Stockhausen. Boulez made his US conducting debut in the 1957 series, premiering *Le Marteau* alongside Stockhausen's *Gesang der Jünglinge*, and Thomas Tallis's *Lamentations I and II* conducted by Robert Craft (Crawford, 1995; Morton, 1993).

A new source of financial support in the United States for new music came about in the 1960s from the Fromm Foundation, directed by German émigré Paul Fromm, which supported a range of commissions and concerts of new music, as well as the journal *Perspectives of New Music*, from 1962. Based at Harvard University from 1972, the foundation had earlier established the annual Festival of Contemporary Music at Tanglewood from 1964 onwards, and an ensemble, the Fromm Fellowship Players, who commissioned new works. They also arranged Seminars in Advanced Musical Studies, modeled in part on Darmstadt, in 1959 and 1962 (Gable, 1988). This was, however, relatively exceptional; new music in the postwar United States, both serial and otherwise, was otherwise primarily supported within universities (Straus, 1999), with Columbia, Harvard, Princeton, Wesleyan, and Yale of particular note in this respect.

In Japan, military defeat and a strong Western presence created a climate in which some Western musical developments that had already established a presence there, including atonality and dodecaphony, could grow further. Groups of composers founded further organizations such as Shinseikai in 1946 that played a major part in increasing exposure to dodecaphonic music to Japan (Galliano, 2002), and then a group of younger figures came together in 1951 to found Jikkenkōbō (Experimental Laboratory). These composers devoured Western music such as they could access, as well as modernist literature, art, and philosophy from Europe. They mounted yearly concerts, including Japanese premieres of such works as Schoenberg's *Pierrot lunaire* and Messiaen's *Quatuor pour la fin du temps*, as well as new works by Yuasa Jōji, Takemitsu Tōru, Fukushima Kazuo, and Suzuki Hiroyoshi, all founding members (Galliano, 2002). This all made possible the establishment of the Gendai Ongakusai new music festival, beginning in 1957. In the 1960s, under the influence above all of Ichiyanagi Toshi, who had spent a period in the 1950s in the United States and become a disciple of Cage, a new type of scene emerged which embraced indeterminacy and other aspects of the "second generation avant-garde" (those who came to prominence from the late 1950s onwards), leading to a significant range of concerts presented at the Sōgetsu Art Centre in Tokyo (Galliano, 2002; Everett, 2009).

New music in Soviet-controlled Eastern Europe was seriously inhibited by the fourth Zhdanov decree in 1948 condemning "formalist" tendencies more emphatically than ever before (Werth, 1949; Hakobian, 2017). This was then adopted at the 1948 Prague Congress, becoming akin to an official policy in much of Eastern Europe and in communist associations further afield (Waters, 2011). In the Soviet Zone of Germany, new music was at first promoted as energetically as in the other three zones (Pace, 2018), but the aesthetic climate changed following Zhdanov and then the establishment of the Deutsche Demokratische Republik (DDR) in 1949, after which the ideals of socialist realism soon came to dwarf the earlier broader culture of new music (Tompkins, 2013).

After Stalin's death in 1953 there was no major growth in new music in the Soviet Union, although some banned or unknown works were played in private or occasionally by students in the Moscow Conservatory (Schmelz, 2009). One of the first, albeit limited, postwar exposures to dodecaphonic/serial traditions came in 1957, when Canadian Glenn Gould was the first North American pianist to play in communist Eastern Europe, including Berg, Webern, and Krenek in his programs, as well as giving a lecture that touched briefly on the Second Viennese School (Schmelz, 2009). The following year, in line with wider de-Stalinization under Khrushchev, the Zhdanov decree was rescinded by the Central Committee and works previously denounced were rehabilitated (Werth, 1961). Nonetheless, Shostakovich denounced his own 1920s "experiments" and dismissed the Western avant-garde more broadly (Werth, 1961), and in 1963, Khrushchev himself spoke at length about music, rejecting "cacophonous" dodecaphonic music and reaffirming a commitment to the principles of socialist realism (Johnson, 1965). As travel restrictions eased during the 1960s, new music composers such as Stravinsky, Boulanger, Boulez, and Nono visited the country, while by the beginning of the Brezhnev era a range of fringe clubs featuring new music in Moscow, Leningrad, Kiev, and elsewhere had become established. But with central authority–issued lists of "recommended" music, the growth of new music remained inhibited (Schmelz, 2009).

In Hungary after an early postwar flourishing including Zenemüvészek Szövétsége (Hungarian Music Week), run in 1951, 1953 and 1956 (Beckles Willson, 2004, 2007; Ignácz, 2017), the climate became as hostile to new music as elsewhere in Eastern Europe, particularly following the Soviet invasion in 1956. The eventual easing of restrictions saw the foundation of two major concert and radio series, entitled Korunk zenéje (Music of Our Time), and Megújhodott Muzsika (Reformed Music) in 1974 and 1977 respectively, while a series of younger composers including Zoltán Jenéy and László Sary founded the Budapest New Music Studio in 1971. Here there was a strong affinity with "experimental" (especially that of Cage), minimal, and other music (Williams 2005).

But a different trajectory for new music was found in Poland, in which new music had its strongest profile of all countries in Eastern Europe, as a political and cultural "thaw" occurred somewhat earlier than elsewhere. There was a Festival of Contemporary Polish Music as early as September 1945, with a strong emphasis on music representing resistance to fascism and liberation, while composers Andrzej Panufnik, Witold Lutosławski and Grażyna Bacewicz were at first able to gain some profile as composers of new music (Thomas 2005). The Polish section of the ISCM was reactivated in 1946, though programming of new music was at first sporadic and centered on Polish composers, then socialist realism was fully implemented, and formalism was attacked, at a conference of composers and critics in 1949 at Łagów Lubuski (Bylander, 1989). The Polish ISCM was suspended until 1957, and the range of contemporary music permitted very limited for several years. But following Stalin's death, the minister of culture and art, Włodzimierz Sokorski, acknowledged the limitations of the aesthetic climate and hostility to innovation, in tandem with a wider political thaw that enabled scores and recordings, for example of Berg, to be brought to the country, a much more open Festival of Polish Music in 1955, more international programming in wider concert series, and increased possibilities for composers to travel outside of the Eastern Bloc. All of this made possible the Warszawska Jesień festival that was founded the following year, initiated primarily by composers Tadeusz Baird and Kazmierz Serocki. This would quickly become the center of radical new music in Eastern Europe (Jakelski, 2017).

Other more isolated events across Europe that promoted new music included a concert of works of the Second Viennese School in Brussels in 1948 (Dufour & Pirenne, 2004), while a range of the European avant-garde were brought together in that city a decade later during the Exposition universelle, leading to the formation of an Association Musiques Nouvelles in 1962 (Dufour & Pirenne, 2004; Pirenne, 2004). In London, William Glock organized new music events in the mid-1950s with the International Musical Association (Wright, 2007), a venture that occurred somewhat on the fringes of his more prominent activities mentioned earlier. A culture for new music did grow in Spain in the later years of the Franco regime, centered on the Grupo Nueva Música of composers in Madrid in 1958, and then important series from soon afterwards sponsored by the organizations Generación del 51, Zaj, and Alea in Madrid, and Música Abierta in Barcelona (Medina, 2001; De Pablo, 2009; Pardo, 2018). The organizations in Scandinavia founded before 1945 came under more radical leadership in the late 1950s and 1960s and hosted major events featuring atonal, indeterminate, and electronic music, as well as hosting artists associated with the Fluxus movement (Herresthal & Pedersen, 2002; nyMusikk, n.d.; Christensen, 2002; Broman, 2002, p. 457; Growth, 2016; Fylkingen, n.d.; Sørensen, 2016). Further afield in Montreal, composer Serge Garant, who had studied with Messiaen in Paris, hosted a series of contemporary music concerts in 1954, 1955, and 1958, placing contemporary Canadian composers in the context of international developments (Lefebvre, 1986; Lefebvre, 2008; SMCQ, n.d.).

In addition to these concerts and influences, as shown in Table 18.1, there was a major growth in many countries (and not only or primarily in Western Europe) in new music festival culture, bequeathed by the events in Donaueschingen and for the ISCM in the 1920s, in Venice in the 1930s, and in Frankfurt and elsewhere in the 1940s, with many new organizations founded.

Table 18.1. Festivals and organizations supporting new music, 1945–1975.
This table does not include various organizations that were founded before 1945
and ran mostly continuously from that point, including the International Society
for Contemporary Music. Composers' organizations are too numerous to include
here. Sources for this and Table 18.3: Howe, 1946; Laux, 1960; Fernández–Cid,
1973; Lefebvre, 1986; Weißbach, 1986; Zintgraf, 1987; Tortora, 1990; Kölner
Gesellschaft für Neue Musik, ed., 1991; Scarpetta, 1992; Morton, 1993; Crawford,
1995; Riedl, 1995; Stefan et al, 1996; Bylander, 1998; Tage der Neuen Musik,
1998; Braas, 2001; Medina, 2001; Neff, 2001; Broman, 2002; Christensen, 2002;
Galliano, 2002; Herresthal, 2002; Dufour & Pirenne, 2004; Herrmann & Weiss,
2004; Marco, 2004; Williams, 2005; Wright, 2005 & 2007; Beal, 2006; Samama,
2006; Besancon, 2007; Flender, 2007; Marti, 2007; Kerry, 2009; Romeo et al,
2013; Sørensen, 2016; Gasser, 2017; Jakelski, 2017; Fugellie, 2018; Cayón, 2019;
Biennale Musica, n.d.; Fylkingen, n.d.; SMCQ, n.d.

Founded	Name and any special focus	Location
1945	Trossinger Musiktage	Trossingen
1945	Musica viva	Munich
1945	Cheltenham Music Festival (initially British composers but became international)	Cheltenham
1945	Stichting Gaudeamus, from 1947 running Gaudeamus Musikwiek	Bilthoven, Netherlands
1946	Concerts of new music at Haus am Waldsee	Berlin
1946	Zeitgenössische Musikwoche; from 1947 Woche für neue Musik.	Bad Nauheim/Frankfurt (from 1947)
resumed 1946	Neue Musik Donaueschingen (re-started from festival in 1920s, only ran 1946 and 1947)	Donaueschingen
resumed 1946	Festival internazionale di musica contemporanea	Venice
resumed 1946	Shin Sakkyokuha Kyōkai and Nihon Gendai Ongaku Kyōkai (GenOn)	Japan
1946	Shinseikai	Tokyo
1946	Ferienkurse für internationale neue Musik	Darmstadt
1946	Abende zeitgenössischer Musik hosted by Kulturbund zur demokratischen Erneuerung Deutschlands	Berlin
resumed 1947	Wittener Kammermusiktage (sporadic until 1960, then annual event)	Witten
1947	Bayreuther Wochen–Neue Musik, then Tagung für Neue Musik und Musikerziehung from 1948	Bayreuth/Darmstadt (from 1951)
1947	Berliner Musiktage	Berlin
1947	Zeitgenössischer Stuttgart Musiktage, later Tage zeitgenössischer Musik	Stuttgart

(Continued)

Table 18.1. Continued

Founded	Name and any special focus	Location
1948	Aldeburgh Festival (limited new music)	Aldeburgh
1948	Bryanston Summer School (became Dartington)	Dorset
1948	Musiktage, later Musica viva	Heidelberg
1949	International Dodecaphonic Congress	Milan
1949	Festliche Tage für Neue Kammermusik	Braunschweig
resumed 1950	Donaueschinger Musiktage für zeitgenössische Tonkunst	Donaueschingen
1951	das neue werk	Hamburg
1951	Konzerte Neuer Musik, from 1952 Musik der Zeit	Cologne
1951	Berliner Festspiele	West Berlin
1951	Studio d'Essai, with Groupe de recherche de musique concrète	Paris
1951	Studio für elektronische Musik, Nordwestdeutscher Rundfunk Köln	Cologne
1951	Jikkenkōbō (Experimental Laboratory)	Tokyo
1951	Festival of Polish Music, second festival in 1955	Warsaw
1952	Berlin Festtage	East Berlin
1952 only	Society for Twentieth Century Music (British composers)	Hampstead
1952	Festtage zeitgenössischer Musik	East Berlin
1952	Tübinger Musiktage	Tübingen
1952	Thuringian Festival of Contemporary Music	Weimar
1952	Pro Arte concert series	Santiago
1953	Dartington International Summer School of Music (previously Bryanston)	Devon
1953	Tonus concert series	Santiago
1954	Caracas Music Festival	Caracas
1954	Musikfest des VDK (Verband deutscher Komponisten) (socialist realism)	Leipzig
1954	Musik unsere Zeit	Stuttgart
1954	Domaine musical concert series	Paris
1955	Festtage neuer Musik (socialist realism)	Leipzig
1955	Musik der Gegenwart	West Berlin
1955	Studio di Fonologia Musicale, RAI	Milan
1955	NHK Studio	Tokyo
1956	Siemens-Studio für elektronische Musik	Munich
1956	Warszawska Jesień (Warsaw Autumn)	Warsaw
1957	Studio de musique electronique	Brussels
1957	Finnish Musical Youth (international and graphic notation)	Helsinki

Table 18.1. Continued

Founded	Name and any special focus	Location
1957	Gendai Ongakusai Festival	Tokyo
1957	Incontri Musicali	Milan
1957	Experimental Radio Studio	Warsaw
1958	Journées Internationales de Musique Experimentale	Brussels
1958	Tage der Neue Musik	Hannover
1958	Pro Musica Nova	Bremen
1960	Contre-Fest	Cologne
1960	Neue Musik München	Munich
1960	Settimane internazionali di Palermo	Palermo
1960	Música Abierta	Barcelona
1961	Music Biennale Zagreb	Zagreb
1961	Helsinki Electronic Music Studio	Helsinki
1962	Association Musiques Nouvelles	Brussels
1962	Reconnaissance des musiques modernes	Brussels
1962	Musica Polonica Nova (Polish music only)	Wrocław
1963	Nuova Consonanza	Rome
1964	Festival of Contemporary Music, Tanglewood	Tanglewood
1964	Festival international d'art contemporain de Royan	Royan
1964	First International Biennial of Contemporary Music	Madrid
1964	Tage zeitgenössischer Musik	Heidelberg
1965	Alea concert series	Madrid
1966	Young Composers Society (AUT) (electronic music)	Århus
1966	Société de musique contemporaine du Québec	Montreal
1968	Musikprotokoll	Graz
1968	Semaines musicales internationales de Paris	Paris
1969	Radio Belgrade Electronic Studio	Belgrade
1969	Min-On Contemporary Music Festival (mostly Japanese composers)	Tokyo
1969	Neue Musik in Delmenhorst	Delmenhorst
1972	Festival d'automne à Paris	Paris
1972	Woche der avantgardistischen Musik	West Berlin
1975	Musique en Armagnac	Pyrenees

Performers and ensembles

A range of solo performers born in the 1920s and 1930s made a reputation for their specialism in new music, including pianists Yvonne Loriod, Marcelle Mercenier, Claude Helffer, David Tudor, Aloys and Alfons Kontarsky, Frederic Rzewski, cellist Siegfried Palm, percussionist Christopher Caskel, singer Cathy Berberian, flautist Severino Gazzelloni, oboist Heinz Holliger, and trombonist Vinko Globokar, Almost all had a background playing more established repertoire, and many continued to do so throughout their careers. Their identity was based as much upon their willingness to tackle some of the immense new challenges in the repertoire they played, and to do so on a regular basis, rather than necessarily through any radical shift in wider performing aesthetic, at least no more so than that which grew in the interwar period. While new music has not always been the exclusive preserve of specialists, few performers whose careers have been based in large measure upon performance of music of the common practice era have taken up works of the first generation postwar avant-garde; the very few exceptions among major international stars include the pianist Maurizio Pollini, and conductors Claudio Abbado, Daniel Barenboim and Christoph Eschenbach.

What is now a staple of new music performance, the new music ensemble, did not really develop significantly until into the 1960s. Two works of Schoenberg provide a template for the type of instrumentation favored: the *Kammersymphonie* in E major, Op. 9, for strings and mostly single wind (though in this exceptional case three clarinets); and the smaller group employed in *Pierrot lunaire*, Op. 21, with flute, clarinet, piano, violin, and cello (and in this case voice too). Leaving aside standard instrumentations such as the string quartet or wind quintet, and works for chamber orchestra with more than one string player to a part, a repertoire had developed from avant-garde composers of the 1950s of works for smaller or larger ensemble, such as:

- Jean Barraqué: *Sequence* (1950–1955);
- Karlheinz Stockhausen: *Kreuzspiel* (1951) and *Kontra-Punkte* (1952–1953);
- Karel Goeyvaerts, *Nr. 2 voor 13 instrumenten* (1951) ;
- Luigi Nono: *Polifonica-monodia-ritmica* (1951), *Liebeslied* (1954), *Canti per 13* (1955);
- Morton Feldman: *Projections 3 and 5* (1951), *Eleven Instruments* (1953), and *Two Pieces for Six Instruments* (1956);
- Elliott Carter, Sonata for flute, oboe, cello, and harpsichord (1952);
- Pierre Boulez: *Le Marteau sans maître* (1953–1955, rev. 1957) and *Improvisations sur Mallarmé I & II* (1959–1962, rev. 1983, 1989);
- Bruno Maderna: *Serenata no. 2* (1954, rev. 1957);
- Earle Brown: *Indices* (1954) and *Penthathis* (1958);
- Henri Pousseur: *Quintette à le Memoire d'Anton Webern* (1955);
- Iannis Xenakis: *ST/10, 1-080262* (1956–1962);
- Luciano Berio: *Serenata* (1957), *Tempi concertante* (1959), and *Différences* (1959) ;
- Harrison Birtwistle, *Monody for Corpus Christi* (1959);

- Louis Andriessen, *Percosse* (1959); and
- Aldo Clementi: *Ideogrammi n. 1* (1959)

There were few fixed groups of players dedicated to this work through the 1950s other than Solistes du Domaine Musical, founded in 1954 in line with the series, and the Viennese Ensemble "die Reihe" (The Series) founded in 1958 (Cerha, 1999). Other ad hoc, but important, groups were Ensemble Incontri Musicali, founded in 1958 by Bruno Maderna in association with the concert series and journal of the same name (Tortora, 1990; Borio & Danuser, 1997, vol. 3), and the Internationale Kranichsteiner Kammerensemble (from 1964 Internationales Kammerensemble Darmstadt), which came together each year for Darmstadt, and was made up of those teaching on the courses (Borio and Danuser, 1997, vol. 2).

From the 1960s, the first major ensembles were formed especially in the United States, UK, France, and the Low Countries, as shown in Table 18.2. Some were more dogmatically

Table 18.2 Ensembles dedicated to new music, 1954–1974. Sources for this and Table 18.4: Fernández–Cid, 1973; Bialosky, 1980; Aguta, 1992; Schönbewrger, 1996; Stefan et al, 1996; Borio & Danuser, 1997; Cerha, 1999; Braas, 2001; Andriessen, 2002; Broman, 2002; Christensen, 2002; Galliano, 2002; Bernbacher, 2003; Madurell, 2003; Dufour & Pirenne, 2004; Pirenne, 2004; Samama, 2006; Kerry, 2009; Dromey, 2012; Sørensen, 2016; Barker, 2017; Fugellie, 2018; Fylkingen, n.d.

Founded	Ensemble name	Base
1954	Solistes du Domaine Musical	Paris
1956	Melos Ensemble	Dartington from 1960
1958	"die Reihe" (The Series)	Vienna
1958	Ensemble Instrumental de Musique Contemporaine	Paris
1960	Schola Cantorum Stuttgart	Stuttgart
1960	Musica nova	Brno
1961	Internationale Kranichsteiner Kammerensemble (from 1964 Internationales Kammerensemble Darmstadt)	Darmstadt
1961	Musica Viva Pragensis	Prague
1962:	The Group for Contemporary Music	New York City
1962	Les Percussions de Strasbourg	Strasbourg
1962	Ensemble Musique Nouvelles	Brussels
1963	Ensemble Ars Nova	Paris
1963	Sonatori di Praga	Prague
1963	Hudba dneška	Bratislava
1963	New Direction	Tokyo

(Continued)

Table 18.2. Continued

Founded	Ensemble name	Base
1964	University of Chicago Contemporary Chamber Players	Chicago
1965	Prague New Music Group	Prague
1966	Amsterdams Studenten Kamer Orkest (later ASKO Ensemble)	Amsterdam
1966	Musique vivante	Paris
1967	Juilliard Ensemble (mostly students)	New York City
1967	The Pierrot Players	London
1967	Budapest Chamber Ensemble	Budapest
1968	Ars Nova	Cluj, Romania
1968	ars nova ensemble nürnberg	Nürnberg
1968	London Sinfonietta	London
1970	Budapest New Music Studio	Budapest
1970	Ensemble "Trial and Error"	Cologne
1970	The Fires of London	London
1970	Gruppe Neue Musik	Leipzig
1971	Speculum Musicae	New York City
1971	2e2m	Paris
1971	De Volharding	Amsterdam
1972	Ensemble Intercontemporain	Paris
1973	Ensemble l'Itinéraire	Paris
1973	Les Rencontres internationales d'art contemporain	La Rochelle
1973	Music Today	Tokyo
1973	Kronos Quartet	San Francisco
1974	Arditti Quartet	London
1974	Schönberg Ensemble	Amsterdam
1974	Wilhelm Breuker Kollektif	Amsterdam

oriented toward serial music than others and some might include medieval or Renaissance music into their programs. As time went on, the American ensembles became less open to European composers, preferring an attitude of "America first"; likewise, with the exception of Solistes du Domaine Musical, French ensembles would show preferences for French music and, although a relatively broad repertoire was performed in Britain, British composers were granted greater prominence as time passed. It was in the UK that the all-black attire of *The Pierrot Players* formed by Harrison Birtwistle and Peter Maxwell Davies in 1967 would emerge as the standard stage dress for many new music ensembles.

While only a few ensembles were formed in Germany in the decades before the establishment of Ensemble Modern in 1980, one group that had a profound effect was the Schola Cantorum Stuttgart, a 16–18-part vocal ensemble founded by conductor and musicologist and radio producer Clytus Gottwald in 1960, and running for thirty years. This group was at the forefront of generating and performing a new repertoire involving increasing hyper-virtuosity and defamiliarization of multiple solo voices, pioneering multiple works including Ferneyhough's *Time and Motion Study III* (1974), which epitomizes an intensified culmination of everything the Schola had achieved (see Figure 18.1).

Debates and performance issues

During the 1960s, debate about the extent to which new music should be incorporated into mainstream programs was articulated particularly strongly in the Netherlands. In Amsterdam, a group of students came together to form the Amsterdams Studenten Kamer Orkest in 1966 (Schönberger, 1996), partially in response to highly politicized campaigns for a much greater commitment to new music in Dutch musical life (Adlington, 2013). The professional ensemble that would emerge from this group in 1966 and flourish, Ensemble ASKO, became a regular presence at the Concertgebouw. Yet some wanted an even greater commitment to new music, stimulating public debate. Opinion was divided over the fundamental questions of whether new music should be integrated into the mainstream or whether much more significant reforms were needed to the latter. Many of the arguments resembled those associated with the *Neue Sachlichkeit* and *Gebrauchsmusik* (utility music) in Germany in the 1920s and involved a significant number of artists or other figures with vested interests in the art worlds presuming to speak for the needs and wishes of the people. In 1966, conductor Bruno Maderna, who had become something of a totemic figure for young Dutch radicals, pronounced that the evolution of the avant-garde was "an unbreakable course of events; the public must learn to see this" (cited in Adlington, 2013, p. 81). Earlier, the composer Ton de Leeuw had advocated a "mobile ensemble" that would respond to changing public needs, and while initially rejected by most of the younger composers for simply relegating new music to the margins, it proved to be the way forward; although not without ongoing protests, the young composers to some extent acquiesced, seeking their own "mobile ensembles" (Adlington, 2013).

These groups, including De Volharding founded by Louis Andriessen in 1971 (Andriessen, 2002), went as far as any before them in forging a style—dry, pointed, with prominent driving rhythms, eschewing blended sonorities—that positioned itself as far away from mainstream performing cultures as anyone had done before, or arguably since. Their approach did however strongly resemble the new styles for performing Renaissance and Baroque music that had themselves been developed by groups in the Netherlands. The other major parallel could be found in minimalist groups formed by young composers to perform their music, notably Steve Reich and Musicians in 1966 and the Philip Glass Ensemble in 1968.

Various other events in the 1960s caused, and were designed to cause, some friction within what was already becoming an "established" culture of new music. In Cologne, a

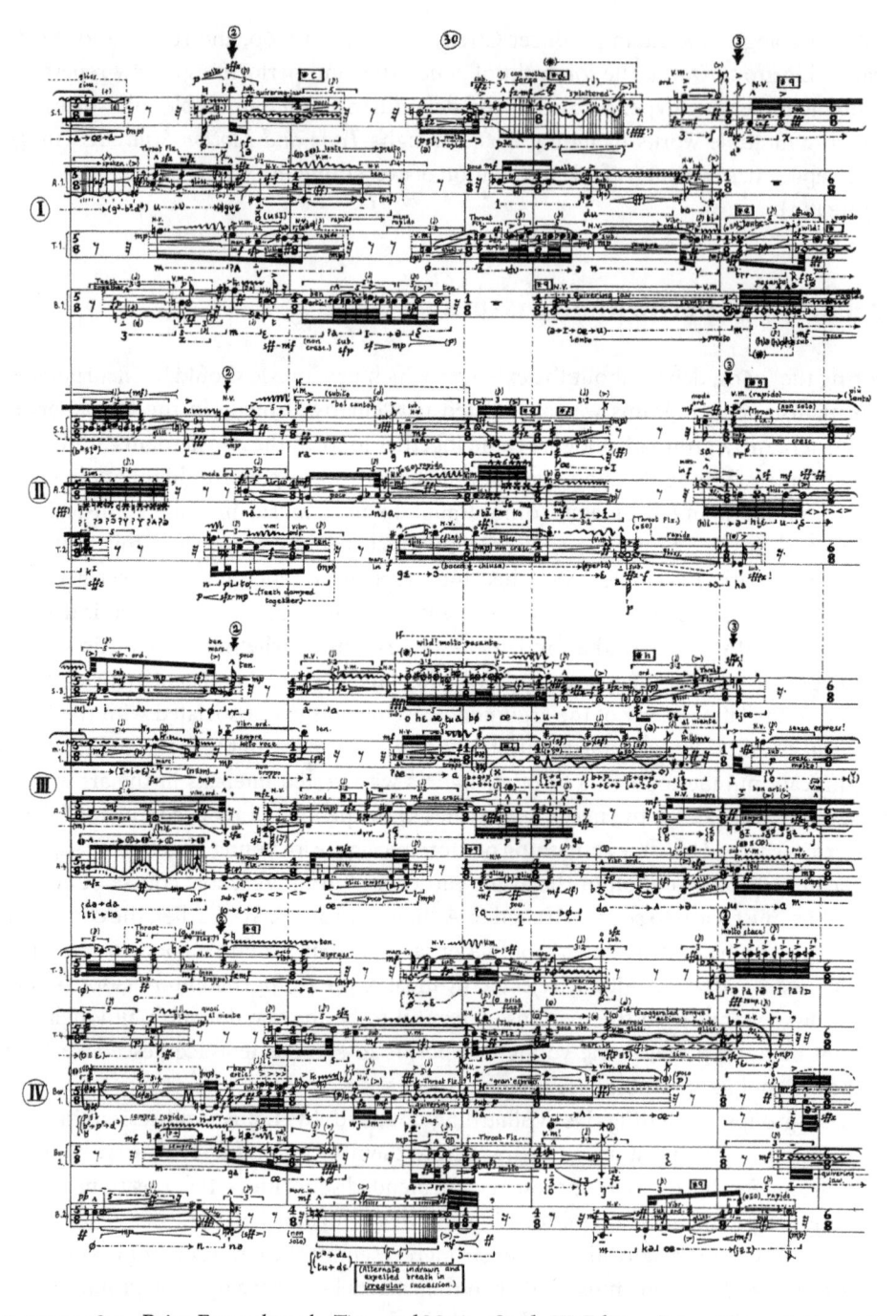

FIGURE 18.1. Brian Ferneyhough, *Time and Motion Study III*, Edition Peters No. 7148, © 1974 by Peters Edition Limited, London. Reproduced by permission of the Publishers.

Contre-Fest taking place at the studio of artist Mary Bauermeister, featuring figures such as Heinz-Klaus Metzger, Hans G. Helms, Sylvano Bussotti, and others, was deliberately scheduled to clash with the ISCM festival in June 1960 (Historisches Archiv der Stadt Köln, 1993), while later that year the concert series Neue Musik München was mounted, with a similar aesthetic agenda, as an alternative to the Musica Viva series (Riedl, 1995). Both of these new events evinced a much greater openness to the indeterminacy of John Cage and others (Beal, 2006). From this point onwards, in the northern parts of Western Europe, new music performance culture came to embrace indeterminacy, music-theater, graphic and text-based works, spatial music, vocal works based upon a search for fundamentals based upon phonetics, and musical quotation (Borio, 1993).

A new dimension to performance was provided by a series of works for live performers together with tape or other pre-recorded source, beginning with Maderna's *Musica sa due dimensioni* for flute and tape (1952, rev. 1958), prepared together with electronic music pioneer Werner Meyer-Eppler. Maderna wanted to effect an interaction between these "two dimensions" of music making (Fearn, 1990). Here and in a range of diffuse subsequent works, from Nono's *La fabbrica illuminata* (1964) for soprano and tape to Steve Reich's *Vermont Counterpoint* (1982) for flute and tape, the performer is constrained arguably like never before—throughout they have to adapt, certainly in terms of rhythm and pitch, to the requirements of the tape, with no possibility of a reciprocal relationship. Such a situation would change with greater use of live electronic performance combined with acoustic instruments, so that the performer on the electronics would play a creative and interactive role themselves, but in general, most performers who have worked with electronics have had to learn a new type of discipline and a degree of self-negation in performance.

Conductors

The most prominent early postwar conductors of new music were Scherchen, Hans Rosbaud, Maderna, and Roger Désormière (for a strong example of the latter, Orchestre de chambre André Girard & Désormière, 2007). The recorded legacies of all four are of defining importance in establishing a sense of mid-century modernist performance, especially Rosbaud, whose absolutely acute sense of fine orchestral detail and clarity in his 1950s recordings of Berg's Three Orchestral Pieces, Op. 6; Webern's Six Orchestral Pieces, Op. 6; and concern for finely etched differentiation of notes with stronger or weaker rhythmic placement in Messiaen's *Turangalîla Symphony*, have rarely been equaled (SWF-Sinfonieorchester Baden-Baden & Rosbaud, 1958; 1992). These four were soon joined by Boulez, considerably younger than all the others besides Maderna, and who saw an opening that he developed primarily first through his work for the Domaine concerts, then when he often came to replace Rosbaud (Jameux, 1991; Boulez, 1976; Vermeil, 1996; Häusler, 1996).

In works conducted by Boulez, one encounters a powerful sense of phrasing, line, and continuity combined with a sensitivity to timbre, preferring more pointed timbres in earlier performances, more lush and expansive blended sounds in later years. While avoiding the *espressivo* approach to the Second Viennese School associated with many earlier performers, his own early performances were anything but dry and mechanical, as will be discussed in the context of Schoenberg's Suite, Op. 29. While highly respectful of musical texts, Boulez was clear that he did not believe there was such a thing as an "objective" interpretation, while realizing that certain attributes associated with that term were not new but were characteristic of earlier generations of conductors, including Ernst Ansermet, who were in turn influenced by Stravinsky and Ravel. But to Boulez, objectivity was "a problem for any generation traumatized by the excessive subjectivity of the generation preceding it," thus distancing himself from the aesthetic ideals of the *Neue Sachlichkeit* (Vermeil, 1996, pp. 74–75).

Reinventing instruments, techniques, voices, notation

The use of unusual playing techniques was an occasional feature in various interwar music, as, for example, through Cowell's use of plucking and scraping piano strings in *Aeolian Harp* (c. 1923) and *The Banshee* (1925), Varèse's use of key-slaps on the flute in *Density 21.5* (1936), Bartók's snap pizzicato in his String Quartet No. 4 (1928), or Berg's use of left-hand pizzicato in his Violin Concerto (1935). But a number of composers who became prominent in the postwar era elevated these and other techniques to a central role in their work. Among the most important early examples of this were John Cage in his works for prepared piano from *Bacchanale* (1938) onwards, and Xenakis's use of continuous string glissandi, for periods appearing to negate stable pitches in *Metastaseis* (1953–1954) and *Pithoprakta* (1955–1956).

As momentum gathered, composers called for sul ponticello and sul tasto, tremoli and glissandi, including multiple simultaneous glissandi on different strings of the same instrument, at different rates. Helmut Lachenmann's idea of a *musique concrète instrumentale*, echoing the transformations of "concrete" sounds but using the widest spectrum of possible timbres that can be made by traditional instruments, calls for an unprecedented degree of unconventional playing techniques and results in music permeated by acerbic, uncompromising timbres. In their most concentrated form (as, for example, in the cello piece *Pression* [1969, rev. 2010] or the string quartet *Gran Torso* [1971–1972]), these appear to negate almost all semblances of a traditional sonic vocabulary. Lachenmann was far from alone in a concentration on extended techniques, which was also pioneered by Mauricio Kagel, Holliger, Salvatore Sciarrino, Hans-Joachim Hespos, and others, with radically different expressive aims, from Sciarrino's phantasmagoric evocations of distant, ungraspable phenomena, to Hespos's Artaud-inspired assaults on the senses. Globokar's *Voix instrumentalisée* (1973) for bass clarinet calls for the mouthpiece to be removed and the player to use their voice as a replacement. Others ask wind players to sing into their instrument while playing, while vocalists are called upon to emit potentially any sound, or to utter syllables and phonemes rather than words, as in Dieter Schnebel's *Für stimmen (. . . missa est . . .)* (1956, rev. 1968) or György

Ligeti's *Aventures* (1962). Ferneyhough's *Time and Motion Study II* (1974) combines a singing cellist with electronics and Holliger's *Scardanelli-Zyklus* (1975) asks vocalists to sing to the beat of their own pulses, or while breathing inwards. Sometimes, performers might not only be asked to acquire new technical prowess, or to move between multiple instruments, but also to adopt a new stage persona that goes beyond the traditional theatricality of live performance, not least in the work of Schnebel, Kagel, or Sylvano Bussotti. Microtonality continued to be explored but would later come to be associated primarily with music associated with the "new complexity," *musique spectrale*, or a certain body of other work employing non-tempered tuning systems.

Overarchingly, the application of extended techniques and idiosyncratic approaches not only reflected a fascination with the quality of sound, its creation, and presentation, but also called for continuity to be achieved between "normal" sounds and extended techniques. Similarly, new forms of notation were devised that relied upon tradition for their gestation but might incorporate different colors to distinguish lines or materials, as in Boulez's *Constellation-Miroir* from the Piano Sonata No. 3 (1955–1957), Gilbert Amy's Piano Sonata (1961), and later Thomas Adès's *Darknesse Visible* for piano (1992). Others might include elaborate written instructions or graphics, or produce entire scores comprising these. But the problems associated with creating an enduring performance tradition for such works contributed to the reduction of interest in graphic scores from the mid-1960s.

Since the 1970s, few works have exceeded the degree of defamiliarization of instruments and voices as those achieved by Schnebel, Holliger, Lachenmann, Globokar, and Sciarrino; but ironically, as mastery of such techniques has become a standard requirement for performers of new music, they may have lost much of the meaning they once had, from explosively disruptive approaches to timbre and theater to part of a new music *lingua franca*.

Indeterminacy

The thirst for experimentation extended beyond exploring sound to include a reconceptualization of the process of musical creation, particularly the relationship between composer and performer. With precedents in Ives's obfuscatory notations at the beginning of the twentieth century, and Cowell's "Mosaic" Quartet (1935), it is Cage who is considered the foremost proponent of indeterminacy in music. Creating specific instructions that belie any putative association with improvisation, his primary impetus was to erase both composer and performer's individual desires and tastes from the music. While few others went so far as Cage himself in this respect, and some of his associates, including in different ways Earle Brown or Morton Feldman, would gradually make evident the importance of their own choices and preferences, nonetheless the gauntlet thrown down by Cage garnered strong interest across the world from the late 1950s onwards, with composers creating entirely indeterminate works or combining aleatoric instructions in otherwise traditionally determinate scores. The major protagonist for this was Cage's *Concert for Piano and Orchestra* (1957–1958), performed at Darmstadt in 1958, involving a set of graphics for the pianist with some "rules" that can nonetheless be interpreted in manifold different ways (see Iddon & Thomas, 2020; Holzaepfel, 2020). Sylvano Bussotti, in his *Five Piano Pieces for David Tudor* (1959) and *pre tre sul piano* (1959) (see Figure 18.2), invites the pianist to find creative responses as much to the overall graphic implications of the scores as the specific but highly ambiguous details contained therein.

In his *Mobile für Shakespeare* (1960), Roman Haubenstock-Ramati, like Bussotti, combines fragments of complex traditional notation with graphic notation, with each part instructed to read their section of the graphic in either clockwise or anticlockwise order, starting anywhere (Haubenstock-Ramati, 1980). Other forms of performer indeterminacy could be found in the text works of Dieter Schnebel such as *raum-zeit y* (1958) or *glossolalie* (1959–1961) that require performers to construct the piece from written instructions, in more absurd textual scores associated with the Fluxus movement at the beginning of the 1960s, and in the work of Stockhausen, whose much more ambiguous and somewhat "spiritualist" indications in *Aus den sieben Tagen* (1968) have been interpreted in many different ways. No performer was more closely associated with composers engaging with indeterminacy than pianist David Tudor, and while it would be rash to assume that Tudor's interpretations (many of them carefully notated before performance) are somehow "definitive," they are certainly informative for all others seeking to perform this work (Holzaepfel, 1994).

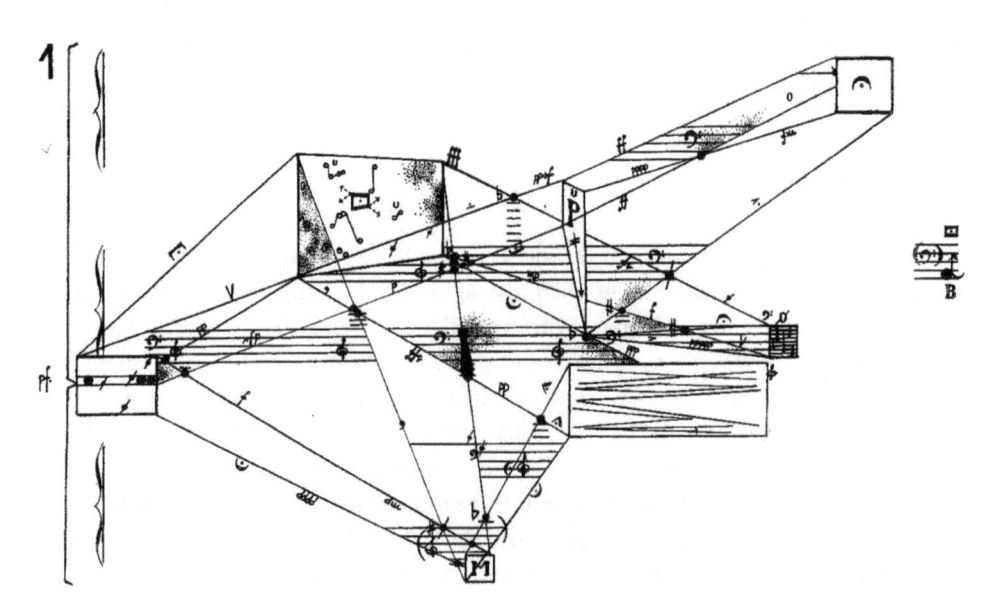

FIGURE 18.2. Sylvano Bussotti, per tre sul piano (1959). Published by Ricordi. Reproduced by permission of the Publishers.

Complexity and new virtuosity

Instrumental challenges that involved a new type of virtuosity that exceeded anything previously asked for had the potential for creating transcendental experiences for performers. Early examples of such extreme demands could be found in such works as:

- Boulez: Sonata No. 2 for piano (1948)
- Stockhausen: *Kontra-Punkte* (1952–1953) (especially the quasi-concertante piano part), *Klavierstück X* (1954–1955, rev. 1961), and *Zyklus* (1959)
- Berio: *Sequenzas I* (1958, rev. 1992) for flute, *II* (1963) for harp, and *III* (1965) for female voice
- Bussotti: *Sette fogli* (1959) and *Pour Clavier* (1961)
- Maderna: Oboe Concerto No. 1 (1962–1963)
- Xenakis: *Herma* (1961), *Eonta* (1964) (see Figure 18.3) and *Nomos Alpha* (1965–1966)

Various subsequent works of Xenakis in particular can fairly be described as having been written with only a relatively small amount of attention to their physical practicality and have provoked ferocious and sometimes competitive debates between performers as to the feasibility of rendering anything approximating to the level of information in the score (see Hill, 1975; Takahashi & Pruslin, 1975; Couroux, 2002; Howard, 2004; and various essays in Kanach, 2010). Moreover, the exploration of extreme virtuosity became a more focused aspect of contemporary composition in the 1960s, inspired above all by the virtuosity of Berberian, Holliger, and Globokar.

A "decoupling" of different aspects of conventional performance could be found early on in two works for recorder, both written for Franz Brüggen: Louis Andriessen's *Sweet* (1964) and Berio's *Gesti* (1966) (see Figure 18.4). In the latter case, the music has separate parts for mouth and fingers. This possibility would be developed by a range of "complex" composers, not least Brian Ferneyhough in his *Time and Motion Study II* (1973–1976) and *Unity Capsule* (1973–1976).

John Cage pursued his own extremes of virtuosity in the *Etudes Australes* (1974–1975) for piano, the *Freeman Etudes* (1977–1980, 1989–1990) for violin, and *Etudes Boreales* (1978) for cello and/or piano, written for and in collaboration with pianist Grete Sultan, violinist Paul Zukofsky, and cellist Jack Kirstein respectively. In each, Cage derived a gamut of possible micro-materials; in the *Etudes Australes*, for example, he gives chords and aggregates for each hand separately.

Although most of its protagonists reject the term, a movement that has come to be known as the "New Complexity," renowned for scores of extreme density and especially rhythmic complexity, was inaugurated by Ferneyhough and Michael Finnissy in the later 1960s (though neither had any conscious intention of founding a "school"), drawing the interest of younger composers such as James Dillon, Richard Barrett, Klaus K. Hübler, Claus-Steffen Mahnkopf, Alessandro Melchiorre, and many others. The movement reached something of a peak with Ferneyhough's *Time and Motion Study*

FIGURE 18.3. Iannis Xenakis, *Eonta* (1964), mm. 193–198. Copyright 1967 by Boosey & Hawkes Music Publishers Ltd. Reproduced by permission of Boosey & Hawkes Music Publishers Ltd. All Rights Reserved. Unauthorized Reproduction is illegal.

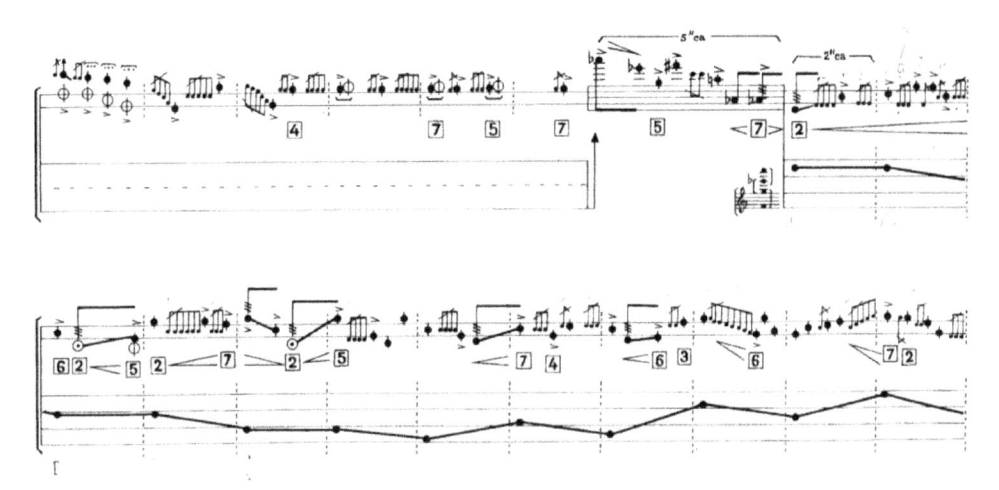

FIGURE 18.4. Luciano Berio, *Gesti* (1966), separate parts for the mouth (*above*) and fingers (*below*).

III (1974) for sixteen solo voices and *Unity Capsule* (1975–1976) for solo alto flute, and Finnissy's *English Country-Tunes* (1977, rev. 1982–1985) and Piano Concerto No. 4 (1978, rev. 1996). These have often been viewed, for better or worse, as epitomizing two quite distinct aesthetic directions: a "Finnissy faction" that takes its cue from Stockhausen, Xenakis, and Bussotti, often focusing on textural factors, with the ranges of instruments exploited to the point of saturation; and a "Ferneyhough faction" that is closer to the work of Schoenberg, Webern, and Boulez, more focused on gestural language, discursive and contrapuntal formulations, and micro-rhythmic detail, together with a greater inclination toward the employment of extended instrumental techniques, including "decoupling" (see Hawkins, 2010).

What end does the virtuosity in this tradition serve? In the case of the Finnissy of the 1970s, it is not difficult to see how the piano works have to do with a breadth and expansiveness of texture and gesture, married to a certain rhetoric of mannered excess. For Ferneyhough, on the other hand, it provides a means of eschewing reified musical gesture and language. But others have been more skeptical, maintaining that the detail of the notation is excessive, unrealizable, and sometimes thus redundant. Roger Marsh, Christoph Keller, and to a lesser extent Klaus Lippe have transcribed actual performances of the works, attempted to notate what they hear, and compared these with the actual scores, in each case finding their own transcriptions to be considerably simpler (Marsh, 1994; Keller, 1997; Lippe, 2013). But this sort of eliding of the distinction between prescriptive and descriptive approaches to notation has been criticized by many (e.g., Feller, 1994; Cross, 1996; Duncan, 2010), noting not least that "simpler" scores would bring about a quite different set of results if provided for performers, and a range of younger composers including Wieland Hoban, Aaron Cassidy, Evan Johnson, and Maxim Kolomiiets have continued to produce scores sometimes of even greater complexity than their older counterparts, and found a small but dedicated range of players prepared to undertake them.

THE CONSOLIDATION OF NEW MUSIC AND ITS MODEST INCORPORATION INTO MAINSTREAM REPERTOIRE

The period from 1945–1960 saw the birth of a particular new music culture that gradually moved away from the more moderate interwar traditions, such as those represented by Hindemith, Milhaud, Prokofiev, Shostakovich, or Hartmann. The period from 1960 until around the mid-1970s was the heyday of avant-garde *composition*, during which various uncompromising tendencies were pursued relentlessly, sometimes to extremes, to an extent not matched since, and probably paralleled only in the 1920s. Yet new music performance remained a fringe activity, sustained by a relatively small few during these times. The period from the mid-1970s until the present day has been one essentially of consolidation, dispersion, and re-integration of disparate, sometimes less radical, compositional tendencies. Even such aesthetic developments as the new forms of quietism and mysticism in the work of Nono and Feldman in the 1980s, combined with the rediscovery of Giacinto Scelsi around the same time (Wilson, 1992), appear as an extension and distillation of earlier tendencies rather than any particular break, while the work of the *Neue Konzeptualismus* after 2000 is not striking in its novelty to those well familiar with earlier work from the Dada or Fluxus movements. At the same time, new music performance has significantly expanded in its scope, leading to some degree of rapprochement with mainstream performance culture, though this has been relatively modest.

With some relaxation of the climate for new music in parts of Eastern Europe, particularly after the end of communism, Dresden became an important East German center for new music (Herrmann & Weiss, 2004), while new music has continued to thrive in Poland, in the Czech Republic, and elsewhere. New music festivals continued and continue to grow in most Western countries, and increasingly further afield. A significant number have become high-prestige institutions whose commissions and opportunities for performance are becoming an essential aspect of composers' careers, and where many new music performers aspire to play. Table 18.3 shows the most prominent of these.

Occasionally, festivals were created by musicians with an equal foot in mainstream music making, as with Claudio Abbado's founding of Wien Modern (Schreiber, 2019). That these organizations, once viewed as fringe institutions, had come to form a type of "establishment" of their own became apparent with the foundation in 1999 of a new consortium of sixteen new music festivals and organizations from eleven European

Table 18.3. Major new music festivals since 1975.

Founded	Name	Location
1975	June in Buffalo	Buffalo
1975	Festival Neue Musik	Lüneburg
1977	Tage der Neue Musik	Würzburg
1977	Gulbenkian Encounters of Contemporary Music	Lisbon
1978	Huddersfield Contemporary Music Festival	Huddersfield
1979	New Music America	New York City then various
1980	Tage für Neue Musik Stuttgart (from 1997 ECLAT)	Stuttgart
1981	Helsinki Biennale (later Musica nova Helsinki)	Helsinki
1982	Berlin Atonal	Berlin
1983	Musica	Strasbourg
1984	L'Espace du son	Brussels
1985	Music Factory (Borealis Festival from 2006)	Bergen
1987	Dresdner Tage der zeitgenössischen Musik (TONLAGEN– Dresdner Tage der zeitgenössischen Musik from 2009)	Dresden
1987	Tage der Neuen Musik	Bamberg
1987	Tage für Neue Musik	Rottenburg/Neckar
1987	Exposition of New Music	Brno
1988	Wien Modern	Vienna
1988	Münchener Biennale	Munich
1988	Wochenende für Neue Musik, from 2000 Zeit für Neue Musik	Bayreuth
1988	Tage Neuer Musik	Weimar
1989	Ars Musica Brussels	Brussels
1990	Kreuzberger Klangwerkstatt (Klangwerkstatt Berlin from 2000)	Berlin
1990	Stockholm New Music	Stockholm
1990	Kyiv Music Fest	Kiev
1990	Takefu International Music Festival	Takefu, Japan
1990	Daegu International Contemporary Music Festival	Daegu, S. Korea
1990	Sydney Spring International Festival	Sydney
1991	Présences	Paris
1991	Ultima Oslo Contemporary Music Festival	Oslo
1992	Festival Archipel	Geneva
1992	Bang on a Can Summer Music Festival	New York City
1993	November Music	's-Hertogenbosch
1994	New Music Marathon	Prague
1994	Festival Atempo Caracas-Paris	Caracas, Paris
1994	Seoul International Computer Music Festival	Seoul

(Continued)

Table 18.3. Continued

Founded	Name	Location
1995	Two Days and Two Nights of New Music	Odessa
1996	Bienal Internacional de Música Eletroacústica de São Paulo	São Paulo
1997	Biennale Neue Musik	Hannover
1997	Deutsches Minimal Music-Festival, from 2007 Internationales Minimal Music Festival	Kassel
1997	Colorado Springs New Music Symposium	Colorado Springs
1998	Festival ton-art	Esslingen
1999	Ultraschall	Berlin
2000	TRANSIT Festival	Leuven
2000	Ostrava Days	Ostrava
2000	KlangZeit Münster, later Musik unsere Zeit, then Klangzeit*Werkstatt	Münster
2000	brandenburgisches fest der neue musik	Potsdam
2000	Opening—Internationales Festival für aktuelle Klangkunst	Trier
2000	Weimarer Frühjahrstage für zeitgenössische Musik	Weimar
2001	Sonemus Fest	Sarajevo
2001	International Festival of New Music, Pristina, from 2005 ReMusica	Pristina
2002	MaerzMusik	Berlin
2002	pyramidale—festival für neue musik und interdisziplinäre kunstaktionen	Berlin
2002	Frankfurter Herbsttage für Neue Komposition	Frankfurt
2002	Cal State Fullerton New Music Festival	Fullerton
2002	Tongyeong International Music Festival (part new music)	Tongyeong, South Korea
2003	Montréal/Nouvelles Musiques	Montreal
2004	Internationales Klangkunstfest Berlin	Berlin
2004	Festliche Tage Neuer Musik	Braunschweig
2005	klub kararakt—Internationales festival für experimentelle Musik	Hamburg
2005	next_generation—Treffen Elektronischer Studios	Karlsruhe
2005	Cortona Contemporary Music Festival (2005), later soundSCAPE, later highSCORE	Maccagno
2006	Sonic Fusion Festival	Edinburgh
2006	Festival champs libres	Strasbourg
2006	Störung Festival	Barcelona
2006	MusicNOW	Cincinnati
2007	soundON Festival of Modern Music	La Jolla
2008	Musik 21 Niedersachsen	Hannover

Table 18.3. Continued

Founded	Name	Location
2008	Impuls—Festival für Neue Musik Sachsen-Anhalt	Various locations in Sachsen-Anhalt
2008	SinusTon—Magdeburger Tage der elektroakustischen Musik	Magdeburg
2008	Melbourne International Biennale of Exploratory Music	Melbourne
2008	Adelaide Contemporary Music Festival	Adelaide
2008	Contempuls	Prague
2009	Dallas Festival of Modern Music	Dallas
2010	Festival Musica Poetovionis	Ptuj, Slovenia
2011	IMATRONIC Festival, later Giga-Hertz-Preis Festival	Karlsruhe
2011	NOW! Festival für Neue Musik	Essen
2011	HEAR NOW Music Festival	Venice, CA
2011	Etchings Festival	Auvillar, France
2012	Tectonics Music Festival	Glasgow
2013	LCMF (London Contemporary Music Festival)	London
2013	Multiphonics Festival	Cologne
2014	Louth Contemporary Music Society Festival	Louth, Ireland
2014	mikromusik—Festival experimenteller Musik und Sound Art	Berlin
2014	Klangbrücken—Festival für zeitgenössische Musik	Hannover
2015	KONTAKTE—Internationales Festival für elektronakustische Musik und Klangkunst	Berlin
2016	Tehran Contemporary Music Festival	Tehran
2018	Beyond: Microtonal Music Festival	Pittsburgh

countries, the Réseau Varèse (Marco, 2004). This enabled a degree of coordination of activities, which some might view as something of a cartel.

The number of new music ensembles created since the early 1970s is also huge, although attrition rates are relatively high. Many have been set up by composers, with repertoire centered on their own works and those with whom they feel a kinship. Table 18.4 lists just some of the most prominent and longest-lasting of these, a significant number of which have dominated European new music through to the present day. Many are modeled on the likes of the Domaine musical and London Sinfonietta.

Among this list of ensembles, the Arditti and Kronos quartets maintained very high profiles up until the mid-1990s. With mutually exclusive repertoire, the latter favoring minimalism and the former championing virtuosity and atonality, it was not until the foundation of Quatuor Diotima (1996), Flux Quartet (1998), and especially the Jack Quartet (2005) that Arditti's and Kronos's preeminence in their fields was seriously challenged. The style of Arditti's leader Irvine Arditti encapsulates archetypal aspects of new music performance: a clear inclination toward extremes of dynamics and tempo (and

Table 18.4. Major new music ensembles created since 1975.

Founded	Name	Based
1975	Österreichisches Ensemble für Neue Musik	Salzburg
1976	Michael Nyman Band	London
1976	New York New Music Ensemble	New York
1976	Hyperion Ensemble	Bucharest
1977	Divertimento Ensemble	Milan
1978	Suoraan, later Ensemble Exposé	London
1978	Group 180	Budapest
1980	Ensemble Contrechamps	Geneva
1980	Ensemble Modern	Frankfurt am Main
1980	Ensemble für Intuitive Musik Weimar	Weimar
1980	Nieuw Ensemble	Amsterdam
1980	Xenakis Ensemble	Middleburg
1980	Toimii	Helsinki
1981	Accroche Note	Strasbourg
1984	Neue Vokalsolisten Stuttgart	Stuttgart
1985	Klangforum Wien	Vienna
1985	Ensemble Recherche	Freiburg im Breisgau
1986	Ives Ensemble	Amsterdam
1986	Oslo Sinfonietta	Oslo
1986	ELISION Ensemble	Melbourne
1987	Birmingham Contemporary Music Group	Birmingham
1987	Kammerensemble Neue Musik Berlin	Berlin
1987	Ensemble Fa	Paris
1988	Champ d'Action	Antwerp
1988	ALEA Ensemble	Graz
1989	BIT20 Ensemble	Bergen
1989	Nouvel Ensemble Moderne	Montreal
1989	Icebreaker	London
1989	Ensemble Avantgarde	Leipzig
1990	Ensemble Musikfabrik	Cologne
1990	Athelas Sinfonietta	Copenhagen
1990	Moscow Contemporary Music Ensemble	Moscow
1990	Alpha Centauri Ensemble (later Sydney Alpha Ensemble)	Sydney
1991	Ensemble Court-Circuit	Paris
1992	Bang on a Can All-Stars	New York City
1992	Ensemble SurPlus	Freiburg im Breisgau

Table 18.4. Continued

Founded	Name	Based
1994	Ictus Ensemble	Brussels
1995	Apartment House	London
1997	Crash Ensemble	Dublin
1997	Ensemble NOMAD	Tokyo
1998	Uusinta Chamber Ensemble (later Uusinta Ensemble)	Helsinki
2000	EarPort Ensemble	Duisburg
2001	International Contemporary Ensemble	New York City and Chicago
2001	ConTempo	Beijing
2005	Jack Quartet	New York City
2005	American Modern Ensemble	New York City
2005	Ensemble Dal Niente	Chicago
2008	Ensemble Prague Modern	Prague
2008	Hong Kong New Music Ensemble	Hong Kong
2009	Riot Ensemble	London

a concomitant reticence toward the use of their more moderate equivalents), and emphasis upon clarity and definition of line, extreme, somewhat unhinged, virtuosity, and no compunction toward articulation of stark contrasts, in terms of the earlier parameters but also accentuation and articulation, celebrating and championing modernist discontinuity and angularity. In the quartet, some of these factors have been moderated by personnel changes, with Arditti himself the sole founding member remaining at the time of writing, but its enduring legacy as one of the last groups to emerge from the heyday of the avant-garde, and its enormous capacity for repertoire building, are renowned. Certainly, some of their uncompromising nature could be found in groups such as Suoraan or the ELISION Ensemble, while these musicians' extreme virtuosity has certainly been matched by later groups, but often in a more controlled and clearly "prepared" fashion that has transformed works of Ferneyhough, Lachenmann, and others into something more akin to "contemporary classics" rather than works sounding almost fresh off the page with each performance. The contrasts between the Ardittis and the "mainstream" Juilliard Quartet performing the quartets of Carter, for example, can be startling (see further, Pace, 2009a).

Since the 1970s the number of soloists specializing in new music has increased, with some of these becoming known especially for a focus upon works considered to entail transcendental virtuosity. Some, like pianists Alexander Abercrombie and James Clapperton, maintained this focus for a period while others who continue to do so include pianists Jonathan Powell and myself; flautists Kathryn Lukas, Nancy Ruffer, and

Mario Caroli; oboists Christopher Redgate and Peter Veale; clarinettists Harry Sparnaay, Armand Angster, and Carl Rosman; violinist Mieko Kanno; and percussionist Steve Schick. To a large degree, the modernist repertoire played by these and other types of performers of new music is rarely undertaken by their mainstream contemporaries. A few exceptions to this tendency include: Berio's *Sequenzas*, the *Sinfonia* and a few other pieces; the later works of Ligeti, especially the *Études* for piano; as well as some works of Elliott Carter, Harrison Birtwistle, and Takemitsu Tōru.

In terms of larger ensembles, Ensemble Modern Orchestra is one of a tiny number of orchestras who play exclusively new music. Nonetheless, a few mainstream conductors such as Claudio Abbado or Simon Rattle have regularly championed a significant amount of new music, while composer-conductors such as Giuseppe Sinopoli, Oliver Knussen, Esa-Pekka Salonen, Thomas Adès, and Jörg Widmann have championed a more eclectic range of new music as part of a broad repertoire.

Social and cultural changes

There is little indication that the performers of the 1960s and 1970s were overly concerned about their distance, even estrangement, from mainstream musical culture and many were able to carve out careers that might or might not bridge the two. But with Western liberal democracies subsequently moving closer toward right-wing economic policies, with a concomitant distrust of culture that could not be sustained by market forces alone, critical discourse around performance of new music began to adopt an aesthetic position that privileged those approaches that minimized the "otherness" of new music, in favor of those which in terms of both repertoire and performance style could be more obviously situated within established traditions (Pace, 2009b).

But in the second decade of the twenty-first century, this situation may have changed again, in a paradoxical situation whereby an increased institutionalization of new music has generated new composers with a more limited engagement with Western art music traditions than their counterparts from earlier generations. These new composers are sometimes utterly immersed in post-1945 new music, but more inclined to legitimize their work through allusion to recent popular and improvised traditions than the longer art music traditions that formed the background of others before them. There is also an increasing trend to bring extra-musical allusions to topical political and other issues into contemporary new music, as in the earlier work of Nono, Cornelius Cardew, Rzewski and others. These might include incorporating natural found sounds to promote an environmentalist agenda, or simply providing program notes that overtly assert some agenda with claims for social justice. Some composers have been able to attain prestigious reputations within institutions for new music with such approaches, which can render unconvincing some of these figures' attempts to position themselves as anti-establishment. Yet, it is almost impossible to imagine mainstream orchestras, chamber groups, choirs, or soloists performing their works. These various factors distinguish them even from the likes of Bussotti, Kagel, Schnebel, or Globokar, all of whom may have taken a highly askew position with respect to art music traditions, but whose work derived a good deal of its meaning specifically in terms of these relationships.

Where does this leave a performance culture for new music? It may be too early to say, but it is hard to see much of an active role for performers in music defined more by its conceptual rather than sonic content. The alternative—a deferential attitude on the part of performers toward musical texts and their composers, which Kolisch described at Schoenberg's Verein (Kolisch, 2009c) as lying somewhere between *Werktreue* and *Texttreue*—has been challenged but not wholly displaced at the time of writing. But what must have seemed vital in 1918, at a time of major societal upheaval throughout Europe in the aftermath of war and revolution, and corresponding upheavals in music, or for that matter in the period of reconstruction after 1945, looks quite different in 2021 New music performance remains on the fringes of the wider culture of Western art music and is even more marginal relative to wider cultural arenas. In light of changing economic circumstances, not least in the wake of the COVID-19 pandemic beginning in 2020, the extent to which the financial support to maintain such a separate infrastructure will remain is unknown. If not, new approaches to presentation, programming, and performance style will be required and no doubt derived, but their relationships to other forms of music making may be significantly realigned, to such an extent that the concept of "new music" no longer satisfactorily demarcates this range of endeavor.

PRACTICAL IMPLICATIONS

As has been argued elsewhere in this chapter, a prescriptive approach to learning how to perform new music is inappropriate. Nevertheless, guidance can be obtained by considering how repertoire has been performed in the past. With this in mind, the first part of this section highlights the value of recordings as a resource, by considering six brief case studies. The later section considers a range of performance issues spanning the entire repertoire.

Kolisch Quartet and Schoenberg's String Quartets

Schoenberg's admiration for the Kolisch Quartet was immense, calling them the "best string quartet I ever heard." He worked intensely with them on his own music, and they premiered the String Quartet No. 4 (1936) and recorded the full set between 1936 and 1937 in the composer's presence (Feisst, 2011). The recordings use highly extravagant continuous wide vibrato and some selective portamento, especially in highly expressive solos for individual players. They also emphasize continuity, line, and rounded tone, avoiding choppy off-string articulations. In the Quartet No. 3, for example, the opening staccato ostinati in the second violin and viola are executed relatively lightly and unobtrusively, not aiming for a major transformation of timbre as would later players but ensuring that the cantabile lines in the outer parts always come clearly to the foreground. Yet the logic of their phrasing and dynamics does not always correspond to a literalist reading of the score; the opening of the Quartet No. 2 does not embody any obvious swell to the center of the one-bar groups, as indicated by Schoenberg (see Figure 18.5), but more of a consistent tone tapering off just a little at the end of the bar.

In various places in the quartet, the precise dynamics appear in the score as one possible type of rendition, but the Kolisch players are not afraid to substitute their own alternatives.

Peter Stadlen—Webern and Schoenberg

One of the most compelling pieces of evidence relating to Webern performance comes from the publication of the instructions provided by Webern to pianist Peter Stadlen (Stadlen, 1979) for performance of the Variations, Op. 27, all pointing to a desire for an extremely flexible, highly diaphanous, and almost expressively overloaded approach (see Figure 18.6) that is borne out by a recording of a performance by Stadlen in 1948 at Darmstadt (Stadlen, 1948).

If somewhat less extreme in its expression, Stadlen's performance of Schoenberg's *Fünf Klavierstücke*, Op. 23 from the same Darmstadt concert also shows a large degree of flexibility, not least in terms of desynchronization between hands and parts, highly individuated rhythm especially in the third piece, and a degree of impulsiveness, even recklessness, in the second, which contrasts with later more "disciplined" approaches to this music.

Boulez conducting Schoenberg

Boulez's 1960 recording of the Schoenberg Suite, Op. 29 (1925–1926), with the ensemble Domaine musical, if in places lacking some of the rhythmic precision and synchronization found in Boulez's later recordings, has a strong sense of forward momentum and urgency (with very brisk tempi), even in the broader passages, with little of the type of expansive rubato, heavy vibrato, or other expressive signifiers of pathos that are still to be found in, say, the Kolisch Quartet's performances of Schoenberg (Kolisch Quartet, 1992). The pointed and unsentimental pianism of Yvonne Loriod also contributes greatly to this effect.

Hauptstimmen are certainly in the foreground, but not so as to overwhelm the detail in the middleground parts. Schoenberg's detailed articulations are contained within longer lines. The music certainly dances, but there is little in the way of noticeable attempts to replicate other stylistic traits associated with the genres in question, which might have taken Boulez closer to neo-Classicism than he would likely have found comfortable. During passages such as in Figure 18.7 from the third movement, Boulez and his players achieve a remarkable level of timbral definition with the *spiccato* and

2. Streichquartett

für Sopran und Streichorchester op. 10
(1907–1908/1929)

Arnold Schönberg
(1874–1951)

Universal Edition UE 32857

FIGURE 18.5. Arnold Schoenberg, String Quartet No. 2 in F sharp minor, Op. 10 (1908), opening.

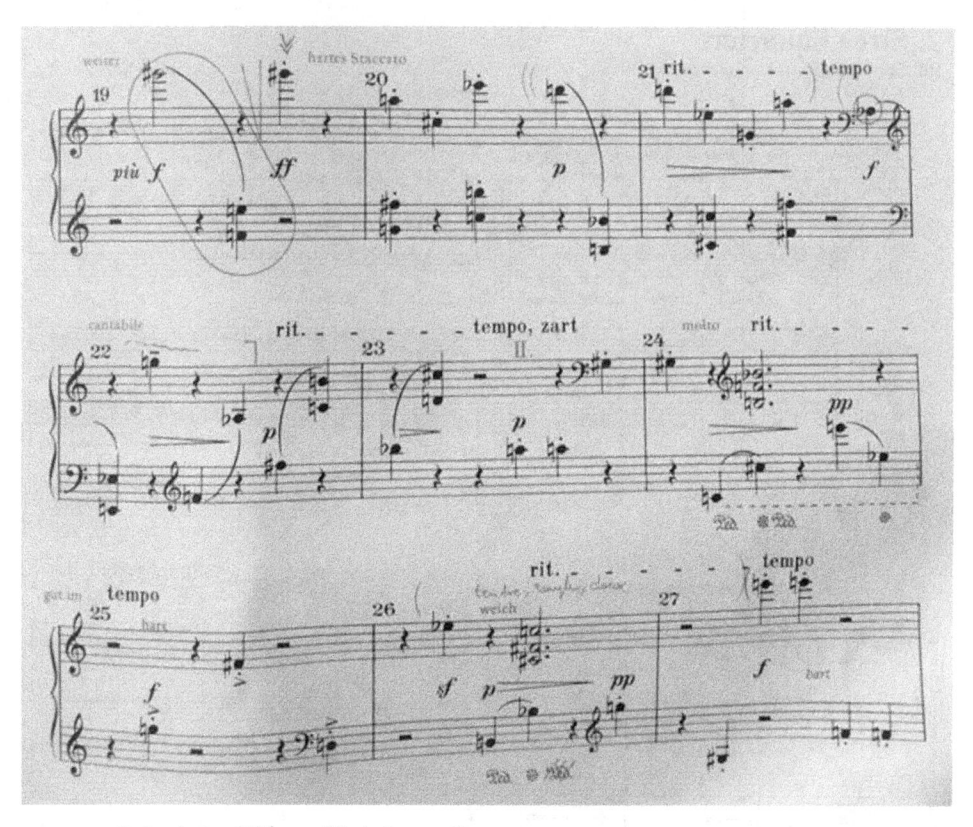

FIGURE 18.6. Anton Webern, *Variationen*, Op. 27, mm. 19–27.

springbogen playing, while maintaining a hushed dynamic and balancing the strings and winds, all so that the sudden sforzando and piano entry has immense dramatic power here and in subsequent passages.

Many of the same qualities can be found in Boulez and the *Domaine*'s 1962 recording of Schoenberg's Serenade, Op. 24 (though the ensemble is tighter), adding a new level of intensity and timbral focus compared to the earlier recordings conducted by Dmitri Mitropoulos (1949) and Robert Craft (1958). Comparison with the recording of Mitropoulos demonstrates a marked shift of style: Mitropoulos still grants a degree of rhythmic flexibility for individual players, with a degree of rubato, less exactly calibrated ritardandi, and a more leisurely tempo in the Minuet, not to mention a more pronounced hierarchy between *Hauptstimme* and other parts (less concerned about absolute contrapuntal clarity) than Boulez. Mitropoulos's strings continue to apply a degree of portamento to their lines, combined with a slower and more obvious vibrato, while all players detach and distinguish slurred units within phrases to a much greater degree than in Boulez's *melos*-oriented approach. In all of this, Mitropoulos creates some connection with an older style of playing that is mostly absent in Boulez's performance.

UE 8685

FIGURE 18.7. Schoenberg, Suite, Op. 29 (1960), third movement, mm. 20–32.

John Cage, *Song Books*

Cage's *Song Books* (1970) ask a considerable amount of effort and many choices from the performer(s) in order to arrive at a rendition of the scores. They incorporate graphic, text, and more traditional forms of notation, as well as gamuts of notes and numbers. Some are with electronics, some are theatrical, some both. They can be sung by single or multiple singers, and in combination with other indeterminate works of Cage or others.

No performance can ever be free of a performer's intentions or desires, however much they attempt to displace these. The recording of *Song Book 11* (the score for which takes the form of a text from Henry David Thoreau's *Walden*, in varying fonts: "blacK WITH THE CAPILLACEous leaves and stems of THE WATER-MARI gold, etc.") by Lore Lixenberg and Gregory Rose, voices, and Robert Worby, electronics (2012), is highly personalized, with electronically modified voices that resemble swanee whistles, in an integrative, dancing texture that gradually gains momentum, while Lixenberg's vocal style at times in this and other pieces approaches the operatic. Other performers might produce a wholly different effect, while equally personalized. The key question for such performers to ask is the extent to which they can relax about the reflection of their preferences, without seeming to contravene Cage's wider aesthetic?

Helmut Lachenmann, *Gran Torso*

As discussed earlier, Lachenmann's *Gran Torso* pushes the four members of the string quartet and the instruments to their limits, with notorious passages including an extended viola solo executed primarily on the tailpiece of the instrument. Figure 18.8 shows a passage soon after the opening. The techniques are specific rather than indeterminate, but what is the musical end to be sought by the players?

The Bern Quartet (1986) enact quite extreme dynamic contrasts but emphasize the results of sonic superimposition, so that some parts emerge out from others rather than always being heard as individual lines. In a recording from twenty-one years later, the Arditti Quartet (2007) allow a greater amount of pitched content to emerge from the techniques they use, and somewhat uncharacteristically present less of the stark contrasts of dynamics and texture of the Bern, attaining a more integrated and continuous sound earlier in this passage. In their recording, the Jack Quartet (2014) return to the more extreme dynamics of the Bern, and with a lesser degree of pitch projection than the Ardittis, but at the same time project less of a sense of fracturing in the texture, almost with some stronger sense of longer "phrasing." Each of these approaches conveys a different sense of the work's relationship to more traditional forms of playing, but also even with the arguably somewhat less acerbic and more auratic world of Lachenmann's two later quartets.

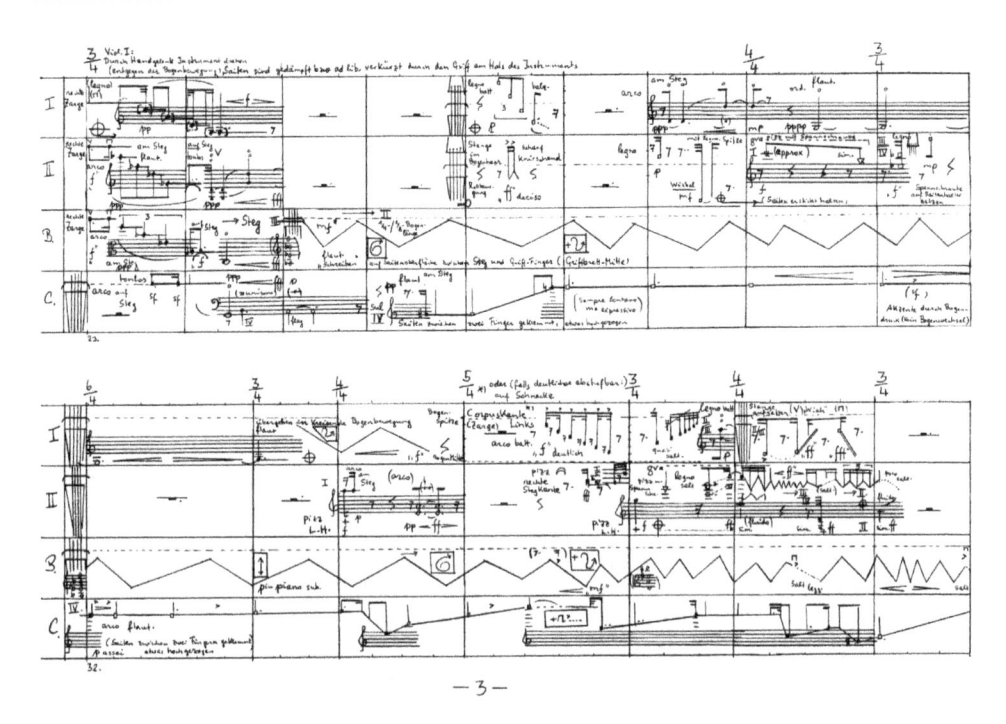

— 3 —

FIGURE 18.8. Helmut Lachenmann, *Gran Torso*, p. 3. © 1972 by Musikverlage Hans Gerig, Köln, 1980, assigned to Breitkopf & Härtel, Wiesbaden.

James Dillon, *The Book of Elements*

Dillon's *The Book of Elements* (1997–2002) is a set of five books of pieces, ranging from eleven miniatures in Book 1, through a progressively smaller number of longer pieces in Books 2–4, to a single piece in Book 5. Throughout, Dillon's range of allusion is extensive, if generally "veiled"—to harmonies, textures, and figurations of Debussy, Scriabin, Szymanowski, Varèse, Messiaen, Xenakis, and others, as well as structural allusions to miniatures including those of Byrd, Beethoven, and Schumann. Yet the various pieces, even the longer ones, remain fragmentary and incomplete in nature, often characterized by striking discontinuities, while the various types of allusions are sometimes blurred through some of the pitch content, overlaying of materials, or simply being given only a brief exposition. The dynamics inhabit a relatively wide spectrum on the page; should one emphasize this, in the manner of an established rhetoric of new music, or seek greater forms of continuities and use fewer extremes or forms of "spikiness"? Similar questions can be asked about voicing, pedaling, tempi, all in terms of relationship to established, traditional practices. In her elegant recording, Noriko Kawai (2004) generally opts for approaches with a clear provenance in earlier pianistic traditions, without using so many extremely quiet sonorities (e.g., in the aphoristic third piece of Book 3) as might be more archetypally associated with new music, while projecting a broad sweep across the pieces in Books 4 and 5 through a variety of means. This music allows a plurality of approaches in this respect: the performer needs to ask what it is that they find most valuable in the score, in what context do they wish it to be heard, and which of the plural expressive possibilities most closely resembles their own perspective as a result.

Approaches to performance

The most advanced music of the 1950s presented its own set of issues, some of which had existed in the interwar period, but were now intensified. One was for the performer(s) to negotiate varying degrees of continuity and discontinuity—works of Boulez and Stockhausen (and Messiaen) certainly embodied plenty of the latter, as had earlier that of Stravinsky, Varèse, Antheil, and others, not to mention, in more pointillistic music, micro-discontinuities between individual pitches. All these factors were diametrically opposed concerns to the Wagnerian *melos* or other approaches emphasizing seamless lines and an avoidance of angular or thorny manners of playing. Overall, one can identify a greater aptitude and inclination toward such an approach, combined with a greater willingness to explore extreme dynamics and dynamic contrasts, among postwar new music specialists, though arguably less so than would be found in later generations.

Other performance questions relate to some quite fundamental questions of the balance between the requirements of small-scale musical material and more macroscopic, structural concerns. In the works of Scelsi and Feldman, particularly, but also Berio and others, long passages are indicated at a uniform dynamic or with relatively unchanging textures, rhythms, or other aspects. In such passages, is the performer to aim for other forms of differentiation, using other parameters, or might this temper the sense of stasis, important to preserve in order to maximize the contrast with what follows? Should rhythms be played quite strictly, even metronomically, in line with earlier objectivist traditions, in order to foreground particular metrical relations (e.g., in the metric modulations in the music of Elliott Carter), or is there room for some flexibility here? These are questions that do not invite easy answers even today, and performers associated with such repertoire have employed and continue to employ a plurality of approaches.

Cage claimed to conceive his etudes in utopian terms, making them "as difficult as possible so that a performance would show that the impossible is not impossible" (cited in Pasler, 1994, p. 140). But I would maintain a distinction between pieces that are literally impossible such as some of those of Xenakis, at least at the stated tempo, and those which stretch the boundaries of possibility, but whose rendition is conceptually possible.

The two traditions of New Complexity evolving from the approaches of Finnissy and Ferneyhough, and elements within either, present very different challenges to performers. Finnissy and Dillon's relationship to pre–new music traditions has become clearer over time, as has Ferneyhough's adherence to a received gestural language (especially from the Second String Quartet and *Lemma-Icon-Epigram* onwards). Yet composers in the latter tradition continue to defamiliarize this language through ever more intricate parameterization, something that goes to other extremes in the increased focus on "decoupling" in Hübler and others. In all these cases, the performer needs on one hand to situate their interpretations relative to some performance tradition associated with the compositional traditions with which the composers in question engage, but on the other to arrive at strategies to make palpable and clear the ways in which the music defamiliarizes and distances itself from such traditions. Performing both within and without a tradition presents a myriad range of questions applying to all types of parameters. These questions can become even more complicated in the context of musical works employing a large degree of explicit or implicit musical borrowing (of materials, styles, or genres), for which approaches emphasizing the performance norms of the original style, or conversely foregrounding the ways in which the borrowed material is modified to make it into something new, can drastically affect perceptions (see Pace, 2019 for an extended consideration of this in the context of theoretical models on musical borrowing).

Kolisch (1983), upon being confronted with an electronic rendition of a work late in life, was quite shocked by how different this was from anything that might be produced by humans. He concluded from this that while there might not be a *single* correct performance, there was still a *correct* performance (see also Trippett, 2009). I would counter this by saying that one should think instead in terms of what is an *incorrect* performance, and then the range of creative options for the performer constitute all those many, possibly infinite, possibilities that do not stray into this realm.

KEY RESOURCES

Adorno, T. (2006). *Towards a theory of musical reproduction* (W. Hoban, Trans.). Cambridge, UK: Polity Press.

Kanach, S. (Ed.). (2010). *Performing Xenakis*. Hillsdale, NY: Pendragon Press.

Kolisch in Amerika (2009). *Rudolf Kolisch in Amerika—Aufsätze und Dokumente. Musiktheorie—Zeitschrift für Musikwissenschaft*, vol. 24, no. 3.

Stravinsky, I. (1947). *Poetics of music: In the form of six lessons* (A. Kondel & I. Dahl, Trans.). Cambridge, MA: Harvard University Press.

Vermeil, J. (1996). *Conversations with Boulez: Thoughts on conducting* (C. Naish, Trans.). Portland, OR: Amadeus Press.

REFLECTIVE QUESTIONS

1. How might you work from the material presented in this chapter to refine your own approach to performing new music repertoire?

2. In which contexts—in terms of venue, type of concert series or festival, and surrounding program—might you present such music, and what do you know about

a century's worth of experience of doing so somewhat apart from mainstream Western art music?

3. Who are the performers who have helped to forge a performance tradition for such work, and what can one learn from their successes and failures, where there exists recorded evidence for these?

4. In performing new music, do you need to master new techniques, skills, insights, and competencies, or for that matter new aesthetic attitudes that differ from those you might bring to bear upon more traditional repertoire?

5. To what extent should you as performer(s) situate your interpretations so as to foreground continuities with earlier traditions, or conversely emphasize difference and uniqueness?

ACKNOWLEDGMENTS

I am immensely grateful to Stephanie Rocke for her significant help in preparing this chapter for publication. I also thank Robert Adlington, Leo Chadburn, Björn Heile, Barbara Kelly, Isaac Malitz, and Eva Moreda Rodriguez for pointers to and help in locating some obscure but invaluable literature, and Jane Davidson and Gary McPherson for their infinite patience and help.

REFERENCES

Texts

Adlington, R. (2013). *Composing dissent: Avant-garde music in 1960s Amsterdam*. New York and Oxford: Oxford University Press.

Adorno, T. (2006). *Towards a theory of musical reproduction*. (Ed. Lonitz, H.; transl. Hoban, W.). Cambridge, UK: Polity Press.

Adorno, T. (2009). 'Rede zu Rudolf Kolischs 60. Geburtstag.' In *Rudolf Kolisch in Amerika – Aufsätze und Dokumente. Musiktheorie – Zeitschrift für Musikwissenschaft*, 24(3), 238–240.

Adorno, T, & Kolisch, R. (2009). 'Gespräch über Neue Musik und Interpretation zwischen Prof. Dr. Adorno und Prof. R. Kolisch' (1954). In *Rudolf Kolisch in Amerika – Aufsätze und Dokumente. Musiktheorie – Zeitschrift für Musikwissenschaft*, 24(3), 241–246.

Aguila, J. (1992). *Le domaine musical: Pierre Boulez et vingt ans de création contemporaine*. Paris: Fayard.

Andriessen, L. (2002). A brief history of De Volharding (from notes in 1972–3). In M. Zegers (Ed.), *The art of stealing time* (trans. C. Yates), 128–136. Todmorden: Arc Music.

Antokoletz, E. (2013). *A history of twentieth-century music in a theoretic-analytical context*. New York and London: Routledge.

Arlt, C. (2010). *Von den Juryfreien zur musica viva: Karl Amadeus Hartmann und die Neue Musik in München*. Frankfurt: Peter Lang.

Barker, J. W. (2017). *The Pro Arte Quartet: A century of musical adventure on two continents.* Rochester, NY: University of Rochester Press.

Beal, A. C. (2006). *New music, new allies: American experimental music in West Germany from the Zero Hour to Reunification.* Berkeley & Los Angeles: University of California Press.

Beckles Willson, R. (2004). *György Kurtág: The sayings of Peter Bornemisza, Op. 7: A "concerto" for soprano and piano.* Farnham: Ashgate.

Beckles Willson, R. (2007). *Ligeti, Kurtág, and Hungarian Music during the Cold War.* Cambridge: Cambridge University Press.

Bekker, P. (1923). Neue Musik (1919). In *Neue Musik. Gesammelte Schriften III* (pp. 85–118). Stuttgart and Berlin: Deutsche Verlags-Anstalt.

Bernbacher, K. (2003). *Klaus Hashagen.* Tutzing: Hans Schneider.

Besancon, H. (2007). *Festival international d'art contemporain de Royan 1964–1977.* Royan: Éditions Bonne Anse.

Besseler, H. (1927). Grundfragen der Musikästhetik. *Jahrbuch der Musikbibliothek Peters für 1926.* Leipzig: Edition Peters.

Betz, A., ed. (1977). *Auftragskompositionen im Rundfunk 1946–1975.* Frankfurt am Main: Satzstudio Frohberg.

Bialosky, M. (1980). A history of composers' groups in the United States. *College Music Symposium, 20*(2), 29–40.

Biennale Musica. (n.d.). *Festival Internazionale di Musica Contemporanea della Biennale di Venezia. Programmi 1930–1972* – see http://www-5.unipv.it/girardi/2015_DM1/1930-1972_BiennaleMusica.pdf [accessed July 28, 2020]

Blumröder, C. v. (1981). *Das Begriff "Neue Musik" im 20. Jahrhundert.* Munich and Salzburg: Musikverlag Emil Katzbichler.

Borio, G. (1993). *Musikalische Avantgarde um 1960: Entwurf einer Theorie der informellen Musik.* Laaber: Laaber-Verlag.

Borio, G., & Danuser, H. (Eds.) (1997). *Im Zenit der Moderne: Die internationalen Ferienkurse für Neue Musik Darmstadt 1946–1966* (4 vols.). Freiburg im Breisgau: Rombach Verlag.

Boulez, P. (1976). *Conversations with Célestin Deliège.* London: Ernst Eulenburg.

Boulez, P. (1986). Ten Years On. In M. Cooper (Ed. & Trans.), *Orientations* (pp. 434–440). London: Faber & Faber.

Braas, T. (2001). Nederlandse avant-garde in het interbellum. In L. P. Grijp et al. (Eds.), *Een muziek geschiedenis der Nederlanden* (pp. 568–573). Amsterdam: Amsterdam University Press.

Brévignon, P. (2020). *Le Groupe des Six: Une histoire des années folles.* Arles: Actes Sud.

Broman, P. F. (2002). New Music of Sweden. In J. D. White (Ed.), *New music of the Nordic countries* (pp. 445–588). Hillsdale, NY: Pendragon Press.

Busoni, F. (1962). Sketch for a New Aesthetic of Music (1907). In *Three classics in the Aesthetics of Music* (pp. 73–102). New York: Dover.

Busoni, F. (1987). *Selected Letters* (Ed. & Trans. A. Beaumont). London: Faber.

Buxbaum, E. H. (1988). Stravinsky, tempo, and *Le Sacre. Performance Practice Review, 1*(1), 61–8-. https://core.ac.uk/download/pdf/148354857.pdf [accessed August 10, 2020]

Bylander, C. E. (1989). *The Warsaw Autumn International Festival of Contemporary Music, 1956–1961: Its goals, structures, programs, and people.* PhD thesis: Ohio State University.

Carpenter, H. (1996). *The envy of the world: Fifty years of the BBC Third Programme and Radio 3.* London: Phoenix.

Cayón, J. F. (2019). "España es diferente . . . España cambia de piel": Of the Festivals of Spain (1954) to the 1st International Biennale of Contemporary Music of Madrid (1964): Avant-Garde Music for the Francoist Technocracy. *Contemporary Music Review*, *38*(92), 24–43

Cerha, G. (1999). Zur Geschichte der Reihe. *Österreichische Musikzeitschrift*, *54*(6), 4–8.

Cherney, B. I. (1974). *The Bekker-Pfitzner controversy (1919–1920): Its significance for German music criticism during the Weimar Republic (1919–1932)*. PhD thesis: University of Toronto.

Christensen, J. (2002). New Music of Denmark. In J. D. White (Ed.), *New music of the Nordic countries* (pp. 1–120). Hillsdale, NY: Pendragon Press.

Civetta, C. (2012). *The Real Toscanini: Musicians reveal the maestro*. Milwaukee: Amadeus Press.

Cook, N. (2013). *Beyond the score: Music as performance*. New York: Oxford University Press.

Couroux, M. (2002). Evryali and the exploding of the interface: From virtuosity to anti-virtuosity and beyond. *Contemporary Music Review*, *21*(2–3), 53–67.

Crawford, D.L. (1995). *Evenings on and off the roof: pioneering concerts in Los Angeles, 1939-197*. Berkeley, CA, and London: University of California Press.

Cross, J. (1996). A necessary violence. *The Musical Times*, *137*(1841), 21.

Custodis, M. (2010). *Traditionen—Koalitionen—Visionen: Wolfgang Steinecke und die Internationalen Ferienkurse in Darmstadt*. Saarbrücken: Pfau.

Dalhaus, C. (1987). "'New Music' as historical category'. In *Schoenberg and the New Music: Essays by Carl Dahlhaus* (Trans. D. Puffett & A. Clayton). Cambridge: Cambridge University Press, pp. 1–13.

Danuser. H. (2002). Werktreue and Texttreue in der musikalischen Interpretation. In S. Ehrmann-Herfort, L. Finscher, & G. Schubert (Eds.), *Europäische Musikgeschichte* (Band 2, pp. 1115–1165). Kassel: Bärenreiter.

De Pablo, L. (2009). *A Contratiempo*. Madrid: Ediciones Arte y Estética.

Dromey, C. (2012). *The Pierrot Ensemble: Chronicle and catalogue, 1912–2012*. London: Plumbago Books.

Duchesneau, M. (1994). Maurice Ravel et la Société Musicale Indépendante: "Projet mirifique de concerts scandaleux." *Revue de Musicologie*, *80*(2), 251–281.

Duchesneau, M. (1997). *L'avant-garde musicale et ses sociétés à Paris de 1871 à 1939*. Sprimont: Mardaga.

Dufour, V., & Pirenne, C. (2004). Du Séminaire des Arts à l'Exposition universelle, quinze années de lutte pour la musique contemporaine. In C. Pirenne (Ed.), *Les Musiques Nouvelles en Wallonie et à Bruxelles (1960–2003)* (pp. 11–35). Sprimont: Mardaga.

Duncan, S. P. (2010). Re-complexifying the function(s) of notation in the music of Brian Ferneyhough and the "New Complexity." *Perspectives of New Music*, *48*(1), 136–172.

Earle, B. (2013). *Luigi Dallapiccola and musical modernism in Fascist Italy*. Cambridge, UK: Cambridge University Press.

Edmunds, N. (2000). *The Soviet proletarian music movement*. Oxford: Peter Lang.

Erdmann, E (1920). Beethoven und wir Jungen. *Vossische Zeitung*, 16 December, 2–3.

Everett, Y. U. (2009). "Scream against the sky": Japanese avant-garde music in the sixties. In R. Adligton (Ed.), *Sound commitments: Avant-garde music and the sixties* (pp. 187–208). Oxford and New York: Oxford University Press.

Fabian, D. (2001). The meaning of authenticity and the Early Music Movement: A historical review. *International Review of the Aesthetics and Sociology of Music*, *32*, 153–167.

Fabian, D. (2003). *Bach performance practice 1945–1975: A review of sound recordings and literature*. Aldershot: Ashgate Press.

Fabian, D. (2006). Is Diversity in Musical Performance truly in Decline?: The Evidence of Sound Recordings. *Context: A Journal of Music Research, 31,* 165–180.

Fearn, R. (1990). *Bruno Maderna.* Chur: Harwood Academic Publishers.

Feisst, S. (2011). *Schoenberg's new world: The American years.* New York: Oxford University Press.

Feller, R. (1994). *Multicursal labyrinths in the work of Brian Ferneyhough.* DMA diss.: University of Illinois at Urbana-Champaign.

Feneyrou, L., & Poirer, A. (Eds.) (2018). *De la libération au domaine musical: Dix ans de musique en France (1944–1954).* Paris: Vrin.

Fernández-Cid, A. (1973). *La música española en el siglo XX.* Madrid: Rioduero.

Fitzpatrick, S. (1992). *The Cultural Front: Power and Culture in Revolutionary Russia.* Ithaca and London: Cornell University Press.

Flender, R. (Ed.) (2007). *Freie Ensembles für Neue Musik in Deutschland.* Mainz: Schott.

Frolova-Walker, M., & Walker, J. (2012). *Music and Soviet Power 1917-1932.* Woodbridge: The Boydell Press.

Fugellie, D. (2018). *"Musiker unsere Zeit": Internationale Avantgarde, Migration und Wiener Schule in Südamerika.* Munich: edition text + kritik.

Fulcher, J. (2005). *The composer as intellectual: Music and ideology in France 1914–1940.* Oxford and New York: Oxford University Press.

Fylkingen. (n.d.). *Vad är Fylkingen* – see http://fylkingen.se/about [accessed October 14, 2020]

Gable, D. (1988). Paul Fromm in American Musical Life. In D. Gable & C. Wolff (Eds.), *A Life for New Music: Selected Papers of Paul Fromm* (pp. ix–xviii). Cambridge, MA: Harvard University Press.

Galliano, L. (2002). *Yogaku: Japanese music in the 20th century.* Lanham, MD: Scarecrow Press.

Garberding, P. (2014). Strauss und der ständige Rat für die internationale Zusammenarbeit der Komponisten. In W. Werbeck (Ed.), *Richard Strauss Handbuch* (pp. 42–47). Stuttgart: Metzler.

Garst, M. M. (1985). How Bartók performed his own compositions. *Tempo, 155,* 15–21.

Gasser, M. (Ed.) (2017). *Vom Verwirklichen der Träume: Die Music im steirischen Herbst. Herbstbuch 1968–2017.* Graz: Styria Verlag.

Gieseking, W., & Leimer, K. (1972). *Piano technique.* New York: Dover.

Glock, W. (1991). *Notes in advance: An autobiography in music.* Oxford and New York: Oxford University Press.

Grosch, N. (2013). *Neue Sachlichkeit*, mass media and matters of musical style in the 1920s. In R. Grüttermeier, K. Beekman, & B. Rebel (Eds.), *Neue Sachlichkeit and Avant-Garde* (pp. 185–201). Amsterdam & New York: Editions Rodopi.

Growth, S. K. (2016). The Fylkingen Concert Society, 1950–1975. In B. Hjartarson, A. Kollnitz, P. Stounjerg, & T. Ørum (Eds.), *A cultural history of the avant-garde in the Nordic countries 1950–1975* (pp. 122–134). Amsterdam & New York: Editions Rodopi.

Grues, H, Kruttge, E., & Thalheimer, E., Eds. (1925). *Neue Musik.* Cologne: F.J. Marcan-Verlag.

Haas, B. (2004). *Karl Amadeus Hartmann 1905–1963. Zeitzeugen und Dokumente zum 100. Geburtstag des Komponisten.* Wilhelmshaven: Florian Noetzel Verlag.

Haefeli, A. (1982). *Die Internationale Gesellschaft für Neue Musik (IGNM): Ihre Geschichte von 1922 bis zur Gegenwart.* Zürich: Atlantis Musikbuch-Verlag.

Hailey, C. (1994). Rethinking sound: Music and radio in Weimar Germany. In B. Gilliam (Ed.), *Music and performance during the Weimar Republic* (pp. 13–36). Cambridge, UK: Cambridge University Press.

Hass, O. (2004). Musikblätter des Anbruch – see https://www.ripm.org/?page=JournalInfo&ABB=ANB [accessed September 28, 2020]

Hass, O. (2005). Melos – see https://www.ripm.org/?page=JournalInfo&ABB=MEL [accessed September 28, 2020]

Hass, O. (2019). Der Auftakt – see https://www.ripm.org/?page=JournalInfo&ABB=AUF [accessed September 28, 2020]

Hakobian, L. (2017). *Music of the Soviet era, 1917–1991* (2nd ed.). Abingdon: Routledge.

Haubenstock-Ramati, R. (1980). *Musik Grafik . . .: Pre Texte*. Vienna: Ariadne.

Häusler, J. (1996). *Spiegel der Neuen Musik: Donaueschingen. Chronik—Tendenzen—Werkbesprechungen*. Kassel, Stuttgart, & Weimar: Bärenreiter and J. B. Mzler.

Hawkins, R. W. M. (2010). *(Mis)understanding complexity from Transit to Toop: "New Complexity" in the British Context*. PhD diss.: University of Leeds.

Haynes, B. (2007). *The end of early music*. Oxford and New York: Oxford University Press.

Herresthal, H., & Pedersen, M. E. (2002). New Music of Norway. In J. D. White (Ed.), *New music of the Nordic countries* (pp. 383–444). Hillsdale, NY: Pendragon Press.

Herrmann, M., & Weiss, S. (2004). *Dresden und die avancierte Musik im 20. Jahrhundert. Teil III: 1966–1999*. Laaber: Laaber-Verlag.

Hess, C. A. (2005). *Sacred passions: The life and music of Manuel de Falla*. Oxford and New York: Oxford University Press.

Hill, P. (1975). Xenakis and the performer. *Tempo, 112*, 17–22.

Hill, R. (1994). "Overcoming romanticism": On the modernization of twentieth-century performance practice. In B. Gilliam (Ed.), *Music and performance during the Weimar Republic*. Cambridge, UK: Cambridge University Press, pp. 37–58.

Hindemith, P. (1952). *A composer's world: Horizons and Limitations*. Mainz et al: Schott.

Hindemith, P. (1994). Zu unserem Programm (1926). In G. Schubert (Ed.), *Aufsätze, Vorträge, Reden* (pp. 16–18). Zürich and Mainz: Atlantis Musikbuch-Verlag.

Hinton, S. (1989). *The idea of Gebrauchsmusik: A study of musical aesthetics in the Weimar Republic (1919–1933) with particular reference to the works of Paul Hindemith*. New York & London: Garland.

Historisches Archiv der Stadt Köln (Ed.) (1993). *Intermedial—kontrovers—experimentell: Das Atelier Mary Bauermeister in Köln 1960–62*. Cologne: Emons Verlag.

Holzaepfel, J. (1994). *David Tudor and the performance of American experimental music, 1950–1959*. PhD thesis: City University of New York.

Holzaepfel, J. (Ed.) (2020). *David Tudor: Solo for piano by John Cage, second realization*. Middleton, WI: A-R Editions.

Howard, P. (2004). *Evryali*: Beyond the surface (What I learned from *Evryali* by performing it). *Perspectives of New Music, 42*(2), 144–157.

Howe, M. A. D. (1946). *The tale of Tanglewood: Scene of the Berkshire Music Festivals*. New York: Vanguard Press.

Hughes, C. A. (2015). *Branding Brussels Musically: Cosmopolitanism and Nationalism in the Interwar Years*. PhD thesis: University of North Carolina at Chapel Hill.

Iddon, M. (2013). *New music at Darmstadt: Nono, Stockhausen, Cage, and Boulez*. Cambridge and New York: Cambridge University Press.

Iddon, M., & Thomas, P. (2020). *John Cage's Concert for Piano and Orchestra*. New York: Oxford University Press.

Ignácz, A. (2017). "Hungarian in Form, Socialist in Content": The Concept of National Dance Music in Stalinist Hungary (1949–56). In E. Barna & T. Tófalvy (Eds.), *Made in Hungary: Studies in popular music* (pp. 69–76). New York & London: Routledge.

Ivry, B. (2000). *Maurice Ravel: A Life*. New York: Welcome Rain Publishers.

Jakelski, L. (2017). *Making new music in Cold War Poland: The Warsaw Autumn Festival, 1956–1968*. Oakland: University of California Press.

Jameux, D. (1991). *Pierre Boulez* (Trans. S. Bradshaw). London: Faber and Faber.

Johnson, P. (Ed.) (1965). *Khrushchev and the arts: The politics of Soviet culture, 1962–1964*. Cambridge, MA: MIT Press.

Kaes, A., Jay, M., & Dimendberg, E. (Eds.) (1994). *The Weimar Republic sourcebook*. Berkeley & Los Angeles: University of California Press.

Kanach, S. (Ed. and Trans.) (2010). *Performing Xenakis*. Hillsdale, NY: Pendragon Press.

Keller, C. (1997). Die Ferneyhough-Familie. *Dissonanz 51*, 34–36.

Kelly, B. L. (2013). *Music and ultra-modernism in France: A fragile consensus, 1913–1939*. Woodbridge: Boydell and Brewer.

Kelly, B L. (2018). Common canon, conflicting ideologies: Music criticism in performance in interwar France. In B. Kelly & C. Moore (Eds.), *Music criticism in France, 1918–1939* (pp. 121–149). Woodbridge: Boydell and Brewer.

Kenyon, N. (1981). *The BBC Symphony Orchestra: The first fifty years 1930–1980*. London: British Broadcasting Corporation.

Kerry, G. (2009). *New Classical Music: Composing Australia*. Sydney: UNSW Press.

Kliemann, H. (1969). *Die Novembergruppe*. Berlin: Gebr. Mann Verlag.

Kolisch, R. (1983). *Zu Theorie der Aufführung: Ein Gespräch mit Berthold Türke. Musik-Konzepte 29/30*. Munich: edition text + kritik.

Kolisch, R. (2009a). Musical Performance: The Realization of Musical Meaning (1939). In *Rudolf Kolisch in Amerika—Aufsätze und Dokumente. Musiktheorie—Zeitschrift für Musikwissenschaft*, vol. 24, no. 3, pp. 201–207.

Kolisch, R. (2009b). How to rehearse and play chamber music (1940). In *Rudolf Kolisch in Amerika—Aufsätze und Dokumente. Musiktheorie—Zeitschrift für Musikwissenschaft*, vol. 24, no. 3, pp. 207–209.

Kolisch, R. (2009c). Interpretationsprobleme bei Schönberg (1966). In *Rudolf Kolisch in Amerika—Aufsätze und Dokumente. Musiktheorie—Zeitschrift für Musikwissenschaft*, vol. 24, no. 3, pp. 273–281.

Kölner Gesellschaft für Neue Musik (Ed.) (1991). *Klangraum: 40 Jahre Neue Musik in Köln 1945–1985*. Cologne: Wienand Verlag.

Kyora, S. (2013). Concepts of the subject in the avant-garde movements of the 1910s and Neue Sachlichkeit. In R. Grüttemeier, K. Beekman, & B. Rebel (Eds.), *Neue Sachlichkeit and Avant-Garde* (pp. 277–295). Amsterdam & New York: Editions Rodopi.

La Mara (Ed.) (1894). *Letters of Franz Liszt, Volume 1: From Paris to Rome: Years of travel as virtuoso* (Trans. C. Bache). London: H. Greyel & Co.

Laux, K. (Ed.) (1960). *Das Musikleben in der Deutschen Demokratischen Republik*. Leipzig: VEB Deutscher Verlag für Musik.

Leech-Wilkinson, D. (2009a). *The Changing Sound of Music: Approaches to Studying Recorded Musical Performances* – see http://www.charm.rhul.ac.uk/studies/chapters/intro.html.

Leech-Wilkinson. D. (2009b). Recordings and History of Performance Style. In N. Cook, E. Clarke, D. Leech-Wilkinson, & J. Rink (Eds.), *The Cambridge companion to recorded music*. Cambridge, UK: Cambridge University Press, pp. 246–262.

Lefebvre, M.-T. (1986). *Serge Garant et la révolution musicale au Quebec*. Montreal: Louise Corteau.

Lefebvre, M.-T. (2008). Overview. In E. Koskoff (Ed.), *The Garland encyclopedia of world music: The United States and Canada* (pp. 1146–1153). London: Routledge.

Levitz, T. (2013). Igor the Angeleno: The Mexican connection. In T. Levitz (Ed.), *Stravinsky and his World* (pp. 141–176). Princeton and Oxford: Princeton University Press.

Lippe, K. (2013). Komplexität als Programm für ein Beobachten zweiter Ordnung: Zur (Un) Spielbarkeit der Werke Brian Ferneyhoughs mit Anmerkungen zu *On Stellar Magnitudes*. In J. P. Hiekel (Ed.), *Ans Licht gebracht: Zur Interpretation Neuer Musik* (pp. 115–117). Mainz et al: Schott.

Lott, R. A. (1983). "New music for mew ears": The International Composers' Guild. *Journal of the American Musicological Society, 36*(2), 266–286.

Madurell, F. (2003). *L'ensemble Ars Nova: Une contribution au pluralisme esthétique dans la musique contemporaine (1963–1987)*. Paris: L'Harmattan.

Marco, J-D. (2004). Le festival Musica et le Réseau Varèse. *Circuit: Musiques contemporaines, 14*(2), 59–66.

Marsh, R. C. (1962). *Toscanini and the art of Conducting*. (Rev. ed.) New York: Collier.

Marsh, R. (1994). Heroic motives: Roger Marsh considers the relation between sign and sound in "complex" music. *The Musical Times, 135*(1812), 83–86.

Marti, S. (Ed.) (2009). *Ars Musica: 20 ans d'aventures musicales*. Wavre: Mardaga.

Martin, B. G. (2016). *The Nazi-Fascist new order for European culture*. Cambridge, MA, and London: Harvard University Press.

Mawer, D. (2006). "Dancing on the edge of the volcano": French music in the 1930s. In R. L. Smith & C. Potter (Eds.), *French music since Berlioz: Issues and debates* (pp. 249–280). Aldershot: Ashgate.

Mead, R H. (1982). Henry Cowell's New Music Society. *Journal of Musicology, 1*(4), 449–463.

Medina, Á. (2001). Primeras oleadas vanguardistas en el área de Madrid. *Cuadernos de Música Iberoamericana, 8–9*, 337–365. https://revistas.ucm.es/index.php/CMIB/article/view/61223 [accessed October 14, 2020]

Milhaud, D. (1995). *My happy life: An autobiography*. (Trans. D. Evans, G. Hall, & and C. Palmer). London & New York: Marion Boyars.

Morton, L. C. (1993). *Monday evening concerts, 1954–1971*. Los Angeles: Lawrence Morton Fund.

Muziek Encyclopedie. (n.d.). Hedendaags: 1920–1945 – see https://www.muziekencyclopedie. nl/action/genre/hedendaags;jsessionid=aaa12_PCAa-q9dIWYmUdw [accessed October 2, 2020]

Nauck, G. (2004). *Risiko des kühnen Experiments: Der Rundfunk als Impulsgeber und Mäzen*. Saarbrücken: PFAU.

Neff, S. (2001). Speculum Musicae. *Grove Music Online* – see https://0-www-oxfordmusiconline-com.wam.city.ac.uk/grovemusic/view/10.1093/gmo/9781561592630.001.0001/omo-9781561592630-e-0000044932?rskey=Ys8Mgq&result=1 [accessed September 30, 2020]

Nelson, A. (2004). *Music for the revolution: Musicians and power in early Soviet Russia*. University Park: Penn State University Press.

Nicolodi, F. (2011). Musica a Roma nella prima metà del '900. *Analecta musicologica, 45*, 478–498.

Notlingk, J. S. (2017). *The Scottish orchestras and new music, 1945–2015*. PhD thesis: University of Glasgow.

Oja, C. J. (2000). *Making music modern: New York in the 1920s*. New York: Oxford University Press.

Orenstein, A. (1975). *Ravel: Man and musician*. New York and London: Columbia University Press.

Orledge, R. (1987). "Satie, Koechlin and the Ballet 'Uspud'". *Music & Letters*, 68(1), 26–41.

Pace, I. (2007). Review of Theodor W. Adorno, *Towards a Theory of Musical Reproduction, Philosophy of New Music, Letters to his Parents. Tempo* 61(242), 61–68.

Pace, I. (2009a). Notation, time and the performer's relationship to the score in contemporary music. In D. Crispin (Ed.), *Unfolding time: Studies in temporality in twentieth-century music* (pp. 151–192). Leuven: Leuven University Press.

Pace, I. (2009b). Verbal discourse as aesthetic arbitrator in contemporary music. In B. Heile (Ed.), *The modernist legacy: Essays on new music* (pp. 81–99). Farnham: Ashgate.

Pace, I. (2011). The Cold War in Germany as ideological weapon for anti-modernists. Conference paper given in Helsinki, London, Graz – see https://openaccess.city.ac.uk/id/eprint/6482/ [accessed October 25, 2020]

Pace, I. (2017a). The new state of play in performance studies. *Music & Letters*, 98(2), 281–292.

Pace, I. (2018). *The reconstruction of post-war West German new music during the early Allied Occupation (1945–46), and its roots in the Weimar Republic and Third Reich*. PhD thesis: Cardiff University.

Pace, I. (2019). Negotiating borrowing, genre and mediation in the piano music of Finnissy: Strategies and aesthetics. In I. Pace & N. McBride (Eds.), *Critical perspectives on the music of Michael Finnissy: Bright futures, dark pasts* (pp. 57–103). Abingdon and New York: Routledge.

Pace, I. Forthcoming 2021–22. Musical internationalism in Nazi Germany: Provenance and post-war consequences. *Journal of the Royal Musical Association*.

Pardo, I.S.L. (2018). 'Música y Política en la España del Desarrollismo (1962-1970)'. PhD thesis: Universidad de Castilla-La Mancha.

Pasler, J. (1994). Inventing a tradition: Cage's "Composition in Retrospect." In M. Perloff & C. Junkermann (Eds.), *John Cage: Composed in America* (pp. 125–143). Chicago: University of Chicago Press.

Perlemuter, V., and Jourdan-Morhange, H. (1988). *Ravel according to Ravel*. London: Kahn & Averill.

Perry, M. E. (2013). Early Works and Life of Robert Gerhard. In M. Adkins & M. Russ (Eds.), *The Roberto Gerhard companion* (pp. 9–24). Farnham: Ashgate.

Peters, R., & Vogt, H. (1988). Die Berliner Novembergruppe und ihre Musiker. In R. Peters & H. Vogt (Eds.), *Stefan Wolpe: Von Berlin nach New York* (pp. 45–50). Cologne: Kölner Gesellschaft für Neue Musik.

Peters, P. (1995). *Eeuwige jeugd. Een halve eeuw Stichting Gaudeamus*. Amsterdam: Donemus.

Pfitzner, H. (1920). *Die neue Aesthetik der musikalischen Impotenz: Ein Verwesungssymptom?* Munich: Verlag der Süddeutschen Monatshefte.

Pirenne, C. (2004). Histoire de l'ensemble Musiques Nouvelles. In C. Pirenne (Ed.), *Les Musiques Nouvelles en Wallonie et à Bruxelles (1960–2003)* (pp. 37–90). Sprimont: Mardaga.

Plumb, S. (2006). *Neue Sachlichkeit 1918–33: Unity and diversity of an art movement*. Amsterdam & New York: Editions Rodopi.

P.M. On the Coul. (2014). Ruijneman, Daniel (1886–1963). In *Biographical Dictionary of the Netherlands* – see http://resources.huygens.knaw.nl/bwn/BWN/lemmata/bwn1/ruijneman [accessed October 2, 2020]

Pujadas, M. P., & Quadreny, J. M. M. (2014). From Valls to Cambridge: Robert Gerhard's musical aesthetics. In *Perspectives on Gerhard: Selected proceedings of the 2nd and 3rd International Roberto Gerhard Conferences* (pp. 1–11). Huddersfield: University of Huddersfield Press.

Rehding, A. (2006). Magic boxes and *Volksempfänger*: Music on the radio in Weimar Germany. In N. Bacht (Ed.), *Music, theatre and politics in Germany: 1848 to the Third Reich* (pp. 259–276). Aldershot & Burlington, VT: Ashgate.

Riedl, J. A. (1995). *NEUE MUSIK München*, Siemens-Studio für elektronische Musik und *Musica Viva* (1953–1963). In R. Ulm (Ed.), *"Eine Sprache der Gegenwart": Musica Viva 1945–1995* (pp. 65–74). Mainz: Piper Schott.

Roderick, P. (2010). *Rebuilding a culture: Studies in Italian music after Fascism, 1943-1953*. PhD thesis: University of York.

Rodriguez, E. M. (2016). *Music and exile in Francoist Spain*. Abingdon: Ashgate.

Romeo, C., Carapezza, P. E., Titone, A., Violante, P., Romeo, D., Damiani, G., & Modestini, M. (2013). *Nuova Musica: Le Settimane internazionali di Palermo (1960-1968)*. Marina di Patti: Pungitopo.

Royal Concertgebouw Orchestra. (n.d.). *Artistike Archief* – see http://archief. concertgebouworkest.nl/nl/archief/zoeken/ [accessed September 27, 2020]

Ryding, E., & Pechefsky, R. (2001). *Bruno Walter: A world elsewhere*. New Haven and London: Yale University Press.

Saldern, A. v. (2013). *Amerikanismus: Kulturelle Abgrenzung von Europa und US-Nationalismus im frühen 20. Jahrhundert*. Stuttgart: Franz Steiner Verlag.

Samama, L. (2006). *Nederlandse muziek in de 20-ste eeuw: Voorspel tot een nieuwe dag*. Amsterdam: Amsterdam University Press.

Samson, J. (1977). *Music in transition: A study of tonal expansion and atonality, 1900-1920*. London: Dent.

Scarpetta, G. (1992). *Le Festival d'automne de Michel Guy*. Paris: Éditions du Regard.

Scherchen, H. (1919). Neue Musik. *Freie Deutsche Bühne*, 1(2) (9 July 1919), 35–39 & 1(4) (21 September 1919), 80–83.

Schmelz, P. J. (2009). *Such freedom, if only musical: Unofficial Soviet music during the thaw*. New York and Oxford: Oxford University Press.

Schönberger, E. (Ed.) (1996). *Ssst! Nieuwe ensembles voor nieuwe muziek*. Amsterdam: International Theatre and Film Books.

Schoenberg, A. (1944). Autobiographie (26): Conductors (Koussevitzki–Toscanini) – see http://archive.schoenberg.at/writings/edit_view/transcription_view.php?id=1861&word_list=toscanini [accessed August 2, 2020].

Schoenberg, A. (1975a). Mechanical musical instruments (1926). In L. Stein (Ed.), *Style and idea* (pp. 326–330). With translations by L. Black. Berkeley & Los Angeles: University of California Press.

Schoenberg. A. (1975b). Modern music on the radio (1933). In L. Stein (Ed.), *Style and idea* (pp. 151–152). With translations by L. Black. Berkeley & Los Angeles: University of California Press.

Schoenberg, A. (1975c). For a treatise on performance (1923 or 1924). In L. Stein (Ed.), *Style and idea* (pp. 319–320). With translations by L. Black. Berkeley & Los Angeles: University of California Press.

Schoenberg, A. (n.d.a). Theory of performance (interpretation) execution. – see http://archive.schoenberg.at/writings/edit_view/transcription_view.php?id=361&word_list=performance [accessed August 2, 2020]

Schoenberg, A. (n.d.b). Zu: Theory of performance (Notizen) – see http://archive.schoenberg. at/writings/edit_view/transcription_view.php?id=358&word_list=performance [accessed August 2, 2020]

Schreiber, W. (2019). *Claudio Abbado: Der stille Revolutionär*. Munich: C. H. Beck.

Schwarz, B. (1983). *Music and Musical Life in Soviet Russia, 1917-1981*, enlarged edition. Bloomington: Indiana University Press.

Shreffler, A., & Trippett, D. (Eds.) (2009a). Introduction / Zu diesem Heft. In *Rudolf Kolisch in Amerika—Aufsätze und Dokumente. Musiktheorie—Zeitschrift für Musikwissenschaft*, 24(3), 195–199.

Shreffler, A., & Trippett, D. (Eds.) (2009b). Kolisch and the New School for Social Research. In *Rudolf Kolisch in Amerika—Aufsätze und Dokumente. Musiktheorie—Zeitschrift für Musikwissenschaft*, 24(3), 199–201.

Simeone, N. (2002). La Spirale and La Jeune France: Group identities. *The Musical Times*, 143(1880), 10–36.

SMCQ. (n.d.). Société de musique contemporaine du Québec (SMCQ) – see http://smcq. qc.ca/smcq/fr/artiste/smcq_/Soci%C3%A9t%C3%A9_de_musique_contemporaine_du_ Qu%C3%A9bec/biographie [accessed October 15, 2020]

Smith, J. A. (1986). *Schoenberg and his circle: A Viennese portrait*. New York & London: Schirmer.

Sørensen, S. M. (2016). Action Music!—Nam June Paik in Scandinavia, 1961. In T. Ørum & J. Olsson (Eds.), *A cultural history of the avant-garde in the Nordic countries 1950–1975* (pp. 259–272). Brill: Rodopi.

Stadlen, P. (Ed.) (1979). *Anton Webern, Variationen für Klavier*. Vienna: Universal Edition.

Stefan, R., Kessel, L., Tomek, O., Trapp, K., & Fox, C. (Eds.) (1996). *Von Kranichstein zur Gegenwart 1946–1996: 50 Jahre Darmstädter Ferienkurse*. Darmstadt: Daco.

Straus, J. N. (1999) The Myth of Serial "Tyranny" in the 1950s and 1960s. *The Musical Quarterly*, 83(3), 301–343.

Stravinsky, I. (1936). *An autobiography*. New York: Simon & Schuster.

Stravinsky, I. (1947). *Poetics of music: In the form of six lessons*. (Trans. A. Kondel & I. Dahl). Cambridge, MA: Harvard University Press.

Strobel, Heinrich. (1926). "Neue Sachlichkeit" in der Musik. *Musikblätter der Anbruch*, 8(6), 254–256.

Stuckenschmidt, H. H. (1925). Die Mechanisierung der Musik. *Pult und Takstock*, 2(1), 1–8.

Stuckenschmidt, H. H. (1977). *Schoenberg: His life, world and work*. London: John Calder.

Suchoff, B. (2003). *Bela Bartók: A celebration*. Lanham, MD: Scarecrow Press.

Szmolyan, W. (1984). Die Konzerte der Wiener Schönberg-Vereins. In *Musik-Konzepte 36: Schönbergs Verein für musikalische Privataufführungen*. Munich: edition text + kritik.

Tage der Neuen Musik, ed. (1998). *40 Jahre Tage der Neuen Musik Hannover. Dokumentation 1958–1998*. Hannover: Tage der Neuen Musik.

Takahashi, Y., & and Pruslin, S. (1975). Letters to the Editor. *Tempo, 115*, 53–54.

Taruskin, R. (1995). *Text and act: Essays on music and performance*. New York & Oxford: Oxford University Press.

Taruskin, R. (1997). *Defining Russia Musically: Historical and Hermeneutical Essays*. Princeton, NJ: Princeton University Press.

Thomas, A. (2005). *Polish music since Szymanowski*. Cambridge, UK: Cambridge University Press.

Thrun, M. (1995). *Neue Musik im deutschen Musikleben bis 1993* (2 vols.). Bonn: Orpheus.

Toch, E. (1926). Musik für mechanische Instrumente. *Musikblätter der Anbruch*, 8(8–9), 346–349.

Tompkins, D. G. (2013). *Composing the party line: Music and politics in early Cold War Poland and East Germany*. West Lafayette, IN: Purdue University Press.

Tortora, D. (1990). *Nuova consonanza: Trent'anni di musica contemporanea in Italia, 1959–1988*. Lucca: Libreria Musicale Italiana.

Trippett, D. (2009). The composer's rainbow: Rudolf Kolisch and the limits of rationalization. In *Rudolf Kolisch in Amerika—Aufsätze und Dokumente. Musiktheorie—Zeitschrift für Musikwissenschaft*, 24(3), 228–237.

Vermeil, J. (1996). *Conversations with Boulez: Thoughts on conducting*. (Trans. C. Naish). Portland, OR: Amadeus Press.

Walter, B. (1948). *Theme and variations: An autobiography*. London: Hamish Hamilton.

Waterhouse, J. G. (1999). *Gian Francesco Malipiero (1882–1973): The life, times and music of a wayward genius*. London & New York: Routledge.

Waters, J. W. (2011). Marxists, manifestos, and "Musical Uproar": Alan Bush, the 1948 Prague Congress, and the British Composer's Guild. *Journal of Musicological Research*, 30(1), 23–45.

Watson, S. (1995). *Prepare for saints: Gertrude Stein, Virgil Thomson, and the mainstreaming of American modernism*. Berkeley & Los Angeles: University of California Press.

Weber, W. (2008). *The great transformation of musical taste: Concert programming from Haydn to Brahms*. Cambridge, UK: Cambridge University Press.

Weißbach, R. (1986). *Rundfunk und neue Musik. Eine Analyse der Förderung zeitgenössischer Musik durch den Rundfunk*. Dortmund: Barbara Weißbach Verlag.

Wellens, I. (2002). *Music on the frontline: Nicolas Nabokov's struggle against communism and middlebrow culture*. Aldershot: Ashgate.

Werth, A. (1949). *Musical uproar in Moscow*. London: Turnstile Press.

Werth, A. (1961). *Russia under Khrushchev*. New York: Hill and Wang.

Williams, A. (2005). Budapest ♥ NY: The New Music Studio 1971–1980. *Perspectives of New Music*, 43(1), 212–235.

Wilson, P. N. (1992). Sakrale Sehnsüchte: Der Scelsi-Feldman-Nono-Kult. *MusikTexte*, 44, 2–4.

Woodley, R. (2000). Performing Ravel: Style and practice in the early recordings. In D. Mawer (Ed.), *The Cambridge companion to Ravel* (pp. 211–239). Cambridge, UK: Cambridge University Press.

Wright, D. (2005). The London Sinfonietta 1968–2004: A perspective. *Twentieth-Century Music*, 2(1), 109–136.

Wright, D. (2007). Reinventing the Proms: The Glock and Ponsonby Eras, 1959–85. In J. Doctor & D. Wright (Eds.), *The Proms: A new history* (pp. 168–209). London: Thames & Hudson.

Zintgraf, W. (1987). *Neue Musik 1921–1950 in Donaueschingen, Baden-Baden, Berlin, Pfullingen, Mannheim*. Horb am Neckar: Geiger-Verlag.

Recordings

Arditti String Quartet (2007). Helmut Lachenmann, *Grido; Reigen seliger Geister; Gran Torso*. KAIROS 0012662KAI.

Bern String Quartet (1986). Helmut Lachenmann, *Gran Torso*. Col legno 5504 Digital.

Craft, R. (1958). Schoenberg, Serenade, Op. 24. With Sam van Ducen, baritone, and instrumental ensemble. Columbia ML 5244.

Domaine Musical, conducted Boulez, P. (1960). Schoenberg, Serenade, Op. 24 (recording 1962); Suite, Op. 29 (recording 1960). In *Pierre Boulez: Le Domaine Musical, 1956–1967*. Accord 4811510.

ISCM Concert Group, conducted Mitropoulos, D. (1949). Schoenberg, Serenade, Op. 24. Esoteric ES-501.

Jack Quartet (2014). Helmut Lachenmann, Complete String Quartets. Mode – Mode 267.

Kawai, Noriko (2004). James Dillon, *The Book of Elements*. NMCD091.

Kolisch Quartet (1992). Schoenberg, String Quartets 1–4. With spoken comments by the composer and by the performers. Archiphon ARC-103/04.

Lixenberg, Loré; Rose, Gregory; Worby, Robert (2012). John Cage, *Song Books*. Sub Rosa SR 344.

Orchestre de chambre André Girard, conducted Désormière. Roger (2007). Messiaen, *Trois petites liturgies de la présence divine*. In *Les Rarissimes d'Olivier Messiaen*. Yvonne Loriod, piano; Jeanne Loriod, ondes martenot. EMI Classics – 0749 385275 2 7.

Ravel, M. (2003). *Valses nobles et sentimentales*, piano roll by composer. Pierian 13 51:51.

Stadlen, P. (1948). Webern, *Variations*, Op. 27. Schoenberg, *Fünf Klavierstücke*, Op. 23. In *Darmstadt Aural Documents, Box 4: Pianists*. NEOS11630.

SWF-Sinfonieorchester Baden-Baden, conducted Rosbaud, H. (1958). Berg, Three Pieces for Orchestra, Op. 6; Webern, Six Pieces for Orchestra, Op. 6. Westminster, S-9709.

SWF-Sinfonieorchester Baden-Baden, conducted Rosbaud, H. (1992) Messiaen, *Turangalîla Symphonie*. Wergo WER 6401-2.

CHAPTER 19

EMOTION AND PERFORMANCE PRACTICES

STEPHANIE ROCKE, JANE W. DAVIDSON,
AND FREDERIC KIERNAN

INTRODUCTION

WHILE most musicians use the term *performance practice*, it is worthwhile considering what it means in detail. Also labeled *performing practice*, the English adaptation of the German term *Aufführungspraxis* (Brown et al., 2001) describes the choices and methods the performer employs to communicate musical ideas to an audience. While a musician's practice can be distinctly individual, the term *performance practice* refers to the application of established rules and conventions relating to the genre and style of music they are playing. The extent to which a written score will provide guidance depends on the historical period, socio-cultural context, or genre. Quite precise instructions are written into the scores of most modern Western art music but with many earlier examples as well as aleatoric music, jazz, and some non-Western musics, annotations are often partial or rudimentary. With other traditions, there is no need for a score at all because both music and style have been transmitted aurally from person to person across multiple generations. (Brinner, 2001).

Regardless of the form in which music has been transmitted, a musician will perform in a certain way due to a multiplicity of interlocking or inter-related factors including:

- the teaching they have received;
- their motivation and prior music-making experience;
- the extent to which precise instructions have been notated or otherwise provided (and how precisely these are expected to be followed);
- negotiations with an accompanist, conductor, or other performers playing in an ensemble large or small;

- the extent to which the performer wishes to emulate the style of the period the music was composed in or to perform in accordance with the norms of the relevant genre;
- the occasion of the performance; and
- anticipated audience expectations.

This mix of factors manifests itself in *performance expression*, which is shaped by both conscious, interpretive choices and unconscious processes, as well as levels of skill. Skill includes mastery of technical control of the music and interpretation of its structure through the use of expressive devices such as variations in timing, dynamics, and articulation. There is evidence that interpretive choices are also shaped by motion principles. For instance, a musical tempo may correspond to biological motion such as walking, in order to achieve pleasing musical shape. From the opposite tangent, random fluctuations arising from human limitations in mechanical accuracy, or chance events, will also shape the sounds produced. In addition to communicating the structural, melodic, and harmonic elements, expressive performance also serves to communicate emotions to, and arouse emotions in, listeners. To achieve this, the performer both consciously and unconsciously imbues the performance with an emotional character. (Juslin, 2003; see also Schubert, this volume).

Totally spontaneous expressions of emotion in performance are probably quite rare, at least in Western art music (Juslin, 1995; Juslin & Timmers, 2010). This is because performers need to maintain some element of psychological balance or "relaxed concentration" to enable them to coordinate all the contributing factors that make the technical and expressive aspects of the performance successful (Connolly & Williamon, 2004). Musicians can and do differentiate between genuine emotion and emotional portrayal, often achieving the latter in performance by accessing personal memories. As an expressive performance technique, it is rather like applying the principles of method acting where there is a strong identification with genuinely felt emotion (Easty, 1989).

In addition to this, if the performance aspects are deeply learned and automated, there is scope for emotion to be experienced by the musician while performing. This may be the emotion that is being portrayed through the music but need not be. For example, performers who are deeply immersed in the act of performance and portraying a musical emotion such as anger, may experience within themselves a feeling of unbidden joy. In accordance with Abraham Maslow's concept of *peak experience*, such experiences are positive, epiphanic moments of meta-awareness, comprising profound "moments of highest happiness and fulfilment" (Maslow, 1968, p. 73). Such experiences have important consequences for personality development, offering catalysts for positive growth and maximizing the performer's potential. Mihalyi Csikszentmihalyi's concept of *flow* is similar but does not necessarily involve peak experiences. Flow occurs when high skill challenge and high absorption in the activity come together, creating a lack of self-consciousness and pleasure in continuation (Csikszentmihalyi, 1975).

Yet even less exceptional emotion-music experiences have significant value. Indeed, the single most cited example of why people engage in music as performers or listeners is to have some sort of emotional experience (Davidson & Garrido, 2014). Thus, if performers are to maximize their interactions and exchanges with their audiences, some understanding of the relationship between music and emotion is needed. As the relationship has been perceived differently over time and remains both highly contested and poorly understood, this chapter discusses the issues involved and shows how ideas about emotion have informed music making in different historical periods.

The Music-Emotion Relationship

Trying to understand the relationship between emotion and music has perplexed scholars, composers, and performers since antiquity and, despite the advances made and noted in the Introduction, there remains no consensus on the matter. This is partly because the term *emotion* has historically been just one of many other terms. *Humors, passions, sentiment,* and *affect* are earlier terms that each had nuanced meanings in their time but would now fall within the umbrella term of "emotion" (Dixon, 2012). Similarly, the idea that there could be a universal view on the music-emotion relationship is problematized by the wide range of musical styles, cultural norms, and individual circumstances in which music is created, performed, and received (Ayari & Makhlouf, 2010, p. 258; Davidson, Kiernan, & Garrido, 2017, pp. 31–32). For example, the notion that every type of musical instrument and every voice generates its own unique sound, with its own emotional timbre, demonstrates the complexity of constructing a workable generalized theory (Sève, 2017). Nonetheless, the emotion-music relationship remains an enticing field of investigation (see, for example, Imberty, 2010; Frangne, Lacombe, Massin, & Picard, 2017, pp. 9–10). Recent historical approaches have made significant contributions to this debate (Gouk, Kennaway, Prins, & Thormählen, 2019; Spitzer, 2020), but perhaps the most influential output in recent times comes from music psychologists who approach the study of music's expressive capacity by contemplating the biological factors and the mechanisms of cognition that bring emotion responses about.

Their work has resulted in the identification of eight mechanisms that induce an emotion response to music. These are encapsulated in the BRECVEMA model, which is summarized in Table 19.1 (Juslin, 2013; and more comprehensively described in Juslin, 2019). In applying BRECVEMA to a performance of Monteverdi's *Il Combattimento di Trancredi e Clorinda* and comparing audience responses to those contained in historical documents, it was found that individuals from both time periods reported strong emotional responses at similar structural points in the music (Davidson, Kiernan, & Garrido, 2017). This is in accord with other evidence about emotion and music—that emotional experiences are colored by generational principles, autobiographical and culturally shared associations, and contextual factors (Davidson & Garrido, 2014).

The performer who is aware of how emotion is induced through music can use this information to shape meaningful performances that appeal to audiences. Knowing the

Table 19.1. Summary of the BRECVEMA model of emotion mechanisms in music with examples.

Mechanism	Explanation	Example
Brain stem reflexes	The brain stem is the source of unconscious reflexes such as the "startle response" and the physiological (bodily) manifestations of emotion it gives rise to. Emotion is induced when the fundamental acoustic characteristics in the music are perceived as urgent.	Sudden force, e.g., percussive clashes, thuds, loud bangs, extreme dynamic or tempo changes
Rhythmic entrainment	Rhythmic entrainment is the compulsion we feel to move to music. External rhythms interact with internal bodily rhythms so that the internal rhythm adjusts and locks into the common periodicity. Listening to energetic music may cause physiological systems such as our heart rate to begin to match those of the music, thus inducing a feeling of increased excitement.	Strong and regular rhythmic structures, e.g., dance music; marching music
Evaluative conditioning	Emotion is induced because of pairings. Repeated exposure to a pairing of music with an event or thing will eventually lead to the music alone evoking the associated feelings. This is related to the concept of classical conditioning.	Musical figures or gestures known to be culturally significant or used regularly in the same context, e.g., a sports team's club song
emotional Contagion	Emotional contagion is based on the theory that mirror neurons cause us to mirror the emotions of people around us, and we develop parallel and reactive emotions to those we perceive in other people. The theory holds that emotion is induced as the listener perceives the emotional expression of the music and then "mimics" this expression internally.	Musical figures or gestures that mimic expressive utterances, e.g., a falling melodic line that imitates weeping or sobbing can induce sadness in the listener
Visual imagery	Emotion is induced as visual images are conjured up while listening to music. This theory depends on a conception of human imagination as a multi-sensory area where listeners appear to conceptualize the musical structures through a metaphorical non-verbal mapping between music and image schemata—e.g., hearing a melodic movement as upward.	Music structures that evoke iconic visual representations, e.g., rippling passages inducing visual images of flowing water, as in the opening of Smetana's symphonic poem *The Moldau*
Episodic memory	Music that was heard during a specific event in a person's life when heard again activates memories of the earlier circumstances, evoking an emotional response.	A favorite lullaby the person's mother sang to them as a child; or, a song heard the first time a couple danced together (as in, "they're playing our tune")
Musical expectancy	Emotion is induced because a specific feature of the music violates or counters the listener's expectations about how the music is going to behave.	Musical structures setting up expectations which are then thwarted, e.g. interrupted cadence (V-vi) in place of the expected V-I
Aesthetic judgment	Emotion is induced by judgments based upon the subjective evaluation of the aesthetic value of music deemed to be art. Although often interrelated, aesthetically induced emotions are differentiated from emotions associated with "music preference," particularly because aesthetic emotions are more intensely felt (Juslin 2013).	Aesthetic judgments of classical music master works often inspire awe and admiration

impact of sudden dynamic changes, regular rhythms, familiar tunes, imitative gestures, visually evocative musical patterns, and unusual harmonies, musicians can tailor their performance to elicit a strong emotional response from listeners. When the expressive choices are meaningful, the performance may evoke aesthetic judgments that further enhance the value of the experience for the listener and garner a strong sense of achievement in the performers.

Applying History of Emotions Concepts to Performance Practice

The foregoing discussion examines the music-emotion relationship primarily from a psychological perspective and focuses on individual experience as it is manifested in the present. However, in the field of the history of emotions, several key concepts that resonate across different time periods or situations have been created to help frame discussions about emotion, many of which can be applied to music contexts. While some terms are more relevant to musical performance practices than others, each term has some relevance when considering how or why a musician develops or selects a particular practice, and how the musician's performance is received.

From emotionology, emotional regimes, and emotional refuges to emotional communities

Carol and Peter Stearns were among the first scholars to treat emotions as historical phenomena. Their term *emotionology* is useful when considering the ways in which musicians interact with others in public situations, particularly fellow musicians, teachers, relevant institutions, and audiences. Conceptually, emotionology comprises "the attitudes or standards that a society, or a definable group within a society, maintains toward basic emotions and their appropriate expression" (Stearns & Stearns, 1985, p. 813). Emotionology controls the way emotions are expressed. In terms of performance practice, by identifying the norms of emotional expression—the emotionology—of those groups relevant to a musician's professional practice, the performer is better able to situate themselves within these groups and to consciously shape their own emotions either to align with group member expectations (whether musical, theoretical, or social) or to intentionally challenge them.

A similar concept to emotionology is that of the *emotional regime*. In developing the theory underpinning the term, William Reddy defines an emotional regime as comprising "[t]he set of normative emotions and the official rituals, practices, and emotives that express and inculcate them; a necessary underpinning of any stable political regime" (Reddy, 2001, p. 129). Whereas emotionology is concerned with the emotional norms and values of society and its social sub-groups, Reddy's concept places political governance at the center of his theory about emotions. Reddy argues that relaxed political regimes make room for a much greater range of emotional expressions than tightly controlled regimes. The tighter the regime, the harder it will be for subjects to find a place where emotions can be explored and expressed freely; but conversely, the greater such places will be appreciated. Proposing the term *emotional refuge* to describe such havens, Reddy defines the concept as constituting:

> a relationship, ritual, or organization (whether informal or formal) that provides safe release from prevailing emotional norms and allows relaxation of emotional effort, with or without an ideological justification, which may shore up or threaten the existing emotional regime. (Reddy, 2001, p. 129)

The obvious example of an emotional refuge in almost any regime is one's own home. But from a performance perspective, composing, performing, and listening to music can also afford opportunities for constructing or locating an emotional refuge. This is similar to Tia DeNora's notion of 'music asylums' (DeNora, 2013). At each point in the creation of Western art music—the composer's processes of notation, the musician's realization through performance, and the listener's interpretation—there are opportunities for emotional expression to be put into the service of catharsis, or some other beneficial process. For example, a composer in a strict regime may encode their dissatisfaction with imposed social constraints into a score, a performer may vent anger by playing a fast and loud piece, and an audience member's applause might not be simply a display of appreciation for the musical aspects of the performance but could also reflect appreciation for the opportunity for emotions to have flown freely within the relative privacy of a darkened auditorium. In terms of performance practice, musicians might consider how the political implications of emotional expression inform their performing choices (including the timing, location and manner of a performance), which may confirm or subvert political authority. By doing this, music performances can generate emotions in performers and listeners that are imbued with political agency.

Barbara Rosenwein expands upon the terms *emotionology* and *emotional regimes* to create a broad conception of *emotional communities* that goes beyond high-level societal groupings and political concerns. Emotional communities are formed within groups that range from such small social units as families to dramatic societies, school communities, and entire neighborhoods. They also include groups living in diverse geolocations who share a common interest. By approaching the study of communities from an emotion perspective, it becomes possible

> to uncover systems of feeling: what these communities (and the individuals within them) define and assess as valuable or harmful to them; the evaluations that they make about others' emotions; the nature of the affective bonds between people that they recognize; and the modes of emotional expression that they expect, encourage, tolerate and deplore. (Rosenwein, 2002, p. 842)

In thinking about emotional communities from the perspective of the music performer, one fascinating study of band members on tour revealed that the musicians developed a "feel" of their outfit. The emotional synergy that came about enabled the group to gauge the unfurling emotions that arose during performance, both between each other and in interaction with their audience. Moreover, achieving this deep awareness of each other's emotion responses led to bonds that enhanced band members' sense of wellbeing (Geeves, Jones, Davidson, & Sutton, 2020). More broadly, the practices of different musical ensembles (e.g., orchestras, string quartets, and jazz trios) can also be interpreted and understood from the theoretical emotion perspectives outlined here (see Davidson & King, 2004).

In one final music-related example, the Singing Revolution of Estonia, Latvia, and Lithuania (1987–1991), emotional regimes, refuges, and communities are all brought to the fore. Subjected to the tight emotional regime of Soviet rule, the traditional cultural practice of choral singing within these Baltic republics provided an emotional refuge. Subversive protests could be enacted by singing songs and hymns that had attained a patriotic meaning, known to the Balts but hidden to the Soviet authorities. Choirs became powerful emotional communities that projected their collective strength to the community at large. But this was no accident. In the words of Latvian conductor Māris Sirmais:

> A conductor must work with each person individually, teaching that person not only how to sing correctly but how to emotionally project yourself so intensively that what you do as a unit, as a personality, speaks to listeners. So that each person standing in this energy circuit would feel these energetic charges all around, next to themselves on the right and on the left. (As cited in Šmidchens, 2014, p. 323)

In one of many remarkable events that demonstrate the soft power of song, Estonians gathered en masse in 1991 linking arms and singing in the face of Soviet tanks, successfully preventing the destruction of radio and television stations. Through the leadership of choir directors, whose performance practices focused on selecting repertoire and fostering expressive singing that would build patriotic fervor, massed singing became a weapon that would contribute to all three Baltic states achieving freedom from Soviet governance in 1991 (Šmidchens, 2014).

While such stories are inspirational, for performers interested in historical performance practice, gaining an understanding about the types or classes of things that moved the emotions of musical communities of a particular period can add depth to their understanding of historical music and provide interpretive stimulus. For example, the performer might train to step into historical character when they walk onto the stage, using both musical and bodily gestures modeled on historical forms of communication, all the while realizing that they are performing to a contemporary audience who may or may not interpret the gestures in accordance with their historical meanings (Davidson & Maddox, 2017). Whereas nobility and rank might have dictated who the audience was in the past, today individual friendship groups, education levels, and personal taste will be more likely determinators, and so understanding of historical gesture cannot be taken for granted within this cohort.

By engaging with the concepts of emotionology, emotional regimes, and emotional communities, a performer can be stimulated in several beneficial ways. Interpretation of musical works can be approached from new theoretical perspectives and existing assumptions about the performer/audience relationship can be reconsidered and challenged. Performers may also apply these emotions concepts to access a deep understanding of the musical communities they work within or for.

Emotions as practice – actions of the body

Most definitions of emotion currently in use in the fields of psychology, sociology, and anthropology emphasize that emotions involve actions of the body in some way. Observing this, Monique Scheer has argued that Bourdieu's practice theory can enrich our understanding of emotions and their relationship to the body and mind (Scheer, 2012). For Bourdieu, practices are learned over time, literally through "practice" and socialization, and comprise the unconscious strategies that people employ to position themselves within a social field (e.g., family, work, the legal system) by investing and seeking different types of resource, or "capital" (Bourdieu, 1977, 1990).

For Scheer, emotions are precisely the same thing: strategies for navigating social space, that may be learned or unlearned, and which involve the investment and seeking of resources. Emotions involve engagements of internal physiological systems and movements of the body and external objects may also be used in the performance of emotion—such as when a person revs their car aggressively. Crucially, Scheer argues that the physiological experiences of emotion cannot be understood as separate from the practices that give rise to them. Scheer writes that emotional practices are

> practices involving the self (as body and mind), language, material artefacts, the environment, and other people . . . mobilizing, naming, communicating, and regulating emotion . . . [recognizing that] the body is . . . socially situated, adaptive, trained, plastic, and thus historical. . . .
>
> The use of the term "emotional practices" should imply 1) that emotions not only follow from things people do, but are themselves a form of practice, because they are an action of a mindful body; 2) that this feeling subject is not prior to but emerges in the doing of emotion; and 3) that a definition of emotion must include the body and its functions, not in the sense of a universal, pristine, biological base, but as a locus for innate and learned capacities deeply shaped by habitual practices. (Scheer, 2012, p. 193; 220)

For Scheer, emotions are not so much something that we *have* as something that we *do*, and for this reason, emotions are not timeless, ahistorical states of being, but historically and socially specific acts performed by a thinking body that is accumulating knowledge of how to navigate its social environment all the time. This has also led to the suggestion that emotions can be viewed as *creative practices*, since they can generate social change by doing different types of creative work (Kiernan, 2020). The body can become so practiced in certain ways that it need not think consciously in some situations. This theory helps to explain why emotions can be strategically evoked, anticipated, or avoided, because the individual can engage, or not, in emotional practices.

Music performers are arguably in a better position than most people to appreciate the idea that the body can accumulate knowledge through practice and deploy it in precise, learned ways (see Davidson, 2001; and also Davidson, this volume). Moreover, they may also easily grasp the idea that specific feeling states can be induced, scaffolded, manipulated, and diffused by these performances to such an extent that it is difficult to consider those feeling states as separable from the performance that gives rise to them.

An audience member's observations relating to the performance of a recently created pasticcio opera, *Voyage to the Moon*, illuminates how emotion is embodied through the acts of musical performance and listening in quite diverse ways. Created from new and pre-existing music in 2016, and based on the epic poem "Orlando furioso," a range of Baroque arias formed the musical backbone of the new opera (Browning & Davidson, 2019; 2021). The arias were selected for their depiction of specific emotional states.

One particular section, in which a female lead playing a male role sings an aria that is followed by an instrumental interlude, demonstrates how the deliberate integration of expressive musical elements from a repertoire of techniques both historical and ahistorical can have extremely moving impacts on both performer and audience. The vengeful feelings encapsulated in Johann Adolph Hasse's (1699–1783) aria "O placido il mare" (from the opera *Siroe, re di Persia*) were adapted to the *Voyage* narrative, the new text depicting a similarly vengeful Orlando (played by the female lead) ravaging the earth, fighting anyone in sight. Following the aria, "Beautiful unearthly music," represented by George Frideric Handel's "Entrée des Songes agréables" (Entrance of the Pleasant Dreams) from *Alcina* HWV 34 (1735), began. As the orchestra played, a vapor was released to calm and soothe Orlando's mind and restore his sanity, the music also depicting this soothing effect. For the audience, the physiological impact of the transition from the fast-paced rageful music that could set hearts beating faster, to peaceful music that would slow the heartbeat down, was noticeable, but as will be shown, for the singer on the final night of the performance, the effect was profound.

Five key observations relating to emotions as practice were noted by the audience member and later discussed with the singer. First, both singer and orchestra employed historically informed expressive musical techniques, such as *notes inégales*, stylistic ornamentation, and special violin bowing techniques, thereby flagging the new work's historical legacy and shaping listeners' expectations accordingly. Second, as the singer sang the aria, she was brandishing a replica medieval flat sword that was very heavy. Visibly shaking under the effort required to raise it above her head, the struggle was also evident in the sonic quality of her voice. Third, as she ended the aria and started to listen to the Handel, she began crying. Fourth, even after the Handel finished, the singer sat for a long time in a dreamlike state before progressing with the action of the opera. Fifth, the researcher had responded empathetically to the performance.

In discussions between the observer and the singer, it became apparent that the emotion portrayed through the stylistic means of the "rage aria" was fused with the performer's own spontaneous lived emotion. The singer actually felt anger surge through her body as she brandished the sword though the air and high above her head. Then, the transition from the aria to the slow tempo and "unearthly" quality of Handel's music unexpectedly evoked an epiphanic personal response. At the very moment of transition, she was struck by the fact that this was her final performance of the opera, which had toured several cities; the joy of performing in it and the sense of worth that belonging to the close-knit emotional community of performers and support crew gave her was about to come to an end. In combination, the three factors—the physical trauma of the sword wielding, the sudden change in the emotive content of the music, and the recognition of imminent loss in real life—caused a bittersweet sadness to well up in the singer, bringing her to tears. But this was not a private moment: it was witnessed by an audience, one of whom at least—the observer—responded empathetically. She felt her heart pound as the Hasse aria became more and more fiery in its florid high passages, and when the singer began to cry to the slow Handel music, so too did the observer.

This example demonstrates that the history of emotions as a field has fundamentally reconsidered the relationship between emotions and the body. Whereas psychology and physiology have firmly framed emotions as exclusively internal physiological and psychological processes, some history of emotions theories place emotion in the practices that link body and environment, to potentially incorporate movements, attires, places/ spaces, and the entire panoply of human cultural and social activity.

EMOTION IN MUSIC CONTEXTS ACROSS TIME

Musical scores from the early period of Western classical music (encompassing medieval, Renaissance, and the early Baroque eras) provide few or sometimes even no notated clues to how the music might have been imbued with a specific kind of emotional expression, affording present-day performers with opportunities to create imaginative responses. While notation practices changed during the common practice period (spanning the mid-Baroque to mid-twentieth century), with composers becoming ever more explicit, even in the music of today there remains some freedom of expression to the performer.

Of course, the performer may opt to work within the constraints of historically informed performance (HIP) practices, acknowledging, as Tim Carter does, that "it is now widely accepted that music of a given time and place should be performed in a manner consonant with the expectations of its original creators" (2019, p. 53). Nonetheless, Carter also acknowledges that "there are still pockets of resistance" to this position.

Indeed, the debate about HIP continues to be strong (Butt, 2002, pp. 3–50; Davies, 2001; Dodd, 2020; Kivy, 1995; Ravasio, 2019; Taruskin, 1996).

For those who are drawn to HIP, some will be satisfied with following the guidance of experts; however, in the words of renowned historical transverse flautist and teacher Barthold Kuijken, it is important to "view all information, be it from . . . music teachers or from musicology, with a critical eye and a healthy dose of scepticism" and to allow what is learned through performance to "fruitfully interact" with what is learnt through personal academic study (2013, p. 4). Thus, while much can be learnt by performing the music, particularly alongside skilled and knowledgeable others, becoming immersed in all aspects of the culture from which the music emanated can add depth and meaning to any performance. Given music's expressive properties, perhaps the most productive insights can be gained by learning about the conventions of emotional expression of those living at the time and place a work was composed; performances underpinned by such knowledge are likely to lead to more nuanced, and perhaps even more innovative musical expression.

Accordingly, the information in this section is aimed at providing an overview of how thoughts and practices relating to emotion and music have changed over time. It draws particularly from the recent six-volume interdisciplinary publication *A Cultural History of the Emotions* (Broomhall, Davidson, & Lynch, 2019) that covers emotion from antiquity to the twenty-first century, with each volume investigating a relatively discrete period. The chapters on music and dance in each volume provide a particularly invaluable resource for understanding how emotion in music contexts has changed over time and key information from volumes 2 to 6 will be interspersed here (Carter, 2019; Collins & Nevile, 2019; Mews & Williams, 2019; Thormählen, 2019a, 2019b).

Vocal music to the nineteenth century

From an evolutionary perspective, the origins of music are either rooted in or at least closely linked to the emotional expressivity of the human voice, and thinking about how emotion is encoded in the vocalizations of singers has inspired significant thought from philosophers, music theoreticians, as well as other scholars through the ages (Coutinho, Scherer, & Dibben, 2019, pp. 2–3). Much that was written about music during antiquity and the Medieval era relates to religious music—hymns, chants, and liturgical and paraliturgical settings—and gathered inspiration from Latin interpretations of the Greek philosophers. While there was a prevailing view that music should be approached with caution due to its capacity to evoke lascivious responses, it was also acknowledged that music could support devotion. Indeed, Augustine of Hippo (354–430 CE) worries about music being put to immoral use but also confesses that he was "keenly moved by the sweet singing. . . . Those voices flowed into my ears, truth seeped into my heart and feelings of devotion welled up; tears ran down and it was well with me that they did" (Augustine, 1981, pp. 9.6.14, 191). For Hildegard of Bingen (1098–1179), composing liturgical songs enabled her to her apply her creativity to spiritual expression. Thus, for singers of religious medieval music, striving to achieve a purity of sound appears to be an essential ingredient.

A century later, the musical theorist Johannes de Grocheio (c. 1275) divided the music of Paris into three genres: popular song, polyphony, and ecclesiastical music. His ideas reflect a marked shift away from the ancient Greek notion that music reflected a cosmic or celestial harmony, a theory that had infatuated earlier medieval scholars to this point. For Grocheio, each of the three Parisian genres had a specific purpose within the community. Songs of the troubadour and trouvère lyric traditions might assist civic agendas by celebrating boldness and bravery while "the innate trials of humanity may be softened" by the melodies and lyrics of others (Grocheio, 2011, 9.4 p. 69; 9.1 p. 67). For these secular songs, then, a performer's expression should accord with the theme of the song in order to communicate it to the listener. The purpose of the ecclesiastical hymn, on the other hand, is "to rouse [the] hearts and minds [of the congregation] and exhort them to devotion" (Grocheio, 2011 27.7 p. 100), which indicates a more robust performance style might be appropriate. If Paris is indicative of medieval Europe, by the close of the thirteenth century, vocal music articulated cultural values and was also used to stir both body and soul (Mews & Williams, 2019).

Throughout the later-medieval and Renaissance eras, music was crafted according to eight-note modal scales. Although not identical, these "church" modes spanning the octave were based on those of the ancient Greeks. It was believed that each mode conveyed a distinctive mood. The Dorian mode, for example was considered majestic, while music in the Mixolydian mode might convey grief or anxiety. In the sixteenth century, modes that equate to the current major and minor scales were added to the existing eight. The perceived affective properties of the modes were often utilized to underscore the message of a text. For example, French chansons of the late fifteenth and early sixteenth centuries with "sad, grave, languorous or plaintive" lyrics were often associated with the Phrygian mode, while texts with mournful associations were often set to the Lydian mode (Collins & Nevile, 2019, pp. 50–52). Thus, performers of such songs might take their expression cues from the lyrics, accepting that the melodies and harmonies will have been crafted in a mode that was believed to match them, even if to modern ears this might not seem to be the case. In another example that shows this principle extended to religious music, the Franco-Flemish composer Claude le Jeune (c. 1528–1600) based his selection of twelve melodies from the Genevan Psalter by matching the mood of the mode with the emotional ethos of one of the Psalms. In selecting one melody from each of the modes for his cycle, Le Jeune appears to have intentionally presented the full gamut of human emotions with the express intention of depicting social harmony, thereby reflecting the transition toward a more humanistic worldview (Freedman, 2003). The transition from a primarily theological underpinning of society to an increasingly humanist one would have important consequences for the music-emotion relationship.

During most of the Renaissance, musical expression was influenced by the meanings of words (in vocal music) as well as prevailing rules about how multiple melodies ought to be interwoven. These rules meant that vocal texts could sometimes be less readily heard in densely polyphonic music. There seems to have been a "tacit assumption" that settings should reflect the overarching sentiments of the text and composers would also paint individual words to emphasize the emotion content (Collins & Nevile, 2019, pp. 52–53). Accordingly, performers of this repertoire today might scrutinize scores carefully looking for examples of word painting to bring out. For example, Josquin des Prez's (c. 1450/1455–1521) setting of Psalm 50 includes "a piercing Phrygian cadence on a unison e' at 'humiliatum' " (Macey, 2000, p. 511).

As the Renaissance proceeded, vocal music was increasingly constructed and subsequently analyzed in terms of interpretations of the ancient Greek principles of rhetoric that Erasmus and other scholars had revisited in the sixteenth century. Applied to music, the composer would attend to the first two of the five stages of persuasion that comprised the rubric of rhetoric—"invention" and "disposition"—by creating convincing music. Responsibility for the final two stages "memory" and "delivery" were allocated to the performer, while the middle stage "elocution" was the preserve of both. Thus, responsibility for expression was recognized as a joint project between composer and performer. This was later highlighted by Johann Joachim Quantz (1697–1773) and C. P. E. Bach (1748–1788) in the context of instrumental music, as will be discussed later in the chapter.

As the Renaissance transitioned into the Baroque there was a turn towards overtly eliciting listeners' emotional responses to the music. This occurred through stylized gestures as well as the strategic use of expressive musical features (such as dissonance) to emphasize specific words. Both sonic and visual eloquence were important to *seconda pratica* composers such as Monteverdi (c. 1567–1643), whose lament in the opera *Arianna* (1608) brought audience members to tears (Carter, 2019). Accordingly, those in the early seventeenth century who were involved in staging the new theatrical musical form—opera—devised a range of physical gestures involving the whole body to complement the vocal delivery. Through ongoing exposure, audiences would learn the specific, usually emotional meanings of these gestures (Barnett & Massey-Westropp, 1987; Hill, 2017; Kaleva, 2021).

Singing techniques were developed to aid emotional expression, including the *messa di voce* (swelling of volume on a sustained note) and *portamento* (sliding from one written note to the next written note), among others (see Peres Da Costa, this part). These had become widespread across all genres by the early eighteenth century and would continue to be put to use, particularly within the *bel canto* style of opera singing, through to the middle of the twentieth century (Potter, 2006). Portamento's emotional power is believed to arise from its likeness to other sounds that elicit "instinctive emotional reactions" (Leech-Wilkinson, 2006, p. 239; on the psychological mechanisms see Juslin, 2005). Most commonly heard in the "slow, most affecting arias and songs, the most overt and uninhibited expressions of musical love," performers were reflecting the earliest musical sounds an infant is likely to hear—the lullaby—to convey "a sense of warmth, security, and love, and perhaps also nostalgia and some sense of loss," thereby finding applicability in a range of emotion settings (Leech-Wilkinson, 2006, p. 248). Performers of this repertoire are directed to early recordings that offer us intriguing insights into how portamento sounded, with swooping and cooing emotion effects captured in the performances of famous opera artists, some of whom had been performing since the mid-nineteenth century.

Instrumental music to the nineteenth century

Minstrels were generally considered of questionable character by the broader medieval and Renaissance communities, and it would not be until the sixteenth century that cathedrals and churches would employ instrumental musicians. Nonetheless, small ensembles of musicians were engaged in courts, including lutenists for whom very moving solos were composed, and the occasional minstrel might become a prince or king's confidant (Brown & Polk, 2001, pp. 99–100). Another feature of medieval thought and practice with regard to music was that instruments were ascribed emotional characteristics. For example, according to Konrad of Megenberg (1308–1374), outdoor instruments such as the trumpet and shawm were believed to "excite pleasure of the mind in one who is an ally but depresses the spirits of enemies with sadness," while indoor instruments such as harps and other string instruments were believed to "incline human minds to the mildness of piety" (Page, 2009, p. 31). Later, Johannes Tinctoris (1435–1511) asserts that bowed instruments "induce piety and stir my heart most ardently to contemplation of heavenly joys" (Baines, 2009, p. 59). Thus, performers of Renaissance instrumental music should be aware that attitudes of religious devotion permeated all aspects of life—and hence music making—in courts as much as in cathedrals, and think how they might inscribe piety into their playing.

Early seventeenth-century instrumental music was usually conceived as functional rather than expressive. Music provided rhythm for dance, supported ritual such as an organ interlude during a religious service, and bestowed pomp and ceremony to festive occasions such as coronations and processions. Thus, emotions might be calmed or aroused by music that was designed to create a particular mood in a social setting, but there was no expectation that instrumental music expressed a specific feeling, much less a series of feelings. This does not mean that instrumental music in the early sixteenth century was lacking in individual character; merely that character was most commonly achieved by emulation rather than emotional evocation (Carter, 2019, pp. 65–66). Quotations from other musical works and attempts to mimic the sounds of nature would, of course, arouse emotional responses linked to the object of emulation. But in these early days of the *seconda pratica* when the principals of functional harmony were still being worked out, composers were focused more on writing music that responded to the needs of the occasion and resolving technical quandaries than on depicting a series of passions. Thus, performers of early Baroque instrumental music might focus particularly on achieving an overarching mood, rather than trying to identify or single out passages to imbue with specific emotions.

By the later seventeenth century, instrumental solos could be extraordinarily evocative, although this might still relate more to pieces expressing an overarching mood than a series of emotions. Heinrich Biber's (1644–1704) fifteen "Rosary" sonatas (c. 1676) provide an exemplary case. Composed to accompany or invoke Rosary Processions during which the faithful proceeded from one painting or sculpture to the next contemplating a specific key event in the life of Christ or the Virgin Mary, each sonata encapsulates the mood of the respective historical event. Nonetheless, the emphasis on emotional evocation was not ubiquitous at this time; it was just as common for composers to focus on virtuosic displays without thought of passion. Indeed, the German composer and theorist Johann Mattheson (1681–1764) was of the opinion that composers of keyboard music were more often focused on the keyboardist's touch than on touching the heart (Carter, 2019; Harriss, 1981). This would indicate that the more technically difficult a work is, the less any specific emotion or series of emotions might be expected to be expressed.

The extent to which each of these attitudes toward instrumental music prevailed in any particular place is difficult to determine, but certainly by the middle of the eighteenth century, composers were adopting the aesthetics of the *Empfindsamer Stil* that was gaining favor among European writers and artists, seeking to move audiences in accordance with this newly fashionable "sentimental style" (Carter, 2019, p. 68). According to Quantz, a composer "must have a fiery spirit, united with a soul capable of tender feeling; a good mixture, without too much melancholy, of what scholars call the temperaments" (Reilly, 1985, p. 13). In similar vein, C. P. E. Bach considers emotion in his treatise on keyboard performance, instructing musicians to communicate the composer's expressive intentions by actually feeling the passions they hope to arouse in listeners as they perform:

> A musician cannot move others unless he too is moved. He must of necessity feel all of the affects that he hopes to arouse in his audience, for the revealing of his own humor will stimulate a like humor in the listener. In languishing, sad passages, the performer must languish and grow sad . . . in lively, joyous passages, the executant must again put himself into the appropriate mood . . . varying the passions he will barely quiet one before he rouses another. (Mitchell, 1949, p. 152)

While to contemporary performers, such a notion might seem inadvisable, as actually feeling some emotions could result in a reduction in technical control, nonetheless, the instruction provides food for thought. Whether the idea is taken on board to the full extent conceivable or in a more modified form, it is evident that emotion should be expressed with as little reserve as possible when performing the music of this transitionary period and even more so as the nineteenth century approached and progressed.

Indeed, toward the end of the eighteenth century, a tendency toward even more hyperbolic expressions of sentiment developed and was encapsulated in the term *Sturm und Drang* (storm and stress). Thus, as the Romantic era approached, composers were increasingly speaking "directly to the heart and soul," rather than through "coded signifiers" (Carter, 2019, p. 68). Moreover, accompanying the rise of instrumental music as an art form came a belief that music's ineffable expressive capacity rendered music the "highest of the arts" (Thormählen, 2019b, p. 58). What became essential to artistic expression from the early nineteenth century was the ability to connect emotionally to a work, to be sensitive to one's own feelings in order to communicate them clearly to audiences (Torbianelli, 2014, pp. 15–16). Certainly, from a technical perspective, emotion was communicated primarily through phrasing, articulation, and a range of playing techniques (see Peres Da Costa, this part). But as the nineteenth century progressed, instrumental virtuosi began to use their whole bodies to communicate emotion. Indeed, Niccolò Paganini and Franz Liszt placed "the performing body . . . centre stage" (Thormählen, 2019b, p. 68) just as singers had done for centuries. (Also see Kopiez, Volume 2, and Davidson, this volume.)

Moving audiences

The way people listened to music underwent a metamorphosis in the fifteenth century. Whereas music had generally been appreciated for its sonic properties and ability to depict a mood without any widespread interest in understanding how this was achieved, from the later fifteenth century onwards an aesthetic appreciation of the structures and techniques composers employed began to be recorded in treatises and other commentary (Wegman, 2002). Thus, the mood of the music might move most listeners, but others might feel pleasure from apprehending a particularly compelling technical device. Composers studied each other's works and became ever more technically adroit. Indeed, across Europe composers became collegial, as evidenced by the proliferation of pieces composed by one composer mourning the death of another. Johannes Ockeghem commemorated Gilles Binchois's death through his *Mort tu as navré/Miserere* (1460), while Josquin des Prez would mark the passing of Ockeghem with his *Nymphes des bois/ Requiem* (1497) (Collins & Nevile, 2019, pp. 54–55). From this perspective, performers may like to honor the intellect and attitude of these early composers by searching for clever technical devices and bringing them out in their performances. Many among current-day admirers of this music have spent considerable time listening to the repertoire attentively, and even adopted a learned approach to understanding it, so any performance that accentuates evidence of the composer's skill may enhance the aesthetic pleasure of such audience members. Even those less aware of the fine detail of medieval and Renaissance music may appreciate the novelty of an interpretation that contains elements that surprise modern ears.

With the forms of entertainment available to a broader populace expanding to include public concerts and opera in the Baroque era, new emotional communities, practices, and opportunities for expression arose. As noted, much of the vocal music and even instrumental music of the era was informed by the processes of rhetoric, finding particularly evocative expression in opera through both music and gesture. Writing about a recent research project revolving around Ariadne's lament from Monteverdi's opera *Arianna*, Daniela Kaleva (2021) explains how she performed the work both theatrically and in concert to determine the effect of Baroque gesture on contemporary audiences.

She then compared the responses of this audience to those of the seventeenth century by drawing on Emily Wilbourne's (2016) investigation of witness accounts, poetry, and paintings inspired by the premiere of the opera, which had starred *commedia dell'arte* Virginia Ramponi Andreini. Andreini's success in *Ariana* arose from her professional theatrical training; and in turn, the overall success of the opera itself was in no small way attributable to her *stile rappresentativo* performance.

In bringing together rhetoric, *seconda pratica*, and *commedia dell'arte*, Monteverdi and Andreini contributed to revolutionizing opera through engaging with the art of rhetoric. Whereas Kaleva found many within her contemporary audiences reported that they were moved by her performances of the lament, often quite deeply, none shed tears as some had in the sixteenth century; nonetheless, the contemporary audience did all pay close attention. While this was also the case with Andreini's rendition of the aria in 1608, the listening practices of audiences differed at that time from those of audiences in modern concert halls. Indeed, by the eighteenth century, theater boxes had become little ecosystems of entertainment with gambling, flirting, and excessive drinking commonplace, and this remained true through until the nineteenth century. Aware that a composer had to work hard to retain audience attention, Mozart "catered to their tastes by a careful mixture of familiarity and surprise" in order to titivate the emotions (Carter, 2019, p. 54). While some scholars describe these listening practices as evidence of audience boredom or an unwillingness to listen attentively (Johnson, 1995), others characterize it more positively in terms of a "sociable listening aesthetic" (Weber, 1997). Contemporary performers of Western art music rarely experience openly inattentive audiences unless their role is to provide functional background music such as when singing or playing in hotel lobbies, or during receptions. But knowing that audiences of the past were often less single-mindedly attentive to the performers' efforts might inspire a different approach to performing Baroque and Classical music today. It is likely that those performing opera in these eras, both singers and instrumentalists, would have brought out the emotion of the music more ostentatiously to try to hold audience members' attention, and this might inspire modern performers to do likewise.

Although by the middle of the eighteenth century, music—both instrumental and vocal—was expected to move the emotions of audiences at a deeper level than those associated with aesthetic appreciation, there was no theoretical consensus on how this was achieved (Carter, 2019). For English composer Charles Avison (1709–1770), composing expressive music was an intuitive process, a function of "Taste rather than reasoning" (Dubois, 2004, p. 88). Nonetheless, the idea that "hearing is . . . the most effective sense for awakening the emotions," asserted by Swiss mathematician and philosopher Johann Georg Sulzer (1771–1779, III, 421), turned the assumption that music *made* an impression because it mimicked emotion on its head by asserting that music expressed feelings and therefore *was* impression. Whereas the lack of any scientific theory explaining music's ineffability had been largely lamented, in the later eighteenth century the very fact that it was "beyond reason, rationality and explanation," began to be celebrated: "music was divorced from earthly emotions and moved instead into a world of ideals" (Thormählen, 2019b, p. 58).

Working in tandem with this growing sense of music as metaphysical entity, listening practices began to change. Whereas opera audiences continued to take a sociable approach to attending live music, the developing taste for concert music was creating a new mode of listening. Appreciating music's beauty of form and its ability to move the listener to higher realms, concertgoers would sit in silence, listening attentively in a ritualized space that emulated that found in churches and cathedrals. Organizations such as the London-based Philharmonic Society established in 1813, and John Ella's Musical Union founded in 1845, fostered an immersive approach to music listening. Ella provided program notes for forthcoming concerts that included music analysis. He also recommended that Union members take scores with them to read along with the music. The listening practice Ella promoted was aimed at helping listeners gain an understanding of the entirety of the work, as opposed to merely hearing "a series of sense impressions" that might otherwise obfuscate "the true force of the music's meaning" (Thormählen, 2019b, pp. 59–64). The legacy of such listening practices remains today, with many Western art music audience members well versed in particular pieces and keen to learn more about them. Performers might consider following a growing trend to enhance audiences' aesthetic appreciation by providing pre-concert talks and detailed program notes.

As the nineteenth century progressed, then, two types of listening habits had become established among the general populace, one founded on the intellectually oriented idea of "music as text and universal truth" and the other affirming its physical and physiological dimension, absorbing "music as event and experience" (Thormählen, 2019b, p. 69). Whereas in the nineteenth century, the former was largely found within concerts of classical music and the latter in opera and popular forms of musical entertainment, today both approaches can be found within all genres of Western music and—in the case of opera and jazz in particular—might even be combined. In such cases, the primary drivers of emotion—from intellectual and aesthetic concerns to embodied, social ones—collide and catalyze into new listening practices. As a consequence, today, the classical music virtuoso must either straddle two profiles or choose between them. The first follows an elitist model in which the music is acknowledged as the product of an extraordinary intellect and the performer separates themselves from the audience allowing the music to appear to flow through them. The second, a more contemporary model of competitive entertainer, involves engaging with the audience in the spirit of doing "whatever it takes" to sell tickets (Rihtaršič, 2017).

Dismissing music as emotion in art music of the twentieth century

In the nineteenth century, theories about the source of musical expressivity spanned the continuum of creativity, from "conception [to] manifestation [to the] reception" of musical works (Thormählen, 2019a, p. 55). But as the twentieth century approached, those influenced by Freudian ideas such as Arnold Schoenberg (1874–1951) rebelled against cognitive explanations that assumed audiences received music according to coded rules learned from observation or training. Instead, a subliminal root for expressive performance and recognition was asserted. In a related shift, Claude Debussy (1862–1918) shunned "false sentimentality" seeking to produce music that sounded beautiful but was not intended to enrapture. No longer obligatorily tied to its status as the language of the emotions, music was freed from the dictates of expressivity inspiring a "proliferation of different styles of music, different modes of consumption and reception" (Thormählen, 2019b, pp. 73–74). Moreover, the application of the psychological theories of creativity underpinning the burst of stylistic heterogeneity also inspired "a stark opposition between an engagement in music as leisure time, and a serious reception of music through concentrated listening and study" (Thormählen, 2019b, p. 74).

Schoenberg's development of atonality was inspired by the psychological idea of musical sensation not emotional expression, while Varèse sought to challenge the aesthetic notion that music should sound beautiful by creating music that intentionally reflected an industrial soundscape. Meanwhile, and paradoxically in some contexts, following the Lisztian model, performers still felt compelled to manifest their inner feelings visibly through their expressive postures and gestures, as they interpreted the score for the audience. But whether in tandem or in opposition, through music and performance that challenged traditional expectations, both composers and performers were keen to provoke the listener to consciously acknowledge their emotional reaction to the music by awakening an awareness of sensory perceptions (Thormählen, 2019a, pp. 59–62). Thus, even though Impressionist and veristic (realist) composers of the early twentieth century were actively moving away from creating expressive musical gestures, a performer of this repertoire today wishing to present a performance that reflects its created context may be torn between honoring the broad intentions of these composers, or the nineteenth-century performance practices many musicians continued to employ at the time the music was composed.

This move away from understanding music as emotion was taken to extremes by art music composers in the middle of the twentieth century: "if composer, performer and listener had once been linked in an unproblematic chain of creation and reception, and music's emotional effect had been merely a matter of details, this chain had now come apart, and its elements were spread around experience as the central concern" (Thormählen, 2019a, p. 65). Pierre Boulez (1925–2016) created musical works based on complicated systems; from an opposing tangent, John Cage (1912–1992) left the musical outcomes of his compositions to chance and to the interpretations of the performer. Meanwhile, minimalists such as Philip Glass (b. 1937), Steve Reich (b. 1936), and La Monte Young (b. 1935) pared down their scores to intentionally create art that resisted interpretation, including emotional interpretation. Their efforts certainly inspired audiences to think about what they were listening to and invoked emotions relating to the aesthetic quality of the music; nevertheless, any attempt to divorce music from emotional expression proved an interesting but ultimately uncompelling diversion that would run its course.

By the twenty-first century, composers might well take advantage of techniques developed during the diversion, but most would return to admitting music's expressive potential into their works and encouraged performers to bring out emotion through the expressive musical gestures they formulated. Cat Hope's opera *Speechless* uses screaming, electronic sounds, a low tessitura, and a graphic score to give voice to the marginalized members of society and to induce an empathetic response from her audiences (Crotty & Hope, 2021). In a more traditional approach, Karl Jenkins, sometimes dubbed the Mozart of the twenty-first century (Payne, 2004), composes art music that expresses emotions in a language that communicates to a broad audience, as reflected in his *The Armed Man: A Mass for Peace* (2000). Analysis of reception data shows that Jenkins' ability to move emotions was key to *The Armed Man's* success, seeing it rise to thirteenth most popular piece of music by all composers across time in the British commercial radio station *Classic FM's* annual poll in 2008 and continuing to remain high on the chart, being placed number twenty-two in 2020 (see Classic FM, 2020; Rocke, 2010).

Conclusions

This chapter has drawn on recent theoretical and applied work in the history of emotions to reveal how the constructed, learned, practiced, and performed aspects of emotion, including its physiological and material forms, can be used to rethink current musical performance practices of historical music. Approaching music through the lens of emotion practices of the past can help performers discover new ways of relating to historical music. As a starting point, a number of ways in which performers might wish to craft their music to accommodate what has been learned about historical emotion have been laid out.

Encapsulated through its key terms, such as emotionology, emotional communities, emotional refuges and emotional practices, the history of emotions offers an enriching framework that aligns well with the historically informed performance (HIP) movement, and performers of historical repertoire are encouraged to develop their knowledge beyond what has been presented here. While historical practices and performances cannot be entirely re-created, performers can be informed and inspired by historical documents, artifacts, and research that point to musical and emotional styles and meanings, including the interrelationships between music, emotion, body and material environment.

Practical Implications

As outlined throughout this chapter, modern-day performers of historical music can think about the role of these various elements in the reconstruction of an historical emotion and adopt an imaginative approach to conveying its historical meaning to the audience. This might be done in a quasi-literal way, through historically accurate attire, posture, gesture, and performance techniques, or more symbolically by conveying the emotion in accordance with present-day expressive norms, or some combination of the two, including ironic combinations.

While performers remain responsible for deciding how to encode or express emotion within a performance of historical music, a methodology that guides thought on how a performance might be staged in accordance with the emotionology of the historical period of the music is laid out in Table 19.2.

Table 19.2 Developing effective emotion expression in historical Western art music performance

Activity	Method	Rationale
Gather Information		
Discover what emotion meant and how it was practiced in the time and location that the music was composed.	Build a body of knowledge from which performance choices can be made. Take this chapter as a starting point and read the relevant resources in the reference list. These will also identify appropriate treatises and other artifacts (such as paintings and writing) from the period. Search these treatises and other artifacts for mention or depiction of emotion, including humors, passion, sentiment, feeling, affection.	It is not sufficient to know what techniques were involved, and which practices HIP commonly adopts today; it is important to know what emotions or moods the musical materials could be depicting, and how performers and audiences might have expected them to be expressed.
Consider your Audience		
Determine who your audience is and how you want to present the emotion in the music to them.	Think about who you will be performing to—is it a small group of people devoted to the music of the period you are playing, or a more general audience. Will the audience be paying attention to the performance, or will you be performing in the background?	For many musicians, the ideal of any performance is to induce a peak experience in the listener, but what pleases an audience is a complex matter dependent on the social and cultural context, which should be accounted for.
Consider what other resources you might bring to the performance to emphasize its emotion context.	Think about how you could supplement your musical portrayal of the emotional content of the music via other means such as: • The selection of concert venue • Your own posture and gestures • Program notes • Historical attire or other props • Pre-concert (or mid-concert) talk • Post-concert conversations • Audience engagement and behavior	
Decide performance strategy and context.	Decide which supplementary resources you wish to employ, and where on the continuum of catering to the expectations of your audience you wish to position your performance.	

Table 19.2. Continued

Activity	Method	Rationale
Prepare		
Daily practice	As you prepare for the concert, integrate your emotion portrayal into your daily practice to ensure depth of learning and automation of action.	Such an approach maximizes the potential for the concert performance to be convincing and meaningful.
Prepare multiple expressive options	Try out a range of expressive options at key points in the piece and, even if one seems the most appropriate, practice others so that you have a repertoire of options available in performance.	
Self-observation	Explore the depth of personal emotional resource you can give to a particular piece, bearing in mind issues of physical management of your musical instrument. When non-performance of a personally troubling musical work is not an option, identify self-management strategies that could be employed.	Such self-knowledge can guide repertoire selection and provide creative stimulus in the preparation phase. In circumstances in which overt demonstrations of emotion may be called for, knowing your capacity to achieve this objective may help in identifying any works that should or should not be selected.
Perform		
Performing with awareness	Even if repertoire and venue cannot be changed, the manner in which emotive musical and physical gestures are communicated to the audience can be. The performer should retain some awareness of audience responses in order to adjust their performance if that response is not positive.	Despite all the care and thought the performer puts into preparing for the concert, mistakes may have been made, or the audience mood may be affected by external factors that could not have been predicted.
Learning	Actively note what did and did not work in your performance, why this might have been the case, and what could have been added, left out, or improved.	Through performing we learn. Performing provides perhaps the greatest opportunity for learning how emotions are best expressed and communicated to audiences through music.

IMAGINATIVE EXPLORATIONS

Following this methodology, performers may consider using their knowledge of historical emotion to create performances that illuminate changes in the contexts of emotion across time. This can be done by considering issues of staging, posture, attire, performance venue and even audience behaviors, in their treatment of any given emotional practice. For example, a venue that commemorates those who have died for their country, such as a war memorial hall, might be chosen as a performance venue for a program of religious Renaissance music, such as a *L'homme armé* mass. The purpose for doing so might be to highlight that, whereas in sixteenth-century Christendom, reverence was predominantly a religious emotion; today it has also taken on secularized connotations. By aligning the venue and program, and guiding the audience through notes or a pre-concert talk, or by rethinking what an audience may do during a performance, both the performers and audience are given the opportunity to engage in creative and critical meaning-making, reflecting not only the transition in how reverence has been understood over time, but also on the transitions in the practices, places, and media by which reverence is expressed.

Conversely, a performance program may explicitly trace the historical trajectory of emotions associated with enduring cultural or religious icons across several centuries. For example, the reverence and adulation for the Virgin Mary of sixteenth-century motets, the romantic redemption of Brahms's *Marienlieder* (Op. 22, 1859), and the sassy, secular commercialism of the Catholic pop singer Madonna's "Like a Virgin" might be brought together in a concert program to facilitate critical reflection on historical and social issues and their abiding (emotional) impact on us today. By creating new experiences for audiences that reveal tangential relationships between historical and current manifestations of musical emotion, a concert such as this would be grounded in an understanding that emotions not only rely upon ongoing practice for their existence, but they are also contextually defined and have been practiced in different ways.

These examples illustrate how imaginative approaches to crafting musical experiences that have emotion at their core have the capacity to inspire new ways of thinking about music performance practice. When the history of emotions is a fundamental component of the conception and realization of such experiences, and when these experiences are disseminated through musical and scholarly forums, further fruitful insights into changes in the music-emotion relationship can be attained. With audiences often craving novelty while also appreciating the traditions they know, creative historically informed performances are well placed to propitiate both.

Key Resources

Carter, T. (2019). Music and dance. In D. Lemmings, C. Walker, & K. Barclay (Eds.), *A cultural history of the emotions in the Baroque and Enlightenment age (1600–1780)* (pp. 53–70). London: Bloomsbury Publishing.

Collins, D., & Nevile, J. (2019). Music and dance. In A. Lynch & S. Broomhall (Eds.), *A cultural history of the emotions in the late-medieval, Reformation and Renaissance age (1300–1600)* (pp. 49–68). London: Bloomsbury Publishing.

Mews, C., & Williams, C. (2019). Music and dance. In J. Ruys & C. Monagle (Eds.), *A cultural history of the emotions in the medieval age (350–1300)* (pp. 49–64). London: Bloomsbury Publishing.

Thormählen, W. (2019). Music and dance. In S. J. Matt (Ed.), *A cultural history of the emotions in the age of Romanticism, revolution, and empire* (pp. 55–74). London: Bloomsbury Publishing.

Thormählen, W. (2019). Music and dance. In J. W. Davidson & J. Damousi (Eds.), *A cultural history of the emotions in the modern and post-modern age (1920–2000+)* (pp. 53–72). London: Bloomsbury Publishing.

Reflective Questions

1. What mechanisms have been identified to explain the underpinning emotional intentions and experiences of musicians and listeners? Thinking of your own experiences as a performer and listener, do these offer a comprehensive account?

2. What are the key concepts of the history of emotions, and can you identify a piece of music in your own repertoire to which one or more of these concepts can be applied?

3. In what ways can emotions be practiced? How easy is it to create new emotional practices? Can you think of two ways you could practice emotion in a piece of music you are currently working on?

4. Think about two contrasting historical emotions. How were they expressed differently in music you have played?

5. Consider the resources you might use to adopt a history of emotions perspective in a forthcoming performance; what might you attempt to do?

References

Augustine. (1981). *Confessionum libris XIII*. Turnhout: Brepols.

Ayari, M., & Makhlouf, H. (Eds.). (2010). *Musique, signification et émotion*. Paris: Editions Delatour France.

Baines, A. C. (2009). Fifteenth-century instruments in Tinctoris's "De Inventionae et usu musicae." In T. J. McGee (Ed.), *Instruments and their music in the Middle Ages* (pp. 53–60). Farnham: Ashgate. https://doi.org/10.4324/9781315092645-5.

Barnett, D., & Massey-Westropp, J. (1987). *Art of gesture*. Heidelberg: C. Winter.

Bourdieu, P. (1977). *Outline of a theory of practice*. Cambridge; New York: Cambridge University Press. https://doi.org/10.1017/CBO9780511812507.

Bourdieu, P. (1990). *Outline of a theory of practice*. Stanford, CA: Stanford University Press, 1990.

Brinner, B. (2001). Performing practice II: Non-western and traditional music. *Grove Music Online* – see https://doi.org/10.1093/gmo/9781561592630.article.40272.

Broomhall, S., Davidson, J. W., & Lynch, A. (Eds.). (2019). *A cultural history of the emotions*. London: Bloomsbury.

Brown, H. M., Hiley, D., Page, C., Kreitner, K., Walls, P., Page, J. K., Holoman, D. K., Winter, R., Philip, R., & Brinner, B. (2001). Performing practice I: Western. *Grove Music Online* – see https://doi.org/10.1093/gmo/9781561592630.article.40272.

Brown, H. M., & Polk, K. (2001). Instrumental music, c. 1300–c. 1520. In *Music as concept and practice in the late Middle Age* (pp. 97–162). New York; Oxford: Oxford University Press.

Browning, J., & Davidson, J. W. (2019). Between realism and re-enactment: Navigating dramatic and musical "problems" in *Voyage to the Moon. Parergon, 36*(2), 17–38. https://doi.org/10.1353/pgn.2019.0053.

Browning, J., & Davidson, J. W. (2021). Assembling *Voyage to the Moon*: Emotion, creativity, and historicity in a new Australian opera. In J. Davidson, M. Halliwell, & S. Rocke (Eds.), *Opera, emotion, and the antipodes. Volume 2, Applied perspectives: Compositions and performances* (pp. 167-191). Abingdon; New York: Routledge. https://doi.org/10.4324/9781003035930-11.

Butt, J. (2002). *Playing with history: The historical approach to musical performance.* Cambridge, UK: Cambridge University Press. https://doi.org/10.1017/CBO9780511613555.

Carter, T. (2019). Music and dance. In D. Lemmings, C. Walker, & K. Barclay (Eds.), *A cultural history of the emotions in the Baroque and Enlightenment age (1600–1780)* (pp. 53–70). London: Bloomsbury Publishing. https://doi.org/10.5040/9781474207041.ch-003.

Classic FM. (2020). Classic FM hall of fame 2020. Classic FM – see https://halloffame.classicfm.com/2020/.

Collins, D., & Nevile, J. (2019). Music and dance. In A. Lynch & S. Broomhall (Eds.), *A cultural history of the emotions in the late-medieval, Reformation and Renaissance age (1300–1600)* (pp. 49–68). London: Bloomsbury Publishing. https://doi.org/10.5040/9781474207058.ch-003.

Connolly, C., & Williamon, A. (2004). Mental skills training. In *Musical excellence: Strategies and techniques to enhance performance* (pp. 221–245). Oxford: Oxford University Press.

Coutinho, E., Scherer, K. R., & Dibben, N. (2019). Singing and emotion. In G. F. Welch, D. M. Howard, & J. Nix (Eds.), *The Oxford handbook of singing* (Online ed.). Oxford; New York: Oxford University Press. https://doi.org/10.1093/oxfordhb/9780199660773.013.006.

Crotty, J., & Hope, C. (2021). Speechless: An operatic response to human rights abuse in twenty-first-century Australia. In J. Davidson, M. Halliwell, & S. Rocke (Eds.), *Opera, emotion, and the antipodes. Volume 2, Applied perspectives: Compositions and performances*, pp.75–89. Abingdon; New York: Routledge. https://doi.org/10.4324/9781003035930-6.

Csikszentmihalyi, M. (1975). *Beyond boredom and anxiety: Experiencing flow in work and play.* San Francisco: Jossey-Bass.

Davidson, J. W. (2001). The role of the body in the production and perception of solo vocal performance: A case study of Annie Lennox. *Musicae Scientiae, 5*(2), 235–256. https://doi.org/10.1177/102986490100500206.

Davidson, J. W., & Garrido, S. (2014). *My life as a playlist.* Crawley, WA: UWA Publishing.

Davidson, J. W., Kiernan, F., & Garrido, S. (2017). Introducing a psycho-historical approach to the study of emotions in music: The case of Monteverdi's "Il combattimento di Tancredi e Clorinda." *Emotions: History, Culture, Society, 1*(1), 29–58. https://doi.org/10.1163/2208522X-00101003.

Davidson, J. W., & King, E. (2004). Strategies for ensemble performance. In A. Williamon (Ed.), *Musical excellence: Strategies and techniques to enhance performance* (pp. 105–122). Oxford: Oxford University Press. https://doi.org/10.1093/acprof:oso/9780198525356.003.0006.

Davidson, J.W., & Maddox, A. (2017). Gestures. In: S Broomhall (Ed.), *Early modern emotions: an introduction* (III.19). Abingdon: Routledge.

Davies, S. (2001). Authenticity in Western classical music. In *Musical works and performances: A philosophical exploration*. Oxford: Oxford University Press. https://doi.org/10.1093/0199241589.003.0005.

DeNora, T. (2013). *Music asylums: Wellbeing through music in everyday life*. Burlington, V.T.: Ashgate.

Dixon, T. (2012). "Emotion": The history of a keyword in crisis. *Emotion Review, 4*(4), 338–344. https://doi.org/10.1177/1754073912445814.

Dodd, J. (2020). *Being true to works of music*. Oxford: Oxford University Press.

Dubois, P. (Ed.) (2004). *Charles Avison's essay on musical expression*. London: Routledge. https://doi.org/10.4324/9781315095851.

Easty, E. D. (1989). *On method acting*. New York: Ivy Books Random House.

Frangne, P.-H., Lacombe, H., Massin, M., & Picard, T. (2017). *La valeur de l'émotion musicale*. Rennes: Presses Universitaire de Rennes.

Freedman, R. (2003). Le Jeune's "Dodecacorde" as a site for spiritual meanings. *Revue de Musicologie, 89*(2), 297–309.

Geeves, A. M., Jones, S., Davidson, J. W. & Sutton, J. (2020). Between the crowd and the band: Performance experience, creative practice, and wellbeing for professional touring musicians. *International Journal of Wellbeing, 10*(5), 5–26. https://doi.org/10.5502/ijw.v10i5.1509.

Gouk, P., Kennaway, J., Prins, J., & Thormählen, W. (Eds.) (2019). *The Routledge Companion to music, mind and well-being*. Abingdon; New York: Routledge. https://doi.org/10.4324/9781315164717.

Grocheio. (2011). Ars musice. In C. J. Mews, J. N. Crossley, C. Jeffreys, L. McKinnon, & C. J. Williams (Eds.), *Ars musice* (pp. 41–129). Kalamazoo, MI: Medieval Institute Publications.

Harriss, E. C. (Ed.) (1981). *Johann Mattheson's "Der vollkommene Capellmeister": A revised translation with critical commentary*. Ann Arbor, MI: UMI Research Press.

Hill, H. (2017). Gesture study in Australia. *The Guardian* – see http://thecrushedtragedian.blogspot.com.au/2007/09/gesture-study-in-australia.html [accessed July 28, 2020].

Imberty, M. (2010). Avant-propos: Quelques réflexions sur les origines psychologique et biologique de la musique. In M. Ayari & H. Makhlouf (Eds.), *Musique, signification et émotion* (pp. 1–18). Paris: Editions Delatour France.

Johnson, J. H. (1995). *Listening in Paris: A cultural history*. Berkeley: University of California Press.

Juslin, P. N. (1995). A functionalistic perspective on emotional communication in music. *European Society for the Cognitive Sciences of Music, 8*, 11–16.

Juslin, P. N. (2003). Five facets of musical expression: A psychologist's perspective on music performance. *Psychology of Music, 31*(3), 273–302. https://doi.org/10.1177/03057356030313003.

Juslin, P. N. (2005). From mimesis to catharsis: Expression, perception, and induction of emotion in music. In D. Miell, R. Macdonald, & D. Hargreaves (Eds.), *Musical communication* (pp. 361–392). Oxford: Oxford University Press. https://doi.org/10.1093/acprof:oso/9780198529361.003.0005.

Juslin, P. N. (2013). From everyday emotions to aesthetic emotions: Towards a unified theory of musical emotions. *Physics of Life Reviews, 10*(3), 235–266. https://doi.org/10.1016/j.plrev.2013.05.008.

Juslin, P. N. (2019). *Musical emotions explained: unlocking the secrets of musical effect* (Oxford Scholarship Online ed.). Oxford: Oxford University Press. https://doi.org/10.1093/oso/9780198753421.001.0001.

Juslin, P. N., & Timmers, R. (2010). Expression and communication of emotion in music performance. In P. N. Juslin (Ed.), *Handbook of music and emotion: Theory, research, applications* (pp. 453–489). Oxford: Oxford University Press.

Kaleva, D. (2021). "Lamento d'Arianna": A transhistorical study of staged emotions and effective audience responses. In J. W. Davidson, M. Halliwell, & S. Rocke (Eds.), *Opera, emotion, and the antipodes. Volume 2, Applied perspectives: Compositions and performances*, 137–166. Abingdon; New York: Routledge. https://doi.org/10.4324/9781003035930-10.

Kiernan, F. (2020). Emotion as creative practice: Linking creativity and wellbeing through the history and sociology of emotion. *International Journal of Wellbeing, 10*(5), 43–63. https://doi.org/10.5502/ijw.v10i5.1517.

Kivy, P. (1995). *Authenticities: Philosophical reflections on musical performance.* Ithaca, NY: Cornell University Press. https://doi.org/10.7591/9781501731631.

Kuijken, B. (2013). *The notation is not the music: Reflections on early music practice and performance.* Bloomington & Indianapolis: Indiana University Press.

Leech-Wilkinson, D. (2006). Portamento and musical meaning. *Journal of Musicological Research, 25*(3–4), 233–261. https://doi.org/10.1080/01411890600859412.

Macey, P. (2000). Josquin and musical rhetoric: Miserere mei, Deus and other motets. In R. Sherr (Ed.), *The Josquin companion* (pp. 485–530). Oxford: Oxford University Press.

Maslow, A. H. (1968). *Toward a psychology of being.* New York: Van Nostrand Reinhold.

Mews, C., & Williams, C. (2019). Music and dance. In J. Ruys & C. Monagle (Eds.), *A cultural history of the emotions in the medieval age (350–1300)* (pp. 49–64). London: Bloomsbury Publishing. https://doi.org/10.5040/9781474207065.ch-003.

Mitchell, W. J. (Ed.). (1949). *C. P. E. Bach: Essay on the true art of playing keyboard instruments.* New York; London: W. W. Norton.

Page, C. (2009). German musicians and their instruments: A 14th-century account by Konrad of Megenberg. In T. J. McGee (Ed.), *Instruments and their music in the Middle Ages* (pp. 29–38). Farnham: Ashgate.

Payne, T. (2004). Mozart, Beethoven—and Jenkins. *The Telegraph* – see https://www.telegraph.co.uk/culture/music/rockandjazzmusic/3615996/Mozart-Beethoven-and-Jenkins.html.

Potter, J. (2006). Beggar at the door: The rise and fall of portamento in singing. *Music and Letters, 87*(4), 523–550. https://doi.org/10.1093/ml/gcl079.

Ravasio, M. (2019). Historically uninformed views of historically informed performance. *Journal of Aesthetics and Art Criticism, 77*(2), 193–205. https://doi.org/10.1111/jaac.12632.

Reddy, W. M. (2001). *The navigation of feeling: A framework for the history of emotions.* Cambridge, UK: Cambridge University Press. https://doi.org/10.1017/CBO9780511512001

Reilly, E. R. (Ed.) (1985). *Johann Joachim Quantz: On playing the flute* (2nd ed.). Boston: Northeastern University Press.

Rihtaršič, U. (2017). Between body and mind: Classical music performer in the postmodern era. *Muzikoloski Zbornik, 53*(1), 143–164. https://doi.org/10.4312/mz.53.1.143-164.

Rocke, S. (2010). *The Armed Man: A mass for a secular age.* Master's thesis: Monash University, Melbourne.

Rosenwein, B. H. (2002). Worrying about emotions in history. *American Historical Review, 107*(3), 821–845. https://doi.org/10.1086/532498.

Scheer, M. (2012). Are emotions a kind of practice (and is that what makes them have a history)? A Bourdieuian approach to understanding emotion. *History and Theory: Studies in the Philosophy of History, 51*(2), 193–220. https://doi.org/10.1111/j.1468-2303.2012.00621.x.

Šmidchens, G. (2014). *The power of song: Nonviolent national culture in the Baltic singing revolution*. Seattle: University of Washington Press.

Sève, B. (2017). L'Orchestre des émotions. In P.-H. Frangne, H. Lacombe, M. Massin, & T. Picard (Eds.), *La valeur de l'émotion musicale* (pp. 247–260). Rennes: Presses Universitaire de Rennes.

Spitzer, M. (2020). *A history of emotion in Western music: A thousand years from chant to pop*. New York: Oxford University Press. https://doi.org/10.1093/oso/9780190061753.001.0001.

Stearns, C. Z., & Stearns, P. N. (1985). Emotionology: Clarifying the history of emotions and emotional standards. *American Historical Review, 90*(4), 813–836. https://doi.org/10.2307/1858841.

Sulzer, J. G. (1771–1779). *Allgemeine Theorie der schönen Künste: In einzelnen, nach alphabetischer Ordnung der Kunstwörter aufeinanderfolgenden Artikeln abgehandelt*. Leipzig: Weidmannsche Buchhandlung (Leipzig, 1771–1774, 2/1778–1779, enlarged 3/1786–1787 by F. von Blankenberg, 4/1792–1799/R).

Taruskin, R. (1996). *Text and act: Essays on music and performance*. Oxford: Oxford University Press.

Thormählen, W. (2019a). Music and dance. In J. W. Davidson & J. Damousi (Eds.), *A cultural history of the emotions in the modern and post-modern age (1920–2000+)* (pp. 53–72). London: Bloomsbury Publishing. https://doi.org/10.5040/9781474207034.ch-003.

Thormählen, W. (2019b). Music and dance. In S. J. Matt (Ed.), *A cultural history of the emotions in the age of romanticism, revolution, and empire* (pp. 55–74). London: Bloomsbury Publishing. https://doi.org/10.5040/9781474207034.ch-003.

Torbianelli, E. (2014). Playing with images: Character and emotions in the age of romanticism. In E. Torbianelli, J. Roudet, J.-P. Bartoli, D. Seaton, & H. Moßburger (Eds.), *Ohne Worte: Vocality and instrumentality in 19th-century music* (pp. 15–40). Leuven: Leuven University Press. https://doi.org/10.2307/j.ctt14jxto3.4.

Weber, W. (1997). Did people listen in the 18th century? *Early Music, 25*(4), 678–691. https://doi.org/10.1093/em/25.4.678.

Wegman. (2002). "Musical understanding" in the 15th century. *Early Music, 30*(1), 46–66. https://doi.org/10.1093/em/30.1.46.

Wilbourne, E. (2016). A question of character: Artemisia Gentileschi and Virginia Ramponi Andreini. *Italian Studies, 71*(3), 335–355. https://doi.org/10.1080/00751634.2016.1189254.

CHAPTER 20

··

MUSICAL CREATIVITY IN PERFORMANCE

··

DYLAN VAN DER SCHYFF AND ANDREA SCHIAVIO

INTRODUCTION

THE words *music* and *creativity* refer to a vast range of human thought, action, and experience. And the ways these two terms are understood vary culturally and historically (Lubart, 2010; Niu & Sternberg, 2006). What is considered creative today in Berlin or Tokyo would not necessarily have been recognized as such in the same areas a few hundred years ago. Likewise, the artifacts created by different cultures reflect various experiences and conceptions of self, society, and politics, as well as contrasting understandings of the uses and meaning of creativity—across cultures and time, "creativity" can entail different boundaries and assumptions. For example, in modern Western societies our concept of creativity has often been guided by what is sometimes referred to as the "myth of the lone creative genius" (see Montuori & Purser, 1995). This involves the view that creativity—or at least the only kind of creativity worth recognizing—dwells in individuals who are "gifted" (or immanently special in some way or another) and who produce creative products at a distance from the rest of the society. As the composer Aaron Copland (1952) writes in *Music and Imagination*:

> It doesn't matter how many times we tell the familiar story of Bach writing each week for the honest burghers of Leipzig, or Mozart's relations with the courtly musical patrons of his day; audiences still prefer to think of the musical creator as a man closeted with his idea, unsullied by the rough and tumble of the world around him. (p. 47)

But this conception of creativity is a relatively recent development in Western culture. For the ancient Greeks, the types of performances and artifacts we refer to as "creative" (music, sculpture, dance, storytelling) were thought to be driven by forces external to people who make and do them—this involved the influences of the Muses (the daughters of Zeus), or possession by some other god or a divine spirit. In the Middle Ages, art and music making often reflected the will of the Christian God, and human creators were thus understood as touched or "gifted" vehicles of divine inspiration. With the humanistic turn in the late Renaissance, this notion of giftedness turned inward so that by the nineteenth century it had become a special property of the artist himself as a heroic or godlike figure (see Dacey, 1999).

Creativity in Traditional, Modern, and Post-Modern Contexts

Changing notions of creativity are intimately connected to shifting conceptions of the relationship between self and society. Pre-modern and non-Western forms of expression often involve iconographic artifacts and performance traditions that do not bear the image or name of the artists who realize them, but rather are intended to maintain the continuity of the broader culture they are associated with. Modern art and performance, by contrast, are often characterized by self-portraiture, "innovation," and the association of a single name with a creative work (a composer, a film director, a choreographer, a painter, and so on).

With the advent of European exploration and colonization, differing cultural perspectives, traditional and "modern," came into contact with each other. Consider, for example, the African and Oceanic art and music that was admired by European painters and composers in the late nineteenth and early twentieth centuries. When Europeans encountered such artifacts and practices at events such as the Paris Exposition Universelle of 1889, they did so through the lens of a Western colonialist worldview. But the African masks and Javanese gamelan performances that so captivated creators like Picasso and Debussy are not themselves indicative of the bold forms of individual self-expression they inspired in these artists (Briggs, 1988). Rather, these expressions reflect the traditions and shared identities of the people who make and do them—they denote "transpersonal" (Levi-Strauss, 1988) connections to place and people, and the images, sounds, stories, and activities that bind a society together. This is not to say that art, music, and storytelling in traditional cultures exhibit no creativity. Even in contexts that are highly prescribed by traditional norms, the act of bringing forth an artifact or a performance will always involve making adaptations to contingencies—e.g., how master carvers or instrument makers adjust to the grain of wood or other materials they are using (Malafouris, 2013), or how a drummer and singer might adapt to, and influence, the movements of a dancer (and the audience) as they co-realize a traditional performance (Bokor, 2017). Traditional artists also make subtle but unique expressions and variations within age-old forms that reflect their own aesthetic contribution to the culture. However, this does require care as in some social groups too much innovation could result in exclusion (Gardner, 1988).

Today, the use of indigenous and traditional imagery, sound and music, dance, clothing, and story-telling in the creation of works and performances by artists who do not come from the cultures such materials are drawn from is subject to growing scrutiny—issues surrounding appropriation and colonialism loom large in the critical discourse. It is also recognized that modern Western culture itself exhibits forms of exclusion and marginalization with regard to creative practices and products that reflect experiences from outside the mainstream of society. These expressions involve approaches to technique, aesthetics, and performance that sometimes challenge established norms. Additionally, a range of gendered, cross-cultural, and critical perspectives, as well as new hybrid forms of production and performance, are intersecting and changing the cultural landscape around the world (e.g., Keenan, 2015). Developments in global communication, travel, digital technology, and cross-cultural awareness have also led to major shifts in how we plan and realize creative projects. In line with this, postmodern conceptions of selfhood have decentered the presumptions of creative autonomy and originality that characterized modern and romantic thinking—creative agents are no longer assumed to stand apart from the world; they are now co-implicated in a shifting ecology of signs, tropes, and critical discourses that must be continually negotiated (Kearny, 1988). Accordingly, conceptions of "skill," the meaning and value of "virtuosity," and the relationship between composer/creator and performer have also been problematized and transformed (Cook, 1999, 2013; Leech-Wilkinson, 2018). Many artists develop their own techniques and methods, which influence, and are influenced by, the creative process; and, as such, many instances of creativity can be seen as "performative" since they are highly dependent on a range of communicative actions between cooperating agents and the society they are situated within.

In brief, it is now understood that creativity often plays out in explicitly collaborative ways, involving various levels of negotiation, adaptation, and interactivity between creative agents who come from different backgrounds and who use various tools and approaches to realize their projects (Glăveanu, 2014; Sawyer, 2012). Interestingly, this recent recognition of the situated, socially interactive, and collaborative aspects of creativity can shed light on areas of human thought and action that have traditionally been under-researched, including the kinds of shared and in-the-moment creative activity associated with musical performance.

KEY PERSPECTIVES

With all these concerns in mind, we now turn to consider some key perspectives on creativity. As we go, we move from more traditional frameworks that examine the products and processes associated with individual agents, to more recent models that explore creativity as an adaptive multi-agent phenomenon. Here, we place a special focus on current work in embodied cognitive science and ecological dynamics, as these perspectives provide theoretical and analytical tools that can help us to better understand the complexities of musical creativity as it unfolds in action. What follows, then, is not intended as a comprehensive overview of musical creativity. Rather, the chapter aims to offer possibilities for thinking about creativity in musical performance that may be useful to performers who work across a range of musical styles and genres.

Creative products

In musical contexts, researchers often examine creativity in terms of the different qualities exhibited by a musical composition, a performed interpretation, or an improvisation. This process usually involves a report of listener responses (such as surprise), and/or an evaluation of balances between novelty and functionality offered by a panel of experts (see, e.g., Baer & McKool 2009; Sloboda, 1983). As Sloboda (1985) notes, much of this research has tended to place a strong emphasis on how these elements contribute to the final products of such activities. This focus on the outcome of the performative process aligns with trends in creativity studies more generally that categorize the products (ideas, knowledge, procedures, artifacts, or other items) produced by individuals in terms of their utility, novelty, and perhaps, most centrally, their reception by society. For example, a prominent approach explores creative outputs in terms of categories such as "big-C" (major domain-changing outputs), "pro-c" (professional-level outputs), little-c (everyday problem solving), and mini-c (the new abilities and understandings that stem from learning processes) (see Lubart, 2010; Runco, 2014). Other approaches make distinctions between the outputs of *adaptors* and *innovators* (Kirton, 2003). The former involves the novel use, combination, and improvements of existing ideas and methods, while the latter concerns the creation of more revolutionary products that significantly alter a given domain.

This product-based perspective can be applied to the outputs of musical performers. For instance, Jimi Hendrix not only redefined the possibilities of the guitar in the context of rock music, but also played a huge role in transforming what performance entailed in that domain. Hendrix's work might be said to exhibit big-C characteristics and are certainly innovative and transformational—in contrast, perhaps, to the many skilled (pro-c) guitarists who might effectively combine some of the concepts and techniques introduced by Hendrix in their own playing. The Canadian pianist Glenn Gould (1932–1982) provides another noteworthy example. Consider the following passage (Henahan, 1982) that appeared in the *New York Times* shortly after Gould died:

> My first encounter with Gould was in the late 1950's at a recital whose opening half included selections from the harpsichord literature—Byrd and Gibbons, probably. The playing was clean and lucid but awfully fussy and affected. At intermission, some pianists were shrugging their shoulders and asking one another what was so wonderful about this Glenn Gould. But then came half a program of Bach, and it was

Bach of an exalted quality, an unbroken flow of contrapuntal sound in which details of articulation were not only etched sharply but were used intelligently and sensitively to give shape and meaning to phrases. No one could doubt it then: Gould was a Bach pianist in a class by himself. (p. 23)

Gould's performances across the repertoire remain highly regarded among listeners, critics, and scholars. However, it is his interpretations of Bach that made him an international celebrity—and most famously his first recording of Bach's Goldberg Variations (1955). The sales of this recording were extraordinary for a classical music album (Bazzana, 2003). This popularity was due in large part to Gould's innovative technique and vision for the music. He integrated bold new approaches to tempo, phrasing, counterpoint, and dynamics that redefined the performance possibilities of Bach's keyboard repertoire. Notably, Gould also used the recording studio as a creative tool to finely tune his rendering of a given piece and thereby produce a final product that closely matched his aesthetic vision.

Given the reception of Gould's contribution in this area of keyboard performance, one could distinguish him as an *innovator*, place him in the big-C category in this domain of keyboard performance, and so on. But while the qualities and reception of Gould's performances have been described by different authors, the majority of writings on Gould do not provide detailed discussions of the processual aspects involved in his playing style and its evolution. Despite some reports on his personal eccentricities, little has been written on why he opted for certain artistic choices in his performances. Like Hendrix, the creative outcomes Gould produced were guided by a range of factors including forms of exploration, combination, risk-taking, and experimentation while practicing at the instrument. This is to say that although descriptions of the qualities of his artifacts and performances are important aspects to consider, they tell us little about the actual experience of creativity, how it develops and unfolds, and how it can be nurtured or enhanced. Likewise, while the focus on the categorization of creative products and their reception has much to offer—especially for studying and comparing the output of historical figures—this kind of analysis provides only a limited view of what creativity entails.

Creative processes

To address such issues, other approaches to creativity have focused more on the *processes* involved. This orientation characterized post–World War II research in creativity, which was initially concerned with understanding the kinds of cognitive abilities and personalities required of pilots and spies if they were to be effective in highly adverse and unpredictable conditions (see Guilford, 1967). This approach soon developed into a broader research program dedicated to understanding the factors involved in understanding and nurturing the forms of thought that would contribute to scientific, social, and cultural innovation (see Sawyer, 2012). This work revealed that to achieve high-level creative outputs, agents require the capacity (and freedom) to develop multiple possibilities for solving a given problem. These processes are often referred to as "divergent" and "convergent" thinking, which describe how various options and solutions are identified and then combined in ways that function effectively in a specific situation. These forms of thought have since been examined across a range of other contexts (Runco, 2014), resulting in a number of empirically testable hypotheses associated with our ability to "change existing thinking patterns, break with the present, and build something new" (Dietrich & Kanso, 2010, p. 822).

In line with this, other thinkers have explored the combinatorial aspects of creativity and problem solving, examining how seemingly disconnected ideas, concepts, techniques, and "frames of mind" are integrated (Koestler, 1964). Here it is important to note the pioneering work of Wallas (1926), who proposed an influential framework for examining creativity in terms of conscious (explicit) and subconscious (intuitive) processes. These processes involve stages of (a) *preparation*, or the acquisition of knowledge; (b) *incubation*, the subconscious restructuring of knowledge; (c) *illumination*, the flash of insight; and (d) *verification*, the evaluation and application of the new idea. Wallas's approach inspired a number of more complex perspectives that describe forms of creative problem solving in terms of how stages of knowledge generation and exploration influence each other and how this leads to the production of creative outcomes (Finke, Ward, & Smith, 1992; Helie & Sun, 2010). Put very simply, these processes involve the creation of mental structures that are combined and recombined in novel ways at various levels of processing.

Process-based approaches shift the focus from the product to the creative agent. They may therefore be better suited to examining how musical artists go about creating novel performances. Thinking of Wallas's model, for example, one might examine how performers engage in forms of technical and conceptual knowledge acquisition (*preparation*) by practicing at the instrument, by exploring new possibilities and combinations, and by learning about existing performance models and traditions. One could then explore how such knowledge is structured and restructured as various levels of thought. For musical performers, such forms of *incubation* may occur over a range of timescales and across various contexts, including periods when they are engaged in activities away from the instrument. These processes may result in *illuminations*, where new technical, perceptual, and conceptual relationships are revealed, and/or where solutions to aesthetic problems are discovered. Such new understandings and possibilities are then subject to *verification*—they are applied and evaluated in terms of their feasibility and functionality in practice. As we mentioned, more recent models suggest that these "stages" do not need to be understood as unfolding as a linear construct. Rather they influence each other in various ways. For example, a performer's illumination might involve the need to revisit an aspect of their technical ability before the new ability can be effectively applied in performance. Or it might involve the refinement of a novel technique. We can imagine this in the case of Hendrix, for example, as he developed and refined his remarkable use of amplifier feedback; or, how Gould may have engaged in such processes, for instance, when he used the recording studio to evaluate and perfect his recorded performances.

It should also be noted that in all of these cases, creative products and processes are shaped by the unique histories of specific people who think and act in specific environments. The innovations of Hendrix and Gould were guided by their personality traits and the cultural milieux they were situated within—indeed, the latter plays a central role in whether an outcome can be recognized as creative at all. Someone not familiar with the styles of Baroque piano performance might not fully recognize the weight of Gould's contribution. Likewise, Hendrix's innovations might not be appreciated by listeners who have little experience and understanding of rock and blues performance. In other words, products are deemed creative (or not) by communities of practitioners and consumers—how they are received and categorized (e.g., big-C, little-c, and so on) involves a process of "sociocultural validation" (Cropley, 2011). These aspects have been recognized by researchers who, in addition to products and processes, highlight two other "P's." One of these involves "person," which studies the various personal factors that underpin creative outputs. The other is referred to as "press," which examines how the external "pressures" of the cultural context impact the creative person and shape the products they produce (Rhodes, 1961).

Creativity in action

Thus far we have seen that understanding creativity in musical performance requires more than the descriptive analysis of products and their reception by society. We can also consider the developmental history and personal traits of the creative agent, the cultural context, and how these influence and the kinds of processes in which they engage. Admittedly, it can be difficult to tease out how such factors actually played out in the lives of many historical performers. We are dependent on the accounts left to us by historians and musicologists, and therefore we are often left to speculate on such details. Nevertheless, models that integrate product, process, people, and press can help to frame studies of living artists and offer useful frameworks for performers to reflect upon their own creative processes. This said, these models may still provide only a partial story of what creativity entails when they place a focus on individual creators and sometimes ignore the socially interactive (interpersonal, collaborative) and material environmental factors involved (Sawyer, 1998). With this last concern in mind, we now turn to consider another context for creativity: the dynamics of performance as it unfolds in action.

Let's begin by imagining a drummer in a modern jazz ensemble named Kim. Kim is an accomplished musician. She has been playing with her band for two years and they are beginning to make an impact on the local scene. The band performs a mix of original material and arrangements of standards—they are concerned to give the music they play a unique sound, while staying true to certain stylistic models associated with the jazz tradition. Much of their music is up-tempo and high-energy, with many dynamic and rhythmic shifts between sections. These arrangements have formed over time, mostly through the cooperative dynamics of the group as they rehearse and perform—they develop what works, and revise or discard what does not. Kim plays an important part in this process and her role in performance is challenging, as it requires her to maintain the right mix of novelty and stability, of the new and the familiar. Indeed, being a modern jazz drummer is no easy task—it demands precision, technical proficiency, energy, restraint, and coordination. One has to push the music while also supporting it, create grooves that are solid, but not static, and orchestrate dynamics and timbres for the various sections of the arrangements. Kim has to understand, and be able to utilize, combine, and adapt, the various styles that mix together in contemporary jazz performance (e.g., hard bop, free, Afro-Cuban, and so on). She also has to find ways of supporting the evolution of the music by introducing new rhythms and sounds that help to create new moods for each soloist. On a personal level, Kim doesn't want to sound exactly like all other drummers of the jazz scene; she wants to show that she has her own style and identity. However, she also needs to work within and around the recognized constraints of the genre in collaboration with her bandmates; otherwise the elements that characterize this kind of music performance will not emerge, resulting in an unconvincing performance. For Kim, this means finding the right balances of freedom and constraint to offer a performance that is coherent and exciting.

Importantly, engaging with freedom and constraint does not need to be seen as an "either/or" dichotomy. While playing, Kim can explore the space of action that stands between adherence to well-known musical norms and novel possibilities; boundaries can be explored and pushed. For example, as a trumpet solo begins, Kim decides to shift from the common "four-four" swing time she was playing with the saxophone solo. She moves to a more "broken-time" feel employing a mix of dotted quarter and syncopated rhythms to give a more "floating" character to the music (a common creative tactic in modern jazz drumming). However, while these rhythms are more irregular than those of the previous feel, and may imply various polyrhythms from bar to bar, they nevertheless remain connected to the original pulse and to the four-four meter the group is working within. To reinforce this connection, Kim quietly maintains the two and four pulse on hi-hat from the previous pattern. As Kim makes this shift, she notes the sonic, emotional, and physical responses of her bandmates. Most of the band members appear to enjoy the change, as indicated by their smiles and head nods—they adapt musically to the shift introduced by Kim without difficulty. However, while looking at and listening to the piano player, Kim realizes that this change in feel may have come across as too sudden, as it appears to have thrown him off slightly. The rest of the band also begins to sense this dynamic and a moment of discomfort and uncertainty starts to spread through the ensemble. Kim decides to return to the original swing pattern for the rest of the piece. Later on, the band discusses what happened in performance and they practice transitioning into new feels, which also inspires new additions to the arrangement of the piece.

These kinds of experiences should be familiar to anyone who has worked in a cooperative musical setting where communication and collaboration are functioning well. Notably, while the product (the quality of the musical performance) and its reception (the reaction of the audience) are important driving factors here, it is the processual aspects that come to the foreground. Once again, the aspects of the four-part model could be used to analyze this situation in terms of *preparation* (Kim needs to develop the skills and understandings involved in playing with the ensemble), *incubation* (she combines her knowledge in various ways), *illuminations* of new possibilities (e.g., new rhythmic patterns that push the music in new directions), and *verification* (how new ideas are implemented, evaluated, revised, and redeveloped). Additionally, this kind of situation could be explored in terms of the "divergent" and "convergent" thinking processes mentioned earlier. As Kim generated the idea of changing the feel of the music, she diverged from the present state of things to add something new to the perfor-mance. These forms of thinking were then taken up by the group as they collaboratively developed a new arrangement of the piece.

Here it is also worth noting the range of phenomena associated with decision-making and thinking in this context. At certain points in musical performance, decision-making entails intentional cognitive process that imply conscious deliberation. In other cases, the shifts initiated by performers involve more immediately impulsive and adaptive actions. Importantly, the balances of these forms of thought-in-action are constantly in play within the flow of the music—they evolve within the webs of mutual depend-ence that characterize a social musical system. This means that in performance contexts "thinking" and "deciding" are dynamic processes that span a variety of experiences and timescales. These observations also suggest that musical creativity in performance cannot simply be reduced to the thoughts and actions of individual agents.

Creativity as socially distributed

While the foregoing account begins with a focus on Kim, the story quickly evolves to include the social context in which the music happens. Kim's drumming experience changes after an exchange of glances with the piano player, which impacts the unfolding dynamics of the piece being performed; discussion and collaborative experimentation and practice lead to new possibilities, and so on. Again, the creative processes involved here occur over multiple timescales and entail various interactive dynamics that are situated within a social and material environment. These involve bidirectional, or back-and-forth, interactions between performers and instruments; between various stages of development (e.g., as performers discuss and enact possibilities given their abilities, understandings, and what they have experienced); and between various modalities of perception (bodily movement and feeling, emotion and empathy, abstract thinking, im-agination, counterfactuals, and so on). Accordingly, the idea of a creative "product" or an "outcome" can be reconceived of here as an emergent property of dynamic, interper-sonal processes that play out within a socio-cultural context (e.g., jazz performance). The context provides certain constraints (style, sounds, phrasing, and so on) on the de-velopment of the musical system and sets the stage for various goals to arise—for ex-ample, maintaining an enjoyable groove, making the appropriate musical shifts to keep the music exciting, and, more generally, creating a show that will be well received by the audience. Indeed, the audience plays an important part both in how musicians plan their performances and in how their creativity develops in the moment. In some genres, the real-time audience responses and feedback are crucial for guiding musical choices and the overall feeling of the event as it unfolds (see Geeves et al., 2016). Just how this plays out will differ from performance to performance as ensemble and audience adapt to each other and collectively create new shared musical experiences.

The example of Kim and her band reveals an aspect of creativity that has gone relatively under-researched (see Glăveanu, 2014), but that is nevertheless central to participatory activities like music performance. Earlier, we considered the influence of the Western romantic assumption that creativity involves a detached autonomous individual who, in extending their cognitive reach, produces products that impact society to various degrees. More recent product- and process-based approaches have adopted much more nuanced views of creativity, but sometimes still display traces of older assumptions when they limit creativity to the personal domain of individual agents. As we have seen, however, understanding musical creativity in performance requires an interpersonal perspective. Keith Sawyer (2007) makes similar observations with regard to the situated and emergent nature of creativity in the context of jazz improvisation:

> Try to imagine a separate drummer, bassist, pianist, and saxophone player, each playing the same song but in separate rooms and unable to hear each other [. . .]. Imagine then using a recording studio to overlay their four performances to create a single recording; it would sound horrible [. . .]. The real jazz group would win, hands down. (p. 68)

Sawyer therefore posits that "the creativity in improvised innovation isn't additive; it's exponential" (68). By this he means to capture the emergent, evolving, and socially distributed nature of creativity in contexts where "no performer is capable of playing every phrase or rhythm" and how therefore "jazz musicians can play the same song hundreds of times over the course of their career, and each time they play something new" (68).

These insights highlight the kinds of feedback and feedforward loops that characterize creativity in intersubjective contexts, where co-actors stimulate each other in a dance of invitations and challenges, support and surprises, which give rise to outcomes that are not entirely predictable (Sawyer, 2007). While these kinds of dynamics have been documented mostly in jazz and improvised music contexts (Monson, 1996; Borgo, 2005), they play out in all kinds of musical performance. The members of a string quartet, for instance, rely on and make adaptations to each other, solve musical problems on the fly, and push and pull the music in various and sometimes unexpected ways to keep the musical environment exciting and "alive" (see Seddon & Biasutti, 2009). In doing so, they must also maintain certain balances and constraints to ensure that the performance does not fall apart. No two performances of a composed work will be same, as each entails its own challenges and discoveries. Similarly, the members of a Ghanaian drumming ensemble perform within the constraints of the tradition. But within those constraints, they play with different rhythmic combinations, tempi, and other musical factors (and interact with dancers), and the ways they do this varies from ensemble to ensemble, and from performance to performance. Importantly, considering the socially distributed aspects of musical activity decenters the focus on individual agents and the works they produce, and highlights the collaborative, situated, and performative nature of creativity as it plays out in lived experience (Linson & Clarke, 2017). Musical creativity, by this light, is best understood as a relational process, a "social fact" (Frith, 2012).

These insights advance the concerns discussed at the outset where we touched upon the various ways creativity happens across a range of collaborative and cooperative contexts (Montuori & Purser, 1995). Accordingly, this perspective can also cast new light on the work of historical musical creators, who, as Copland points out, are always situated within a social environment. The lives and music of Hendrix and John Coltrane, for example, were enmeshed with the culture of the United States in the 1960s (civil rights, antiwar, black spirituality), but their groundbreaking explorations of the guitar and saxophone, respectively, were also supported and fueled by their interactions with longtime bandmates. Their performances pushed against constraints across personal, instrumental, musical, social, and cultural domains. The "outcomes" of this then feed back into the culture to redefine the possibilities of performance in their respective domains.

Creativity as technologically distributed

The example of Hendrix brings to light yet another important aspect of the environments in which performers work. This, as we have mentioned, includes technologies like musical instruments, recording devices, and other media (television, film, radio, and so on) and the possibilities and constraints they impose on creative processes. Indeed, to listeners equipped with the expectations imposed by previous models of rock guitar playing, Hendrix's bold use of amplifier feedback, distortion, and other novel ways of interacting with the technology may have seemed like incoherent noise. However, a closer inspection reveals that he developed a highly refined set of techniques for producing the sounds he did. This is especially apparent in his famous performance of the "Star-Spangled Banner" at Woodstock, which displays a remarkable soundscape that clearly evokes the sounds of war in juxtaposition with the anthem (see Clarke, 2005b; Maurice & Wadleigh, 1970). The use of technology plays out in a different way with Gould in his use of the recording studio to refine his recorded performances. In both cases, however, the creative processes and outcomes cannot be separated from the technological devices that afforded their creation. Therefore, in addition to being socially distributed, musical creativity in performance is often materially and technologically distributed—where the technology plays a central role in defining the constraints and possibilities of the creative act (Borgo 2016).

An ecological perspective

Taking the socially and materially distributed nature of creativity into account can help us develop a richer perspective on what musical performance entails (see Clarke & Doffman, 2017). However, this perspective also introduces a rather daunting level of complexity. As we have seen, musical creativity in performance may be understood as an emergent property that arises from interactions that span personal (corporeal-emotional-neural), social, cultural, and technological domains and how these play out over developmental, historical, and in-the-moment timescales (Johnson-Laird, 1988; Pressing, 1988). Additionally, the nature of these interactions is "synergistic," meaning that each component of the extended network involved in the act of musical performance influences, and is influenced by, every other component of the system. This synergistic aspect also highlights the fact that when such interactions are functioning well, the system can exhibit certain emergent features that cannot be reduced to the sum of its parts. In line with Sawyer's insights, this means that the properties of a musical performance cannot be fully grasped in terms of an additive or "linear" causal framework. Rather, they emerge from the circular, recursive, or non-linear interactions between a range of components within a complex, evolving, musical ecology (Abraham et al., 2012; Borgo, 2005; Fabian, 2017).

Fortunately, there exist a number of interrelated perspectives associated with current trends in cognitive science that can aid in understanding such phenomena. These perspectives are referred to as "embodied cognitive science," "enactivism," "ecological dynamics," and "ecological psychology" (Hristovski et al., 2011; Kimmel et al., 2018; Kello & Van Orden, 2009; Chemero, 2009). While these approaches support and diverge from each other in various ways, they all examine cognition with an emphasis on the active environmentally situated body. As such, they draw on a number of shared principles and insights that are useful for thinking about musical performance.

Affordances

One of these principles involves the idea of "affordances" (Gibson, 1966; Chemero, 2009). This term describes the possibilities for action an organism discovers through its history of interactions within a given environment. Similar ecological features can offer different affordances to agents exhibiting various physiologies and developmental backgrounds—the manifold ways the affordances of things and situations "show up" and become significant for agents depends on their history of activity within an environment. A chair, for example, implies a different set of affordances for an infant (essentially none), a toddler (as an area of support as they learn to walk), an adult (offers the invitation to sit, or to stand upon for elevation), or for someone skilled in Chinese acrobatics (sitting, stacking, climbing, throwing, and so on). Similarly, for beginning musical performers the affordances offered by an instrument are limited, whereas an expert instrumentalist will be able to discern a much wider and more refined set of possibilities. An advanced trumpet player, for example, will be able to shade the timbre and tuning of sounds the instrument is capable of producing using subtle shifts in embouchure in combination with fine movements of the valves. This trumpeter could also influence the actions of others by communicating shifts in tempo and dynamics. Likewise, the wider range of affordances available to experts means that they can also adjust their playing to meet the needs and invitations of the other members of the ensemble, the acoustics of the performance space, or the specific character of the audience.

In line with this, affordances can also be co-enacted by multiple agents as they develop together in a musical environment. Indeed, the ability to realize and exploit shared affordances is foundational for creativity in performance. Again, such forms of cooperative action and perception do not simply involve responses to environmental causes. They are active, adaptive, or "creative" processes that are guided by the possibilities and constraints inherent to both animal (physiology, growth, learning, perceptual capacities) and the shared socio-material environment (stable features, evolving features). This is to say that the (social) enactment of affordances is guided by processes that play out over various developmental and in-the-moment timescales, and across corporeal and environmental domains. These processes are shaped by the activity of the agents as they develop in interaction with their environment.

Self-organization

This leads to another key principle referred to as "self-organization." Self-organizing systems can be observed across a range of biological and non-biological contexts, from the way wall-mounted pendulums tend to synchronize over time, to the shifting patterns of behavior exhibited by insect swarming, bird flocking, and schooling fish; from the transforming macro-level structures found in weather patterns, to the micro-level behaviors of heated molecules (Haken, 1977; Strogatz, 1994). In each case, the patterns of behavior that characterize these examples are not simply reducible to the sum of components involved. Rather, it is through the ongoing interactivity of these components that these so-called emergent properties arise (Capra, 1996; Schuldberg, 1999). The fields of mathematics referred to as "complexity theory" and "dynamical systems theory" offer useful tools that help to model and describe such phenomena. Here, researchers use nonlinear differential equations to examine how the mutually influencing trajectories of a system unfold over time. Most centrally, this involves mapping the network in terms of relative instantiations of stability and entropy. This mapping is often represented as a topography: periods where trajectories that tend to converge are shown as basins. These so-called attractor basins represent stability and can discerned across a range of contexts.

In brief, this perspective has helped to illuminate how living systems enact new patterns for action through adaptive goal-directed behavior (Kello & Van Orden, 2009). It has also shown how, in realizing these new patterns, agents also often gain more flexibility within a given domain—how they are able to work, think, or move in new and more adaptive ways within a given set of constraints (Amazeen et al.,1996; Dixon et al., 2010). An important aspect that characterizes biological systems is that, in order to survive, they need to engage in forms of behavior that exhibit varying degrees of stability and instability. Indeed, if an animal is to create a niche that remains functional under a range of conditions, then the forms of action and perception it develops must be both patterned and flexible, recurrent and adaptable. This involves striking balances between constraint and freedom: too much constraint and the living system cannot evolve or adapt its repertoire of behavior in relation to perturbations that threaten its wellbeing; too much freedom and the system risks falling into incoherence. This connects with the dynamical systems idea of a "strange" or "chaotic" attractor (Schuldberg, 1999), which describes aspects of a system that are stable, but that nevertheless exhibit degrees of freedom within such stability. Moreover, in certain cases these strange attractors can bifurcate, leading to the development of new attractors and attractor layouts across neural, bodily, and environmental trajectories (Abraham et al., 2012).

As children learn to walk, for example, they trade one set of attractors for another (Thelen & Smith, 1994). In doing so, each child traverses a period of instability from which new body-environment relationships and possibilities for actions and understanding emerge (new attractor layouts). Likewise, as infants make their first connections with the social environment, the communicative (and often music-like) patterns of movement and sound they co-realize with caregivers are not determined only by genetic programming, but rather unfold collaboratively as of repertoires of recurrent yet adaptable behavior emerge between them (see Fantasia et al. 2014; Reddy, 2008). Importantly, these developmental processes can involve challenging periods where the trajectories between neural, emotional, muscular, and environmental (material, social) factors exhibit a high degree of instability, resulting in moments of physical, emotional, and social discomfort (falling, chaotic crying, frustration, and so on). Once new patterns of behavior are stabilized, however, a range of new affordances arise.

CREATIVE PERFORMERS IN PRACTICE

Let's now turn to consider how the ideas and insights discussed in the previous section can help to illuminate aspects of musical performance. The first thing we might note is that musical actions and environments involve self-organizing dynamics that are similar to the developmental contexts just mentioned (Borgo, 2005; Sudnow, 2001). Indeed, human musical performers are living systems and, accordingly, synergetic processes—and the push and pull of constraint and freedom, of stability and instability—are a central feature of the musical environments they participate in and actively shape. For example, learning a new multi-limb pattern on a drum kit requires enacting new ways of engaging bodily with an instrument, and can result in physically uncomfortable and frustrating periods indicative of unstable and dissociated relationships within the body and between the body and the instrument (van der Schyff, 2016). However, this process is necessary to create new relationships between corporeal, neural, and environmental trajectories—new patterns of action that permit a performer to develop a wider range of musical possibilities, to be more flexible and adaptive (new attractor layouts), and to perceive new affordances in the musical instruments one is using. Similarly, musical ensembles need to co-realize the patterns of interactivity that will allow them to work together effectively (Høffding & Satne, 2019; Salice et al., 2017). This involves being able to keep the dynamics of their performance within certain ranges and developing the ability to understand the communicative gestures they make to each other through sound, bodily movement and gestures, facial emotional expression, and so on. And here, too, sometimes a group must experience moments of instability, frustration, and discomfort where these balances break down. These situations need to be understood and solutions must be negotiated. In doing so, the ensemble may develop more flexibility and be able to push the boundaries of their performances in new and sometimes unexpected ways.

These dynamics have begun to be examined empirically. For example, Walton and colleagues (2015) used the mathematical tools of dynamical systems theory to analyze how changes in the structure of a musical environment impacts the experience of creativity for pairs of interacting keyboard improvisers, and how this is reflected in their bodily movements and the ways they adapt to the sonic environment they co-create. Here, musicians performed improvised duets along with different backing tracks while their head, left arm, and right arm movements were recorded, as was the music they made. Variations in the musicians' movements were found that correlated with periods of stability and instability in the audio documents, as well as with the musicians' reports that they felt most creative in environments that afforded a balance of freedom and constraint, where varying degrees of instability could be introduced and resolved cooperatively.

Skilled coping, flow, and risk

Crucially, performing musicians need to develop, both individually and collectively, repertoires of action and perception that can be pushed and pulled in various directions across modalities, that are adaptive, and that can be combined in different ways. Moreover, these dynamics need to be able to play out in the moment, and therefore depend deeply on the knowledge possessed by the body (Gallagher, 2005; Sutton et al., 2011). This idea of "bodily knowledge" is useful as it provides a richer conception of what knowing and understanding entails—one that looks beyond knowledge as a collection of facts, or knowing *this* or *that*, to include the kinds of practical *know-how* that allows us to move, act, and participate effectively within the social and material environments we inhabit.

As experienced basketball players move down the court, they do not need to focus on all of the movements they produce. Nor do they need to objectively account for all the properties of their environment—doing so would impede their performance. Likewise, a performing musician needs to be able to enact the appropriate bodily (e.g., embouchure, fingering, grip) and social (e.g., tuning, rhythmic coordination) configurations without stopping to deliberate on such factors. Such forms of contextual know-how are sometimes referred to as "skilled coping" (Dreyfus, 2013; Høffding, 2014) and are shaped through various developmental processes (exploration, adaptation, learning, experimentation, practice and training, and so on). It is also important to note that recognizing the centrality of the situated body for skilled coping does not necessarily mean that there is no thinking or reflecting involved (Høffding, 2018; Montero, 2016; Sutton et al., 2011). However, as we touched on earlier, performance contexts require a more dynamic and embodied conception of thought-in-action, where more deliberative decision making and problem-solving processes are enmeshed synergistically with movement, context, and feeling. The experience of seamless integration of bodily knowledge and thought-in-action is referred to as "flow" (Csikszentmihalyi, 1996). Flow is related to skilled coping and affordance as it describes an agent's ability to be engaged in contextually situated activities where the actions and equipment involved become transparent with regard to the moment-to-moment goals and contingencies of the event—whereby agents initiate and engage with the invitations and challenges that arise in the course of performance in a fluid way. It is the capacity to enact and maintain this flow, this deep embodied connection with the environment (being "in the zone"), that affords creative action in musical performance.

Affordance, skilled coping, and flow highlight a continuity between cognition, creativity in action, and the objects and tools we use. For example, Merleau-Ponty (2002) discusses how when a blind person uses a uses a cane to navigate an environment, the cane becomes an extension of their perceptual apparatus, that is, how their perception now extends beyond the person's hand to the tip of the cane (see also Malafouris, 2013). Similarly, an expert cellist will feel an important focal point of contact with the instrument where the bow hair engages with the strings—and they will be able to perceive the variations in texture, tension, friction, and so on that are required to express themselves and engage with the music environment through that material extension of their bodily consciousness. This can be seen with the mastery of a musical instrument more generally, where the instrument is no longer experienced simply as an object—rather, it gains a certain transparency as there is a sense in which the (musical) world is enacted and experienced though it. The saxophonist free-improviser Evan Parker discusses this in terms of a "bio-feedback" between himself and the instrument (see Borgo, 2005). He explains that the "instrument teaches you as much you tell it what to do" (Borgo, 2014, p. 95), resulting in a hybrid system where it sometimes becomes difficult to discern who is playing whom. As we began to consider earlier, developing this deep connection between body and instrument involves synergetic self-organizing processes that play out over periods of practice, exploration, reflection, and performance.

One can also consider how these environmentally extended aspects of perception and action unfold in social contexts. Here we can think again of an interacting musical ensemble, where the musicians involved develop shared repertoires of action and perception that allow them to enact rhythmic structures, timing, phrasing, intonation, and dynamics, as well as the various forms of emotional and corporeal coordination required to sustain the music they co-create (Keller, 2001). In doing so, they participate in and shape an extended musical environment by taking on and offloading various tasks to and from each other (e.g., by entraining with a beat provided by a drummer; by adapting to each other's phrasing; by leading or following harmonic and dynamic shifts; and so on). In other words, performing musicians enact affordances for each other, resulting in an interpersonal flow and a certain social transparency where strict distinctions between self and other recede into the background (Krueger, 2019). To be clear, this does not mean that the individual is necessarily effaced in such contexts; that the musicians become the same person, or that they have identical experiences. Rather, these situations highlight how individual embodied minds support, challenge, and "extend into" each other as they engage in the realization of a shared musical world. In connection with this, Høffding (2018) has examined the experiences involved in collective music making through a series of interviews with the Danish String Quartet. Notably, this research develops a richer understanding of what "musical absorption" involves—one that ranges from something close to a total immersion in the shared activity, to "frustrated playing" (associated with overcoming obstacles and challenges), to more reflective experiences while performing. Such insights are helping to revise conceptions of what flow and skilled coping entail to include the forms deliberate thought-in-action mentioned earlier.

Importantly, developing high levels of adaptive skilled coping and flow allows musical performers to trust each other and to take risks by introducing new elements into the system (as with Kim, our drummer). Indeed, risk taking can entail the deliberate initiation of moments of instability as a prompt for creative action—that is, to keep the music evolving, adaptive, and "alive." Such actions can involve the intentional introduction of subtle shifts in phrasing and dynamics, or the use of novel ornamentation (e.g., in the performance of Baroque music). In other contexts, more radical shifts might take place that involve new ways of interacting with instruments and co-performers that break from traditional models of technique, virtuosity, and even what "music" involves. Examples of these kinds of performance can be found in such fields as "new music," "experimental music," and "free improvisation," where musicians become highly adept at pushing the balances of freedom and constraint, stability and instability, to extremes (Borgo, 2005; Clarke, 2005a).

All of this implies that, to be creative in performance, musicians need to develop skills that go beyond the reproduction of style or the musical notes on the page of a composition. They need to understand how the patterns of action and perception they engage in are developed and gain the flexibility to explore how these patterns might evolve. This means that musicians need to take risks, experiment, and be willing to endure uncomfortable periods of instability and negotiation in order to enact new affordances for thought and (inter)action. It seems likely, therefore, that performers who are unwilling to engage in these kinds of processes will not experience, or exhibit, a high degree of creativity, regardless of the musical genre in which they work. It is important to clarify here that "going beyond reproduction" does not mean abandoning the constraints of culture and the community of practice one is situated within. To creatively contribute to, advance, or challenge a form of musical activity, performers need to have a deep grasp of their culture and community, and how their work draws on, informs, and transforms that social environment. Otherwise, the products they create risk being irrelevant and possibly incoherent.

Musical creativity in four dimensions

We have begun to consider how creativity in musical performance may be explored in a holistic context that involves the dynamic interaction of a range of factors distributed across personal and environmental domains (bodily, social, material, technological). Such interactions form a self-organizing network of feedback and feedforward loops that stabilize and evolve over various timescales—from in-the-moment impulses and adaptations, to how creativity unfolds over rehearsals, negotiations, and multiple performances. In general, we can also say that creativity in musical performance involves playing with and within constraints (Johnson-Laird, 1988). These constraints are defined by the physiological possibilities of performers' bodies in interaction with their instruments; the understandings performers can access (both individually and collectively) though experience; the types of meaningful social interactions available; as well as the norms that prescribe communication and meaning at socio-cultural levels. As we have also discussed, constraints can evolve over time through growth, learning, and exploration, leading to new musical affordances. This can entail discovering new ways to move within a recognized musical domain, as Gould did in his performances of Bach. It can also involve developing a new set of constraints in which one performs and creates new ways of moving and interacting with instruments and technology, as Hendrix did with his innovative use of feedback. New affordances emerge as a musical performer adapts to new environmental factors. And these factors can involve the introduction of new technologies and the new modes of interaction they enable, and/or engagements with performers from different cultural backgrounds, resulting in the emergence of new, hybrid forms of expression. Once again, these experiences can involve periods of instability as agents enact cognitive structures that afford new social, emotional, bodily configurations at the intersection of self, technology, and culture.

Researchers associated with embodied and ecological trends in cognitive science have recently proposed a "4E" model (Newen et al., 2018) that may be useful for thinking about the intersecting corporeal and environmental aspects of musical creativity (Glăveanu, 2014; Torrance & Schumann, 2018; Wheeler, 2018) (see Figure 20.1). By this light, cognition is seen as fundamentally *embodied* (since it is based in the ability to move, sense, and feel), environmentally *embedded* (since it always occurs within a contingent socio-material ecology), and *extended* (since it includes factors that go beyond the brains and bodies of individual agents, like tools, musical instruments, and other people). In being embodied, embedded, and extended, cognition is also *enactive* (since it involves the active bringing-forth of a world of meaningful relationships between agent and environment; see Varela et al., 1991).

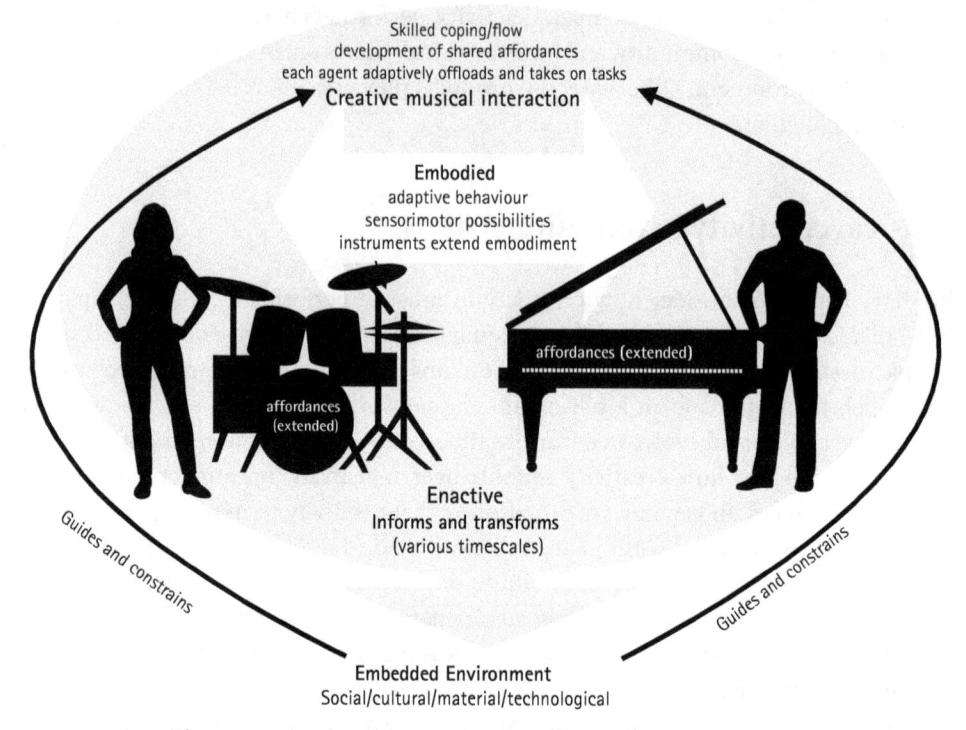

FIGURE 20.1. This image sketches the extended cognitive ecology of two interacting musicians (a drummer and a piano player). They bring forth a musical world by co-enacting patterns of self-organizing behavior that are guided by, and that in turn inform and transform environmental constraints. Musical creativity in performance involves interactions that span neural, corporeal, and environmental domains—it is a dynamic-synergistic process that plays out over various timescales (in-the-moment, developmental, historical). Adapted from van der Schyff et al., 2022.

This model provides a general four-dimensional framework (see van der Schyff et al., 2018, p. 10) for thinking about musical creativity in terms of:

1. The *embodied* dynamics of creative musical action: the motor and affective aspects associated with how musicians simultaneously produce and experience musical sound.
2. The *embedded* dynamics of the shared creative niche: how musicians adaptively situate themselves in relation to the physical, social, and cultural environments they inhabit and actively shape.
3. The *extended* dynamics of the musical event: how musicians use instruments and other technologies as parts of their cognitive domain; and how they adaptively offload and take on various social tasks related to maintaining and manipulating the balance between stability and entropy within an ensemble.
4. The *enactive* dynamics of the performers' relational development: how unique musical identities and environments emerge through the self-organizing activity of musical agents, and how these processes shape relational and creative constraints in an ongoing way.

A 4E approach can help guide researchers in constructing participant questionnaires, or frame behavioral studies (e.g., see Schiavio et al., 2020). This orientation could also be useful in the context of reflective, first-person analysis of skill development. It is especially well suited to explore creativity in the contexts of practice-led research and research-led practice (see Smith & Dean, 2009), where it might help performer-researchers gain new phenomenological insights into the experience of creativity in performance. Additionally, a 4E perspective may also be useful for examining and comparing the contributions of historical figures. As we have touched on, performers like Hendrix and Coltrane were *embedded* within the socio-cultural milieu of the mid-twentieth-century United States. Both artists developed unique approaches to performing that expressed that environment, drawing on, and radically transforming, existing musical conventions. In the process, they and their bandmates *enacted* new sets of relationships and meanings for ensemble and instrumental practice. This revealed new *extended* musician-instrument-ensemble affordances that, in turn, contributed to the evolution of the broader culture.

CONCLUSION

Approaching musical performance from a synergistic/4E orientation opens exciting possibilities for thought and research (van der Schyff et al., 2022). As we have seen, this perspective recasts creative the idea of creative products, processes, people, and press in a more dynamical light—one that seems well positioned to offer new insights into the range of embodied practices and shared experiences associated with musical creativity in performance as it evolves through social, cultural, and technological worlds. Some researcher/performers have begun to use dynamical systems concepts of attractors, entropy, constraint, and self-organization alongside flow, affordance, and skilled coping to examine their creative process from a first-person perspective. Notably, Phil Slater (2020) develops these ideas to offer a rich ecological, embodied, and "constraints-led" account of his practice as an improvising trumpet player. An embodied-ecological approach can also help to address some of the concerns outlined at the start of this chapter. For example, thinking of creativity as an emergent property of multiple interacting agents—and the transformations and adaptation that occur over time in such contexts—could shed light on how creativity unfolds in cross-cultural and cross-disciplinary performance situations. As with the developmental contexts we have discussed, it could also help us anticipate and better understand the periods of instability involved as new shared affordances and understandings stabilize and as new hybrid communities and forms of expression emerge. A 4E model could frame these kinds of processes by highlighting different aspects of the evolving system. Additionally, readers may also be interested to know that historical accounts of musical creativity inspired by 4E thinking have emerged in recent years, such as Le Guin's *Boccherini's Body: An Essay in Carnal*

Musicology (2006), and the treatment of music and song in Tribble and Keene's *Cognitive Ecologies and the History of Remembering* (2011). There is, of course, much more to say about the possibilities of this orientation. And as more research and theory emerges— and as new techniques for analysis and modelling are developed—we can look forward to richer accounts of musical creativity across a range of contexts. For now, we hope that the ideas and insights introduced in this chapter have provided some compelling options for thought that will be useful to musicians of all styles and genres as they engage in their practice as creative performers.

Key Sources

Glăveanu, V. P. (2014). *Distributed creativity: Thinking outside the box of the creative individual.* New York: Springer.

Runco, M. (2014). *Creativity: Theories and themes. Research, development, and practice* (2nd ed.). Amsterdam: Academic Press.

Sawyer, R. K. (2012). *Explaining creativity: The science of human innovation.* (2nd ed.). New York: Oxford University Press.

Reflective Questions

1. How might your experience as a performer be explained in terms of a 4E framework? How do these dimensions interact in your development and practice as a performer? In what ways do you act as part of the embedded and extended world of other creative people?

2. How would you describe the relationship between the absorbed states of consciousness associated with "flow" and "skilled coping" with more detached or analytical forms of thinking as you engage in musical performance?

3. What musical activities might be introduced into individual and ensemble practice that could help develop musical affordances, increase flexibility, and stimulate creativity?

4. How have you experienced "instability" in the musical environments you participate in? In what ways can it foster or impede creativity? How do the ensembles you perform with negotiate novelty, freedom, constraint, and risk taking? How can you make yourself aware of the existing conventions, constraints, and expectations against which your creativity will be measured by others?

5. How might the concepts self-organization and synergy be used as heuristics for thinking about creative development? How might this apply in bodily, social, pedagogical, and cross-cultural contexts? What about interactions with technology?

ACKNOWLEDGMENT

Andrea Schiavio's contribution is supported by the Austrian Science Fund (FWF): project number P 32460.

REFERENCES

Abraham, F. D., Krippner, S., & Richards, R. (2012). Dynamical concepts used in creativity and chaos. *NeuroQuantology*, *10*(2), 177–182. https://doi.org/10.14704/nq.2012.10.2.561.

Amazeen, E. L., Sternad, D., & Turvey, M. T. (1996). Predicting the nonlinear shift of stable equilibria in interlimb rhythmic coordination. *Human Movement Science*, *15*(4), 521–542. https://doi.org/10.1016/0167-9457(96)00025-5.

Bach, J. S. (Composer). (1955). *Bach: The Goldberg Variations* [Recorded by G. Gould.]. CBS Records.

Baer, J., & McKool, S. (2009). Assessing creativity using the consensual assessment technique. In C. Schreiner (Ed.), *Handbook of research on assessment technologies, methods, and applications in higher education*, 65–77. Hershey, PA: IGI Global.

Bazzana, K. (2003). *Wondrous strange: The life and art of Glenn Gould*. New York: Oxford University Press.

Bokor, M. (2017). When the drum speaks: The rhetoric of motion, emotion, and action in African societies. *Rhetorica*, *32*(2), 165–194. https://doi.org/10.1525/RH.2014.32.2.165.

Borgo, D. (2005). *Sync or swarm: Improvising music in a complex age*. New York: Continuum.

Borgo, D. (2014). Ghost in the music, or the perspective of an improvising ant. In G. E. Lewis & B. Piekut (Eds.), *The Oxford handbook of critical improvisation studies*. Oxford Handbooks Online. https://doi.org/10.1093/oxfordhb/9780195370935.013.005.

Borgo, D. (2016). Openness from closure: The puzzle of interagency in improvised music and a meocybernetic solution. In E. Waterman & G. Siddall (Eds.), *Negotiated moments: Improvisation sound and subjectivity* (pp. 113–130). Durham, NC, and London: Duke University Press.

Briggs, J. (1988). *Fire in the crucible: The alchemy of creative genius*. New York: St. Martin's.

Capra, F. (1996). *The web of life: A new scientific understanding of living systems*. New York: Anchor Books.

Chemero, A. (2009). *Radical embodied cognitive science*. Cambridge, MA: MIT Press.

Csikszentmihalyi, M. (1996). *Creativity: Flow and the psychology of discovery and invention*. New York: HarperCollins.

Clarke, E. F. (2005a). Creativity in performance. *Musicae Scientiae*, *9*(1), 157–182. https://doi.org/10.1177%2F102986490500900106.

Clarke, E. F. (2005b). *Ways of listening: An ecological approach to the perception of musical meaning*. New York: Oxford University Press.

Clarke, E. F., & Doffman, M. (2017). *Distributed creativity: Collaboration and improvisation in contemporary music*. New York: Oxford University Press.

Cook, N. (1999). Analyzing performance and performing analysis. In N. Cook & M. Everist (Eds.), *Rethinking music* (pp. 239–261). New York: Oxford University Press.

Cook, N. (2013). *Beyond the score: Music as performance*. New York: Oxford University Press.

Copland, A. (1952). Music and imagination. Cambridge, MA: Harvard University Press.

Cropley, A. (2011). Definitions of Creativity. In M. A. Runco & S. R. Pritzker (Eds.), *Encyclopedia of creativity* (2nd ed., pp. 358–68). Elsevier.

Dacey, J. (1999). Concepts of creativity: A history. In M. A. Runco & S. R. Pritzker (Eds.), *Encyclopedia of creativity, Vol. 1 A–H* 309–322. San Diego, CA: Academic Press.

Dietrich, A., & Kanso, R. (2010). A review of EEG, ERP and neuroimaging studies of creativity and insight. *Psychological Bulletin, 136*(5), 822–848. https://doi.org/10.1037/a0019749.

Dixon, J. A., Stephen, D. G., Boncoddo, R. A., & Anastas, J. (2010). The self-organization of cognitive structure. In B. Ross (Ed.), *The psychology of learning & motivation*, vol. 52, (pp. 343–384). San Diego, CA: Elsevier.

Dreyfus, H. L. (2013). The myth of the pervasiveness of the mental. In J. K. Schear (Ed.), *Mind, reason, and being-in-the-world*, 15–40. London: Routledge.

Fabian, D. (2017). Analyzing difference in recordings of Bach's violin solos with a lead from Gilles Deleuze. *Music Theory Online, 23*(4), 1–23. https://doi.org/10.30535/mto.23.4.4.

Fantasia, V., De Jaegher, H., & Fasulo, A. (2014). We can work it out: An enactive look at cooperation. *Frontiers in Psychology, 5*, 874. https://doi.org/10.3389/fpsyg.2014.00874.

Finke, R. A., Ward, T. B., & Smith, S. M. (1992). *Creative cognition*. Cambridge, MA: MIT Press.

Frith, S. (2012). Creativity as a social fact. In D. J. Hargreaves, D. E. Miell, & R. A. R. MacDonald (Eds.), *Musical imaginations* (pp. 62–72). Oxford: Oxford University Press.

Gallagher, S. (2005). *How the body shapes the mind*. New York: Oxford University Press.

Gardner, H. (1988). Creativity: An interdisciplinary perspective. *Creativity Research Journal, 1*(1), 8–26. https://doi.org/10.1080/10400418809534284.

Geeves, A. M., McIlwain, D. J., & Sutton, J. (2016). Seeing yellow: "Connection" and routine in professional musicians' experience of music performance. *Psychology of Music, 44*(2), 183–201. https://doi.org/10.1177%2F0305735614560841.

Gibson, J. J. (1966). *The senses considered as perceptual systems*. Boston: Houghton-Mifflin.

Glăveanu, V. P. (2014). *Distributed creativity: Thinking outside the box of the creative individual*. New York: Springer.

Guilford, J. P. (1967). *The nature of human intelligence*. New York: McGraw-Hill.

Haken, H. (1977). *Synergetics: An introduction*. Berlin: Springer.

Helie, S., & Sun, R. (2010). Incubation, insight, and creative problem solving: A unified theory and a connectionist model. *Psychological Review, 117*(3), 994–1024. https://psycnet.apa.org/doi/10.1037/a0019532.

Henahan, D. (1982, October 17). What has Glenn Gould left us? *New York Times*, Section 2, p. 23.

Høffding, S. (2014). What is skilled coping? Experts on expertise. *Journal of Consciousness Studies, 21*(9–10), 49–73.

Høffding, S. (2018). *A phenomenology of musical absorption*. New York: Palgrave Macmillan.

Høffding, S., & Satne, G. (2019). Interactive expertise in solo and joint musical performance. *Synthese, 198*, 1–19. https://doi.org/10.1007/s11229-019-02339-x.

Hristovski, R., Davids, K., Araújo, D., & Passos P. (2011). Constraints-induced emergence of functional novelty in complex neurobiological systems: A basis for creativity in sport. *Nonlinear Dynamics Psychology and the Life Sciences, 15*(2), 175–206.

Johnson-Laird, P. N. (1988). Freedom and constraint in creativity. In R. J. Sternberg (Ed.), *The nature of creativity*, pp. 202–219. Cambridge, UK: Cambridge University Press.

Kearny, R. (1988). *The wake of imagination: Toward a postmodern culture*. London: Routledge.

Keenan, E. K. (2015). *Intersectionality in third-wave popular music*. Oxford Handbooks Online. https://doi.org/10.1093/oxfordhb/9780199935321.013.36.

Keller, P. E. (2001). Attentional resource allocation in musical ensemble performance. *Psychology of Music*, 29(1), 20–38. https://doi.org/10.1177%2F0305735601291003.

Kello, C. T., & Van Orden, G.C. (2009). Soft-assembly of sensorimotor function. *Nonlinear Dynamics Psychology and Life Sciences*, 13(1), 57–78.

Kimmel, M., Hristova, D., & Kussmaul, K. (2018). Sources of embodied creativity: Interactivity and ideation in contact improvisation. *Behavioral Sciences*, 8(6), 52. https://doi.org/10.3390/bs8060052.

Kirton, M. J. (2003). *Adaption-innovation: In the context of diversity and change*. New York: Routledge.

Koestler, A. (1964). *The act of creation*. London: Pan Books.

Krueger, J. (2019). Music as affective scaffolding. In D. Clarke, R. Herbert, & E. F. Clarke (Eds.), *Music and consciousness II* (pp. 48–63). New York: Oxford University Press.

Leech-Wilkinson, D. (2018). The danger of virtuosity. *Musicae Scientiae*, 22(4), 558–561. https://doi.org/10.1177%2F1029864918790304.

Le Guin, E. (2006). *Boccherini's body: An essay in carnal musicology*. Berkeley: University of California Press.

Levi-Strauss, C. (1988). *The way of the masks*. Seattle: University of Washington Press.

Linson, A., & Clarke, E. F. (2017). Distributed cognition, ecological theory, and group improvisation. In E. F. Clarke & M. Doffman (Eds.), *Distributed creativity: Collaboration and improvisation in contemporary music*, 52–69. New York: Oxford University Press.

Lubart, T. (2010). Cross-cultural perspectives on creativity. In J. C. Kaufman & R. J. Sternberg (Eds.), *The Cambridge handbook of creativity* (pp. 265–278). Cambridge, UK: Cambridge University Press.

Malafouris, L. (2013). *How things shape the mind: A theory of material engagement*. Cambridge, MA: MIT Press.

Maurice, B. (Producer), & Wadleigh, M. (Director) (1970). *Woodstock* [Motion picture]. Warner Brothers.

Merleau-Ponty, M. (2002). *Phenomenology of perception*. London: Routledge.

Monson, I. T. (1996). *Saying something: Jazz improvisation and interaction*. Chicago: University of Chicago Press.

Montero, B. (2016). *Thought in action: Expertise and the conscious mind*. Oxford: Oxford University Press.

Montuori, A., & Purser, R. (1995). Deconstructing the lone genius myth: Toward a contextual view of creativity. *Journal of Humanistic Psychology*, 35(3), 69–112. https://doi.org/10.1177%2F00221678950353005.

Newen, A., De Bruin, L., & Gallagher, S. (2018). *The Oxford handbook of 4E cognition*. New York: Oxford University Press.

Niu, W., & Sternberg, R. J. (2006). The philosophical roots of Western and Eastern conceptions of creativity. *Journal of Theoretical and Philosophical Psychology*, 26(1–2), 18–38. https://psycnet.apa.org/doi/10.1037/h0091265.

Pressing, J. (1988). Improvisation: Methods and models. In J. A. Sloboda (Ed.), *Generative processes in music* (pp. 129–178). Oxford: Clarendon Press.

Reddy, V. (2008). *How infants know minds*. Cambridge, MA.: Harvard University Press.

Rhodes, M. (1961). An analysis of creativity. *The Phi Delta Kappan*, 42(7), 305–310.

Runco, M. (2014). *Creativity: Theories and themes: Research, development, and practice* (2nd ed). Amsterdam: Academic Press.

Salice, A., Høffding, S., & Gallagher, S. (2017). Putting plural self-awareness into practice: The phenomenology of expert musicianship. *Topoi*, 38, 1–13. https://doi.org/10.1007/s11245-017-9451-2.

Sawyer, R. K. (1998). The interdisciplinary study of creativity in performance. *Creativity Research Journal 11*(1), 11–19. https://doi.org/10.1207/s15326934crj1101_2.

Sawyer, R. K. (2007). *Group genius: The creative power of collaboration*. New York: Basic Books.

Sawyer, R. K. (2012). *Explaining creativity: The science of human innovation*. (2nd Ed.). New York: Oxford University Press.

Schiavio, A., Stupacher, J., Parncutt, R., & Timmers, R. (2020). Learning music from each other. Synchronization, turn-taking, or imitation? *Music Perception*, 37(5), 403–422. https://doi.org/10.1525/mp.2020.37.5.403.

Schuldberg, D. (1999). Chaos theory and creativity. In M. Runco & S. Pritzker (Eds.), *The encyclopedia of creativity* (Vol. 1, pp. 259–272). London: Academic Press.

Seddon, F. A., & Biasutti, M. (2009). A comparison of modes of communication between members of a string quartet and a Jazz sextet. *Psychology of Music*, 37(4), 395–415. https://doi.org/10.1177%2F0305735608100375.

Slater, P. (2020). *The Dark Pattern: Towards a constraints-led approach to jazz trumpet*. Doctoral thesis, University of Sydney, Sydney.

Sloboda, J. A. (1983). The communication of musical metre in piano performance. *Quarterly Journal of Experimental Psychology Section A*, 35(2), 377–396. https://doi.org/10.1080/14640748308402140.

Sloboda, J. (1985). *The musical mind: The cognitive psychology of music*. Oxford: Clarendon Press.

Smith, H., & Dean, R. T. (2009). *Practice-led research, research-led practice in the creative arts*. Edinburgh: Edinburgh University Press.

Strogatz, S. (1994). *Nonlinear dynamics and chaos: With applications to physics, biology, chemistry, and engineering*. Reading, MA: Perseus Books.

Sudnow, D. (2001). *Ways of the hand: A rewritten account*. Cambridge, MA: MIT Press.

Sutton, J., Mcllwain, D., Christensen, W., & Geeves, A. (2011) Applying intelligence to the reflexes: Embodied skills and habits between Dreyfus and Descartes. *Journal of the British Society for Phenomenology*, 42(1), 78–103. https://doi.org/10.1080/00071773.2011.11006732.

Thelen, E., & Smith, L. B. (1994). *A dynamic systems approach to the development of cognition and action*. Cambridge, MA: MIT Press.

Torrance, S., & Schumann, F. (2018). The spur of the moment: What jazz improvisation tells cognitive science. *AI & Society*, 34, 251–268. https://doi.org/10.1007/s00146-018-0838-4.

Tribble, E., & Keene, N. (2011). *Cognitive ecologies and the history of remembering*. New York: Palgrave.

van der Schyff, D. (2016). From Necker cubes to polyrhythms: Fostering a phenomenological attitude in music education. *Phenomenology and Practice*, 10(1), 4–24. https://doi.org/10.29173/pandpr27998.

van der Schyff, D., Schiavio, A., & Elliott, D. (2022). *Musical bodies, musical minds: Enactive cognitive science and the meaning of human musicality*. Cambridge, MA: MIT Press.

van der Schyff, D., Schiavio, A., Walton, A., Velardo, V., & Chemero, A. (2018). Musical creativity and the embodied mind: Exploring the possibilities of 4E cognition and dynamical systems theory. *Music & Science*, 1. https://doi.org/10.1177/2059204318792319.

Varela, F., Thompson, E., & Rosch, E. (1991). *The embodied mind: Cognitive science and human experience*. Cambridge, MA: MIT Press.

Wallas, G. (1926). *Art of thought*. New York: Harcourt-Brace.

Walton, A., Richardson, M. J., Langland-Hassan, P., & Chemero, A. (2015). Improvisation and the self-organization of multiple musical bodies. *Frontiers in Psychology*, 6, 313. https://doi.org/10.3389/fpsyg. 2015.00313.

Wheeler, M. (2018). Talking about more than heads: The embodied, embedded and extended creative mind. In B. Gaut & M. Kieran (Eds.), *Creativity and Philosophy* (pp. 230–250). London: Routledge.

CHAPTER 21

PERFORMING IN THE STUDIO

MARK SLATER

INTRODUCTION

WHILE studio recordings can resemble live performances and draw upon similar reserves of knowledge and skill, the processes and experiences of performing in the studio are notably different from being on stage in front of an audience. The broad sweep of technological development since 1877 has given rise to increasingly powerful and prevalent devices that facilitate the capture of music in increasingly diverse settings. These developments have impacted upon music and its associated practices from all angles, including performance. Such technologies are not passive objects painted into the scenery of music's story; they have been entangled with music in a complex plot that has changed music in all its aspects—sonic, stylistic, social, artifactual, economic, political, and institutional. Reciprocally, the demands of music making throughout the technological era have nudged the trajectory of technological development.

Every recording that exists is an example of a recorded performance in some way. Whether that involves playing musical instruments individually or as an ensemble, triggering drum pads for a remix, sequencing synthesizers and samplers for a soundtrack, shaping the dynamics of sound through compression and equalization, or editing audio on tape or using a digital audio workstation, any conceivable way that musicians might interact with technology to create a recording is arguably a form of performance. The diverse ways that recordings can now be made, the prevalence of the recording process in contemporary musicianship, and the blurring of roles within this whole process underpin the ideas put forward here. Rather than analyzing individual recorded performances or offering technical how-to advice, this chapter situates performance within the technological trappings of the studio and its associated social and musical processes.

To begin, two ideologically opposed cases are introduced, leading to a consideration of key ideas in the field by way of poetics and assemblages; questions about who and what is performing will then be addressed followed by a consideration of the studio environment replete with its tools, objects, and materiality. The final section outlines four proposals relating to the practical implications of the discussion, which encourage: (1) a recognition of the similarities and differences between live and recording performance contexts; (2) an understanding of the ideological underpinnings of why a recording is being made; (3) an acknowledgment of the productive effects of technology; and (4) the necessary admission that recordings construct an illusion of some kind of reality.

THE GOULD-DRUMMOND AXIS

In 1964, Glenn Gould renounced the concert hall and declared he would, from then on, only make recordings. For him, the opportunities heralded by the rapidly improving recording technologies of the time signaled the impending death of the concert hall. Having toured extensively on the international circuit following his debut in 1946, Gould regarded the concert experience as "degrading and humanly damaging" (Gould & Page, 1981, p. 452). Recording offered rich aesthetic possibilities that could not be matched in the fragile immediacy of the concert experience:

> [T]he young pianist, then thirty-one years old [. . .] was tired of what he called the "non-take-two-ness" of the concert experience—the inability of a performer to correct finger slips and other minor mistakes. He pointed out that most creative artists are able to tinker and to perfect, but that the live performer must re-create his work from scratch every time he steps onto a stage. (Page, 1984, p. xii)

In 1962, Gould presaged this position when he wrote that "the most efficacious step which could be taken in our culture today would be the gradual but total elimination of audience response" (Gould, 1962, p. 246). In an article for *Piano Quarterly*, Gould recounts a memorable broadcast for the Canadian Broadcasting Corporation in December 1950 during which he performed sonatas by Mozart and Hindemith. Afterwards, Gould was gifted an acetate disc of the performance.

> [E]ven today, a quarter-century after the fact, I still take [it] down from the shelf on occasion in order to celebrate that moment in my life when I first caught a vague impression of the direction it would take, when I realized that the collected wisdom of my peers and elders to the effect that technology represented a compromising, dehumanizing intrusion into art was nonsense, when my love affair with the microphone began. (Gould, 1974–1975, p. 354)

In an interview with Tim Page in 1981, Gould summarized his position in relation to recording technology and live performance:

> [T]echnology has the capability to create a climate of anonymity and to allow the artist the time and the freedom to prepare his conception of a work to the best of his ability, to perfect a statement without having to worry about trivia like nerves

and finger slips. It has the capability of replacing those awful and degrading and humanly damaging uncertainties which the concert brings with it. (Gould & Page, 1981, p. 452)

Though his prediction about the death of the concert hall has not come to pass, Gould's challenge to the establishment of music practice is formidable. Indeed, Gould (1966) was fully aware that to "reckon with [the concert hall's] obsolescence is to defy the very body of the musical establishment" (p. 333). The concert hall, at the time Gould was writing, was emblematic of the musical establishment's values in the way that performances in such spaces propagated a masterwork mentality along with the perceived qualities of coherence, organicism and authenticity. In his essay "The Prospects of Recording," Gould discusses splicing in relation to the perceived infringement on the supremacy and coherence of an artist's utterance that some considered to run so counter to the in-the-moment, in-person authenticity of concert hall performances. In recounting the process of recording Bach's fugue in A minor from the first volume of *The Well-Tempered Clavier*, Gould testifies to the transcendental possibilities of recording through the act of editing. In his account, takes 6 and 8 had markedly different approaches to articulation—one strident and severe, the other jubilant—but, surprisingly, both had the same tempo, which allowed them to be spliced. Such a version emerged as a result of the speculative process of recording: "By taking advantage of the post-taping afterthought, [...] one can very often transcend the limitations that performance imposes upon the imagination" (p. 339). Recording processes present the possibility of transcending received tradition to achieve new interpretative insights.

Gould's embrace of the rich potential of recording technology and outright rejection of live performance marks out a clear ideological position. The opposite pole is represented by Bill Drummond, who rejected recording technologies in favor of the unrepeatable immediacy of live performance. Drummond had worked in the popular music industry from 1977 as an artist and in business roles, but by 1992 had reached the end of the road with making that kind of technologically mediated music:

The very urge to make recorded music is a redundant and creative dead end, not even an interesting option, fit only for the makers of advertising jingles, ring-tones and motion picture soundtracks. The sheer availability and ubiquity of recorded music will inspire forward-looking music-makers to explore different ways of creating music [. . .] and the very making of recorded music will seem an entirely two-dimensional 20th-century aspiration to the creative music-makers of the next few decades. (Drummond, 2008, p. 5)

Drummond's personal journey led him to reject the stylistic, technological, and commercial imperatives that had dominated his practice up to that point, which he symbolized potently with his renunciation of recording. In 2003, Drummond made his position clear by serving the following notice:

All recorded music has run its course.

It has all been consumed, traded, downloaded, understood, heard before, sampled, learned, revived, judged and found wanting.

Dispense with all previous forms of music and music-making and start again. (Drummond, 2008, p. 3)

The ubiquity of recordings demonstrates, for Drummond, the cheapening and diluting effects of capitalist commodification. Recordings are symbols of consumerist excess devoid of any capacity for profundity. Indeed, it is the very rejection of recordings and all the economic apparatus that necessarily surrounds them that heralds the new horizon. In response, Drummond formed a choir—The17—that would have a variable line-up, would never be recorded, and would not perform for an audience. Instead it would meet for the purpose of collective music making in a particular moment and place in response to a series of text-based scores of Drummond's own hand. The sound of the choir was initially inspired by the "throbbing engine, rattling bits, wind through the wing mirror and the whoosh of the other motorway traffic" (Drummond, 2008, p. 28) as he drove from Hull to Liverpool along the M62 in the north of England. The prospect of such sounds, to be replicated with the human voice somehow, filled the vacuum left by the fatigued rejection of previous forms of music making clustered around recording.

While Gould and Drummond represent polar ideological positions in relation to recording, both sought to navigate tradition (and all the repetition and expectation that brings) and the future prospects of music making hinging on the effects of recording technology. Both adopt a position that has a personal logic and an aesthetic veracity that allows them to make what they regard as their best music. In reality, it is likely that most artists involved in recording adopt a more center-ground position in between the polar extremities of the Gould-Drummond axis. But, certainly, all recordings represent a pivot point between tradition and future, artists and audiences, works (of some kind) and interpretations; and all recordings assume the form they do through aesthetic and ideological positioning as much as instrumental, technical, imaginative, and economic prowess.

TRANSPARENT POETICS AND MUSICAL ASSEMBLAGES

Capturing a performance for a recording is a poetic moment. The term *poetics*, derived from the Greek *poiesis*, means to create, produce, or make. David Bordwell (2008) summarizes the term in relation to cinema: "The poetics of any artistic medium studies the finished work as the result of a process of construction—a process that includes a craft component [. . .], the more general principles according to which the work is composed, and its functions, effects, and uses" (p. 12). Henry Stobart (2006), in his ethnographic study of an agrarian community in South America, prises the meaning of poetics out of its entrenched Romantic literary meaning (e.g., "poets" and "poetry") by stressing "the mutual interdependence of musical and socio-economic production" (p. 5).

> The word "production" is also commonly heard in reference to the creation or preparation of something for (public) presentation, such as a piece of music, play, film or radio broadcast. It is notable that this term is often associated with presentational aspects of a work, object or a phenomenon and its reception, rather than earlier stages of its creation. (p. 7)

Indeed, in the case of music recordings, the beguiling aesthetic effects of the music's presentation obliterate the earlier preparatory, poetic stages of its making. Recordings obscure the technical, technological, and ideological story of their making just as live performances obscure the considerable time and effort that goes into the preparation, practice, rehearsal, thought, and decision-making that shapes the musical utterance. As in Stobart's example, the earlier stages of the creation of a recording (or a live performance) are disguised by the presentational aspects of performers', artists', composers', or producers' public-facing image and reception.

Consider the microphone: "Invisible to the listener and a tool of the trade for the producer or engineer, the microphone is the representative of potentially countless future audiences" (Greig, 2009, p. 16). Other technological devices notwithstanding, this indispensable piece of equipment is the channel through which sound to be recorded must pass. Yet, though we undoubtedly hear it, we do not *hear* it. Instead, we listen *through* it, passing our attention onwards to the source of the sound—the work, the artist, and perhaps the place of the performance. The microphone simultaneously senses, transmits, mediates, inflects, and represents: it is positioned "between the attempt and the realization" (Gould, 1974-75, p. 354) as an object whose function and character places "special demands" (Gould, 1966, p. 336) on performers because "recording's attention to detail creates a distinct kind of pressure" (Greig, 2009, p. 19).

While rendering the musician audible, the recording process (as symbolized by the microphone) makes musicians and audiences invisible to one another, which "removes an important channel of communication, for performers express themselves not only through the sound of their voices or instruments but with their faces and bodies" (Katz, 2004, p. 20). "Whole sets of kinesic and paralinguistic components which reinforce the acoustic content of the recording—including facial expression, gesture, phatic language and rhythmic indicators—are no longer available" (Greig, 2009, p. 19). Reciprocal in-the-moment audience responses during a live performance, upon which a performer may thrive, are absent during a studio recording, which creates a particular kind of non-present relationship between performer and audience.

By making tangible what is transient, a recording transports music from its fragile, ephemeral existence to other times and places; it allows repeatable access to what would otherwise be an unrecoverable event. As a microscope reveals previously hidden micro-worlds, the microphone brings those distant, perhaps revered and elusive figures into an intimate, aural proximity. "The microphone had the same function as the close-up in film history—it made stars knowable, by shifting the conventions of personality, making singers sound sexy in new ways, [...] and moving the focus from the song to the singer" (Frith, 1986, p. 270). Crooners such as Frank Sinatra and Bing Crosby built their musical identities on the sense of intimacy created by the proximity of their bodies to the microphone, which also had the perceived benefit of masculinizing their vocal sound via the proximity effect that boosts bass frequencies (below 200 Hz) when within about three centimeters of most microphones. Their sound was made *with* and *by* technology; we hear its effects, but we listen through it.

The simple act of pressing "play" sweeps away all of the complexity, angst, fatigue, and sheer human effort that went into making the recording whose every sound was pored over by a team of skilled musicians and music technology specialists in order to put forth the best music that time, resources, technique, and imagination could render: a version worthy of a place among an infinite library of offerings. The ease and ubiquity of experiencing recordings flattens the complexity of the poetic conditions of their making and can make them appear as cold, indifferent objects of consumption. But recordings are not inoculated against the flow of ideas, predilections, and material constraints. They do not stand outside history and society but are infused with significance for those who make them and for those who listen to them.

The poetic event of capturing a performance in a studio gathers together a complex and specific combination of factors. A recording session is an example of "an aggregation of sonic, social, corporeal, discursive, visual, technological and temporal mediations—a musical assemblage" (Born, 2011, p. 377). Such an assemblage provides an ideal case-in-point for considering music through the lens of "subject-object relations" (p. 377) because people and technologies are necessarily entangled. An assemblage made manifest for the purposes of making, an act of labor, is a *poetic assemblage*, which distinguishes this work of producing from that of symbolic, interpretative exegesis carried out by listeners that continues to "make" the work once it is publicly available. A recording session, understood as a point of confluence, might typically include and draw upon: individual subjectivities (biographies, predilections, tastes, skills); interpersonal collaboration (between similarly and differentially skilled groups of people, such as musicians and engineers); interpretative exegeses (drawing upon historical and subjective positioning in relation, say, to notions of genre or received performance practices); tools and objects (instruments, computers, microphones, scores, acoustic panels); economic imperatives (which may be commercial, non-commercial, or even anti-commercial in nature); legal frameworks (copyright control, licensing, union guidelines); institutions (record labels, publishers, venues); organizations (orchestras, bands, arts funding bodies); and imagined communities (audiences, critics, other non-present musicians). Assemblages, then, are complex constructs of varying stability that draw together a large body of knowledge, skills, imperatives, perspectives, and materials.

Music and mediation theories go hand in hand because of music's particular (and perhaps peculiar) material and nonmaterial existence as a form of art.

> Music has no material essence but a plural and distributed materiality. Its multiple simultaneous forms of existence—as sonic trace, discursive exegesis, notated score, technological prosthesis, social and embodied performance—indicate the necessity of conceiving of the musical object as a constellation of mediations. (Born, 2011, p. 377)

A musical object, then, is not a singular, identifiable entity but something that is constituted plurally across time and in many places. Music's significance, meaning, and powers of affect derive from a constellation of relations. Recordings of performances are certainly among this constellation and, to a certain extent, endow music with a kind of "material essence." Georgina Born's writing has the explanatory capacity to trace a musical object's cultural life (how its meaning changes over time and alters for different groups of people, for example) and the theoretical apparatus that her work assembles is relevant to a consideration of performance in the studio because of the sensitivity it has to notions of mediation, particularly in terms of music's sociality and materiality. A recording session is emblematic of the social, musical, economic, cultural, and technological relations that constitute the poetic reality of how music is made.

WHO (AND WHAT) IS PERFORMING

Recordings require complicity. No matter how compelling the recording of Debussy's string quartet in G minor (Op. 10), those four musicians are not present in your lounge. So much is obvious. The veracity of the recording may be praised because of the way it conjures the sense of the moment, the resonance of the place, the impression of the musicians' movements and physical exertions. In his exploration of Trent Reznor's combination of real and synthetic instruments, Virgil Moorefield (2005) neatly summarizes the verisimilar quality of recordings:

> This blurring of the distinction between recordings of real instruments and recordings of recordings is an interesting game, and it fits right in with Reznor's overall strategy of playing a kind of push-and-pull with the two poles of record production, the *illusion of reality* [. . .] and the *reality of illusion*. (p. 74; emphases added)

Recordings conjure an illusion of some kind of reality; and that constructed, illusory quality is a fundamental part of the reality of recordings. Recordings that seek to present a "real" situation—the sense of musicians actually playing their instruments in an appropriate acoustic in an uninterrupted and feasible temporal flow—would be described as transparent. That is, the technical means of capturing, shaping, and reproducing the performance are rendered barely perceptible; the music "passes through" the technological processes, seemingly unimpeded and unchanged, to resemble closely what might be expected in a live performance. Such transparency aligns with the masterwork mentality in which the audience may hear the genius of the composer *through* the performer. Set against that is the notion of opacity: when a recording lays bare or allows its technical poetic origins to be heard, its production aesthetics could be described as opaque.

Transparency and opacity—and all degrees in between—are states that are achieved via very particular means and for very particular reasons. Such means might include microphone selection and placement, choice of recording location and its acoustic properties, post-capture processing (such as equalization and application of reverb), and the quantity and audibility of edits. Transparent production aesthetics obscure the technological reality of the illusion being created while exemplifying the comprehensive effectiveness of this sophisticated ruse. Opaque production aesthetics exploit and celebrate the particularities of the tools and processes in operation by amplifying them and absorbing them into the sonic signature of the music. In their analysis of Los Sampler's "La Vida es Llena de Cables," Ragnhild Brøvig-Hanssen and Anne Danielsen (2016) trace the glitchy stuttering of brutal, numerous cut-and-paste actions that are possible as a direct result of digital technology's capacity for manipulating audio as data. The track begins with a solo Spanish guitar playing a Cuban-style riff presented in what seems to be a straightforward, transparent way. But just four seconds into the track, we hear a stutter that, at first, sounds like a mistake in editing or the CD skipping (which cannot be the case, as we are listening on YouTube). Within a few more seconds, the recurrence of these skips and their close alignment with the underlying metrical frame quickly establishes these features as integral to the track. "The skips and stutters of 'La Vida es Llena de Cables,' then, are powerfully incongruent with our deep roots in understanding music as a spatiotemporally coherent singular performance" (p. 88). So, "[t]he cut-up techniques thus make the listener aware of the recording/production medium's double function, to mediate and to *be* that which is mediated—it presents itself while it mediates or represents something else" (p. 89, original emphasis). The signature of the digital technology used to make the music is laid bare, incorporated, and celebrated.

The guitarist on Los Sampler's track once sat down in a room and recorded this performance. We hear that performance, but we also hear the performance of the producers coaxing particular effects out of their technological apparatus through various interactions (keyboard, mouse, trackpad, synths, controllers). We hear many kinds of performance simultaneously layered though differentially perceptible and symbolic. As Michael Dellaira (1995) puts it:

> [T]he recording studio is itself an instrument, one step further removed from the original sound sources yet requiring no less technique and sensitivity in bringing those sounds to life. [. . .] For the recording studio is "played" too, though not on stage and in real time. But it *is* played for an audience, an audience who, in the very act of bringing the concert hall to its living room, gladly embraces the illogical and willingly submits to illusion. (p. 200; original emphasis)

The claim that the use of technologies is akin to a performance, based on specialized knowledge and skill required to carry out a task that we readily admit for musicians, sits equitably with the necessarily collaborative social construct of recording performances in which the star performer or ensemble is embedded in a wider team of contributors.

Dellaira (1995) makes another useful distinction "between recorded objects which serve to document live musical performances and those which do not document but which *are* performances in and of themselves" (p. 193; original emphasis). The distinction might be summarized in binaries such as documentation-generation or capture-invention, both of which rather bluntly downplay the complexity of the situation but are nonetheless useful for explaining different approaches that might be taken in a recording studio. Verbs like "document" and "capture" imply a passivity on the part of recording technologies in that what is being documented and captured is going on already, regardless of the act of recording the performance, and in which the people and technologies assembled have little bearing on the thing being recorded. Similarly, terms like "generate" and "invent" might imply a valorization of such acts of creativity in contradistinction to the servile execution of extant music. A performance of a Haydn piano sonata does not need to generate the score from which the melodic, rhythmic, harmonic, and structural progress is decoded. Instead, the musician concentrates on the interpretative versioning that will be enshrined in the recording. In the case of popular music bands, it is conceivable that no melodic, harmonic, rhythmic, or structural material exists prior to the recording session, which serves as a meeting point to improvise, experiment, and gradually fix the musical ideas in recorded form. Whatever kind of music is being recorded and whatever function the process of recording serves, each constructs an illusion on a spectrum of verisimilitude through very particular technical means in alignment with the aesthetic and ideological tenets of the music being recorded.

THE STUDIO ENVIRONMENT

One way of understanding the history of recording technologies is to divide the time since 1877 into three broad categories, which are defined by the kinds of technology used to transfer acoustic energy into a stable, repeatable form: acoustical/mechanical, electrical, and digital. George Brock-Nannestad (2009) provides a very useful discussion of the various ways that the history of the development of recording and reproduction technologies (since 1850) can be traced through mechanical, magnetic, and optical principles. In the acoustical (or mechanical) era (from 1877 to the mid-1920s), vibrations of the air were transferred to a stylus via a large horn to amplify the sonic energy to be engraved on some kind of membrane (originally wax, but later mica or glass; Katz, 2004). As this process entirely depended on a physical, mechanical process, the musicians had to be arranged in relation to the horn according to the power of their instrument's sound so that the sum of the ensemble reached the horn in a balanced way.

The resulting configurations were often cramped, uncomfortable, and at odds with the norms of live performance (see Figure 21.1): "Whether jostling for space or standing barely within shouting distance, performers were thus often forced to work in unnatural arrangements that hindered the interaction between musicians" (Katz, 2004, p. 83). Instruments that produce higher sound-pressure levels (such as trumpets and trombones) are placed at the rear of the space, while strings are placed next to the horn. Note also the Stroh violin (with the addition of the amplifying horn attached to the body) and the elevated position of the cellist that brings the sound-emitting F-holes in line with the sound-capture horn.

The electrical era (1924 onwards) was marked by the introduction of microphone and amplification technologies that enabled wider frequency and dynamic ranges to be captured, giving improved resolution and sense of depth. The pace of technological innovation accelerated due to the competition that radio posed to a recording industry that relied upon physical sales and due to scientific research taking place in telecommunications industries. The improved fidelity of recording technologies allowed musicians to resume a configuration more akin to the live performance situation, with

FIGURE 21.1. Music director Rosario Bourdon conducting Victor Symphony Orchestra (precise date unknown, c. 1920–1930). George H. Clark Radioana Collection, Archives Center, National Museum of American History, Smithsonian Institution. Used by permission.

the first recording of a live concert performance occurring in 1926 (Beardsley & Leech-Wilkinson, 2009). Throughout the first part of the electrical era, the means of playback also changed from shellac to vinyl to tape.

Finally, the digital era began to flourish in the mid-1980s with the development of computer technologies that could meet the exacting demands of audio processing. The history of music production technologies becomes aligned with the history of computer technologies, as both were fueled by the capacities of microprocessor and storage technologies. Each technological innovation brought with it a significant shift in associated practices.

Throughout the digital era (which is currently still in progress), two profound effects are notable: (1) the ability to manipulate sound significantly increases in terms of quantity, quality, resolution, and ease; and (2) music production processes become available to a much wider group of people through decreasing costs of technologies. In the early 1970s, the prohibitive costs of studio equipment meant that only "star performers" could assemble such home set-ups "to experiment and create while relatively unfettered by the constraints of time and money" imposed by commercial studios (Théberge, 1997, pp. 52–53). The trend for setting up project studios began in the mid-1980s in response to the inversely proportional pattern of technologies becoming cheaper while their functionality improved. While the technologies required to record performances are still expensive, they are within reach of more people than before. As "technologies have continued to get smaller, lighter, cheaper and more powerful" (Slater, 2016, p. 168), music recording practices have expanded across socio-demographic planes and can take in "[g]eographic locations previously unusable for sonic creativity" (Slater & Martin, 2012, p. 72). Studio set-ups vary considerably in form, location, quality, and size depending on practical factors such as budget and space as well as the purpose they need to serve. The apparatus of a studio will be assembled for very particular purposes and the entirety of the fabric of the studio environment—everything within it and acting upon it—is part of a complex relational interplay. To understand this complexity, the concepts of actors, agency, and affordance are instructive.

Performances take place within a network of relations. The most obvious manifestation of such a network is made up of the people carrying out the various specialized roles during the recording session: the human actors. Edward Kealy (1979) notes in his discussion relating to popular music production that the division of labor in recording sessions reflects three main components: "the music, the commercial system for promoting and distributing it to a mass audience, and the technology for recording and reproducing it" (p. 208). Kealy goes on to say that the "*art of recording* was not to compete for the public's aesthetic attention to *the art that was being recorded*" (p. 211; original emphases); in other words, an artful recording rendered the "little understood" (p. 207) technical roles even more transparent and even less detectable.

Kealy's study of roles in the making of a recording makes space for considering the collaborative connections across a large team of people, with the performer occupying only one, albeit prominent, position. Such a collaborative team might include: producer, engineer, assistant engineer, tape operator, mix engineer, mastering engineer, performer, composer, songwriter, arranger, publicist, agent, artist and repertoire representative, and other ancillary roles. A team like this gathers significant specialist expertise and knowledge, with each person exerting influence; they are human actors whose agency affects and shapes not only the final product but also the nature of the relations across the whole team.

Actor-network theory (ANT) embraces the agency of human actors and also points to the capacity of objects, or "nonhuman actors," to act upon a given moment: "If action is limited a priori to what 'intentional,' 'meaningful' humans do, it is hard to see how a hammer, a basket, a door closer, a cat, a rug, a mug, a list, or a tag could act [. . .]. By contrast, [. . .] *any thing* that [modifies] a state of affairs by making a difference is an actor" (Latour, 2005, p. 71; original emphases). Thinking about the studio, this claim is not controversial: consider the physical placement of musicians caused by the acoustical and mechanical capacities of the megaphone horn in early recording sessions or the transcendental claims of Gould's aesthetic discoveries that were facilitated by the microphone and magnetic tape. Differences in the act of making a recording, and the resulting musical outcome, are propagated by the agencies of nonhuman actors (styluses, microphones, instruments). As Christopher Haworth (2018) puts it in his study of microsound: "If something leaves a trace—if it makes a difference in some way—then it is an 'actor,' and it is this directive that leads to the inclusion of 'nonhuman' actors amongst those entities that carry agency and are able to produce effects" (p. 608).

In a case study of Danish dance-music producer and performer DJ Static, Mads Krogh (2018) explains how the "teeming mosaic" (p. 529) of Static's studio—"furniture, instruments, computers, turntables, records, CDs and movies, posters, magazines, a vocal booth" (p. 541)—constitutes the "material semantics of his work" (p. 544) in a complex, productive relation that attunes, aligns, and affects Static as he produces his music. The proximity of records (from which he can derive samples) and posters (that conjure the affective community that is his future audience) provide a navigational nudge, forging relations between pasts and futures made present by those objects, and reminding us that musical practices are material in nature.

Inanimate objects, then, have agency because they make a difference; they "authorize, allow, afford, encourage, permit, suggest, influence, block, render possible, forbid" (Latour, 2005, p. 72). Objects afford certain uses in a dynamic relation with the user, who recognizes the properties and potential uses of something (a chair, a cup, a brick, a microphone, a piano, a laptop) and then puts it to use. Eric Clarke (2005) points out that "although affordances depend on the properties of the object, they don't depend solely on them: affordances are the product both of objective properties and the capacities and needs of the organism that encounters them" (p. 37). Alan Williams (2012) considers the effects of a single piece of equipment that occupies pride of place in most studios—the visual display of the digital audio workstation (DAW)—in terms of its affordances in the musical and social moment of making a recording:

> Consider the enormous amount of information that is conveyed by the computer monitor. DAW waveforms can be expanded to illustrate milliseconds of sonic activity or condensed to represent a recording in its entirety. This has the obvious benefit of making the ephemeral "real," as a song appears to exist as a kind of object. (p. 1)

The computer monitor invites participation, demands attention, educates participants about technological processes and possibilities, and democratizes the process of music recording through its accessible graphical depictions of the captured audio scene. In this sense, the computer monitor affords a kind of flattened social hierarchy in which roles previously segregated by specialist knowledge become commingled.

In addition to the affordances of individual objects, the architectural setting in which recordings take place can also be considered as affording certain uses. In his article "What Studios Do," Eliot Bates (2012) proposes six key functions of a studio, the first five of which outline the territory of socio-architectural affordances:

1. They affect/effect sound during both tracking and mixing, and may become the focus of audition or the subject of critical listening;
2. They isolate studio workers from the outside world, and the world from studio work, while possessing a visual and audible difference from other work environments;
3. They constrain lines of sight and focus visual attention on key places or objects within the studio;
4. They constrain paths of audibility and precipitate the need for [. . .] technologies of audition; and
5. They cultivate new practices and shape social interactions. (pp. 2–3)

Architectural features of a studio render it unique in terms of its acoustic properties and of the experience of being in that space. The pool table, sofas, and tea and coffee facilities play into the situated experience of being in the recording studio as much as its acoustic characteristics and quality of hardware. Studios are constructed in order to focus attention on the task at hand, notably through the way that they constrain paths of audibility by controlling the flow of sound to facilitate a critical mode of listening. Social interactions are also afforded by architectural capacity. In its simplest terms, the physical dimensions of the recording space determine the kinds of ensembles that can perform there. In more complex ways, the physical layout of a recording space may constrain lines of sight between performing musicians in a way that makes the intervention of technology palpable (e.g., headphone monitoring systems); social relations are carried out *through* and *with* technologies. In sum, the studio environment cannot be thought of as a passive container of human experience, but instead exerts a traceable, shaping force upon the creative work that goes on there.

Practical Implications

For those familiar with performing in the studio, the ideas mapped out here might offer ways to interrogate the moment of recording particularly if the quotidian act of recording performances obscures its critical, conceptual dimensions. For those unfamiliar with the studio environment, and indeed those who fear it, the ways of thinking offered here about what is happening when a recording is being made are intended to help situate and differentiate recording *in relation* to the wider (perhaps more familiar) modes of music-making practices rather than as being something adjunctive; a kind of purge of anxiety through critical familiarity, or knowing better the nature of the beast. By understanding the technological and social processes at play during a recording session, the creative potential of the recording process is more likely to be fully harnessed; the presentation of sounds, regardless of musical style or mode of operation, is likely to be more compelling because all involved in the process of making a recording will be equipped with a shared vocabulary and the ability to negotiate confidently in the service of achieving the best musical results possible.

The value of such knowledge, fluency, and skill is exemplified in the following extended interview extract with pianist Clare Hammond as she describes her experiences of recording with engineer Thore Brinkmann for BIS Records:

> I really enjoy the recording process—both with the solo stuff that I do and also ensemble or concerto works. [...] I think it's a different kind of discipline, a different kind of challenge. You're listening in a different way when you listen back to a recording, and you're listening in a much more precise way. So, you have to be much more aware of yourself in the sessions. And also, it's a more collaborative thing in that not only do you have all the performers involved, but also you have to trust, and you have to have, really excellent engineers because the kind of sound they [produce] can make or break a recording. I really think that people who haven't recorded, or people who don't understand the set-up, [don't] have any conception at all about what difference the placement of a microphone can make or how important the engineer's role is. They really are of equal importance to the performers [...]. You're always slightly nervous and slightly intrigued to see what kind of sound they'll create; [...] it will always be different and then you'll always have to make different modifications to your playing to optimize the sound that's coming through on the recording, which is very different from what you can hear in the hall. And that often brings new aspects of the texture, or new aspects of the rhetoric and the way that you space the line, to light. [...] I really quite enjoy that—it's very, very different from live performance. (Personal interview with Clare Hammond, August, 2016)

Hammond draws out the differences between recording and live performance settings, along with the dynamic and productive relationships between musicians, their instruments, engineers, microphones, the recorded sound, acoustics, and emerging musical ideas relating to texture and melodic lines. Hammond describes the fine-tuned modifications that she makes in her performance in response to what she hears in the sound as captured by the technologies through the efforts of the recording engineer; she plays the piano differently and recognizes new possibilities in the composed material as a result of the sound of the highly specific poetic assemblage in which the recording is being made. Hammond's words convey the importance of understanding the inextricably entwined nature of technical, musical, and social understanding in the moment of performing for a recording.

By way of conclusion and to provide a summary of the practical implications of the discussion set out in this chapter, four proposals are offered. These are intended to be very general in nature, as the reader's positioning in terms of genre, experience, knowledge, and skill will largely determine how relevant or already familiar each one is. They are intended to have some practical applicability for those involved, or soon-to-be-involved, in recording performances.

First, recognize the similarities and differences between musicianship in the recording studio and musicianship in the live performance setting. Critical aspects of studio performance—such as preparation, technical control, and interpretative clarity—remain the same as for live performance, but the situated context of performing in the studio places different demands on the performer. Most notably, the audience is replaced by inanimate technological objects, which requires an imaginative leap in the moment of performance to connect with distant, future listeners. The performer may need to find some way of conjuring the idea of an audience if that in-person energy normally enlivens their performances. While the absence of an audience may serve to lower to physical and emotional strain of performance anxiety, the recording process may require a degree of physical stamina not normally experienced in the live domain because of the numerous takes that are likely to be captured.

Second, understand the ideological purpose that underpins the making of the recording and recognize that there may be competing ideologies at play. Gould and Drummond represent extreme positions in terms of the possible mixtures of recorded and live performance activities, but both are ideologically driven. While Hammond invokes the trust she has in Brinkmann as her engineer, it may be that in other partnerships the motivations, intentions, and ideological goals of the performer differ from those of the engineer, producer, agent, or record label. All recordings are made with a specific purpose in mind and take the form they do accordingly, but different parties involved in the process may have varying ideas about how this should take place and what the eventual finished outcome should be. Such ideologies might inform the degree to which technological interventions are permitted to be perceived (transparency and opacity), which might open up a consideration for notions clustering around authenticity, presentational realism, veracity, and the like. The ideological positioning of the recording will relate to how the recording, with its specific sonic qualities, aligns with wider conditions of the music culture, including performance locations, practices, norms, and expectations.

Third, acknowledge the agency and affordances of technology. While the efficiency of technology renders its presence and functioning less detectable and makes it appear somewhat silent and invisible, its effects are no less significant. All technologies exert a shaping force by what they afford and by what they inhibit. Each microphone, for example, carries out the same basic function, but the specifics of the design of each model affects the sonic characteristics that will be achieved (e.g., via polar patterns and frequency response curves). As a result, different microphones suit different purposes. The microphone is the ideal example of technological mediation: what passes through the microphone is inflected, colored, or *mediated* by the particular properties of the object.

Digital audio workstations now permit copious editing interventions at extremely fine scales of magnification, which allows a very high degree of control over the temporal and rhythmic flow of the recorded music. Equalization and complex pitch-correction tools help shape and morph the frequency profile of a recording at both a general level across the whole recording and also within textures, which means melodic and harmonic content can be altered, perhaps corrected, after the fact. And the application of reverb alongside spatialization in the stereo domain (or in higher-order spatial contexts such as ambisonics) means that the illusion of location and the exploitation of the significance of a sense of space can form part of the expressive force of the recorded performance. The practical implication of this point is both simple and complex: on the one hand, musicians recording in the studio might be well advised to gain a basic understanding of the technologies being used and how they contribute to and inflect the final outcome; on the other hand, the relationship between musicians and technologies is far more complex than an active-passive binary. The most compelling studio recordings may be those in which performers have attended to and understood the inflecting effects of technology, have adjusted their instrumental performance accordingly, or have sought new ways to generate and combine sounds. This kind of understanding, derived from experience, takes time.

Finally, admit the reality of the illusion that is fundamental to what a recording is. Complex issues around persona, authenticity, authority, coherence, and integrity are brought into relief by recordings. Indeed, what makes recording so powerful a medium is the sense of the performer in such close proximity to the listener. But such a culture of individualism in which a single artist can gain credit for the totality of the work undermines the necessarily complex collaborative sociality of recordings, which is further compounded by the powerful capacity of computer technologies to intervene imperceptibly in audio—in music—as data. Such an illusory construct, though, does not undermine the value of musicianship and skill; recordings, instead, resituate the locus of value from the pristine musical performance given flawlessly and seamlessly to the performance given by the whole, complex crew that constructs the compelling illusions embodied in recordings.

Key Sources

Born, G. (2011). Music and the materialization of identities. *Journal of Material Culture, 16*(4), 376–388. https://doi.org/10.1177%2F1359183511424196.

Gould, G. (1966). The prospects of recording. In T. Page (Ed.), *The Glenn Gould reader* (pp. 331–353). New York: Vintage Books.

Katz, M. (2004). *Capturing sound: How technology has changed music.* Los Angeles: University of California Press.

Théberge, P. (1997). *Any sound you can imagine: Making music/consuming technology.* Middletown, CT: Wesleyan University Press.

Williams, A. (2012). Putting it on display: The impact of visual information on control room dynamics. *Journal of the Art of Record Production, 6*, 1–8.

REFLECTIVE QUESTIONS

1. How might you perform differently in a recording studio compared to being in front of an audience for a live performance?
2. What influence does technology exert upon you as a performing musician during a recording session?
3. How do recordings contribute to and challenge your understanding of the forms of music's existence?
4. How would you characterize the relationships between the people and the technologies assembled for the creation of a recording?
5. When you listen to a recording, what does its sense of realism (or not) tell you about the priorities and ideologies of those who made it?

REFERENCES

Bates, E. (2012). What studios do. *Journal on the Art of Record Production, 7*, 1–25.

Beardsley, R., & Leech-Wilkinson, D. (2009). *A brief history of recording to ca. 1950.* Centre for the History and Analysis of Recorded Music, Royal Holloway, University of London, UK – see http://www.charm.rhul.ac.uk/history/p20_4_1.html [accessed April 30, 2020]

Bordwell, D. (2008). *Poetics of cinema.* New York: Routledge.

Born, G. (2011). Music and the materialization of identities. *Journal of Material Culture, 16*(4), 376–388. https://doi.org/10.1177/1359183511424196.

Brock-Nannestad, G. (2009). The development of recording technologies. In N. Cook, E. Clarke, D. Leech-Wilkinson, & J. Rink (Eds.), *The Cambridge companion to recorded music* (pp. 149–176). Cambridge, UK: Cambridge University Press.

Brøvig-Hanssen, R., & Danielsen, A. (2016). *Digital signatures: The impact of digitization on popular music sound.* Cambridge, MA: MIT Press.

Clarke, E. F. (2005). *Ways of listening: An ecological approach to the perception of musical meaning.* Oxford: Oxford University Press.

Dellaira, M. (1995). Some recorded thoughts on recorded objects. *Perspectives of New Music, 33*(1–2), 192–207.

Drummond, B. (2008). *17.* London: Beautiful Books.

Frith, S. (1986). Art versus technology: The strange case of popular music. *Media, Culture and Society, 8*(3), 263–279. https://doi.org/10.1177/016344386008003002.

Gould, G. (1962). Let's ban applause! In T. Page (Ed.), *The Glenn Gould reader* (pp. 245–250). New York: Vintage Books.

Gould, G. (1966). The prospects of recording. In T. Page (Ed.), *The Glenn Gould reader* (pp. 331–353). New York: Vintage Books.

Gould, G. (1974–1975). Music and technology. In T. Page (Ed.), *The Glenn Gould reader* (pp. 353–357). New York: Vintage Books.

Gould, G., & Page, T. (1981). Coda: Glenn Gould in conversation with Tim Page. In T. Page (Ed.), *The Glenn Gould reader* (pp. 451–461). New York: Vintage Books.

Greig, D. (2009). Performing for (and against) the microphone. In N. Cook, E. Clarke, D. Leech-Wilkinson, & J. Rink (Eds.), *The Cambridge companion to recorded music* (pp. 16–19). Cambridge, UK: Cambridge University Press.

Haworth, C. (2018). Protentions and retentions of Xenakis and Cage: Nonhuman actors, genre and time in microsound. *Contemporary Music Review*, 37(5-6), 606–625. https://doi.org/10.1080/07494467.2018.1577639.

Katz, M. (2004). *Capturing sound: How technology has changed music*. Los Angeles: University of California Press.

Kealy, E. R. (1979). From craft to art: The case of sound mixers and popular music. In S. Frith & A. Goodwin (Eds.), *On record: Rock, pop, and the written word* (pp. 207–220). London: Routledge.

Krogh, M. (2018). A beat is a hybrid: Mediation, ANT and music as material practice. *Contemporary Music Review*, 37(5-6), 529–553. https://doi.org/10.1080/07494467.2018.1575125.

Latour, B. (2005). *Reassembling the social: An introduction to actor-network-theory*. Oxford: Oxford University Press.

Moorefield, V. (2005). *The producer as composer: Shaping the sounds of popular music*. Cambridge, MA: MIT Press.

Page, T. (1984). Introduction. In T. Page (Ed.), *The Glenn Gould reader* (pp. xi–xvi). New York: Vintage Books.

Slater, M. (2016). Locating project studios and studio projects. *Journal of the Royal Musical Association*, 141(1), 167–202. https://doi.org/10.1080/02690403.2016.1151241.

Slater, M., & Martin, A. (2012). A conceptual foundation for understanding musico-technological creativity. *Journal of Music, Technology and Education*, 5(1), 59–76. https://doi.org/10.1386/jmte.5.1.59_1.

Stobart, H. (2006). *Music and the poetics of production in the Bolivian Andes*. Aldershot: Ashgate.

Théberge, P. (1997). *Any sound you can imagine: Making music/consuming technology*. Middletown, CT: Wesleyan University Press.

Williams, A. (2012). Putting it on display: The impact of visual information on control room dynamics. *Journal of the Art of Record Production*, 6, 1–8.

CHAPTER 22

DIVERSITY, INCLUSION,
AND ACCESS

TAWNYA D. SMITH AND KARIN S. HENDRICKS

INTRODUCTION

IT might be presumed that performance opportunities in classical music are equally accessible to anyone who chooses to participate. The reality, however, is that the field has a long and troubled history of discrimination and marginalization. Currently, representation of performers and administrators in major symphony orchestras in Europe, the UK, Australia, and United States is overwhelmingly white, with recent increases only in the proportion of Asian individuals (League of American Orchestras, 2016; Wise & Lewin, 2015). Black and minority individuals constitute less than 7 percent of the music and performing visual arts workforce in England and Wales, compared to 14 percent of the population as a whole (Warwick Commission, 2015). Similarly, commissioned works come from as little as 6 percent from black or ethnic minority composers, compared to 14 percent black and minority individuals in the UK population (BASCA, 2016).

Despite being equally represented (or even overrepresented) in music degree programs, women in the UK and Germany still tend to be underrepresented in classical music professions (Arts Council England, 2014; Scharff, 2018). The gender balance in US professional orchestras has more recently begun to represent the population at large (Goldin & Rouse, 2000; League of American Orchestras, 2016). However, overrepresentation of men to women is especially high in classical music positions with more social status, such as conductors, artistic directors, principal positions, conservatory teachers, and/or members of the most prestigious orchestras or competitions (McCormick, 2009; Scharff, 2018).

Class distinction is also a double-edged sword, with those reared in working-class families both underrepresented and underpaid in comparison to individuals from more privileged backgrounds (O'Brien et al., 2016). Pay inequity is also experienced by women and persons of color in multiple countries including the UK, Germany, and United States (Scharff, 2018).

Finally, the plight of those with varying levels of physical ability, mental health, and/ or neurodiversity is just beginning to be understood within classical performance contexts. Notably, many diversity reports by major arts organizations do not even include such categories for consideration. According to the Arts Council England (2014), "one of the challenges for arts and cultural sector organizations is to understand that the support needs of people with disabilities in their workforce can vary substantially" (p. 5). Few professional organizations have traditionally been concerned with the prevalence of situational or ongoing mental health challenges including music performance anxiety (Kenny, 2011; McGrath, Hendricks & Smith, 2017). Considering that lower-income and minority persons are statistically at higher risk for mental and physical health challenges (Khullar & Chokshi, 2018), such a lack of concern may perpetuate barriers to equal opportunity.

This chapter addresses some of the challenges and possibilities faced by a variety of individuals who aspire to perform Western classical music. We focus on the social structures that have led to discrimination and/or marginalization for individuals who identify within certain social categories (e.g., gender, race, ethnicity, class, sexual orientation, ability). However, we avoid sole reliance upon social identifiers to describe issues of diversity and inclusion for three reasons. First, human classifications are themselves socially constructed and culturally relative (Boyce-Tillman, 2018; Ramsey, 2007; Zuberi, 2001). Second, no person or social group is monolithic, and each individual's social identity is constructed by a unique formula of intersectional sub-identities, which may play out differently in different contexts (Bell, 2016). Third, it would be counterproductive and potentially hurtful to draw upon categorical distinctions that could unnecessarily essentialize or stigmatize certain people or populations.

Our aim in this chapter is to encourage reflection about various differences and potentials that exist in every individual, and to emphasize particular ways in which institutional practices within classical performance might become more inclusive for those who value it. Therefore, we address diversity, inclusion, and access through four perspectives: first by surveying historical trends, then by discussing social cognition, third by examining social constructionism, and finally by considering critical and postmodern philosophies. This four-lens approach is intended to offer multidimensional ways to envision possibilities for music learning and performance for a broader range of individuals and contexts.

HISTORICAL TRENDS

Since the eighteenth century, classical music has been viewed as an art form for the elite, associated with individuals from higher-class backgrounds and with performance opportunities generally reserved for "educated" people (Johnson, 2002). As Wang

(2016) stressed, "classical music has served as a tool of class distinction" (p. 200) and has in many cases attained social value precisely by virtue of its limited social access. Unsurprisingly, then, its long history is intertwined with a history of social restriction, oppression, and marginalization that has extended over centuries and across the world.

Imperialist theories and practices

Theories of biological race differences stemmed from European expansion and colonization as early as the fifteenth century, and were further crystallized through slavery practices in the Americas and late nineteenth-century nationalism in Europe (Ramsey, 2007). Although European classical music performance groups have not historically given place for individuals of minority races and ethnicities, colonization nevertheless led to the appropriation of various musics and styles of the colonized. Imperialistic musical practices have ranged from exotic references of other cultures' musics within European classical music repertoire (Locke, 2009), to more extreme measures whereby displaced people (including prisoners of war) and their musics were systematically collected and studied along with other elements of scientific research to support post-Darwinian narratives of white supremacy (Bohlman, 2007). Such "imperialist projects of collection and control" led to a "displacement of musical otherness" (p. 14) that put non-white Europeans and their music at odds with their white counterparts. In some cases, classical music has played a less overt role in social theories of white supremacy, but in others—such as the legendary anti-Semitism of Richard Wagner (Brown, 2007), or the entanglements of the Vienna Philharmonic with national socialism (Rathkolb, 2019)—it has helped to weave racialized and gendered narratives that Western society at large is still attempting to unravel.

The racial discourse surrounding European Romani musicians has been compared to that of African Americans: both groups have been historically and inaccurately labeled by supremacists as racially inferior to whites, yet simultaneously essentialized for having a so-called innate gift of affective musicianship, which has been celebrated in classical music more often through musical arrogation and mimicry than through inclusion (Currid, 2007). Accomplished black performers have often been met with surprise or praised for their musical "whiteness" (Lefferts, 2013)—attributions that worked to maintain the narrative of white superiority and reinforced systematic marginalization. Over the centuries, however, some musicians of color have strategically navigated the world of classical music and challenged white narratives (Hill, 2015). Black vocalists such as Roland Hayes, Marian Anderson, Simon Estes, and Jessye Norman, to name just four, have been able to circumvent the "ugly racial politics that opera could not avoid" (Thurman, 2014, p. 568) through the performance of German lieder, where they could side-step controversial casting of a black persons in "white" roles, especially in cases where black men might be in the position of being paired with a white female partner (Sandow, 1997).

Performers with Asian backgrounds have been essentialized in a different direction, such as the stereotype of having musical prowess that is allegedly technical yet robotic (Peynircioğlu, Bi, & Brent, 2018). Although some critics have claimed that a new generation of Asian performers is bringing new lifeblood to classical music (Lipsyte & Morris, 2002), Asian classical performers in the West are subject to the same kind of power inequities and objectification as are Asian inhabitants of Western-colonized countries, facing "alternating pressures of assimilation and cultural retention and struggling to create a viable self against the backdrop of hegemonic Orientalist representations" (Yang, 2007, p. 11). Such representations have often been more generous with Asian instrumentalists, leaving less welcome for Asian vocalists in opera, for instance, where "people claim they can hear races" (Chung, 2016, para. 6). The Asian-female intersectionality has been particularly essentialized as the innocent/aloof child prodigy, the sensuous/sexy young performer, and/or the mature/exotic woman stereotype—all depictions that detract attention away from the musical performance itself (Yoshihara, 2007).

Hypothetical narratives of racial superiority and associated oppressive practices have continued through the twentieth century to the present. Classical music has, in many ways, been a mirror for these social trends, as evidenced in racial discourses of the pre-Nazi era that attempted to relate composer and performer styles with an individual's national and/or ethnic identity (Brown, 2007; Lajosi, 2014). American classical music historiographies at the turn of the twentieth century followed a similar evolutionary narrative to that of their European counterparts, proclaiming the decline of society due to industry, urbanization, immigration, and increasing diversity, and alleging that classical music was a mark of culture and societal progress (Paul, 2016). Ironically, such ideas were put forward by white female music teachers and middle-class women who created music clubs in order to assert a greater role in civic life, even after centuries of their own musical discrimination (see Campbell, 2003; Gagné & McPherson, 2016; Pendle, 1991).

Hiring practices

Hiring practices for professional orchestras have become more inclusive in recent decades, particularly for females. Pre-1950 approaches typically involved the handpicking of instrumentalists by the ensemble's conductor from a relatively small pool of well-known studios, at a time where gender bias existed not only in performers' and conductors' perceptions of an "ideal" musician but also in formal policies of some major orchestras (Goldin & Rouse, 2000). In the 1970s and 1980s, however, extensive efforts began to reduce selection bias in some orchestras, including a broader dissemination of opening announcements, expansion of audition committees, and "blind" and "screen" auditions whereby the auditioning party could not be identified.

Despite improvements in hiring practices, audition procedures remain inconsistent between major orchestras (Goldin & Rouse, 2000; Green, 2007; Tsioulcas, 2018). Additionally, improved hiring practices do not address systemic issues that prevent minority and low-income individuals from attaining resources and experiences sufficient to qualify for an audition in the first place (see Chung, 2016). Furthermore, discrepancies in pay remain unequal for males and females in some countries. For example, a recent lawsuit in the United States revealed that the female principal flautist of the Boston Symphony Orchestra made only 75 percent the salary of her closest male peer, despite that she had soloed more with the orchestra than any other principal and was frequently targeted for media promotion (Tsioulcas, 2018).

Emergence of social programming

In the past five decades, Western art music has experienced an astounding wave of excitement in Latin America due to the rise of the El Sistema movement, which was initiated in Venezuela in 1975 as an educational approach to music with a mission to foster positive social change among disadvantaged and/or at-risk youth (Creech et al., 2016). Excitement for the program has spread to over 277 programs in 58 countries worldwide, primarily in disadvantaged areas. Although El Sistema has received an overwhelmingly positive global reception including numerous honors and awards, its assimilation into other countries and cultures has been criticized by some scholars who view it as "a moral project in the form of a middle-class civilizing mission" (Bull, 2016a, p. 121; see also Baker, 2018).

Another thriving classical music program with a social emphasis emerged in the latter part of the twentieth century: the Sphinx Organization, a United States–based program with an aim to increase opportunities for black and Latinx performers and composers. Developed in 1996 by violinist Aaron Dworkin, Sphinx's mission is to (a) increase black and Latinx participation in music schools; (b) promote music education in underserved communities; and (c) advance the work of composers of color (Gilroy, 2011). Despite the organization's success, black and Latinx representation in major professional orchestras remains low—a concern that, according to Dworkin, could negatively affect attendance and appreciation for classical music in a culture that is becoming increasingly ethnically diverse (Knowles, 2014).

Finally, a number of classical music ensembles have recently emerged that celebrate and promote the artistry of minority musicians, such as the Harlem Quartet (Gilroy, 2011); Imani Winds (Tsioulcas, 2005); and choirs for social justice (de Quadros, 2019). Differently abled musicians have found a musical home in such organizations as BSO Resound in the UK (Davis, 2019). Prison choirs have also brought hope and healing to incarcerated individuals—arguably some of the most marginalized and oppressed people in the world (Cohen, 2012).

SOCIAL COGNITION

The lens of social cognition provides a psychological perspective for viewing how individuals function within their social environment. Certain human behaviors have been explained by personal, social, cognitive, and environmental factors (Bandura, 1986). In the social cognitive view, people are neither driven by inner forces nor automatically shaped and controlled by external stimuli. Rather, human functioning is explained in terms of a model of triadic reciprocality in which behavior, cognitive and other personal factors, and environmental events all operate as interacting determinants of each other.

Self-efficacy belief, or task-based confidence, fits into the triadic reciprocality model as a personal factor (Bandura, 1997). Competence beliefs affect behavior by influencing a person's choice of tasks, effort, and perseverance. However, behavior reciprocally affects an individual's perception of self-efficacy, because success or failure will lead people to develop certain beliefs, attitudes, or cognitive strategies regarding similar tasks.

The role of social cognition has scarcely been considered with minority musicians in classical music performance (Hendricks, 2016). This lack of research is surprising, considering the profound impact that an awareness of the interplay between environmental and interpersonal catalysts could have on the persistence of musicians to achieve in these settings, despite myriad socially imposed constraints. Research has revealed differences in the relative influence of the sources of self-efficacy among males versus females in classical music performance (Hendricks, 2014; Hendricks, Smith, & Legutki, 2016). It is likely that differences exist among musicians who are differently abled and/or from various racial/ethnic and/or cultural backgrounds, given that such differences have been found in other settings (Usher & Pajares, 2008).

Social influences upon the sources of self-efficacy

Each of the four sources of self-efficacy (e.g., enactive mastery experience, vicarious experience, verbal/social persuasion, physiological/affective states) might hypothetically interact with the biases and systemic barriers that minority musicians face in classical music performance. Concerning *vicarious experience*, underrepresentation may limit a minority performer's exposure to positive models from similar backgrounds. The more similar the model, the more influential it will be on an individual's self-efficacy belief (Bandura, 1997). Therefore, a relative lack of positive role models may limit self-efficacy boosts for individuals who are less likely to see people like themselves in classical performance settings.

Enactive mastery experiences may likely play a role in the case of preferential treatment or bias against performers because of their race or gender—a concern that has been demonstrated through decades of research (Abeles, 2009; Davidson & Edgar, 2003; Van Weelden & McGee; 2007; Peynircioğlu et al., 2018). Race or gender biases may have an inappropriate impact on performer achievement and related future opportunities, or on task-based beliefs that lead to persistence after such setbacks.

Gender, age, (dis)ability, or neurodiversity may interact with *physiological/affective states*. For example, Disney (2018) highlighted the physical limitations faced by short and/or female drumline percussionists who wore harnesses created for eighteen-year-old males. One pianist with physical disabilities described physical limitations that were first "disabling" but became "affirmative" through creative and innovative techniques such as removing leg braces, using a mechanical foot pedal extension, playing from a wheelchair, and using alternative fingering techniques (Honisch, 2009). Deaf percussionist Evelyn Glennie, known for performing barefoot to feel acoustic vibration, is a similar example.

Verbal/social persuasion can also play a role in the self-efficacy beliefs and subsequent persistence of those deemed different from the so-called "ideal" classical musician. For instance, the social "othering" of non-white performers has been associated with a kind of "double-consciousness" within the psyche of some African Americans that "only lets him see himself through the revelation of the other world . . . of measuring one's soul by the tape of a world that looks on in amused contempt and pity (Du Bois, 1903, p. 9). Double-consciousness—spawned by living in a culture with white value systems, traditions, and norms—can play a role toward people of color coming to doubt their own place within society.

In classical music specifically, some performers of color may start to believe repeated narratives of inferiority, taking on themselves the measures, stereotypes, and expectations established by white individuals (Hildebrand, 2010; Robinson & Hendricks, 2018). This is not to suggest that all people of color feel a sense of double-consciousness, or are stymied by it. Rather, such as in the case of African American composer William Grant Still, a multiplicity of perspectives (or "universal idiom") might allow for a freedom and enhancement of musical style and creativity (DjeDje, 2011).

LGBTQ+ individuals often face their own kind of self-belief crisis when attempting to fit within social norms (Bergonzi, 2015; Hendricks & Boyce-Tillman, 2018). Although classical music has historically been a place of refuge and/or expression for gay performers and composers (Brett, Wood, & Thomas, 2006; Hendricks & Boyce-Tillman, 2018), heteronormative narratives in the music culture—and even within some classical works themselves—may create a sense of isolation and inadequacy among those who do not embody expected archetypes (Cayari, 2019; Hendricks & Boyce-Tillman, 2018).

From a cursory glance, it may be incorrectly assumed that a lack of achievement among some classical musicians could be simply ascribed to a lack of self-efficacy. However, there are many environmental catalysts that affect opportunities, perceptions, biases, and expectations for "ideal" classical musicians, some of which are not simply surmountable by a boost in self-efficacy belief. An understanding of the ways in which minority musicians face marginalization and discrimination—and the different ways in which individuals develop task-based beliefs that aid in persistence against social barriers—can, therefore, help stakeholders understand how to promote equal opportunity.

Social Constructionism

The social constructionist perspective asserts "that all knowledge, and therefore all meaningful reality [is] constructed in and out of interaction between human beings and their world, and developed and transmitted within an essentially social context" (Crotty,

2015, p. 42). Musical performance runs parallel with the performance of social identity, and both influences and is influenced by the performance of race, gender, and other social classifications (McCormick, 2009, p. 57). In other words, musical performers are not only involved in creation and re-creation of aural phenomena, but of social narratives as well.

A common perception among scholars and practitioners is that individuals who have more financial and social capital have more access to provisions that enhance a musical career. Less often considered, however, are the ways in which classical music performance and middle-class culture work reciprocally to reinforce social norms through implicit association (either through active performance or consumerism); shared values of long-term investment, hard work, and accumulation; norms of restraint and control; respect for authority; and gendered narratives (Bull, 2016a, 2016b, 2019).

Classical music is not only inherently connected to the bourgeoisie, but also to whiteness. Performances of non-white musicians have been essentialized and/or fanaticized in ways that maintain the white performer as normative and the non-white as "other" (Brown, 2007; Leppänen, 2015). Such narratives also apply when classical music is considered as an educational, civilizing, or therapeutic tool to somehow "lift up" or "save" non-whites or those otherwise considered less fortunate (Bull, 2016a; Chung, 2016). Hurtful and inaccurate narratives of superiority/inferiority persist as individuals continue to normalize or trivialize structural impediments that exist for differently abled, classed, gendered, or raced musicians—through a practice of silence or resignation that even marginalized people may continue to reinforce (Scharff, 2018).

Music performance may be a particularly insightful means for understanding gender performance and negotiation because music is also culturally constructed (Moisala, 1999). Music "allows, or may even require, different gender roles than do other aspects of culture" (para. 7) and may therefore offer a fresh perspective to study gender negotiation. Delineated meanings (those that convey contextual or symbolic material) inform how classical music is performed and received by an audience—and that audience is most often presumed to be male (Green, 1997). Delineated meanings therefore influence how music is received depending upon the gender of the performer, and whether the performer is a vocalist or instrumentalist. For example, female vocalists tend to invoke "affirmative gesture[s] that concord with patriarchal definitions of femininity" (Green, 1997, p. 132), as do female instrumentalists when performing as soloists on "feminine" instruments such as the harp or piano (which require demure postures). Female instrumentalists invoke negative delineations when performing in the more mechanistic and "masculine" realm of the ensemble or when performing larger instruments.

Culture in competition

One celebrated pinnacle of achievement in the classical music profession is the international solo competition, which is commonly viewed as a springboard for an individual's virtuoso career. In an analysis of the Cliburn International Piano Competition,

McCormick (2009) made a case for how this competition—although used as an identifier for those allegedly "'worthy of support' because it is believed to be fair and democratic" (p. 11)—is in itself a social performance in which pianists, adjudicators, and audience members take place in an interactive musical experience to make meaning of their social circumstances.

The roles of musical competitors and other stakeholders are considered within two different narrative levels: (a) the mundane narrative of musical champions, where performers are viewed as contenders and compared with athletes vying against one another for a top spot; and (b) the mythical narrative of artist-interpreter, where the performer is assumed to transcend beyond the score to communicate cultural and eternal truths through music. The latter narrative encapsulates the story of musical genius, with an associated expectation to sacrifice one's life to perfect the art and further bless those who will be enriched by the virtuoso's career.

Music competitions are both games and rituals. They are games in that there is a clear distinction of superior and inferior at the conclusion (McCormick, 2009). However, competitions are also "ritual-like" (p. 25) in the way that they create a union between performers and audience, and solidify cultural norms and understandings through shared meaning-making and symbolic interpretation. This ritual, in turn, reinforces the masculine notions of combat (mundane narrative) as well as heroism (mythical narrative)—both of which may be problematic for female performers, who have been traditionally expected in Western societies to perform roles of softness and subjugation.

Female classical musicians face a further conundrum in that successful musical artistry involves the art of self-promotion, something that women have been socialized against (Scharff, 2018). Self-promotion is a necessity in freelance or "precarious" music endeavors, which are more often distributed among those with less prestigious full-time musical positions, where a gender and race/ethnicity gap already exists. Because a knack for self-promotion aligns with beliefs of entitlement prevalent among the middle and upper class, it can further enhance the advantages for those who are more affluent.

Blatant racism and sexism can occur in media coverage of competitions, with norms of masculinity and/or whiteness reinforced through reviews that objectify or sexualize non-white and/or female performers, thereby shifting the attention from technical achievements (Leppänen, 2015; Yoshihara, 2007). Similarly, discriminatory or simplistic narratives that include physique as a part of how one "makes the cut" in a competitive musical arena do not account for the attitudinal barriers and/or insufficient educational and assistive support that places individuals with disabilities at an unfair disadvantage (Darrow, 2015).

CRITICAL AND POSTMODERN PHILOSOPHIES

Critical/feminist and postmodern/post-structuralist/queer philosophies challenge many of the assumptions and ideologies that were prevalent during the construction of the classical canon, so these perspectives work to disrupt and deconstruct the social basis upon which this music was created. We would be remiss not to include these perspectives, considering that they reflect the current body of philosophical thought that has emerged in the Western world in which classical music continues to operate.

These philosophical perspectives are largely applied by musicologists and music educators to challenge existing paradigms surrounding musical engagement. There are also some composers creating from these perspectives, and performers who apply these perspectives in the performance of more recent compositions as well as the reconceptualization of the classical canon. Space allows only a cursory treatment of these philosophies, and our introductory descriptions do not reflect the complexity, depth, or breadth of this evolving literature. However, our aim is to elucidate contradictions and conflicts that arise when these ideas confront cultural material from the past, in order to situate the essence of present challenges.

Feminism

Feminism is often caricatured by its critics through derogatory and essentialist notions of feminist ideas. Like many of the perspectives in this section, within each feminist tradition there are various strands of thought that—albeit sometimes similar in aim— are often divergent and even contradictory (Tong, 1995). One commonality, however, is the notion that the world is patriarchal and that masculinist culture has been passed from our predecessors. Although feminists tend to reject classification, within feminism there are liberal, Marxist, radical, psychoanalytic, existential, and postmodern strands that each approach the project of deconstructing dualisms such as "reason/emotion, beautiful/ugly, self/other" (Crotty, 2015, p. 168).

Feminist critique of classical music has challenged the classist undertones we have mentioned, as well as colonial ideologies that assert classical music's superiority to other musics. For example, Boyce-Tillman (2012) argued that the enmeshed history of classical music and that of Christianity has led to shared imperial values and patriarchal hierarchies. Similarly, McClary (2002) argued that classical music is "bound up with issues of gender construction and the channeling of desire" (p. 54), and noted that a patriarchal tendency to deny the body has influenced the ways that music is created, performed, promoted, and received.

Whereas "second wave" feminists reject objectification of the female body, "third wave" feminists might contradict these notions by dawning sexy attire to "sell" a musical product (Citron, 2004)—a reflection upon postmodern capitalist views of classical music discussed later in this chapter. On the other hand, feminists might view musical scores as performance scripts to meet audience members' expectations of gender metaphors, which mirror gender roles performed in society (Cusick, 1994)— a point similar to Green's (1997) delineated meanings concept addressed previously. No matter (or perhaps because of) the differences in individual feminist perspectives, feminist critiques work to deconstruct or subvert structures and practices that disadvantage women because they impose or assume masculine values.

Critical inquiry

A broad movement of thought that includes feminist philosophy, critical inquiry is typically attributed to Marx, Durkheim, and others of the Frankfurt School including Horkheimer who first used the term *critical theory* (Crotty, 2015). Composer and musicologist Theodor Adorno critiqued the domination ideas that served "to perpetuate the system" (Crotty, 2015, pp. 136–137). Similarly, Habermas was concerned with the limitations of language and advocated for speech "free of systematic distortion," which he posited would allow for "unimpaired self-presentation" rather than "one-sided norms" (pp. 143–144). Critical inquiry, then, stands to deconstruct prevalent ideas and the language in which they are conveyed in order to free individuals and societies from blind adherence to oppressive thought that has been passed from generation to generation.

Also concerned with emancipation, Brazilian Paulo Freire (1996) advocated for the conscientization of learners, to reflect and act on oppressive powers and structures. Critical approaches have informed recent critiques of taken-for-granted structures in classical performance, such as Hess's (2018) critique of educators who take schoolchildren to classical concerts without contextualizing classical music and its performance norms in order to situate that genre as only one of many possibilities for study.

Postmodernism and post-structuralism

Postmodernism connotes the literary and cultural movements that stand in opposition to those in the modern era (Milner, 1991). Lyotard, a self-professed postmodernist, posited that the grand narratives of modernity previously used to legitimize practice were now being fractured into more local and discrepant ones (Crotty, 2015). In postmodernism, ideas of absolutism and unified human reason are replaced with a plurality of reasons and bases for truth claims. Using a postmodern perspective, Peters and Lankshear (1996) explained that labels such as "high art" and "culture" are seen as a "hostile" force when claiming intellectual superiority over other art forms (p. 23). On the other hand, counternarratives in music discourse challenge hegemonic or "majoritarian" narratives that perpetuate discrimination and marginalization of "other" people and musics (Hendricks, in press).

Post-structuralism and *postmodernism* are sometimes conflated terms; some authors argue they are distinct, while others argue they overlap or are an outgrowth of the other (Crotty, 2015). Post-structuralism is associated with the philosophies of French philosophers such as Foucault, Derrida, and Lacan, who were opposed to structuralist ideas including humanism, existentialism, and phenomenology (Slattery, 2013). Post-structuralists resist categorizations, notions of "progress," and historical continuity, giving way instead to openness, spontaneity, and change (Crotty, 2015). Higgins (2012) used Derrida's conception of *hospitality* as a model for community music making, demonstrating possibilities for openness and exchange that stand in sharp contrast to the often exclusive and competitive nature of classical music culture. The works of Derrida also inspired Boyce-Tillman (2012) to critique classical music's "inequitable distribution of power" that can result in the "disempowerment of many groups . . . by means of an encroaching mono-culture" (p. 40). Her argument challenges the ways in which powerful classical music stakeholders might "other" or disenfranchise musicians and musical cultures that they consider less notable in comparison.

Queer theory

Queer theory should be distinguished from the study of LGBTQ+ individuals, which could occur within any other stance presented in this chapter. Rather, it represents a movement that challenges and/or disrupts taken-for-granted norms, resists positivistic notions or frameworks, and offers radical liberation (Hendricks & Boyce-Tillman, 2018). Queer perspectives in music performance might involve the disruption of normative aspects of performance (music and/or social), and re-envisioning the past, present, and/or future (see Gould, 2016). One example of post-structural feminism and queer theory in music performance is the work of Morillas (2014), who recontextualized vocal performance to disrupt traditional, heteronormative entertainment boundaries by interspersing the performance of traditional classical vocal pieces with feminist poetry and prose, euphonium music, a narrator describing biological research, and a plot twist involving a switch of assumed love partners.

It is important to emphasize that critical/postmodern scholars are less apt to challenge classical music itself, but rather the social structures surrounding it—a challenge that classical performers may or may not find problematic. For example, Rihtaršič (2017) defined the postmodern virtuoso as one who must balance traditional classical traditions (e.g., elitist, intellectual, separated from the audience) with those of a postmodern world (e.g., branding oneself as an entertainer and having to connect with the audience to compete with other contemporary art forms). Similarly, Wang (2016) reflected upon postmodern and post-structuralist thought to suggest that converting classical music to a "culture in common" would further require a shift in the meaning and value of this genre: "Not only would the lines of education be transformed, but the institution and meaning of classical music would become an 'ordinary' aspect of culture" (p. 197). Such reworking of the social structures around classical music would necessarily de-center the tradition and place it as equal among other musical traditions, with implications for where, to whom, and by whom classical music is performed.

PRACTICAL IMPLICATIONS

It is not only important to offer strategies for diversity, inclusion, and access, but to articulate why they are necessary. There are at least four reasons why discussions regarding inequality matter in the context of cultural and creative industries (Scharff, 2018). First, equality is a social concern that determines how our society views itself, particularly given the visibility of the arts in culture and their perpetuation of cultural distinctions. Second, progress is not a given from year to year (and we would add that "progress" itself is a subjective term). Specifically, so-called societal progress does not coincide with progress in equal opportunity. Therefore, it is important to name and document trends of equality, rather than assuming they exist.

Third, diversity in membership and administration increases "breadth and depth of creative perspectives, audiences, and consumers" (Warwick Commission, 2015, p. 21, as cited in Scharff, 2018, p. 15). As the world's population becomes more globalized and racially and ethnically integrated, Western classical performers face a dilemma: separate off from the rest of society, or integrate with the world all around us. In our view, it makes sense for Western art music to reflect the diversity in perspective and cultural background that reflects our twenty-first-century world. Otherwise, as the population of potential concertgoers becomes more diverse, the art risks becoming obsolete. Finally, understandings about diversity in the arts can help to enhance broader understandings about diversity in society (Scharff, 2018).

Considering Moisala's (1999) argument that musical performance can be a unique way to understand social construction in society, the study of music performance might similarly offer a space for better understanding negotiated meanings with a variety of individuals and in a variety of settings. The remaining discussion is aimed at offering implications for practice that are gleaned from the ideas we have presented thus far.

Start with education

The importance of education cannot be underestimated in helping to understand, appreciate, and promote the growth and achievement of all individuals in musical performance. However, formal learning structures are insufficient to promote diversity, inclusion, and access when they continue to promote oppressive norms (Hendricks, 2018). Curricula and pedagogical practices need to be reconsidered, including the "hidden curriculum" that extends to lessons students learn through social and cultural interactions (Slattery, 2013). Such curricular reconsiderations must, then, expand beyond passive, unquestioned transmission of musical culture and practices to include an active critique of oppressive forces and a creative reimagining of the art form.

Considering the ways that bias, stereotype, and "othering" narratives exist in music performance understructures (Disney, 2018), we might turn to dialogue and experience-based inquiry in formal schooling and beyond to learn about ourselves and others and to challenge preconceived assumptions (O'Neill, 2011). Furthermore, it is important to challenge systemic barriers that prevent minority individuals from having sufficient access to education, and/or opportunity to become teachers and educational leaders themselves (see Elpus, 2015). The importance of supporting the advancement of minority music educators cannot be overstated, not only as a means of broadening perspectives but in providing role models for students who may not otherwise relate to white and/or male instructors.

Promoting diversity in and through education also goes beyond more diverse programming, a potentially good start (and one for which a large array of resources is now available), but one that must be done with care to avoid stigmatizing, essentializing, and/ or misrepresenting. Social change involves education and performance that actively challenges oppressive structures (Hess, 2019). Bergonzi (2015) offered suggestions for how music educators might make "classrooms and programs . . . not only spaces of safety, but also spaces where Otherness is embraced, and where normalcy is not assumed, but contested" (p. 225). Recommendations for supporting LGBTQ+ performers specifically include detaching gender expression from categories of vocal range or choral part, developing travel policies that are gender-sexual diverse, and allowing for gender-fluid concert dress policies. Educators might further consider ways in which they notice curricula that perpetuate narratives of "otherness," educate *about* the other, and teach critical thinking to challenge societal othering.

Welcome different narratives

Counternarratives can challenge majoritarian music narratives that reinforce societal norms and marginalize those who do not embody a so-called "ideal" classical musician archetype (Hendricks, in press). Each black/Latinx orchestral musician, each female conductor, each differently abled pianist, each Asian opera singer (and so forth) helps to challenge majoritarian narratives. When met with an open rather than stereotypical response, each counternarrative can create new visions of possibility for all musicians.

Simplistic notions of being "innately" born with a specific talent can be discriminatory and create false narratives about the ways in which musical competencies are attained. New narratives might also challenge the simplistic myth of meritocracy, and consider the systemic barriers that disallow some individuals from achievement. We might similarly challenge "hero" or "genius" narratives that promote dualistic notions of superiority/inferiority or helper/helpless, and that do not account for the various ways that individuals inspire and strengthen one another (Hendricks, 2021).

New narratives might simply begin by directly calling out old ones, such as in this recent advertisement: "Rhiannon Giddens curates a dynamic concert to rediscover the great Black composers who have been hiding in plain sight" (Boston Pops, 2019). New narratives in music performance can also unfold as performers use music as a vehicle for unique identity expression (Drake, 2018; Krell, 2014; Manovski, 2012). Finally, considering that "deficit" perspectives focus attention on weakness and limitation, empowerment can come by changing to a perspective of unique strengths, flexibility, and creativity. As Honisch (2009) asserted about narratives of (dis)ability:

> To view mainstream Western art traditions as predominantly oppressive is simplistic and indeed "disabling." On the contrary, music performance offers exciting potential for promoting the inclusion of disability into the culture of Western art music. . . . These fluid narratives are about the constant probing of real and perceived limitations, as well as the accommodation of differing views of physical impairment and even impairment itself. (para. 27–28)

The importance of a "strengths" over "deficits" perspective is also emphasized by Hammel and Hourigan (2011), who advocate for a "label-free approach" to (dis)ability that views every individual as a unique set of strengths and weaknesses. Taking such a perspective would also apply in situations such as where minorities might be unnecessarily pitied and not challenged to the same extent as their majoritarian counterparts.

Name, reflect, act

There is much to be done among classical music performance stakeholders to diversify representation of participants, from education of the youngest members of societies, to decisions and policies put forward by boards of major professional performing organizations to attract more minority musicians. However, merely opening the gates of inclusion will not suffice to substantially diversify the field. Instead, it will require that individuals across the social spectrum be given equal opportunities for education, access, and provisions so that the particular language and idioms associated with this art are accessible as well (Wang, 2016).

Drawing from Wink's (2011) critical pedagogy approach, we offer a simple formula for educational and structural change, as follows: (a) name experiences; (b) reflect critically upon them; and (c) act accordingly. This formula can be used at every level, from individual music studios and classrooms to organizational boardrooms and political arenas where structural barriers, majoritarian narratives, and other systemic constraints can be named, reflected upon, and changed. Particular attention might be paid to issues of intersectionality (Bell, 2016) to focus on the complex ways that such narratives might influence individuals differently.

According to Aaron Dworkin of the Sphinx Organization, diversifying the classical music field will take active, intentional steps such as (a) recognizing and naming problems as they arise; (b) creating specific diversity initiatives, similar to what corporate and academic institutions have done; (c) budgeting for diversity outreach; (d) hiring black and Latinx administrative staff; (e) challenging persistent negative attitudes and stereotypes; (f) actively recruiting people of color for auditions; and (g) simply making an effort to include diversity in programming, scholarships, and competitions (Knowles, 2014).

Accessibility and interest in classical music participation is attained through societal systems that promote equal opportunity for all its members through educational provisions, occupational levels, income equality, and appropriate physical and linguistic supports—but first by naming and reflecting upon what those things might mean for different people. For example, DiMaggio and Ostrower (1992) found that whites who did not participate in artistic pursuits (e.g., performance, concert attendance) cited lack of time and availability, whereas non-participating black and Latinx individuals expressed interest in participating but cited cost and/or lack of access (e.g., inadequate transportation, child care, language barriers).

It is clear from recent scholarship and institutional reports that there is an interest in most classical music organizations to more fully encourage and embrace diversity of musicians as well as audiences. As expressed by the League of American Orchestras:

> The work of orchestras is shifting and intensifying, as orchestras recognize and respond to sweeping cultural, social, political, economic, technological, and demographic change within the communities they serve. For all cultural institutions, knowledge and information are becoming critical tools in the work of navigating a course through this new landscape. In particular, there is a recognized value in learning from the past in order to inform action for the future. (League of American Orchestras, 2016, p. 1)

Learning from the past requires not only studying our own history, but also re-contextualizing classical music narratives with awakened perspectives, with courage to recognize and name taken-for-granted cultural norms that permeate music performance. Perhaps, as Ramsey (2007) articulated, "the next step in our re-contextualisation of the past will involve revealing some of our own secrets and lies and how they have shaped the music and work to which we are undeniably devoted" (p. 36).

KEY SOURCES

Bandura, A. (1997). *Self-efficacy: The exercise of control*. New York: W. H. Freeman.

Brown, J. (2007). (Ed.). *Western music and race*. Cambridge, UK: Cambridge University Press.

Bull, A. (2019). *Class, control, and classical music*. New York: Oxford University Press.

Hendricks, K. S., & Boyce-Tillman, J. (Eds.). (2018). *Queering freedom: Music, identity, and spirituality*. Oxford: Peter Lang.

Scharff, C. (2018). *Gender, subjectivity, and cultural work*. London: Routledge.

Reflective Questions

1. What is a prevalent concern of diversity or inclusion in your own music community? How might you act to create a more equitable situation?
2. Which individuals in your musical community are often "unseen" or otherwise marginalized? What structures and practices may contribute to this?
3. How does your institution set goals and track progress for diversity and inclusion? What might they do better?
4. What social narratives have you taken for granted that might reinforce hurtful stereotypes or biases? How might these narratives be countered?
5. Considering that individuals may interpret majoritarian narratives through the intersections of their unique identities, in what ways might attempts to create new narratives from single identities be harmful?

Acknowledgments

We acknowledge Jessandra Kono, Amanda Tumbleson, Gary McPherson, Brita Heimarck, and Harvey Young for their support and insight.

References

Abeles, H. (2009). Are musical instrument gender associations changing? *Journal of Research in Music Education, 57*(2), 127–139. https://doi.org/10.1177/0022429409335878.

Arts Council England. (2014). *Equality and diversity within the arts and cultural sector in England*. Arts Council England – see https://www.artscouncil.org.uk/sites/default/files/download-file/Equality_and_diversity_within_the_arts_and_cultural_sector_in_England.

Baker, G. (2018). El Sistema, "The Venezuelan musical miracle": The construction of a global myth. *Latin American Music Review, 39*(2), 160–193. https://doi.org/10.7560/LAMR39202.

Bandura, A. (1986). *Social foundations of thought and action: A social cognitive theory*. Englewood Cliffs, NJ: Prentice Hall.

Bandura, A. (1997). *Self-efficacy: The exercise of control*. New York: W. H. Freeman.

BASCA. (2016). *Equality and diversity in new music commissioning*. London: British Academy of Songwriters, Composers, & Authors.

Bell, L. A. (2016). Theoretical foundations. In M. Adams & L. A. Bell (Eds.), *Teaching for diversity and social justice* (3rd ed., pp. 3–26). New York: Routledge.

Bergonzi, L. S. (2015). Gender and sexual diversity challenges (for socially just) music education. In C. Benedict, P. Schmidt, G. Spruce, & P. Woodford (Eds.), *The Oxford handbook of social justice and music education* (pp. 221–237). New York: Oxford University Press.

Bohlman, P. V. (2007). Erasure: Displacing and misplacing race in twentieth-century music historiography. In J. Brown (Ed.), *Western music and race* (pp. 3–23). Cambridge, UK: Cambridge University Press.

Boston Pops. (2019). Rhiannon Giddens and friends rediscover the incredible black composer – see https://www.bso.org/brands/pops/features/2019-spring-pops/rhiannon-giddens-and-friends-rediscover-the-incredible-black-composer.aspx.

Boyce-Tillman, J. (2012). Music and the dignity of difference. *Philosophy of Music Education Review*, 20(1), 25–44.

Boyce-Tillman, J. (2018). The myths we live by. In K. S. Hendricks & J. Boyce-Tillman (Eds.), *Queering freedom: Music, identity, and spirituality* (pp. 3–34). Oxford: Peter Lang.

Brett, P., Wood, E., & Thomas, G. C. (Eds.). (2006). *Queering the pitch: The new gay and lesbian musicology*. New York: Routledge.

Brown, J. (2007). (Ed.). *Western music and race*. Cambridge, UK: Cambridge University Press.

Bull, A. (2016a). El Sistema as a bourgeois social project: Class, gender, and Victorian values. *Action, Criticism and Theory for Music Education*, 15(1): 120–153.

Bull, A. (2016b). Gendering the middle classes: The construction of conductors' authority in youth classical music groups. *Sociological Review*, 64(4): 855–871. https://doi.org/10.1111%2F1467-954X.12426.

Bull, A. (2019). *Class, control, and classical music*. New York: Oxford University Press.

Campbell, G. J. (2003). Classical music and the politics of gender in America, 1900–1925. *American Music*, 21(4), 446–474.

Cayari, C. (2019). Musical theater as performative autoethnography: A critique of LGBTQIA+ representation in school curricula. *International Journal of Education and the Arts*, 20(10). https://doi.org/10.26209/ijea20n10/.

Chung, J. (2016, March 15). Race and classical music. *Uchicago magazine* – see https://mag.uchicago.edu/law-policy-society/race-and-classical-music.

Citron, M. J. (2004) Feminist waves and classical music: Pedagogy, performance, research, women and music. *A Journal of Gender and Culture*, 8, 47–60. https://doi.org/10.1353/wam.2004.0004.

Cohen, M. (2012). Safe havens: The formation and practice of prison choirs in the US. In L. Cheliotis (Ed.), *The arts of imprisonment: Control, resistance, and empowerment* (pp. 1–26). Aldershot, UK: Ashgate.

Crotty, M. (2015). *The foundations of social research*. London: Sage.

Creech, A., González-Moreno, P., Lorenzino, L., Waitman, G., Sandoval, E., & Fairbanks, S. (2016). El Sistema and Sistema-inspired programmes: A literature review of research, evaluation, and critical debates (2nd Ed.). San Diego, CA: Sistema Global.

Currid, B. (2007). "Gypsy violins" and "hot rhythms": Race, popular music, and governmentality. In J. Brown (Ed.), *Western music and race* (pp. 37–48). Cambridge, UK: Cambridge University Press.

Cusick, S. G. (1994). Feminist theory, music theory, and the mind/body problem. *Perspectives of New Music*, 32(1), 8–27. https://doi.org.10.2307/833149.

Darrow, A. A. (2015). Ableism and social justice. In C. Benedict, P. Schmidt, G. Spruce, & P. Woodford (Eds.), *The Oxford handbook of social justice and music education* (pp. 204–220). New York: Oxford University Press.

Davidson, J. W., & Edgar, R. (2003). Gender and race bias in the judgement of Western art music performance. *Music Education Research*, 5(2), 169–181. https://doi.org/10.1080/1461380032000085540.

Davis, E. (2019, March 26). *Meet BSO Resound, the ensemble of disabled musicians changing the classical music world*. Classic FM Discover Music – see https://www.classicfm.com/discover-music/bso-resound-disabled-led-ensemble/.

de Quadros, A. (2019). *Choral music in global perspective*. London: Routledge.

DiMaggio, P., & Ostrower, F. (1992). *Race, ethnicity, and participation in the arts: Patterns of participation by Hispanics, whites, and African-Americans in selected activities from the 1982 and 1985 surveys of public participation in the arts* (No. 25). Santa Ana, CA: Seven Locks Press.

Disney, K. D. (2018). *Understructures, gender roles, and performativity in a high school percussion section*. Doctoral dissertation, Boston University. https://hdl.handle.net/2144/32697.

DjeDje, J. C. (2011). Context and creativity: William Grant Still in Los Angeles. *Black Music Research Journal*, *31*(1), 1–27.

Drake, R. M. (2018). *Musical performance and trans identity: Narratives of selfhood, embodied identities, and musicking*. Doctoral dissertation, University of California, Santa Barbara.

Du Bois, W. E. B. (1903). *The souls of black folk*. Chicago: A. C. McClurg and Co.

Elpus, K. (2015). Music teacher licensure candidates in the United States: A demographic profile and analysis of licensure examination scores. *Journal of Research in Music Education*, *63*(3), 314–335. https://doi.org/10.1177%2F0022429415602470.

Freire, P. (1996). *Pedagogy of the oppressed*. (Rev. ed.). London: Penguin.

Gagné, F., & McPherson, G. E. (2016). *Analyzing musical prodigiousness using Gagné's Integrative Model of Talent Development*. In G. E. McPherson (Ed.), *Music prodigies: Interpretations from psychology, education, musicology and ethnomusicology* (pp. 3–114). Oxford: Oxford University Press.

Gilroy, M. (2011). Sphinx organization promotes diversity in classical music. *The Hispanic Outlook in Higher Education*, *21*(20), 10–12.

Goldin, C., & Rouse, C. (2000). Orchestrating impartiality: The impact of "blind" auditions on female musicians. *American Economic Review*, *90*(4), 715–741. https://doi.org/10.1257/aer.90.4.715.

Gould, E. (2016). Ecstatic abundance: Queer temporalities in LGBTQ studies and music education. *Bulletin of the Council for Research in Music Education*, *207–208*, 123–138.

Green, L. (1997). *Music, gender, education*. Cambridge, UK: Cambridge University Press.

Hammel, A. M., & Hourigan, R. M. (2011). *Teaching music to students with special needs: A label-free approach*. New York: Oxford University Press.

Hendricks, K. S. (2014). Changes in self-efficacy beliefs over time: Contextual influences of gender, rank-based placement, and social support in a competitive orchestra environment. *Psychology of Music*, *42*, 347–365. https://doi.org/10.1177/0305735612471238.

Hendricks, K. S. (2016). The sources of self-efficacy: Educational research and implications for music. *Update: Applications of Research in Music Education*, *35*(1), 32–38. https://doi.org/10.1177/8755123315576535.

Hendricks, K. S. (2018). *Compassionate music teaching: A framework for motivation and engagement in the 21st century*. Lanham, MD: Rowman and Littlefield.

Hendricks, K. S. (2021). Authentic connection in music education. In K. S. Hendricks & J. Boyce-Tillman (Eds), *Authentic connection: Music, spirituality, and wellbeing* (pp. 237–253). Peter Lang.

Hendricks, K. S. (in press). Counternarratives: Troubling majoritarian certainty. *Action, Criticism, and Theory for Music Education*, in press.

Hendricks, K. S., & Boyce-Tillman, J. (Eds.). (2018). *Queering freedom: Music, identity, and spirituality*. Oxford: Peter Lang.

Hendricks, K. S., Smith, T. D., & Legutki, A. R. (2016). Competitive comparison in music: Influences upon self-efficacy belief by gender. *Gender and Education*, *28*(7), 918–934. https://doi.org/10.1080/09540253.2015.1107032.

Hess, J. (2018). Interrupting the symphony: Unpacking the importance placed on classical concert experiences. *Music Education Research*, 20(1) 11–21. https://doi.org/10.1080/146138.2016.1202224.

Hess, J. (2019). *Music education for social change*. New York: Routledge.

Higgins, L. (2012). *Community music: In theory and in practice*. New York: Oxford University Press.

Hildebrand, J. (2010). "Two souls, two thoughts, two unreconciled strivings": The sound of double consciousness in Roland Hayes's early career. *Black Music Research Journal*, 30(2), 273–302.

Hill, A. K. (2015). *Clarence Cameron White: Classical violin performance and pedagogy in the African American community*. Doctoral dissertation, West Virginia University.

Honisch, S. S. (2009). "Re-narrating disability" through musical performance. *Music Theory Online*, 15(3 and 4). http://www.mtosmt.org/issues/mto.09.15.3/mto.09.15.3.honisch.html.

Johnson, J. (2002). *Who needs classical music? Culture choice and musical value*. New York: Oxford University Press.

Kenny, D. T. (2011). *The psychology of music performance anxiety*. Oxford: Oxford University Press.

Khullar, D., & D. A. Chokshi (2018, October 4). Health, income, and poverty: Where we are and what could help. Health Affairs Health Policy Brief – see https://www.healthaffairs.org/do/10.1377/hpb20180817.901935/full/.

Knowles, D. (2014). Classical music's color bind. *Strings*, 28(7), 34–37.

Krell, E. D. (2014). *Singing strange: Transvocality in North American music performance*. Doctoral dissertation, Northwestern University.

Lajosi, K. (2014). National stereotypes and music. *Nations and Nationalism*, 20(4), 628–645. https://doi.org/10.1111/nana.12086.

League of American Orchestras. (2016). *Racial/ethnic and gender diversity in the orchestra field: A report by the League of American Orchestras with research and data analysis by James Doeser, Ph.D.* League of American Orchestras – see http://www.ppv.issuelab.org/resources/25840/25840.pdf [accessed May 27, 2019]

Lefferts, P. M. (2013). U.S. Army black regimental bands and the appointments of their first black bandmasters. *Black Music Research Journal*, 33(2), 151–175.

Leppänen, T. (2015). The West and the rest of classical music: Asian musicians in the Finnish media coverage of the 1995 Jean Sibelius Violin Competition. *European Journal of Cultural Studies*, 18(1), 19–34. https://doi.org/10.1177/1367549414557804.

Locke, R. P. (2009). *Musical exoticism: Images and reflections*. Cambridge, UK: Cambridge University Press.

Lipsyte, R., & Morris, L. B. (2002, October 22). *Hated music, but hear him now; from cultural revolution chaos to Metropolitan fame*. New York Times – see https://www.nytimes.com/2002/10/22/arts/hated-music-but-hear-him-now-from-cultural-revolution-chaos-to-metropolitan-fame.html.

Manovski, M. P. (2012). *Finding my voice: [Re] Living, [re] learning, and [re] searching becoming a singer in a culture of marginalization*. Doctoral dissertation, Oakland University.

McClary, S. (2002). *Feminine endings: Music, gender, and sexuality*. Minneapolis: University of Minnesota Press.

McCormick, L. (2009). Higher, faster, louder: Representations of the international music competition. *Cultural Sociology*, 3(1), 5–30. https://doi.org/10.1177%2F1749975508100669.

McGrath, C., Hendricks, K. S., & Smith, T. D. (2017). *Performance anxiety strategies.* Lanham, MD: Rowman & Littlefield.

Milner, A. (1991). *Contemporary cultural theory: An introduction.* North Sydney: Allen & Unwin.

Moisala, P. (1999). Musical gender in performance. *Women & Music: A Journal of Gender and Culture, 3,* 1ff.

Morillas, M. V. (2014). *Recontextualizing music for social change.* Doctoral dissertation, Arizona State University.

O'Brien, D., Laurison, D., Miles, A., & Friedman, S. (2016). Are the creative industries meritocratic? An analysis of the 2014 British labour force survey. *Cultural Trends, 25*(2), 116–131. https://doi.org/10.1080/09548963.2016.1170943.

O'Neill, S. (2011). Learning in and through music performance: Understanding cultural diversity via inquiry and dialogue. In M. S. Barrett (Ed.), *A cultural psychology of music education* (pp. 179–200). New York: Oxford University Press.

Paul, D. C. (2016). Consensus and crisis in American classical music historiography from 1890 to 1950. *Journal of Musicology, 33*(2), 200–231. https://doi.org/10.1525/jm.2016.33.2.200.

Pendle, K. (1991). *Women and music: A history.* Bloomington: Indiana University Press.

Peters, M., & Lankshear, C. (1996). Postmodern counternarratives. In H. Giroux, C. Lankshear, P. McLaren, & M. Peters (Eds.), *Counternarratives: Cultural studies and critical pedagogies in postmodern spaces* (pp. 1–39). New York: Routledge.

Peynircioğlu, Z. F., Bi, W., & Brent, W. (2018). The "Asian bias" illusion in musical performance: Influence of visual information. *American Journal of Psychology, 131*(3), 295–305.

Ramsey, G. P., Jr. (2007). Secrets, lies and transcriptions: Revisions on race, black music and culture. In J. Brown (Ed.), *Western music and race* (pp. 24–36). Cambridge, UK: Cambridge University Press.

Rathkolb, O. (2019). Honours and awards (Honorary members, rings of honour, the Nicolai Medal and the "Yellow" List) – see http://wphdata.blob.core.windows.net/documents/Documents/pdf/NS/ns_rath_ehrungen_en_v03.pdf.

Rihtaršič, U. (2017). Between body and mind. Classical music performer in the postmodern era. *Muzikoloski Zbornik, 53*(1), 143–164.

Robinson, D., & Hendricks, K. S. (2018). Black keys on a white piano: A Negro narrative of double-consciousness in American music education. In B. C. Talbot (Ed.), *Marginalized voices in music education* (pp. 28–45). New York: Routledge.

Sandow, G. (1997). The classical color line. *The Village Voice, 8,* 71–72.

Scharff, C. (2018). *Gender, subjectivity, and cultural work.* London: Routledge.

Slattery, P. (2013). *Curriculum development in the postmodern era.* New York: Routledge.

Thurman, K. (2014). The German Lied and songs of black Volk. In Ronyak, J. (Ed.), Studying the Lied: Hermeneutic traditions and the challenge of performance (565–569). *The Journal of the American Musicological Society, 67*(2), 543–582.

Tong, R. (1995). *Feminist thought: A comprehensive introduction.* New York; London: Routledge.

Tsioulcas, A. (2005). Music: Classical score – Imani winds blow for quality and diversity. *Billboard – The International Newsweekly of Music, Video and Home Entertainment, 117*(5), 14–46.

Tsioulcas, A. (2018, July 5). *Seeking pay equity, female flutist sues Boston Symphony Orchestra.* NPR Music News – see https://www.npr.org/2018/07/05/626125374/seeking-pay-equity-female-flutist-sues-boston-symphony-orchestra.

Usher, E. L., & Pajares, F. (2008). Sources of self-efficacy in school: Critical review of the literature and future directions. *Review of Educational Research, 78*(4), 751–796. https://doi.org/10.3102/0034654308321456.

Van Weelden, K., & McGee, I. R. (2007). The influence of music style and conductor race on perceptions of ensemble and conductor performance. *International Journal of Music Education, 25,* 7–17.

Wang, J. (2016). Classical music: A norm of "common" culture embedded in cultural consumption and cultural diversity. *International Review of the Aesthetics and Sociology of Music, 47*(2), 195–205.

Warwick Commission. (2015). *Enriching Britain: Culture, creativity and growth.* Coventry, UK: University of Warwick – see https://warwick.ac.uk/research/warwickcommission/futureculture/finalreport/warwick_commission_report_2015.pdf.

Wink, J. (2011). *Critical pedagogy: Notes from the real world* (4th ed). Upper Saddle River, NJ: Pearson.

Wise, B., & Lewin, N. (2015). *American orchestras grapple with lack of diversity.* WQXR New York Public Radio – see https://www.wqxr.org/story/american-orchestras-grapple-diversity/.

Yang, M. (2007). East meets West in the concert hall: Asians and classical music in the century of imperialism, post-colonialism, and multiculturalism. *Asian Music, 38*(1), 1–30.

Yoshihara, M. (2007). *Musicians from a different shore: Asians and Asian Americans in classical music.* Philadelphia: Temple University Press.

Zuberi, T. (2001). *Thicker than blood: How racial statistics lie.* Minneapolis: University of Minnesota Press.

PART IV

PSYCHOLOGY

CHAPTER 23

SELF-REGULATED LEARNING MUSIC MICROANALYSIS

GARY E. MCPHERSON

INTRODUCTION

As a musician, how do you react when encountering situations that are challenging and difficult, or that seem out of your control? To what degree do you always persist and persevere, and how resolute are you when faced with failure? And perhaps even more important, how do you feel and what do you think when you fail to perform at a level you had hoped to achieve, or when a new piece of music seems beyond your reach or insurmountable to master?

The toolkit of strategies that help individuals adapt their behaviors to break through, feel energized, and perform successfully collectively embody the concept of being a self-regulated learner (Cleary, 2018). This toolkit of strategies is what this chapter is about, and its purpose is to help musicians more skilfully infuse ideas and principles from the Self-Regulated Learning (SRL) literature into their musical development. As we will see in the following sections, this toolkit encompasses the ability to monitor one's own thoughts and actions, navigate and control your own emotions especially when you feel frustrated or anxious, and focus your efforts to select the most efficient solutions that will enable you to perform at your personal best. Put another way, becoming self-regulated with your mastery of music involves being able to recognize a challenge, understand the scope and nature of this challenge, focus your motivation to deal with the challenge, enact strategies and plans to overcome the challenge, and evaluate your own progress toward overcoming the challenge (Cleary, 2018). Put more simply, becoming master of your own musical learning involves drawing on and enacting a number of self-directive processes that allow you to transform your mental abilities into skills (Zimmerman, 2000).

SELF-REGULATED LEARNING

The early seeds of Self-Regulated Learning (SRL) emerged in the 1970s and 1980s when researchers sought to devise strategies for helping students take more control of their own learning by proactively setting themselves goals, choosing strategies, and self-monitoring their own effectiveness at their attempts to perform challenging tasks (Zimmerman, 2005). In many of the early studies, students were coached to apply a strategy such as imagery or goal setting to aid their performance. Researchers who undertook these studies found that students actually improved their performance but also that their improvements were often short-lived because they seldom used the strategies spontaneously in other contexts such as when undertaking practice or homework outside of the lesson (Zimmerman, 2005).

SRL emerged as a concept when educational psychologists began to change the focus from coaching students to apply certain strategies to studying how they learn to proactively become "metacognitively, motivationally, and behaviorally active participants in their own learning process" (Zimmerman, 2005, p. 167).

This quote, from the influential educational psychologist Barry Zimmerman, defines an important way that musicians can learn to *direct their actions* in order to *exceed their expectations* to *fulfill their intentions*. In this way, self-regulation involves how individuals develop the self-regulatory skills and accompanying self-motivational beliefs to push themselves to an even higher level of performance. The principles upon which SRL is based therefore seek to lay a foundation from which to become much more efficient with one's own learning.

We may be motivated to improve, but improvements are unlikely to occur unless we do something concrete to act on our motivations. This is where SRL strategies play a role. These strategies involve turning internal cues into external actions and positive feelings. To improve, we need to be goal-directed, purposeful with our efforts, and mindful of our intentions. Our thoughts, feelings, and actions all need to be coordinated in a way that allows us to perform at our personal best.

Self-regulation is more than self-control. Every time we attempt to inhibit impulses to act in a certain way we are exercising self-control. Self-regulation, on the other hand, is about reducing the incidence and intensity of our impulses in the first place. It is about how we control our thoughts, feelings, and actions in order to concentrate on short- and long-term goals. To do this we need to manage disruptive emotions and impulses we may have that distract us from what we are doing.

Music is unique in the way we refine our craft. As musicians we typically learn from a master teacher, but then have days between lessons when the strategies covered in lessons are refined during solitary (often mindless) practice. It is these solitary practice episodes that are solely under our control. For this reason, learning how to monitor, direct, and regulate one's self-regulatory process is integral to the development of musical expertise (Zimmerman, 2006).

In this chapter I explain how musicians can learn how to monitor, direct, and regulate their own self-regulatory processes by applying techniques aimed at improving those parts of their playing where they are experiencing problems. All are based on a philosophy that success starts with self-discipline. Even though most of the suggestions are about practice, they can be easily expanded to include other types of music performance, rehearsals, and skill development.

COMPONENTS OF SELF-REGULATED LEARNING

Figure 23.1 summarizes the cyclical feedback loop that Zimmerman (2000; Zimmerman & Campillo, 2003; Zimmerman & Moylan, 2009) developed to explain the processes that are characteristic of successful learners. It begins with a *Forethought Phase* in which you, as a musician, set goals, plan actions, and motivate yourself to master a new performance technique, or to perform at your personal best. These "pre-action" processes set the context for helping you focus your efforts to ensure that practice or performance is more purposeful and productive. Thinking ahead in this way is an important part of enhancing the impact on the quality of how you will strategically engage with the music you are practicing, once your performance begins.

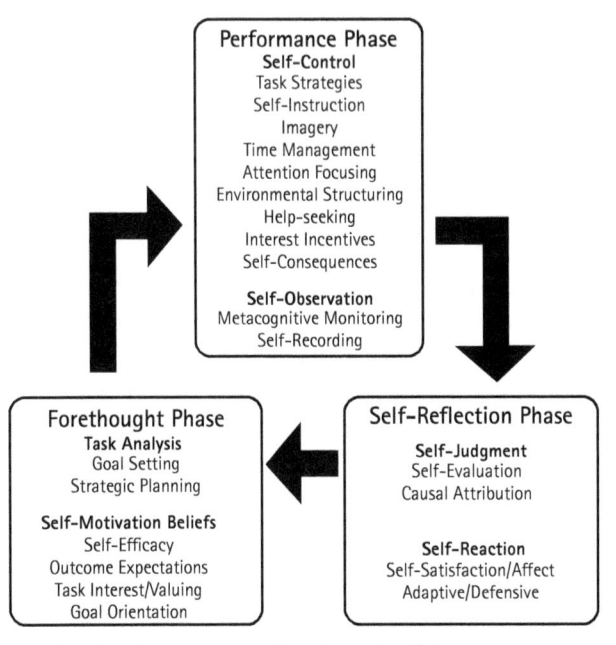

FIGURE 23.1. Phases and sub-processes of self-regulated learning in music. Adapted from Zimmerman & Moylan (2009); Zimmerman & Campillo (2003).

In the *Performance Phase* you act on the tactics and strategies you set for yourself beforehand, monitor your progress, and manage your emotions. *Self-Reflection* is where you reflect on how well you performed (either by pausing during the learning process or after the task has been completed), and as a result of this analysis comes the natural reactions of finding reasons to explain why you were unsuccessful or ineffective, and experienced either positive or negative feelings, such as satisfaction at performing beyond the level you set for yourself, or the frustration you felt at not being able to cope. These self-reflection phase processes exert an important influence on your future attempts at the same repertoire or performance, especially when they involve proactive decisions about what most needs improving in your next attempt at the same or a similar performance task (Cleary, 2018). In this way of thinking, our motivation to achieve does not come from the goals we set ourselves but instead from how we react to these experiences as we try to fulfill our goals (Zimmerman & Kitsantas, 2005).

This explanation provides the basic elements of the three-phase model. However, each process listed in Figure 23.1 is underpinned by a great deal of research that has been undertaken in different areas of learning. By summarizing a number of key sources (Cleary, 2018; Cleary & Callan, 2017; Cleary, Peters-Burton, Gergel, & Willet, 2018; Dembo & Seli, 2020 Kitsantas & Zimmerman, 2002; McPherson, Evans, & Miksza, 2017; McPherson & Zimmerman, 2011; O'Neill & Conzemius; 2006; Zimmerman, 2006; Zimmerman & Campillo, 2003; Zimmerman & Kitsantas, 2005; Zimmerman & Moylan, 2009), the following sections attempt to explain the main elements for optimizing one's potential to become a self-regulated musician.

Forethought Phase

This phase utilizes processes that can either enhance or impede our performance.
Task Analysis:

Ways of organizing practice or preparing for a performance

> *Goal Setting:* "What do I want to achieve in this practice session?" Goals can be conceptualized in terms of three dimensions: immediate (focused on the next attempt), short-term (aiming to achieve mastery within the practice session or a week), or long-term (aiming to reach a certain level for a major recital or performance). The ones that are the most important for individual practice are the first two of these. To make sure immediate and short-term goals are achieved goals also need to be SMART: specific (what you want to accomplish), **m**easurable (how your success can be evaluated), **a**ction-oriented (focused on actions rather than personal feelings), **r**ealistic (what you are capable of achieving), and **t**imely (if needed, breaking longer-term goals into shorter-term goals and setting specific deadlines for each of these to be achieved). It is better to set goals that are typically

just out of your reach, in order to push yourself forward and to maximize your ability to focus on being better than yourself. As a general rule, it is better to concentrate on *process goals* first (i.e., the parts of the actions and small steps needing to be mastered) and as the skill becomes automatized switch to *outcome goals* (i.e., the big picture, the end result, what it should sound like when you perform).

Strategic Planning: "How do I go about realizing my goals?" Begin by clarifying your vision of what you want to achieve, then analyze the task and what needs further attention in order to identify any specific or advantageous approaches that would aid your learning or mastery of certain components of the task. This also involves managing time allocations to ensure sufficient attention to priority aspects of the practice session.

Self-Motivation Beliefs:

Beliefs related to feelings of confidence, outcome expectations, interest, and passion that are based on the *want* ("I want to do this") and *can* ("I can do this") parts of motivation.

Self-Efficacy: "How confident am I that I *can* do this?" This includes the beliefs you hold about your own capacity to perform at an expected level of attainment (self-efficacy for performance) or your beliefs about your own capacity to implement or learn the types of processes that will allow you to master a musical challenge within a practice session (self-efficacy for learning). We perform best when we are confident, which is why self-efficacy beliefs are critical to expert performance. The emphasis is on believing you *can* do something (rather than *will* do something). We tend to overestimate our capacity to achieve and perform (which is not necessarily bad, but our evaluations need to be realistic because of this). When personal self-efficacy is high, we are more likely to set challenging goals for ourselves, and search for strategies to achieve these.

Outcome Expectations: "What do I expect to be able to do?" What types of actions will I need to adopt in order to achieve a particular outcome? Outcome expectations precede your action (in contrast to outcomes that arise from our actions) and are therefore important if you want to change your behavior. Outcome expectations involve being able to visualize an outcome and then determining whether you have sufficient capacity to perform this imagined outcome, and whether you believe that the outcome that you anticipate will occur because you performed (or failed to perform) a particular behavior.

Task Interest/Valuing: "Do I want to do this?"; "Why am I doing this?" What drives you to want to achieve certain outcomes? Is the emphasis intrinsic or extrinsic? Personal interest can range from an *intrinsic* desire to want to do something based on a valuing of the music that is being rehearsed or performed or love for performing in front of an audience, through to an *extrinsic* focus where you seek endorsement from some other outcome, such as praise by a teacher or audience (see further, Evans & Ryan, this part).

Goal Orientation: "What are the reasons why I'm practicing today?" Goal orientation refers to the cognitive representations of the general goals we wish to pursue.
Put another way, they are the reasons for pursuing a goal or a task rather than the
goal itself. We measure our success by how well we have mastered the task, how
much we have improved, and how proficient we feel our abilities are. Our goal
orientations help us focus on mastering tasks that we wish to master as we utilize
the skills and abilities we possess at that particular time. This is because competition drives our egos to want to achieve at a higher level than others.

Performance Phase

This phase utilizes processes linked to how we monitor and control our performance.
Self-Control:

Processes that impact on our performance by improving concentration. These processes
are varied with some overlap evident within the following list:

Task Strategies: "Which method will help optimize my musical skills and proficiency
during practice?" Strategies that are advantageous to your learning or practicing,
such as playing difficult sections of the music slower and softer, and other forms of
varied practice. The usefulness of the strategy needs to be constantly monitored to
ensure that it is employed optimally.

Self-Instruction: "To what extent do I employ inner speech to focus my efforts to perform better?" Athletes often use positive self-talk (inner speech, verbal thinking)
such as saying, "come on" or "let it go" to motivate themselves, while musicians
can try to perform with their ears—hearing and feeling the flow of the music
in anticipation of their playing—in order to more faithfully express their musical intentions to themselves and their audience. To work most effectively, self-
talk should be related to the task being mastered and then reduced as the skill is
mastered. These types of self-talk serve an important cognitive regulation function by helping musicians focus on the performance strategies being employed
and the positive emotions that appropriate inner speech will generate (Lee, Wang
& Ren, 2020).

Imagery: "How often do I recall a mental image of the work I am about to perform?"
Creating or recalling a mental image of a model performance by another performer
or imagining your own idealized performance as a way of guiding and assisting
practice or performance are two examples of imagery. To maximize the benefits
of imagery, the mimicry of the task should be vivid and detailed, incorporate all
senses (e.g., see, feel, move), occur in "real-time" through mental rehearsal of the
event, and involve a positive focus (i.e., the mental rehearsal should mimic a realistic performance) (Cumming, 2020).

Time Management: "How can I organize my day to complete all of my practice?"; "To what extent do I organize each practice session to achieve the goals I set for my-self?" Managing time by scheduling appropriate times in the day to practice and estimating how long to spend on each task or piece during a practice session helps to ensure that the time spent practicing is productive and efficient.

Attention Focusing: "How do I increase my concentration and focus while per-forming?" Strategies designed to improve concentration and block out distractions such as phone calls and messages from friends and not ruminating about poor past performance are integral to this dimension. To facilitate motor coordination, it is better to attend to an external focus (e.g., on the effects of movement) rather than on an internal focus (e.g., on the body movements themselves) in order to avoid disrupting the automaticity of a movement (Vaz, Avelar, & Resende, 2019).

Environmental Structuring: "To what extent do I actively choose a practice environ-ment that minimizes distractions?" Selecting or creating the optimal conditions to ensure the quality and quantity of practice time. This can be achieved by practicing at the most effective time of the day such as during the morning to avoid other distractions, blocking out distractions that might interfere with practice, or practicing with a metronome to help concentrate your mind on the goals you are trying to achieve.

Help-Seeking: "How often do I energetically seek help from other sources or re-sources?" Seeking out models, teachers, or resources to obtain assistance with your learning as you seek to correct a specific flaw in your playing. Adaptive help seeking can be compared to social dependence on aids because it is self-initiated, has a se-lective focus, and is generally limited to a specific part of your technique that you are trying to improve. Knowing what recordings to listen to can also help. Adaptive help-seeking involves proactively seeking assistance from multiple sources about something you are trying to master, rather than relying on a single source (such as your teacher).

Interest Incentives: "How can I pace and shape my practice to maximize my interest across the session?" Studies with musicians show that their practice is more effi-cient if they start with repertoire they are still learning or find most challenging and finish with repertoire they enjoy and know how to play. This general principle of focusing on the most challenging things first, before rewarding oneself with opportunities to perform works for their intrinsic enjoyment, can help to sustain motivation across long, arduous practice sessions.

Self-Consequences: "To what extent do I reward myself for accomplishing my goals?" Motivation can be enhanced by setting rewards for oneself, such as putting off opportunities to relax or socialize and not answering emails or text messages from friends until after practice is completed.

Self-Observation: Processes that impact on concentration and involve monitoring and observing the above self-control mechanisms.

Metacognitive Monitoring: "How can I mentally track what I am doing?" Tracking your own performance by observing and reflecting on what you have done, and analyzing the results, relative to your other performances or an idealized performance. Experts tend to be selective in their metacognitive monitoring because the goals they set themselves for practicing and performing are typically specific and focused on helping them drill down and analyze problems.

Self-Recording: "To what extent do I regularly self-record my practice efforts?" Taking notes on the most and least positive aspects of your performance or checking off from a list of priorities challenges that you have now mastered helps increase the accuracy of feedback you provide for yourself. These types of self-recording techniques allow you to make the process your own and to see over time what you have achieved as you build on the procedures that have worked best for you in the past. In this way they help to optimize your learning.

Self-Reflective Phase

This phase utilizes processes linked to our own personal responses to the performance.
Self-Judgment:

Reflecting on the degree to which you chose to engage in aspects of your performance that were satisfying or avoid those aspects that you find frustrating or stressful.

Self-Evaluation: "Did I improve?"; "How do I know?" Strive to set appropriate and achievable standards of performance from which you can then compare your performance with these or other model performances. You can avoid the frustration of not being able to repeatedly demonstrate your mastery of a musical challenge and therefore the negative consequences of making errors by assuming beforehand that you will make a certain number of errors and then gradually trying to reduce the number of errors within each practice session.

Causal Attribution: "Why did I perform well/struggle?" Assigning reasons to explain success or failure. If these reasons are due to a perception of a lack of ability, then future efforts will be stymied because you will feel that no amount of effort will help. In contrast, if your focus is on attributions aligned to causes within your control then you will attribute your failures to a lack of effort and be more inclined to try harder the next time. Another example would be attributing poor performance to a deficient strategy (e.g., poor time management), and then feeling motivated to change this to improve future performance.

Self-Reaction: Giving direction to your actions and creating self-incentives to persist with your efforts.

Self-Satisfaction/Affect: "Was I satisfied?" Our personal feelings of satisfaction/dissatisfaction about what we have just accomplished. We tend to work harder and focus our efforts when we experience positive feelings about what we have just achieved. Feeling satisfied after practicing or performing is an outcome of our efforts to actively attribute the causes of our success on aspects of our approach to performing music in which we have control, such as the goals we set ourselves and the plans we devise to accomplish our goals.

Adaptive/Defensive: "What should be my approach for the next practice session?" Adaptive inferences about prior performance occur when we proactively set about planning more effective strategies to use into the future. Defensive inferences serve the function of protecting us from further dissatisfaction and failure that can result in feelings of helplessness, procrastination, avoidance of the task, disengagement, and apathy.

It is self-evident from studying the foregoing dimensions that all of these strategies involved in cognition (thinking), affect (feeling), or behaving (acting) need to be practiced, preferably on an ongoing basis. Like any skill, musicians employ each of these at various times in their learning.

Practical Implications

At the beginning of this chapter, I referred to studies from the 1970s and 1980s where researchers studied coaching and teaching sessions in which students were actively trained to employ more efficient or task-appropriate strategies when undertaking challenging tasks. Although students improved when exposed to these training programs, they often failed to spontaneously use these strategies in their subsequent efforts, especially when working on their own.

Such findings are in many ways similar to typical instrumental learning, where a performance student will rely on their studio teacher to guide their learning of a new strategy during a lesson yet fail to apply the same strategy adequately or consistently when practicing on their own, or even a week later during the next lesson. This point highlights an important aspect of becoming a self-regulated musician. To succeed, a musician needs much more than basic talent and high-quality instruction. For those musicians who are willing to make the investment, SRL offers an important toolkit of strategies they can draw upon in order to learn how to change their practice behaviors. In this way, SRL is about how to focus your *will*, in parallel to your *skills*, on the types of strategies that will most efficiently allow you to master a new technique or musical challenge.

Becoming a self-regulated musician

The technique proposed here to describe how performing musicians can master complex skills is based on research showing that the learning of complex skills is more efficient if it moves through a continuing spiral process, moving from social guidance (e.g., observation, instruction) to self-directed strategies (e.g., taking responsibility, monitoring and controlling personal progress) in a hierarchical learning cycle (Zimmerman, 2000; Zimmerman & Kitsantas, 2005):

1. *Observation*: watching/listening to a musician who is teaching you the skill/technique. A critical part of observation is being able to focus your attention to discern differences between your performance and the model performance.
2. *Emulation*: Imitating the musician's performance under the assistance of the performance teacher. When learning something new or difficult, learners seldom perform the task exactly as it was modeled to them but emulate the general style or pattern of functioning in order to blend these into their own repertoire of responses.
3. *Self-Control*: Independently performing the new skill/technique during structured conditions such as during isolated practice, all the time being aware of the original, target model. During this stage we aim for automaticity in order to perform the task accurately across repeated attempts. Automaticity is best achieved by focusing on the fundamental processes or techniques (i.e., the elements that come together in order to be able to perform the task), rather than on task outcomes. Such an emphasis minimizes inefficient trial-and-error practice.
4. *Self-Regulation*: Spontaneously and independently adaptation of the newly acquired skill or technique in different musical contexts. When this level is attained, we are able to make mindful adjustments in how to perform the task because the skill has been automatized and we are therefore able to practice with minimal attention to the task. This allows us to adapt our playing to changing personal conditions and outcomes as we concentrate more on developing our own distinctive style of performing.

Observation and emulation typically occur in a music lesson where the studio teacher provides the model for the developing musician to observe, analyze, and emulate their performance or from an idealized model such as a recording. But in the ways I have described, students often fail or have difficulty applying what they have learned in the lesson or rehearsal during their isolated practice or ensemble experience. Consequently, difficulties often arise between the second and third (moving from emulation to self-control), and third and fourth (moving from self-control to self-regulation) phases of the learning cycle.

Microanalysis

In a growing body of literature in other areas such as sport, academic learning, medical training, and more recently in music, the use of a technique known as *microanalysis* has been developed to help learners proactively initiate, manage, and adapt strategies that can improve those parts of their behaviors (actions), cognition (thoughts), and affect (feelings) that are not optimal, and would benefit from extra attention (Cleary & Callan, 2017).

Five steps are followed when using the microanalysis technique (Cleary et al., 2012):

Step 1: *Selecting* a well-defined task, for example, a specific section of a piece you are trying to master or even a complete music practice session.

Step 2: *Identifying* target SRL processes that need most attention from the three-phase SRL model shown in Figure 23.1.

Step 3: *Developing* SRL microanalytic strategies that align to the specific self-regulated learning technique that is being targeted.

Step 4: *Linking* cyclical phase processes to task dimensions, from the Forethought Phase before practice begins, to the Performance Phase, which might be a complete performance of repertoire or techniques during practice or a performance beyond the practice session, to the Self-Reflection Phase immediately after the performance takes place.

Step 5: *Evaluating* and planning for the next attempt, practice session, or performance.

In a series of studies, McPherson and his colleagues adapted the microanalysis technique to help refine the practice habits of conservatory-level performance students (McPherson, Osborne, Evans, & Miksza, 2019; Osborne, McPherson, Miksza, & Evans, 2020) by identifying parts of the musicians' practice that were not optimal, and studying how these aspects of their practice could be enhanced by applying different behaviors, thoughts, and feelings. Results using the protocol they devised (McPherson et al., 2015) show that these musicians were capable of understanding and completing the diary entries during their practice sessions. General findings were also consistent with results obtained when using the microanalysis in other fields of learning. In general, they found that the more productive, self-regulated *proactive musicians* tended to focus on the Forethought Phase of the SRL model in contrast to the less self-regulated *reactive learners*, who relied less on Forethought processes and often reacted negatively to what they had just accomplished after their performance or practice session had finished.

Interpreting the literature on proactive versus reactive learners, suggests important differences between these two approaches to learning, which can be summarized as follows:

Proactive Learners: By placing an emphasis on the Forethought Phase, proactive learners are more likely to:

- plan ahead to eliminate or minimize problems before they occur;
- anticipate what needs to be accomplished, the problems they might encounter, and the possible outcomes that might be achieve during the practice session or performance; and
- foresee potential obstacles and exert more effort into identifying ways to overcome these obstacles before they turn into roadblocks.

Reactive Learners: By emphasizing the Self-Reflection Phase and reacting afterwards, reactive learners are more like to:

- respond to problems after they have occurred;[1]
- view their progress negatively because of their focus on negative affect (feelings) rather than positive cognitions and actions; and
- avoid or delay further practice on the problems they find most difficulty, give up and move on to something different, and develop feelings of helplessness or lack of ability.

The musicians' use of our microanalysis protocol demonstrated the highly individualized and complex nature of encouraging changes to practice habits for students who have already been learning for a number of years. It is self-evident that breaking old, unproductive practice habits is not easy, and will require weeks and months of constant attention to update and redefine them into more optimal practice schedules. Young musicians will continue to rely heavily on cues from their performance teacher in the form of constant reminders about key aspects of their rehearsal of new works, which are often in the form of comments that build awareness of certain issues they need to take into account while refining their performance skills on specific repertoire. Self-regulated learning theory recognizes the need for learners' efforts to be regulated in this way (i.e., socially by others such as a teacher) in addition to the need for learners to self-direct their own learning through self-awareness, self-motivation, and behavioral skills in ways that will enable them to take charge of their own learning (Zimmerman, 2002).

Applying the SRL microanalysis technique

The following passages provide two contrasting examples of how musicians can use the SRL microanalysis strategies described earlier to refine their practice, performance, and rehearsal strategies. Both of these contrasting profiles start with a short vignette about each developing musician and are followed by an explanation of how their behavior, cognition, and affect can be optimized through a music microanalysis intervention.

Scenario 1

John is a second year Bachelor of Music performance major who realizes that his piano practice is characterized by poor habitual strategy use and that he often doesn't accomplish as much as he knows he is capable of achieving. He typically begins his practice with only a vague idea of what he wants to achieve by the end of the session, other than

---

[1] "Reaction" is an integral part of SRL and not necessarily bad. However, it will be ineffective if this is one's general approach to learning.

comments provided from the teacher at the last lesson (Goal Setting). He also has no clear sense of what will be achieved in the practice session and does not pre-plan his use of time across the practice session (or day, or week) to allow sufficient time to work on those aspects of the piece that need the most attention (or that pose the most difficult performance challenges) (Strategic Planning).

John's confidence level is mixed. Although he feels confident that he can master the new piece by the end-of-semester performance recital (Self-Efficacy), he doubts himself at times because he is unable to visualize himself performing the work accurately at the performance recital. This uncertainty has created further confusion and doubt about the types of actions he will need to implement in order to provide a performance that exceeds his previous personal best (Outcome Expectations). John chose the work to be performed and has performed other works from the same composer. He values and likes the new piece to be learned (Task Interest/Valuing) but lacks an internalized cognitive representation of the goals he wishes to pursue, or the effort needed to learn this new repertoire (Goal Orientation).

When playing the new piece or sections of the new repertoire during his practice, John uses inner talk, such as saying, "Come on, I'm going to get it this time" to try to focus his repeats of the piece (or sections of the piece) (Self-Instruction). John hasn't heard any other performances of the work other than his teacher's model during lessons so does not possess a complete mental image from which to model his performance (Imagery). He is often distracted during practice and will give up or move on to another section after a few unsuccessful attempts (Attention Focusing). John has a limited number of strategies to vary his practice and tends to fall back on ineffective strategies if the current one isn't achieving results (Task Strategies). He rarely seeks out one of the quieter practice rooms at the conservatory to practice and doesn't maintain regular tuning of his piano at home (Environmental Structuring). He also typically does not come to lessons with questions or issues about the piece that can be discussed with the teacher (Help-Seeking). During his practice, there is little analysis or drilling down to work out why something is going wrong (Metacognitive Monitoring), and he has no orderly method (e.g., practice diary) to keep track of progress or questions and issues to discuss with his teacher (Self-Recording).

After each practice segment during his practice or at the end of the practice session, John moves quickly on to other activities, so there is little reflection about what was achieved during the practice, or what needs more focused attention in the next practice session (Self-Evaluation). John possesses a positive self-esteem about music and is an average performance student in his year cohort. He believes that he has ability and that if he worked hard, he could master the piece (Causal Attributions). As the weeks go by, and he does not see sufficient improvement, John starts to feel more frustrated that he does not have sufficient time to master the piece by the performance recital (Self-Satisfaction/Affect). Even though John got a good mark for his last semester performance examination he starts to feel that other students are overtaking him and because his confidence is starting to wane avoids volunteering to perform in his teacher's weekly studio workshops (Adaptive/Defensive).

Microanalysis intervention

If this profile leans in your direction, then applying the microanalysis technique to change your practice habits could involve work on a variety of dimensions, though not necessarily all at the same time. For example, to work on Goal Setting for each practice session, you could start a practice diary to define what you want to achieve in the next practice session, what technical challenges will receive priority attention, what you might reasonably expect to be able to do by the end of the practice session, and how much time you can allocate to each individual component that needs work. At all times, it's wise to think of mastery as a journey and to map where you feel you are along the road to mastering the challenge each time you begin practicing a section of a piece or complete work (e.g., "My playing in that middle section is only about 30%, and I want to get it to 35% by the end of today's practice"). To improve your Strategic Planning, you could try mapping out what needs to be accomplished across the ten weeks allocated for learning the new work and then defining each small step that would help put the piece together and aid mastery, such as focusing on each specific technical difficulty (e.g., by the end of this week I want to be achieve 40% mastery of that section involving tricky fingerings, by the end of next week 50% mastery through to the last two weeks before the recital when I want to play it 100% accurate to make sure I feel confident in the final performance).

To become more aware of the actions you will need to perform the work at your personal best (Outcome Expectations) and focus your efforts to ensure continual progress (Goal Orientation), listen to model recordings of the work to develop a more complete mental picture of the work (Imagery), and try to outdo yourself in each performance or practice of a segment in order to make your progress visible to yourself. You can do this through Attention Focusing processes such as removing distractions and ensuring that you do not leave a section you are having difficulty with until you can hear that the segment has improved, to at least some degree. Using Self-Instruction techniques of inner talk (e.g., "Come on, I can do this") will also help Attention Focusing processes. Purposefully searching out other ways of tackling a deficiency using a strategy that you haven't previously attempted or monitoring the effectiveness of the current strategy (Task Strategies) is important for efficient learning. This form of drilling down (Metacognitive Monitoring) and reflecting on your actions needs to be catalogued in some way, such as Self-Recording what went well and what went poorly in a Practice Diary, or writing out a list of specific issues that you can ask your teacher about (Help-Seeking) during the next lesson.

At the end of each practice session it is wise to also spend a minute or two thinking about how well the session went (Self-Evaluation) in terms of what you did (behavior), what you were thinking while practicing (cognition), and how you felt (affect). Was it better than the last session? What needs the most attention in the next practice session? How can you turn your negative feelings of frustration or even hopelessness into attributions (Causal Attribution) that are focused on a growth mindset and attitude that progress will be made, if you focus your efforts and practice even more deliberately?

Balance your affect on parts of the practice that went well as compared to those that went poorly, remembering also that you are more likely to feel satisfied with your practice when you feel you are in control of your learning, and able to shape your own progress. Most important, think about what you might plan to do next based on how you feel at that particular moment (Adaptive/Defensive). How can your next session be even better than this one?

Scenario 2

Katy is also in the second year of the Bachelor of Music performance strand. Her previous teacher had stressed the importance of using a practice diary so before each practice session, she has a quick think of what needs most practice (Goal Setting), and before practice begins she takes a mental note of what pieces, and in which priority order, she wants to work on in the session so she can move to them one by one. During her practice she marks the parts of the piece that she still cannot perform and understands the deficiencies that need extra attention to be mastered or refined for her next lesson and for her end-of-semester recital (Strategic Planning).

Katy feels confident that she can master the new piece of repertoire by the end-of-semester performance recital (Self-Efficacy) although she sometimes gets frustrated during practice because of technical problems that impede her progress. She has heard two other recordings of the work being learned by pianists she admires and has listened carefully to these and her teacher's performance of the same work. These mental models have helped her to visualize how the work should be played and how she might provide her own interpretation (Outcome Expectations). Katy chose the work to be performed and has learned other works by the composer who is one of her favorites (Task Interest). She knows that she has time to master the piece and solve a number of technical challenges before her recital (Goal Orientation), and during her playing she often motivates herself to perform better by using positive Self-Instruction such as saying to herself, "Come on, I can get it this time" as an aid to focus her repetitions of repeated sections of the piece during the practice period. She has listened to other recordings of the work being learned, as well as her teacher's model during lessons and now has a clear mental image of the work and how it should be performed (Imagery).

While practicing and playing, Katy tries to feel the flow of the music based on the mental image she has captured from recordings she admires (Attention Focusing). She also has a few basic strategies for refining different technical problems (Task Strategies) beyond those she has previously discussed with her teacher, which she applies when having difficulties. In addition, she understands how important it is to master the piece at least two weeks before the final recital, in order to leave the last couple of weeks for polishing off the work so that it can be performed confidently. Katy tries to organize her days by practicing around the same time each day. She makes practice a priority by completing at least 2 hours practice away from distractions Monday to Friday and 3 hours on Saturdays and Sundays (Environmental Structuring). She comes to lessons with a list of questions about problems she wishes to discuss with her teacher (Help-Seeking). During her practice, she drills down to work out why something is going wrong (Metacognitive Monitoring) by asking herself questions immediately after practicing sections of the work such as "Why didn't I get that this time?," "My left hand fingers aren't in sync with my right hand because that passage isn't drilled into them yet." Her use of a practice diary also involves keeping track of her own progress by listing the areas in which she had most and least difficult in each particular practice session (Self-Recording).

After each practice session, Katy spends one to two minutes thinking about how she progressed on the most challenging parts of the new piece (Self-Evaluation), but often her self-evaluations turn to negative comparisons with others such as "I heard Suzie play this during the last masterclass and she's so much better than me in the presto section of the third page" or "If I don't get this I'm going to muck it up next week in the masterclass." When Katy performs works in front of others, she also tends to be extremely self-critical and feels that she did not perform as well as she wanted. After performances, she will typically also ask her friends or even her teacher, "How did I go?"

In addition, in the days leading up to the performance and during the performance, Katy can often feel anxious about how she will go and how others will judge her performance, especially her closest "rivals" in her year cohort. Katy possesses a positive self-esteem about music and her abilities as a pianist in comparison with other students in her year cohort. She knows she is among the top three piano students in her cohort. However, she seems to be more motivated by wanting to please her teacher and get better marks than the other students than by an intrinsic desire to perform well for herself (Causal Attributions). As the weeks go by, Katy's confidence about her ability to perform the piece during the performance recital increases (Self-Satisfaction/Affect). She obtained a high mark for her previous semester performance examination and this is partly responsible for her wanting to perform at least to this level in the upcoming recital (Adaptive/Defensive).

Microanalysis intervention

On one level, the narrative above illustrates the many ways Katy's actions successfully utilizes a number behavioral and cognitive aspects that are part of the repertoire of self-regulated learning strategies shown in Figure 23.1. But it would be wrong to think that all is well in Katy's profile and that there are only minor adjustments and enhancements to be made for her to optimize her performance.

In many teaching situations, the foregoing description might be handled by trying to reduce Katy's anxiety, while being unaware of the underlying problem. As we will see in the following explanation, this would be akin to focusing on the symptom rather than the causes of Katy's performance anxiety.

If you can see any of Katy in your approach to rehearsing and performing music, then one approach for the microanalysis intervention would involve concentrating on the self-motivation beliefs component of the Forethought Phase, and the self-judgment and self-reaction components of the Self-Reflection Phase. From the scenario description, it would seem that there are at least three ways Katy could think through her current approach to practicing and performing music. On one level, her personal belief in her own ability is relatively strong. She knows she is a good musician and among the top pianists in her year cohort. And she has obviously devoted a lot of time and effort into developing her skills to this level. But unpacking these perceptions of her own ability reveals that she is driven by *social comparisons* whereby she compares her performance to that of others. Over time, this type of mindset can reduce one's self-concept of ability, especially in situations where the competition becomes tougher and she ends up starting to feel that she is in the middle rather than top of the group. Right now, she is a big fish in a little pond, but over time, and especially when she enters the profession, she might start to feel less confident about her abilities; that is, a little fish in a large pond. Such perceptions can reduce one's motivation for an activity (Wigfield, Eccles, & Möller, 2020). The challenge for Katy is to move from this *social comparison* mindset to one that is more focused on *temporal comparisons*. This type of change would reposition her to concentrate more on what she has learned and can do now, as compared to what she was able to do previously.

Recall, in the Self-Reflective Phase we observed that Katy's self-evaluations often turn to negative comparisons with others, such as when she compares her own progress with that of her peers and tends to catastrophize about how well she might play in an upcoming masterclass. Moving to a focus more aligned with *temporal comparisons* would see her using more positive self-talk when self-evaluating her own practice through such self-talk as "I'm only 40% there today, I need to get to over 45% when I practice that section again tomorrow," "I couldn't do that last week but I got it right that time; I just now need to make sure I can get it right every time I play it," or "Because I was methodical in the way I practiced this piece during the past eight weeks, I can now play this without errors; I just now need to consolidate on this during the last couple of weeks leading up to the performance so it's secure during the performance"; or even, "I'll play this to my friends and family to ensure I can also perform well during the performance." Adopting a *temporal comparisons* mindset motivates musicians to focus on their own personal best, because they start to see learning as a journey, and their own development as having reached a particular point along this journey (see McPherson & Hattie, this volume; see also Evans & Ryan, this part).

Another aspect Katy could work on concerns her approach to her practice. A close examination of what she does and the feelings she experiences shows that, like many other young musicians, her practice habits are focused on *what* she plans to do in the practice session and *how* she will achieve her personal goals and through which strategies. Katy would do well to reposition this mindset to focus more on the *why* of her own learning. As McPherson and Hattie show in Part I of this handbook, refocusing on why (or even starting with why) has the advantage of bolstering one's own personal belief in oneself and what can be achieved into the future.

Katy's expertise as a musician includes more than the competence of being able to demonstrate a skill or perform a piece to her teacher (i.e., *what*), or her willingness (i.e., *how*) to incorporate certain self-regulated learning strategies in her practice or performing, or even to act on her teacher's advice in order to master a certain skill or repertoire. What needs to be added is her ability to contextualize the learning so it is clear to her *why* this new skill or piece of music is being learned, *what* the next level of success looks like, and *how* this newly developed knowledge or competency can be transferred in other musical situations.

As suggested earlier, in many ways Katy's performance anxiety is the symptom not the cause so by implementing these mindset changes, we would hopefully see a reduction in her anxiety during public performance, even though it may never be eliminated (see further, Osborne, Part VI in Volume 2).

Designing your own music microanalysis intervention

These two scenarios provide only a brief glimpse of how the microanalysis technique might be utilized to optimize one's own performance. Everyone is different, so to use the technique effectively requires that we design our own, tailored version. For musicians, one way of designing an appropriate microanalysis strategy would be to start by writing out your own personal vignette that comments on all the dimensions mentioned in the three-phase model shown in Figure 23.1. Once this is completed, you can show it to your teacher to discuss, or share it with a peer with whom you feel comfortable discussing information about your abilities.

When writing your own vignette, it is important to reflect on all the things you typically do in your practicing and performances (i.e., your behavior), what you think about when practicing and performing (i.e., your cognition), and also how you feel (affect). So, it is always a good idea to start the vignette with a paragraph that reflects on *why* you have chosen to devote yourself to music and what this means for you well into the future. What is it that you want to do with music, where will your music studies take you, and what are the types of career options to which you aspire? As Evans and Ryan show (see Evans & Ryan, this part) one's intrinsic motivation depends on the three psychological needs of feeling able to do an activity (*competence*), feeling that you can talk and relate to your teacher and your peers (*relatedness*), and, most important, a sense of *autonomy*, especially in terms of your willingness to take control of your own musical journey instead of feeling controlled by external factors that can cause frustrations and result in feelings of being controlled by others. This is important because as we saw in the second vignette, Katy's motivations as a performer were more extrinsically controlled rather than intrinsically embedded. In ten or twenty years from now, she will probably hardly remember how well her peers played in masterclasses and end-of-semester performance examinations, or even the comments that were made to her after good and poor performances. But it is likely also that she will remember some of her negative reactions and the performance anxiety she experienced that diminished her abilities to perform to her own personal best.

Once your vignette is completed, designing a music microanalysis intervention would follow the five-step guide suggested earlier by *selecting* a well-defined task, *identifying* target SRL processes, *developing* SRL microanalysis strategies, *linking* these to the three-phase SRL model, and *evaluating* and planning for the next event. At the start it is better to concentrate on only a few of aspects rather than every aspect in the three-phase model. Over time, and with more practice using the microanalysis technique, you will build up your own toolkit of strategies and be able to integrate more and more of these into your own unique way of practicing and performing.

CONCLUSIONS

It is insufficient to know what you want to achieve, set some immediate goals to accomplish these, and have a sense that they need to be fully mastered for a performance or recital. These are all about the *what* and the *how* of improving and progressing. Added to these must be an overarching sense of *why* you value these goals in your own development. What values—mindsets and beliefs—govern how you learn as a musician, and to what degree do these align with your own overarching beliefs about music? Are they related to a love of music, something to do with how you want to shape your career, or how far you want to get in your career (such as a principal position in an orchestra)? Are they related to relationships and friendships you have established as a musician (that is, the joy of making music with others), or something you want to do because you have your heart set on being a musician? These are some of the values that govern our desire to achieve in music. The main point is that you need to sort these out for yourself, and then use them as the basis from designing your own learning to fulfill your own aspirations and desires in music. It is therefore important to ask ourselves: "To what extent are the goals that govern my life musical, occupational, social or personal?" Importantly, overarching values are most effective when they include items that will sustain your career as a musician (rather than, for example, just wanting to play well at the next concert).

"Time on task" is a saying that is often used as a measure of how busy students have been learning material as they strive to fulfill a learning goal. A more sophisticated understanding of this concept, however, does not mean that learners are merely occupied during the learning process but rather that they spend their time working productively and are challenged and willing to push themselves further during the process of working on the task. Practice, practice, practice is not the ideal; but practice that is based on goal setting, strategic monitoring, feeling empowered, and goal-oriented is the ideal. "Time on task" is therefore best viewed as a sense of both "deliberateness" and "purposefulness" in the use of the available time so that your efforts on a learning activity are not wasted but spent productively.

So, what can musicians do in order to optimize their own performance abilities? Using the self-regulated learning approach, such optimization would result from:

1. asking yourself *why* you chose a career in music, and using this to ground learning and performances on your love of music;
2. focusing on comparisons of yourself (e.g., "Last week I couldn't do this, now I can"), rather than comparisons with others (e.g., "I'm not able to play as well as Suzie");

3. understanding the different types of behavior (doing), cognition (thinking), and affect (feeling) that enhance and impede your performance;

4. constantly expanding the repertoire of strategies and microanalysis techniques that you apply when practicing and performing in order to help break old practice and performance habits; and

5. realizing that improvements often occur gradually and over long periods of time, which is the reason why you need to be patient and persist even when improvements are not immediately obvious.

"Play the ball before it plays you!" is a common saying in sport that applies equally well to music. When musicians embrace the philosophy behind this saying, they cue themselves to proactively take charge of what they do (behavior), think (cognition), and feel (affect), and in so doing their efforts capture the essence of what self-regulated learning is all about.

Key Sources

Cleary, T. J. (2018). *The self-regulated learning guide.* New York: Routledge.

López-Íñiguez, G., & McPherson, G. E. (2020). Applying self-regulated learning and self-determination theory to optimize the performance of a concert cellist. *Frontiers in Psychology, 11,* 385. https://doi.org/10.3389/fpsyg.2020.00385.

McPherson, G. E., Osborne, M. S., Evans, P., & Miksza, P. (2015). *Self-regulated learning micro-analysis protocol for university musicians.* The University of Melbourne, Australia. Retrieved from www.optimalmusicperformance.com.

McPherson, G. E., Osborne, M. S., Evans, P., & Miksza, P. (2019). Applying self-regulated learning microanalysis to study musicians' practice. *Psychology of Music, 47*(1), 18–32. https://doi.org/10.1177/0305735617731614.

Osborne, M. S., McPherson, G. E., Miksza, P., & Evans, P. (2020). Using a microanalysis intervention to examine shifts in musicians' self-regulated learning. *Psychology of Music.* https://doi.org/10.1177/0305735620915265.

Reflective Questions

1. List up to ten points that summarize *why* you chose music as a career. Separate these points into two columns, one focusing on the intrinsic reasons and the other on extrinsic reasons. What do you see? How would someone else interpret this profile of intrinsic and extrinsic reasons? Can you identify what you believe to be the most powerful reasons that you can use to guide your aspirations into the future?

2. Design your own vignette using the SRL three-phase model described in this chapter that describes what you tend to do, think about, and feel when practicing (or performing, rehearsing). Once finished, share this with peers who are also designing their own microanalysis intervention and then revise accordingly based on this feedback and your further reflections. How can you turn this vignette into a tailored microanalysis intervention aimed at updating and redefining your own practice (or performing)? Can you identify a schedule over the days, weeks, or months for developing each of the main target deficiencies you aim to improve?

3. Reflect critically on your own development, and particularly the types of strategies you habitually employ when practicing and performing. If you had your time over, is there anything you might change? What worked well and what could you have done?

4. Reflect on the best performance teachers you have come in contact with up to this point. What do you most admire in their abilities as musicians? What do they *do*, *think*, and *feel* that depicts them as self-regulated learners? What would you highlight from observing and knowing these people that you can incorporate into your own musical development?

5. Reflect on someone who isn't a musician that you greatly admire. What do you most admire about this person? What do they *do*, *think*, and *feel* that depicts them as self-regulated learners? What would you highlight from observing and knowing these people that you can incorporate into your own musical development?

Acknowledgments

This chapter was supported by an ARC Discovery Grant DP150103330. The author is grateful to Timothy Cleary and Dale Schunk for their valuable comments and helpful suggestions on an earlier version of this chapter.

References

Cleary, T. J. (2018). *The self-regulated learning guide*. New York: Routledge.

Cleary, T. J., & Callan, G. L. (2017). Assessing self-regulated learning using microanalytic methods. In D. Schunk & J. Greene (Eds.), *Handbook of self-regulation of learning and performance* (2nd ed., pp. 338–351). New York: Routledge.

Cleary, T. J., Callan, G. L., & Zimmerman, B. J. (2012). Assessing self-regulation as a cyclical, context-specific phenomenon: Overview and analysis of SRL microanalytic protocols. *Education Research International*, 2012, 1. https://doi.org/10.1155/2012/428639.

Cleary, T. J., Peters-Burton, E., Gergel, C., & Willet, K. (2018). Applications of cyclical self-regulated learning principles to life science. In *Connecting Self-regulated Learning and Performance with Instruction Across High School Content Areas*, 127–162). Springer International Publishing. https://doi.org/10.1007/978-3-319-90928-8_5

Cumming, J. (2020, November 1). *Sport imagery training.* Association for Applied Sport Psychology – see https://appliedsportpsych.org/resources/resources-for-athletes/sport-imagery-training]=/.

Dembo, M. H., & Seli, H. (2020). *Motivation and learning strategies for college success: A focus on self-regulated learning.* New York: Routledge.

Kitsantas, A., & Zimmerman, B. J. (2002). Comparing self-regulatory processes among novice, non-expert, and expert volleyball players: A microanalytic study. *Journal of Applied Sport Psychology, 14*(2), 91–105. https://doi.org/10.1080/10413200252907761.

Lee, S., Want, T., & Ren, X. (2020). Inner speech in the learning context and the prediction of students' learning strategy and academic performance. *Educational Psychology: An International Journal of Experimental Educational Psychology, 40*(5), 535–549. https://doi.org/10.1080/01443410.2019.1612035.

McPherson, G. E., Miksza, P., & Evans, P. (2017). Self-regulated learning in music practice and performance. In D. H. Schunk & J. A. Greene (Eds.), *Handbook of self-regulation of learning and performance* (2nd ed, pp. 181–193). New York: Routledge.

McPherson, G. E., Osborne, M. S., Evans, P., & Miksza, P. (2015). *Self-regulated learning microanalysis protocol for university musicians.* The University of Melbourne – see www.optimalmusicperformance.com.

McPherson, G. E., Osborne, M. S., Evans, P., & Miksza, P. (2019). Applying self-regulated learning microanalysis to study musicians' practice. *Psychology of Music, 47*(1), 18–32. https://doi.org/10.1177/0305735617731614.

McPherson, G. E., & Zimmerman, B. J. (2011). Self-regulation of musical learning: A social cognitive perspective on developing performance skills. In R. Colwell & P. Webster (Eds.), *MENC handbook of research on music learning, volume 2: Applications* (pp. 130–175). New York: Oxford University Press.

O'Neill, J., & Conzemius, A. (2006). *The power of SMART goals: Using goads to improve student learning.* Bloomington, IN: Solution Tree Press.

Osborne, M. S., McPherson, G. E., Miksza, P., & Evans, P. (2020). Using a microanalysis intervention to examine shifts in musicians' self-regulated learning. *Psychology of Music.* https://doi.org/10.1177/0305735620915265.

Wigfield, A., Eccles, J. S., & Möller, J. (2020). How dimensional comparisons help to understand linkages between expectancies, values, performance, and choice. *Educational Psychology Review, 32*, 657–680. https://doi.org/10.1007/s10648-020-09524-2.

Vaz, D. V., Avelar, B. S., & Resende, R. A. (2019). Effects of attentional focus on movement coordination complexity. *Human Movement Science, 64*, 171–180. https://doi.org/10.1016/j.humov.2019.01.012.

Zimmerman, B. J. (2000). Attaining self-regulation: A social cognitive perspective. In M. Boekaerts, P. R. Pintrich, & M. Zeidner (Eds.), *Handbook of self-regulation* (pp. 13–40). San Diego, CA: Academic Press. https://doi.org/10.1016/B978-012109890-2/50031-7.

Zimmerman, B. J. (2005). Investigating self-regulation and motivation: Historical background, methodological developments, and future prospects. *American Educational Research Journal, 45*(1), 166–183. https://doi.org/10.3102/0002831207312909.

Zimmerman, B. J. (2006). Development and adaptation of expertise: The role of self-regulatory processes and beliefs. In K. A. Ericsson, N. Charness, P. J. Feltovich, & R. R. Hoffman (Eds.), *The Cambridge handbook of expertise and expert performance* (pp. 705–722). Cambridge, UK: Cambridge University Press. https://doi.org/10.1017/CBO9780511816796.039.

Zimmerman, B. J., & Campillo, M. (2003). Motivating self-regulated problem solvers. In J. E. Davidson & R. J. Sternberg (Eds.), *The psychology of problem solving* (pp. 233–262). New York: Cambridge University Press.

Zimmerman, B. J., & Kitsantas, A. (2005). The hidden dimension of personal competence: Self-regulated learning and practice. In A. J. Elliot & C. S. Dweck (Eds.), *Handbook of competence and motivation* (pp. 509–526). New York: Guilford Publications.

Zimmerman, B. J., & Moylan A. R. (2009). Self-regulation: Where metacognition and motivation intersect. In D. J. Hacker, J. Dunlosky & A. C. Graesser (Eds.), *Handbook of metacognition in education* (pp. 299–315). New York: Routledge.

....

CHAPTER 24

INTRINSIC AND EXTRINSIC MOTIVATIONS FOR MUSIC PERFORMANCE

....

PAUL EVANS AND RICHARD M. RYAN

INTRODUCTION

....

MOTIVATION for music can be seen as something of a paradox. On the one hand, music is a source of immense joy. Throughout history and across cultures, people have gained intrinsic pleasure from musical activities, through performing, singing, creating, listening, or moving to music. Beyond the sheer joy it provides, people find a deep sense of personal connection with music, and with other people through music. There are few people who do not find some meaning in musical activity.

Yet on the other hand, anyone who has attempted to learn and develop their musical skills knows that music can also be demanding, difficult, and effortful. It can often require hard work, dedication, and sacrifice. Keeping up a regular practice routine requires substantial motivational resources. Developing musicians can be presented with challenges to their motivation: teachers can be demanding, evaluations can be stressful, and competitions can shift the focus from creating an aesthetic experience to outshining others. Performance anxiety cripples many— hardly an experience associated with an activity that otherwise seems so personally meaningful and enjoyable.

In this chapter, we provide a motivational model of music performance, one that recognizes it as both an intrinsically motivated joy and passion, but also as a discipline that can be arduous, frustrating, or depleting. To capture this complexity, we apply *Self-Determination Theory* (SDT; Ryan & Deci, 2017), a broad psychological theory of human motivation, personality development, and wellness. We begin by discussing how engagement in music is often intrinsically motivated, and how interest in playing music can, under nurturing conditions, develop into an avocation or career. We then address how music performance also requires internalized motivation, as it demands self-regulated learning and meaningful practice. We also look at the darker side of music engagement—conditions that undermine the enjoyment of music and can even be detrimental to motivation and wellbeing. SDT provides a framework for understanding the internalization of the attitudes, practice habits, and sacrifices that musical performance requires, as well as how social environments can either support or undermine musicians' intrinsic motivation and internalization. Specifically, SDT argues that contexts that support the fulfillment of performers' *basic psychological needs* for autonomy, competence, and relatedness help sustain high-quality motivation and performance over time. To conclude, we summarize the implications of this model for musicians, parents, educators, and researchers.

The Joy and Discipline of Music

Intrinsic motivation and the joy of music

There can be no doubt that motivation to experience and produce music is a fundamental part of human nature. Despite varying definitions between cultures about what is and is not counted as "music," and the vastly different forms music can take across cultures, people are moved to produce music almost everywhere in the world (Nettl, 2001). In Brown's (2017) survey of anthropological literature on human universals, music is listed not only by itself as "music" but also in more specific forms such as children's music, vocal music, music in relation to dance, music as an art form, and music associated with religious activity. These associations are supported by recent evidence examining large-scale ethnomusicological corpuses of text and recorded music from hundreds of cultures around the world (Mehr et al., 2019). Indeed, singing and other music activities have been proposed as an evolutionary adaptation for social connection—through mother-infant bonding during pregnancy and in the acquisition of social and emotional capital throughout life (Cross, 2001; Davidson & Garrido, 2019; Parncutt, 2016).

In addition to being found in human cultures all over the world, motivation for music performance is present across the lifespan (Hargreaves & Lamont, 2017). From a very young age (possibly before birth), infants identify, remember, and respond to music (Parncutt, 2016; Trehub & Degé, 2015). Children spontaneously and intuitively play games involving singing and movement (Marsh & Young, 2015). Later, adolescents become particularly involved in music at a time when they are developing their identities and establishing independence in the social world (Hargreaves et al., 2015). For those adolescents who develop an interest in music performance, they begin to think about the role it might have in their lives and careers (Evans & McPherson, 2015). And at the end of life, music is used as therapy to improve the experience of ageing and in some cases, at least temporarily, reverse cognitive decline (Särkämö, 2018).

It seems that humans all over the world, and in all stages of life, find interest and enjoyment in music. This "naturally" rewarding nature of musical experience is, at a psychological level, described by the phenomenon of *intrinsic motivation*, which refers to activities that are done for their own sake—for the inherent enjoyment and satisfaction that arises from the activity itself (Ryan & Deci, 2017). As shown with other manifestations of intrinsic motivation (Di Domenico & Ryan, 2017), musical experiences have positive neural correlates, including striatal responses such as those evidenced with other attractive stimuli (Chanda & Levitin, 2013; Levitin, 2013). Music also appears to play a self-regulatory, even self-soothing, function. For example, a study of patients post-surgery showed lower stress, pain, anxiety, and blood pressure when listening to music—an effect even greater for those who chose the music themselves (Leardi et al., 2007). In short, music is something people find inherently satisfying and well as beneficial to wellness. Even the concept of "playing" an instrument (in English, at least) conveys that intrinsic motivation plays a fundamental role in the act of music making.

Intrinsic motivation in music performance

Whenever researchers study musicians and music students, they find intrinsic motivation in abundance. Indeed, because music is so fundamental to human nature, we might expect that the experience of intrinsic motivation pervades efforts to develop musical skills and become a musician. Moreover, intrinsic motivation in music students in high school and university is associated with a range of positive outcomes, including their intentions to continue studying music during high school or university (Comeau et al., 2019; Freer & Evans, 2019; Freer & Evans, 2018; Kingsford-Smith & Evans, 2019; Lacaille et al., 2007); their intentions to commence or continue a music performance career (Bonneville-Roussy et al., 2017; Miksza et al., 2019; Parkes, 2012; Parkes & Jones, 2011; Schmidt et al., 2006); the quantity and quality of their practice (Evans & Bonneville-Roussy, 2016; Renwick, 2008); and the quality of their music performance (Bonneville-Roussy et al., 2017; Lacaille et al., 2007). Intrinsic motivation is also associated with how involved people outside schools are with music activities. For example, amateur musicians in community ensembles generally report high amounts of intrinsic motivation (Dale, 2018), and comparisons between musically disengaged, amateur, and professional music performers show an increasing level of intrinsic motivation according to the level of involvement (Appelgren et al., 2019).

It appears that serious engagement in music requires a heavy dose of intrinsic motivation. As we alluded to earlier, music performance begins with an interest and enjoyment that is cultivated through activities that might not always themselves seem to be interesting and enjoyable, but which are necessary for skill development. Nonetheless, we maintain that few music students or music artists would be able to sustain high-quality work without a high degree of intrinsic motivation.

Sustaining (or undermining) intrinsic motivation for music performance

For an activity where intrinsic motivation is found in such abundance, we might well ask, why isn't everyone doing it? Most people participate in musical culture by listening, consuming, and attending live music events, but the same cannot be said for creating, composing, and performing music. Few people attain even rudimentary music performance skills, and even fewer become proficient musicians in pursuit of a professional career, or even for the sake of a hobby.

Intrinsic motivation in any activity is an experience that can either be supported or undermined by particular social and environmental conditions. SDT provides a long-standing and empirically supported "mini-theory" of this phenomenon called *cognitive evaluation theory* (Deci & Ryan, 1985; Ryan & Deci, 2017). Within this theory, intrinsic motivation is dependent on experiences of *competence* (feeling able to do an activity rather than incompetent or lost) and *autonomy* (feeling willing and volitional rather than forced or controlled). In their early work, Deci and Ryan (1985) specifically argued that early childhood interests (such as music) are nourished by experiences of competence and autonomy in the activity, and by social supports that enable those experiences to occur. Insofar as activities and social environments support the satisfaction of these needs, intrinsic motivation for an activity becomes enhanced and sustained. Conversely, salient or chronic frustrations of either of these needs (e.g., by excessive challenges or external control) can undermine intrinsic motivation.

Cognitive evaluation theory therefore provides a way to explain why such an intrinsically motivating activity is also one that is only pursued seriously beyond childhood by relatively few people. Later in this chapter, we explore in greater detail the potential for music to satisfy or frustrate people's needs and thus affect their motivation. Meanwhile, it is clear that intrinsic motivation is a necessary condition in the pursuit of music learning and performance. Music learning contexts can either provide early feelings of competence and autonomy that develop ongoing intrinsic motivation, particularly so if they also experience parental involvement and support for the activity itself. Or they can fail to supply these satisfying experiences, leading children to cease the activity altogether (Evans et al., 2013). For musicians who eventually become performers, these processes are relevant from a relatively young age, as depending on the instrument, many children begin lessons before six years of age (Comeau et al., 2015; McPherson et al., 2015). Of course, even though the experience of music can be intrinsically motivating, there are many activities involved in developing musical skills are not themselves intrinsically motivating. We now turn to the phenomenon of extrinsic motivation to elaborate on these experiences.

Extrinsic motivation and the discipline of music

Although music performance can be intrinsically motivated, the efforts required to develop musical skills and expertise are not always so. Singing may emerge spontaneously and happily for young children, but their mandated involvement in a school choir might feel dissatisfying or uninteresting. Playing a musical instrument can be immensely satisfying, but anyone who has attempted to learn has known the frustrations of initial efforts whose payoffs seem distant and even unattainable. Music lessons, practice, rehearsals,

Motivation	AMOTIVATION	EXTRINSIC MOTIVATION				INTRINSIC MOTIVATION
		Controlled Motivation Lower Motivational Quality (e.g., performance and wellness)		**Autonomous Motivation** Higher Motivational Quality (e.g., performance and wellness)		
Regulatory Style		External Regulation	Introjection	Identification	Integration	
Attributes	• Lack of perceived competence, or • Lack of value	• External rewards or punishments • Compliance • Reactance	• Ego Involvement • Focus on approval from self and others	• Personal importance • Conscious valuing of activity • Self-endorsement of goals	• Congruence • Synthesis and consistency of identifications	• Interest • Enjoyment • Inherent satisfaction
Perceived Locus of Causality	Impersonal	External	Somewhat External	Somewhat Internal	Internal	Internal

FIGURE 24.1. Continuum of motivation ranging from amotivation, through four types of extrinsic motivation, and intrinsic motivation. Adapted from Ryan & Deci, 2000; © 2017 Center for Self-Determination Theory.

participation in ensembles, and even public performances are all examples of activities that developing musicians might not find *inherently* enjoyable, and that require time and persistence. And there are many activities not so fundamental to music itself, but that are necessary for music learning and performance, that might be described as particularly *unenjoyable*—consider dragging heavy equipment from vans to venues, sleepless nights on tour in unfamiliar places, or managing time and resources in relation to multiple teaching and performing jobs.

Extrinsic motivation is a broad class of behavior defined by instrumentality. Any behavior driven by a goal separate from the activity itself is considered to be extrinsically regulated (Ryan & Deci, 2000; 2017). Extrinsic motivation is therefore a large category of behaviors and can take a variety of forms. Within SDT these varied forms of extrinsic motivation are seen as falling on a continuum, reflecting the extent to which the motivation is well-internalized and self-regulated, as shown in Figure 24.1.

At one end of this extrinsic motivation continuum is external regulation, where the motivation and instigation of the activity comes from something phenomenally outside the self. At the other end of the extrinsic motivation continuum is integration, a fully internalized form of motivation in which one's behavior is aligned or congruent with one's values and interests, as when one is wholeheartedly and volitionally engaged. The continuum therefore spans a dimension from *controlled* to *autonomous* regulation, or the extent to which the motivation emerges from external forces as opposed to emerging from the self. Because all of the motivations on this continuum are highly relevant to music performance, in what follows we shall describe each of them briefly.

External regulation

A highly controlled form of motivation is *external regulation*—when a person is driven or motivated by external rewards, pressures, or controls. In music performance, external regulation can appear at any age or skill level, as there are often external mandates, pressures, and rewards for participating or achieving.

In musical development, the fostering of external regulation is exemplified by parents who use external rewards and sanctions to motivate their children to practice or achieve. In the broader literature on self-determination theory, the effects of monetary rewards were one of the first phenomena to be investigated. They tend to have primarily short-term effects and tend to undermine intrinsic motivation. For example, a meta-analysis of 127 studies found that in educational settings, the provision of extrinsic rewards reduced free-choice behavior and interest, relative to comparable no-reward conditions (Deci et al., 2001). In music, similar findings have emerged. For example, in Faulkner, Davidson, and McPherson's (2010) study, all of the children who were given monetary rewards to practice had ceased learning within twelve months of starting to learn an instrument, suggesting that the use of tangible extrinsic rewards to get children to practice music may actually increase the risk of dropping out of music. Similarly, Comeau, Huta, Lu, and Swirp (2019) found that the parental strategy of giving extrinsic tangible rewards for practice and achievement predicted high levels of external regulation in their children.

External regulation is problematic not because it is not successful in energizing behavior—in fact, external regulations can be particularly effective for moving people to action. But external regulation incurs a cost in the quality of outcomes for the behavior and for the person. It tends to elicit either compliance or defiance in relation to the salient demands—resulting in a relatively impoverished form of behavior. For this reason, it may impact the amount and quality of music performance activities. For example, Comeau et al. (2019) found that external regulation, in contrast to intrinsic motivation, was unrelated to the amount or quality of their practice and was associated with children reporting that they practiced for no other reason than because they were forced or pressured.

Introjected regulation

Introjected regulation is a common and salient form of motivation among music performers. It is motivation driven by desires for approval, or to avoid disapproval, from the self and from others. While external regulation involves pressure from others, introjection represents ego-involvement and can be thought of as pressure from oneself. The foregrounding of the ego in introjected regulation means that when a musician is motivated by pride, adoration, and praise, their motivation could be sustained when things are going well. But when things go badly, the fragility of the ego is revealed, and a musician is likely to respond with defensiveness, aggression, or withdrawal. Ego involvement is also evident in avoidance behaviors, where behavior is regulated by the avoidance of shame or guilt (as when a student practices just to avoid feel guilty for not practicing, or to avoid disappointing a parent or teacher). By definition, then, these ego-driven introjection effects are unstable, because introjection relies on conditional regard.

Accordingly, research findings have found mixed results for introjected regulation. Introjected regulation for music learning can be positively (but mildly) related to children's intentions to continue music learning in the short, medium, and long term

(Liu, 2019), parents' estimates that children would continue well into the future (Comeau et al., 2019), and a desire to learn (Macintyre & Potter, 2014). But these relationships tend to be fairly weak, suggesting not that introjection has a small influence, but that its influence is unstable and contingent on the extent to which activities fuel or threaten the ego.

The decline of singing as a feature of everyday life, particularly in developed Western societies, may also be linked to introjected regulation. The ubiquity of recorded music in daily life means an abundance of "perfect" singing and performance, much of it impossible without either extensive experience and training, a large amount of studio engineering, or sometimes both. This point of comparison for one's own singing in everyday life is a highly unattainable standard, so many people may therefore unconsciously conclude that they are simply not cut out for it and may even feel potentially embarrassed to sing in social settings. This phenomenon was observed in a case study (Ruddock & Leong, 2005) of adults who had imposed bans on themselves singing in public situations (such as singing "Happy Birthday" with family or friends). The adults in the study had needs-frustrating experiences earlier in their lives, such as a choir teacher telling them to be quiet, or someone laughing at them being off-key. Of course, this phenomenon is not experienced by everybody, and there are many stark exceptions in contemporary social life (karaoke bars, evangelical churches, and even chanting at sports games)—but it does illustrate how a relatively intrinsic behavior such as singing can be externalized and feel controlled by ego-contingent behavioral regulations.

Identification and integration

As we step into the realm of high-quality motivation, we first encounter *identified motivation*, when people are motivated because they value the activity as being important and are personally invested in what they are doing. Identification—knowing that something is worthwhile and having a solid rationale for doing it—is hypothesized to be particularly important as a motivation to persist at the arduous or taxing tasks that enhance performance. These tasks may not be inherently enjoyable, but one can be willing to engage in them anyway, so long as they are perceived as being important to more intrinsic goals. Among the advantages of identification is that musicians will mobilize greater effort and focus when facing obstacles, be more flexible in strategies to achieve them, and feel good having done something that they personally experienced as being worthwhile. Clearly this is a high-quality form of motivation.

Identified regulation is necessary, but not sufficient, for fully internalized motivational regulation. In a study of high-performing musicians in high school, Evans and McPherson (2017) investigated how the students were describing their identities and looking ahead to the role music would play in their lives. One of the students, Margaret, played exceptionally well, and was passionate about music. Margaret had identified the value of music, and this led to her persisting with music as a potential choice for studying at university. In Margaret's case, though, identification was not enough—and it was not possible to integrate plans with external factors like feeling the need to enter a more lucrative career, and pressure from parents to stay close to the family home. The result was a delay in selecting a university course, and rumination and anxiety around planning for the future. Thus, although identified regulation is a high-quality type of motivation, Margaret's case illustrates why identification may not be enough to sustain ongoing motivation, especially in the face of ongoing external pressures.

SDT also specifies an even more autonomous form of extrinsic motivation, called *integrated regulation*. When integrated, a strong identification with music performance is also consistent and unified with the person's other identifications and values. In integrated regulation, the person is then unconflicted in pursuing an activity. In the case of Margaret, the identified value of music in her life could not be integrated with the external pressures of her career choice and not moving away from home. In the same study, another student, Brian, demonstrated a more integrated motivational profile (Evans & McPherson, 2017). Brian had considered a range of possible career options, but envisaged music as an ongoing leisure interest alongside pursuing a law degree in line with his passion for philosophy. In thinking about his future, Brian had integrated the possibilities ahead and reconciled a sense of personal identity but was flexible approaching how these plans might play out in the more distant future. In integrated regulation, activities are undertaken volitionally and are compatible with one's other values and sense of self, which is why it resembles intrinsic motivation in its degree of autonomy.

Quantity and quality of motivation

The previous section reviewed a number of motivation types, which fall on a continuum ranging from *controlled* to *autonomous* motivation, as shown in Figure 24.1 (Ryan & Deci, 2000; 2017). But motivation for a task, or even for music more broadly, cannot generally be described by a single type of regulation. People tend to hold different types of motivations at the same time, and depending on the circumstances, different types of motivation might become more or less salient. Nonetheless, it is beneficial to be able to describe people's overall motivational profiles for an activity or task. There are two ways this can be done. *Relative autonomy* refers to the idea that although people may hold different types of motivational regulations in different amounts, what really matters is the degree to which their overall motivation is relatively internal or external—a general indication of where their motivation fits on the continuum from controlled to autonomous. In this way, it is proposed that relative autonomy, or the overall internalization of motivation, is much more important than the overall quantity of motivation. In contrast, a *multiple motives* approach recognizes that people simultaneously hold different types of motivation and preserves the various configurations of these motivation types instead of reducing them to a single point. Using a multiple motives approach, researchers attempt to identify groups of people who represent common motivation profiles, maintaining the qualitative distinctions between the categories. In the following sections we review research on these two approaches—relative autonomy and multiple motives—and how they help to better understand the quantity and quality of musicians' motivation and behavior.

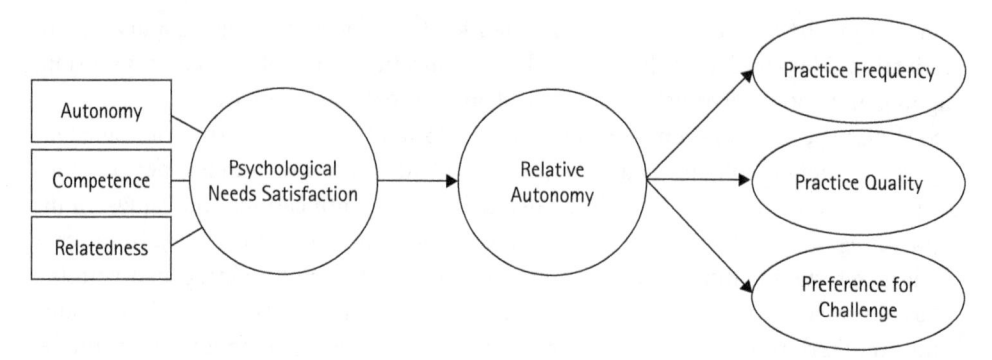

FIGURE 24.2. A study of university music students found the predictive value of relative autonomy for a range of music learning outcomes. Adapted from Evans & Bonneville-Roussy, 2016.

Relative autonomy

SDT predicts that what matters most in predicting optimal outcomes is not the total amount of motivation involved, but the quality of motivation, operationalized as relative autonomy. Considerable empirical support stands behind the idea that more autonomous forms of motivation contribute to higher-quality outcomes, whereas controlled forms do not, and can even yield negative effects (Ryan & Deci, 2017, 2020).

The pattern that emerges from relationships between the various types of motivational regulations results in a "simplex" (see Ryan & Connell, 1989). This is evident in a pattern of inter-correlations, in which motivation types adjacent along the continuum are most highly statistically correlated, a pattern that has been widely replicated in SDT measures across domains. This reliable structure in the pattern of correlations allows researchers to form a composite value for the overall level of relative autonomy. Various ways of calculating relative autonomy have been applied, including simple contrasts of autonomous versus controlled motives and various weightings that involve subtracting scores of controlled regulations from scores of autonomous regulations (Litalien et al., 2017; Sheldon et al., 2017). This was demonstrated in a study of university musicians shown in Figure 24.2, where their relative autonomy predicted a range of outcomes that were indicative of the quality of their engagement in music practice (Evans & Bonneville-Roussy, 2016).

In an important recent study, Comeau, Huta and Swirp (2019) developed a *Motivation for Music Learning* (MLM) scale comprising five subscales: intrinsic motivation, identification and integration, introjection, external regulation, and amotivation. In their validation work on children (ages 6-17) learning piano and violin, they administered the scale with the children and their parents. The MLM showed a systematic pattern of relationships that was consistent with the simplex model hypothesized by SDT. As with studies on relative autonomy in other contexts and domains, the MLM demonstrated consistent predictive validity. For example, experiences of external pressure correlated positively with amotivation and external regulation, and negatively with autonomous regulations. In contrast, freely choosing to play one's instrument outside of practice sessions showed an opposite pattern, being connected most strongly with intrinsic motivation and most weakly with amotivation. Interestingly, the parents' report of how much their child practiced was positively related to identified motivation, but unrelated to intrinsic motivation. This suggests that the difficult work of regular weekly practice was sustained not by intrinsic motivation, but by identified regulation, consistent with SDT findings on tasks that are not inherently enjoyable and thus require autonomous extrinsic motivation (Losier & Koestner, 1999; Niemiec & Ryan, 2009). Finally, long-term commitment to music was associated negatively with amotivation and positively to autonomous motives.

Multiple motives

An alternative approach to studying the quality of motivation is to maintain distinct, qualitatively different combinations of the motivation regulations, rather than collapsing the motivation categories to form a unidimensional indicator of relative autonomy. This approach preserves the important principle that people can hold different types of motivational regulations at the same time. For example, an orchestral musician might be autonomously motivated by the thrill of public performances, the feeling that they are being themselves through the career they have chosen, and the enjoyment of a team effort produced with their peers. But at the same time, they might also feel controlled by crippling performance anxiety stemming from introjected standards, or by a pushy section leader whose management style is based on external evaluations and control. In this example, the person has a high quantity of motivation—both autonomous and controlled forms. In contrast, another musician might have strong autonomous motivation, but none of the controlled motivation. They have less motivation overall, but their motivation is of a higher quality, being exclusively of the autonomous type, absent of the control and pressure.

SDT researchers have been able to examine these combinations of the quality versus the quantity of motivation through *person-centered analysis*—a statistical technique that identifies groups of people who share similar characteristics. Person-centered analysis has been used to compare people who have high quantity of motivation (i.e., high autonomous and high controlled motivation) with people who have high quality of motivation (i.e., high autonomous motivation and low controlled motivation). Figure 24.3 depicts these various configurations of motivation. This approach has already been used in other educational settings—for example, with high school students to find differences in self-regulated learning, procrastination, achievement, and attitudes toward cheating (Vansteenkiste et al., 2009), and with university students to find differences in dropout intentions, critical thinking, organization, affect, and achievement (Gillet et al., 2017).

In music, similar findings have emerged (Bonneville-Roussy & Evans, in preparation; Evans et al., in preparation). The results demonstrate that the overall amount of motivation can be influential in regulating behavior, but provides no advantages and may even undermine outcomes, depending on the qualities of motivation that are predominant. Consistent with SDT, motivation profiles characterized by more controlled motives can instigate behavior (e.g., they might move musicians to practice longer or

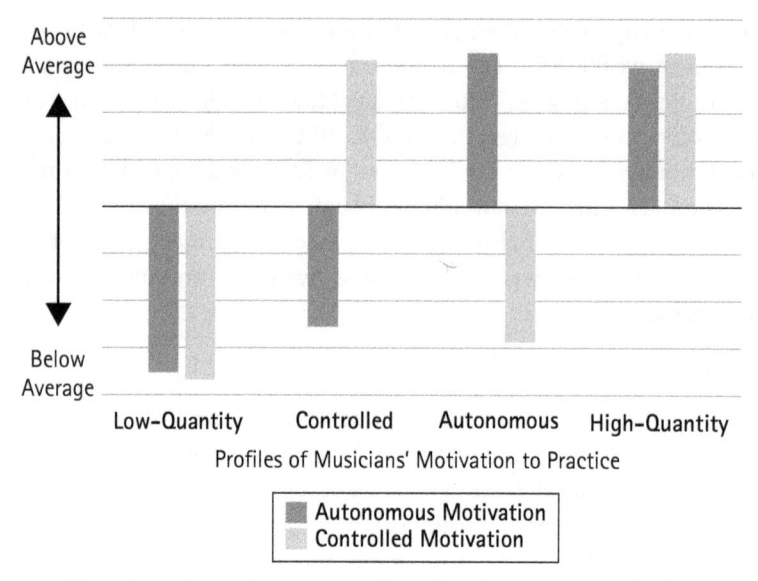

FIGURE 24.3. These hypothesized motivational profiles demonstrate multiple motives with respect for musicians' motivation to practice. Evans et al., in preparation.

more regularly), but they can have consequences for the quality of behavior (e.g., their practice might be less effective). The multiple motives approach also provides a way to understand how various types of motivation can change over time in response to the environment—for example, toward preparation for a high-stakes music performance examination. The profiles of students could start out with relatively high quality (i.e., strong autonomous motivation, low controlled motivation) but shift as they near the time of their performance assessment (Evans et at., in preparation). Although they might maintain their autonomous motivation, the increase in controlled motivation could add stress and anxiety, shift their focus away from high-quality practice, and undermine their performance. Such dynamics, common in music training, are thus illuminated through studies of profiles over time.

Summary: The joy and discipline of music

It is clear that music is universal to humans, suggesting that to some degree, it is an inherently interesting and enjoyable activity. However, learning music and being a professional musician both involve many types of activities that are arduous, difficult, or even unenjoyable, and impose demands and constraints that seem to undermine intrinsic motivation. SDT offers an explanation for this conundrum by identifying the importance of intrinsic motivation as a behavioral orientation to an activity characterized by interest and enjoyment, and the potential for internalizing activities such that they represent relatively autonomous types of motivation. In this way, motivation for these activities can become relatively internalized, to the extent that a musician can identify with why the activities are important, personally relevant, or necessary for other self-endorsed goals, and even to integrate the activities within a sense of self and identity as a performing musician. Research clearly supports the SDT predictions that a high dose of intrinsic motivation is necessary for sustained engagement in meaningful music learning and performance. And for those aspects that are not intrinsically motivating, the overall quality of a person's motivation—the extent to which it is internalized and autonomous—is an important predictor of music related outcomes.

Psychological Needs and Supports for Intrinsic Motivation and Internalization

Having established the various types of motivational regulations leading to various music learning and performance outcomes, we now turn to the social and environmental conditions that support (or undermine) the internalization of motivation. Intrinsic motivation and more autonomous forms of extrinsic regulation, as well as greater wellbeing, are more likely to be sustained and enhanced when conditions support the satisfaction of musicians' basic psychological needs (Ryan & Deci, 2017).

Basic psychological needs are so named because they are essential for thriving. Much like physical needs such as food and water, basic psychological needs are nutrients required for psychological integration, regulation, and growth (Ryan & Deci, 2017). Social environments can provide affordances for the fulfillment of basic psychological needs, in which case needs become fulfilled, directly predicting personal adjustment, growth, wellbeing, and thriving. Conversely, the environment can be impoverished of needs fulfillment, or worse, can provide structures that actively impede or frustrate psychological needs—leaving people vulnerable to maladjustment, disintegration, and psychological illbeing. This requirement of basic psychological needs fulfillment is evident across the lifespan, has been demonstrated cross-culturally, and is present regardless of whether or not a person explicitly values these basic needs (Chen et al., 2015).

SDT has specifically identified three basic psychological needs (Ryan & Deci, 2017):

Competence—at its most basic form, the need to feel that one has an effect on one's environment (as in the joy of an infant when learning that the movement of a rattle makes a sound; White, 1959), and in a more elaborate form, the need to feel effective and masterful in the development of skills and abilities (as in the excitement of a pianist when finally "nailing" a difficult passage of music).

Autonomy—the need to feel that one is the agent or cause of one's behavior and actions. Autonomy is present in music activity when a musician has a willingness and authentic interest in doing it. It is experienced as self-expression and volition, and with it comes a sense of ownership and identity. Autonomy stands in contrast to control—a feeling that something outside the self is determining one's actions and involvement in an activity.

Relatedness—the need to feel that one's activities occur within an environment of security, connection, or belonging with others. As an inherently social activity, engaging in music naturally affords many such opportunities for social connectedness, including the act itself (singing in a karaoke bar, playing in an orchestra, or improvising in a jazz ensemble) and the preparation for it (learning from a teacher, or rehearsing a large orchestral work with other players).

By its nature, music performance lends itself to the fulfillment of psychological needs for competence, relatedness, and autonomy, as noted in the examples cited earlier. In many contexts, this may be the case, but as with other activities, the fulfillment of psychological needs in music depends on the affordances of the activity, particularly the social environment in which it occurs. This SDT formulation translates directly into a number of key assumptions about how parental, educational, and professional environments will affect musicians' wellness and motivation. Most important, social contexts that support autonomy, competence, and relatedness are expected to help maintain and enhance internalization and intrinsic motivation, whereas social contexts that thwart these needs will undermine both sustained persistence and wellbeing.

This general formulation is illustrated in the study shown in Figure 24.2, where psychological needs fulfillment predicts the internalization of motivation for studying music at university (as indicated by relative autonomy). Needs satisfaction drives internalization in a synergistic way—the fulfillment of all three psychological needs is required for autonomous motivation. Piano performers, for example, can feel competence if they are performing well, and relatedness if they have good connections with their friends and colleagues, but if they also have a lack of autonomy (by feeling pressured by a manager, locked in by their touring schedule, or doing everything because they "have to"), they will likely not be able to advance their motivation beyond introjected regulation to more fully internalized regulations.

In the following sections, we review salient research on basic psychological needs satisfaction (and frustration) in various music contexts. These studies have looked at basic psychological needs in music contexts in two ways. First, researchers study the affordances of the social environment and how they fulfill basic needs, operationalized as *needs support*. In SDT, support for the fulfillment of autonomy has a particular role. When a parent or instructor provides autonomy support, their starting point is seeking to understanding the perspective and experience of the person whose motivation they are attempting to support. From this stance, they are attuned to the needs of the musician they are working with. Because of the interrelated nature of the psychological needs as well as the central role played by autonomy in internalization, autonomy support in this sense is fulfilling of all basic psychological needs. Second, researchers measure people's experiences of needs satisfaction (vs. needs frustration) in music performance activities, and these are shown to be predictive of internalized motivation and, as noted earlier in our discussion of internalization, a range musical and nonmusical outcomes. These two perspectives—needs support provided by musical environments, and the experience by musicians of needs satisfaction (or frustration)—have been studied in the various contexts where musicians work.

Needs support from parents

Studies of parenting environments within the SDT framework have typically focused on three dimensions: autonomy support (supporting volition), involvement (supporting engagement and relatedness), and structure (supporting competence and optimal challenges; e.g., Grolnick et al., 1997). All three dimensions are relevant to music performers insofar as learning to master an instrument or voice usually begins in childhood. Parents are therefore involved in diverse ways in their children's music learning, from transport to lessons, purchasing equipment, and attending concerts, to involvement in the lessons themselves, helping with the child's practice at home, and seeking out opportunities to extend their child's learning (Creech, 2010; McPherson, 2009). In an illustrative study of the role of parental involvement, Davidson et al. (1996) concluded that the students of higher ability tended to have parents who started out being highly supportive and involved, and maintained consistent, increasing involvement in response to their children's growing sense of musicianship. The students in their study with lower ability, in contrast, had parents who appeared to be more directive. The parents' own motivations therefore become influential.

In a more direct examination of parents' self-determined goals for their children's musical outcomes, Liu et al. (2015) studied interactions between what they termed "intrinsic" reasons why parents support their child's learning ("I want to develop my child's interests in music") and "extrinsic" reasons ("I want my child to get awards or become famous"). The interaction results suggest that while parents' extrinsic motivations appeared to energize their children's practice behavior, there was a cost both in the psychological pressure placed on them and in the quality of their practice.

One strategy typically used to motivate children's music and practice behavior is to connect the relevant activity to some kind of tangible extrinsic reward. As we reviewed earlier, studies suggest that this could result in higher externalized regulation, where the main reason why the child practices is because they felt forced by others or themselves (Comeau et al., 2019), leading to lower persistence in learning beyond a short period (Faulkner et al., 2010). In relation to psychological needs, the reason why tangible rewards undermine motivation is because they reduce autonomy. They communicate to the recipient not that the person is interested in their perspective or experience, but that the person is interested in controlling their behavior. It can also convey to the musician that the target behavior is indeed not enjoyable—otherwise the reward would not be required.

More generally, we suggest that parents who supports their child's autonomy while also being actively involved in supporting music activities provide the most nurturing and optimal backdrop for a developing musician. Needs-supportive parents are better positioned to help their children negotiate the inevitable highs and lows of music engagement and performance. In addition, providing structure can help organize the learner's time and balance their engagement with other demands and interests.

Needs support in studio lessons

One of the most common ways children and adolescents can be involved in music performance is by learning to sing or play a musical instrument from a studio teacher. In these contexts, vocal and instrumental teachers instruct and coach the development of music performance skills and provide direction for practice between lessons. A large literature on the effects of academic teachers (e.g., Ryan & Deci, 2020) and sport coaches (e.g., Standage & Ryan, 2019) is the main source of evidence for how needs support might operate in the music studio.

Needs support can be communicated by teachers and experienced by students on a moment-to-moment basis. Kupers, Van Dijk, Van Geert, and McPherson (2015) looked at such interactions between teachers and children over the course of a lesson. Controlling teachers (the study used the term *directive teachers*) appeared to respond negatively to resistance from the students, whereas the less directive teachers had regarded students' expressions of resistance as opportunities to respond with autonomy support. The study found that students responded differentially to autonomy-supportive versus directive teaching. Teachers who were more autonomy-supportive had students who responded to their efforts with greater engagement, but only if they themselves were autonomously motivated. If the student had a controlled orientation, teachers' attempts to provide autonomy support were often met with resistance. As noted in much SDT literature, when students lack any autonomy for learning, it can "pull" teachers to become controlling, which unfortunately does not inspire greater engagement (Pelletier et al., 2002). The micro-level analysis of these moment-to-moment interactions illustrates the complexity of interactions between teachers' general disposition to be autonomy-supportive (or otherwise), the specific strategies teachers use to support autonomy from moment to moment, and the students' own autonomous or controlled motivation (Kupers et al., 2015).

Another perspective on needs support in studio lessons comes from studying teachers' controlling behaviors, which frustrate the learner's need for autonomy, foster external regulation (Ryan & Deci, 2020), and induce stress responses such as increased cortisol (Reeve & Tseng, 2011). Teacher control is indicated in students who report that their teacher tries to control what they do, is inflexible, uses forceful language, or puts pressure on the student (Jang et al., 2009). Reports from studio musicians on their level of teacher control in this way have been associated with increased feelings of controlled motivation and with socially prescribed perfectionism—the feeling of external pressure to play perfectly and the belief that others hold unrealistically high expectations of one's behavior (e.g., see Miksza, Evans, & McPherson, 2019).

Needs support in school music programs

In most school systems around the world, music at some point becomes a subject among many, and students have to make choices about which subjects to study. Music education researchers have therefore been interested in whether students want to or intend to keep studying music. Freer and Evans (2019) found that needs satisfaction was strongly related to high school students' intentions to continue studying music, and was predicted by perceived needs support provided in their classroom. Longitudinal work (Kingsford-Smith & Evans, 2019) has upheld this finding and suggested that students' internalization of motivation for studying music was an important predictor of their intentions to continue. In that study, psychological needs satisfaction explained why the value was internalized, but students' intentions to continue studying music were more closely associated with their experiences of psychological needs fulfillment rather than their value of the subject as useful or important. Similarly, in a high school orchestra program, psychological needs satisfaction strongly predicted intentions to continue (Evans & Liu, 2019). And in a retrospective study of students who had recently completed high school (Evans et al., 2013), respondents were asked to report on their psychological needs satisfaction throughout childhood and adolescence. The reasons cited as to why they ceased learning clearly reflected psychological needs frustration, or at least, a lack of needs fulfillment—both quantitatively and qualitatively.

The role of the teacher and the teacher's experience in school music programs is also relevant to their students' motivation. In particular, teachers' perceptions of their ability to teach have arisen as issues related to their motivational practices. Figueiredo (2019) found that among music teachers in Brazil, those who had formal music teaching qualifications in addition to music qualifications were less controlling than those who had only music qualifications. They speculated that the training in music pedagogy helped the teachers understand that controlling teaching practices may not be effective. In many other places around the world, the primary (elementary) school music curriculum is often taught by non-specialists with minimal training in music. In an Australian study (Freer, 2018), students who reported a low-quality primary school music program were unlikely to have high intentions to continue pursuing music—even when their early high school music experience was needs-fulfilling. Together these studies speak to not only the need for music to be taught by experienced specialists, but also the need to consider the teacher's perspective about how difficult and unenjoyable it is to teach something one does not feel confident in teaching, and how this competence-frustrating experience can manifest in controlling teaching and be passed on to students.

A case study of teachers in the UK may illustrate ways to address these concerns. In Garrett's (2019) qualitative case study in the UK, a primary school provided a workshop for teachers to acknowledge that they may not have requisite music teaching skills, and to share ideas about how they might wish to acquire them. These teachers developed their music teaching abilities while feeling safe to air their concerns and anxieties, suggesting that an autonomy-supportive environment helped teachers who otherwise may have been vulnerable to competence frustration. Indeed, it is clear from meta-analytic research on high school teachers across the full range of school subjects that teachers are receptive to learning about autonomy support and can adopt autonomy-supportive teaching techniques, with lasting positive effects on their teaching practices, their own motivation, and the motivation of their students (Su & Reeve, 2010). There does not appear to be substantial work on such interventions with music teachers, but carefully designed professional development opportunities could have substantial efficacy.

Needs support in elite-level music performance programs

Gaining a place in an elite music program—particularly schools and conservatories emphasizing Western classical, jazz, or art music—tends to be competitive and based on advanced prior music performance attainment. Here, musicians are honing and perfecting their craft at a high level, competence perceptions are foregrounded, and the specific goal of a long-term music performance career is more salient. It is not surprising that these environments can be competitive, and students experience high amounts of pressure to continue developing their performance in an environment that demands excellence.

Competitiveness in these environments may pose a threat to high-quality motivation. In studying this hypothesis, Miksza et al. (2019) examined musicians in higher education music schools in Australia, the UK, and the United States. They found competitiveness was associated positively with controlled motivation, as predicted. But competitiveness was also associated positively (though to a lesser extent) with autonomous motivation. For the students in these institutions, it may be that the competitive nature of the social context provided motivation-relevant information about their level of competence, helping them to position their ongoing motivation. Autonomous motivation (but not controlled motivation) in turn predicted the students' career intentions—their commitment to music as a profession. Such results fit with SDT's formulation that competition has both informational and controlling aspects, and it is the relative salience of these aspects that determines the effects of competitive contexts on motivational outcomes (Ryan & Deci, 2017)

As noted earlier, musicians in elite contexts may also be prone to perfectionism—a trait clearly concerned with the pursuit of competence satisfaction, but probably more associated with competence frustration, since perfectionism is characterized by the inability to live up to exceedingly demanding standards. Controlling conditions in particular are thought to exacerbate the impact of perfectionistic concerns on competence frustrations. If the music learning environment is perceived as particularly controlling, it may leave music students more vulnerable to needs frustration (Haraldsen et al., 2019).

It seems that in response to highly demanding educational environments, the development of general psychological skills might be valuable, like adaptability to a chaotic environment, or resilience in the face of adversity. Undoubtedly, these traits are associated with positive outcomes for students (for a review, see Martin & Evans, this part). But although this may be the case, it is also important to study whether the demanding environments are having an impact. Miksza, Evans, and McPherson (2019) studied whether this might be the case for adaptability, peer relationships, and perfectionism. They hypothesized that these traits might mitigate (or aggravate, in the case of perfectionism) the negative effects of stress on students' wellbeing. None of the traits did, suggesting that although they are valuable in themselves, they do not negate the experience of stress. Further study of this type of phenomenon is crucial, because it suggests that any focus on intervening to alleviate the causes of stress should focus on the characteristics of the social environment, rather than attempts to develop psychological meta-skills as protective factors.

Although the previous research suggests that elite educational institutions are treacherous contexts for motivation and wellbeing, studies show mixed results. Earlier we mentioned that everywhere researchers study motivation in music, they find intrinsic motivation, and elite music education contexts are no exception. Wellbeing and health-promoting behaviors appeared to be higher than the general population in a study of students in UK conservatoires (Araújo et al., 2017). But a study of students in comparable US institutions found high levels of depression, anxiety, and stress on a standardized instrument (Koops & Kuebel, 2019). Within the domain of music, performance anxiety is also particularly salient for students as they prepare for increasingly frequent public performances, many of them coupled with the stress of formal evaluation (see also Osborne, Volume 2). As noted by Ascenso et al. (2018) in their study of professional classical musicians, it is important to measure and model music students' motivations and wellbeing-related concerns with precision, rather than relying on stereotypes of dramatically poor mental health.

Non-professional musicians and community music organizations

One way to be involved in music performance, particularly if music is not a central occupation or professional pursuit, is through participation in community bands, orchestras, choirs, or other types of ensembles. Naturally these groups tend to have a social focus, and they are voluntary activities, suggesting high amounts of relatedness and autonomy. They are often amateur groups, so unlike in the elite music performance contexts we described earlier, participation does not depend so highly on perceptions of ability, and competence motivation may be more easily fulfilled. Community music groups often consist of participants with a range of abilities and motivational profiles—some might be beginners, some taking up an instrument they had learned in childhood, some professional musicians. In a qualitative study of people's motivations in these settings, Murray (2017) found common ground, in that all participants were "driven" by the fulfillment of their basic psychological needs. Within the activity, it is also possible that participants experience a range of different needs satisfactions. Of course, the fact of participating in such a group is indicative of a high level of autonomy, but there can also be variation experienced in needs support within the activity. Dale's (2018) study of community band participants demonstrates this: participants who reported greater needs fulfillment also reported greater valuing of music, belief in the importance of music for children, and present wellbeing.

More recently, Krause et al. (2019) investigated needs satisfaction in Australian adults actively participating in music. They found that music activities were associated with competence and relatedness satisfactions and that these satisfactions were in turn associated with benefits to emotional and social wellbeing. In addition, being autonomously engaged in music, as indicated by relative autonomy, predicted higher mood, self-esteem, and self-actualization. It seems that even outside of formal education and career settings, music can satisfy people's basic psychological needs.

Implications for Music Performers

As we have noted throughout this chapter, the support for high-quality motivation is crucial for developing musicians and for music performers. The environments in which musicians learn, work, and perform can either support or thwart psychological needs fulfillment, and impact the quality of motivation. The previous section outlined some of the implications for the various social contexts in which music happens. Here, we more explicitly highlight some of the major implications for how high-quality motivation can be managed for two major features of the lives of musicians: the need to practice as the primary means of improving performance, and the management of potentially difficult and challenging music performance careers.

A note on practice

Performing musicians face a range of motivational challenges, including the need for sustained engagement and regular practice to develop skills, and the necessity of maintaining a real passion and interest in their craft. A critical element in developing mastery in music performance is *deliberate practice* (Ericsson et al., 1993; Lehmann et al., 2018; cf. Burgoyne, Hambrick & Harris, this volume). Music practice is for students the single most proximal activity within their control to improve their performance ability, but it is difficult to do. In defining deliberate practice, Ericsson et al. (1993) noted that it is inherently difficult and effortful, and that the ability to sustain large amounts of high-quality deliberate practice is constrained by motivational resources. As we have reviewed throughout this chapter, becoming and being a musician involves many activities that are themselves not intrinsically motivating, and practice can often be one of them.

Two dimensions are particularly relevant for self-determination theory: the amount of practice behavior that is undertaken (practice quantity), and the degree to which that behavior is attentive, deliberate, and focused on improving performance (practice quality). In terms of practice quantity, more frequent and longer practice is strongly associated with autonomous motivation (e.g., Bonneville-Roussy & Bouffard, 2015; Evans & Bonneville-Roussy, 2016), but has mixed relationships with controlled motivation. In terms of practice quality, autonomous motivation is much more clearly predictive, leading students to practice with higher behavioral, cognitive, and emotional engagement (e.g., Evans et al., in preparation), more self-regulated learning strategies (McPherson et al., 2017), and a higher preference by students for challenging tasks from which they have an opportunity to extend their learning (Evans & Bonneville-Roussy, 2016). In fact, one study (Bonneville-Roussy & Bouffard, 2015) found a strong effect of practice quality on achievement, and when this was taken into account, practice quantity was negatively predictive of achievement, a result speaking to the importance of understanding the quality of behavior rather than merely the amount of it. Teachers can play a role in supporting high-quality practice in their students: In analyzing data from expert teachers, Krause and Davidson (2018)summarized a range of best-practice skills. Latent among these skills was teachers' recognition of the need to support basic psychological needs in educational settings.

Self-Regulated Learning is a term used to describe the ways in which learners (or in this case, music performers) plan, monitor, and evaluate their own progress toward learning goals (McPherson, Miksza, & Evans, 2017; see also McPherson, this part). The use of the term *self-regulated* overlaps with the SDT concept of self-regulation in the sense of behaviors that emanate from or are determined by oneself as opposed to external forces. The high-quality behaviors described by the self-regulated learning framework are a way to consider the kinds of practice quality outcomes predicted by self-determination theory.

Professional musicians and their careers

Although our focus has been on developing musicians and musical training, professional musicians face ongoing challenges to their motivation and wellbeing. One can find many biographies of famous musicians where an absence of need support from managers, handlers, and contractual relationships led to negative outcomes, including burnout, addiction, and even suicide. Such stories extend from Mozart to Michael Jackson. Despite the prevalence of these stories, it may be tempting to form a view that great music requires artists who endure negative or traumatic experiences for the sake of their art. We know of no empirical evidence supporting that view. Indeed, in the examples just listed, both Mozart and Michael Jackson paid a considerable psychological price for the controlled motivations they experienced during their lives, which surely also limited their creative abilities. Although the genius of many artists appears to emerge from troubling circumstances or mental illness, there does not seem to be a compelling case that chronic or acute needs frustration is a necessary condition for creative artistic output.

One area of research of potential relevance to professional musicians is another mini-theory within SDT called *Goal Contents Theory* (GCT; Ryan & Deci, 2017). The theory grows out of research on people's life aspirations or long-term goals (Kasser & Ryan, 1996; Martela et al., 2019). According to GCT, when people strongly aspire to or value intrinsic goals such as having loving relationships, giving to community, or personal growth, this tends to facilitate the satisfaction of their basic psychological needs and enhance their wellbeing. In contrast, placing a strong emphasis or value on extrinsic goals, such as a desire for fame, wealth, or image, can thwart the fulfillment of basic needs and lead to greater ill-being. This seems also to be true even when considering whether the goals were realized: Attainment of intrinsic goals has been directly linked with greater wellness, while attainment of extrinsic goals is not (e.g., Niemiec et al., 2009). Because many musicians may pursue a professional career out of a desire for fame, money, or image, they may be particularly at risk for lower basic need satisfaction. To date, aspirations research testing GCT among career musicians has not to our knowledge emerged, but it seems like an important set of questions to study.

Yet despite such hazards and challenges, those who are able to establish a professional music career may find high psychological needs satisfaction and self-actualization. For example, as noted earlier, Ascenso et al. (2018) profiled the wellbeing of hundreds of classical musicians and found that it was actually much higher than that of the general population on all dimensions that were measured. Pursuing one's passions and finding through them a sense of autonomy, competence, and relatedness is of course one of the great draws of an artistic life (Bonneville-Roussy et al., 2011; Bonneville-Roussy & Vallerand, 2018a, 2018b). Nonetheless, our review of motivation and psychological needs support showed a dearth of research at the professional level, with most of the research having studied these phenomena in educational settings such as the studio, high school and university, and in community organizations.

CONCLUSION

Music is an enormously pervasive phenomenon across human cultures, and engaging in music is for almost all people is an intrinsically motivated activity. However, becoming a music performer requires not only an intense interest and enjoyment of music, but also the development of skills, talents, and discipline. SDT addresses the complexities of music performance by conceptualizing how both the intrinsically and extrinsically motivated aspects of performing music can be enhanced or undermined.

In this chapter we focused especially on how parents, teachers, mentors, and professional pressures can enhance or undermine high-quality, autonomous engagement in music, and lead either to great psychological needs satisfaction, or alternatively to frustration and burnout.

Given the pervasive role of music in people's lives, and the near universal interest in music education and talent development, it is remarkable to us how relatively neglected has been the study of music motivation and career development, especially relative to domains such as sport coaching and work motivation. That said, as we have reviewed herein, there is a burgeoning set of research findings emerging from within the self-determination theory perspective that investigate issues of both theoretical and practical significance. Many of these findings have direct implications for music education, talent development, and personal self-regulation. We hope this summary of the field as it stands inspires more work in this area, using a framework already providing a clear set of theoretical principles with robust empirical support.

Key Sources

Ryan, R. M., & Deci, E. L. (2017). *Self-determination theory*. New York: Guilford Press.
McPherson, G. E., Miksza, P., & Evans, P. (2017). Self-regulated learning in music practice and performance. In D. H. Schunk & J. A. Greene (Eds.), *Handbook of self-regulation of learning and performance* (2nd ed., pp. 181–193). New York: Routledge.

Reflective Questions

1. When and how did you develop your passion for music learning, and what were the circumstances that led to it?
2. Why do you practice? List reasons for practicing and consider whether they represent autonomous or controlled reasons for doing so.
3. Think about the instructors or teachers who have been most motivating for you—what characterized their approach? Conversely, think about those who were the most demotivating or discouraging—how did they affect your autonomy, competence, and relatedness?
4. This chapter has outlined why the quality of motivation is much more important than the quantity of motivation. Can you think of circumstances where you had a high amount of motivation, but it was not of high quality? What were the consequences?
5. Music performance careers can have many external demands. In what ways can you recognize the inner motivational resources that can sustain difficult times in a performance career while external demands are salient?

ACKNOWLEDGMENTS

This chapter was supported by an ARC Discovery Grant DP150103330. The authors are grateful to Andrew Kingsford-Smith, who assisted with the literature search and review.

REFERENCES

Appelgren, A., Osika, W., Theorell, T., Madison, G., & Bojner Horwitz, E. (2019). Tuning in on motivation: Differences between non-musicians, amateurs, and professional musicians. *Psychology of Music, 47*(6), 864–873. https://doi.org/10.1177/0305735619861435.

Araújo, L. S., Wasley, D., Perkins, R., Atkins, L., Redding, E., Ginsborg, J., & Williamon, A. (2017). Fit to perform: An investigation of higher education music students' perceptions, attitudes, and behaviors toward health. *Frontiers in Psychology, 8*, 1558. https://doi.org/10.3389/fpsyg.2017.01558.

Ascenso, S., Perkins, R., & Williamon, A. (2018). Resounding meaning: A PERMA wellbeing profile of classical musicians. *Frontiers in Psychology, 9*, 1895. https://doi.org/10.3389/fpsyg.2018.01895.

Bonneville-Roussy, A., & Bouffard, T. (2015). When quantity is not enough: Disentangling the roles of practice time, self-regulation and deliberate practice in musical achievement. *Psychology of Music, 43*(5), 686–704. https://doi.org/10.1177/0305735614534910.

Bonneville-Roussy, A., & Evans, P. (in preparation). *Motivational profiles of music practice from a self-determination theory perspective.*

Bonneville-Roussy, A., Evans, P., Verner-Filion, J., Vallerand, R. J., & Bouffard, T. (2017). Motivation and coping with the stress of assessment: Gender differences in outcomes for university students. *Contemporary Educational Psychology, 48*, 28–42. https://doi.org/10.1016/j.cedpsych.2016.08.003.

Bonneville-Roussy, A., Lavigne, G. L., & Vallerand, R. J. (2011). When passion leads to excellence: The case of musicians. *Psychology of Music, 39*(1), 123–138. https://doi.org/10.1177/0305735609352441.

Bonneville-Roussy, A., & Vallerand, R. J. (2018a). Passion at the heart of musicians' well-being. *Psychology of Music, 48*(2), 266–282. https://doi.org/10.1177/0305735618797180.

Bonneville-Roussy, A., & Vallerand, R. J. (2018b). The role of passion in the development of expertise: A conceptual model. In D. Z. Hambrick, G. Campitelli, & B. N. Macnamara (Eds.), *The science of expertise: Behavioral, neural, and genetic approaches to complex skill* (pp. 376–398). New York: Routledge.

Brown, D. E. (2017). *Human universals.* New Yok: McGraw-Hill.

Chanda, M. L., & Levitin, D. J. (2013). The neurochemistry of music. *Trends in Cognitive Sciences, 17*(4), 179–193. https://doi.org/10.1016/j.tics.2013.02.007.

Chen, B., Vansteenkiste, M., Beyers, W., Boone, L., Deci, E. L., Van der Kaap-Deeder, J., Duriez, B., Lens, W., Matos, L., Mouratidis, A., Ryan, R. M., Sheldon, K. M., Soenens, B., Van Petegem, S., & Verstuyf, J. (2015). Basic psychological need satisfaction, need frustration, and need strength across four cultures. *Motivation and Emotion, 39*, 216–236. https://doi.org/10.1007/s11031-014-9450-1.

Comeau, G., Huta, V., & Liu, Y. (2015). Work ethic, motivation, and parental influences in Chinese and North American children learning to play the piano. *International Journal of Music Education*, 33(2), 181–194. https://doi.org/10.1177/0255761413516062.

Comeau, G., Huta, V., Lu, Y., & Swirp, M. (2019). The Motivation for Learning Music (MLM) questionnaire: Assessing children's and adolescents' autonomous motivation for learning a musical instrument. *Motivation and Emotion*, 43(5), 705–718. https://doi.org/10.1007/s11031-019-09769-7.

Creech, A. (2010). Learning a musical instrument: the case for parental support. *Music Education Research*, 12(1), 13–32. https://doi.org/10.1080/14613800903569237.

Cross, I. (2001). Music, cognition, culture, and evolution. *Annals of the New York Academy of Sciences*, 930, 28–42. https://doi.org/10.1111/j.1749-6632.2001.tb05723.x.

Dale, D. (2018). *Community bands of Kentucky: Participation, engagement and the fulfillment of basic psychological needs*. Doctoral dissertation, Boston University.

Davidson, J. W., & Garrido, S. (2019). Singing and psychological needs. In G. F. Welch, D. M. Howard, & J. Nix (Eds.), *The Oxford handbook of singing* (pp. 902–918). Oxford: Oxford University Press. https://doi.org/10.1093/oxfordhb/9780199660773.013.017.

Davidson, J. W., Howe, M. J. A., Moore, D. G., & Sloboda, J. A. (1996). The role of parental influences in the development of musical performance. *British Journal of Developmental Psychology*, 14(4), 399–412. https://doi.org/10.1111/j.2044-835X.1996.tb00714.x.

Deci, E. L., Koestner, R., & Ryan, R. M. (2001). Extrinsic rewards and intrinsic motivation in education: Reconsidered once again. *Review of Educational Research*, 71(1), 1–27. https://doi.org/10.3102/00346543071001001.

Deci, E. L., & Ryan, R. M. (1985). *Intrinsic motivation and self-determination in human behavior*. New York: Plenum.

Di Domenico, S. I., & Ryan, R. M. (2017). The emerging neuroscience of intrinsic motivation: A new frontier in self-determination research. *Frontiers in Human Neuroscience*, 11.

Ericsson, K. A., Krampe, R. T., & Tesch-Römer, C. (1993). The role of deliberate practice in the acquisition of expert performance. *Psychological Review*, 100(3), 363–406. https://doi.org/10.1037/0033-295X.100.3.363.

Evans, P., & Bonneville-Roussy, A. (2016). Self-determined motivation for practice in university music students. *Psychology of Music*, 44(5), 1095–1110. https://doi.org/10.1177/0305735615610926.

Evans, P., & Liu, M. Y. (2019). Psychological needs and motivational outcomes in a high school orchestra program. *Journal of Research in Music Education*, 67(1), 83–105. https://doi.org/10.1177/0022429418812769.

Evans, P., & McPherson, G. E. (2017). Processes of musical identity consolidation during adolescence. In D. J. Hargreaves, R. M. R. MacDonald, & D. Miell (Eds.), *Oxford handbook of musical identities* (pp. 213–232). Oxford: Oxford University Press.

Evans, P., McPherson, G. E., & Davidson, J. W. (2013). The role of psychological needs in ceasing music and music learning activities. *Psychology of Music*, 41(5), 600–619. https://doi.org/10.1177/0305735612441736.

Evans, P., Vansteenkiste, M., & Ryan, R. (in preparation). *Motivational profiles of music students over the course of a university term and their associations with practice quantity and quality*.

Faulkner, R., Davidson, J. W., & McPherson, G. E. (2010). The value of data mining in music education research and some findings from its application to a study of instrumental learning during childhood. *International Journal of Music Education*, 28(3), 212–230. https://doi.org/10.1177/0255761410371048.

Figueiredo, E. A. de F. (2019). Associations between training, employment, and motivational styles of Brazilian instrumental music teachers. *International Journal of Music Education*, 37(2), 198–209. https://doi.org/10.1177/0255761419839170.

Freer, E. G. (2018). *Intentions to study music as a subject in high school: A self-determination theory perspective.* Doctoral dissertation, University of New South Wales.

Freer, E. G., & Evans, P. (2018). Psychological needs satisfaction and value in students' intentions to study music in high school. *Psychology of Music*, 46(6), 881–895. https://doi.org/10.1177/0305735617731613.

Freer, E. G., & Evans, P. (2019). Choosing to study music in high school: Teacher support, psychological needs satisfaction, and elective music intentions. *Psychology of Music*, 47(6), 781–799. https://doi.org/10.1177/0305735619864634.

Garrett, B. (2019). Confronting the challenge: The impact of whole-school primary music on generalist teachers' motivation and engagement. *Research Studies in Music Education*, 41(2), 219–235. https://doi.org/10.1177/1321103X18814579.

Gillet, N., Morin, A. J. S., Huyghebaert, T., Burger, L., Maillot, A., Poulin, A., & Tricard, E. (2017). University students' need satisfaction trajectories: A growth mixture analysis. *Learning and Instruction*, 60, 275–285. https://doi.org/10.1016/j.learninstruc.2017.11.003.

Grolnick, W. S., Deci, E. L., & Ryan, R. M. (1997). Internalization within the family: The self-determination theory perspective. In J. E. Grusec & L. Kuczynski (Eds.), *Parenting and children's internalization of values: A handbook of contemporary theory* (pp. 135–161). New York: J. Wiley.

Haraldsen, H. M., Halvari, H., Solstad, B. E., Abrahamsen, F. E., & Nordin-Bates, S. M. (2019). The role of perfectionism and controlling conditions in Norwegian elite junior performers' motivational processes. *Frontiers in Psychology*, 10, 1366. https://doi.org/10.3389/fpsyg.2019.01366.

Hargreaves, D., & Lamont, A. (2017). *The psychology of musical development.* Cambridge, UK: Cambridge University Press. https://doi.org/10.1017/9781107281868.

Hargreaves, D. J., North, A. C., & Tarrant, M. (2015). How and why do musical preferences change in childhood and adolescence? In G. E. McPherson (Ed.), *The child as musician: A handbook of musical development* (2nd ed., pp. 303–322). Oxford: Oxford University Press. https://doi.org/10.1093/acprof:oso/9780198744443.003.0016.

Jang, H., Reeve, J., Ryan, R. M., & Kim, A. (2009). Can self-determination theory explain what underlies the productive, satisfying learning experiences of collectivistically oriented Korean students? *Journal of Educational Psychology*, 101(3), 644–661. https://doi.org/10.1037/a0014241.

Kasser, T., & Ryan, R. M. (1996). Further examining the American dream: Differential correlates of intrinsic and extrinsic goals. *Personality and Social Psychology Bulletin*, 22(3), 280–287. https://doi.org/10.1177%2F0146167296223006.

Kingsford-Smith, A., & Evans, P. (2019). A longitudinal study of psychological needs satisfaction, value, achievement, and elective music intentions. *Psychology of Music*, 49(3), 382–389. https://doi.org/10.1177/0305735619868285.

Koops, L. H., & Kuebel, C. R. (2019). Self-reported mental health and mental illness among university music students in the United States. *Research Studies in Music Education*, 1321103X19863265. https://doi.org/10.1177/1321103X19863265.

Krause, A. E., & Davidson, J. W. (2018). Effective educational strategies to promote life-long musical investment: Perceptions of educators. *Frontiers in Psychology*, 9, 1977. https://doi.org/10.3389/fpsyg.2018.01977.

Krause, A. E., North, A. C., & Davidson, J. W. (2019). Using self-determination theory to examine musical participation and well-being. *Frontiers in Psychology*, *10*, 405. https://doi.org/10.3389/fpsyg.2019.00405.

Kupers, E., Van Dijk, M., Van Geert, P., & McPherson, G. E. (2015). A mixed-methods approach to studying co-regulation of student autonomy through teacher-student interactions in music lessons. *Psychology of Music*, *43*(3), 333–358. https://doi.org/10.1177/0305735613503180.

Lacaille, N., Koestner, R., & Gaudreau, P. (2007). On the value of intrinsic rather than traditional achievement goals for performing artists: A short-term prospective study. *International Journal of Music Education*, *25*(3), 245–257. https://doi.org/10.1177/0255761407083578.

Leardi, S., Pietroletti, R., Angeloni, G., Necozione, S., Ranalletta, G., & Del Gusto, B. (2007). Randomized clinical trial examining the effect of music therapy in stress response to day surgery. *British Journal of Surgery*, *94*(8), 943–947. https://doi.org/10.1002/bjs.5914.

Lehmann, A. C., Gruber, H., & Kopiez, R. (2018). Expertise in music. In K. A. Ericsson, R. R. Hoffman, A. Kozbelt, & A. M. Williams (Eds.), *The Cambridge handbook of expertise and expert performance* (2nd ed., pp. 535–549). Cambridge, UK: Cambridge University Press. https://doi.org/10.1017/9781316480748.028.

Levitin, D. J. (2013). Neural correlates of musical behaviors: A brief overview. *Music Therapy Perspectives*, *31*(1), 15–24. https://doi.org/10.1093/mtp/31.1.15.

Litalien, D., Morin, A. J. S., Gagné, M., Vallerand, R. J., Losier, G. F., & Ryan, R. M. (2017). Evidence of a continuum structure of academic self-determination: A two-study test using a bifactor-ESEM representation of academic motivation. *Contemporary Educational Psychology*, *51*, 67–82. https://doi.org/10.1016/j.cedpsych.2017.06.010.

Liu, L., Harris Bond, M., Guan, Y., Cai, Z., Sun, J., Yu, Q., Fu, R., & Wang, Z. (2015). Parents' music training motivation and children's music learning achievement: An investigation in the Chinese context. *Psychology of Music*, *43*(5), 661–674. https://doi.org/10.1177/0305735614532703.

Losier, G. F., & Koestner, R. (1999). Intrinsic versus identified regulation in distinct political campaigns: The consequences of following politics for pleasure versus personal meaningfulness. *Personality and Social Psychology Bulletin*, *25*(3), 287–298. https://doi.org/10.1177/0146167299025003002.

Macintyre, P. D., & Potter, G. K. (2014). Music motivation and the effect of writing music: A comparison of pianists and guitarists. *Psychology of Music*, *42*(3), 403–419. https://doi.org/10.1177/0305735613477180.

Marsh, K., & Young, S. (2015). Musical play. In G. E. McPherson (Ed.), *The child as musician: A handbook of musical development* (2nd ed., pp. 462–484). Oxford: Oxford University Press. https://doi.org/10.1093/acprof:oso/9780198744443.003.0025.

Martela, F., Bradshaw, E. L., & Ryan, R. M. (2019). Expanding the map of intrinsic and extrinsic aspirations using network analysis and multidimensional scaling: Examining four new aspirations. *Frontiers in Psychology*, *10*, 2174. https://doi.org/10.3389/fpsyg.2019.02174.

McPherson, G. E. (2009). The role of parents in children's musical development. *Psychology of Music*, *37*(1), 91–110. https://doi.org/10.1177/0305735607086049.

McPherson, G. E., Davidson, J. W., & Evans, P. (2015). Playing an instrument. In G. E. McPherson (Ed.), *The child as musician: A handbook of musical development* (2nd ed., pp. 401–421). Oxford: Oxford University Press.

McPherson, G. E., Miksza, P., & Evans, P. (2017). Self-regulated learning in music practice and performance. In D. H. Schunk & J. A. Greene (Eds.), *Handbook of self-regulation of learning and performance* (2nd ed., pp. 181–193). New York: Routledge.

McPherson, G. E., Osborne, M. S., Evans, P., & Miksza, P. (2017). Applying self-regulated learning microanalysis to study musicians' practice. *Psychology of Music*, 47(1), 18–32. https://doi.org/10.1177/0305735617731614.

Mehr, S. A., Singh, M., Knox, D., Ketter, D. M., Pickens-Jones, D., Atwood, S., Lucas, C., Jacoby, N., Egner, A. A., Hopkins, E. J., Howard, R. M., Hartshorne, J. K., Jennings, M. V., Simson, J., Bainbridge, C. M., Pinker, S., O'Donnell, T. J., Krasnow, M. M., & Glowacki, L. (2019). Universality and diversity in human song. *Science*, 366(6468). https://doi.org/10.1126/science.aax0868.

Miksza, P., Evans, P., & McPherson, G. E. (2019). Motivation to pursue a career in music: The role of social constraints in university music programs. *Psychology of Music*, 49(1), 50–68. https://doi.org/10.1177/0305735619836269.

Murray, S. S. (2017). *Basic psychological needs and the New Horizons musician: A cross-case analysis of six older adults participating in a New England New Horizons ensemble*. Doctoral dissertation, Boston University.

Nettl, B. (2001). Music. In *Grove Music Online*. Oxford University Press – see https://doi.org/10.1093/gmo/9781561592630.article.40476.

Niemiec, C. P., & Ryan, R. M. (2009). Autonomy, competence, and relatedness in the classroom: Applying self-determination theory to educational practice. *Theory and Research in Education*, 7(2), 133–144. https://doi.org/10.1177/1477878509104318.

Niemiec, C. P., Ryan, R. M., & Deci, E. L. (2009). The path taken: Consequences of attaining intrinsic and extrinsic aspirations in post-college life. *Journal of Research in Personality*, 43(3), 291–306. https://doi.org/10.1016/j.jrp.2008.09.001.

Parkes, K. A. (2012). Motivational constructs influencing undergraduate students' choices to become classroom music teachers or music performers. *Journal of Research in Music Education*, 60(1), 101–123. https://doi.org/10.1177/0022429411435512.

Parkes, K. A., & Jones, B. D. (2011). Students' motivations for considering a career in music performance. *Update: Applications of Research in Music Education*, 29(2), 20–28. https://doi.org/10.1177/8755123310397005.

Parncutt, R. (2016). Prenatal development. In G. E. McPherson (Ed.), *The child as musician: A handbook of musical development* (2nd ed., pp. 3–30). Oxford: Oxford University Press. https://doi.org/10.1093/acprof:oso/9780198744443.003.0001.

Pelletier, L. G., Séguin-Lévesque, C., & Legault, L. (2002). Pressure from above and pressure from below as determinants of teachers' motivation and teaching behaviors. *Journal of Educational Psychology*, 94(1), 186–196. https://doi.org/10.1037/0022-0663.94.1.186.

Reeve, J., & Tseng, C. M. (2011). Cortisol reactivity to a teacher's motivating style: The biology of being controlled versus supporting autonomy. *Motivation and Emotion*, 35(1), 63–74. https://doi.org/10.1007/s11031-011-9204-2.

Renwick, J. M. (2008). *Because I love playing my instrument: Young musicians' internalized motivation and self-regulated practising behavior*. Doctoral dissertation, University of New South Wales.

Ruddock, E., & Leong, S. (2005). "I am unmusical!": The verdict of self-judgement. *International Journal of Music Education*, 23(1), 9–22. https://doi.org/10.1177%2F0255761405050927.

Ryan, R. M., & Connell, J. P. (1989). Perceived locus of causality and internalization: Examining reasons for acting in two domains. *Journal of Personality and Social Psychology*, 57, 749–761. https://psycnet.apa.org/doi/10.1037/0022-3514.57.5.749.

Ryan, R. M., & Deci, E. L. (2000). Self-determination theory and the facilitation of intrinsic motivation, social development, and well-being. *American Psychologist*, 55(1), 58–78.

Ryan, R. M., & Deci, E. L. (2017). *Self-determination theory*. New Yok: Guilford Press.

Ryan, R. M., & Deci, E. L. (2020). Intrinsic and extrinsic motivation from a self-determination theory perspective: Definitions, theory, practices, and future directions. *Contemporary Educational Psychology, 61*, 101860. https://doi.org/10.1016/j.cedpsych.2020.101860.

Särkämö, T. (2018). Music for the ageing brain: Cognitive, emotional, social, and neural benefits of musical leisure activities in stroke and dementia. *Dementia, 17*(6), 670–685. https://doi.org/10.1177/1471301217729237.

Schmidt, C. P., Zdzinski, S. F., & Ballard, D. L. (2006). Motivation orientations, academic achievement, and career goals of undergraduate music education majors. *Journal of Research in Music Education, 54*(2), 138–153. https://doi.org/10.1177%2F002242940605400205.

Sheldon, K. M., Osin, E. N., Gordeeva, T. O., Suchkov, D. D., & Sychev, O. A. (2017). Evaluating the dimensionality of self-determination theory's relative autonomy continuum. *Personality and Social Psychology Bulletin, 43*(9), 1215–1238. https://doi.org/10.1177/0146167217711915.

Standage, M., & Ryan, R. M. (2019). Self-determination theory in sport and exercise. In G. Tenenbaum & R. C. Eklund (Eds.), *Handbook of sport psychology* (4th ed), 37–56. Hoboken, NJ: Wiley.

Su, Y.-L., & Reeve, J. (2010). A meta-analysis of the effectiveness of intervention programs designed to support autonomy. *Educational Psychology Review, 23*(1), 159–188. https://doi.org/10.1007/s10648-010-9142-7.

Trehub, S. E., & Degé, F. (2015). Reflections on infants as musical connoisseurs. In G. E. McPherson (Ed.), *The child as musician: A handbook of musical development* (2nd ed., pp. 31–51). Oxford: Oxford University Press. https://doi.org/10.1093/acprof:oso/9780198744443.003.0002.

Vansteenkiste, M., Sierens, E., Soenens, B., Luyckx, K., & Lens, W. (2009). Motivational profiles from a self-determination perspective: The quality of motivation matters. *Journal of Educational Psychology, 101*(3). 671–688. https://doi.org/10.1037/a0015083.

White, R. W. (1959). Motivation reconsidered: The concept of competence. *Psychological Review, 66*(5), 297–333. https://doi.org/10.1037/h0040934.

....

CHAPTER 25

PERSONALITY AND INDIVIDUAL DIFFERENCES

....

EMESE HRUSKA AND ARIELLE BONNEVILLE-ROUSSY

INTRODUCTION

THE music profession is full of personalities who are larger than life, and every one of them seems to have their own persona that attracts their own audiences. Franz Liszt's legendary flamboyant, virtuosic showman-like performances were unprecedented for his time, while Jascha Heifetz regarded flair and showmanship to be in bad taste and ensured a stage presence that was dignified and unassuming. Martha Argerich may well be one of the greatest pianists of the past century, but she shunned media attention, while Maria Callas, in the middle part of her career, was obsessed with her diet and a controversial media figure whose personal life was complex and multifaceted. Within orchestras, string and woodwind players are thought to be introverted, in comparison with brass players who tend to possess extraverted qualities (Kemp, 1996), while string players perceive the brass as "heavy boozers" and "slightly oafish and uncouth" and brass players perceive string players as "oversensitive and touchy," "weaklings," and feel they "think they are God's gift to music" (Davies, 1978, p. 203).

As this brief listing shows, there is no shortage of interesting personality quirks among prominent classical musicians, and although we might all know someone who is a meek violinist or a boozy trumpeter, examples such as these all focus on either superficial personality features and stereotypes, or the eccentric behaviors of prominent musicians as they exist in media and in the public imagination. This is because music itself is closely linked to the affective experiences and meanings that underlie and form our very selves. Consequently, any explanation of what makes us human, as well as what makes us individuals, needs to take into account the roles of personality and individual differences.

There are many stereotypes about musicians that are held both by the general community and by musicians about each other, and we might well ask how, and in what ways, the personal lives of musicians we most admire are actually like the way they are depicted in the media or through their performances. In this chapter, we instead move our focus to a scientific, psychological perspective, to examine whether musicians really are that different from each other and from the rest of the population. The concept of individual differences includes the enduring psychological characteristics that distinguish one person from another (Baumeister & Vohs, 2007). Therefore, individual differences are defined as systematic variations in different segments of the population according to their specific characteristics.

The most important individual difference characteristics that have been researched in music performance are personality, gender, age, and experience (Hargreaves & Lamont, 2017). The study of individual differences in music has traditionally focused on psychometric assessments, usually through paper or web-based testing through questionnaires. Recently, the increased availability of genetic testing has allowed music psychologists to uncover some biological bases to individual differences in musical behavior (Hambrick et al., 2018). In addition, other individual differences in music performance, such as musicians' motivation and anxiety, have gained widespread attention because they are thought to be more malleable with the right support and training.

Our chapter starts with a description of the roles of personality as one of the major influences on musicians' development and choices. Next we discuss the roles of gender, age, and experience as determinants of musical behavior. We then detail traits that are thought to be more fixed such as the role of genes, and some that may be more subject to external influences, such as propensity to experiencing flow, motivation, perfectionism, and anxiety. Finally, we provide some practical implications of these individual differences in musical contexts.

PERSONALITY

Canadian pianist Glenn Gould and American composer and conductor Leonard Bernstein provide interesting case studies of personality in prominent classical music performers. Indeed, they were two of the most iconic Western musicians of the twentieth century. While they were both highly celebrated by the public, their relationships with their audiences contrasted. Bernstein's personality was one that relished in the company of the audience:

> The original energizing motor that makes me compose is the urge to communicate—and to communicate with as many people as possible. Because what I love about the world and life is people, I like them as much as I like music, if not more. (Rosen, 1978)

Practically, Bernstein never stopped working with the public as, at the age of seventy-two, he announced his retirement from conducting five days before his death (Kozinn, 1990). Even though Gould and Bernstein loved working together, their personalities were completely different. Gould was a much more private person. He was known for his eccentricities, from his unorthodox musical interpretations on the piano to aspects of his behavior outside music. His interpretations ranged from brilliantly creative to outrightly bizarre. Experts have speculated that his abnormally delicate personality derived from the fact that he was lonely, and this might have caused him to feel huge pressure from audiences (Glass, 1993). For this reason, at the age of thirty-one, Gould stopped giving concerts. From that time on, he only worked as a recording artist in search of capturing the perfect interpretation of the musical pieces he chose to perpetuate. "I can honestly say that I do not recall ever feeling better about the quality of a performance because of the presence of an audience," said Gould (Konieczny, 2009, p. 52).

Gould and Bernstein's seemingly opposite personalities illustrate how much individual differences can affect the behaviors of musicians. But beyond public commentary on prominent performances, are there more systematic ways to understand personality? The most widely accepted definition of personality is an organized system of psychological traits that is expressed in a person's actions that is relatively constant over time and also independent of context (Matthews, Deary, & Whiteman, 2003). Within this conception, personality can be simplified as a pattern of repeatable behavior. The distinctly different careers of Gould and Bernstein are just two examples of how much personality is an important predictor of a musician's career path. For Gould, the personality patterns involved a particularly reclusive lifestyle suggestive of an introverted personality, but also a considerable openness and challenging of pre-existing norms that led him to develop performance characteristics that extended and challenged previous practices. Bernstein, on the other hand, had a highly extraverted and gregarious personality—characteristics that lent themselves to a much greater level of cooperation and working together with other musicians in a position of leadership.

The five-factor model of personality

Theoretical and empirical investigations of personality have increasingly focused on a framework of five factors of personality (named the "Big Five," McCrae & Costa, 2008). The acronym "OCEAN" is often used to describe these Big Five factors:

Openness to experience (or simply openness) describes individual differences in proactively seeking experiences for their own sake and possessing a positive attitude to new things. People high in openness are typically described as unconventional, innovative, and intellectual.

Conscientiousness reflects the degree of one's organization, persistence, and goal-directed behavior. Individuals high in conscientiousness are organized, thorough, efficient, self-disciplined, responsible, and attend to details.

Extraversion relates to the quantity and intensity of one's interpersonal interaction and need for stimulation, thus it is related to sociability. Extraverted people are talkative, assertive, enthusiastic, and energetic.

Agreeableness refers to pleasantness and affability. People high in agreeableness are typically described as kind, warm, considerate, helpful, and generous.

Neuroticism is a trait that refers to individual differences in psychological maladjustment versus emotional stability, and identifies individuals who are prone to psychological distress, dysfunctional beliefs, and maladaptive coping responses. Individuals high in neuroticism are typically described as nervous, anxious, emotional, and moody (Stoeber et al., 2018).

Figure 25.1 represents the Big Five personality model and its interpretation from two aspects: how personality operates at a particular moment, and how it operates across the life span as personality develops (McCrae & Costa, 2008). It has three main components:

1. Basic tendencies are specific personality traits (e.g. neuroticism) that are considered as abstract psychological potentials. Basic tendencies have biological bases, such as the genetic material.

2. Characteristic adaptations are the concrete manifestations of the basic tendencies, the intrapsychic and interpersonal features that develop over time as expressions of the personality traits. These manifestations include habits, attitudes, skills, or roles (e.g., if someone is high in neuroticism, it may be expressed as negative perfectionistic beliefs and pessimistic attitudes).

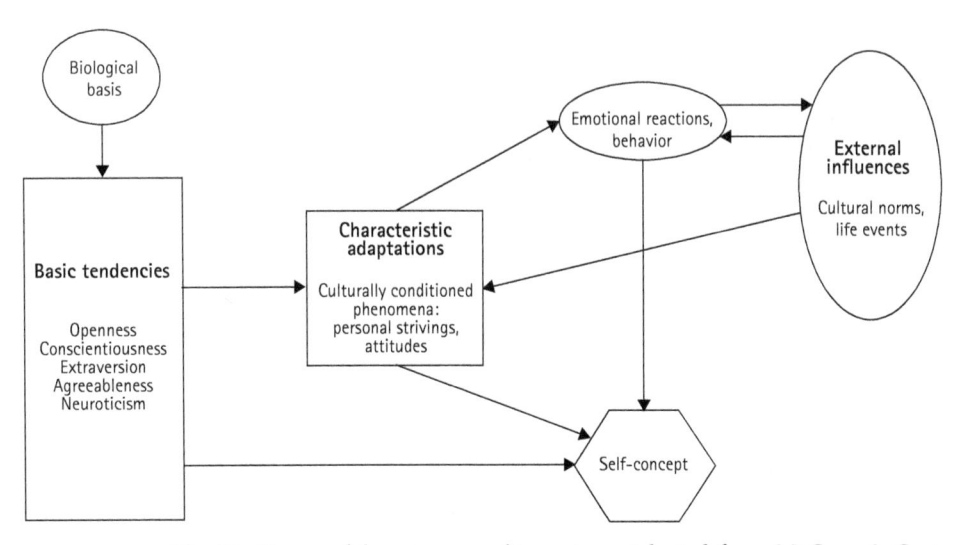

FIGURE 25.1. The Big Five model as a personality system. Adapted from McCrae, & Costa (2008, p. 163). Empirical and theoretical status of the five-factor model of personality traits.

3. External influences come from societies, communities, and social groups. The arrows in the model indicate the most important paths through which personality components interact. For instance, the basic tendencies and characteristic adaptations of individuals influence their self-concept (such as perceptions of competence) and emotional reactions to an event, as well as their behavior. External influences also play a role in shaping characteristic adaptations as well as emotional reactions and behavior.

We can interpret Figure 25.1 from the young Gould and Bernstein's perspectives. Their *external influences* were different. Gould was a child of musical parents, and his mother was protective of him and introduced him to lone practice very early with the explicit goal of making a concert pianist of him (Girard, 1993). In contrast, Bernstein's parents were not musicians. However, they supported their son's music education with a special request which was that the young Bernstein had to give piano lessons to younger children so that the family could afford his own music lessons (Burton, 1988). As a result of the distinct norms and life events, the characteristic adaptations manifested themselves differently for the two musicians. It could be that Bernstein's naturally extraverted basic tendencies led him to enjoy teaching at a young age and shaped his attitude toward music, and this in turn affected his career later on. On the other hand, Gould's basic introverted tendency and the protective parenting style of his parents may have influenced his lonely attitude through lone practice, which, in the long run, may have contributed to Gould's more isolated musical career and personal life. As we can see, different personalities can affect career paths greatly.

PERSONALITY IN MUSIC PERFORMANCE

Research on personality in music performance finds that out of the five factors of personality, two are consistently associated with musicians: extraversion (or low extraversion, sometimes called introversion) and openness to experience. Kemp (1996) found that classical musicians tend to be introverted (as opposed to extraverted). In some ways, this is not surprising: the sheer amount of lone practice that classical musicians do seems better aligned with an introverted personality. Nonetheless, studies of the last two decades have failed to replicate Kemp's result. For example, compared to visual arts students, music students tend to be more extraverted (Haller & Courvoisier, 2010). Also, classical and heavy metal musicians seem to be less introverted than the general population (Butkovic & Dopudj, 2017).

Overall, openness to experience seems to be the strongest link to musicianship out of all of the personality traits. Musicians appear to be more open to new experiences than non-musicians (Corrigall et al., 2013; Rose et al., 2019; Vaag et. al, 2018). This difference is not genre-specific, as, for instance, both heavy metal and classical musicians show higher levels of openness when compared to non-musicians (Butkovic & Dopudj, 2017).

Openness seems to be a general trait in music and related to musical ability both in individuals who play and do not play a musical instrument (Greenberg et al., 2015). This relationship between openness to experience and musicality may be due to openness being linked with aesthetics sensitivity, such as appreciating beauty or art. Openness is also associated with creativity, interest and enjoyment in intellectual activities, traits that are also associated with musicians (Corrigall & Schellenberg, 2015).

Personality differences across musical styles

It seems that personality can at least partly explain the choice of styles of musicians. When classical music students are compared with traditions characterized by a higher amount of improvisation (e.g., jazz, rock, pop), such musicians are higher in sensation seeking (a facet of openness to experience), are more easily bored, and are less prone to experiencing anxiety on stage (Vuust et al., 2010). They also seem to have higher risk taking (associated with both openness to experience and extraversion; Wopereis et al., 2013). But these differences in personality traits across musical styles are by no means universal. Butkovic and Dopudj (2017), for example, could not find any differences between genres—even between such contrasting styles as heavy metal and classical music. Together, these findings suggest that differences in personality traits between musicians who specialize in different types of music may not be associated with the "personality" of the music itself (e.g., classical music vs. heavy metal). Instead, it may be more associated with the kinds of musical activity within the tradition (e.g., highly pre-composed music such as classical, compared with highly improvised music such as jazz). But again, the research on these more subtle distinctions is as yet relatively inconclusive, and such differences seem to be minimal.

Personality differences across musical instruments and voice

Have you ever wondered how your own personality has shaped the way you chose which instrument you wanted to play? Players of different families of instruments do tend to differ from each other, particularly in terms of lay beliefs about personality traits that appear in the form of stereotypes (a general and pervasive, often oversimplified, belief about a particular group of people). For instance, pianists are seen as more introverted, perhaps because they are often depicted as practicing alone, and bassists as more agreeable, again possibly due to the image people have of bassists being chatty and relaxed, both in classical and popular music (Cameron et al., 2014; Butkovic & Modrusan, 2019). Perhaps the most prevalent stereotype is that singers are more extraverted than instrumentalists, a stereotype that is often due to the seemingly extravagant persona of singers. This can be explained by the fact that singers are most of the time at the center of stage and this requires them to be more assertive and comfortable in the spotlight (Greenberg et al., 2015). There is no conclusive evidence, however, that players of different musical instruments and singers are as strikingly different as the stereotypes would suggest (Langendorfer, 2008). That is, stereotypes do not necessarily translate into real personality differences in musicians. In sum, for outsiders, musicians who play different instruments may appear to be vastly different, such as singers being seen as extraverted and pianists as introverted. However, musicians seem to have more in common with regard to their personalities than what the stereotypes would suggest.

The role of personality on musical skill-acquisition

Personality might also affect the way we learn music. The duration of children's involvement in formal music training can be foreseen when they are higher in the conscientiousness and openness personality traits (Corrigall et al., 2013). Highly conscientious and open people are often more organized and tend to be self-disciplined, tend to persist in the face of difficulty, and to be curious—all traits that lend themselves to effective learning in any domain, particularly music. Children who display all of these traits may find music more enjoyable and therefore are able to engage more, and for longer. Because children depend so heavily on their parents in their early experiences of music, their parents' personalities can also have an influence. In the early stages of development, parents' openness-to-experience appears to be an important factor that determines the commencement of their children's musical education (Corrigall & Schellenberg, 2015). As we have seen, openness to new experience is associated with curiosity and artistic and aesthetic dispositions, so parents who are higher in openness may be more inclined to expose their children to artistic activities like music from an early age. Musicians who are more open also tend to practice a greater number of hours per week (Butkovic et al., 2015), possibly because their inner curiosity make them want to explore music more, and more often.

Personality may also impact particular kinds of musical skills. In a study of sight-reading ability, conservatory students who took a more analytical approach to sight-reading tended to be more emotionally stable, agreeable, and conscientious (Bogunovic, 2018). The study also found that the latter two personality traits were possessed by students who achieved higher levels of expertise in music performance. In practice, this may be because the emotional insight leads to a better aesthetic understanding of musical works, and conscientiousness leads to more attention to details. Combined with more frequent practice, these personality characteristics seem to be advantageous for the development of a skill like sight-reading. However, while the research to date seems reasonably conclusive in terms of the associations between skills and personality characteristics, precise explanations for the underlying mechanisms are still speculative.

In sum, in this section, we have seen that different personality traits are associated with different outcomes in music performance. Of the five personality dimensions comprised in the "Big Five," openness to new experiences seems to be the most significant to musicians. Musicians tend to be more open than non-musicians, parents who are more open tend to involve their children in more musical activities, and children who are more open tend to practice more and to stay involved in music for longer. Conscientiousness is also important in music making, as it allows musicians to pay attention to details and to be more self-disciplined—characteristics that are essential to be able to practice frequently and deliberately, and to be resilient in the face of challenge and difficulty. Importantly, many perceived or assumed personality differences in musicians are not necessarily observed, and most of the popular or folk understandings of different types of musicians and their personalities appear to be little more than crude stereotypes (Kuckelkorn, Manzano, & Ullén, 2021).

Gender

The occurrence of gender differences in music performance manifests in several forms such as the type of musical activity, the choice of musical instruments, career, and general musical practice and performance (see further, Blackwell & McPherson; Smith & Hendricks, both this volume). Gender stereotypes are formed early in schoolchildren's choices of starting to play a musical instrument (Dibben, 2002). High-pitched and soft-sounding instruments (e.g., flute and harp) are seen as feminine and low-pitched and louder instruments (e.g., tuba and electric guitar) are seen as masculine (Hallam et al., 2008; Rose et al., 2019). This may explain why most girls choose harp and boys the tuba if asked to pick between the two instruments (Hallam et al., 2017). The social consequences of diverging from those stereotypes seem important to children, and they may fear being excluded if not conforming to those stereotypes (O'Neill, 1997). In popular genres, boys tend to be more highly represented (Baker & Cohen, 2007), while in school music programs, girls are more highly represented. One study in the UK concluded that school-aged girls chose music as an elective more often than boys with a ratio of 3:2 (Hallam, Rogers, & Creech, 2008). Although this figure may seem trivial at first glance, especially compared with other subject areas, it leads to many thousands more girls than boys receiving a school music education in the UK, which is an important material difference.

In the professional music scene, males are found in greater numbers (Bonneville-Roussy, Hruska, & Trower, 2020; Kenny, Driscoll, & Ackermann, 2018). This gender imbalance in professional orchestras has been well documented (Scharff, 2018). Before the second half of the twentieth century, in the majority of classical orchestras worldwide, hiring practices were such as that female musicians were explicitly not allowed to audition and almost never hired (Goldin & Rouse, 2000). In 2003, Ursula Plaichinger made headlines as the first female musician to be hired at the Vienna Philharmonic, in the orchestra's more than 150 years of existence (Burgermeister, 2003). In recent years, the introduction of double-blind auditions has decreased the gender imbalance regarding hiring of female professional musicians in orchestras (Scharff, 2018). On the other hand, there are other issues that women face in music such as the effects of pregnancy and maternity leave (or parental leave) that are less documented but may have an important impact on female musicians' performing careers.

There are also some gender differences with regard to motivation, practice time, and performance, though to a smaller extent (Bonneville-Roussy & Bouffard, 2015; Bonneville-Roussy et al., 2017; Hallam et al., 2018). Considering practice strategies of musicians, females tend to practice more systematically, even though they use both effective and ineffective strategies, while males use less effective strategies. Despite this, at higher levels of expertise, male musicians do not appear to organize their practice sessions as much or as effectively as female musicians (Hallam et al., 2017).

Gender imbalances also exist in some of the more indirect influences on music performance such as stress, anxiety, and coping. Females tend to be more negatively affected by these issues than males. Among university music students, disengagement-orientated coping strategies like procrastinating, drinking, and drug use, or ignoring the problem, were more frequently found at male musicians. But a closer look at the outcomes is necessary: females were less affected by disengagement coping in relation to their wellbeing and examination results, but more affected in relation to their longer-term career intentions. Female musicians reported higher stress in the context of performance examinations, and this stress impacted their wellbeing more greatly than it did for males (Bonneville-Roussy et al., 2017). These results illustrate that gender differences do not exist just in amount, but also in the different ways that various factors impact on outcomes. A better understanding of the differences and similarities in which male and female musicians experience music performance can help music schools and professional music scenes to understand how to promote more equal musical development and career opportunities.

Age and experience

Naturally, age, and experience are related to one another (Hallam et al., 2016)—indeed, it is not really possible to gain experience over time without aging! Some development in musical skills can be seen as a gradual, linear phenomenon (like aging)—musicians progress from being complete novices, and over time, gradually acquire increasingly sophisticated skills as they progress toward expertise and long-term performing careers. In contrast, a stage-based perspective identifies qualitatively different periods—musicians commence with initial experiences in childhood, working with a teacher during adolescence, studying at an advanced level in a conservatory or university, and the commencement of an independent performance career. In music, the stage-based perspective is often more useful than simply looking at age (Bonneville-Roussy & Vallerand, 2018; Hallam, 2013; Hallam et al., 2016), probably because of the differences in when people commence learning music and the precise timing of when they undergo each of the stages.

The particular stages identified are often based on qualitative shifts in the level of experience and expertise demonstrated by musicians (Hallam et al., 2016). There are different perspectives about precisely what the stages are, and there is probably no universal agreement about stages that apply usefully to performing musicians of all kinds. But most stage perspectives seem to agree on an exploration stage (when different activities and musical instruments are explored), a specialization stage (when a specific musical instrument is chosen), and a refinement stage (when musicians refine their skills to a professional level). In the exploration stage, nearly half of children aged five to six years old express an interest in playing a musical instrument, but this rate steadily decreases to about 4 percent by the time they become teenagers (McPherson, 2000). The interaction between starting age and different types of musical instruments is a good example of why the stage perspective provides more explanation of musical outcomes than does looking purely at age. Piano and the violin can be studied from a very young age due to their size and physical demands. The tuba and other wind instruments, especially larger wind instruments, tend to be started much later, some not even before adolescence (McPherson, Davidson, & Evans, 2006). In this example, a tubist would potentially reach the specialization stage of expertise at a much later age than a violinist.

Bearing both perspectives in mind, starting age may be crucial in musical performance ability because an earlier start enables both a greater accumulation of practice, and an advantage in progressing through the various stages earlier in life. By the time a pianist reaches eighteen years of age, they could potentially have accumulated thousands more hours of practice if they started playing the piano at the age of five years old, as compared with a pianist who started in their teenage years. This accumulation of practice is likely to have a substantial impact on music performance as musicians enter adulthood (Ericsson & Lehmann, 1996; Krampe & Ericsson, 1996), as it corresponds with better performing skills (Vaquero et al., 2016). Among experts, though, there are individual differences in the speed of their development, and the advantages conferred by their accumulated practice (Simonton, 2014; Gagné & McPherson, 2016). There is also an interaction between starting age and various other biological and neurodevelopmental processes (which themselves occur in stages). Pianists who start at an earlier age seem to show greater music-related neuroplasticity and temporal precision as compared with non-musicians or pianists who start later (Vaquero et al., 2016).

The interaction of age and stage is also associated with practice, and provides a useful perspective on the importance of both total accumulated practice, as well as the quality of that practice. For school-aged children in the exploration to specialization stages, practice time tends to be a good predictor of performance (Hallam, 2013). At conservatory levels and beyond, the quality of the practice strategies used seems to be more related to performance quality than the quantity of that practice (Bonneville-Roussy & Bouffard, 2015). Part of the explanation for this is that musicians in these high-performance environments are homogeneous—the reason they are there is because all of them have generally acquired large amount of practice. But it also shows that at the highest levels of expertise, "empty practice" that lacks efficient practice strategies (e.g., structured practice with focused attention and clear goals) can even be detrimental to performance as the quality of the performance is not likely to improve, despite the time and effort invested in it (Bonneville-Roussy & Bouffard, 2015; McPherson, this part).

Age and experience are therefore two useful ways of studying the development of musical performance. It is clear that an earlier start to music performance is an advantage in the sheer accumulation of practice time before entering adulthood, but this depends on the instrument played. Research also supports that qualitative differences in stages of development are also important considerations: Engaging in meaningful music activities from early childhood may have important neurological implications for later in life, and aiming to develop at a conservatory level may require a particular kind of practice that builds on prior experiences. So, it is not just a matter of catching up on the total amount of practice, but the structure and quality of practicing can enhance music performance skills just as much.

Genetic and inheritable traits and practice

It may seem odd in a chapter on "personality and individual differences" to include a section on practice. After all, practice can be considered to be simply a behavior—something that one does, not something that is a relatively immutable personal characteristic. However, as we will describe, practice may be more than simply a behavior, and the propensity to undertake practice may be an expression of some heritable, even genetic, component. Practice is obviously one of the main activities undertaken to improve music performance ability (see Miksza, this volume). However, here we expand on practice as an activity in the context of individual differences that may influence and interact with it.

"Natural" abilities and practice

Our understanding of the complexities of genes, heritability, their expression, and the effects of environment has advanced considerably in the last century. Traditionally, this had often been expressed as a nature-nurture distinction: the "nature" view considered musical ability as in some way genetically configured, while the "nurture" view stresses that events over the life course like practice and training are more important (Hambrick et al. 2018). It is now known that this distinction, although somewhat intuitive, appears to be flawed, and that the "nature" part—the expression of particular genes or configurations of genes—cannot be understood in isolation from the "nurture" part—the environments in which this occurs. In relation to musical practice, individual differences can actively facilitate both "better faster" as a genetic factor and "more bang for the buck" as an environmental effect in developing performing expertise (Simonton, 2014).

However, looking back at the development of our understandings in this area, there is a relatively clear distinction between the two. On the "nurture" side, it has been nearly thirty years since Ericsson and his colleagues published their influential article stating that deliberate practice can lead to high levels of expertise (Ericsson,

Krampe, & Tesch-Römer, 1993). Ericsson's stance was mainly that *practice makes perfect*, that is, the main explanation for how experts acquired their expert performance was the accumulated practice they had undertaken throughout the course of their lives. In a similar vein, the publication of a paper titled "Innate talent: Reality or myth?" generated considerable debate and argued strongly against the existence of talent, instead emphasizing the effects of the home environment, economic resources, and practice (Howe, Davidson, & Sloboda, 1998).

The "nature" perspective has focused on exactly what particular skills and subskills might constitute musical ability. Since the early twentieth century, researchers have developed various measures and tests purporting to assess this underlying capacity known as musical aptitude (see McPherson, Blackwell & Hallam, this volume). Some of these assessments prove to be effective measures, although it is difficult to attribute their effectiveness to aptitude, exclusive of the effects of music training or exposure (itself an illustration of the problem of the nature-nurture distinction). In the last decade, there are indications that other factors, such as biological influences, potentially contribute to developing expert music expertise and performance skills (Hambrick et al. 2018; see further, Burgoyne, Hambrick, & Harris, this volume).

Gene-environment interactions

In the field of music performance, the Multifactorial Gene-Environment Interaction Model (MGIM, Ullén et al., 2016) of expertise, illustrated in Figure 25.2, describes that both domain-general traits and domain-specific knowledge/skills can indirectly and directly influence expertise. In the model, genetic and environmental factors both play an important role in each individual path to performance. The MGIM suggests that genetically influenced innate abilities may predict not only one's initial dispositions but also the ultimate performances later in life (Hambrick et al., 2018).

The central concept of the MGIM is the *gene-environment interplay*. This interplay can be considered as *passive* when one possesses genetically inherited musical aptitude and is being raised in a musically rich environment but does not take action. In contrast, this interplay is *active* when individuals seek out opportunities to develop their musical ability, such as through engaging with a teacher in music lessons and practicing. The interplay can also be defined as *evocative* when one's genotype, in the form of musical talent, induces certain reactions in other people, such as the attention of music teachers whose role can be highly beneficial (Hambrick et al., 2018).

In line with this multidimensional model, athletes' deliberate practice may explain only 18 percent of their athletic skills and success (Hambrick et al. 2018). Similarly, in a large study in which twins completed musical aptitude tests, results showed that heritability ("nature") was accountable for at least half of their accumulated amount of music practice and musical skills such as rhythm and melody discrimination (Ullén et al., 2014). Therefore, heritability seems to play a substantial role in one's musical achievement and willingness to undertake music practice (Hambrick et al., 2018), and genetic models can potentially explain why some musicians become exceptionally skilled virtuosi and others remain "average" musicians. In simple terms, commitment to

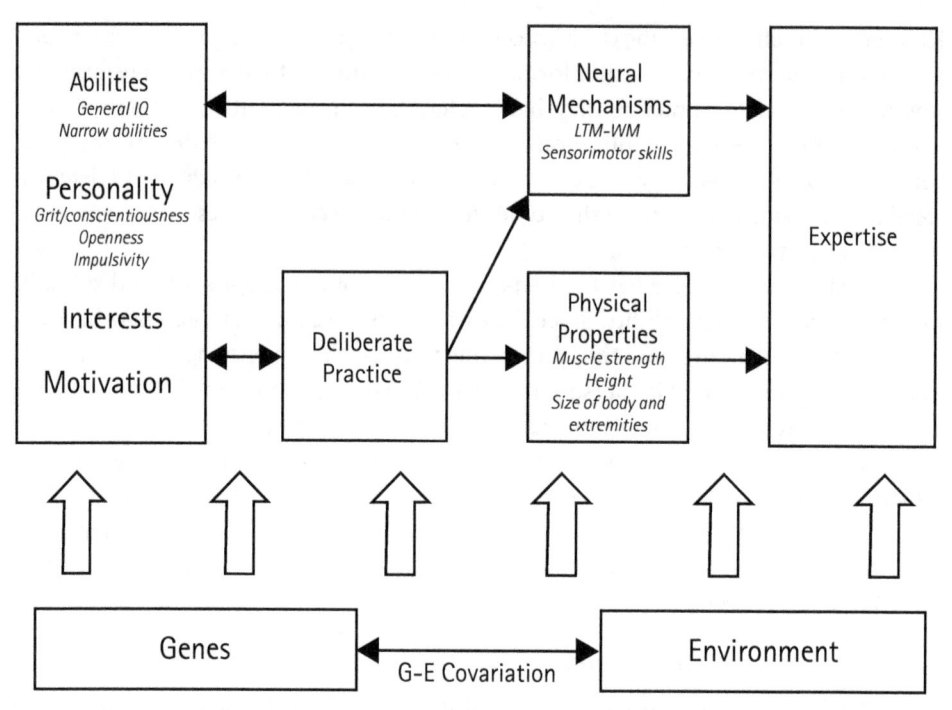

FIGURE 25.2. Multifactorial Gene-Environment Interaction Model of expertise: Schematic summary of main elements of the Multifactorial Gene-Environment Interaction Model (MGIM). Reprinted with permission from Ullén, Hambrick, & Mosing (2016, p. 437).

> Note. At the phenotypic level (upper part), the MGIM assumes that psychological traits such as abilities, personality, interests, and motivation are associated with the domain and intensity of practice. Specific examples of variables that have been shown to be involved in various forms of expertise are provided in italics under each general heading. According to the model, practice will cause adaptations of neural mechanisms involved in expertise and can also influence relevant physical body properties, and neural mechanisms related to these trait differences may impact expertise independently of practice. Both genetic and non-genetic factors (lower part) influence the various variables that are involved in expertise at the phenotypic level. These influences are likely to be complex and involve both gene-environment interaction effects and covariation between genes and environment (G-E covariation).

practice may partly be an inheritable trait that can explain deliberate practice. Burgoyne, Hambrick, and Harris (this volume) provide more details on the debates going on between genetic and environmental influences in expertise.

Many Olympic athletes seem to carry a particular genotype for the gene *ACTN3*. This gene is responsible to code the protein (α-actinin-3) in fast-twitch muscles when short, sudden movements in performance are required (for details, see Hambrick et al., 2018). What are the specific genetic influences that might be associated with music performance? Associations were found between specific genes and a wide range of music-related traits (e.g., music perception, musical creativity, singing accuracy; see Tan, McPherson & Wilson, 2017). For instance, the variants of the gene *EPHA7* may be linked to absolute pitch (the ability to identify the pitch of musical tones) and synesthesia (a condition that results in a joining or merging of senses that are not normally connected such as hearing, thus sound is simultaneously perceived like sight). The skills involved in the most fundamental aspects of perceiving and producing music are many and complex, and even more so when considering the ways in which the practice of music itself varies between societies, traditions, and genres. Despite many promising attempts to disentangle this complexity, our understanding of individual differences in musical ability and practice is still in its infancy.

Flow proneness

Have you ever found yourself so deeply involved in a particular piece of music that you practiced and played it for many hours, losing track of time, forgetting to eat or to attend to other daily activities, feeling immune to distraction, and being completely consumed by the task? Afterwards, you may have felt exhausted, but also elated, and maybe a feeling of great productivity and having learned or accomplished something worthwhile. The experience of *flow*, also described as optimal experience or being in the zone, is a psychological state in which individuals are fully immersed in an activity (Csikszentmihalyi, 2008). It is difficult to predict the precise environmental circumstances under which flow occurs, but it seems to partly rely on an optimal balance between one's skills and the challenge of the task. It has been linked with peak performance and high achievement in various domains such as competitive sports and music performance.

Flow in musicians has been associated with numerous positive outcomes. Flow experience is related to musical persistence, self-esteem, perceived musical ability, life satisfaction, intrinsic motivation, lower anxiety, sense of control, and intrinsic motivation (Butkovic et al., 2015; Eriksson et al., 2017). These relations potentially interact with personality traits. For example, individuals with higher flow-proneness and lower impulsivity tend to be more emotionally stable and conscientious, which may partly be explained by the differences found in the brain's dopamine system (Butkovic et al., 2015).

Flow also appears to increase persistence and future musical intentions (Butkovic et al. 2015; Eriksson et al., 2017). Individuals who are active in music making until adulthood are likely to be more prone to experience flow during their musical activities. This may help us understand why some individuals like to practice more than others. Since music practice is not inherently enjoyable but flow is, musicians who experience flow while practicing may be inclined to practice more. Flow has also been associated with personality traits, mostly openness to new experience, emotional stability (e.g., low neuroticism), and conscientiousness (Ullén et al., 2016). In this sense, typical flow-prone musicians are likely to be more emotionally stable, conscientious, and open to new experiences than musicians who do not experience flow regularly. The frequent experience of flow would obviously confer many advantages, not only because it is enjoyable, but it means that substantial amounts of time can be spent highly engaged in the improvement of musical ability.

In sum, musical abilities and musical behavior seem to partly depend on the tendencies of musicians to experience flow in music practice and performance (Butkovic et al. 2015). This flow proneness may also be partly genetic and is related to other individual differences such as personality. It is worth noting that flow is often dependent on the quality and quantity of motivation, which is the subject of the following section.

Motivation

Motivation is a powerful individual difference that acts as a drive to music performance and persistence. It has been of particular interest to researchers who try to understand the development of musical ability, because although a love of music and even music performance can come naturally for most people, the development of high levels of musical performance skills requires hard work and the ability to deal with many types of setbacks and challenges. For this reason, other chapters of this volume also visit the topic of motivation comprehensively. Here, we briefly describe two aspects of motivation—passion and grit—that may not have been touched upon in other chapters of this volume.

Passion has been conceptualized as a strong propensity toward an activity that people value, love, and consider central to their identity, and in which they allocate substantial amounts of their time and energy (Bonneville-Roussy et al., 2011). The Dualistic Model of Passion (Vallerand et al., 2003) defines two types of passion: harmonious (the "adaptive" one, i.e., when the passionate activity is in harmony with other aspects of one's life) and obsessive (the "maladaptive" one, i.e., when the activity is in conflict with other life events). Using this classification, passion has been linked with various outcomes in musicians. Harmonious passion has been associated with future music-related career intentions and musical persistence (Bonneville-Roussy, Vallerand, et al., 2013), with higher levels of musical performance and life satisfaction (Bonneville-Roussy et al., 2011) and with musicians' general sense of wellbeing (Bonneville-Roussy & Vallerand, 2020). In contrast, obsessive passion does not always lead to positive consequences and can even lead to ill-being in musicians. That is, contrary to the general belief, although passion can often lead to positive consequences, unhealthy passion in musicians can hinder not only performance, but also well-being.

A related concept of "adaptive" motivation is grit, defined as "perseverance and passion for long-term goals" (Duckworth, Peterson, Matthews, & Kelly, 2007, p. 1087). The concept of grit assesses perseverance of effort and sustained interest, but not the affective and motivational components of love and importance of the activity into one's life. For instance, grit is strongly related to flow, practice efficiency, and self-efficacy in musicians (Miksza & Tan, 2015). It is therefore likely to be a useful characteristic, although it is important to note that the construct of grit has been criticized due to insufficient differentiation from trait conscientiousness, the internal consistency of the measure and its factor structure, and its purported benefits (Credé, Tynan, & Harms, 2017).

Perfectionism

Music performance is an exacting activity. Concert performance has evolved such that highly precise and technically flawless performances are the norm. For these reasons, it is not surprising that many musicians experience some kind of perfectionism at some point through their performance careers. The demands of excellence and flawlessness have high stakes. Not meeting these demands can result in negative professional and personal consequences: orchestral musicians who make a serious mistake during a concert could be demoted or lose their job. While seemingly necessary in music, perfectionism is defined as a "personality disposition characterized by striving for flawlessness and setting exceedingly high standards of performance accompanied by overly critical evaluations of one's behavior" (Stoeber, 2018, p. 3).

Inherent in the definition of perfectionism is a negative connotation, suggesting that it is rarely a psychologically adaptive tendency. The negative type, *evaluative concerns perfectionism* captures the aspects of perfectionism that are related to unhealthy evaluation concerns such as the tendency to perceive others as demanding perfection (socially prescribed perfectionism), reacting negatively to perceived failures, and worrying about the consequences of errors (concern over mistakes), or having doubts about performance quality (doubts about action). It is worth noting that while this type of perfectionism is preferable to the social concerns and pressure of failures that characterize the evaluative concerns type, it is not without its dangers: musicians' perfectionism related to evaluative concerns are associated with music performance anxiety and psychological distress. It demonstrates mixed results with pressured forms of motivation (extrinsic motivation when one is motivated to perform an activity to earn a reward or avoid punishment; Stoeber and Eismann, 2007) and in some cases is positively associated with negative psychological outcomes such as depression and anxiety (Smith, Saklofske, & Yan, 2015).

Other kinds of perfectionism can be more conducive to adaptive outcomes. *Personal standards perfectionism*, typically known as a more adaptive form of perfectionism, is a tendency to set and strive for high personal standards and for perfection without having concerns (Stoeber et al., 2018). It is usually associated with better performance outcomes and less risk of burnout and, for musicians, successfully achieving their performance goals (Stoeber & Eismann, 2007). Notably, both forms of perfectionism are present in every individual, but to a different degree (Stoeber et al., 2018). In practice, a musician can both be striving for excellence in performance, which is positive, and have doubts and worries about their ability to achieve this excellence, which is more negative.

Perfectionism is linked with four of the Big Five personality dimensions: neuroticism, extraversion, agreeableness, and conscientiousness (Stoeber, 2018). It seems that while both the negative and positive aspects of perfectionism are related to conscientiousness, the more positive side of perfectionism is also linked to extraversion and agreeableness. In contrast, musicians who tend to be more anxious (neurotic) and introverted may also be more inclined to experience the negative aspects of perfectionism. The perfectionistic tendencies of music students tend to develop along with increasing levels of expertise, thus making perfectionism a likely characteristic of elite performers (Araújo et al., 2017). It seems that elite musicians' levels of perfectionistic strivings are higher than their tendency to react negatively to mistakes. As such, as expertise and professional experience develop, musicians may be more prone to experience the more adaptive side of perfectionism. It could also be that musicians who overwhelmingly experience the negative side of perfectionism tend to quit music before they become experts.

Anxiety

Like other performance-based domains, musicians can experience considerable anxiety in the context of public performance or assessment. Music performance anxiety (MPA) is the experience of chronic, distressing anxiety that may be accompanied by an impairment of performance skills in the public context to an unjustified degree given the capacity, experience, and preparation level of the individual (Salmon, 1990). Some musicians experience MPA more than others, making it a key topic in the theme of individual differences.

However, not all musicians find anxiety harmful when performing. A positive type of anxiety, "performance boost," helps musicians conceptualize their experience of performing on stage as a challenge, and it elevates their mood to perform even better because they perceive the situation as appropriately balanced to their abilities (Simoens et al., 2015). The more negative aspect of stage fright is MPA, in which musicians perceive the performance as threat as they feel that the situation exceeds their skills and abilities. One would assume that the two lie at the two ends on the same continuum. However, they proved to be on two distinct spectrums of performance-related factors. This means that musicians can naturally experience both general MPA and performance boost at the same time. Also, it seems that only a minority of musicians perceive anxiety as a boost (Simoens et al., 2015).

MPA has been associated with health-related factors and perceived pressure, whereas boost is linked to better perceived support (Simoens et al., 2015). In practice, this suggests that anxiety is linked to musicians' psychosocial environment. This may not be surprising, as when we feel anxious, we naturally tend to seek support from peers and loved ones, as do anxious musicians. On the other hand, "performance boost" may be closely related to self-efficacy beliefs (confidence in the ability to accomplish something successfully), since musicians who perceive themselves as efficacious tend to experience higher boost. And perhaps due to their higher "boost" levels, efficacious musicians also tend to rate their performance as more successful (Gonzáles et al., 2018).

Finally, personality and the tendency to experience MPA are likely to be related since undergraduate conservatory students' performance anxiety experiences depended on their optimism and pessimism levels (Orejudo et al., 2017). In other words, students' feelings of helplessness and their performance anxiety could be explained by how much they were optimistic or pessimistic generally in life. In sum, although MPA is a real issue in musicians that needs thorough attention, not all anxiety is harmful. To some extent, both social (perceived support versus pressure) and personality (optimism and pessimism) factors seem to be linked to the development of MPA and performance boost in a positive way.

PRACTICAL IMPLICATIONS

We all have distinctive personalities and are born and raised in diverse contexts, so we have different tendencies in how we behave. Sometimes, these are only a small part of explaining who we are. Nevertheless, personality and individual differences are interesting because some of them have a bearing on how music performance learning and careers play out. While many musical traits and talent are relatively stable, some individual differences are malleable, so the implications are far-reaching. The implications discussed in this section mainly concern the roles of social environment, such as teachers and parents, and the roles musicians themselves can play, in order to make the best out of the various individual differences mentioned in this chapter. We start with the individual differences that are considered to be less changeable and then discuss the more malleable ones.

Among the most stable of individual differences, by definition, are personality factors. It can be useful for teachers, parents, and even adult musicians to know that extravert and high-sensation-seeking musicians may find it difficult to engage in rigorous practice routines for prolonged hours (Vuust et al., 2010). Instead, they may prefer more intuitive and improvising types of lessons. Teachers may benefit from knowing about certain research outcomes, such as the fact that improvisational skills require a willingness to take risks that may not suit all personality types. On the other hand, introvert or low-sensation-seeking students may prefer more structured lessons and a more traditional style of teaching (Bogunovic, 2018). Also, students may find out that their teacher's personality does not seem to fit them. The good news is that experienced music teachers tend to be very flexible in their teaching style, even if their personalities are not easily changeable, so communication is a good starting point. In this sense, many teachers can adapt their teaching styles (and not their personality) to better fit the needs of the students.

Another less malleable individual difference is gender. Exposing children with role models of musicians who do not adhere to the gender stereotypes mentioned earlier could contribute to reduce gender bias in music. For example, music teachers and parents may want to introduce the tuba with a female tuba player, or the flute with a male player, so that boys and girls are exposed to a less stereotyped choice of instruments early on.

Some components of musical talent may also be genetically determined (Hambrick et al., 2018), and therefore less malleable. As we have mentioned, our understanding of the genetic components contributing specifically to musical ability is in its infancy. A great amount of the variation in one's ultimate performance level is not due to genes, so there is hope! Despite recent challenges to research on deliberate practice (e.g., Hambrick et al, 2018), no greater influence on music performance expertise has been found than practice.

We now turn to some of the more malleable individual differences. Music teachers and musicians may be relieved to know that experience greatly affects performance ability, and it might help to think about this as being an *intra-individual* difference as well as an *inter-individual* difference. Novice musicians tend to start out disorganized and unable to conduct focused practice. They would benefit from teachers who provide a strong structure to their lessons, with a focus not only on the teaching of musical skills, but the teaching of practice skills, so that the student learn how to practice more efficiently early on. It is common that beginner musicians practice very little. Even the pianist Evgeny Kissin described that in the first year of his musical studies he could not practice more than twenty minutes daily, and the rest of the time he enjoyed himself (Nupen, 1998). As he explained, his practice time linearly increased with the years of learning the piano. Research has underpinned that, as for beginners, quantity (and particularly frequency) seems to be important, whereas for expert musicians, quantity distinguishes them less from their peers than quality (Bonneville-Roussy & Bouffard, 2015). Therefore, as musical skills develop, musicians may become more efficient in balancing effective practice time with other life activities. This should be a relief to many experienced musicians who are no longer able to practice many hours a day due to other life engagements and who may feel guilty about it.

While we recognize that even the more malleable individual differences have a biological basis, the right type of support from teachers, parents, and colleagues can facilitate positive outcomes stemming from these differences. In particular, music educators play an important role in shaping the futures of young musicians. The majority of the most exceptional musicians have encountered at rigorous, yet supportive, teachers. For instance, Bernstein studied with Isabelle Vengerova, a renowned musician known for possessing great psychological insight that brought out the best in her students. In a television documentary, Bernstein recalled that he was terrified of her during his first year of tuition until he realized what she was striving for: a flawless technique, a beautiful sound, and a relaxed manner. He recalled: "I think that I owe her an enormous debt" (in Burton, 1988). The narrative between Bernstein and Vengerova shows how much the personality and behavior of educators matters.

We briefly explained two types of motivation that can be changed with the right type of social support: passion and grit. Music teachers and parents are in a good position to promote their students' harmonious passion by fostering a healthy view of music and by using supportive behavior and speech, and avoid controlling ones (Bonneville-Roussy, Hruska, Trower, 2020). Teachers can also promote music practice as a process integrated into other activities instead of promoting music as a form of obsession. Controlling motivational factors, such as a pressuring teacher, the stress of examinations or evaluations, and anxiety around public performances can all lead to obsessive passion. In terms of grit, persistence in the face of difficulty is also associated with motivation (for a fuller review of skills that deal with setback and difficulty, see Martin & Evans, this part).

Similarly, characteristics of perfectionism can be subject to change. Music teachers and parents are in the best position to prevent the emergence of harmful perfectionistic traits or to reduce them if already developed. Because the negative reactions to mistakes perfectionism trait (frustration) is the most problematic among music students and professionals (Stoeber et al., 2018), teachers can help their students by explaining the detrimental effects of this type of perfectionism. In this context, teaching acceptance and optimism may help musicians to acknowledge and recognize their skills in performance, which can reduce anxiety and increase focus, and in turn improve their overall performances (Orejudo et al., 2017).

So far, we have discussed how the environments of musicians can impact their more (and less) malleable individual differences as they develop. Musicians themselves also have much control over how certain individual differences impact their music performance and themselves as people. Musicians who are highly conscientious may have an advantage, as they are more likely to spend time on activities that increase their competence and ability, and to take on challenging and flow-promoting tasks (Ullén et al., 2016). But even though conscientious musicians tend to be motivated in this way, they may not have the practical skills to carry out effective practice. Whether high in conscientiousness or not, it is possible to learn the suite of self-regulated behaviors that seem to come naturally to some (see McPherson, this part). Neuroticism is generally associated with negative outcomes, and in music it can be detrimental to experiencing flow, and associated with feelings of anxiety, worry, fear, and frustration. Being high in the neurotic personality traits can also reduce the tendency to participate in challenging activities. Of course, this can generate a vicious circle for musicians. Because anxious performers doubt themselves, their neuroticism stops them from gaining valuable performing experiences and experiencing flow. While neuroticism is difficult to change, health practitioners can help to address some of the anxiety issues using problem-specific interventions (e.g., Cognitive Behavioral Therapy; see also Osborne & Kirsner, Volume 2). The ultimate goal for musicians is to give more positive experiences that will protect them from being negatively affected by failure in the future. Participating in a greater number of musical activities that are challenging but not stressful may help musicians acquire greater control that reduces performance anxiety.

The topic of personality and individual differences focuses on a range of characteristics: from those that are relatively stable to those that change over time; from those that seem to be predetermined to those that respond readily to influences from the social environment; and from those that distinguish different types of musicians from each other, to those that more meaningfully distinguish musicians from non-musicians. And in this final section, we looked at some of the implications of these differences. Although many of these are not seemingly within our control, sometimes simply knowing about them and how they work can give a greater understanding of ourselves as people and as musicians.

Key Sources

Butkovic, A., & Modrusan, I. (2019). Personality differences among musicians: Real differences or stereotypes? *Psychology of Music, 49*(2), 216–226. https://doi:10.1177/0305735619849625.

Hambrick, D. Z., Burgoyne, A. P., Macnamara, B. N., & Ullén, F. (2018). Toward a multifactorial model of expertise: Beyond born versus made. *Annals of the New York Academy of Sciences, 1423*(1), 284–295. https://doi.org/10.1111/nyas.13586.

Hargreaves, D., & Lamont, A. (2017). *The psychology of musical development*. Cambridge, UK: Cambridge University Press.

Matthews, G., Deary, I. J., & Whiteman, M. C. (2003). *Personality traits*. Cambridge, UK: Cambridge University Press.

Stoeber, J., Corr, P. J., Smith, M. M., & Saklofske, D. H. (2018). Perfectionism and personality. In J. Stoeber (Ed.), *The psychology of perfectionism: Theory, research, applications* (pp. 68–88). London: Routledge. pp. 68–88.

Reflective Questions

1. How do themes and ideas from this chapter relate to what you already thought prior to reading this chapter?

2. As you reflect on the content of the chapter, what have you learned about yourself and your musician peers?

3. Many musicians are concerned that they may not have the "raw talent" required for high levels of success. While there may not be such a thing in music, there may be other individual differences at play. What are some of the differences that come to mind when you consider the way you practice, your motivation, interests in music, relationships with your teachers, and aesthetic interpretation of musical works?

4. Have you ever wondered how your own personality has shaped the musical choices you have made? If so, how and in what ways?

5. What kind of healthy and unhealthy aspects of perfectionism do you experience in your practice? How do these affect you?

References

Araújo, L. S., Wasley, D., Perkins, R., Atkins, L., Redding, E., Ginsborg, J., & Williamon, A. (2017). Fit to perform: An investigation of higher education music students' perceptions, attitudes, and behaviors toward health. *Frontiers in psychology, 8*, 1558. https://doi.org/10.3389/fpsyg.2017.01558.

Baker, S., & Cohen, B. M. Z. (2007). From snuggling and snogging to sampling and scratching: Girls' nonparticipation in community-based music activities. *Youth & Society, 39*(3), 316–339. https://doi.org/10.1177/0044118X06296696.

Baumeister, R. F., & Vohs, K. D. (2007). *Encyclopedia of social psychology* (Vol. 1). Thousand Oaks, CA: Sage.

Bogunovic, B. (2018). Sight-reading strategies and personality dimensions. In R. Parncutt & S. Sattmann (Eds.), *Proceedings of ICMPC15/ESCOM10*, 85–90. Graz, Austria: Centre for Systematic Musicology, University of Graz.

Bonneville-Roussy, A., & Bouffard, T. (2015). When quantity is not enough: Disentangling the roles of practice time, self-regulation and deliberate practice in musical achievement. *Psychology of Music, 43*(5), 686–704. https://doi.org/10.1177/0305735614534910.

Bonneville-Roussy, A., Evans, P., Verner-Filion, J., Vallerand, R. J., & Bouffard, T. (2017). Motivation and coping with the stress of assessment: Gender differences in outcomes for university students. *Contemporary Educational Psychology, 48*, 28–42. https://doi.org/10.1016/j.cedpsych.2016.08.003.

Bonneville-Roussy, A., Hruska, E., & Trower, H. (2020). Teaching music to support students: How autonomy-supportive music teachers increase students' well-being. *Journal of Research in Music Education, 68*(1), 97–119. https://doi.org/10.1177/0022429419897611.

Bonneville-Roussy, A., Lavigne, G. L. G. L., & Vallerand, R. J. (2011). When passion leads to excellence: The case of musicians. *Psychology of Music, 39*(1), 123–138. doi:10.1177/0305735609352441

Bonneville-Roussy, A., & Vallerand, R. J. (2018). The role of passion in the development of expertise: A conceptual model. In D. Z. Hambrick, G. Campitelli, & B. N. Macnamara (Eds.), *The science of expertise: Behavioral, neural, and genetic approaches to complex skill* (pp. 376–397). London: Routledge.

Bonneville-Roussy, A., & Vallerand, R. J. (2020). Passion at the heart of musicians' well-being. *Psychology of Music, 48*(2), 266–282. https://doi.org/10.1177/0305735618797180.

Bonneville-Roussy, A., Vallerand, R. J., & Bouffard, T. (2013). The roles of autonomy support and harmonious and obsessive passions in educational persistence. *Learning and Individual Differences, 24*(3), 22–31. doi:10.1016/j.lindif.2012.12.015

Burgermeister, J. (2003). *First woman takes a bow at Vienna Philharmonic. The Guardian* – see https://www.theguardian.com/world/2003/jan/10/gender.arts.

Burton, H. (1988). *Teachers and teaching: An autobiographical essay* [Television documentary]. Unitel – see https://www.youtube.com/watch?v=5m7Ky4VtNIU.

Butkovic, A., & Dopudj, D. R. (2017). Personality traits and alcohol consumption of classical and heavy metal musicians. *Psychology of Music, 45*(2), 246–256. https://doi.org/10.1177/0305735616659128.

Butkovic, A., & Modrusan, I. (2019). Personality differences among musicians: Real differences or stereotypes? *Psychology of Music, 49*(2), 216–226. https://doi.org/10.1177/0305735619849625.

Butkovic, A., Ullén, F., & Mosing, M. A. (2015). Personality related traits as predictors of music practice: Underlying environmental and genetic influences. *Personality and Individual Differences, 74*, 133–138. https://doi.org/10.1016/j.paid.2014.10.006.

Cameron, J. E., Duffy, M., & Glenwright, B. (2014). Singers take center stage! Personality traits and stereotypes of popular musicians. *Psychology of Music, 43*(6), 818–830. https://doi.org/10.1177/0305735614543217.

Credé, M., Tynan, M. C., & Harms, P. D. (2017). Much ado about grit: A meta-analytic synthesis of the grit literature. *Journal of Personality and Social Psychology, 113*(3), 492–511. https://doi.org/10.1037/pspp0000102

Corrigall, K. A., & Schellenberg, E. G. (2015). Predicting who takes music lessons: Parent and child characteristics. *Frontiers in Psychology*, *6*, 282. https://doi.org/10.3389/fpsyg.2015.00282.

Corrigall, K. A., Schellenberg, E. G., & Misura, N. M. (2013). Music training, cognition, and personality. *Frontiers in Psychology*, *4*, 222. https://doi.org/10.3389/fpsyg.2013.00222.

Csikszentmihalyi, M. (2008). *Flow: The psychology of optimal experience*. New York: HarperPerennial Modern Classics.

Curran, T., & Hill, A. P. (2019). Perfectionism is increasing over time: A meta-analysis of birth cohort differences from 1989 to 2016. *Psychological Bulletin*, *145*(4), 410. https://psycnet.apa.org/doi/10.1037/bul0000138.

Davies, J. B. (1978). *The psychology of music*. London: Hutchinson & Co.

Dibben, N. (2002). Gender identity and music. In R. A. MacDonald, D. J. Hargreaves, & D. Miell (Eds.), *Musical identities* (pp. 117–133). Oxford: Oxford University Press.

Duckworth, A. L., Peterson, C., Matthews, M. D., & Kelly, D. R. (2007). Grit: Perseverance and passion for long-term goals. *Journal of Personality and Social Psychology*, *92*(6), 1087–1101. https://doi.org/10.1037/0022-3514.92.6.1087.

Eriksson, H., Harmat, L., Theorell, T., & Ullén, F. (2017). Similar but different: Interviewing monozygotic twins discordant for musical practice. *Musicae Scientiae*, *21*(3), 250–266. https://doi.org/10.1177%2F1029864916649791.

Ericsson, K. A., Krampe, R. T., & Tesch-Römer, C. (1993). The role of deliberate practice in the acquisition of expert performance. *Psychological Review*, *100*(3), 363–406.

Ericsson, K. A., & Lehmann, A. C. (1996). Expert and exceptional performance: Evidence of maximal adaptation to task constraints. *Annual Review of Psychology*, *47*, 273–305. https://doi.org/10.1146/annurev.psych.47.1.273.

Gagné, F., & McPherson, G. E. (2016). Analyzing musical prodigiousness using Gagné's Integrative Model of Talent Development. In G. E McPherson (Ed.), *Musical prodigies: Interpretations from psychology, education, musicology and ethnomusicology* (pp. 3–114). Oxford: Oxford University Press.

Girard, F. (Director) (1993). *Thirty two short films about Glenn Gould* [Biographical anthology film]. Rhombus Media – see https://www.youtube.com/watch?v=2ySdvaLUt-s.

Glass, H. (1993) *Essentials of that eccentric Glenn Gould*. Los Angeles Times, May 30., ca–41362–story.

Goldin, C., & Rouse, C. (2000). Orchestrating impartiality: The impact of "blind" auditions on female musicians. *American Economic Review*, *90*(4), 715–741. https://doi.org/10.1257/aer.90.4.715X.

González, A., Blanco-Piñeiro, P., & Díaz-Pereira, M. P. (2018). Music performance anxiety: Exploring structural relations with self-efficacy, boost, and self-rated performance. *Psychology of Music*, *46*(6), 831–847.

Greenberg, D. M., Müllensiefen, D., Lamb, M. E., & Rentfrow, P. J. (2015). Personality predicts musical sophistication. *Journal of Research in Personality*, *58*, 154–158. http://dx.doi.org/10.1016/j.jrp.2015.06.002.

Hallam, S. (2013). What predicts level of expertise attained, quality of performance, and future musical aspirations in young instrumental players? *Psychology of Music*, *41*(3), 267–291. https://doi.org/10.1177/0305735611425902.

Hallam, S., Creech, A., Papageorgi, I., Gomes, T., Rinta, T., Varvarigou, M., & Lanipekun, J. (2016). Changes in motivation as expertise develops: Relationships with musical aspirations. *Musicae Scientiae* 20(4), 528–550. https://doi.org/10.1177/1029864916634420.

Hallam, S., Creech, A., & Varvarigou, M. (2018). Are there differences in practising and motivation between beginners playing different musical. instruments? *ORFEU*, *3*(1), 54–84. https://doi.org/10.5965/2525530403012018036.

Hallam, S., Rogers, L., & Creech, A. (2008). Gender differences in musical instrument choice. *International Journal of Music Education*, *26*(1), 7–19. https://doi.org/10.1177/0255761407085646.

Hallam, S., Varvarigou, M., Creech, A., Papageorgi, I., Gomes, T., Lanipekun, J., & Rinta, T. (2017). Are there gender differences in instrumental music practice? *Psychology of Music*, *45*(1), 116–130. https://doi.org/10.1177/0305735616650994.

Haller, C. S., & Courvoisier, D. S. (2010). Personality and thinking style in different creative domains. *Psychology of Aesthetics, Creativity, and the Arts*, *4*(3), 149–160. https://doi.org/10.1037/a0017084.

Hambrick, D. Z., Burgoyne, A. P., Macnamara, B. N., & Ullén, F. (2018). Toward a multifactorial model of expertise: beyond born versus made. *Annals of the New York Academy of Sciences*, *1423*(1), 284–295. https://doi.org/10.1111/nyas.13586.

Hargreaves, D., & Lamont, A. (2017). *The psychology of musical development*. Cambridge, UK: Cambridge University Press.

Howe, M. J., Davidson, J. W., & Sloboda, J. A. (1998). Innate talents: Reality or myth?. *Behavioral and brain sciences*, *21*(3), 399–407. https://doi.org/10.1017/S0140525X9800123X

Kemp, A. E. (1996). *The musical temperament: Psychology and personality of musicians*. Oxford: Oxford University Press.

Kenny, D., Driscoll, T., & Ackermann, B. (2018). Effects of aging on musical performance in professional orchestral musicians. *Medical Problems of Performing Artists*, *33*(1), 39–46. https://doi.org/10.21091/mppa.2018.1007.

Konieczny, V. (2009). *Glenn Gould: A musical force*. Toronto: Dundurn.

Kozinn, A., (1990, October) *Bernstein retires from performing, citing poor health. New York Times*, Oct. 10., Section C, p. 15.

Krampe, R. T., & Ericsson, K. A. (1996). Maintaining excellence: Deliberate practice and elite performance in young and older pianists. *Journal of Experimental Psychology. General*, *125*(4), 331–359.

Kozinn, A., (1990, October) *Bernstein retires from performing, citing poor health*. The New York Times, Oct. 10., Section C, p.15).

Kuckelkorn, K., Manzana, O., & Ullén, F. (2021). Musical expertise and personality: differences related to occupational choice and instrument categories. *Personality and Individual Differences*, *173*, 110573. https://doi.org/10.1016/j.paid.2020.110573.

Langendorfer, F. (2008). Personality differences among orchestra instrumental groups: Just a stereotype? *Personality and Individual Difference*, *44*, 610–620. https://doi.org/10.1016/j.paid.2007.09.027.

Matthews, G., Deary, I. J., & Whiteman, M. C. (2003). *Personality traits*. Cambridge, UK: Cambridge University Press.

McCrae, R. R., & Costa Jr., P. T. (2008). Empirical and theoretical status of the five-factor model of personality traits. In G. J. Boyle, G. Matthews, & D. H. Saklofske (Eds.), *The SAGE handbook of personality theory and assessment, Vol 1: Personality theories and models* (pp. 273–294). Thousand Oaks, CA: Sage. https://doi.org/10.4135/9781849200462.n13.

McPherson, G. E. (2000). Commitment and practice: Key ingredients for achievement during the early stages of learning a musical instrument. *Bulletin of the Council for Research in Music Education*, *147*, 122–127.

McPherson, G. E., Davidson, J. W., & Evans, P. (2006). Playing an instrument. In G. E. McPherson (Ed.), *The child as musician: A handbook of musical development* (pp. 331–351). Oxford: Oxford University Press.

Miksza, P., & Tan, L. (2015). Predicting collegiate wind players' practice efficiency, flow, and self-efficacy for self-regulation: An exploratory study of relationships between teachers' instruction and students' practicing. *Journal of Research in Music Education*, 63(2), 162–179. https://doi.org/10.1177/0022429415583474.

Nupen, C. (Director). (1998). *The gift of music*. [Documentary]. Allegro Films.

O'Neill, S. A. (1997). Gender and music. In D. J. Hargreaves & A. C. North (Eds.), *The social psychology of music* (p. 46–63). Oxford: Oxford University Press.

Orejudo, S., Zarza-Alzugaray, F. J., Casanova, O., Rodríguez-Ledo, C., & Mazas, B. (2017). The relation of music performance anxiety (MPA) to optimism, self-efficacy, and sensitivity to reward and punishment: Testing Barlow's theory of personal vulnerability on a sample of Spanish music students. *Psychology of Music*, 45(4), 570–583. https://doi.org/10.1177%2F0305735616674791.

Rose, D., Bartoli, A. J., & Heaton, P. (2019). Formal-informal musical learning, sex and musicians' personalities. *Personality and Individual Differences*, 142, 207–213. https://doi.org/10.1016/j.paid.2018.07.015.

Rosen, P. (Director). (1978). *Leonard Bernstein: Reflections* [Documentary]. EuroArts.

Salmon, P. G. (1990). A psychological perspective on musical performance anxiety: A review of the literature. *Medical Problems of Performing Artists*, 5, 2–11.

Scharff, C. (2018). *Gender, subjectivity, and cultural work: The classical music profession*. London: Routledge. https://doi.org/10.4324/9781315673080.

Simoens, V. L., Puttonen, S., & Tervaniemi, M. (2015). Are music performance anxiety and performance boost perceived as extremes of the same continuum? *Psychology of Music*, 43(2), 171–187. https://doi.org/10.1177%2F0305735613499200.

Simonton, D. K. (2014). Creative performance, expertise acquisition, individual differences, and developmental antecedents: An integrative research agenda. *Intelligence*, 45, 66–73. https://doi.org/10.1016/j.intell.2013.04.007.

Smith, M. M., Saklofske, D. H., Yan, G., & Sherry, S. B. (2015). Perfectionistic strivings and perfectionistic concerns interact to predict negative emotionality: Support for the tripartite model of perfectionism in Canadian and Chinese university students. *Personality and Individual Differences*, 81, 141–147. https://doi.org/10.1016/j.paid.2014.09.006

Stoeber, J. (2018). An introduction. In J. Stoeber (Ed.), *The psychology of perfectionism: Theory, research, applications* (pp. 3–17). London: Routledge.

Stoeber, J., Corr, P. J., Smith, M. M., & Saklofske, D. H. (2018). Perfectionism and personality. In J. Stoeber (Ed.). *The psychology of perfectionism: Theory, research, applications* (pp. 68–88). London: Routledge.

Stoeber, J., & Eismann, U. (2007). Perfectionism in young musicians: Relations with motivation, effort, achievement, and distress. *Personality and Individual Differences*, 43(8), 2182–2192. https://doi.org/10.1016/j.paid.2007.06.036.

Tan, Y. T., McPherson, G. E., & Wilson, S. J. 2017. The molecular genetic basis of music ability and music-related phenotypes. In D. Z. Hambrick, B. N. Macnamara, & G. Campitelli (Eds.), *The science of expertise: Behavioral, neural, and genetic approaches to complex skill* (pp. 283–304). New York: Routledge.

Ullén, F., Hambrick, D. Z., & Mosing, M. A. (2016). Rethinking expertise: A multifactorial gene-environment interaction model of expert performance. *Psychological Bulletin, 142*(4), 427–446. https://psycnet.apa.org/doi/10.1037/bul0000033.

Ullén, F., Mosing, M. A., Holm, L., Eriksson, H., & Madison, G. (2014). Psychometric properties and heritability of a new online test for musicality, the Swedish Musical Discrimination Test. *Personality and Individual Differences, 63*, 87–93. https://doi.org/10.1016/j.paid.2014.01.057.

Vaag, J., Sund, E. R., & Bjerkeset, O. (2018). Five-factor personality profiles among Norwegian musicians compared to the general workforce. *Musicae Scientiae, 22*(3), 434–445. https://doi.org/10.1177/1029864917709519.

Vallerand, R. J., Blanchard, C. M., Mageau, G. A., Koestner, Léonard, M., Gagne, M., & Marsolais, J. (2003). Les passions de l'âme: On obsessive and harmonious passion. *Journal of Personality and Social Psychology, 85*(4), 756–767. https://doi.org/10.1037/0022-3514.85.4.756.

Vaquero, L., Hartmann, K., Ripollés, P., Rojo, N., Sierpowska, J., François, C., Camara, E., van Vugt, F. T, Mohammadi, B., Samii, A., Münte, T. F., Rodríguez-Fornells, A., Altenmüller, E. (2016). Structural neuroplasticity in expert pianists depends on the age of musical training onset. *NeuroImage, 126*, 106–119. https://doi.org/10.1016/j.neuroimage.2015.11.008.

Vuust, P., Gebauer, L., Hansen, N. C., Jørgensen, S. R., Møller, A., & Linnet, J. (2010). Personality influences career choice: Sensation seeking in professional musicians. *Music Education Research, 12*(2), 219–230. https://doi.org/10.1080/14613801003746584.

Wopereis, I. G. J. H., Stoyanov, S., Kirschner, P. A., & Van Merriënboer, J. J. G. (2013). What makes a good musical improviser? An expert view on improvisational expertise. *Psychomusicology: Music, Mind, and Brain, 23*(4), 222–235. https://doi.org/10.1037/pmu0000021.

CHAPTER 26

BUOYANCY, RESILIENCE, AND ADAPTABILITY

ANDREW J. MARTIN AND PAUL EVANS

INTRODUCTION

THE path to becoming and being an accomplished musician is challenging and plagued by uncertainty. As with other performance domains, there are two broad types of adversity facing musicians: everyday adversity and major adversity. Everyday adversity includes difficult practice regimes, challenging repertoire, busy or short timelines under which to practice and perform, and the management of a career that can often include a range of business management, employment, and contract work. Research has identified *buoyancy* as the attribute helpful for dealing with this kind of everyday adversity. It is not uncommon for musicians to also experience major adversity at some stage in their career. Major adversities can include poor physical and/or mental health, periods of unemployment or underemployment, and chronically onerous performance pressures. Research has identified *resilience* as the attribute important for dealing with these major adversities. Alongside the need to navigate adversity, music performers will also be faced with a great deal of uncertainty, novelty, change, and variability in their lives. For example, they will need to meet and work with musicians, learn new musical pieces, play to different audiences, constantly adjust practice and rehearsal regimes, and work under different conductors and directors. Recent research has identified individuals' *adaptability* as an attribute critical to navigate uncertainty, novelty, change, and variability.

When musicians are better able to respond to minor adversity with buoyancy, major adversity with resilience, and uncertainty and change with adaptability, they are ideally placed for optimal performance. To the extent that this is the case, this trio of psychological skills—buoyancy, resilience, and adaptability—play an important part in musicians' lives. This chapter reviews theory and research relevant to buoyancy, resilience, and adaptability in music and identifies directions for practice to promote these important psychological attributes.

Our approach to buoyancy, resilience, and adaptability is an asset-oriented or strengths-based approach to musicians' responses to adversity, change, and uncertainty (Martin & Marsh, 2009). This is in line with theorizing and research into positive psychology, wellbeing, and mental health. As Martin and Marsh (2009) point out, researchers have extended from the more defensive "risk" and "protective" factors to also encompass "enabling" factors (Bandura, 2006) and positive adaptations whereby "individuals play a proactive role in their adaptation rather than simply undergo happenings in which environments act upon their personal endowments" (Bandura, 2006, p. 28). Relatedly, positive psychology proposes the "broaden-and-build" theory of positive emotion (Fredrickson, 2001; see also Martin, 2004) positing that boosting positive emotions and narrowing negative ones can expands one's behavioral and psychological repertoire to enhance buoyancy, resilience, and adaptability at times of stress and change. Along similar lines, theory and research also propose that mental wellbeing is not only the absence of mental illness but also the capacity to "flourish" (Keyes, 2007)— consistent with asset-oriented attributes such as buoyancy, resilience, and adaptability. Following from these conceptions, we propose that musicians can learn to be more buoyant, resilient, and adaptable through developing positive cognitive, behavioral, and emotional orientations to their performance life. In this chapter, we explore these ideas and their implications for enhancing musicians' capacity to successfully navigate adversity and change.

BUOYANCY AND RESILIENCE

The idea that it is important to be motivated and engaged to attain optimal performance is uncontroversial. Indeed, to be motivated and engaged through relatively smooth and successful phases of life is not too difficult a task. The reality, however, is that life is not always smooth and successful. It is punctuated by challenge, setback, adversity, and pressure. A musician's life is no exception (Martin, 2018). The process of learning music from childhood through adulthood and establishing a career as a performing musician are laden with unique kinds of challenge, setback, adversity, and pressure. In order to understand the factors that optimize a musician's capacity to effectively function, it is important to understand the adversities that are implicated in musical performance and the psychological skills required for navigating and managing those adversities.

Defining buoyancy and resilience

In considering adversity experienced in performance domains, Martin and Marsh (2009) identified two typical types of adversity. The first refers to "everyday" adversity that connotes low-level setback and challenge. Musicians face such everyday adversity with the need to maintain daily rehearsal regimes, learning new repertoire, and maintaining expensive and delicate instruments and equipment (Martin, 2018). The second type of adversity refers to more major and substantial adversity. This might involve chronic adversity that is ongoing in a musician's life. Or, it may involve acute adversity that emerges at short notice and is particularly aversive and challenging. Musicians can encounter much more significant adversity in the context of high-stakes competitions, extensive (e.g., season-long) performance regimes, ongoing performance anxiety, chronic self-doubt, and markedly uncertain and non-linear performance and career pathways.

Martin and Marsh (2009) identified "buoyancy" as the attribute necessary to effectively deal with low-level everyday adversity, and "resilience" as the attribute necessary for successfully navigating major adversity (the latter being in keeping with the "classic" definitions of resilience; e.g., Luthar & Cicchetti, 2000; Masten, 2001; Werner, 2000). As relevant to the music domain, Martin (2018) identified buoyancy and resilience as important attributes that musicians might look to for building and sustaining their performance outcomes.

The bulk of research literature has tended to focus on resilience in response to major, acute, or chronic adversity. Resilience is the process of, capacity for, or outcome of successful adaptation despite challenging or threatening circumstances (Howard & Johnson, 2000). These circumstances are not minor or insubstantial; they tend to be "acute," "chronic," and "major assaults" on development (e.g., see Garmezy, 1981; Lindstroem, 2001; Luthar & Cicchetti, 2000; Masten, 2001; Werner, 2000). The focus of most resilience research has been on "life" events such as being raised in a disadvantaged context, receiving poor parenting, or divorce (Lindstroem, 2001; Luthar & Cicchetti, 2000; Masten, 2001). There is less domain-specific resilience research—including in music.

Because resilience has usually referred to major adversities, not so much attention had been given to challenges and adversities that are typical of daily life and relevant to most individuals (Martin & Marsh, 2009). Thus, typical constructions of resilience relate to a relatively small number of individuals experiencing rather extreme adversity. The need to intervene to assist such individuals is obvious. However, these constructions of resilience do not refer to a relatively large number of individuals experiencing "everyday" adversities, who are arguably equally in need of intervention or assistance. As relevant to music, for example, resilience might refer to chronic performance anxiety that threatens to disrupt a career-making (or -breaking) concert event, but it does not speak to musicians who experience minor events that might not threaten the outcome of a performance but do shake their preparation or have other consequences for their mental wellbeing. For this reason, it is important to differentiate resilience and buoyancy as responses to, respectively, major adversity and everyday adversity (Martin & Marsh, 2009).

Indeed, by proposing the concept of buoyancy, Martin and Marsh (2008a, 2008b, 2009) aimed to bridge the gap between "classic" treatments of resilience of acute and chronic adversity experienced by the relative few (e.g., Garmezy, 1981; Lindstroem, 2001; Luthar & Cicchetti, 2000; Martin, 2013a; Masten, 2001; Werner, 2000) and the everyday adversities experienced by the many. Accordingly, they demarcated buoyancy and resilience predominantly in terms of differences of degree (Martin & Marsh, 2008a, 2008b, 2009). Adapting some of the examples provided by them to the music domain, resilience and buoyancy might be juxtaposed in the ways shown in Table 26.1.

Buoyancy may be a necessary but not sufficient condition for resilience (Martin & Marsh, 2008a, 2008b, 2009). There may be something of a hierarchical or directional ordering of buoyancy and resilience. Put another way, perhaps an ongoing capacity to deal with everyday and low-level adversity may reduce the chances of major risk emerging in one's life. Indeed, Martin (2013) investigated this, finding that buoyancy was more salient in negatively predicting low-level maladaptive outcomes (higher buoyancy associated with less low-level risk such as fear of failure), whereas resilience was more salient in negatively predicting major maladaptive outcomes (higher resilience associated with less major risk such as disengagement). He further found that the effect of buoyancy on major maladaptive outcomes was mediated by resilience. Extrapolating this to the music domain, it may be that promoting buoyancy (a capacity to navigate low-level everyday adversity) is vital not only for dealing with everyday setback typical of most musicians' lives, but also as a foundation for resilience when more substantial adversity strikes.

Table 26.1. Examples of low–level, minor adversity (buoyancy) and high–level, chronic adversity (resilience) for performing musicians.

	Isolated, minor setbacks	Chronic, major setbacks
Domain	*Buoyancy*	*Resilience*
Intrapersonal	• One-off injury requiring a short bout of treatment • Dissatisfaction with a performance event	• Ongoing physical ailment or repetitive strain injury affecting performance • Major, ongoing self-doubts or lack of confidence
Interpersonal	• Disagreement with a teacher or manager • Minor fallout with another ensemble member	• Breakdown in relationship with a teacher or manager • Chronically poor relationships in ensembles
Musical/technical	• Minor equipment failure (e.g., reed breaking just before a concert) • Scores supplied in an unfamiliar clef or key	• Major equipment issue (e.g., theft of a valuable instrument)
Professional	• Managing cancellation or rebooking of a gig • Managing a touring schedule	• Running a small business • Integrating a challenging range of diverse activities (e.g., teaching, performing, accompanying)
Educational	• Taking longer than usual to learn challenging repertoire	• Needing to find a new teacher or coach

Major resilience frameworks also emphasize a process (or cycle) where resilience and risk are closely connected. They suggest that individuals are able to move out of risk and into resilience—and vice versa (Catterall, 1998). For example, Rutter (1987) identified the process of building resilience that involved reducing risk and also promoting individuals' capacity to deal with it. In similar vein, Morales (2000) identified a resilience cycle that involves recognizing and reducing risk and at the same time learning how to better respond to it (see also Brooks, 2010; Compas, 2004; Iwaniec, Larkin, & Higgins, 2006; Martin & Marsh, 2009; Rutter, 2006). In this chapter, we focus on individuals' capacity to respond to risk (namely, their buoyancy and resilience).

Measuring and identifying buoyancy and resilience

There have been two predominant approaches to studying resilience: variable-focused and person-focused approaches (Masten, 2001). The *variable-focused approach* examines the associations among measures of risk/adversity, buoyancy/resilience, and the factors that may protect the individual from negative consequences or adverse events. Approaches to variable-focused research typically involve regression-based and path analyses, and structural equation modeling. The *person-focused approach* identifies distinct groups of people in terms of their responses to risk and seeks to differentiate resilient from non-resilient individuals. Approaches to person-focused research typically involve cluster analysis and latent profile analysis. Variable- and person-focused approaches are complementary, with the former identifying *factors* to target to promote buoyancy and resilience and the latter identifying *individuals* to target or assist (e.g., Morin et al., 2017).

Arguably, the most straightforward variable-focused means of assessing buoyancy and resilience is via self-report measures. For example, in relation to buoyancy, Martin (2008a; see also Martin & Jackson, 2008) adapted the Academic Buoyancy Scale to the music domain to ask young musicians how they deal with music-related adversity and challenge (e.g., performance pressure, occasional poor performances). This measure can be operationalized as a *predictor* of music performance outcomes, but it can also be identified as a desirable end (*outcome*) in itself. It is also possible to use this unidimensional buoyancy measure to enable tests of *moderation*. This determines the extent to which, for example, high levels of music-related buoyancy can buffer the negative effects of performance anxiety in relation to a concert performance. Indeed, Martin and Marsh (2019) tested the moderating role of buoyancy in the academic domain and found that high levels of buoyancy reduced the negative effects of academic risk. How this buffering role of buoyancy generalizes to the music domain is worth exploring further. Alongside moderation analyses, variable-focused approaches also permit tests of *mediation* that seek to determine the effects of hypothesized antecedents on outcomes via buoyancy and resilience (see Baron & Kenny, 1986). In the music domain, for example, there may be dispositional (e.g., personality) and contextual (e.g., family support) antecedents that impact performance outcomes via buoyancy and resilience. This would allow insights into the extent to which these antecedents boost (or diminish) musicians' responses to adversity and challenge, which in turn boost (or diminish) their performance outcomes.

Person-focused approaches seek to identify distinct groups of individuals deemed as buoyant and resilient (or not) with a view to identifying key factors that determine their group membership. In such cases we purposefully research the very groups in which one is interested (e.g., resilient musicians). This approach also presents an opportunity to study groups of buoyant and resilient individuals as they occur "naturally"—these groups are not created or manipulated; they are identified through their own responses and characteristics (Masten & Powell, 2003). In the scheme of buoyancy and resilience research, the person-focused approaches have received much less attention than the variable-focused approaches, including in music. However, this is changing with an increasing body of research attending to person-focused considerations. These are now recognized as particularly important because they overcome some of the limitations inherent in variable-focused approaches. For example, a variable-focused approach might find that particular aspects of personality are associated with buoyancy—indeed, Martin, Nejad, Colmar, and Liem (2013) found that neuroticism negatively predicted buoyancy. But person-focused analyses can arrive at a more nuanced picture: for example, such analyses might find that there are some musicians who are high in neuroticism but do not experience lower buoyancy, provided that they are also high in conscientiousness and family support. Thus, person-focused analyses can uncover critical insights about a phenomenon that variable-focused analyses cannot. We thus recommend person-focused approaches to buoyancy and resilience in the music domain. (For a similar contrast of variable-centered and person-centered approaches in the domain of motivation, see Evans & Ryan, this volume).

Buoyancy and resilience research findings

The bulk of domain-specific work into buoyancy and resilience has been conducted in the academic and workplace domains, traversing: (1) research identifying links between buoyancy/resilience and other constructs (e.g., coping, adaptability, grit, control, anxiety, fear; Fong & Kim, 2019; Martin et al., 2013; Putwain & Aveyard, 2019; Putwain, Chamberlain, Daly, & Sadreddini, 2014, 2015; Putwain, Connors, Symes, & Douglas-Osborn, 2012; Putwain & Daly, 2013; Putwain, Daly, Chamberlain, & Sadreddini, 2015; Symes, Putwain, & Remedios, 2015); (2) research on predictors of buoyancy/resilience (e.g., motivation predictors; Collie, Martin, Malmberg, Hall, & Ginns, 2015; Martin, Colmar, Davey, & Marsh, 2010; Martin & Marsh, 2006); (3) research on outcomes predicted by buoyancy/resilience (e.g., engagement and achievement; Martin, 2013a; Martin & Marsh, 2008a); (4) intervention research (e.g., Puolakanaho et al., 2018; Putwain, Gallard, & Beaumont, 2019); and (5) research of buoyancy/resilience among different samples and contexts (e.g., cross-cultural comparisons; Collie, Ginns, Martin, & Papworth, 2017; Datu & Yang, 2018; Martin, Yu, Ginns, & Papworth, 2017; Yun, Hiver, & Al-Hoorie, 2018).

However, there is an emerging body of work in the music domain that sheds preliminary light on music-related buoyancy and resilience. For example, in a study of young musicians' motivation and engagement, Martin (2008a) identified numerous factors correlated with their music-related buoyancy (music-related buoyancy was assessed using the Academic Buoyancy Scale adapted to music). Factors positively correlated with their buoyancy included their self-efficacy (feeling confident in music), valuing (regarding music as important and useful), mastery orientation (developing musical skill for its own sake rather than to be seen as impressive), and their self-regulation and persistence in music. Factors negatively correlated with music-related buoyancy included music-related anxiety (particularly), a low sense of control, fear of failure, and disengagement in music. In a subsequent publication, Martin and Jackson (2008) found that flow in music was positively correlated with music-related buoyancy.

Other researchers have found that these key correlates of music-related buoyancy are implicated in musicians' performance and experiential outcomes. For example, when musicians have a sense of control and are given greater autonomy, they demonstrate more persistence in the face of setback and challenge (Renwick & McPherson, 2002). In terms of self-efficacy, musicians benefit from positive music-related self-appraisals (McCormick & McPherson, 2003; McPherson & McCormick, 2006). Relatedly, their expectations for success are important for positive performance outcomes (McCormick & McPherson, 2007). In similar vein, Evans and McPherson (2015) found that there were some children who, when they first started their instrument, articulated a long-term view of themselves as musicians. Ten years later, these students were more likely to be still learning and playing music—suggesting that the long-term musical identity they had of themselves was associated with persistence through the ups and downs of their music career. The evidence on self-regulated learning suggests positive outcomes among musicians who plan, set goals, monitor progress, and revise their approach where necessary (McPherson & Renwick, 2011; see also McPherson, this part). In terms of persistence in music, it is evident that ongoing and cumulative practice is key to navigating challenge (Evans & McPherson, 2015). These findings demonstrate that although the role of buoyancy has not been directly studied, it is implicated indirectly through the importance of these closely related performance factors.

When responding to music-related adversity, it is also important to recognize there are maladaptive psychological dimensions that must be effectively managed. One classic construct is anxiety. Anxiety is a pervasive factor in the music domain and can be a significant impediment to one's performance experience and outcomes (see Osborne & Kirsner, Volume 2). Indeed, anxiety appears to be one of the most significant threats to buoyancy (Martin, Colmar, et al, 2010). At the same time, however, anxiety can be managed and indeed harnessed such that it may assist performance. For example, there is evidence that anxiety, combined with effective self-management and skill development, can enhance music performance (Osborne & Kirsner, Volume 2). Another threat to the musician is the threat to self-esteem following a poor performance or an unfavorable review/assessment (Dunkel, 1989). This is not uncommon in competitive environments (Hendricks, 2014), and the loss of confidence can lead to helplessness

(O'Neill & Sloboda, 1997). There is also the pressure of external factors such as others' beliefs and expectations. Sometimes, exceedingly high expectations can be onerous and present significant psychological risk. At the other end of the expectation spectrum, low expectations or negative beliefs can represent significant threat and affect behavior. For example, others' views that one is not musically capable can lead to a lifetime of avoidance to play and reluctance to be involved in music (Ruddock & Leong, 2005).

Boosting buoyancy and resilience

It is possible to enhance individuals' ability to deal with setback because there are "alterable processes or mechanisms that can be developed and fostered" (Waxman, Huang, & Padron, 1997, p. 137). Here we point to three lines of research that provide guidance for boosting buoyancy and resilience. The first draws on research by Martin and colleagues that has identified the "5Cs" that are implicated in buoyancy (Martin & Marsh, 2006; Martin, Colmar, et al., 2010): confidence (self-efficacy), coordination (planning), commitment (persistence), control, and composure (low anxiety). Cross-sectional (Martin & Marsh, 2006) and longitudinal research (Martin, Colmar et al., 2010) found these factors to significantly predict individuals' buoyancy. Notably, in the preceding discussion, we reported research showing that each of these factors is also implicated in young musicians' buoyancy (Martin, 2008a). Accordingly, these five factors have been suggested as useful points for practitioners seeking to enhance individuals' responses to adversity. Indeed, there is a well-established evidence base on interventions successfully addressing each of these five factors (e.g., see Craven, Marsh, & Debus, 1991; Hattie, 2009; Martin, 2005, 2008b; McInerney, McInerney, & Marsh, 1997; O'Mara, Marsh, Craven & Debus, 2006).

In addition to psychologically oriented (or, intrapersonal) intervention aimed at enhancing responses to risk and setback, a second line of research has identified interpersonal factors that may promote buoyancy (Martin & Marsh, 2008a). Consistent with seminal research into risk (Masten, 2001), good teacher-student relationships are vital for promoting buoyancy (Martin & Marsh, 2008a). Extrapolating from this, we would suggest the importance of positive interpersonal relationships between musicians and their instructors, coaches, mentors, and directors/conductors. Indeed, as Martin (2018) noted, there is a need for more research into interpersonal relationships in the music domain, and this work might be extended to consider the buoyancy and resilience of musicians. Martin (2018) observed that given the inter-individual and group processes central to most musical performances, it is plausible to explore the extent to which interpersonal connectedness is influential in musicians' capacity to navigate performance-related adversity (Martin, 2018).

A third line of intervention pertains to the relative priority given to a focus on risk or a focus on buoyancy and resilience. There has been a lack of clarity as to whether resilience is developed through exposing individuals to adversity in the same way that exposing individuals to a low-level dose of a virus inoculates against future infection (Coleman

& Hagell, 2007; Olsson, Bond, Burns, Vell-Brodrick, & Sawyer, 2003). This aligns with the "stress inoculation" and "just manageable challenge" approaches to coping and resilience (e.g., Jaremko & Meichenbaum, 2013; Nakamura & Csikszentmihalyi, 2009; Slade, 2010; Spreitzer & Quinn, 2006; Zimmer-Gembeck & Skinner, 2008). In the context of music, this would imply that it is important to introduce some (manageable) difficulty and setback to the musician in order to increase their buoyancy and resilience. On the other hand, it may be the case that it is better to increase musicians' buoyancy and resilience (not their risk) in order to reduce any subsequent risk and adversity. Martin and Marsh (2019) explored these two possibilities in the academic setting. The dominant finding was that high school students' buoyancy led to lower subsequent levels of academic risk and setback. They found that risk and adversity could lead to lower subsequent levels of risk and adversity, provided that the individual was already high in buoyancy. But if they were low in buoyancy, this risk and adversity led to higher levels of subsequent risk and adversity. In the music domain, then, promoting buoyancy and resilience seems to be the optimal strategy for reducing subsequent risk and adversity; introducing or escalating adversity in a musician's life would only be indicated if that musician was already buoyant/resilient.

ADAPTABILITY

It has recently been emphasized that it is important to distinguish adversity from cognate factors such as uncertainty, change, novelty, and transition (Martin, Nejad, et al., 2012, 2013). The former (i.e., adversity) is relevant to buoyancy/resilience, whereas the latter (i.e., change, etc.) is related to "adaptability." Indeed, Martin (2017) recently made the point that not all novelty is a threat; not all change is adverse; and not all uncertainty is a challenge. Change, novelty, uncertainty, and transition may be quite positive, providing opportunities for growth and new beginnings. Indeed, research has shown that adaptability and buoyancy are correlated, but distinct—with the bulk of variance between them being unshared and the two of them predicting performance outcomes in different ways (Martin, Nejad, et al., 2013). Martin (2017), however, did also recognize that change, novelty, uncertainty, and transition are not always growth opportunities and not always positive. In fact, they can be difficult, challenging, and adverse, which is why disentangling adaptability from buoyancy/resilience is vital (Martin, 2017). Doing so helps us know when adaptability is needed and when both adaptability and buoyancy/resilience are needed. Without clarity on definitions and constructs, targeted and nuanced intervention may not be possible.

There is now a growing body of research into adaptability in numerous performance domains, including school, university, and work. But there remain important questions to address as researchers explore the potential of this construct in other performance domains. The music domain is no exception, as it too comprises uncertainty, change, novelty, and transition, as the examples in Table 26.2 illustrate. Uncertainty is not uncommon, especially with regard to upcoming musical programs and venues—and even one's medium- to longer-term career; change is evident in terms of the different musicians with whom one will play and the numerous mentors, instructors, and conductors/directors one will encounter along the way; novelty is evidenced in the large range of repertoire that a musician must learn and master; with regard to transition, as musicians become more proficient, they will move from one level of technical difficulty to another and often one performance context to another. Uncertainty, change, novelty, and transition along these lines disrupt routines and create new circumstances to which individuals must habituate (Pinquart & Silbereisen 2004; Tomasik & Silbereisen 2009; Tomasik, Silbereisen, & Heckhausen, 2010). Adaptability has been identified as a critical factor for helping individuals to do so.

The yields of adaptability are found across diverse outcomes and across multiple countries (e.g., Australia, the United States, the United Kingdom, China; Collie & Martin, 2017a, 2017b; Liem & Martin, 2015; Martin, Nejad et al., 2013, 2015; Collie, Holliman, & Martin, 2017; Holliman, Collie, & Martin, 2018). In the academic domain, adaptability is linked to heightened achievement, motivation and engagement, effective goal setting, and a growth mindset. Moving beyond academic outcomes, adaptability is associated with positive personal wellbeing outcomes, including a greater sense of life satisfaction, meaning and purpose in life, and self-esteem. In the workplace, research has demonstrated that when employees are more adaptable, they tend to experience greater wellbeing at work, higher organizational commitment, and lower levels

Table 26.2. Examples of adaptability in response to novelty, change, and transition for performing musicians.

	Uncertainty, change, novelty, and transition
Domain	*Adaptability*
Intrapersonal	• Transitioning from a university music performance program into a professional career • Managing impact of external personal events on role as a musician (e.g., having children, relocation)
Interpersonal	• Commencing a job in an orchestra and establishing relationships with new colleagues and section principal • Managing changing expectations of clients
Musical/technical	• Playing in an unfamiliar genre (e.g., an orchestral musician used to the concert hall filling in for a musical theater pit orchestra)
Professional	• Understanding a new conductor/director • Commencing in a leadership role (e.g., principal, conductor) • Retiring from a performance career into a teaching job • Negotiating new contracts
Educational	• Teacher or coach moving away • New repertoire that requires different strategies to learn

of disengagement (Collie & Martin, 2017b). Taken together, adaptability is linked with important outcomes. In this chapter we explore its potential in the music domain.

Defining adaptability

The American Psychological Association (APA) defines adaptability as "the capacity to make appropriate responses to changed or changing situations; the ability to modify or adjust one's behavior in meeting different circumstances or different people" (VandenBos, 2015, p. 18). This conceptualization of adaptability reflects a predominantly behavioral perspective, but can be expanded to include cognitive and emotional regulation (Martin et al., 2012, 2013). There are thus three dimensions of regulation underlying adaptability: cognitive regulation, which refers to adjusting one's thoughts or thinking patterns; behavioral regulation, which refers to adjusting the nature and/or degree of one's responses or behavioral patterns; and emotional regulation, which refers to emotional reframing and adjusting one's emotion (Burns & Martin, 2014; Martin, Nejad, et al., 2013). Collectively, this represents the "tripartite perspective" on adaptability (Martin et al., 2013). Hence, this recent conceptualizing has built on the behaviorally focused APA definition of adaptability to also consider cognitive and emotional responses to uncertainty, change, novelty, and transition (Martin, Nejad et al., 2012), bringing the concept into line with other major tripartite self-system frameworks (e.g., Fredricks, Blumenfeld, & Paris, 2004).

For musicians, cognitive regulation might involve thinking about a new situation in different ways to find an effective response, such as thinking about a change in band members as an opportunity for further musical development or stimulation. Regulation of one's behavior might involve trying new actions such as seeking help or different resources in the face of a new musical piece. Regulation of one's emotions might entail downward regulation of negative emotions such as anxiety or frustration in an unexpected event such as the cancellation of a performance. As Holliman, Collie, and Martin (2020) argue, each of these dimensions—cognition, behavior, emotion—is vital for maintaining a positive alignment between oneself and one's (changing) environment.

Definitional and operational dimensions of adaptability draw on numerous theoretical traditions that have sought to inform human functioning. These include the lifespan theory of control (e.g., Heckhausen & Schulz, 1995), models of change (e.g., Parker, Martin, Martinez, Marsh, & Jackson, 2010; Prochaska & Velicer, 1997), models of adaptation (e.g., Diener, Lucas, & Scallon, 2006), evolutionary theorizing (e.g., Barrett, Dunbar, & Lycett, 2002), and positive psychology (e.g., Fredrickson, 2001). Of particular relevance to music, another major line of theory and research is that related to self-regulation and self-regulated learning (e.g., Zimmerman, 2002; see McPherson, this part).

Self-regulated learning involves monitoring, directing, and controlling actions aimed at attaining learning goals, improving one's expertise, and building one's skills (Boekaerts & Corno, 2005; Zimmerman, 2002, McPherson, this part). Models of self-regulated learning typically articulate a process by which individuals make the appropriate self-related adjustments in order to perform a task or adjust to their environment.

For example, Winne and Hadwin's (2008) four phases of self-regulation lead to an adaptation phase where the individual evaluates their performance and identifies what modifications are needed to improve on their performance. Martin, Nejad, et al. (2013) extended the "classic" self-regulatory models of cognition and behavior to also explicitly encompass regulation of emotion (see also Pekrun, 2012). Moreover, whereas "classic" self-regulatory models focus on learning tasks and demands, adaptability is focused on uncertainty, change, novelty, and transition and the adjustments and modifications needed to deal with these. Accordingly, Martin, Nejad, et al. (2013) proposed adaptability as a distinct dimension under the self-regulation umbrella.

Positioning adaptability as a self-regulation perspective brings into consideration a line of music-related self-regulation research. For example, Davidson (2005) assessed the behavioral and self-regulatory aspects of music and found clear benefits for musicians who planned, set goals, and self-monitored progress (see also McCormick & McPherson, 2003; McPherson & Renwick, 2011). Martin (2008a) found that self-regulation in music (operationalized via planning and task management) was significantly correlated with musicians' participation, enjoyment, and positive future intentions/aspirations. More recently, McPherson, Osborne, Evans, and Miksza (2019) used microanalysis to study two university music students' practice from moment to moment, finding stark contrasts in their self-regulatory abilities that were related to their performance. These self-regulatory processes also appear to be somewhat malleable in response to targeted interventions (Osborne, McPherson, Miksza, & Evans, 2020). Although there is relatively little direct research on adaptability among musicians, these findings highlight the importance of self-regulation more broadly, so a more nuanced examination of adaptability (conceived as a self-regulation in response to change) may be fruitful (see McPherson, this part).

Measuring and identifying adaptability

The measurement of adaptability—as conceptualized here—has been conducted by way of the Adaptability Scale (Martin, Nejad, et al., 2013). Using a Likert response format, the scale includes nine items to assess individuals' cognitive adjustment (e.g., "I am able to adjust my thinking or expectations to assist me in a new situation"), behavioral adjustment (e.g., "In uncertain situations, I am able to develop new ways of going about things [e.g. a different way of asking questions or finding information] to help me through"), and emotional adjustment (e.g., "I am able to reduce negative emotions [e.g., fear] to help me deal with uncertain situations"). Thus, the scale captures the tripartite model of adaptability. Evaluations have thus far shown the scale to be highly reliable and valid (e.g., Martin, Nejad, et al., 2012, 2013). Subsequently, Collie and Martin (2016) developed a domain-specific template that could be applied to specific performance areas. They demonstrated its application to the work domain, but equally the items can be applied to the music domain. There is thus a self-report form available to administer to musicians to explore their adaptability and its implications for their performance life.

Over the past five years, there has been a growing evidence base for adaptability. Research has identified antecedents and consequences of adaptability in longitudinal research (Martin, Nejad, et al., 2013), investigated adaptability among at-risk student populations (Burns & Martin, 2014; Martin & Burns, 2014), located adaptability in major models of human functioning (e.g., Bandura's social-cognitive theory; Burns, Martin, & Collie, 2018), explored the link between adaptability, engagement, and achievement (Collie, Holliman, & Martin, 2017; Holliman et al., 2018, 2020), modeled the role of adaptability in young people's responses to climate change (Liem & Martin, 2015), identified the role of adaptability in reducing students' failure dynamics (Martin, Nejad, et al., 2015), and shown how significant others' perceptions of students' adaptability impact students' achievement outcomes (Collie & Martin, 2017a).

Large-scale cross-national research has also now been conducted, scoping adaptability across the United States, the United Kingdom, and China (Martin, Yu, Ginns, & Papworth, 2017), while at a more granular level, neuroscientific research has been harnessed to identify potential neural networks and mechanisms that may be implicated in adaptability (Burns, Martin, & Lipton, 2020). Recent adaptability research has also extended to the workplace, showing that an autonomy supportive workplace is associated with higher employee adaptability and that this in turn is associated with better psychological functioning in the workplace (Collie & Martin, 2017b).

Adaptability was examined in one study as a potential mitigator of the effects of stress in a music conservatory environment on feelings of vitality (a sense of aliveness and energy, as opposed to feeling drained and depleted; Ryan & Deci, 2017). The findings from that study showed that indeed students who were higher in adaptability were also higher in vitality, suggesting a strong role for adaptability in maintaining this important psychological state. Notably, though, adaptability in this study did not moderate the relationship of stress on vitality. In other words, although it may be a positive factor for vitality, it was not a protective factor against the effects of stress. But this is consistent with Martin and colleagues' theorizing about adaptability: it is an attribute relevant to navigating change, uncertainty, etc., not an attribute relevant to adversity, stress, etc. For the latter, buoyancy and resilience are warranted (Martin, Nejad, et al., 2013).

Boosting adaptability

Adaptability is considered an alterable construct (van Rooij, Jansen, & van de Grift, 2017) and thus is hypothesized to be responsive to intervention and practice efforts. Holliman et al. (2020) have suggested two implications for practice as relevant to adaptability (which we here extrapolate to the music domain). First, adaptability may be part of a screening exercise in order to identify musicians who may need assistance in navigating novelty, change, and uncertainty. As noted, the Adaptability Scale (Martin, Nejad, et al., 2013) and its domain-specific modifications (Collie & Martin, 2016) may be helpful here. Second, adaptability-based interventions might be applied for those who are struggling to adjust to novelty, change, and uncertainty. As we describe next, addressing the cycle of adaptability (as one would address the risk and resilience cycle; Morales, 2000; Martin & Marsh, 2008a) may be helpful here.

To promote resilience, Morales (2000; see also Martin & Marsh, 2008a) suggested the importance of addressing the cycle of risk and resilience. We can infer from this to propose a process for addressing a cycle of change, novelty, and adaptability. According to Martin (2013b), this approach would involve the following steps: (1) the musician is taught how to recognize change, uncertainty, and novelty that are likely to require some form of cognitive, behavioral, and/or emotional adjustment; (2) the musician is explicitly taught how to adjust his/her behavior, cognition, and/or emotion appropriate to this change; (3) change, uncertainty, and novelty are successfully accommodated or navigated; (4) the musician recognizes the benefits of these adjustments; and (5) he/she internalizes the motivation to implement behavioral, cognitive, and/or emotional adjustment as a means to deal with subsequent change, uncertainty, and novelty in his/her music domain. Importantly, there is a considerable body of research showing that individuals can change behavior, cognition, and emotion in order to more effectively function in a given domain (e.g., Craven et al., 1991; Hattie, 2009; Martin, 2005, 2008b; McInerney et al., 1997; O'Mara et al., 2006). These interventions thus may be a basis for assisting the behavioral, cognitive, and emotional adjustments required to successfully respond to change, uncertainty, and novelty experienced by musicians.

The adaptability research conducted among school leaders may also be informative for developing practice guidelines for musicians' instructors, mentors, directors, and conductors. Research in the workplace has shown that supportive principal leadership—in particular, autonomy-supportive leadership—is important for promoting teachers' adaptability (Collie & Martin, 2017b). Autonomy-supportive leadership is that which promotes teachers' self-determination and empowerment—typically by inviting teachers' input in decision-making, listening to teachers' perspectives, conveying confidence in teachers' abilities to undertake their work in a self-directed manner, and encouraging teachers' initiative. Holliman et al. (2020) report that these positive outcomes likely occur because these teachers feel self-determined and empowered to make appropriate and necessary adjustments when faced with novelty, change, and uncertainty in their work. We might speculate the same for musicians who are under the autonomy-supportive leadership of an instructor, mentor, director, and conductor. Autonomy-supportive leadership by these people would involve allowing musicians' input in decision-making, considering musicians' perspectives, communicating confidence in musicians' capacity to conduct themselves in a self-directed manner, and encouraging musicians to take initiative. Research is now needed to determine the extent to which autonomy-supportive leadership practices along these lines can promote musicians' adaptability.

Finally, just as there is a role for professional development (or in-servicing) of teachers to help them adapt to novelty, change, and uncertainty (e.g., Collie & Martin, 2017b; Holliman et al., 2020; Parsons et al., 2018), there may also be a role for music teachers, coaches, or mentors to promote musicians' adaptability. This might involve the musician and mentor collaboratively identifying a novel or unexpected situation recently occurring in the musician's performance life, reflecting on and talking through the extent to which they did or could have adjusted their thoughts, actions, and/or emotions to successfully navigate that adversity, and then planning for appropriate cognitive, behavioral, and emotional adjustments in the event a similar situation arises in the future. This is aimed at assisting musicians to become aware of adaptability, when it might be helpful, and ways to implement it when needed. Again, however, there is a need for research among musicians to evaluate and potentially finesse these ideas.

CONCLUSION

There is a large body of research and theorizing around "life" or "general" resilience, but there has been relatively little work into resilience in the music domain—and much less research on buoyancy and adaptability in the music domain. As relevant to music, this chapter has sought to scope the conceptual and operational terrain relevant to these three under-investigated constructs. The ideas and research hold substantive and methodological implications for researchers studying buoyancy, resilience, and adaptability in music and are also relevant to musicians who are required to frequently and effectively respond to setback, adversity, and change in their performance lives.

KEY SOURCES

Collie, R. J., & Martin, A. J. (2016). Adaptability: An important capacity for effective teachers. *Educational Practice and Theory, 38*, 27–39. https://doi.org/10.7459/ept/38.1.03.

Martin, A. J., & Marsh, H. W. (2008). Academic buoyancy: Towards an understanding of students' everyday academic resilience. *Journal of School Psychology, 46*(1), 53–83. https://doi.org/10.1016/j.jsp.2007.01.002.

Martin, A. J., & Marsh, H. W. (2009). Academic resilience and academic buoyancy: Multidimensional and hierarchical conceptual framing of causes, correlates, and cognate constructs. *Oxford Review of Education, 35*(3), 353–370. https://doi.org/10.1080/03054980902934639.

Martin, A. J., Nejad, H. G., Colmar, S., & Liem, G. A. D. (2013). Adaptability: How students' responses to uncertainty and novelty predict their academic and non-academic outcomes. *Journal of Educational Psychology, 105*, 728–746. https://psycnet.apa.org/doi/10.1037/a0032794.

KEY QUESTIONS

1. What are the *minor* sources of adversity you face in your day-to-day experiences of music learning or managing a music performance career? Does your everyday management and responses to these issues reflect low buoyancy or high buoyancy?

2. What has been a *major* or ongoing source of adversity that has impacted on your music learning or performance career? How do you manage this?

3. Think of a major change event that has occurred during your learning or performance career. How did you and the people around you respond to the change? What factors influenced your adaptability? How might you better respond to change in the future?

4. What are the environmental circumstances like in your music study environment (teachers, peers, school) or professional environment (managers, leaders, colleagues) that impact on the psychological skills of buoyancy, resilience, and adaptability?

REFERENCES

Bandura, A. (2006). Adolescent development from an agentic perspective. In F. Pajares & T. Urdan (Eds.), *Self-efficacy beliefs*, 1–43. Greenwich, CT: Information Age Press.

Baron, R. M., & Kenny, D. A. (1986). The moderator-mediator variable distinction in social psychological research: Conceptual, strategic and statistical considerations. *Journal of Personality and Social Psychology*, 51(6), 1173–1182.

Barrett, L., Dunbar, R., & Lycett, J. (2002). *Human evolutionary psychology*. New York: Palgrave.

Boekaerts, M. & Corno, L. (2005). Self-regulation in the classroom: A perspective on assessment and intervention. *Applied Psychology: An International Review*, 54(2), 199–231. https://doi.org/10.1111/j.1464-0597.2005.00205.x.

Brooks, J. E. (2006). Strengthening resilience in children and youths: Maximizing opportunities through the schools. *Children & Schools*, 28(2), 69–76. https://doi.org/10.1093/cs/28.2.69.

Burns, E. C., & Martin, A. J. (2014). ADHD and adaptability: The roles of cognitive, behavioural, and emotional regulation. *Australian Journal of Guidance and Counselling*, 24(2), 227–242. https://doi.org/10.1017/jgc.2014.17.

Burns, E. C., Martin, A. J., & Collie, R. J. (2018). Adaptability, personal best (PB) goal setting, and gains in students' academic outcomes: A longitudinal examination from a social cognitive perspective. *Contemporary Educational Psychology*, 53, 57–72. https://doi.org/10.1016/j.cedpsych.2018.02.001.

Burns, E. C., Martin, A. J., & Lipton, P. A. (2020). Adaptability, its neural foundations, and implications for education and neuroscience. *Submitted for publication*.

Catterall, J. S. (1998). Risk and resilience in student transitions to high school. *American Journal of Education*, 106, 302–333.

Coleman, J., & Hagell, A. (Eds) (2007). *Adolescence, risk, and resilience*. London: Wiley.

Collie, R. J., Ginns, P., Martin, A. J., & Papworth, B. (2017). Academic buoyancy mediates academic anxiety's effects on learning strategies: A cross-cultural investigation. *Educational Psychology*, 37(8), 947–964. https://doi.org/10.1080/01443410.2017.1291910.

Collie, R. J., Holliman, A. J., & Martin, A. J. (2017). Adaptability, engagement, and academic achievement at university. *Educational Psychology*, 37(5), 632–647. https://doi.org/10.1080/01443410.2016.1231296.

Collie, R. J., & Martin, A. J. (2016). Adaptability: An important capacity for effective teachers. *Educational Practice and Theory*, 38, 27–39. https://doi.org/10.7459/ept/38.1.03.

Collie, R. J., & Martin, A. J. (2017a). Students' adaptability in mathematics: Examining self-reports and teachers' reports and links with engagement and achievement outcomes. *Contemporary Educational Psychology*, 49, 355–366. https://doi.org/10.1016/j.cedpsych.2017.04.001.

Collie, R. J., & Martin, A. J. (2017b). Teachers' sense of adaptability: Examining links with perceived autonomy support, teachers' psychological functioning, and students' numeracy achievement. *Learning and Individual Differences*, 55, 29–39. https://doi.org/10.1016/j.lindif.2017.03.003.

Collie, R. J., Martin, A. J., Malmberg, L-E., Hall, J., & Ginns, P. (2015). Academic buoyancy, student achievement, and the linking role of control: A cross-lagged analysis of high school students. *British Journal of Educational Psychology*, 85(1), 113–130. https://doi.org/10.1111/bjep.12066.

Compas, B. E. (2004). Processes of risk and resilience during adolescence: Linking contexts and individuals. In R. M. Lerner & L. Steinberg (Eds.), *Handbook of adolescent psychology* (pp. 263–296). Hoboken, NJ: Wiley.

Craven, R. G., Marsh, H. W., & Debus, R. L. (1991). Effects of internally focused feedback and attributional feedback on the enhancement of academic self-concept. *Journal of Educational Psychology*, 83(1), 17–26. https://psycnet.apa.org/doi/10.1037/0022-0663.83.1.17.

Datu, J. A. D., & Yang, W. (2018). Psychometric validity and gender invariance of the academic buoyancy scale in the Philippines: A construct validation approach. *Journal of Psychoeducational Assessment*, 36(3), 278–283. https://doi.org/10.1177%2F0734282916674423.

Davidson, J. W. (2005). Bodily communication in musical performance. In D. Miell., R. MacDonald, & D. J. Hargreaves (Eds.), *Musical communication* (pp. 215–238). Oxford: Oxford University Press.

Diener, E., Lucas, R., & Scollon, C. N. (2006). Beyond the hedonic treadmill: Revising the adaptation theory of well-being. *American Psychologist*, 61(4), 305–314. http://doi.org/10.1037/0003-066X.61.4.305.

Dunkel, S. E. (1989). *The audition process: Anxiety management and coping strategies*. Stuyvesant, NY: Pendragon Press.

Evans, P., & McPherson, G. E. (2015). Identity and practice: The motivational benefits of a long-term musical identity. *Psychology of Music*, 43(3), 407–422. https://doi.org/10.1177/0305735613514471.

Fong, C. J., & Kim, Y. W. (2019). A clash of constructs? Re-examining grit in light of academic buoyancy and future time perspective. *Current Psychology*, 40(1), 1–14. https://doi.org/10.1007/s12144-018-0120-4.

Fredrickson, B.L. (2001). The role of positive emotions in positive psychology: The broaden-and-build theory of positive emotions. *American Psychologist*, 56(3), 218–226. https://psycnet.apa.org/doi/10.1037/0003-066X.56.3.218.

Fredricks, J. A., Blumenfeld, P. C., & Paris, A. H. (2004). School engagement: Potential of the concept, state of the evidence. *Review of Educational Research*, 74(1), 59–109. https://doi.org/10.3102%2F00346543074001059.

Garmezy, N. (1981). Children under stress: Perspectives on antecedents and correlates of vulnerability and resistance to psychopathology. In A. I. Rabin, J. Aronoff, A. Barclay, & R. A. Zucker (Eds.), *Further explorations in personality* (pp. 196–269). New York: Wiley.

Hattie, J. (2009). *Visible learning: A synthesis of over 800 meta-analyses relating to achievement*. London: Routledge.

Heckhausen, J., & Schulz, R. (1995). A life-span theory of control. *Psychological Review*, 102(2), 284–304. https://psycnet.apa.org/doi/10.1037/0033-295X.102.2.284.

Hendricks, K. S. (2014). Changes in self-efficacy beliefs over time: Contextual influences of gender, rank-based placement, and social support in a competitive orchestra environment. *Psychology of Music, 42*(3), 347–365. https://doi.org/10.1177/0305735612471238.

Holliman, A. J., Collie, R. J., & Martin, A. J. (2020). Adaptability and academic development. In S. Hupp & J. D. Jewell (Ed). *The encyclopedia of child and adolescent development*, 1–11. London: Wiley.

Holliman, A. J., Martin, A. J., & Collie, R. J. (2018). Adaptability, engagement, and degree completion: A longitudinal investigation of university students. *Educational Psychology, 38*(6), 785–799. https://doi.org/10.1080/01443410.2018.1426835.

Howard, S., & Johnson, B. (2000). Resilient and non-resilient behavior in adolescents. In A. Graycar (Ed.), *Trends and issues in crime and criminal justice series* (pp. 1–6). Canberra: Australian Institute of Criminology.

Iwaniec, D., Larkin, E., & Higgins, S. (2006). Research review: Risk and resilience in cases of emotional abuse. *Child & Family Social Work, 11*(1), 73–82. https://doi.org/10.1111/j.1365-2206.2006.00398.x.

Jaremko, M., & Meichenbaum, D. (Eds.). (2013). *Stress reduction and prevention*. New York: Springer Science & Business Media.

Keyes, C. L. M. (2007). Promoting and protecting mental health as flourishing. *American Psychologist, 62*(2), 95–108. https://psycnet.apa.org/doi/10.1037/0003-066X.62.2.95.

Liem, G. A. D., & Martin, A. J. (2015). Young people's responses to environmental issues: Exploring the role of adaptability and personality. *Personality and Individual Differences, 79*, 91–97. https://doi.org/10.1016/j.paid.2015.02.003.

Lindstroem, B. (2001). The meaning of resilience. *International Journal of Adolescent Medicine and Health, 13*(1), 7–12. https://doi.org/10.1515/ijamh.2001.13.1.7.

Luthar, S. S., & Cicchetti, D. (2000). The construct of resilience: Implications for interventions and social policies. *Development and Psychopathology, 12*(4), 857–885. https://psycnet.apa.org/doi/10.1017/S0954579400004156.

Martin, A. J. (2004). The role of positive psychology in enhancing satisfaction, motivation, and productivity in the workplace. *Journal of Organizational Behavior Management, 24*(1–2), 113–133. https://doi.org/10.1300/J075v24n01_07.

Martin, A. J. (2005). Exploring the effects of a youth enrichment program on academic motivation and engagement. *Social Psychology of Education, 8*(2), 179–206. https://psycnet.apa.org/doi/10.1007/s11218-004-6487-0.

Martin, A. J. (2008a). How domain specific are motivation and engagement across school, sport, and music? A substantive-methodological synergy assessing young sportspeople and musicians. *Contemporary Educational Psychology, 33*(4), 785–813. https://doi.org/10.1016/j.cedpsych.2008.01.002.

Martin, A. J. (2008b). Enhancing student motivation and engagement: The effects of a multidimensional intervention. *Contemporary Educational Psychology, 33*(2), 239–269. https://doi.org/10.1016/j.cedpsych.2006.11.003.

Martin, A. J. (2013a). Academic buoyancy and academic resilience: Exploring "everyday" and "classic" resilience in the face of academic adversity. *School Psychology International, 34*(5), 488–500. https://doi.org/10.1177%2F0143034312472759.

Martin, A. J. (2013b). The Personal Proficiency Network: Key self-system factors and processes to optimize academic development. In D. M. McInerney, H. W. Marsh., R. G. Craven, & F. Guay (Eds). *Theory driving research: New wave perspectives on self-processes and human development*, 251–286. Charlotte, NC: Information Age Publishing.

Martin, A. J. (2017). Adaptability—What it is and what it is not: Comment on Chandra and Leong (2016). *American Psychologist, 72*(7), 696–698. https://psycnet.apa.org/doi/10.1037/ampooo0163.

Martin, A. J. (2018). Preparation, perseverance, and performance in music: Views from a program of educational psychology research. In G. E. McPherson & G. Welch (Eds.), *Music and music education in people's lives: An Oxford handbook of music education*, 661–666. Oxford: Oxford University Press.

Martin, A. J., & Burns, E. C. (2014). Academic buoyancy, resilience, and adaptability in students with ADHD. *The ADHD Report, 22*(6), 1–9. https://doi.org/10.1521/adhd.2014.22.6.1.

Martin, A. J., Colmar, S. H., Davey, L. A., & Marsh, H. W. (2010). Longitudinal modeling of academic buoyancy and motivation: Do the "5Cs" hold up over time? *British Journal of Educational Psychology, 80*(3), 473–496. https://doi.org/10.1348/000709910X486376.

Martin, A. J., & Jackson, S. A. (2008). Brief approaches to assessing task absorption and enhanced subjective experience: Examining "Short" and "Core" flow in diverse performance domains. *Motivation and Emotion, 32*, 141–157. https://doi.org/10.1007/s11031-008-9094-0.

Martin, A. J., & Marsh, H. W. (2006). Academic resilience and its psychological and educational correlates: A construct validity approach. *Psychology in the Schools, 43*(3), 267–282. https://doi.org/10.1002/pits.20149.

Martin, A. J., & Marsh, H. W. (2008a). Academic buoyancy: Towards an understanding of students' everyday academic resilience. *Journal of School Psychology, 46*(1), 53–83. https://doi.org/10.1016/j.jsp.2007.01.002.

Martin, A. J., & Marsh, H. W. (2008b). Workplace and academic buoyancy: Psychometric assessment and construct validity amongst school personnel and students. *Journal of Psychoeducational Assessment, 26*(2), 168–184. https://doi.org/10.1177%2F0734282907313767.

Martin, A. J., & Marsh, H. W. (2009). Academic resilience and academic buoyancy: Multidimensional and hierarchical conceptual framing of causes, correlates and cognate constructs. *Oxford Review of Education, 35*(3), 353–370. https://doi.org/10.1080/03054980902934639.

Martin, A. J., & Marsh, H. W. (2019). Investigating the reciprocal relations between academic buoyancy and academic adversity: Evidence for the protective role of academic buoyancy in reducing academic adversity over time. *International Journal of Behavioral Development, 44*(4), 301–312.

Martin, A. J., Nejad, H. G., Colmar, S., & Liem, G. A. D. (2012). Adaptability: Conceptual and empirical perspectives on responses to change, novelty and uncertainty. *Australian Journal of Guidance and Counselling, 22*(1), 58–81. https://psycnet.apa.org/doi/10.1017/jgc.2012.8.

Martin, A. J., Nejad, H. G., Colmar, S., & Liem, G. A. D. (2013). Adaptability: How students' responses to uncertainty and novelty predict their academic and non-academic outcomes. *Journal of Educational Psychology, 105*, 728–746. https://psycnet.apa.org/doi/10.1037/a0032794.

Martin, A. J., Nejad, H. G., Colmar, S., Liem, G. A. D., & Collie, R. (2015). The role of adaptability in promoting control and reducing failure dynamics: A mediation model. *Learning and Individual Differences, 38*, 36–43. https://doi.org/10.1016/j.lindif.2015.02.004.

Martin, A. J., Yu, K., Ginns, P., & Papworth, B. (2017). Young people's academic buoyancy and adaptability: A cross-cultural comparison of China with North America and the United Kingdom. *Educational Psychology, 37*(8), 930–946. https://doi.org/10.1080/01443410.2016.1202904.

Masten, A. S. (2001). Ordinary magic: Resilience processes in development. *American Psychologist*, 56(3), 227–238.

Masten, A. S., & Powell, J. L. (2003). A resilience framework for research, policy, and practice. In S. S Luthar (Ed.), *Resilience and vulnerability*, 1–25. Cambridge: Cambridge University Press.

McCormick, J., & McPherson, G. E. (2003). The role of self-efficacy in a musical performance examination: An exploratory structural equation analysis. *Psychology of Music*, 31(1), 37–50. https://doi.org/10.1177%2F0305735603031001322.

McCormick, J., & McPherson, G. E. (2007). Expectancy-value motivation in the context of a music performance examination. *Musicae Scientiae*, 11(2), 37–52. https://doi.org/10.1177%2F102986490701100S203.

McInerney, V., McInerney, D. M., & Marsh, H. W. (1997). Effects of metacognitive strategy training within a cooperative group learning context on computer achievement and anxiety: An aptitude-treatment interaction study. *Journal of Educational Psychology*, 89(4), 686–695.

McPherson, G. E. & McCormick J. (2006). Self-efficacy and music performance. *Psychology of Music*, 34(3), 322–336. https://doi.org/10.1177%2F0305735606064841.

McPherson, G. E., Osborne, M. S., Evans, P., & Miksza, P. (2019). Applying self-regulated learning microanalysis to study musicians' practice. *Psychology of Music*, 47(1), 18–32. https://doi.org/10.1177%2F0305735617731614.

McPherson, G. E., & Renwick, J. (2011). Self-regulation and mastery of musical skills. In B. Zimmerman & D. Schunk (Eds.), *Handbook of self-regulation of learning and performance* (pp. 234–248). New York: Routledge.

Morales, E. E. (2000). A contextual understanding of the process of educational resilience: High achieving Dominican American students and the "Resilience Cycle." *Innovative Higher Education*, 25(1), 7–22. https://doi.org/10.1023/A:1007580217973.

Morin, A. J., Boudrias, J. S., Marsh, H. W., McInerney, D. M., Dagenais-Desmarais, V., Madore, I., & Litalien, D. (2017). Complementary variable- and person-centered approaches to the dimensionality of psychometric constructs: Application to psychological wellbeing at work. *Journal of Business and Psychology*, 32(4), 395–419. https://doi.org/10.1007/s10869-016-9448-7.

Nakamura, J., & Csikszentmihalyi, M. (2009). The concept of flow. In C. R. Snyder & S. J. Lopez (Eds.), *Oxford handbook of positive psychology*, 195–206. Oxford: Oxford University Press.

Olsson, C., Bond, L., Burns, J., Vella-Brodrick, D., & Sawyer, S. (2003). Adolescent resilience: A concept analysis. *Journal of Adolescence*, 26(1), 1–11. https://doi.org/10.1016/S0140-1971(02)00118-5.

O'Mara, A. J., Marsh H. W., Craven, R. G., & Debus, R. (2006). Do self-concept interventions make a difference? A synergistic blend of construct validation and meta-analysis. *Educational Psychologist*, 41(3), 181–206. https://doi.org/10.1207/s15326985ep4103_4.

O'Neill, S. A., & Sloboda, J. A. (1997). The effects of failure on children's ability to perform a musical test. *Psychology of Music*, 25(1), 18–34. https://doi.org/10.1177%2F0305735697251003.

Osborne, M., McPherson, G. E., Miksza, P. J., & Evans, P. (2020). Using a microanalysis intervention to examine shifts in musician's self-regulated learning. *Psychology of Music*, 0305735620915265. https://doi.org/10.1177%2F0305735620915265.

Parker, P. D., Martin, A. J., Martinez, C., Marsh, H. W., & Jackson, S. A. (2010). Stages of change in physical activity: A validation study in late adolescence. *Health Education and Behavior*, 37(3), 318–329. https://doi.org/10.1177%2F1090198109333281.

Parsons, S. A., Vaughn, M., Scales, R. Q., Gallagher, M. A., Parsons, A. W., . . . & Allen, M. (2018). Teachers' instructional adaptations: A research synthesis. *Review of Educational Research, 88*(2), 205–242. https://doi.org/10.3102%2F0034654317743198.

Pekrun, R. (2012). Emotion regulation. In N. Seel (Ed.), *Encyclopedia of the sciences of learning*, 1117–1119. New York: Springer.

Pinquart, M., & Silbereisen, R. K. (2004). Human development in times of social change: Theoretical considerations and research needs. *International Journal of Behavioral Development, 28*(4), 289–298.

Prochaska, J. O., & Velicer, W. F. (1997). The transtheoretical model of health behavior change. *American Journal of Health Promotion, 12*(1), 38–48. https://doi.org/10.4278%2F0890-1171-12.1.38.

Puolakanaho, A., Lappalainen, R., Lappalainen, P., Muotka, J. S., Hirvonen, R., Eklund, K. M., . . . & Kiuru, N. (2018). Reducing stress and enhancing academic buoyancy among adolescents using a brief web-based program based on acceptance and commitment therapy: A randomized controlled trial. *Journal of Youth and Adolescence, 48*(2), 1–19. https://doi.org/10.1007/s10964-018-0973-8.

Putwain, D. W., & Aveyard, B. (2019). Is perceived control a critical factor in understanding the negative relationship between cognitive test anxiety and examination performance? *School Psychology Quarterly, 33*(1), 65–74. https://psycnet.apa.org/doi/10.1037/spq0000183.

Putwain, D., Chamberlain, S., Daly, A. L., & Sadreddini, S. (2014). Reducing test anxiety among school-aged adolescents: A field experiment. *Educational Psychology in Practice, 30*(4), 420–440. https://doi.org/10.1080/02667363.2014.964392.

Putwain, D. W., Connors, L., Symes, W., & Douglas-Osborn, E. (2012). Is academic buoyancy anything more than adaptive coping? *Anxiety, Stress & Coping, 25*(2), 349–358. https://doi.org/10.1080/10615806.2011.582459.

Putwain, D. W., & Daly, A. L. (2013). Do clusters of test anxiety and academic buoyancy differentially predict academic performance? *Learning and Individual Differences, 27*, 157–162. https://doi.org/10.1016/j.lindif.2013.07.010.

Putwain, D. W., Daly, A. L., Chamberlain, S., & Sadreddini, S. (2015). Academically buoyant students are less anxious about and perform better in high-stakes examinations. *British Journal of Educational Psychology, 85*(3), 247–263. https://doi.org/10.1111/bjep.12068.

Putwain, D. W., Gallard, D., & Beaumont, J. (2019). A multi-component wellbeing programme for upper secondary students: Effects on wellbeing, buoyancy, and adaptability. *School Psychology International, 40*(1), 49–65. https://doi.org/10.1177%2F0143034318806546.

Renwick, J. M., & McPherson, G. E. (2002). Interest and choice: Student-selected repertoire and its effect on practising behaviour. *British Journal of Music Education, 19*(2), 173–188. https://doi.org/10.1017/S0265051702000256.

Ruddock, E., & Leong, S. (2005). "I am unmusical!": The verdict of self-judgement. *International Journal of Music Education, 23*(1), 9–22. https://doi.org/10.1177%2F0255761405050927.

Rutter, M. (1987). Psychosocial resilience and protective mechanisms. *American Journal of Orthopsychiatry, 57*(3), 317–331. https://doi.org/10.1111/j.1939-0025.1987.tb03541.x.

Rutter, M. (2006). *Genes and behavior: Nature-nurture interplay explained*. London: Blackwell.

Ryan, R. M., & Deci, E. L. (2017). *Self-determination theory*. New York: Guilford Press.

Slade, M. (2010). Mental illness and well-being: The central importance of positive psychology and recovery approaches. *BMC Health Services Research, 10*(1), 26. https://doi.org/10.1186/1472-6963-10-26.

Spreitzer, G. M., & Quinn, R. E. (2006). Entering the fundamental state of leadership: A framework for the positive transformation of self and others. In R. Burke & C. Cooper (Eds.), *Inspiring leaders* (pp. 83–99). New York: Routledge.

Symes, W., Putwain, D. W., & Remedios, R. (2015). The enabling and protective role of academic buoyancy in the appraisal of fear appeals used prior to high stakes examinations. *School Psychology International*, 36(6), 605–619. https://doi.org/10.1177%2F0143034315610622.

Tomasik, M. J., & Silbereisen, R. K. (2009). Demands of social change as a function of the political context, institutional filters, and psychosocial resources. *Social Indicators Research*, 94(1), 13–28. https://psycnet.apa.org/doi/10.1007/s11205-008-9332-6.

Tomasik, M. J., Silbereisen, R. K., & Heckhausen, J. (2010). Is it adaptive to disengage from demands of social change? Adjustment to developmental barriers in opportunity-deprived regions. *Motivation and Emotion*, 34(4), 384–398. https://doi.org/10.1007/s11031-010-9177-6.

VandenBos, G. R. (Ed). (2015). *American Psychological Association (APA) dictionary of psychology* (2nd ed.). Washington, DC: American Psychological Association.

van Rooij, E. C. M., Jansen, E. P. W. A., & van de Grift, W. J. C. M. (2017). Secondary school students' engagement profiles and their relationship with academic adjustment and achievement in university. *Learning and Individual Differences*, 54, 9–19. https://doi.org/10.1016/j.lindif.2017.01.004.

Waxman, H. C., Huang, S. L., & Padron, Y. N. (1997). Motivation and learning environment differences between resilient and non-resilient Latino middle school students. *Hispanic Journal of Behavioral Sciences*, 19(2), 137–155. https://doi.org/10.1177%2F07399863970192003.

Werner, E. (2000). Protective factors and individual resilience. In J. P. Shonkoff & S. J. Meisels (Eds.), *Handbook of early childhood intervention* (2nd ed., pp. 115–132). New York: Cambridge University Press.

Winne, P. H., & Hadwin, A. F. (2008). The weave of motivation and self-regulated learning. In D. H. Schunk & B. J. Zimmerman (Eds.), *Motivation and self-regulated learning: Theory, research, and applications* (pp. 297–314). Lawrence Erlbaum Associates Publishers.

Yun, S., Hiver, P., & Al-Hoorie, A. H. (2018). Academic buoyancy: Exploring learners' everyday resilience in the language classroom. *Studies in Second Language Acquisition*, 40(4), 805–830. https://psycnet.apa.org/doi/10.1017/S0272263118000037.

Zimmer-Gembeck, M. J., & Skinner, E. A. (2008). Adolescents coping with stress: Development and diversity. *The Prevention Researcher*, 15(4), 3–8.

Zimmerman, B. J. (2002). Achieving self-regulation: The trial and triumph of adolescence. In F. Pajares & T. Urdan (Eds), *Academic motivation of adolescents*, 1–27. Greenwich, CT: Information Age Publishing.

CHAPTER 27

IDENTITY AND THE PERFORMING MUSICIAN

JANE OAKLAND AND RAYMOND MACDONALD

INTRODUCTION

PERFORMANCE can be anything from the most fulfilling experience in a musician's career, through to an activity that is the most feared. Whether performing to an audience of three or three thousand, musicians are faced with numerous personal and professional challenges every time they step onto a stage—challenges that can impact not only on performance, but also on their daily lives. Issues such as managing performance anxiety (see Osborne & Kirsner, Volume 2), desire for perfection, social isolation, psychological pressure, fear of failure, or even fear of success (Pecan et al., 2016) are just some of the issues that can impact on a musician's overall sense of self and wellbeing. In addition, in order to remain employable, contemporary performing musicians often need to adapt to a *protean* career (see also & Burland & Bennett, Volume 2). This can involve embracing many different activities, including non-musical activities that require a broad-based approach to identity formation.

The psychological processes underpinning the way performing musicians negotiate and maintain their identities are crucial in managing the numerous challenges musicians encounter within a performing career (Wilson & MacDonald, 2017). However, the nuances of these identity processes are often taken for granted while young musicians are training and are rarely discussed by professional players engaged in day-to-day music making. In an increasingly competitive and constantly changing profession, greater understanding of these processes can help produce a healthy and sustainable approach to music performance and contribute to the overall wellbeing of the performing musician. It is our contention that understanding the development and maintenance of "healthy" musical identities should be a stated aim that is covered within the tertiary education of all performing musicians.

Self and Identity

The construction of self and the components of what can loosely be termed identity has been a major concern of psychology since the birth of the discipline. Indeed, William James (1890), one of the founding theorists of modern psychology, claimed that identity was "the most puzzling puzzle with which psychology has to deal" (p. 330). To this day, social and behavioral scientists have largely avoided attempting to deal with defining and understanding the "self" more broadly, instead preferring to focus on component constructs and processes (such as self-esteem, self-concept, and self-regulation; Leary & Tangney, 2012). Nonetheless, music is a social phenomenon, and part of understanding music is understanding our own self and identity in relation to others. Here we articulate a social constructionist perspective as a broad backdrop to our subsequent discussion of how our musical identity develops, and the identity processes that are relevant to performing musicians.

The social construction of identity

Identity does not always place exclusive emphasis on the individual. Social identity theory (Tajfel & Turner, 1979) posits that identity is a combination of social interactions and experiences that link individuals to the groups and institutions to which they belong. This sense of belonging can promote social status, influence behavior and discourse, and has been found to be important in motivation and wellbeing (Martin & Dowson, 2009).

The development of self relies upon a reciprocal relationship between self and society (Stryker, 1980). The social constructionist paradigm (Mead, 1934) views the self as a social process, created through interactions between self and the society an individual inhabits, and where language is the medium of negotiating these interactions. In this chapter, we also contend that, like language, music is also a medium for instigating this social process of forming self. Stets and Burke (2003) concur with this view, adding that self consists of multiple concepts, which they call identities, and that in order to fully understand the self, it is also necessary to understand the society in which the self operates. Thus, an important aspect of identity is maintaining a coherent sense of self in differing social contexts (Spychiger, 2017).

Taking the perspective that the self provides a link between the individual and the larger social structure, the self can then be viewed as a construction of roles or role-identities (Callero 1985). Some roles or allegiances may be more prominent than others and therefore become a salient identity. For example, a person may identify as a musician, a parent, a sibling, or a gardener. Identifying as a musician, particularly for a professional musician, is likely to be a salient identity even if they are a hobby gardener, due in part to the amount of time spent in musical activities and levels of commitment to the role of musician. Role salience also influences role behavior, and leads people to prioritize values and actions that are perceived to enhance a chosen identity. It is therefore important to acknowledge and value other dimensions of self in the interests of a healthy approach to maintenance of self. The most obvious example is a professional musician whose sense of self is perceived to be linked to the perceived standard of their performance.

Validation of identity

In order to justify a claim to a particular identity, validation is required. For example, it would be difficult to claim an identity as a surgeon if you had never been to medical school. Mills (2004) approached this issue by differentiating between an individual's sense of professional identity and private identity. The professional identity is externally validated by others, usually through work and the associated status and success of work. The private identity is internally validated and represents what a person feels they are, irrespective of work or the perception of others. The professional identity can be vulnerable, particularly if it is constructed with firm ideas about the kind of professional life a musician might want to have. For example, a performing musician may feel their identity is in doubt if they are required to spend more time teaching or engaged in non-musical activities than performing. Developing a strong, internally validated sense of self is crucial to maintaining a stable sense of self within a constantly changing environment.

Recent years have seen an explosion of interest in identities, particularly in relation to gender, global politics, and climate change (Appiah, 2018). As people constantly negotiate evolving identities through conversations and interactions with social institutions, issues of identity and its complexities will remain central to daily life for the foreseeable future. With this in mind, identity can be viewed as a constituent of an overall sense of self that is influenced by social environments, group affiliations, and commitment to specific roles.

How does music shape identity?

Aligned with this ubiquitous interest in identities is compelling evidence that music is a universal and fully accessible channel of communication (Miell, MacDonald, & Hargreaves, 2005). Music is therefore inextricably linked to a whole range of important aspects of daily life such as emotional regulation (Juslin & Sloboda, 2010), health, and wellbeing (MacDonald, Kreutz & Mitchell, 2012), aesthetic experiences (De Nora, 2013), and creativity (Hargreaves, Miell & MacDonald, 2012). These aspects of daily life are contributors to an individual's sense of self, which makes music an influential factor in identity formation.

There is a considerable and growing amount of published work that deals with how these identity-relevant musical factors interact with psychological and social factors to influence the identities of musicians (MacDonald et al., 2002, 2017). In line with the social constructionist paradigm we have outlined (Mead 1934), early research into music and identity proposed that music acts in a similar way to language in the negotiation and maintenance of an identity and that a musical identity is just one of many identities a person may negotiate. Hargreaves et al. (2002) showed how musical identities can be negotiated and maintained in two distinct yet inter-connected ways: the ways in which our experiences of music shape our personal sense of self and identity (music in identity), and the ways we identify in relation to the musical activities and roles we undertake in our interactions with society (identity in music).

Music in identity

There are few people who can say that music does not impact in some way on their public and private lives (de Nora, 2000; MacDonald et al., 2017). Preferences for certain genres of music and the social groups associated with those preferences help us to construct and negotiate our sense of self. Musical tastes are utilized to help shape our identity in the same way that an individual may define themselves using factors such as where they live, their type of employment, who their friends are, their sexuality, or their political and religious beliefs. Thus music becomes a medium through which we can shape and form our personal and collective identities and choose how we present ourselves to others (Hargreaves et al., 2017). For example, attending a concert by the Scottish Symphony Orchestra in Glasgow is likely to initiate a different presentation of self to attending the Coachella festival in California. Musical preferences and tastes are inextricably linked to a collection of social and psychological variables such as feeling part of a particular sub-section or cultural group within society and adopting certain behavioral traits attached to such groups (Zilman & Gan, 1997). Music is therefore an important psychological resource that influences how we negotiate our constantly evolving sense of self.

Identity in music

The second category identified by Hargreaves et al. (2002) is the way in which an identity develops in relation to music participation, most broadly in the way we view ourselves as *musical* or *nonmusical* in relation to culturally defined roles and the expectations that are attached to these roles. More specifically, consider the ways in which we may identify with more specific categories: violinist, flautist, or vocalist; performer, composer, or producer; classical pianist, jazz drummer, or bluegrass fiddler; professional, amateur, or hobbyist. Expressing an identity using any of these terms, particularly contrasting with others, suggests something about the way the person sees themselves and defines their musical role. These well-established roles tend to be reinforced by musical institutions, especially specialist music schools and conservatories. An identity in music can also refer to less obviously performative identities such as individuals who may see themselves as non-musical or who only engage in musical activities on certain occasions. Pascale (2013) describes the case of a woman born in Barbados but living in the United States. She considered herself to be a non-singer in the United States because she was expected to be able to sing solos and perform. However, in Barbados she felt able to call herself a singer because singing was an activity conducted in a less formal environment.

In line with social identity theory, an identity in music is also shaped by the ensembles (orchestras, choirs, and bands) or other group activities to which people become affiliated. A primary means of self-definition for many professional musicians is their employment; for example, "I play with the Scottish Symphony Orchestra." More recently, social identity theory has been utilized to highlight how social media and new technologies play a crucial role in the development of musical identities (Auh & Walker, 2017).

In summary, we all have musical identities. *Music in identity* refers to how music, consciously or otherwise, shapes aspects of our identities through our experiences of music in social life. *Identity in music* refers to the extent to which we see ourselves as musical, the nature of this musicality, and the specific musical roles we have in society.

IDENTIFYING AS A PERFORMING MUSICIAN

Throughout this section, we consider what it might mean to identify as a performing musician. Status as a musician is often conferred by the attainment of a performance career (Bennett, 2008). This was particularly evident in a study of the learning cultures of UK conservatories, where aspiring to be a specialized, high-quality performer remained a dominant feature of the conservatory culture and therefore influenced the beliefs and values developed by students (Perkins, 2013). Within these learning cultures, students aspired to a full-time, professional music performance career as the prototypical example of what it is to be a musician, to cultural interpretations and the perceived importance of the identity. However, this image of the professional musician in the imagination of the conservatory students does not always match with the kind of lives lived by the majority of professional musicians (Bennett, 2009).

Most professional musicians, of course, have more than one role—they may be employed in an orchestra, be a member of a chamber group, perform occasionally at weddings, teach students of various ages and stages, or lead a community ensemble. Each role implies a particular identity or combination of identities—orchestral musician, chamber musician, wedding musician, teacher, and community leader. Among the most common combinations is of *performer* and *teacher*, and several studies have found tensions among the two. For example, people who are both teachers and performers may express either side of their identities more prominently, depending on which role was seen as more valued in their workplace (Triantafyllaki, 2010). For students in the same situation, one study found that most had not committed to either identity, but that more actively exploring each role would lead to a more successful negotiation of the roles of both identities, and a better integration of their professional identity (Gonzalez, 2018). Both studies suggested the importance of integrating the multiple roles or identities to the self (a process involved in *identity work*, discussed later in this chapter).

In contrast, however, it may also be important to maintain distinctiveness of each role. Parkes et al. (2015) found that while several participants in their study considered themselves to be talented teachers, they gained more satisfaction from performing. They concluded that teacher and performer identities should be seen as separate because career satisfaction was determined by different factors. This separation of identities was also apparent in a focus group study (Bennett, 2008), where participants felt that being a musician was an "umbrella" term to encompass a variety of musical roles, whereas being a performer was a specialist role akin to being a teacher or composer. Viewed through this lens, a performer identity is a specialist role and a sub-identity of the broader musician identity.

Music and the performing musician

The role played by music in the life of a musician would appear to be a strong determiner in choosing a performance career. Burland (2005) explored the emergence of a performer identity when she followed a group of undergraduate music students during the transition to professional musician. Through interviews with thirty-two musicians, she found that the way students perceived themselves in relation to music was the strongest influence on a choice to become a professional performer. Similarly, Papageorgi and Welch (2016) provide interview data to link the musician identity with the performer identity when they proposed that a strong, internal concept as a musician is highly significant when learning about performance because it signifies a deep love for music and is a strong motivator toward becoming successful.

There are, however, potential difficulties associated with strong identification with music, including problems separating personal identity from musical ability (Kemp, 1996). Kemp cites links between musical identity and self-esteem, observing that many musicians believe that they must be competent performers in order to be worthwhile people.

Further identity tensions can arise between music as an expression of self and the task of performing music for public consumption. Lack of personal expression through music has long been recognized as a source of frustration, particularly among orchestral musicians (Allmendiger et al., 1996; Brodsky, 2006; Parasuraman & Purohit, 2000). In a comparison study between classical string players and jazz musicians, Dobson (2010) notes clear distinctions in the way these two different types of musician interact with self and music in performance. The jazz musicians in that study felt able to impose much greater levels of self-expression in their performances than their classical counterparts. They felt that improvisation and creativity served as a manifestation of self rather than the self being judged by the accuracy of performance, whereas the classical string players expected to behave more like workers, giving accurate renditions of a piece while conforming with the artistic direction of the group and its director, and imposing very little of their own artistic identities on the final product.

Although distinguishing between the job of music performance and music as a manifestation of self may be more significant for certain types of musician than others, awareness of the differences and taking steps to manage any tensions can help all performers aspire to wellbeing and adapt to changing working environments. To investigate this issue further, we now turn to a case study by the first author (Oakland et al., 2014) that demonstrates the importance for performing musicians to regularly monitor their relationship to music and the impact it may have on the way they identify as a performer and an individual.

Case study: Joe

Joe had been an opera singer for twenty-five years when he became physically disabled, temporarily losing the use of his legs. Despite several years of medical investigations, there was no diagnosis to explain his disability. A dominating feature of Joe's story was an extremely strong controlling relationship with music that was integral to his self-concept as a servant to music: "Music is master! That is how I was brought up." Joe felt that his love for music and technical expertise gave him certain rights over how the music should be performed or (in his words) served. This perception led to several conflicts with colleagues throughout his career. When Joe felt victimized by a group of singers within one organization, he approached management for support in dealing with the situation. He believed that his commitment and ability to serve the music was superior to those singers and therefore his value as an employee should be acknowledged. When this was not the case and the management sided with his colleagues, Joe's whole concept of self was put under threat: "You give everything, you give your body and soul to make the music wonderful and you believe that and suddenly it doesn't care for you as a person." In Joe's eyes, it was the music that had let him down, rather than the management.

A musician's love or passion for music can explain a large proportion of the individual differences concerning the wellbeing of musicians, dependent upon whether that passion is harmonious (implying an intrinsic enjoyment of music) and contributes to a healthy relationship with music, or obsessive (fueled by controlling environments and internal or external pressures), which can be detrimental to wellbeing (Bonneville-Roussy & Vallerand 2018). Joe displayed signs of obsessive passion for music to the point where his physical health became affected. He described the moment he realized his musical abilities did not give him the security and recognition he expected from his employers: "I felt that my musical legs had been literally taken away from me."

Joe's musician and performer identities were inextricably linked to his self-worth as a person. For this reason, he declined an offer of alternative work in the company believing it would have lowered his self-worth even further. Part of Joe's recovery was realizing what he could and could not control, primarily in his music but also in everyday life. He was ultimately able to walk again with no clinical interventions and resume his career as an operatic performer. He attributed much of his recovery to gaining a greater understanding of how his sense of self and relationship to music had contributed to the disruption to his life.

While this may be an extreme case of a detrimental relationship with music, in the interests of performer wellbeing, Joe's case highlights the need for performers to be aware of the expectations they have with regard to self-investment in the music they perform.

The performer as a communicator

Research has also explored the way performers use identity to communicate with an audience and the need (particularly for a solo performer) to develop a projected persona that is "focused, confident, and larger than would be appropriate in a one-to-one conversation" (Davidson, 2002, p. 103) in order to present music to an audience. Video analysis of performances by solo and chamber artists (Davidson, 2017) has expanded this concept by demonstrating a variety of performing techniques and sub-identities such as "narrator" and "manipulator" that contributed to this projected persona. Freddie Mercury, well known for his lively stage performances and the ability to engage even very large audiences, explained the relationship between an internal, private identity and an external, performed persona: "I'm so powerful on stage that I seem to have created a monster. When I'm performing I'm an extrovert, yet inside I'm a completely different man" (Myers, 1991). Mercury used his highly theatrical, flamboyant style of performance as lead singer for the band Queen to "tease, shock and ultimately charm his audience with various extravagant versions of himself" (Blaike, 1996).

Mercury projected a performer identity that was distinct from his personal identity. In this way, he embodies the idea of a musician who is a "bold introvert" (Kemp, 1996). Musicians are inclined to identify with their internal, imaginative lives in order to spend long hours practicing but at the same time, be able to emerge from the practice room with sufficient confidence and autonomy to convey aspects of that internal world to a public.

For Mercury, these magnified, and at times controversial versions of self were conveyed to the public through music but in such a way that he could manipulate the reactions of his audiences as opposed to falling victim to them (Jones, 2012).

Identity work

Although some musicians may be more genetically suited to performing music (Davidson, 2002), Mercury shows how musicians themselves can take proactive steps to develop the skills needed to manage their identities as performers through what is termed *identity work*. In this context, *identity work* is used to refer to psychological processes that an individual engages with to modify a constantly evolving sense of self. The term *work* is used because it is an active process that involves psychological resources for the individual. For example, a failed audition may require an individual to reassess their career aspirations. Alternatively, a particularly well received performance for an amateur musician may precipitate thoughts of becoming professional. These are both examples of *identity work* (MacDonald & Wilson, 2020).

Identity within contemporary society may be a more important and difficult issue for people to engage in (Giddens, 1991). We all have to make choices about our lives, from mundane questions about what to wear or when we get up in the morning, to life-changing decisions about relationships and career paths. In earlier times, traditional social order with clearly defined roles gave much more specific guidance regarding our life choices. These decisions were much easier to make, and in some ways, were made for us. However, in post-traditional societies, particularly in industrialized democracies, there are many more options open to us, and thus a lot more identity work needs to be done. The focal questions of what to do, how to act, and who to be need to be addressed by everyone living in circumstances of late modernity—and ones that, on some level or another, all of us answer, either discursively or through day-to-day social behavior (Giddens, 1991).

Musical identities are performative and social because they "represent something we do rather than something we have" (MacDonald et al., 2017, p. 3). This implies that the construction of a musical identity (in line with other identities including a performer identity) can be an agentic process open to personal choice, behavior, and decision-making (Jutti, 2012). In this way, *identity work* is a process of adapting or modifying notions of self in relation to specific and ongoing events. An individual can also choose to maintain a certain identity by adopting specific traits and behavior that characterize a desired identity (MacDonald et al., 2005).

Despite this emphasis on personal choice in the way identities can be formed and maintained, performing musicians are often constrained by environments over which they may have little control, such as institutional managements or peer evaluation. In situations such as these, the performer can, through a process of reflexivity, realign the self in order to fit with an environment they cannot influence. The following case study of Helen shows how working with identity enabled her to renegotiate her sense of self as a singer following the loss of full-time performance work (Oakland et al., 2012, 2013).

Case study: Helen

Helen had been a professional opera chorister with the same company for twenty years when redundancy forced her to reflect on how her sense of self was constructed:

> I definitely rode on the fact that I was an opera singer, nothing to do with singing but the name of the job and the level of the job. I got a lot of my identity from being part of a national company.

For Helen, group affiliation in the form of being a member of a prestigious opera company validated her identity as a performer of opera rather than just a singer. She relied on the external validation of work to justify the title of opera singer, which meant that her sense of self was reliant on factors beyond her immediate control. When Helen's position in the opera company was no longer available, her loss of status initiated a process of reflection where she considered the meaning and limitations of her identity as an opera singer:

> I never got comfortable with myself. The only version there was, was me in my jeans and scruffy tee-shirt and a costume at night. I never developed any kind of identity of my own.

In this extract, Helen realizes how little autonomy she had over her self-concept. Her one "version" of self was dictated by the job, to the detriment of other possible identities. If we cannot influence external environments that may restrict personal growth and development, we can, through the reflexive self, influence the way we fit and interact with these environments (Giddens, 1991). In other words, we can change the way we perceive that which we cannot change. A strategy ultimately used by Helen to adapt to her loss of social identity and status was to re-evaluate the role of singing in her life: "Singing means energy and expression, not identity. "It was identity for years; it isn't identity now."

It was not possible for Helen to reclaim her former identity as an opera singer through alternative work, and her case demonstrates the way she engaged in identity work by reviewing the meaning of singing in her life. Singing became the catalyst to move away from a sense of self that relied on the external validation of status to a more internally validated concept of self where singing became an act of personal self-expression.

To summarize, the performer identity can be seen as a two-way construction.

First, the meanings that are assigned to being a performer of music are instrumental in maintaining a healthy performing career contributing to the general wellbeing of the performer. As the two case studies demonstrate, these meanings need to be adaptable if a performer is to negotiate the professional challenges and find a "fit" within a constantly changing industry. Second, an identity or persona is needed to portray confidence and authority during the act of music performance. Adopting this type of performer identity can protect the self from the vulnerability of public scrutiny as well as helping the performer to convey emotions rather than experience them during music performance.

Practical Implications

It should be the aim of all performing musicians to strive toward a healthy approach, not only to the job of performing music but also to their career trajectory and personal lives. Ascenso and colleagues (2017) explored the wellbeing profiles of a number of solo and collaborative performing musicians and found identity negotiation to be an overarching sustainer of wellbeing. Identity can therefore have an enormous impact (both beneficial and detrimental) on personal, professional, psychological, and physical wellbeing. From a practical stance, musicians who are helped toward developing an in-depth but flexible approach to understanding the nuances of identity formation are better placed to negotiate the successes and the disappointments experienced throughout a performing career.

Accommodating artistic integrity with the business of performance

In this chapter, we have highlighted identity tensions between music making as a definer of self, and music as a professional business activity (Ascenso et al., 2017). Both these areas are rooted in the distinctions and interactions between music in identity and identity in music. Aspiring to a balance between the way music can shape and influence the self and the expectations that arise from such perceptions is at the heart of a healthy approach to performance. Helping musicians to develop a greater awareness of the meanings they attach to their musician and performer identities and to exercise compromise where necessary are essential in order to accommodate the tensions (identified by Dobson, 2010) between playing music for self-expression and playing music under the direction of others.

A musician in the clinical practice of the first author provides an example of this sort of work. The musician in question found herself in conflict between her artistic interpretation of a piece, guided by instruction from one teacher, and the criticism that another teacher had made about her playing. This was further complicated by the fact that the second teacher was also her examiner. She was presented with the dilemma of deciding whether to be true to her own musical identity and risk a low assessment, or to compromise that identity and adopt some of the techniques advised by the examiner. During the clinical session, one solution discussed was to point out that if she were to gain a place in a professional orchestra, she was likely to find herself in a similar situation where the wishes of the conductor or section leader would take priority over her own musical values. Therefore, her dilemma could be turned around into a learning opportunity to prepare for such a scenario in the form of compromise and adaptability. This compromise and adaptability thus became a part of her music performer identity—she began to identify as a professional musician who was able to balance her own artistic integrity with adaptations to the professional circumstances as required.

Variety of repertoire and ensembles appear to feature prominently in the wellbeing of musicians (Ascenso, Williamon, & Perkins, 2017) and one advantage of the protean career (Bennett, 2009) is that performing musicians have more choice in the work they undertake. It is therefore easier to combine a variety of skills and roles to promote a balanced career. For contract players, longer-term strategies may need to be found if frustrations are not to emerge through lack of autonomy over musical expression. Some strategies employed have been to organize extracurricular activities such as recitals, chamber concerts, conducting amateur groups, or music arranging as a means to increase levels of creativity (Oakland, 2014).

Aligned with creativity and self-expression is a performer's own emotional involvement with music. Emotions can heighten the experience of performance for musicians or become a distracting force that impacts on their enjoyment of performance (Renfrew, 2014). Reaching an emotional state whereby a performer can convey the emotions of music rather than experience them can enhance the mental and physical skills needed to execute the music and is essential to evoke an emotional response from an audience (Woody & McPherson, 2010). Clearly, this level of engagement will be individually biased. Some orchestral musicians in the study by Renfrew (2014) admitted to deliberately detaching themselves from their own emotional involvement with music in favor of focusing on the job of performing music. Renfrew called this "forming a professional performing identity." But for other musicians, particularly those in the popular field (see Dobson, 2010), detaching themselves from any emotional investment in the music would seem unnecessary and unacceptable. A performing identity should then be negotiated, taking into consideration the musical context and individual biases of the musician.

Validation of self

All performers wish to be received positively by audiences, but when the performance becomes the primary measure of self-worth (see Kemp, 1996) it can put enormous pressure on them to set unrealistically high expectations on their performances. The resulting stress can initiate wide-ranging anxiety conditions such as unhelpful perfectionist tendencies, increased risk of physical injury through added psychological pressure, or the avoidance of performance completely (see Osborne & Kirsner, Volume 2). A study of the coping strategies of "soon to be retired" orchestral musicians (Oakland, 2014), highlights the immense pressure players can exert on themselves in the search for perfection and self-worth through music performance. Roger had been a principal wind player for thirty years:

> It's like a vendetta against yourself, even the smallest blemish, it goes straight to the heart, you want to go home and slash your wrists. It's personal pressure, not pressure from anyone else.

Although Roger denies feeling pressure from external sources, in the following quotation he shows how the pressure he exerts on himself is nevertheless instigated by the need to feel valued by others through his musical abilities: "I never take a week off, because someone else will be playing my part and you think, do they still want me anymore?"

Other players were able to find practical coping solutions to counteract potential low self-worth. Sally, a rank-and-file string player found greater self-worth by developing other aspects of her life, in this case gaining a pilot's license: "It did help my self-esteem getting into flying. As a musician you always seem to be told you're wrong. As a pilot I only had compliments. That helped enormously in the orchestra." The lack of self-worth experienced by Sally as an orchestral performer had a negative impact on her musician self as well as her private self. Engaging in an activity outside of music that boosted self-confidence helped her retain a more positive approach to orchestral playing. Learning to acknowledge and value different dimensions of self is highly advantageous in lessening the degree to which self-worth is performance-contingent.

Work-life balance

With reference to the concept of multiple selves and in the interests of the wellbeing of performing musicians, consideration should also be given to the balance between musical roles and personal roles. *Work-life balance* is a popular term in modern society and an understanding, supportive family is considered to be a key factor for professional success (Vaag, Giaver, & Bjerkeset, 2013).

Frank, a principal wind player with thirty-five years' experience, described the balance he has achieved between striving for perfection in performance while still feeling grounded in his private life:

> You realize there is more to life than being perfect. You want to be perfect but if it goes wrong you can still look forward to going home and seeing the grandchildren. It's the other side of life that keeps me going.

Taking time out of music, even for one day a week, should be viewed as an opportunity to nurture the personal self. Many musicians can be afraid to take this time for fear of not being technically prepared or fully committed. Physical and psychological consequences that have a negative impact on their wellbeing as performers can be the result. They are also in danger of denying the rich experiences that activities outside of music can contribute to the individuality of performance. Consequently, there may be times when a greater investment in personal identities is required in order to keep performance fresh.

The ability to switch consciously between the performer self and the private self is essential to maintain a balanced sense of self. Stepping into the performer role can be perceived as stepping into a character. Alter egos have been used for many years in sport and are designed to give athletes the characteristics and personality traits needed for success in their field (see Perry, 2020, p.198). For the musician, performance clothing can be representative of this switch. Some performers even give their performer self a different name. For example, the golfer Tiger Woods was born Eldrick Woods. He was given the name Tiger by his father to help embody what he needed to do on the golf course. Any symbolic undertakings utilized can be left behind, physically or psychologically, after the performance is finished in a process that actors call "de-roling." This technique can be practiced as part of a performance simulation exercise and can lessen the impact, positive or negative, that performance has on personal life.

CONCLUSION

The way we perceive ourselves as musical performers can have an enormous impact on the quality of our performances and our ability to manage a career trajectory. This is because our self-perceptions are sometimes the only control we have in a changing and competitive professional environment.

Performance is a dynamic process influenced not only by the music and the way we perform it but also by outside interests and our personal lives, which, together with our individual characteristics and values, shape and color the music we perform. Balancing the reciprocal relationship between public performer, private self, and musician is crucial to developing a healthy approach to performance and therefore to the wellbeing of the performer. These relationships are individually biased and always subject to change. Performers should therefore be constantly attentive to matters of self-perception and adapt when necessary to "fit" with their performing environment. Although this chapter has focused primarily on classical music performers, the issues discussed have universal relevance. If more attention can be given to the understanding of self-formation during training, the seeds of a healthier approach to performing may bear fruit throughout a performing career.

KEY SOURCES

Kemp, A. E. (1996). *The musical temperament: Psychology and personality of musicians*. Oxford: Oxford University Press.

MacDonald, R. A. R., Hargreaves, D. J., & Miell, D. E. (Eds.) (2002). *Musical identities*. Oxford: Oxford University Press.

MacDonald, R. Hargreaves, D. J. & Miell, D. (Eds.) (2017). *Handbook of musical identities*. New York: Oxford University Press.

Papageorgi, I., & Welch, G. (2016) How do musicians develop their learning about performance? In I. Papageorgi & G. Welch (Eds.), *Advanced musical performance: Investigations into higher education learning* (pp. 171–185). London: Routledge.

REFLECTIVE QUESTIONS

1. Interactions between self and music are just one of the aspects of a performer identity. How might the relationship you have with your instrument impact on this identity?

2. What specific performance identity issues might you encounter if you compose and perform your own music?

3. What factors do you consider to be important in achieving a balance between your personal and professional identities and your musician and performer identities?
4. In what ways might you need to adapt or modify your solo performing identity to a collaborative context?
5. What does "being a performer of music" mean to you?

References

Allmendinger, J., Hackman, J. R., & Lehman, E. V. (1996). Life and work in symphony orchestras. *The Musical Quarterly, 80*(2), 194–219. https://doi.org/10.1093/mq/80.2.194.

Appiah, K. A. (2018). *The lies that bind: Rethinking identity* New York: Liveright Publishing.

Ascenso, S., Williamon, A., & Perkins, R. (2017). Understanding the wellbeing of professional musicians through the lens of Positive Psychology. *Psychology of Music, 45*(1), 65–81. https://doi.org/10.1177%2F0305735616646864.

Auh, M. S., & Walker, R. (2017). Musical identities in Australia and South Korea and new identities emerging through social media and digital technology. In R. A. R. MacDonald, D. J. Hargreaves, & D. E. Miell, (Eds.), *The handbook of musical identities* (pp. 789–806). Oxford: Oxford University Press.

Bennett, D. (2008). Identity as a catalyst for success. In M. Hannah (Ed.), *Educating musicians for a lifetime of learning: Proceedings of the 17th International Seminar of the Commission for the Education of the Professional Musician, International Society for Music Education* (pp. 1–4). Spilamberto, Italy: International Society for Music Education.

Bennett, D. (2009). Academy and the real world: Developing realistic notions of career in the performing arts. *Arts and Humanities in Higher Education, 8*(3), 309–327. https://doi.org/10.1177%2F1474022209339953.

Blaike, T. (1996). Camping at a high altitude – see https://archive.spectator.co.uk/issue/7th-december-1996 [accessed April 1, 2019]

Bonneville-Roussy, A., & Vallerand, R. J. (2018). Passion at the heart of musicians' well-being. *Psychology of Music, 48*(2), 266–282. https://doi.org/10.1177/0305735618797180.

Brodsky, W. (2006). In the wings of British orchestras: A multi-episode interview study among symphony players. *Journal of Occupational and Organizational Psychology. 79*(4), 673–690. https://doi.org/10.1348/096317905X68213.

Burland, K. (2005). *Becoming a musician: A longitudinal study investigating the career transitions of undergraduate music students.* Unpublished doctoral dissertation, University of Sheffield.

Callero, P. L. (1985). Role-identity salience. *Social Psychology Quarterly, 48*(3), 203–215. https://doi.org/10.2307/3033681.

Davidson, J. W. (2002). The solo performer's identity. In R. A. R. MacDonald, D. J. Hargreaves, & D. Miell (Eds.). *Musical identities* (pp. 99–113). Oxford: Oxford University Press.

Davidson, J. W. (2017). Performance identity. In R. MacDonald, D. J. Hargreaves, & D. Miell (Eds.), *Handbook of musical identities* (pp. 364–382). New York: Oxford University Press.

DeNora, T. (2000). *Music in everyday life.* Cambridge, UK: Cambridge University Press.

DeNora, T. (2013). *Music asylums: Wellbeing through music in everyday Life.* Farnham, UK: Ashgate.

Dobson, M. C. (2010). Performing yourself: Autonomy and self-expression in the work of jazz musicians and classical string players. *Music Performance Research, 3*(1), 42–60.

Giddens, A. (1991 *Modernity and self-identity: Self and society in the late modern age*. Cambridge, UK: Polity Press.

Gonzales, M. J. F. (2018). Undergraduate students' strategies for negotiating emerging performer and teacher identities. *Psychology of Music*, 46(6) 813–830. https://doi.org/10.1177030573561726594.

Hargreaves, D. J., Miell, D. E., & MacDonald, R. A. R. (2002). What are musical identities and why are they important? In R. A. R. MacDonald, D. J. Hargreaves, & D. E. Miell (Eds.), *Musical identities* (pp.1–20). Oxford: Oxford University Press.

Hargreaves, D. J., Miell, D. E., & MacDonald, R. A. R. (2017). The changing identity of musical identities. In R. A. R. MacDonald, D. J. Hargreaves, & D. E. Miell (Eds.), *Handbook of musical identities* (pp. 3–27). Oxford: Oxford University Press.

Hargreaves D. J., Miell D. E., & MacDonald, R. A. R. (Eds.). (2012). *Musical imaginations*. Oxford: Oxford University Press.

James W. (1890). *The principles of psychology*. New York: Cosimo Books.

Jones, L-A. (2012). *Mercury: An intimate biography of Freddie Mercury*. New York: Touchstone.

Juslin, P. N., & Sloboda, J. A. (Eds.). (2010). *Handbook of music and emotion: Theory, research, applications*. Series in Affective Science. New York: Oxford University Press.

Jutti, S. (2012). *Piano musicians' identity negotiations in the context of the academy and transition to working life: A socio-cultural approach*. Unpublished doctoral dissertation, University of Helsinki.

Kemp, A. E. (1996). *The musical temperament: Psychology and personality of musicians*. Oxford: Oxford University Press.

Leary, M., & Tangney, J. P. (2012). The self as an organizing construct in the social and behavioral sciences. In M. Leary & J. P. Tangney (Eds.), *Handbook of self and identity* (pp. 1–21). New York: Guilford.

MacDonald, R. A. R, Hargreaves, D. J, & Miell, D. E. (Eds.). (2002). *Musical identities*. Oxford: Oxford University Press.

MacDonald, R., Hargreaves, D. J., & Miell, D. (Eds.). (2017). *Handbook of musical identities*. New York: Oxford University Press

MacDonald, R. A. R, Kreutz, G., & Mitchell, L. A. (Eds.). (2012). *Music, health and wellbeing*. Oxford: Oxford University Press.

MacDonald, R. A. R., &. Wilson, G. B. (2005). The musical identities of professional jazz musicians: A focus group investigation. *The Psychology of Music*, 33(4), 395–419. https://doi.org/10.1177%2F0305735605056151.

MacDonald, R. A. R., &. Wilson, G. B. (2020). *The art of becoming: How group improvisation works*. New York: Oxford University Press.

Martin, A. J., & Dowson, M. (2009). Interpersonal relationships, motivation, engagement, and achievement: Yields for theory, current issues, and educational practice. *Review of Educational Research*, 79(1), 327–365. https://doi.org/10.3102%2F0034654308325583.

Mead, G. H. (1934). *Mind, self and society*. Chicago: University of Chicago Press.

Miell, D., MacDonald, R. A. R., & Hargreaves, D. J. (Eds). (2005). *Musical communication* Oxford: Oxford University Press.

Mills, J. (2004). Working in music: Becoming a performer-teacher. *Music Education Research*, 6(3), 245–261. https://doi.org/10.1080/1461380042000281712.

Myers, P. (1991). Queen star dies after AIDS statement. *The Guardian* – see https://www.theguardian.com/ heguardian/2011/nov/25/archive-queen-star-dies-after-aids-statement [accessed April 19, 2019]

Oakland, J. (2014). *Ageing and retirement: Towards an understanding of the experiences of orchestral musicians as they approach retirement* [Unpublished research report sponsored by Musicians Union]. London.

Oakland, J., MacDonald, R. A., & Flowers, P. (2012). Re-defining "Me": Exploring career transition and the experience of loss in the context of redundancy for professional opera choristers. *Musicae Scientiae, 16*(2), 135–147. https://doi.org/10.1177/2F1029864911435729.

Oakland, J., MacDonald, R., & Flowers, P. (2013). Identity in crisis: The role of work in the formation and renegotiation of a musical identity. *British Journal of Music Education, 30*(2), 261–276. https://doi.org/10.1017/S026505171300003X.

Oakland, J., MacDonald, R., & Flowers, P. (2014). Musical disembodiment: A phenomenological case study investigating the experiences of operatic career disruption due to physical incapacity. *Research Studies in Music Education, 36*(1), 39–55. https://doi.org/10.1177/2F1321103X14521355.

Papageorgi, I., & Welch, G. (2016). How do musicians develop their learning about performance? In I. Papageorgi & G. Welch (Eds.), *Advanced musical performance: Investigations into higher education learning* (pp. 171–186). London: Routledge.

Parkes, K. A., Daniel, R., West, T., & Gaunt, H. (2015). Applied music studio teachers in higher education: Exploring the impact of identification and talent on career satisfaction. *International Journal of Music Education, 33*(3), 372–385. https://doi.org/10.1177%2F0255761415581281.

Parasuraman, S., & Purohit, Y. S. (2000). Distress and boredom among orchestra musicians: The two faces of stress. *Journal of Occupational Health Psychology, 5*(1), 74–83. https://psycnet.apa.org/doi/10.1037/1076-8998.5.1.74.

Pascale, L. (2013). "I'm really NOT a singer": Examining the meaning of the word singer and non-singer and the relationship their meaning holds in providing a musical education in schools. In A. Rose & K. Adams (Eds.), *The phenomenon of singing III*, 164–170. St. John's, NF: Memorial University Press.

Pecen, E., Collins, D., & MacNamara, Á. (2016). Music of the night: Performance practitioner considerations for enhancement work in music. *Sport, Exercise, and Performance Psychology, 5*(4), 377–395. https://doi.org/10.1037/spy0000067.

Perkins, R. (2013). Learning cultures and the conservatoire: An ethnographically-informed case study. *Music Education Research, 15*(2), 196–213. https://doi.org/10.1080/14613808.2012.759551.

Perry, J. (2020). *Performing under pressure: Psychological strategies for sporting success*. Oxford: Routledge.

Renfrew, M. E. (2014). *The musical identities of professional orchestral musicians*. Unpublished doctoral dissertation, University of Edinburgh.

Spychiger, M. B. (2017). From musical experience to musical identity: Musical self-concept as a mediating psychological structure. In R. A. R. MacDonald, D. J. Hargreaves, & D. E. Miell (Eds.), *The handbook of musical identities* (pp. 267–287). Oxford: Oxford University Press.

Stets, J. E., & Burke, P. J. (2003). A sociological approach to self and identity. In M. R. Leary & J. P. Tangney (Eds.), *Handbook of self and identity* (pp. 128–152). New York: Guildford Press.

Stryker, S. (1980). *Symbolic interactionism: A social structural version*. Menlo Park, CA: Benjamin Cummings.

Tajfel, H., & Turner, J. C. (1979). An integrative theory of inter-group conflict. In S. Worschel & W. Austin (Eds.), *Psychology of intergroup relations* (pp. 33–47). Pacific Grove, CA: Brookes/Cole.

Triantafyllaki, A. (2010). Performance teachers' identity and professional knowledge in advanced music teaching. *Music Education Research*, *12*(1), 71–87. https://doi.org/10.1080/14613800903568254.

Wilson, G., & MacDonald R. (2017). The ear of the beholder: Improvisation, ambiguity, and social contexts in the constructions of musical identities. In R. A. R. MacDonald, D. J. Hargreaves, & D. E. Miell (Eds.), *The handbook of musical identities* (pp. 105–122). Oxford: Oxford University Press.

Woody, R. H., & McPherson, G. E. (2010). Emotion and motivation in the lives of performers. In P. H. Juslin & J. Sloboda (Eds.), *Handbook of music and emotion: Theory, research, application* (pp. 401–425). Oxford: Oxford University Press.

Vaag, J., Giaver, F., & Bjerkeset, O. (2013). Specific demands and resources in the career of the Norwegian freelance musician. *Arts & Health*, *6*(3), 205–222. https://doi.org/10.1080/17533015.2013.863789.

Zillmann, D., & Gan, S.-l. (1997). Musical taste in adolescence. In D. J. Hargreaves & A. C. North (Eds.), *The social psychology of music* (pp. 161–187). New York: Oxford University Press.

CHAPTER 28

SYNESTHESIA AND MUSIC PERFORMANCE

SOLANGE GLASSER

INTRODUCTION

> I'd be lost. It's my only reference for understanding. I don't think I would have what some people would call talent and what I would call a gift. The ability to see and feel (this way) was a gift given to me that I did not have to have. And if it was taken from me suddenly I'm not sure that I could make music. I wouldn't be able to keep up with it. I wouldn't have a measure to understand.
>
> Pharrell Williams, in Seaberg, 2011

> It's the only way that I can identify what something sounds like. I know when something is in key because it either matches the same color or it doesn't. Or it feels different and it doesn't feel right.
>
> Pharrell Williams, in Greene, 2013

THESE two quotes, taken from interviews with the Grammy Award–winning producer, performer, and entrepreneur Pharrell Williams, provide a fascinating window into the lived experience of a musician whose perceptual experiences of music are profoundly different from most. By his own accounts, Williams has synesthesia: a rare neurological condition that in his case means that he sees colors when listening to or thinking about music. Williams in not alone. Pianist and composer Franz Liszt demanded, "O please, gentlemen, a little bluer, if you please! This key requires it! That is a deep violet, please, depend on it! Not so rose!" (Mahling, 1926). The American big-band leader, composer, and pianist Duke Ellington stated, "If Harry Carney is playing, D is dark blue burlap. If Johnny Hodges is playing, G becomes light blue satin" (George, 1981). Williams, Liszt, and Ellington are among many more well-known and highly decorated musicians reported as having synesthesia. Indeed, for a small number of musicians, their musical journey is shaped by the way they connect music and sounds with color, shape, taste, or any other perceptual modality. This chapter therefore attempts to provide information on the impact of synesthesia on music performance, choices, and preferences by describing the lived experiences of musicians with synesthesia and highlighting the multiplicity of experiences and behavioral outcomes of this unique group of musicians.

A number of questions arise when reflecting on the individual differences evident among such musicians: In what ways does a musical performance differ for a musician with synesthesia? Which musical tasks are aided or hindered by the synesthetic experience, and do these differences lead to specific engagement or avoidance behaviors? Are there any practical applications that arise for musicians who possess synesthesia? And finally, what can we all learn from these cases of exceptional musical perception?

The explanations provided in this chapter are drawn from the existing literature on synesthesia more generally. These are supplemented using quotes from interviews I have undertaken with musicians who have synesthesia to provide specific details on how synesthesia expresses itself in varied and rich ways within music-related contexts (Glasser, 2018, 2020).

SYNESTHESIA

Defining synesthesia

The word 'synesthesia' (also spelt 'synaesthesia') is derived from the Greek words *syn* (union or join) and *aesthesis* (sensation or perception): literally meaning joint perception, or a union of the senses (Cytowic, 1989, 2002). *Synesthesia* is a neurological condition in which the stimulation of one sensory or cognitive pathway leads to an automatic, involuntary experience in a second sensory or cognitive pathway (Cytowic, 1989, 2002). Although it is referred to as a neurological condition due to the neurological basis of the perceptual differences it characterizes, synesthesia rarely interferes with normal functioning (Baron-Cohen & Harrison, 1999).

People with synesthesia are called *synesthetes*, and the range and variety of their experiences is vast and highly idiosyncratic. A synesthete may, for example, perceive numbers and letters as colored (known as grapheme → color synesthesia), or perceive musical pitches as having distinct flavors (musical note → flavor synesthesia). Learned semantic categories such as letters, numbers, or days of the week are the most frequent stimuli, which then lead to sensory experiences such as the perception of synesthetic color or flavor (Hochel & Milán, 2008). The inducer (triggering stimulus) and the concurrent (resultant synesthetic experience) often belong to different sense modalities, such as in sound → color synesthesia (auditory → visual), but many of the most prevalent forms of synesthesia occur when both the inducer and concurrent belong to the same sense, such as in grapheme → color synesthesia (visual → visual; Simner, 2012). As such, a common misrepresentation of synesthesia as a joining or union of the senses is not always technically valid.

Types of synesthesia

There are currently more than eighty documented types of synesthesia. Importantly, synesthetes can experience several types of synesthesia concurrently, with a reported 81 percent of the synesthetic population possessing multiple forms of synesthesia (Niccolai et al., 2012).

By far the most prevalent type is grapheme → color synesthesia with between 82–88 percent of all forms of synesthesia being triggered by language units such as graphemes, phonemes, and words (Niccolai, Jennes, Stoerig, & Van Leeuwen, 2012; Simner, Glover, & Mowat, 2006; Simner, Mulvenna, et al., 2006). The second most prevalent type is spatial-sequence synesthesia, whereby time-related words such as days of the week or months of the year are perceived in a spatial location; and this has been found to occur in up to 62 percent of cases (Niccolai et al., 2012).

While less prevalent than both grapheme → color and spatial-sequence synesthesia, this chapter will focus on auditory or music induced types of idiopathic synesthesia. The most prevalent music inducing type of synesthesia is broadly categorized as music → color synesthesia, in which a musical stimulus (the inducer) elicits a color perception (the concurrent). This type of truly cross-modal linking is often considered a paradigmatic example of synesthesia, even though it is less common than other types. Estimations on the prevalence of music → color synesthesia within the synesthete population vary between studies, being reported at 41 percent in a study by Niccolai and colleagues (2012), which is higher than the 25 percent and 18.7 percent reported by Rich and colleagues (2005) and Barnett and colleagues (2008), respectively. General sound → color synesthesia is also common, and has been found to occur in 33 percent of synesthetic occurrences (Niccolai et al., 2012). Other types of music-induced synesthesia include inducers such as musical notes, keys or tonalities, instruments, musical styles or genres, and non-music specific aspects such as color, flavor, or spatial location (Glasser, 2018).

Prevalence

Idiopathic synesthesia is a relatively rare condition. Estimates concerning the prevalence of synesthesia vary widely, with early studies estimating ranges from as low as 1 in 25,000–100,000 (Cytowic, 1993, 1997), to 1 in 2,000 (Baron-Cohen, Burt, Smith-Laittan, Harrison, & Bolton, 1996), and to 1 in 200 (Ramachandran & Hubbard, 2001a) in studies based on self-referral. In the first random sampling study of the condition, synesthesia was estimated to occur in as high as 4.4 percent of the population (Simner, Mulvenna, et al., 2006). It is this latter statistic that is generally used when discussing overall prevalence of synesthesia in the general population, although it is widely accepted that further random sampling studies are needed to encourage the diversification of population groups studied.

Synesthesia is more commonly reported among artistic professionals and people with creative hobbies (Cytowic, 1989; Domino, 1989; Niccolai et al., 2012; Ramachandran & Hubbard, 2001b); a large-scale study established that 24 percent of the synesthetes questioned were professionally engaged in the arts (Rich, Bradshaw, & Mattingley, 2005), as compared to a general population rate of only 2 percent (Hochel & Milán, 2008). Furthermore, it has been suggested that synesthesia may be more prevalent in arts student populations, with one study finding that 7 percent of the sample were synesthetes, as compared to 2 percent of the control sample (Rothen & Meier, 2010). Apart from professional engagement, Niccolai and colleagues (2012) indicated that 68 percent of the respondents in their study were artistically active, and an interest in the arts was frequently reported. Moreover, 78 percent of participants indicated that their synesthesia was an advantage in creative jobs, memorizing, learning, or calculating. Participants further described themselves as skilled at painting, learning foreign languages, and memorization. Indeed it has been proposed that links between synesthesia, metaphor, creativity, and the origins of language may exist, with interdisciplinary research debating whether idiopathic synesthesia can actively contribute to an artist's ability (Domino, 1989; Mulvenna, 2007; Ramachandran & Hubbard, 2001b; Sitton & Pierce, 2004). Yet apart from general studies of synesthesia, creativity, and artistic ability, studies that specifically look at the influence of synesthesia on musical abilities are scarce.

SYNESTHESIA AND ITS
IMPACT ON MUSICIANS

Does the possession of synesthesia influence the musical performance, choices, or preferences of a musician synesthete, are any musical tasks aided or hindered by the synesthetic experience, and do these potential impacts lead to specific engagement or avoidance behaviors? As we shall see, the response to these questions is highly idiosyncratic. There are, however, behavioral manifestations that are reported as more common than others.

Having established that synesthesia is relatively more prominent among arts professionals and those involved in the creative and performing arts, we now turn our attention to how it might impact musicians using examples drawn from interviews with ten synesthetes: Charlotte (flautist), Xavier (violinist), Thomas (oboist), Ethan (pianist), Ruby (soprano and cellist), Isabella (composer and pianist), Mason (violinist),

Mia (soprano), Lily (soprano), and Benjamin (musicologist and pianist). In the following sections, comments from these ten synesthetes are used to elaborate on six underlying features of how the possession of synesthesia influences musicians' musical performances, choices, and preferences, and shapes the ways musicians experience, create, and perform music (Glasser, 2018).

Stylistic preferences and repertoire choices

Synesthetic percepts can strongly influence musical style preferences and repertoire decisions, with decisions being made based explicitly on the synesthetic color percepts—or lack thereof—induced by a particular piece or style. One example of this decision-making process comes from the flautist Charlotte, who suggested that her preference for playing avant-garde music was largely due to her enjoyment of the "huge bursts of color" it provokes, with avant-garde music inducing "stronger" colors than those induced by other forms of music: "I don't actually like that much typical classical Mozart type stuff to play myself. . . . I don't see much. I feel like I don't see much from it. It's very 'flat.' There's not a lot I would get from it." This divide between classical and modern music, resulting from qualitative differences in the saturation of concurrent color percepts, was similarly noted by the violinist Xavier, who has a comparable preference for multicolored synesthetic percepts that fundamentally affects his repertoire and listening choices:

> It definitely affects my choice. I don't enjoy classical music (as in the classical era) because it's so single-colored. It's very mechanical: here's this and the next color's this in twenty minutes. It's on the same thing but very technical, whereas I really enjoy twentieth century modern music. I love impressionism because it's very progressive, very colorful in the choices of chords, notes, melodies, even within the orchestration. So, I think that's also why I love jazz, because there are so many different chords and notes. It's very colorful in my head. I wouldn't be as engaged in an electronic dance song because it's very singular in color, unless it was very progressive and there was more musicality to it where I can enjoy the color and the beat. I definitely think it's impacted my choice of music. I still enjoy baroque music even though it's still pretty singular as well. I think that the colors and that are still quite defined and that's also helped me enjoy that music more.

It is important to recall the highly personal nature of synesthetic percepts, and although both Charlotte and Xavier indicated a relative dislike for classical music, based on the resulting flatness of induced synesthetic colors, this is by no means observed across the board for musician synesthetes. Indeed, comments made by the oboist Thomas indicate he does not enjoy complex musical forms such as jazz, as "it doesn't have a nice color. . . . It's quite a lot darker than other music and I think that's based off the sound of the drums and the low string bass. But then it's like juxtaposed with this bright trumpet sound and I don't like it." Thomas made a similarly strong pronouncement in relation to non-Western music, which he indicated is all the same browny-yellow color: "it really got to me that it was just all the same color. It didn't matter what I did. I couldn't discern a different thing. It was all just the same. Really annoying!"

From their comments, we can conclude that Charlotte and Xavier appear to be focusing on the intricate color combinations induced by the harmonic complexity of colors induced by individual notes or tonalities, while Thomas's assertions appear to suggest that individual styles (such as jazz) may induce individual colors, and that certain stylistic synesthetic colors are preferable to others. Thomas's comments, however, highlight the interplay of a wide variety of musical influences on the resulting synesthetic percepts. Besides stylistic color associations, he mentioned the influence of timbre (drums, string bass, and trumpet), along with the assertion that any "non-Western" music was the same browny-yellow color, implying that familiarity might also be a factor. Stylistic preferences may therefore be more appropriately viewed as occasionally resulting from a constellation of factors.

Extending the conversation around stylistic preferences and repertoire choices further, these preferences are often translated into concert programming decisions. The pianist Ethan, for example, insists on a balanced color palette within a concert program. Here Ethan describes how he chooses and orders concert repertoire based on the interaction of the resulting synesthetic colors:

> I tend to choose repertoire that's going to interest me in the way of color and it's also going to balance itself out in a program together. So I'm not going to choose a whole lot of pieces in E major because it's going to be all these pieces in this same color. . . . For example, the pieces I'm doing this semester—one of them is in F sharp minor, one's in E major, one's in F minor and one's in D major. Together they create a really nice color for me.

Crafting the "right" balance of synesthetic colors in a program can therefore play a crucial role in concert program choices and repertoire orderings.

Along with influencing specific choices, synesthetic percepts can enhance the enjoyment of particular musical styles and lead to stronger engagement with these styles. Ruby, a soprano, appeared surprised when asked whether her synesthesia influenced her stylistic preferences:

> [Laughs] Yes, yes, yes [laughs]! That's really funny! Yeah, I think it has. I love early music. Yes, that's [laughs] strange. I love Bach and Monteverdi and people like that and their colors are definitely very rich. There are lots of pinks, reds, yellows and beautiful greens in there. It's very rich and full of jewels, whereas I think a lot of the time I really dislike *bel canto* opera. I find it a lot blander a lot of the time. So yes, I think that's true. I probably would choose things that I think have much more vivid colors. That's interesting [laughs].

As a singer, Ruby's preference for performing baroque and early music repertoire over *bel canto* opera centered on the former's richness of color, as opposed to the blandness of the latter; this preference for a richer color palette was a driving factor in Ruby's decision to specialize as an early music singer.

Music listening preferences and aversions

As with the aforementioned repertoire and programming choices, the link between synesthesia and listening preferences is strongly emphasized in discussions with synesthetes. For the composer Isabella, the synesthetic colors induced by individual tonalities influence her listening choices to the point where she indicates her listening choices were often based on the desire to "see" (or not see) a specific synesthetic color, rather than to "hear" a specific piece of music: "Like, *Don Giovanni* overture I know is in D minor, and that song is really deep red, so if I don't feel like listening to deep dark red then I won't, or if I do . . . you know." Choosing to listen to a known piece of music to explicitly experience a particular color percept was also noted by the composer Olivia: "The Bach *Brandenburg Concerto*, I think the No. 3, I've wanted to listen to because it's so bright. When I've wanted to engage in that brightness, I've deliberately chosen that. . . . The color and the sound are bright. They're that yellow color again. They're very, very sunny. It's an extraordinary piece of music."

Synesthetes reported frequently listening to music that "matches" a desired synesthetic output. A good example of this comes from the pianist Ethan, who (among other forms) has grapheme → color synesthesia: "The majority of my listening time I spend on post-rock, which is like the Icelandic band [Sigur Rós], like a Scottish band called Mogwai. They're kind of orchestral huge bands that just create waves of sound. It's almost like they're painting my numbers for me. It's just amazing." Ethan described these bands as "painting" his grapheme-induced synesthetic percepts and acknowledged his enjoyment of this music stems in large part from the propitious ability of these groups to match his internally perceived colored percepts. Like Ethan, the violinist Mason similarly indicated he "might be in search for a particular mood or a particular color or aesthetic on a particular day and then be like, "Yeah, this is what I want right now," thus choosing a particular piece that will induced the synesthetic percepts he wishes to experience. Hence the desired outcomes of Mason's music listening choices are habitually the ensuing synesthetic percepts.

Music listening preferences founded on the desire to experience specific synesthetic percepts can also be extended to include music playlists. The soprano Mia, for example, had compiled a playlist of pieces, specifying: "sometimes I'll just want something that has a particular atmosphere. I have a playlist of blue things which, if I'm in a particular mood, I might prefer." Mia indicated "blue" is "not a doing thing, this color," thus Mia's blue playlist is preferred by her when she is in a calm mood, and "not particularly active." While the pieces in this playlist are not all in the same key, a higher percentage of them are "in the A keys." Mia indicated she physically perceives differing shades of blue in her mind's eye while listening to this playlist.

The choice to listen to a particular piece, based on its corresponding synesthetic percepts, is not, however, always a conscious one. Comparable to Mia's blue playlist, the oboist Thomas indicated his favorite color is blue, and that tonalities that engender synesthetic variants of blue are keys he most often composes in. When asked if this preference for "blue" tonalities also influenced his music listening preferences, he initially indicated he had never "thought about that," before acknowledging "a lot of the pieces on my iPod and stuff are in minor keys so they're more around C, D and G minor": keys that induce variants of the color blue. Thomas furthermore conceded that there are "not very many bright red pieces" on his iPod—a noteworthy admission, as reds and oranges are his least favorite synesthetic colors. Thomas stipulated his iPod playlist choices were made "unintentionally," thus suggesting they were made instinctively and spontaneously.

While the desire to engage with satisfying synesthetic percepts can influence a synesthetes music listening choices, so too can the desire to avoid certain induced percepts, as the flautist Charlotte reveals:

> I don't like Wagner and people have shown me parts of some Wagner compositions that in theory are quite nice and I can't, I just can't like it. I see the same color every single time and it's that murky, browny green color. And it's just something about how he composes or something about. . . . I just . . . yeah! I can't do it! . . . A lot of the time with Wagnerian opera, it's so full on, that's where I describe it's like noise in my head. I see horrible color, and it's noisy and I can't hear anything. It's just too much.

A synesthete may therefore be aware of the musical merits of a composition yet cannot overcome the synesthetic "dissonance" that arises from compositional aspects of the piece.

Compositional choices

Composition is an activity central to the lives of many musicians, and the role of synesthesia on the compositional process can occur on three levels: enriching the compositional process through decisions based on synesthetic percepts; the potentiality for synesthetic percepts to be restrictive when composing; and the use of synesthesia as a practical aid during the composition process.

Enriching the compositional process

The complementarity of synesthetic colors can prime over musical considerations, with synesthete composers frequently reporting compositional choices made based on the synesthetic colors (or other percepts) they wished to "compose" with. One good example comes from the pianist Ethan, who stated he makes compositional choices "based on colors, all the time," which occurs more frequently than choices based on musical considerations. Ethan noted that when composing, he will often find himself working from a single chord, as "the chord itself for me is interesting enough," implying the synesthetic percepts induced by the chord add a further dimension to the auditory aspect of the composition that greatly enhances its interest. Indeed, some musical features, such as octave or fifth parallels "*look* fantastic," and are therefore tools Ethan enjoys writing with, even if they are disapproved of in traditional compositional practice.

Ultimately, compositions can be written to center completely on a specific synesthetic percept. The oboist Thomas provided the example of a piece he composed at school entitled "Cold Blue," which was composed entirely of tonalities that induced variants of the color blue for him: "I wrote the piece that only had blue in it. I . . . pick colors that I like and colors that go well together. . . . D and D minor are blue; A flat and A flat major; F minor is also that darker blue, but they're the kind of chords and I write in those keys more often because they're that color." Here we see that in addition to having a general stylistic preference for music that induces the color blue, it is also a factor that influences his decision to employ his synesthetic percepts as a compositional framework.

Restricting the compositional process

While synesthetes may enjoy or find it rewarding to compose music based on their synesthetic percepts, this can be limiting and restrict the compositional process. The violinist Xavier, for example, always starts his compositional process with chords, instead of melodies, as his synesthesia is stronger for chords than for individual notes. He is led by his synesthesia to focus—at least initially—on the colors engendered by specific chordal progressions and tonalities. But he understands that from a compositional standpoint, this is restrictive, and there may be more effective means of composing. Synesthetes are often compelled by an internal drive that cannot be easily overridden if or when desired. In this sense synesthetic percepts can be observed as being potentially limiting in certain compositional situations.

A practical aid to the compositional process

Some composers can balance the way their synesthesia enriches the compositional process with the way it restricts it, making it a practical aid during the composition process. Lily's synesthesia facilitates her ability to write serial music, whereby her induced synesthetic colors enable her to formulate twelve-tone rows and compose in diminished or whole-tone harmony. Not only does Lily indicate this is possible purely from an internal compositional perspective, but she states she is able to actively use her synesthesia to derive inspiration from external sources:

> I've written pieces of music based on paintings: got the tone rows from the paintings and then written pieces using that which is quite useful. . . . I was using Kandinsky (he's my favorite painter) and I think he's my favorite painter because of the colors that he uses. When I look at Kandinsky, I do actually sort of hear the colors in a more direct way. Without necessarily thinking: for orange, that's a perfect fourth. It has more immediacy for me. It seems to bypass that connection a little bit. A lot of his paintings look to me like graphic scores, even when they're not using color.

Using paintings by Kandinsky as an additional source of material for her compositions holds special significance for Lily, as she has heard Kandinsky may be a synesthete himself. The utilization of her synesthesia in these instances is an "active utilization," indicating that it is a practical aid to her compositional decision-making process.

Instrument preferences

One of the more commonly reported forms of music-related synesthesia is instrument sound → color synesthesia, where different instruments or timbral qualities will induce specific color percepts. Consequently, the effect of synesthetic percepts on choice, preference, or aversion to certain instruments warrants consideration. This effect can appear at a very young age and impact the desire or choice of instrument of a child even before the onset of instrumental lessons. Ruby recounted how she initially learned the flute as a child but noted the instrument "didn't suit me. It didn't gel," while also mentioning she had always wanted to learn the cello. When asked if her synesthesia played a role in these instrumental preferences, Ruby replied:

> Yes, I think it has. I didn't want to play the flute. I didn't like its color. . . . I always wanted to play the cello and that definitely felt right and it felt like the right color. So yes, I think it has—definitely. . . . I think it would have been a motivation to stop doing what I was doing. I remember [laughs] I really, really hated the flute. . . . It was just this utter loathing of it. I hated everything about it.

Ruby indicated the disagreeable color induced by the flute was a reason "to stop doing what I was doing," while the pleasurable red color induced by the cello "would certainly mean an attraction" toward it.

The attraction or repulsion of certain instrument "colors" extends beyond the instrument played by the synesthete; these same instrument preferences or aversions can impact the musical (and indeed personal) partnerships entered into by synesthete musicians. A good example of this comes from the soprano Lily, who has several forms of synesthesia, including instrument sound → color, with her strongest color associations being for instrument timbres that she dislikes, like the saxophone, which produces a horrible muddy-yellow color. For Lily, any instrument that produces a nasal sound quality will engender a strong color association, and it is both the sound and corresponding color that she dislikes. She refers to the induced colors in these instances as a "distraction," and also notes they provoke a strong aversion to these instruments. For Lily the color of an instrumental tone that she does not like—such as the muddy-yellow of the saxophone—overrides any intervallic or individual note color that she would normally experience due to her musical note → color synesthesia. As such, any note or interval played on the saxophone induces the same overriding muddy yellow color. This, she estimates, is because the color is so "strong." The overbearing nature of the color greatly affects her ability to work with saxophonists (whom she admitted to not wanting in her band), or to play or listen to the saxophone. She admitted, tongue in cheek, that she would not even date a saxophonist.

Individual instruments may induce idiosyncratic synesthetic percepts (such as a direct instrument sound → color pairing), but so too can timbral groupings of like-sounding instruments or sound sources. For the flautist Charlotte, the "oboe that's not played well," chimes, and vibraphone all induce the same horrible yellow color as the saxophone: "If I think about saxophone—I don't really like them very much. They're always this horrible—it feels like it hurts—this shade of bright highlighter yellow." Lily and Charlotte share a strong dislike of the yellow color induced by the saxophone, but Lily's yellow is "muddy," while Charlotte's yellow is "bright." In both cases, this strong perception of yellow overrides all other forms of synesthesia. For preferred timbres, the color induced by the timbre and the colors induced by other elements of the music (such as tonality or pitch) form layers of colors in the mind's eye. For disliked timbres, this layering effect is stifled: in Charlotte's case, "if it's something I don't like—I don't like saxophone—that's all I see. I see that color that is that instrument and everything else feels like it's been blocked out. I can't hear the music in any other way than that." This aversion to the saxophone in particular strongly influences her interest in playing the instrument: "No, there's no way [laughs]!"

These synesthete musicians offer striking examples of how their synesthetic percepts not only influence their instrumental preferences, but also create strong and in some cases extreme avoidance behaviors toward certain instruments or timbral qualities—or even toward musicians who play them.

Interpretation

The interpretation of a musical work is a process that requires musicians to decide how to perform music that has been previously composed. As is shown in the first three chapters of Part III in this handbook, interpretation is a fundamental aspect of any performance. Music-induced synesthetic percepts can influence the perceived mood, and therefore interpretation, of musical compositions. Associating specific moods with synesthetic colors impacts how a piece is learned, and how it is interpreted. When synesthetes see associated colors and images with the music, they are more expressive in their musical interpretations, and furthermore note that if they do not perceive a color for a certain section of the music they are performing, or if the color is not as expected, this can prompt them to change their interpretation to maximize the potentiality to pro-duce the desired synesthetic effect. For the flautist Charlotte, "when it's not there [the synesthetic percept], then something is wrong. I need to be doing something to make it appear to me in the way it would." The success of specific interpretations is therefore often judged on the precision of the color a synesthete perceives when performing.

The synesthetic colors perceived by a synesthete are often used as an aesthetic tem-plate, with synesthetes modifying their musical interpretation to fit the internally perceived colors of that template. As an interpretational process, this is particularly true with regard to the tonality of a piece. For the oboist Thomas, a piece performed in C major is "more boring" than if it were performed in C sharp or D, as these two keys induce synesthetic color percepts while C major "is just clear." In most classical music, adjusting the tonality of a piece is not generally acceptable as an interpretation, but Thomas indicated he would make smaller adjustments, like placing "more emphasis on the color of individual notes than on the overall phrase" if the piece is composed in an unfavorable key. Focusing on individual notes instead of on the "boring" tonality as a whole enables Thomas to interpret the piece more successfully.

Synesthetic percepts, including colors, shapes, odors, or tastes, can change the emotional connection with, and interpretation of, music as it is performed. But as with compositional choices, the reliance on these synesthetic percepts when interpreting music can be inhibiting. Rapid changes of tonality engender equally rapid changes in color or other percepts, and these changes may hinder the ability of some synesthetes to transition smoothly through these changes of color and mood.

To further compound this difficulty, synesthetes may find that their individual (and highly idiosyncratic) percepts may not match the perceived mood of a piece they are performing. The mismatch between synesthetic percepts and perceived mood can be frustrating for a synesthete and restrict their interpretational options. The potentially restrictive aspect of synesthetic percepts was highlighted by the composer and pianist Isabella, who reported an example of how her synesthetic percepts did not match the mood of a piece she was learning to play:

> It's funny, I was playing this Rachmaninoff etude and it was in E flat. I associate that key with probably the more light Mozart stuff. This piece was really pounding. You've got to be attacking the note: a completely different touch, but I was playing more with a lighter touch and trying to make everything smooth.

For Isabella, the key of E flat induces a synesthetic light blue color, which did not match the character of the music:

> Maybe that piece being in that key was a bit—it should be in a harsher color. . . . I think if that piece had been in D, which is red and angry, I would have probably been more inclined to bash it out.

The synesthetic colors she perceives therefore influence the way Isabella shapes her expressivity and sound production, while the "ideal sound to color characteristics" she wishes to achieve guide her interpretational decisions.

Overall, synesthetes note that plotting their musical interpretations in terms of colors or other synesthetic percepts, and the strength and fit of these perceived percepts, is an important guide that is frequently followed when interpreting music. This process can enhance interpretations, specifically when synesthetic colors are perceived as being fulfilled or matched in a performance setting, while the mismatch or absence of colors can be seen as an indication of a poor interpretation. Synesthetes report the interpretation of certain pieces based on their synesthetic percepts can be restrictive, specifically in relation to the tonality of the piece.

Technique

We generally think of technical proficiency in terms of the fine motor skills needed to perform music. It may seem somewhat counterintuitive to consider how synesthesia might impact musical technique. Yet synesthete musicians report that synesthetic percepts affect them in a range of ways and can either enhance or hinder instrumental technique and learning.

Synesthesia is credited as aiding in sound production and is strongly tied to our earlier discussion on interpretation. From a technical perspective, a synesthete's desire to match the ideal synesthetic percept to the sound they are producing manifests itself in changes to their technique, such as in the sound envelope and speed of vibrato, or through bow control on a stringed instrument, as described by the violinist Mason:

> In terms of the synesthesia, it forces me to think about how I produce my sound. With violin, the main thing's vibrato, but also the bow control. Then just thinking about, "Is the sound too hot? Do I want it to be this way?" Say I didn't want it to be that way, I might make a lighter vibrato that's not so fast. Just the characteristics of the sound in terms of flavor but also temperature, as I mentioned. Then figuring out if it's too much one way or the other and doing what I can to adjust.

Mason feels a sense of satisfaction if he is able to adjust his playing to match the "ideal picture" of how he wants his playing to sound but that conversely, if he is unable to match his desired synesthetic output, he feels "quite bothered or annoyed," and can have a sense of "disapproval or discomfort." This constant striving for the musical translation of his ideal synesthetic percepts flows into his practice regime, which is often focused on aspects of sound production: "I'll have a very specific sound quality in mind. Sometimes I might spend ages just trying to get that right sound rather than thinking that the note sounds fine and going on to the next section." Mason therefore views achieving a level of proficiency through the application of his synesthetic percepts in his practice regime as positive.

But if we were to turn our attention in the opposite direction, in what ways could synesthesia be detrimental to instrumental technique and learning? When asked to imagine what might be different had she not had synesthesia, the flautist Charlotte responded:

> I almost feel like I would have been a more technique-focused player, more technically adept. I feel like that has always been something that I haven't quite conquered. I'm not the most technical player. I think maybe if I didn't have synesthesia, my focus on that would have been different because everything is so related to expression and color and these images and things that it's all about the sound. It's not so much about how my fingers work and that sort of thing. Whether my embouchure's right! I feel like that would have made a difference.

A focus on "other," non-technical aspects of performance was therefore suggested as being detrimental to technical development. It must be noted, however, that reports of technical enhancements or hindrances by synesthete musicians are scarce. Thus, while attention must be given by both performers and teachers for occasions where these effects manifest, the examples from this section are not indicative of the broader synesthete population.

Practical Implications

Synesthesia can impact various facets of music performance and composition. If you are reading this chapter because you identify as a synesthete, chances are you are interested in increasing your understanding of your condition and the impact it may have on your performance. In my work with synesthetes, I have found that many have never shared the personal nature of their associations and internal lived experiences with anyone else. They are often both relieved and enlightened given this opportunity. Reflecting more deeply and introspectively on the experiences, outcomes, and mechanisms that underly the synesthetic experience can foster a greater level of understanding and an ability to harness that knowledge in all aspects of musical decision-making.

Others of you reading this chapter may be more interested in the implications of research on how musicianship is taught to students with synesthesia. Translating the highly idiosyncratic learning and developmental trajectories of synesthetes into complex teaching environments is admittedly challenging. Yet understanding the unique strengths and struggles of individuals with this condition enables practical adaptions to be made to the design of educational approaches. Defining musical development and learning in terms of neurological and psychological processes enables music curriculums to be adapted to the perceptual experiences and needs of students, rather than futilely trying to adapt the students to any particular curriculum (for a discussion of neuro-pedagogical practices in music, see Hodges & Gruhn, 2018).

The maladaptation of specific teaching styles to the learning of synesthetes can be frustrating and furthermore undermine a synesthete's capacity to understand. This was exemplified by an incident that happened to one synesthete—the soprano, Lily—in the first year of her music studies:

> We did one of the classes called "Harmonic Devices" and you do a lot of interval aural training. In talking about the chords, the notes in the chords and chord extensions, my teacher talked about sound colors. He used these terms so often when he would talk about chords—added colors to the chords. It started to really throw me. One day I was obviously just frowning and going, "What?!" He was talking about opposite colors to use to play outside the chord tones and I was like, "Whaaaaat?!" And he said, "What's wrong?" And I said, "That sounds purple to me! That sounds red and you've just said that they're green and red!" . . . And so, then he said, "Ah! You've got synesthesia!" And I was like, "Oh okay."

While Lily had previously heard of synesthesia as a condition, she was unaware that her unique perceptual experiences could be classified as such. This incident was therefore her first realization that she potentially had synesthesia. This newfound realization subsequently enabled Lily to discuss her learning difficulties with her teacher, who was able to adapt his teaching to account for her needs.

Even in non-music-related subject areas, examples of specific instances where difficulties were faced when synesthetic expectations were not met abound. One thought-provoking example worth highlighting concerning difficulties experienced in a classroom setting was provided by the musicologist and pianist Benjamin, who it is worth noting has both absolute pitch and synesthesia:

> I was in Year 9. I was in English class and we were watching a film. In the film, they played an excerpt from the second movement of Beethoven's fifth piano concerto, which I was learning at the time. So, I was particularly sensitive and attuned to it. They'd transposed it up a semitone into C major. [Pauses] I had to leave the room. I had a panic attack, and I don't want to sound melodramatic or anything, but it was so painful—it was physically painful. I had a headache; I just couldn't think; the lights in the room suddenly got too bright and it was painful on my eyes. It was like fingernails down the blackboard: it was the worst kind of [pauses] dissonance—in that metaphoric sense—that you can possibly imagine. It was horrible.

The level of pain Benjamin reported experiencing was so intense that he had to physically remove himself from the room. What is intriguing in this recollection is his insistence on the physical nature of the pain he was experiencing, provoked by the juxtaposition of his aural memory of the correct pitch of the piece and its induced synesthetic color, with the actual external rendition of the same music and ensuing conflicting color. Indeed, he characterized this as "the worst kind of dissonance." This is not the first of such episodes, but it is the most memorable for Benjamin, potentially because of the situation that he was in (a school classroom), and the fact that his teacher was confused by what Benjamin was experiencing. While the examples from Lily and Benjamin are highly personal and idiosyncratic, they do highlight the need for teachers across disciplines to be educated on the unique learning enhancements and difficulties experienced by possessors of conditions such as synesthesia.

CONCLUSION

No two synesthetes experience, perceive, or interpret music in the same way, and the statements from individual synesthete musicians outlined in this chapter are highly idiosyncratic. There are, however, examples of both positive and negative behavioral manifestations that have been reported as more common than others. Throughout this chapter, statements from musician synesthetes affirm that their synesthetic percepts play an important role in performance aspects of their music engagement. This includes such factors as music interpretation and technical aspects of performance, as well as musical preferences and choices, including repertoire choices, programming decisions, listening choices, and stylistic preferences.

At this point it is worth remembering, however, that research into music-induced forms of synesthesia is still in its infancy (Glasser, 2018, 2020, 2021). The comments made by synesthete musicians in my research reveal that there is still much to be discovered about the nature and scope of the impact of conditions like synesthesia on the whole gamut of musical abilities and potential, including in areas of music performance. Even so, it is clear that by including synesthesia more directly in explanations of musical development, we can expand how we define and think about human musical ability and potential more broadly.

The French composer Olivier Messiaen once qualified his synesthetic sound-color relationship as "the most important characteristic of my language" (Samuel, 1994, p. 21). While Messiaen was aware that his unique synesthetic percepts were not shared by the vast majority of his public or fellow musicians, the color percepts he saw were so important to his compositional language that he would meticulously write them into his compositions and writings in great detail. They shaped Messiaen's relationship with music, inspired him, and drove his compositional choices (Glasser, 2016). It is hoped that through fostering a greater understanding of music-related types of synesthesia, other musicians can—like Messiaen—enhance their understanding of their, or their students' or colleagues', unique musical perceptions and creative insights.

Key Sources

General Literature

Cytowic, R. E., & Eagleman, D. M. (2011). *Wednesday is indigo blue: Discovering the brain of synesthesia*. Cambridge, MA: MIT Press. *Provides an easy-to-read summary of research into synesthesia for a general audience.*

Simner, J., & Hubbard, E. M. (Eds.). (2013). *The Oxford handbook of synesthesia*. Oxford: Oxford University Press. *Provides a comprehensive overview of synesthesia, including a discussion of its neurological underpinnings; it does not, however, include a chapter on synesthesia and music.*

The UK Synaesthesia Association (https://uksynaesthesia.com/). *Brings scientists, researchers, students, and synesthetes together and provides verifiable and reliable information regarding the condition for the media and any other interested parties.*

Music Literature

Glasser, S. (2018). *The impact of synaesthesia and absolute pitch on musical development*. Doctoral Dissertation, University of Melbourne, Australia. *The first known investigation into the impact of synesthesia on musical development.*

Glasser, S. (2020). Music and synaesthesia. In A. V. Sidoroff-Dorso, S. A. Day, & J. Jewanski (Eds.), *Synaesthesia: Opinions and perspectives. 30 interviews with leading scientists, artists and synaesthetes* (pp. 204–216). Münster: Westfälische Wilhelms-Universität. *A discussion of the current and future directions of research into music related forms of synesthesia.*

REFLECTIVE QUESTIONS

1. How has reading about the idiosyncratic perceptual experiences of synesthete musicians broadened your understanding of the range of perceptual responses to music that all musicians experience?
2. Think about the musicians that you work with or teach. Have there ever been indications that any of these musicians may have experienced music in a multisensory or multimodal way? How could the information included in this chapter influence your understanding of their lived-world experiences?
3. Can you think of any ways you might implement the information in this chapter into your own performance practice, regardless of whether you are a synesthete or not?
4. The synesthetic experience can impact a musician's performance, choices, and preferences in both positive and negative ways. What aspects of your own perceptual experience of music can you identify that impact your performance practice, choices, and preferences?
5. What was of most interest to you when reading about the ways that synesthesia can manifest among members of the musical community? Why?

REFERENCES

Barnett, K. J., Finucane, C., Asher, J. E., Bargary, G., Corvin, A. P., Newell, F. N., & Mitchell, K. J. (2008). Familial patterns and the origins of individual differences in synaesthesia. *Cognition, 106*(2), 871–893. https://doi.org/10.1016/j.cognition.2007.05.003.

Baron-Cohen, S., Burt, L., Smith-Laittan, F., Harrison, J., & Bolton, P. (1996). Synaesthesia: Prevalence and familiality. *Perception, 25*(9), 1073–1079. https://doi.org/10.1068%2Fp251073.

Baron-Cohen, S., & Harrison, J. (1999). Synesthesia: A challenge for developmental cognitive neuroscience. In H. Tager-Flusberg (Ed.), *Developmental cognitive neuroscience. Neurodevelopmental disorders* (pp. 491–503). Cambridge, MA: MIT Press.

Cytowic, R. E. (1989). *Synaesthesia: A union of the senses:* New York: Springer-Verlag.

Cytowic, R. E. (1993). *The man who tasted shapes.* New York: Putnam.

Cytowic, R. E. (1997). Synaesthesia: Phenomenology and neuropsychology—a review of current knowledge. In S. Baron-Cohen & J. E. Harrison (Eds.), *Synaesthesia: Classic and contemporary readings* (pp. 17–42). Oxford: Blackwell.

Cytowic, R. E. (2002). Touching tastes, seeing smells—and shaking up brain science. *Cerebrum, 4*(3), 7–26.

Domino, G. (1989). Synesthesia and creativity in fine arts students: An empirical look. *Creativity Research Journal, 2*(1–2), 17–29. https://doi.org/10.1080/10400418909534297.

George, D. (1981). *Sweet man: The real Duke Ellington.* New York: Putnam.

Glasser, S. (2016). Synaesthesia and child prodigiousness: The case of Olivier Messiaen. In G. E. McPherson (Ed.), *Musical prodigies: Interpretations from psychology, musicology and ethnomusicology* (pp. 453–470). Oxford: Oxford University Press.

Glasser, S. (2018). *The impact of synaesthesia and absolute pitch on musical development.* Doctoral thesis, University of Melbourne, Australia.

Glasser, S. (2020). Music and synaesthesia. In A. V. Sidoroff-Dorso, S. A. Day, & J. Jewanski (Eds.), *Synaesthesia: Opinions and perspectives. 30 interviews with leading scientists, artists and synaesthetes* (pp. 204–216). Münster: Westfälische Wilhelms-Universität.

Glasser, S. (2021). Perceiving Music Through the Lens of Synaesthesia and Absolute Pitch. *Perception, 50*(8), 690–708. https://doi.org/10.1177/03010066211034439

Greene, D. (2013). Radio interview with Pharrell Williams for the program: "Pharrell Williams on juxtaposition and seeing sounds," *Morning Edition*, PBS radio; December 31, 2013.

Hochel, M., & Milán, E. G. (2008). Synaesthesia: The existing state of affairs. *Cognitive Neuropsychology, 25*(1), 93–117. https://doi.org/10.1080/02643290701822815.

Hodges, D., & Gruhn, W. (2018). Implications of neurosciences and brain research for music teaching and learning. In G. E. McPherson (Ed.), *The Oxford handbook of music education* (2nd ed., Vol. 1, pp. 206–224). Oxford: Oxford University Press.

Mahling, F. (1926). *Das Problem der "Audition colorée": Eine historische-kritische Untersuchung.* Archiv für die Gesamte Psychologie. Leipzig: Akademische Verlagsgesellschaft M.B.H.

Mulvenna, C. M. (2007). Synaesthesia, the arts and creativity: A neurological connection. *Frontiers of neurology and neuroscience, 22,* 206–222. https://doi.org/10.1159/000102882.

Niccolai, V., Jennes, J., Stoerig, P., & Van Leeuwen, T. M. (2012). Modality and variability of synesthetic experience. *American Journal of Psychology, 125*(1), 81–94.

Ramachandran, V. S., & Hubbard, E. M. (2001a). Psychophysical investigations into the neural basis of synaesthesia. *Proceedings of the Royal Society of London, B, 268* (1470), 979–983. https://doi.org/10.1098/rspb.2000.1576.

Ramachandran, V. S., & Hubbard, E. M. (2001b). Synaesthesia: A window into perception, thought and language. *Journal of Consciousness Studies, 8*(12), 3–34.

Rich, A. N., Bradshaw, J. L., & Mattingley, J. B. (2005). A systematic, large-scale study of synaesthesia: Implications for the role of early experience in lexical-colour associations. *Cognition, 98*(1), 53–84. https://doi.org/10.1016/j.cognition.2004.11.003.

Rothen, N., & Meier, B. (2010). Higher prevalence of synaesthesia in art students. *Perception, 39*(5), 718–720. https://doi.org/10.1068%2Fp6680.

Samuel, C. (1994). *Olivier Messiaen: Music and color—Conversations with Claude Samuel* (E. T. Glasow, Trans.). Portland, OR: Amadeus.

Seaberg, M. (2013). *Tasting the universe: People who see colors in words and rainbows in symphonies.* Newburyport, MA: Red Wheel/Weiser.

Simner, J. (2012). Defining synaesthesia. *British Journal of Psychology, 103*(1), 1–15. https://doi.org/10.1348/000712610X528305.

Simner, J., Glover, L., & Mowat, A. (2006). Linguistic determinants of word colouring in grapheme-colour synaesthesia. *Cortex, 42*(2), 281–289. https://doi.org/10.1016/S0010-9452(08)70353-8.

Simner, J., Mulvenna, C., Sagiv, N., Tsakanikos, E., Witherby, S. A., Fraser, C., Scott, K., & Ward, J. (2006). Synaesthesia: The prevalence of atypical cross-modal experiences. *Perception, 35*(8), 1024–1033. https://doi.org/10.1068%2Fp5469.

Sitton, S. C., & Pierce, E. R. (2004). Synesthesia, creativity and puns. *Psychological Reports, 95*(2), 577–580. https://doi.org/10.2466%2Fpr0.95.2.577-580.

INDEX